Argentina

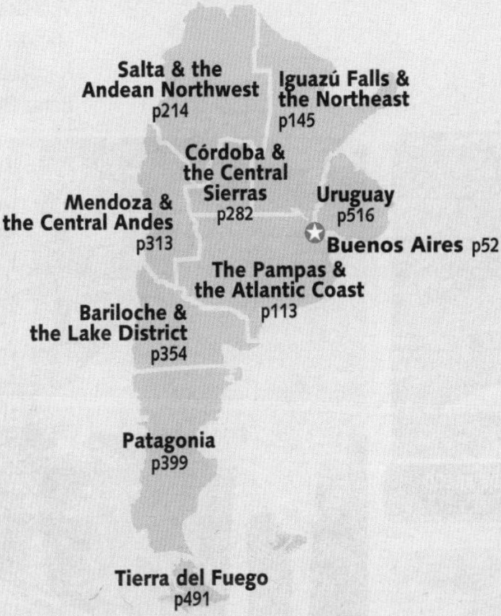

Isabel Albiston, Cathy Brown, Gregor Clark, Alex Egerton, Michael Grosberg, Anna Kaminski, Carolyn McCarthy, Anja Mutić, Adam Skolnick

PLAN YOUR TRIP

ON THE ROAD

BY FELICITAS MOLINA/GETTY IMAGES ©
SAN ANTONIO DE ARECO P119

ELOJOTORPE/GETTY IMAGES ©
FARO JOSÉ IGNACIO P558

PATAGONIALANDSCAPES/SHUTTERSTOCK ©

Contents

LA BOCA, BUENOS AIRES
P64

COVID-19

We have re-checked every business in this book before publication to ensure that it is still open after the COVID-19 outbreak. However, the economic and social impacts of COVID-19 will continue to be felt long after the outbreak has been contained, and many businesses, services and events referenced in this guide may experience ongoing restrictions. Some businesses may be temporarily closed, have changed their opening hours and services, or require bookings; some unfortunately could have closed permanently. We suggest you check with venues before visiting for the latest information.

ON THE ROAD

MENDOZA P315

VILLA LA ANGOSTURA P377

Contents

UNDERSTAND

SURVIVAL GUIDE

SPECIAL FEATURES

Right: Glaciar Perito Moreno, p464

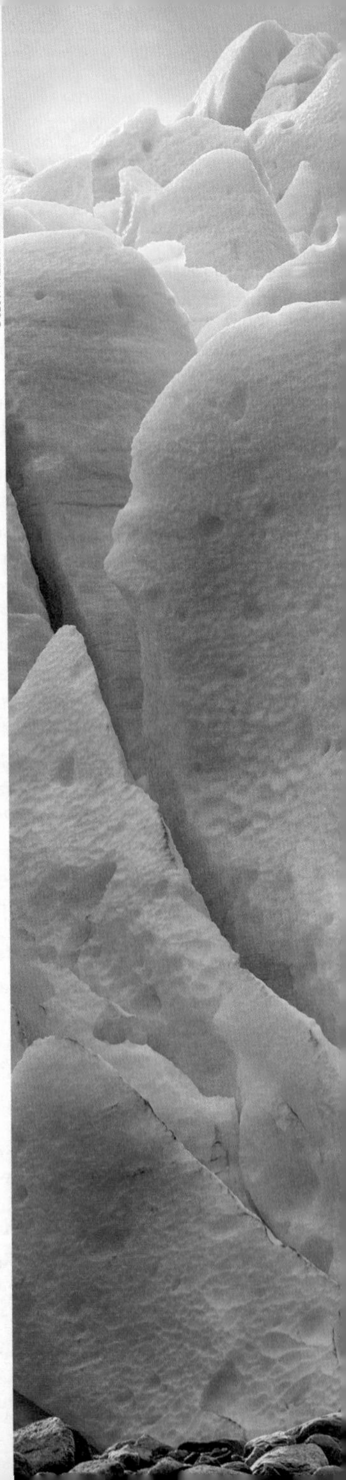

WELCOME TO

Argentina

During the years that I lived in Argentina, and during many visits since, I've felt enlivened by this colorful land where dogs wear soccer shirts and septuagenarians dance tango until dawn. It's a country whose cultural riches are ever present and always accessible; a land of superlatives and such sublime natural wonders it's almost too much to take in. Life in Argentina can be challenging, but everyday absurdities are met with humor, resilience and kindness.

By Isabel Albiston, Writer
For more about our writers, see p640.

Argentina & Uruguay

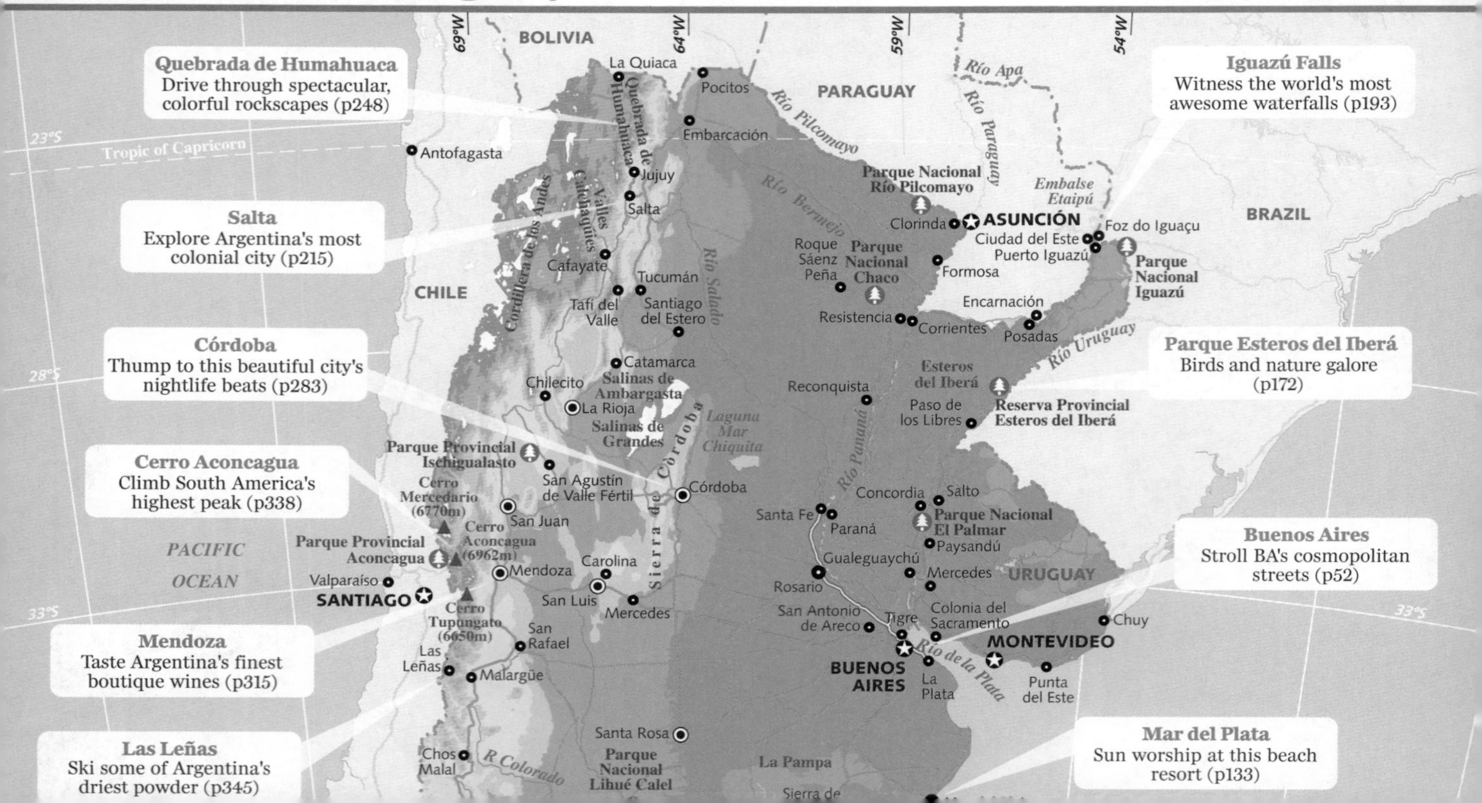

Quebrada de Humahuaca
Drive through spectacular, colorful rockscapes (p248)
Salta
Explore Argentina's most colonial city (p215)
Córdoba
Thump to this beautiful city's nightlife beats (p283)
Cerro Aconcagua
Climb South America's highest peak (p338)
Mendoza
Taste Argentina's finest boutique wines (p315)
Las Leñas
Ski some of Argentina's driest powder (p345)
Iguazú Falls
Witness the world's most awesome waterfalls (p193)
Parque Esteros del Iberá
Birds and nature galore (p172)
Buenos Aires
Stroll BA's cosmopolitan streets (p52)
Mar del Plata
Sun worship at this beach resort (p133)
0 500 km
0 250 miles
69°W
64°W
59°W
54°W
23°S
28°S
33°S
Tropic of Capricorn
BOLIVIA
PARAGUAY
BRAZIL
CHILE
URUGUAY
PACIFIC OCEAN
La Quiaca
Pocitos
Embarcación
Antofagasta
Jujuy
Salta
Valles Calchaquíes
Cafayate
Cordillera de los Andes
Tucumán
Tafí del Valle
Santiago del Estero
Río Salado
Río Pilcomayo
Río Bermejo
Río Apa
Río Paraguay
Parque Nacional Río Pilcomayo
Clorinda
ASUNCIÓN
Embalse Etaipú
Foz do Iguaçu
Ciudad del Este
Puerto Iguazú
Parque Nacional Iguazú
Roque Sáenz Peña
Parque Nacional Chaco
Formosa
Encarnación
Posadas
Resistencia
Corrientes
Río Uruguay
Catamarca
Chilecito
Salinas de Ambargasta
La Rioja
Salinas de Grandes
Laguna Mar Chiquita
Esteros del Iberá
Reconquista
Paso de los Libres
Reserva Provincial Esteros del Iberá
Parque Provincial Ischigualasto
San Agustín de Valle Fértil
Córdoba
Sierra de Córdoba
Río Paraná
Cerro Mercedario (6770m)
Cerro Aconcagua (6962m)
San Juan
Parque Provincial Aconcagua
Mendoza
Carolina
San Luis
Mercedes
Valparaíso
SANTIAGO
Cerro Tupungato (6650m)
San Rafael
Las Leñas
Malargüe
Santa Fe
Paraná
Concordia
Salto
Parque Nacional El Palmar
Paysandú
Gualeguaychú
Mercedes
Rosario
San Antonio de Areco
Tigre
Colonia del Sacramento
Chuy
MONTEVIDEO
BUENOS AIRES
Río de la Plata
La Plata
Punta del Este
Santa Rosa
Chos Malal
R Colorado
Parque Nacional Lihué Calel
La Pampa
Sierra de

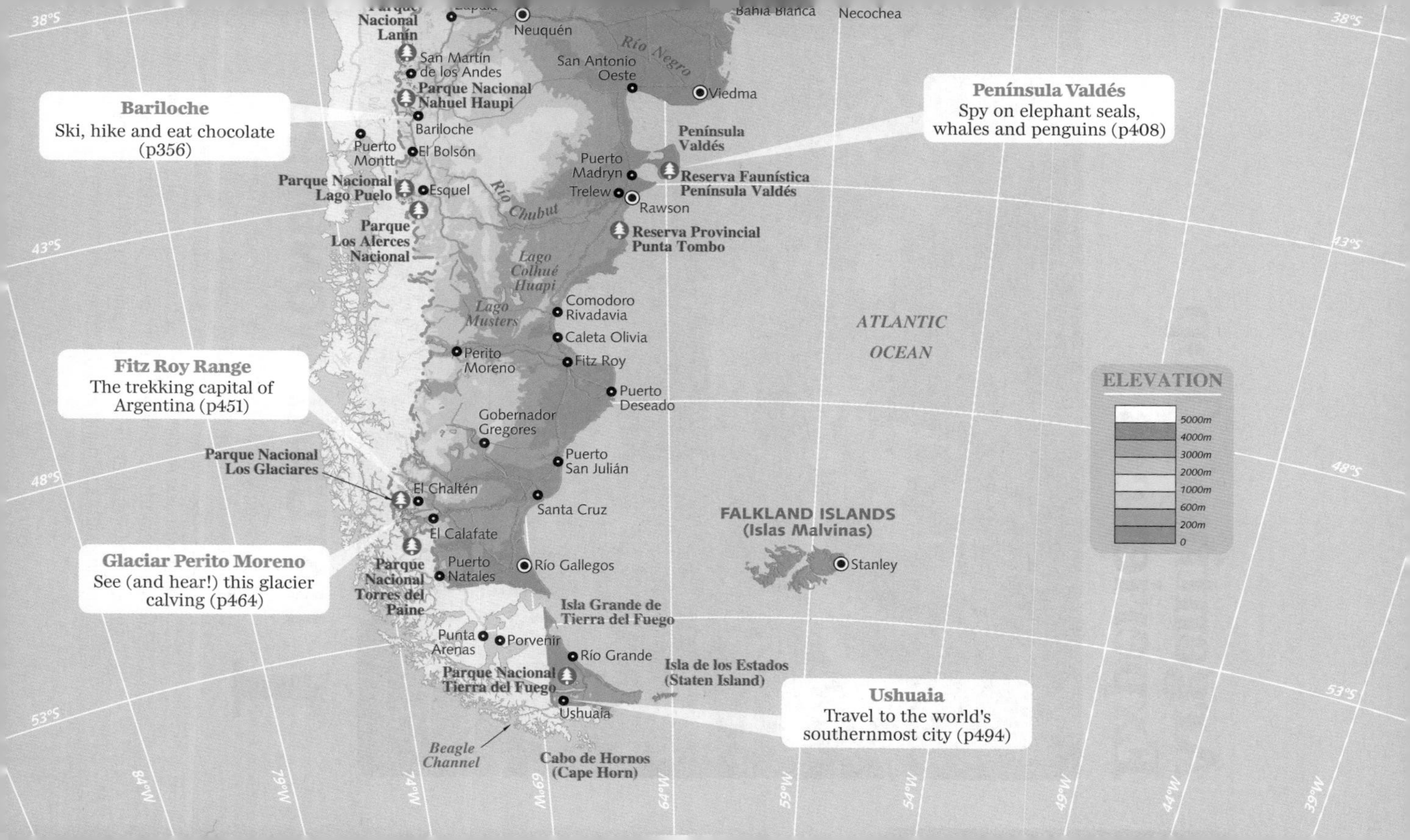
Bariloche
Ski, hike and eat chocolate (p356)
Fitz Roy Range
The trekking capital of Argentina (p451)
Glaciar Perito Moreno
See (and hear!) this glacier calving (p464)
Península Valdés
Spy on elephant seals, whales and penguins (p408)
Ushuaia
Travel to the world's southernmost city (p494)
Nacional Lanín
San Martín de los Andes
Parque Nacional Nahuel Haupi
Bariloche
Puerto Montt
El Bolsón
Parque Nacional Lago Puelo
Esquel
Parque Los Alerces Nacional
Neuquén
Bahía Blanca
Necochea
Río Negro
San Antonio Oeste
Viedma
Península Valdés
Puerto Madryn
Reserva Faunística Península Valdés
Trelew
Rawson
Río Chubut
Reserva Provincial Punta Tombo
Lago Colhué Huapi
Lago Musters
Comodoro Rivadavia
Caleta Olivia
Perito Moreno
Fitz Roy
Puerto Deseado
Gobernador Gregores
Puerto San Julián
Parque Nacional Los Glaciares
El Chaltén
El Calafate
Santa Cruz
Parque Nacional Torres del Paine
Puerto Natales
Río Gallegos
Isla Grande de Tierra del Fuego
Punta Arenas
Porvenir
Río Grande
Parque Nacional Tierra del Fuego
Ushuaia
Isla de los Estados (Staten Island)
Beagle Channel
Cabo de Hornos (Cape Horn)
ATLANTIC OCEAN
FALKLAND ISLANDS (Islas Malvinas)
Stanley
ELEVATION
5000m
4000m
3000m
2000m
1000m
600m
200m
0
38°S
43°S
48°S
53°S
84°W
79°W
74°W
69°W
64°W
59°W
54°W
49°W
44°W
39°W

Argentina's Top Experiences

1 NATURAL WONDERS

From the mighty Iguazú Falls in the subtropical north to the thunderous, crackling advance of the Glaciar Perito Moreno in the south, Argentina is home to a vast natural wonderland. The country with the Andes' highest snowbound peaks is also home to rich wetlands, rust-hued desert, deep-blue lakes, lichen-clad Valdivian forests and Patagonia's arid steppes. In this vast land, stunning sights abound and big adventure awaits.

Above: Fitz Roy Range (p451)

Iguazú Falls

The Río Iguazú, flowing through the jungle between Argentina and Brazil, plunges suddenly over a basalt cliff in a spectacular display. Iguazú Falls are a primal experience for the senses: the roar, the spray and the sheer volume of water. p193

Right: Iguazú Falls, Brazil side

Parque Nacional Los Glaciares

Perito Moreno (pictured above) is one of the most dynamic and accessible glaciers on the planet. Its slow but constant motion creates incredible suspense, as building-sized icebergs calve from the face and spectacularly crash into Lago Argentino. p451

Parque Provincial Aconcagua

The tallest peak in the western hemisphere, Aconcagua is an awe-inspiring sight. If you reach the top (not a task to be taken lightly), you'll be granted bragging rights as one of a select group who have touched the 'roof of the Americas.' p336

Above: Parque Provincial Aconcagua

2 PORTEÑO PASSIONS

Arriving in Buenos Aires is like jumping aboard a moving train. The modern metropolis whizzes by, alive with street life, from sidewalk cafes to parks carpeted in purple jacaranda blooms in springtime. *Porteños* (people from Buenos Aires) savor public life, whether it's meeting friends for a steak or a late-night gelato. Passion-fueled activities abound, from dancing tango to chanting and stomping alongside other stadium fanatics at a *fútbol* (soccer) game.

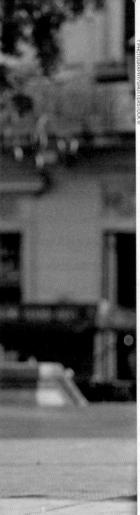

T PHOTOGRAPHY/SHUTTERSTOCK ©

JERSEAN GOLATT/LONELY PLANET ©

LUCIANA SILVA RODRIGUES/SHUTTERSTOCK ©

Tango at a Milonga

Nothing captures the essence of Buenos Aires like the sensual and melancholy tango. To experience the dance in its most authentic form, head to a *milonga* (a tango club or event). p100

Above: Tango dancers in San Telmo

Football Games

In Buenos Aires, *fútbol* (soccer) inspires intense passion. The atmosphere is particularly boisterous when Boca Juniors and arch-rivals River Plate face off at La Bombonera stadium (pictured above). p69

Steak Dinners

Feast at one of the capital's many *parrillas* (steakhouses), where waiters carve generous cuts of prime beef. *Parrilla*s run the gamut from roadside grills to neighborhood joints to upscale restaurants, so there's a price for every pocket. p88

Top: Don Julio (p91)

3 HITTING THE TRAIL

Hiking is a fantastic way to experience Argentina's mesmerizing landscapes. Opportunities abound, from stomping through cactus-filled deserts to scaling mountain peaks to backpacking past deep-blue lakes and through verdant forests. Bariloche is a popular hiking destination, with outstanding day and multiday hikes. Lining Argentina's western edge like a bumpy spine, the Andes rise to nearly 7000m at Aconcagua's peak and offer some of the continent's finest hiking and mountaineering.

KAVRAM/SHUTTERSTOCK ©

PAWEL TOCZYNSKI/GETTY IMAGES ©

Volcán Lanín

Trails at Parque Nacional Lanín include the ascent up the perfect cone of Volcán Lanínis, one of Argentina's most spectacular trekking challenges. p386

Above: Parque Nacional Lanín

Torres del Paine

This exceptional Chilean park abuts the Argentine border, with some of the world's best hiking. p481

Top left: Torres del Paine

Fitz Roy Range

With rugged wilderness, glaciers and shark-tooth summits, the Fitz Roy Range (pictured above) is the trekking capital of Argentina. p451

4 ANDEAN CULTURE

YADID LEVY /ALAMY STOCK PHOTO ©

OBSCUR/SHUTTERSTOCK ©

Northwestern Argentina has a distinctly Andean feel. The striking red-rock landscape is dotted with dusty villages, where you'll find pretty adobe churches, cobbled streets, and stalls laid out with colorful textiles, ponchos and handicrafts. Through it all drifts the sounds of folk music and the smells of *locro* (stew). Experience Andean culture at the local Carnaval celebrations in February and March, or year-round at a *peña* (folk music club).

Folk music at Salta's peñas

The beautiful city of Salta is set in a fertile valley that acts as a gateway to the impressive Andean cordillera. Experience Salta's lively folkloric music scene at the city's excellent *peñas*. p228

Left: La Casona del Molino (p228)

Quebrada de Humahuaca

This spectacular valley of scoured rock impresses visually with its tortured formations and artist's palette of mineral colors. The Quebrada's settlements are traditional and indigenous in character, with typical Andean dishes supplanting steaks on the restaurant menus, and llamas, not herds of cattle, grazing the sparse highland grass.Quebrada de Humahuaca p254

Left: Quebrada de Humahuaca

5 WINE COUNTRY

With so much fantastic wine on offer, it's tempting just to pull up a bar stool and work your way through the menu, but getting out there and seeing how the grapes are grown and processed is almost as enjoyable as sampling the finished product. Wine tasting in Argentina and Uruguay isn't just for the wine snobs – experiences range from DIY bike tours to tasting-and-accommodations packages at exclusive wineries.

Mendoza

The Mendoza wine region produces the majority of Argentina's grapes and has countless wineries. It's the best place to taste malbec, the dark, robust, plum-flavored wine that has solidly stamped the region of Mendoza on every oenophile's map. p322

Below: Wine sampling at a Mendoza bodega

San Juan

The lesser-known wine region of San Juan (pictured above) has exceptional syrah and bonarda varieties. Sample them along the San Juan Wine Route. p347

Uruguay

The area around the town of Carmelo in Uruguay has a number of vineyards offering tastings of their well-regarded tannats. p544

Right: Tannat grapes

6 WILDLIFE WATCHING

FEDERICO CABRERA/GETTY IMAGES ©

In Argentina, wildlife comes in spectacular variety. The country's diverse environments translate into homes for many creatures, including flightless, grasslands-loving ñandú (rheas); Andean condors and pumas; and desert-dwelling camelids such as llamas and guanacos. Coastal walks offer ample opportunities to spot whales and other sea life, while diving and kayak tours take you deeper into their world. Boat trips through the wetlands provide sightings of alligators and other swamp dwellers.

Whale-watching

Península Valdés is a hub for wildlife watching. The main attraction is endangered southern right whales, but you can also spot orcas, penguins and elephant seals. p408

Above: Southern right whale, Península Valdés

Wetland Wonders

Parque Esteros del Iberá offers astonishing wildlife-watching opportunities around shallow vegetation-rich lagoons. Head out in a boat to spot alligators, exotic bird species, monkeys, swamp deer and capybaras. p172

Penguins in Ushuaia

Colonies of cormorants, sea lions and penguins flank this stepping-off point to Antarctica. Ushuaia p494

7 GAUCHO CULTURE

An enduring Argentine icon, the intrepid gaucho came to life after Spaniards let their cattle loose on the grassy pampas centuries ago. These nomadic cowboys lived by taming wild horses (introduced by the Spaniards), hunting errant herds and drinking *mate* (a tea-like beverage) under the shade of the Ombú tree. It's a living tradition. Look out for modern-day gauchos, riding across the pampas in their *boinas* (a kind of beret).

KSENIA RAGOZINA/SHUTTERSTOCK ©

NIARKRAD/SHUTTERSTOCK ©

Feria de Mataderos

Gauchos demonstrate their horseback-riding skills by playing *sortija*, a game where they ride at full speed to spear a tiny dangling ring. p81

Above: Stalls at Feria de Mataderos

Pampas Traditions

If you want to experience gaucho culture in all its glory, don't miss November's Fiesta de la Tradición (pictured top) in San Antonio de Areco. p121

Visit an Estancia

Soak up gaucho culture at an *estancia* (ranch). Activities on offer include horseback riding and elaborate *asados* (barbecues). p122

Above: Gaucho preparing *mate*

8 HITTING THE ROAD

SAIKO3P/GETTY IMAGES ©

MATTHEW WILLIAMS-ELLIS /GETTY IMAGES ©

Seven Lakes Route

A journey of extraordinary beauty, the Ruta de los Siete Lagos (Seven Lakes Route) is a not-to-be-missed road trip. Your vehicular adventure winds through lush forests, past waterfalls and dramatic mountain scenery, and skirts the various crystal-blue lakes that give it its name. p385

Top left: Parque Nacional Nahuel Huapi (p367)

The Cactus Road

The road trip from Salta to the enchanting towns of Cachi and Cafayate begins with a cruise through the spectacular Parque Nacional Los Cardones (pictured left), which takes its names from the cardón (candelabra cactus) that dominates the landscape. p231

Taking a road trip is an excellent way to experience the beauty of Argentina's varied landscapes. And since some parts of the country are not accessible by public transport, getting behind the wheel is one of the best ways to get off the beaten track. Road trips are particularly worthwhile in Patagonia, where distances are vast and buses infrequent. Put on some tunes and prepare for an unforgettable adventure.

Need to Know

For more information, see Survival Guide (p601)

Currency
Argentine peso (AR$)

Language
Spanish

Visas
Generally not required for stays of up to 90 days. Canadians must pay a 'reciprocity fee' before entering.

Money
ATMs are widely available, though tend to run out of money in tourist destinations. Credit cards are accepted in most hotels and restaurants.

Cell Phones
It's best to bring your own unlocked tri- or quad-band GSM cell phone to Argentina, then buy an inexpensive SIM chip (you'll get a local number) and credits (or *carga virtual*) as needed.

Time
Argentina Standard Time (GMT/UTC minus three hours)

When to Go

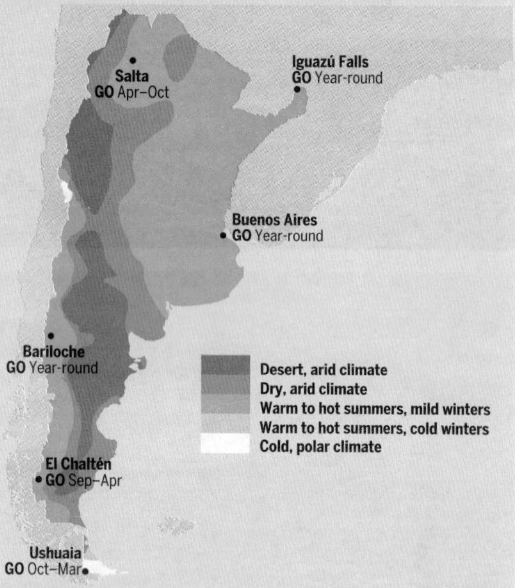

High Season (Nov–Feb & Jul)

- Patagonia is best (and most expensive) December to February.
- Crowds throng to the beaches from late December through January.
- Snow falls at ski resorts from June to August.

Shoulder (Sep–Nov & Mar–May)

- Temperature-wise the best times to visit Buenos Aires.
- The Lake District is pleasant; leaves are spectacular in March and April.
- The Mendoza region has its grape harvests and wine festival.

Low Season (Jun–Aug)

- Good time to visit the north.
- Many services close at beach resorts, and mountain passes can be blocked by snow.
- July is a winter vacation month, so popular destinations get busy.

Useful Websites

Argentina Independent (www.argentinaindependent.com) Current affairs and culture, plus much more.

The Bubble (www.thebubble.com) Dissects current events in Argentina and Latin America, with a dose of pop and media culture.

Pick up the Fork (http://pickupthefork.com) Savvy guide to Buenos Aires food and more.

Ruta 0 (www.ruta0.com) Handy driving tips, such as distance/duration between cities, gas consumption, road conditions and tariffs.

Lonely Planet (www.lonelyplanet.com/argentina) Destination information, traveler forum and more.

Important Numbers

Argentina country code	☎54
Directory assistance	☎110
International access code	☎00
National Tourist Information (in BA)	☎11-4312-2232
Police	☎101; ☎911 in some large cities

Exchange Rates

Australia	A$1	AR$14.81
Canada	C$1	AR$15.18
Chile	CH$100	AR$3.11
Euro	€1	AR$22.65
Japan	¥100	AR$15.39
NZ	NZ$1	AR$13.48
UK	UK£1	AR$25.53
Uruguay	UR$1	AR$0.66
USA	US$1	AR$18.81

For current exchange rates see www.xe.com.

Daily Costs

Budget: Less than US$60

- Dorm bed: US$15–22
- Double room in good budget hotel: US$65
- Cheap main dish: under US$11

Midrange: US$60–200

- Three-star hotel room: US$75–150
- Average main dish: US$10–16
- Four-hour bus ticket: US$30

Top End: More than US$200

- Five-star hotel room: US$165+
- Fine main dish: over US$17
- Taxi trip across town: US$12

Opening Hours

General opening hours:

Banks 8am to 3pm or 4pm Monday to Friday; some till 1pm Saturday

Bars 8pm or 9pm to between 4am and 6am nightly

Cafes 6am to midnight or much later; open daily

Clubs 1am to 2am to between 6am and 8am Friday and Saturday

Office business hours 8am to 5pm

Post offices 8am to 6pm Monday to Friday, 9am to 1pm Saturday

Restaurants Noon to 3:30pm and 8pm to midnight or 1am (later on weekends)

Shops 9am or 10am to 8pm or 9pm Monday to Saturday

Arriving in Argentina

Aeropuerto Internacional Ministro Pistarini ('Ezeiza'; Buenos Aires) Shuttle buses (AR$240) travel frequently to downtown BA in 40 to 60 minutes; local buses take two hours. Use official taxi services only; avoid touts.

Aeroparque Jorge Newbery ('Aeroparque,' airport with mostly domestic flights; Buenos Aires) Shuttle buses (AR$75) travel frequently to downtown BA in 10 to 15 minutes; or take local bus 33 or 45. Taxis available (AR$160 to downtown).

Getting Around

Air Argentina is a huge country, so flights are good for saving time. Delays happen occasionally, however.

Bus Generally the best way to get around Argentina; they're fast, frequent, comfortable, reasonably priced and cover the country extensively.

Car Renting a car is useful (but expensive) for those who want the most travel independence in remote regions such as Patagonia.

Train A few train lines can be useful for travelers, but generally this is not the most efficient method of transportation.

For much more on **getting around**, see p615

Month by Month

TOP EVENTS

Carnaval, February

Fiesta Nacional del Lúpulo, February

Fiesta Nacional de la Vendimia, March

Fiesta Nacional del Chocolate, March–April

Tango BA Festival y Mundial, August

January

January is peak summer in Argentina. *Porteños* (residents of Buenos Aires) escape the sweltering heat at beach resorts, making them crowded and expensive. It's also high season in Patagonia, so expect top prices there, too.

Festival Nacional del Folklore

Near the city of Córdoba, the town of Cosquín hosts the National Festival of Folk Music during the last week of January. It's the country's largest and best-known *folklórico* (folk music) festival. (p297)

February

Summertime crowds at the beaches and in Patagonia thin later in the month. The Andean deserts and the Iguazú region continue to be very hot, but the Lake District is ideal. Mendoza's grape harvest begins.

Carnaval

Though not as rockin' as it is in Brazil, the celebration is very rowdy in the northeast, especially in Gualeguaychú (p182) and Corrientes (p169). Montevideo, the capital of Uruguay, is another party spot (p528). Dates vary depending on the city.

El Lúpulo al Palo

El Bolsón's hop festival honors the key ingredient for its artisanal craft beers. Expect musical performances, activities, food and plenty of beer tasting (of course). (p373)

March

Autumn is starting and Buenos Aires is balmy, though rainy. Prices fall at the beaches and in Patagonia, but the weather remains decent. The north starts cooling, and Iguazú Falls is less hot and humid.

Fiesta Nacional de la Vendimia

Mendoza city's week-long Fiesta Nacional de la Vendimia kicks off with parades, *folklórico* events and a royal coronation – all in honor of Mendoza's wines. (p319)

DÍA DE LA MEMORIA

Held on March 24 (the date a military coup took over the Argentine government in 1976), this public holiday commemorates the victims of Argentina's military dictatorship. Over seven years, tens of thousands of people 'disappeared' and were never heard from again.

April

Lake District forests start changing from verdant green to fiery hues. Patagonia is clearing out but you might get lucky with decent hiking weather. Buenos Aires heads into

Top: Fiesta Nacional de la Vendimia, Mendoza (p319)

Bottom: Fiesta de la Tradición, San Antonio de Areco (p121)

low season, with still-pleasant temperatures.

Festival Internacional de Cine Independiente

Independent film buffs shouldn't miss this festival in Buenos Aires, which screens more than 100 films from Argentina and Uruguay.

Fiesta Nacional del Chocolate

Happening during Easter week (dates vary annually), Bariloche's chocolate festival often highlights a 9m tall chocolate egg, cracked and consumed on Easter Sunday. Look for the world's longest chocolate bar, too.

May

It's late autumn and Buenos Aires is cool as the rains ebb. It's a good time to visit Iguazú Falls. The crowds also leave Mendoza, though vineyards are still a gorgeous red from autumn leaves.

Día de Virgen de Luján

On May 8 thousands of devout believers make a 65km pilgrimage to the pampas town of Luján in honor of the Virgin Mary. Other pilgrimages take place in early October, early August, late September and on December 8.

June

Winter begins. Beach resorts and Patagonia close down, but it's an ideal

time to visit the deserts of the Andean Northwest and Iguazú Falls, which have less rain and heat at this time of year.

Anniversary of Carlos Gardel's death

On June 24, 1935, tango legend Carlos Gardel died in a plane crash in Colombia. Head to Buenos Aires' Chacarita cemetery to see fans pay their respects at his grave and statue.

Festival Nacional de la Noche Más Larga

Ushuaia celebrates the longest night of the year with about 10 days' worth of music and shows. (p499)

July

Ski season is at its peak, so skiers head off to the resorts around Bariloche, San Martín de los Andes and Mendoza. Whale-watching season starts heating up in the area around Península Valdés.

Día de la Independencia

Argentina's Independence Day is July 9, and celebrations are especially strong in Tucumán, where the country's independence was first declared.

August

Beach resort towns are dead and Patagonia is desolate and cold. Buenos Aires is still cool, but it's a great time to explore the theaters, museums and art galleries.

Tango BA Festival y Mundial

World-class national and international tango dancers perform throughout Buenos Aires during this two-week festival. It's a great way to see some of the country's best tango dancers and musicians do their thing. (p81)

September

Spring has sprung, and it's peak season for whale watching (both southern right whales and orcas) around Península Valdés. Polo season begins in Buenos Aires and the ski slopes wind down.

Vinos y Bodegas

Lovers of the grape shouldn't miss this huge Buenos Aires event, which highlights vintages from bodegas (wineries) all over Argentina. (p81)

October

It's a fine time to visit Buenos Aires and central Argentina. The season is just starting in Patagonia, but the crowds haven't quite descended. Flowers are blooming in the Lake District.

Bariloche a la Carta

This week-long food festival represents the Lake District's best culinary offerings. Dozens of restaurants take part, showcasing special menus, and numerous food stalls and microbreweries set up shop in the main square.

Oktoberfest

Join the swillers and oompah bands at Argentina's national beer festival, Villa General Belgrano's Oktoberfest in the Central Sierras. (p307)

November

Buenos Aires' weather is perfect, its jacaranda trees dazzling with purple blooms. It's a good time to visit the beach resorts and Patagonia, since the crowds and peak prices are still some weeks away.

Fiesta de la Tradición

This festival salutes the gaucho and is especially significant in San Antonio de Areco (p119), the most classically gaucho of towns. However, it is also important (and much less touristy) in the mountain town of San José de Jáchal.

December

Summer begins and it's excellent beach weather at the resorts (just before the January peak). It's also ideal weather for outdoor activities in the Lake District, and penguin and hiking seasons start in Patagonia.

Buenos Aires Jazz

This big jazz festival takes place over five days in venues all over the city in either November or December, attracting tens of thousands of spectators.

Itineraries

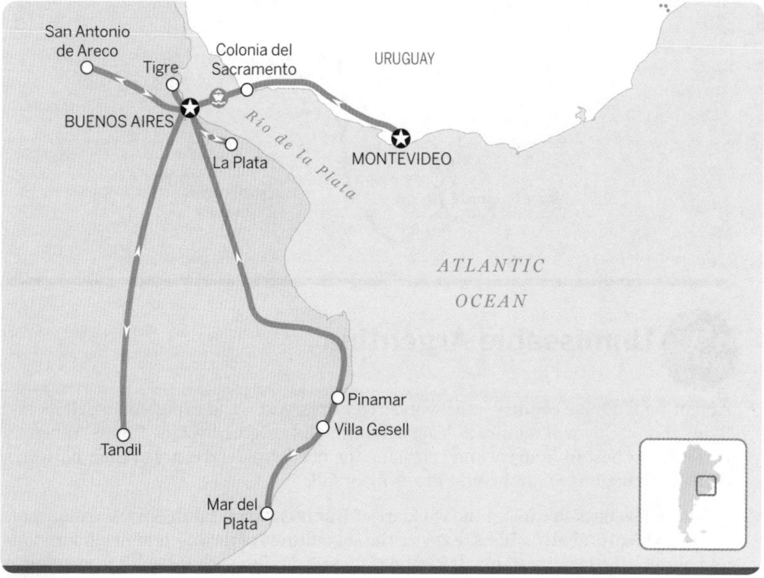

1 WEEK A Week Around Buenos Aires

Seen Buenos Aires from top to bottom and wondering where else to visit? There's plenty of choice just outside Argentina's capital, from small and alluring cobblestoned towns to bigger, more exciting cities and bustling soft-sand beach resorts.

Tigre, with its hidden waterways and busy delta, is a popular *porteño* (resident of Buenos Aires) getaway for a day or two. Take a day trip to peaceful **San Antonio de Areco**, which has a history of gaucho culture, or tidy **La Plata**, with its huge cathedral.

Perhaps you'd prefer a weekend at the beach? **Pinamar** and **Villa Gesell** make great summer escapes, as does **Mar del Plata**, the biggest Argentine beach destination of them all. Or head inland to **Tandil** for a couple of days; it's a pretty town near scenic hills and a large recreational reservoir.

And then there's Uruguay, just a (relatively) short boat ride away. **Colonia del Sacramento** is truly charming; filled with cobbled streets and atmospheric colonial buildings it makes a great day trip. Or stay overnight in **Montevideo**; like BA's little sister, it's smaller and less frantic, with a historic downtown with a thriving cafe and nightlife scene and a long Río de la Plata beachfront on the Rambla.

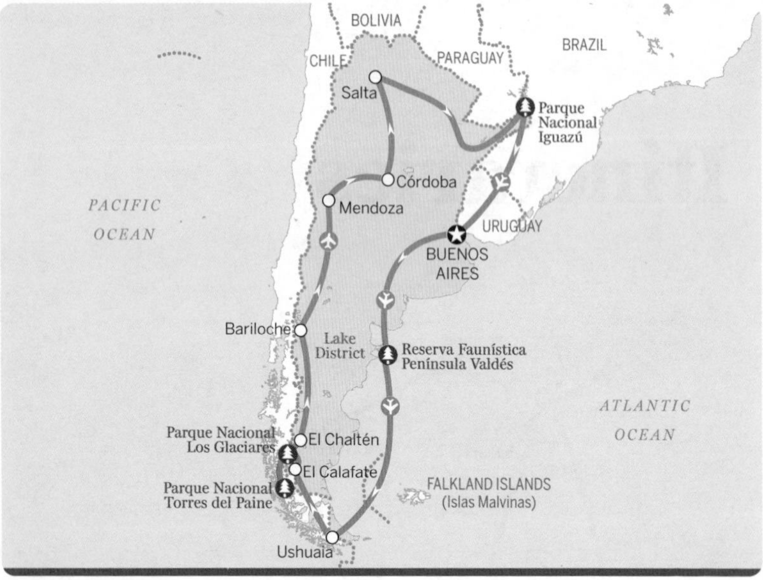

5 WEEKS Unmissable Argentina

Argentina is a huge country – the world's eighth largest – and experiencing all its highlights thoroughly will require at least a month, plus several airplane flights. Whereas Patagonia is best in January and February, the northern deserts are at their hottest, so doing both regions might be best in spring or fall.

Take a few days to explore the wonders of **Buenos Aires**, taking in the restaurants, parks and cultural attractions. Explore the subcultures of its different neighborhoods and admire the big-city sights. If it's the right season, fly south for wildlife viewing at **Reserva Faunística Península Valdés**. From here hop another flight to **Ushuaia**, the southernmost city in the world with skiing, dogsledding and penguin viewing. It's also a prime jumping-off point to Antarctica (for this side trip, add another two weeks and *minimum* US$5000).

Now you'll head north to **El Calafate**, where the stunning Glaciar Perito Moreno of **Parque Nacional Los Glaciares** is one of the world's most spectacular sights. If you adore the outdoors, cross the border to Chile's **Parque Nacional Torres del Paine**, to hike its awe-inspiring landscapes. Back in El Calafate, your next stop should be **El Chaltén**, another world-class trekking destination.

Further up the Andes is Argentina's Lake District, where a chocolate stop in **Bariloche** is a must. Gorgeous scenery, outdoor activities and lovely nearby towns can easily add days to your itinerary. Your next destination is **Mendoza**, Argentina's wine mecca, which also offers great outdoor adventures and mind-blowing Andean scenery. Tour the wineries by bicycle or on a driving tour. A 10-hour bus ride lands you in **Córdoba**, the country's second-largest city, with amazing colonial architecture and cutting-edge culture. From here go north to pretty **Salta**, a colonial masterpiece where you can explore colorful desert canyons, charming villages and rust-colored panoramas.

Pack your bags again and head east to **Parque Nacional Iguazú**, where the world's most massive falls will astound you. Fly back to Buenos Aires and party till your plane leaves.

Top: Glaciar Perito Moreno (p464)

Bottom: Tigre (p111)

JOPSTOCK / GETTY IMAGES ©

Top: Lago Nahuel Huapi (p367)

Bottom: Farm in Tandil (p123)

30 DAYS Ruta Nacional 40

Argentina's quintessential road trip, RN 40 travels the length of the country. To do this adventure independently you'll need to rent a vehicle. If you plan to get off the beaten path, a 4WD comes in handy.

Start near the colorful mountainsides of **Quebrada de Humahuaca** before hitting **Salta** to take in the colonial charms and the wildly scenic villages of **Valles Calchaquíes**. Pause at lovely **Cafayate** and **Chilecito** before the long trip down to **Mendoza** to suss out the wine scene.

Continue south, stopping to check out the lagoons and hot springs around **Chos Malal**. Explore the lovely national parks of **Lanín** and **Nahuel Huapi** before hitting **San Martín de los Andes** and **Bariloche**, both of which offer fantastic outdoor opportunities. Further on, sidetrack to **Cueva de las Manos** for indigenous rock art.

Enjoy world-class hiking at **El Chaltén**, then experience **Glaciar Perito Moreno**. Cross the border to Chile to explore the stunning **Parque Nacional Torres del Paine** before your last stop, **Ushuaia** – the windswept finale of the world's most southern highway.

18 DAYS Patagonian Passage

Jaw-dropping Andean peaks, adorable mountain villages and exotic coastal wildlife – you'll hit them all on this spectacular Patagonian adventure.

Start in **Puerto Madryn** in springtime to see the whales, elephant seals and penguins at **Reserva Faunística Península Valdés**. From nearby **Trelew**, check out the world's largest dinosaur at the Museo Paleontologico Egidio Feruglio and catch a flight south.

Arrive in **Ushuaia** and hop on a boat to cruise around the Beagle Channel. Nearby **Parque Nacional Tierra del Fuego** offers hiking at the end of the world.

Now hop to **El Calafate** and lay your eyes on the spectacular **Glaciar Perito Moreno**. Outdoors lovers should cross the border and trek in Chile's famous **Parque Nacional Torres del Paine**. Hit **El Chaltén** for world-class hiking and camping.

Return to El Calafate to fly to **Bariloche**, gateway to the gorgeous national parks of **Nahuel Huapi** and **Lanín**. If you have a couple of days extra, overnight in the hippie enclave of **El Bolsón** or the cute village of **Villa Traful**.

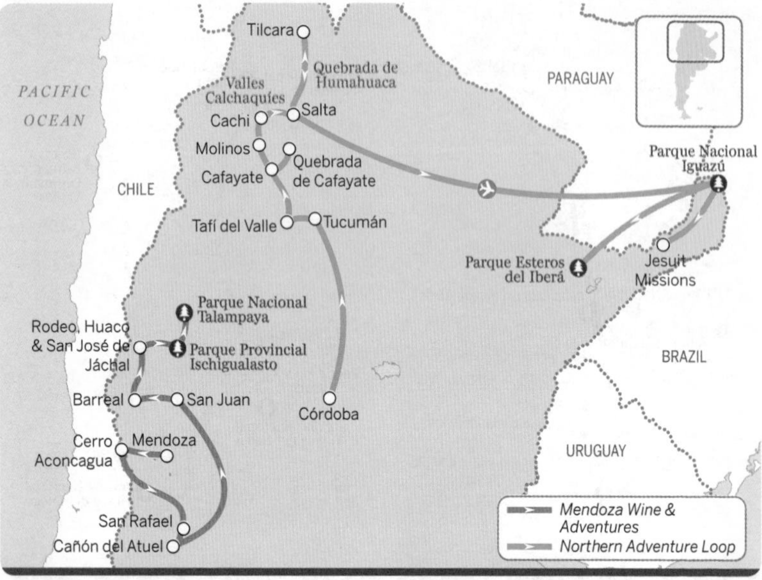

2 WEEKS Mendoza Wine & Adventures

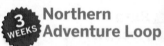

Few getaways hold more appeal than a journey to South America's most scenic wine country. Whether you're cycling through the vineyards or sipping malbecs, it's a fabulous way to unwind.

Start in beautiful **Mendoza**, on the flanks of the Andes with world-class vineyards surrounding the city. White-water rafting and skiing in the area are superb, and **Cerro Aconcagua** (the western hemisphere's highest peak) isn't too far away.

Now take a crack-of-dawn bus to **San Rafael**, where you can rent a bike and ride out to the city's wineries. The area is also home to scenic **Cañon del Atuel**, a colorful mini Grand Canyon. Then backtrack up north to **San Juan** to try the excellent syrah and regional whites. Rent a car and head west to ethereal **Barreal** for rafting, mountaineering and land sailing, then go further north to explore the remote, traditional villages of **Rodeo**, **Huaco** and **San José de Jáchal**.

Finally, visit the amazing landscapes of **Parque Provincial Ischigualasto** and **Parque Nacional Talampaya**; both boast spectacular rock formations, along with petroglyphs and dinosaur fossils.

3 WEEKS Northern Adventure Loop

Argentina's north feels otherwordly, with pretty towns and cities, colorful mountains and desert scenery. To the east are incredible waterfalls and wildlife-filled wetlands.

Start in **Córdoba**, and explore one of the country's finest colonial centers.

Now head north to historic **Tucumán** to see where Argentina declared its independence from Spain. Over to the west is pretty **Tafí del Valle**. A bit further north is beautiful **Cafayate**, the place to knock back some aromatic torrontés wine. Sober up and day-trip to the epic **Quebrada de Cafayate**, then head to otherworldly **Valles Calchaquíes** and the adobe villages of **Molinos** and **Cachi**.

Historic **Salta** is a great base for stellar excursions into the Andes. Now journey north through the magnificently eroded valley of **Quebrada de Humahuaca**, where you can overnight in lively little **Tilcara**.

Return to Salta and fly to the incredible **Parque Nacional Iguazú**. With time, head to **Parque Esteros del Iberá**, an amazing wetlands preserve full of capybaras, caimans and birds, or pay a visit to the evocative ruins of the **Jesuit missions**.

Top: Catedral de la Plata (p115)

ttom: Ruta Nacional 40 (p452), Patagonia

KAVRAM/SHUTTERSTOCK ©

Off-piste skiing, Cerro Chapelco (p38

Plan Your Trip

Argentina Outdoors

Mountaineering, hiking and skiing have long been Argentina's classic outdoor pursuits, but these days locals and visitors alike are doing much more. They're kiteboarding in the Andes, paragliding in the Central Sierras, diving along the Atlantic coast and pulling out huge trout in the Lake District.

Best Bases for Thrill Seekers

Bariloche

One of Argentina's premier outdoor cities, with a hut-to-hut hiking tradition thanks to its Swiss-German roots. There's also fine skiing, biking, fishing, rafting and even paragliding.

Mendoza

One word: Aconcagua. Here at the highest section of the Andes there's also outstanding skiing and rafting and rock climbing in summer months.

El Chaltén

At the edge of the southern ice field, there's no location more dramatic for world-class hiking, mountaineering, ice-hikes and rock climbing.

Puerto Madryn

Check out the outstanding marine wildlife, including sea lions and whales, by going diving, kayaking or windsurfing.

Junín de los Andes

In the drier part of the Lake District you will find lovely hiking and gorgeous rivers offering some of the world's best fly-fishing with huge trout.

Córdoba

The closest city to Los Gigantes, Argentina's rock-climbing mecca (80km away).

Hiking & Trekking

Argentina is home to some superb stomping. The Lake District is probably the country's most popular hiking destination, with outstanding day and multiday hikes in several national parks, including Nahuel Huapi and Lanín. Bariloche is the best base for exploring the former, San Martín de los Andes the latter.

Patagonia, along the Andes, has out-of-this-world hiking. South of Bariloche, El Bolsón is an excellent base for hiking both in the forests outside of town and in nearby Parque Nacional Lago Puelo. Parque Nacional Los Glaciares offers wonderful hiking in and around the Fitz Roy Range; base yourself in El Chaltén and wait out the storms (in the brewery, of course).

Head to Parque Nacional Torres del Paine, in Chile but not far from El Calafate in Argentina, for epic hiking. Tierra del Fuego also has good routes in Parque Nacional Tierra del Fuego.

Then there are the high Andean peaks west of Mendoza. Although these areas are more popular for mountaineering, there's some great trekking here as well. The northern Andes around Quebrada de Humahuaca are also good.

Bariloche, Ushuaia, El Bolsón and Junín de los Andes have a hiking and mountaineering club called Club Andino, which is good for local information, maps and current conditions.

Mountaineering

The Andes are a mountaineer's dream, especially in the San Juan and Mendoza provinces, where some of the highest peaks in the western hemisphere are found. While the most famous climb is Aconcagua, the highest peak in the Americas, there are plenty of others in the Andes – many of them more interesting and far more technical. Near Barreal, the Cordón de la Ramada boasts five peaks more than 6000m high, including the mammoth Cerro Mercedario, which tops out at 6770m. The region is less congested than Aconcagua, offers more technical climbs and is preferred by many climbers. Also near here is the majestic Cordillera de Ansilta, with seven peaks scraping the sky at between 5130m and 5885m.

The magnificent and challenging Fitz Roy Range, in southern Patagonia near El Chaltén, is one of the world's top mountaineering destinations, while the mountains of Parque Nacional Nahuel Huapi offer fun for all levels.

Rock Climbing

Patagonia's Parque Nacional Los Glaciares, home to Cerro Torre and Cerro Fitz Roy, is one of the world's most important rock-climbing destinations. Cerro Torre is

SUZIE HALL / GETTY IMAGES ©

Top: Bike riding near Cerro Catedral (p370)

Bottom: Lago Puelo (p376)

MUSH, FIDO, MUSH!

You can't say you've done it all until you've tried dogsledding, and Argentina's a great place to start. Obviously, this activity is possible only when there's snow, during the winter months of June to October – though in Ushuaia the season might be longer. Here are a few places to check out:

Caviahue A village on the flanks of Volcán Copahue.

San Martín de los Andes A picturesque town north of Bariloche.

Ushuaia The southernmost city in the world!

onsidered one of the five toughest climbs n the planet. The nearby town of El Chalén is a climber's haven, and several shops ffer lessons and rent equipment. If you on't have the time or talent for climbs of erro Torre's magnitude, there are plenty f other options.

Los Gigantes, in the Central Sierras, fast becoming the country's de facto ock-climbing capital and has lots of igh-quality granite. There's also climbing around Carolina.

In Mendoza province, Los Molles is a nall, friendly hub for rock climbing, and ere's more nearby at Chigüido (near alargüe). Around Mendoza city are the aws of Los Arenales and El Salto.

There's good climbing around Bariloche – erro Catedral especially has popular crags. nally, in the Pampas, there's some climbg in Tandil and Mar del Plata.

ishing

gether, Patagonia and the Lake District nstitute one of the world's premier flyshing destinations, where introduced out species (brown, brook, lake and inbow) and landlocked Atlantic salmon ach massive sizes in cold rivers surunded by spectacular scenery. It's an gler's paradise.

In the Lake District, Junín de los Andes the self-proclaimed trout capital of Arntina, and lining up a guide to take you to Parque Nacional Lanín's superb trout streams is easy. Nearby Aluminé sits on the banks of Río Aluminé, one of the country's most highly regarded trout streams. Bariloche and Villa la Angostura are other excellent bases.

Further south, Parque Nacional Los Alerces (near Esquel) has outstanding lakes and rivers. From El Chaltén, you can do day trips to Lago del Desierto or Laguna Larga. Río Gallegos is a superb fly-fishing destination. Other important Patagonian rivers include Río Negro and Río Santa Cruz.

The city of Río Grande, on Tierra del Fuego, is world famous for its fly-fishing. Its eponymous river holds some of the largest sea-run brown trout in the world.

Deep-sea fishing is possible in Camarones and Puerto Deseado; near Gobernador Gregores there's a lake with salmon and rainbow trout.

In subtropical northeast Argentina, the wide Río Paraná attracts fly-fishers, spin fishers and trollers from around the world, who pull in massive river species, such as surubí (a huge catfish) and dorado (a troutlike freshwater game fish). The dorado, not to be confused with the saltwater mahimahi, is a powerful swimmer and one of the most exciting fish to catch on a fly.

Guides & Services

In smaller towns such as Junín de los Andes, you can usually go to the local tourist office and request a list of local fishing guides or operators. Another good option for independent anglers heading to the Lake District is the Asociación de Guías Profesionales de Pesca Parque Nacional Nahuel Huapi y Patagonia Norte (www.guiaspatagonicos.com.ar), which maintains a list and contact details of licensed guides for northern Patagonia and the Lake District. For information about fly-fishing, contact Asociación Argentina de Pesca con Mosca (www.aapm.org.ar).

Many anglers use tour agencies based outside Argentina for guided fishing excursions.

Rules & Regulations

In the Lake District and Patagonia, the season runs from November through April or May. In the northeast, the season runs from February to October. Certain lakes and streams on private land may stay open longer.

Trout fishing is almost always mandatory catch and release. Throughout Patagonia (including the Lake District), native species should *always* be thrown back. These are usually smaller than trout and include perca (perch), puyen (common galaxias, a narrow fish native to the southern hemisphere), Patagonian pejerrey and the rare peladilla.

Fishing licenses are required and available at tackle shops, *clubs de caza y pesca* (hunting and fishing clubs), and sometimes at tourist offices and YPF gas stations.

Skiing & Snowboarding

Argentina's mountains have outstanding skiing, offering superb powder and plenty of sunny days. Many resorts have large ski schools with instructors from all over the world, so language is not a problem. At some of the older resorts, equipment can be a little antiquated, but in general the quality of skiing more than compensates.

There are three main snow-sport areas: Mendoza, the Lake District and Ushuaia. Mendoza is near Argentina's premier resort, Las Leñas, which has the best snow and longest runs; the resort Los Penitentes is also nearby. The Lake District is home to several low-key resorts, including Cerro Catedral, near Bariloche, and Cerro Chapelco, near San Martín de los Andes. Although the snow doesn't get as powdery here, the views are superior to Las Leñas.

NORBERTO MARIO LAURIA/SHUTTERSTOCK ©

Paragliding, Bariloche (p356)

And Esquel, further south in Patagonia, has great powder at La Hoya.

The world's most southerly commercial skiing is near Ushuaia. The ski season everywhere generally runs from mid-June to mid-October.

CATCHING THE WIND

From around the world, windsurfing and kiteboarding fanatics drag an insane amount of gear to an isolated spot in the central Andes: Dique Cuesta del Viento, literally 'slope of the wind reservoir.' The reservoir, near the small village of Rodeo in San Juan province, is one of the best wind-sports destinations on the planet. Its consistent and extremely powerful wind blows every afternoon, without fail, from October to early May. We checked it out and it blew us away!

Cycling

Cycling is a popular activity among Argentines, and spandex-clad cyclists are a common sight along many roads (despite a decided lack of bike lanes in the country). There are some outstanding paved routes, especially in the Lake District and, to a lesser extent, in the Andean northwest.

In the northwest, there are several excellent road routes, including the highway from Tucumán to Tafí del Valle, the direct road from Salta to Jujuy, and, arguably most spectacular of all, RN 68, which takes you through the Quebrada de Cafayate. The Central Sierras are also great candidates for cycling, and the mostly paved network of roads rolls past a countryside that is at times reminiscent of Scotland. Mendoza boasts some epic routes through

ALEX EGGERMONT / GETTY IMAGES ©

Top: Las Leñas (p345)

Bottom: Rock climbing in El Chaltén (p445)

SAILING...ON LAND?

In San Juan province's Parque Nacional El Leoncito, the lake bed of Pampa El Leoncito has become the epicenter of *carrovelismo* (land sailing). Here, people zip across the dry lake bed beneath Andean peaks in so-called sail cars. If you're interested, head straight to Barreal.

the Andes, but most are doable only for the seasoned cyclist – those lacking thighs of glory can entertain themselves by pedaling between wineries in Maipú.

In the Lake District's Parque Nacional Nahuel Huapi, there are several excellent loops (including the Circuito Chico) that skirt gorgeous lakes and take in some of Patagonia's most spectacular scenery. Cyclists often take their bikes on the Cruce de Lagos, a famous two-day boat-bus journey across the Andes to Chile.

Patagonia is a popular and mythical destination, with its desolate, beautiful landscapes and wide-open skies. However, be ready for fierce, multidirectional winds and rough gravel roads. Take four-season gear, even in summer, when long days and relatively warm weather make for the best touring. The classic road down here is RN 40, but cycling is tough because of the winds and lack of water; most cyclists alternate sections with Chile's Carretera Austral.

In recent years, Buenos Aires has become a more bike-friendly destination, with an expanding system of dedicated bike lanes, along with a free bike-share program. Mendoza and Córdoba also have some dedicated bike lanes.

Mountain Biking

Mountain biking is fairly undeveloped in Argentina and you'll find few places have true single tracks for mountain bikers. However, at most outdoor hubs (such as Bariloche) you can rent a mountain bike for a day of independent pedaling or for guided mountain-bike rides – a fantastic way to see parts of an area you wouldn't otherwise explore.

Good places with mountain-bike rentals include San Martín de los Andes, Villa la Angostura, Bariloche and El Bolsón in the Lake District; Esquel in Patagonia; Mendoza and Uspallata in Mendoza province; Barreal in San Juan province; Tilcara in the Andean Northwest; and Tandil in La Pampa province.

White-Water Rafting & Kayaking

Currently, Río Mendoza and Río Diamante in Mendoza province are the reigning white-water destinations, while Río Juramento near Salta is an exciting alternative.

If you want great scenery, however, it's all about Patagonia. The Río Hua Hum and Río Meliquina, near San Martín de los Andes, and Río Limay and Río Manso, near Bariloche, are all spectacular. So is Río Aluminé, near wee Aluminé. From the Patagonian town of Esquel, you can join a rafting trip on the incredibly scenic, glacial-fed Río Corcovado. A relatively unknown rafting destination is Barreal, but it's more about the epic Andean scenery than the rapids. Scenic Class II to III floats are possible on most of these rivers, while Class IV runs are possible on the Ríos Mendoza, Diamante, Meliquina, Hua Hum and Corcovado. Experience is generally unnecessary for guided runs.

Kayaking is possible on many of the rivers mentioned, and also around Ushuaia, El Chaltén, Viedma, Puerto Madryn, Paraná, Rosario and Salta. Sea kayakers have options at Río Deseado and the *estancia* (ranch) at Bahía Bustamante.

Paragliding & Skydiving

Paragliding is popular in Argentina and it's a great place to take tandem flights or classes. Many agencies in Bariloche offer paragliding. Tucumán is especially big on this sport, but Salta, La Rioja and Merlo also have options in or near the Andean Northwest. Perhaps the best place is La Cumbre, in Córdoba's Central Sierras, also a thrilling place to try skydiving.

Grilled beef steak (p41)

Plan Your Trip

Eat & Drink Like a Local

Argentines are artists at the grill. Pasta and gnocchi is invariably fresh, while the best pizzas vie with those of New York and Naples. Pair any of this with some fabulous Argentine wines. Mate, that iconic tea, doubles as a social bond between family and friends. And don't skip a scoop or two of gelato, preferably with *dulce de leche*.

Tips for Eating Out

Reservations

Only necessary on weekends at better restaurants (or high season at Mar del Plata or Bariloche, for example).

Budgeting

To save a few bucks at lunch, opt for the *menú del día* or *menú ejecutivo*. These 'set menus' usually include a main dish, dessert and drink.

Large, modern supermarkets are common, and they'll have whatever you need for self-catering, including (usually) a takeout counter.

Paying the Bill

Ask for your bill by saying, *'la cuenta, por favor'* ('the bill, please') or making the 'writing in air' gesture. Some restaurants accept credit cards, but others (usually smaller ones) only take cash. This is especially true outside big cities.

At fancier restaurants, your final bill may arrive with a *cubierto* (small cover charge for bread and use of utensils). This is not a tip, which is usually around 10% and a separate charge.

Staples & Specialties

Beef

When the first Spaniards came to Argentina, they brought cattle. But efforts to establish a colony proved unfruitful, and the herds were abandoned in the pampas. Here the cows found the bovine equivalent of heaven: plenty of lush, fertile grasses on which to feed and few natural predators. After the Europeans recolonized, they bred these cattle with other bovine breeds.

Traditionally, free-range Argentine cows ate nutritious pampas grass and were raised without antibiotics and growth hormones. But this culture is being lost, and today most beef in restaurants comes from feedlots.

Average beef consumption in Argentina is around 59kg per person per year – though in the past, they ate much more.

Italian & Spanish

Thanks to Argentina's Italian heritage, the national cuisine has been highly influenced by Italian immigrants who entered the country during the late 19th century. Along with an animated set of speaking gestures, they brought their love of pasta, pizza, gelato and more.

Many restaurants make their own pasta – look for *pasta casera* (handmade pasta). Some of the varieties of pasta you'll encounter are *ravioles*, *sorrentinos* (large, round pasta parcels similar to ravioli), *ñoquis* (gnocchi) and *tallarines* (fettuccine). Standard sauces include *tuco* (tomato sauce), *estofado* (beef stew, popular with ravioli) and *salsa blanca* (béchamel). Be aware that occasionally the sauce is *not* included in the price of the pasta – you choose and pay for it separately.

Pizza is offered at pizzerias, many with stone or brick ovens, though restaurants offer it too. It's generally excellent and cheap.

Spanish cooking is less popular than Italian, but forms another bedrock of Argentine food. In Spanish restaurants here you'll find paella and other typical Spanish dishes. Most of the country's *guisos* and *pucheros* (types of stew) are descendants from Spain.

Local Specialties

Although *comidas típicas* can refer to any of Argentina's regional dishes, it often refers to food from the Andean Northwest. Food from this region, which has roots in pre-Columbian times, has more in common with the cuisines of Bolivia and Peru than with the Europeanized food of the rest of Argentina. It's frequently spicy and hard to find elsewhere (most Argentines can't tolerate anything spicy). Typical dishes can include everything from *locro* (a hearty corn or mixed-grain stew with meat) and tamales to *humitas* (sweet tamales) and fried empanadas.

In Patagonia, lamb is as common as beef. Along the coast, seafood is a popular choice and includes fish, oysters and king crab – though seafood is often overcooked. In the Lake District, game meats such as venison, wild boar and trout are popular. In the west, the provinces of Mendoza, San Juan and La Rioja pride themselves on *chivito* (young goat). River fish, such as the dorado, pacú (a relative of the piranha) and surubí (a type of catfish), are staples in the northeast.

Snacks

Kioscos (kiosks) are all over town and provide sweets, cookies, ice cream and packaged sandwiches. On the streets, *pancho* (hot dog) and *garrapiñadas* (sugar-roasted peanuts) sellers prepare and sell their treats from carts.

Sandwiches de miga (thin, crustless sandwiches, usually with cheese and ham) are popular tea-time snacks. *Lomitos* (steak sandwiches) are the pinnacle of Argentine sandwiches, while the *choripán* is a classic barbecue sausage sandwich.

Empanadas – small, stuffed turnovers ubiquitous in Argentina – are prepared differently throughout the country (you'll find spicy ground-beef empanadas in the Andean Northwest, while in Patagonia lamb is a common filling). They make for a tasty, quick meal and are especially good for bus travel.

Desserts & Sweets

Two of Argentina's most definitive treats are *dulce de leche* (a creamy milk caramel) and *alfajores* (round, cookie-type sandwiches often covered in chocolate). Each region of Argentina has its own version of the *alfajor*.

Because of Argentina's Italian heritage, Argentine *helado* is comparable to the best ice cream anywhere in the world. There are *heladerías* (ice-cream stores) in every town, where the luscious concoctions will be swirled into a peaked mountain and handed over with a plastic spoon stuck in the side. Don't miss this special treat.

In restaurants, fruit salad and ice cream are often on the menu, while *flan* is a baked custard that comes with either cream or *dulce de leche* topping.

THE SKINNY ON BEEF

You walk into a traditional *parrilla* (steak restaurant), breeze past the sizzling grill at the entrance and sit down. You've never had to choose between more than two or three cuts of steak in your life, but the menu has at least 10 choices. What to do?

If you want to try a bit of everything, go for the *parrillada* (mixed grill). It often includes chorizo (beef or pork sausage), *costillas* (ribs) and *carne* (beef). It can also come with more exotic items such as *chinchulines* (small intestines), *mollejas* (sweetbreads) and *morcilla* (blood sausage). Order a *parrillada* for as many people as you want and the *parrilla* will adjust servings accordingly.

Prime beef cuts include the following:

Bife de chorizo Sirloin; a thick and juicy cut.

Bife de costilla T-bone or Porterhouse steak.

Bife de lomo Tenderloin; a tender though less flavorful piece.

Cuadril Rump steak; often a thin cut.

Ojo de bife Rib eye; a choice smaller morsel.

Tira de asado Short ribs; thin crispy strips of ribs.

Vacío Flank steak; textured, chewy and tasty.

If you don't specify, your steak will be cooked *a punto* (medium to well done). Getting a steak medium rare or rare is more difficult than you'd imagine. If you want a little pink in the center, order it *jugoso*; if you like it truly rare, try *vuelta y vuelta*. Often it comes overcooked, however; try showing your server a photo of a cut steak, cooked the way you want it.

Don't miss *chimichurri*, a tasty sauce often made of olive oil, garlic and parsley. Occasionally you can get *salsa criolla*, a condiment made of diced tomatoes, onion and parsley.

If you're lucky enough to be invited to an *asado* (family or friends' barbecue), do attend – here the art of grilling beef has been perfected, and the social bonding is priceless.

Mate (a tea-like beverage)

Drinks

Nonalcoholic Drinks

Argentines love their coffee, and you can order several versions. A *café con leche* is half coffee and half milk, while a *cortado* is an espresso with a little milk. A *café chico* is an espresso and a *lagrima* is mostly milk with a few drops of coffee.

Té negro or *té común* is black tea; herbal tea is usually *manzanilla* (chamomile). Chocolate lovers should try a *submarino*, a bar of chocolate melted in hot milk. Fresh-squeezed orange juice is *jugo de naranja exprimido*. A *licuado* is fruit blended with milk or water.

Even in big cities like Buenos Aires, the *agua de canilla* (tap water) is drinkable. In restaurants, however, most people order bottled mineral water – ask for *agua con gas* (with bubbles) or *agua sin gas* (without). In older, more traditional restaurants, carbonated water in a spritzer bottle (*un sifón de soda*) is a great for drinking. *Gaseosas* (soft drinks) are very popular in Argentina.

Alcoholic Drinks

Mendoza is Argentina's premier wine region and well known for its robust malbec, but other provinces also produce excellent wines. San Juan is famous for its syrah and Cafayate for its torrontés, a crisp, dry white wine. Meanwhile, the Patagonia region is becoming a stronghouse for pinot noir.

If Argentina has a national beer, it's Quilmes. Order a *porrón* and you'll get bottled beer (a half-liter bottle in BA; a big bottle up north); a *chopp* is a mug of draft.

Most fine restaurants have a wine list, called *la carta de vinos*. Sommeliers are scarce. At the harder end of the spectrum, it's all about Fernet Branca, a bitter, herbed Italian digestif originally intended as medicine. Fernet con Coke is Argentina's favorite cocktail and, despite claims that it won't give you hangover, it will (trust us).

Where to Eat & Drink

Restaurants are generally open from noon to 3.30pm for lunch and 8pm or 9pm to midnight for dinner, though exact hours will vary depending on the restaurant.

For the best meats, head to a *parrilla* (steak restaurant). *Panaderías* are bakeries. *Confiterías* (cafes serving light meals) are open all day and into the night, and often have a long list of both food and drinks. Cafes, bars and pubs usually have a more limited range of snacks and meals available, though some can offer full meals. A *tenedor libre* (literally, 'free fork') is an all-you-can-eat restaurant; quality is usually decent, but a minimum-drink purchase is often mandatory and costs extra.

Argentines eat little for breakfast – usually just a coffee with *medialunas* (croissants – either *de manteca*, sweet, or *de grasa*, plain). *Tostadas* (toast) with *manteca* (butter) or *mermelada* (jam) is an alternative, as are *facturas* (pastries). Higher-end hotels and B&Bs tend to offer heartier breakfasts.

Vegetarians & Vegans

Health foods, organic products and vegetarian restaurants are available in Argentina's biggest cities, but outside of them you'll have to search harder. A recent surge in alternative diets means that more gluten-free and vegan options are now available, though selections will seem poor compared to North America or Europe.

Most restaurant menus include a few vegetarian choices, and pastas are a nearly ubiquitous option. Pizzerias and *empanaderías* (empanada shops) are good bets – look for empanadas made with *acelga* (chard) and *choclo* (corn). If you're stuck at a *parrilla*, your choices will be salads, omelets, pasta, baked potatoes, *provoleta* (a thick slice of grilled provolone cheese) and roasted vegetables. *Pescado* (fish) and *mariscos* (seafood) are sometimes available for pescatarians.

Sin carne means 'without meat,' and the words *soy vegetariano/a* ('I'm a vegetarian') will come in handy when explaining to an Argentine why you don't eat their nation's renowned steaks.

The word for vegan is *vegano/a*. Vegans can be challenged in Argentina. Make sure homemade pasta doesn't include egg, and that bread or vegetables aren't cooked in lard (*grasa*; *manteca* means butter in Argentina). Some breads are made with milk or cheese. You'll need to be creative. One tip: look for accommodations offering kitchen use. Good luck.

MATE & ITS RITUAL

The preparation and consumption of mate (pronounced mah-tay) is more than a simple drink. It's an elaborate ritual shared among family, friends and coworkers.

Yerba mate is the dried, chopped leaf of Ilex paraguayensis, a relative of the common holly. Argentina is one of the world's largest producers and consumers of the stuff, and its citizens down an average of 5kg per person per year.

Preparing and drinking mate is a ritual in itself. One person, the cebador (server), fills the mate gourd almost to the top with yerba, and then slowly pours hot water as he or she fills the gourd. The cebador then passes the mate to each drinker, who sips the liquid through the bombilla, a silver straw with a filter at the end. Each participant drinks the gourd dry each time. Remember it's bad form to touch the bombilla, and don't hold the mate too long before passing it on! A simple 'gracias' will tell the server to pass you by.

An invitation to partake in mate is a cultural treat and not to be missed, although the drink is an acquired taste and novices will find it very hot and bitter at first (adding sugar can be an option).

Mate is rarely served in restaurants or cafes, but you can buy a thermos, mate gourd, bombilla and a bag of herb at any large supermarket. Cure your gourd by filling it with hot water and yerba and letting it soak for 24 hours. Nearly all restaurants, cafes and hotels are used to filling thermoses, sometimes charging a small amount. Simply whip out your thermos and ask: '¿Podía calentar agua para mate?' ('Would you mind heating water for mate?'). And start making friends.

Top: Empanadas (p41)

Bottom: *Alfajores* (cookie-type sandwiches, p41)

Plan Your Trip

Travel with Children

Argentina has plenty to offer little ones, from dinosaur museums to beach resorts and plenty of outdoor activities to use up all that extra energy. With a culture that is very family-friendly, you'll find Argentina makes a good, interesting and, yes, at times challenging, but fun, family destination.

Argentina for Kids

Argentina is remarkably child-friendly in terms of general travel safety and people's attitudes toward families. This is a country where family comes first.

Argentine parents will often send unaccompanied pre-adolescents on errands or neighborly visits. While you're not likely to do this, you can usually count on your children's safety in public.

Argentina's numerous plazas and public parks, many with playgrounds, are popular gathering spots for families. Argentines frequently touch each other, so your children may be patted on the head by friendly strangers. Kids are a great ice-breaker and certainly make it easier for you to meet the locals.

And remember that families stay out very late in this country – it's common to see young kids and babies out past midnight with their parents. There's no early curfew and everyone's out having fun, so consider doing the same!

Best Regions for Kids

Buenos Aires

Argentina's capital provides plenty of museums, parks and shopping malls, many with fun areas for kids.

Atlantic Coast

Beaches and more beaches – bring swimsuits and sunscreen, and start building castles. Wildlife watching is also a plus.

Iguazú

Waterfalls and wildlife galore, plus thrilling boat rides that guarantee a fun soaking.

Península Valdés

Rich with wildlife, such as splashy whales, smelly elephant seals and supercute penguins.

Bariloche

Outdoor activities are the draw here – go hiking, rock climbing, horseback riding and rafting.

Mendoza

Wine tasting is off-limits for the kids, but you can take them skiing and white-water rafting.

Children's Highlights

Watching Wildlife

Güirá Oga (p195) Zoo in the Iguazú Falls area.

Parque Esteros del Iberá (p172) Full of marsh deer, black caimans and adorable capybaras.

Península Valdés (p408) Check out whales, elephant seals and suit-wearing penguins.

Jardín de los Niños (p149) Rosario's fun discovery park offers activities and puzzles for the little ones.

Energy Burners

Parque de la Costa (p111) Theme-park fun ust outside BA in Tigre.

Complejo Termal Cacheuta (p333) Outside Mendoza; is a thermal-baths complex with wave pool and waterslides.

The Andes mountains Offer great skiing around Bariloche and Mendoza.

Rainy Days

Museo Paleontológico Egidio Feruglio (p415) Kids can overnight in their pajamas at Trelew's dinosaur museum.

Museo de La Plata (p115) Argentina's best natural history museum; the taxidermy and skeletons are especially awesome.

Glaciarium (p456) El Calafate's slickest museum; highlights the wonders of glaciers.

Shopping centers The bigger ones often have playgrounds, video arcades, toy stores and ice-cream shops.

Museo Municipal Ernesto Bachmann (p396) Marvel at the world's largest predator, as well as the spectacular skeletons of other locally found dinosaurs.

Outdoor Fun

Glaciar Perito Moreno (p464) El Calafate's superactive glacier is a wonder to behold for all ages.

Beaches Argentina's Atlantic coast beaches are family-friendly, and offer up plenty of sand, surf and sun.

Estancias Horseback rides and folkloric shows are highlights during your stay on an *estancia* (ranch).

Planning

➡ Outdoor activities are best experienced outside the winter months of June through August (with the exception of skiing, of course).

➡ Small kids often get discounts on such things as motel stays, museum admissions and restaurant meals.

➡ Supermarkets offer a decent selection of baby food, infant formulas, disposable diapers, wet wipes and other necessities. Big pharmacies such as Farmacity also stock some of these items.

➡ Strollers on crowded and uneven sidewalks can be a liability, so consider bringing a baby carrier.

➡ Public bathrooms are often poorly maintained, and baby changing tables are not common.

➡ For all-round information and advice, check out Lonely Planet's *Travel with Children*.

Sleeping

➡ The great majority of hotels accept children without any problems; the most upscale may even offer babysitting services.

➡ The only places with possible minimum age restrictions are small boutique hotels or guesthouses.

➡ Hostels are usually not the best environment for kids, but a few welcome them.

➡ During summer, reserving a hotel with a pool can be a good idea. Also look for places with kitchenettes.

➡ Apartments are available, especially in BA; in less-urban holiday destinations you can look for *cabañas* (cabins) with full kitchens.

➡ Larger campgrounds often have *cabañas*, common cooking facilities and sometimes play structures.

Eating

➡ Most restaurants offer a selection of food suitable for children, such as vegetables, pasta, pizza, chicken and *milanesas* (breaded meat cutlets).

➡ Empanadas make good, healthy snacks that are fun to eat, and don't forget to take the kids out for ice cream – it's a real Argentine treat!

Regions at a Glance

As the eighth-largest country in the world, Argentina boasts nearly every kind of environment, from glaciated mountain peaks and cacti-dotted deserts, to wildlife-dense swamplands and shrubby, arid steppes. Outdoor-fun-seekers will find their blissful adventures, beachcombers their warm stretches of sand and wine lovers their luscious vineyards.

The bigger cities, such as Buenos Aires and Córdoba, boast endless nightlife, entertainment, shopping and restaurants, along with doses of culture, such as excellent museums, tango dance halls and colonial history. Argentina offers pretty much everything you might be looking for in a destination, so choose your desires, set aside enough time to experience them all, and just take off!

Buenos Aires

Food
Nightlife
Tango

Steaks & More

There are plenty of fine steak houses in Buenos Aires. But you'll also find trendsetters banking on the latest international tendencies as well as ethnic restaurants serving up cuisines from China to the Middle East.

Burn the Midnight Oil

After dinner – which often ends after midnight on weekends – *porteños* (Buenos Aires residents) head out for a drink, then hit the nightclubs after 2am. Other events happen at a more 'reasonable' hour, but you get the idea – this city is nocturnal.

Sultry Dancing

Ah, the tango. There's no denying the attraction of this sexy dance. And BA boasts countless dance venues and classes, along with world-class competitions. Put on your dancing shoes and get ready to fall in love. It all started here.

p52

The Pampas & the Atlantic Coast

Beaches
Gauchos
Hiking

Life's a Beach

In January, coastal cities such as Mar del Plata, Pinamar and Necochea become heaving hubs of sun-bronzed Argentines lying on hot sands during the day and partying all night long.

Gaucho Culture

This quintessential icon's heyday was centuries ago, but today the culture is kept alive in San Antonio de Areco, where an annual festival celebrates gaucho life. You can also visit an *estancia* (ranch), where horseback riding, gaucho demonstrations and *asados* (barbecues) are highlights.

Hiking & Landscapes

The ancient, worn-down mountain ranges of the Pampas aren't as spectacular as the youthful Andes. But around Sierra de la Ventana are some hikes offering dramatic views of surrounding landscapes – including one where you peek through a rock 'window.'

p113

Iguazú Falls & the Northeast

Water Features
Wildlife
Historic Missions

Wide Rivers, Mighty Iguazú

Towns and cities along the region's two major rivers often boast great waterside strips for boating, strolling, eating and partying, while large fish attract anglers. Up north, Iguazú, the world's most impressive waterfalls, will leave you in awe.

Cute Capybaras

The Esteros del Iberá wetlands hold an astonishing wealth of creatures, including snapping caimans, colorful birdlife and roly-poly capybaras. A long hop north, Iguazú's national park and jungle ecosystem is equally rich in distinct wildlife species.

Jesuit Ruins

Built by Jesuits in the 17th and 18th centuries, remote *reducciones* (missions) were created to educate, evangelize and protect local Guaraní populations. They flourished for about 150 years before the Jesuits' expulsion left the missions exposed to slave raids and colonization.

p145

Salta & the Andean Northwest

Indigenous Culture
Colonial Cities
Activities

Before Columbus

The northwestern peoples witnessed the Inca; then the Spanish arrived. Centuries later, the ruins of cities remain, but the food, daily life and handicrafts speak of a persisting, living and changing culture.

Historical Towns

The northwestern cities are Argentina's oldest, and there's an unmistakable time-honored feel to them. Venerable churches, stately facades and handsome plazas planted with lofty trees – together with the relaxed pace of life – give these places an ambience unlike any other.

Out & About

The Andes dominate the geography here and boast excellent climbing, walking and 4WD excursions. But there are also subtropical national parks replete with bird and animal life, and top-notch hang gliding and paragliding offer the opportunity to see how things look from above.

p214

Córdoba & the Central Sierras

Historic Buildings
Nightlife
Paragliding

Oldies but Goodies

The Jesuit legacy in Córdoba extends beyond winemaking and higher education – they also constructed some fabulous buildings. Córdoba city boasts an entire block of well-preserved Jesuit architecture, and further examples are scattered around the province.

Bring on the Night

Catch an independent movie or a play, dance the night away or grab a few quiet drinks in a cozy bar – whatever you're looking for, Córdoba's young population and vibrant cultural scene make finding it a snap.

Take to the Skies

If you've ever even been vaguely tempted to try paragliding, this is the place to do it – the world-famous launch sites of La Cumbre and Merlo are home to scores of instructors offering tandem flights that will have you soaring with the condors.

p282

Mendoza & the Central Andes

Wine
Mountains
Rafting

Hear It on the Grapevine

Get to the heart of Argentina's magnificent wine culture by visiting the vineyards, talking to the winemakers and seeing how it all comes together, from planting the vine to tasting the final, delicious product.

Lofty Ambitions

Snowcapped year-round and dominating the horizon, the Andes are one of Argentina's iconic images. Get up close and personal with them by climbing Aconcagua, the Americas' highest peak, or hitting the slopes in Mendoza's world-class ski resorts.

Wet & Wild

All that snowmelt from the Andes does more than just irrigate the grapevines. It also feeds a couple of rivers that gush down from the mountains, giving rafters the ride of their lives.

p313

Bariloche & the Lake District

Activities
Village Life
Paleontology

Get Out There

There's always something to do in the Lake District, a true year-round destination. Powder hounds hit the slopes in season at the province's top-notch ski resorts while the rest of the year the mountain trails, hikers' refuges and expansive vistas make it a trekker's paradise.

Kicking Back

One of the joys of traveling through this region is discovering small alpine villages nestled in the forest, surrounded by breathtaking mountain scenery – the perfect remedy for big-city blues.

Jurassic Parks

Some truly huge animals used to roam these parts – including the world's largest dinosaur and the world's largest carnivore. The sites where they were discovered are open to the public to teach a humbling lesson in size.

p354

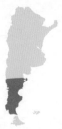

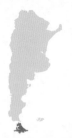

Patagonia

Hiking
Wildlife Watching
Adventure

Wild Hiking

Iconic hikes around Fitz Roy and Torres del Paine bring deserved fame to the trails of Patagonia. But if you have time, check out the millennial forests of Parque Nacional Los Alerces and the electric turquoise lakes of ultra-remote Parque Nacional Perito Moreno.

Wildlife on the Steppe

Abundant marine life makes the coast, and Península Valdés in particular, the hub for watching wildlife, but there's also the subtle allure of Patagonia's guanaco herds, soaring condors and ñandús that sprint across the steppe.

Real Adventure

Riding on an *estancia,* driving RN 40, glacier chasing or just getting deep into the Andean wilderness: Patagonia is all about unfettered freedom and the allure of the unexpected.

p399

Tierra del Fuego

Hiking
Sea Travel
Winter Sports

Hoof It

Austral summer's long days make for backpacking bliss. Alpine lagoons and snowy basins comprise an iconic Fuegian trek. For a quick dose of big nature, hit the enchanted forests of Parque Nacional Tierra del Fuego.

Set Sail

You don't have to round Cape Horn to find magic in these southern seas. Sail the Beagle Channel in search of marine life and indigenous ruins, boat through the Chilean fjords or paddle a sea kayak.

Winter Wonderland

Brave a winter journey to the frozen ends of the earth. From June to October, snow makes Ushuaia adventure central. Whoosh down the slopes of Cerro Castor, ski cross-country or race across the snowdrifts driven by sled dogs. Crackling bonfires, seafood banquets and comfy lodges cap the day.

p491

Uruguay

Beaches
Estancias
Food & Wine

A Beach for Every Taste

Beachside bliss wears many faces on Uruguay's Atlantic coast: chasing the perfect surf break at La Pedrera, getting friendly with sea lions at Cabo Polonio or scanning the sands for international celebrities at Punta del Este.

Wide Open Skies

Uruguay's gaucho soul lies in its vast interior landscapes. For a taste of traditional ranch life, spend a few nights on an *estancia,* riding horseback into an endless horizon by day and savoring the warmth of the fire and the brilliance of the stars by night.

Dinner's all Fired Up

Something's always grilling in Uruguay. The classic *parrillada* (mixed grill) of steak, pork chops, *chorizo* and *morcilla* (blood sausage) is enough to make any carnivore swoon, especially when accompanied by a glass of tannat from one of the country's up-and-coming wineries.

p516

On the Road

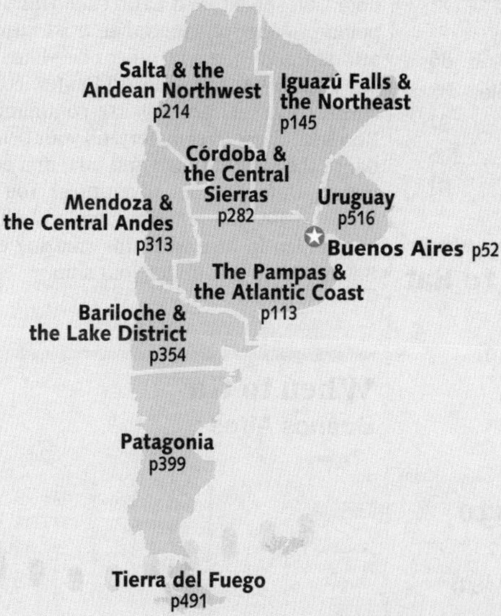

Salta & the Andean Northwest p214
Iguazú Falls & the Northeast p145
Córdoba & the Central Sierras p282
Mendoza & the Central Andes p313
Uruguay p516
Buenos Aires p52
The Pampas & the Atlantic Coast p113
Bariloche & the Lake District p354
Patagonia p399
Tierra del Fuego p491

Buenos Aires

Includes ➡

Best Places to Eat

- Café San Juan (p89)
- La Carnicería (p91)
- i Latina (p92)
- Cadore (p87)

Best Places to Stay

- Poetry Building (p84)
- Faena Hotel + Universe (p82)
- Magnolia Hotel (p85)
- Casa Calma (p82)
- Le Petit Palais (p85)

Why Go?

Buenos Aires combines faded colonial architecture with Latin passion. Whip together a beautiful metropolis with gourmet cuisine, a packed cultural agenda and frenzied nightlife – and you get Buenos Aires. It's a rough-hewn mix of Paris' architecture, Rome's traffic and Madrid's late-night hours, all spiked with Latin American flavor. BA is cosmopolitan, seductive, emotional, frustrating and chock-full of attitude, and there's no other place like it in the world. Seek out classic BA: the old-world cafes, colonial architecture, curious markets and diverse communities. Visit Evita at Recoleta's famous cemetery, fill your belly with tasty steaks, dance the soulful tango and take in a crazy *fútbol* (soccer) match. Unforgettable adventures? You'd better believe it. Come to BA and you'll understand why so many people have fallen in love with this amazing city. Sexy and alive, Buenos Aires gets under your skin.

When to Go

Buenos Aires

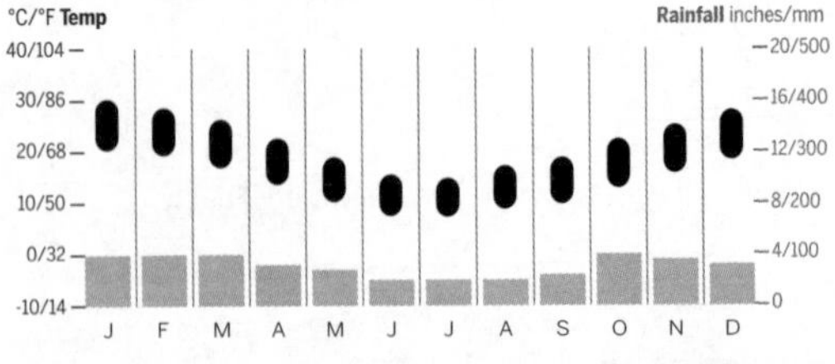

Oct-Dec Spring and early summer mean warm days to enjoy outdoor restaurant patios and bars.

Aug Winter's peak brings BA's tango festival; or visit museums, art galleries and cultural centers.

Mar-May Explore BA during fall's pleasant days.

History

Buenos Aires was first settled in 1536 by Spaniard Pedro de Mendoza, but food shortages and attacks by indigenous groups prompted his hasty departure in 1537. Meanwhile, other expedition members left the settlement, sailed 1600km upriver and founded Asunción (now the capital of Paraguay). Then in 1580 a new groups of settlers moved back south and repopulated Mendoza's abandoned outpost.

For the next 196 years BA was a backwater and smuggler's paradise due to trade restrictions imposed by mother Spain. All the same, its population had grown to around 20,000 by 1776, the year Spain decreed the city as capital of the new viceroyalty of Río de la Plata.

BA's *cabildo* (town council) cut ties with Spain on May 1810, but decades of power struggles between BA and the other former viceregal provinces ensued, escalating into civil war. Finally, in 1880 the city was declared the federal territory of Buenos Aires and the nation's capital.

Agricultural exports soared for the next few decades, which resulted in great wealth accumulating in the city. Well-heeled *porteños* (Buenos Aires citizens) built opulent French-style mansions, immigrants arrived from Europe in their millions, and the government spent lavishly on public works. But the boom times didn't last. The 1929 Wall Street crash dealt a big blow to the country's markets, and soon the first of many military coups took over. It was the end of Argentina's Golden Age.

Poverty, unemployment, decaying infrastructure, a series of military dictatorships and a roller-coaster economy beset the city in the following decades, but Argentina continues to bounce back. Today BA remains a vibrant city with resilient and adaptable citizens – just like their ancestral settlers.

Sights

Ever since Juan de Garay came ashore from his ship in 1580, founding Buenos Aires for the second time, the area that is now Plaza de Mayo has been Buenos Aires' symbolic and political heart. The city's key institutions – political (the Casa Rosada), economic and religious – remain in the same location to this day; naturally, you'll find some of the city's best museums and important historical sights in this area, with further key political buildings lying on the other side of superwide Av 9 de Julio.

To the south, the neighborhoods of San Telmo and La Boca have color and grit as well as some cutting-edge art galleries and atmospheric streets and plazas. The docks of La Boca were abandoned in favor of Puerto Madero, a relatively new neighborhood with a couple of museums and a nature reserve nearby.

The flavor changes as you go north to Retiro and Recoleta, past the vast mansions built by Argentina's elite at the peak of the country's wealth, to the equally elaborate tombs in Recoleta Cemetery they commissioned to house them in death. Continue north and you'll reach Palermo, where the main sights surround the neighborhood's green parks.

The Center

Buenos Aires' Center (geographically on the edge of the city and not in the middle) is where endless lines of business suits move hastily along the narrow streets in the shadow of skyscrapers and old European buildings. Stretching from Retiro to San Telmo, this downtown area is the heart and brains of the city, and is made up of the sub-neighborhoods of the Microcentro and Montserrat.

★Plaza de Mayo PLAZA

(Map p58; cnr Av de Mayo & San Martín; Línea A Plaza de Mayo) Surrounded by the Casa Rosada, the Cabildo and the city's main cathedral, Plaza de Mayo is the place where Argentines gather in vehement protest or jubilant celebration. At the center is the **Pirámide de Mayo**, a white obelisk built to mark the first anniversary of independence from Spain.

If you happen to be here on Thursday at 3:30pm, you'll see the Madres de la Plaza de Mayo gather and circle the pyramid, holding photographs of their missing children. These mothers of the 'disappeared' (Argentines abducted by the state during the military dictatorship of 1976 to 1983) continue to march as a reminder of the past and for other social justice causes.

★Casa Rosada NOTABLE BUILDING

(Pink House; Map p58; 011-4344-3804; https://visitas.casarosada.gob.ar; Plaza de Mayo; tours in Spanish 10am-6pm Sat & Sun, in English 12:30pm & 2:30pm Sat & Sun; Línea A Plaza de Mayo) FREE On the eastern side of Plaza de Mayo stands the Casa Rosada, named for its distinctive

Buenos Aires Highlights

1. **Cementerio de la Recoleta** (p69) Meandering through narrow lanes lined with elaborate mausoleums.
2. **Tango** (p99) Experiencing the sensual and melancholy dance at an authentic *milonga*, such as La Catedral.
3. **La Bombonera Stadium** (p69) Braving the crowds to embrace the excitement of a *fútbol* game.
4. **Grilled meats** (p91) Savoring a steak dinner at one of BA's many *parrillas* (steak houses), such as Don Julio.
5. **Plaza de Mayo** (p53) Absorbing some history and seeing the President's office.
6. **San Telmo** (p63) Wandering the cobbled streets and shopping for antiques.
7. **Street Art** (p80) Admiring the city's graffiti and murals.
8. **Palermo's Parks** (p72) Exploring BA's greenery on two wheels.
9. **Reserva Ecológica Costanera Sur** (p60) Taking a nature walk in the shadow of Puerto Madero's skyscrapers.
10. **Feria de Mataderos** (p81) Celebrating country traditions at this folk market and fair.

0 2 km
0 1 mile
Río de la Plata
Pier
Av Costanera R Obligado
Aliscafos (Hydrofoils)
Estación Saldías
PALERMO CHICO
Av del Libertador
Av Figueroa Alcorta
Estación Maritima
Av General Las Heras
See Retiro, Recoleta & Barrio Norte Map (p70)
RECOLETA
Dársena A
1 Cementerio de la Recoleta
Av del Libertador
Retiro
Austria
Av Callao
BARRIO NORTE
Av 9 de Julio
RETIRO
Av Eduardo Madero
Dársena Norte
Gallo
Av Santa Fe
Florida
Av Córdoba
Av Córdoba
TRIBUNALES
Av Pueyrredón
Av Corrientes
MICROCENTRO
Laguna de las Gaviolas
Av Int Hernan M Giralt
ONCE
5 Plaza de Mayo
Reserva Ecológica Costanera Sur
Estación Once
Pasco
Av de Mayo
Plaza Miserere
Alberti
CONGRESO
Av Paseo Colón
Laguna de los Patos
9 Reserva Ecológica
BALVANERA
Av Belgrano
Av 9 de Julio
Av Ing Huergo
MONTSERRAT
Reserva Ecológica Costanera Sur (southern entrance)
Av Independencia
See The Center, Congreso & San Telmo Map (p58)
San Telmo 6
PUERTO MADERO
Club Gricel
General Urquiza
Jujuy
Pichincha
CONSTITUCIÓN
See La Boca Map (p65)
Av Brasil
Av Entre Ríos
Av Juan de Garay
Estación Constitución
Bernardo de Irigoyen
Autopista La Plata–Buenos Aires
Dársena Sur
Av Martín García
Av Almirante Brown
Av Jujuy
LA BOCA
Av Patricios
3 La Bombonera Stadium
Av Chiclana
Av Caseros
Av Amancio Alcorta
BARRACAS
Brandsen

color. It was from the balcony here that Eva Perón famously addressed the throngs of impassioned supporters packed into Plaza de Mayo. The building houses the Argentine President's offices; the presidential residence is in the suburb of Olivos, north of the center. Free hour-long guided tours are given at weekends and must be booked online in advance; bring ID.

One theory goes that the Casa Rosada's pink hue represented President Sarmiento's attempts to make peace during his 1868–74 term (by blending the red of the Federalists with the white of the Unitarians), but the more likely explanation is that it was caused by mixing white paint with bovine blood, a common practice in the late 19th century.

The building occupies the site where colonial riverbank fortifications once stood; today, however, after repeated landfills, the palace stands more than 1km inland. The Museo Casa Rosada is located behind the palace.

Museo Casa Rosada MUSEUM

(Map p58; 011-4344-3802; cnr Av Paseo Colón & Hipólito Yrigoyen; 10am-6pm Wed-Sun; Línea A Plaza de Mayo) FREE Behind the Casa Rosada you'll notice a glass wedge that's the roof of this bright and airy museum, housed within the brick vaults of the old *aduana* (customs house). Head down into the open space, which has over a dozen side rooms, each dedicated to a different era of Argentina's tumultuous political history. There are videos (in Spanish) and a few artifacts to see, along with an impressive restored mural by Mexican artist David Alfaro Siqueiros.

Catedral Metropolitana CATHEDRAL

(Map p58; 7:30am-6:30pm Mon-Fri, 9am-6:45pm Sat & Sun, museum 10am-1:30pm Mon-Fri; Línea D Catedral) This cathedral was built on the site of the original colonial church and not finished until 1827. It's a significant religious and architectural landmark, and carved above its triangular facade and neoclassical columns are bas-reliefs of Jacob and Joseph. The spacious interior is equally impressive, with baroque details and an elegant rococo altar. There's a small museum (AR$50) dedicated to the cathedral's history. For Pope Francis souvenirs, visit the small gift shop near the entrance.

The cathedral is also a national historical site that contains the **mausoleum of General José de San Martín**, Argentina's most revered hero, who led the country to independence in 1816. In the chaos that followed, San Martín chose exile in France, never again returning to Argentina; his remains were brought to Buenos Aires in 1880, 30 years after his death. Outside the cathedral you'll see a flame keeping his spirit alive.

Cabildo MUSEUM

(Map p58; 011-4342-6729; https://cabildonacional.cultura.gob.ar; Bolívar 65; 10:30am-5pm Tue, Wed & Fri, to 8pm Thu, to 6pm Sat & Sun; Línea A Perú) FREE This mid-18th-century town hall building is now an interesting museum largely dedicated to the revolution of May 1810, when Argentina declared independence. Exhibits cover the history of the Cabildo during colonial times (when it was also a prison) through to the British invasions of 1806 and 1807 and independence three years later. There are good views of Plaza de Mayo from the 2nd-floor balcony.

Manzana de las Luces NOTABLE BUILDING

(Block of Enlightenment; Map p58; 011-4342-6973; Perú 222; 10am-7:30pm Mon-Fri, 2-8pm Sat & Sun; Línea E Bolívar) FREE In colonial times, the Manzana de las Luces was Buenos Aires' most important center of culture and learning and today the block still symbolizes education and enlightenment. Two of the five original buildings remain; Jesuit defensive tunnels were discovered in 1912. Tours in Spanish (AR$50) are given at 3pm daily and also at 4:30pm and 6pm at weekends, but you can go inside and see the main patio area for free.

★Centro Cultural Kirchner CULTURAL CENTER

(Map p58; 0800-333-9300; www.culturalkirchner.gob.ar; Sarmiento 151; 1-8pm Wed-Sun; Línea B Alem) FREE It was Néstor Kirchner who, in 2005, first proposed turning the abandoned former central post office into a cultural center. He died in 2010 before the project was completed, but the breathtaking cultural center was named in his honor. Within the vast beaux-arts structure – which stands eight stories tall and takes up an entire city block – are multiple art galleries, events spaces and auditoriums. The highlight, however, is the Ballena Azul, a concert hall with world-class acoustics that seats 1800.

The original building, which was modeled on New York City's main post office, took nearly 30 years to complete (in 1928).

BUENOS AIRES IN...

Two Days

Start with a stroll in **San Telmo** and duck into some antiques stores. Walk north to **Plaza de Mayo** (p53) for a bit of history, then wander the **City Center**, perhaps veering east to **Puerto Madero** – a great spot for a break.

Keep heading northward into **Retiro** and **Recoleta**, stopping off at the **Museo Nacional de Bellas Artes** (p71) to admire some impressionism. Be sure to visit the **Cementerio de la Recoleta** (p69), to commune with BA's bygone elite. For dinner and nightlife, **Palermo Viejo** is hard to beat.

On day two take in the **Congreso** neighborhood or head to **La Boca**. Shop in **Palermo Viejo** and at night catch a **tango show** or a performance at the **Teatro Colón** (p62).

Four Days

On your third day consider taking a day trip to **Tigre**. On the fourth day you can take a **tango lesson**, check out **Palermo's parks** or head to the **Feria de Mataderos** (p81), if it's a weekend. Be sure to find yourself a good steak restaurant for your last meal.

Restoration for the cultural center began in 2009 and it opened in May 2015. The architects used glass and stainless steel to maintain and add to the beauty of the original structure.

The result is one of BA's grandest buildings, and it's well worth a visit. It's free to enter and there may be exhibitions to see that don't require tickets, but there are a host of activities (such as yoga and dance classes as well as concerts) that are free but ticketed – check the website to see what's on and act quickly if you want to book. Free guided tours of the center in Spanish are given at 2pm and 3:30pm at weekends with advance online bookings.

Museo Etnográfico Juan B Ambrosetti MUSEUM

(Map p58; ☎011-5287-3050; www.museoetnografico.filo.uba.ar; Moreno 350; adult/child AR$30/free; ⏲1-7pm Tue-Fri, 3-7pm Sat & Sun; Ⓢ Línea A Plaza de Mayo) This worthwhile anthropological museum was created by Juan B Ambrosetti not only as an institute for research and university training but also as an educational center for the public. On display are archaeological and anthropological collections from the Andean Northwest and Patagonia. Beautiful indigenous costumes are also featured, while an African and Asian room showcases some priceless pieces.

Galerías Pacífico NOTABLE BUILDING

(Map p58; ☎011-5555-5110; www.galeriaspacifico.com.ar; cnr Florida & Av Córdoba; ⏲10am-9pm, food court to 10pm; Ⓢ Línea B Florída) Covering an entire city block, this beautiful building inspired by Le Bon Marché in Paris has fulfilled the commercial purpose that its designers envisioned when they constructed it in 1889. Galerías Pacífico is now a shopping center – dotted with lovely fairy lights at night – and boasts upscale stores along with a large food court. Self-guided audio tours are available in English and Spanish; inquire at the information kiosk. The excellent Centro Cultural Borges (p98) takes up the top floor.

Museo Mitre MUSEUM

(Map p58; ☎011-4394-8240; www.museomitre.gob.ar; San Martín 336; ⏲1-5:30pm Mon-Fri; Ⓢ Línea B Florida) FREE This museum is located in the colonial house where Bartolomé Mitre – Argentina's first legitimate president elected under the constitution of 1853 – resided with his family from 1859 to 1906. Mitre's term ran from 1862 to 1868, and he spent much of it leading the country's armies against Paraguay. Two courtyards, salons, an office, a billiards room and Mitre's old bedroom are part of this complex. Since part of the museum is open-air, it sometimes closes when it rains.

Museo Histórico y Numismático Héctor Carlos Janson MUSEUM

(Central Bank Museum; Map p58; ☎011-4348-3882; www.bcra.gov.ar; San Martín 216; ⏲10am-4pm Mon-Fri; Ⓢ Línea D Catedral) FREE Housed in the former Buenos Aires Stock Exchange (1862), this interesting little museum tells the story of Argentina through its money.

The Center, Congreso & San Telmo

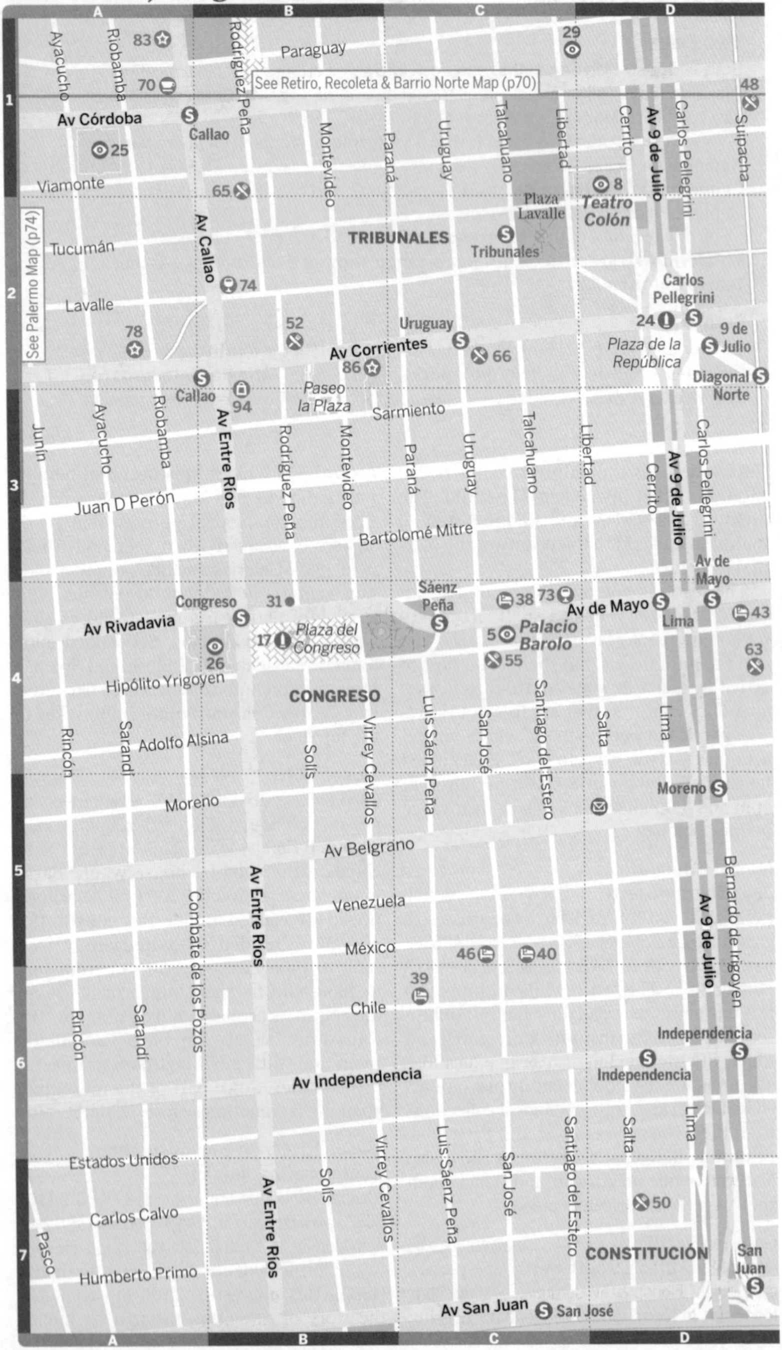

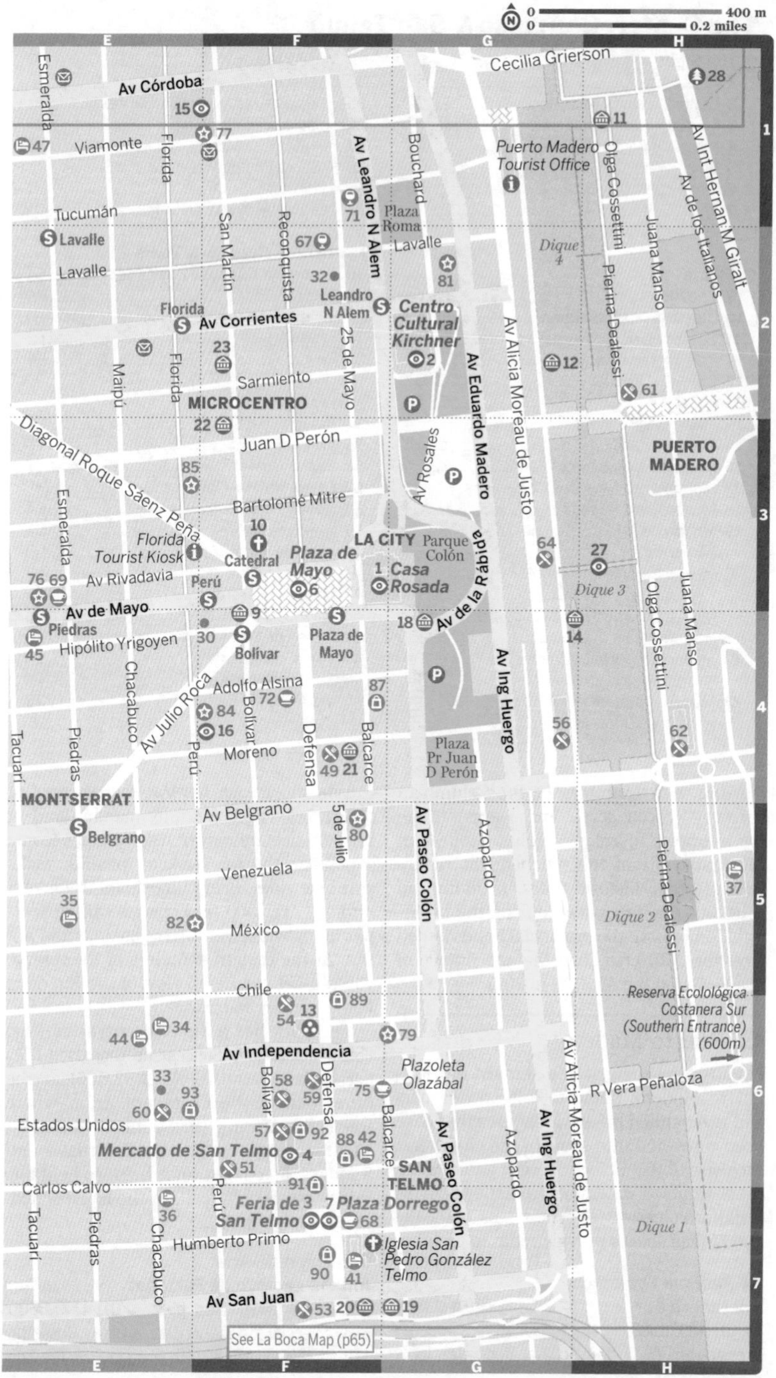
0
400 m
0
0.2 miles
E
F
G
H
1
2
3
4
5
6
7
Av Córdoba
Cecilia Grierson
Esmeralda
15
77
11
28
47
Viamonte
Florida
Av Leandro N Alem
Bouchard
Puerto Madero Tourist Office
Olga Cossettini
Av Int Hernan M Giralt
Av de los Italianos
Tucumán
San Martín
Reconquista
71
Plaza Roma
Lavalle
67
Lavalle
Dique 4
Pierina Dealessi
Juana Manso
32
81
Leandro N Alem
Centro Cultural Kirchner
Florida
Av Corrientes
23
2
Av Eduardo Madero
Av Alicia Moreau de Justo
25 de Mayo
Maipú
Sarmiento
12
61
MICROCENTRO
22
Juan D Perón
Av Rosales
PUERTO MADERO
Diagonal Roque Sáenz Peña
85
Bartolomé Mitre
10
LA CITY
Parque Colón
64
27
Florida Tourist Kiosk
Catedral
Plaza de Mayo
1
Casa Rosada
Av de la Rábida
76
69
Av Rivadavia
Perú
6
Dique 3
Av de Mayo
9
18
14
Piedras
30
Bolívar
Plaza de Mayo
45
Hipólito Yrigoyen
Chacabuco
Av Ing Huergo
Adolfo Alsina
72
87
Av Julio Roca
84
16
56
62
Tacuarí
Piedras
Moreno
Defensa
Balcarce
49
21
Plaza Pr Juan D Perón
MONTSERRAT
Av Belgrano
5 de Julio
80
Belgrano
Av Paseo Colón
Azopardo
Venezuela
37
35
82
México
Dique 2
Chile
89
13
54
Reserva Ecolológica Costanera Sur (Southern Entrance) (600m)
34
44
79
Av Independencia
Plazoleta Olazábal
33
58
59
75
R Vera Peñaloza
93
60
Estados Unidos
57
92
88
42
Mercado de San Telmo
4
51
SAN TELMO
Carlos Calvo
91
36
Feria de San Telmo
3
7
Plaza Dorrego
68
Dique 1
Humberto Primo
Iglesia San Pedro González Telmo
90
41
Av San Juan
53
20
19
See La Boca Map (p65)

The Center, Congreso & San Telmo

Starting with examples of Pre-Columbian currency (cocoa seeds and leaves), there are examples of colonial coins, replicas of the first coins of the independent republic and other historic notes, including an AR$1,000,000 bill issued during the hyperinflation of 1981, the provincial bonds issued after the 2001 crisis and the appearance of Eva Perón on the AR$100 in 2012.

◉ Puerto Madero

Buenos Aires' newest and shiniest barrio is Puerto Madero, home to lofty skyscrapers and regenerated brick warehouses that have been converted into some of the city's most exclusive lofts, offices, hotels and restaurants. Cobbled waterside promenades make walking a pleasure for pedestrians, while the open green spaces provide room to breathe.

★ Reserva Ecológica Costanera Sur
NATURE RESERVE

(☏011-4893-1588; visitasguiadas_recs@buenos aires.gob.ar; Av Tristán Achaval Rodríguez 1550; ☉8am-7pm Tue-Sun Nov-Mar, to 6pm Apr-Oct; ☐2) FREE The beautifully marshy land of this 350-hectare nature reserve has become a popular site for weekend picnics, walks and bike rides. Bring binoculars if you're a birder – over 300 bird species can be spotted, along with river turtles, iguanas and nutria. At the eastern shoreline of the reserve you can get a close-up view of the Río de la Plata's muddy waters.

The park has a second entrance (Map p58; cnr Mariquita Sánchez de Thompson & Av Intendente Hernán M Giralt; ☐92, 106) at the other end of the Costanera, from where free guided tours (in Spanish) depart at 10:30am and 3:30pm on Saturdays and Sundays. Free night tours are also held one Friday per month (call for the latest schedule; reserve ahead).

Colección de Arte Amalia Lacroze de Fortabat
MUSEUM

(Museo Fortabat; Map p58; ☏011-4310-6600; www.coleccionfortabat.org.ar; Olga Cossettini 141; adult/child AR$80/40; ☉noon-8pm Tue-Sun,

Eating

48	180 Burger Bar	D1
49	Aldo's Restoran & Vinoteca	F4
50	Aramburu	D7
51	Bar El Federal	F6
52	Cadore	B2
53	Café San Juan	F7
54	Cantina San Juan	F6
55	Chan Chan	C4
56	Chila	G4
57	Chin Chin	F6
58	El Banco Rojo	F6
59	El Desnivel	F6
60	El Refuerzo Bar Almacen	E6
61	i Central Market	H2
62	i Fresh Market	H4
63	Latino Sandwich	D4
64	Le Grill	G3
	Lo de Freddy	(see 4)
65	Parrilla Peña	B1
66	Pizzería Güerrín	C2
	Vita	(see 30)

Drinking & Nightlife

67	Bahrein	F2
68	Bar Plaza Dorrego	F7
69	Café Tortoni	E3
70	Clásica y Moderna	A1
	Coffee Town	(see 4)
	El Gato Negro	(see 52)
71	La Cigale	F1
72	La Puerto Rico	F4
73	Los 36 Billares	C4
74	Los Galgos	B2
75	Pride Cafe	F6

Entertainment

76	Academia Nacional del Tango	E3
77	Centro Cultural Borges	F1
78	El Beso	A2
79	El Viejo Almacén	G6
80	La Ventana	F5
81	Luna Park	G2
82	Maldita Milonga	E5
83	Notorious	A1
84	Patio de Tango	F4
85	Piazzolla Tango	E3
	Rojo Tango	(see 37)
	Tango Queer	(see 82)
86	Teatro San Martín	B2

Shopping

87	Arte y Esperanza	F4
88	L'Ago	F6
89	Materia Urbana	F6
90	Punto Sur	F7
91	Puntos en el Espacio	F6
92	Vinotango	F6
93	Walrus Books	E6
94	Zivals	B3

tours in Spanish 5pm; S Línea B Alem) Prominently located at the northern end of Puerto Madero is this stunning art museum showcasing the private collection of the late billionaire, philanthropist and socialite Amalia Lacroze de Fortabat. There are works by Antonio Berni and Raúl Soldi, as well as pieces by international artists including Dalí, Klimt, Rodin and Chagall; look for Warhol's colorful take on Fortabat herself in the family portrait gallery.

The building was designed by renowned Uruguayan architect Rafael Viñoly, and is constructed from steel, glass and concrete – the last a most appropriate material considering its patron (Fortabat was the major stockholder of Argentina's largest cement company).

Corbeta Uruguay MUSEUM

(Map p58; ☎011-4314-1090; Dique 4; AR$10; ⏰10am-7pm; S Línea B Alem) This 46m-long military ship conducted surveys along Argentina's coast and supplied bases in Antarctica until it was decommissioned in 1926, after 52 years of service. Displayed below the main deck are interesting relics from Antarctica expeditions, such as crampons and snowshoes, along with historical photos and nautical items. Check out the tiny kitchen, complete with *mate* (tea-like beverage) supplies (of course).

Puente de la Mujer BRIDGE

(Women's Bridge; Map p58; Dique 3; S Línea A Plaza de Mayo) The striking Puente de la Mujer is Puerto Madero's signature monument. Unveiled in 2001, this gleaming white structure spans Dique 3 and resembles a sharp fishhook or even a harp – it's supposed to represent a couple dancing the tango. Designed by acclaimed Spanish architect Santiago Calatrava and mostly built in Spain, this 160m-long pedestrian bridge cost US$6 million and rotates 90 degrees to allow water traffic to pass.

Fragata Sarmiento MUSEUM

(Map p58; ☎011-4334-9386; Dique 3; AR$10; ⏰10am-7pm; S Línea A Plaza de Mayo) Over 23,000 Argentine naval cadets and officers have trained aboard this 85m sailing vessel, which traveled around the world 37 times between 1899 and 1938. On board are detailed records of its lengthy voyages, a gallery of commanding officers, plenty of nautical items including old uniforms, and even the stuffed remains of Lampazo (the ship's pet dog). Peek into the ship's holds, galley and engine room and note the hooks where sleeping hammocks were strung up.

Congreso & Tribunales

The streets surrounding the Congress building (home to the legislative branch of government) are full of an interesting mix of old-time cinemas, theaters and bustling commerce. It's the city's top entertainment district, home to the Teatro Colón and the bright lights of Av Corrientes, BA's Broadway. On Av de Mayo the buildings still hold a European aura, but this area has more faded-glory atmosphere and grittiness than in the Center.

★Teatro Colón THEATER
(Map p58; ☎011-4378-7100; www.teatrocolon.org.ar; Tucumán 1171, Cerrito 628; tours AR$300; ⏰tours 9am-5pm; Ⓢ Línea D Tribunales) This impressive seven-story building is one of BA's most prominent landmarks. It's the city's main performing-arts venue and a world-class forum for opera, ballet and classical music with astounding acoustics. Occupying an entire city block, the Colón can seat 2500 spectators and provide standing room for another 500. The theater's real beauty lies on the inside, so if you can't get hold of tickets to a performance, take one of the frequent 50-minute backstage tours to view the stunning interior.

Tours in English are at 11am, 1pm and 3pm.

Palacio del Congreso NOTABLE BUILDING
(Congress Building; Map p58; ☎011-2822-3000; www.senado.gov.ar; Hipólito Yrigoyen 1849; ⏰tours 12:30pm & 5pm Mon, Tue, Thu & Fri; Ⓢ Línea A Congreso) FREE The green-domed Palacio del Congreso was modeled on the Capitol Building in Washington, DC and was completed in 1906. Worthwhile free tours of the Senate chamber, the Chamber of Deputies and the gorgeous, walnut-paneled Congress library are given in English and Spanish. The tour also includes the pink room where until 1951 women met to discuss policies; their notes were then passed to a male deputy. Go to the entrance on Hipólito Yrigoyen and bring photo ID.

Separate tours in Spanish only are run by the Chambers of Deputies, accessed via the entrance on Av Rivadavia.

Note the stone statues on either side of the steps at the front of the palace, facing the square; these were sculpted by the controversial artist Lola Mora and caused a scandal when they were erected in 1907. Conservatives insisted that they be removed; in 2014 President Cristina Kirchner returned replicas of the sculptures to their original location.

Across the way, the **Monumento a los Dos Congresos** (Map p58; Plaza del Congreso, cnr Avs Rivadavia & Entre Rios; Ⓢ Línea A Congreso) honors the assembly of 1813 and the 1816 Congress in Tucumán, when independence was declared.

★Palacio Barolo NOTABLE BUILDING
(Map p58; ☎011-4381-1885; www.palaciobarolotours.com; Av de Mayo 1370; tours AR$245; ⏰tours 10am-7pm Wed-Sun; Ⓢ Línea A Sáenz Peña) One of Buenos Aires' most beautiful buildings is this 22-story office block, whose unique design was inspired by Dante's *Divine Comedy;* its height (100m) is a reference to each canto (or song), the number of floors (22) to verses per song, and its divided structure to hell, purgatory and heaven. To see Palacio Barolo you'll need to book a guided tour, during which you'll get to ride in the 1920s elevator and admire the panoramic views from the rooftop lighthouse.

Completed in 1923, Palacio Barolo was BA's tallest skyscraper until the construction of Edificio Kavanagh in 1936. In Montevideo, Uruguay is Palacio Barolo's 'twin,' the Palacio Salvo, a similar building that was also designed by the architect Mario Palanti. Night tours, including musical recitals and wine tastings, are also available; see the website for details.

Teatro Nacional Cervantes NOTABLE BUILDING
(Map p58; ☎011-4815-8883; www.teatrocervantes.gov.ar; Libertad 815; tours AR$90; Ⓜ Línea D Tribunales) From the grand tiled lobby to the red-and-gold-hued main theater, you can smell the long history of the ornately decorated Cervantes. Though it's definitely showing its age, there is an undeniable faded elegance to the place.

BUENOS AIRES FOR FREE

Buenos Aires has a surprising range of free things to do. Many cultural centers offer free or inexpensive events, and some museums have free or half-off days. Search www.bue.gob.ar for upcomig festivals and events.

Cementerio de la Recoleta (p69) BA's most popular tourist attraction and a must-visit for its decorative tombs and statues.

Centro Cultural Kirchner (p56) Catch a concert at this magnificent venue housed in the former central post office.

La Glorieta (p104) Dance the tango at this romantic open-air *milonga* (dance school) in a bandstand at the Barrancas de Belgrano.

Museo Nacional de Bellas Artes (p71) Spend an afternoon at this large and excellent national art museum.

Casa Rosada (p53) Book your place on a free weekend tour of the Presidential Palace.

Hipódromo Argentino (Map p74; ☎011-4778-2800; www.palermo.com.ar; Av del Libertador 4101; 🚌29, 152, 160) FREE Head to Palermo's horse-racing track and place some bets.

Feria de San Telmo See street performers among the stalls at this famous Sunday street market.

Reserva Ecológica Costanera Sur (p60) Marshy lands located in Puerto Madero near the city center, but miles away in atmosphere.

Free City Tour (p81) Locals who love their city offer free walking tours in English (tips appreciated).

Take it in on entertaining guided tours led by actors (in Spanish only), or catch a play, musical show or dance performance.

Palacio de las Aguas Corrientes NOTABLE BUILDING
(Map p58; ☎011-6319-1104; www.aysa.com.ar; Riobamba 750; ⏰museum 9am-1pm Mon-Fri; S Línea D Callao) FREE Completed in 1894 when Buenos Aires was booming, this gorgeous, palace-like waterworks building has an elaborate exterior intended to convey the importance of the purified water it housed in huge tanks. On the 1st floor is the small and quirky **Museo del Agua y de la Historia Sanitaria** (Map p58; Riobamba 750, 1st fl; ⏰9am-1pm Mon-Fri, tours in Spanish 11am Mon, Wed & Fri; S Línea D Callao) FREE, where the collection of ornate tiles, faucets, ceramic pipe joints, and old toilets and bidets is displayed. Guided visits offer a backstage glimpse of the building's inner workings.

Obelisco MONUMENT
(Map p58; cnr Avs 9 de Julio & Corrientes; S Línea B Carlos Pellegrini) One of the city's most iconic monuments is the needle-like Obelisco, which soars 67m above the oval Plaza de la República and was erected in 1936 on the 400th anniversary of the first Spanish settlement on the Río de la Plata. To celebrate major soccer victories, boisterous fans gather at the Obelisco to sing, jump in unison and honk horns.

San Telmo

Full of charm and personality, San Telmo is one of BA's most attractive neighborhoods, with narrow cobbled streets and low-story colonial houses. This is where some of the first homes were built in the early years of the colony and these elaborate mansions later became *conventillos* (tenement housing) for European immigrants. Amid the melancholy of homesickness and the merging of musical traditions in the shared patios of the *conventillos,* tango music was born. Take a walk around; history oozes from every corner of this barrio.

★ **Feria de San Telmo** MARKET
(Map p58; Defensa; ⏰10am-6pm Sun; 🚌10, 22, 29, 45, 86) On Sundays, San Telmo's main drag is closed to traffic and the street is a sea of both locals and tourists browsing craft stalls, waiting at vendors' carts for freshly squeezed orange juice, poking through the antique glass ornaments on display on Plaza Dorrego, and listening to street performances by myriad music groups. Runs from Avenida San Juan to

Plaza de Mayo. It's a tight and crowded scene, so be prepared to bump into people and watch your bag carefully.

★Plaza Dorrego PLAZA

(Map p58; 24, 29, 111) After Plaza de Mayo, Plaza Dorrego is the city's oldest plaza. It dates to the 18th century and was originally a pit stop for caravans bringing supplies into BA from the Pampas. At the turn of the 19th century it became a public square surrounded by colonial buildings that survive to this day. There's still a wonderful old-time atmosphere here and cafe-restaurants that will definitely take you back in time – if you can ignore the nearby chain coffee shops.

Plaza Dorrego is the heart of San Telmo's famous Sunday *feria* (street market).

★Mercado de San Telmo MARKET

(Map p58; btwn Defensa & Bolívar, Carlos Calvo & Estados Unidos block; 8am-8:30pm; S Línea C Independencia) This market was built in 1897 by Juan Antonio Buschiazzo, the same Italian-born Argentine architect who designed Cementerio de la Recoleta. It occupies the inside of an entire city block, though you wouldn't be able to tell just by looking at the modest sidewalk entrances. The wrought-iron interior (note the beautiful original ceiling) makes it one of BA's most atmospheric markets; locals shop here for fresh produce and meat. Peripheral antique stalls offer old treasures.

El Zanjón de Granados ARCHAEOLOGICAL SITE

(Map p58; 011-4361-3002; www.elzanjon.com.ar; Defensa 755; tours Mon-Fri AR$250, Sun AR$200; tours noon, 2pm & 3pm Mon-Fri, every 30min 11am-5:30pm Sun; S Línea C Independencia) One of the more unusual places in BA is this amazing urban architectural site. A series of old tunnels, sewers and cisterns (built from 1730 onwards) were constructed above a river tributary and provided the base for one of BA's oldest settlements, which later became a family mansion and then tenement housing and shops.

Museo de Arte Moderno de Buenos Aires MUSEUM

(MAMBA; Map p58; 011-4361-6919; www.museodeartemoderno.buenosaires.gob.ar; Av San Juan 350; AR$30, Tue free; 11am-7pm Tue-Fri, to 8pm Sat & Sun; 29, 24, 111) Housed in a former tobacco warehouse, this spacious, multistory museum shows off the works of (mostly) Argentine contemporary artists. Expect exhibitions showcasing everything from photography to industrial design, and from figurative to conceptual art. There's also an auditorium and gift shop.

Museo de Arte Contemporáneo Buenos Aires MUSEUM

(MACBA; Map p58; 011-5263-9988; www.macba.com.ar; Av San Juan 328; AR$60, Wed AR$40; noon-7pm Mon & Wed-Fri, 11am-7:30pm Sat & Sun; 24, 29, 111) Art lovers shouldn't miss this fine museum, which specializes in geometric abstraction drawn from the technology-driven world that surrounds us today (think architecture, maps and computers). So rather than traditional paintings, you'll see large, colorful and minimalist pieces meant to inspire reflection.

Museo Histórico Nacional MUSEUM

(Map p65; 011-4300-7530; https://museohistoriconacional.cultura.gob.ar; Defensa 1600; 11am-6pm Wed-Sun, tours in English noon Thu & Fri; 29) FREE Located in **Parque Lezama** (Map p65; cnr Defensa & Av Brasil; 29, 24, 111) is the city's national historical museum. It's mostly dedicated to Argentina's revolution of May 25, 1810, though there is some coverage of precolonial times. There are several portraits of presidents and other major figures of the time, along with a beautifully lit generals' room. Peek into the re-created version of José de San Martín's bedroom – military hero and liberator of Argentina (along with other South American countries).

Highlights include an Argentine flag taken by General Belgrano to Alto Perú (now Bolivia) in 1812 and, best of all, a sword belonging to San Martín himself, now guarded by grenadiers; you'll need to walk through a tunnel displaying other revolutionary heroes' swords, lit up like a nightclub, to reach it.

La Boca

Blue collar and raffish to the core, La Boca is very much a locals' neighborhood. Its colorful shanties are often portrayed as a symbol of Buenos Aires, while El Caminito is the barrio's most famous street, full of art vendors, buskers and tango dancers twirling for your spare change.

★El Caminito STREET

(Map p65; Av Don Pedro de Mendoza, near Del Valle Iberlucea; 33, 64, 29, 168, 53) FREE La

La Boca

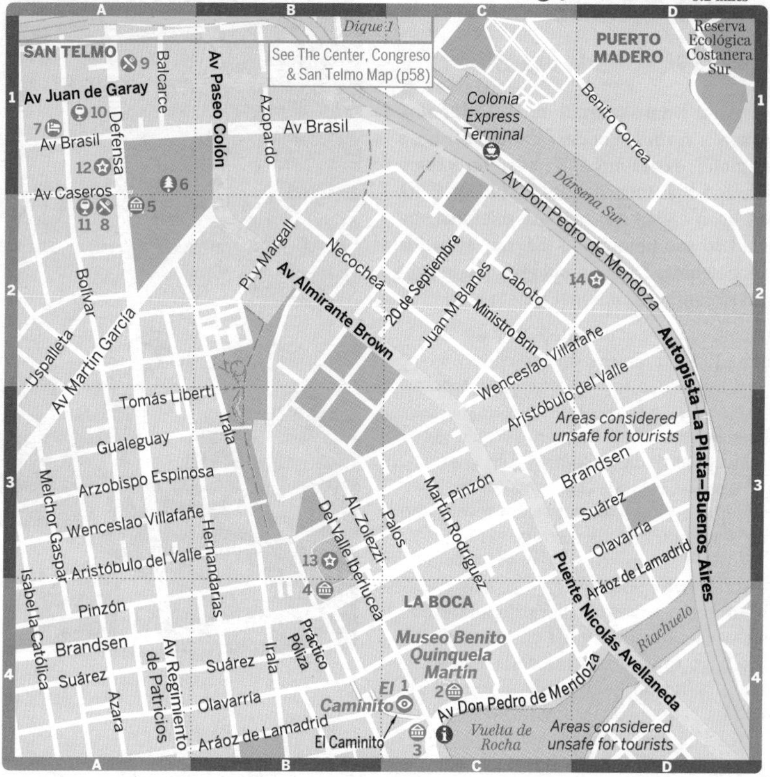

La Boca

Top Sights
1 El Caminito ... C4
2 Museo Benito Quinquela Martín ... C4

Sights
3 Fundación Proa ... C4
4 Museo de la Pasión Boquense ... B4
5 Museo Histórico Nacional ... A2
6 Parque Lezama ... A1

Sleeping
7 L'Adresse ... A1

Eating
8 Hierbabuena ... A2
Proa Cafe ... (see 3)
9 Pulpería Quilapán ... A1

Drinking & Nightlife
10 Doppelgänger ... A1
11 On Tap ... A2

Entertainment
12 Centro Cultural Torquato Tasso ... A1
13 La Bombonera Stadium ... B3
14 Usina del Arte ... D2

Boca's most famous street and 'open-air' museum is a magnet for visitors, who come to see its brightly painted houses and snap photographs of the figures of Juan and Eva Perón, Che Guevara and soccer legend Diego Maradona, who wave down from balconies. (Expect to pay a few pesos to take pictures of tango dancers or pose with props.) Sure, it could be called a tourist trap, but don't let that put you off.

The houses here represent the neighborhood's typical tenement shacks, covered in corrugated zinc and originally brushed with leftover paint that Genoese port

Going to a Fútbol Game

In a land where Maradona is God, going to see a *fútbol* (soccer) game can be a religious experience. The *superclásico* between the Boca Juniors and River Plate has been called the number one sporting event to see before you die, but even the less-celebrated games will give you insight into Argentina's national passion.

Attending a regular match isn't too difficult. Keep an eye on the clubs' websites, which inform when and where tickets will be sold; often they're sold at the stadium before the game. You'll get a choice between *populares* (bleachers) and *plateas* (seats). Try to avoid the *populares;* these can get really rowdy and can sometimes be dangerous.

If you want to see a *clásico* – a match between two major teams – getting a ticket is much harder. Boca doesn't even put tickets for its key matches on sale; all tickets go to *socios* (members). Instead, you're better off going with an agency such as Tangol or via organizations like www.fcbafa.com or www.landingpadba.com. It won't be cheap, but it's much easier getting a ticket this way (and safer, with less chance of fake tickets).

However, if you do want to chance getting your own *clásico* or *superclásico* ticket, you can always look online at www.buenosaires.craigslist.org or www.mercadolibre.com.ar. If you're confident in your bargaining skills, scalpers exist, too.

Dress down, and try to look inconspicuous when you go. Take minimal cash and keep your camera close. You probably won't get in with water bottles, and food and drink in the stadium is meager and expensive. Arrive early to enjoy the insane build-up to the game. Most importantly – don't wear the opposing team's colors.

1

TEAMS

Buenos Aires has two dozen professional football teams – the most of any city in the world. Here are some of them:

Boca Juniors (☎011-5777-1200; www.bocajuniors.com.ar)

Racing (☎011-4371-9995; www.racingclub.com)

River Plate (☎011-4789-1200; www.cariverplate.com.ar)

Independiente (☎011-4229-7600; www.clubaindependiente.com/en)

San Lorenzo de Almagro (☎011-4016-2600; www.sanlorenzo.com.ar)

1. River Plate supporters 2. Crowd at Boca Juniors and River Plate match 3. La Bombonera stadium (p69), Buenos Aires

TIAGO_FERNANDEZ/GETTY IMAGES ©

TERRY CARTER/LONELY PLANET ©

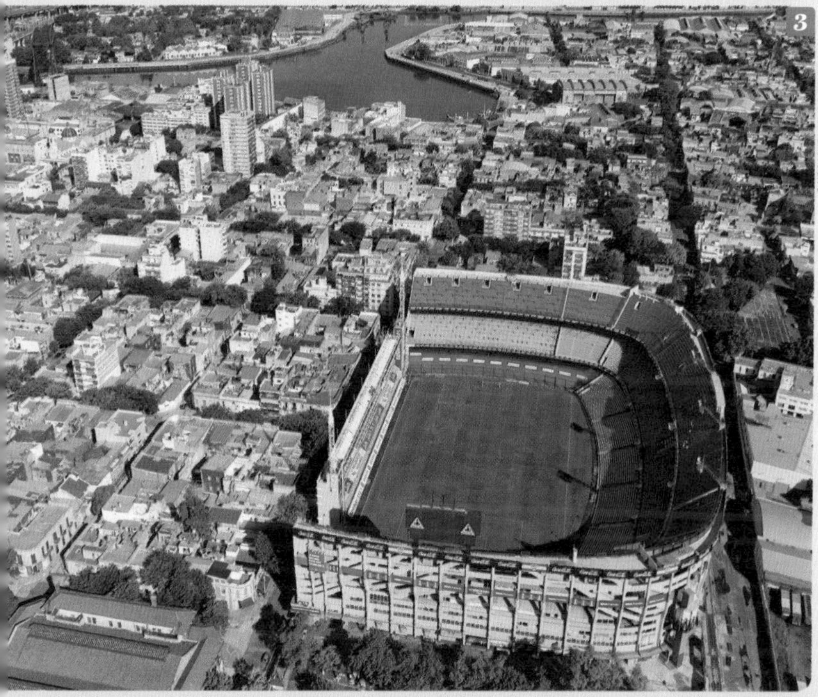

SUNSINGER/SHUTTERSTOCK ©

LA BOCA WARNING

La Boca is not the kind of neighborhood for casual strolls. Don't stray too far from the riverside walk, El Caminito and La Bombonera stadium, especially with expensive cameras. Be discreet, stick close to the busier streets and you should be fine. The **tourist information** (p108) booth is a good place to start your visit. It runs free walking tours of La Boca in English and Spanish (reserve in advance).

workers got from the ships. Caminito (or 'little path') was named after a 1926 tango song, which tells of a love lost. This song inspired Benito Quinquela Martín, La Boca's most famous artist, to help create Caminito in 1955.

★Museo Benito Quinquela Martín MUSEUM
(Map p65; ☎011-4301-1080; www.buenosaires.gob.ar/museoquinquelamartin; Av Don Pedro de Mendoza 1835; AR$40; ⏲10am-6pm Tue-Fri, 11:15am-6pm Sat & Sun; 🚌33, 64, 29) Once the home and studio of painter Benito Quinquela Martín (1890–1977), this fine-arts museum exhibits his works and those of other Argentine artists. Quinquela Martín used silhouettes of laboring men, smokestacks and water reflections as recurring themes, and painted with broad, rough brushstrokes. Don't miss the colorful tiles of his former kitchen and bathroom, his hand-painted piano and the sculptures on the rooftop terraces; the top tier has awesome views of the port.

In keeping with the museum's maritime theme, there's also an excellent permanent collection of painted wooden bowsprits *(proas)*, which are the carved statues projecting forward at the front of ships.

Fundación Proa GALLERY
(Map p65; ☎011-4104-1000; www.proa.org; Av Don Pedro de Mendoza 1929; AR$50; ⏲11am-7pm Tue-Sun; 🚌33, 64, 29) Only the most cutting-edge national and international artists are invited to show at this contemporary art center, with its high ceilings, white walls and large display halls. The innovative installations utilize a wide variety of media and themes, while the rooftop terrace cafe (p89) is the most stylish place in La Boca for pausing for a drink or snack as you take in the spectacular views of the Riachuelo.

Museo de la Pasión Boquense MUSEUM
(Map p65; ☎011-4362-1100; www.museoboquense.com; Brandsen 805; museum AR$210, museum & stadium tour AR$240; ⏲10am-6pm; 🚌29, 53, 152) This high-tech *fútbol* museum chronicles the history of the boisterous neighborhood of La Boca and its famous soccer team Boca Juniors with displays on the club's idols, championships and trophies and, of course, the gooooals. There's a 360-degree theater in a giant soccer-ball auditorium and a good gift shop. It's worth paying the few extra pesos for the stadium tour, which includes the chance to step onto the pitch. Located at La Bombonera stadium, three blocks north of El Caminito.

Retiro

Sandwiched between the Center and Recoleta, Retiro was once the most exclusive neighborhood in Buenos Aires. Vast mansions dating from BA's early-20th-century heyday along with art-deco apartments and other landmark buildings characterize this area. The centerpiece is Plaza San Martín – a pleasant grassy park on a hill overlooking Retiro train and bus stations and the Torre Monumental clock tower.

★Palacio Paz NOTABLE BUILDING
(Map p70; ☎011-4311-1071, ext 147; www.palaciopaz.com.ar; Av Santa Fe 750; tours AR$200; ⏲tours in English 3:30pm Thu, in Spanish 3pm Tue, 11am & 3pm Wed-Fri; Ⓢ Línea C San Martín) Once the private residence of José C Paz – founder of the newspaper *La Prensa* – this opulent, French-style palace (1909) is the grandest in BA. Inside its 12,000 sq meters are ornate rooms with marble walls, salons gilded in real gold and halls boasting beautiful wood-tiled floors. The pièce de résistance is the circular grand hall with mosaic floors, marble details and stained-glass cupola.

Look for the Paz family tomb at Recoleta Cemetery.

Plaza San Martín PLAZA
(Map p70; Ⓢ Línea C San Martín) French landscape architect Carlos Thays designed the leafy Plaza San Martín, which is surrounded by some of Buenos Aires' most impressive public buildings. The park's most prominent monument is an equestrian **statue of José de San Martín**; visiting dignitaries often come to honor the country's liberator by leaving wreaths at its base. On the downhill side of the park you'll see the **Monumento**

a los Caídos de Malvinas (Map p70; Ⓢ Línea C Retiro), a memorial to the young men who died in the Falklands War.

Retiro was the site of a monastery during the 17th century, and later became the country *retiro* (retreat) of Agustín de Robles, a Spanish governor. Since then, Plaza San Martín – which sits on a bluff – has played host to a slave market, a military fort and even a bullring.

At the southern end of the plaza is Estación Retiro (Retiro train station), which was built in 1915 by the British.

Torre Monumental LANDMARK
(Map p70; Plaza Fuerza Aérea Argentina; Ⓢ Línea C Retiro) FREE Standing prominently across from Plaza San Martín, this 76m-high clock tower was a donation from the city's British community in 1916 and built with materials shipped over from England. The tower is only open to the public on occasional free guided tours; check www.ba.tours for upcoming dates.

Museo de Arte Hispanoamericano Isaac Fernández Blanco MUSEUM
(Palacio Noel; Map p70; ☎011-4327-0228; www.museofernandezblanco.buenosaires.gob.ar; Suipacha 1422; AR$10, Wed free; ⏲1-7pm Tue-Fri, 11am-8pm Sat & Sun; Ⓢ Línea C San Martín) This museum is in a 1920s mansion in the neocolonial Peruvian style that developed as a reaction against French influences in turn-of-the-19th-century Argentine architecture. Its exceptional collection of colonial art includes silverwork from Alto Perú (present-day Bolivia), religious paintings and baroque instruments (including a Guarneri violin). The curved ceiling in the main salon is beautifully painted, and there's also a peaceful garden. Signage is in Spanish.

Recoleta & Barrio Norte

It's easy to see how Buenos Aires could be called the Paris of the south in this grand neighborhood. Recoleta is where the rich live in luxury apartments and mansions while spending their free time sipping coffee at elegant cafes and shopping in expensive boutiques. Full of lush parks, grand monuments, art galleries and French architecture, Recoleta is also famous for its cemetery.

★**Cementerio de la Recoleta** CEMETERY
(Map p70; ☎0800-444-2363; visitasguiadasrecoleta@buenosaires.gob.ar; Junín 1760; ⏲7am-5:30pm; Ⓢ Línea H Las Heras) FREE This cemetery is perhaps BA's top attraction. You can wander for hours in this incredible city of the dead, where the 'streets' are lined with impressive statues and marble mausoleums. Peek into the crypts and check out the dusty coffins and try to decipher the history of its inhabitants. Past presidents, military heroes, influential politicians and the just plain rich and famous have made it past the gates here.

Free tours are offered in Spanish at 11am from Tuesday to Sunday and also at 3pm on Saturday and Sunday (weather permitting). For a great map and information, order Robert Wright's PDF guide (www.recoletacemetery.com); touts also sell maps at the entrance.

Basílica de Nuestra Señora del Pilar CHURCH
(Map p70; ☎011-4806-2209; www.basilicadelpilar.org.ar; Junín 1904; museum adult/child AR$25/free; ⏲museum 10:30am-6pm Mon-Sat, 2:30-6pm Sun; Ⓢ Línea H Las Heras) The centerpiece of this gleaming white colonial church, built by Franciscans in 1732, is a Peruvian

DON'T MISS

LA BOMBONERA STADIUM

Seeing Boca Juniors play at **La Bombonera** (Map p65; ☎011-5777-1200; www.bocajuniors.com.ar; Brandsen 805; 🚌29, 53, 152) is one of the world's top spectator sports experiences, especially if the game happens to be the *'superclasico'* derby match against River. Tickets are hard to come by – it's best to go via an agent like LandingPadBA (http://landingpadba.com). You can see the stadium during a visit to the Museo de la Pasión Boquense.

On match days the streets around La Bombonera are a sea of yellow and blue (the colors of Boca's strip, inspired by the flag of a Swedish ship back in 1905). Across the neighborhood, the impassioned voices of match commentators drift out from TVs and radios, above the sound of the fans singing and cheering at the ground; when Boca scores you'll be sure to know about it.

Retiro, Recoleta & Barrio Norte

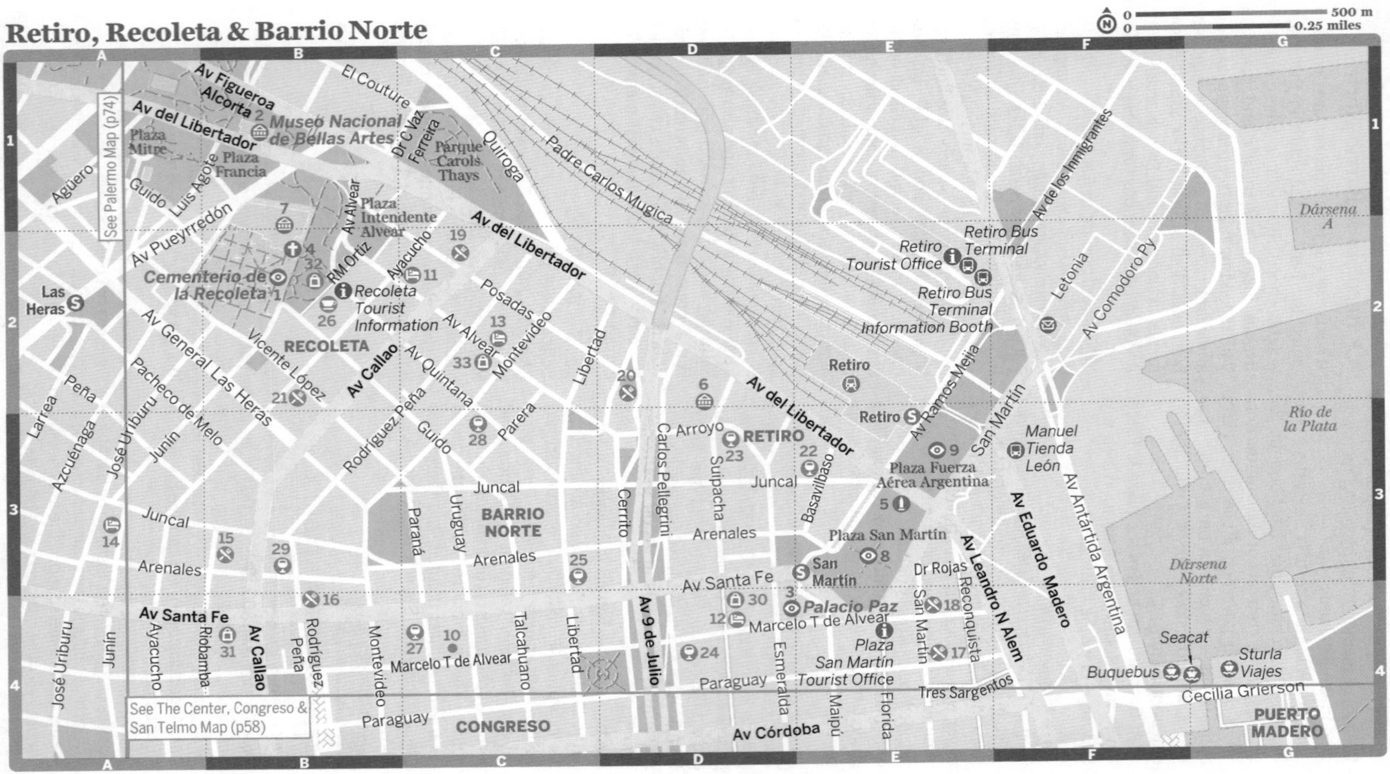

Retiro, Recoleta & Barrio Norte

Top Sights
1 Cementerio de la Recoleta....................B2
2 Museo Nacional de Bellas Artes B1
3 Palacio Paz...D4

Sights
4 Basílica de Nuestra Señora del Pilar B2
5 Monumento a los Caídos de Malvinas E3
6 Museo de Arte Hispanoamericano Isaac Fernández Blanco.....................D2
7 Museo Participativo de Ciencias............B1
8 Plaza San Martín E3
9 Torre Monumental..................................E3

Activities, Courses & Tours
10 VOS C4

Sleeping
11 Alvear Palace Hotel................................C2
12 Casa Calma..D4
13 Palacio Duhau – Park Hyatt...................C2
14 Poetry Building.......................................A3

Eating
15 Como en Casa..B3
16 Cumaná..B4
17 Dadá E4
18 El Federal E4
19 El Sanjuanino...C2
20 Elena...D2
21 Rodi Bar B2

Drinking & Nightlife
22 BASA Basement Bar...............................E3
23 Florería Atlántico D3
24 Flux D4
25 Gran Bar Danzón C3
26 La Biela...B2
27 Milión..C4
28 Presidente C3
29 Shamrock B3

Shopping
30 Autoría..D4
31 El Ateneo Grand Splendid B4
32 Feria Artesenal Plaza Francia B2
33 Fueguia...C2

altar adorned with silver from Argentina's northwest. Inside, head to the left to visit the small but historic cloisters museum; it's home to religious vestments, paintings, writings and interesting artifacts, and there are good views of Recoleta cemetery.

On the left-hand side of the courtyard as you enter the church, look for a ceramic tiled artwork depicting Buenos Aires as it was in 1794, back when the church stood in open countryside outside the town.

★ Museo Nacional de Bellas Artes MUSEUM

(Map p70; ☎011-5288-9900; www.mnba.gob.ar; Av del Libertador 1473; ⊙11:30am-7:30pm Tue-Fri, 9:30am-7:30pm Sat & Sun; 🚌130, 92, 63) FREE This is Argentina's most important fine art museum and contains many key works by Benito Quinquela Martín, Xul Solar, Eduardo Sívori and other Argentine artists, including a whole room of works by Antonio Berni. There are also pieces by European masters such as Cézanne, Degas, Picasso, Rembrandt, Toulouse-Lautrec and van Gogh. Worthwhile free tours in English (focusing on Argentine art) are given on Tuesday, Wednesday and Friday at 1pm.

The museum's building is a former pump house for the city waterworks, and was designed by architect Julio Dormala. It was later modified by Alejandro Bustillo, famous for his alpine-style civic center in the northern Patagonian city of Bariloche.

Palermo

Palermo's large, grassy parks – regally punctuated with grand monuments – are popular destinations on weekends, when families fill the shady lanes, cycle the bike paths and paddle on the peaceful lakes. The sub-neighborhood of Palermo Viejo (itself subdivided into Soho and Hollywood) is home to dozens of restaurants, bars, nightclubs and shops, along with the city's largest selection of boutique hotels.

★ Museo de Arte Latinoamericano de Buenos Aires MUSEUM

(MALBA; Map p74; ☎011-4808-6500; www.malba.org.ar; Av Figueroa Alcorta 3415; adult/student Thu-Mon AR$120/60, Wed AR$50/free; ⊙noon-8pm Thu-Mon, to 9pm Wed; 🚌102, 130, 124) Sparkling inside its glass walls, this airy modern art museum is one of BA's most impressive. It displays the fine collection of Latin American art of millionaire and philanthropist Eduardo Costantini, including works by Argentines Xul Solar and Antonio Berni, as well as pieces by Mexicans Diego Rivera and Frida Kahlo. The temporary exhibitions here are usually world class. A cinema screens art-house films.

LOCAL KNOWLEDGE

PALERMO PARKLIFE

On sunny weekends Palermo's residents flock to Parque 3 de Febrero (known locally as the *bosques*). Don't forget to bring your *mate*, yerba tea and thermos of hot water.

To catch a glimpse of BA's famous dog walkers and their charges, head to Parque Las Heras, at the corner of Avs Las Heras and Coronel Díaz. The best time to see them is late morning during the week.

Grab a bike and make use of the kilometers of protected bike paths along Palermo's green parks. It's a great way to see the area's many spread-out sites while breathing in some fresh air and getting exercise. The bike paths also exist within Palermo Soho and Hollywood. Bike rentals are available at a few bike-touring companies and on nice weekends near Av de la Infanta Isabel and Av Pedro Montt. Or sign up to use the yellow city bikes (p110) for free!

Tours in Spanish of the temporary exhibitions are given on Thursday, Friday and Sunday at 5pm; tours of the permanent collection are on Wednesday and Sunday at 4pm.

★Parque 3 de Febrero PARK

(Map p74; cnr Avs del Libertador & de la Infanta Isabel; 10, 34, 130) Also known as Bosques de Palermo (Palermo Woods), this sweeping open parkland abounds with small lakes and pretty gazebos. Stands rent bikes and in-line skates, and joggers and power walkers circle the ponds – if you don't have the energy to join them, lie back under a tree and people-watch. There's also a monument to literary greats called El Jardín de los Poetas (the Garden of Poets), and the exquisite Rosedal (rose garden).

Jardín Japonés GARDENS

(Map p74; 011-4804-4922; www.jardinjapones.org.ar; Av Casares 2966; adult/child AR$95/free; 10am-6pm; 67, 102, 130) First opened in 1967, these well-maintained Japanese gardens are a peaceful spot for a stroll, unless you're averse to the gentle chimes of Japanese music that emanate from speakers around the grounds. Inside there's a Japanese restaurant along with ponds filled with koi and spanned by pretty bridges.

Museo Evita MUSEUM

(Map p74; 011-4807-0306; www.museoevita.org; Lafinur 2988; AR$90; 11am-7pm Tue-Sun; S Línea D Plaza Italia) Argentina's iconic first lady and wife of President Juan Domingo Perón has this fine museum devoted to her. Housed in a gorgeous 1923 mansion that from 1948 belonged to Eva Perón's social foundation, Museo Evita celebrates the Argentine heroine with videos, historical photos, books and posters. However, the prize memorabilia has to be her wardrobe: dresses, shoes, handbags, hats and blouses are all on display. Look for the picture of her kicking a soccer ball – in heels.

Museo Nacional de Arte Decorativo MUSEUM

(Map p74; 011-4802-6606; www.mnad.org; Av del Libertador 1902; AR$25, tours AR$60; 2-7pm Tue-Sun, closed Sun in Jan; 130, 63, 92) This museum is housed in the stunning beaux-arts Residencia Errázuriz Alvear (1917) mansion, once the residence of Chilean aristocrat Matías Errázuriz and his wife, Josefina de Alvear. It now displays their art collection and other extravagant belongings, and is worth visiting for a glimpse into the world of Argentina's wealthy aristocratic families in the early 20th century, for whom these grand palaces with their elaborate marble staircases and ballrooms inspired by the Palace of Versailles were a status symbol.

Everything from renaissance religious paintings and porcelain dishes to Italian sculptures and period furniture was owned by Errázuriz, and some artwork by El Greco, Manet and Rodin can also be seen. Don't miss the wood-paneled Gothic-style central hall, created to complement the style of the religious tapestries it houses; concerts are sometimes held here. There are guided tours in English and French daily at 2:30pm.

Museo Xul Solar MUSEUM

(Map p74; 011-4824-3302; www.xulsolar.org.ar; Laprida 1212; AR$60; noon-8pm Tue-Fri, to 7pm Sat; S Línea D Agüero) Xul Solar was a painter, inventor, poet and friend of Jorge Luis Borges. This museum (located in his old mansion) showcases over 80 of his unique and colorful, yet muted, paintings. Solar's Klee-esque style includes fantastically themed, almost cartoonish figures placed in surreal cubist landscapes. It's great stuff, and bizarre enough to put him in a class of his own.

Guided tours in Spanish are given at 4pm on Tuesdays and Thursdays, and at 3:30pm on Saturdays.

Belgrano, Nuñez & the Costanera Norte

Though the affluent and largely residential northern neighborhoods of Belgrano and Nuñez don't feature on most travelers' itineraries, they are home to a number of worthwhile museums, parks and plazas, as well as a pleasant weekend market, that make for a great day trip. The Costanera Norte on the river's edge provides open spaces where you can walk next to the water as well as a number of attractions – including a kitschy religious theme park and a water park – that may appeal to families.

Tierra Santa AMUSEMENT PARK

(011-4784-9551; www.tierrasanta.com.ar; Av Costanera R Obligado 5790; adult/child AR$170/70; 9am-9pm Fri, noon-10pm Sat & Sun Apr-Nov, 4pm-midnight Fri-Sun Dec-Mar, last entry 2hr before close; ; 33, 42, 160) This wonderfully tacky 'Holy Land' theme park is roughly based on Jerusalem. Though many people who visit are devout Catholics, others go for the kitschy spectacle of the animatronic dioramas of Adam and Eve and the Last Supper among others; photo opportunities abound. Tierra Santa's pièce de résistance is a giant Jesus rising from a fake mountain – aka the resurrection – every half-hour.

Museo Larreta MUSEUM

(011-4784-4040; www.buenosaires.gob.ar/museolarreta; Juramento 2291; AR$20, Thu free; noon-7pm Tue-Fri, 10am-8pm Sat & Sun; S Línea D Juramento) Hispanophile novelist Enrique Larreta (1875–1961) resided in this elegant colonial-style house opposite Plaza Belgrano that now displays his private art collection. It's a grand and spacious old building containing classic Spanish art, period furniture, wood-carved religious items, and shields and armor. The tiled floors are beautiful and the art is well-lit. Be sure to stroll the lovely gardens out back.

Tours in Spanish are given at 2pm, 3pm and 4:30pm on Saturday and Sunday and in English at 3pm on the last Friday of the month.

South of Palermo

The largely residential, middle-class neighborhoods south of Palermo are part of the 'real' Buenos Aires not much affected by the tourist trade. Villa Crespo is increasingly hip, benefiting from its proximity to Palermo; Almagro is full of alternative theaters, underground music venues and good local restaurants and bars; Abasto and Once are cultural melting pots and busy commercial districts; and Boedo has bohemian flavor and some very traditional cafes.

ESPACIO MEMORIA Y DERECHOS HUMANOS: A MEMORIAL TO THE DISAPPEARED

Human rights groups estimate that during the military dictatorship of 1976 to 1983 up to 30,000 people were 'disappeared' by the state: kidnapped and taken to secret detention centers where they were tortured and killed. One such detention center was at the former naval campus known as the ESMA, where some 5000 men and women were held. Today the complex serves as a memorial to the victims and houses museums, cultural centers and the offices of several human rights organizations. It's located in the neighborhood of Nuñez in the north of the city.

The building where the secret detention center was located, the Casino de Oficiales (officers' club), is now an excellent – though harrowing – **museum** (011-4702-9920; www.espaciomemoria.ar; Av del Libertador 8151, Nuñez; 10am-5pm Tue-Sun; 15, 29, 130) FREE. Due to the disturbing subject matter, children under 12 are not permitted.

The loft space where more than 5000 detainees were kept hooded and chained has been preserved, as has the 'nursery' where some 30 pregnant women gave birth to babies that were then taken and secretly given to families (often with military links) to raise as their own. Also part of the museum is the basement where detainees selected for a 'transfer' were taken before being put onto a plane and thrown alive into the Río de la Plata. Audio guides in English are available.

Palermo

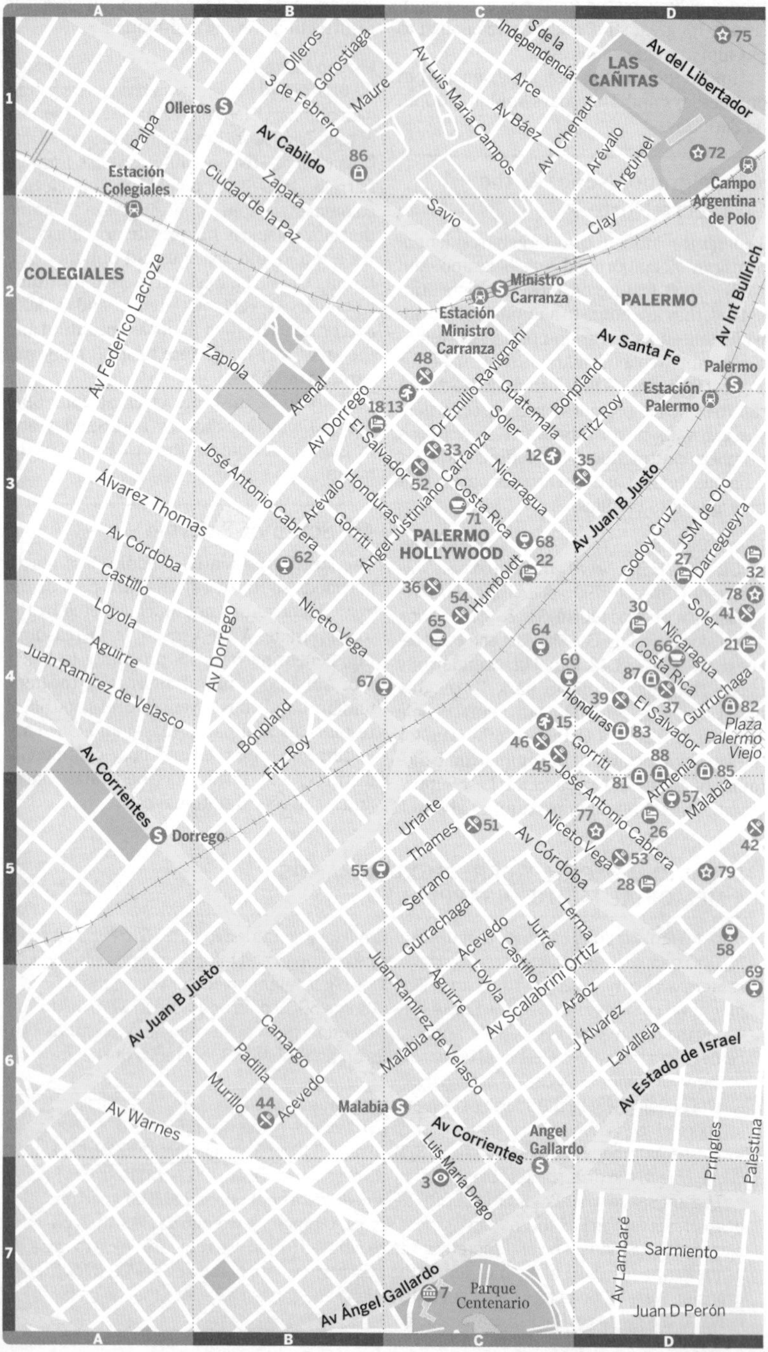

LAS CAÑITAS
COLEGIALES
PALERMO
PALERMO HOLLYWOOD
Av del Libertador
Av Cabildo
Av Federico Lacroze
Av Santa Fe
Av Int Bullrich
Av Juan B Justo
Av Dorrego
Av Corrientes
Av Córdoba
Av Estado de Israel
Av Warnes
Av Ángel Gallardo
Av Scalabrini Ortiz
Olleros
Estación Colegiales
Ministro Carranza
Estación Ministro Carranza
Palermo
Estación Palermo
Campo Argentina de Polo
Dorrego
Malabia
Angel Gallardo
Plaza Palermo Viejo
Parque Centenario
Sarmiento
Juan D Perón
Av Lambaré
Pringles
Palestina
BUENOS AIRES

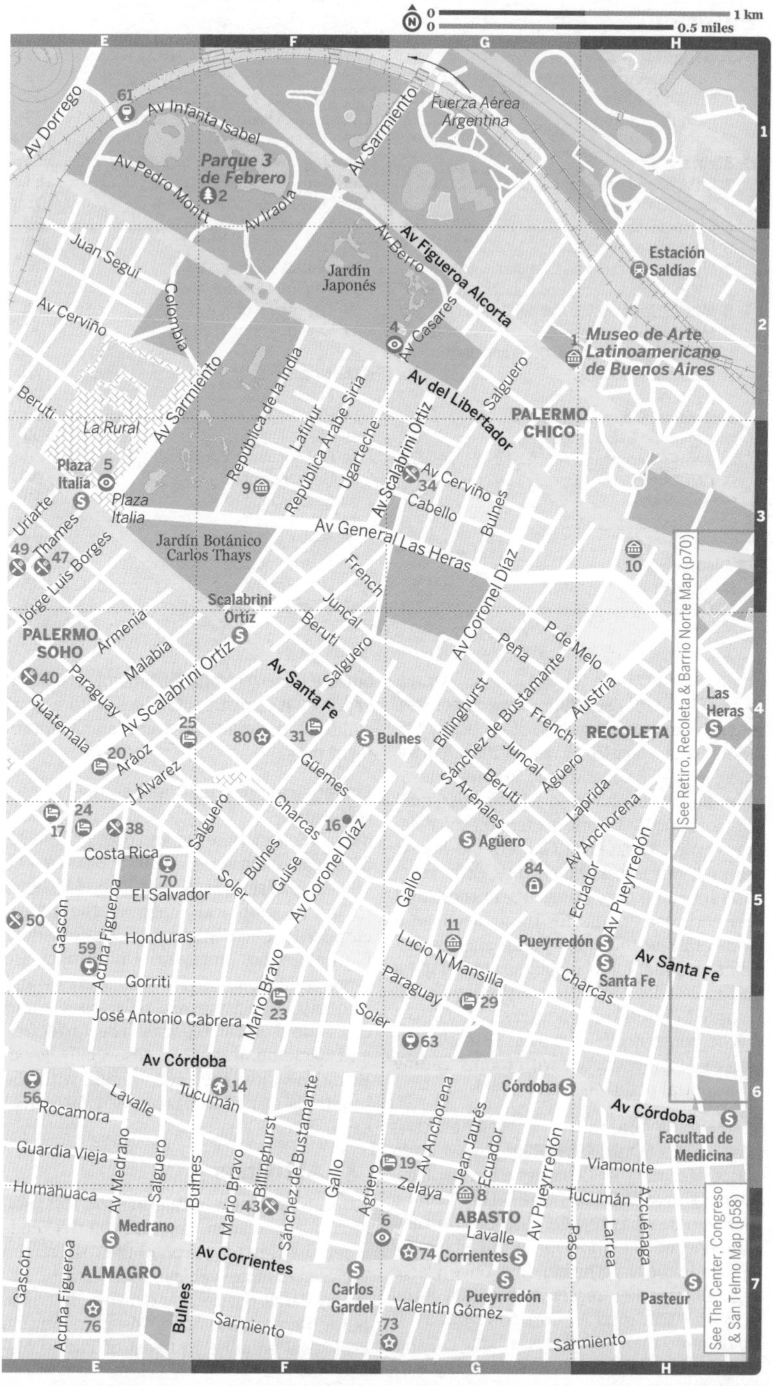

Parque 3 de Febrero
Jardín Japonés
Museo de Arte Latinoamericano de Buenos Aires
Fuerza Aérea Argentina
Estación Saldías
PALERMO CHICO
La Rural
Plaza Italia
Jardín Botánico Carlos Thays
Scalabrini Ortiz
PALERMO SOHO
RECOLETA
Las Heras
Bulnes
Agüero
Pueyrredón
Santa Fe
Córdoba
Facultad de Medicina
ABASTO
ALMAGRO
Medrano
Carlos Gardel
Corrientes
Pasteur
Av Dorrego
Av Infanta Isabel
Av Pedro Montt
Av Iraola
Av Sarmiento
Av Figueroa Alcorta
Av Berro
Av Casares
Av del Libertador
Av Cerviño
Av General Las Heras
Av Scalabrini Ortiz
Av Santa Fe
Av Coronel Díaz
Av Córdoba
Av Corrientes
Av Pueyrredón
Av Anchorena
Av Medrano
See Retiro, Recoleta & Barrio Norte Map (p70)
See The Center, Congreso & San Telmo Map (p58)
BUENOS AIRES

Palermo

Top Sights

1	Museo de Arte Latinoamericano de Buenos Aires	G2
2	Parque 3 de Febrero	F1

Sights

3	Casa Brandon	C7
4	Jardín Japonés	G2
5	La Rural	E3
6	Mercado de Abasto	G7
7	Museo Argentino de Ciencias Naturales	C7
8	Museo Casa Carlos Gardel	G7
9	Museo Evita	F3
10	Museo Nacional de Arte Decorativo	H3
11	Museo Xul Solar	G5

Activities, Courses & Tours

12	Argentine Experience	C3
13	Bar du Marché	C3
14	DNI Tango	F6
15	Pain et Vin	C4
16	Vamos	F5

Sleeping

17	Art Factory Palermo	E5
18	CasaSur	B3
19	Chill House	G6
20	Duque Hotel	E4
21	Eco Pampa Hostel	D4
22	Hotel Clasico	C3
23	Le Petit Palais	F6
24	Magnolia Hotel	E5
25	Mansilla 3935 B&B	E4
26	Mine Hotel	D5
27	Miravida Soho	D3
28	Palermo Viejo B&B	D5
29	Reina Madre Hostel	G6
30	Rugantino Hotel	D4
31	The 5th Floor	F4
32	Vain Boutique Hotel	D3

Eating

33	Artemisia	C3
34	Big Sur	G3
35	Bio	D3
36	Buenos Aires Verde	C4
37	Burger Joint	D4
38	Casa Coupage	E5
39	Chori	D4
40	Don Julio	E4
41	El Preferido de Palermo	D4
42	Gran Dabbang	D5
43	Guarda la Vieja	F7

Museo Casa Carlos Gardel MUSEUM
(Map p74; ☎011-4964-2015; www.buenosaires.gob.ar/museocasacarlosgardel; Jean Jaurés 735; AR$10; ⊙11am-6pm Mon & Wed-Fri, 10am-7pm Sat & Sun; Ⓢ Línea B Carlos Gardel) Recent renovations have brought fresh life to this small but noteworthy tribute to tango's most famous voice. Located in Gardel's old house, the museum traces the singer's early years in France and Argentina, his musical and cinematic career, and his tragic death in a plane crash at the height of his success. Exhibits include audio displays, memorabilia and tablets loaded with every song Gardel recorded – a total of 893 tracks.

The house itself – a typical *casa chorizo* (sausage-like) residence with rooms leading off a central patio – is worth a look.

Mercado de Abasto NOTABLE BUILDING
(Map p74; ☎011-4959-3400; www.abasto-shopping.com.ar; Av Corrientes 3247; ⊙10am-10pm; Ⓢ Línea B Carlos Gardel) The historic Mercado de Abasto (1895) has been turned into one of the most beautiful shopping centers in the city. The building, once a large vegetable market, received an architectural prize in 1937 for its Av Corrientes facade. It holds more than 200 stores, a large cinema, a food court and the only kosher McDonald's outside Israel (the one upstairs next to Burger King). It's great for families, with a good children's museum and even a small amusement park.

Museo Argentino de Ciencias Naturales MUSEUM
(Natural Science Museum; Map p74; ☎011-4982-6595; www.macn.gov.ar; Av Ángel Gallardo 490; AR$40; ⊙2-7pm; 👪; Ⓢ Línea B Ángel Gallardo) In the geographical center of the city at circular Parque Centenario is this excellent natural-science museum. On display are large collections of meteorites, rocks and minerals, Argentine seashells, insects and dinosaur-skeleton replicas. The taxidermy and skeleton rooms are especially good. Bring the kids; they can mingle with the hundreds of children who visit on school excursions.

Activities

Extensive greenery in Palermo provides good areas for recreation, especially on weekends when the ring road around the rose garden is closed to motor vehicles. Recoleta also has grassy parks, but not as extensive. Best of all is the Reserva Ecológica Costanera Sur, an ecological paradise just east of Puerto Ma-

44	i Latina	B6
45	La Cabrera	C4
46	La Cabrera Norte	C4
47	La Carnicería	E3
48	La Mar Cebicheria	C2
49	Las Pizarras	E3
50	NoLa	E5
51	Sarkis	C5
52	Siamo nel Forno	C3
53	Steaks by Luis	D5
54	Sunae Asian Cantina	C4
	Drinking & Nightlife	
55	878	B5
56	Amerika	E6
57	Antares	D5
58	Bach Bar	D5
59	Benaim	E5
60	Boticario	C4
61	Crobar	E1
62	Frank's	B3
63	Glam	G6
64	Kika	C4
65	LAB Training Center & Coffee Shop	C4
66	Lattente Espresso & Brew Bar	D4
67	Niceto Club	B4
68	On Tap	C3
69	Sitges	D6
	Uptown	(see 48)
70	Verne	E5
71	Vive Café	C3
	Entertainment	
72	Campo Argentino de Polo	D1
73	Ciudad Cultural Konex	G7
74	Esquina Carlos Gardel	G7
75	Hipódromo Argentino	D1
	La Bomba de Tiempo	(see 73)
76	La Catedral	E7
77	La Viruta	D5
78	Los Cardones	D4
79	Salón Canning	D5
80	Thelonious Bar	F4
	Shopping	
81	Bolivia	D5
82	Elementos Argentinos	D4
83	Feria Plaza Serrano	D4
84	Galeria Patio del Liceo	G5
85	Humawaca	D4
86	Instituto Geográfico Nacional	B1
87	Lo de Joaquín Alberdi	D4
88	Rapsodia	D4

dero that might just make you forget you're in a big city.

Cycling

The city's bike lanes make cycling in the city a safer proposition. Bike paths run along many roads in Parque 3 de Febrero (p72), or head to the Reserva Ecológica Costanera Sur (p60), along the coast. This green and tranquil space has some flat dirt paths that are great to bike on. Pick up one of the free city bikes (p110) or hire one from a tour company such as Biking Buenos Aires (p80).

Horseback Riding

★Caballos a la Par HORSEBACK RIDING
(☎011-15-5248-3592; www.caballos-alapar.com; Villa Elisa; per person AR$2950-4150) If you want to get out of town for a few hours and hop on a horse, check out Caballos a la Par. Guided rides are given in the woods of a provincial park about an hour's drive from Buenos Aires. Even if you've never ridden before, you might be cantering by sundown. Prices include transportation to and from Buenos Aires.

Fútbol

Inspired by watching professional *fútbol* teams play the game? Well, you can partake yourself – just contact **Buenos Aires Fútbol Amigos** (www.fcbafa.com) to join fellow travelers and locals for fun on the pitch. There's a modest charge for the experience, but post-match beers often lie at the end of the *fútbol* rainbow – and the sporty memories can be priceless.

Polo

Argentina Polo Day POLO
(☎011-15-6738-2422; www.argentinapoloday.com.ar; RP 39, Km11.2, Capilla del Señor; full day/half-day polo US$185/130) Learn to play polo with a two-hour class then watch the pros play a four-chukka game at an *estancia* about 100km northwest of BA. The price includes transportation, snacks and an *asado* (barbecue grill) with wine.

Swimming

Parque Norte SWIMMING
(☎011-4787-1382; www.parquenorte.com; Avs Cantilo & Guiraldes; adult/child Mon-Fri AR$195/105, Sat AR$230/135, Sun AR$250/135; ⊙pool 9am-8pm, park 9am-midnight; 👪; 🚌33, 42, 160) When the temperatures and humidity skyrocket, head to this large water park. It's great for families with huge shallow pools, plus a large waterslide and lots of umbrellas and lounge chairs (both cost extra). There

1

STUART DEE/GETTY IMAGES ©

2

4

SPECTRAL-DESIGN/SHUTTERSTOCK ©

1. El Caminito (p64)
Boca's most famous street and 'open-air museum' is lined with brightly painted houses.

2. Puerto Madero (p60)
Cobbled waterside promenades make walking a pleasure for pedestrians in Buenos Aires' newest and shiniest barrio.

3. Plaza de Mayo (p53)
This is the place where Argentines gather in vehement protest or jubilant celebration.

4. Parque 3 de Febrero (p72)
This sweeping open parkland abounds with small lakes and pretty gazebos.

ANTON_IVANOV/SHUTTERSTOCK ©

are plenty of grassy areas in which to enjoy a picnic or *mate*. Bring your own towels, and make sure you're clean – quick 'health' inspections are done to check for such unpleasantries as athlete's foot or lice.

Tango

★DNI Tango DANCING
(Map p74; ☎011-4866-6553; https://dni-tango.com; Bulnes 1101; group class per person AR$100; Ⓢ Línea B Medrano) This excellent tango school offers group and private classes in English and Spanish for all levels. For those starting out, the Saturday afternoon *práctica* is a friendly place to dance with different partners without the pressure of taking to the floor at a more formal *milonga*. DNI is located in a beautiful old building in the neighborhood of Almagro.

Courses

Spanglish LANGUAGE
(☎011-5252-9523; www.spanglishexchange.com; AR$150) For something different, try Spanglish. It's set up like speed dating; you'll speak five minutes in English and five in Spanish, then switch partners. Check the website for upcoming events, usually held in bars in Palermo or San Telmo.

Vamos LANGUAGE
(Map p74; ☎011-5984-2201; www.vamospanish.com; Av Coronel Díaz 1736; ⏲9:30am-5:30pm Mon-Fri; Ⓢ Línea D Bulnes) This Spanish-language school in Palermo offers a crash course for travelers as well as group and private classes.

VOS LANGUAGE
(Map p70; ☎011-4812-1140; www.vosbuenosaires.com; Marcelo T de Alvear 1459; ⏲9am-7pm Mon-Fri; Ⓢ Línea D Callao) Offers a range of group and private classes as well as intensive courses and conversation classes.

Rayuela LANGUAGE
(Map p58; ☎011-4300-2010; www.spanish-argentina.com.ar; Chacabuco 852, 1st fl, No 11; Ⓢ Línea C Independencia) San Telmo–based language school offering a range of courses, with both group and private classes.

Expanish LANGUAGE
(Map p58; ☎011-5252-3040; www.expanish.com; 25 de Mayo 457, 4th fl; Ⓢ Línea B Alem) Centrally located Spanish school offering a range of courses.

Academia Buenos Aires LANGUAGE
(Map p58; ☎011-4345-5954; www.academiabuenosaires.com; Hipólito Yrigoyen 571, 4th fl, Microcentro; Ⓢ Línea A Perú) Located in an attractive old building near Plaza de Mayo this well-established Spanish-language school offers intensive courses.

Tours

Graffitimundo TOURS
(☎011-15-3683-3219; www.graffitimundo.com; tours US$20-33) Excellent tours of some of BA's best graffiti are offered by this nonprofit organization that supports the local urban art scene. Learn artists' history and the local graffiti culture. Several tours available; stencil workshops too.

Buenos Aires Street Art TOURS
(www.buenosairesstreetart.com; tours US$20-35) Group and private walking tours with knowledgeable guides highlighting some of BA's most interesting street art in the northern and southern city suburbs. Supports local artists, too.

Tango Trips DANCING
(☎011-5235-4923; www.tangotrips.com; tour for 1/2/3 people US$160/190/240) Private tours to *milongas* with experienced and passionate *tangueros* (tango dancers). The venues visited depend on which is the best place to go on any particular night. Start with a private tango lesson to gain confidence before hitting the salons; if you're not a dancer, just sit back and watch tango danced in its most authentic form.

Buenos Tours WALKING
(www.buenostours.com; full-/half-day tour for 1-3 people US$235/125) Well-run private walking tours guided by friendly, knowledgeable and responsible native English speakers living long-term in Buenos Aires.

Biking Buenos Aires CYCLING
(Map p58; ☎011-4300-5373; www.bikingbuenosaires.com; Perú 988; ⏲9am-6pm; Ⓢ Línea C Independencia) Friendly American and Argentine guides take you on various tours of Buenos Aires; tour themes include graffiti and architecture. Recommended.

Foto Ruta TOURS
(☎011-15-3331-7980; www.foto-ruta.com; per person US$120) On Foto Ruta's 'streetscape' workshops a professional photographer offers pro tips before sending folks out into

neighborhoods with a few themes to photograph – afterwards everyone watches the slide show over a glass of wine. The company also offers a number of private tours and photography workshops.

BA Free Tour WALKING
(Map p58; ☎011-4420-5897; www.bafreetour.com; cnr Av Rivadavia & Rodríguez Peña; by donation; ⏰11am Mon-Sat) Free (donations recommended) walking tours given by enthusiastic young guides who love their city. Even if you can't give anything, you're welcome to join.

BA Walking Tours WALKING
(☎011-5626-9888; www.ba-walking-tours.com; 2hr group tour per person US$37.50) Group and private tours covering all the main sights on day tours, night tours, historic tours and tango tours.

Buenos Aires Pub Crawl FOOD & DRINK
(☎011-3678-0170; www.pubcrawlba.com; AR$200) If you like to party with young, heavy-drinking crowds, check out the Buenos Aires Pub Crawl. Held every night, it usually starts at 10pm in a bar in Palermo or San Telmo and includes some food and drinks, as well as club entry; see the website for details of current events.

Festivals & Events

Arte BA ART
(www.arteba.org; ⏰May) Popular event highlighting contemporary art, introducing exciting new young artists, and showing off top gallery works. Held at **La Rural** (Map p74; www.larural.com.ar; Av Sarmiento 2704; Ⓢ Línea D Plaza Italia).

Tango BA Festival y Mundial DANCE
(http://festivales.buenosaires.gob.ar; ⏰mid-Aug) Masterful tango performances, tango movies, classes, workshops, conferences and competitions in venues all over Buenos Aires. The final of the *mundial* (tango world cup) is held at **Luna Park** (Map p58; ☎011-5279-5279; www.lunapark.com.ar; cnr Bouchard & Av Corrientes; Ⓢ Línea B Alem).

Vinos y Bodegas WINE
(☎011-4777-5557; admission incl tastings AR$500; ⏰Sep) A can't-miss event for wine aficionados, offering vintages from over 100 Argentine bodegas (wineries). The entrance fee includes your own glass to use for tastings. Usually held at La Rural.

WORTH A TRIP

FERIA DE MATADEROS

In the working-class barrio of Mataderos is this excellent **folk market and fair** (☎011-4342-9629; www.facebook.com/feriademataderos; cnr Avs Lisandro de la Torre & de los Corrales; ⏰11am-8pm Sun Apr–mid-Dec, 6pm-midnight Sat late Jan–mid-Mar; 🚌126, 55). Merchants offer handmade crafts and regional cuisine including *locro* (a spicy stew of maize, beans, beef, pork, and sausage) and *humita* (stuffed corn dough, resembling Mexican tamales). Folk singers, dancers and gauchos on horseback entertain, and there's a small gaucho museum nearby. Call ahead in between seasons to make sure it's open. From downtown take bus 126 or from Palermo take bus 55; the journey takes about one hour.

You can also take a taxi to and from Mataderos if you're pinched for time.

Campeonato Abierto de Polo SPORTS
(Map p74; www.aapolo.com; Arévalo 3065; ⏰Nov-Dec; Ⓢ Línea D Ministro Carranza) Watch the world's best polo players and their gorgeous horses thunder up and down Palermo's polo field, the **Campo Argentino de Polo**.

Sleeping

The Center

★**Portal del Sur** HOSTEL $
(Map p58; ☎011-4342-8788; www.portaldelsurba.com.ar; Hipólito Yrigoyen 855; dm from US$13, s US$35, d with/without bathroom from US$44/39; ❄@📶; Ⓢ Línea A Piedras) Located in a charming old building, this is one of the city's best hostels. Beautiful dorms and hotel-quality private rooms surround a central common area, which is rather dark but open. The highlight is the lovely rooftop deck with views and attached bar. A relaxed but sociable place with plenty of activities on offer including *asados* and tango classes.

Milhouse Youth Hostel HOSTEL $
(Map p58; ☎011-4345-9604; www.milhousehostel.com; Hipólito Yrigoyen 959; dm from US$14, r from US$48; ❄@📶; Ⓢ Línea A Av de Mayo) BA's premiere party hostel, this popular spot offers a plethora of activities and

BUENOS AIRES FOR CHILDREN

For a megalopolis, BA is remarkably child-friendly. On sunny weekends Palermo's parks bustle with families taking walks and picnicking, while shopping malls fill with strollers. Museums and theme parks are also popular destinations – and don't forget those fun street fairs!

Buenos Aires has numerous plazas and public parks, many with playgrounds. If you're downtown and need a nature break, try Reserva Ecológica Costanera Sur (p60), a large nature preserve with good bird watching, pleasant dirt paths and no vehicular traffic. Up north, the most attractive green spots are the wide open spaces of Palermo, especially Parque 3 de Febrero (p72). This huge park has a planetarium and a Japanese garden (p72). Here you can rent bikes, boats and in-line skates and range freely without worrying about cars.

Head to Tigre, just north of the center, for a great day excursion. Hop on the fun Tren de la Costa to get to Parque de la Costa (p111), a typical amusement park with rides and activities. Kids might enjoy Tierra Santa (p73), a religious theme park unlike anywhere you've ever been. Parque Norte (p77), a large water park, is perfect on a hot day.

In the Centro Cultural Recoleta, the **Museo Participativo de Ciencias** (Map p70; 011-4806-3456; www.mpc.org.ar; Centro Cultural Recoleta, Junín 1930; AR$100; 10am-5pm Tue-Fri, 3:30-7:30pm Sat & Sun; ; S Línea H Las Heras) has interactive displays that focus on fun learning – signs say *'prohibido no tocar'* (not touching is forbidden). Outside the center in Caballito is the excellent natural history museum (p76), with myriad rooms containing giant dinosaur bones, dainty seashells, scary insects and amusing stuffed animals and birds.

Many large modern shopping malls have indoor playgrounds (often on the top floor), along with video arcades, multiplexes and toy shops. On rainy days, these are great places to be with little ones. The Mercado de Abasto (p76) boasts a full-blown 'Museo de los Niños' (more like a playground than a museum) where kids enter a miniature city complete with post office, hospital and even TV station. It also has a mini amusement park.

services. Dorms are good and private rooms can be very pleasant; most surround an appealing open patio. Common spaces include a bar-cafe (with pool table) on the ground floor, a TV lounge on the mezzanine and a rooftop terrace. A gorgeous annex building nearby offers similar services.

V & S Hostel Club HOSTEL **$**
(Map p58; 011-4322-0994; www.hostelclub.com; Viamonte 887; dm from US$15, d from US$49; ; S Línea C Lavalle) This attractive, central hostel is located in a pleasant older building. The common space, which is also the dining and lobby area, is good for socializing, and there's a kitchen for guests. The spacious dorms are carpeted and the private rooms are excellent; all have their own bathroom. A nice touch is the tiny outdoor patio out back.

★ **Casa Calma** BOUTIQUE HOTEL **$$$**
(Map p70; 011-4312-5000; www.casacalmahotel.com.ar; Suipacha 1015; r from US$200; ; S Línea C San Martín) Hidden behind a living wall of greenery is this ecoconscious hideaway in central BA. The 17 rooms are pristine and relaxing with Jacuzzi baths and a serene ambience; some have small balconies. Yoga mats and bamboo bikes available; discount without breakfast.

Puerto Madero

★ **Faena Hotel + Universe** HOTEL **$$$**
(Map p58; 011-4010-9000; www.faena.com/buenos-aires; Martha Salotti 445; r from US$500; ; 111, 43, 143) Located in a renovated storage mill, this Philippe Starck–designed fantasy hotel is more than just a place to stay. Traipse through the plush main hallway, lined with two top-notch restaurants, a sultry bar-lounge, a basement cabaret and – outside – a slick swimming pool. The luxurious rooms feature claw-foot beds and glass-walled bathrooms. Also has a Turkish bath and spa.

Congreso & Tribunales

Hostel Estoril HOSTEL $
(Map p58; ☎011-4382-9684; www.hostelestoril3.com; Av de Mayo 1385, 1st & 6th fl; dm/s/d from US$15/34/51; ❄@📶; Ⓢ Línea A Sáenz Peña) This well-run hostel is located across two floors in a beautiful old building. It's stylish and clean, with pleasant, good-sized dorms and hotel-quality doubles. There's also a decent kitchen for guests, but the hostel's biggest draw has to be the awesome rooftop terrace overlooking the Palacio Barolo and Av de Mayo; the owners organize regular *asados* and yoga classes.

The same family runs a cheaper hostel on the 3rd floor.

Sabatico Hostel HOSTEL $
(Map p58; ☎011-4381-1138; www.sabaticohostel.com.ar; México 1410; dm from US$16, d with/without bathroom from US$56/47; ❄@📶; Ⓢ Línea E Independencia) This friendly hostel is located off the beaten tourist path in an atmospheric neighborhood. Rooms are small but fine, and the pleasant common areas include a nice kitchen, dining and living room, airy patio hallways and a great rooftop terrace with hammocks, *parrilla* (grill) and soaking tub. There's also a ping-pong table, bike rentals and a daily schedule of group activities.

Hotel Bonito BOUTIQUE HOTEL $
(Map p58; ☎011-4381-2162; www.bonitobuenosaires.com; Chile 1507, 3rd fl; r US$38-50; ❄@📶; Ⓢ Línea E Independencia) Lovely boutique hotel with just five artsy, gorgeous rooms mixing the traditional and contemporary. Some have loft beds and small balconies; floors are wooden or acid-finished concrete. There's a warm, homey atmosphere, with a small bar area and a good breakfast. It's in a nontouristy, very local neighborhood within walking distance of Congreso and San Telmo.

★**Imagine Hotel** BOUTIQUE HOTEL $$
(Map p58; ☎011-4383-2230; www.imaginehotelboutique.com; México 1330; s/d/tr from US$90/110/160; ❄@📶; Ⓢ Línea E Independencia) This beautiful guesthouse in a traditional *casa-chorizo*-style house offers nine appealing rooms, all individually decorated with rustic, yet upscale, furniture. The rooms open onto three outdoor patios with original tiles and leafy plants; the last one has a grass lawn. It's a peaceful little place in a nontouristy neighborhood. Fully wheelchair accessible. Reserve ahead.

San Telmo

Located within walking distance of the Center and surrounded by bars and restaurants, San Telmo is a popular area in which to stay. Some of the city's best hostels are located here, as well as a few good guesthouses and boutique hotels.

★**América del Sur** HOSTEL $
(Map p58; ☎011-4300-5525; www.americahostel.com.ar; Chacabuco 718; dm from US$15, d from US$45; ❄@📶; Ⓢ Línea C Independencia) This gorgeous boutique-like hostel – the smartest of its kind in BA – was built especially to be a hostel. Beyond reception is a fine bar area with a large wood-decked patio. Sparklingly clean dorms with four beds all have well-designed bathrooms, while private rooms are tastefully decorated and better than those at many midrange hotels. Wide range of services on offer.

Circus Hostel & Hotel HOSTEL $
(Map p58; ☎011-4300-4983; www.hostelcircus.com; Chacabuco 1020; dm from US$15, r from US$47; ❄@📶🏊; Ⓢ Línea C Independencia) From the flash lounge at the front to the wooden deck–surrounded wading pool in back, this hotel-hostel exudes hipness. Both dorms and private rooms, all small and simple, have basic furniture and their own bathrooms. There's a pool table and slick TV area, but no kitchen.

L'Adresse BOUTIQUE HOTEL $
(Map p65; ☎011-4307-2332; https://ladressehotel.com; Bolívar 1491; r from US$55; ❄📶; 🚌29, 33, 159, 130) French couple Clara and Romain spent more than three years painstakingly restoring an 1880s mansion turned run-down tenement house into this character-filled boutique hotel. The 15 rooms are simple but comfortable and lead off the house's original tiled passageways; much of the furniture was salvaged and upcycled by the owners themselves. Great bar and breakfast area, too.

Art Factory Hostel HOSTEL $
(Map p58; ☎011-4343-1463; www.artfactoryba.com.ar; Piedras 545; dm from US$17, d from US$47; ❄@📶; Ⓢ Línea E Belgrano) Friendly and art-themed, this fine hostel offers more private rooms than most – and all feature huge murals, painted and decorated by different artists. Even the hallways and water tanks have colorful cartoonish themes, and the 1850s rambling mansion adds some charm. There's

a large rooftop terrace with hammocks and separate bar-lounge area with pool table.

Patios de San Telmo — BOUTIQUE HOTEL $$

(Map p58; ☑ 011-4307-0480; http://patiosde santelmo.com.ar; Chacabuco 752; r US$105-138; ✳ @ 🛜 🏊; Ⓢ Línea C Independencia) Located in an 1860 former *conventillo* (tenement house) is this pleasant boutique hotel with 30 spacious, elegant rooms surrounding several patios. There's a lovely 'library' room decorated with artwork, a back patio with hanging basket chairs and a tiny rooftop pool with wood deck.

Mansión Vitraux — BOUTIQUE HOTEL $$

(Map p58; ☑ 011-4878-4292; www.mansion vitraux.com; Carlos Calvo 369; r from US$110; ✳ @ 🛜 🏊; Ⓢ Línea C Independencia) Almost too slick for San Telmo, this glass-fronted boutique hotel offers 12 beautiful rooms, all in different designs. All have either flat-screen or projection TV, and bathrooms have a contemporary design. The breakfast buffet is in the basement wine bar. There is also a large Jacuzzi, a sauna, an indoor pool and a slick rooftop terrace with a second pool.

🛏 Recoleta & Barrio Norte

★Poetry Building — APARTMENT $$$

(Map p70; ☑ 011-4827-2772; www.poetry building.com; Junín 1280; apt US$280-390; ✳ 🛜 🏊; Ⓢ Línea D Pueyrredón) These gorgeous studios and one-bedroom apartments are perfect for families. Each one is different, eclectically decorated with reproduction antique furniture, and all come with plenty of mod cons and a fully equipped kitchen (stocked with groceries on request). Some apartments have a private outdoor balcony or patio, but there's also a beautiful common terrace with soaking pool.

Best of all is the rooftop vegetable garden, where guests can help themselves to homegrown kale, hot peppers, chard, beans and tomatoes.

★Palacio Duhau – Park Hyatt — HOTEL $$$

(Map p70; ☑ 011-5171-1234; https://buenosaires. park.hyatt.com; Av Alvear 1661; d from US$520; ✳ @ 🛜 🏊; 🚌 130, 111, 62) If it's good enough for presidents, diplomats and Tom Cruise, it's good enough for us. The luxurious Park Hyatt takes up a city block and consists of two wings, including the Palacio Duhau, a renovated mansion with a separate reception. There's a gorgeous terraced garden with fountains and patios, plus a fine spa, indoor pool and the fabulous Oak Bar.

Alvear Palace Hotel — HOTEL $$$

(Map p70; ☑ 011-4808-2100; www.alvearpalace. com; Av Alvear 1891; r from US$630; ✳ @ 🛜 🏊; 🚌 130, 93, 62) The classiest, most traditional hotel in BA oozes old-world sophistication and has the service and all the facilities you would expect of a five-star hotel, with in-room luxuries such as Hermès toiletries and Egyptian-cotton bed sheets. The recently added top-floor suites have stunning views across Recoleta to the river; the new roof bar and indoor pool are equally impressive.

There's also an excellent restaurant, wine-tasting room, elegant tea room, champagne bar and fine spa.

🛏 Palermo

About a 20-minute taxi ride from the city center (and also well connected by bus and Subte lines), Palermo is the top choice for many travelers. Not only is it full of extensive parklands – which are great for weekend jaunts and sporting activities – but you'll have heaps of cutting-edge restaurants, designer boutiques and dance clubs at your door. Most of these places are located in the extensive sub-neighborhoods of Palermo Soho and Palermo Hollywood.

★Reina Madre Hostel — HOSTEL $

(Map p74; ☑ 011-4962-5553; www.rm hostel.com; Av Anchorena 1118; dm US$15-20, s/d US$40/44; ✳ @ 🛜; Ⓢ Línea D Pueyrredón) This wonderful hostel is clean, safe and well run. It's in an old building,with high ceilings and original tiles, and all rooms are comfortable (and share bathrooms). There's a cozy living room and small kitchen, plus lots of dining tables, but the highlight is the wooden-deck rooftop with *parrilla*. Pet cat on premises.

★Palermo Viejo B&B — GUESTHOUSE $

(Map p74; ☑ 011-4773-6012; www.palermo viejobb.com; Niceto Vega 4629; s US$55, d US$60-75, tr US$85; ✳ @ 🛜; 🚌 140) This friendly B&B is located in a remodeled *casa chorizo* dating from 1901 that was once the clothes factory of the owner's father. The six rooms all front a leafy outdoor patio and are decorated with local artwork; two have lofts. All come with a fridge and a good breakfast. Call ahead.

Art Factory Palermo — HOSTEL $

(Map p74; ☑ 011-2004-4958; www.artfactorypaler mo.com.ar; Costa Rica 4353; dm US$14-18, r with/

without bathroom US$57/50; ❄@📶; Ⓢ Línea D Scalabrini Ortiz) This decent, no-frills hostel is well located close to Palermo's restaurants and nightlife. Like its sister hostel in San Telmo, it's in an old house and decorated with artsy murals and stencils. There's a small kitchen, ping-pong table and living room area, and a limited number of bathrooms – so their use can get tight.

Rugantino Hotel GUESTHOUSE **$**
(Map p74; ☎011-6379-5113; www.rugantinohotelboutique.com; Uriarte 1844; r US$64-68; ❄@📶; Ⓢ Línea D Palermo) This intimate, homey guesthouse is located in a 1920s building. Various terraces and catwalks connect the seven simple rooms, all decked out in hardwood floors and modern styling, combined with a few antiques. The climbing vine and greenery in the small central courtyard is soothing, and there's a guitar on hand for impromptu music sessions. Reserve ahead.

Mansilla 3935 B&B B&B **$**
(Map p74; ☎011-4833-3821; www.mansilla3935.com; Mansilla 3935; s/d US$35/50; ❄@📶; Ⓢ Línea D Scalabrini Ortiz) Family-run B&B in a homey, darkish house, offering great value. Each of the six simple rooms comes with its own bathroom. Ceilings are high, and a few tiny patios add charm.

Eco Pampa Hostel HOSTEL **$**
(Map p74; ☎011-4831-2435; www.hostelpampa.com.ar; Guatemala 4778; dm US$13-17, s/d US$50/60; @📶; Ⓢ Línea D Plaza Italia) 🍃 Buenos Aires' first 'green' hostel is this casual spot sporting vintage and recycled furniture, low-energy light bulbs and a recycling system. The rooftop is home to a small veggie garden, compost pile and solar panels. Dorms are a good size and each of the eight private rooms comes with bathroom and flat-screen TV (most have air-con). Also has a kitchen.

★Le Petit Palais B&B **$$**
(Map p74; ☎011-4962-4834; www.lepetitpalais-buenosaires.com; Gorriti 3574; s/d from US$75/85; ❄📶; Ⓢ Línea D Agüero) Small but charming, this French-run B&B offers just five simple but pleasant rooms, all with private bathrooms. The highlight is the pretty little terrace on the 2nd floor, where possibly BA's best breakfast is served in warm weather – fresh yogurt, jams and breads (all homemade), along with eggs, *medialunas* (croissants) and cereals. Friendly cats on premises.

The 5th Floor B&B **$$**
(Map p74; ☎011-4827-0366; www.the5thfloorba.com; near Vidt & Santa Fe; r US$90-170; ❄@; Ⓢ Línea D Scalabrini Ortiz) This upscale B&B offers six elegant rooms, two with private balconies. All are tastefully decorated with art-deco furniture and modern amenities. The common living room is great for chatting with the English owner, a polo enthusiast, and there's also a pleasant back patio with lovely tile details. Excellent breakfast. Address given upon reservation; three-night minimum stay.

Duque Hotel BOUTIQUE HOTEL **$$**
(Map p74; ☎011-4832-0312; www.duquehotel.com; Guatemala 4364; s US$130, d US$145-175; ❄@📶≋; Ⓢ Línea D Scalabrini Ortiz) All 14 rooms at this charming boutique hotel are well designed, though some can be a bit small – go for a superior or deluxe if you need more space. Pluses include a large Jacuzzi, sauna, basement spa, buffet breakfast, afternoon tea with pastries, and a great little backyard garden with a tiny pool. Online discounts available.

Hotel Clasico HOTEL **$$**
(Map p74; ☎011-4773-2353; www.hotelclasico.com; Costa Rica 5480; r US$120-160; ❄📶; Ⓢ Línea D Palermo) Attractive hotel with 33 tasteful 'classic' rooms, some with tiny balconies but all with wood floors, modern conveniences and earthy color schemes; a local photographer was specially commissioned to take the photos of BA that adorn the walls. Go for the penthouse with terrace for something special. Creative elevator with one glass wall facing an artsy mural.

★Magnolia Hotel BOUTIQUE HOTEL **$$$**
(Map p74; ☎011-4867-4900; http://magnoliahotelboutique.com/palermo-buenosaires; Julián Álvarez 1746; r US$154-195; ❄@📶; Ⓢ Línea D Scalabrini Ortiz) This classy boutique hotel is in a gorgeously restored old house. Its eight impeccably groomed rooms are bathed in muted colors and fitted with elegant furniture; some have a patio or balcony. Other pluses include a welcome drink and a little patio for breakfast. Discounts available online.

CasaSur HOTEL **$$$**
(Map p74; ☎011-4770-9452; http://casasurhotel.com/palermo; Costa Rica 6032; r US$165-265; ≋; Ⓢ Línea D Ministro Carranza) Beginning

with its airy, contemporary lobby fitted with oversized bookshelves, the CasaSur is a stylish place to stay. The elegant rooms have graphic wallpaper and a monochrome color scheme; those on floors one to four have balconies. There's a small outdoor pool, spa and gym and – best of all – a spacious roof terrace with great views.

Vain Boutique Hotel BOUTIQUE HOTEL $$$
(Map p74; ☎011-4776-8246; www.vainuniverse.com; Thames 2226; r US$145-300; ❄@📶; Ⓢ Línea D Plaza Italia) Fifteen elegant rooms, most with high ceilings and wooden floors, can be found at this nicely renovated building. All are modern in that white, minimalist way, with sofas and small desks. The highlight is the wonderfully airy, multilevel living room with attached wooden-decked terrace and Jacuzzi. Discounts available online.

Miravida Soho GUESTHOUSE $$$
(Map p74; ☎011-4774-6433; www.miravidasoho.com; Darregueyra 2050; r US$220-300; ❄@📶; Ⓢ Línea D Plaza Italia) This gorgeous guesthouse comes with six elegant rooms, one with a private terrace. There's a wine cellar, bar-lounge area for evening wine tastings, a small and relaxing patio, and even an elevator. It serves good, full breakfasts; reserve ahead.

Mine Hotel BOUTIQUE HOTEL $$$
(Map p74; ☎011-4832-1100; www.minehotel.com; Gorriti 4770; d US$160-235; ❄@📶🏊; 🚌140, 110, 55) 🍃 This hip boutique hotel offers 20 good-sized rooms; some come with Jacuzzis and balconies and all have desks and natural decor touches. Get one overlooking the highlight of the hotel: the peaceful backyard with a small wading pool. There's a small bistro for the buffet breakfast.

South of Palermo

★Chill House GUESTHOUSE $
(Map p74; ☎011-4861-6175; www.chillhouse.com.ar; Agüero 781; s US$45, d US$55-65; @📶; Ⓢ Línea B Carlos Gardel) This relaxed and friendly guesthouse is in a remodeled old house with high ceilings and a rustic artsy style, and has 10 private rooms (number 6, with a balcony and air-con, is especially nice). There's also an awesome rooftop terrace where *asados* take place, with DJs and occasional live music.

Well-located close to public transportation and within easy reach of Palermo and the Center.

Eating

The Center

180 Burger Bar BURGERS $
(Map p58; ☎011-4328-7189; www.facebook.com/180burgerbar; Suipacha 749; burgers AR$110-135; ⏰noon-4pm Mon-Fri; Ⓢ Línea C Lavalle) Hankering for a hamburger? Then join the young crowd that will likely be lined up at this small diner. Choose a 'salsa' (mayochimi, tzatziki, barbacoa) and add cheese if you wish. Chow down within the confines of concrete walls, clunky furniture and blasting music.

Latino Sandwich SANDWICHES $
(Map p58; ☎011-4331-0859; www.latinosandwich.com; Tacuari 185; sandwiches AR$75-100; ⏰8am-5pm Mon-Fri; Ⓢ Línea A Piedras) Some of the best eateries in BA are holes-in-the-wall – and here's a case in point. This is the downtown place to grab sandwiches such as Argentine *milanesa* (breaded cutlet) but with rocket and guacamole!), barbecue pork with cheddar cheese, or grilled zucchini and eggplant. There's only one communal table, as they cater to a mostly to-go business clientele.

Vita VEGAN $
(Map p58; ☎011-4600-8164; Hipólito Yrigoyen 583; mains AR$85-110; ⏰8am-8pm Mon-Wed, to 1am Thu & Fri, 10:30am-1am Sat, 11am-7pm Sun; 🖉; Ⓢ Línea E Bolívar) Here's a hippie-ish, casual and health-oriented eatery offering tasty vegan dishes such as risotto, lentil burgers and vegetable calzones, as well as a selection of vegan cakes. Various freshly mixed juices are available and there are plenty of salads. Another branch is in Palermo.

Aldo's Restoran & Vinoteca ARGENTINE $$$
(Map p58; ☎011-4334-2380; www.aldosvinoteca.com; Moreno 372; mains AR$360-490; ⏰noon-midnight Sun-Thu, to 1am Fri, 7pm-1am Sat; Ⓢ Línea A Plaza de Mayo) This restaurant and wine shop is an upscale eatery serving a small but tasty menu of meat, seafood and pasta dishes, all amid walls lined with wine. Look out for wine tastings held on Tuesday evenings, or ask your server to recommend one of the nearly 600 bottles in stock.

There is a second branch in Palermo.

Puerto Madero

i Central Market ARGENTINE $$
(Map p58; ☎011-5775-0330; www.icentralmarket.com.ar; Av Macacha Güemes 302; mains AR$105-215; ⏰8am-10pm; 📶; Ⓢ Línea B Alem) Especially

pleasant on sunny days is this modern restaurant on the waterfront – the tables on the promenade are great for people-watching. Order espresso and scones for breakfast, and panini (Italian-style sandwiches) or contemporary Argentine dishes for lunch. There's also more casual seating at the gourmet deli, plus a kitchenwares shop to poke around.

Another branch (not on the water, however) is **i Fresh Market** (Map p58; ☎011-5775-0335; www.icentralmarket.com.ar; Olga Cossettini 1175; mains AR$90-160; ⏰8am-10pm; Ⓢ Línea A Plaza de Mayo).

★Chila MODERN ARGENTINE **$$$**
(Map p58; ☎011-4343-6067; www.chilaweb.com.ar; Alicia Moreau de Justo 1160; 6-course menu AR$1900; ⏰8-11pm Tue-Sun; Ⓢ Línea A Plaza de Mayo) Some of Buenos Aires' best and most original cuisine is created by chef Pedro Bargero. His six-course, haute-cuisine dishes utilize only the best seasonal ingredients, and the restaurant also works closely with quality producers. Expect beautifully presented food, a professional staff and – if you're lucky – a table with a romantic view of the docks.

Le Grill PARRILLA **$$$**
(Map p58; ☎011-4331-0454; www.legrill.com.ar; Alicia Moreau de Justo 876; mains AR$210-750; ⏰12:30-3pm & 7pm-midnight Mon-Fri, 7pm-1am Sat, 12:30-3.30pm Sun; Ⓢ Línea A Plaza de Mayo) No surprise – grilled meat is the specialty at this sophisticated *parrilla*. Go for the rack of lamb or the house specialty, dry-aged beef. There are a few seafood and pasta dishes for noncarnivores. Try to reserve a table in the atrium, with a full view of Puente de la Mujer.

Congreso & Tribunales

★Cadore ICE CREAM **$**
(Map p58; ☎011-4374-3688; http://heladeriacadore.com.ar; Av Corrientes 1695; ice cream from AR$100; ⏰noon-1am Mon-Thu, to 2am Fri-Sun; Ⓢ Línea B Callao) This, one of BA's classic *heladerías* (ice-cream parlors), was founded by the Italian Olivotti family in 1957 and gets busy with the post-theater crowds late into the night. Try the *dulce de leche* (milk caramel), made using a process that involves boiling *dulce leche* (sweetened milk) for 14 to 16 hours.

★Pizzería Güerrín PIZZA **$**
(Map p58; ☎011-4371-8141; www.facebook.com/pizzeriaguerrin; Av Corrientes 1368; pizza slices AR$28-38; ⏰11am-1am Sun-Thu, to 2am Fri & Sat; Ⓢ Línea B Uruguay) This much-loved pizza joint on Av Corrientes has been feeding the masses since 1932. For a quick pit stop (and the cheapest prices), order a slice of thick, doughy *muzzarella* at the counter and eat standing up at the benches. Add a portion of *fainá* (chickpea-based flatbread) and wash it down with Moscato and soda.

There are also tables with waiter service where you can choose a freshly baked pizza from a more extensive menu. Empanadas and plenty of desserts are available, too.

Chan Chan PERUVIAN **$**
(Map p58; ☎011-4382-8492; Hipólito Yrigoyen 1390; mains AR$70-142; ⏰noon-4pm & 8pm-12:30am Tue-Sat, to 11:30pm Sun; Ⓢ Línea A Sáenz Peña) Thanks to fair prices and quick service, this colorful Peruvian eatery is usually packed with office workers devouring plates of ceviche (seafood cured in citrus) and *ajiaco de conejo* (rabbit and potato stew). There are also *arroz chaufa* (Peruvian-style fried rice) dishes, easily washed down with a tangy pisco sour or a pitcher of *chicha morada* (a sweet fruity drink).

Parrilla Peña PARRILLA **$$**
(Map p58; ☎011-4371-5643; www.parrillapenia.url.ph; Rodríguez Peña 682; mains AR$130-390; ⏰noon-4pm & 8pm-midnight Mon-Sat; Ⓢ Línea D Callao) This simple, traditional, long-running *parrilla* is well-known for its excellent quality meats and generous portions. The service is fast and efficient and it's great value. Also on offer are homemade pastas, salads and *milanesas,* along with several tasty desserts and a good wine list.

★Aramburu MODERN ARGENTINE **$$$**
(Map p58; ☎011-4305-0439; www.arambururesto.com.ar; Salta 1050; 18-course tasting menu AR$1750, with wine pairings AR$2600; ⏰8:30-11pm Tue-Sat; Ⓢ Línea E San José) Chef Gonzalo Aramburu's seasonal 18-course 'molecular' meal is astounding; each artistically created plate is just a few bites of gastronomic delight. Expect enlightening tastes, textures and smells, plus unique presentations – all will translate into a highly memorable dining experience. Located in the edgy but up-and-coming neighborhood of Montserrat.

San Telmo

★El Banco Rojo INTERNATIONAL **$**
(Map p58; ☎011-4040-2411; www.elbancorojo.wordpress.com; Bolívar 866; mains AR$60-110;

RAISING THE STEAKS

Going to a *parrilla* is probably on every BA visitor's to-do list, but if you want to eat meat in a different way, try these options:

Argentine Experience (Map p74; ☎011-4778-0913; www.theargentineexperience.com; Fitz Roy 2110; per person US$105-140; ⏰6:30-11:30pm Mon-Sat; Ⓜ Línea D Palermo) Learn the meaning of local hand gestures, the story of Argentina's beef and how to make empanadas and *alfajores* (cookie-type sandwiches usually stuffed with dulce de leche). Plus you'll eat a supremely tender steak.

Steaks by Luis (Map p74; ☎011-4776-0780; www.steakbuenosaires.net; Malabia 1308; 5 courses with wine US$89; ⏰8pm Mon, Tue, Thu & Sat; 🚌140, 15, 168) An upscale *asado* experience where you'll nibble on cheese and sip boutique wine while watching large hunks of meat being grilled.

Parrilla Tour (☎011-15-4048-5964; www.parrillatour.com; per person US$79; ⏰Palermo tour noon & 7:30pm Tue, noon Fri & Sat, San Telmo tour noon Mon & Wed) Meet your knowledgeable guide at a restaurant for a *choripán* (traditional sausage sandwich), then an empanada. You'll finish at a local *parrilla*.

⏰noon-12:30am Tue-Sat, to 11:30pm Sun; Ⓢ Línea C Independencia) A San Telmo youth magnet, this trendy joint serves up sandwiches, falafels, burgers and tacos, as well as a range of beers and spirits. Try the *empanada de cordero* (lamb turnover) if they have it. This place, Banco Rojo's new digs (one block over from the old one), has more space to eat-in but the same grungy vibe.

Chin Chin PUB FOOD $
(Map p58; Estados Unidos 500; mains AR$100-250; ⏰5:30pm-midnight Tue-Thu, 6pm-2am Fri & Sat, 10am-10:30pm Sun) This corner bar with grungy vibes and craft beer on tap has been making a name for itself as the place to go for flavorsome, good-value bar food. Generous sandwiches served in crusty baguettes, green and yellow curries and crunchy polenta with roasted vegetables are among the dishes on offer.

Lo de Freddy PARRILLA $
(Map p58; Bolívar 950; choripanes AR$50, vaciopanes AR$100; ⏰1:30-5:30pm & 8-11:30pm Mon-Fri, 1-11:30pm Sat & Sun; 🚌29) Near the entrance to San Telmo market is this hole-in-the wall *parrilla* serving some of the best-value *choripanes* (sausage sandwiches) and *vaciopanes* (beef sandwiches) in town. It's a rustic joint with just one bench and a few sidewalk stools (which are likely to be occupied by the regulars), but for a filling feed it can't be beat.

Pulpería Quilapán ARGENTINE $
(Map p65; ☎011-4307-6288; http://pulperiaquilapan.com; Defensa 1344; set menu AR$150, mains AR$120-290; ⏰noon-midnight Wed-Sun; 📶; 🚌29) Get a taste of life in the rural pampas without leaving the city at Pulpería Quilapán, a former colonial-era house that has been transformed into the kind of bar that's traditionally frequented by gauchos. Typical Argentine meats, pastas and stews are served; it's also a good place to try *mate*.

Check the social calendar online for the week's events, which might include all-you-can-eat gnocchi and bingo nights. There's also a great little *almacén* (grocery store) selling cheeses, jams, wines from small vineyards and *pingüinos* (penguin-shaped wine jugs).

Bar El Federal ARGENTINE $
(Map p58; ☎011-4361-7328; Carlos Calvo 599; mains AR$92-295; ⏰8am-2am Sun-Thu, to 4am Fri & Sat; 📶; Ⓢ Línea C Independencia) Dating from 1864, this historical bar is a classic, with original wooden features, black-and-white floor tiles, and an eye-catching antique bar and cash register. The specialties here are sandwiches and *picadas* (shared appetizer plates), but there are also lots of pastas, salads, desserts and tall mugs of icy beer.

El Desnivel PARRILLA $$
(Map p58; ☎011-4300-9081; Defensa 855; mains AR$106-381; ⏰noon-1am Tue-Sun, 7pm-1am Mon; Ⓢ Línea C Independencia) This long-running, low-key *parrilla* joint packs in both locals and tourists, serving them treats such as *chorizo* (sausage) sandwiches and *bife de lomo* (tenderloin steak). The delicious smells from the sizzling grill out front are torturous as you wait for a table – get here early, especially on weekends.

★Café San Juan INTERNATIONAL **$$$**

(Map p58; ☎011-4300-1112; www.facebook.com/CafeSanJuanrestaurant; Av San Juan 450; mains AR$300-390; ⏲12:30-4pm & 8pm-midnight Sun & Tue-Thu, to 1am Fri & Sat; Ⓢ Línea C San Juan) Having studied in Milan, Paris and Barcelona, TV-chef Leandro Cristóbal now runs the kitchen at this renowned San Telmo bistro. Start with fabulous tapas, then delve into the grilled Spanish octopus (AR$1100), *molleja* (sweetbreads) cannelloni and amazing pork *bondiola* (deliciously tender after nine hours' roasting). Reserve ahead for lunch and dinner.

El Refuerzo Bar Almacen ARGENTINE **$$$**

(Map p58; ☎011-4361-3013; www.facebook.com/elrefuerzobaralmacen; Chacabuco 872; mains AR$230-450; ⏲10am-2am Tue-Sun; Ⓢ Línea C Independencia) The small dining room fills up quickly at this *almacén*-style restaurant. There's an excellent wine list to match the menu of top-notch dishes written on blackboards on the walls – think cured meats, cheeses, homemade pastas and bistro-style casseroles. It's a casual, friendly place that's popular with locals.

Hierbabuena VEGETARIAN **$$$**

(Map p65; ☎011-4362-2542; www.hierbabuena.com.ar; Av Caseros 454; mains AR$190-410; ⏲9am-midnight Tue-Sun, to 5pm Mon; ✍; 🚌29, 33, 159, 130) Offering a wide selection of healthy vegetarian dishes, smoothies and juices, Hierbabuena is a good option for those looking for a satisfying, non-meat-based meal. It's in a pretty spot, too, looking out onto Av Caseros. Also serves a few chicken and fish dishes.

Cantina San Juan ARGENTINE **$$$**

(Map p58; ☎011-4300-9344; www.facebook.com/CafeSanJuanrestaurant; Chile 474; mains AR$270-370; ⏲12:30-4pm & 8pm-midnight Sun-Thu, to 1am Fri & Sat; Ⓢ Línea C Independencia) At this casual joint chef Leandro Cristóbal sticks with simple dishes such as antipasto, mini pizzas, fresh pastas and a few meat and fish mains – but it's all excellent. Afterwards, try the in-house vermouth from the '*vermuteria*' bar.

La Boca

Proa Cafe CAFE **$$**

(Map p65; ☎011-4104-1003; www.proa.org/eng/cafe.php; Av Don Pedro de Mendoza 1929; set lunch AR$280, sandwiches AR$90-150; ⏲cafe 11am-7pm, kitchen noon-3:30pm Tue-Sun; 🚌33, 64, 29) Located on the top floor of Fundación Proa (p68; free access) is this airy cafe. Stop in briefly for a fresh juice and gourmet sandwich, or stay longer and order a meat, seafood or pasta dish. Don't miss the rooftop terrace on a sunny day – you'll get good views of the Riachuelo, hopefully without its corresponding scents.

Retiro

Dadá INTERNATIONAL **$$**

(Map p70; ☎011-4314-4787; San Martín 941; mains AR$198-318; ⏲noon-4am; Ⓢ Línea C San Martín) Tiny bohemian Dadá, with walls painted red and a bar cluttered with wine bottles, feels like an unassuming neighborhood bar in Paris. Order something savory, such as a stir-fry, off the bistro menu during the day; at night you can dine on grilled salmon and down an expertly mixed cocktail.

El Federal ARGENTINE **$$$**

(Map p70; ☎011-4313-1324; www.elfederalrestaurante.com; San Martín 1015; mains AR$220-389; ⏲11am-midnight; 📶; Ⓢ Línea C San Martín) This traditional downtown eatery is something of a neighborhood institution. You'll find Argentine comfort food – simple pastas, steaks and empanadas – as well as higher-end specialties including Patagonian lamb, ñandu *milanesas* (cutlets of the emu-like, flightless ñandu) and northern river fish served here. Elaborate desserts top things off, and a rustic wooden bar adds charm.

Recoleta & Barrio Norte

★El Sanjuanino ARGENTINE **$**

(Map p70; ☎011-4805-2683; www.elsanjuanino.com.ar; Posadas 1515; empanadas AR$27, mains AR$110-290; ⏲noon-4pm & 7pm-1am; 🚌130, 93, 124) This long-running, cozy little joint has some of the cheapest food in Recoleta, attracting both penny-pinching locals and thrifty tourists. Order spicy empanadas, tamales or *locro* (a spicy stew of maize, beans, beef, pork, and sausage).

The curved brick ceiling adds to the atmosphere, but many take their food to go – Recoleta's lovely parks are just a couple of blocks away.

Cumaná ARGENTINE **$**

(Map p70; ☎011-4813-9207; Rodríguez Peña 1149; mains AR$93-156; ⏲noon-1am; Ⓢ Línea D Callao) To sample Argentina's regional cuisine, check out this colorful, budget-friendly eatery with huge picture windows and an old-fashioned adobe oven. Cumaná specializes in delicious *cazuelas* – stick-to-your-ribs stews filled with squash, corn, eggplant, potatoes and meat. Also popular are the empanadas, *locro* (a spicy stew of maize, beans, beef, pork, and sausage) and *humita* (stuffed corn dough, like Mexican tamales).

Rodi Bar ARGENTINE **$$**
(Map p70; ☎011-4801-5230; Vicente López 1900; mains AR$150-350; ⏲8am-1am Mon-Sat; 📶; Ⓢ Línea H Las Heras) A great option for well-priced, unpretentious food in upscale Recoleta. This traditional neighborhood restaurant with a fine old-world atmosphere and extensive menu offers something for everyone, from inexpensive combo plates to relatively unusual dishes such as marinated beef tongue.

Como en Casa ARGENTINE **$$**
(Map p70; ☎011-4816-5507; www.tortascomoencasa.com; Riobamba 1239; mains AR$100-240; ⏲11am-5pm Mon, 11am-5pm & 8-11pm Tue-Sat; 📶; Ⓢ Línea D Callao) This gorgeous, upscale cafe-restaurant has a very elegant atmosphere and attracts Recoleta's wealthiest. Its best feature is the shady patio, complete with large fountain and surrounded by grand buildings, great on a warm day. For lunch there are sandwiches, salads, vegetable tarts and gourmet pizzas, while dinner options include goulash and homemade pastas. Plenty of luscious cakes and desserts, too.

★ **Elena** ARGENTINE **$$$**
(Map p70; ☎011-4321-1728; www.elenaponyline.com; Posadas 1086, Four Seasons; mains AR$310-580; ⏲7am-3:30pm & 7:30pm-12:30am; 🚌130, 62, 93) If you're looking to splurge on a night out, Elena should be your destination. Located at the Four Seasons Hotel, this highly rated restaurant uses the best-quality ingredients to create exquisite dishes. Order its specialty – the dry-aged meats – for something really special. The cocktails, desserts and service are five-star.

Casa Saltshaker INTERNATIONAL **$$$**
(www.casasaltshaker.com; set menu incl wine pairings US$80; ⏲8:45pm Tue-Sat) Ex–New Yorker Dan Perlman is the chef behind this respected place, which is a *puerta cerrada* (closed-door restaurant) in his own home. You'll need to book ahead, arrive at an appointed hour and sit at a communal table, which can be a lot of fun – especially for solo diners. Address and phone number given upon reservation.

Palermo

★ **NoLa** CAJUN **$**
(Map p74; www.nolabuenosaires.com; Gorriti 4389; mains AR$100-145; ⏲12:30pm-midnight Sun-Thu, to 1am Fri & Sat; 🚌140, 141, 110) The brainchild of American Lisa Puglia is this small, popular place serving New Orleans Cajun cuisine. Everything is homemade, from the fried chicken sandwich to the *chorizo* gumbo and the spicy, vegetarian red beans and rice. The jalapeño cornbread and bourbon-coffee pecan pie are the bomb, as is the microbrewed beer. Happy hour until 8pm.

Chori ARGENTINE **$**
(Map p74; ☎011-3966-9857; www.facebook.com/Xchorix; Thames 1653; choripán AR$90-110; ⏲12:30pm-12:30am; 📶; 🚌55, 39) Elevating the humble Argentine *chori* (sausage) to new heights is this hip new joint in Palermo, its bright yellow walls decorated with smiling cartoon sausages. The quality, 100% pork *choris* and *morcillas* (blood sausages) hang on display – choose from a range of gourmet toppings and homemade breads for a *choripán* sandwich.

Also serves craft beer and a selection of sides.

Big Sur BURGERS **$$**
(Map p74; ☎011-4806-7264; www.facebook.com/BigSurBA; Av Cerviño 3596; burgers AR$90, meals AR$220; ⏲noon-midnight Wed-Mon; Ⓢ Línea D Scalabrini Ortiz) This casual, industrial-style joint serves great hamburgers, fried chicken, hot dogs and fries in baskets, as well as quality craft beer.

Burger Joint BURGERS **$**
(Map p74; ☎011-4833-5151; www.facebook.com/BurgerJointPalermo; Jorge Luis Borges 1766; burgers AR$100; ⏲noon-midnight; Ⓢ Línea D Plaza Italia) For some of the juiciest burgers in BA, head to this popular, graffiti-covered spot. NYC-trained chef Pierre Chacra offers just four kinds to choose from, but they're all stellar. Try the Mexican (jalapeños, guacamole and hot sauce) or Jamaican (pineapple, cheddar and bacon).

Buenos Aires Verde VEGETARIAN **$$**
(Map p74; ☎011-4775-9594; www.bsasverde.com; Gorriti 5657; mains AR$210-265; ⏲9am-12:30am Mon-Sat; 🖉; 🚌111, 140, 39) Long-running organic, vegetarian restaurant serving wraps, salads, soups and sandwiches; wash them down with a wheatgrass juice or fruit smoothie. Small grocery too.

Gran Dabbang FUSION **$$**
(Map p74; 011-4832-1186; www.facebook.com/grandabbang; Av Scalabrini Ortiz 1543; small plates AR$120-230; 8pm-midnight Mon-Sat; 141, 15, 160) The rule-breaking, experimental fusion food conjured up by Mariano Ramón, one of the rising stars of the BA food scene, can be sampled in the small, packed dining room of this unassuming restaurant. Choose three small plates to share between two and get ready for a wild-eyed blend of Indian, Thai and Paraguayan flavors (among others), drawn from Ramón's travels.

Siamo nel Forno PIZZA **$$**
(Map p74; 011-4775-0337; Costa Rica 5886; pizzas AR$240-370; 8pm-midnight Tue-Thu & Sun, to 1am Fri & Sat; 111, 93, 39) Possibly the city's best Naples-style pizzas, made with quality ingredients and finished in a hot wood-fired oven so the thin crusts char beautifully. Try the margherita, with tomatoes, fresh mozzarella, basil and olive oil; the champignon and prosciutto comes with mushrooms, ham and goat cheese. Also bakes excellent calzone.

El Preferido de Palermo ARGENTINE **$$**
(Map p74; 011-4774-6585; Jorge Luis Borges 2108; mains AR$130-260; 9am-11:30pm Mon-Sat; S Línea D Plaza Italia) You can't get much more traditional than this atmospheric, family-run joint. Order tapas, meat platters, homemade pastas and seafood soups, or try one of its specialties – the tortillas, *milanesas* and Cuban rice with veal and polenta. Hanging hams, jars of olives and high tables with blocky wood stools add to the charm.

Bio VEGETARIAN **$$**
(Map p74; 011-4774-3880; www.biorestaurant.com.ar; Humboldt 2192; mains AR$175-290; 10am-midnight; ; S Línea D Palermo) Tired of meat? Then make a beeline for this casual family-run restaurant, which specializes in healthy, organic and vegetarian fare. Try the quinoa hamburgers, Mediterranean couscous or lentil *milanesa,* washed down with refreshing ginger lemonade. Caters to celiacs, vegans and raw foodists. Also runs cooking classes.

★ **La Carnicería** PARRILLA **$$$**
(Map p74; 011-2071-7199; www.facebook.com/xlacarniceriax; Thames 2317; mains AR$360-380; 8pm-midnight Tue-Fri, 1-3:30pm & 8pm-midnight Sat & Sun; S Línea D Plaza Italia) The menu at this modern *parrilla* is limited, but everything on it is spectacular, from the crispy *provoleta* (barbecued cheese), to the homemade *chorizo* and *morcilla,* to the tenderloin and rib cuts. This is a place for serious meat lovers who won't be put off by the butcher-themed decor. Portions are huge. Reserve ahead.

★ **Don Julio** PARRILLA **$$$**
(Map p74; 011-4832-6058; www.parrilladonjulio.com.ar; Guatemala 4691; mains AR$296-657; noon-4pm & 7:30pm-1am; S Línea D Plaza Italia) Classy service and a great wine list add an upscale bent to this traditional – and very popular – corner steak house. The *bife de chorizo* (sirloin steak) is the main attraction here, but the baked goat cheese provolone, *bondiola de cerdo* (pork shoulder) and gourmet salads are a treat as well, and portions are large. Reserve ahead.

Las Pizarras INTERNATIONAL **$$$**
(Map p74; 011-4775-0625; www.laspizarrasbistro.com; Thames 2296; mains AR$310-365; 8pm-midnight Tue-Sun; S Línea D Plaza Italia) At this simple, unpretentious, excellent restaurant, Chef Rodrigo Castilla cooks up an eclectic range of dishes, such as grilled venison or rabbit stuffed with cherries and pistachios. Those with meeker stomachs can choose the asparagus and mushroom risotto or any of the homemade pastas.

Artemisia VEGETARIAN **$$$**
(Map p74; 011-4773-2641; www.artemisianatural.com; Costa Rica 5893; mains AR$220-330; 10am-4:30pm & 8:30-11pm Tue-Sat, 10am-4:30pm Sun; ; S Línea D Ministro Carranza) At this gorgeous corner restaurant you'll want to linger over the tasty organic, vegetarian food (there are a few fish options available, too). The large windows let in tonnes of light, and local artwork and a sunny, internal patio packed with plants add to the ambience. Meals come with a basket of excellent, freshly baked bread.

Sunae Asian Cantina ASIAN **$$$**
(Map p74; 011-4776-8122; www.sunaeasiancantina.com; Humboldt 1626; mains AR$265-420; 8-11:30pm Mon-Thu, to midnight Fri & Sat; ; 111, 108, 140) After honing her skills at her popular closed-door restaurant, chef Christina Sunae has moved on to open a sophisticated Asian cantina in Palermo Hollywood. The menu spans Southeast Asia, featuring Malaysian *rendang* (meat curry), Filipino pork buns, Vietnamese dishes, tangy Thai salads and fiery curries from the Chiang Mai region.

La Cabrera PARRILLA $$$

(Map p74; ☎011-4832-5754; www.lacabrera.com.ar; José Antonio Cabrera 5099; mains AR$388-562; 12:30-4:30pm & 8:30pm-midnight Sun-Thu, to 1am Fri & Sat; 140, 34) Hugely popular for grilling up some of BA's most sublime meats, so soft they can be cut with a spoon. Steaks weigh in at 400g or 800g and arrive with many little complimentary side dishes. Come at 7pm for happy hour, when everything is 40% off – arrive early to score a table; reservations are taken from 8:30pm only.

Has a **second location** (Map p74; ☎011-4832-5754; http://lacabrera.com.ar/; José Antonio Cabrera 5127; mains AR$244-400; 12:30-4:30pm & 8:30pm-midnight Sun-Thu, to 1am Fri & Sat; 140, 34) nearby.

South of Palermo

Sarkis MIDDLE EASTERN $

(Map p74; ☎011-4772-4911; Thames 1101; mains AR$60-190; noon-3pm & 8pm-1am; 140, 111, 34) The food is fabulous and well-priced at this long-standing Middle Eastern restaurant – come with a group to sample many exotic dishes. Start with the roasted eggplant hummus and *boquerones* (marinated sardines), then follow up with kebabs or lamb in yogurt sauce. Less busy at lunchtime; there's usually a wait for a table at dinner.

Guarda la Vieja ARGENTINE $$

(Map p74; ☎011-4863-7923; Billinghurst 699; mains AR$125-235; 6pm-2am Sun-Thu, to 4am Fri & Sat; ; Línea B Carlos Gardel) With a reliable menu of tasty pizzas, salads, pastas and *milaneses,* it's no surprise that this corner restaurant-bar in Abasto is so popular. Sit at one of the pavement tables and order a few *raciones* (snacks) or a *picada* (shared appetizer plate) – they come laden with calamari, ham, cheeses, olives, sweet potato and homemade bread.

★ **i Latina** SOUTH AMERICAN $$$

(Map p74; ☎011-4857-9095; www.ilatinabuenosaires.com; Murillo 725; 7-course tasting menu AR$1600, wine pairing AR$900; 8-11pm Tue-Sat; Línea B Malabia) Located south of Palermo in Villa Crespo is one of BA's best restaurants: i Latina. The set menu consists of seven courses, all exquisitely prepared and presented. Flavors are incredibly stimulating and complex; this isn't a place to simply fill your tummy, but rather to savor a gustatory experience that will dazzle your taste buds. Reservations required.

Drinking & Nightlife

Buenos Aires' nightlife is legendary. What else could you expect from a country where dinner rarely starts before 10pm? In some neighborhoods, finding a good sports bar, classy cocktail lounge, atmospheric old cafe or upscale wine bar is as easy as walking down the street. And dancers will be in heaven, as BA boasts spectacular nightclubs showcasing top-drawer DJs.

The Center

Café Tortoni CAFE

(Map p58; ☎011-4342-4328; www.cafetortoni.com.ar; Av de Mayo 829; Línea A Piedras) BA's oldest and most famous cafe, Tortoni has become so popular with foreigners that the bus loads of tourists detract from its charm. Still, it's practically an obligatory stop for any visitor to town: order a couple of *churros* (fried pastry dough) with your hot chocolate and forget about the inflated prices. There are also nightly tango shows – reserve ahead.

La Puerto Rico CAFE

(Map p58; ☎011-4331-2215; www.lapuertoricocafe.com.ar; Adolfo Alsina 416; 7am-8pm Mon-Fri, 8am-7pm Sat, noon-7pm Sun; Línea E Bolívar) La Puerto Rico has been going strong since 1887. Located a block south of Plaza de Mayo, the place serves coffee and great pastries, the latter baked on the premises. Pope Francis used to come here for his morning *café con leche* (coffee with milk) and *medialunas* (croissants) when he was Archbishop of Buenos Aires.

Bahrein CLUB

(Map p58; ☎011-4314-8886; www.bahreinba.com; Lavalle 345; Fri & Sat; Línea B Alem) Attracting a good share of BA's tattooed youth, Bahrein is a hugely popular downtown club housed in an old bank (check out the 'vault' in the basement). On the ground floor is the lounge-like Funky Room where resident DJs spin house music and electronica. Downstairs is the Xss discotheque, an impressive sound system and a dance floor for hundreds.

La Cigale BAR

(Map p58; ☎011-4893-2332; www.facebook.com/lacigalebar; 25 de Mayo 597; noon-3pm & 6pm-3am Mon-Fri, 9:30pm-3am Sat; Línea B Alem) This upstairs bar-restaurant is popular with office workers during the week, and fusion foods are served for both lunch and dinner.

LGBTIQ+ BUENOS AIRES

Despite the fact that Argentina is a Catholic country, Buenos Aires is one of the world's top gay destinations, with dedicated hostels and guesthouses, bars and nightclubs. In 2002 BA became the first Latin American city to legalize same-sex civil unions, and in July 2010 Argentina became the first Latin American country to legalize same-sex marriage. Today the city is home to South America's largest **gay pride parade** (www.marchadelorgullo.org.ar; ⌚Nov).

Look out for the free map of local gay-friendly businesses, Circuitos Cortos BSAS Gay (www.mapabsasgay.com.ar). Good general websites are www.thegayguide.com.ar and www.nighttours.com/buenosaires.

An especially gay-friendly accommodation is **Lugar Gay** (Map p58; ☎011-4300-4747; www.lugargay.com.ar; Defensa 1120; dm US$25, s US$45-60, d US$65-80; ❄📶; 🚌29, 24, 111), a casual guesthouse that also acts as an information center.

Check out the gay bars **Sitges** (Map p74; www.facebook.com/SitgesBuenosAires; Av Córdoba 4119; ⌚11pm-6am Thu-Sun; 🚌140, 109, 24), **Flux** (Map p70; ☎011-5252-0258; www.facebook.com/FluxBarBsAs; Marcelo T de Alvear 980; ⌚7pm-2am Sun-Wed, to 3am Thu-Sat; Ⓢ Línea C San Martín) and **Pride Cafe** (Map p58; ☎011-4300-6435; Balcarce 869; ⌚9am-8pm; 📶; 🚌29, 24, 33). The best nightclubs are **Glam** (Map p74; ☎011-4963-2521; www.glambsas.com.ar; José Antonio Cabrera 3046; ⌚midnight-7am Thu & Sat; 🚌29, 109), Rheo at Crobar (p97) and Amerika (p97). A long-running lesbian bar is **Bach Bar** (Map p74; ☎011-5184-0137; www.facebook.com/bach.bar; José Antonio Cabrera 4390; ⌚11pm-6am Fri & Sat, 10pm-6am Sun; 🚌140, 141, 110).

Casa Brandon (Map p74; ☎011-4858-0610; www.brandongayday.com.ar; Luis Maria Drago 236; ⌚8pm-3am Wed-Sun; Ⓢ Línea B Ángel Gallardo) is an art gallery/cultural center. And for a fun night of guided drinking and partying, there's **Out & About Pub Crawl** (☎011-3678-0170; www.outandaboutpubcrawl.com/buenosaires; AR$200; ⌚10pm Sat).

Finally, gay tango classes and *milongas* are given at La Marshall at El Beso (p104) and Tango Queer (p104).

Come on the second Monday of the month for the Buenos Aires Pub Quiz (www.buenosairespubquiz.com). Happy hour is from 6pm to 10pm.

Congreso & Tribunales

★Los Galgos BAR

(Map p58; ☎011-4371-3561; www.facebook.com/LosGalgosBarNotable; Av Callao 501; ⌚8am-1am Mon-Sat; Ⓢ Línea B Callao) This classic neighborhood bar – formerly frequented by the neighborhood's elderly *señores* – has been immaculately restored and transformed into a sophisticated bar and restaurant serving modern Argentine food. It's open all day, for breakfast, lunch, *merienda* (afternoon tea) and dinner. Come from 6pm for a cocktail in the candlelight accompanied by a *picada* of meats, olives and cheeses.

El Gato Negro TEAHOUSE

(Map p58; ☎011-4374-1730; Av Corrientes 1669; ⌚9am-10pm Mon, to 11pm Tue, to midnight Wed & Thu, to 2am Fri & Sat, 3-11pm Sun; Ⓢ Línea B Callao) Tea-lined wooden cabinets and a spicy aroma welcome you to this pleasant little sipping paradise. Enjoy imported cups of coffee or tea, along with breakfast and dainty *sandwiches de miga* (thin, crustless sandwiches, traditionally eaten at tea time). Imported teas and coffees are sold in bulk, and a range of exotic herbs and spices are also on offer.

Los 36 Billares BAR

(Map p58; ☎011-4122-1500; www.los36billares.com.ar; Av de Mayo 1271; ⌚7am-2am Mon-Thu, to 3am Fri, to 4am Sat, to 1am Sun; Ⓢ Línea A Lima) Dating from 1894, this is one of the city's most historic cafe-bars and serves a good selection of pizzas and empanadas. As its name implies, it's big on billiard tables (check out the basement).

San Telmo

★Bar Plaza Dorrego CAFE

(Map p58; ☎011-4361-0141; Defensa 1098; ⌚8am-midnight Sun-Thu, to 3:30am Fri & Sat; 🚌29, 24, 33) You can't beat the atmosphere at this traditional joint; sip your *submarino*

WINE TASTING & MORE

By now you've probably heard: Argentine wines are world-class. Most famous is malbec, that dark, robust plum-flavored wine that has solidly stomped the region of Mendoza on every oenophile's map (the Mendoza region produces 60% of the country's wine). But Argentina has other fine varietals that are very worthy of a sip or three – fresh torrontés (a dry white), fruity bonarda and earthy pinot noir.

So which to try? They say there's a perfect Argentine wine for every occasion and a good *vinoteca* (wine boutique) will help you find it. In Palermo, try Lo de Joaquín Alberdi (p107), in San Telmo there's **Vinotango** (Map p58; 011-4361-1101; www.vinotango.com.ar; Estados Unidos 488; 10:30am-9pm; 29). Aldo's Vinoteca (p86) is a restaurant and wine store with some 600 different labels in stock, to drink in or take away.

Supermarket selections are usually adequate, though you miss out on the tailored advice. Among the mainstay brands are Norton, Trapiche, Zuccardi and Santa Julia, with different lines that cater to every price range. Spend a bit more to try the elegant Rutini (from Bodega La Rural), Nicasia or Luigi Bosca.

For wine tastings, inquire at **Pain et Vin** (Map p74; 011-4832-5654; www.facebook.com/painevin; Gorriti 5132; tastings per person AR$550; noon-10pm Tue-Sat, to 7pm Sun; 140, 34, 111), a casual wine and bread shop. **Bar du Marché** (Map p74; 011-4778-1050; www.bardumarchepalermo.com; Nicaragua 6002; wine tasting AR$195; 10am-midnight Mon-Sat; S Línea D Ministro Carranza) is a low-key bistro offering 50 wines by the glass, while Gran Bar Danzón is an upscale lounge-restaurant that also has a good selection of wines by the glass.

Contact sommelier Sorrel Moseley-Williams for private tastings and customized tours of local wine bars; she writes about local wines on her blog www.comewinewith.me and organizes a monthly pop-up wine event, Come Wine With Us.

Many *puertas cerradas* (closed-door restaurants) offer fine wines with their meals; **Casa Coupage** (Map p74; 011-4777-9295; www.casacoupage.com; Acuña de Figueroa 1790; 6-/8-course tasting menu AR$770/935; 8:30-11pm Wed-Sat; S Línea D Palermo), run by an Argentine sommelier, is especially wine-oriented.

(hot milk with chocolate) by a picturesque window and watch the world pass by, or grab an outdoor table next to the busy plaza. Meanwhile, traditionally suited waiters, piped-in tango music, antique bottles and scribbled graffiti on the walls and counters might take you back in time.

Doppelgänger COCKTAIL BAR
(Map p65; 011-4300-0201; www.doppelganger.com.ar; Av Juan de Garay 500; 7pm-2am Tue-Thu, to 4am Fri, 8pm-4am Sat; 29, 24) At this cool, emerald-hued corner bar you can count on being served a perfectly mixed martini. That's because Doppelgänger specializes in vermouth cocktails. The lengthy menu is full of creative concoctions: start with the journalist, a martini with a bitter orange twist, or go for the bar's best seller – an old fashioned.

Coffee Town COFFEE
(Map p58; 011-4361-0019; http://coffeetown-company.com; Bolívar 976, Mercado de San Telmo; 8am-8:30pm; S Línea C Independencia) For some of BA's best coffee, drop by this coffee shop inside the Mercado de San Telmo (p64) – enter via Carlos Calvo. Experienced baristas serve up organic, fair-trade coffee derived from beans from all over the world – Colombia, Kenya, Sumatra and Yemen. A few pastries help the java go down.

Retiro

★ **Florería Atlántico** COCKTAIL BAR
(Map p70; 011-4313-6093; http://floreriaatlantico.com.ar; Arroyo 872; 7pm-2am Mon-Wed, to 2:30am Thu, to 4am Fri, 8pm-4am Sat, 8pm-2am Sun) This basement speakeasy is located within a flower shop, which adds an air of mystery and is likely a key reason for its success. Hipsters, artists, chefs, businesspeople and foreigners all flock here for the excellent cocktails, both classic and creative, accompanied by delicious tapas.

If you're a gin lover, note that the owner, Renato Giovannoni, produces and sells his own brand – called Príncipe de los

Apóstoles – aromatically infused with mint, grapefruit, eucalyptus and *yerba mate*. Reserve ahead for dinner.

BASA Basement Bar BAR

(Map p70; ☎011-4893-9444; www.basabar.com.ar; Basavilbaso 1328; ⏰noon-3:30pm & 7pm-close Mon-Fri, 8pm-close Sat; Ⓢ Línea C San Martín) This fashionable and classy spot sets the mood with open spaces, dim lighting and sofas. Check out its cocktail list – the refreshing Moscow mule is a pleasant surprise, especially on warm days. DJs provide the sounds from 10pm.

Recoleta & Barrio Norte

Gran Bar Danzón BAR

(Map p70; ☎011-4811-1108; www.granbardanzon.com.ar; Libertad 1161; ⏰7pm-2am Mon-Fri, from 8pm Sat & Sun; Ⓢ Línea D Tribunales) Upscale restaurant-wine bar with a good selection of wines by the glass as well as fresh fruit cocktails, exotic martinis and Euro- and Asian-inspired dinner selections. It's very popular, so come early and snag a good seat on a sofa.

Milión COCKTAIL BAR

(Map p70; ☎011-4815-9925; www.milion.com.ar; Paraná 1048; ⏰noon-2am Mon-Wed, to 3am Thu, to 4am Fri & Sat, 8pm-2am Sun; Ⓢ Línea D Callao) One of BA's most elegant bars, this sexy spot takes up three floors of a renovated old mansion. The garden out back is a leafy paradise, overlooked by a solid balcony that holds the best seats in the house. Nearby marble steps are also an appealing place to lounge with a frozen mojito or basil daiquiri.

Clásica y Moderna CAFE

(Map p58; ☎011-4812-8707; www.clasicaymoderna.com; Av Callao 892; ⏰9am-1am Mon-Sat; Ⓢ Línea D Callao) Catering to the literary set since 1938, this cozy and intimate bookstore-restaurant-cafe oozes history from its atmospheric brick walls. It's nicely lit, serves fine, simple meals and offers nightly live performances of folk music, jazz, bossa nova and tango (after 9pm). The late Mercedes Sosa, tango singer Susana Rinaldi and Liza Minnelli have all performed here.

Presidente BAR

(Map p70; ☎011-4811-3248; http://presidentebar.com.ar; Quintana 188; ⏰8pm-2am Tue-Thu, to 3am Fri & Sat; Ⓢ Línea D Callao) Join Recoleta's well-heeled residents for a cocktail beneath chandeliers in an elegant space that's fit for a president. Order from the extensive drinks list, or ask the mixologists to create a cocktail that's tailored to your tastes. Book ahead to bag your place in one of the dark-wood booths. DJs play most nights.

La Biela CAFE

(Map p70; ☎011-4804-0449; www.labiela.com; Av Quintana 600; ⏰7am-2am Mon-Thu, to 3am Fri & Sat, 8am-2am Sun; 🚌130, 62, 93) A Recoleta institution, this classic cafe has been serving the *porteño* elite since the 1950s – when race-car champions used to frequent the place. The outdoor front terrace is unbeatable for a coffee or beer on a sunny afternoon. Just know that the privilege of seating here will cost 20% more.

The huge *gomero* (rubber tree) opposite across from La Biela was planted by a Franciscan monk in around 1800.

Shamrock CLUB

(Map p70; ☎011-4812-3584; www.theshamrock.com.ar; Rodríguez Peña 1220; ⏰6pm-3am Tue & Wed, to 5:30am Thu, to 6:30am Fri, 10pm-6:30am Sat; Ⓢ Línea D Callao) The Shamrock Basement is an unpretentious subterranean club known for its first-rate DJ lineups, pounding house music and diverse young crowd. Thanks to the ever-popular Irish pub upstairs, the place sees plenty of traffic throughout the night. Come at 3am to see the club in full swing, or just descend the stairs after enjoying a few pints at ground level.

Women beware: this is a serious pick-up joint.

Palermo

★Uptown BAR

(Map p74; ☎011-2101-4897; www.uptownba.com; Arévalo 2030; ⏰8:30pm-2am Tue & Wed, to 3am Thu-Sat; Ⓢ Línea D Ministro Carranza) Descend the graffiti-strewn stairwell and step aboard the carriage of an actual New York subway train to reach BA's hottest bar, a cavernous underground space with DJs and dancing, and a smaller, cozier room styled as a pharmacy. It's a popular place; call ahead to put your name on the guest list.

Uptown's menu reflects NY's diverse food scene, with dishes themed around the city's culinary hot spots – think Midtown bacon cheeseburgers, tagliatelle from Little Italy and ribs from the Meatpacking District (mains AR$240 to AR$360).

★Verne COCKTAIL BAR
(Map p74; ☎011-4822-0980; http://vernecocktailclub.com; Av Medrano 1475; ⏰9pm-2am Sun-Tue, 8pm-2am Wed, 8pm-3am Thu, 8pm-4am Fri, 9pm-4am Sat; 🚌160, 15) This upscale yet casual bar has a vague Jules Verne theme. Cocktails are the house specialty, whipped up by one of BA's best bartenders, Fede Cuco. A few tables, some cushy sofas and an airy outdoor patio offer a variety of seating options, but plant yourself at the bar to watch the mixologists work their magic.

★LAB Training Center & Coffee Shop CAFE
(Map p74; ☎011-4843-1790; www.labcafe.com.ar; Humboldt 1542; ⏰8am-8pm Mon-Fri, from 10am Sat; 🚌111, 140, 39) The high ceilings, exposed brick wall and industrial aesthetic here are such hallmarks of a hipster cafe that the place borders on self-parody, but the coffee *is* excellent. Choose your house-roasted beans and have them run through a Chemex, AeroPress, V60, Kalita, syphon or Clever Dripper. Mostly counter seating.

★Niceto Club CLUB
(Map p74; ☎011-4779-9396; www.nicetoclub.com; Niceto Vega 5510; ⏰Tue-Sat; 🚌111, 140, 34) One of the city's biggest crowd-pullers, the can't-miss event at Niceto Club is Thursday night's Club 69, a subversive DJ extravaganza featuring gorgeously attired showgirls, dancing drag queens, futuristic video installations and off-the-wall performance art. On weekend nights, national and international spin masters take the booth to entertain lively crowds with blends of hip-hop, electronic beats, cumbia and reggae.

Boticario COCKTAIL BAR
(Map p74; www.boticariobar.com; Honduras 5207; ⏰8pm-2am Tue-Thu, to 4am Fri & Sat; 🚌55, 34) With walls draped in leafy vines and wooden shelves lined with glass bottles and jars, Boticario takes its inspiration from an old-time apothecary. The mixologists work their magic to create cocktails with botanical touches, like lemongrass and fresh mint. DJs spin the tunes at weekends.

Vive Café CAFE
(Map p74; ☎011-4774-5461; www.facebook.com/ViveCafeTienda; Costa Rica 5722; ⏰9:30am-8pm Mon-Fri, 11am-8pm Sat, 2-7pm Sun; 📶; Ⓢ Línea D Palermo) If you're fussy about coffee, head to Vive for your flat white or cold brew fix – it'll be made with quality Colombian beans and prepared with a smile by the friendly owners, a young Colombian-Argentine couple. There are a few pastries available too, but the coffee is the star of the show.

Benaim BAR
(Map p74; www.facebook.com/BenaimBA; Gorriti 4015; ⏰6pm-12:30am Mon-Thu, to 3am Fri, noon-3am Sat, noon-12:30am Sun; 🚌140, 39, 99) Order a pint of IPA or golden ale from the caravan bar and drink it under the fairy lights and hanging plants in Benaim's attractive beer garden. There's also a kitchen serving good-value Jewish street food, such as hummus and falafel, kebabs and pastrami. Happy hour is from 6pm to 8pm.

On Tap CRAFT BEER
(Map p74; ☎011-4771-5424; www.ontap.com.ar; Costa Rica 5527; ⏰5pm-midnight Mon-Wed & Sun, to 1am Thu-Sat) This popular pub has 20 Argentine microbrews on tap, including IPAs, pilsners, stouts, wheat porters and honey beers. It's more of a place to enjoy beers than to hang out – there's only counter seating and a communal table, though a few burgers and other pub food are available. Bring a growler for refills; happy hour runs from 5pm to 8:30pm.

There's another **On Tap** (Map p65; Av Caseros 482; ⏰5pm-midnight Sun, Tue & Wed, to 1am Thu-Sat; 🚌29) in San Telmo.

Lattente Espresso & Brew Bar CAFE
(Map p74; ☎011-4833-1676; www.cafelattente.com; Thames 1891; ⏰9am-8pm Mon-Sat, 10am-8pm Sun; Ⓢ Línea D Plaza Italia) Riding on BA's java boom is this modern coffee shop serving house-roasted beans. Order your espresso, cappuccino, Americano or latte (via AeroPress or V60) and have a seat at one of the tall communal tables along with other caffeine junkies. A few cookies and brownies are also on offer.

Antares BAR
(Map p74; ☎011-4833-9611; www.cervezaantares.com; Armenia 1447; ⏰6pm-2am Mon-Thu, 6pm-4am Fri, 7pm-4am Sat, 7pm-2am Sun; 🚌140, 15, 110) Craft beer may be all the rage in BA right now, but Antares has been brewing ales at its Mar del Plata factory since the current crop of beer-makers were in diapers. Its Palermo branch is a modern but relaxed space serving the brewery's famous porters, stout and barley wine.

Kika CLUB
(Map p74; www.kikaclub.com.ar; Honduras 5339; ⏰1am-late Tue-Sun; 🚌111, 34, 140) Being su-

premely well located near the heart of Palermo's bar scene makes Kika's popular Tuesday-night 'Hype' easily accessible for those up for a party. It's a mix of electro, rock, hip-hop, drum and bass, and dubstep, all spun by both local and international DJs. Other nights see electronica, raggaeton, Latin beats and live bands ruling the roost.

Frank's COCKTAIL BAR

(Map p74; www.facebook.com/FranksBar.ar; Arévalo 1445; ⌚9pm-3am Tue-Thu, to 4am Fri & Sat; 🚌111, 140, 39) This plush speakeasy bar requires a password (via telephone booth) to get in – follow the clues on the Facebook page. Inside it's an elegant space with crystal chandeliers, billowy ceiling drapes and an exclusive feel. Classic cocktails from before the 1930s are stirred – never blended – and served to a crowd of locals and foreigners.

Crobar CLUB

(Map p74; ☎011-4778-1500; www.crobar.com.ar; cnr Av de la Infanta Isabel & Freyre; ⌚11:30pm-7am Fri & Sat; 🚌10, 33, 111) Stylish and spacious Crobar remains one of BA's most popular clubs. On Fridays international DJs mash up the latest techno selections at Be Techno, while on Saturdays there's trance at Pixel in the main room, as well as the gay party Rheo. Bring a full wallet – this is a top-end spot.

Jet CLUB

(☎011-4872-5599; www.jet.com.ar; Av Rafael Obligado 4801; ⌚10pm-6am Thu-Sat; 🚌33, 45, 160) Jet definitely has an exclusive vibe that attracts celebrities and fashionistas, so put on your best get-up or you won't make the dress code. Early on you can hang in the swanky cocktail lounge, nibble on tapas or sushi and enjoy the marina view. As the night progresses, however, the hip young clubbers start making their appearance.

South of Palermo

Las Violetas CAFE

(☎011-4958-7387; http://lasvioletas.com; Av Rivadavia 3899; ⌚8am-2am; Ⓢ Línea A Castro Barros) Dating back to 1884, this historic coffeehouse's stained-glass awnings, high ceilings and gilded details make it one of the most beautiful cafes in the capital. Come for the luxurious afternoon tea and be sure to pick something up in the cake shop on the way out.

878 COCKTAIL BAR

(Map p74; ☎011-4773-1098; www.878bar.com.ar; Thames 878; ⌚7pm-3am Mon-Thu, to 4:30am Fri, 8pm-4:30am Sat & Sun; 🚌55) Hidden behind an unsigned door is this 'secret' bar, but it's hardly exclusive. Enter a wonderland of elegant, low lounge furniture and red-brick walls; for whiskey lovers there are over 80 kinds to try, but the cocktails are tasty too. If you're hungry, tapas are available (reserve for dinners). Vermouth happy hour is 7pm to 9pm Monday to Friday.

Amerika CLUB

(Map p74; ☎011-4865-4416; www.ameri-k.com.ar; Gascón 1040; ⌚Fri-Sun; Ⓢ Línea B Medrano) BA's largest and feistiest gay nightclub, long-running Amerika attracts all kinds of folks – but Saturdays are especially popular with gay guys. There are two music floors, one electronica and one Latina, plus *barra libre* (all-you-can-drink) on Fridays and Saturdays. Large video screens, stripper shows, four bars and a wild dark room keep things interesting.

☆ Entertainment

The entertainment scene in Buenos Aires has always been lively, but there was an outburst of creative energy in the decade following the economic crisis of 2001. Filmmakers began producing quality works on shoestring budgets, troupes performed in new avant-garde theaters and live-music groups played in more mainstream venues. Today nearly every neighborhood offers great entertainment options.

Major entertainment venues often require booking through **Ticketek** (☎011-5237-7200; www.ticketek.com.ar; Av Santa Fe 4389; ⌚1-8pm Mon-Sat; Ⓢ Línea D Plaza Italia). The service charge is about 10% of the ticket price.

Carteleras (discount-ticket offices) sell a limited number of discounted tickets for many events, such as movies, theater and tango shows, with savings of 20% to 50%. Try **Cartelera Baires** (☎011-4372-5058; Av Corrientes 1382, Galería Apolo; ⌚10am-6pm Mon, 1-8pm Tue-Thu, 1-9pm Fri, 2-9pm Sat; Ⓢ Línea B Uruguay), **Cartelera Vea Más** (☎011-6320-5319; http://carteleraveamas.com.ar; Av Corrientes 1660, Local 2; ⌚10am-8pm Mon, to 9:30pm Tue-Wed & Sun, to 10:30pm Thu, to 11pm Fri & Sat; Ⓢ Línea B Callao) or **Cartelera Espectáculos** (☎011-4322-1559; www.123info.com.ar; Lavalle 742; ⌚noon-9pm Mon-Sat, to 8pm Sun; Ⓢ Línea C Lavalle). Buy tickets as far in advance as possible.

WORTH A TRIP

SAN ISIDRO

About 20km north of Buenos Aires is peaceful and residential San Isidro, a salubrious suburb of leafy cobblestone streets lined with some luxurious mansions, as well as more modest houses. The historic center is at Plaza Mitre with its beautiful neo-Gothic cathedral; on weekends the area buzzes with a **crafts fair**. There are a number of worthwhile museums with sweeping river views that make for a pleasant day trip from the city. The suburb is easily reached by train from Buenos Aires; it's also possible to stop here on the way to or from Tigre.

San Isidro is steeped in history dating back to the first settlement of Buenos Aires in 1580, when Juan de Garay divided a 20km stretch of coastline into narrow strips of land that were divvied up among the group of 40 who had made the journey from Spain.

Once owned by Argentine icon, General Pueyrredón, the **Museo Pueyrredón** (011-4512-3131; www.museopueyrredon.org.ar; Rivera Indarte 48; 10am-6pm Tue & Thu, 3-8pm Sat & Sun; San Isidro) FREE is an old colonial villa set on spacious grounds with faraway views of the Río de la Plata. Note the algarrobo (carob tree) under which Pueyrredón and San Martín planned strategies against the Spanish. To get here from the cathedral, follow Av Libertador south five blocks, turn left on Peña and after two blocks turn right onto Rivera Indarte.

Even more glamorous is the Unesco site **Villa Ocampo** (011-4732-4988; http://unescovillaocampo.org/; Elortondo 1837; AR$70; 12:30-7pm Fri-Sun, guided tours 3pm & 4:30pm; Beccar), a wonderfully restored mansion. Victoria Ocampo was a writer, publisher and intellectual who dallied with the literary likes of Borges, Cortázar, Sabato and Camus. The gardens are lovely here; guided tours are offered in English and Spanish.

Also worth a visit is **Quinta Los Ombúes** (www.quintalosombues.com.ar; Adrián Beccar Varela 774; 10am-6pm Tue & Thu, 2-6pm Sat & Sun; San Isidro) FREE, a historical house with some period items once owned by prominent local figures. It's located one block behind the cathedral.

The Tigre branch of the Mitre line train from Retiro stops at San Isidro and Beccar stations (with/without SUBE card AR$5/12, 35 minutes).

Tango Shows

If there's one thing Buenos Aires isn't short of it's tango shows. The best known are the expensive, tourist-oriented spectacles that are very entertaining and awe-inspiring, and showcase amazing feats of grace and athleticism. However, they are highly glamorized and not what purists consider 'authentic' tango.

The theatrical shows usually include various tango couples, an orchestra, a couple of singers and possibly some folkloric musicians. They last about 1½ hours and come with a dinner option – the food is usually good. VIP options mean a much higher price tag for better views, meal choices and refreshments. Nearly all of them require reservations; some offer modest online discounts and pick-up from your hotel. (Many hotels will book shows for you, which is fine, since sometimes the price is similar to what you'd pay at the venue anyway.)

More modest shows cost far less; some are even free but require you to order a meal or drink at the restaurant. If you don't mind eating there, this is a decent deal. For free (or rather, donation) tango, head to San Telmo on a Sunday afternoon – or sometimes other days. Dancers do their thing in the middle of Plaza Dorrego (p64), though you have to stake out a spot early to snag a good view. Another sure bet is weekends on El Caminito (p64) in La Boca; some restaurants have couple dancing for customers. Many *milongas* (dance halls) also have good, affordable shows.

★**Centro Cultural Borges** TANGO

(Map p58; 011-5555-5359; www.ccborges.org.ar; cnr Viamonte & San Martín; shows US$22-25; Línea C Lavalle) This excellent cultural center has many quality offerings, including recommended, reasonably priced tango shows several times per week. Bien de Tango, on Friday and Saturday nights at 8pm, is especially good and comparable to other tango shows that are triple the cost. Check the cultural center's website or stop in beforehand to see what's on and get an advance ticket.

Café de los Angelitos TANGO
(☎011-4952-2320; www.cafedelosangelitos.com; Av Rivadavia 2100; show from US$90, show & dinner from US$130; ⊙cafe 8am-midnight; SLínea A Congreso) Originally called Bar Rivadavia, this cafe was once the haunt of poets, musicians and even criminals, which is why a police commissioner jokingly called it *los angelitos* (the angels) in the early 1900s. As well as being an elegant hangout for a coffee or tea, come evening time Los Angelitos puts on one of the best tango shows in Buenos Aires.

Rojo Tango TANGO
(Map p58; ☎011-4952-4111; www.rojotango.com; Martha Salotti 445, Faena Hotel; show US$220, show & dinner US$290; 🚌111, 43, 143) This sexy performance is the tango show to top all others, though it comes with a hefty price tag. Offering only 100 seats, the Faena's cabaret room is swathed in blood-red curtains and gilded furniture. The show itself loosely follows the history of the tango, starting from its cabaret roots to the modern fusions of Ástor Piazzolla.

Esquina Carlos Gardel TANGO
(Map p74; ☎011-4867-6363; www.esquinacarlosgardel.com.ar; Carlos Gardel 3200; show from US$96, show & dinner from US$140; SLínea B Carlos Gardel) One of the fanciest tango shows in town plays at this impressive 430-seat theater right next to the lovely Mercado de Abasto (p76) shopping mall. This fine show highlights passionate, top-notch musicians and performers in period costumes, though a modern segment involving a skin suit is cutting-edge, athletic and memorable.

The Abasto neighborhood was once Carlos Gardel's stomping ground, and he even hung out at this locale.

Piazzolla Tango TANGO
(Map p58; ☎011-4344-8200; www.piazzollatango.com; Florida 165, Galaría Güemes; show from US$55, show & dinner from US$100; SLínea D Catedral) This beautiful art-nouveau theater, just off pedestrian Calle Florida, used to be a red-light cabaret venue. The show here is based on the music of Ástor Piazzolla, a *bandoneón* (small accordian) player and composer who revolutionized tango music by fusing in elements from jazz and classical music. Be aware most tables are communal. Free tango class before the show.

El Viejo Almacén TANGO
(Map p58; ☎011-4307-7388; www.viejoalmacen.com; Balcarce 799; show from US$90, show & dinner from US$140; 🚌29, 24, 111) One of BA's longest-running shows (since 1969), this venue is a charming old building from the 1800s. Dinner is served at a multistory restaurant in the main building, then everyone heads across the street to the small theater with an intimate stage, highly athletic dancers and plenty of glitz.

La Ventana TANGO
(Map p58; ☎011-4334-1314; www.laventanaweb.com; Balcarce 431; show from US$70, show & dinner from US$120; SLínea E Belgrano) This long-running basement venue is located in an old converted building with rustic brick walls in San Telmo. The tango show includes a folkloric segment with Andean musicians and a display of *boleadores* (gaucho hunting weapons). There's also a patriotic tribute to Evita, and the dinner offers a wide variety of tasty main dishes – unusual for tango shows.

Academia Nacional del Tango TANGO
(Map p58; ☎011-4345-6967; www.facebook.com/academianacionaldeltango; Av de Mayo 833; SLínea A Piedras) Hosts *milongas* and tango concerts; check the Facebook page for details.

Milongas

Milongas are dance events where people strut their tango skills. The atmosphere at these events can be modern or historical, casual or traditional.

Milongas either start in the afternoon and run until 11pm, or start at around midnight and run until the early-morning light. Classes are often offered beforehand. For a current list of *milongas,* see www.hoy-milonga.com.

★**La Catedral** MILONGA
(Map p74; ☎011-15-5325-1630; www.lacatedralclub.com; Sarmiento 4006; SLínea B Medrano) This grungy warehouse space is very casual, with unusual art on the walls, thrift-store furniture, dim, atmospheric lighting and the occasional cat wandering among the tables. It's very bohemian and there's no implied dress code – you'll see plenty of jeans. A great place for beginners since even non-expert dancers can feel comfortable on the dance floor.

The most popular night here is Tuesday.

Maldita Milonga TANGO
(Map p58; ☎011-15-2189-7747; www.facebook.com/malditamilonga1; Perú 571, Buenos Ayres Club; ⊙class 9pm, milonga 10:30pm Wed; SLínea E Belgrano) Maldita Milonga, held

(Continued on page 104)

The Tango

A lone woman, dressed in slit skirt and high heels, sits at a small table. She glances around, in search of the subtle signal. Her gaze suddenly locks onto a stranger's eyes, and there it is: the *cabeceo*. She nods and rises to meet him, and the new pair head toward the dance floor.

History of Tango

The tango hasn't always been quite so mysterious, but it does have a long and somewhat complex history. Though the exact origins can't be pinpointed, some believe the dance started in Buenos Aires in the 1880s. Legions of European immigrants, mostly lower-class men, arrived in the great village of Buenos Aires to seek their fortunes. Missing their motherlands and the women they left behind, they sought out bars, cafes and bordellos to ease the loneliness. Here the men cavorted with waitresses and prostitutes, helping to evolve a dance blending machismo, passion and longing, with an almost fighting edge to it.

Small musical ensembles were soon brought in to accompany early tangos, playing tunes influenced by pampas *milonga* verse, Spanish and Italian melodies (dance hall) and African *candombe* drums. (The *bandoneón,* a small accordion, was brought into these sessions and has since become an inextricable part of the tango orchestra.) Here the tango song was also born. It summarized the new urban experience for the immigrants and was permeated with nostalgia for a disappearing way of life. Themes ranged from profound feelings about changing neighborhoods to the figure of the mother, male friendship and betrayal by women. Sometimes raunchy lyrics were added.

The perceived vulgarity of the dance was deeply frowned upon by the reigning elites, but it did manage to influence some brash young members of the upper classes, who took the novelty to Paris and created a craze – a dance that became an acceptable outlet for human desires,

1

1. Tango dancers, San Telmo (p63) **2.** Tango dancers, La Boca (p64) **3.** Dancing at a *milonga*, Palermo (p71)

2

3

1

expressed on the dance floors of elegant cabarets. The trend spread around Europe and even to the US, and 1913 was considered by some to be 'the year of the tango.' When the evolved dance returned to Buenos Aires, now refined and famous, the tango finally earned the respectability it deserved. The golden years of tango were just beginning.

Tango at a Milonga Today

Buenos Aires is full of *milongas* (tango dance events), from classic venues with old-time atmosphere to hip warehouse spaces where dancers wear jeans – in other words, there's something for everyone.

At an established *milonga*, finding a good, comparable partner involves many levels of hidden codes, rules and signals that dancers must follow. In fact, some men will only proposition an unknown woman after the second song, so as not to be stuck with a bad dancer. After all, it's considered polite to dance at least to the end of a set (four songs) with any partner; if you are given a curt '*gracias*' after just one song, consider yourself excused.

Your position in the area surrounding the dance floor can be critical. Ideally, you should sit where you have easy access to the floor and to other dancers' line of sight. You may notice singles sitting in front, while couples sit further back. Generally couples are considered 'untouchable' – for them to dance with others, they either enter the room separately, or the man may signal his intent by asking another woman to the floor. Now 'his' woman becomes available to others.

The *cabeceo* – the quick tilt of the head, eye contact and uplifted eyebrows – can happen from way across the room. The woman to whom the *cabeceo* is directed either nods yes and smiles, or pretends not to have noticed. If she says yes, the man gets up and escorts her to the floor. If she pretends not to have seen him, it's considered a rejection. When you're at a *milonga* and don't want

1. Tango class **2.** Musician playing the *bandoneón*

to dance with anyone, don't look around too much – you could be breaking some hearts.

Don't be surprised to see different *milongas* put on at a single venue, depending on the time or day. Each *milonga* can be run by a different promoter, so each will have its own vibe, style, music and table arrangement, as well as age levels and experiences.

For good information on Buenos Aires' tango scene and how to navigate it, get a copy of Sally Blake's practical guide *Happy Tango: Sallycat's Guide to Dancing in Buenos Aires, 2nd edition* (www.sallycatway.com/happytango). You can pick up free tango magazines at *milongas* and tango shoe shops (of which there are many in Buenos Aires).

Tango classes are often available in the same venue as *milongas,* in the hours before they start. But you can find them everywhere from youth hostels to cultural centers – some are even included free when you book a fancy tango show. Tourist-oriented classes are often taught in English.

So what is the appeal of the tango? Experienced dancers will say that the rush from a blissful tango connection with a stranger can lift you to exhilarating heights. But the dance can also become addictive – once you have fallen for the passion and beauty of the tango's movements, you can spend your life trying to attain a physical perfection that can never be fully realized. The true *tanguero* simply attempts to make the journey as graceful as possible.

TOP MILONGAS

- **Patio de Tango** (p104)
- **Salón Canning** (p104)
- **La Catedral** (p99)
- **Maldita Milonga** (p99)
- **La Viruta** (p104)
- **La Glorieta** (p104)

(Continued from page 99)

on Wednesdays at Buenos Ayres Club, is a well-run and popular event, and one of the best places to see tango being danced by real couples. The highlight of the night is when the dynamic orchestra El Afronte plays at 11pm; at midnight there's a professional dance demonstration.

Tango Queer TANGO
(Map p58; ☎011-15-3252-6894; www.tangoqueer.com; Perú 571, Buenos Ayres Club; ⏱class 8:30pm, milonga 10pm-2am Tue; S Línea E Belgrano) On Tuesday nights anyone can dance with anyone, leading or following as they choose, at this excellent gay tango class and *milonga*.

La Glorieta TANGO
(www.facebook.com/milonga.glorieta; Echeverría 1800, Barrancas de Belgrano; ⏱7-11pm daily Nov-Mar, once weekly Apr-Oct; 🚌15, 29, 42) FREE It's hard to imagine a more romantic setting for an outdoor *milonga* than the park bandstand at the Barrancas de Belgrano, where on summer evenings dancers of all ages and levels come to tango. There's usually a free lesson beforehand from 6pm to 7pm.

See website for the winter schedule.

Patio de Tango TANGO
(Milonga de la Manzana de las Luces; Map p58; ☎011-4343-3260; www.facebook.com/PatioDeTangoManzana; Perú 222; by donation; ⏱class 7:30-9pm, milonga 9pm-midnight Fri; S Línea E Bolívar) FREE This wonderfully atmospheric *milonga* takes place in the outdoor patio and surrounding salons of the historic Manzana de las Luces (p56), one of the city's oldest buildings. There's no entrance fee but you may wish to contribute a little money 'to the hat,' which goes to the teachers and musicians.

El Beso TANGO
(Map p58; ☎011-4953-2794; http://elbeso.com.ar; Riobamba 416, 1st fl; S Línea B Callao) This small, intimate dance salon hosts various different *milongas;* the most popular is **Milonga Cachirulo** on Tuesdays from 9pm to 5am. The Cachirulo attracts some very good dancers – you should be confident of your skills if you plan to take to the floor. On Friday nights, El Beso hosts **La Marshall Milonga Gay** (https://lamarshallmilonga.com.ar) from 10:30pm to 4am.

La Viruta TANGO
(Map p74; ☎011-4774-6357; www.lavirutatango.com; Armenia 1366; 🚌141, 15, 110) Popular basement venue. Good beginner tango classes are available before the *milongas* – translating into many inexperienced dancers on the floor earlier on – so if you're an expert get here late (after 2am). Music can run the gamut from tango to rock to cumbia to salsa earlier in the evening, with more traditional tunes later.

If you're still there when the breakfast *medialunas* (croissants) are brought out at 4am it's probably been a good night.

Salón Canning TANGO
(Map p74; ☎011-15-5738-3850; www.parakultural.com.ar; Av Scalabrini Ortiz 1331; 🚌141, 140, 15) Some of BA's finest dancers (no wallflowers here) grace this traditional venue with its great dance floor. Well-known tango company Parakultural stages good events on Monday, Tuesday and Friday, involving orchestras, singers and dance performances; check the website for class times and the *milonga* musical lineup. Expect big crowds and plenty of tourists.

Club Gricel TANGO
(☎011-4957-7157; www.clubgriceltango.com.ar; La Rioja 1180; S Línea E General Urquiza) This old classic in the San Cristóbal neighborhood (take a taxi) often has big crowds. It attracts an older, well-dressed, mostly local clientele – avoid Sundays if you're alone, as it's mostly for couples. There's a wonderful springy dance floor and occasional live orchestras.

Live Music

There are some fine venues that only feature live music, but many theaters, cultural centers, bars and cafes also put on shows. Centro Cultural Torquato Tasso is a good choice for tango-music performances.

Usina del Arte CONCERT VENUE
(Map p65; www.buenosaires.gob.ar/usinadelarte; Agustín R Caffarena 1; 🚌130, 86, 8) FREE This former power station has been transformed into a spectacular concert venue in an effort to regenerate a somewhat sketchy area of La Boca. It's a gorgeous red-brick building complete with scenic clock tower and the two concert halls have top-notch acoustics. Nearly all the art exhibitions, concerts and dance performances here are free; check the website for upcoming events.

Ciudad Cultural Konex CULTURAL CENTER
(Map p74; ☎011-4864-3200; www.ciudadculturalkonex.org; Av Sarmiento 3131; S Línea B Carlos Gardel) Cutting-edge cultural center offering

multidisciplinary performances that often fuse art, culture and technology. Famous for its fantastic Monday night percussion shows **La Bomba de Tiempo** (AR$90; ⏲7-10pm Mon), which attract a young crowd.

Notorious JAZZ
(Map p58; ☎011-4813-6888; www.notorious.com.ar; Av Callao 966; ⏲10am-midnight Mon-Thu, 10am-2am Fri, 5pm-2am Sat, 5pm-midnight Sun; **S** Línea D Callao) This stylish, intimate joint is one of Buenos Aires' premier jazz venues, with a restaurant-cafe (overlooking a verdant garden) hosting live shows nearly every night at 9pm. Check the website for schedules; most performances are jazz, but there's also blues and Brazilian music.

Thelonious Bar JAZZ
(Map p74; ☎011-4829-1562; www.thelonious.com.ar; Jerónimo Salguero 1884, 1st fl; ⏲8:30-11:30pm Wed & Thu, to 12:45am Fri & Sat; **S** Línea D Bulnes) Upstairs in an old mansion lies this dimly lit jazz bar, with high brick ceilings and a good sound system. Come early to snag a seat (or reserve one) and choose something from the typically Argentine food menu and good range of cocktails.

It's known for its classic and contemporary Argentine jazz lineups, though international musicians sometimes play here.

Centro Cultural Torquato Tasso LIVE MUSIC
(Map p65; ☎011-4307-6506; www.torquatotasso.com.ar; Defensa 1575; 🚌29, 168, 24) One of BA's best-loved live-music venues, with top-name tango music performances – keep an eye out for Rodolfo Mederos and La Chicana. Attracts bands that mix genres, such as fusing tango or *folklórico* with rock.

Los Cardones LIVE MUSIC
(Map p74; ☎011-4777-1112; www.cardones.com.ar; Jorge Luis Borges 2180; ⏲9pm-4am Wed-Sat; **S** Línea D Plaza Italia) Come to this friendly, low-key *peña* (folk club) for mellow guitar shows, audience-participatory jam sessions (and possible dancing), hearty regional cuisine from northern Argentina and free-flowing red wine. A great place to hear traditional Argentine folklore music. Check the website for details on the current lineup and reserve ahead for a good table.

Theater

Av Corrientes, between Avs 9 de Julio and Callao, has traditionally been the capital's center for theater, but there are now dozens of venues throughout the city. Check to see what's on at Teatro Colón (p62) and Teatro Nacional Cervantes (p62).

Teatro San Martín THEATER
(Map p58; ☎0800-333-5254; www.complejoteatral.gob.ar; Av Corrientes 1530; **S** Línea B Uruguay) Now reopened after extensive renovations, this major venue has several auditoriums (the largest seats over 1000 people) and showcases international cinema, theater, dance and classical music, covering conventional and more unusual events.

Shopping

Buenos Aires is laced with shopping streets lined with clothing and shoe stores, leather shops and nearly everything else you can think of. Large shopping malls are modern and family-friendly, offering designer goods, food courts and even children's play areas. But perhaps the city's best shopping is in Palermo Viejo, where you'll find upscale boutiques. San Telmo is where antiques aficionados flock.

The Center & Congreso

★ **Autoría** ARTS & CRAFTS
(Map p70; ☎011-5252-2474; www.autoriabsas.com.ar; Suipacha 1025; ⏲9:30am-8pm Mon-Fri, 10am-6pm Sat; **S** Línea C San Martín) This gallery-like store, stocked with edgy art books, fashion, accessories, whimsical leather desk sculptures, original artworks and unique handmade jewelry, strives to promote Argentine designers. Especially interesting are the recycled materials – check out the bags made of Tyvek, inner tubes, fire hoses or even old sails. Products are of high quality and prices are accessible.

Arte y Esperanza ARTS & CRAFTS
(Map p58; ☎011-4343-1455; www.arteyesperanza.com.ar; Balcarce 234; ⏲10am-6pm Mon-Fri; **S** Línea A Plaza de Mayo) This store sells fair-trade, handmade products that include many made by Argentina's indigenous craftspeople. Shop for silver jewelry, pottery, ceramics, textiles, *mate* gourds, baskets, woven bags, wood utensils and animal masks.

Zivals MUSIC
(Map p58; www.facebook.com/Zivals; Av Callao 395; ⏲9:30am-9:30pm Mon-Sat; **S** Línea B Callao) This is one of the better music stores in town, especially when it comes to tango, folk, jazz and classical music. Listening stations are a big plus, and there are also books for sale.

San Telmo

Punto Sur CLOTHING
(Map p58; 011-4300-9320; www.feriapuntosur.com.ar; Defensa 1135; noon-8pm Mon-Sat, 11am-8pm Sun; 29) This is a great clothing store highlighting the works of a number of local independent designers. Creativity is rampant and it's a fun walk-through for one-of-a-kind threads including interesting knitwear, colorful skirts, printed T-shirts, jewelry and accessories, cool handbags and even kids' stuff.

Walrus Books BOOKS
(Map p58; 011-4300-7135; www.walrus-books.com.ar; Estados Unidos 617; noon-8pm Tue-Sun; S Línea C Independencia) Run by an American photographer, this tiny shop is probably the best English-language bookstore in BA. Thousands of new and used literature and nonfiction books line the shelves here, and there's a selection of Latin American classics translated into English. Bring your quality books to trade; literary workshops are offered, too.

L'Ago HOMEWARES
(Map p58; 011-4362-4702; Defensa 970; 11am-8pm; 29) Kitschy-cool home decor – from fluorescent-hued *mate* sets and fun pillows to Frida Kahlo kitchen magnets, eclectic lighting, recycled Elvis wallets and Marilyn Monroe handbags – can be found at cute-as-a-button L'Ago.

Puntos en el Espacio FASHION & ACCESSORIES
(Map p58; 011-4307-7906; www.puntosenelespacio.com.ar; Carlos Calvo 450; 11am-8pm) With over 40 designers represented, this store is a good place to check out edgy women's collections by rising stars in the local fashion world. There are also kids' and men's clothes, handbags, jewelry and a few shoes.

Materia Urbana ARTS & CRAFTS
(Map p58; 011-4361-5265; www.materiaurbana.com; Defensa 702; 11am-7pm Wed-Fri, from 2pm Sat & Tue, 11am-6pm Sun; 29) This innovative design shop shows the work of over 100 local artists; cool finds include leather animal organizers, retro tote bags, plastic *mate* sets and jewelry made from metal, wood and leather.

Recoleta & Barrio Norte

★ **El Ateneo Grand Splendid** BOOKS
(Map p70; 011-4813-6052; www.yenny-elateneo.com/local/grand-splendid; Av Santa Fe 1860; 9am-10pm Mon-Thu, to midnight Fri & Sat, noon-10pm Sun; S Línea D Callao) This glorious bookstore in a converted theater continues to flourish in the age of the Kindle. The Grand Splendid theater opened in 1919 and was converted into a bookstore in 2000. Most of the seating was replaced with bookshelves, but the original features have been preserved, including the beautiful painted cupola and balconies.

Browse through potential purchases in one of the theater boxes or have a cup of coffee at the on-stage cafe.

Fueguia PERFUME
(Map p70; 011-4311-5360; www.fueguia.com; Av Alvear 1680; 11am-8pm; 130, 62, 93) On Recoleta's most *cheto* (posh) avenue you'll find this suitably upmarket perfumery selling a large selection of in-house scents and candles. Pop in to smell the latest creations.

Feria Artesenal Plaza Francia MARKET
(Map p70; www.feriaplazafrancia.com; Plaza Intendente de Alvear; 11am-8pm Sat & Sun; S Línea H Las Heras) Recoleta's popular artisan fair has dozens of booths and a range of creative, homemade goods. Hippies, mimes and tourists mingle. It's at its biggest on weekends, though there are usually a few stalls open during the week. Despite its name, the market is located just outside the Cementerio de la Recoleta in Plaza Intendente de Alvear.

Palermo

★ **Elementos Argentinos** HOMEWARES
(Map p74; 011-4832-6299; www.elementosargentinos.com.ar; Gurruchaga 1881; 11am-7pm Tue-Sat; S Línea D Plaza Italia) The high-quality carpets, rugs and blankets sold here are hand-dyed, hand-woven on a loom and fair trade; the owners work with cooperatives and NGOs to help the communities in northwestern Argentina where the textiles are produced. Have larger items mailed home, or pick up a super soft llama wool blanket to squeeze into your suitcase.

Humawaca FASHION & ACCESSORIES
(Map p74; 011-4832-2662; www.humawaca.com; El Salvador 4692; 11am-8pm Mon-Sat, 2-7pm Sun; 141, 15, 39) Award-winning designer handbags, tote bags and wallets made with Argentine leather, all with clean modernist lines and colorful hues. Visit this tiny boutique – with the tagline 'todo cow' – and you'll always find something different and

DON'T MISS

BUENOS AIRES STREET MARKETS

Wandering through a weekend *feria* is a quintessential BA experience. Artisans display their wares while buskers, mimes and tango dancers entertain. Often there are nearby restaurants with sidewalk tables for people-watching. At some of the more touristed markets, especially Feria de San Telmo, watch for pickpockets.

Check out Feria Artesenal Plaza Francia in Recoleta, Feria de Mataderos (p81) in Mataderos, San Telmo's Feria de San Telmo (p63) and Palermo's Feria Plaza Serrano (Map p74; cnr Honduras & Jorge Luis Borges; 10am-8pm Sat & Sun; 140, 141, 34).

eye-catching. Bags cost around AR$2000 to AR$5000.

Lo de Joaquín Alberdi FOOD & DRINKS
(Map p74; 011-4832-5329; www.lodejoaquinalberdi.com; Jorge Luis Borges 1772; wine tastings AR$850; 11am-9:30pm Mon-Sat, noon-9pm Sun; Línea D Plaza Italia) Nationally produced wines for every taste and budget line the racks and cellar of this attractive wine shop; ask friendly owner Joaquín for his recommendations. Tastings happen Thursday and Friday at 7:30pm (book online ahead of time) and include at least six wines and some cheeses.

Galeria Patio del Liceo MALL
(Map p74; http://patiodelliceo.com; Av Santa Fe 2729; most stores 2-8pm Mon-Sat; Línea D Agüero) Eclectic little shopping mall with a bohemian vibe. In the past few years, young independent artisans have taken over and created an artistic hub here, filling it with various small boutiques, exhibition spaces and workshops. You'll find a couple of bookshops, **Los Hermanos** ukulele store and some great design stores, including **Greens** and sustainable specialists **Tienda Raiz**. Hours vary.

Rapsodia FASHION & ACCESSORIES
(Map p74; 011-4831-6333; www.rapsodia.com; Honduras 4872; 10am-9pm; 140, 110, 15) With gorgeous printed fabrics and details such as fringes and sequins, this large and popular boutique is a must for fashion mavens. Old and new are blended into creative, colorful styles with exotic and bohemian accents. Locals covet the dresses and jeans. There are over a dozen branches in the city.

Bolivia CLOTHING
(Map p74; 011-4832-6284; www.bolivia-divina.com; Gurruchaga 1581; 10:30am-8:30pm Mon-Sat, from 3pm Sun; 141, 110, 15) There's almost nothing here that your young, hip brother wouldn't love, from the fitted shirts to the skin-tight jeans and the military-style jackets. Metrosexual to the hilt, and paradise for the man who isn't afraid of patterns, plaid or pastels. Six other branches in the city.

Information

CONCIERGE SERVICES

BA Cultural Concierge (011-15-3876-5937; www.baculturalconcierge.com) Madi Lang's concierge service helps you plan itineraries, book flights, arrange airport transportation, run errands, get a cell phone, reserve theater tickets, scout out a potential apartment and do a thousand other things that'll help your trip run smoothly. She also offers customized day tours of Buenos Aires, tango tours and outings to Mataderos fair.

MEDICAL SERVICES

Dental Argentina (011-4828-0821; www.dental-argentina.com.ar; Laprida 1621, 2B; 9am-7pm Mon-Fri; Línea D Agüero) Dental services with English-speaking professionals.

Hospital Británico (011-4309-6400; www.hospitalbritanico.org.ar; Perdriel 74; 28, 50, 59)

Hospital Italiano (011-4959-0200; www.hospitalitaliano.org.ar; Juan D Perón 4190; Línea B Medrano)

MONEY

ATMs *(cajeros automáticos)* are everywhere in BA and are the handiest way to get money; they can also be used for cash advances on major credit cards. There's often an English-translation option if you don't read Spanish.

There may be limits per withdrawal, but you may be able to withdraw several times per day – just beware of per-transaction fees. A fee is charged on ATM transactions by the *local* bank (not including charges by your home bank, which are extra). Note that this is a *per transaction* fee, so consider taking out your maximum allowed.

POST

Andreani (Map p58; 0810-122-1111; www.andreani.com.ar; Av Belgrano 1211; 9am-7pm Mon-Fri, to 1pm Sat; Línea C Moreno) A reliable international and domestic postal service, with several branches around the city.

Correo Internacional (Map p70; 011-4891-9191; www.correoargentino.com.ar; Av

TRAVELING SAFELY IN BUENOS AIRES

Buenos Aires is generally pretty safe and you can comfortably walk around at all hours of the night in many places, even as a lone woman. Some areas where you should be careful at night, however, are around Constitución's train station, the eastern border of San Telmo, some parts of Once and La Boca – where, outside tourist streets, you should be careful even during the day. Using your head is good advice anywhere: don't flash any wealth (including expensive jewelry), always be aware of your surroundings and look like you know exactly where you're going (even if you don't).

Like all big cities, BA has its share of problems. As a tourist you're much more likely to be a target of petty crimes such as pickpocketing than armed robbery or kidnapping.

Be careful on crowded buses, on the Subte and at busy *ferias* (street markets). Don't put your bag down without your foot through the strap (especially at sidewalk cafes), and even then keep a close eye on it. Be especially careful at Retiro bus station.

The Tourist Police (p609) can provide interpreters and help victims of robberies.

Antártida Argentina 1100; 9am-3:30pm Mon-Fri; S Línea C Retiro) For international parcels weighing 2kg to 20kg. Bring an open box or parcel as contents will be checked; boxes are also sold here. Look for the building with the yellow facade.

DHL Internacional (Map p58; 0810-122-3345; www.dhl.com.ar; Av Córdoba 783; 9am-7pm Mon-Fri; S Línea C Lavalle) One of many branches around town.

Fedex (Map p58; 0810-333-3339; www.fedex.com; Av Corrientes 654; 9am-6pm Mon-Fri; S Línea B Florida)

OCA (Map p58; 011-4311-5305; www.oca.com.ar; Viamonte 526; 8am-6pm Mon-Fri; S Línea C Lavalle) For domestic packages.

TOURIST INFORMATION

There are several tourist offices and kiosks in Buenos Aires. Staff speak English and can provide maps and information about free guided walks and other activities.

Ezeiza airport (011-5480-6111; Terminal A arrivals, 1st fl, Ezeiza Airport; 8:15am-7:15pm)

Florida (Map p58; cnr Florida & Roque Sáenz Peña; 9am-6pm; S Línea D Catedral)

La Boca (Map p65; for WhatsApp messages 011-2851-8074; https://turismo.buenosaires.gob.ar; Av Don Pedro de Mendoza 1901; 9am-6pm; ; 33, 64, 29)

Plaza San Martín (Map p70; cnr Av Florida & Marcelo T de Alvear; 9am-6pm; S Línea C San Martín)

Puerto Madero (Map p58; Dique 4, Juana M Gorriti 200; 9am-6pm; S Línea B Alem)

Recoleta (Map p70; for WhatsApp 011-2851-8047; https://turismo.buenosaires.gob.ar; Av Quintana 596; 10am-6pm; 130, 62, 93)

Retiro (Map p70; Retiro Bus Station; 7am-4pm; S Línea C Retiro)

TRAVEL AGENCIES

Anda Responsible Travel (011-3221-0833; www.andatravel.com.ar; Billinghurst 1193, 3B; 9am-5pm Mon-Fri; S Línea D Agüero) Recommended outfit that's most notable for its La Boca tour, which introduces travelers to local organizations working toward improving the lives of its citizens. Also offers many tours around Argentina that benefit locals.

Say Hueque (011-5258-8740; www.sayhueque.com; Thames 2062; 9am-6pm Mon-Fri, 10am-1pm Sat; S Línea D Plaza Italia) This recommended independent travel agency specializes in customized adventure trips all around Argentina, and will also make air, bus and hotel reservations. It offers various BA tours as well. Also has a branch in San Telmo (011-4307-2614; www.sayhueque.com; Chile 557; 9am-6pm Mon-Fri, 10am-1pm Sat; S Línea C Independencia).

Tangol (011-4363-6000; www.tangol.com; Defensa 831; 9am-6pm Mon-Sat, 10am-7pm Sun; S Línea C Independencia) Travel and tour agency that offers a little bit of everything: city tours, tango shows, guides to *fútbol* games, air tickets, hotel reservations and countrywide packages.

Getting There & Away

Buenos Aires is well connected by air, with direct international flights to cities all over the world including New York, Miami, London, Madrid, Frankfurt, Amsterdam and Auckland, as well as most major cities within South America.

If you are traveling overland, you'll most likely arrive by bus at Retiro bus station, from where long-distance buses depart for destinations across Argentina as well as Chile and Paraguay.

A small number of infrequent trains link the capital with Rosario, Córdoba, Tucumán, Bahía Blanca, Tandil and Mar del Plata. Tickets are cheap but often sell out well in advance.

Ferries link Buenos Aires with Colonia and Montevideo in Uruguay.

AIR

Most international flights arrive at Buenos Aires' **Aeropuerto Internacional Ministro Pistarini** (Ezeiza; ☎ 011-5480-6111; www.aa2000.com. ar), about 35km south of the Center. Ezeiza is a modern airport with ATMs, restaurants, a pharmacy, duty-free shops and a small **post office** (⊙ 9am-5pm Mon-Fri).

There's a **t**ourist information booth immediately after passing through customs.

When departing Buenos Aires, get to Ezeiza at least two to three hours before your international flight out; security and immigration lines can be long. And be aware that traffic is often bad *getting* to Ezeiza; it can take an hour or more.

Most domestic flights arrive at **Aeroparque Jorge Newbery airport** (☎ 011-5480-6111; www. aa2000.com.ar; Av Rafael Obligado; ☐ 33,45) a short distance from downtown Buenos Aires.

BOAT

There's a regular ferry service to and from Colonia and Montevideo, both in Uruguay. **Buquebus** (Map p70; ☎ 011-4316-6530; www.buquebus. com; Av Antártida Argentina 821; ☐ 92, 106) and **Seacat** ferries leave from the same terminal in Puerto Madero. The terminal is a 15-minute walk from Alem Subte station on Línea B. **Colonia Express** (Map p65; ☎ 011-4317-4100; www.coloniaexpress.com; Av Don Pedro de Mendoza 330; ☐ 130, 8, 86) is the cheapest company but has limited departures; its terminal is in an industrial neighborhood near La Boca; take a taxi. Book online in advance for the best prices.

BUS

Buenos Aires' modern **Retiro bus terminal** (Retiro; Map p70; ☎ 011-4310-0700; www.retiro. com.ar; Av Antártida Argentina; ⑤ Línea C Retiro) is 400m long and has bays for 75 buses. The bottom floor is for cargo shipments and luggage storage, the top for purchasing tickets, and the middle for everything else.

There's an **information booth** (Map p70; ☎ 011-4310-0700; ⊙ 24hr) that provides general bus information and schedules, plus a tourist office near Puente 3 on the main floor, on the same level as bus bay 36. Other services include ATMs, telephone offices (some with internet access), cafes and many small stores. There's also a booth where you can buy a SUBE card (p110).

You can buy a ticket to practically anywhere in Argentina and departures are fairly frequent to the most popular destinations. You can buy tickets online using the booking services **Omnilíneas** (www.omnilineas.com) or Plataforma 10 (www.plataforma10.com.ar), or from the bus company's website (depending on your route).

TRAIN

There is a limited train service connecting Buenos Aires with nearby provinces. Book ahead; tickets often sell out in advance.

➡ The northern suburbs including San Isidro and Tigre are served by **Línea Mitre** (☎ 0800-222-8736; www.trenmitre.com.ar) trains from Retiro.

➡ Trains to Rosario, Córdoba and Tucumán also depart from Retiro; see www.sofse.gob.ar.

➡ The southern suburbs and La Plata are served by **Línea Roca** (☎ 0800-222-8736; www.trenroca.com.ar) trains from Constitución.

➡ The southwestern suburbs and Luján are served by **Línea Sarmiento** (☎ 0800-222-8736; www.trensarmiento.com.ar) trains from Once. Take Subte Línea C to Retiro and Constitución and Línea A to Plaza Miserere for Once.

ⓘ Getting Around

TO/FROM THE AIRPORT
Ezeiza Airport

If you're traveling alone, the best option is to catch a shuttle with a transfer company such as **Manuel Tienda León** (MTL; Map p70; ☎ 011-4315-5115; www.tiendaleon.com; Av Eduardo Madero 1299; ⑤ Linea C Retiro). You'll see its stand immediately as you exit customs, in the transportation 'lobby' area. Frequent shuttles cost AR$240 per person to the Center, run all day and night, and take 40 to 60 minutes, depending on traffic. They'll deposit you at the MTL office in Retiro (from where you can take a taxi).

Another service is **ArBus** (☎ 011-4897-4258; http://arbus.com.ar), which stops in the city center, Retiro and Palermo (AR$200 per person).

A shuttle service directed at independent travelers, is **Hostel Shuttle** (☎ 011-4511-8723; www.hostelshuttle.com.ar; US$13). Check the website for schedules and drop-off destinations (only certain hostels), and try to book ahead.

To catch a taxi, go past the transportation 'lobby' area immediately outside customs, walk past the taxi touts, and you'll see the freestanding city taxi stand (with a blue sign saying **Taxi Ezeiza** (☎ 011-5480-0066; www.taxiezeiza. com.ar; from Ezeiza to Center AR$780; ⊙ 24hr).

Aeroparque Airport

Manuel Tienda León and ArBus offer hourly transfers from Ezeiza to Aeroparque. To get from Aeroparque to the Center, take public bus 33 or 45 (don't cross the street; take them going south); you'll need a loaded SUBE transportation card, though, as the buses no longer accept cash.

SUBE CARD

- To use BA's public-transportation system, you'll need a SUBE card (☎0800-777-7823; www.sube.gob.ar); it's no longer possible to pay for buses with cash.
- Purchase one at any of the city tourist information booths, some kioskos and Correo Argentino or OCA post offices around the city; check the website for locations or look for the SUBE logo at businesses.
- Ezeiza airport and Retiro bus station also have SUBE booths where you can purchase and recharge cards.
- To purchase a SUBE card, you'll need your passport or a copy of it.
- Charging the card is easy, and can be done at many kiosks or Subte stations.

A taxi to the Center costs around AR$160.

BICYCLE

For those comfortable with the trials of cycling in a major city, bicycle is often the fastest and most pleasant way of getting around Buenos Aires. The city is almost completely flat, most streets are one-way, and you can use the 130km network of interconnected bike lanes. Just remember to watch out for traffic (if in doubt, always give way, be prepared for the odd running of a red traffic light and be especially careful of buses – assume they haven't seen you). If you are cycling on one of the main, one-way avenues (eg Av Corrientes), use the lane on the far left (but watch out for motorcycles).

The city government has a free **city bike** (Eco-Bici; ☎0800-333-2424; www.buenosaires.gob.ar/ecobici/sistema-ecobici/turistas; ⏲24hr) scheme, called EcoBici, which tourists can use. Complete the registration form online or via the app – you'll need to upload a photo of your passport. Once you're registered, you can use the Eco-Bici app to hire a bike by entering an access code at any of the (unstaffed) bike stations. You'll need data on your cell phone to use the app while at the bike stations. The free bike hire period is one hour on weekdays and two hours at weekends.

Ask in any of the city tourist offices for a copy of the city government cycle map *(mapa de ciclovías de la Ciudad de Buenos Aires)*, which shows the bike lanes and location of city bike stations and repair shops *(bicicletarías)*. You can also use http://comollego.ba.gob.ar to plot your route. You can also join city bike tours – try **Biking Buenos Aires** (p80) – which include bicycle and guide.

BUS

Buenos Aires has a huge and complex bus system. Luckily the city government has set up the website Como Llego (http://comollego.ba.gob.ar) to help you plot your journey; there's also a free app you can download to your smartphone.

To use the buses, you must have a SUBE card – coins are no longer accepted. The best place to get one of these cards is at any of the city tourist booths; bring your passport.

Most bus routes (but not all) run 24 hours; there are fewer buses at night. Seats up front are offered to the elderly, pregnant women and those with young children.

Metrobus

The new Metrobus system is a network of dedicated bus lanes and stations along several of city's main thoroughfares. These include **Metrobus 9 de Julio** (from Contitución to Recoleta), **Metrobus Norte** (from Plaza Italia in Palermo along Avenida Cabildo to Belgrano), **Metrobus Juan B Justo** (from Palermo to Liniers), **Metrobus Sur** (from Contitución to General Paz), **Metrobus San Martín** (from Avenida Juan B Justo to General Paz) and **Metrobus Del Bajo** (running along Paseo Colón and Alem from Avenida Independencia to Retiro).

CAR

Anyone considering driving in Buenos Aires should know that it can be challenging. Problems include aggressive drivers, unpredictable buses, potholes, traffic, difficulty parking and the fact that pedestrians cross the road haphazardly. Reconsider your need to have a car in this city; public transportation will often get you anywhere faster, cheaper and with much less stress.

SUBTE (SUBWAY)

BA's Subte opened in 1913 and is the quickest way to get around the city, though it can get mighty hot and crowded during rush hour (from 8am to 10am and 6pm to 8pm). It consists of *líneas* (lines) A, B, C, D, E and H. Four parallel lines run from downtown to the capital's western outskirts, while Línea C runs north–south and connects the two major train stations of Retiro and Constitución. Línea H runs from Las Heras south to Hospitales, with plans to expand it.

To use the Subte you'll need a **SUBE card**. The best place to get one of these cards is at any of the city tourist booths; Each journey is AR$7.50.

Trains operate from 5am to around 8:30pm Monday to Saturday and 8am to around 8pm on Sundays and holidays, so don't rely on the Subte to get you home after dinner. Service is frequent on weekdays; on weekends you'll wait longer. At some stations platforms are on opposite sides, so be sure of your direction *before* passing through the turnstiles.

TAXI & REMISE

The city's numerous (about 40,000) and relatively inexpensive taxis are conspicuous by their black-and-yellow paint jobs. They click every 200m (or every minute of waiting time) and cost 20% more after 6pm. Make sure that the meter's set to the current price when you start your ride. Drivers do not expect a big tip, but it's customary to let them keep small change. Taxis looking for passengers will have a red light lit on the upper right corner of their windshield.

Most cab drivers are honest workers making a living, but there are a few bad apples in the bunch. Try to have an idea of where you're going or you might be taking the 'scenic' route (though also be aware there are many one-way streets in BA, and your route to one place may be quite different on the way back).

Finally, make an attempt to snag an 'official' taxi. These are usually marked by a roof light and license number printed on the doors; the words *radio taxi* are usually a good sign. Official drivers must display their license on the back of their seat or dashboard.

Many locals will recommend you call a *remise* instead of hailing cabs off the street. A *remise* looks like a regular car and doesn't have a meter. It costs a bit more than a street taxi but is considered more secure, since an established company sends them out. Most hotels and restaurants will call a *remise* for you; expect a short wait for them to show up.

TRAIN

Trains connect Buenos Aires' center to its suburbs and nearby provinces. They're best for commuters and only occasionally useful for tourists. To get to Tigre or San Isidro, take the **Línea Mitre** (p109) from Retiro station.

TIGRE & THE DELTA

The city of Tigre (35km north of Buenos Aires) and the surrounding delta region is a popular weekend getaway for weary *porteños*. Latte-colored waters, tinted by sediment that results from large quantities of water from South America's great rivers being forced through smaller tributaries, flow through what is the third-largest river delta in the world. Enjoy a glimpse into how locals live along peaceful canals, with boats as their only transportation. All along the shorelines are signs of water-related activity, from kayaking to canoeing to sculling.

Sights

Tigre city itself is very walkable and its main sights are easily reached on foot.

★Museo de Arte Tigre MUSEUM

(☎011-4512-4528; www.mat.gov.ar; Paseo Victorica 972; adult/child AR$50/free; ⏰9am-7pm Wed-Fri, noon-7pm Sat & Sun) Tigre's grandest museum is located in a magnificent 1912 social club. Inside, it showcases the work of famous Argentine artists from the 19th and 20th centuries. Guided tours in Spanish are given at 11am and 5pm Wednesday to Friday and more frequently on weekends.

Museo Naval MUSEUM

(Naval Museum; ☎011-4749-0608; Paseo Victorica 602; AR$20; ⏰8:30am-5:30pm Mon-Fri, 10:30am-6:30pm Sat & Sun) This worthwhile museum traces the history of the Argentine navy with an eclectic mix of historical photos, old maps and artillery displays. The intricate scale models of various naval ships are impressive.

Museo del Mate MUSEUM

(☎011-4506-9594; www.elmuseodelmate.com; Lavalle 289; AR$60; ⏰11am-6pm Wed-Sun) This niche museum with over 2000 items is dedicated to the national drink. The visit begins with a short film explaining the history of *mate* and Argentine *yerba* production.

Parque de la Costa AMUSEMENT PARK

(☎011-4002-6000; www.parquedelacosta.com.ar; Vivanco 1509; rides from AR$70, gold pass AR$662; ⏰11am-6:30pm Fri-Sun) Near to Puerto de Frutos is Tigre's amusement park with some fun attractions including roller-coaster rides and waterslides. Opening hours vary between seasons; call ahead.

Tours

Frequent commuter launches depart from Estación Fluvial (behind the tourist office) for various destinations in the delta (AR$70 to AR$190 one-way). A popular destination is the **Tres Bocas** neighborhood, a half-hour boat ride from Tigre, where you can take residential walks on thin paths connected by bridges over narrow channels. There are several restaurants and accommodations here. The **Rama Negra** area has a quieter and more natural setting with fewer services, but is an hour's boat ride away.

Several companies offer inexpensive boat tours (one-hour trips from AR$150), but commuter launches give you flexibility if you want to go for a stroll or stop for lunch at one of the delta's restaurants.

Bonanza Deltaventura ADVENTURE

(☎011-4409-6967; http://bonanza.com.ar; Stand 16, Estación Fluvial, Bartolomé Mitre 305; ⏰9am-

5pm) Adventures include canoe trips, guided nature walks and horseback rides. Also offers overnight accommodations. Located a one-hour boat ride from Tigre.

El Dorado Kayak KAYAKING
(011-4039-5858; www.eldoradokayak.com; half-/full day US$50/85) Kayaking tours deep inside the delta; all equipment and lunch included. Also offers full-moon night kayaking trips.

Sleeping & Eating

Tigre's huge delta region is dotted with dozens of accommodations, including camping, B&Bs, *cabañas* (cabins) and beach resorts. Since many are reached only by boat, meals are often provided. If you opt for self-catering you'll need to bring all your own supplies, including drinking water.

Tigre's **tourist office** (011-4512-4080; www.vivitigre.gov.ar; Bartolomé Mitre 305; 9am-6pm) has information on all accommodations and many are listed on its website. Book ahead on weekends and holidays, when prices can rise significantly.

Hotel Villa Victoria GUESTHOUSE $$
(011-4731-2281; www.hotelvillavictoria.com; Av Liniers 566; r US$100-150;) Just six elegant rooms make up this welcoming guesthouse, located in a peaceful spot. The owner has gone all-out on the Swedish decoration theme; several rooms have balconies or private terraces. Best of all, there's a large grassy garden with a pool.

Casona La Ruchi GUESTHOUSE $$
(011-4749-2499; www.casonalaruchi.com.ar; Lavalle 557; d/tr with shared bathroom US$85/95;) This family-run guesthouse is in a beautiful 1893 mansion. Most of the four romantic bedrooms have balconies; all have shared bathrooms with original tiled floors. There's a pool and large garden out back.

Boulevard Sáenz Peña INTERNATIONAL $$
(011-5197-4776; www.boulevardsaenzpena.com.ar; Blvd Sáenz Peña 1400; mains AR$180-220; 10:30am-7pm Wed-Sat, 8:30pm-1am Fri & Sat, 10:30am-5pm Sun) Occupying a prime corner spot on an attractive avenue is this appealing cafe with a patio, serving salads, sandwiches, coffee and cakes. There's also a **shop** here, selling art, books and homewares.

María del Luján ARGENTINE $$$
(011-4731-9613; www.ilnovomariadellujan.com; Paseo Victorica 611; mains AR$145-365; 8am-1am) For an upscale meal on Paseo Victorica, the city's pleasant riverside avenue, try María del Luján. Serves the usual Argentine fare as well as a number of seafood dishes.

Getting There & Away

BOAT

Sturla Viajes (Map p70; in BA 011-4314-8555, in Tigre 011-4731-1300; www.sturlaviajes.com.ar; Cecilia Grierson 400; one-way/return AR$520/750; 92, 106) You can take the Sturla boat straight to Tigre from Puerto Madero. Boats leave Puerto Madero at 10am (journey time two hours) and make the return trip from Tigre's Estación Fluvial at 4pm.

BUS

Certain branches of the 60 bus go to Tigre from Constitución station via Plaza Italia in Palermo; check with the driver. Look for the bus marked 'Panamericana' which takes the highway (1½ hours).

TRAIN

You can take the Tigre branch of the Mitre line train (with/without SUBE AR$6/12) from Retiro (one hour) or Belgrano C (45 minutes).

The most scenic way to reach Tigre is via the **Tren de la Costa** (0800-222-8736; www.trendelacosta.com.ar; tickets AR$20), whose southernmost station (Maipú) is in the suburb of Olivos. The Mitre train from Retiro will take you to Maipú (get off at Mitre station at the end of the line and cross the pedestrian bridge to Maipú). You can also reach Maipú station on the 152 bus, which stops at Plaza Italia in Palermo.

The Pampas & the Atlantic Coast

Includes ➜

Best Places to Eat

- Época de Quesos (p127)
- Tisiano (p139)
- Don Atilio (p142)
- Gambrinus (p143)
- Tante (p131)

Best Places to Stay

- Hospedaje del Bosque (p141)
- La Vieja Hostería (p130)
- Hotel Sirenuse (p137)
- Paradores Draghi (p121)
- Estancia Ave María (p126)

Why Go?

There's Buenos Aires, and then there's the province of Buenos Aires. Home to more than a third of the country's population, this is the nation's economic powerhouse: these fertile grasslands financed Argentina's turn-of-the-century golden age and still produce most of the country's famous beef.

While the region isn't packed with tourist attractions, simple pleasures and traditional gaucho culture are waiting to be discovered. Charming San Antonio de Areco offers a glimpse of Argentina's real-life cowboys in action, while the picturesque hills around Tandil are lovely for hiking and feasting on locally produced *picadas* (shared appetizer plates). Beach towns on the Atlantic coast provide a breezy escape from the summer heat.

If you have a few days to spare, check into one of the region's historic *estancias* (ranches), where you can ride a criollo horse under an expansive sky – and experience the faded elegance of Argentina's past.

When to Go

Mar del Plata

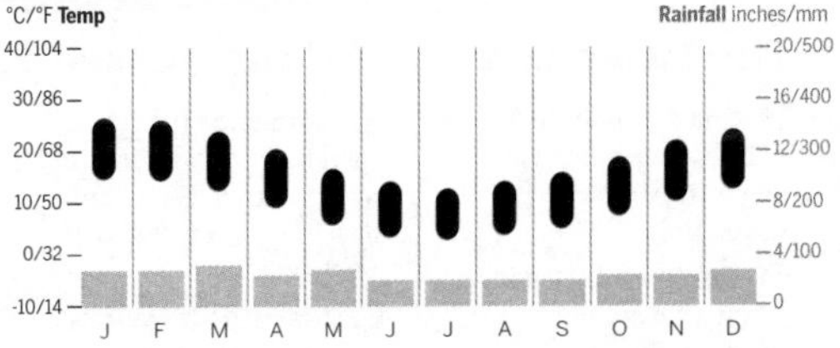

Jan–Feb Summer brings sunny weather and big crowds to the beaches.

Oct–Nov & Mar–Apr Spring and fall are perfect for exploring Tandil.

Early Nov San Antonio de Areco hosts the gaucho festival Fiesta de la Tradición.

NORTHERN PAMPAS

Dotted with rambling *estancias* (ranches), many of them steeped in history, the northern pampas offers a taste of the rural idyll within easy reach of Buenos Aires. The area's rich soil and lush natural grasses make it Argentina's best cattle-raising country, and the region yields hides, beef, wool and wheat for global markets. Horseback riding and polo playing are just some of the activities on offer here.

This is the homeland of the gaucho, the skilled, nomadic horsemen who are a symbol

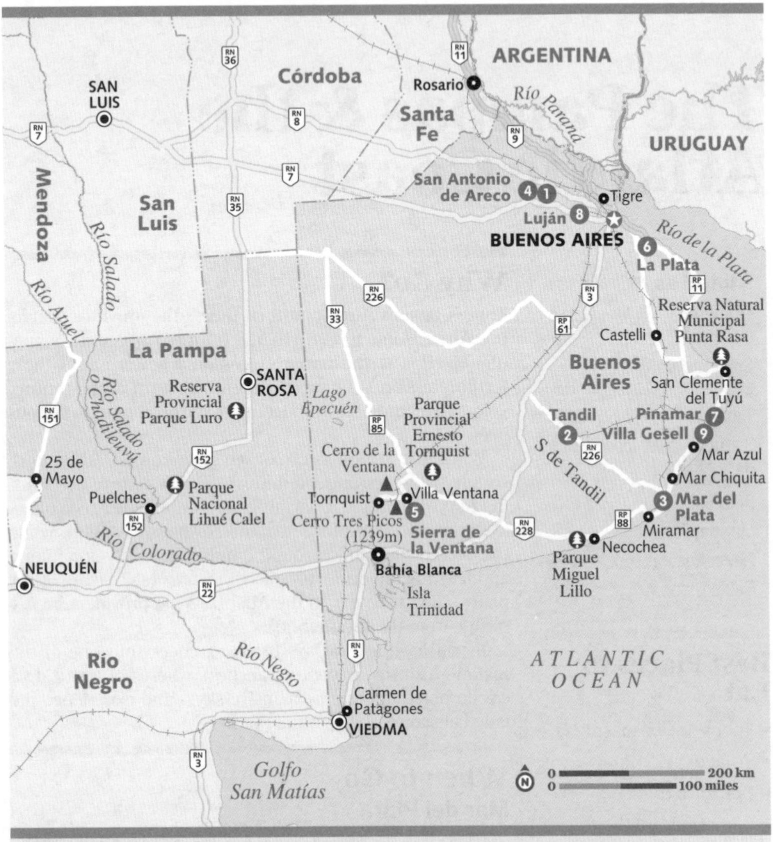

The Pampas & the Atlantic Coast Highlights

1. **San Antonio de Areco** (p119) Going gaucho in the prettiest town in the pampas.
2. **Tandil** (p123) Heading out on a savory hunt for locally produced prosciutto, salami and cheese.
3. **Mar del Plata** (p133) Soaking up sun and a vibrant cultural scene in the 'Pearl of the Atlantic.'
4. **Estancias** (p122) Spending the weekend riding horses and relaxing at one of the region's traditional ranches.
5. **Sierra de la Ventana** (p128) Peeking through a natural rock 'window' with a view.
6. **La Plata** (p115) Wandering the streets of South America's first fully planned city.
7. **Pinamar** (p130) Windsurfing, swimming or cycling in this stylish beach resort.
8. **Luján** (p118) Following the footsteps of generations of Catholic pilgrims.
9. **Villa Gesell** (p132) Strolling the quaint wooden boardwalk and enjoying a bit of beach life.

of Argentina; look out for their distinctive *boinas* (berets) and traditional silver work, including knives and *mates* (gourds for drinking *yerba mate*, a bitter tea-like beverage). Several good museums explore the history of the gaucho, who is also celebrated in San Antonio de Areco's annual Fiesta de la Tradición. At the heart of gaucho culture is the *asado*, an elaborate barbecue stacked high with generous cuts of beef.

La Plata

0221 / POP 654,000

Just over an hour from Buenos Aires, the bustling university city of La Plata is notable for being South America's first planned city. The leafy streets of the capital of Buenos Aires province follow an elaborate plan of diagonal avenues crossing a regular 5km-square grid pattern to connect the major plazas, creating a distinctive star design.

It's a pleasant city with a vibrant nightlife, expansive parkland and a number of worthwhile sights, including an excellent natural history museum (great for kids) and an imposing neo-Gothic cathedral – the largest in Argentina. Architecture buffs won't want to miss peeking inside a house designed by Le Corbusier, his only completed work in Latin America.

Sights

La Plata's main sights are all within walking distance of each other.

★Catedral de la Plata CATHEDRAL

(0221-423-3931; www.catedraldelaplata.com; Plaza Moreno, Calles 51 & 15; museum AR$60; 10am-7pm, museum 11am-7pm Tue-Sun) Construction began on La Plata's spectacular neo-Gothic cathedral in 1885, but the building wasn't inaugurated until 1932, and the twin steeples were only completed in 1999. The design was inspired by medieval churches in Cologne and Amiens, and the cathedral has fine stained-glass windows, gargoyles and polished granite floors.

In the basement is an interesting **museum** with exhibits on the construction of the cathedral; entry includes an elevator ride to the top of the left-hand tower.

★Casa Curutchet ARCHITECTURE

(0221-421-8032; www.capbacs.com; Av 53, No 320; AR$75; 10am-5pm Tue-Fri, 1-5pm Sat & Sun) The famed French-Swiss architect Le Corbusier only built two structures in the Americas: Carpenter Center for the Visual Arts at Harvard, and Casa Curutchet. The strikingly modern house, commissioned by the Argentine surgeon Pedro Curutchet in 1948, is a prime example of Le Corbusier's five points of architecture.

The house was featured in the award-winning film *El hombre de al lado* (The Man Next Door; 2009).

Museo de La Plata MUSEUM

(0221-425-7744; www.museo.fcnym.unlp.edu.ar; Paseo del Bosque s/n; adult/child AR$40/free, Tue free; 8am-4pm Tue-Fri, 10am-5pm Sat & Sun;) Founded in 1884, this excellent museum features the paleontological, zoological, archaeological and anthropological finds of famous Patagonian explorer Francisco P Moreno. The eclectic collection includes Egyptian tomb relics, Jesuit art, amusing taxidermy, and an impressive array of skeletons, fossils, rocks and minerals, scary insects and reconstructed dinosaurs. There's also a **cafe**.

The neoclassical building has a grand pillared entrance and fabulous stained-glass windows, sweeping wooden staircases and tiled floors inside.

Paseo del Bosque PARK

Plantations of eucalyptus, gingko, palm and subtropical hardwoods cover Paseo del Bosque, parkland expropriated from an *estancia* at the time of the city's founding. It attracts a collection of strolling families, smooching lovers and sweaty joggers, and contains various interesting sights: a small lake with paddleboats for rent; a **planetarium** (0221-423-6593; www.planetario.unlp.edu.ar; Paseo del Bosque; shows Sat & Sun); the open-air Teatro Martín Fierro, which hosts music and drama performances (closed for renovations at research time); and the star attraction, Museo de La Plata.

THE PAMPAS

The pampas is both a general term for a large geographic region of fertile plains and the name of the province that lies to the west of Buenos Aires (La Pampa). The pampas grasslands roll southwards from the Río de la Plata to the banks of the Río Negro, stretching west toward the Andes and all the way up to the southern parts of Córdoba and Santa Fe provinces, taking in the entire Buenos Aires and La Pampa provinces.

La Plata

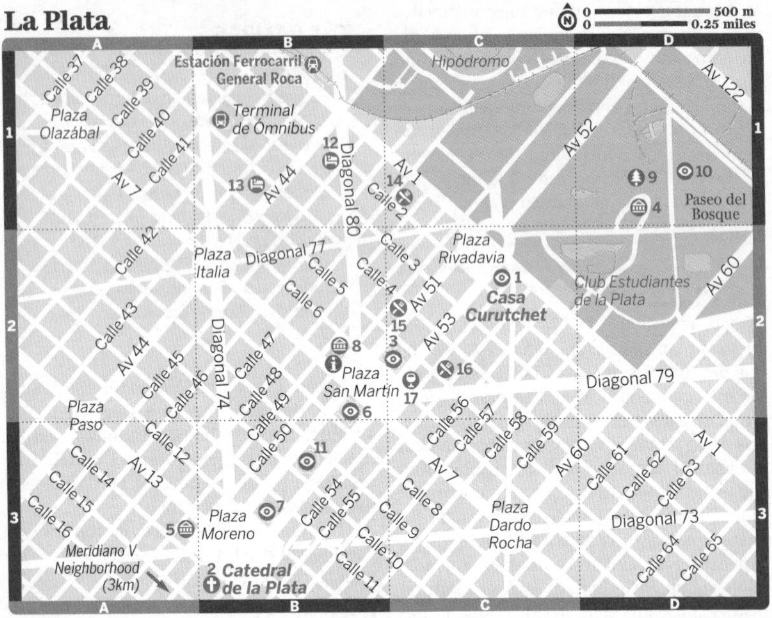

La Plata

Sleeping & Eating

Único Ecohostel HOSTEL $

(☎0221-423-2626; www.hostelunico.com; Calle 4 No 565, btwn Calle 43 & Av 44; dm/d from US$17/50;) A backpackers' favorite, this gleaming modern hostel is conveniently located only a block from the bus station. Highlights include a pair of common kitchens, a patio and garden, and ecofriendly amenities, including solar hot water. Fills up when there's a concert or event happening in town; book ahead.

★Benevento Hotel HOTEL $$

(☎0221-423-7721; www.hotelbenevento.com.ar; Calle 2, No 645; s/d/ste US$63/92/120; @) This charmingly renovated hotel, housed in an elegant French-inspired building that dates from 1915, offers pretty rooms with high ceilings and cable TV. Most have wood floors, plus balconies overlooking the busy street; top-floor rooms are the most modern and offer great views over the city. It's a few blocks from the bus station.

Carne BURGERS $

(☎0221-421-9817; www.carnehamburguesas.com; Calle 50, No 452, btwn Calles 4 & 5; burgers AR$135-185; noon-midnight) Mauro Colagreco, a chef from La Plata whose French restaurant Mirazur is currently ranked number four in the world, caused a buzz when he opened this sleek, monochrome burger bar in his hometown. Made with mostly organic produce, the burgers live up to the marketing – which includes Carne-branded aprons, baseball caps and bottled craft beer.

★**Big Siberia** CAFE $$
(☎0221-423-2759; www.facebook.com/bigsiberia; Calle 2, No 786, btwn Calles 47 & 48; sandwiches & salads AR$140-160, brunch incl drink AR$230-380; ⏰9am-8pm Mon-Fri, 12:30-8pm Sat) Seriously good coffee, sandwiches made with freshly baked bread, satisfying brunches and a selection of more than 10 different homemade cakes are among the array of treats on offer at this airy cafe-cum-bookstore. Hot food served until 4pm.

Cervecería Modelo ARGENTINE $$
(☎0221-421-1321; www.cerveceriamodelo.com.ar; cnr Calles 5 & 54; mains AR$135-360; ⏰8am-1am Sun-Thu, to 3am Fri & Sat; 📶) Dating from 1894, its ceiling hung with hams, this classic place serves snacks, meals and ice-cold ales to a happy crowd. There are great sidewalk tables, and it's not too old to boast a big-screen TV and wi-fi.

Drinking & Nightlife

There's no shortage of watering holes and cafes dotted around the city center. Further afield, a 10-minute taxi ride from the center in the bohemian neighborhood of **Meridiano V**, you'll find several bars and live-music venues, plus theater, cinema and cultural centers catering to university students.

Molly's Beer House CRAFT BEER
(☎0221-482-1648; www.facebook.com/mollysbeerhouse; Calle 53, No 538, btwn Calles 5 & 6; ⏰6pm-2am Sun-Thu, to 4am Fri & Sat) Sample some of the 35 different craft beers on tap at Molly's, an elegant bar in a beautifully restored old house. The outdoor tables in the beer garden are the perfect spot for a summer's night.

Ciudad Vieja BAR
(☎0221-452-1674; www.ciudadviejaweb.com.ar; cnr Calles 17 & 71; ⏰7pm-1:30am Wed & Thu, 7pm-4:30am Fri, noon-4:30am Sat, noon-1:30am Sun) This corner venue in Meridiano V attracts a range of musicians, from jazz to tango to swing and blues; check the website to see what's on.

Information

Tourist Office (☎0221-427-1535; cnr Av 7 & Calle 50, Pasaje Dardo Rocha; ⏰10am-8pm) Just off Plaza San Martín.

Getting There & Away

La Plata's **bus terminal** (☎0221-427-3198; www.laplataterminal.com; Calle 41, btwn Calles 3 & 4) has plenty of connections to other parts of Argentina, plus a helpful website with links and information.

Costera Metropolitana (☎0221-489-2084) runs frequent buses (AR$40, 1½ to two hours) between Buenos Aires and La Plata's bus station. Though the buses stop at many locations in Buenos Aires, the easiest place to get on and off is at Retiro, the start/end of the line. Buses

DON'T MISS

ARCHITECTURE OF LA PLATA

Architecture fans plan trips to La Plata just to see Le Corbusier's Casa Curutchet (p115). But the city skyline has several other highlights you'll spot on a quick stroll around the center.

Opposite the cathedral is the **Palacio Municipal** (cnr Av 51 & Calle 11), designed in German Renaissance style by Hanoverian architect Hubert Stiers. On the west side of the plaza, the **Museo y Archivo Dardo Rocha** (☎0221-427-5591; Calle 50, No 935; ⏰9am-2pm Mon & Fri, to 5pm Tue-Thu, 3-6pm Sat) FREE was the vacation home of the city's creator and contains period furniture and many of his personal knickknacks.

Two blocks northeast, the **Teatro Argentino** (www.gba.gob.ar/teatroargentino; Av 51, btwn Calles 9 & 10) is a concrete monolith, but boasts great acoustics – ideal for the lineup of ballet, symphony orchestras and opera. Two blocks further northeast, in front of Plaza San Martín, is the ornate **Palacio de la Legislatura**, also in German Renaissance style. Nearby, catch the French Classic **Pasaje Dardo Rocha** (☎0221-427-1296; www.facebook.com/PasajeDardoRocha; cnr Av 6 & Calle 50), once La Plata's main railroad station and now the city's major cultural center, containing two museums. Also close by is the Flemish Renaissance **Casa de Gobierno** (Plaza San Martín), housing the provincial governor and his retinue.

leave approximately every 20 to 30 minutes until 10pm, with fewer departures on weekends.

La Plata is also served by Buenos Aires' **Línea Roca** (Train Station; www.trenroca.com.ar; 535 N Owensby) suburban train line, with half-hourly services from the Constitución station (with/without SUBE card AR$4/8, one hour 10 minutes).

Luján

02323 / POP 106,000

Luján is a small riverside town that famously overflows several times per year as pilgrims make their way here to visit Argentina's most important shrine. It boasts a huge Spanish-style plaza with an imposing neo-Gothic cathedral, as well as a couple of interesting museums. The riverside area is lined with restaurants and barbecue stands.

Sights

★Basílica Nuestra Señora de Luján CHURCH
(02323-420058; www.basilicadelujan.org.ar; San Martín 51; crypt weekday/weekend AR$40/45; basilica 8am-7pm, crypt 11am-4pm Mon-Fri, 10am-6pm Sat & Sun) Luján's undisputed focal point is this imposing neo-Gothic basilica, built from 1887 to 1935 and made from a lovely rose-colored stone that glows in the setting sun. The venerated **statue of the Virgin** sits in the high chamber behind the main altar. Under the basilica you can tour a **crypt** that's inhabited by Virgin statues from all over the world. Masses take place in the basilica several times a day.

Complejo Museográfico Enrique Udaondo MUSEUM
(02323-420245; http://museo-udaondo.tumblr.com/; Torrezuri 917; AR$20; 12:30-5pm Wed, 11:30am-5pm Thu & Fri, 10:30am-6pm Sat & Sun) On the west side of Luján's gargantuan basilica plaza, this gorgeous colonial-era museum complex rambles with several display rooms, pretty patios and gardens. The Sala General José de San Martín showcases Argentina's battles for independence, while the Sala de Gaucho contains some beautiful *mate* gourds, horse gear and other gaucho paraphernalia.

Museo del Transporte MUSEUM
(Torrezuri 917, Complejo Museográfico Enrique Udaondo; AR$20; 12:30-5pm Wed, 11:30am-5pm Thu & Fri, 10:30am-6pm Sat & Sun) Luján's transportation museum displays a remarkable collection of horse-drawn carriages from the late 1800s, the first steam locomotive to serve the city from Buenos Aires, and a monster of a hydroplane that crossed the Atlantic in 1926. The most offbeat exhibits, however, are the stuffed and scruffy remains of Gato and Mancha, the hardy Argentine criollo horses ridden by adventurer AF Tschiffely from Buenos Aires to New York. This trip took 2½ years, from 1925 to 1928.

Festivals & Events

On the first Saturday in October, throngs of the faithful walk the 60km from the Buenos Aires neighborhood of Liniers to Luján – a journey of up to 16 hours – to pay tribute to the Virgen de Luján. Other large gatherings occur on May 8 (Virgin's Day), the first weekend in August for the colorful **Peregrinación Boliviana**, the last weekend in September for the 'gaucho' pilgrimage (watch for horses) and December 8 for **Immaculate Conception Day**.

Sleeping & Eating

Hotel Hoxón HOTEL $$
(02323-429970; www.hotelhoxon.com; 9 de Julio 760; s US$60-70, d US$90-120, ste US$140;) The biggest and best in town, this place two blocks north of the basilica has modern, clean rooms. Superiors are carpeted and come with fridge and air-con. There's also a heated swimming pool with raised sundeck, a Jacuzzi and a steam room.

★L'Eau Vive FRENCH $$
(02323-421774; www.leauvivedeargentina.com; Constitución 2112; mains AR$110-195; noon-2:30pm & 8:30-10pm Tue-Sat, noon-2:15pm Sun) It's not every day you have the chance to dine on French cuisine – prepared by Carmelite nuns from around the world – in small-town Argentina. L'Eau Vive is on the town outskirts, but many foodies consider the friendly restaurant worth a detour. Every evening and at Sunday lunchtime the nuns gather in the dining room to sing 'Ave Maria'. Reservations recommended.

Take a taxi from the center.

1800 Restaurant ARGENTINE $$
(02323-433080; www.restaurant1800.com; Rivadavia 705; mains AR$100-220) In a charming building dating from the early 18th century, this friendly neighborhood restaurant serving typical Argentine grilled meats, chicken and fish dishes and pastas is a safe bet for a tasty and satisfying meal.

LA VIRGENCITA

Argentina's patron saint is a ubiquitous presence – you can spot her poster on butcher-shop walls, her statue in churches throughout the country and her image on the dashboards of taxis. She wears a triangular blue dress, stands on a half-moon and radiates streams of glory from her crowned head.

In 1630, a Portuguese settler in Tucumán asked a friend in Brazil to send him an image of the Virgin for his new chapel. Unsure what style of Virgin was required, the friend sent two – including one of the Immaculate Conception. After setting out from the port of Buenos Aires, the cart bearing the statues got bogged down near the river of Luján and only moved when the Immaculate Conception was taken off. Its owner took this as a sign, and left the statue in Luján so that a shrine could be built there. The other statue continued its journey to the northwest.

Since then the Virgin of Luján has been credited with a number of miracles – from curing tumors to protecting the province from a cholera epidemic. Every year millions of pilgrims from throughout Argentina visit Luján's basilica, where the original 17th-century statue is still displayed, to honor the Virgin for her intercession in affairs of peace, health, forgiveness and consolation. If you arrive here during the massive pilgrimage on the first Sunday in October, you'll spot families of exhausted pilgrims snoozing in the square, enjoying barbecues by the river and filling plastic bottles with holy water from the fountain.

Information

Tourist Office (☎ 02323-427082; www.turismolujan.com.ar; San Martín 1; ⌚ 9am-5pm Mon-Fri, 10am-6pm Sat & Sun)

Getting There & Away

Luján's **bus terminal** (Av de Nuestra Señora de Luján & Almirante Brown) is three blocks north of the basilica. From Buenos Aires, take bus 57 (AR$42, two hours), operated by **Atlántida** (☎ 02323-434957). It leaves every half-hour from Plaza Italia (in Palermo) and Plaza Miserere (outside the Once train station, with a bus stop on Av Rivadavia).

San Antonio de Areco

☎ 02326 / POP 20,000

San Antonio de Areco is the prettiest town in the pampas. Located 113km northwest of Buenos Aires, it welcomes many day-trippers from BA, who come for the peaceful atmosphere and picturesque colonial streets. The town dates from the early 18th century and preserves many gaucho and criollo traditions, including the fine silverwork and saddlery of its artisans. Gauchos from all over the pampas gather here for November's Fiesta de la Tradición (p121), when you can catch them, and their horses, strutting the cobbled streets in all their finery.

San Antonio de Areco's compact town center is very walkable. Around the Plaza Ruiz de Arellano, named in honor of the town's founding *estanciero* (ranch owner), are several historic buildings, including the **iglesia parroquial** (parish church).

Like many other small towns in this part of Argentina, Areco shuts down during the afternoon siesta.

Sights

★Museo Gauchesco Ricardo Güiraldes MUSEUM
(☎ 02326-455839; www.facebook.com/museoguiraldes; Camino Ricardo Güiraldes; ⌚ 10am-5pm) FREE This sprawling museum in Parque Criollo dates from 1936 and is largely dedicated to Ricardo Güiraldes, author of the novel *Don Segundo Sombra,* and local gaucho history and culture in general. The entrance is in a re-created *pulpería* (tavern), set up as it would have been when it first opened in 1850, while the museum's main displays are housed in a 20th-century reproduction of an 18th-century *casco* (ranch house).

These well laid-out exhibits include gaucho money belts, silverwork and paintings (a number of them by Eduardo Sívori) and there are several rooms dedicated to Güiraldes – items include his old poncho and writing desk. Within the museum complex is a workshop and loom used to weave traditional woolen ponchos and blankets, which are also available to buy.

Museo Las Lilas de Areco MUSEUM
(☎ 02326-456425; www.museolaslilas.org; Moreno 279; AR$100; ⌚ 10am-7pm Thu-Sun) Florencio Molina Campos is to Argentines what

San Antonio de Areco

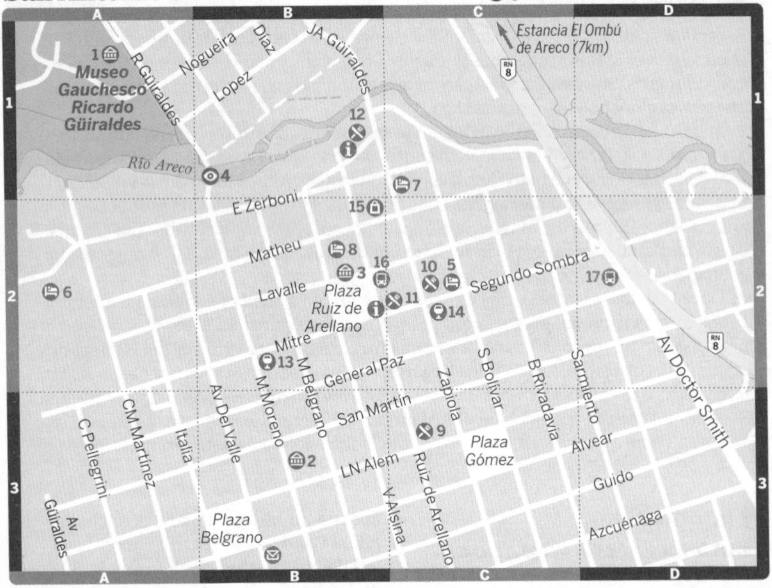

San Antonio de Areco

Top Sights

1 Museo Gauchesco Ricardo Güiraldes A1

Sights

2 Museo Las Lilas de Areco B3
3 Museo y Taller de Platería Draghi B2
4 Puente Viejo B1

Sleeping

5 Antigua Casona C2
6 Estancia La Cinacina A2
7 Hostal de Areco C1
8 Paradores Draghi B2

Eating

9 Almacén de Comidas C3
10 Almacén Ramos Generales C2
11 La Esquina de Merti C2
12 Puesto La Lechuza B1

Drinking & Nightlife

13 Almacén Los Principios B2
14 Boliche de Bessonart C2

Shopping

15 La Olla de Cobre B2

Transport

16 Areco Bus B2
17 Chevallier D2
Terminal de Ómnibus .... (see 17)

Norman Rockwell is to Americans – a folk artist whose themes are based on comical caricatures. This pretty courtyard museum displays an extensive collection of his famous works. As well as the gallery there is also a **Sala de Carruajes** (carriage room) to look at and a gaucho-themed sound-and-light show.

Museo y Taller de Platería Draghi MUSEUM
(☎02326-454219; www.draghiplaterosorfebres.com; Lavalle 387; AR$100; ⊙10am-12:30pm & 4-7pm Mon-Sat, 10am-12:30pm Sun) This small museum contains an exceptional collection of 19th-century silver *facones* (gaucho knives), beautiful horse gear and intricate *mate* paraphernalia. It's attached to the silversmith workshop of the locally renowned Draghi family. Mariano Draghi's jewelry and silverwork are for sale in the attached shop.

Puente Viejo BRIDGE
The pink *puente viejo* (old bridge) spanning the Río Areco dates from 1857 and follows

the original cart road to northern Argentina. Once a toll crossing, it's now a pedestrian bridge leading to San Antonio de Areco's main attraction, the Museo Gauchesco Ricardo Güiraldes.

Festivals & Events

★Fiesta de la Tradición CULTURAL
(www.sanantoniodeareco.com; ⊙Nov) Areco is the symbolic center of Argentina's vestigial gaucho culture, and for the Fiesta de la Tradición the town puts on the country's biggest celebration of criollo traditions. The weekend event is held in early to mid-November, and includes displays of horsemanship, folk dancing, live music, craft exhibitions and plenty of grilled meat. If you're in the area, don't miss it.

Sleeping

Hostal de Areco HOTEL $
(☎02326-456118; www.hostaldeareco.com.ar; Zapiola 25; d/tr from US$55/66; ❄📶) This simple place has a pleasant salon and a nice large grassy garden out back. Rooms are dated but comfortable.

★Paradores Draghi GUESTHOUSE $$
(☎02326-455583; www.paradoresdraghi.com.ar; Matheu 380; d/tr US$105/120; ❄@📶🏊) It's worth staying over in Areco just so you can check in here. Lovingly run by a mother-daughter team and conveniently located near the main plaza, this nine-room boutique guesthouse has spacious rooms, breezy patios, a grassy garden with a beautiful pool, a lovely continental breakfast, and a private silver workshop and museum where you can learn about silverware-making.

Antigua Casona GUESTHOUSE $$
(☎02325-15-416030; www.antiguacasona.com; Segundo Sombra 495; d US$120; ❄📶🏊) A wonderful place to stay in Areco, this restored traditional home offers five high-ceilinged rooms with wooden floors; all are set around covered tile hallways and leafy patios. There's a communal *parrilla*, should you be tempted to grill your own steak, and a small but picturesque swimming pool set in a brick-lined courtyard.

Eating & Drinking

★La Esquina de Merti ARGENTINE $
(www.esquinademerti.com.ar; cnr Arellano & Segundo Sombra; mains AR$125-250; ⊙9am-midnight) Located right on the plaza, this corner bar and restaurant is one of San Antonio de Areco's most traditional and atmospheric. Stop in for coffee, empanadas (pastries), sandwiches, a glass of wine, or a steak grilled on the *parrilla*. When the weather's nice, the outdoor tables are a prime spot for gaucho-watching.

Almacén de Comidas ARGENTINE $
(☎02326-455244; www.facebook.com/AlmacenDeComidasAreco; Arellano 285; mains AR$100-150; ⊙5-11pm Tue-Fri, noon-2pm & 6-11pm Sat) Supremely tasty, freshly made salads, pastas, pies, burgers and a cabinet-full of tempting desserts are on offer at this deli-style restaurant, which has just one bench for eating-in. Pick up a sandwich made with freshly baked bread or a slice of homemade cheesecake or lemon pie to eat by the river.

Almacén Ramos Generales ARGENTINE $$
(www.ramosgeneralesareco.com.ar; Zapiola 143; mains AR$130-350; ⊙noon-4pm & 8pm-midnight; 📶) Another of San Antonio's historic dining venues, this elegantly restored space was once a general store. Today, it offers a quaintly rustic setting and quality, traditional Argentine fare – grilled meats from the *parrilla, milanesas* (fried breaded cutlets) and some specialty rabbit dishes.

Puesto La Lechuza PARRILLA $$
(☎02326-470136; www.facebook.com/puestolalechuza; Victorino Althaparro 423; mains AR$90-170; ⊙12:30-5pm & 9:30pm-2am Sat, 12:30-5pm Sun) Open weekends only, this charming riverside spot is ideal on a warm day, when you can savor a lunch of *empanadas* or grilled steak under the trees. There's live guitar music on Saturday nights starting around 9:30pm.

★Boliche de Bessonart BAR
(cnr Zapiola & Segundo Sombra; ⊙11am-3pm & 7pm-midnight Tue-Sun) This weather-beaten corner building full of dusty bottles was originally a general store and is more than 200 years old. These days it's a family-run bar popular with gauchos and young people alike, who come for the excellent *picadas* (sharing boards of cold cuts and cheese) washed down with copious beers, red wine or Fernet (a bitter aromatic spirit).

Almacén Los Principios BAR
(Moreno 151; ⊙8:30am-1pm & 5-9:30pm Mon-Sat) Stop for a beer at this charming general store and bar, which remains much as it was when it first opened in 1922. Dusty

WORTH A TRIP

HOME ON THE RANGE

One of the best ways to spend a few days in the region – and soak up a bit of traditional gaucho culture while remaining within easy reach of Buenos Aires – is to visit an *estancia* (ranch). Once the private homes of wealthy landowners, many of the province's grandest mansions are now open to the public. Choose between a *día de campo* (country day; an access pass to the ranch that typically includes an elaborate lunch and afternoon tea, plus horseback riding and other outdoor activities) or stay for a night or two.

Near San Antonio de Areco, upscale **Estancia El Ombú de Areco** (02326-492080, in Buenos Aires 011-4737-0436; www.estanciaelombu.com; RP 31, Cuartel VI, Villa Lía; día de campo US$100, s/d with full board US$325/410;) is a 300-hectare ranch with a gorgeous colonial mansion that dates from 1880. It's named after the massive ombú *(Phytolacca dioica)* tree casting shade over the gardens. At El Ombú, it's old-fashioned hospitality all the way. In addition to horseback riding, you can watch (and even take part in) rounding up cattle herds.

A slightly more affordable option – and one that's closer to town – is **Estancia La Cinacina** (02326-452045; www.lacinacina.com.ar; Zerboni & Martínez; d from US$170;). With thematic gaucho shows, the *estancia* is on the touristy side, but it's popular with travelers. Also near San Antonio de Areco is **La Porteña** (011-5626-7347; www.laporteniadeareco.com; RN 8, Km 110; día de campo adult/child US$70/35, d with full board US$288; @), the *estancia* where Ricardo Güiraldes wrote his gaucho epic *Don Segundo Sombra*. It's 10km east of town.

Located 100km southwest of Buenos Aires near San Miguel del Monte is **Candelaria del Monte** (02271-442431; www.candelariadelmonte.com.ar; Ruta 41, San Miguel del Monte; r with full board per person from US$250;), a working cattle ranch with a charming main house, a swimming pool, forested grounds, and meals featuring homemade breads and pastries. Polo enthusiasts should check out **Puesto Viejo Estancia** (011-5279-6893; www.puestoviejoestancia.com.ar; RP 6, Km 83, Cañuelas; día de campo adult/child US$85/43, r with full board per person from US$225;), a chic 100-hectare ranch and polo club located 75km south of Buenos Aires, near Cañuelas, or **La Candelaria** (02227-494132; www.estanciacandelaria.com; RN 205, Km 114.5, near Lobos; día de campo from US$83, d with full board from US$350;), 120km southwest of Buenos Aires, near Lobos.

Private transfers directly from Buenos Aires to most *estancias* are available for an extra charge.

jars and tins line the wooden shelves and vintage advertisements adorn the walls.

Shopping

Even on the shortest stroll around town you can't miss the silversmith workshops and stores lining the streets of San Antonio de Areco. Local artisans are known throughout the country – *mate* paraphernalia, *rastras* (silver-studded belts), knives and leather goods are the most traditional items to buy.

La Olla de Cobre CHOCOLATE
(www.laolladecobre.com.ar; Matheu 433; 10am-1pm & 3-8pm Wed-Sun, 10am-1pm Mon) Pick up an edible gift of artisanal chocolates or *alfajores* (cookies filled with *dulce de leche*) at the chocolate factory and store, La Olla de Cobre (The Copper Pot).

Information

There are a few banks with ATMs along Alsina.

Post Office (02326-455609; cnr Alvear & Av Del Valle; 9am-5pm Mon-Fri)

Tourist Information Booth (cnr Arellano & Segundo Sombra; 10am-2pm Mon-Fri, to 7pm Sat & Sun) Additional booth at the main square.

Tourist Office (02326-453165; www.sanantoniodeareco.com; cnr Zerboni & Arellano; 8am-8pm) The main tourist office is located next to the river, and can provide maps and information.

Getting There & Away

Areco's **bus terminal** (Av Dr Smith & Gral Paz) is five blocks east of the central square. **Chevallier** (02326-453904; www.nuevachevallier.com; Av Dr Smith & Gral Paz) runs frequent buses to/from Buenos Aires (AR$160, two hours).

A more expensive option, but a useful one if you're trying to connect to one of the area's *estancias* is the shuttle service operated by independent companies like **Areco Bus** (www.arecobus.com.ar; bus stop cnr Arellano & Lavalle; roundtrip AR$500; ⏲ Sat & Sun). On weekends, the service offers roundtrip transportation between Buenos Aires and San Antonio de Areco (AR$500) with pick-up and drop-off at certain *estancias*, including **Estancia El Ombú de Areco**. Check the website for the latest itineraries and to make reservations.

SOUTHERN PAMPAS

Spreading out from the capital, the pampas region extends south beyond the borders of Buenos Aires province and west into the province of La Pampa. These are the hearty flatlands that feed a carnivorous nation thanks to local livestock, which outnumber people by a wide margin. When you drive these two-lane ribbon highways that parallel irrigation ditches and canals, and where water fowl light above the pasture in breathtaking murmurations, you'll be forgiven if you lose all train of thought and become hypnotized, if only for a moment. Such is the poetry of monotony in the Argentine plains.

In southern Buenos Aires province, however, the endlessly flat plain is punctuated by the Sierras de Tandil, an ancient mountain range, worn to low summits that barely reach 500m. A little to the west, Sierra de la Ventana's jagged peaks rise to 1300m, attracting hikers and climbers from BA and beyond.

Tandil

☎0249 / POP 124,000

Pretty Tandil is a leafy, walkable, endearing city with world-class delis, public orange trees, wonderful period architecture, upstart craft breweries and nearby trails to explore. It sits at the northern edge of the Sierras de Tandil, a 2.5-million-year-old mountain range worn down to gentle, grassy peaks and rocky outcroppings – perfect for bouldering and mountain biking.

The town center is leafy and relaxed, with many places observing the afternoon siesta. Later in the evening, however, locals crowd the squares and streets, shopping and partaking in the city's cultural offerings. Going out for *picadas* – wooden boards piled high with locally produced cheeses and cured meats – is a local tradition, and Tandil is known throughout Argentina for its excellent salamis.

Something else Tandil is known for? Nurturing a disproportionate number of

THE GLORIOUS GAUCHO

If the melancholy *tanguero* (tango dancer) is the essence of the *porteño* (resident of Buenos Aires), then the gaucho represents the pampas: a nomadic cowboy-like figure, pitted against the elements, with only his horse for a friend.

In the early years of the colony, the fringe-dwelling gauchos lived entirely beyond the laws and customs of Buenos Aires, eking out an independent and often violent existence in the countryside. They slaughtered the cattle that roamed free and unsupervised on the fertile grasslands and drank *mate*, the caffeine-rich herbal tea.

As Argentina grew, cattle became too valuable to leave unprotected. Foreign demand for hides increased and investors moved into the pampas to take control of the market, establishing the *estancia* (ranch) system in which large landholdings were handed out to a privileged few. Many freewheeling gauchos became exploited farmhands, while those who resisted domestication were threatened with prison or the draft.

Like so many heroes, the gaucho only won love and admiration after his demise. His physical bravery, honor and lust for freedom are celebrated in José Hernández's 1872 epic poem *Martín Fierro* and Ricardo Güiraldes' novel *Don Segundo Sombra*. His rustic traditions form part of Argentina's sophisticated folk art, with skilled craftspeople producing intricate silver gaucho knives and woven ponchos, while his image is endlessly reproduced – most amusingly in Florencio Molina Campos' classic caricatures.

These days, the gaucho-for-export is much easier to spot than the real deal, especially in folkloric shows at many *estancias*. But the gaucho's descendants can be found on cattle farms throughout the pampas, riding over the plains in their dusty *boinas* (a kind of beret) and *bombachas* (riding pants). And on special occasions, such as the Fiesta de la Tradición (p121), they sport their best horse gear and show off their riding skills.

M G THERIN WEISE / GETTY IMAGES ©

1. Traditional gaucho *rastra* (silver-studded belt) and *facón* (long-bladed knife) **2.** An *asado* (barbecue) **3.** La Candelaria, near Lobos **4.** Gaucho herding cattle

2

ROCHARIBEIRO/SHUTTERSTOCK ©

4

Staying on an Estancia

One of the best ways to enjoy the open spaces of the pampas is to visit an *estancia* (ranch). Argentina's late-19th-century belle epoque saw wealthy families adorn their ranches with lavish homes and gardens.

Those glorious days being long gone, many of these establishments are open to tourists. The *día de campo* (day in the country) usually includes a huge *asado* (barbecue) with drinks, a tour of the historic home and use of the property's horses, bicycles and swimming pool. Some places offer a *show gauchesco,* featuring folk dances and feats of horsemanship, while others host polo matches. *Estancias* are a sustainable tourism option, helping to preserve part of the country's past while providing an impressive guest-to-tree ratio. Most offer overnight stays, which include meals and activities.

Estancia Options

These are all within a few hours' drive of Buenos Aires.

Los Dos Hermanos (☎011-5577 8829; www.estancialosdoshermanos.com) This down-to-earth ranch is best for day trips and horseback riding.

La Candelaria (p122) At sunset, this extravagant French-style castle is the ultimate photo op.

Estancia Ave María (p126) A refined rural getaway outside of Tandil.

Candelaria del Monte (☎02271-442-431; www.candelariadelmonte.com.ar; Ruta 41, San Miguel del Monte; r with full board per person from US$250;) Laid-back and elegant, with a beautiful swimming pool.

Puesto Viejo Estancia (☎11-5279-6893; www.puestoviejoestancia.com.ar; RP 6, Km 83, Cañuelas; día de campo adult/child US$85/43, r with full board per person US$225;) Learn to play polo at this chic ranch and polo club.

Argentina's tennis stars, including Juan Martín del Potro.

Sights

The walk to **Parque Independencia** from the southwestern edge of downtown offers good views of the city, particularly at night, while the central **Plaza de Independencia**, surrounded by the typical municipal buildings and an uplit church, is where the locals go for a stroll in the evenings.

Parroquia Santísimo Sacramento CHURCH
(Templo de la Inmaculada Concepción; Belgrano 514) Built in 1878, Tandil's gorgeous central Catholic Church is decked out with arts-and-crafts era tiled floors, floral mosaic ceilings and a gilded altar. The domes are formed like budding tulips, and the stained glass is special. Sit for a while on one of the worn pews and take it all in.

Cerro El Centinela PARK
(www.cerrocentinela.com.ar; Cerro El Centinela s/n) For great views over Tandil and a relaxing afternoon hike, head 6km west of town to this hilltop park. There's a **bakery**, a **restaurant** with outdoor tables, and a **chairlift** (per person AR$130) that can whisk you further up the ridgeline (only open on weekends outside warm months). You can also rent a mountain bike (per hour AR$180) and roam the trails from the parking lot. Take a taxi.

Cerro La Movediza HILL
(www.lapiedramovediza.com.ar; Av Campos s/n) At the north edge of town, the Piedra Movediza, a 300-tonne stone, teetered precariously atop Cerro La Movediza for many years before finally falling in 1912. A 'replica' (non-moving) stone was built in 2007; like its predecessor, it's still a major tourist draw (and a fun photo op). Take a taxi or bus 503.

Museo Tradicionalista Fuerte Independencia MUSEUM
(☎0249-443-5573; 4 de Abril 845; AR$50; ⏲2:30-6:30pm Tue-Sun Mar-Nov, 4-8pm Tue-Sun Dec-Feb) This historical museum, worth a walk-through for context, exhibits a large and varied collection on Tandil's history. Photographs commemorate major events, and the place is filled with relics – from carriages to ladies' gloves – donated by local families.

Activities

The **Lago del Fuerte**, only 12 blocks south of Plaza de Independencia, is a huge reservoir that you can easily walk around in a couple of hours. In summer, you can rent **canoes** and **kayaks** and hang around for lunch or *merienda* (afternoon snack with tea, coffee or *mate*) at one of the restaurants along the shoreline.

For details on the plentiful outdoor activities around town, including bike rentals, trekking, canoeing, rappeling, mountain biking and rock climbing, ask the tourist office (p128) for its comprehensive list of tour operators and rental agencies.

Gabriel Barletta HORSE RIDING
(☎0249-450-9609; www.facebook.com/Gaulibar; 4hr tour from AR$400 per person, minimum 2 people) Gabriel Barletta offers excellent four-hour horseback rides in the Reserva Natural Sierra del Tigre or other surrounding areas.

Sleeping

Reservations are a must during summer, Easter week and holiday weekends. Many Argentines come here specifically for the experience of staying in one of the many *cabaña* (cabin) complexes in the area – many have terraces, fireplaces and/or swimming pools, so they're great places to unwind. But they're only convenient if you have a car.

Gran Hotel Roma HOTEL $
(☎0249-442-5217; www.hotelromatandil.com.ar; Alem 452; sUS$47-53, d/tr US$71/82; wi-fi) Family owned for three generations and recently renovated, rooms here are small but well-appointed with small flat screens, minifridge, crown mouldings and air-con. The location, only a block from Tandil's main plaza, is ideal.

Casa Chango HOSTEL $
(☎0249-442-2260; www.casa-chango.com.ar; 25 de Mayo 451; dm US$21, ste US$47-53, d US$56; @ wi-fi) The best parts of this hostel are the bright and attractive common areas, including the communal dining room and kitchen, with colorful tiles, high ceilings and historical charm. Dorms are just so-so, and service can be spotty. Suites include a private bathroom.

★ **Estancia Ave María** ESTANCIA $$$
(☎0249-442-2843; www.avemariatandil.com.ar; Paraje La Porteña; d from US$251; @ wi-fi pool) Just a few kilometers outside of town and practically next door to Cerro El Centinela, Estancia Ave María is a wonderful traditional retreat that travelers rave about. The historic and beautiful 300-hectare *estancia* offers spacious rooms with views of the hills, and elegant living areas for reading a book or enjoying afternoon tea.

Prices include breakfast and dinner, plus activities such as horseback rides. Be sure to book ahead: it's rightfully popular.

Hotel Mulan BOUTIQUE HOTEL **$$$**
(☎0249-422-1718; www.mulentandil.com; Av Santamarina 380; s & d US$106-118;) This attractive brick-and-glass tower is Tandil's newest and best in show. Rooms are large and bright with modern wood furnishings, balconies and minibar, and there's a top-floor dipping pool, gym and sauna.

Eating

Tandil's tourism office has created the Circuito de Salami y Queso (Salami and Cheese Circuit). Pick up a map and a list of participating delis and restaurants, and you can eat your way across Tandil and around its outskirts. The charcuterie is so good here, you may want to avoid the restaurant scene and simply stock up at the deli case and gorge on *picada* platters night and day.

Bar Firpo SPANISH **$**
(☎0249-443-2214; 14 de Julio 201; mains AR$100-160; ⏲11am-1am) An atmospheric, locally loved, Spanish-themed brick house-bar with tasty, affordable bites. You'll love the memorabilia mounted on the walls and displayed on the built-in bookcases behind the bar, which stocks a killer beer selection. The kitchen is open all day.

Naturísima VEGETARIAN **$**
(☎0249-444-2004; www.facebook.com/NaturisimaTandil/; 585 Chacabuco; dishes AR$35-150; ⏲9am-9pm;) Tandil's little health-food hut offers vegetarian fare, bulk foods, and a range of natural health and beauty products. Its superb deli offers assorted flatbreads, Spanish tortillas and salads for take away. It also bakes vegan pastries and empanadas made with whole-wheat flour.

★**Época de Quesos** ARGENTINE **$$**
(☎0249-444-8750; www.epocadequesos.com/tandil; cnr San Martín & 14 de Julio; picadas for 1/2 people from AR$160/370; ⏲9am-midnight) An essential, exquisite stop, and the most romantic restaurant in Tandil. It's got rustic style to spare, but the food is the thing, thanks to piles of succulent *picadas,* craft beer and wine. The shop in front presents it wide variety of local cheeses and cured meats – ask for samples – sold by the kilo, perfect for a picnic.

It's worth perusing the shop and sampling the goods, before grabbing a table in the cozy, tumbledown dining room (candlelit at night) or leafy patio.

Parrilla El Trébol PARRILLA **$$**
(☎0249-444-2333; cnr Mitre & 14 de Julio; mains AR$60-276; ⏲8pm-midnight Tue-Fri, noon-midnight Sat, noon-3pm Sun) Fun and flavorful, this simple *parrilla,* specializing in perfectly grilled steaks and top-notch salads, is a locals' favorite. The sausage and blood sausage are wonderful, as is the short rib. There's a reason locals gather in this brick-house corner restaurant for birthday dinners.

Bodegón del Fuerte ARGENTINE **$$$**
(☎0249-442-4219; Belgrano 589; mains AR$210-360; ⏲11:30am-4pm & 7pm-3am;) A popular, upscale dinner haunt thanks to that exquisite back patio. It serves more of that mixed grill *típica* and local *picada* platters made to order. Lunch specials are offered for under AR$140.

Drinking & Entertainment

★**Cervecería Harriz** CRAFT BEER
(Maipú 501; beers AR$90, bites AR$100-180; ⏲6:30pm-4:30am Tue-Sat, to midnight Sun) One of Argentina's new microbreweries, and Tandil's best, is set in a cool stone building with standing bar tables on the street side and a chalkboard menu inside scrawled with the night's offerings. Think ambers, porters, triple IPAs, honey and cream brews. There are always tasty tunes on the sound system, and a hip, young crowd.

Ogham Cervecería CRAFT BEER
(☎0249-443-0666; www.cervezaogham.com; Pinto 636; ⏲6pm-1:30am Mon-Thu, to 3:30am Fri-Sun;) Another of Tandil's craft-beer halls. This is a link in an Argentine chain, with eight beers on tap at all times. It also does a range of pub grub, from burgers and tacos to nachos and pizza, all of which lures a preppy local crowd.

★**Teatro Bajosuelo** THEATER
(☎0249-421-3639; www.teatrobajosuelo.com; Rodríguez 457) Everything about this place is cool. From the name, to the location on the Plaza Independencia, to the original plays it stages nearly every weekend and the charming beer hall upstairs. If you enjoy the theater, and speak some Spanish, give it a look.

Shopping

Syquet FOOD
(www.syquet.com.ar; cnr Gral Rodríguez & Mitre; ⏲9am-1pm & 5-9pm Mon-Fri, 9am-9pm Sat, 10am-

9pm Sun) This charming corner emporium sells a tantalizing array of local cheeses, salamis and hams, along with other gourmet regional products. You'll spot several other businesses offering similarly tempting spreads around town, and most are happy to offer free samples.

Information

There are plenty of banks with ATMs in the center.

Tourist Office (☎0249-444-8698; www.tandil.gov.ar; Rodríguez 445; ⊙9am-8pm Mon-Sat, 9am-1pm Sun) Opposite Tandil's central plaza. There's another branch at the bus terminal.

Getting There & Away

Tandil's **bus terminal** (☎0249-432092; Av Buzón 400) is located 12 blocks east of the main plaza. Walk or take a taxi (about AR$60) from in front of the terminal.

Trains from Buenos Aires' Constitución station (*primera*/Pullman class AR$100/582, five to seven hours) arrive at Tandil's train station, **Estación Tandil** (☎0249-423002), on Sunday, Monday, Thursday and Friday, and head back on Thursday, Saturday and Sunday. Double-check the schedule online, as service can be suspended.

Buses from Tandil

DESTINATION	COST (AR$)	TIME (HR)
Buenos Aires	533	5½
Córdoba	1300-1545	14-15
Mar del Plata	297	3
Necochea	233	3

Getting Around

Tandil's excellent public transportation system (rides AR$10) reaches every important sight. Bus 500 (yellow) goes to Lago del Fuerte, buses 501 (red) and 505 (brown) go to the bus terminal, and bus 502 (white) goes to Cerro La Movediza, the university and the bus terminal.

Sierra de la Ventana

☎0291 / POP 2200

There's no point in pretending otherwise, Sierra de la Ventana is a third-rate mountain-resort town, though one with access to some striking mountain scenery and within range of Buenos Aires. This explains why Argentine weekenders roll into town with their kids and dogs all summer. Still, most foreign visitors ignore it since there is much more dramatic and beautiful mountains scenery elsewhere. However, the rocky hills and nearby park offer hiking, trout fishing and a respite from the monotony of the flatlands.

Activities

Lots of outdoor pursuits are on offer in this region. You can tackle many on your own. For hiking guides, rappeling, horseback riding and other tours, stop in to the offices of the agencies conveniently located on Av San Martín.

El Tornillo CYCLING

(☎0291-15-431-1812; Roca 142; bike rental per hr/day AR$30/120; ⊙10am-7pm, closed in afternoons during hot weather) For bike rentals, find this reliable vendor in the town center.

Sleeping & Eating

Some restaurants close one or more days per week outside the December to March summer months. Self-caterers will find supermarkets and artisanal food shops on the main street.

Alihuen Hotel HOTEL $

(☎0291-491-5074; www.lasierradelaventana.com.ar/alihuen; cnr Tornquist & Frontini; d US$52; P 📶 🏊) Sierra de la Ventana's mini–Grand Budapest Hotel is 'an enchanted old ruin' set about four blocks from the main drag and strategically positioned on the banks of the river. It's not exactly luxurious, with creaky wood floors and simple furnishings, but there's plenty of atmosphere at this vine-covered Victorian.

Las Golondrinas CABAÑAS $$

(☎0291-15-443-4630; www.posadayspalasgolondrinas.com; Cerro Ceferino s/n; cabañas US$100-129; P 📶 🏊) Arguably the nicest setting in the area, this collection of condo-like *cabañas* rests on a hilltop accessed by a dirt road about 1km outside and above town. Digs are modern, with two double rooms upstairs and a larger room that sleeps four downstairs. There's a nice pool and a spa.

El Molino de la Casa Azul ARGENTINE $$

(☎0291-414-2322; www.facebook.com/El-Molino-de-la-casa-Azul-472603566233528; San Martín 480; mains AR$164-298; ⊙noon-3pm & 8:30-11pm Thu-Sun; 📶) A slightly progressive kitchen set in a gorgeous, historic blue house with a windmill (hence the name). The interior is alive with art and the menu offers creative takes on Argentine classics. It's not cheap, but it is the most fun dining room in town.

Atero PIZZA $$
(☎0291-491-5002; San Martín & Güemes; mains AR$140-260, pizzas AR$180-269; ⊙8am-4pm & 8pm-11pm) Set in the ground floor of a three-star hotel but independently operated, this is the spot for casual, well-prepared meals all day long. It's best known for its breakfasts and pizzas.

Orientation

The town is divided into two sections by Río Sauce Grande. The main street, Av San Martín, lies south of the river, as do the bus and train stops and most other services.

Information

A good resource for information about activities, accommodations, and transportation in the region is www.sierrasdelaventana.tur.ar (in Spanish).

Banco Provincia (Av San Martín 260; ⊙9am-5pm Mon-Fri) Has ATMs.

Tourist Office (☎0291-491-5303; www.sierradelaventana.org.ar; Av del Golf s/n; ⊙8am-8pm) Across the tracks from the train station, which is now defunct. Staff offer maps and some helpful tips, all in Spanish.

Getting There & Away

Condor Estrella (☎0291-491-5091; www.condorestrella.com.ar) has buses to Buenos Aires (AR$840 to AR$980, nine hours, six times weekly) and Bahía Blanca (AR$179, 2½ hours, twice daily), leaving from a small office on Av San Martín, a block from the YPF gas station. Condor Estrella also runs a daily bus between Sierra de la Ventana and Villa Ventana (AR$17, 20 minutes) and between Sierra de la Ventana and Parque Provincial Ernesto Tornquist (AR$27, one hour).

Transporte Silver (☎0291-491-5383; Av San Martín 156) runs a door-to-door service between Sierra de la Ventana and Tornquist (AR$43, one hour), stopping at Villa Ventana (AR$20, 25 minutes) and Parque Provincial Ernesto Tornquist (AR$32, 40 minutes). The minibuses run two or three times daily (more in summer, December to March).

Villa Ventana

Just 17km northwest of Sierra de la Ventana is the peaceful village of Villa Ventana. There's nothing much to do here except poke around the *artesano* shops and wander the dusty streets, which meander through pretty residential neighborhoods full of pine trees.

You can also investigate the ruins of South America's first casino, by guided tour only; see the **tourist office** (☎0291-491-0095; Cruz del Sur s/n; ⊙8am-6pm Mon-Thu, to 7pm Fri-Sun, to 8pm daily Jan & Feb), located at the town's entrance. Villa Ventana is a closer base than Sierra de la Ventana from which to visit Parque Provincial Ernesto Tornquist (p131).

Sleeping & Eating

There are several places to stay, though none are particularly budget-friendly. A convenient option is **Cabañas Piuque-Lom** (☎0291-491-0079; www.piquelom.com.ar; Cruz del Sur s/n; d/tr from US$78/95). Its headquarters is on the main commercial strip, where it books lodging at an assortment of comfortable *cabañas* in the area. If you don't have your own wheels, **Cabañas La Ponderosa** (☎Whatsapp 0291-15-578-0640; www.villalaponderosa.com.ar; cnr Cruz del Sur & Hornero; cabañas for 2/3/4/5 people US$59/65/71/76; 📶) is conveniently located on the main strip. Prices drop on weekdays and from April to mid-December.

★**Hotel Água Pampas** BOUTIQUE HOTEL $$$
(☎0291-491-0210; www.aguapampas.com.ar; Las Piedras btwn Hornero & Canario; r from US$110; ❄@📶🏊) The town's best stay, this place is built from local stone and recycled wood, right down to the hollow-log bathtubs. It also boasts a gray-water system to irrigate its extensive lawns. This doesn't mean luxury takes a back seat – rooms are gorgeous, each with its own deck, and there are wonderful indoor and outdoor pools, spa services and a **restaurant**.

Getting There & Away

Condor Estrella runs a daily bus between Sierra de la Ventana and Villa Ventana (AR$17, 20 minutes); you can catch a ride to Parque Provincial Ernesto Tornquist by catching the same bus (AR$27, 30 minutes) to Tornquist. If you want to get to the park before 9am to join a group hike, you should take a *remise* (private taxi), which costs AR$200 to AR$300 for up to three passengers.

ATLANTIC COAST

Outside of Patagonia, Argentina's beaches often get an undeserved bad rap. Yet, as a rule, the sand is wide, clean and often rolling with picturesque dunes. There's some terrific surf here and the cold water is pleasant in the summertime, which is why each January and February the beaches attract droves from all across the country.

To avoid the summertime crush visit in the shoulder months of December and March, when the weather is still warm enough to enjoy the beaches and their activities, and the surf is pumping. In the dead of winter, the coastal towns feel abandoned, and the gray weather is depressing. Mar del Plata is an exception – the coast's largest city is a buzzing cultural capital, with plenty to do year-round.

Pinamar

02254 / POP 30,000

Located about 120km up the coast from Mar del Plata, Pinamar is a popular destination for style-conscious *porteños* who'd rather not make the trip to the beaches of Uruguay. The city was founded and designed in 1944 by architect Jorge Bunge, who figured out how to stabilize the shifting dunes by planting pines, acacias and pampas grass. It was once the refuge for the country's upper echelons, but is now somewhat less exclusive and more laid-back.

Activities

The main activity in Pinamar is relaxing and socializing on the beach, which stretches all the way from north of the town down to Cariló. But the area also offers a wealth of outdoor activities, from windsurfing and waterskiing to horseback riding and fishing. You can also ride bicycles in the wooded areas near the golf course or through the leafy streets of nearby Cariló.

For bike rentals, try **Leo** (02254-488855; Av Bunge 1111; bike rental per hr AR$100; 9am-9pm), on the main street near the tourist office. If you want to learn how to kiteboard, go to Sport Beach, the last *balneario* (river beach) located about 5km north of Av Bunge. There are many more options for activities – ask at the **tourist office** (02254-491680; www.pinamar.tur.ar; cnr Av Bunge & Shaw; 8am-8pm Mon-Fri, 10am-8pm Sat, 10am-5pm Sun).

Festivals & Events

Pinamar's film festival, **Pantalla Pinamar** (www.pantallapinamar.gov.ar; Mar), takes place in March, and there are concerts and parties on the beach around New Year.

Sleeping

Reservations are a must in January, when some places have a one-week minimum stay. Best options for the budget-minded are near the southern beaches of Ostende and Valeria, though you'll also find some cheaper hotels and *hospedajes* (family homes) along Calle del Cangrejo, north of the tourist office. There are steep discounts across the board during the off-season.

Hotel Yarma HOTEL **$**
(02254-405401; www.hotelyarma.com.ar; Del Tuyú 109; d US$46; P) The stone-and-stucco exterior helps this one stand out, and there's some interesting art on the interior walls, too. The rooms are a bit dated, yet they are superclean and great value at this price.

Playas Hotel HISTORIC HOTEL **$$**
(02254-482236; www.playashotel.com.ar; Bunge 250; standard/superior r US$118/129; P) Pinamar's original hotel is a shingled, whitewashed eye-catcher, right on the main drag, three blocks from the beach. The parlor floors and sculpture in the lobby are nice. The wood floors are a bit drab upstairs, but all else is updated. The location is ideal, the rooms are a good size, and the terrazzo pool area is romantic.

Hotel Mojomar HOTEL **$$**
(02254-407300; www.hotelmojomar.com.ar; De las Burriquetas 247; d from US$83;) The Mojomar is upscale, if not luxurious, with a great location three blocks off Av Bunge, and only a block from the beach. The look is modern but warm; guest rooms are small but comfortable, and some have sea views.

Hotel Arenas BOUTIQUE HOTEL **$$**
(02254-482621; www.hotelarenaspinamar.com.ar; Bunge 700; s/d US$53/94; P) Looking like something out of Crete, and about six long blocks from the beach, this aging four-star has its charms. Rooms are good sized with wood furnishings, private terrace, flat screens and Jacuzzi tubs. Plus there are two pool tables in the games room downstairs.

La Vieja Hostería BOUTIQUE HOTEL **$$$**
(02254-482804; www.laviejahosteria.com.ar; Del Tuyú 169; d from US$129;) In a beautifully remodeled 1940s house, Pinamar's best boutique hotel has elegantly appointed rooms, inviting common areas (including a poolside deck and a patio with massage tents) and a perfect location, just south of the main street and two blocks in from the beach.

WORTH A TRIP

PARQUE PROVINCIAL ERNESTO TORNQUIST

This 67-sq-km **park** (☎0291-491-0039; entry per person AR$50; guided treks per person AR$140-200; ⊙9am-5pm daily), 22km from Sierra de la Ventana, draws visitors from throughout the province. There are two entrances. The first is 5km west of Villa Ventana and home to the **Centro de Visitantes**, which has a small display on local ecology. The park's highlight, however, is at its other entrance, 3km further west. Consider making two day trips to the park (camping is forbidden), during which time you can enjoy two or three hikes. You can also visit with a guided tour, available from various agencies around Sierra de la Ventana, such as **Juanjo Navarro** (☎0291-15-507-0319; Navarro.juanjo@hotmail.com), or through the local guide cooperative, **Guías de Ventanía** (☎0291-414-5113; www.guiasdeventania.com).

The park's highlight, the five-hour (roundtrip) guided hike to 1150m **Cerro de la Ventana**, which leads to a window-shaped rock formation near its peak, is accessed via the westernmost entrance. The climb offers dramatic views of surrounding hills and the distant pampas. Register with rangers before 9am at the trailhead, and take plenty of water and sun protection. That hike costs an additional AR$140 per person.

Less-demanding destinations accessible from the Cerro de la Ventana trailhead include **Piletones** (2½ hours roundtrip) and **Garganta Olvidada** (one hour roundtrip). To visit the gorge and waterfall pool at **Garganta del Diablo** (AR$200 per person, six hours roundtrip), you need a guide, arranged by rangers at 9am at the trailhead, or you can book with a tour company out of Sierra de la Ventana.

Condor Estrella (p129) serves Tornquist from Sierra de la Ventana (AR$27, one hour) three times daily – tell the driver you want to get off at the park entrance. For better timing, to catch the park opening, arrange a *remise* (taxi) to the park from Sierra de la Ventana or Villa Ventana.

Eating

★Los Troncos ARGENTINE $$

(cnr Eneas & Lenguado; mains AR$140-400; ⊙noon-3pm & 8pm-midnight Thu-Tue; 📶) In business for four decades, this beloved backstreet eatery is often packed with locals even in low season. There's a casual but convivial old-school ambience, and the menu includes everything from roast meats to seafood stews to homemade pastas, all well executed.

Nelson Resto Bar PUB FOOD $$

(☎02254-517550; Bunge 68; mains AR$110-240; ⊙noon-3pm & 7pm-midnight; 📶) This vibrant, corrugated tin shack is packed with memorabilia, rocks with reggae and salsa, and serves gourmet burgers (including veggie burgers), tacos and pizza to vintage vinyl booths, and tables made from reclaimed wood. Quirky and fun, with bars and dining areas inside and out, this place packs them in.

Tante INTERNATIONAL $$

(De las Artes 35; mains AR$115-320; ⊙noon-midnight) This elegant tearoom, restaurant and bar – a few blocks in from the beach, just off Av Bunge – was once the home of a well-known 1950s soprano. Nowadays it serves up German, French and Alpine specialties such as fondue, crepes, goulash, wurst and sauerkraut. Afternoon teas are a delight.

There's a second location in Cariló.

Cantina Tulumei SEAFOOD $$

(Bunge 64; mains AR$100-290; ⊙noon-4pm & 8pm-1am) Hit the outdoor deck at this main-street eatery, one block in from the waterfront, for reasonably priced, quality seafood. Fish is prepared in at least a dozen different sauces; homemade pastas are also a good choice.

Getting There & Away

Pinamar's **bus terminal** (☎02254-403500; Jason 2250) is about eight blocks north of the town center, just off Av Bunge. Buses run eight times a day to Buenos Aires (AR$493-AR562, five hours) and thrice daily to Mar del Plata (AR$225, 2½ hours).

There are frequent buses to nearby Villa Gesell (AR$75, 30 minutes). For the southern beaches of Ostende, Valeria del Mar and Cariló, catch a Montemar local bus just outside the long-distance terminal.

ALONG THE COAST

If you have a rental car, excursions to the following beach enclaves – particularly popular with Argentine families – are a snap.

Starting in the north, just south of Pinamar, there are the tranquil and largely residential villages of **Ostende** and **Valeria**. Further down the coast is woodsy **Cariló**, a favorite of well-off Argentines. A jumble of luxury posadas, elegant inns and hotels and homes fit for architectural digest, it's a worthwhile detour at night for its fashionable restaurants or for a stroll under the trees, ice-cream cone in hand.

On the other side of Villa Gesell, continuing down the coast, are **Mar de las Pampas** and **Mar Azul**, exclusive beach neighborhoods with expensive lodging (rented only by the week in summer) and upscale services, all dropped into a pine forest that runs to the rolling dunes at the beach. The wide beach here is less crowded, too, making the area a good day-trip destination, even if you're staying in busier Villa Gesell. All of it is linked by a network of sandy roads that snake through the pines, which only adds to the charming, isolated feel. Of these two, Mar de las Pampas has more shopping and dining options.

Villa Gesell

☎02255 / POP 34,000

Smaller and less flashy than Mar del Plata, if less tasteful and louder than Pinamar, laid-back Villa Gesell is a hit with the younger crowd. Unlike the other coastal towns, it offers a wood-planked beach boardwalk, making walks along the sand much easier. It's also known for summer concerts (classical, folk and rock), and there are plenty of outdoor activities to enjoy. In the spring, you may glimpse migrating whales, penguins and sea otters.

In the 1930s, merchant, inventor and nature lover Carlos Gesell designed this resort of zigzag streets, planting acacias, poplars, oaks and pines to stabilize the shifting dunes. He envisioned a town merging with that woodland, but it wasn't long before high-rise vacation shares began their malignant growth and trees disappeared.

The town sprawls outward from its leafy nucleus, with most services located on Av 3, three blocks in from the beach.

Sights & Activities

Piñar del Norte PARK

(Alameda 201; Casa Histórica per person AR$20; ⏲Casa Histórica 9am-4pm Mon-Sat, 9am-2pm Sun) The nucleus of what became Villa Gesell can be found among the trees in the town center, planted long ago by founder Carlos Gesell. Among the shade trees is his old house, Casa Histórica, now a small museum. It contains archives from the town's inception and some old photos. The surrounding park is now threaded with trails and remains a wonderful spot for a picnic.

Feria Artesanal MARKET

(Crafts Fair; Av 3 btwn Paseos 112 & 113) There's a nightly handicrafts fair in mid-December to mid-March. Expect lots of handmade jewelry, carved wood, paintings and souvenirs. The rest of the year it's a weekend-only event.

Windy Playa Bar SURFING

(www.windyplayabar.com.ar; cnr Paseo 104 & beach; ⏲8am-dusk in summer) You can't miss it: just look for the faux pirate ship parked on the sand. At Windy, you can rent surf gear or sign up for lessons; the beach bar is also one-stop shopping for renting beach equipment or just grabbing some cold drinks and sandwiches with a view.

Casa Macca CYCLING

(Av Buenos Aires 449; per hr AR$50) For bicycle rentals, try Casa Macca. It's located between Paseo 101 and Av 5.

Sleeping

La Deseada Hostel HOSTEL $

(☎02255-473276; www.ladeseadahostel.com.ar; cnr Av 6 & Paseo 119; dm/d from US$30/75; @📶) Teeming with young Argentines in January, and shuttered in the off-season, this ultra-homey hostel sits atop a sloping, evergreen-fringed lawn in a residential area between the bus terminal and the center, six blocks from the beach. Eight-bed dorms are complemented by spacious common areas and a nice guest kitchen. Breakfast is served till 1pm.

★**Hostería Santa Barbara** BOUTIQUE HOTEL **$$**
(02255-463143; www.hosteriasantabarbara.com; Av 1, No 938; d from US$76; Oct-Apr;) This four-floor walk-up offers a sparkling-clean, three-star habitat. Rooms aren't huge, but they are bright, and the best situated have balconies. The top floor *comedor* (dining room) where you'll have breakfast overlooks the sea, and there's a gorgeous brick *parrilla* here, too.

Hotel de la Plaza HOTEL **$$**
(02255-468793; www.delaplazahotel.com; Av 2, No 375; d/tr from US$100/140) Centrally located between the beach and Villa Gesell's commercial center, this tidy hotel is professionally run and open 365 days of the year – a great pick if you happen to be passing through out of season. Several restaurants are located less than a block away.

Eating & Drinking

Rancho Hambre EMPANADAS **$**
(Av 3, No 871; empanadas AR$35, 4 for AR$110-170; 11:30am-3pm & 7-11pm) This main street hot spot features 36 varieties of empanadas, from the humble (minced beef) to the more elaborate (arugula, parmesan and walnuts, or bacon with mozzarella and muscat-infused prunes). Pick up a dozen to go. There's a second location on the corner of Av 3 and Paseo 125.

El Náutico ARGENTINE **$$**
(02255-461806; Paseo 102 & Playa; mains AR$110-250; 8am-11pm;) This charming jumble of wood festooned with fishing nets is set on the sand like a barge in dry dock. And though it looks like a fish house, it's actually known for its steaks, especially the *bife de chorizo*. It does burgers, sandwiches, salads and a lovely grilled fish, too.

El Viejo Hobbit PUB FOOD **$$**
(Av 8 btwn Paseos 11 & 12; snacks AR$60-110, fondue AR$200-340; 6pm-late Fri & Sat Apr-Nov, daily Dec-Mar;) An obligatory stop for beer lovers and Tolkien fans, this whimsical backstreet bar plunges you straight into hobbit-land from the minute you pass through the round front door. Several beers brewed on-site complement a menu focused on fondue. There's a cozy 2nd floor, plus a backyard with a miniature hobbit house for kids to play in.

★**Castillo de Ilusiones** FUSION **$$$**
(02255-473055; www.facebook.com/ilusionesresto.castillo; Costanera & Paseo 103; mains AR$150-350; 6pm-2am Thu-Sun;) Come to this funky, colorful dining room in the lobby restaurant of a condo tower, for an ever-changing international fusion menu courtesy of an inventive chef, Patrick Lechner. He rose to Argentine prominence thanks to a popular television show similar to *Master Chef*. Expect seafood towers, Indonesian noodle and seafood dishes, tantalizing paella and much more.

★**La Ventola** SEAFOOD **$$$**
(02255-572222; Laventola@telpin.com.ar; Calandria 1551, Cariló; mains AR$244-340; 8pm-midnight Thu-Sun) Tucked away in tiny Cariló, here's a locally beloved fish house, famous for its platters of grilled seafood, piled with salmon, sea bass, shrimp, mussels and calamari. It also does paellas, pastas and roast chicken if you aren't into fish. Book ahead in peak season.

Information

Tourist Office (02255-478042; www.turismo.gesell.gob.ar; Paseo 107, btwn Avs 2 & 3; 8am-8pm Mar-Dec, to midnight Jan & Feb) Conveniently located in the center. There's another branch at the bus terminal.

Getting There & Away

The **bus terminal** (cnr Av 3 & Paseo 140; 5am-midnight mid-Dec–Easter, 8am-8pm rest of year) is 30 blocks south of the town center. Destinations include Buenos Aires (AR$596, 5½ hours) and Mar del Plata (AR$205, two hours). You can buy bus tickets in the town center at **Central de Pasajes** (02255-472480; cnr Av 3 & Paseo 107; 9am-1pm & 5-8:30pm), saving you a trip to the terminal. You'll have to buy tickets for more local destinations, such as Pinamar (AR$75, 30 minutes), at the station itself.

Local buses into town (AR$10, 15 minutes) leave regularly from a shelter just across Av 3 from the long-distance terminal, or you can grab a taxi.

Mar del Plata

0223 / POP 621,000

'Mardel' is the classic Argentine beach destination, and popular with people from all over the country. A little too popular, in fact. If you end up here on a summer weekend, the string of beaches that fringe the shoreline are shoulder-to-shoulder sunburned bodies: not exactly a relaxing getaway. Out-of-season visitors, however, will find that Mardel, once a glamorous seaside resort in the 1920s and 1930s, and again during a midcentury development boom, has become a large and interesting city with stunning architecture and plenty of cultural attractions that have nothing to do with the beach. Many of them are connected by attractive pedestrian thoroughfares that link to an oceanfront promenade that winds along the city's gorgeous arced coastline.

History

Europeans were slow to occupy this stretch of the coast, so Mardel was a late bloomer. Not until 1747 did Jesuit missionaries try to evangelize the indigenous people of the southern pampas; the only reminder of their efforts is a chapel replica near Laguna de los Padres.

More than a century later, Portuguese investors established El Puerto de Laguna de los Padres. Beset by economic problems in the 1860s, they sold out to Patricio Peralta Ramos, who founded Mar del Plata proper in 1874. Peralta Ramos helped develop the area as a commercial and industrial center, and later as a beach resort. By the turn of the 20th century, many wealthy *porteño* families owned summer houses here, some of which still grace Barrio Los Troncos.

Since the 1960s the 'Pearl of the Atlantic' has lost some of its exclusivity, with the Argentine elite seeking refuge in resorts such as nearby Pinamar or Punta del Este (Uruguay). Still, Mar del Plata remains a thriving Argentine beach town. As a local taxi driver recently explained to us, 'There's enough hotel rooms for everyone, and if it rains, there's a lot to see and do aside from the beach.'

Sights

For a look at Mar del Plata's golden age, go for a stroll down Av Alvear: you'll see some of the city's finest old mansions, some of which now house museums and cultural spaces.

Plaza Mitre is an urban plaza with manicured lawns and gardens, a play area for kiddos, and a captivating local scene. It's a great spot for a picnic and some people-watching at all hours.

★ Puerto Mar del Plata PORT
(www.puertomardelplata.net; 533, 581) Mar del Plata is one of Argentina's most important fishing centers. Its port area, 8km south of the city center, is worth a visit, though public access to the jetty – and its graveyard of ruined ships, half-sunken and rusting in the sun – is now restricted. You can still watch the fishing boats come and go from the **Banquina de Pescadores**, the port's scenic, rather aromatic and slightly touristy wharf.

Grab some calamari and a beer here and watch the massive, shaggy sea lions who snooze, flirt and fight on the dock. Forget the aquarium, this is the real show!

To get to the port from downtown, you have two options. You can take local bus 581 or 533 (which stop at various points downtown and along the oceanfront road) all the way to the wharf (AR$10). You'll need a magnetic card to board. A taxi from downtown costs between AR$120 and AR$160. If you're going by taxi, consider arranging your return, as it's not easy to flag a taxi heading the other way. Note that the wharf mentioned here is not to be confused with the **Centro Comercial de Mar del Plata**, a cluster of high-end restaurants located near the entrance to the larger port complex.

Torre Tanque TOWER
(0223-451-4681; Falucho 995; 8am-5pm Mon-Fri, 2-5pm holiday weekends) FREE This interesting medieval-style water-storage tower, atop Stella Maris hill, was finished in 1943 and is still functioning. It's 88m high (that's 194 stairs), but has just two floors! The top floor is glassed in, but still offers spectacular views over Mar del Plata and further out to sea. Free guided tours (in Spanish) are available at 2pm, 3pm and 4pm. It's lit up like a landmark lavender night-light after the sun drops each evening.

Museo Municipal de Arte Juan Carlos Castagnino MUSEUM
(0223-486-1636; www.mardelplata.gob.ar; Av Colón 1189; AR$40; noon-6pm Mon & Wed-Fri, 2-7pm Sat & Sun) Built in 1909 as the summer residence of a prominent Argentine family, the turreted Villa Ortiz Basualdo now houses this fine arts museum; its interior exhibits paintings, photographs and sculptures by Argentine artists.

Torreón del Monje HISTORIC BUILDING
(0223-486-4000; www.torreondelmonje.com.ar; cnr Viamonte & Paseo Jesús de Galindez; 8am-10pm) Grand and castle-like, positioned on a cliff over the ocean, Torreón del Monje is hard to miss – look for the red domes and the stone footbridge straddling the oceanfront road. This classic landmark is a throwback to Mar del Plata's glamorous heyday. The Argentine businessman Ernesto Tornquist, intent on beautifying the area around

his own summer getaway, had the medieval-style lookout tower built in 1904. Stop for the view, and perhaps a coffee break on the terrace.

Centro Cultural Villa Victoria CULTURAL CENTER

(☎0223-492-0569; www.mardelplata.gob.ar; Matheu 1851; AR$20; ⏰2-8pm Wed-Mon) Victoria Ocampo (p138), founder of the literary journal *Sur,* hosted literary salons with prominent intellectuals from around the world – Borges, Le Corbusier, and Rabindranath Tagore were among more distinguished guests – here at her summer chalet, its gardens still bursting with lavender. It's now a cultural center that features changing art and cultural exhibitions, plus seminars and workshops on photography, illustration, literature, conflict resolution, drama and comedy.

Catedral de los Santos Pedro y Cecilia CHURCH

(www.catedralmardelplata.org.ar; Plaza San Martín; ⏰8am-8pm) Facing the leafy Plaza San Martín, this neo-Gothic building features gorgeous stained glass, an impressive central chandelier from France, English tiled floors and occasional choral concerts.

Beaches

Mar del Plata's beaches are mostly safe and swimmable, though thanks to the nearby harbor, the water isn't all that pristine. Downtown faces onto the most central beach, **Playa Popular** (formerly Playa Bristol), with its wharf and restaurant and several breakwaters. The boardwalk here, next to the casino area, is always packed with activity thanks to its centerpiece skate park – replete with bowls and rails. The next beach to the north is **Playa La Perla**, favored by a younger crowd and filled with *balnearios* (bathing resorts, or sections of beach with services such as beach chairs and parasols). To the south of Punta Piedras are **Playa Varese** and **Cabo Corrientes**, a pair of small beaches that are protected by small rocky headlands.

South of these beaches, at the more fashionable end of town, lies **Playa Grande**, also crowded with *balnearios*. About 11km south of the center, just past the port, you'll find the huge **Punta Mogotes** complex – slightly more relaxed and favored by families, who fill the *balnearios* to overflowing in January. This is also the location of **Playa Waikiki**, a popular spot for surfing.

Beyond the lighthouse is a less urbanized area. Though the beaches here are still filled with yet more *balnearios* in the summer, they're a quieter option. And for the adventurous, there's **Playa Escondida**, some 25km south of Mardel, which claims to be Argentina's only legal nude beach.

Activities

Mar del Plata and its surrounds offer plenty of opportunities to enjoy outdoor activities and adventure sports.

Biking is a good way to get around town – just remember that the city is hilly! The streets of Los Troncos are relatively calm and pleasant for cycling. Rent bicycles at a classic stand: **Bicicletería Madrid** (☎0223-494-1932; Yrigoyen 2249; per hr from AR$90; ⏰9am-5:30pm Mon-Fri, 10am-6pm Sat) has been in operation on Plaza Mitre for more than six decades.

Surf is best in March or April. Visit www.mardelplata.com/tour/surf.html for more information in English on surf breaks and conditions.

As the sea lions attest, Mar del Plata is one of the best spots for fishing in Argentina. The rocky outcrop at **Cabo Corrientes**, just north of Playa Grande, is a good spot to try, as are the two breakwaters – **Escollera Norte** and **Escollera Sur** – at the port. Freshwater fishing is popular at Laguna de los Padres, while **Mako Team** (☎0223-493-5338; www.makoteam.com.ar) offers ocean fishing excursions.

The rocky cliffs by the sea and the hills of Sierra de los Padres make for excellent climbing and rappelling. **Acción Directa** (☎0223-474-4520; www.facebook.com/acciondirecta.mdp; Av Libertad 3902; ⏰10am-1pm & 5-9pm Mon-Fri, 10am-1pm Sat) runs a school – it also offers mountain biking, canoeing and overnight active camping trips.

Más Vida YOGA

(☎0223-495-1189; www.masvidayoga.com.ar; Bolívar 2976; prices vary) A popular yoga space in the vibrant Plaza Mitre area offering Hatha, Ashtanga and aerial yoga classes. It can also arrange massages and yoga and SUP sessions in the summertime. The schedule is online, but call to confirm before turning up.

Kikiwai Surf School SURFING

(☎0223-485-0669; www.clubdesurfkikiwai.wix.com/kikiwaisurfclub; Av Martínez de Hoz 4100, Playa Kikiwai; 1-day class per person AR$690) This long-running surf school offers board rental and four-hour surf classes at Waikiki Beach, an 11km drive south of town.

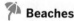

Mar del Plata

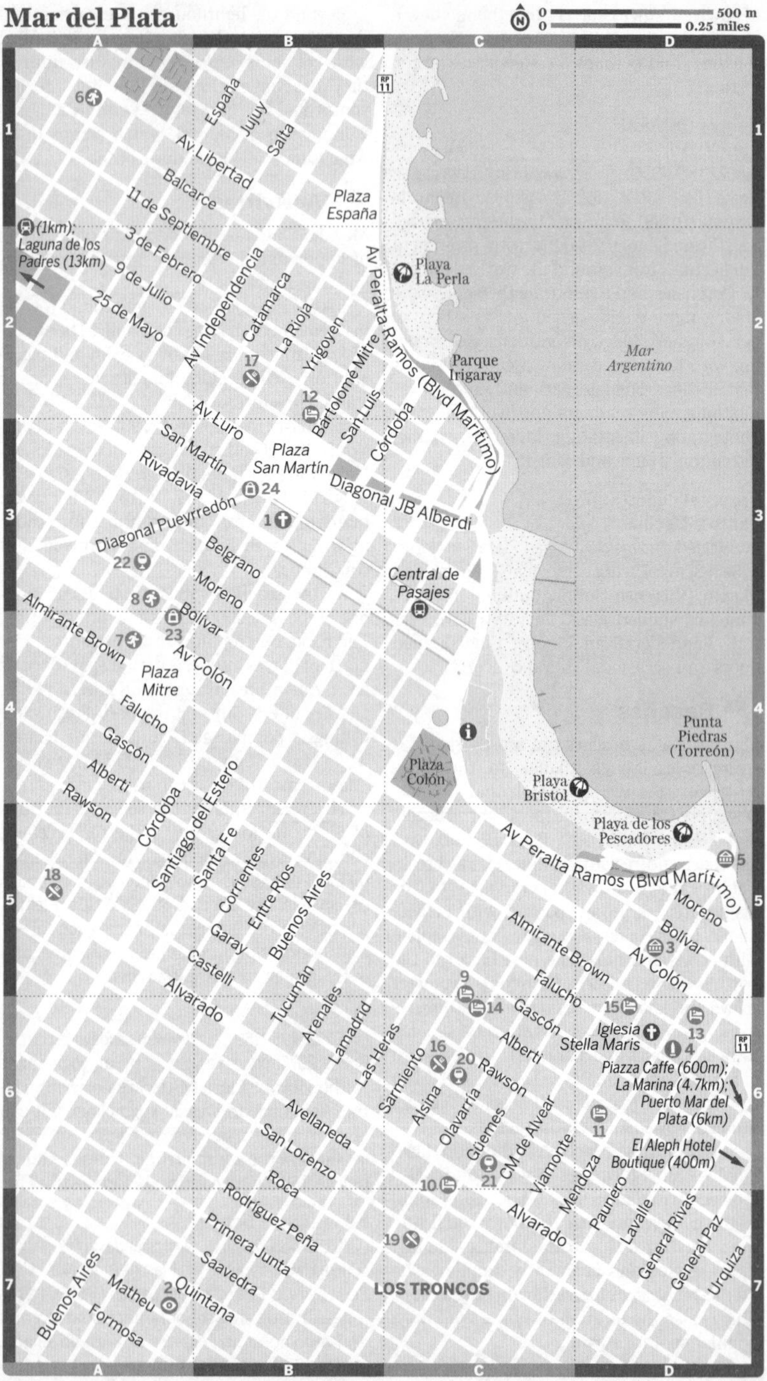

0 500 m
0 0.25 miles
España
Jujuy
Salta
Av Libertad
Balcarce
11 de Septiembre
3 de Febrero
9 de Julio
25 de Mayo
(1km); Laguna de los Padres (13km)
Plaza España
Av Independencia
Catamarca
La Rioja
Yrigoyen
Bartolomé Mitre
San Luis
Córdoba
Av Peralta Ramos (Blvd Marítimo)
Playa La Perla
Parque Irigaray
Mar Argentino
Av Luro
San Martín
Rivadavia
Plaza San Martín
Diagonal JB Alberdi
Diagonal Pueyrredón
Belgrano
Moreno
Bolívar
Central de Pasajes
Almirante Brown
Av Colón
Plaza Mitre
Falucho
Gascón
Alberti
Rawson
Plaza Colón
Punta Piedras (Torreón)
Playa Bristol
Playa de los Pescadores
Santiago del Estero
Santa Fe
Corrientes
Entre Ríos
Buenos Aires
Garay
Castelli
Alvarado
Tucumán
Arenales
Lamadrid
Las Heras
Sarmiento
Alsina
Olavarría
Güemes
CM de Alvear
Viamonte
Mendoza
Paunero
Lavalle
General Rivas
General Paz
Urquiza
Iglesia Stella Maris
Piazza Caffe (600m); La Marina (4.7km); Puerto Mar del Plata (6km)
El Aleph Hotel Boutique (400m)
Avellaneda
San Lorenzo
Roca
Rodríguez Peña
Primera Junta
Saavedra
Quintana
Matheu
Formosa
LOS TRONCOS

Mar del Plata

Sights
1 Catedral de los Santos Pedro y Cecilia B3
2 Centro Cultural Villa Victoria A7
3 Museo Municipal de Arte Juan Carlos Castagnino D5
4 Torre Tanque D6
5 Torreón del Monje D5

Activities, Courses & Tours
6 Acción Directa A1
7 Bicicletería Madrid A4
8 Más Vida A3

Sleeping
9 Che Lagarto Hostel C5
10 Dodo C6
11 Hostería Lucky Home D6
12 Hotel 15 de Mayo B2
13 Hotel Sirenuse D6
14 On Tap C6
15 Villa Nuccia D6

Eating
16 Crucoli Caffe C6
17 Montecatini B2
18 Sur A5
19 Tisiano C7

Drinking & Nightlife
20 Almacén Estación Central C6
21 La Bodeguita del Medio C6
On Tap .... (see 14)
22 Pueblo A3

Shopping
23 Casa El Gaucho A4
24 Diagonal de los Artesanos B3

Tours

Crucero Anamora BOATING
(☎0223-489-0310; www.cruceroanamora.com.ar; adult/child under 10yr AR$220/150) This 30m boat offers 70-minute harbor tours four times daily in summer and twice daily on weekends in winter from Dársena B at the port – just past the Banquina Pescadores at the Puerto Mar del Plata (p134).

Festivals & Events

Fiesta Nacional de los Pescadores CULTURAL
(Fisherman's Festival; www.patronespescadores.com.ar; ⊙Jan) Mar del Plata celebrates Fiesta Nacional de los Pescadores, which sees locals cooking up seafood feasts, along with a traditional procession.

Fiesta Nacional del Mar CULTURAL
(National Sea Festival; www.mardelplata.com/fiesta-nacional-del-mar.html; ⊙Feb) A large maritime celebration that includes the election and coronation of a 'Sea Queen.'

International Film Festival FILM
(www.mardelplatafilmfest.com; ⊙Nov) Launched in 1950, the city's International Film Festival is considered South America's most important film festival.

Sleeping

Prices start climbing in November and December, peak in January and February, then drop off in March. Reserve ahead in summer. In the off-season, some accommodations close their doors. If you love Airbnb, seek an apartment near Plaza Mitre, a fashionable local district.

Hotel Sirenuse HOTEL $
(☎0223-451-9580; www.hotelsirenuse.com.ar; Mendoza 2240; d from US$58; ❄@☜) Friendly, and family-run, this small hotel with 31 rooms on Stella Maris hill, just a few blocks from Playa Varese, is one of Mardel's best-value choices. With dark-wood furnishings and a hearty breakfast, the place feels more like a mountain lodge than a beach getaway. Travelers rave about the kind owners who speak English; you'll need to book well ahead.

Che Lagarto Hostel HOSTEL $
(☎0223-451-3704; www.chelagarto.com; Alberti 1565; dm/d from US$17/47; ⊙Sep 15-Apr; @☜) This popular branch of the Che Lagarto chain has it all: friendly staff, a central location close to Mardel's best nightlife and shopping, and squeaky clean (fan-cooled) private rooms and dorms. There's also a guest kitchen and a pleasant living area and cocktail bar. It's closed in the Argentine winter.

Hostería Lucky Home INN $
(☎0223-451-9978; www.hotelluckyhome.com; Alberti 1092; d from US$65; ⊙Oct-Apr; ❄☜) A newer, seasonal inn operated by the wonderful family behind Hotel Sirenuse this converted stone and wood house, just 500m from Playa Varese, offers cozy and bright rooms with wood furnishings, cheery paint jobs and a tasty breakfast every

LITERARY LADIES OF LA PLATA

Beloved by French novelist Pierre Drieu, and the great Jorge Luis Borges alike, in the 1920s and 1930s Victoria Ocampo gathered writers and intellectuals from around the globe to her home, Villa Victoria, creating a formidable literary and artistic salon.

Ocampo never went to university, but her voracious appetite for knowledge and love of literature led her to become Argentina's leading lady of letters. She founded the literary magazine *Sur,* which introduced writers such as Virginia Woolf and TS Eliot to Argentine readers. She was also an inexhaustible traveler and a pioneering feminist, and was loathed for her lack of convention. A ferocious opponent of Peronism, chiefly because of Perón's interference with intellectual freedom, Ocampo was arrested at Villa Victoria at the age of 63. She entertained her fellow inmates by reading aloud and acting out scenes from novels and cinema.

If Victoria is remembered as a lively essayist and great patron of writers, her younger sister, Silvina, was the literary talent, writing both short stories and poetry. Silvina won several literary prizes for her works, and in 1940 married Adolfo Bioy Casares, a famous Argentine writer and friend of Jorge Luis Borges.

morning. Management speaks English, but the *hostería* doesn't operate year-round.

On Tap B&B $
(☎0223-622-1394; www.ontap.com.ar; Alsina 2583; d US$48; ❄📶) A popular *cervecería* with small, well-imagined rooms on the floor above. Fashioned from reclaimed wood and polished concrete, each has a private bath, cable TV and wi-fi, as well as access to bicycles to tool around town. In this case the 'b&b' means 'bed and beer'.

Dodo BOUTIQUE HOTEL $
(☎0223-451-1479; www.hoteldodo.com.ar; Güemes 3041; s/d US$58/66; ❄📶) A cute boutique sleep in the heart of Mardel's fashionable Los Troncos district. Set in a three-story, whitewashed brick walk-up, rooms are all dressed in creams and whites, with white leather headboards and wall-mounted flat screens. Great value for money here.

Villa Nuccia GUESTHOUSE $$
(☎0223-451-6593; www.villanuccia.com.ar; Almirante Brown 1134; d from US$141; ❄@📶🏊) This beautiful guesthouse offers a small range of elegant and spacious rooms. Some are in a renovated house, others are in a modern annex; all are individually decorated. There's a rear garden with a swimming pool and Jacuzzi, and guests rave about the breakfast and afternoon tea, both featuring homemade cakes. It's often closed off-season.

Hotel 15 de Mayo HOTEL $$
(☎0223-495-1388; www.hotel15demayo.com; Mitre 1457; s from US$59, d from US$82-105; ❄📶) Conveniently located between Plaza San Martín and La Perla beach, this modern, four-star hotel is great value for its spotless, decent-sized guest rooms, spa, professional service, breakfast buffet and fast wi-fi.

El Aleph Hotel Boutique GUESTHOUSE $$$
(☎0223-451-4380; www.elalephmdq.com.ar; LN Alem 2542; d from US$155; ❄@📶) Located on a residential street a couple of blocks south of Playa Varese, this upscale guesthouse considers itself Mar del Plata's first boutique hotel. El Aleph, a converted historic home, features individually decorated rooms with hardwood floors, antique furnishings (you'll love those marble-topped vanities), wide flat-screen TVs and a well-stocked minibar, set around a grassy yard. The atmosphere is exclusive but relaxed.

Eating

For fresh seafood, head to the port. At the entrance, just off the busy oceanfront road, you'll see a large cluster of seafood restaurants surrounding a parking lot. This area is known as the **Centro Comercial del Puerto**.

And for a glimpse at one of the city's more stylish neighborhoods, head inland along Av Alvear to **Barrio Los Troncos**. The upscale barrio is filled with adorable cafes, bars and restaurants.

★**Crucoli Caffe** CAFE $
(☎0223-451-2386; Garay 1511; dishes AR$40-120; ⏲8am-8pm Mon-Fri, to 9pm Sat & Sun) This dreamy little cafe in Los Troncos is like a portal into the brain of artist, designer and baker, Maria Bertone. She has crafted or

painted everything on the walls – the mermaids and sailors, the sailboat napkin dispensers and fishy place mats, as well as the mixed-media art.

It all has a marine vibe and, oh, the pies and cupcakes, brownies and coconut-corn muffins are delicious. Same goes for the coffee. It does wok stir-fries and sandwiches, too.

Montecatini ARGENTINE **$**
(☎0223-492-4299; www.montecatini.com.ar; cnr La Rioja & 25 de Mayo; mains AR$110-190; ⏲noon-3pm & 8pm-midnight;) For solid, good-value dishes, make like the locals and head to this large, modern and popular restaurant – one of three branches in town. There's something for everyone on the menu (meat, fish, pasta, *milanesas,* sandwiches) and portions are generous. The weekday lunch special (AR$120, including dessert and a drink) is a steal. Good for families and large groups.

La Marina SEAFOOD **$$**
(☎0223-489-9216; 12 de Octubre 3147; mains AR$90-390; ⏲noon-4pm & 8pm-midnight Thu-Mon, noon-4pm Tue) You won't find seafood any fresher or more affordable than at this down-to-earth place a few blocks inland from the entrance to the port. In business since 1957, its specialty is the delicious *cazuela especial La Marina,* a seafood stew packed with fish, shrimp, squid and mussels simmered in white wine, cream and saffron.

Sur SEAFOOD **$$**
(☎0223-493-6260; Alvarado 2763; mains AR$95-350; ⏲8pm-midnight) The hype around Sur creates high expectations: many locals still consider it the best seafood restaurant in town. There's an extensive wine list and decadent desserts.

Piazza Caffe CAFE **$$**
(☎0223-451-9939; www.piazzacaffe.com.ar; Alem 2427; mains AR$88-390; ⏲8am-1am Mon-Sat, to 8pm Sun) A perfect perch over the boulevard and the bay upon which you may peruse a wide-ranging menu of pizzas, salads, pastas, grilled fish, chicken and steaks and tasty desserts. Sit in the cozy dining room or on the sun-splashed patio outside.

★**Tisiano** ITALIAN **$$$**
(☎0223-486-3473; San Lorenzo 1332; mains AR$196-384; ⏲8pm-late Mon-Fri, noon-3pm & 8pm-late Sat & Sun) You have two dining choices here. Up front is the craft cocktail bar where they rotate four *platos del día,* at fixed and affordable prices. However, you'll need to step a bit further off the street and into the stone dining room if it's the sensational housemade pasta that you crave, and it should be.

It offers three raviolis daily, and a range of succulent sauces. The pizzas are wood-fired and have thin crusts. You'll see the chef spinning his dough in front of the oven. The wine list is extensive and even the soundtrack is perfect. There's a reason

OFF THE BEATEN TRACK

MAR CHIQUITA

A humble and windy little gem, the village of Mar Chiquita is home to **Albúfera Mar Chiquita** (www.reservamarchiquita.com.ar), a 35km-long lagoon with an impressive range of wildlife. The word *albúfera* comes from the Arabic phrase *al-buhayra,* or 'the small sea' – which is, of course, also the meaning of the name 'Mar Chiquita.' Fed by creeks from the Sierras de Tandil and sheltered by a chain of sand dunes, the lagoon alternately drains into the ocean or absorbs seawater, depending on the tides. This creates a uniquely biodiverse ecosystem, and is the only lagoon of its kind in Argentina.

It's a paradise for bird watchers, with over 220 feathered species, 86 of which are migratory, including flamingos. Fishermen love it too, thanks to over 55 fish species. You can rent kayaks at the mouth of the lagoon. The nearby beach is also popular for windsurfing, kiteboarding or just hanging out for a while.

The **visitors center** (☎0223-469-1288; saladeinterpretacion@hotmail.com; cnr Belgrano & Rivera del Sol; ⏲9am-8pm Dec-Easter, 9am-4pm Mon-Fri, 10am-6pm Sat & Sun rest of year) is beside the lagoon, a few blocks inland from the beach. Between December and March staff can help arrange accommodations.

Bring cash, as the closest ATM is 4km away in Mar de Cabo.

Mar Chiquita is 34km north of Mar del Plata, and is best accessed by car. A taxi (one-way, AR$250, 40 minutes) from Mar del Plata will drop you at the lagoon's edge, where you'll find food and a bed within a few steps.

it's renowned across Argentina. After dinner, wander around the neighborhood; it's filled with bars and pubs.

Drinking & Nightlife

Many recommended venues are located in chic Barrio Los Troncos and the area along Irigoyen and LN Alem, between Almafuerte and Rodríguez Peña, a section of the city that's thick with cocktail bars and nightlife. Wander around the neighborhood for yourself and see what appeals.

Pueblo BEER HALL

(La Rioja 2068; ⌚7pm-4am Tue-Sun) Thanks to a recent change in ownership, there's a youthful crowd and free-flowing *cerveza* at this stylish pub with a corrugated facade and a cool, front door that rolls open to expose the pub directly to the street. There are surf videos on the flat screens, 11 beers on tap and a menu of pub grub on the blackboard. Food is priced to share.

On Tap CRAFT BEER

(www.ontap.com.ar; 2585 Alsina; ⌚6:30pm-1:30am Mon-Sat) A fantastic new craft-beer bar with a minimum of 10 beers on tap at any one time. Design is creative minimalist with wood-paneled walls and speckled-concrete tile floors. It's frequently standing room only.

La Bodeguita del Medio BAR

(Castelli 1252; ⌚6pm-4am) A classic rum-soaked dive, named after one of Hemingway's favorite haunts in Havana, serving famously delicious mojitos (choose among seven varieties), Cuban-inspired food and occasional live music.

Almacén Estación Central BAR

(cnr Alsina & Garay; ⌚7pm-late) This glitzy pub is set in a quaint and thoughtfully restored antique building – an old corner store where the former president of Argentina, Marcelo Torcuato de Alvear, reportedly did his shopping. Expect gourmet pub food, frequent happy-hour deals (even on weekends), and a mostly conservative crowd.

Shopping

Forgot your swimsuit? Calle Güemes, in Barrio Los Troncos, is lined with upscale shops and boutiques, while downtown has more mainstream chains and department stores.

Casa El Gaucho CLOTHING

(Yrigoyen 2140; ⌚9am-noon & 4-8pm) A gaucho-themed shop stocking leather goods galore, as well as ponchos, scarves, handbags, some nice shoes and berets – not to mention some lovely artisan necklaces as well as rope, saddles and stirrups. Family owned since 1924, everything in the shop has been handmade in Argentina.

Diagonal de los Artesanos CRAFTS, MARKET

(Plaza San Martín; ⌚6pm-1am mid-Dec–late Feb, 3-8pm Sat & Sun Mar-Nov) This long-running craft fair features nearly 200 vendors: they set up their stalls on Plaza San Martín and along Diagonal Pueyrredón to sell everything from *mate* gourds and knives to sweaters and silverwork. The fair happens daily (and starts in the evening) during the summer; outside the peak season, it only runs on Saturday and Sunday.

Information

Find **Jonestur** (www.jonestur.com; San Martín 2574), **La Moneta** (☎0223-494-0535; www.lamoneta.com; Rivadavia 2615) and other money exchanges and banks along San Martín and Rivadavia.

There are several branches of the city's official tourist information office around town. The **tourist office** (☎0223-495-1777; www.turismomardelplata.gov.ar; Blvd Marítimo 2270; ⌚10am-8pm Mar-Dec, to 10pm Jan & Feb) is centrally located and exceptionally helpful.

Getting There & Away

AIR

From Mardel's **Ástor Piazzolla International Airport** (☎0223-478-0744), 10km north of town, **Aerolíneas Argentinas** (☎0223-496-0101; www.aerolineas.com.ar; Moreno 2442; ⌚10am-6pm Mon-Fri) has several daily flights to Buenos Aires.

BUS

Mar del Plata's sparkling bus terminal is next to the **train station** (☎0223-475-6076; www.sofse.gob.ar; Av Luro 4700 at Italia; ⌚6am-midnight), about 2km northwest of the beach. To reach the center, cross Av Luro in front of the terminal and take local bus 511 or 512 heading southeast; taxis to downtown cost around AR$50.

In the city center, the ticket agency **Central de Pasajes** (☎0223-493-7843; cnr San Martín & Corrientes; ⌚10am-8pm) sells long-distance bus tickets for most companies, saving you a trip to the terminal.

Buses from Mar del Plata

DESTINATION	COST (AR$)	TIME (HR)
Bahía Blanca	819	8
Bariloche	1688	19
Buenos Aires	630-730	5½
Córdoba	1575-1800	16-18
Mar Chiquita	30	40min
Mendoza	1250-1785	18-21
Pinamar	225	2½
Puerto Madryn	1436-1735	16
Tandil	217	4
Villa Gesell	205	1½

TRAIN

The train station is adjacent to the bus terminal, 2km from the beach. Trains with *primera*-class service (US$40) run between Mar del Plata and Buenos Aires' Constitución station (six hours) three times weekly (on Monday, Wednesday, and Friday) in each direction.

Getting Around

The airport is 10km north of the city. Take bus 715 (AR$10, 30 minutes) from the corner of Blvd Marítimo and Belgrano. Taxis cost from around AR$150, depending on where you're going.

Despite Mar del Plata's sprawl, frequent buses reach just about every place in town. However, most buses (including the airport bus) require *tarjetas de aproximación* (magnetic cards) that must be bought ahead of time at *kioscos* (newsstands) and charged up.

The webpage www.cualbondi.com.ar/mar-del-plata provides useful maps of all local bus routes. The tourist office can also help with transportation details.

Car rentals are available downtown at **Alamo** (0223-493-3461; Córdoba 2270).

Necochea

02262 / POP 87,000

Totally pumping in summer and near dead in winter, Necochea has a beach-town feel and remains relatively undisturbed by the high-rises that keep springing up. It's not the most charming of the towns along the central Atlantic coast, but with such a long and wide beach, it's fairly certain that you'll find a spot to lay your towel – and Necochea has some of the best-value lodging on the coast.

Activities

With some of the best waves along the Atlantic coast, Necochea is a hit with surfers; it also attracts windsurfers year-round. At the north end of the town's wide beach are picturesque dunes that roll along the coast until the industrial port begins at the river mouth. Given the presence of the port, pollution could be an issue here.

Speaking of the **Río Quequén Grande**, there's easy rafting and kayaking upstream, particularly around the falls at **Saltos del Quequén**. Local outfitters organize both river and ocean kayak trips in summertime; just take a stroll downtown to see what's on.

The dense pine woods of **Parque Miguel Lillo**, a large greenbelt along the beach, are popular for cycling, horseback riding, walking and picnicking. Horses and bikes can be rented inside the park.

Monte Pasubio Surf Camp SURFING
(cnr Av 502 & Calle 529; 8am-6pm summer only) They rent boards and offer surf lessons during the summer. No reservations needed, simply wander down to the sand and they will hook you up.

Sleeping

Dyd Hotel HOTEL **$**
(02262-425560; www.dydnecochea.com.ar; Calle 77, No 314; s/d from US$54/63; P) Simple but colorfully decorated, this friendly hotel has small but well-equipped rooms. The best part is the location, two long blocks from the beach and a few blocks north of the main plaza – it's relatively quiet here in high season. Note that rooms are fan-cooled, not air-conditioned.

Hotel Tres Reyes HOTEL **$**
(02262-526419; www.hotel-tresreyes.com.ar; Calle 4, No 4123; s/d US$44/56;) A cute, pastel-brushed, four-floor hotel on the plaza with simple, three-star digs. Rooms are a bit cramped but cozy, furnished with both a full-sized bed and love seat. Some overlook the plaza and there's a cute lobby bar downstairs.

★**Hospedaje del Bosque** HOTEL **$$**
(02262-420002; www.hosteria-delbosque.com.ar; Calle 89, No 350; s/d from US$88/100; @) Four blocks in from the beach, this homey yet elegant family-run Tudor inn is by far the most atmospheric place to stay in Necochea. Rooms are large and comfortable, the decor reveals a keen eye for design, and some rooms have views of Parque Miguel Lillo across the street. There's a lovely garden and a good buffet breakfast.

WORTH A TRIP

MIRAMAR

If you've read *The Motorcycle Diaries*, or seen the film based on Ernesto 'Che' Guevara's memoir, you might remember Miramar. The beach resort was the first stop that the future revolutionary and his traveling companion, Alberto Granado, made on their epic trip around South America – Guevara's girlfriend, Chichina, was vacationing here with her family at the time.

Today, it's still a family-friendly destination with a long, wide beach, known for its surf, more easily accessible at the north end of town where there are a few surf schools and pumping waves. Compared to Mar del Plata, 45km to the north, Miramar is fairly low-key, but like any other Argentine resort it does get crowded in summer.

The **tourist office** (02291-420190; www.miramar.tur.ar; cnr Calle 21 & Costanera; 8am-9pm), located at the beach, has details about various activities around town, including horseback riding, golfing and fishing.

For accommodations, try **Hotel Danieli** (02291-432366; www.hoteldanielimiramar.com.ar; Calle 24, No 1114; d from US$60;), **Aventureiro Hostel** (02291-572-4320; www.aventureiro.com.ar; Calle 16, No 1067; dm US$12-15, r US$29-35; @), or one of the other basic but comfortable hotels a few blocks inland from the beach in the pedestrian zone. The towers along the beachfront road are all privately owned apartments, some of which will be for rent via Airbnb.

From Mar del Plata, buses (AR$50, one hour) run regularly to Miramar's bus terminal at Av 40 and Calle 15, within six blocks of the center.

Travelers looking for downright isolation can head to **Mar del Sud**, a small town 16km south of Miramar. It's known for its rustic atmosphere, empty beaches backed by rolling dunes, and good fishing.

It's popular, so reserve well ahead in the summer months.

Eating & Drinking

Sabe La Tierra HEALTH FOOD $
(02262-645224; www.sabelatierra.com; Calle 89, No 352-356; mains AR$75-160; 8am-8pm Tue-Sun;) A sleek eatery and the only vegetarian-friendly option in town. Expect green juices, veggie lasagna, huge salads, and among its range of wraps and sandwiches is the rare (to Argentina) vegan burger! It also has a wonderful tea selection and shelf space where it stocks local oils, vinegars, olives, cookies and all-natural beauty products.

Don Atilio EUROPEAN $$
(02262-440509; Calle 81, No 263; mains AR$140-290; noon-3pm, 8-11pm) A fabulous, if overly illuminated, family-run Italian and Spanish dining room. House-made pastas include cannelloni stuffed with beef, squid-ink spaghetti, and spinach-and-calf-brain (yes, really) ravioli, which you may pair with one of nine sauces. It also does do a tasty paella – packed with fish, shrimp, mussels and calamari, and a popular seafood *cazuela*.

Ernnan's CAFE $$
(02262-521427; Calle 83, No 284; mains AR$98-189; 8am-late;) Sitting on the edge of Necochea's main square, this high-ceilinged resto-bar with sidewalk seating, hip soundtrack, and free wi-fi makes a great place for a snack any time of day. It serves everything from *medialunas* (croissants) and gourmet sandwiches to pizza and paella.

Information

Tourist office (02262-438333; www.necochea.tur.ar; cnr Avs 2 & 79; 8am-9pm Dec-Mar, 10am-4pm Apr-Nov) On the beach.

Getting There & Away

The **bus terminal** (Av 58, btwn Calle 47 & Av 45) is 3.5km from the beach; taxis to the center cost AR$40-50, or take a local bus marked 'playa.' Buses run seven times daily to Mar del Plata (AR$139, two hours) and Buenos Aires (AR$748-AR853, 7½ hours) and thrice daily to Tandil (AR$233, three hours).

Bahía Blanca

0291 / POP 297,000

With grandiose period buildings, tiled sidewalks, a gorgeous plaza and boulevards thrumming with mom-and-pop businesses,

Bahía Blanca looks as if it emerged intact from a mid-century slumber. However, it remains a relatively prosperous port city thanks to a perfectly formed, natural harbor that gave life to the city, and the hordes of sailors who dock at what is now South America's largest naval base.

In an early effort to establish military control on the periphery of the pampas, Colonel Ramón Estomba situated the Fortaleza Protectora Argentina at that natural harbor in 1828. By 1885, when the present-day port was first opened, it had become a vital link to both North America and Europe.

Sights

Downtown, attractions are mostly of the architectural variety, thanks to the wave of construction by European immigrants in the early 20th century, followed by another wave of construction at mid-century. Go for a stroll past the city's neoclassical performing arts center, **Teatro Municipal** (☎0291-456-3973; www.facebook.com/TeatroMunicipalBahiaBlanca; Alsina 425), and the **Museo de Arte Contemporáneo** (☎0291-459-4006; Sarmiento 450; ⏱2-8pm Mon-Fri, 1-8pm Sat & Sun) FREE.

Contrary to popular expectation, the city center is not close to the port, and to get a good sense of Bahía Blanca, you'll want to see both sections.

★Museo Taller Ferrowhite HISTORIC BUILDING
(☎0291-457-0335; www.ferrowhite.bahiablanca.gov.ar; Juan B Justo 3883; by donation; ⏱9am-1pm Mon-Fri, 3-7pm Sat & Sun) Ferrowhite is the kind of ghostly landmark you see from far away and no matter how eerie, you can't stop yourself from inching closer and closer. The castle-like power plant, built by Italians in the 1930s, sits beside massive grain elevators on the edge of the bay. There's a **museum** and **cafe**, but half the fun is strolling around the abandoned structure with its elegant architecture, shattered windows and purported paranormal activity.

Puerto Bahía Blanca PORT
(☎0291-401-9000; Guillermo Torres 4200) FREE The working port is now open for entry, and includes the new **Paseo Portuario** – a drive which takes you past two overlooks: Balcón Del Mar, accessed by a concrete path studded with the original shipping bit, and another dating from 1901, which is the most interesting. This section is part of the original dock, and today stretches over a muddy beach.

Museo del Puerto MUSEUM
(☎0291-457-3006; www.museodelpuerto.blogspot.com; cnr Guillermo Torres & Carrega; donation requested; ⏱9am-noon Mon-Fri, 4-8pm Sat & Sun) Housed in a colorfully painted former customs building dating from 1907, this small but engaging museum is a tribute to the region's immigrants. The rooms include archives and photographs, and mock-ups of an old *peluquería* (barber shop) and bar. In the yard outside, a wooden fishing boat and other artifacts harken back to the port's intriguing past.

Sleeping

Hotel Muñiz HOTEL $
(☎0291-456-0060; www.hotelmuniz.com.ar; O'Higgins 23; standard/intermediate/superior US$43/56/78; ❄@📶) A downtown landmark, the Muñiz is located in a beautiful 90-year-old building. Upstairs, three levels of guest rooms are linked by long hallways. Superior rooms are the largest and best of the bunch, and service is impeccable.

Yes, you'll feel its age, but it's still an enjoyable (and affordable) choice only steps away from the central plaza.

Hotel Land Plaza HOTEL $$
(☎0291-459-9000; www.landplaza.com.ar; Saavedra 41; s/d US$105/128; P❄📶) There's nothing especially charming about the newest and most modern hotel in town, but rooms are well-appointed, large, bright and quite comfortable if a touch overpriced. Parking brings an additional fee of AR$180.

Apart Hotel Patagonia Sur HOTEL $$
(☎0291-455-2110; www.apartpatagoniasur.com.ar; Italia 64; s/d from US$72/85; 📶) A popular pick for families and budget travelers, this friendly aparthotel has dated but functional apartment-style rooms with kitchenettes. An added bonus: the included continental breakfast features fresh fruit and a surprising variety of homemade cakes and pastries. It's a short walk south of the plaza, near the intersection of O'Higgins and Italia.

Eating & Drinking

El Encuentro ARGENTINE $
(☎0291-451-9265; Sarmiento 307; empanadas AR$18; ⏱7:30-11pm) Set in a glorious period building, this kitchen specializes in regional empanadas for takeout and dining in.

★Gambrinus ARGENTINE $$
(www.gambrinus1890.com; Arribeños 174; mains AR$65-270; ⏱noon-3pm & 8pm-1am) Located

GETTING TO THE PORT

Unless you have a rental car, you have two options for getting to Ingeniero White (the port neighborhood) from downtown Bahía Blanca. Option one is to take bus 500 (30 to 40 minutes) from the south side of Plaza Rivadavia. Option two is to take a 20-minute taxi ride (AR$200 one-way). Coming back, there are also taxis available, parked at the stand near Museo del Puerto (p143).

in a lovely 19th-century corner building, on a side street a few blocks south of the main plaza, the menu features Spanish- and Italian-inspired Argentine classics. There's a good wine list and a number of beers on tap; the vivacious local crowd and walls plastered with vintage ads and Argentine basketball memorabilia contribute to the welcoming atmosphere.

Pelicano Bar PUB FOOD **$$**
(0291-451-2758; Alsina 226; mains AR$100-225;) A popular, music-themed bar and cafe. Each booth has been assigned its own decade and the table is plastered in artwork and photographs from famous albums and bands of that era. It serves coffee, Argentine beer and wine, pizzas and hot sandwiches all day and night. Sports or music videos stream on four flat screens.

★**Tributo** COCKTAIL BAR
(0291-453-3300; Yrigoyen 401; noon-3pm & 8:30pm-midnight Mon-Thu, to 12:30am Fri & Sat, noon-3pm Sun) If you're after craft beer and high-end cocktails, find this sleek spot with wood-paneled walls and a granite slab bar. The attached **restaurant** is also popular, but the bar is where you want to be.

Information

Tourist Kiosk (0291-459-4000; www.turismo.bahiablanca.gov.ar; Alsina 65, Municipalidad de Bahía Blanca; 9am-6pm Mon-Fri, 9:30am-1pm & 2:30-6pm Sat)

The bus terminal also has a tourist office.

Getting There & Away

AIR

Aerolíneas Argentinas (0291-456-0561; www.aerolineas.com.ar; San Martín 298; 10am-6pm Mon-Fri) and **LATAM** (0810-999-9526; www.latam.com; Chiclana 344; 9am-6pm Mon-Fri) offer flights from Bahía Blanca's airport, 15km east of town (AR$250 by taxi; there are no buses).

BUS

Bahía Blanca's **bus terminal** (Brown 1700) is 2km southeast of Plaza Rivadavia. Taxis to the city center cost around AR$60-AR$70; local buses 514 and 512 run to the bus station from Plaza Rivadavia, but you'll need to acquire a SUBE bus card from a municipal **kiosk** (Colón & Drago) before you ride, which makes catching a bus into town from the terminal a challenge. On the way out, however, it's easy enough, provided you've procured that SUBE card, which won't cost anything, but you will need your passport to get one. After that you'll need to hit a *kiosco* to add money to the card. It's all doable with some patience.

There are several businesses around the south end of Plaza Rivadavia that sell long-distance bus tickets, saving you a trip to the bus terminal. These businesses sell different bus companies' tickets, so ask around if you want a particular schedule, company or price..

Travelers to Sierra de la Ventana have two options: Condor Estrella (p129) runs two daily buses (AR$160, 2½ hours) and **Norte Bis** (0291-15-468-5101; www.elnortebis.com) operates a door-to-door shuttle (AR$200, one hour) with two or three departures per day. Call ahead to reserve a spot.

Buses from Bahía Blanca

DESTINATION	COST (AR$)	TIME (HR)
Bariloche	1031-1175	12-14
Buenos Aires	1053	9
Córdoba	1150	13-15
Mar del Plata	829-921	7
Neuquén	551	7½
Sierra de la Ventana	160	2½
Tandil	562	5-6
Trelew	1000	10-12

TRAIN

Trains run from the **Estación Ferrocarril Roca** (0291-452-9196; Cerri 750) to Buenos Aires' Constitución station several days of the week (AR$58 to AR$66, 14 hours). Check the website for more details
on routes and fare options, and to make reservations.

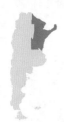

Iguazú Falls & the Northeast

Includes ➡

Best Places to Eat

- ➡ De La Fonte (p199)
- ➡ Zazpirak Bat (p154)
- ➡ La Rueda (p199)

Best Places to Stay

- ➡ La Alondra (p169)
- ➡ Rancho de los Esteros (p175)
- ➡ Boutique Hotel de la Fonte (p197)

Why Go?

Northeast Argentina is defined by water. Muscular rivers roll through plains that they flood at will, while fragile wetlands support myriad birdlife, snapping caimans and cuddly capybaras. The peaceful Río Iguazú, meandering through jungle between Brazil and Argentina, dissolves in fury and power in the planet's most awe-inspiring waterfalls.

The river then flows into the Paraná, one of the world's mightiest watercourses, which surges southward, eventually forming the Río de la Plata near Buenos Aires. Along it are some of the country's most interesting cities: elegant Corrientes, colonial Santa Fe and booming Rosario, as well as Posadas, gateway to the ruined splendor of the Jesuit missions.

Dotted throughout are excellent parks that represent the region's biological diversity. The Esteros del Iberá harbor a particularly astonishing richness of wildlife.

When to Go

Puerto Iguazú

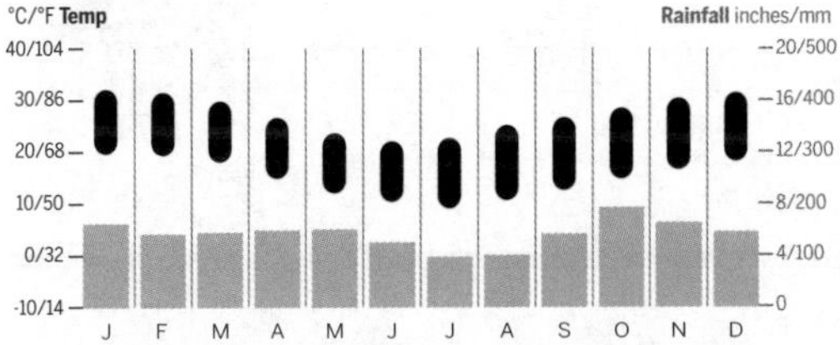

Feb Hot weather and flashy Carnaval celebrations in Gualeguaychú, Corrientes and Posadas.

Aug Cool and dry; good for wildlife watching as water sources are scarcer.

Sep–Oct Moderate temperatures, not too crowded. Iguazú flowing well but flooding and rain less likely.

Iguazú Falls & the Northeast Highlights

1 Iguazú Falls (p193) Dropping your jaw in stunned amazement at the beauty and power of the continent's greatest waterfalls.

2 Rosario (p148) Getting personal with the mighty Paraná in this livable, lovable city.

3 Parque Esteros del Iberá (p172) Cooing at the cute capybaras and getting up close to countless caimans chilling in the wetlands.

4 Colón (p180) Munching delicious freshwater fish by the Río Uruguay in this relaxed and pretty town.

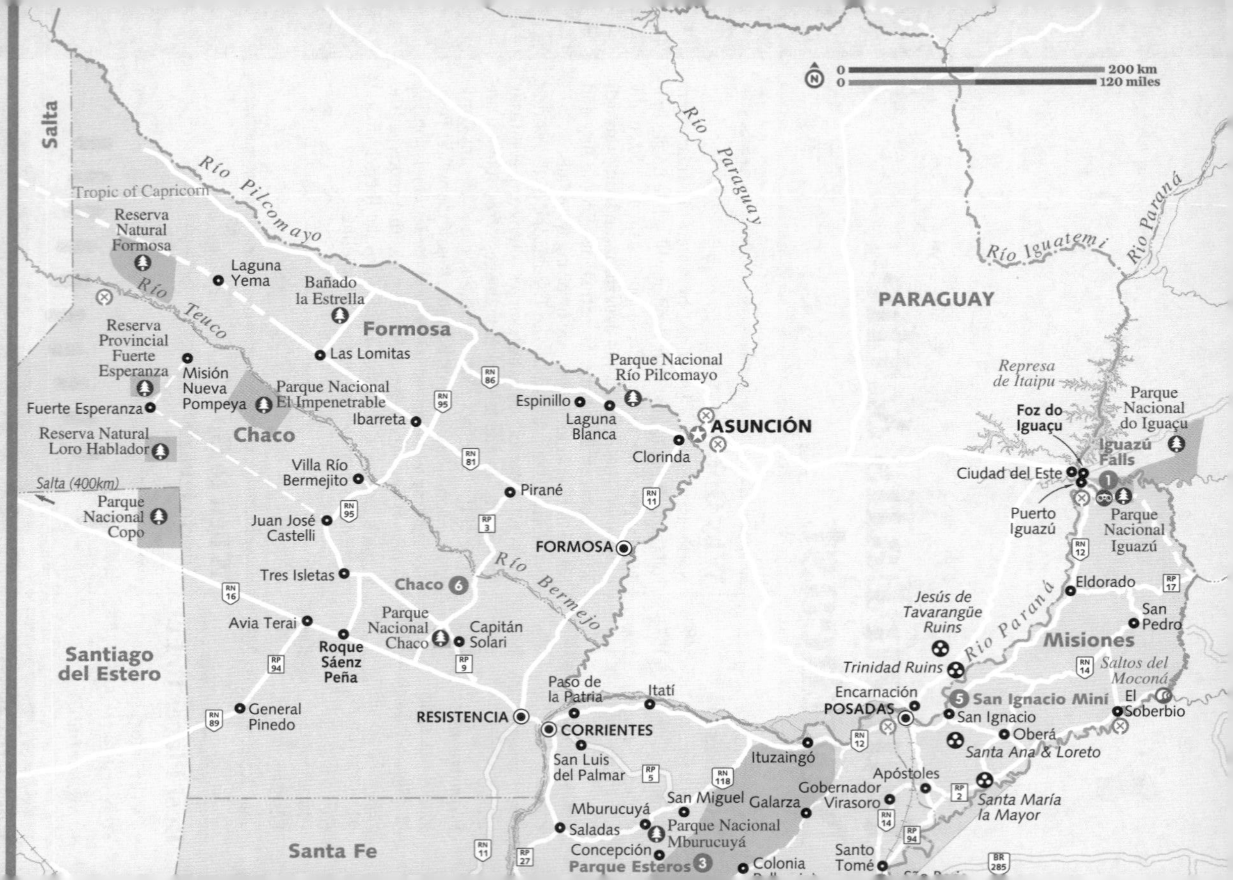

5 San Ignacio Miní (p189) Pondering a unique experiment in humanity while wandering among the ruins of this and other Jesuit missions.

6 Chaco (p212) Admiring the sculptures in arty Resistencia then hitting the 'impenetrable', a bastion of traditional indigenous culture.

7 Gualeguaychú (p182) Living it up at one of the region's classic Carnaval celebrations, like Carnaval de Gualeguaychú.

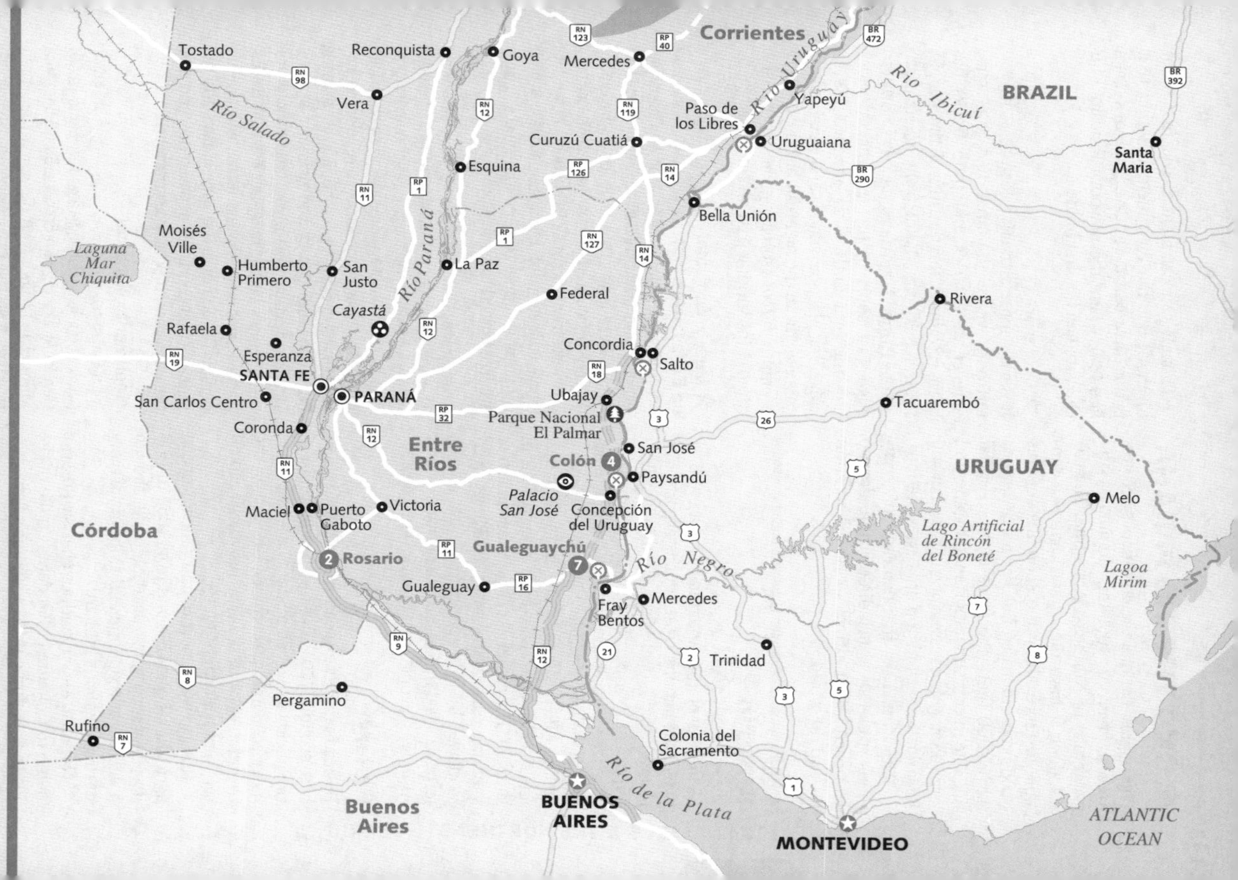

ALONG THE RÍO PARANÁ

The mighty Paraná, the continent's second-longest river at 4000km, dominates the geography of Northeast Argentina. The cities along it have their town centers a sensible distance above the shorelines of this flood-prone monster, but have a *costanera* (riverbank) that's the focus of much social life. The river is still important for trade, and large oceangoing vessels ply it to and beyond Rosario, the region's top urban destination.

The Paraná is the demesne of enormous river fish – including surubí, dorado and pacú – that attract sports fishers from around the world.

Rosario

☎0341 / POP 1.27 MILLION

Birthplace of the Argentine flag as well as two of the nation's most famous exports, Che Guevara and Lionel Messi, Rosario is still an important river port but has done a great job of regenerating its center. The derelict buildings of the long *costanera* have been converted into galleries, restaurants and skate parks, and river beaches and islands buzz with life in summer. The center – a curious mishmash of stunning early-20th-century buildings overshadowed by ugly apartments – has a comfortable, lived-in feel, and the down-to-earth *rosarinos* (people from Rosario) are a delight.

History

Rosario's first European inhabitants settled here around 1720. After independence Rosario quickly superseded Santa Fe as the province's economic powerhouse, though, to the irritation of *rosarinos,* the provincial capital retained political primacy.

Rosario was a port of entry for European agricultural colonists and from 1869 to 1914 its population grew nearly tenfold, though a decline of economic and shipping activity during the 1960s hit hard.

Nationalistic Argentines cherish Rosario, home to Cuna de la Bandera (Cradle of the Flag), a monument to the nation's flag.

Sights

Many of Rosario's main attractions are found along the *costanera* and around the Parque Independencia, an expansive green space just south of the center where locals come to hang out and picnic, sip *mate* (a tea-like beverage) and play football.

Though you can't enter, you may want to check out the apartment building that is the **Casa Natal de 'Che' Guevara** (Entre Ríos 480), where the newborn Ernesto 'Che' Guevara had his first home.

★Costanera WATERFRONT

Rosario's most attractive feature is its waterfront, where the area that was once derelict warehouses and train tracks has been reclaimed for the fun of the people. It stretches some 15km from its southern end at Parque Urquiza to the city's northern edge, just short of the suspension bridge crossing into Entre Ríos province. It's an appealing place to wander and watch what's going on, from the plentiful birdlife and impromptu *fútbol* (soccer) games to massive cargo ships surging past on the river.

★Museo Municipal de Bellas Artes GALLERY

(www.museocastagnino.org.ar; cnr Av Carlos Pellegrini & Blvd Oroño; AR$10; 2-8pm Wed-Mon) This gallery is worth a visit for its inventive displays of contemporary and 20th-century artworks from the MACRO collection, and its small collection of European works, which contains a couple of very fine pieces. There are free guided tours at 6pm.

Costanera Sur WATERFRONT

The grassy zone below downtown includes plenty of space for jogging and courting, as well as the **Estación Fluvial** (La Fluvial; ☎0341-447-3838; www.estacionfluvial.com; noon-5pm Mar-Oct, 10am-6pm Nov-Feb) building, offering boat trips and eating and drinking options. Heading further north, you pass various cultural venues before reaching **Parque de España** (Paraná riverbank) and its mausoleum-like edifice. Beyond here is a zone of bars and restaurants that gets lively at weekends, and then the city's contemporary-art museum.

Monumento Nacional a La Bandera MONUMENT

(www.monumentoalabandera.gob.ar; Santa Fe 581; elevator AR$20; 9am-6pm Tue-Sun, 2-6pm Mon) Manuel Belgrano, who designed the Argentine flag, rests in a crypt beneath this colossal stone obelisk built where the blue-and-white stripes were first raised. If rampant nationalism isn't your thing, it's nevertheless worth taking the elevator to the top for great views over the waterfront, Paraná and islands. The attractive colonnade houses an eternal flame commemorating those who died for the fatherland.

Paraná Delta ISLAND

Rosario sits on the banks of the Río Paraná upper delta, a 60km-wide area of mostly uninhabited, subtropical islands and winding *riachos* (streams). It's rich in bird and animal life, and even the closest islands feel miles from anywhere, though you can see the city's buildings looming close at hand. Various boat services and tours reach the islands and/or explore the delta.

From Estación Fluvial, boats run weekends from mid-September to May and daily from December to February across to the island beaches at the Banquito de San Andrés (AR$130 return).

Museo de Arte Contemporáneo de Rosario GALLERY

(MACRO; www.macromuseo.org.ar; cnr Av de la Costa & Blvd Oroño; AR$10; 2-8pm Wed-Mon) Housed in a brightly painted grain silo on the waterfront, this is part of Rosario's impressive riverbank renewal. It features temporary exhibitions, mostly by young local artists, of varying quality, housed in small galleries spread over eight floors. There's a good view of river islands from the mirador (viewpoint) at the top and an attractive cafe-bar by the river.

On Fridays at 5pm there are free guided tours in Spanish.

Museo de la Memoria MUSEUM

(www.museodelamemoria.gob.ar; Córdoba 2019; AR$20; 2-8pm Tue-Fri, 4-8pm Sat & Sun) A former army HQ, not far from where police held, tortured and killed people during the Dirty War, this museum seeks to remember the violence and victims. If you can read Spanish, you'll find it's a small but very moving display, with witness descriptions, photos of the 'disappeared' and an attempt to look at the wider history of man's inhumanity to man. There are temporary exhibitions upstairs.

Museo Histórico Provincial MUSEUM

(www.museomarc.gob.ar; Av del Museo, Parque Independencia; 9am-6pm Tue-Fri, 2-7pm Sat & Sun, 3-8pm Sat & Sun Dec-Mar) FREE The well-presented collection features plenty of post-independence exhibits plus excellent displays on indigenous cultures from many parts of Latin America. Particularly interesting is the collection of baroque religious art from the southern Andes. Information is in Spanish only. It's closed when Newell's Old Boys are playing at home in the adjacent stadium.

Museo de la Ciudad MUSEUM

(www.museodelaciudad.gob.ar; Blvd Oroño 2300; 9am-3pm Tue-Fri, 2-7pm Sat, 8:30am-1:30pm Sun) FREE Opposite the racetrack in a tin-roofed bungalow, one of Rosario's loveliest buildings, this enthusiastically run museum in Parque Independencia has good-quality temporary exhibitions, a reconstructed 19th-century pharmacy, a cute exhibition space in a former greenhouse, and an involved, bring-it-out-to-the-people attitude.

The museum has an excellent bilingual leaflet to guide you around the park, making it a good place to begin a tour of the area.

Activities

Jardín de los Niños AMUSEMENT PARK

(0341-480-2421; Parque de la Independencia; AR$20; 2-7pm Fri-Sun) This former zoo has been converted into a marvelous activity park for kids, with a wide variety of innovative puzzles, climbing frames, a great pirate ship and a flying machine. It's good fun for parents too. Two other (also excellent) child-oriented places in town – La Granja de la Infancia and La Isla de los Inventos – make up the 'Tríptico de la Infancia.'

Courses

Spanish in Rosario LANGUAGE

(0341-15-560-3789; www.spanishinrosario.com; Catamarca 3095) Rosario is a great base for learning Spanish; this place offers enjoyable language programs and can arrange family stays and volunteer work placements.

Tours

★**Rosario Kayak & Motor Boat Tours** TOURS

(Paseos en Lancha y Kayak; 0341-15-571-3812; www.boattours.com.ar; Estación Fluvial) A friendly, professional, recommended, multilingual set-up with great boat trips around the Paraná delta (AR$300, one to 1½ hours) with an optional lunch stop on a delta island. You can also explore the islands by kayak. It also offers water-taxi service to the delta islands and rents bikes for AR$250 per day. Book by phone or at the Estación Fluvial.

Ciudad de Rosario BOATING

(0341-449-8688; www.barcocr1.com; cruise AR$225) Near the Estación Fluvial, this converted barge offers two-hour cruises on the Paraná. Inside it's air-conditioned but the open-air decks give better views. It leaves on weekends and holidays at 2:30pm and 5pm,

Rosario

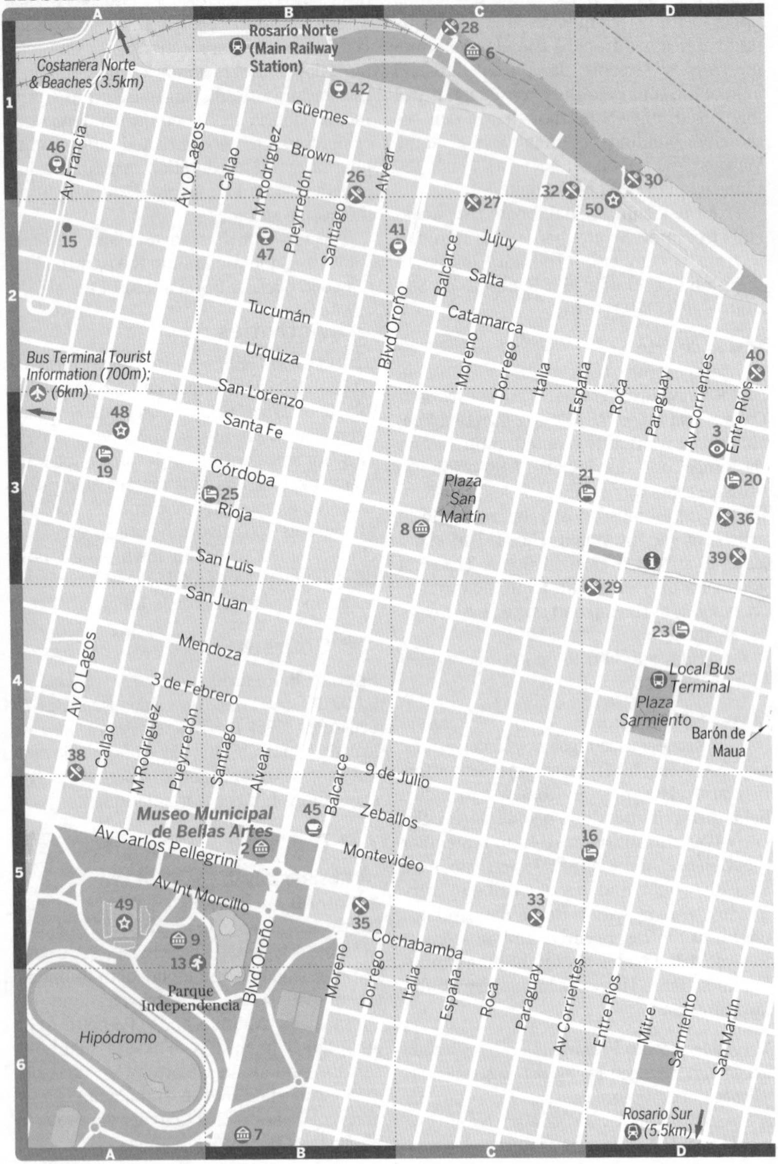

or 5pm and 7:30pm in summer. Vulnerable to cancellation if windy.

Rosario Free Tour WALKING

(☎0341-560-3789; www.rosariofreetour.com; cnr Maipú & Urquiza; ⏲tours 10am Sat) Two-hour walking tours in Spanish and English. Meet on the steps of the old customs building at the end of Maipú. Though it's technically free, a donation is appropriate.

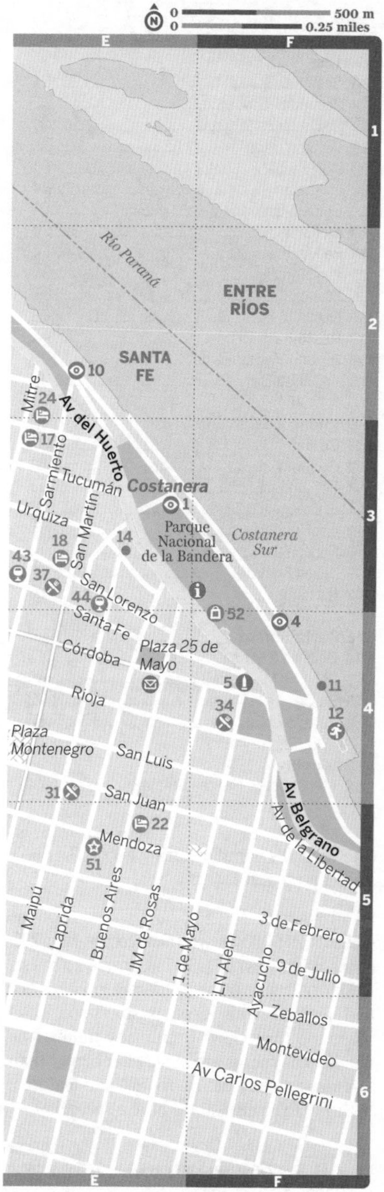

Festivals & Events

Fiesta de las Colectividades CULTURAL

(Nov) A 10-day festival celebrating the cultural diversity of Rosario with groups representing immigrant communities presenting concerts, dances, workshops and culinary arts. It finishes with a major fireworks display.

Sleeping

There are dozens of hostels, but they're often block-booked by groups of police or other government workers. There's also a herd of average midrange hotels. Prices generally drop midweek.

Residence Boutique Hostel HOTEL, HOSTEL $

(0341-421-8148; www.residenceboutique.com.ar; Buenos Aires 1145; dm/d US$17/51;) Rather a special place, this lovely early-20th-century building houses a serene, beautiful hotel and hostel. Public spaces are full of art-nouveau flourishes, and the compact, stylish private rooms offer great value for this level of comfort. Dorms are similarly upmarket, and the little garden patio and breakfast area are lovely places to relax. Original and striking.

Avoid the private rooms at the front if you're a light sleeper.

La Casa de Arriba HOSTEL $

(0341-430-0012; www.lacasadearriba.com.ar; Córdoba 2889; dm weekend/weekday US$15/18;) A designer's flair has made a fabulous hostel from this old house. Exposed brick, creative use of space, modern shelf-style bunks and a welcoming attitude make this a comfortable, stylish Rosario base. Its distance from the center is offset by its relative proximity to bars and nightlife.

La Casa de Pandora HOSTEL $

(0341-679-9314; www.lacasadepandora.com.ar; San Lorenzo 1455; dm/r US$15/32;) Arty and welcoming, this fine hostel has moved to expansive new digs in a classic older building but it remains clean and comfortable with a relaxed vibe. Air-conditioned dorms are roomy and comfortable and the cafe out the front is a good place to hang out. Various workshops and events – yoga, dance, folk music – are held on-site.

Rosario Global House HOSTEL $

(0341-424-4922; www.rosarioglobalhouse.com.ar; Rodríguez 863; dm US$13-15, r US$35-41;) On a fairly suburban street, this peaceful budget retreat is within striking distance of nightlife options. High-ceilinged dorms have comfortable bunks and fancy light fittings, while the lounge and patio spaces make great chill-out spots. Management is very friendly.

Rosario

Top Sights
1 Costanera ... E3
2 Museo Municipal de Bellas Artes ... B5

Sights
3 Casa Natal de 'Che' Guevara ... D3
4 Costanera Sur ... F4
5 Monumento Nacional a La Bandera ... F4
6 Museo de Arte Contemporáneo de Rosario ... C1
7 Museo de la Ciudad ... B6
8 Museo de la Memoria ... C3
9 Museo Histórico Provincial ... A5
10 Parque de España ... E2

Activities, Courses & Tours
11 Ciudad de Rosario ... F4
12 Estación Fluvial ... F4
13 Jardín de los Niños ... A5
14 Rosario Free Tour ... E3
Rosario Kayak & Motor Boat Tours ... (see 12)
15 Spanish in Rosario ... A2

Sleeping
16 1412 ... D5
17 Catamarca Suites Land ... E3
18 Esplendor Savoy Rosario ... E3
19 La Casa de Arriba ... A3
20 La Casa de Pandora ... D3
21 Plaza Real ... D3
22 Residence Boutique Hostel ... E5
23 Roberta Rosa de Fontana Suites ... D4
24 Ros Tower ... E2
25 Rosario Global House ... B3

Eating
26 Ceviche ... B1
27 Comedor Balcarce ... C2
28 Davis ... C1
29 De Buen Humor ... D4
30 Don Ferro ... D1
31 El Ancla ... E4
32 El Viejo Balcón ... C1
33 La Estancia ... C5
34 La Marina ... F4
35 Los Potrillos ... B5
36 Monreal ... D3
37 Nuria ... E3
38 Restaurant Bruno ... A4
39 Rincón Vegetariano ... D3
40 Zazpirak Bat ... D2

Drinking & Nightlife
41 Bound ... C2
42 Costello ... B1
43 El Cairo ... E3
44 El Diablito ... E3
45 Espiria ... B5
46 Fenicia ... A1
Jekyll & Hyde ... (see 17)
47 Pichangú ... B2

Entertainment
48 Distrito Siete ... A3
49 Estadio Marcelo Bielsa ... A5
50 La Casa del Tango ... D2
51 Teatro El Círculo ... E5

Shopping
52 Mercado de Pulgas del Bajo ... F4

Catamarca Suites Land HOTEL $$
(☎0341-440-0020; www.catamarcasuitesland.com.ar; Catamarca 1219; r US$79; ❄📶) These spacious apartment-style doubles with breakfast bar, microwave and minibar have plenty of style, while big comfy beds and powerful showers add value. Rooms have a balcony looking down the street to the Paraná and there's a small roof terrace with a Jacuzzi. Breakfast is brought up to your room. Cash only.

Esplendor Savoy Rosario HOTEL $$
(☎0341-429-6000; www.esplendorsavoyrosario.com; San Lorenzo 1022; standard/superior r US$122/147, ste US$185; P❄@📶🏊) Even among Rosario's many elegant early-20th-century buildings, this art-nouveau gem is a standout. It's a flawless contemporary conversion; rooms feature modern conveniences that blend well with the centenarian features. An indoor pool, elegant cafe-bar and roof garden are among the attractions. It's popular during events, so don't expect a peaceful stay.

Ros Tower HOTEL $$
(☎0341-529-9000; www.rostower.com.ar; Mitre 295; deluxe/deluxe-plus r US$132/158, junior/executive ste US$184/210; P❄@📶🏊) Offering great service and facilities, this sleek business-spa hotel offers top river views from many rooms. The deluxe-plus rooms are somewhat bigger than the first-category deluxe rooms, and feature a bathtub. Executive suites have a Jacuzzi.

1412 HOTEL $$
(☎0341-448-7755; www.1412.com.ar; Zeballos 1412; s/d US$82/106; ❄📶) Comfortably stylish, this decent-value modern hotel is perfectly located for sorties to the busy restaurant strip on Av Carlos Pellegrini. The handsome lobby offers free tea, coffee and cakes all day, while rooms are pleasingly and flawlessly modern. Throw in friendly and enthusiastic young staff and it's a winner.

Plaza Real HOTEL $$

(☎0341-440-8800; www.plazarealhotel.com; Santa Fe 1632; standard/superior r US$138/163; P❄@📶≋) Luxurious rooms, apartments and suites are to be had in this business hotel with rooftop pool. Fine facilities – gym, sauna, pool, open-air Jacuzzi – a cracking breakfast and polite, friendly service make it a reliable choice.

Roberta Rosa de Fontana Suites APARTMENT $$

(☎0341-449-6767; www.rrdfsuites.com.ar; Entre Ríos 914; s/d US$76/88; ❄📶) Situated very centrally above a colorful cafe, these rooms are modern and commodious, with brushed-concrete ceilings, black floors and a small kitchenette. They come in various sizes, making it a good family option.

Puerto Norte Hotel HOTEL $$$

(☎0341-436-2700; www.puertonortehotel.com; Carballo 148; city/executive/premium r US$185/205/235; P❄@📶≋) In a new riverside development north of the center, this flashy hotel is built atop 14 former grain silos, whose circular spaces house the reception and bar. Rooms are handsome and well-equipped, with coffee-pod machines and beds backed by whole-wall photos of old Rosario. The restaurant and rooftop spa complex, including outdoor and indoor pools, have spectacular panoramas.

Cheapest-category city views are more interesting than those from executive rooms. For brilliant river views, you'll need to upgrade to a premium room or suite.

Eating

Central Rosario seems empty come suppertime. That's because half the city is out on Av Carlos Pellegrini. Between Buenos Aires and Moreno there's a vast number of family-friendly eateries, including barn-like *parrillas* (steak restaurants), dozens of pizza places, buffets, bars and excellent ice-creameries. Just stroll along and take your pick. Most places have street terraces.

For meals outside standard times, check out the city's many classic cafes.

La Marina SPANISH, SEAFOOD $

(1 de Mayo 890; mains AR$79-138; ⏲noon-4pm & 8pm-midnight Mon-Sat) Just above the flag monument, this basement place decorated with faded Spanish tourism posters is a top spot for inexpensive and really delicious seafood, like *rabas* (calamari) or succulent river fish on the grill. Wash it all down with a bottle of imported cider from Asturias. No bookings, so be prepared to wait, as it's deservedly popular. Don't confuse with the restaurant above it.

Monreal SANDWICHES $

(☎0341-421-9356; www.sandwichesmonreal.com.ar; cnr San Lorenzo & Entre Ríos; sandwiches AR$90-150; ⏲9am-10pm Mon-Fri, 8am-1pm & 6-10pm Sat, 6-10pm Sun; 🖉) A Rosario institution, this no-nonsense corner place serves up a wide variety of delicious hot and cold sandwiches which are widely regarded as the best in town. It's more a take-out place than somewhere to hang out. Grab some for a picnic on the *costanera*. Also offers delivery.

De Buen Humor ICE CREAM $

(www.debuenhumorhelados.com.ar; Rioja 1560; cones AR$28-58; ⏲10am-11pm; 📶🖉👪) Ice cream here comes from happy cows, they say. We can't vouch for that, but anyone with a sweet tooth will be mooing contentedly at the optimism-filled decor, patio seating, and tasty cones, concoctions and fruit salads. *Rosarinos* eat 7kg of ice cream each per year, so you've got some catching-up to do.

Nuria BAKERY $

(www.nuria.com.ar; Santa Fe 1026; pastries from AR$15; ⏲7am-9pm Mon-Sat, 7am-7pm Sun) This much-loved Rosario institution – now with several more modern outlets around town – is still a seductively old-fashioned place to pick up delicious pastries and cakes.

Comedor Balcarce ARGENTINE $

(cnr Balcarce & Brown; mains AR$80-220; ⏲noon-3pm & 8:15pm-midnight Mon-Sat) In business for decades, this typical corner *bodegón* (traditional diner) is one of a fast-disappearing breed. Home-style Argentine cooking comes in big portions. Quality is average to good, prices are great and it's an authentic, friendly experience. Don't let its affectionate nickname, El Vómito (The Vomit), put you off.

Rincón Vegetariano VEGETARIAN $

(www.turinconvegetariano.blogspot.com; Mitre 720; mains AR$58-85, buffet AR$80; ⏲9am-4pm Mon-Sat; 🖉) This mostly vegetarian place offers a huge range of meat-free hot and cold dishes to eat in or take out. There are always all sorts of deals going, with an all-you-can-eat buffet at lunchtime. It's unsophisticated but a decent cheap feed.

GOING TO A GAME

Rosario has two rival *fútbol* teams with several league titles between them. Newell's Old Boys plays in red and black at **Estadio Marcelo Bielsa** (☎0341-425-4422; Parque Independencia) and has a long, proud history of producing great Argentine players. Rosario Central plays in blue-and-yellow stripes at **Estadio 'El Gigante de Arroyito'** (☎0341-421-0000; cnr Blvd Avellaneda & Génova). Buy tickets from the stadiums from two hours before the match.

★Escauriza SEAFOOD **$$**
(☎0341-454-1777; cnr Bajada Escauriza & Paseo Ribereño; mains AR$280; ⏲noon-3:30pm & 8pm-midnight) Backing Florida beach, this legendary place is one of Rosario's best spots for fish. The enormous indoor-outdoor dining area is redolent with the aromas of chargrilling river catch like surubí; start with some delicious seafood empanadas (pastries). Service, quality and quantity are all highly impressive. Book, get there at noon, or wait and wait at summer weekend lunchtimes. No credit cards. Awful coffee.

★Zazpirak Bat BASQUE **$$**
(☎0341-421-7670; www.zazpirakbat.com; Entre Ríos 261; mains AR$160-380; ⏲8pm-12:30am Tue-Sat, 12:30-4pm Sun) From outside, this Basque cultural center gives few clues that there's a restaurant inside, and the menu seems a little humdrum at first glance. But what a place this is. Fish and seafood are prepared to give maximum expression to the natural flavors; it's all delicious, quantities are enormous and the salads are particularly praiseworthy.

Restaurant Bruno ITALIAN **$$**
(☎0341-421-2396; Montevideo 2798; pasta AR$125-185; ⏲8pm-midnight Tue-Sat, noon-3:30pm & 8-11pm Sun) An elegant villa a block from Pellegrini is decorated with dark wood and tasteful gondolier prints. Well-heeled locals flock here for homemade pasta, which has a huge reputation. Go for gnocchi, lasagna or cannelloni over fettuccini, but the combination of stylish interior with trattoria-style comfort works. Portions are large.

Don Ferro PARRILLA **$$**
(☎0341-15-320-1122; riverbank near España; mains AR$155-380; ⏲7:30am-1am; 📶) The most handsome restaurant in town, Don Ferro is exquisitely set in an old brick railroad shed, with a delightful terrace on the platform, excellent service and seriously delicious meat. The menu is wide-ranging, though, and has mixed-grilled vegetables and more meaty options than most. Wines are very overpriced.

El Viejo Balcón PARRILLA **$$**
(☎0341-425-5611; cnr Italia & Wheelwright; mains AR$129-329; ⏲noon-3pm & 8pm-midnight) Be prepared to wait for a table at this long-time Rosario favorite in a *parrilla*-rich zone by the river. The meat is generously proportioned and of excellent quality: staff even listen to how you want it cooked. But there's enough on the menu here – crepes, pastas – to cater for all tastes.

La Estancia PARRILLA **$$**
(☎0341-449-8052; Av Carlos Pellegrini 1501; mains AR$155-295; ⏲noon-3:30pm & 8pm-1am, to 2am Fri & Sat; 📶) A sound choice on the Pellegrini strip, this typical upmarket grillhouse has really excellent cuts of meat – the *vacío* (flank steak) is special – allied with enough waiters that you'll never have to, er, wait. The only downsides are closely spaced tables and a limited wine list.

El Ancla ARGENTINE **$$**
(☎0341-411-4142; Maipú 1101; mains AR$120-295; ⏲7am-1am Mon-Fri, 8am-4pm & 7pm-1am Sat, 10am-4pm & 7pm-1am Sun) One of Rosario's many beloved corner restaurants, this much-frequented local has an appealingly venerable interior and an authentic feel. The food – with lots of inexpensive single-plate meals – is reliably good and you always seem to receive a friendly welcome.

Ceviche SUSHI **$$$**
(☎0341-689-2899; www.cevicherosario.com.ar; Jujuy 2378; mains AR$250-390; ⏲8:30pm-1am, to 3am Fri & Sat) This ultra-fashionable restaurant all decked out in black in the heart of the nightlife district is popular for its lively atmosphere, quality plates and mixed drinks. In addition to four types of ceviche there is an extensive selection of sushi and sashimi. Turns into a sociable bar later on.

Los Potrillos PARRILLA **$$$**
(☎0341-482-4027; www.lospotrillos.com.ar; cnr Av Carlos Pellegrini & Moreno; mains AR$232-348; ⏲noon-3:30pm & 8pm-1am; 📶) Decorated with warm colors and a sweeping horse mural, this *parrilla* offers plenty more than just grilled meat, with a fine selection of river

fish and other seafood dishes, tasty homemade pasta and a decent wine list. It's high on quality and quantity and the menu is reasonably translated. Good service.

Davis ARGENTINE **$$$**
(☎0341-435-7142; www.complejodavis.com; Av de la Costa 2550; mains AR$160-375; ⊙noon-3pm & 8:30pm-midnight; 📶) Occupying Rosario's most charming position, right on the river below the contemporary-art museum with 180-degree views, Davis offers minimalist-chic design with a smart restaurant inside a glass cube and outdoor riverside seating. The menu features well-executed beef, pasta, chicken and river-fish dishes. Try the fish platter for two (AR$470).

If possible, grab a spot on the deck to make the most of the location. Outside mealtimes, it's open for drinks.

Drinking & Nightlife

Rosario has a great number of *restobares,* which function as hybrid cafes and bars and generally serve a fairly standard selection of snacks and plates. Many are good for a morning coffee, an evening glass of wine – or anything in between.

★ **Fenicia** BREWERY
(www.feniciabrewing.com.ar; Francia 168; ⊙noon-late Tue-Fri, 6pm-late Sat & Sun; 📶) You can smell the malt at this brewpub, where the delicious ales are produced right beneath your feet. It's a fine place to start exploring this bar-rich nightlife zone, and it also does a handy line in quesadillas, burgers and salads. The roof terrace is good on a warm evening. It's northwest of the city center, near the train station.

Espiria CAFE
(www.facebook.com/culturaespiria; Montevideo 2124; ⊙8am-1am Mon-Thu, 9am-2am Fri & Sat, 10am-1am Sun; 📶) Perfect for combining with a visit to the nearby art gallery, this enchanting cafe-bookshop-gallery occupies a beautiful house with stained glass and an enticing patio. Tasty sandwiches, snacks and breakfasts (light meals AR$160 to AR$190), coffees and delicious juices make this one of Rosario's most relaxing spots, and it's a cocktail venue later, too.

Pichangú BAR
(cnr Salta & Rodríguez; ⊙6pm-1am Mon-Wed, 6pm-2am Thu, 7pm-3am Fri & Sat) Brightly lit and cheerful, this inviting corner space is a cooperative that puts on regular music and other cultural events. It's a social, slightly chaotic scene and a good place to meet locals. It does a reasonable line in pizzas and the like, with several vegan options.

El Cairo BAR
(www.barelcairo.com; cnr Sarmiento & Santa Fe; ⊙8am-1am Mon-Thu, 8am-2am Fri & Sat, 10am-1am Sun; 📶) High-ceilinged and elegant, with huge panes of glass for people-watching (and vice versa), this classic Rosario cafe is good at any time of day, but especially in the evening, when it mixes a decent cocktail and puts on good Argentine pub grub. This is also one of the rare places that serve *mate.*

El Diablito PUB
(Maipú 622; ⊙9pm-3:30am Tue-Sat) With a red-lit interior true to its origins as a brothel, this place has an atmosphere all of its own. The soundtrack is 1970s and 1980s rock, and the decor is sumptuous with stained-glass panels and age-spotted mirrors. A classic place to drink.

Costello CLUB
(Rivadavia 2455; ⊙6-4:30am Thu, 10pm-5:30am Fri & Sat, 9-2:30am Sun) An expansive club out near the river that gets packed with hard partying *rosareños.* Regularly hosts fun theme nights that are all lasers, fluoro markers and confetti. Unpretentious and welcoming.

Jekyll & Hyde BAR
(www.jekyllhyde.com.ar; Mitre 343; ⊙7am-1am Mon-Fri, 10am-2am Fri & Sat; 📶) With even more identities than its namesake, this bar occupies a noble building left artfully semi-restored. Checkerboard tiles, exposed brick and antiques make for an appealing ambience for breakfast, lunch, after-workers or an evening drink accompanied by cultural offerings ranging from comedy to live rock.

LOCAL KNOWLEDGE

PICHINCHA

Between Oroño and Francia, and north of Urquiza, the barrio of Pichincha is the city's most interesting for nightlife. The leafy streets and wide pavements make it seem a sleepy suburb by day, but at night every corner seems to have a quirky bar or hipster restaurant. The city's best *boliches* (nightclubs) are also found here.

Bound CLUB
(Blvd Oroño 198; 9pm-late Fri & Sat) One of Rosario's fanciest *boliches* (nightclubs) this stylish spot is in the heart of the liveliest nightlife zone. Strict door policy,.

Entertainment

There are regular tango events; grab the monthly listings booklet from the tourist office and check www.rosarioturismo.com.

La Casa del Tango TANGO
(www.facebook.com/casadeltangorosario; Av Illia 1750; 9am-noon Mon-Fri) This tango center has info on performances and classes around town, often offers fun, very cheap evening lessons, and stages various events. Regular 9pm Saturday concerts (AR$100) are a great deal. There's also a good cafe and restaurant. It's on the riverbank road near the junction with España.

Distrito Siete LIVE MUSIC
(www.facebook.com/distritosie7e; Av Lagos 790; 9am-1am Mon-Thu, 9am-4:30am Fri & Sat, 6pm-1am Sun;) This warehouse-like space is run by the Giros local social movement and has plenty of live acts as well as classes, activities, a cheap daily meal and a bar.

Teatro El Círculo THEATER
(0341-424-5349; www.teatroelcirculo.com.ar; Laprida 1235; performances AR$150-500; box office 10am-12:30pm & 4-7:30pm Mon-Fri, 10am-12:30pm & 5pm-performances Sat) This noble old theater is known for excellent acoustics. Performances are regular and range from folk and classical concerts to opera. Guided visits run from December to March at 10:30am and 5:30pm Monday, Wednesday and Friday and at 10:30am Saturday, costing AR$125.

Shopping

Mercado de Pulgas del Bajo MARKET
(Av Belgrano; 2-8pm Sat, noon-8pm Sun) A small handicrafts market by the tourist office where dealers sell everything from silverwork to leather goods. There are several other weekend markets along the riverbank, including an excellent **Sunday retro market** near where Oroño meets the 'coast' part of the bigger Pichincha market.

Information

Bus Terminal Tourist Information (www.rosario.tur.ar; Terminal de Ómnibus; 9am-7pm)

Hospital Clemente Álvarez (0341-480-8111; Av Carlos Pellegrini 3205) Southwest of the city center.

Post Office (www.correoargentino.com.ar; Córdoba 721; 8am-8pm Mon-Fri)

Tourist Kiosk (Córdoba, near Av Corrientes; 8am-7pm Mon-Fri, 9am-7pm Sat, 10am-6pm Sun) On the main pedestrian street.

Tourist Office (0341-480-2230; www.rosario.tur.ar; Av del Huerto; 8am-7pm Mon-Fri, 9am-7pm Sat, 9am-6pm Sun) The office is on the riverbank in the city center. It's very helpful, and the website is excellent.

Getting There & Away

AIR

Aerolíneas Argentinas (0810-2228-6527; www.aerolineas.com.ar; España 840; 10am-6pm Mon-Fri, 9am-noon Sat) Flies several times daily to Buenos Aires. Also offers direct flights to Córdoba, El Calafate, Mendoza, Puerto Iguazú and Salta.

Avianca (www.avianca.com) Offers flights to Buenos Aires.

Copa (www.copa.com) Flies direct to Panama.

Gol (www.voegol.com.br) Serves Rio de Janeiro.

Latam (www.latam.com) Flies to Lima in Peru, São Paulo in Brazil and Santiago in Chile.

Sky (www.skyairline.com) Flies to Santiago de Chile.

BUS

The modernized **long-distance bus terminal** (0341-437-3030; www.terminalrosario.gob.ar; cnr Cafferata & Santa Fe) is 25 blocks west of downtown. To get there, any bus along Santa Fe will do the trick. To get into town from there, take a bus marked 'Centro' or 'Plaza Sarmiento.' It's about AR$80 to AR$110 in a taxi. There are direct daily services to nearly all major destinations, including international services.

Buses from Rosario

DESTINATION	COST (AR$)	TIME (HR)
Buenos Aires	440	4
Córdoba	550	5½-7
Corrientes	1150	9-11
Mendoza	760	12-15
Paraná	235	3-3½
Posadas	1215	14-15
Salta	2150	14-17
Santa Fe	207	2½-3½
Tucumán	1436	11-13

CAR & MOTORCYCLE

Budget (0341-421-3594; www.budget.com.ar; Mitre 320; 9am-1pm & 3-7pm Mon-Fri, 9am-1pm Sat)

Hertz/Thrify (0341-426-3400; www.hertz.com.ar; Mitre 747; 8am-8pm)

TRAIN

Slow air-conditioned trains leave from **Rosario Norte train station** (www.trenesargentinos.gob.ar; Av del Valle 2750; ticket office 8-2:30am Mon & Fri, 8am-1:30pm Tue-Thu, 5:30pm-1:30am Sat, noon-1:30am Sun) for Buenos Aires (2nd class AR$255/210, seven hours) daily at 1:23am passing Rosario Sur train station (www.trenesargentinos.gob.ar; cnr San Martín & Battle y Ordóñez; ticket office 6pm-2am), 7.5km south of the city center, on the way. From Buenos Aires, trains depart 4:40pm from El Retiro.

Other less frequent services on the route between Buenos Aires and Córdoba, and Buenos Aires and Tucumán, call at Rosario Norte only. They book out well in advance.

Bus 140 runs south down Sarmiento to the Rosario Sur station. Take bus 134 north up Mitre to a block from the Rosario Norte train station.

Getting Around

Rosario's public transportation system is efficient and comprehensive; once you learn the ropes there should be no need to take taxis.

TO/FROM THE AIRPORT

For the **airport** (Fisherton; 0341-451-3220; www.aeropuertorosario.com; Av Jorge Newbery s/n, Fisherton), 8km west, bus 115 runs west along Santa Fe. A taxi will charge around AR$300.

BICYCLE

Visitors are able to use the Mi Bici Tu Bici public bicycle scheme, which has posts all over town. A daily subscription costs AR$12.50 but each trip is limited to 30 minutes before you have to dock and check out again. You'll need a smartphone and a credit card. Download the Mi Bici Tu Bici app on your phone and generate a code which you enter into the panel at the station. Note that you'll need a local data plan or to find a station near a wi-fi hot spot as the codes expire rapidly.

To rent a bike, Rosario Kayak & Motor Boat Tours (p149) at the Estación Fluvial, has well-equipped town bikes for AR$150 per day. You'll need your passport and an AR$300 deposit.

BUS

Local buses run from the terminal on Plaza Sarmiento (see www.rosario.gov.ar for a journey planner). You can pay the AR$10.50 fare in coins, but unless you've broken a piggy bank, it's much easier to buy a rechargeable Tarjeta Movi card for AR$30 from the little booths at many major central bus stops. Trips then cost AR$9.70.

Santa Fe

0342 / POP 569,118

There's quite a contrast between Santa Fe's relaxed center, where colonial buildings age gracefully in the humid heat and nobody seems to get beyond an amble, and a Friday evening in the Recoleta district, where university students in dozens of bars show the night no mercy. Capital of its province, but with a small-town feel, Santa Fe is an excellent place to visit for a day or two.

Santa Fe's remaining colonial buildings are within a short walk of Plaza 25 de Mayo. Av San Martín, north of the plaza, is the major commercial street and part of it forms an attractive *peatonal* (pedestrian street) with palms and terraces.

To the east, a bridge crosses the river, then a tunnel beneath the Paraná connects Santa Fe with its twin city of Paraná in Entre Ríos.

History

Santa Fe (de la Veracruz) moved here in 1651 from its original location at Cayastá, 75km to the north. In 1853, Argentina's first constitution was ratified by an assembly meeting here; these days ambitious riverfront rehabilitation has added extra appeal to this historic city.

Sights

★Convento y Museo de San Francisco MONASTERY

(Amenábar 2257; AR$20; 8am-12:30pm & 3:30-7pm Tue-Fri, 8am-noon & 4-7pm Sat) Santa Fe's principal historical landmark is this Franciscan monastery and museum, built in 1680. While the museum is mediocre, the church is beautiful, with an exquisite wooden ceiling. The lovely cloister has a real colonial feel and is full of birdsong and the perfume of flowers. The monastery is still home to a handful of monks.

On your left as you enter the church is a fine polychrome Christ by grumpy Spanish master Alonso Cano, sent as a sympathy gift by the Queen of Spain when the town moved in 1649. By the altar, a stone marks the tomb of a priest killed by a jaguar taking refuge in the church during 1825 flooding.

★Museo Histórico Provincial MUSEUM

(www.museobrigadierlopez.gob.ar; Av San Martín 1490; 8:30am-12:30pm & 2:30-8:30pm Tue-

Santa Fe

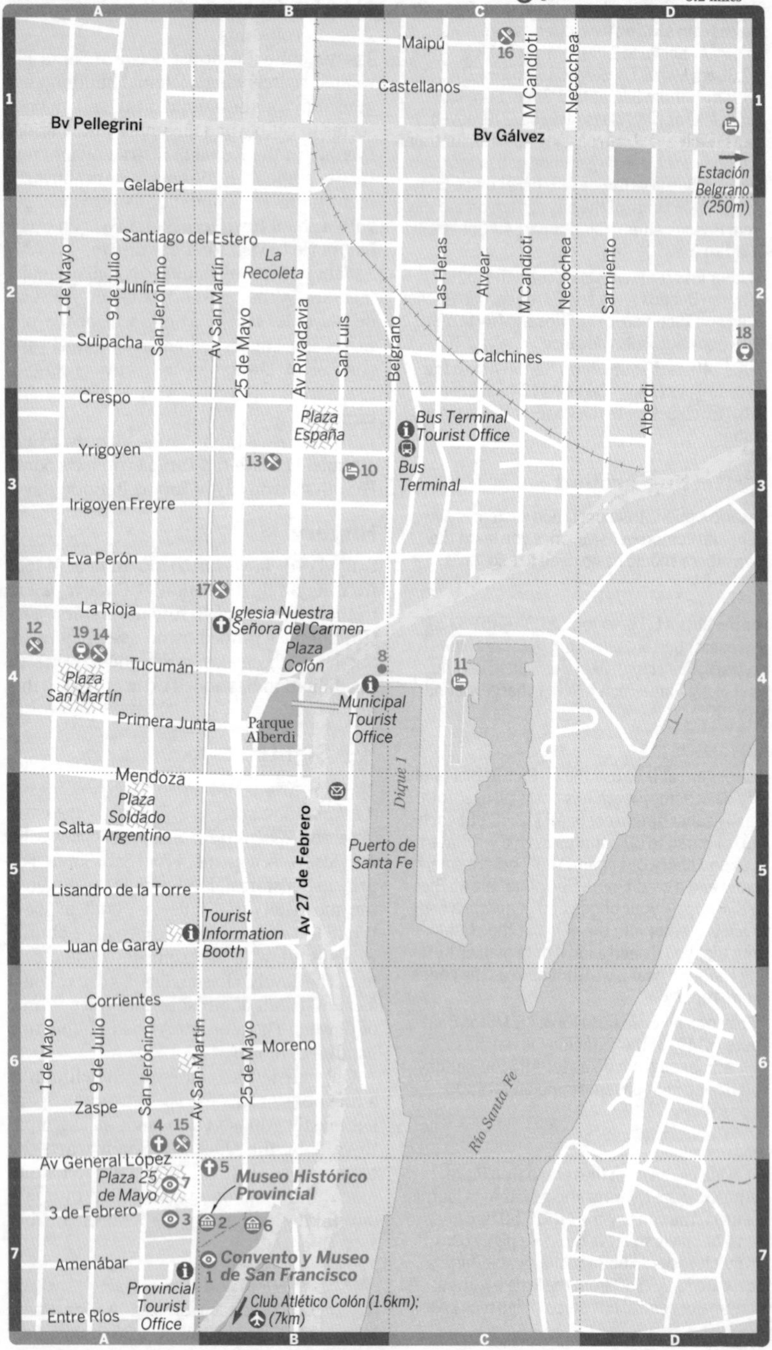
0 400 m
0 0.2 miles
Maipú
Castellanos
M Candioti
Necochea
Bv Pellegrini
Bv Gálvez
Estación Belgrano (250m)
Gelabert
Santiago del Estero
La Recoleta
1 de Mayo
9 de Julio
Junín
San Jerónimo
Av San Martín
25 de Mayo
Av Rivadavia
San Luis
Belgrano
Las Heras
Alvear
M Candioti
Necochea
Sarmiento
Suipacha
Calchines
Crespo
Alberdi
Plaza España
Bus Terminal Tourist Office
Yrigoyen
Bus Terminal
Irigoyen Freyre
Eva Perón
La Rioja
Iglesia Nuestra Señora del Carmen
Plaza Colón
Tucumán
Plaza San Martín
Municipal Tourist Office
Primera Junta
Parque Alberdi
Mendoza
Plaza Soldado Argentino
Dique 1
Salta
Puerto de Santa Fe
Av 27 de Febrero
Lisandro de la Torre
Tourist Information Booth
Juan de Garay
Corrientes
Moreno
1 de Mayo
9 de Julio
San Jerónimo
Av San Martín
25 de Mayo
Zaspe
Río Santa Fe
Av General López
Plaza 25 de Mayo
Museo Histórico Provincial
3 de Febrero
Amenábar
Convento y Museo de San Francisco
Provincial Tourist Office
Entre Ríos
Club Atlético Colón (1.6km); (7km)

Santa Fe

Fri, 5:30-8:30pm Sat & Sun) FREE In a lovable 17th-century building, this museum has a variety of possessions and mementos of various provincial governors and *caudillos* (provincial strongmen), as well as religious art and fine period furnishings, including a sedan chair once used to carry around the Viceroy of Río de la Plata. Opening hours are for summer: it doesn't close mid-afternoon the rest of the year.

Museo Etnográfico y Colonial Provincial MUSEUM
(www.museojuandegaray.gob.ar; 25 de Mayo 1470; donation AR$5; 8:30am-12:30pm & 3-7pm Tue-Fri, 8:30am-12:30pm & 4-7pm Sat & Sun) Run with heartwarming enthusiasm by local teachers, this museum has a chronological display of stone tools, Guaraní ceramics, jewelry, carved bricks and colonial objects. Highlights include a set of *tablas* (a colonial game similar to backgammon) and a scale model of both original Santa Fe settlements. Afternoon opening hours vary.

Plaza 25 de Mayo SQUARE
The center of colonial Santa Fe is a peaceful square framed by fine buildings. The vast **Casa de Gobierno** was built in 1909 and replaced the demolished *cabildo* (town council building), seat of the 1852 constitutional assembly. On the square's east side, the exterior simplicity of the Jesuit **Iglesia de la Compañía** masks an ornate interior. The **cathedral** is a little underwhelming by comparison, and dates from the mid-18th century.

Estación Belgrano NOTABLE BUILDING
(Bulevar Gálvez) This magnificent old train station close to the river serves to show just how much of a busy regional powerhouse Santa Fe used to be. It's now been turned into a convention center but visitors are free to duck inside and check it out.

Tours

Costa Litoral BOATING
(0342-456-4381; www.costalitoral.info; Dique 1) From the redeveloped harbor area, a large catamaran runs trips around the river islands. Both two-hour trips (adult/child AR$250/130, 5pm Saturday) and one-hour loops (adult/child AR$180/130, 5pm Sunday) are available. Also runs excursions to Paraná (adult/child AR$350/150, 5½ hours, 2pm Sunday) with a couple of hours to explore the city. Book tickets in the cafe opposite the dock.

Sleeping

The area around the bus terminal is the budget-hotel zone. Nearly all hotels offer a discount for cash payment.

Hotel Constituyentes HOTEL $
(0342-452-1586; www.hotelconstituyentes.com.ar; San Luis 2862; s/d/tr US$38/47/59, without bathroom US$20/29/35; P @) Spacious rooms, low prices and proximity to the bus terminal are the main drawcards of this relaxed place. It's not luxury, but the owners are always looking to improve things and it makes a pleasant budget base. Rooms at the front suffer from street noise. Breakfast is extra.

★ **Ámbit Boulevard** BOUTIQUE HOTEL $$
(0342-455-7179; www.ambithotel.com.ar; Blvd Gálvez 1408; superior/premium r US$100/112; P) An early-20th-century mansion has been converted into this compact,

WORTH A TRIP

CAYASTÁ RUINS

An interesting day trip from Santa Fe takes you to Cayastá, a pleasant little place on the banks of the Río San Javier that is the site of the city's original location. The ruins of the settlement on the outskirts of town have been converted into a **museum** (Santa Fe la Vieja; ☎03405-493056; www.santafelavieja.gob.ar; RP 1, Km 78; AR$25; ⏱9am-1:30pm & 3-7:30pm Tue-Fri, 10am-1pm & 4-7pm Sat & Sun Oct-Mar, 9am-1:30pm & 2-6:30pm Tue-Fri, noon-6pm Sat & Sun Apr-Sep).

The river has eroded away a good portion of the ruins and there's ongoing archaeological excavation, but the most fascinating find by far has been the **Iglesia de San Francisco**. The Spanish and mestizo inhabitants of old Santa Fe were buried directly beneath the earth-floored church, and nearly 100 graves have been excavated. The skeletons have now been replaced by replicas, but it's still a spooky, atmospheric place.

Graves include those of Hernando Arias de Saavedra ('Hernandarias'), the first locally born governor of Río de la Plata province, and his wife, Jerónima, daughter of Juan de Garay, who founded Santa Fe and Buenos Aires.

You can also see the remains of two other churches (there were originally six) and the *cabildo* (town council), as well as a handsome reconstructed period house. Near the site entrance is an attractive museum housing finds, including fine indigenous pottery with parrot and human motifs. Last entry is strictly one hour before closing.

Cayastá is 76km northeast of Santa Fe on RP 1 and served regularly from Santa Fe's bus terminal (AR$96, 1½ hours) by Paraná Medio. Ask the driver to drop you at *las ruinas*, 1km short of Cayastá itself.

If you want to visit the ruins in the morning, you'll have to get the 6am, 7am or 9am bus from Santa Fe.

rather lovely hotel. Exquisitely decorated rooms were each designed as a charity project by different architects; all are charming. Premium category rooms have high ceilings and venerable floorboards. A little spa-style plunge pool sits between floors.

Los Silos HOTEL **$$**
(☎0342-450-2800; www.hotellossilos.com.ar; Dique 1; s/d from US$94/109; P ❄ @ ☎ ≋) Santa Fe's decaying waterfront has been smartened, and this creatively designed hotel is a centerpiece. Brilliantly converted from grain silos, it features original, rounded rooms with marvelous views and plenty of modern comfort, though some seem in need of a touch-up. Vistas from the rooftop pool, spa and sundeck are super, and service is excellent throughout.

Eating

The best zones for cheap eats are across from the bus terminal, and the nightlife zone of La Recoleta.

Merengo BAKERY **$**
(Av General López 2632; alfajores from AR$24; ⏱8am-10pm) In 1851, Merengo stuck two biscuits together with *dulce de leche* (milk caramel) and invented the *alfajor,* now Argentina's favorite snack. It's still going strong: this cute little shop on the plaza is one of several branches.

Makánun Diáafah MIDDLE EASTERN **$**
(cnr Tucumán & 9 de Julio; dishes AR$15-100; ⏱11:30am-2:45pm & 7:30-11:45pm Tue-Sat) Excellent-value, super-tasty Lebanese food. It's a cheerful, brightly lit corner spot with generous portions and great prices. Very popular but takes no reservations so get in early.

★ **La Boutique del Cocinero** INTERNATIONAL **$$**
(☎0342-456-3864; www.laboutiquedelcocinero.com; Yrigoyen 2443; set meals AR$170-210, mains AR$250; ⏱9pm-1am Mon-Sat) This innovative, welcoming chef-driven restaurant has an open kitchen right beside the dining area and a sociable vibe. On Monday it offers a set house meal while on Tuesday and Wednesday it serves a set Italian meal, including an appetizer, main plate and dessert. On other nights there is a small menu of high-quality dishes from various international cuisines. Great atmosphere.

Nesta ARGENTINE **$$**
(☎0342-15-595-1983; www.facebook.com/nesta.restobar; Maipú 1964; mains AR$170-240; ⏱9pm-12:30am Wed-Sun; ☎) The hippie decor and inviting rear patio of this handsome house

in a quiet leafy barrio make a welcome evening retreat. A small but interesting menu of tacos, salads, pizzas, vegetarian options and a couple of well-prepared gourmet takes on traditional meat dishes are all prepared with fresh, healthy ingredients. Meals are accompanied by reggae or chillout beats. Good drinks. Worth booking at weekends.

El Quincho de Chiquito ARGENTINE **$$**
(☎0342-460-2608; cnr Brown & Obispo Principe; set menu AR$270; ⏲11:30am-3pm & 8pm-midnight) This legendary local institution is *the* place for river fish, on the *costanera* 6km north of downtown. There are few frills and no choice: four or five courses of delicious surubí, sábalo or pacú are brought out; you can repeat as often as you want. Drinks are extra but cheap.

It's around AR$120 each way in a taxi (staff will phone one to take you back) or catch bus 16 from any point on the waterfront road.

Restaurante España ARGENTINE **$$**
(☎0342-455-2471; www.lineaverdehoteles.com.ar; Av San Martín 2644; mains AR$175-260; ⏲11:30am-3pm & 8pm-midnight; 📶) This hotel restaurant on the pedestrian street is a lovely space, with high ceilings, attentive waistcoat-and-tie staff and an old-fashioned feel. There's a huge menu that covers the range of fish (both locally caught and from the sea), steaks, pasta, chicken and crepes, with a few Spanish dishes thrown in to justify the name. The wine list is a winner, too.

El Aljibe ITALIAN **$$**
(☎0342-456-2162; Tucumán 2950; mains AR$175-240; ⏲noon-2:30pm & 9pm-12:30am Tue-Sat, noon-2:30pm Sun & Mon; 📶) Warmly lit and cordial, this appealing neighborhood Italian eatery uses great ingredients to create flavor-filled salads, pasta and meat dishes.

Drinking & Nightlife

Santa Fe's nightlife centers on the intersection of 25 de Mayo and Santiago del Estero, the heart of the area known as La Recoleta, which goes wild on weekend nights – a crazy contrast to the sedate pace of life downtown. Places change name and popularity rapidly, so just take a look around the dozens of bars and clubs.

Uh Lala BAR
(☎0342-455-7633; Tucumán 2832; ⏲8am-12:30pm & 4:30-11pm Mon-Wed, 8am-12:30pm & 4:30pm-late Thu-Sat) A chilled bohemian cafe-bar with friendly staff, Uh Lala is a good place to mix it with locals over a coffee or an evening drink. From Thursday to Saturday there's stand-up comedy and live music performances.

Patio de la Cerveza BREWERY
(cnr Calchines & Lavalle; ⏲6pm-1am) Part of the Santa Fe brewery opposite, this picturesque beer garden has its lager piped across the road via a 'beerduct' bridge. It's a great outdoor setting for *liso,* as draft beer, traditionally served in 8oz cylindrical glasses, is known hereabouts, and there's a menu of deli plates, sandwiches, salads, etc to accompany it.

Entertainment

The city's best *fútbol* team, Colón (www.clubcolon.com.ar), is an overachiever considering the size of the city. It's a regular in the Argentine top division and often graces South American cups. It plays at the Brigadier Estanislao López Stadium, where you can pick up tickets.

Information

Bus Terminal Tourist Office (☎0342-457-4124; www.santafeturismo.gov.ar; Belgrano 2910; ⏲8am-8pm)

Hospital Provincial José María Cullen (☎0342-457-3340; Av Freyre 2150)

Municipal Tourist Office (☎0342-457-4123; www.santafeturismo.gov.ar; Dique 1, Puerto de Santa Fe; ⏲7am-8pm Mon-Fri, 10am-4pm Sat & Sun) Under the old steel crane at the entrance to the port.

Post Office (Mendoza 2430; ⏲8am-8pm Mon-Fri)

Getting There & Away

Aerolíneas Argentinas (www.aerolineas.com.ar; 25 de Mayo 2287; ⏲9:30am-5:30pm Mon-Fri, 9am-noon Sat) flies to Buenos Aires. The

Buses from Santa Fe

DESTINATION	COST (AR$)	TIME (HR)
Buenos Aires	680	6-7½
Córdoba	625	5
Corrientes	908	6½-8
Paraná	26	¾
Posadas	1036	12
Resistencia	908	6½-8
Rosario	207	2
Tucumán	1085	11½

1

ANIBAL TREJO/SHUTTERSTOCK ©

2

4

AWAKENING/BARCROFT MEDIA/BARCROFT MEDIA VIA GETTY IMAGES ©

. Monumento Nacional a La Bandera (p148), Rosario
Built where the Argentine blue-and-white flag was irst raised, this obelisk also marks the resting ılace of the flag's designer, Manuel Belgrano.

. Carnaval, Gualeguaychú (p182)
'his otherwise mellow riverside town kicks off in ummer with the country's longest and flashiest Carnaval celebration.

. Parque Esteros del Iberá (p172)
stunning 18,000-hectare wetland reserve, this s among South America's finest places to see vildlife, including marsh deer.

. San Ignacio Miní (p189)
hese atmospheric mission ruins are the most omplete of those in Argentina.

MATYAS REHAK/SHUTTERSTOCK ©

airport is 7km south of town on RN 11. A *remise* (taxi) costs about AR$200.

From the **bus terminal** (☑ 0342-457-4124; www.terminalsantafe.com; Belgrano 2910) there are services throughout the country. Buses to nearby Paraná are frequent but often oversubscribed: prepare for long queues. It's AR$600 in a *remise*.

ℹ Getting Around

Free **bicycle hire** (☉ 9am-7pm) is offered by the local tourism authorities at the old Belgrano train station. You'll need to bring ID and a business card from the hotel that you're staying in.

Paraná

☑ 0343 / POP 367,792

Unpretentious Paraná, capital of Entre Ríos province, is a sleepy, slow-paced city perched on the hilly banks of its eponymous river. There's a lovely riverbank for strolling and a few minor attractions. Paraná was the capital of the Argentine Confederation (which didn't include Buenos Aires) from 1853 to 1861.

A tunnel beneath the main channel of the Paraná connects the city to Santa Fe.

◉ Sights

★ Museo y Mercado
Provincial de Artesanías HANDICRAFTS
(Av Urquiza 1239; ☉ 7am-1pm & 4-8pm Mon-Fri, 9am-noon Sat) 🏆 FREE Promoting handicrafts from throughout the province, this is a likable little place that is part museum, part shop. Ask the curator to explain things to you; you'll be amazed by the intricacy of some of the work, like the hats made from tightly woven palm fibers. Those items available for purchase are identified by a sticker.

Museo Histórico de Entre Ríos MUSEUM
(cnr Buenos Aires & Laprida; donation AR$10; ☉ 8am-12:30pm & 3-8pm Tue-Fri, 9am-noon & 4-7pm Sat, 9am-noon Sun) Flaunting local pride, this modern museum on Plaza Alvear contains information on the short-lived Republic of Entre Ríos and the battle of Monte Camperos, as well as *mate* paraphernalia and numerous solid wooden desks and portraits of Urquiza. Much of it was the collection of a local poet.

Costanera WATERFRONT
From the northern edge of downtown, Parque Urquiza slopes steeply downward to the banks of the Río Paraná. During summer, the waterfront fills with people strolling,

fishing and swimming. There's a public beach, **Playa El Parque**, west of the Paraná Rowing Club's private strand, but a better strip of sand, **Playas de Thompson**, is 1km further east, beyond the port.

☞ Tours

Regular small-boat trips (AR$150–AR$200) leave at weekends (daily in summer) from behind the tourist office on the *costanera,* but make sure you're happy safety-wise before making your choice.

Costa Litoral BOATING
(☑ 0343-423-4385; www.costalitoral.info; Buenos Aires 212) This outfit runs weekend one-hour cruises on the river (AR$180) in a large catamaran in addition to one-way transportation across the river to Santa Fe. Trips leave from near the tourist office on the *costanera*.

🛏 Sleeping

★ Las Mañanitas HOTEL $
(☑ 0343-407-4753; www.lasmanianitas.com.ar; Carbó 62; s/d US$35/50; ❄@🛜🏊) There's a summer-house feel about this delightfully relaxed little budget place, which has nine rooms alongside a courtyard and garden with pool. The rooms are colorful and comfortable; they differ widely from darkish duplexes to simpler, lighter chambers – but it's the grace and friendliness of the whole ensemble that makes this a winner.

Paraná Hostel HOSTEL $
(☑ 0343-422-8233; www.paranahostel.com.ar; Pazos 159; dm/d US$13/31; 🅿❄@🛜) Right in the mix in central Paraná, this tranquil traveler-focused hostel has good security, a tree-shaded back patio and garden with barbecue, as well as smart furnishings, decent facilities and comfy single-sex dorms. Upstairs are attractive, airy private rooms that share a bathroom.

Entre Ríos Apart Hotel APARTMENT $
(☑ 0343-484-0906; www.aparthotel-entrerios. com; Montevideo 55; r/t US$67/81; 🅿❄🛜) Spotless, spacious apartments here have stove, microwave and fridge, as well as a foldout sofa, decent bathroom and attractive bedroom. It's in a clean-lined modernized building and rates include breakfast and parking, making this a great deal.

Maran Suites HOTEL $$
(☑ 0343-423-5444; www.maran.com.ar; cnr Alameda de la Federación & Mitre; s US$106-115, d

US$124-138; P ❄ @ ☎ ≋) Towering over the western end of Parque Urquiza, this sleek modern hotel has a rare combination of style and personal service. Try for a room as high as possible, for city or river views. All are very spacious and decorated with flair; 'presidential' suites (US$380) are big enough to get lost in and boast a Jacuzzi with memorable water vistas.

Howard Johnson Mayorazgo HOTEL **$$**
(☎0343-420-6800; www.hjmayorazgo.com.ar; Etchevehere; r from US$109; P ❄ ☎ ≋) The long, curved facade of this remodeled five-star dominates the waterfront from above. All rooms face the river, are very spacious, and offer great views from large windows. A little extra gets you a balcony, but these are lower down. There's an indoor and outdoor pool, a spa, a gym and a large casino.

Eating & Drinking

★**La Pastelería** CAFE **$**
(☎0343-422-2339; 25 de Junio 100; light meals AR$80-200; ⏱8:30am-12:30pm & 5-9pm) You might have to wait for a table at this popular little corner cafe where locals go for their *merienda* to plug the gap between lunch and the late Argentine dinner. Enjoy tasty light meals and big portions of delicious cakes and pastries as well as good coffee, milkshakes and fresh juices. The blueberry lassi is a winner.

Flamingo Grand Bar CAFE **$**
(cnr Av Urquiza & José de San Martín; light meals AR$63-160, mains AR$150-240; ⏱8am-midnight; ☎) Smart seats and a plaza-side location make this a favorite throughout the day, from morning croissants and juices through to *lomitos* (steak sandwiches) and lunch specials, to decent à la carte dishes and *picadas*. Menu includes some vegetarian and diet options. Service could be better.

Giovani ARGENTINE **$$**
(☎0343-423-0527; Av Urquiza 1045; mains AR$140-315; ⏱noon-3pm & 8pm-midnight Mon-Fri, to 1am Sat, to 11:30pm Sun; ☎) With as-it-should-be service and thoughtful touches such as free coffee, this stylish restaurant in the center of town serves excellent meats from the *parrilla* and delectable pasta. There's a good line in river fish and a rather refined, romantic atmosphere.

Don Charras PARRILLA **$$**
(☎0343-422-5972; cnr José de San Martín & San Lorenzo; mains AR$150-280; ⏱11:30am-3pm & 8:30pm-midnight Tue-Thu, 11:30am-3pm & 8:30pm-1am Fri-Sun; ☎) Thatched and atmospheric, this *parrilla* is a popular Paraná choice. Fridays and Saturdays see special fire-roasted options, otherwise just enjoy the usual chargrilled selection and solicitous service. Deep-pan stews are designed to share between three or more. Starters, drinks and the salad bar are overpriced, but the meat comes out to the table in most generous portions.

Pasaje 501 PUB
(Alameda de la Federación 501; ⏱7pm-2am Tue-Sun) A polished, spacious corner bar with a youthful atmosphere and small beer garden, 501 is a fine place to settle in for an evening of drinking. It also serves good meals including nachos, burritos, salads and wraps that offer respite from the normal Argentine fare.

Shopping

A recommended place to buy quality handicrafts is the Museo y Mercado Provincial de Artesanías.

Centro de Artesanos ARTS & CRAFTS
(☎0343-422-4493; www.facebook.com/centrodeartesanosparana; cnr Av 9 de Julio & Carbó; ⏱9am-1pm & 4-8pm Mon-Sat Apr-Oct, 9am-1pm & 5-9pm Mon-Sat Nov-Mar) Traditional *artesanías* (handicrafts) are on display and for sale here. There's some very high-quality ware, and prices are fair. Next door, the cultural center has temporary art and photographic exhibits and workshops.

Information

The helpful **Tourist Office** (☎0343-423-0183; www.turismoparana.com.ar; Plaza 1 de Mayo s/n; ⏱8am-9pm Mon-Fri, 9am-8pm Sat & Sun) has good brochures. There are other branches by the **Río Paraná** (☎0343-420-1837; Laurencena & San Martín; ⏱8am-8pm), and in the **bus terminal** (☎0343-420-1862; ⏱8am-8pm).

Hospital San Martín (☎0343-423-4545; www.hospitalsanmartin.org.ar; Presidente Perón 450)

Post Office (www.correoargentino.com.ar; cnr 25 de Mayo & Monte Caseros; ⏱8am-8pm)

Getting There & Away

The airport is 6km south of town and is accessible by bus 14, which leaves from in front of the post office. A *remise* (taxi) will cost around AR$200. Aerolineas Argentinas serves Buenos Aires.

Paraná

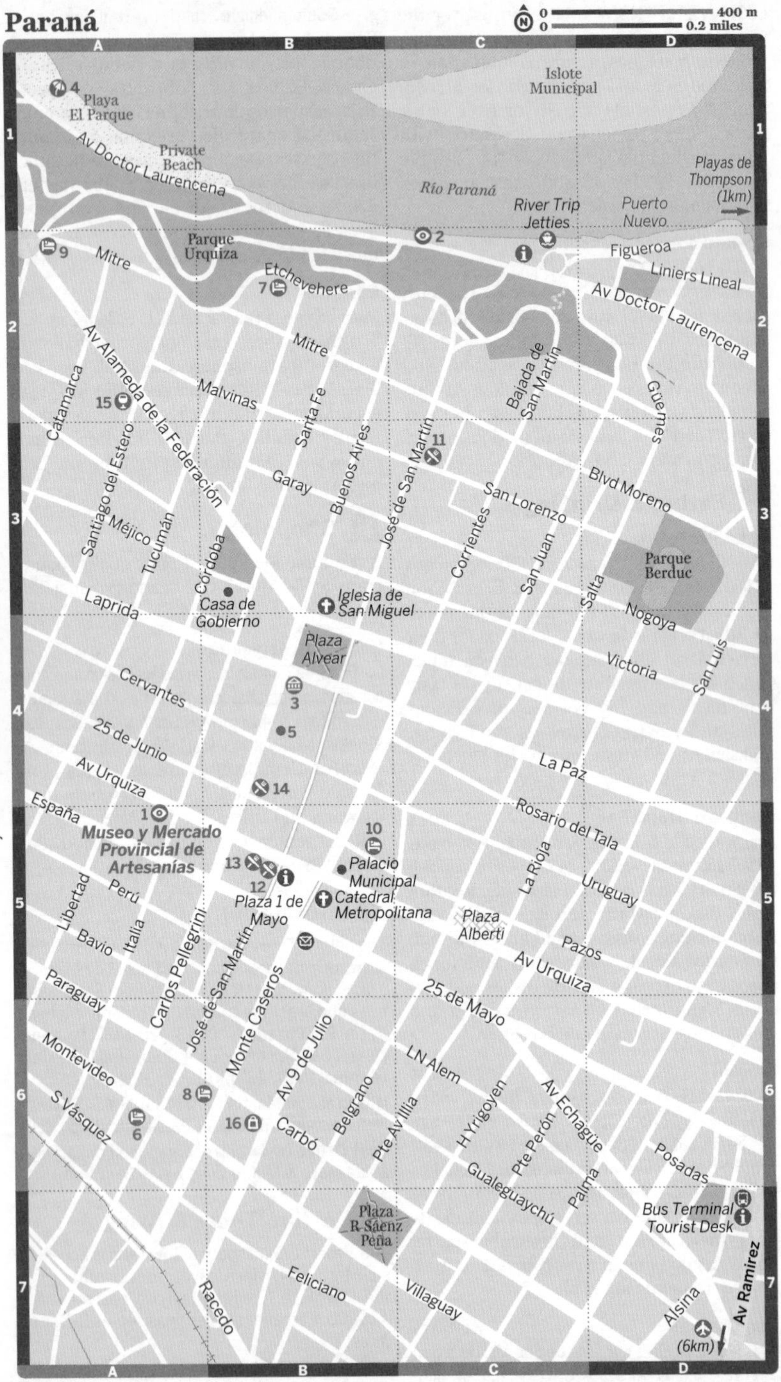

400 m
0.2 miles
Islote Municipal
Playa El Parque
Private Beach
Av Doctor Laurencena
Río Paraná
River Trip Jetties
Puerto Nuevo
Playas de Thompson (1km)
Parque Urquiza
Mitre
Etchevehere
Figueroa
Liniers Lineal
Av Doctor Laurencena
Av Alameda de la Federación
Catamarca
Malvinas
Santa Fe
Buenos Aires
José de San Martín
Bajada de San Martín
Güemes
Garay
Blvd Moreno
San Lorenzo
Santiago del Estero
Méjico
Tucumán
Córdoba
Corrientes
San Juan
Salta
Parque Berduc
Casa de Gobierno
Iglesia de San Miguel
Laprida
Nogoya
Plaza Alvear
Victoria
San Luis
Cervantes
25 de Junio
La Paz
Av Urquiza
España
Museo y Mercado Provincial de Artesanías
Rosario del Tala
Palacio Municipal
Catedral Metropolitana
La Rioja
Uruguay
Plaza 1 de Mayo
Plaza Alberti
Libertad
Perú
Italia
Bavio
Carlos Pellegrini
José de San Martín
Pazos
Av Urquiza
Paraguay
Monte Caseros
25 de Mayo
Montevideo
Av 9 de Julio
LN Alem
S Vásquez
Carbó
Belgrano
Pte Av Illia
H Yrigoyen
Av Echagüe
Pte Perón
Posadas
Gualeguaychú
Palma
Plaza R Sáenz Peña
Bus Terminal Tourist Desk
Av Ramírez
Feliciano
Villaguay
Racedo
Alsina
(6km)

Paraná

The **bus terminal** (☎0343-422-1282) is eight blocks southeast of the central square. Buses 1, 4, 5 and 9 run downtown.

From the bus terminal, buses leave every 30 minutes for Santa Fe (AR$26, 40 minutes). There are two companies running the route; Etacera is more comfortable and has space for bags in the hold.

Buses from Paraná

DESTINATION	COST (AR$)	TIME (HR)
Buenos Aires	700	7-8
Colón	260	4-5
Concordia	205	4-5
Córdoba	685	6
Paso de los Libres	588	6-7
Rosario	235	3-3½

Getting Around

Urban buses in Paraná use the Sube card which also operates in many other cities. Each trip costs AR$8.75.

Corrientes

☎0379 / POP 398,163

Stately Corrientes sits below the confluence of the Paraná and Paraguay rivers, just across the water from its twin city, Resistencia. One of the nation's most venerable cities, it has elegant balconied buildings dating from the turn of the 20th century that lend a timeworn appeal to its colorful streets. The *costanera* is everybody's destination of choice for strolling, eating ice creams, jogging or sipping *mate* with friends.

Corrientes is a center for regional indigenous crafts and Guaraní culture. The city is famous for its Carnaval. Graham Greene's novel *The Honorary Consul* was set here.

Sights

★Costanera WATERFRONT

The *costanera* of Corrientes is one of the most attractive along the entire Río Paraná with shady park areas, gold-sand beaches and a variety of bars and restaurants. It is right on the edge of the old town and comes to life in the early evening when it seems like the entire population is down here exercising, drinking or just relaxing.

Museo de Artesanías Tradicionales Folclóricas MUSEUM

(Quintana 905; ⌚8am-noon & 3-7pm Mon-Fri, 9am-noon & 4-7pm Sat) FREE This intriguing museum in a converted colonial house has small displays of fine traditional *artesanía* (handicrafts) plus a good shop, but the highlight is watching students being taught to work leather, silver, bone and wood by master craftspeople. Other rooms around the courtyard are occupied by working artisans who will sell to you directly. Museum guides are enthusiastic, knowledgeable and friendly.

The best time to visit is in the mornings when there's a greater variety of artisans working. There's also a shop here.

Teatro Juan de Vera THEATER

(☎0379-442-7743; www.teatrovera.com; San Juan 637; ⌚ticket office 9am-12:30pm & 6-9pm Tue-Fri, 10am-1pm & 6-8pm Sat) FREE A striking belle-époque building; ask at the ticket office if you can have a peek inside to see the beautiful treble-galleried theater and its painted ceiling.

Museo Histórico de Corrientes MUSEUM

(9 de Julio 1044; ⌚8am-noon & 4-8pm Tue-Fri) FREE This museum is set around an

Corrientes

attractive patio and exhibits weapons, antique furniture, coins and items dealing with religious and civil history. It's a little bit higgledy-piggledy, but staff are proud of the exhibition and keen to chat. The room on the War of the Triple Alliance is the most interesting.

Museo Casa Martínez NOTABLE BUILDING
(Quintana 971; ⏱8am-noon & 3-7pm Tue-Fri, 9am-noon & 4-7pm Sat) FREE Located in one of the oldest buildings in Corrientes, this small museum has threadbare displays on traditional local architecture and some anthropological objects including Guaraní funeral urns.

Activities

Various operators run boat trips on the Paraná; the tourist office (p171) has a list.

★Experiencia Corrientes KAYAKING
(☎0379-15-450-1702; www.experienciacorrientes.com) A recommended adventure tour operator offering a variety of kayaking trips on the Río Paraná ranging from short sightseeing jaunts and night tours to longer adventures. Also runs excursions in the Esteros del Iberá and Mburucuyá.

Playa Arazaty BEACH
(Costanera Sur; ⏱late Nov-Mar) FREE This wide stretch of sand south of the Resistencia bridge is the city's best river beach. Don't dip until it's officially open – currents are dangerous. A bit of terraforming is done each season to make it safer for bathing, and there are lifeguards.

Turistas Con Ruedas CYCLING
(cnr Costanera & 9 de Julio; ⏱8am-noon & 3-7pm) FREE Head down to the riverside tourist office with your passport, and grab a free bike to explore the Costanera. You are restricted to the riverside areas and rentals are only for an hour, so you'll need to go back and check in again if you want to ride in both directions.

Corrientes

Top Sights
1 Costanera ... B2

Sights
Museo Casa Martinez ... (see 2)
2 Museo de Artesanías Tradicionales Folclóricas ... C1
3 Museo Histórico de Corrientes ... C2
4 Teatro Juan de Vera ... C2

Activities, Courses & Tours
5 Playa Arazaty ... A4
6 Turistas Con Ruedas ... B2

Sleeping
7 Astro Apart Hotel ... C3
8 Bienvenida Golondrina ... C1
9 Don Suites ... C1
10 La Alondra ... C3
11 La Rozada ... C1
12 Ñanderoga ... D2

Eating
13 Cristobal del Puerto ... C1
14 El Mirador del Paraná ... A2
15 Ginger ... A2
16 Martha de Bianchetti ... C2

Drinking & Nightlife
17 Confiteria Panambi ... C2
18 El Flotante ... C1
19 Sherwood ... A3

Entertainment
20 Cantalicio ... B3

Shopping
Museo de Artesanías Tradicionales Folclóricas ... (see 2)
21 Super Disco ... D2

Festivals & Events

★ **Carnaval Correntino** CARNIVAL
Corrientes' traditionally riotous Carnaval competes with Gualeguaychú's as the country's showiest. Celebrated over four consecutive weekends starting nine weeks before Easter, parades along the *costanera* attract participants from neighboring provinces and countries, with huge crowds.

Sleeping

Bienvenida Golondrina HOSTEL $
(☎ 0379-443-5316; www.hostelbienvenidagolondrina.com; La Rioja 455; dm/r US$25/48; P ❄ @ 📶) Occupying a marvelous centenarian building, all high ceilings, stained glass and artistic flourishes, this hostel makes a great base a few steps from the *costanera*. Comfortable wide-berthed dorm beds have headroom and common areas are inviting. Warmly-welcoming management are helpful.

Astro Apart Hotel HOTEL $
(☎ 0379-446-6112; www.astroapart.com; Bolívar 1285; s/d US$59/73; P ❄ @ 📶) Top value is to be had at this modern place, featuring sizable, handsome white rooms with great beds and large windows. They come with simple kitchen and offer plenty of handy facilities as reasonably priced extras. Parking included; breakfast is brought to the room.

Ñanderoga GUESTHOUSE $
(☎ 0379-455-2138; www.nanderogacorrientes.com.ar; Pellegrini 1765; d/tr US$65/75; ❄ 📶) A short walk from the center, this small, quiet hotel has just a handful of spacious comfortable rooms set in a converted house. Beds and bathrooms are very comfortable and the staff are very helpful. There's an attached tour office offering trips with a natural slant throughout the region.

La Rozada BOUTIQUE HOTEL $$
(☎ 0379-443-3001; www.larozada.com; Plácido Martínez 1223; s/d US$73/88; P ❄ 📶) An excellent option near the riverfront, this hotel has commodious apartments and suites unusually set in a tower in the courtyard of an appealing, 19th-century, battleship-gray historic building. Fine views are on offer from most rooms. A balcony room is slightly more expensive. There's an attractive bar area; guests can use the pool at the nearby rowing club.

Don Suites HOTEL $$
(☎ 0379-442-3433; www.donsuites.com.ar; La Rioja 442; s/d US$86/98, superior s/d US$104/116; P ❄ @ 📶 🏊) Paces from the *costanera*, the Don offers pleasingly modern rooms with fridge and microwave. Rooms higher up are better, with river views and a fresher feel – those on the ground floor can feel a bit musty. Pleasant pool area and helpful staff.

★ **La Alondra** BOUTIQUE HOTEL $$$
(☎ 0379-443-5537; www.laalondra.com.ar; Av 3 de Abril 827; r US$150, ste US$200-225; P ❄ @ 📶 🏊) Sumptuously furnished with darkwood antiques, this wonderfully renovated

house is an oasis of relaxation from the unappealing main road. Most rooms surrounding the small finger-shaped pool are suites boasting plush king-sized beds and characterful bathrooms with claw-foot tubs. A second area is craftily created from a former industrial butchery. Strikingly handsome public spaces, excellent food and classy service complete a most impressive package.

✕ Eating

★ Martha de Bianchetti CAFE, BAKERY $

(cnr 9 de Julio & Mendoza; pastries from AR$16; ⊘7am-1pm & 4-10pm Mon-Sat; 🔊) This old-fashioned Italian-style bakery and cafe serves mind-altering pastries and excellent coffee accompanied by *chipacitos* (little cheese scones). It's all warm when the doors open and the lovely smell wafts halfway down the block. Ice cream too.

Ginger ARGENTINE $$

(☑0379-443-4516; Junín 84; mains AR$140-250; ⊘8pm-1am Tue-Sun) Across the road from the river, this popular place has a varied menu featuring the normal meat mains as well as gourmet sandwiches, pizzas, salads and some Asian-influenced rice dishes. The decor feels a little out of a packet but the food is good and it draws a friendly crowd.

Cristóbal del Puerto ARGENTINE $$

(☑0379-442-4229; Martínez 1102; mains AR$120-250; ⊘5:30pm-4am; 🌐) A popular restaurant down near the port with a large air-conditioned dining room and a big bunch of tables out on the sidewalk that's famous for its *picadas*. There are also crepes and tacos alongside standard restaurant fare. The lively atmosphere makes it worth sticking around for drinks after dinner.

El Mirador del Paraná ARGENTINE $$

(☑0379-442-9953; www.facebook.com/elmirador delparana; cnr Costanera & Edison; mains AR$135-270; ⊘noon-3pm & 8:30pm-12:30am; 🔊) Perched right above a river beach, the lovely bow-shaped deck here makes a great lunchtime destination. There's a fairly unsophisticated menu of *parrilla* and Argentine staples, but quality is good. Specialty surubí dishes go a step beyond: *al paquete* is very succulent, cooked in foil with walnuts. Edison is a continuation of Bolívar.

🍷 Drinking & Nightlife

The *costanera* has lots of action, with several bars and *boliches* (nightclubs) in the Costanera Sur zone south of the Resistencia bridge and bars strung out north of it. Near the intersection of Junín and Buenos Aires, several bars and clubs pump along at weekends.

El Flotante BAR

(Centro Cultural Siete Corrientes; ☑0379-405-7604; ccflotante@gmail.com; Puerto de Corrientes; ⊘7pm-1am Fri-Sun) Set atop an old barge moored behind the port, this friendly alternative bar with river views is a fantastic place for a drink and to tap into Corrientes culture. Outside colorfully painted wooden tables overlook the masts of the yachts docked below while inside there's an events area that hosts concerts and theater. Serves local craft beer and bar food.

Getting here adds to the atmosphere: cross the car park next to the local bus terminal, push the unmarked white metal gate in the corner and follow the elevated walkways around. The empty waterside corridors make it feel like you're heading into a shootout at the end of a B-grade action movie but it's perfectly safe.

Confitería Panambi CAFE

(Córdoba 932; ⊘7am-1pm & 4:30-9:30pm) This cozy cafe just off the Junín mall serves good coffee alongside a mouthwatering array of quality handmade chocolates and pastries. Also a good spot for breakfast.

Sherwood BAR

(www.sherwoodrestobar.com.ar; Quevedo 11; ⊘7pm-2am; 🔊) This massive complex on the *costanera* does a bit of everything – food, DJs, etc – but is best for a mojito or negroni on its spacious front deck or upstairs for better river views. It tries for the upmarket image with front-of-house staff in suits, but is actually very relaxed once you're in. Quevedo is an extension of Belgrano.

☆ Entertainment

★ Cantalicio LIVE MUSIC

(☑3794-751-005; Chaco 1236; ⊘9:30pm-2am Thu-Sat) This welcoming traditional-style bar a couple of blocks off the *costanera* is the place to go to get to know *chamamé* with live performances and a colorful energetic crowd. The tables are packed in but the aficionados still manage to find places to dance once things heat up. Also serves meals with an emphasis on typical plates of the region.

CHAMAMÉ

Tango? What's that? Up here it's all about *chamamé*, one of the country's most intoxicating musical forms. Rooted in the polka, introduced by European immigrants, it's also heavily influenced by Guaraní culture. Its definitive sound is the accordion, traditionally accompanied by the guitar, *guitarrón* (an oversized guitar used for playing bass lines), the larger *bandoneón* (accordion) and the *contrabajo* (double bass). Of course, a *conjunto* (band) is hardly complete without a singer or two.

Chamamé is a lively dance for a couple, except when the man takes his solo *zapateo* (tap dance). Corrientes province is the heart of *chamamé* and therefore the easiest place to find a live performance. Check out Spanish-only website www.corrienteschamame.com.ar for upcoming performances and online tunes to introduce you to the genre. Corrientes holds a fortnight-long *chamamé* festival in early January. **Super Disco** (9 de Julio 1781; ⏲8:30am-12:30pm & 5-9pm Mon-Sat) specailizes in Corrientes *chamamé* CDs.

Information

There are various irregularly open information offices around town, including at the airport and bus terminal.

Casa Ibera (www.parqueibera.com; Pellegrini 501; ⏲8am-1pm & 4:30-9pm) Offers assistance in organizing trips to the Esteros del Iberá wetlands.

Municipal Tourist Office (☎0379-447-4733; www.ciudaddecorrientes.gov.ar; cnr Av Costanera & 9 de Julio; ⏲8am-9pm) The main municipal tourist office, though opening hours can be patchy.

Post Office (www.correoargentino.com.ar; San Juan 1098; ⏲7:30am-7:30pm Mon-Fri)

Provincial Tourist Office (☎0379-442-7200; http://turismo.corrientes.gob.ar; 25 de Mayo 1330; ⏲7:30am-2pm & 4:30-8:30pm Mon-Fri) Helpful for information about the province.

Getting There & Away

Aerolíneas Argentinas (☎0379-442-3918; www.aerolineas.com.ar; Junín 1301; ⏲8am-12:30pm & 4:30-8pm Mon-Fri, 9am-noon Sat) flies to Buenos Aires daily. It also flies there from nearby Resistencia.

The **long-distance bus terminal** (☎0379-447-7600; Av Maipú 2400) is 3km southeast of the town center. Resistencia has better long-distance bus connections to the west and northwest.

Buses to Resistencia (AR$8–AR$10, 40 minutes) leave frequently from the **local bus terminal** (cnr Av Costanera General San Martín & La Rioja). Make sure to take the one marked 'Chaco–Corrientes Directo' or 'Sarmiento' to avoid a prolonged journey.

Shared taxis that zip you into Resistencia for AR$35 are faster but you'll have to wait for them to fill. They leave from two locations: one **by the river** (Plácido Martínez 1016), and one on the **main road** (Av 3 de Abril 953).

Buses from Corrientes

DESTINATION	COST (AR$)	TIME (HR)
Buenos Aires	1450	12-14
Córdoba	1100	11-14
Mercedes	278	3-4
Paso de los Libres	430	5
Posadas	375	4-4½
Puerto Iguazú	730	9-10
Rosario	1148	9-11
Salta	1235	13
Santa Fe	640	6½-8

Getting Around

Local bus 109 goes to the **airport** (☎0379-445-8684; RN 12, Km 10), 10km northeast of town on the Posadas road. A taxi costs around AR$200.

Bus 103 runs between the local bus terminal and the long-distance bus terminal via downtown. A taxi to/from the long-distance bus terminal will cost AR$80 to AR$90.

Buses cost AR$8, payable only with a Sube charge card, available from some kiosks and usable in many other cities around the country. If you don't have a card other passengers are usually willing to swipe their card if you give them the cash fare.

Mercedes

☎03773 / POP 43,895

The main access point for the spectacular Esteros del Iberá wetlands, Mercedes is a rather handsome gaucho town with a mighty easy pace to life. Its claim to fame is the nearby – and completely surreal – roadside shrine to gaucho Antonio Gil, an enormously popular religious phenomenon.

Prices are low here, and there are appealing places to stay.

Sleeping & Eating

Casa de China B&B $

(☎03773-15-627269; lacasadechina@hotmail.com; Beltrán 599; r per person US$30;) This enchanting 19th-century mansion offers magnificently characterful rooms with miles-high ceilings, large beds and antique furniture. Gardens, original artworks, gorgeous veranda spaces and a generous breakfast add enchantment. Best, though, is China herself, a warm-hearted, cultured and interesting host with a fund of stories and a lovably informal style. If you're not looking for hotel-style amenities, you won't want to leave.

Hostel Gitanes HOSTEL $

(☎03773-421558; hostelgitanes@gmail.com; Av San Martín 224; r per person US$18;) A fantastic option for the budget traveler, this self-contained hostel out the back of a family home has decent basic rooms with air-conditioning and private bathrooms. There are also two kitchens, and a yard with a barbecue for guest use. The owners couldn't be more helpful or welcoming.

Hotel Manantiales Mercedes HOTEL $$

(☎03773-421700; www.manantialeshoteles.com; cnr Pujol & Sarmiento; s/d/tr US$60/94/139;) Right on the plaza, this modern hotel is Mercedes' most upmarket, with well-equipped rooms sporting contemporary color schemes, a restaurant, a casino, a spa and a gym. Service is polite and helpful. Rates are reasonable for this quality and include parking.

Che Rhoga ARGENTINE $

(☎3773-407272; Av San Martín 2296; mains AR$160-170; 8:30pm-midnight Tue, 11:30am-2:30pm & 8:30pm-midnight Wed-Sun;) It's a bit of a hike out to this homey restaurant on the roundabout at the entrance, but it's worth it for toothsome homemade pasta, steaks in tasty sauces and low prices. Service tries hard to be formal. A great place.

Sal y Pimienta ARGENTINE $

(Gómez 665; mains AR$85-165; 24hr Mon-Sat, 11:30am-3pm & 8-11:30pm Sun;) A local favorite, this uncomplicated joint near the bus terminal is almost always open and has a wide-ranging menu and unbeatable prices for tasty meats, river fish, pastas and pizzas. Sometimes has live music in the evenings.

Shopping

Manos Correntinas ARTS & CRAFTS

(San Martín 487; 9am-noon & 5-8pm Mon-Fri, 9am-noon Sat) A friendly handicrafts gallery and shop that displays the work of a cooperative of local craftspeople. There's some excellent basketwork and leatherwork. English spoken.

Information

Most services are along San Martín, which links the bus terminal with the plaza.

Centro de Interpretación (☎03733-15-400572; www.mercedescorrientes.gov.ar; cnr Gómez & Caá Guazú; 7am-1pm & 3-9pm Mon-Fri, 9am-noon & 4-8pm Sat & Sun) Three blocks north and a block east of the bus terminal, this cultural information office in the grounds of the old hospital is helpful. There's a small museum about *correntino* culture out the back.

Tourist Information (☎03733-15-438769; www.guiadigitalmercedes.com.ar; Estación de Ómnibus; 6am-midnight Mon-Fri, 7am-noon & 4-8pm Sat & Sun) The handiest of the tourist information places, this is at the bus terminal. The best for info on transportation to Colonia Pellegrini.

Getting There & Away

The **bus terminal** (☎03773-420165; cnr San Martín & Perreyra) is six blocks west of the plaza. Destinations include Buenos Aires (AR$1100 to AR$1400, eight to 10 hours), Paso de los Libres (AR$120, two hours) and Corrientes (AR$278, three to four hours).

Parque Esteros del Iberá

This stunning 18,000-hectare wetland reserve is home to an abundance of bird and animal life, and is among South America's finest places to see wildlife. Although tourism has increased substantially in recent years, Los Esteros del Iberá remains comparatively unspoiled.

Donations of tracts of land by the late American conservationist Douglas Tompkins and his wife Kristine have seen the boundaries of the park expanded from the original provincial reserve to include four new national park zones to form the Gran Parque Iberá.

The main base for visiting the park is the sleepy village of Colonia Pellegrini, 120km northeast of Mercedes. With the creation of the new Gran Parque Iberá, which adds several stretches of national park to the

GAUCHITO GIL

Spend time on the road anywhere in Argentina and you're bound to see roadside shrines surrounded by red flags and votive offerings. These pay homage to Antonio Gil, a Robin Hood–like figure whose burial place 9km west of Mercedes attracts hundreds of thousands of pilgrims yearly.

Little is certain about 'El Gauchito,' as he is affectionately called, but romantic tales have sprung up to fill the gaps. What is known is that he was born in 1847 and joined the army – some versions say to escape the wrath of a local policeman whose fiancée had fallen in love with him – to fight in the War of the Triple Alliance.

Once the war ended, Gil was called up to join the Federalist Army, but went on the run with a couple of other deserters. The trio roamed the countryside, stealing cattle from rich landowners and sharing them with poor villagers, who in turn gave them shelter and protection. The law finally caught up with them, and Gil was hung by the feet from the espinillo tree that still stands near his grave, and beheaded.

So how did this freeloading, cattle-rustling deserter attain saint-like status? Moments before his death, Gil informed his executioner that the executioner's son was gravely ill. He told the soldier that if he were buried – not the custom with deserters – the man's son would recover.

After lopping off Gil's head, the executioner carried it back to the town of Goya where – of course – a judicial pardon awaited Gil. On finding that his son was indeed seriously ill, the soldier returned to the site and buried the body. His son recovered quickly, word spread and a legend was born.

'Gauchito' Gil's last resting place is now the site of numerous chapels and storehouses holding thousands of votive offerings – including T-shirts, bicycles, pistols, knives, license plates, photographs, cigarettes, hair clippings and entire racks of wedding gowns – brought by those who believe in the gaucho's miracles. January 8, the date of Gil's death, attracts the most pilgrims.

existing provincial park, a number of alternative access points have been developed that offer differing landscapes and experiences. Rural *estancias* in the larger area also make enticing bases.

Sleeping

The greatest concentration of accommodations in the greater reserve are in Colonia Pellegrini where the hotels either border the estuary or are just a short walk away. There are several charming more isolated rural properties adjoining other areas of the park.

Iberá Lodge LODGE **$$$**
(☎0379-423-0228; www.iberaexplorer.com; RP 29 Km 50; d incl full board & activities US$360; P 📶 🏊) This handsome complex has a totally rural location by the lakeshore, 50km north of Mercedes via RP 29. Rooms are furnished in elegant country style; riding and boat trips are included. Grassy grounds and a plethora of facilities, including games room, spa and excellent food, make this a fine retreat. It's a popular spot for sportfishing enthusiasts.

Colonia Pellegrini

☎03773

Gloriously tranquil Pellegrini is the perfect place from which to explore Los Esteros: the wetlands surround the settlement on several sides. The town's wide sand streets have almost no traffic and the only noise you'll hear most of the time is a chorus of birdsong.

Here you can organize excellent boat trips around the lagoons, explore the wetlands by kayak or hike along dedicated trails. But you don't even need to leave your hotel to get up close to the Esteros' fabulous wildlife – many hotels are constructed right on the edge of the *laguna* and capybaras stroll leisurely through their grounds while caimans loiter at the water's edge.

Sights

The best place to check out Pellegrini's famous sunset is from the bridge at the exit to Mercedes.

Visitor Center WILDLIFE WATCHING
(RP 40; ⏰7am-7pm) The reserve's visitor center, on the Mercedes side of the causeway,

WILDLIFE OF LOS ESTEROS DEL IBERÁ

The lakes and *esteros* (lagoons) of Parque Esteros del Iberá are shallow, fed only by rainwater, and thick with vegetation, which accumulates to form *embalsados* (floating islands); this fertile habitat is home to a stunning array of life. Sinister black caimans bask in the sun while capybaras feed around them. Other mammals include the beautiful orange-colored marsh deer, howler monkeys (officially the world's noisiest animal), the rare maned wolf, coypu, otters and several species of bat.

The birdlife is simply extraordinary; there are some 350 species present in the reserve, including colorful kingfishers, delicate hummingbirds, parrots, spoonbills, kites, vultures, several species of egret and heron, cormorants, ducks, cardinals and the plump southern screamer, which would really light up Big Uncle Bob's eyes at a Christmas roast.

has a good exhibition on local wildlife (in Spanish) and an audiovisual presentation. The short path opposite gives you a sporting chance of seeing howler monkeys; and other paths and boardwalks introduce you to the area's different plants and habitats.

Activities

Lodges can organize most activities; they are usually included in the accommodations price. Otherwise, the best place to organize boat trips and other excursions is the campsite (from where most trips leave). Note that few guides speak English; if you want an English-speaking guide, it's best to go through one of the lodges.

Hiking

There are several short hiking trails leaving from the visitor center, the longest of which is about 2km. During the day you are free to hike at your leisure although its worth taking a guide (AR$150 to AR$200 per visitor) in order to learn about the ecosystem and to point out wildlife you may otherwise miss. For nocturnal exploration, guides are obligatory.

Water Activities

You can rent kayaks and canoes (per hour AR$100) at the municipal campground for exploring the *laguna* at your own pace.

Horseback Riding

Horseback rides (AR$280) are also offered around town, although these are more for the ride's sake than for wildlife spotting.

Tours

★Boat Trips BOATING

(per person AR$250-300) The best way to appreciate the area. The classic trip is a two- to three-hour excursion in a *lancha* (boat) around the Laguna Iberá and its *embalsados*. You'll see myriad bird and animal life, elegant lilies, water hyacinths and other aquatic plants. The guide will punt you remarkably close to the creatures. You can also take night trips; take plenty of insect repellent.

Boats leave with a minimum of four clients but you can pay any remaining seats if you're in a hurry or want a private cruise.

Sleeping

Colonia Pellegrini's numerous accommodations are divided between *hospedajes*, usually simple rooms behind a family home, and posadas or *hosterías*, comfortable lodges that offer full-board rates and excursions. Multiday packages are offered by most lodges, which can also book transfers from Mercedes or Posadas.

Camping Iberá CAMPGROUND $

(☎03773-15-412242; www.ibera.gob.ar; Mbiguá s/n; campsite per person 1st/subsequent days US$6/5, per vehicle US$3; P) This municipal campground by the lake is a great place with grassy pitches, nearly all with their own covered barbecue/eating area. Boat trips leave from here, and it's worth checking out the view as the sun sets. Book ahead as it's not huge. Also rents kayaks and canoes.

Posada Rancho Jabirú GUESTHOUSE $

(☎03773-15-474838; www.posadaranchojabiru.com.ar; Yaguareté s/n; s/d/tr US$26/44/66; ❄📶) The best of the budget options. Set in a carefully tended flowery garden, it has spotless rooms sleeping up to five in a pretty bungalow. It's run by the friendly folk of Yacarú Porá (p176) restaurant next door.

Hospedaje San Cayetano GUESTHOUSE $

(☎03773-15-628763, 03773-15-400929; iberasancayetano@hotmail.com; cnr Guazú Virá & Aguapé; s/d US$44/56; ❄📶🏊) This friendly choice with plunge pool offers small but comfortable twins, doubles and family rooms with decent beds. There's a good open social area with a kitchen and barbecue for guest use and spacious grounds. Rooms can be shared if others want to, and prices are a little negotiable. Runs good boat trips. Beethoven, the parrot, covers front-of-house.

Casa Santa Ana LODGE $$
(☑03773-15-475114; www.iberaexpora.com; Capibara s/n; d US$320; ❄) Right by the lakeshore, this simple but elegant lodge is an appealing choice with expansive grounds. Artistic flourishes and comfortable furnishings make it feel more like visiting a rural home than a hotel. It has just four rooms and two *cabañas* (cabins) for families; rooms are a bit on the small side but are cozy and well decorated. Prices include all meals and activities.

★Rancho de los Esteros LODGE $$$
(☑03773-15-493041; www.ranchodelosesteros.com.ar; cnr Ñangapiry & Capivára; s incl full board & activities US$318, d standard/superior US$407/424; P❄🛜❄) This exquisitely peaceful lakeside retreat is run with traditional Argentine country hospitality. Four gorgeous, super-spacious rooms (they can fit a family) surround a beautifully maintained wetland garden full of birdsong. Traditional architecture, attentive hosts, tasty meals and lakeside shelter to watch the spectacular sunsets make this a very special place. Minimum two-night stay.

★Estancia Rincón del Socorro LODGE $$$
(☑03782-15-475114; www.rincondelsocorro.com.ar; RP 40, Km 83; s/d incl full board & activities US$335/454; P🛜❄) This former cattle ranch turned nature reserve, 31km south of Pellegrini, is a wonderful place in which to come to terms with the big sky and abundant wildlife. It's substantial country comfort rather than luxury; the pretty rooms in the main house interconnect, making them great for family stays, while freestanding cabins sleep two. Beyond, vast lawns blend into pastureland and contemplation.

Excursions from here are great and include hikes, horseback riding, boat trips and night safaris. More than 350 bird species have been recorded here and it's a good spot to try to observe the reintroduced giant anteater.

Meals here are good and include fresh vegetables from the gardens.

Ecoposada del Estero LODGE $$$
(☑03773-15-443602; www.ecoposadadelestero.com.ar; Yaguareté s/n; 3 nights incl full board & activities s/d US$482/824; P🛜❄) 🌿 Best in town for bird watching, this place is warmly run by a couple who know the area intimately. Ecological design has resulted in comfortable cool adobe buildings with wide verandas, hammocks and attractive home-made recycled wooden furnishings. House excursions are fantastic but you'll also see plenty from here: the lodge sits on the edge of the water and has abundant birdlife.

Aguapé Lodge LODGE $$$
(☑03773-499412, reservations 011-4742-3015; www.iberaesteros.com.ar; Yacaré s/n; s/d incl full board & activities US$340/540, incl full board US$160/230; P✳🛜❄) This luxurious, long-established colonial-style posada is in a beautiful setting above the lake. It has attractive, high-ceilinged rooms, all-white walls and dark wood. Rooms are along a veranda looking over the lawn to the water and there's a wide variety of excursions. Ask for a room in the main building, as those in the annex are smaller. Service and meals here are excellent.

Posada de La Laguna LODGE $$$
(☑03773-499413; www.esterosibera.com; Guazú Virá s/n; d incl full board & activities US$400; P✳🛜❄) Simple and elegant, in wide lakeside grounds, this lodge has bright white rooms with great beds and paintings by the owner. The emphasis is on relaxation (no TV), and staff pull it off, with friendly service, guided trips and good meals. You can really feel the nature here with capybaras wandering the grounds and caimans sunning themselves by the dock.

✕ Eating

Lodges provide meals for their guests; many allow nonguests if you ask in advance. There are other simple options in town. Eating hours are early for Argentina.

IGUAZÚ FALLS & THE NORTHEAST PARQUE ESTEROS DEL IBERÁ

> **ⓘ SWIMMING IN PARQUE ESTEROS DEL IBERÁ**
>
> Swimming in any of the bodies of water in the area is not advised because of the presence of piranhas – which while they won't devour you entirely like in the movies – can give a nasty bite. Locals say as long as you keep moving you shouldn't get bitten.

Comedor Don Marcos ARGENTINE $
(cnr RN40 & Guasúvira; mains AR$120; ⌚7am-10pm) Take a seat under the thatched roof on the porch at this simple place and tuck into huge portions of delicious home-cooked meals. There's no menu – they'll tell you what's fresh. It's always open – ring the bell on the door for service.

Yacarú Porá ARGENTINE $
(cnr Caraguatá & Yaguareté; mains AR$90-230; ⌚noon-2:30pm & 8-10:30pm; 📶) Run with charm and enthusiasm, this bungalow guarantees a warm welcome. Food is prepared to order and features generous portions of meat, chicken dishes, river fish, pasta, salads, omelets and *milanesas*. They also prepare typical dishes from the region with advanced notice.

Information

There is no bank or ATM, so take cash.

Wi-fi is widespread but unreliable – don't plan on downloading movies or even perusing web pages.

The **Municipal Tourist Office** (☎03773-401575; www.ibera.gov.ar; RP 40; ⌚8am-noon & 2-7pm) is at the Mercedes entrance to the village, just after crossing the causeway.

The reserve's visitor center (p173) is on the Mercedes side of the causeway.

Getting There & Away

Transport options change regularly: check at Mercedes bus terminal tourist information.

The road from Mercedes to Colonia Pellegrini (120km) is driveable in a normal car except after rain.

Cruce del Norte runs one rickety bus a day between Pellegrini and Mercedes (AR$190, three hours). It leaves Pellegrini at 4am and returns from the terminal in Mercedes at 12:30pm. There's no terminal in Pellegrini – just tell the driver where you're staying and he'll drop you at the door. Heading back you'll need to arrange a pick-up in advance.

More expensive than the bus are the scheduled minibus/van services.

Chartered transfers in 4WD pickups between the towns cost around AR$2000 from Mercedes for up to four people. If it hasn't been raining, you could also get a *remise*.

The road from Posadas is worse (take the turning between Gobernador Virasoro and Santo Tomé in a normal car). It's sometimes difficult to find a driver willing to take the trip. If you find one, expect to pay at least AR$3000 for a charter to Posadas, or AR$2500 to Gobernador Virasoro, from where frequent buses travel the 80km on to Posadas.

There's no gas station in Pellegrini; the closest are in Mercedes and the main road junction near Santo Tomé. Fill up before you head in. A couple of places in Pellegrini can sell you gas and diesel if necessary.

Be aware that car-rental companies may refuse you service if you mention that the Iberá is one of your destinations.

Daniel Ortiz (☎03773-15-431469) Runs daily from Mercedes (AR$300) at 7:30am to 8:30am, stopping outside the bus terminal but also doing hotel pick-ups. Returns from Pellegrini at around 3pm. Price a little variable.

Iberá Bus (Mario Azcona; ☎03773-15-462836; cnr Aguará & Pindó) Leaves from the market on Pujol between Gómez and Alvear in Mercedes at midday to 12:30pm Monday to Friday and 9:30am Saturdays; the trip costs AR$300. Returns from Pellegrini 4am Monday to Saturday.

Martín Sandoval (☎03773-15-466072) Reliable for private vehicle transfers to Mercedes and Posadas if road conditions permit.

Maxi Ojeda (☎03773-15-450486) Based in Pellegrini; runs private vehicle transfers to Mercedes and Posadas if the road conditions permit.

Portal Carambola

☎03794

Accessed by the town of Concepción, Portal Carambola is the best place in the park to get a feel for the culture and traditional life in *los esteros*. It's also a great place to take boat trips thanks to its diverse aquatic ecosystems.

Unlike the other portals on this side of the reserve, here there is a small community right beside the park boundary. Traditional houses surrounded by trees sit atop clumps of high ground surrounded by the flooded plains, and barefoot gauchos guide their horses through wetlands, swimming alongside them when the crossings get deep.

Sights & Activities

Portal Carambola is a fine place to spot wildlife. Almost all the action here is on the water – there are not yet any trails through the park itself so you'll need to go on a boat or kayak trip to fully experience *los esteros* here.

Around the port the river is full of small channels winding their way through walls of high grasses that make for a scenic journey.

You'll also see plenty of animals along the road that runs from the park entrance down to the river.

Museo Histórico MUSEUM
(☎03782-610008; Mitre & Vernengo, Concepción; ⏲8-11am & 3-6pm Wed-Sat, 3-6pm Tue & Sun) FREE Set in the old church, this museum has fairly interesting displays on the history of the region. Check out the *balsa,* a small boat made of cow's hide that locals use to drag their belongings through the wetlands behind their horses, and Antonio Maria who was a mysterious medicine man and outlaw who hid out in the *esteros.*

Asociación de Guias Iberá Pora BOATING
(☎03782-477339; guiasdesitioiberapora@gmail.com; RP 6, Concepción; ⏲8am-noon) A cooperative of local guides that organizes a variety of activities within the Portal Carambola including a full-day cultural trip with a traditional meal and a trip through the wetlands in a canoe pulled by a horse – a traditional method of transportation in the region.

Sleeping

Nido de Pajaros BOUTIQUE HOTEL $
(☎03756-614370; www.nidodepajarosposada.com.ar; Mitre 820, Concepción; s/d/tr US$71/88/106) In a meticulously restored house, this elegant boutique hotel has just three rooms and offers outstanding value. Polished floors, high ceilings, exposed brickwork and period furnishings give it a classic vibe while quality bedding and gleaming modern bathrooms add comfort. Management are enthusiastic and can arrange activities throughout the region.

★**Alondra'i Casa de Esteros** BOUTIQUE HOTEL $$$
(www.laalondra.com.ar; Independencia 402, Concepción; d US$580; ❄📶) A wonderfully atmospheric boutique hotel set in a restored old house, Alondra perfects the rustic-chic vibe with antique furnishings and unobtrusive artworks adding flavor throughout. Comfortable rooms are set around a grassy courtyard and framed maps and battered leather suitcases on the shelves make it feel like a frontier lodge for explorers in another era. Facilities are top notch. Prices include full board and ecological activities in Esteros del Iberá.

Eating

If you stay in the park refuge there is a kitchen area for guests. Another option is to purchase meals from locals in the village next to the park but these need to be organized in advance.

Dining out is the one weak link in Concepción's push to get into tourism but there are some *comedores* (basic cafeterias) in town that serve filling meals at a good price.

Information

Oficina Municipal de Turismo (☎03782-444886; Terminal de Buses; ⏲8am-1pm & 1:30-6pm Mon-Fri, 3-6pm Sat & Sun) Plan your visit at this municipal tourism office in the bus station.

There's an ATM on the plaza in Concepción.

Getting There & Away

Portal Carambola is 27km from Concepción down a sandy road – you'll need 4WD – that passes through farmland before reaching the national park nucleus. After around 22km you'll reach a ranch called 'El Transito' – take the right-hand road to enter the park and continue for another 5km to reach the port. There may be a couple of locked gates along the road so ask in town before heading out.

Concepción is 120km east of Corrientes and is served by two buses a day from the terminal.

Portal San Nicolás

☎0379

Accessed through the sleepy town of San Miguel, Portal San Nicolás offers the chance to explore both on land and in the water and is a good option for those who want to explore nature at their own pace and spend the night inside the park boundaries.

Alongside multitudes of *carpinchos* (capybaras) and caimans there are also monkeys, deer and a plethora of birdlife here. The flat terrain, lack of trees and distance from settlements mean that on clear nights the stars here are absolutely phenomenal.

San Miguel is a pleasant Guaraní-speaking rural community with sand streets and friendly locals. It's a comfortable base if you don't want to rough it in a tent in the park.

Sights & Activities

Motorized transportation is prohibited on the water here. From the port you can explore the wetlands in a canoe pushed by a boatman with a pole (AR$300 for up to three visitors) or under your own power in a guided kayak trip. Both need to be arranged in advance in San Miguel before heading down to the park. Guides for canoe trips can be found at the shop next to the chapel on the road out of town.

Centro de Visitantes San Nicolás NATIONAL PARK
(day use per person AR$35, campsite per person AR$50) The visitors center has two hiking trails, the best of which is the **Sendero Curupí**, which winds through the bush for 2km and offers the chance to spot plenty of wildlife. The shorter **Sendero La Cañada** runs through grassland and is more monotonous. There's a nice expanse of green grass for pitching a tent and individual kiosks with barbecues and picnic tables as well as power outlets and decent toilet facilities.

Sleeping

The visitors center at San Miguel has a nice grassy yard for setting up tents and good bathrooms. In San Miguel there are a couple of basic *hospedajes* as well as an excellent rural lodge.

Posada Mboy Cua LODGE **$$$**
(☎0379-401-6618; www.posadamboycua.com; Av Itatí s/n, Salida a Los Esteros, San Miguel; s/d US$186/266; ❄≋) The most comfortable place to stay in the area, this lodge is set on 12 hectares of bushland on the road between San Miguel and the park. It boasts traditional country-style design and six very comfortable modern rooms. There's a nature trail on the property but you can also spot plenty of birdlife from the porch or the refreshing pool.

Shopping

Casa del Artesano ARTS & CRAFTS
(☎3794-023726; Circunvalación, San Miguel; ⏱10am-1pm & 5-9pm) Run by a local artisans' cooperative, this gallery-shop has some fine baskets woven from grasses found in Los Esteros as well as wood carvings, rugs and wines made from local fruits.

Information

There are a couple of ATMs in San Miguel.

Oficina de Turismo (Mitre s/n, San Miguel; ⏱8am-8pm) Friendly local tourism office that can assist with accommodations and transportation

Getting There & Away

Two buses a day run from the terminal in Corrientes to San Miguel (AR$170, four hours) leaving at 4:45am and 7:30pm and returning at 4:30am and 12:45pm.

From San Miguel to the visitors center at Portal San Nicolás it's a 17km drive along a very soft sandy road that resembles a beach in some places. The first 15km are dominated by monotonous pine plantations after which the road emerges in farmland before reaching the red gate of the park. The port is another 10km drive from the visitors center. A private transfer in a 4WD pickup, such as the one run by **Sebastian Gonella** (☎03781-403761), costs AR$1300 for up to four visitors.

Portal Cambyretá

☎03786

Also known as the Portal Norte, this is the most accessible point to get into the wetlands – it's just 30km off the paved Ruta Nacional 12 that runs up to Iguazú Falls close to the pleasant vacation town of Ituzaingó. Unlike other entry points it has no navigable waterways but it is one of the best areas in the park for bird watching; the wetlands here are absolutely teeming with caimans and fish.

The visitors center at Hacienda Monte Rey has a short trail through a small section of forest that is home to howler monkeys and reintroduced scarlet macaws. Another longer trail is in the pipeline.

Ituzaingó has over 12km of inviting river beaches and a laid-back atmosphere, and is a good base to spend a couple of days.

Tours

The principal activity here is wildlife watching from a vehicle or on foot. Guided tours can be arranged in Ituzaingó. You can contract a tour with transportation or organize a guide to jump into your own vehicle. It's well worth taking a professional guide as they know where to find the wildlife and spot animals a casual observer may miss.

Turismo Diversidad WILDLIFE WATCHING
(☎03786-420024; www.turismodiversidad.com; Centenario 2014, Ituzaingó) A recommended outfit based in Ituzaingó offering interesting guided tours into northern regions of the park in comfortable vehicles with experienced, knowledgeable guides. It will tailor excursions according to visitor interests.

Sleeping

Hotel Puerto Valle LODGE **$$$**
(☎03786-425700; www.puertovalle.com.ar; RN 12, Km 1282; s/d incl full board, transfers & activities from US$620/890; P❄@≋) This luxurious secluded option does not actually connect with the reserve but is rather on the banks of the Paraná – huge here, above the

OFF THE BEATEN TRACK

PARQUE NACIONAL MBURUCUYÁ

Less well known than neighboring Parque Esteros del Iberá, this compact **national park** (☎03782-498907; www.parquesnacionales.gob.ar; ⌚7am-8pm) **FREE** contains more than 100 small lakes and boasts thriving communities of deer, capybaras and caimans in addition to a phenomenal array of birdlife. While the wildlife is similar to Los Esteros, the landscapes here are more varied with more forest cover.

There are two trails leading out from the visitors center – the park guards will give you a leaflet containing a map. The **Yatay path** is a 7km roundtrip to a lookout point overlooking the lovely Estuario Santa Lucía while the **Che Rhoga path** is a 4km circuit ideal for bird watching and spotting larger fauna.

At the visitors center there is an area to pitch tents with hot showers and wi-fi. The nearest hotels are located in the town of Mburucuyá. If you are staying the night you need to be back in the services area by park closing. Free barbecues are found at the visitors center but you'll need to bring in all your supplies. In town there are a couple of good, cheap places to eat but it's a long way to go for a meal.

The visitors center of Parque Nacional Mburucuyá is 25km from the town of Mburucuyá. There's no public transportation to the park. A private transfer from town runs at AR$600–AR$700. The road can be impassable when it's wet so check before heading out. It's possible to hike in and it's common to see locals hitchhiking on this stretch. The staff in the park office in Mburucuyá town can assist with finding transportation.

Yacyreta dam – near the Esteros' northeastern tip. Rooms, some in the historic original building, others in annexes, are impeccable, with great river views. Meals and service are excellent.

Getting There & Away

The 30km access road from RN 12 to the visitors center is a firm dirt track that is suitable for most types of vehicles although you'll need to cross numerous private farms along the way, which makes taking a local guide indispensable. The turnoff is at Km 1242, 15km to the west of Ituzaingó.

Ituzaingó is served by regular buses running between Posadas (AR$124, one hour), Puerto Iguazú (AR$460, six hours) and Corrientes (AR$268, three hours).

ALONG THE RÍO URUGUAY

The lesser of the two great rivers that converge to form the Río de la Plata, the Uruguay divides the country of the same name from Argentina, and also forms part of the border with Brazil. Bridges provide access to these neighbors, whose influences have blended with those of indigenous and immigrant groups in the area. The Argentine riverside towns have lots to offer and are popular summer and weekend destinations.

Concepción del Uruguay

☎03442 / POP 109,975

Set around a stately plaza, Concepción is a typical riverside town, wondering what to do with itself now that trade on the Río Uruguay has died off. It makes a decent stopover, has good sleeping and eating choices, and boasts the Palacio San José outside town.

Sights

The principal sights in the town itself are around the noble main plaza, where the earthy-pink-colored basilica holds the remains of Justo José de Urquiza.

★**Palacio San José** PALACE
(☎03442-432620; www.palaciosanjose.com; RP 39, Km 30; ⌚8am-7pm Mon-Fri, 9am-6:30pm Sat & Sun; 🐾) **FREE** Topped by twin towers and surrounded by elegant gardens, Justo José de Urquiza's ostentatious pink palace is 33km west of Concepción. Set around an arched patio, with a walled garden out back, it was built partly to show up Urquiza's archrival in Buenos Aires, Juan Manuel de Rosas, and partly to show the power and wealth of Entre Ríos province. Local *caudillo* Urquiza was largely responsible for Rosas' 1852 downfall and the eventual adoption of Argentina's modern constitution.

Sometime allies such as Domingo Sarmiento and Bartolomé Mitre supped at

Urquiza's 8.5m dining-room table and slept in the palatial bedrooms. The bedroom in which Urquiza was murdered by a mob sent by Ricardo López Jordán is a permanent shrine, created by Urquiza's wife.

Free guided tours in Spanish leave daily at 10am, 11am, noon, 2pm, 3pm and 4pm. There's a restaurant on-site and picturesque grounds for picnicking.

From Concepción, **Servimas** (03442-427777; Belgrano 465) or other *remise* companies will take up to four people there and back, including a two-hour wait, for AR$550. Another option is a tour – **Turismo Pioneros** (03442-433914; www.facebook.com/pionerosturismo; Mitre 908) organizes guided visits. You could also jump off a Caseros-bound bus and walk 3km to the palace.

Sleeping & Eating

★Antigua Fonda HOTEL $
(03442-433734; www.antiguafonda.com.ar; España 172; s/d/tr US$38/47/56;) Though you wouldn't know it, this has been created from part of what was once a historic Concepción hotel. Pleasing, spacious rooms in shades of cream surround a small grassy garden, with artistic touches and a relaxing vibe. It's one block west and three blocks south of the plaza. Great value.

Antigua Posta del Torreón BOUTIQUE HOTEL $$
(03442-432618; www.postadeltorreon.com.ar; Almafuerte 799; s/d/superior r US$56/82/109;) This intimate hotel one block west and four blocks south of the plaza offers a real haven for a relaxing stay, although service is not its strong point. It's an elegantly refurbished 19th-century mansion with original features and rooms surrounding a postcard-pretty courtyard complete with fountain and small heated pool. Superiors are worth the upgrade: much more spacious, with lovely furniture.

Danube Azul ARGENTINE $
(03442-423244; San Martín 763; mains AR$75-210; 8am-11:30pm) An unpretentious local restaurant on a corner of the park, Danube Azul is popular for its generous portions of local dishes. It's not fancy but it's clean and tasty; you won't find a better deal in town.

Bella Vista CAFE $
(cnr 9 de Julio & Urquiza; mains AR$70-145; 8am-midnight) A bright and inviting cafe on the plaza serving good-quality meals including breakfasts, filling brunch and an excellent-value daily special. Also has a full range of beverages, delicious desserts and great tunes.

El Conventillo de Baco ARGENTINE $$
(03442-15-549695; España 193; mains AR$180-260; 11am-3pm & 8pm-midnight Tue-Sun) This handsome and recommended spot has both indoor and outdoor dining in an attractive patio space and specializes in well-prepared river fish and seafood. Good value.

Information

The handiest **tourist office** (03442-425820; www.concepcionentrerios.tur.ar; cnr Galarza & Supremo Entrerriano; 7am-1pm & 2-8pm) is a block east of the plaza.

Getting There & Away

Buses from Concepción

DESTINATION	COST (AR$)	TIME (HR)
Buenos Aires	420	4
Colón	40	45min
Concordia	125	2¾
Paraná	245	5
Rosario	325	4

Getting Around

The **bus terminal** (03442-422352; cnr Galarza & Chiloteguy) is 10 blocks west of the plaza. Bus 1 runs between them; a *remise* costs AR$35.

Colón

03447 / POP 72,630

The most appealing destination for riverside relaxation in Entre Ríos, Colón's population almost doubles with Argentine holidaymakers in January, but the pretty town takes it all in its stride. With numerous places to stay, a thriving handicrafts scene and worthwhile, out-of-the-ordinary restaurants, it's a great place to be. It's also a base for visiting Parque Nacional El Palmar.

Colón is connected to Paysandú in Uruguay by bridge. The center of the action is Plaza San Martín, a block back from the river, and the street 12 de Abril running up to it.

Sights & Activities

Strolling around the riverbank, the beach and quiet leafy streets is the highlight here.

ENTERING URUGUAY

Three main crossings link Argentina with its eastern neighbor Uruguay. From south to north these are Gualeguaychú–Fray Bentos, Colón–Paysandú (cars pay an AR$130 toll on these two bridges) and Concordia–Salto. All three are open 24 hours.

Numerous *artesanía* shops sell everything from *mate* gourds to pickled coypu (rodent).

Tours

Ita i Cora Aventura BOATING
(☎03447-423360; itaicora@gmail.com; San Martín 97; 2hr tour adult/child AR$400/200) The best option for getting out on the river. The standard tour is a charismatic two-hour affair taking in sand flats and a forest trail in the middle of the Río Uruguay. Excellent English spoken.

Naturaleza Yatay BUS
(☎03447-15-465528; naturalezayatay@gmail.com; El Palmar tour AR$450) Runs good guided trips to the El Palmar national park. Can organize tailored bird-watching trips. English spoken.

Festivals & Events

Fiesta Nacional de la Artesanía HANDICRAFTS
(www.fiestadelaartesania.com.ar) This crafts fair in February in Parque Quirós features high-standard live folkloric entertainment.

Sleeping

There are numerous summer campgrounds, cabins, bungalows and apartments available for rent. Look for signs saying *'Alquilo a turistas.'* The tourist office can supply you with a list of official accommodations: there are several hundred.

★**Hostería 'Restaurant del Puerto'** HOTEL $
(☎03447-422698; www.hosteriadecolon.com.ar; Alejo Peyret 158; r US$74; ❄@🛜🏊) In what has a strong claim to be Colón's loveliest house, this has characterful rooms decorated faithfully in the style of the 1880 building, with enormous windows, plenty of wood and noble rustic furniture. Family duplexes (US$110) are a good deal, as are midweek discounts. The restaurant serves good dinners, and there's an outdoor heated pool and Jacuzzi out back. No cards.

Hostería El Viejo Almacén GUESTHOUSE $
(☎03447-422216; Av Urquiza 108; s/d US$40/52; P❄🛜) In the restaurant of the same name, this is ultra-friendly and has well-furnished neat rooms with both fan and air-con plus plenty of space. Facilities are in excess of what is the norm for the price: massive flat screens, Jacuzzi baths and quality bedding. Go for one near the front if in-room wi-fi is important.

Hotel Costarenas HOTEL $$
(☎03447-425050; www.hotelcostarenas.com.ar; cnr Av Quirós & 12 de Abril; r US$128, with view US$150, superior r US$141-175; P❄@🛜🏊) A favorite of weekending *porteños,* this offers smart, very well-kept riverside accommodations. The handsome downstairs spa/pool complex is included; there's also an outdoor pool and a good restaurant. Rooms are bland cream with pine furniture but well-equipped; those with views are lighter and larger, while superior rooms add a few more square meters. Service is personable. Breakfast is served in the 4th-floor dining area, which affords great views of the river.

Hotel Plaza HOTEL $$
(☎03447-421043; www.hotel-plaza.com.ar; cnr 12 de Abril & Belgrano; standard/superior d US$101/128; P❄@🛜🏊) This Colón staple has been around for a century, but now looks modern and glistening. The rooms, which are available with exterior or internal pool views, aren't quite as posh; the superiors (Neo) have much more space and quality bathrooms. But the combination of plaza-side location and top facilities including fine indoor and outdoor pools make it a winner. Four-night minimum stay in high summer.

Eating

Heladería Italia ICE CREAM $
(12 de Abril 173; ⏰10am-midnight) Ice-cream parlors are all over Colón but this locally run place is the pick of the bunch for its delicious home-style flavors. Go early in your visit because you'll want to go back.

El Sótano de los Quesos DELI $
(www.elsotanodelosquesos.com.ar; cnr Chacabuco & Av Costanera; mixed plates for 1-2 people AR$150; ⏰9:30am-8:30pm Mon-Tue, to 10:30pm Thu-Sun; 🖋) This intriguing spot serves artisanal cheeses and other delicacies at pretty thatched tables on a lawn overlooking the port. There's also locally made wine and beer, and a cellar shop whose aromas will almost compel you to

GUALEGUAYCHÚ CARNAVAL

A mellow riverside town, Gualeguaychú is quiet out of season but kicks off in summer with the country's longest and flashiest **Carnaval celebration** (www.carnavaldelpais.com.ar). Any weekend from mid-January to late February you'll find things in full swing. The main venue is the Corsódromo, where admission is AR$230 to AR$290 most nights.

There's a string of decent budget hotels along Bolívar between Bartolomé Mitre and Monseñor Chalup, and several hostels in town. During Carnaval things fill up so make plans in advance.

Gualeguaychú is easily reached by bus from Buenos Aires (3½ hours), Paraná and other Río Uruguay towns. Gualeguaychú is also a crossing point to Uruguay: Fray Bentos lies just across the bridge.

buy. Opening hours extend in summer. Flooding sometimes forces it to close.

El Viejo Almacén ARGENTINE $
(☎03447-422216; cnr Urquiza & Paso; mains AR$119-269; ⏰11:30am-3pm & 8pm-midnight; 📶) 🌿 A block from the plaza and offering a quiet, brick-walled interior decorated with old-time photos, this has a wide-ranging menu including great homemade pasta, delicious empanadas, river fish and *parrilla* options. Portions aren't as big as in some places – probably a good thing – but prices are right and vegetables come from their organic garden. Offers soy *milanesas* and other veg options.

★ **La Cosquilla del Ángel** ARGENTINE $$
(☎03447-423711; cnr San Martín & Balcarce; pasta AR$165; ⏰noon-4pm & 8pm-midnight Wed-Sun; 📶) Colón's best restaurant combines elegant, romantic decor and service with a whimsical and unpretentious approach, particularly in the curiously named dishes and the intriguing restaurant name: The Angel's Tickle. Many dishes combine sweet and savory flavors; try the *mollejitas* (sweetbreads). The pasta is recommended and the wine list is above average.

Restaurant del Puerto ARGENTINE $$
(☎03447-422698; www.hosteriadecolon.com.ar; Peyret 158; mains AR$130-250; ⏰8pm-midnight Thu-Tue; 📶) In a lovely old building near the river, this restaurant does tasty evening meals with good service and plenty of imaginative river-fish dishes. It's good for a lighter dinner, with plenty of salad vegetables and fruit used. No cards.

Cala Bistro ARGENTINE $$
(☎03447-15-40224; 3 de Febrero 37; mains AR$170-230; ⏰noon-3:30pm & 8pm-midnight) A cozy split-level restaurant in an old, stone-walled house decorated with antiques, this great little place serves fantastic flavorful meals that are a bit more adventurous than the standard fare around town. Ask about the off-menu seafood *sorrentinos* with portobello mushrooms. Meals take a while to come out because everything is freshly prepared.

ℹ Information

Tourist Office (☎03447-423000; www.colonturismo.tur.ar; cnr Gouchón & Av Costanera; ⏰8am-8pm) Occupies the former customs building, built by Urquiza. There is also a helpful office in the bus terminal (open 8am to 7pm).

ℹ Getting There & Away

Colón's **bus terminal** (☎03447-421716; cnr Rocamora & 9 de Julio) is eight blocks north of the main shopping and entertainment street, 12 de Abril. A *remise* downtown costs around AR$50.

Destinations include Buenos Aires (AR$480, 4½ to six hours), Gualeguaychú (AR$53, two hours) via Concepción (AR$40, 40 minutes), Concordia (AR$95, two hours) via Ubajay (AR$48, one hour) and Paysandú, Uruguay (AR$75, 45 minutes, three to five Monday to Saturday, one Sunday).

ℹ Getting Around

Bicicletas Puerto (☎011-15-5417-2068; Urquiza 168; per 3hr/day AR$150/250; ⏰9am-1pm & 3-8pm) is a friendly rental shop offering cycles for exploring around town and the *costanera*.

Taxi companies include **Remis Colón** (☎03447-422221; Alem 13) and **Remises Palmares** (☎03447-424808; Paso 30).

Parque Nacional El Palmar

☎03447

On the Río Uruguay's bank, midway between Colón and Concordia, 8500-sq-km **Parque Nacional El Palmar** (☎03447-493049; www.parqueelpalmar.com.ar; RN 14, Km 199; Argentines/

foreigners AR$120/250) preserves the last extensive stands of yatay palm on the Argentine littoral. In the 19th century, the native yatay covered large parts of Entre Ríos, Uruguay and southern Brazil, but intensive agriculture, ranching and forestry destroyed much of the palm savanna.

Reaching a maximum height of about 18m, the larger specimens clustered throughout the park create a striking and soothing subtropical landscape that lends itself to photography. Grasslands and gallery forests along the watercourses shelter much wildlife.

Park admission (valid for 48 hours) is collected at the entrance from 7am to 10pm, but those spending the night in the park will be given a card that permits after-hours access if they want to come and go.

Sights & Activities

Facilities are 12km from the highway entrance down a good dirt road. Here, the **visitors center** (8am-6pm) has displays on natural history; you can organize canoeing, cycling and horseback-riding trips. Roads lead off the main access road to three viewpoints. **Arroyo Los Loros**, a short distance north of the campground, is a good place to observe wildlife. South of the visitor center is Arroyo El Palmar, a pleasant stream accessed at two viewpoints, **La Glorieta** and **El Palmar**. These have short marked trails; the latter has a bird-watching hide. There are three other short trails near the visitor center, and another hide by the river. Visitors are free to explore the trails on their own; guided walks are available by prior arrangement.

There is river access for swimming and boating from the campground.

Sleeping & Eating

There's a restaurant in the park next to the visitor center as well as a small shop selling sandwiches and basic supplies.

Camping El Palmar CAMPGROUND $
(03447-493031; campsites per adult/child/tent US$7/3.50/4) This sociable campground by the visitor center is the park's only place to stay, with shady, level campsites, hot showers and electricity. The shop sells snacks and food, including slabs of beef for the barbecues; opposite, there's a restaurant. Checkout is at a very reasonable 6pm.

La Aurora del Palmar LODGE, CAMPGROUND $$
(03447-15-431689, 0345-490-5725; www.auroradelpalmar.com.ar; RN 14, Km 202; campsites per adult/child/tent US$11/5/11, r US$128-159; P) Near the park entrance, this cattle ranch and citrus farm has a protected palm forest as spectacular as the national park itself. It's an original, well-run place with shady campsites, family duplexes in a pretty bungalow, and attractive rooms in renovated railway carriages. There's a good swimming pool and a restaurant. Canoeing, horseback riding and palm safaris are available (AR$250 per activity).

Packages with meals and excursions are offered.

Getting There & Away

El Palmar is on RN 14, a major national highway, with frequent north–south bus services. Most buses will drop you at the park entrance, 12km from the visitors center, but double-check with the driver as it's technically prohibited. You could walk or hitchhike from here or else get off 6km north at Ubajay, from where a *remise* will cost you around AR$300 to the visitors center.

The easiest way to get here is by tour from Colón. You can also charter a *remise* from Colón: a return trip plus two hours at the park, covering all the trails, costs AR$850 (up to four people). Remises Palmares is recommended.

Concordia

0345 / POP 185,592

This pleasant agricultural service town on the Río Uruguay won't keep you spellbound for weeks, but it makes a convenient stop for a night. It's a citrus town – you can smell the tang in the air at times – and has a fine central plaza, riverside beaches and fishing. It also offers a border crossing, across a hydroelectric dam, to the pretty Uruguayan city of Salto.

Sights

Museo Judío de Entre Ríos MUSEUM
(0345-421-4088; www.museojudioer.org.ar; Entre Ríos 476; donation AR$50; 8:30am-12:30pm Sun-Tue, Thu & Fri) Three rooms detailing the arrival and struggles of the Jewish gauchos, their way of life and the Holocaust seen through the eyes of those who experienced it. Also temporary exhibitions. One block west and 2½ blocks south of the plaza.

Castillo San Carlos RUINS
(AR$30; 10am-noon & 2-5pm, 3-6pm Nov-Feb) In riverside Parque Rivadavia, northeast of town,

DON'T MISS

THERMAL SPAS

Many towns along the Río Uruguay – Gualeguaychú, Colón and Concordia for starters – have tapped the region's abundant geothermal aquifers to create appealing thermal spa complexes: a major focus of domestic tourism in these parts. They are well-equipped places with several indoor and outdoor pools of various temperatures. Entry to most of them is around AR$100 to AR$200. Check www.termasdeentrerios.com for a complete list.

this ruined mansion was built in 1888 by a French industrialist who mysteriously abandoned the property years later. Writer Antoine de Saint-Exupéry briefly lived here; there's a monument to *The Little Prince* nearby. Bus number 2 will drop you by the entrance from where it's a pleasant walk to the ruins.

Sleeping

Hotel Salto Grande HOTEL $
(0345-421-0034; www.hotelsaltogrande.net; Urquiza 581; turista s/d US$56/70, standard r US$84/105; P ❄ @ ☎ ≋) Just south of the main plaza, this hotel offers excellent service and fair prices. It's showing its age but is gradually being renovated. There are two grades of room; the 'standard' ones are being remodeled; if you get a new one it's worth the extra but the original ones aren't much better than regular *turista* rooms. Above-average breakfast and parking included.

Hotel Centro Plaza HOTEL $
(0345-422-9642; www.centroplazahotel.com.ar; La Rioja 543; s/d US$39/51) Offering good value just a couple of blocks from the plaza, this corner hotel has small but decent enough rooms with good beds. Rooms opening onto the internal patios are quieter.

Eating & Drinking

El Reloj PIZZA $
(Pellegrini 580; pizza AR$95-265; 11am-3:30pm & 7pm-1am Mon-Sat; ☎) This spacious pizzeria has a good ambience and a staggering selection of thin-base pizzas. Half-and-half? No problem. It also does *parrilla, milanesas* and the like. Look out for special deals.

El Ciervo ARGENTINE $$
(0345-422-4867; 1 de Mayo 59; mains AR$135-290; noon-3pm & 6pm-2am) A fashionable eatery on the plaza serving a small menu of well-prepared Argentine favorites. Good-quality fare and a jovial ambience. Worth sticking around for drinks once the plates are cleared away.

Bar Ideal CAFE
(0345-421-2668; 1 de Mayo 51; 24hr) Right on the main plaza, this typical Argentine corner cafe is always open and always pulls a crowd. It's good for drinks, snacks or something more substantial. One of the few places to get a solid plate outside meal times.

Information

Tourist Office (0345-421-3905; www.concordia.tur.ar; cnr Pellegrini & Mitre; 8am-8pm) On the plaza. The bus terminal info desk can also help.

Getting There & Away

The **bus terminal** (0345-421-7235; cnr Justo & Hipólito Yrigoyen) is 13 blocks north of Plaza 25 de Mayo. Four daily buses (none Sunday) go to Salto, Uruguay (AR$130, 1¼ hours).

From the port beyond the east end of Carriego, launches cross the river to Salto, although they are frequently out of service. Check at the tourism office before heaving your luggage down here.

Buses from Concordia

DESTINATION	COST (AR$)	TIME (HR)
Buenos Aires	670	5½-6
Colón	95	2
Concepción	125	2¾
Corrientes	792	9
Paraná	205	4½
Paso de los Libres	318	4
Posadas	695	8

Getting Around

Local buses cost AR$10. Bus 2 takes Hipólito Yrigoyen south from the bus terminal to the town center. On its northward run catch it on Pellegrini in front of Banco de la Nación. A taxi should cost about AR$60.

Paso de los Libres

03772 / POP 52,780

The name ('Crossing of the Free') is the most romantic thing about this border town on the Río Uruguay. It faces the larger Brazilian city of Uruguaiana opposite, and is connected to it by a well-used bridge. There's little to detain the traveler, but the town has plenty of cross-border life, a picturesque central plaza, and acceptable sleeping and eating options.

Sleeping & Eating

Hotel Alejandro Primero HOTEL $

(03772-424100; www.alejandroprimero.com.ar; Coronel López 502; s/d US$56/59; P ❄ @ ☎ ≋) Ageing but reliable, this hotel has an elegant and old-fashioned lobby and restaurant and less impressive but very spacious rooms. Ask for one with views over the river and Uruguaiana. There's also a pleasant outdoor pool and garden area. Card payments cost extra.

El Nuevo Mesón ARGENTINE $

(Colón 587; mains AR$100-190; 11:30am-3pm & 8pm-midnight; ☎) Still the best place to eat in Libres, with waiters smartly turned out in black-and-white and a wide range of decent dishes. There's pizza, *parrilla*, the river fish pacú and more elaborate creations, but it's all fairly priced – unlike a couple of tourist traps in town – and tasty.

Information

There's no tourist office, but there are maps posted around the town center and there are helpful traffic cops on many corners.

You can change money on the international bridge. There are several banks with ATMs around the main plaza.

Brazilian Consulate (03772-425444; Mitre 894; 9am-5pm) Processes visas for land entry into Brazil.

Getting There & Away

The **bus terminal** (03772-425600) is 1km from downtown. There are services to Buenos Aires (AR$775 to AR$1080, eight to nine hours), Posadas (AR$417 to AR$440, five to six hours) and Corrientes (AR$430, five hours) via Mercedes (AR$118, three hours).

Buses to Uruguaiana (AR$25), Brazil, leave frequently, stopping on Av San Martín at Colón and opposite the bus terminal (by the castle-like building). Get off to complete migration formalities and get on the same bus to continue on to the bus terminal.

The frontier is open 24 hours. Travelers have reported that you can transit to Uruguay without requiring a Brazilian visa here, but don't bank on it.

Getting Around

Buses and minibuses (AR$7) run from the corner below the bus terminal into town. A taxi downtown is AR$80.

MISIONES

The narrow northeastern province of Misiones juts out like an Argentine finger between Brazilian and Paraguayan territory and is named for the Jesuit missions whose ruins are now a major attraction. Buses churn through Misiones en route to the Iguazú Falls in the north of the province, but

THE GAUCHO JUDÍO

The gaucho is an archetypal Argentine image, but it's little-known that many were of Jewish origin. The first known mass Jewish immigration was in the late 19th century, when 800 Russian Jews arrived, fleeing persecution from Tsar Alexander III.

The Jewish Colonization Association, funded by a German philanthropist, began distributing 100-hectare parcels of land to immigrant families; the first major colony was Moisés Ville in Santa Fe province, which became known at the time as Jerusalem Argentina. Today there are only about 300 Jewish residents left in town (15% of the population), but many traditions prevail: the tiny town boasts four synagogues, the bakery sells Sabbath bread, and kids in the street use Yiddish slang words like 'schlep' and 'schlock.'

These rural Jews readily assimilated into Argentine society, mixing their own traditions with those of their adopted country, so it was not unusual to see a figure on horseback in baggy pants, canvas shoes and skullcap on his way to throw a hunk of cow on the *asado* (barbecue). Many descendants have since left the land in search of education and opportunities in the cities. Argentina's Jews number about 200,000, making them Latin America's largest Jewish community.

To learn more about the *gauchos judíos*, visit Concordia's Museo Judío de Entre Ríos (p183).

OFF THE BEATEN TRACK

YAPEYÚ

This delightfully peaceful place is no one-horse town: there are many horses, and the sound of their hooves thumping the reddish earth in the evening is one of the nicest things about it. Yapeyú is a great spot to relax with its tree-filled plaza and lovely quiet grassy riverfront. It's the sort of place where locals will greet you on the street.

An hour north of Paso de los Libres by bus, Yapeyú was founded in 1626 as the southernmost of the Jesuit missions. It's also famous for being the birthplace of the great Argentine 'Liberator,' José de San Martín.

You can examine the Jesuit ruins – the **museum** (Sargento Cabral s/n; 8am-noon & 3-6pm Tue-Sun) FREE here has a comprehensive overview of all the missions – and admire the ornate **Casa de San Martín** (8am-noon & 2-6pm) FREE, a pavilion that now shelters the ruins of the house where San Martín was born in 1778.

Four daily buses (AR$55, one hour) run to/from Paso de los Libres and to Posadas (AR$275, 4½ hours) in the other direction. More buses stop on the highway at the edge of the town.

The **Terminal de Transporte** (Sargento Cabral s/n) is just two blocks from the main plaza.

a detour will take you to another stunning cascade – the Saltos del Moconá on the Río Uruguay.

The landscape here is striking; you will see a change to gently rolling low hills, stands of bamboo, and fields of papaya and manioc. Plantations grow from the region's trademark red-brown soil – the province is the main producer of *mate*, Argentina's national drink.

Posadas

0376 / POP 358,986

Capital of Misiones, and a base for visiting the Jesuit ruins after which the province is named, Posadas is a modern city that gazes across the wide Río Paraná to Encarnación in Paraguay. It's a stopover on the way north, and though it offers few in-town sights, it has a pleasant riverbank and an enjoyable vibe.

Sights

The Jesuit missions are the area's main attraction.

★Costanera WATERFRONT

In the afternoon, the *costanera* comes alive with joggers, cyclists, dog walkers, *mate* sippers, hot-dog vendors and young couples staring at Paraguay across the water. Pride of place goes to 'Andresito,' a huge stainless-steel **sculpture** of Guaraní provincial strongman Andrés Guacarurí (Guazurary).

Tours

Many operators offer tours to Iguazú Falls, the Jesuit missions and Los Esteros del Iberá (p172).

Yacaré Tours TOURS

(0376-442-1829; www.yacaretours.com.ar; Bolívar 1419) Offers half-day trips to Argentine (AR$1850 per vehicle) and Paraguayan (AR$2200 per vehicle) missions. Also has trips to *mate* plantations, Saltos del Moconá, Los Esteros del Iberá and more.

Misión Paraná CRUISE

(0376-440-2216; www.misionparana.com; San Lorenzo & Bolívar, Posadas Plaza Shopping; cruise AR$550-690; tickets sold 9am-9pm) Runs regular lunch and dinner cruises on the Paraná in addition to shorter afternoon cruises, party events and longer trips up to the beaches of San Ignacio. Food, drinks and dancing included. Book at the booth in the shopping center on the corner of San Lorenzo and Bolívar.

Guayrá TOURS

(0376-443-3415; www.guayra.com.ar; San Lorenzo 2208) Very helpful agency (inside the Grand Crucero hotel) offering half-day tours to the Jesuit missions, Paraguayan missions, Saltos del Moconá and more.

Sleeping

Posadeña Linda HOSTEL $

(0376-443-9238; www.hostelposadasmisiones.com; Bolívar 1439; dm/r US$12/29;) Run with a caring attitude, this narrow hostel a short walk from the plaza offers a genuine welcome, comfortable bunkrooms with bathroom and a patio with a tiny plunge pool. En-suite private rooms are a little musty but a decent deal. It's colorful and relaxing with a compact but OK kitchen. Despite the address, it's between 1411 and 1419.

La Misión HOTEL $
(☎0376-445-1222; www.lamisionposadashotel.com; Av Quaranta 6150; s/d US$58/70;) A fair way out of town but convenient for the bus terminal and airport, this modern hotel offers real value with smart spacious rooms decked out with king beds and great bathrooms and an inviting pool area. A good option if you're just passing through and don't actually want to see Posadas. It's a AR$200 taxi from downtown.

★Hotel Posadas Urbano HOTEL $$
(☎0376-444-3800; http://alvarezarguelles.com/hotel/hotel-urbano; Bolívar 2176; r/ste from US$111/156;) This smartly renovated hotel has rapidly become top dog with its wide array of facilities and great central location. Bright, very large, carpeted chambers all have gleaming bathrooms, balconies and big windows with views over town. Suites add space but little else. The atrium pool area, art exhibitions, gym and spa facilities, and appealing lounge add points.

Grand Crucero Posadas Express HOTEL $$
(☎0376-443-6901; www.grandcrucero.com; San Lorenzo 2208; s/d US$68/90;) Owned by a bus company, this smart reconversion of an older hotel in the center has resulted in crisp modern rooms with local art on the walls and a fresh feel. All come with safe, mini-fridge and good-looking bathrooms, while suites are large, have two flat-screen TVs and coffee machines. Staff are professional and friendly and there's a bar-restaurant. Top value.

Eating & Drinking

A delicious specialty is *galeto* (chargrilled chicken pieces stuffed with bacon, red peppers and butter). A string of popular places along Bolívar west of the plaza do *lomitos* (steak sandwiches), sandwiches and other cheap eats.

★La Tradicional Rueda PARRILLA $$
(La Ruedita; cnr Arrechea & Av Costanera; mains AR$140-200; 11am-3:30pm & 8pm-midnight;) Stylish and traditional in feel, with uniformed waiters and sturdy wooden seats, this two-level grillhouse has a prime riverside position: look for the wooden wheel outside. There's excellent service; quality meats and nice lines in salads and river fish put this a class above most *parrilla* places. If you go for *galeto,* make sure to get it encrusted with Parmesan.

La Querencia PARRILLA $$
(www.laquerenciarestaurante.com; Bolívar 1867; meals AR$290; noon-2:30pm & 8pm-12:30am Mon-Sat, noon-2:30pm Sun;) On the plaza, this upmarket *parrilla* specializes in delicious *galeto.* Also memorable are the brochettes (giant spikes with various delicious meats impaled upon them). Salads are also unusually well prepared. Service is great and the atmosphere a highlight.

Astillero ARGENTINE $$
(Av Costanera s/n; mains AR$180-220; noon-2pm & 8pm-midnight;) Tucked away behind foliage on the riverbank strip, this has a treehouse feel with three levels and a balcony with limited Paraná vistas. The food is a bit up-and-down but the setting is romantic and the menu has potential. The wine list is full of good things.

La Nouvelle Vitrage CAFE
(Bolívar 1899; 6am-1am;) This traditional, amiable cafe on the plaza has a comfy interior and a terrace perfect for watching everyday life in Posadas go by. It serves an excellent Fernet and cola: you know you want one.

Shopping

Fundación Artesanías Misioneras GALLERY
(www.famercosur.com.ar; cnr Álvarez & Arrechea; 8:30am-noon & 5-8pm Mon-Fri, 9:30am-12:30pm Sat) Guaraní culture is strong in this part of Argentina; particularly fine indigenous crafts are displayed and sold here. There's another branch on the *costanera* near the train station, which is open in the evenings and on weekends when the main branch is closed.

Information

Misiones Tourist Office (☎0376-444-7539; www.misiones.tur.ar; Colón 1985; 7am-8pm) There are other tourist kiosks around town, but this is the most efficient.

Paraguayan Consulate (☎0376-442-3858; http://paraguay.int.ar; San Lorenzo 1561; 7am-2pm Mon-Fri) A single-entry visa (US$65, but US$160 for Americans) from the Paraguayan consulate in Posadas can be ready

Posadas

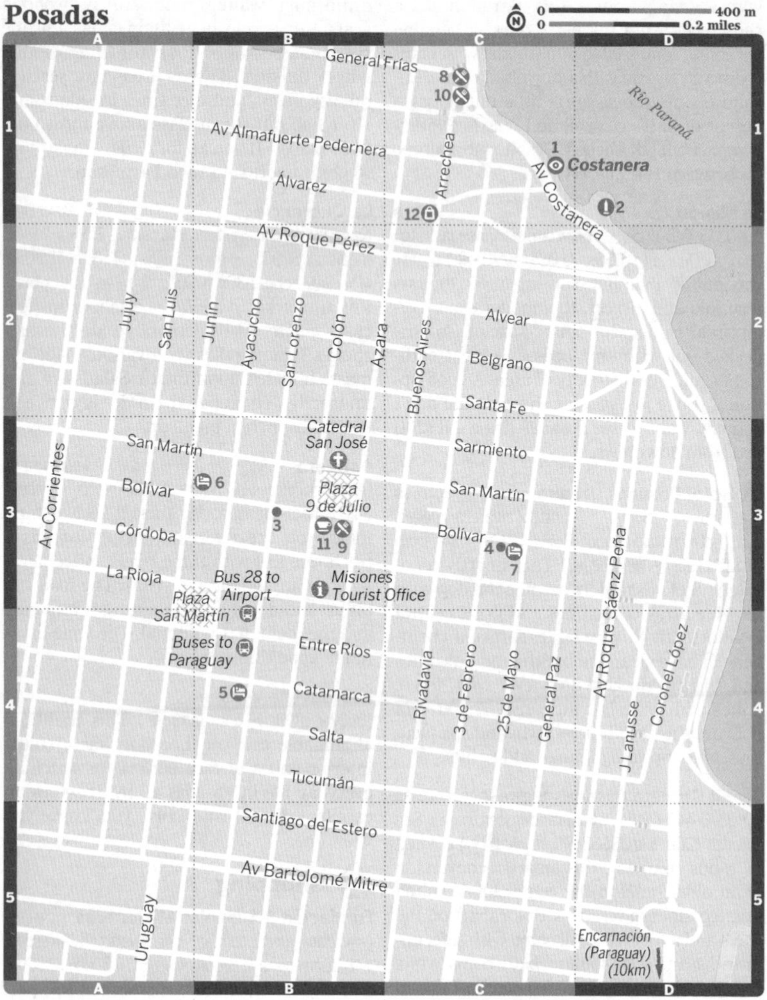

Posadas

Top Sights
1 Costanera C1

Sights
2 Andresito statue D1

Activities, Courses & Tours
Guayrá .... (see 5)
3 Misión Paraná B3
4 Yacaré Tours C3

Sleeping
5 Grand Crucero Posadas Express B4
6 Hotel Posadas Urbano B3
7 Posadeña Linda C3

Eating
8 Astillero C1
9 La Querencia B3
10 La Tradicional Rueda C1

Drinking & Nightlife
11 La Nouvelle Vitrage B3

Shopping
12 Fundación Artesanías Misioneras C1

in around two hours if they're not busy. You'll need two passport photos, a copy of your passport, plus possibly proof of an onward ticket and sufficient funds (a credit card may do).

Getting There & Away

AIR

Aerolíneas Argentinas (0810-222-86527; Sarmiento 2280; 8am-noon & 4-8pm Mon-Fri, 8am-noon Sat) flies daily to Buenos Aires.

BUS

Buses to Encarnación (AR$22), Paraguay, leave every 20 minutes, stopping at the corner of San Lorenzo and Entre Ríos. With queues and border formalities, the trip can take more than an hour.

Everyone gets out to clear Argentine emigration. If the bus leaves without you, keep your ticket and catch the next one. The same happens on the Paraguayan side. There are fairly honest moneychangers hanging out by Paraguayan immigration. Get small denominations: a 100,000 guaraní note is hell to change.

TRAIN

Buses from Posadas

DESTINATION	COST (AR$)	TIME (HR)
Buenos Aires	1188	12-14
Corrientes	375	4-4½
Paso de los Libres	417	5-6
Puerto Iguazú	360	4½-5½
Resistencia	400	4½-5
Rosario	1215	14-15
San Ignacio	65	1
Tucumán	1683	15

A shiny modern rail service connects Posadas and Encarnación in Paraguay, leaving Posadas every 30 minutes from 7:15am to 6:15pm (AR$35, eight minutes). You clear both Argentine and Paraguayan authorities at the **Apeadero Posadas station** (www.sofse.gob.ar).

Getting Around

Posadas' bus terminal is 5km south of town and can be reached from downtown by bus 8, 15 (from Junín), 21 or 24 (AR$12). It costs about AR$150 in a taxi. From the bus terminal, catch local buses out in front or from the adjacent metropolitan terminal.

Bus 28 (AR$12) goes to the airport from San Lorenzo (between La Rioja and Entre Ríos). A *remise* costs around AR$250.

Buses 7 and 12 (AR$12) go to the Apeadero Posadas station.

San Ignacio

0376 / POP 6800

The best preserved of the Argentine missions, San Ignacio Miní is the central attraction of this small town north of Posadas. You could visit from Posadas or on your way to Iguazú, but making this a stopover appeals: there are some decent places to stay, and you'll have a chance to check out the excellent sound-and-light show at the ruins. San Ignacio is a good base for visiting other mission ruins, both in Argentina and Paraguay.

San Ignacio is 56km northeast of Posadas via RN 12. From the highway junction, Av Sarmiento leads 1km to the town center, where Rivadavia leads six blocks north to the ruins.

Sights & Activities

★**San Ignacio Miní** RUINS

(www.misiones.tur.ar; entrance Alberdi s/n; combined missions ticket foreigners/Latin Americans/Argentines AR$200/170/130; 7am-5:30pm Apr-Oct, 7am-7pm Nov-Mar) These mission ruins are the most complete of those in Argentina: atmospheric and impressive for the quantity of carved ornamentation still visible and for the amount of restoration. There's a small museum and the ruins themselves feature interactive panels providing multilingual audio (although not all are in operation). Admission includes entry to nearby ruins at Santa Ana (p192) and Loreto (p192) and to **Santa María la Mayor** (RP 2, Km 43; combined missions ticket foreigners/Latin Americans/Argentines AR$200/170/130; 7am-5:30pm Apr-Oct, 7am-7pm Nov-Mar) further afield. There's a worthwhile sound-and-light show (foreigners AR$200) at the ruins every nonrainy night.

Founded in 1610 in Brazil, but abandoned after repeated slaver attacks, San Ignacio was established here in 1696 and functioned until the Jesuit expulsion. The ruins, rediscovered in 1897 and restored between 1940 and 1948, are a great example of 'Guaraní baroque.' At its peak, the settlement had a Guaraní population of nearly 4000.

There are free guided tours (in English and Spanish) of the ruins which leave once a group builds up – usually every half hour or so. You pass between rows of Guaraní houses before arriving at the **plaza**, on one side of which is the enormous red sandstone **church**. Impressive in its dimensions, it is

WORTH A TRIP

VISITING THE PARAGUAYAN MISSIONS

From Posadas (or San Ignacio) there's a very rewarding day trip to two Jesuit missions in Paraguay. The ruined but majestic churches at Trinidad and Jesús de Tavarangüe have been carefully restored and preserve fabulous stonework.

From Posadas, bus or train it to Encarnación. From the bus terminal (buses stop here, or bus here from the Encarnación train station; G2500), buses (most marked Ciudad del Este) run roughly half-hourly to Trinidad (G10,000, 50 to 60 minutes). Get the driver to let you off at the turnoff to the ruins; it's then a 700m walk.

The **Trinidad ruins** (Trinidad, Paraguay; combined mission ticket G25,000; ⏲7am-9pm) are spectacular, with the church's red-brown stone contrasting strongly with the flower-studded green grass and surrounding hillscapes. There is much decoration preserved: scalloped niches still hold timeworn sculptures, and the font and elaborate baroque pulpit are impressive. Doorways are capped with fine carved decoration. An earlier church and bell tower have also been restored. There's a hotel and restaurant by the ruins.

Walk back to the main road and turn right. At the gas station 200m along is the turnoff to Jesús de Tavarangüe, 12km away. Shared taxis (G7500) wait here to fill, but during the day there's usually little traffic, and buses pass every two hours. You can get a taxi to take you, wait for you and bring you back to the turnoff for about G50,000 to G60,000.

The restored church at **Jesús** (Paraguay; combined mission ticket G25,000; ⏲7am-7pm Apr-Sep, 7am-6pm Oct-Mar) was never finished. It boasts spectacular trefoil arches (a nod to Spain's Moorish past) and carved motifs of crossed swords and keys. The treble-naved church with green grass underfoot is on a similarly monumental scale as Trinidad and is the most complete structure of any of the Jesuit churches. However, perhaps because it was never used, it lacks decoration and feels less atmospheric than the ragged church at Trinidad. Entry includes a free guided tour in Spanish, German and a bit of English. If you take the tour you are permitted to climb the tower for views of the surrounding countryside.

Back on the main road, Encarnación-bound buses stop by the gas station. From Encarnación, Posadas-bound buses stop outside the bus terminal, opposite the school.

A joint ticket for the main Paraguayan ruins at Trinidad, Jesús and San Cosme (southwest of Encarnación) is G25,000; it's valid for three days.

Some nationalities need a visa to enter Paraguay (check before you go). A single-entry visa (US$65, but US$160 for Americans) from the Paraguayan consulate in Posadas (p187) can be ready in about an hour. You'll need two passport photos, a copy of your credit card or similar proof of funds.

Things on the Paraguayan side of the border are pretty relaxed so you could try remaining on the bus and going through without stamping in. While you risk a fine if caught, when we visited the fine was significantly less than the visa fee!

You can also visit the ruins from San Ignacio: get the bus to Corpus, then cross to Paraguay on the ferry (8am to 5pm Monday to Friday).

Tour operators in both Posadas and San Ignacio offer day trips to the Paraguayan ruins.

the focal point of the settlement. While the red-brown stone picturesquely contrasts with the green grass, the buildings were originally white. Before lime was available, it was obtained by burning snail shells.

Check out the **Cotiguazú** on the far corner of the site beside the graveyard where widows and women whose husbands had left the mission were secluded along with adulterous females and spent their time spinning wool.

The small **museum** has panels providing unbiased information (in Spanish with small print English translations to one side) about the missions from both Jesuit and Guaraní perspectives, in addition to some finely detailed wood and stonework found among the ruins. There's a scale model of San Ignacio as it would have been at its peak.

Times for the nightly **show** vary according to the number of groups. It's a touching, at times haunting, experience played out in various locations using projections onto a mist of water spray, giving a ghost-like quality. Headsets offer a variety of languages.

Casa de Horacio Quiroga MUSEUM
(Av Quiroga s/n; AR$100; ⊙10am-6pm) Uruguayan writer Horacio Quiroga was a get-back-to-nature type who found his muse in the rough-and-ready Misiones backwoods lifestyle. He built his simple stone house at the southern end of town (a 30-minute walk) himself. Spanish-speaking guides will lead you through the sugarcane fields to the house and inform you about Quiroga's deeply tragic life, so full of shotgun accidents and doses of cyanide it almost seems to be out of the movies.

Parque Provincial Teyú Cuaré OUTDOORS
FREE Head down to this protected peninsula on the Río Paraná for forest walking – there are three marked interpretive trails – and cycling, views from riverside clifftops and beaches. There are several small Guaraní settlements that welcome visitors and sell handicrafts. A local will show you around for a fee or tip.

There is a dedicated zone on the peninsula where you can pitch a tent for free.

Another chunk of wilderness just outside the park boundaries, the Reserva Natural Osusunú is managed by the Fundación Temaikèn, which is working with the local indigenous communities to develop ecotourism here.

Tours

★Tierra Colorada TOURS
(☎0376-437-3448; tierracoloradaturismo@gmail.com; RN 12; ⊙8am-8:30pm Mon-Sat, 9am-4pm Sun) This all-round helpful operator just below the bus terminal runs tours to the Paraguayan missions (US$60 per person) and Moconá Falls (AR$6000 for up to four people), plus good-value packages to Los Esteros del Iberá. It also hires bikes (per day AR$150), arranges river kayaking and visits to Guaraní settlements, sells discount bus tickets and provides impartial tourist information.

Sleeping & Eating

Adventure Hostel HOSTEL $
(☎0376-447-0955; www.sihostel.com; Independencia 469; dm US$10-12, d US$40, campsites per person US$7; P❄@🛜≋) This well-run, motivated place has comfortable dorms with either three beds or four bunk-berths, decent private rooms with renovated bathrooms, and excellent facilities. Added perks include pool (both kinds), ping-pong and spacious grounds. Tasty homemade breakfasts are included. The restaurant does decent pasta-pizza-type meals; there are also powered campsites.

It's next to the plaza, two blocks south of the church.

Posada Madre America GUESTHOUSE $
(☎0376-447-0778; Sarmiento 605; s/d/tr US$38/44/50, dm/s/d without bathroom US$12/16/32) Right in the middle of town, this welcoming new place has spacious but sparsely decorated hotel rooms with spotless bathrooms and cheaper hostel rooms with shared facilities. There's good fast wi-fi throughout and the staff are very obliging. It's set back from the road so is fairly tranquil.

Hotel La Toscana HOTEL $
(☎0376-447-0777; www.hotellatoscana.com.ar; cnr H Irigoyen & Uruguay; s/d/tr/q US$29/38/41/44; P❄🛜≋) In a less developed part of town half a block from the highway, this simple, welcoming Italian-run place is a relaxing retreat indeed. Cool, spacious, basic rooms surround a great pool, deck and garden area. It's a top spot to relax and offers excellent value although the distant highway noise somewhat dampens the tranquil vibe. Plans are afoot to add an on-site restaurant.

La Misionerita ARGENTINE $$
(☎0376-437-6220; RN 12; mains AR$150-280; ⊙5am-midnight; 🛜) On the highway opposite the town entrance, this has impressive opening hours, friendly service and a decent range of burgers, *milanesas* and the like, along with grill options and river fish. One of the few evening options.

Information

Tourist Office (⊙7am-9pm) At the highway junction. Not very useful.

Getting There & Away

The bus terminal is on the main road near the town entrance. Services between Posadas (AR$65, one hour) and Puerto Iguazú (AR$220, four to five hours) are frequent.

Buses leave four times a day to El Soberbio (AR$200, four hours) near the Saltos de Moconá.

Local buses to Loreto and Santa Ana leave every hour on weekdays and every two hours on Saturday from the bus terminal. In the other direction they run up to Corpus which has a ferry connection to Paraguay.

Getting Around

A local urban bus service runs down to Parque Provincial Teyú Cuaré passing close to the Casa de Horacio Quiroga, but it's very infrequent.

A free bicycle scheme run by the municipal government is located on the west side of the ruins but is more often than not closed. Ask your hotel to call in advance.

Santa Ana & Loreto

Atmospherically decaying in the humid forest, these two Jesuit missions are both off RN 12, between Posadas and San Ignacio.

Admission for both is via a combined missions ticket that includes San Ignacio Miní (p189) and Santa María la Mayor (p189). Both sites have small museums with models of how the missions once looked and some pieces unearthed around the locations. Guided tours – sometimes in English – are included in the admission price.

Sights

Santa Ana RUINS

(www.misiones.tur.ar; combined missions ticket foreigners/Mercosur/Argentines AR$200/170/130; 7am-6pm Apr-Oct, 7am-7pm Nov-Mar) At Santa Ana, which was founded in 1633 but moved here in 1660, dense forest has been partially removed to reveal a settlement that had over 7000 Guaraní inhabitants at its peak. The enormous 140-sq-meter plaza attests to its importance. The muscular church's thick walls and surrounding photogenic strangler figs lend a dramatic effect to what must have been a magnificent building, though none of its decorative embellishments remain. The cemetery, used into the latter half of the 20th century, is now neglected.

Nuestra Señora de Loreto RUINS

(www.misiones.tur.ar; combined missions ticket foreigners/Mercosur/Argentines AR$200/170/130; 7am-5:30pm Apr-Oct, 7am-7pm Nov-Mar) Loreto, founded in 1632, has few visible remains but is atmospheric. There are plans for further excavation and restoration, but for now the jungle is king here and for the most part it's difficult to interpret the tumbled mossy stones among the trees, so the free guided tour is worthwhile. It was one of the more important missions; a printing press was built here, the first in the southern part of the continent.

Getting There & Away

Regular buses heading north from Posadas or south from San Ignacio stop at the turnoffs on RN 12 for both sites. Santa Ana's is at Km 1382.5, from where it's a 700m walk to the ruins. Loreto's is at Km 1389, with a 2.5km walk. It can be intensely hot, so take plenty of water.

From San Ignacio, a local bus (AR$15 to Loreto, AR$20 to Santa Ana) leaves hourly from 8am to noon and 3pm to 7pm weekdays and every two hours on Saturday, calling right beside the Loreto ruins and then at the Santa Ana intersection. This makes it easy to see both in a day trip from San Ignacio. You can get a *remise* from San Ignacio to take you to both, including waiting time, for about AR$800.

If you don't have private transportation a good option is busing it to Santa Ana first where you'll find **Remises Castro** (0376-449-7317; RN 12) right by the bus stop, whose drivers will take you to both ruins and back to the bus stop for AR$250 including waiting time.

Tierra Colorada (p191) in San Ignacio offers transport to both missions plus a visit to Parque Provincial Tayú Cuaré for AR$350 per visitor (two-client minimum).

Saltos del Moconá

Like Iguazú, the remote and unusual Saltos del Moconá at Misiones' eastern edge also live long in the memory. A geological fault in the bed of the Río Uruguay divides the river lengthwise and water spills over the shelf between the two sections, creating a waterfall some 3km long and up to 15m high, depending on the water level.

The falls aren't always visible; if the river is high, you're out of luck.

The gateway to the falls is El Soberbio, an interesting town that is a service center for a lush agricultural area growing tobacco, citronella and manioc. It has a short, pretty riverfront with views across the Río Uruguay. There's a ferry crossing to Brazil, and blond heads are everywhere, a legacy of German and Eastern European immigrants joining the native Guaraní population. Oxcarts are still commonly used for transportation.

Sights

Parque Provincial Moconá PARK

(http://saltosdelmocona.tur.ar; RP 2; foreigners/Argentines AR$30/15; 9am-5:30pm) At the end of the road from El Soberbio you cross the Río Yabotí and arrive in the Parque Provincial Moconá. There's a visitors center, walking trails and a restaurant. Boat trips (AR$250) are essential if you want to get a good look at the falls as they flow from the Argentine side of the river toward Brazil; from land here you are just able to see the top where the water drops off. January to March is normally the best time to visit.

The park website tells you the visible height of the falls; it's crucial to check before coming. When water levels are high the Yabotí may be impassable.

For good views of the upper Río Uruguay hike the 1.8km **El Chachi trail**. The shorter but more challenging **La Gruta trail** leads to a small cave with a narrow waterfall.

Sleeping & Eating

Posada Guatambú CABAÑAS **$**
(03756-434725; RP 2, Km 35; cabins US$67; P) Two sweet, roomy cabins make for a romantic retreat at this spot 3km off the road midway between El Soberbio and the falls. It's a spectacular property, with ample forested grounds and a river to bathe in. Hosts are engaged and welcoming, and provide tasty home-style meals.

Puro Moconá Lodge LODGE **$**
(www.puromocona.com.ar; Av Corrientes 1000, El Soberbio; s/d/tr US$56/68/100, ste from US$91) Located on the edge of Soberbio just a short walk from the bus station, this appealing lodge combines easy access with a peaceful riverside location. The ample grounds make it feel quite remote and there are all kinds of activities for guests. *Cabañas* are spacious and comfortable with elegant dark-wood furniture. Go for a suite with a balcony.

The attractive on-site restaurant with river views is a fine place to dine.

Don Enrique Lodge LODGE **$$$**
(011-15-5932-6262; www.donenriquelodge.com.ar; Colonia La Flor; r US$212; P) Beautiful wooden bungalows in a very remote location with the river below make for a romantic getaway. Delicious food and welcoming hosts seal the deal. The rate is for full board, with guided walks and other activities included. The turnoff is 16km from El Soberbio, then another 16km up a rough road. A pickup will take you the last stretch.

Information

Oficina de Turismo (03755-495206; cnr Avs San Martín & Rivadavia, El Soberbio; 8am-8pm) The friendly tourism office in El Soberbio can help sort out logistics for a trip to the falls.

Getting There & Away

The falls are roughly equidistant from Posadas and Puerto Iguazú. They are best accessed by public transportation from Posadas or San Ignacio.

From Posadas, several daily buses leave for El Soberbio (AR$200, five hours), calling at San Ignacio on the way. From El Soberbio it's 63km to the falls. There is just one daily bus service (AR$90, one hour) on this road, leaving El Soberbio at 8am and returning at 5pm, so plan on spending the whole day in the park.

A *remise* from Soberbio to the falls with waiting time costs AR$1300.

IGUAZÚ FALLS

One of the planet's most awe-inspiring sights, the Iguazú Falls are simply astounding. A visit is a jaw-dropping, visceral experience, and the power and noise of the cascades – a chain of hundreds of waterfalls nearly 3km in extension – live forever in the memory. An added benefit is the setting: the falls lie split between Brazil and Argentina in a large expanse of national park, much of it rainforest teeming with unique flora and fauna.

The falls are easily reached from either side of the Argentine–Brazilian border, as well as from nearby Paraguay.

History

According to Guaraní tradition, the falls originated when a warrior named Caroba incurred the wrath of a forest god by escaping downriver in a canoe with a young girl, Naipur, with whom the god was infatuated. Enraged, the god caused the riverbed to collapse in front of the lovers, producing a line of precipitous falls over which Naipur fell and, at their base, turned into a rock. Caroba survived as a tree overlooking it.

Geologists have a more prosaic version. The Río Iguazú's course takes it over a basaltic plateau that ends abruptly just short of the confluence with the Paraná. Where the lava flow stopped, thousands of cubic meters of water per second now plunge down as much as 80m into sedimentary

Iguazu Falls

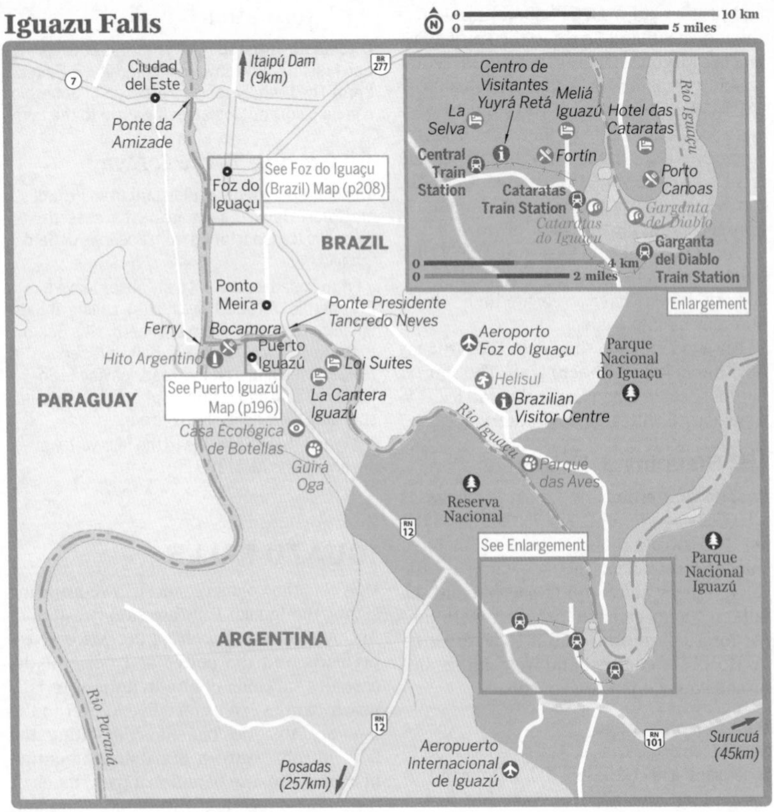

terrain below. Before reaching the falls, the river divides into many channels with rocks and islands separating the many distinct cascades that together form the famous 2.7km-long *cataratas* (waterfalls).

Seeing the Falls

The Brazilian and Argentine sides offer different views and experiences. Go to both (perhaps to the Brazilian first for the grand first impression) and hope for sun. The difference between a clear and an overcast day at the falls is vast: ideally plan a multiple-day stay to have a better shot at optimal conditions.

While the Argentine side, with its variety of trails and boat rides, offers many more opportunities to see individual falls close up, the Brazilian side yields the more panoramic views. You can easily make day trips to both sides of the falls, no matter which side of the border you base yourself on. Some choose to see both sides in one day, but it's a rush and not recommended.

National Parks

Both the Argentine and Brazilian sides of the falls are national parks: Parque Nacional Iguazú and Parque Nacional do Iguaçu, respectively. High temperatures, humidity and rainfall encourage a diverse habitat: the parks' rainforest contains more than 2000 identified plant species, countless insects, 400 species of birds, and many mammals and reptiles.

The Iguazú forests consist of multiple levels, the highest a 30m canopy. Beneath are several additional levels of trees, plus a dense ground-level growth of shrubs and herbaceous plants.

Pumas, jaguars and tapirs all reside in the parks, but you won't see them. Most common is the coati, a relative of the raccoon, and capuchin monkeys. Iguanas are common, and watch out for snakes.

Tropical bird species add color, with toucans and various parrot species easily seen. The best time to see birds is early morning along the forest trails.

Despite regular official denials, the heavy impact of so many visitors to the area has clearly driven much of the wildlife further into the parks, so the more you explore the region away from the falls themselves, the more you'll see.

Safe Travel

River currents are strong and swift; tourists have been swept downriver and drowned. Of course, don't get too close to the falls proper.

Heat and humidity are often intense and there's plenty of hungry insect life, so pack sunscreen and repellent. Take your own water.

On both sides, you'll encounter coatis. Keep food well away from them; though these clownish omnivores seem tame, they become aggressive around food and will bite and scratch to rob you of it. Both parks have medical points in case of coati attack.

You are likely to get soaked, or at least very damp, from the spray at the falls, so keep documents and cameras protected in plastic bags. You can buy plastic ponchos on both sides.

Stamps for sale on the Argentine side of the park cannot be posted anywhere but in the park itself or large cities.

Puerto Iguazú

03757 / POP 94,994

At the end of the road in Argentina, Puerto Iguazú sits at the confluence of the Ríos Paraná and Iguazú and looks across to Brazil and Paraguay. There's little feeling of community: everyone is here to see the falls or to make a buck out of them, and planning laws seem nonexistent as hotels go up on every street. Still, it's not unattractive and is quiet, safe and has good transportation connections; there are also many excellent places to stay and eat.

Sights & Activities

Hito Argentino VIEWPOINT

(Map p194; Av Tres Fronteras) FREE A kilometer west of the center, this is a great viewpoint with a small obelisk painted in Argentine colors at the impressive confluence of the Ríos Paraná and Iguazú. From here you can see Brazil and Paraguay, with similar markers on their sides. It's usually pretty empty during the day but gets busy in the evening when visitors descend to watch the light show at 7:30pm which features colorful fountains and hologram like videos of folk dancers projected onto the mist.

Güirá Oga ANIMAL SANCTUARY

(Map p194; www.guiraoga.com.ar; RN 12, Km 5; adult/child AR$200/150; 9am-6pm, last entry 5pm) On the way to the falls, this is an animal hospital and center for rehabilitation of injured wildlife. It also carries out valuable research into the Iguazú forest environment and has a breeding program for endangered species. You get walked around the jungly 20-hectare park by one of the staff, who explains about the birds and animals and the sad stories of how they got there. The visit takes about 90 minutes.

Casa Ecológica de Botellas ARCHITECTURE

(Map p194; http://lacasadebotellas.googlepages.com; RN 12, Km 5; AR$100; 9am-6:30pm) About 300m off the falls road, this fascinating place is well worth a visit. The owners have taken used packaging materials – plastic bottles, juice cartons and the like – to build not only an impressive house, but furnishings and a bunch of original handicrafts that make unusual gifts. The guided visit talks you through their techniques.

Tours

Numerous local operators offer day tours to the Brazilian side of the Iguazú Falls, some taking in the Itaipú dam and Paraguay shopping as well. Many have offices at the bus terminal. At the port, there are various options for boat trips around the junction of the Paraná and Iguazú rivers. Boats leave every 30 minutes during peak periods. Expect to pay around AR$150 for a one-hour cruise in a small boat.

Iguazú Bike Tours CYCLING

(03757-15-678220; www.iguazubiketours.com.ar) These guys run anything from gentle jaunts through the nearby forest to long vehicle-supported rides through the less-visited corners of Parque Nacional Iguazú.

Sleeping

There are numerous sleeping options for all budgets, including a string of resort-type hotels between the town and Parque Nacional Iguazú and lots of cabin accommodations south of this road. In the streets around the bus terminal are many hostels. Many places don't accept credit cards or may add a hefty surcharge.

Puerto Iguazú

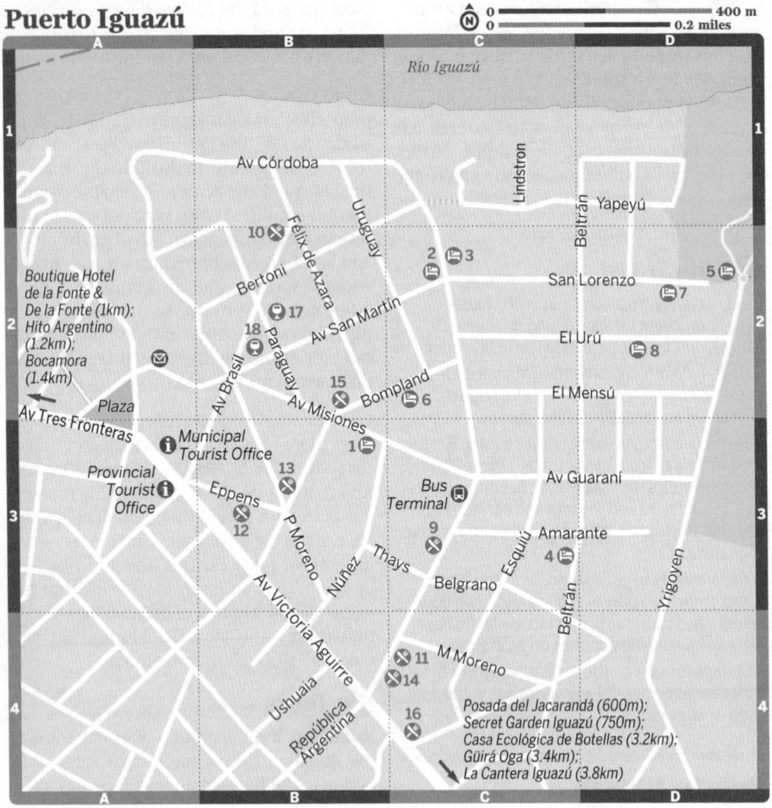

Puerto Iguazú

Sleeping

1 125 Hotel B3
2 Bambú Hostel C2
3 Hotel La Sorgente C2
4 Hotel Lilian C3
5 Iguazú Jungle Lodge D2
6 Jardín de Iguazú C2
7 Jasy Hotel D2
8 Porämbá Hostel D2

Eating

9 Color C3
10 Feria B2
11 La Dama Juana C4
12 La Misionera B3
13 La Misionera Casa de Empanada B3
14 La Rueda C4
15 Lemongrass B2
16 Tatu Carreta C4
Terra .... (see 1)
Trattoria La Toscana .... (see 3)

Drinking & Nightlife

17 Cuba Libre B2
18 Quita Penas B2

125 Hotel HOSTEL $
(Map p196; 03757-422346; Misiones 125; dm/d US$16/35;) With a fine location, a social vibe and friendly staff, this hostel is a decent budget base. Private rooms are a bit poky but they're modern, clean and good value. Dorms are some of the best in town, with each bunk sectioned off by curtains, and the shared bathrooms are well maintained. Has a good pool area.

Porämbá Hostel HOSTEL $
(Map p196; 03757-423041; www.porambahostel.com; El Urú 120; dm US$10-11, r/tr US$34/40;

) In a very peaceful location but an easy walk from the bus terminal, this is a popular choice for its variety of noncrowded dorms, private rooms with or without bathroom and small pool. It's a chilled place with a kitchen and a super laid-back atmosphere.

Hotel Lilian HOTEL $
(Map p196; 03757-420968; hotellilian@gmail.com; Beltrán 183; s US$42, standard/superior d US$47/59, q US$106;) Run by a hospitable family which isn't out to rip off tourists, this friendly place offers plenty of value, with decent rooms around a couple of plant-filled patios. Most superiors – worth the small extra outlay – have a balcony and heaps of natural light. All bathrooms are spacious and spotless. Things get done the way they should here.

Bambú Hostel HOSTEL $
(Map p196; 03757-425864; www.hostelbambu.com.ar; cnr Avs San Martín & Córdoba; dm US$16, r with/without bathroom US$50/56) A popular choice close to the bus station, this well-run hostel has friendly staff and a social vibe. Accommodations are just OK for the price: private rooms are comfortable but fairly plain and the dorms are a bit tight for space. However, there's an excellent, loungey street-side bar that is the perfect place to hang out in the evenings.

★**Boutique Hotel de la Fonte** HOTEL $$
(03757-420625; www.bhfboutiquehotel.com; cnr Corrientes & 1 de Mayo; r from US$142;) The mark of a good hotel is constant improvement, and this place adds great features so fast we can barely keep up. It's a secluded, enchanting spot, featuring characterful, individually decorated rooms and suites around a tree-filled courtyard garden that is romantically lit at night. One of the welcoming owners is an architect, and it shows in the numerous small decorative touches and artistic design.

Outdoor hot tubs, a saltwater pool and all-over style and elegance are other attractive features. The other owner is a chef who runs the town's best restaurant on-site, so you're in luck there too. A standout.

★**Jasy Hotel** HOTEL $$
(Map p196; 03757-424337; www.jasyhotel.com; San Lorenzo 154; d/q US$95/110;) Original and peaceful, these 10 two-level rooms, with a great design for family sleeping, climb a hill like a forest staircase and are all equipped with a balcony gazing over plentiful greenery. Artful use of wood is the signature; you'll fall in love with the bar and deck area. Prepare to stay longer than planned. There's a decent restaurant open evenings.

Secret Garden Iguazú B&B $$
(03757-423099, 03757-539571; www.secretgardeniguazu.com; Los Lapachos 623; s/d US$95/125;) Down the back of a garden full of birds and greenery is a bungalow with three spacious, enchanting rooms at this welcoming off-track B&B. Crosscut timber furniture and well-selected nature prints make for a relaxing environment. Breakfast and afternoon tea are standout moments, featuring homemade jams, chutneys and banana bread. Both host and staff are helpful, making this a fabulously personalized stay.

Posada del Jacarandá HOTEL $$
(03757-423737; www.posadadeljacaranda.com; cnr Andresito & Caraguatá; r US$90;) Harmonious rooms, a terrific attitude toward guests, gleaming polished floors and a peaceful ambience make this a worthwhile midrange choice in the quiet streets to the southeast of town. There's a pretty pool area, above-average breakfast and attractive use of wood throughout. More than the sum of its parts.

Jardín de Iguazú HOTEL $$
(Map p196; 03757-424171; www.jardindeiguazu.com.ar; Bompland 274; s/d US$108/118;) Appealing for its handy central location, professional staff, pleasant pool and Jacuzzi, and comfortably bland modern rooms. The standards aren't super-spacious, so if that's important to you, upgrade to a superior, which costs very little extra. Reliable and well-run.

Hotel La Sorgente HOTEL $$
(Map p196; 03757-424252; www.lasorgentehotel.com; Av Córdoba 454; s/d/tr US$71/97/115;) Life couldn't be easier at this hotel, set around a verdant garden – if you can't face the long walk around the pool, take the bridge across it. Attractively remodeled and spacious, if a little dark, rooms surround it. Breakfast, served in the authentic Italian restaurant, gets the seal of approval, too. The only downside is the tiny showers.

★**La Cantera Iguazú** LODGE $$$
(Map p194; 03757-493016; www.hotellacanteraiguazu.com; Selva Iryapú s/n; r US$164-272;

P❄@🛜≋) Nestled in forest 1.5km off the falls road, this intimate lodge has appealing 'tierra' rooms with mosquito-proof balconies in wooden buildings, some with trees growing through them. Upper-level 'jungle' rooms offer better views and have hammocks. Cheaper 'forest' rooms are less rustic, while harmonious wooden 'villa' rooms sleep four and have balcony Jacuzzis. Good pool area and excellent service.

A series of wireless routers deliver high-speed internet throughout the property. A forest walk with a Guaraní guide is included and transportation service to both sides of the falls can be organized.

Loi Suites RESORT **$$$**
(☎03757-498300; www.loisuites.com.ar; Selva Iryapú s/n; r US$314-440; P❄@🛜≋) Spectacularly set in the jungle, yet just a few kilometers from town, this giant complex has several buildings connected by walkways. It's decorated in a relaxed country style and features a huge tree-surrounded, triple-pool area as its highlight. Rooms are spacious and comfortable; upgrade to a balcony for bird watching opportunities. There's a spa complex too. Online prices are usually lower.

Iguazú Jungle Lodge HOTEL **$$$**
(Map p196; ☎03757-420600; www.iguazujungle lodge.com; cnr Yrigoyen & San Lorenzo; r/f US$210/301; P❄🛜≋) A little corporate in feel, but with a secluded ambience, considering its comparatively central location, this hotel offers spacious, well-equipped accommodations with quality beds and jungle balconies in a resort-style complex surrounding a large pool. Some come with lounge and kitchen. Staff are multilingual and very helpful. It's a great option for families, with a games room and suites. Good on-site restaurant.

Eating

★Feria MARKET **$**
(Feirinha; Map p196; cnr Av Brasil & Félix de Azara; picadas for 2 AR$200-225; ⏲8am-midnight) A really nice place to eat or have a beer is this market in the north of town. It's full of stalls selling Argentine wines, sausages, olives and cheese to visiting Brazilians, and several of them put out *picadas,* grilled meats, other simple regional dishes and cold beer. There's folk music some nights and a good evening atmosphere.

Lemongrass CAFE **$**
(Map p196; Bompland 231; light meals AR$65-150; ⏲8:30am-2:30pm & 5-9:30pm Mon-Sat; ✎) One of few decent cafes in Puerto Iguazú, this offers good fresh juices, decent coffee, delicious sweet temptations, sandwiches, pizzas and tasty savory tarts. Beers, mint-dependent mojitos and caipirinhas are also available.

La Misionera ARGENTINE **$**
(Map p196; Eppens 227; per 100g AR$22; ⏲11:30am-3pm & 7-11pm Tue-Sat, 7-11pm Sun, 11:30am-3pm Mon) A good budget option in the heart of town, this per-kilo buffet has a small but tasty selection of hot dishes alongside pastas, salads and great vegetable pies. Every time you visit the buffet take the plate to the counter to be weighed and it'll be added to your bill. Staff are very friendly.

La Misionera Casa de Empanada EMPANADAS **$**
(Map p196; ☎03757-424580; P Moreno 228; empanadas AR$20; ⏲11:30am-midnight Mon-Sat) Excellent empanadas with a big variety of fillings, as well as a delivery option.

Tatu Carreta ARGENTINE **$$**
(Map p196; ☎03757-575643; Av Victoria Aguirre 773; mains AR$120-460; ⏲noon-midnight) Located in a big barn-like structure a block away from the main restaurant strip, this popular grill serves up big portions to a mostly Argentine crowd. The outside terrace seating fills up first and is a good place to down some beers and watch the grill masters at work. Make sure to order some of the house special potato skins.

Bocamora ARGENTINE **$$**
(Map p194; ☎03757-420550; www.bocamo ra.com; Av Costanera s/n; mains AR$145-250; ⏲noon-11pm Tue-Sun; 🛜) A romantic location overlooking two rivers and three nations is reason enough to come to this place just down the hill from the Argentine border marker. It specializes in grilled meats and well-prepared plates of river fish; the food is competent, service is very hospitable and the view is just breathtaking.

Color PARRILLA, PIZZA **$$**
(Map p196; ☎03757-420206; www.parrilla pizzacolor.com; Av Córdoba 135; mains AR$175-325, pizza AR$160-285; ⏲11:30am-midnight; 🛜) This popular indoor-outdoor pizza 'n' *parrilla* packs them into its tightly spaced tables, so don't discuss state secrets. Prices are OK for

this strip, and the meat comes out redolent of wood smoke; the wood-oven pizzas and empanadas are also very toothsome. You'll have to wait for a seat during high season, or reserve online.

Terra ASIAN $$
(Map p196; ☑03757-421931; Av Misiones 125; mains AR$145-280; ⊙4pm-midnight; 🖥🍴) Chalked signatures of myriad satisfied customers mark the walls of this chilled bar-restaurant that specializes in wok dishes, with teriyaki salmon, pasta and salads as other options. Dishes are solid rather than spectacular and portions can be a little small, but it remains a good choice if you're looking for some variety. The streetside terrace fills fast.

La Dama Juana ARGENTINE $$
(Map p196; ☑03757-424051; www.facebook.com/ladamajuanaiguazu; Av Córdoba 42; mains AR$240-316; ⊙11:30am-11:30pm; 🖥) Offering a compact interior and pleasant balcony terrace, this is more informal than most of this strip and offers significant value. Service comes with a smile; abundant meat or fish plates with innovative sauces, and colorful salads, make for pleasant dining. While prices for mains are similar to elsewhere, it often has specials and the pastas dishes are well priced.

★ De La Fonte GASTRONOMY, ITALIAN $$$
(☑03757-420625; www.bhfboutiquehotel.com; cnr Corrientes & 1 de Mayo; mains AR$480-550; ⊙7-11:30pm Mon-Sat; 🖥) This exquisite hotel restaurant, domain of a maverick creative talent, is super-strong on presentation, whether homemade pasta or inventive creations with a touch of molecular gastronomy. The imagination on display presents local tropical flavors seamlessly intertwined with prime cuts of carefully sourced fish or meat. The homemade bread is a delight. The degustation menu (AR$1250) showcases great culinary ability: leave room for dessert.

The menu always includes an innovative vegan option. Reservations are essential.

★ La Rueda ARGENTINE $$$
(Map p196; ☑03757-422531; www.larueda1975.com; Av Córdoba 28; mains AR$245-480; ⊙5:30pm-midnight Mon-Tue, from noon Wed-Sun; 🖥) A mainstay of upmarket eating in Puerto Iguazú, this culinary heavyweight still packs a punch. The salads are inventive and delicious, as are the imaginative river-fish (mostly pacú and surubí) creations. Meat with a variety of sauce options is reliably

good; the homemade pasta is cheaper but doesn't disappoint. Service is good but slow. The wine list has a high flagfall.

Trattoria La Toscana ITALIAN $$$
(Map p196; ☑03757-422756; www.trattorialatoscana.com; Córdoba 454; mains AR$216-338; ⊙7-11:30pm) A genuine Italian-run outfit, La Toscana offers delectable homemade pasta, flavorful risotto and a full selection of beef and river fish. Try the pumpkin, cinnamon and pine-nut ravioli. The mix-and-match combination plates (AR$338) featuring steak and pasta are an excellent deal. Reservations are essential.

🍷 Drinking & Nightlife

Quita Penas BAR
(Map p196; ☑03757-458223; Av Brasil 120; ⊙6pm-late) A happening open-air bar in the middle of Puerto Iguazú's little nightlife strip, Quita Pena has an elevated deck and a variety of other spaces below. It serves good food and is a fine place to hit some beers and watch the action. Often has live music.

Cuba Libre CLUB
(Map p196; www.facebook.com/cuba.megadisco; cnr Av Brasil & Paraguay; ⊙11pm-late Wed-Sun) This unsubtle but fun nightclub just off the Av Brasil strip fills up with Brazilians looking for a big night out on the weak peso. The dance floor fills late but fast.

ℹ️ Information

Brazilian Consulate (☑03757-420192; https://scedv.serpro.gov.br; Córdoba 278; ⊙visas 8am-1:30pm Mon-Fri) Visa processing (Australia/USA/other AR$2400/3600/1600) takes 24 to 72 hours so visit as soon as you arrive in town. Apply online first and print out the receipt before visiting the consulate with a bank statement, a photograph with a light background and a ticket out either from Brazil or Argentina.

Hospital (☑03757-420288; cnr Av Victoria Aguirre & Ushuaia)

Macro (cnr Av Misiones & Bompland) Has an ATM.

Municipal Tourist Office (Map p196; ☑03757-423951; www.iguazuturismo.gob.ar; Av Victoria Aguirre 337; ⊙8am-2pm & 4-9pm)

Paraguayan Consulate (☑03757-424230; http://paraguay.int.ar; P Moreno 236; ⊙7am-3pm) Paraguayan visas cost US$65 for most nationalities but US$160 for Americans at the time of research. Visa processing takes three hours, and you'll need your passport, two photos and a copy of your credit card.

Post Office (Map p196; www.correoargentino.com.ar; Av San Martín 384; ⌚8am-1pm & 4-7pm Mon-Fri)

Provincial Tourist Office (Map p196; ☎03757-420800; www.misiones.tur.ar; Av Victoria Aguirre 311; ⌚8am-9pm) The most helpful information office in town.

Currency-exchange places are along Av Victoria Aguirre downtown. If you've got Brazilian reals, you're much better off changing them in Brazil or buying services with them here rather than changing at official rates.

Getting There & Away

Aerolíneas Argentinas (☎03757-420168; www.aerolineas.com.ar; Av Victoria Aguirre 295; ⌚8am-noon & 3-7pm Mon-Fri, 8am-1pm Sat) flies from Iguazú to both Buenos Aires airports, Mendoza via Córdoba or Rosario, Salta and El Calafate (via BA). LAN (www.lan.com) and Andes (www.andesonline.com) also fly the Buenos Aires route.

The **bus terminal** (Map p196; cnr Avs Córdoba & Misiones) has departures for all over the country.

There are many Brazilian domestic services across the border in Foz do Iguaçu. There are a couple of direct buses from Puerto Iguazú to São Paulo and Rio de Janeiro but it's usually cheaper to pick up a service in Foz.

Buses from Puerto Iguazú

DESTINATION	COST (AR$)	TIME (HR)
Buenos Aires	1200-1730	19-10
Córdoba	1295	22
Corrientes	600	9-10
Posadas	250	5-6
Resistencia	700-750	10-11
San Ignacio	220	4-5

Getting Around

Four Tourist Travel (☎03757-420681, 03757-422962; www.ftt.tur.ar) runs an airport shuttle for AR$130 per person that meets most flights; from town, it needs to be booked in advance. A *remise* costs AR$350 to or AR$450 from the airport, which is 25km from town.

Frequent buses cross to Foz do Iguaçu, Brazil (AR$25 or R$5, 40 minutes, every 20 minutes 6:30am to 7:30pm), and to Ciudad del Este, Paraguay (AR$40, one hour, hourly 6:50am to 5:45pm), from the local side of the bus terminal. There are also buses direct to the Brazilian side of the Iguazú Falls (AR$80 return, hourly 8:30am to 2:30pm, last return 5pm), which are inexplicably much cheaper than the bus to the local park.

A taxi to Foz costs around AR$450; to the Brazilian side of the Iguazú Falls it's AR$600 return. Avoid the *remise* office at the bus terminal: it's more expensive than others. Always negotiate. We particularly like the taxi stop on Córdoba opposite El Mensú, which has some knowledgeable multilingual drivers and metered cabs.

Ostensibly air-conditioned local buses cost AR$15 and are useful for reaching hotels and attractions located along the falls road, or the triple frontier marker.

Another option is the hop-on, hop-off double-decker **Bus Turistica** (www.busturisticoiguazu.com.ar; ⌚8:30am-6:30pm) although service is fairly infrequent, which means long stops at the attractions it visits.

Run by the local government, **Eco Bicis** (cnr Av Victoria Aguirre & San Martín; ⌚11am-5pm) offers free bicycle rental near the plaza. For a more solid ride **Jungle Bike** (☎03757-423720; www.junglebike.com.ar; Av Victoria Aguirre 262, Local 7 Galeria Plaza Pueblo; bike hire per hr/day AR$50/200; ⌚9am-8:30pm) offers bikes for hire, as well as guided excursions to rarely visited local nature reserves. Mountain bikes are available for AR$350 to AR$400 per day.

Parque Nacional Iguazú

☎03757

On the Argentine side of the marvelous Iguazú Falls, this **park** (☎03757-491469; www.iguazuargentina.com; adult foreigners/Mercosur/Argentines AR$500/400/260, child AR$130/100/80, parking AR$100; ⌚8am-6pm) has plenty to offer, and involves a fair amount of walking.

The spread-out complex at the entrance has various amenities, including lockers (AR$70-200), two ATMs – you have to pay in cash in pesos – and a restaurant. There's also an exhibition, Yvyrá-retã, with a display on the park and Guaraní life essentially aimed at school groups.

There's enough at the park to detain you for a couple of days; admission is reduced by 50% if you visit the park again the following day. Get your ticket stamped when leaving on the first day to receive the discount.

Last entry is at 4:30pm.

Sights

It really is worth getting here by 9am: the gangways are narrow and getting stuck in a conga line of tour groups in searing heat and humidity takes the edge off the experience.

Three circuits provide the falls viewing via a series of trails, bridges and *pasarelas* (boardwalks).

Close to the Circuito Inferior trailhead, the old park hotel houses a small **falls museum** but it won't hold your attention for long considering what awaits outside.

★Circuito Inferior WATERFALL
This circuit (1400m) descends to the river, passing delightfully close to falls on the way. At the end of the path prepare for a drenching at the hands of **Salto Bossetti** if you're game. Just short of here, a free launch makes the short crossing to Isla San Martín . At the same junction you can buy tickets for the popular boat rides under the falls.

★Circuito Superior WATERFALL
The **Paseo Superior** (1750m) is entirely level and gives good views of the tops of several cascades and across to more. A recently constructed final section crosses a large swath of the Iguazú river, ending above the powerful Salto San Martín before wending its way back across river islands.

Isla San Martín ISLAND
From the end of the **Paseo Inferior**, a free launch takes you across to this island with a trail of its own that gives the closest look at several falls, including Salto San Martín, a huge, furious cauldron of water. It's possible to picnic and paddle on the lee side of the island, but don't venture too far off the beach. When the water is high – and this is the case more often than not – island access is shut off.

A decision is made on access at 10:30am each morning – ask at any of the stations or information points. The last boat across to the island leaves at 3:15pm but it's best to visit early on while you wait for the crowds to dissipate in busier parts of the park.

Garganta del Diablo WATERFALL
A 1.1km walkway across the placid Río Iguazú leads to one of the planet's most spectacular sights, the 'Devil's Throat.' The lookout platform is perched right over this amazingly powerful, concentrated torrent of water, a deafening cascade plunging to an invisible destination; vapors soaking the viewer blur the base of the falls and rise in a smoke-like plume that can be seen several kilometers away. It's a place of majesty and awe, and should be left until the end of your visit.

From Cataratas train station, train it or walk the 2.3km to the Garganta del Diablo stop. The last train to the Garganta leaves at 4pm, and we recommend taking it, as it'll be a somewhat less crowded experience. If you walk, you'll see quite a lot of wildlife around this time of day, too. Another option is to visit at lunchtime, as most organized tours stop to eat for an hour around 1:30pm.

The entire trail is wheelchair acessible.

Activities

Relatively few visitors venture beyond the immediate falls area to appreciate the park's forest scenery and wildlife, but it's well worth doing. On the falls trails you'll see large lizards, coatis, monkeys and birds, but you'll see much more on one of the few trails through the dense forest.

Sendero Macuco WALKING
This 3.5km jungle trail leads through dense forest to a nearly hidden waterfall. It's a rare opportunity to explore the park independently. Six interpretive stations explain the flora, including bamboo, palmitos and pioneer plants. The white-bearded manakin and toco toucan live in these parts, as does a troupe of brown capuchin monkeys.

The trail ends at the **Arrechea waterfall**, a 20m cascade that has gouged out a lovely natural pool below. The first 3km to the top of the waterfall is almost completely level, but there is a steep, muddy drop to the base of the falls and beyond to the Rio Iguaçu, about 650m in all. Figure on about 1¼ hours each way from the trailhead.

You can swim at the base of the waterfall but take care and don't head out into the river. Early morning is best, with better opportunities to see wildlife. Last entry is at 3pm. There's a map-guide available at the information desks.

Tours

Safaris Rainforest JUNGLE TOUR
(☎03757-491074; www.rainforest.iguazuargentina.com) Using knowledgeable guides, this is the best option for appreciating Parque Nacional Iguazú's flora and fauna. It offers combined driving-walking excursions: the Expedición a la Cascada takes you to the Arrechea waterfall (AR$560, 90 minutes); better is the Expedición en la Selva (AR$660, two hours), a trip in a less-touristed part of the park that includes explanations of Guaraní culture.

Groups are small and you don't need the falls admission ticket; morning departures can include hotel pick-up, and afternoon departure includes a transfer back to Puerto Iguazú. Best to book in advance by phone or online but you can also sign up at information booths at the falls.

Iguazú Jungle Explorer BOATING
(☎03757-421696; www.iguazujungle.com) Offers three adventure tours: most popular is the short boat trip leaving from the Paseo Inferior that takes you right under one of the waterfalls for a high-adrenalin soaking (AR$550). The Gran Aventura combines this with a jungle drive (AR$950), while the Paseo Ecológico (AR$300) is a wildlife-oriented tour in inflatable boats upstream from the falls.

Children under 12 are not permitted on the boat ride. Borderline kids will be asked for an identity document.

Full Moon Walks WALKING
(☎03757-491469; www.iguazuargentina.com/en/luna-llena) For five consecutive nights per month, these guided walks visit the Garganta del Diablo (p201). There are three departures nightly. The first, at 8pm, offers the spectacle of the inflated rising moon; the last, at 9:30pm, sees the falls better illuminated. Don't expect wildlife. The price (AR$850) includes admission and a drink; dinner is extra (AR$300). Book in advance as numbers are limited..

Extra buses from Puerto Iguazú cater for moonwalkers. If the weather is bad the tour is postponed to the following night or a refund is offered, so allow some flexibility in your plans.

Sleeping & Eating

There's one hotel within Parque Nacional Iguazú.

Meliá Iguazú HOTEL $$$
(☎03757-491800; www.melia.com; standard r with forest/falls view from US$414/503; P ❄ @ ☜ ≋) With a privileged position within Parque Nacional Iguazú itself and looking right upriver to the Garganta del Diablo, this hotel has spacious rooms with balconies, all recently renovated. The jungle-side view is pretty too. There's a good outdoor pool area, as well as an indoor pool and spa. These rates reflect online reality: rack tariffs are double.

The restaurant has a limited selection of fairly pricey mains. In-room wi-fi costs extra. There's no legal park access after hours. You have to pay one park entrance fee per stay.

La Selva BUFFET $$$
(www.iguazuargentina.com; buffet AR$320; ⊙11am-3:30pm) During your visit, this restaurant, close to the Parque Nacional Iguazú's main entrance, will get talked up so much you'll fear the worst, but it's actually OK, with a buffet of hot and cold dishes that includes *parrillada*. It's pricey but information kiosks give out vouchers offering a substantial discount depending on how busy they are, so head there first.

Information

There are two ATMs on-site, one by the ticket counter and another inside the park gates. If the machine outside is out of service ask one of the staff to accompany you inside. Better still, arrive with enough pesos to avoid any complications.

WORTH A TRIP

MISIONES JUNGLE WITHOUT THE CROWDS

The Iguazú jungle is a fabulous habitat of birds, plants, insects and mammals, but mass tourism at the falls means you're unlikely to see as much wildlife as you might wish. One option for seeing more is to head east to the other end of the park. Around the *mate*-growing town of Andresito are several lodges, including excellent **Surucuá** (☎0376-15-437-1046; www.surucua.com; Andresito; s/d/tr incl transfers & full board US$217/352/480, 2 days US$390/634/864; P ☜ ≋) . Run by a welcoming young Misiones couple, this is right in the jungle. Comfortable rustic accommodations and delicious home-cooked meals featuring local ingredients are supplemented by activities including jungle walks and memorable kayak trips among river islands. It's a birdwatcher's paradise, with over 200 species recorded including trogons, toucans, hummingbirds and manakins. Relaxation is guaranteed with a swimming pool and no mobile coverage, though there is wi-fi. Multinight stays are cheaper. You will be picked up from Andresito, which is served by four daily buses from Puerto Iguazú (AR$150, 2½ hours).

BORDER CROSSINGS: ENTERING BRAZIL

Many nationalities require visas to enter Brazil. At the time of writing, these included citizens of the USA, Australia, Canada and Japan. EU citizens did not. Download the application form at https://scedv.serpro.gov.br and take it to a Brazilian consulate. The one in Puerto Iguazú (p199) will likely be cheaper than in your home country. You'll need a return ticket (from Argentina will do), photo and a bank or credit card statement. While they say it takes 24 to 72 hours to process, if you get there early, it can often be ready by the next working day.

That said, it is usually – but not always – possible to take a day trip by bus to the Brazilian falls without a visa. You'll have to catch the Foz do Iguaçu–bound bus, not the one that goes direct to the Brazilian falls. Argentine officials will stamp you out; stay on the bus when it passes Brazilian immigration and don't blame us if you're out of luck that day. Taxi drivers also may be able to get you through without a visa but not all are willing to risk it. Bear in mind that this isn't officially sanctioned, so if you get caught, you may be fined.

Getting There & Away

Parque Nacional Iguazú is 20km southeast of Puerto Iguazú. From Puerto Iguazú's bus terminal, buses leave every 20 minutes for the park (AR$75, 40 minutes) between 7:20am and 7:20pm, with return trips between 7:50am and 8pm. Three additional late-night return services run when full-moon tours operate. The buses make flag stops along the road.

A taxi from town to the park entrance is AR$300 (AR$550 return).

Getting Around

The park complex ends at a train station, from which a train runs every half-hour to the Cataratas train station, where the waterfall walks begin, and to the Garganta del Diablo. Overcrowding is a serious problem in peak periods and you may have to wait a long while for a spot. Seek out a printed return ticket as soon as you arrive. You may prefer to walk: it's only 650m along the Sendero Verde path to the Cataratas station, and a further 2.3km to the Garganta, and you may well see capuchin monkeys along the way.

To see all the falls involves quite a lot of walking although you'll have many breaks as you gawk at individual cascades, and there are not many strenuous climbs.

Most of the trails are at least 90% wheelchair/pusher accessible; while there are some stairs in parts it's possible to reach all the viewpoints by navigating some of the trails in reverse or using dedicated special access paths.

Parque Nacional do Iguaçu (Brazil)

This Brazilian **park** (☎045-3521-4400; www.cataratasdoiguacu.com.br; adult foreigners/Mercosur/Brazilians R$62/49/36, child R$10; ⏲9am-5pm) is entered via an enormous visitor center with a snack bar, ATMs and lockers (R$19), among other amenities. Parking here costs R$22.

Tickets can be purchased by card or a variety of currencies. All catering outlets take cards, so day-trippers won't need to obtain Brazilian currency. Double-decker buses await to take you into the park proper. Keep your eyes peeled for animals. The last bus back to Puerto Iguazú from the falls is at 6pm (and from Foz do Iguaçu at 7pm).

Sights & Activities

The double-decker bus into Parque Nacional do Iguaçu makes two stops before the main falls stop (R$10). These are trailheads for excursions that cost extra. If you plan to do any of these, chat with one of the agents touting them around the park visitor center; they can get you a discount. There are several other combinations and boat trips available. Some of these excursions need to be booked the day before.

★**Cataratas do Iguaçu** WATERFALL
(www.cataratasdoiguacu.com.br; Parque Nacional do Iguaçu) The main waterfall observation trail provides unforgettable vistas. It is the third, and principal, bus stop on the route that takes you into the national park. From here you walk 1.5km down a paved trail with brilliant views of the falls on the Argentine side, the jungle and the river below. Every twist reveals a more splendid vista until the path ends right under majestic Salto Floriano, which will give you a healthy sprinkling via the wind it generates.

The Iguazú Falls

There are few more impressive sights on the planet than this majestic array of cascades on the border of Argentina and Brazil. Set in luxurious tropical jungle, the falls are accessible, and provide a primal thrill that will never be forgotten.

Brazilian Side

Hit the Brazilian side (p203) first to appreciate the wide panorama from its short viewing path within a birdlife-rich national park. Cascade after cascade is revealed, picturesquely framed by tropical vegetation before you end up below the impressive Salto Floriano.

Garganta del Diablo

The highlight of the falls is the 'Devil's Throat' (p201). Stroll out over the placid Iguazú river before gazing in awe as it drops away beneath you in a display of primitive sound and fury that leaves you breathless.

Argentine Side

Two spectacular walkways, one high, one low, get you in close to torrents of water of extraordinary power. Expect awesome photos, expect to get wet, and expect to be exhilarated (p200).

Boat Trips

Not wet enough yet? Then prepare to be absolutely drenched. Zippy motorboats take thrillseekers right in under one of the biggest waterfalls on the Argentine side (p201). More sedate kayaking and rafting excursions are also available on the Brazilian side (p206).

Jungle Trails

The waterfalls aren't the only thing on offer. National parks on both sides of the river offer various easy-to-medium trails through the jungle that give great wildlife-watching opportunities (p201 and p206).

Clockwise from top left

1. Iguazú Falls, Brazilian side 2. Rainforest trail, Argentine side 3. Coati

R.M. NUNES/SHUTTERSTOCK ©

2

ALEKSANDRA H. KOSSOWSKA/SHUTTERSTOCK ©

A catwalk leads out to a platform with majestic views, with the Garganta del Diablo close at hand, and a perspective down the river in the other direction. If the water's high, it's unforgettable.

From here, an elevator heads up to a viewing platform at the top of the falls at Porto Canoas, the last bus stop. Porto Canoas has boat excursions, a gift shop, a couple of snack bars and a buffet restaurant.

Trilha do Poço Preto HIKING, BOAT
(045-3574-4244; www.macucosafari.com.br; Av das Cataratas Km 25, Parque Nacional do Iguaçu; R$150) This easy 9km trail takes you on a guided journey through the jungle on foot, by bike or vehicle. It ends above the falls, where you can kayak then take a boat cruise around river islands to Porto Canoas. You can also return via the Bananeiras Trail. First stop on the park bus route.

Bananeiras Trail WALKING
(045-3574-4244; www.macucosafari.com.br; Av. das Cataratas Km 25, Parque Nacional do Iguaçu; incl boat ride R$150) This is a 1.6km walk passing lagoons and observing aquatic wildlife, which ends at a jetty where you can take boat rides or silent 'floating' excursions in kayaks down to Porto Canoas. Second stop on the park bus route.

Macuco Safari BOATING
(045-3574-4244; www.macucosafari.com.br; Av das Cataratas, Km 25, Parque Nacional do Iguaçu; adult/child R$323/161) This two-hour safari includes a 3km trailer ride through the jungle, a 600m walk to a small waterfall and then a boat ride (half-price without this) to the falls for a soaking. Don't confuse with Macuco Trail on the Argentine side. Second stop on the park bus route.

Helisul SCENIC FLIGHTS
(045-3529-7327; www.helisulfoz.com.br; Rodovia das Cataratas, Km 16.5; flights R$430; 9am-5:30pm) By the park visitor center, this setup runs 10-minute chopper jaunts over the Brazilian side of the falls. Environmental impact is questionable, but it's undeniably exhilarating. There are open panels in the windows for photography.

Sleeping & Eating

★Hotel das Cataratas HOTEL $$$
(045-2102-7000; www.belmond.com; BR 469, Km 32; r without/with view from R$1079/1679, ste with view from R$2279; P ❄ @ 🛜 ≋) In the Parque Nacional do Iguaçu near the falls, the location of this excellent hotel appeals enormously, though only a few rooms have falls views, and those only partial. It's decorated throughout in understated, elegant Portuguese colonial style, with tiling in the bathrooms and dark wood in the bedrooms. Public areas have cozy appeal, and the fine pool area is surrounded by birdsong. Service is excellent.

After-hours falls access is a major perk. Make sure you climb the belvedere for the view. Online rates are much better.

Restaurante Porto Canoas BUFFET $$
(www.cataratasdoiguacu.com.br; Parque Nacional do Iguaçu; buffet R$59; noon-4pm) Situated at the end of the main trail at the Parque Nacional do Iguaçu, this restaurant has a long pleasant terrace overlooking the river just before it descends into maelstrom – a great spot for a beer or caipirinha – and an OK buffet lunch with plenty of salads and hot dishes.

Getting There & Around

From Foz, catch the 120 bus from the urban bus terminal or stops along Av Juscelino Kubitschek; the trip takes 30 to 40 minutes, stops at the airport and costs R$3.45, paid as you enter the terminal.

Taxis from Foz to the park entrance cost R$55 to R$70. Haggle.

From Puerto Iguazú, there's a direct bus to the Brazilian falls hourly (AR$80 return, 40 minutes), with departures from 8:30am to 2:30pm and returns from 10am to 5pm (Brazilian time). This stops at Brazilian immigration and collects passports. You can also take the regular bus to Foz do Iguaçu (AR$25 or R$5, 40 minutes, every 20 minutes 6:30am to 7:30pm) and get off a couple of stops after crossing the international bridge. Cross the road, and wait for the Parque Nacional bus. Repeat at the same stop on the way back.

Foz do Iguaçu (Brazil)

Hilly Foz is base camp for the Brazilian side of the Iguazú Falls, and gives you a chance to get a feel for a Brazilian town. It's much bigger and more cosmopolitan than Puerto Iguazú, and has a keep-it-real feel that its Argentine counterpart lacks.

Sights

Itaipu DAM
(045-3576-7000; www.turismoitaipu.com.br; Tancredo Neves 6702; panoramic/special

tour R$38/82; ⌚regular tour hourly 8:30am-3:30pm Sun-Thu, half-hourly 8:30am-3:30pm Fri-Sat) This bi-national dam is the world's second-largest hydroelectric power station and, at some 8km long and 200m high, is a memorable sight, especially when a vast torrent of overflow water cascades down the spillway.

The visitor center, 12km north of Foz, has regular tours and the more detailed *circuito especial* (minimum age 14), taking you into the power plant itself.

Buses (R$3.45, 30 minutes) head here quarter-hourly from the urban bus terminal.

The project was controversial: it plunged Brazil into debt and necessitated large-scale destruction of rainforest and the displacement of 10,000 people. But it cleanly supplies most of Paraguay's energy needs, and 20% of Brazil's.

A variety of other attractions within the complex include a museum, wildlife park and river beaches.

Parque das Aves BIRD SANCTUARY
(Bird Park; www.parquedasaves.com.br; Av das Cataratas, Km 17.1; admission R$45; ⌚8:30am-5:30pm) This 5-hectare bird park, located 300m from the entrance to Parque Nacional do Iguaçu, is home to nearly 150 species of birds (over 1300 in total), including red ibis, bare-throated bellbird, and flamingos galore. They live in 8m-high aviaries that are constructed right in the forest, some of which you can walk through. The park has good information in English and Spanish. Well worth it.

Sleeping

Normally you'll get a rate up to 50% lower than rack rates. Don't be afraid to ask for a discount: it's expected.

★**Tetris Container Hostel** HOSTEL $
(☎045-3132-0019; www.tetrishostel.com.br; Av das Cataratas 639; dm R$55-65, d from R$160; ❄@🛜🏊) Brazil's coolest hostel is crafted from 15 shipping containers – even the pool is a water-filled shipping container! – and makes full use of other industrial by-products as well, like sinks made from oil drums. Colorful bathrooms brighten the dorms (a four-bed female plus 10- and 12-bed mixed) and the patio/bar area is tops. Adorable staff – and a free nightly caipirinha! – to boot.

Pousada Sonho Meu GUESTHOUSE $
(☎045-3573-5764; www.pousadasonhomeufoz.com.br; Mem de Sá 267; s/d R$210/249; P❄@🛜🏊) This is a delightful oasis barely 50m from the urban bus terminal. Rooms are simply decorated with bamboo; there's a standout pool (complete with a mini *catarata!*), breakfast area and outdoor guest kitchen, and a warm welcome throughout. Prices can be half those indicated.

Iguassu Guest House HOSTEL $
(☎045-3029-0242; www.iguassuguesthouse.com.br; Naipi 1019; dm from R$55, d without/with bathroom from R$145/180; P❄@🛜🏊) Great facilities and welcoming management mark this out from the Foz hostel herd. There's a small pool out the back, it's spotless, and there's a really good open kitchen and lounge area. Dorms vary in size; private rooms are very compact but comfortable. The local bus station is just around the corner.

Hotel Rafain Centro HOTEL $$
(☎045-3521-3505; www.rafaincentro.com.br; Marechal Deodoro da Fonseca 984; s/d from R$118/215; ❄@🛜🏊) Much more appealing than some of the hulking megahotels around town, the Rafain is an excellent-value, four-star business-like hotel with plenty of style, artistic detail and friendly staff. Rooms are simple with large balconies and there's a cracking pool and terrace. Nice poolside Happy Hour and Saturday *feijoada* (Brazil's national dish) in winter (R$40; March to September).

Hotel Del Rey HOTEL $$
(☎045-2105-7500; www.hoteldelreyfoz.com.br; Tarobá 1020; s/d R$280/315; ❄@🛜🏊) Friendly, spotless and convenient hotel with a fresh new facade that's more intimate than most of the big guns around. The completely modernized rooms are spacious and comfortable, facilities are excellent and the breakfast buffet is huge.

Eating

It's easy to eat cheaply. Many places will serve you a soft drink and *salgado* (baked or fried snack) for as little as R$5, and cheap

> **CHANGING THE CLOCKS**
>
> From mid-October to mid-February, southern Brazil changes the clocks for summer, putting it an hour ahead of Argentina, which doesn't observe daylight saving time.

Foz do Iguaçu (Brazil)

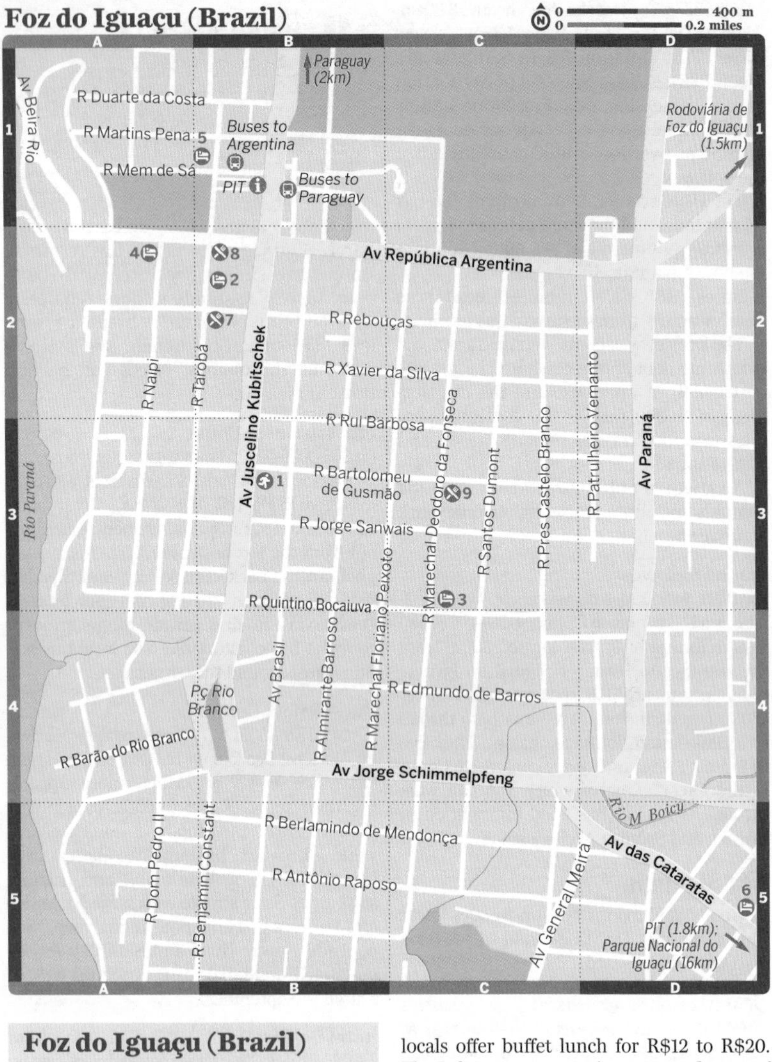

Foz do Iguaçu (Brazil)

Activities, Courses & Tours

1 Central de Passagens B3

Sleeping

2 Hotel Del Rey B2
3 Hotel Rafain Centro C3
4 Iguassu Guest House A2
5 Pousada Sonho Meu B1
6 Tetris Container Hostel D5

Eating

7 Búfalo Branco B2
8 Churrascaria do Gaúcho B2
9 Vó Bertila C3

locals offer buffet lunch for R$12 to R$20. The Lebanese community ensures dozens of shawarma (kebab) places.

Churrascaria do Gaúcho STEAK $
(www.churrascariadogaucho.com.br; Av República Argentina 632; all-you-can-eat buffet R$40; 11:30am-11pm;) Near the local bus terminal, this isn't a refined spot, but offers excellent value for its tasty cuts of meat and reasonable salad options.

★ **Vó Bertila** PIZZA $$
(www.facebook.com/vobertila; Bartolomeu de Gusmão 1116; pizza R$50-77, pasta for 2 R$55;

⌚6:30pm-11:30am, closed Mon) This informal, family-run cantina churns out wood-fired pizza – even in personal sizes! – and authentic pastas in heaping portions. All homey and hardwoods, it's the kind of down-home Italian spot Brazil does so very well. Expect it to be packed.

Búfalo Branco CHURRASCARIA $$
(☎045-3523-9744; www.bufalobranco.com.br; Rebouças 530; all-you-can-eat buffet R$90; ⌚noon-11pm; 📶📝) This spacious Foz classic certainly isn't Brazil's best *churrascaria* (grilled meat), but it's said to be the best in town and continues to draw locals and tourists alike for its decent *rodízio,* which features solid roast meats, including excellent *picanha* (sirloin) and filet mignon topped with crispy fried garlic.

Drinking & Nightlife

Brazil is all about an ice-cold bottle of beer in a plastic insulator served in a no-frills local bar with red plastic seats. Unbeatable. For a healthier tipple, juice bars give you the chance to try exotic fruits such as *acerola, açaí* or *cupuaçu.*

Nightlife centers on Av Jorge Schimmelpfeng. A row of big indoor-outdoor bars here all specialize in *chopp* (draft beer) and do decent food designed to share.

Orientation

Foz is at the confluence of the rivers Iguaçu (Iguazú) and Paraná; international bridges connect it to Puerto Iguazú, Argentina and Ciudad del Este, Paraguay. Av das Cataratas leads 20km to the Brazilian side of the Iguazú Falls, passing the Argentina bridge on the way.

Information

Other currencies are widely accepted, but it's cheaper to pay in Brazilian reais. The ATM closest to the urban bus terminal is a block beyond, under the Muffato supermarket.

PIT (☎0800-451516; www.pmfi.pr.gov.br/turismo; Av das Cataratas 2330, Vila Yolanda; ⌚8am-8pm) Between the town and the falls. There's a handier office in the **urban bus terminal** (☎045-3523-7901; www.pmfi.pr.gov.br/turismo; Juscelino Kubitschek 1385; ⌚7:30am-6pm).

Getting There & Away

There are daily flights to Rio de Janeiro, Porto Alegre, Curitiba and São Paulo, among other Brazilian cities.

Long-distance buses include to Curitiba (10 hours), São Paulo (16 hours) and Rio de Janeiro (22 hours). Buy tickets at downtown **Central de Passagens** (☎045-3523-4700; www.centraldepassagens.com; Av Juscelino Kubitschek 526; ⌚8am-6pm Mon-Fri, to 2pm Sat).

Getting Around

The **long-distance bus terminal** (☎045-3522-2590; Av Costa e Silva 1601) is 5km northeast of downtown. To get to downtown, grab a taxi for R$20 to R$25 or catch bus 105 or 115 (R$3.45).

For the airport, catch the falls bus (bus 120) or a taxi R$50 to R$55.

Buses to Puerto Iguazú (R$7 to R$9) run along Rua Mem de Sá alongside the urban bus terminal half-hourly from 7am until 7:15pm; they stop along Av Juscelino Kubitschek, and the trip takes an hour. Buses making the 40-minute trip to Ciudad del Este, Paraguay (R$5 to R$6), run every 15 minutes (half-hourly on Sundays) from 6:15am to 11:45pm; catch them on Av Juscelino Kubitschek opposite the urban bus terminal. Fares vary due to currency fluctuations.

THE GRAN CHACO

The Gran Chaco is a vast alluvial lowland, stretching north from Santa Fe and Córdoba provinces, across the entirety of Chaco and Formosa, and into Paraguay, Bolivia and Brazil. The western side, known as the Chaco Seco (Dry Chaco), has been dubbed the Impenetrable, due to its severe lack of water across an endless plain of thorn scrub. The eastern side is attractively fertile, and an important wildlife habitat.

Deforestation continues apace here, with vast areas being cleared to plant soya, Argentina is now one of the world's major soya producers. This has seriously affected Toba tribes, whose traditional environment is being destroyed.

Crossing the Gran Chaco from Formosa to Salta along the northern RN 81 is an interesting option on mostly decent paved road.

Protests from indigenous and other community groups often temporarily close roads in the Chaco – be patient and chat to the protesters while you wait.

Resistencia

☎0362 / POP 425,922

This provincial capital is perched on the edge of the barely populated Chaco, northern Argentina's 'outback'. It isn't the most likely candidate for the garland of artistic center of the north, yet its streets are studded with several hundred sculptures and there's a strong boho-cultural streak that represents a complete contrast to the tough cattle-and-scrub solitudes that characterize the province.

Sights

At last count, more than 650 sculptures graced the city, a number that increases with every **Bienal** (www.bienaldelchaco.com). The streets are packed with them, especially around the plaza and north up Avenida Sarmiento. Every Bienal, a brochure is printed with a sculpture walking tour around the city. Locals can buy pieces at a symbolic cost, but they have to display them streetside.

Download the CulturApp Resistencia application for smartphones for a self-guided tour of the artworks.

★ MusEUM GALLERY
(www.bienaldelchaco.com; Av de los Inmigrantes 1001; 9:30am-1:30pm & 4-8pm Mon-Sat) FREE The headquarters of the sculpture Bienal and the venue for it, this exhibition room and grounds houses many of the most impressive pieces from past festivals. It's well worth a visit. It also distributes brochures in English and Spanish on sculptural walking tours in town. The avenue is a northward continuation of Wilde. If going by taxi, mention the adjacent Domo del Centenario.

Museo del Hombre Chaqueño MUSEUM
(http://museohombrechaco.blogspot.com; JB Justo 280; 8am-1pm & 3-8:30pm Mon-Fri) FREE This small but excellent museum is run by enthusiastic staff (some English spoken) who talk you through displays covering the three main pillars of Chaco population: indigenous inhabitants (there are some excellent ceramics and Toba musical instruments here); Criollos who resulted from interbreeding between the European arrivals and the local populations; and 'Gringos', the wave of mostly European immigration from the late 19th century onward. Best is the mythology room upstairs, where you'll get to meet various quirky characters from Chaco popular religion.

El Fogón de los Arrieros CULTURAL CENTER
(www.fogondelosarrieros.com.ar; Brown 350; AR$10; 8am-noon & 4-7pm Mon-Fri) Founded in 1943, this is a cultural center and gallery that for decades has been the driving force behind Resistencia's artistic commitment. It's famous for its eclectic collection of objets d'art from around the Chaco and Argentina. The museum also features the wood carvings of local artist and cultural activist Juan de Dios Mena. Check out the irreverent epitaphs to dead patrons in the memorial garden; it's called 'Colonia Sálsipuedes' (leave if you can).

Sleeping

Casa Mía HOTEL $
(0362-442-5026; www.casamiahotel.com.ar; Santa María de Oro 368; s/d US$37/53; P ❄ @ 📶) Easily the best of the cheaper lodgings, Casa Mia is bright and neat with modern rooms boasting wooden floorboards and good bathrooms. Nice touches such as some art and plants about the place, and helpful service make it stand out from the crowd. Limited but free parking spaces.

★ Amerian Hotel Casino Gala HOTEL $$
(0362-445-2400; www.hotelcasinogala.com.ar; Perón 330; s/d US$127/141; P ❄ @ 📶 🏊) The city's smartest choice, with various grades of room and slick service. Rooms are excellent for these rates: very spacious, attractively stepped and with a dark, elegant, vaguely Asian feel to the decor. As well as slot machines, there's a sauna, gym and self-contained spa complex. The huge outdoor pool with bar is a highlight.

Eating & Drinking

No Me Olvides ARGENTINE, BAR $
(Laprida 198; mains AR$90-175; 6am-3am; 📶) Huge windows and a high-ceilinged interior make this hip corner spot feel much larger than it is. Verve and color are added by vibrant paintings, paper lampshades and arty touches. As the heroic opening hours suggest, it does everything from breakfasts to late-night cocktails. The pasta, ciabattas and *lomitos* are really excellent.

Coco's Resto ARGENTINE $$
(0362-442-3321; Av Sarmiento 266; mains AR$188-218; noon-2:30pm & 8:30pm-midnight Mon-Sat, noon-2:30pm Sun; 📶) Stylishly occupying the front rooms of a house, this intimate, well-decorated restaurant is popular with suited diners from the nearby state parliament. A wide-ranging menu of pastas, meats soused in various sauces, river fish and a long wine list make this a pleasant

Resistencia

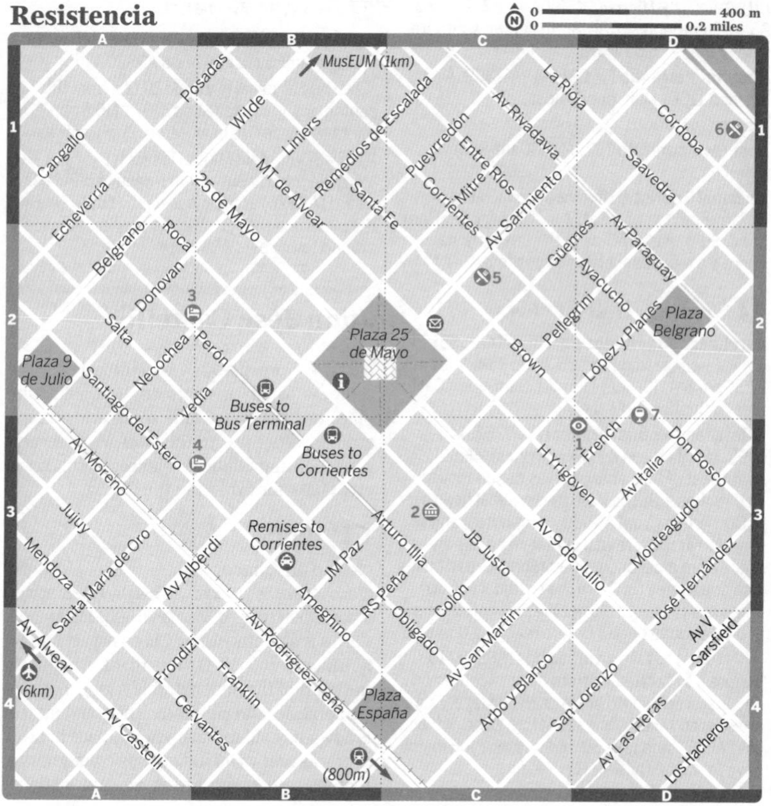

Resistencia

Sights

1 El Fogón de los Arrieros C3
2 Museo del Hombre Chaqueño C3

Sleeping

3 Amerian Hotel Casino Gala A2
4 Casa Mía B3

Eating

5 Coco's Resto C2
6 No Me Olvides D1

Drinking & Nightlife

7 Guana y Velasquez D2

Chaco choice. Some good options for vegetarian diners.

Guana y Velasquez BAR

(cnr French & Don Bosco; 7pm-late) This groovy corner bar is an excellent place for some drinks. Head inside for wooden floors, mosaic walls and fashionably mismatched wooden chairs or pick a table outside under the trees beneath the murals. The music is as interesting as the decor and a large Jim Morrison portrait keeps an eye over proceedings.

Information

Banco de Patagonia (Justo 152)

Centro Cultural Leopoldo Marechal (0362-445-2738; Pellegrini 272; 9am-2pm & 4:30-7:30pm Mon-Fri) The place to go to learn about indigenous issues and visiting Toba communities. There's a small display of Toba handicrafts.

City Tourist Office (☎0362-445-8289; Roca 20; ⊙7am-noon & 2:30-8pm) On the southern side of Plaza 25 de Mayo.

Hospital Perrando (☎0362-444-2399; Av 9 de Julio 1100) Main public hospital

Macro (Justo 160)

Post (Av Sarmiento 102; ⊙8:30am-8pm Mon-Fri)

Terminal Tourist Office (www.chaco.travel; ⊙7am-8pm Mon-Fri Sat, 7-9:30am & 6-8:30pm Sat & Sun) Useful office in the bus terminal. There's a municipal office opposite it.

Getting There & Away

Aerolíneas Argentinas (☎0362-444-5551; www.aerolineas.com.ar; JB Justo 184; ⊙8am-12:30pm & 4:30-8pm Mon-Fri, 8am-noon Sat) flies to Buenos Aires daily.

Resistencia's **bus terminal** (☎0362-446-1098; cnr MacLean & Islas Malvinas), 4km southwest of the center, serves destinations in all directions. Buses from the terminal head over to Corrientes (from AR$30, 35 minutes) and will drop you at the terminal in that city a fair distance from most accommodations. Urban buses also apparently run from the terminal to Corrientes from Platform 15 but are very infrequent and take a long detour before reaching that city.

It's better to take an urban bus (AR$10, 40 minutes) to Corrientes from the city center, on Av Alberdi just south of Plaza 25 de Mayo. Faster are **shared taxis** (Obligado 111; ⊙24hr), which cost AR$35 and take 30 minutes, but you might have to wait a while for them to fill.

Getting Around

Aeropuerto San Martín is 6km south of town on RN 11; a *remise* costs around AR$200.

The bus terminal is a AR$120 taxi from the center, or you can take bus 3, 9 or 110 from Santa María de Oro near Perón. Don't walk it: travelers have reported muggings.

To ride the city buses you'll need to purchase a card (AR$26) at the office on the south side of the plaza and then load it with credit. Each ride around town costs AR$8.50.

Juan José Castelli

☎0364 / POP 27,200

A fairly prosperous agricultural service center, Castelli is a green, fertile-looking place but gateway to the more arid Impenetrable wilderness to the west. With several good accommodations choices, it makes a great base for exploring the Chaco.

Tours

★ **EcoTur Chaco** DRIVING
(Carlos Aníbal Schumann; ☎0364-446-8128; ecoturchaco@gmail.com; Av San Martín 500) Personable Carlos is an enthusiastic Chaco expert and offers memorable 4WD tours that get right into the heart of the Impenetrable region, both geographically and culturally. The standout trip is a two-day affair that eschews roads in favor of tracks and visits indigenous communities, remote settlements, reserves and national

OFF THE BEATEN TRACK

NORTH TO FORMOSA & PARAGUAY

If you're heading to Paraguay, buses run from Resistencia to Asunción, Paraguay's capital, crossing in Argentina's far north at **Clorinda**, a chaotic border town with little of interest beyond bustling markets.

A better stop is baking-hot **Formosa**, a medium-sized provincial capital two hours' bus ride north of Resistencia. Hotels, restaurants and services can be found along Av 25 de Mayo, which links the sleepy plaza with the Río Paraguay waterfront – the best place to stroll once the temperatures drop. **Laguna Oca** offers good bird watching 6km from town, but the rest of Formosa province has even more.

Formosa province's standout attraction is **Bañado la Estrella** (www.banadolaestrella.org.ar; ⊙8am-6pm). This stunning wetland area is a floodplain of the Río Pilcomayo and harbors an astonishing range of birdlife, as well as alligators, capybaras, sizeable serpents and beautiful water plants. From the roads that cross this 200km-long finger-shaped area, it's easy to spot a huge variety of wildlife: pack binoculars.

One of the highlights of the park is **Fortín Soledad** where local residents organize canoe trips among the lush landscapes. The handiest town for the Bañado is Las Lomitas, 300km west of Formosa on RN 81 and accessed by regular bus (AR$300, 5½ to six hours). From here, paved RP 28 heads north and cuts across the wetlands on a causeway, starting 37km north of Las Lomitas and extending for some 15km. In Las Lomitas, there is a range of accommodations, the best of which are out on the highway.

OFF THE BEATEN TRACK

PENETRATING 'EL IMPENETRABLE'

If you have a yen to get off the beaten track, the more remote areas of the Chaco are for you. From Castelli, you can head west along *ripio* (gravel) roads to remote Fuerte Esperanza (buses and shared *remises* run this route), which has two nature reserves in its vicinity – **Reserva Provincial Fuerte Esperanza** and **Reserva Natural Loro Hablador**. Both conserve typical dry Chaco environments, with algarrobo and quebracho trees, armadillos, peccaries and many bird species. Loro Hablador, 40km from Fuerte Esperanza, has more vegetation, a good campground and short walking trails. It adjoins similar **Parque Nacional Copo** in Santiago del Estero province. Fuerte Esperanza has simple *hospedajes* (guesthouses).

Further north, **Parque Nacional El Impenetrable** (☎03644-201831; www.parquesnacionales.gob.ar; ⏲8am-6pm) is Argentina's newest national park and protects 130,000 hectares of *bosque chaqueño* forest, which is home to an impressive array of fauna including jaguars, tapirs and armadillos. Nearby **Misión Nueva Pompeya** was founded in 1899 by Franciscans who established a mission station for Matacos in tough conditions. The main building, with its square-towered church, is a surprising sight in such a remote location. There are cheap lodgings in town.

One of the best ways to visit is via a tour from Castelli. Be warned, summer temperatures can be uncomfortably warm out here.

parks. Day trips and excursions camping on ranches are also possible.

Sleeping

Portal del Impenetrable HOTEL $

(☎0364-15-470-8848; www.hotelportaldelimpenetrable.com; RP 9; s/d US$24/32/44; P ❄ @ ☏) At the entrance to town, this spacious – almost too spacious – modern hotel offers interesting artworks, efficient service and capacious rooms. It's a commodious Chaco base at less than half the price of many Argentine hotels of this standard. An extra few pesos gets you a superior room, with a king-size bed and minibar.

Getting There & Away

Castelli is served by five daily buses from Resistencia (AR$260, five hours), and more regular services from Roque Sáenz Peña (AR$110, two hours).

There are half a dozen daily services to Miraflores (AR$40, 45 minutes) for access to Parque Nacional El Impenetrable. Only three buses a week run to Nueva Pomeya (AR$210, three hours) leaving at 11:30am Monday, Thursday and Sunday and returning at 6am the following day. There is also a van service running the route at around 11am on weekdays leaving from outside the terminal.

Upon arrival in town get off the bus at the old hospital, which is in the center, rather than continuing all the way to the terminal.

Salta & the Andean Northwest

Includes ➡

Best Places to Eat

- Chirimoya (p226)
- Sopra Tutto (p272)
- Piattelli (p242)
- Pacha (p242)

Best Places to Stay

- El Cortijo (p232)
- Descanso de las Piedras (p266)
- Balcón de la Plaza (p225)
- Posada El Arribo (p245)
- Antigua Tilcara (p252)

Why Go?

Argentina's hardscrabble northwest sits beneath the mighty snowcapped Andes, where a confluence of wind, water, ice and time has conjured weird, wonderful rockscapes, streaked with minerals and glowing red in the sun. Nature speaks powerfully here, lending the region a certain mystery.

Argentina is known worldwide for its European influence, but there's an Andean feel in the northwest. This is thanks to the creativity and endurance of indigenous communities here – descendants of empires, they are people of the *puna* (Andean highlands), which stretch into Chile and Bolivia.

The region's cities were Argentina's first colonial settlements, and it's here where independence was claimed. There's much to see: national parks aplenty, and century-old, high-altitude vineyards producing some of Argentina's finest wine.

When to Go

Salta

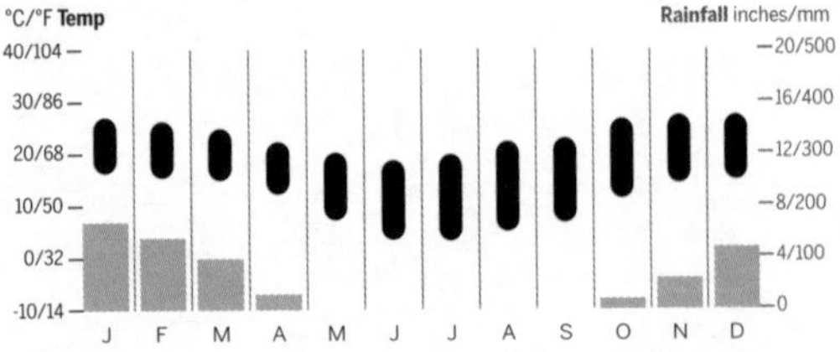

Feb Temperatures are high but Carnaval celebrations are worth seeing.

Jul & Aug Chilly up on the puna (Andean highlands), but pleasant around the Salta region.

Sep & Oct Top compromise: fewer tourists in Salta and acceptable spring temperatures.

SALTA & JUJUY PROVINCES

Intertwined like yin and yang, Argentina's northwestern provinces harbor an inspiring wealth of natural beauty and traditional culture. Bounded by Bolivia to the north and Chile to the west, the zone climbs from sweaty cloud forests westward to the puna highlands and some of the most majestic peaks of the Andes cordillera.

The two capitals, especially colonial Salta, which is beloved by travelers, are launchpads for exploring the jagged chromatic ravines of the Quebrada de Cafayate and Quebrada de Humahuaca, and the villages of the Valles Calchaquíes, rich in artisanal handicrafts and laced with high-altitude vineyards. Not to mention the stark puna scenery, the national parks of Calilegua and El Rey, and the aromatic Cafayate torrontés, Argentina's signature white wine.

Salta

☎0387 / POP 520,700 / ELEV 1187M

Sophisticated Salta is a favorite, engaging active minds with its outstanding museums and lighting romantic candles with its plazaside cafes and the live *música folklórica* of its vibrant *peñas* (folk-music clubs). It offers the facilities (and the traffic and noise) of a larger city, and aside from the morning gridlock, retains the comfortable pace of a smaller town that happens to have preserved more colonial architecture than most Argentine destinations.

Founded in 1582, it's now the most touristed spot in northwest Argentina, and offers numerous accommodations options. The center bristles with tour agents: this is the place to get things organized for onward travel. A popular option is to hire a car here, hit the road and explore the wild northwest.

Sights

★Museo de Arqueología de Alta Montaña MUSEUM

(MAAM; www.maam.gob.ar; Mitre 77; adult/student & senior AR$130/40; ⏲11am-7:30pm Tue-Sun) One of northern Argentina's premier museums, MAAM has a serious and informative exhibition focusing on Inca culture and, in particular, the child sacrifices (p218) left on some of the Andes' most imposing peaks. The centerpiece is the mummified body of one of three children (rotated every six months) discovered at the peak of Llullaillaco in 1999. It was a controversial decision to display the bodies and it is a powerful experience to come face-to-face with them.

Intricately plaited hair and clothes are perfectly preserved, and their faces reflect – you decide – a distant past or a typical 21st-century Salta face; a peaceful passing or a tortured death.

The grave goods impress by their immediacy, with colors as fresh as the day they were produced. The *illas* (small votive figurines of animals and humans) are of silver, gold, shell and onyx, and many are clothed in textiles. It's difficult to imagine that a more privileged look at pre-Columbian South American culture will ever be offered to us. Also exhibited is the 'Reina del Cerro,' a tomb-robbed mummy that ended up here after a turbulent history. Good videos give background on the sacrifices and on the Qhapaq Ñan, the Inca road system given Unesco status in 2014.

There's a shop and library as well as a cafe-bar with terrace.

Centro Cultural América ARCHITECTURE

(☎0387-431-6700; Mitre 23; ⏲9am-9pm) FREE A former church built in French academia style between 1721 and 1732, in 1913 it became Salta's most important social club until the government took it over in 1987. In 1994 it was declared a national landmark. It's now an administrative building focused on arts and culture and visitors are welcome to enjoy rotating art exhibits in the lobby.

Catedral Basilica de Salta CATHEDRAL

(España 590; ⏲6:30am-12:15pm & 4:30-8:15pm Mon-Fri, 7:30am-12:15pm & 4:30-8:15pm Sat, 7:30am-1pm & 5-9pm Sun) Salta's pink cathedral was consecrated in 1878 and harbors the ashes of (among other notables) General Martín Miguel de Güemes, a *salteño* (resident of Salta) and independence hero. It's been a national monument since 1942, and looks spectacular when it's illuminated after dark.

Museo Histórico del Norte MUSEUM

(Caseros 549; requested donation AR$20; ⏲9am-1:30pm & 3-8pm Mon-Fri, 2:30-6:30pm Sat) Set on the plaza in the lovely *cabildo* (town hall), this collection ranges from pre-Columbian ceramics to colonial-era religious art. The endless portraits of Salta's governors wouldn't be out of place in a Brooklyn beard-and-mustache museum, while the transportation collection includes an enormous 1911 Renault that puts Hummers to shame.

Salta & the Andean Northwest Highlights

1 Quebrada de Humahuaca (p248) Wondering at nature's palette in this vivid landscape.

2 Valles Calchaquíes (p230) Observing weavers at work in this memorable rural region.

3 Tafí del Valle (p265) Cleansing your lungs in the crisp air of this hill town.

4 Cachi (p231) Nesting in a boutique hotel room and strolling around this adorable adobe town.

5 Chilecito (p278) Hitting this appealing base for uplifting mountain excursions.

6 Salta (p215) Soaking up this sophisticated town's colonial ambience.

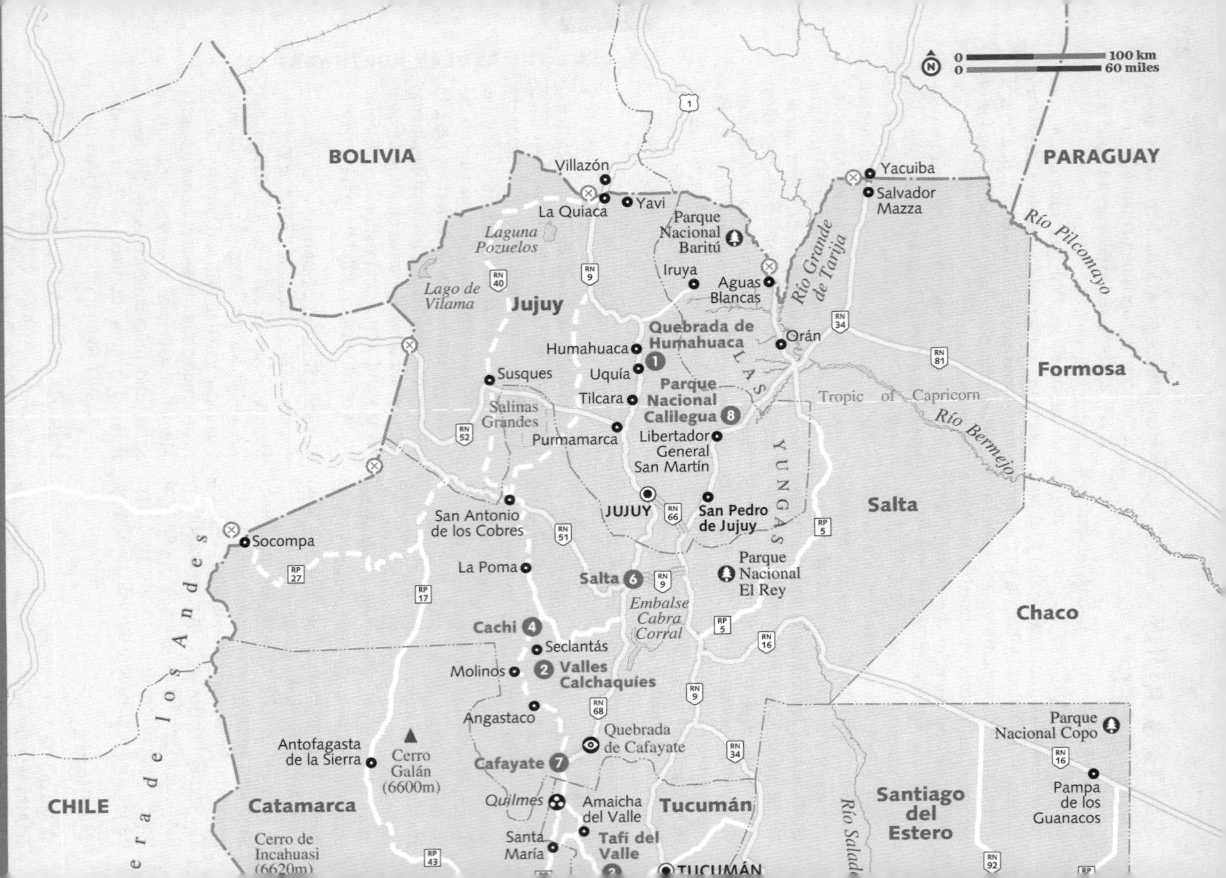

7 Cafayate (p235)
Quaffing torrontés and malbec in north Argentina's wine hub.

8 Parque Nacional Calilegua (p248)
Experiencing subtropical forest while ascending through this steamy national park.

9 Western Catamarca (p274)
Gazing over crater lakes, 6000m volcanoes and awesome Andean scenery in the far west.

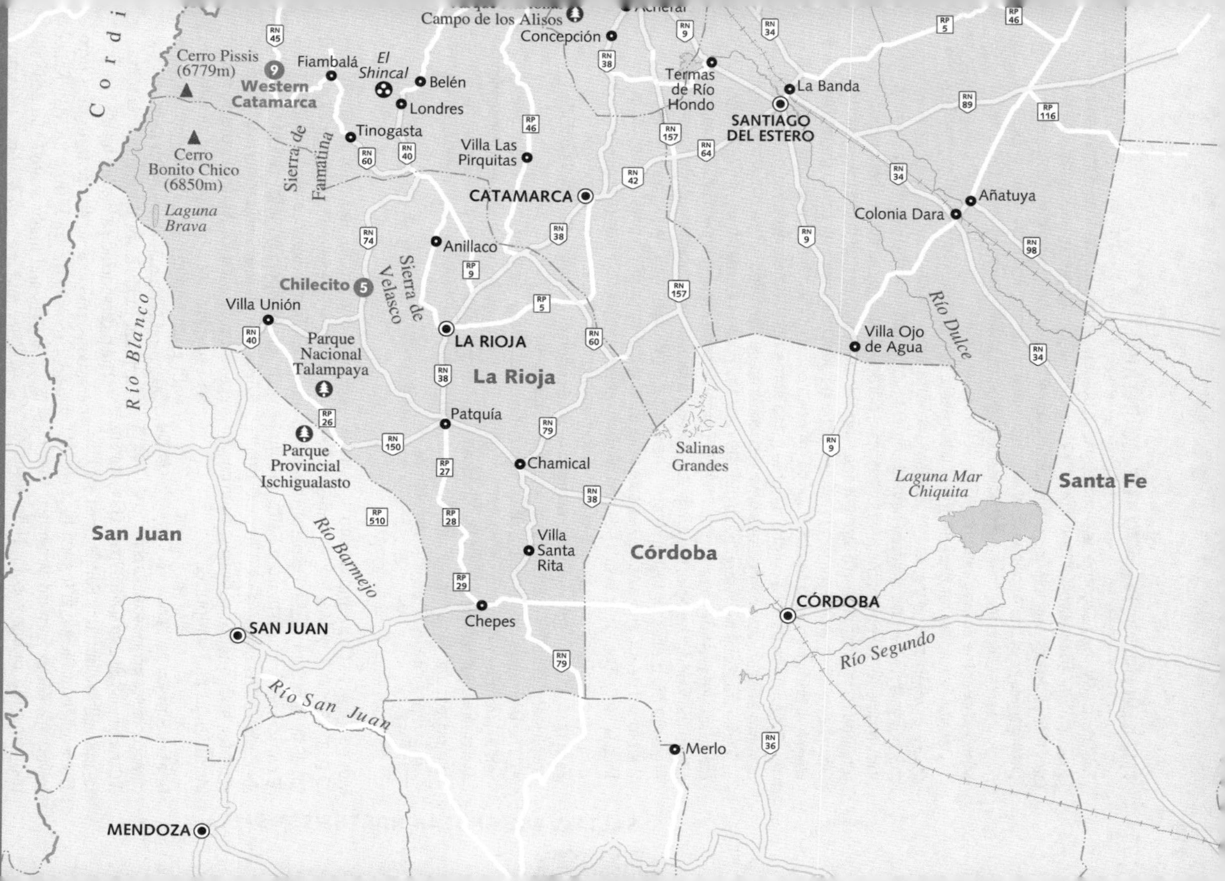

THE CHILDREN GIVEN TO THE MOUNTAIN

The phrase 'human sacrifice' is sensationalist, but it is a fact that the Inca culture sometimes sacrificed the lives of high-born children to please or appease their gods. The Inca saw this as an offering to ensure the continuing fertility of their people and the land. The high peaks of the Andes were always considered sacred, and were chosen as sacrifice sites; the Inca felt that the children would be reunited with their forefathers, who watched over the communities from the loftiest summits.

Carefully selected for the role, the children were taken to the ceremonial capital Cuzco, Peru, where they were central to a large celebration – the *capacocha*. Ceremonial marriages between the children helped cement diplomatic links between tribes across the empire. At the end of the fiesta, they were paraded around the plaza, then were required to return home in a straight line – an arduous journey that could take months. Once home, they were feted and welcomed, then taken into the mountains. There they were fed, and given quantities of *chicha* (maize alcohol). When they passed out, they were taken up to the peak of the mountain and entombed, sometimes alive, presumably never to awaken, and sometimes having been strangled or killed with a blow to the head.

Three such children were found in 1999 near the peak of **Llullaillaco**, a 6739m volcano 480km west of Salta, on the Chilean border. It's the highest known archaeological site in the world. The cold, the low pressure and a lack of oxygen and bacteria helped preserve the bodies almost perfectly. The Doncella (Maiden) was about 15 years old at the time of death, and was perhaps an *aclla* (a 'virgin of the sun'), a prestigious role in Inca society. The other two, a boy and girl both aged from six to seven (the girl damaged by a later lightning strike), had cranial deformations that indicate they came from high-ranking families. Each was accompanied by a selection of grave goods, which included textiles and small figurines of humanoids and camelids.

The mummies' transfer to Salta was controversial. Many felt they should have been left where they were discovered; but once their location was known, this was impossible. Whatever your feelings about the children, and the role of archaeology, the dig was a daring feat and amazing accomplishment, and the children offer an undeniably fascinating glimpse into Inca religion and culture.

Museo de Arte Contemporáneo GALLERY
(☎0387-437-0498; Zuviría 90; ⏲9am-8pm Tue-Sat, 10am-2pm Sun) FREE Displays the work of contemporary artists from Salta and further afield. The space is well lit and usually exhibits high-quality canvases, multimedia installations and sculpture.

Iglesia San Francisco CHURCH
(www.conventosanfranciscosalta.com; cnr Caseros & Córdoba; ⏲8am-1pm & 2-6:30pm) This magenta-and-yellow church is Salta's most striking. The exuberant facade is topped by a slender tower; inside are several venerated images, including the rather spooky Niño Jesús de Aracoeli. There's a lovely garden cloister, accessed via tours (English available; AR$40; from 10am to 1pm and 2pm to 6:30pm Tuesday to Saturday) that include a mediocre museum of religious art and treasures.

Pajcha – Museo de Arte Étnico Americano MUSEUM
(☎0387-422-9417; 20 de Febrero 831; AR$100; ⏲10am-1pm & 4-8pm Mon-Fri, 4-8pm Sat) This eye-opening private museum is worth seeing if you're interested in indigenous art and culture. Juxtaposing archaeological finds with contemporary and recent artisanal work from all over Latin America, it encourages a broad view of Andean culture and is an exquisite dose of color and beauty run with great enthusiasm. The collection is revealed on bilingual tours (with flair!) by the charming English-speaking management.

The pieces include amazing macaw-feather creations, religious sculpture from the Cuzco School, tools of the trade from Bolivian Kallawaya healers and finely crafted Mapuche silver jewelry, and are high quality – testament to decades of study and collection by the anthropologist founder.

Convento de San Bernardo CONVENT
(Caseros s/n; ⏲pastries for sale 9am-noon & 4-6pm Mon-Sat) Only Carmelite nuns may enter this 16th-century convent, the oldest building in Salta (though it was rebuilt into its current form in the 1840s after falling into ruin).

Visitors can approach the handsome adobe building to admire its carved, 18th-century algarrobo-wood door and buy nun-made pastries. The church can be visited before Mass (from 7am to 8:30am weekdays and Sunday mornings, and 7pm to 8pm Saturday evenings).

Cerro San Bernardo HILL

For outstanding views of Salta, take the **teleférico** (☎0387-431-0641; 1 way/roundtrip AR$100/200; ⏰9am-7pm) from Parque San Martín to the top of this hill, a 1km ride that takes eight minutes. Alternatively, take the trail starting at the **Güemes Monument**. Atop is a rather unique wine bar (p227), a watercourse and *artesanía* (handicraft) shops.

Museo Antropológico MUSEUM

(www.antropologico.gov.ar; cnr Ejército del Norte & Polo Sur; AR$20; ⏰8am-7pm Mon-Sat) Has good representations of local ceramics, especially from the Tastil ruins (Argentina's largest pre-Inca town), and some well-designed displays in its attractive, purpose-built spaces.

Iglesia Nuestra Señora de la Candeleria de la Viña CHURCH

(☎0387-421-3237; Alberdi 485) Closed for renovations at research time, this gorgeous, pastel-blue and peach domed sanctuary was built in 1854 and became a shelter during Salta's civil war. In 1982 it was declared a national monument. Even if you cannot enter, it's worth strolling to the gates and taking it in.

☞ Tours

Salta is the base for a range of tours, offered by numerous agencies, with a high concentration of companies on Buenos Aires and Caseros near the plaza. Popular trips head to Cafayate, Cachi, San Antonio de los Cobres (the Tren a las Nubes route), Salinas Grandes, Purmamarca and more.

Operators such as Altro Turismo, Socompa and **Tastil** (☎0387-322-0897; www.turismotastil.com.ar; Caseros 468) are reliable, but we also recommend newer and more creative tour companies for interesting trips beyond the standard excursions.

★**Origins** TREKKING

(☎0387-431-3891; www.originsargentina.com; Zorrilla 171; ⏰9am-8pm Mon-Fri, to noon Sat) A top-rated, community-based tour operator that combines well-planned trekking, horseback-riding and other active cultural itineraries with farm stays. Responsible tourism is its ethos, and the company can even help you learn Spanish. Guides speak English and French as well as Spanish.

Altro Turismo TOURS

(Marina Turismo; ☎0387-431-9769; www.altroturismo.com.ar; Caseros 489) Reliable organizer of excursions, with frequent departures (combined with other operators) to Cafayate, Cachi, the Quebrada de Humahuaca, and Salinas Grandes, including San Antonio de los Cobres and Purmamarca. Options that are harder to do by yourself include a three-day excursion to Tolar Grande and the Llullaillaco volcano.

Socompa TOURS

(☎0387-431-5974; www.socompa.com; Balcarce 998) This professional setup runs recommended tours into the Andean highlands. Its flagship five-day Puna Experience takes in the best of the highland scenery of Catamarca and Salta provinces using comfortable accommodations and multilingual guides. Another tour covers highlights of the northwest, including a sally into Chile. Book well ahead. Tours are private: you can't join a group.

Dexotic ADVENTURE SPORTS

(www.dexotic.com; Güemes 569; ⏰7:30am-12:30pm & 3-8pm) An all-purpose travel agency attached to the Las Rejas hostel (p221), with a range of tours including cultural jaunts into Jujuy; bodega and vineyard tours in Cafayate; and adventure itineraries featuring trekking, mountain biking, horseback riding, paragliding and white-water rafting, all within a few hours of Salta.

Quechua Cicloturismo CYCLING

(☎0387-15-50-56771; www.saltabiking.com) A friendly and motivated couple who run worthwhile cycling tours, ranging from an easy 90-minute spin around Salta city (AR$420) to multiday excursions to the Valles Calchaquíes.

AlterNativa Salta DRIVING

(☎0387-425-0276, 0387-15-502-5588; www.alternativasalta.com) Runs multiday 4WD trips into the remote highlands of northwestern Argentina and down into the Mendoza wine country.

Clark Expediciones BIRDWATCHING

(☎0387-421-5390, 0387-15-489-0118; www.clarkexpediciones.com; Caseros 121) A professional agency offering trips with English-speaking guides to national parks and remote

Jujuy & Salta Provinces

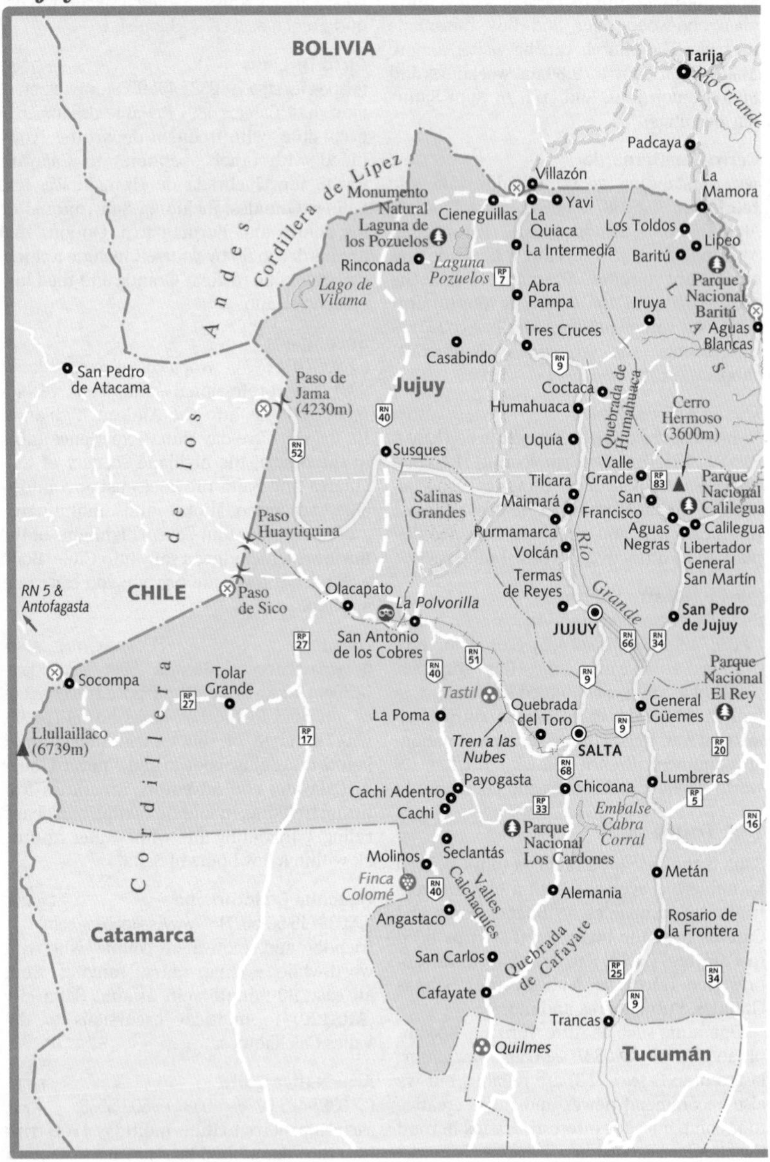

uplands. This outfit is serious about bird watching; trips include a half-/full day in the Reserva del Huaico, a 60-hectare cloud-forest reserve 8km west of Salta, two days to Parque Nacional El Rey and multi-day tailored itineraries.

Salta Rafting RAFTING

(☎0387-421-3216; www.saltarafting.com; Caseros 177) Salta's original white-water outfitter runs two-hour white-water rafting trips on the Class III Río Juramento,

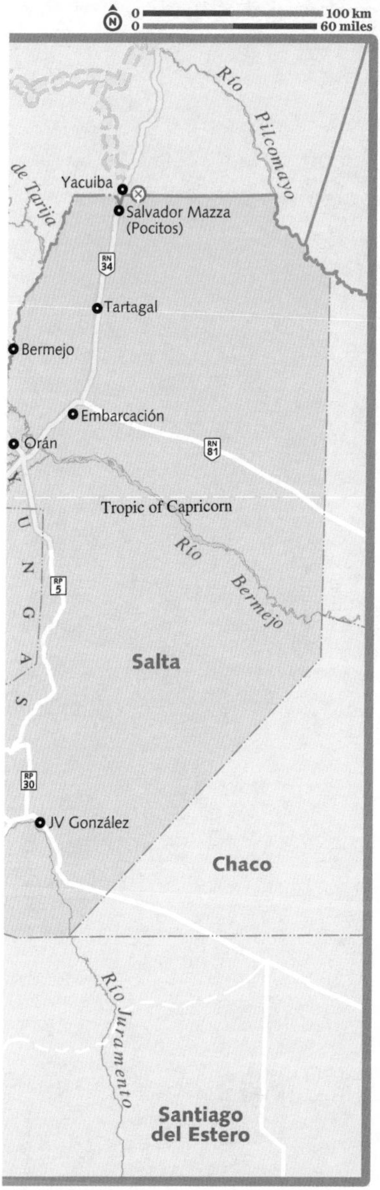

100km from Salta (AR$720 including barbecue lunch; transportation AR$550 extra). You can also click into a 400m zip line across a canyon (four-line trip AR$600). A combo with lunch is AR$1300.

Norte Trekking HIKING
(0387-431-6616; www.nortetrekking.com; Güemes 265) Runs trips to national parks, multiday treks and luxury 4WD adventure trips throughout the mountains of northwest Argentina. Its website lists a handful of itineraries, but staff can cobble together bespoke trips too.

Tren a las Nubes TOURS
(www.trenalasnubes.com.ar; cnr Ameghino & Balcarce; roundtrip AR$2150; Sat Apr–mid-Dec) The 'Train to the Clouds,' Argentina's most famous rail trip, heads from Salta down the Lerma Valley then ascends multicolored Quebrada del Toro, continuing past the Tastil ruins and San Antonio de los Cobres, before reaching a stunning viaduct spanning a desert canyon at La Polvorilla (altitude 4220m).

Sleeping

Salta has dozens of hostels, some cleaner than others, and competition keeps prices low. Ditto for boutique hotels, of which there are a plethora. It's not hard to find a comfortable and stylish nest here.

★ **Espacio Mundano** B&B $
(0387-572-2244; www.espaciomundano.com.ar; Güemes 780; r US$58-82;) An artistic oasis in the heart of Salta. The setting is a 200-year-old house, converted into an art studio and B&B that is a riot of color and imagination. Rooms have timber floors, are decked out with vintage vanities and wrought-iron beds, and open onto a leafy courtyard.

It's owned by an artist/architect. You'll love her work and her gallery.

Hostal Prisamata HOSTEL $
(0387-431-3900; www.hostalprisamata.com; Mitre 833; dm US$10-15, d US$25-35; @) Hammocks on the patio and a great location a street away from the Calle Balcarce action make this friendly, stylish, well-kept hostel a top spot. The kitchen is decent and there's a barbecue out the back; it's worth the extra spend for the dorms with fewer beds.

Las Rejas HOSTEL $
(0387-422-7959; www.lasrejashostel.com; Güemes 569; d/d $US15/47;) Occupying an older building with character to spare, this hostel has trendy exposed brick in the common areas, and two levels of rooms and dorms. The combination of the central location and a relaxed vibe works. The staff speak good English, and there are bike rentals on-site.

Salta

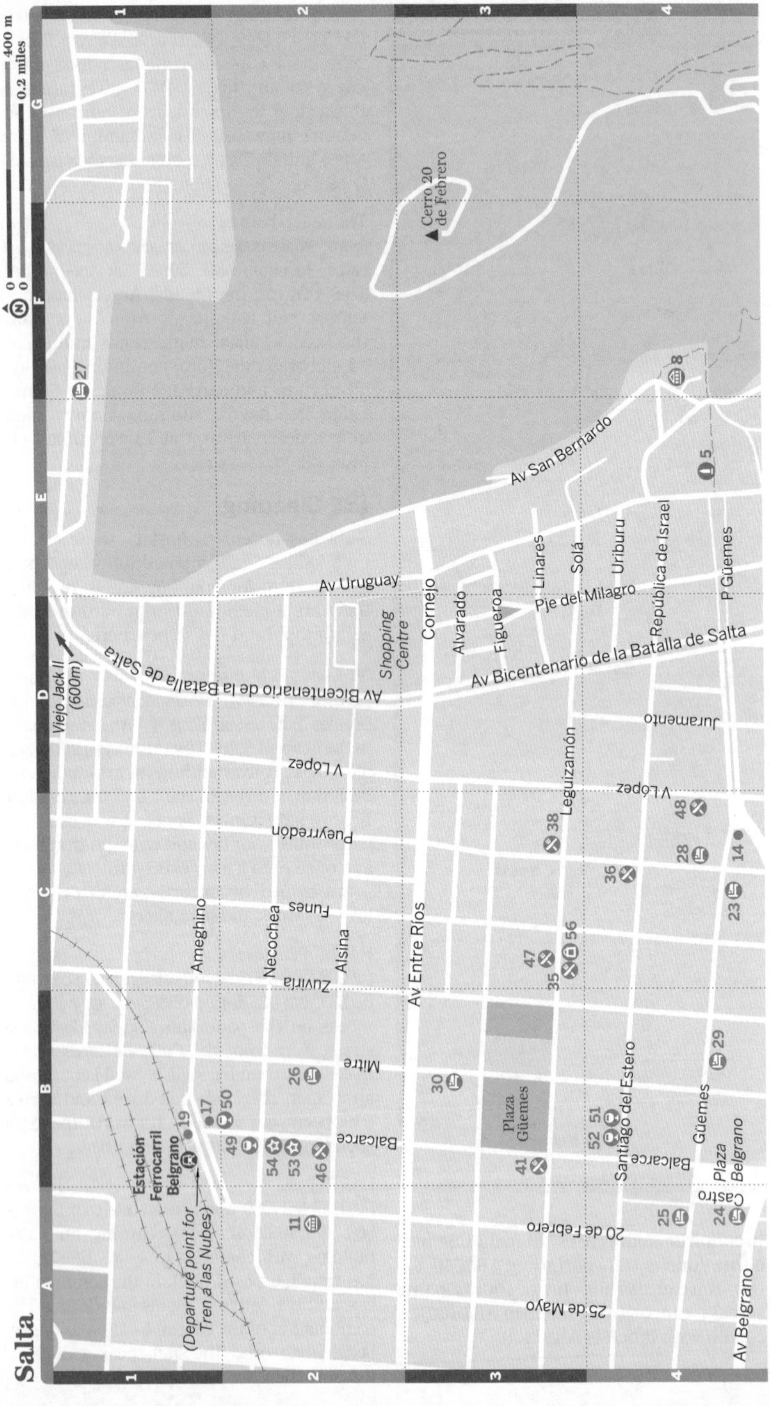
400 m
0.2 miles
Cerro 20 de Febrero
Av San Bernardo
Av Uruguay
Av Bicentenario de la Batalla de Salta
Viejo Jack II (600m)
Shopping Centre
Cornejo
Alvarado
Figueroa
Linares
Solá
Uriburu
República de Israel
Pje del Milagro
P Güemes
Juramento
V López
Leguizamón
Pueyrredón
Funes
Alsina
Necochea
Ameghino
Zuviría
Av Entre Ríos
Mitre
Balcarce
Santiago del Estero
Güemes
Plaza Güemes
Plaza Belgrano
Castro
20 de Febrero
25 de Mayo
Av Belgrano
Estación Ferrocarril Belgrano
(Departure point for Tren a las Nubes)
5
8
11
14
17
19
23
24
25
26
27
28
29
30
35
36
38
41
46
47
48
49
50
51
52
53
54
56

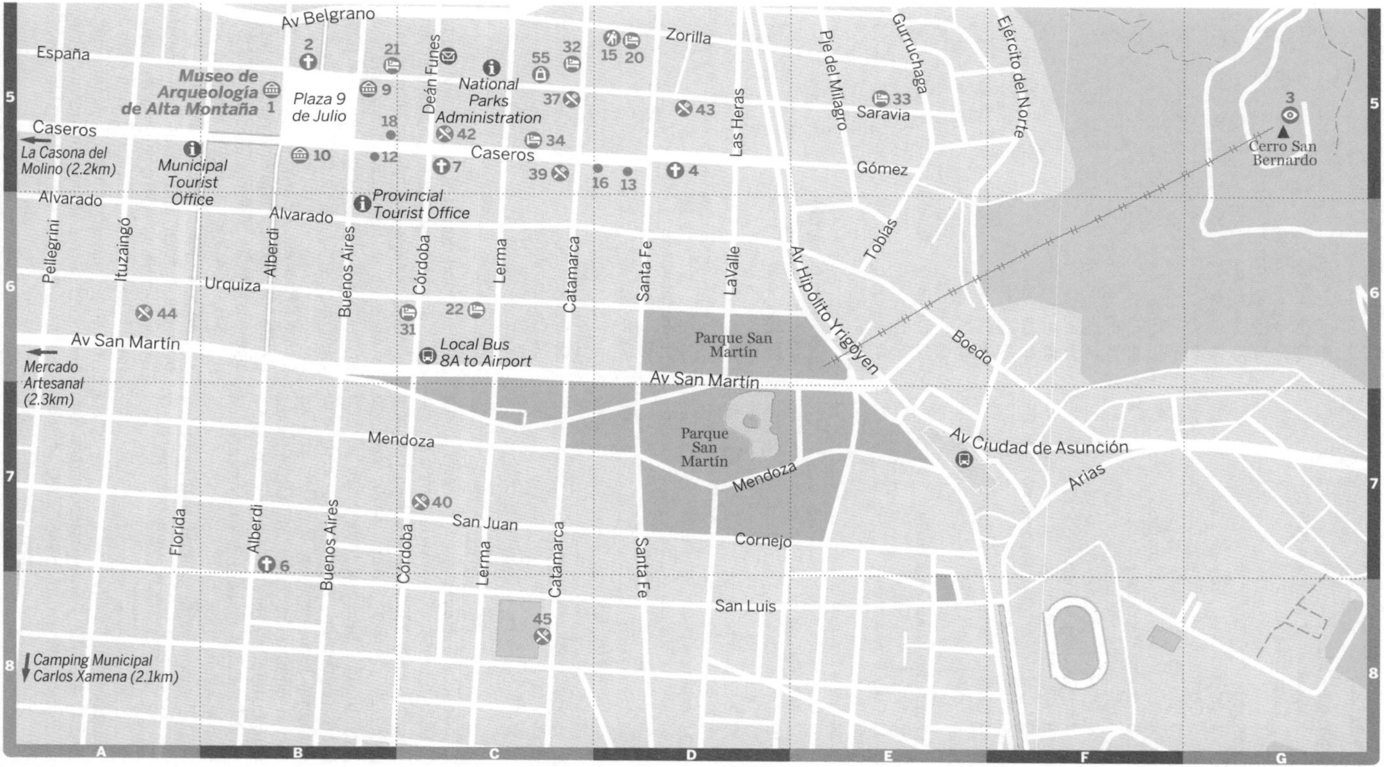
Av Belgrano
España
Zorilla
Museo de Arqueología de Alta Montaña
Plaza 9 de Julio
Deán Funes
National Parks Administration
Caseros
La Casona del Molino (2.2km)
Municipal Tourist Office
Provincial Tourist Office
Alvarado
Pellegrini
Ituzaingó
Alberdi
Buenos Aires
Córdoba
Lerma
Catamarca
Santa Fe
LaValle
Las Heras
Urquiza
Local Bus 8A to Airport
Av San Martín
Mercado Artesanal (2.3km)
Parque San Martín
Mendoza
San Juan
Cornejo
San Luis
Florida
Camping Municipal Carlos Xamena (2.1km)
Pje del Milagro
Gurruchaga
Saravia
Gómez
Ejército del Norte
Tobías
Av Hipólito Yrigoyen
Boedo
Av Ciudad de Asunción
Arias
Cerro San Bernardo
1
2
3
4
6
7
9
10
12
13
15
16
18
20
21
22
31
32
33
34
37
39
40
42
43
44
45
55
A
B
C
D
E
F
G
5
6
7
8

Salta

Top Sights
1 Museo de Arqueología de Alta Montaña ... B5

Sights
2 Catedral Basilica de Salta ... B5
Centro Cultural América ... (see 1)
3 Cerro San Bernardo ... G5
4 Convento de San Bernardo ... D5
5 Güemes Monument ... E4
6 Iglesia Nuestra Señora de la Candeleria de la Viña ... B7
7 Iglesia San Francisco ... C5
8 Museo Antropológico ... F4
9 Museo de Arte Contemporáneo ... B5
10 Museo Histórico del Norte ... B5
11 Pajcha – Museo de Arte Étnico Americano ... A2

Activities, Courses & Tours
12 Altro Turismo ... B5
13 Clark Expediciones ... D5
Dexotic ... (see 29)
14 Norte Trekking ... C4
15 Origins ... D5
16 Salta Rafting ... D5
17 Socompa ... B1
18 Tastil ... B5
19 Tren a las Nubes ... B1

Sleeping
20 Ankara Suites ... D5
21 Balcón de la Plaza ... B5
22 Carpe Diem ... C6
23 Coloria Hostel ... C4
24 Design Suites ... A4
25 Espacio Mundano ... A4
26 Hostal Prisamata ... B2
27 Kkala ... F1
28 La Candela ... C4
29 Las Rejas ... B4
30 Legado Mítico ... B3
31 Posada de las Farolas ... C6
32 Prisamata Boutique ... C5
33 Residencial El Hogar ... E5
34 Villa Vicuña ... C5

Eating
35 Bartz ... C3
36 Bonnie Parker ... C4
37 Chirimoya ... C5
38 Dubai ... C3
39 El Charrúa ... C5
40 La Céfira ... C7
41 La Esquina ... B3
42 La Tacita ... C5
43 Ma Cuisine ... D5
44 Mercado Central ... A6
45 Paseo de la Familia ... C8
46 Umai ... B2
47 Vaikuntha ... C3
48 Viracocha ... C4

Drinking & Nightlife
49 Café del Tiempo ... B2
50 Macondo ... B2
51 Peke's Bar ... B4
52 Ruta Norte ... B4
Wine & Bike ... (see 3)

Entertainment
53 La Vieja Estación ... B2
54 Nora Julia ... B2

Shopping
55 CUM ... C5
56 Espacio Urbano ... C3

Residencial El Hogar GUESTHOUSE $
(☎0387-431-6158; www.residencialelhogar.com.ar; Saravia 239; d with/without bathroom US$51/26; P❄☜) Run with genuine warmth, this pleasing little place is on a quiet residential street with Cerro San Bernardo looming over it, and is still an easy stroll into the center. Attractive rooms with tasteful touches, helpful owners and a good breakfast make this a recommended base at a fair price.

The rooms with shared bathroom are the best budget deal in town, but they don't come with breakfast.

Posada de las Farolas HOTEL $
(☎0387-421-3463; www.posadalasfarolas.com.ar; Córdoba 246; s/d/tr US$46/65/82; P❄☜) This place is good value for its neat, clean and air-conditioned rooms in the center, some of which look onto tiny garden patios. It's a spotless and reliable choice. A few extras such as big fluffy towels and hairdryers put it above most in its price band. Cash only.

Coloria Hostel HOSTEL $
(☎0387-431-3058; http://coloria-hostel.hotels-argentina.net/en/; Güemes 333; dm US$10-12, d US$41; P❄☜≋) Upbeat, engaged staff and an open-plan common area that looks over the garden and small pool are the major highlights of this enjoyable central hostel. It's colorful and quite upmarket by Argentine hostel standards; cleanliness is good; and dorms, though there's not a huge amount of space, are comfortable. Private rooms are very tight.

Camping Municipal Carlos Xamena CAMPGROUND $
(0387-496-0506; Av Libano; per person/tent/car US$1.50/2/2; P Wi-Fi pool) This place has 400 tent sites and a huge lakelike pool (it takes 10 days to fill). It's typically loud in summer and on weekends. To get here take bus 3B from Ituzaingó between San Martín and Mendoza. There's a supermarket near the campground.

★**Design Suites** HOTEL $$
(0387-422-4466; www.designsuites.com; Pasaje Castro 215; r/ste from US$104/154; P A/C @ Wi-Fi pool) You may wonder whether the look of this place – all exposed concrete and urban-trendy design – works in colonial Salta, but its excellent, large and quiet rooms are undeniably attractive. They have hydromassage tubs and almost-floor-to-ceiling windows that offer super town views. The rooftop pool-and-spa space is another great spot to linger over splendid views of pretty, old Salta. Service is willing and the restaurant is very good.

Ankara Suites APARTMENT $$
(0387-421-3969; www.ankarasuites.com; Zorrilla 145; apt US$116; P A/C @ Wi-Fi) Inviting luxury apartments in the center of Salta. They come with polished floors, breakfast bar (food is brought to your room), fully equipped kitchens and comfortable double bedrooms. Bathrooms are attractive and modern, with spacious showers. There's a top-floor Jacuzzi and sauna, as well as free laundry facilities.

Finca Valentina ESTANCIA $$
(0387-592-0099, 0387-15-415-3490; www.finca-valentina.com.ar; RN 51, Km6; s/d standard US$115/140, superior US$120/155; P Wi-Fi pool) Only the chirping of birds and cicadas breaks the silence at this peaceful ranch 6km beyond Salta's airport and a 20-minute drive from the town center. The comfortable, homey elegance focuses on cool white spaces and the abundant lounging potential of their verandas. An excellent breakfast is included and other meals are available.

La Candela HOTEL $$
(0387-422-4473; www.hotellacandela.com.ar; Pueyrredón 346; standard/superior d US$87/104; P A/C @ Wi-Fi pool) Decked out like a country villa with an L-shaped pool and a grassy garden, this central and inviting boutique sleep offers cozy and cute rooms with high ceilings, wood floors and tasteful furnishings. Superior rooms have bigger bathrooms, but standard rooms are comfortable too.

Carpe Diem B&B $$
(0387-421-8736; www.bedandbreakfastsalta.com; Urquiza 329; d US$88; @ Wi-Fi) There's a homey feel about this B&B that's full of thoughtful touches, such as home-baked bread at breakfast, enticing places to sit with a book, and attractive rooms, which are stocked with antique furniture. Book well ahead.

Prisamata Boutique BOUTIQUE HOTEL $$
(0387-422-7449; www.prisamataboutique.com; Vicente López 129; d US$94; A/C @ Wi-Fi) Book ahead to grab one of the six rooms at this stylish yet comfortable boutique sleep. The rooms all have tiled floors, Moroccan lanterns and recessed lighting, and the back garden is a chilled-out delight.

★**Balcón de la Plaza** BOUTIQUE HOTEL $$$
(0387-421-4792; www.balcondelaplaza.com.ar; España 444; r US$151-169; P A/C @ Wi-Fi) Polite and genuine, helpful service, an appealing genteel ambience, and 10 understated and elegant rooms with handsome bathrooms and king-sized beds – all this points to a wonderful boutique nest crafted from a converted family home. All rooms come with beamed ceilings, terra-cotta sinks and other tasteful details. You can often get lower rates (and some wonderful deals) in the low season.

★**Legado Mítico** BOUTIQUE HOTEL $$$
(0387-422-8786; www.legadomitico.com; Mitre 647; d from US$210; P A/C @ Wi-Fi) The elegant rooms, some faithful to the style of this noble old Salta house, some with a subtle indigenous theme, are reason enough to book in at this tranquil central retreat. Courteous service and an atmosphere of refined relaxation are other high points. Children aren't allowed.

Kkala BOUTIQUE HOTEL $$$
(0387-439-5962, 0387-439-6590; www.hotelkkala.com.ar; cnr Las Higueras & Las Papayas; r US$128-297; P A/C @ Wi-Fi pool) Tucked away in the upmarket residential barrio of Tres Cerritos, this peaceful place makes relaxation easy. Exquisite rooms, suites and public areas surround a small garden with a heated pool; the higher-grade options come with views and their own Jacuzzi. Decks with city vistas make perfect spots for a sundowner from the bar. Service is top-notch.

Villa Vicuña BOUTIQUE HOTEL $$$
(0387-432-1579; www.villavicuna.com.ar; Caseros 266; r US$154-174; P A/C Wi-Fi pool) Beautifully realized in a central location, this hotel boasts luminous rooms, dressed with

antiques and old-style floor tiles, in a typically elegant Salta house. There's a feeling of light and space throughout; the back garden with pool is a highlight, as is the pleasant service.

Eating

It's a toss-up between Salta and Tucumán for Argentina's best empanadas. Locals debate the merits of fried (in an iron skillet – juicier) or baked (in a clay oven – tastier) offerings.

Vaikuntha VEGAN $

(0387-421-2453; www.facebook.com/pg/vaikuntha.life.food; Leguizamón 450; mains AR$100-130; noon-3pm & 8pm-midnight Mon-Sat;) An adorable vegan joint with pastel brushed chairs, exposed brick walls, rattan lanterns, and classic rock on the sound system. It does a small menu of burgers (made from lentils and rice and piled with tomatoes, pickles and grilled onions), vegan pizzas, pastas and salads. There's a Thai stir-fry too.

More home-style than chef-driven, it's a welcome diversion for herbivores.

Viejo Jack II PARRILLA $

(Catolicos 1465; mains AR$78-325; 12:30-3:30pm & 8pm-1am or later;) Far enough out of the tourist zone to be authentic, this down-to-earth *parrilla* (steak restaurant) in Tres Cerritos is popular with locals for its *parrillada* (mixed grill) and pasta. The servings are huge – designed for two to four – but you'll get a single portion (still enough for two!) for 70% of the price. This is a dynamite place to taste *bife de chorizo* (sirloin steak).

There's another location, closer to the center of town, but this kitchen does it better.

La Tacita EMPANADAS $

(Caseros 396; empanadas AR$15; 8am-11pm Mon-Sat, 10am-11pm Sun) This basic little eatery offers some of the city's best empanadas, all baked, in a welcoming no-frills setting. Great for a quick stop while sightseeing.

Dubai MEDITERRANEAN $

(0387-431-6140; www.facebook.com/Dubaicomidasarabes; Leguizamón 474; mains AR$95-150; noon-3pm & 9pm-midnight;) Family-owned and set in a charming corner dining room, this Syrian kitchen offers a welcome break from *parrilla* fare. Expect solid falafel, hummus and baba ghanoush, shawarma, kebabs and much more served in tasteful upscale environs at fair prices. Free delivery to your hotel.

Mercado Central MARKET $

(Florida & Av San Martín; 8am-4pm) This large, lively market is very interesting, as well as one of the cheapest places to eat in town. You can supplement inexpensive pizza, empanadas and *humitas* (stuffed corn dough, resembling Mexican tamales) with fresh fruit and vegetables.

Paseo de la Familia STREET FOOD $

(Catamarca btwn San Luis & La Rioja; meals AR$70-90, parilla for 4 AR$350; most stalls 8am-3pm) A simple and enjoyable local eating scene can be found on the 'Paseo de la Familia,' occupying a block of Catamarca south of San Luis. Street-food stalls dole out grilled chicken, sausages and rabbit, pizza, tamales and *lomitos* (steak sandwiches). This is a great spot to get the full, affordable *parrilla* treatment, at plastic tables under a long awning.

La Esquina BURGERS $

(0387-432-9476; www.facebook.com/LaEsquinSandwicheria; Balcarce 499; mains AR$35-80; 10am-7am) A greasy corner grill packed with locals who stroll up day and night (it's open 21 hours a day) for burgers, chicken, *lomo* (sirloin) and chorizo sandwiches, all of it grilled or fried to perfection. Congratulations, you've achieved Salta junk-food nirvana. Cash only.

★**Chirimoya** VEGAN $$

(0387-431-2857; España 211; mains AR$130-170; 10:30am-3pm & 8pm-1am Mon-Sat;) Colorful and upbeat, this artsy, world-class vegan restaurant is the most inventive and consistently excellent kitchen in the entire region. Here pasta is fashioned from zucchini, cannelloni are made from corn flour and stuffed with cauliflower florets, they make savory soups and meat-like quinoa patties, and turn mushrooms into high culinary art.

Even the beer and wine are all natural and well curated. Portions are generous, and it's all delicious. It does take-out orders and delivery too.

La Céfira ITALIAN $$

(0387-421-4922; Córdoba 481; mains AR$135-250; 7pm-midnight Mon-Sat, noon-3pm Sun;) This cute hole-in-the-wall, well-lit and decorated with original art, is set a few blocks south of the center, but it's worth the walk here for the menu of house-made pasta combined with inventive ingredients including squid ink, curried pumpkin, coconut milk and poppy seeds. There are some meat and fish dishes too, such as beef stuffed with figs and sun-dried tomatoes.

The range of pasta sauces is tempting, and the wine selection is affordable and delicious.

Bonnie Parker CAFE **$$**
(☎0387-422-2521; www.facebook.com/bonnieparkerhouse; Estero 310; mains AR$130-250; ⏰7am-1am Mon-Sat; 📶) A stylish corner coffeehouse, with arts-and-crafts tiled floors, exposed brick walls, and vintage *vitrolas* (vintage record players) stacked on shelves. The menu offers everything from house-baked pies, juices and smoothies to meal-sized salads, quinoa burgers, grilled salmon and pizza. The kitchen is open all day, which is useful if you need an early dinner.

Bartz TAPAS **$$**
(☎0387-486-3291; www.facebook.com/bartzrestaurant; Leguizamón 465; tapas AR$80-220; ⏰noon-1am Mon-Sat; 📶) An eclectic tapas list is the lure at this cafe-restaurant north of the center. Influences include Spanish, Greek, Japanese and more. The chef puts together attractive but unpretentious combinations that include delicious salmon and tuna options. Dishes are generously proportioned – think three to four of them to feed two.

Viracocha PERUVIAN **$$**
(☎0387-421-2916; www.restaurantviracocha.com.ar; Vicente López 353; dishes AR$90-240; ⏰7pm-1am Mon-Sat; 📶) This noble high-ceilinged Salta building has likably rustic Andean decor and makes a nice change of scene. There's tasty ceviche among other Peruvian dishes, which are generally well presented. It's also a nice spot to drop by for a drink.

Umai SUSHI **$$**
(☎0387-620-4820; www.facebook.com/umaisushibistro; Alsina 710; dishes AR$150; ⏰7:30pm-midnight Mon-Sat) A sushi spot with a stylish minimalist dining room near Plaza Güemes. It does a range of classic and creative rolls, including a list of *panko*-encrusted hot rolls. Don't expect a huge menu of fish, as almost all of the items utilize salmon, tuna or steak, but the food gets high marks from diners.

El Charrúa ARGENTINE, PARRILLA **$$**
(www.parrillaelcharrua.com.ar; Caseros 221; mains AR$180-380; ⏰noon-3:30pm & 7pm-12:30am Mon-Fri, to late Sat & Sun; 📶) Bright and homey, this popular restaurant goes beyond the normal *parrilla* focus and includes some regional dishes, specials and decent pasta. Service and quality are reliable, and the price is fair for this standard.

Ma Cuisine FUSION **$$**
(☎0387-421-4378; www.facebook.com/MaCuisineResto; España 83; mains AR$90-220; ⏰8pm-midnight Mon-Sat; 📶) The refreshing crisp interior of this likable place sees a variety of changing dishes – pasta, fish and meat, all well prepared and served with noodles or stir-fried vegetables – chalked up on the board. The friendly couple that runs it lived in France, so there's a certain Gallic influence at work.

🍷 Drinking & Nightlife

Peñas (p228) are the classic Salta nighttime experience. The two blocks of Balcarce north of Alsina, and the surrounding streets, are the main zone for these and other nightlife. Bars and clubs around here follow the typical 'boom/bust/reopen with new name' pattern, so just follow your nose.

★Café del Tiempo BAR
(www.facebook.com/CafeDelTiempo; Balcarce 901; ⏰6pm-3am Mon-Sat, 8am-2am Sun; 📶) Decked out to resemble a Buenos Aires cafe, this place has prices to match and offers a stylish terrace in the heart of the Balcarce zone; it's a top spot for a drink and makes a mean mojito. Expect some sort of performance or live music every night. The menu includes llama dishes and international offerings such as chop suey.

Wine & Bike WINE BAR
(☎0387-610-1590; www.facebook.com/winebikesalta; Cerro San Bernardo; ⏰11am-6pm) Part wineshop, part wine bar, operated out of a tricked-out bicycle and wagon parked on Cerro San Bernardo (p219). Fair prices, well-curated stock, and you can opt to taste, buy a bottle for the road, or order a bottle and some glasses and find a place to relax, sip and enjoy the view.

Ruta Norte KARAOKE
(☎0387-471-7001; Estero 690; ⏰8pm-4am Tue-Sat, to midnight Sun) An atmospheric dive with dusty tiled floors, exposed brick walls and a tiny bandstand near the brick bar where you and all your new friends will belt out your favorite karaoke numbers. Dark and tawdry, tucked away and damn inviting, this is the perfect place to torch your stage fright to cinders. Nobody knows you here!

Peke's Bar BAR
(☎0387-576-1304; www.facebook.com/PekesBarSalta; Estero 686; ⏰7:30pm-1:30am Mon-Wed, to 2:30am Thu-Sat, to midnight Sun) A locally loved

SALTA'S PEÑAS

Salta is famous Argentina-wide for its *folklórica* (folk music), which is far more national in scope than tango. A *peña* is a bar or social club where people eat, drink and gather to play and listen, traditionally in the form of an impromptu jam session.

These days, the Salta *peña* is quite a touristy experience, incorporating a dinner-show with CD sales and tour groups; nevertheless, it's a great deal of fun. Traditional fare such as empanadas and red wine are served but most places offer a wider menu of regional dishes.

Peña heartland is Calle Balcarce, between Alsina and the train station. There are several here, along with other restaurants, bars and *boliches* (nightclubs) – it's Salta's main nightlife zone.

La Casona del Molino (0387-434-2835; www.facebook.com/lacasonadelmolino; Burela 1; cover charge varies; 9pm-4am Tue-Sun) This former mansion, about 20 blocks west of Plaza 9 de Julio, is a Salta classic. Several spacious rooms feature performers who work around the tables rather than on a stage, as well as spontaneous jams and lots of dancing. The food is good quality (mains cost AR$70 to AR$180). Get there earlyish to guarantee a table. There's a cover on weekend nights.

La Vieja Estación (0387-421-7727; Balcarce 885; cover charge AR$150; 7pm-3am;) The best-established of the Balcarce *peñas*, this place is a professional operation featuring an atmospheric dining room with twinkling rattan lanterns and some terrific photography on the walls, along with a menu that includes children's, gluten-free and vegetarian options among the mostly Andean fusion fare (mains from AR$100 to AR$190). Music starts at 10pm.

Nora Julia (Balcarce 887; cover charge AR$60) This brick and adobe haunt is a good choice for *peña* music. The singers all wear traditional garb and a crew of dancers entertain as well. You'll need to buy drinks or dinner in addition to the cover charge.

two-story bar with well-priced cocktails and cheap eats. It's a good spot for a quiet drink before or after burning down the night.

Macondo BAR

(www.facebook.com/macondo.barensalta; Balcarce 980; 8pm-late Wed-Sun;) With all the *folklórica* music on this street, the mostly indie mix in this trendy bar might come as a relief. Popular with locals and tourists, it keeps it lively until late and has a good streetside terrace. There's live music most nights.

Shopping

An artisans market sets up every Sunday along Balcarce, stretching a couple of blocks south from the station. Av Alberdi is a walking street in the center of town popular with local families who enjoy shopping and snacking here on weekend evenings.

Mercado Artesanal ARTS & CRAFTS

(Av San Martín 2555; 9am-9pm) Good for souvenirs, this provincially sponsored market is set in a centuries-old complex that was once Salta's main flour mill. Within it are a collection of independent kiosks selling handicrafts such as hammocks, string bags, ceramics, basketry, leatherwork, jewelry and the region's distinctive ponchos. To get here take bus 5A from downtown.

Across the street is the much less charming jumble that is Féria Artesano, which operates the same hours. Don't be fooled into coming here by cabbies looking for payola.

CUM CLOTHING

(Comunidades Unidas de Molinos; España 268; 9am-1pm & 5-9pm) The unfortunate English acronym should not keep you away from this charming boutique that trades in top-quality wool sweaters, shawls, blankets, throw pillows, gloves, hats and yarns. All of it is sourced straight from community mills and tradespeople.

Espacio Urbano FASHION & ACCESSORIES

(www.facebook.com/espaciourbano.salta; Leguizamón 445; 10am-1:30pm & 5-9pm) Espacio Urbano is a gorgeous courtyard boutique trading in hip styles from international brands. Think Bensimon swimwear, Bolivia chinos and much more. Sales associates are eager to help, and it's just a fun and fashionable browse.

Information

Calle España, at the corner of Plaza 9 de Julio, was the money changers' hangout when we last visited. You'll get a better deal with clean US$100 bills than with US$20 bills.

Bolivian Consulate (☎0387-421-1040; www.embajadadebolivia.com.ar; Boedo 34; ⌚8am-1pm Mon-Fri) If you plan on crossing the Bolivian border, stop here to apply for your visa first.

Chilean Consulate (☎0387-431-1857; http://chileabroad.gov.cl; Estero 965; ⌚9am-1pm Mon-Fri) This consulate also issues visas.

Hospital San Bernardo (☎0800-444-4111; www.hospitalsanbernardo.gob.ar; Tobías 69)

Municipal Tourist Office (Caseros 711; ⌚8am-9pm Mon-Fri, 9am-9pm Sat & Sun) Gives out maps. Also runs desks in the bus terminal and at the airport, open roughly 9am to 9pm, depending on staffing.

National Parks Administration (APN; ☎0387-431-2683; www.parquesnacionales.gov.ar; España 366; ⌚8am-2pm Mon-Fri) On the 3rd floor of the Aduana building; offers information and advice on the region's national parks.

Post Office (www.correoargentino.com.ar; Deán Funes 160; ⌚8:30am-7:30pm Mon-Fri)

Provincial Tourist Office (☎0387-431-0950; www.turismosalta.gov.ar; Buenos Aires 93; ⌚8am-9pm Mon-Fri, 9am-8pm Sat & Sun) This office gets top marks – it's friendly, efficient and multilingual. Ask staff about provincial road conditions.

Getting There & Away

AIR

Salta's **Martín Miguel de Güemes Airport** (SLA; ☎0387-424-3115; RN 51, Km 5) is 9.5km southwest of town.

Aerolíneas Argentinas (☎0810-222-8652; www.aerolineas.com; Caseros 475; ⌚8am-12:45pm & 4-6:45pm Mon-Fri, 9am-12:45pm Sat) Flies several times daily to Buenos Aires; also serves Córdoba and Mendoza.

Andes (☎0-810-7772-6337; www.andesonline.com; Caseros 459; ⌚8am-1pm & 4:30-7pm Mon-Fri, 9:30am-1pm Sat) Two to three weekly flights to Buenos Aires with connection to Puerto Madryn.

BoA (☎0387-471-1558; www.boa.bo; Mitre 37, Shop 24; ⌚9am-1pm & 3-6pm) Has an office in a shopping arcade off Plaza 9 de Julio. Flies to Santa Cruz (Bolivia) once a week.

LATAM (☎0-810-999-9526; www.latam.com; Caseros 476; ⌚9am-1pm & 5-8pm Mon-Fri) Flies to Buenos Aires and Lima (Peru)

BUS

Salta's **bus terminal** (☎0387-431-5022; Av Hipólito Yrigoyen; ⌚information 6am-10pm) has ATMs, tourist information and left-luggage services.

Three companies run to San Pedro de Atacama, Chile (AR$700, nine to 10 hours), with daily departures at 7am via Jujuy and Purmamarca. They continue to Calama (AR$850), Antofagasta (AR$900), Iquique (AR$1050) and Arica (AR$1150).

Ale Hermanos runs two to three times daily to San Antonio de los Cobres (AR$208, 5½ hours) and Cachi (AR$210, 4½ hours).

OFF THE BEATEN TRACK

PARQUE NACIONAL EL REY

East of Salta, this **national park** (☎in Salta 0387-431-2683; www.parquesnacionales.gob.ar/areas-protegidas/region-noroeste/pn-el-rey) FREE is at the southern end of the Yungas subtropical corridor and protects a glorious, biologically diverse habitat. It's a beautiful, varied landscape ranging from meadowlands and low scrub forest to subtropical cloud forest. From its well-marked trails, some accessible by vehicle, you'll see lots of birdlife, and mammals such as peccaries and brown brocket deer are often spotted.

Laguna Los Patitos, 2km from park headquarters, offers opportunities to observe waterbirds. Longer trails lead to moss-covered Pozo Verde, a three- to four-hour climb to an area teeming with birdlife. Other trails are of similar day-trip length and involve multiple river crossings. Shorter 2km Sendero La Chuña heads out from the campground and is a good introduction to this ecosystem. There is free camping at the park's headquarters, with a huge grassy area for tents, with toilets, drinkable water, cold showers and evening power, but no shop. Contact the National Parks Administration office in Salta for up-to-date info. The closest noncamping accommodations are at a curious ecological community 4km down the park road from the turnoff.

For Puerto Iguazú, change in Resistencia. For Bariloche, change in Mendoza. Companies sell through-tickets.

Buses from Salta

DESTINATION	COST (AR$)	TIME (HR)
Buenos Aires	2259-2616	18-22
Cafayate	215	4
Córdoba	1197-1995	11-14
Jujuy	175	2
La Quiaca	360	7½
La Rioja	1275-1332	10
Mendoza	2445-2550	18-20
Resistencia	1205-1381	10-12
Salvador Mazza	725	6½
Santiago del Estero	624	7
Tucumán	372-500	4¼

CAR

There are dozens of car-rental agencies: get several quotes. Typically, it's AR$800 to AR$1000 per day, and triple that for a 4WD.

There are often advance-booking specials online. Most offer discounts for paying cash.

Companies, including international names, can be slipshod operations. Mechanical problems are common (we had a car break down on us at the Bolivian border!), and don't expect state-of-the-art roadside assistance: you're often better off sorting out minor problems yourself. Complaints are frequent.

A list of providers is available at http://turismo.salta.gov.ar. **Alto Valle** (☎0387-431-0796; www.altovallerentacar.com.ar; Zuviria 524; ⏰9am-6pm) is considered a solid service – well priced and professional.

Always check with the Provincial Tourist Office (p229) for current road conditions. Punctures are common, so check the spare kit of your vehicle before leaving Salta.

You can't take rental cars into Bolivia, but it's possible to head into Chile by paying a bit extra and giving a few days' notice.

Getting Around

Local bus 8A from San Martín by Córdoba runs to the airport, otherwise it's AR$180 to AR$220 in a taxi from downtown.

Grab a rechargeable *tarjeta magnética* bus card, available from some kiosks. Fares cost AR$8 per ride.

Several local buses connect downtown with the bus terminal; it's not a long walk, either.

From Parque San Martín the teleférico cable car (p219) zips you up to the top of Cerro San Bernardo in less than 10 minutes.

Valles Calchaquíes

One of Argentina's most seductive rural zones is a winning combination of rugged landscapes, traditional weavers' workshops, striking adobe villages and top vineyards. Small but sophisticated Cafayate, with its wineries and paved highway, presents quite a contrast to more remote settlements such as Angastaco or Molinos, while Cachi, accessible from Salta via a spectacular road that crosses the Parque Nacional Los Cardones, is a peaceful, adorable and increasingly popular base. Vernacular architecture merits special attention: even modest adobe houses sport neoclassical columns or neo-Moorish arches.

The indigenous Diaguita (Calchaquí) put up some of the stiffest resistance to Spanish rule.

Getting There & Away

The RN 40, a mostly rugged, unpaved road, stretches 157km from Cafayate to Cachi, but is still passable in most passenger cars. Buses from Salta access both ends of the road (Cachi and Cafayate), but at research time they had stopped running from Angastaco north to Cachi on RN 40, which means the best way to do the circuit is to rent your own wheels.

Chicoana

☎0387 / POP 4200

Tucked away near the junction of the Cafayate and Cachi roads, just 41km south of Salta, the likable country town of Chicoana, with its shady plaza and inviting green mountains rising from surrounding horse pastures, makes a fine stop for lunch, for the night (a tempting final stop if you're flying out of Salta the next morning), or for a spot of horseback riding.

Activities

Sayta HORSEBACK RIDING
(☎0387-15-683-6565; www.saltacabalgatas.com.ar; Chicoana) This *estancia* (ranch) near Chicoana runs excellent horseback-riding day tours, offering a blast of gaucho culture and optional *asado* (barbecue grill). A half-day with/without lunch costs US$85/60; a full day US$120 to US$140 (with overnight accommodations US$150). A two-day/one-

PARQUE NACIONAL LOS CARDONES

Flanking the winding RP 33 from Salta to Cachi across the Cuesta del Obispo, **Parque Nacional Los Cardones** (www.parquesnacionales.gob.ar; RP 33) takes its name from the cardón (candelabra cactus), the park's dominant plant species. In the treeless Andean foothills and puna, the cardón has long been an important source of timber for rafters, doors, windows and more. You'll see it often in the region's traditional buildings.

The most picturesque part of the park is the Valle Encantado, accessed via a drivable 4km track at Km 61. A few further miradores (viewpoints) are signposted along the road, along with a couple of short interpretative trails from along the straight stretch in Recta de Tin-Tin. The modern **national park office** (☑ 03868-15-452879; loscardones@apn.gov. ar; Payogasta; ⊘ 8am-3pm Mon-Fri) is in Payogasta, 11km north of Cachi.

This is gorgeous high-desert territory, with rounded peaks crowning velvety mountains, where cactus groves stand tall at elevations that eclipse 3000m. Take plenty of water and protect yourself from the sun. Buses between Salta and Cachi will stop for you, but verify times in advance. It's much better to have your own wheels.

night package is US$250. Prices include transfers from Salta.

🛏 Sleeping & Eating

★ **Bo Hotel & Spa**　　　BOUTIQUE HOTEL **$$**
(☑ 0387-490-7068; www.facebook.com/bo.chicoa na; 25 de Mayo 25; d from US$75; ［P］❄@🛜🏊) This smart place on substantial grassy grounds offers eight spacious rooms decorated in an upbeat style with modern fabrics and colors. Enjoy a range of facilities, including free bikes, a spa, an in-house chef and restaurant, and helpful service.

Finca Las Margaritas　　　ESTANCIA **$$$**
(☑0387-15-592-9194; www.fincalasmargaritas.com. ar; RP 49, Paraje Bella Vista; d/f US$163/185; ［P］🛜🏊) Located 8km from Chicoana, signposted off the RN 33, this divine *estancia* has the lot: elegant rooms themed on the farm's crops, wide verandas, a classic rural Argentine ambience and good food. It has a pool too, and can happily arrange excursions in the area. Oh, and it's nestled up against rolling jade hills.

Bocha　　　ARGENTINE **$**
(Güemes 90; meals AR$70; ⊘noon-4:30pm) This very simple family-run *comedor* (basic cafeteria) is the town's favorite eating place. Big round tables are parked across a concrete floor. Choose from three or four daily specials, all delicious. Soup is offered after the mains. Lunch and cash only.

❶ Information

Tourist Office (www.chicoanasalta.org; cnr Córdoba & El Carmen; ⊘8am-8pm) On a corner of the square; very helpful.

❶ Getting There & Away

Chicoana is connected to Salta via local buses (interurban route 5, AR$20, 60 minutes), which run east along Belgrano and west along San Martín. You'll need a Salta bus card.

Cachi

☑ 03868 / POP 2600 / ELEV 2280M
An enchanting adobe town, backed by snow-capped Andean peaks and fringed with high-altitude vineyards that produce world-class wine, Cachi will make your heart quiver. It's the biggest place hereabouts by some distance – you'll hear locals refer to it as 'the city' – but it's more of a *pueblo* (small town). A damn handsome *pueblo*. One with fresh highland air, sunny days and crisp nights. The cobblestones, adobe architecture, tranquil plaza and the opportunities on hand to explore the surrounding wilds mean that it's the sort of place that can easily eat extra days out of your carefully planned itinerary. Go ahead and torch that thing. Cachi will make everything alright.

◉ Sights & Activities

A short walk from Cachi's plaza brings you to a **viewpoint**, then a picturesque hilltop **cemetery**; nearby is an unlikely airstrip.

A handful of unremarkable **archaeological sites** dotted around the valley make destinations for hikes or drives with views. There's a winery in town, and others within easy driving distance.

Many locals rent horses for **horseback riding**; look for signs or ask at the tourist office.

Iglesia San José CHURCH
(Plaza 9 de Julio s/n; ⏲9am-9pm) This endearing adobe church (1796) has graceful arches and a barrel-vaulted ceiling of cardón wood. The confessional and other features are also cardón, while holy water lives in a large *tinaja* (oil jar).

Museo Arqueológico MUSEUM
(☎03868-491080; Calchaquí s/n; AR$60; ⏲9am-6pm Tue-Sun) This well-presented and professionally arranged museum on the plaza gives an account of the surrounding area's cultural evolution, with good background information (in Spanish) on archaeological methods. Don't miss the wall in the secondary patio, composed of stones with petroglyphs.

Valley Walking WALKING
Around 6km from Cachi, Cachi Adentro is a tiny village where not a lot happens: ride the seesaws in the demi-plaza or sip a soda from the store. It's a particularly lovely walk in summer, when streams and cascades are alive with running water.

From here, you could return a longer way (20km total): bear left past the church and then take a left down the road signposted Las Trancas. This winds around the valley and eventually crosses the river; 400m later, turn left (heading right leads 2km up to the lovely Algarrobal campground). This will lead you back to Cachi via the hamlet of La Aguada. This last section is splendid in the late afternoon.

Tours

★Urkupiña OUTDOORS
(☎03868-491317; www.urkupinatur.wix.com/cachi; Zorrilla 237) An excellent agency offering trips to nearby archaeological sites, and longer jaunts along RN 40 in both directions, toward Cafayate or San Antonio. But it's best known for enjoyable hiking tours into the Nevado de Cachi mountains or the red sandstone cave formations of Acsibi. Call or email for current prices.

Sleeping

Casa Blanca INN $
(☎03868-840417; www.facebook.com/casajaguarcachi; Güemes s/n; d from US$65, apt US$118; 📶🏊) Set a few blocks from Cachi's plaza, this converted home is now an upmarket inn. Rooms are simple but nice, with polished wood furnishings, high ceilings and crown moldings. There's also a stand-alone apartment that sleeps four, and makes a great choice for families. There's a pool and a sweet garden bursting with lavender.

Viracocha HOSTEL $
(☎03868-15-491713; Ruiz de los Llanos s/n; dm US$18, d with/without bathroom US$54/43; 📶) Central and relaxed, this likable hostel has good dorms featuring sturdy bunk beds with plenty of headroom. Private rooms are colorful and comfortable; mattresses throughout are decent. There's no kitchen, but there's courtyard space and tea- and coffee-making facilities. A romantically lit restaurant serving decent regional specialties and Andean cuisine is attached.

Camping Municipal CAMPGROUND, HOSTEL $
(☎03868-491902; oficinadeturismo.cachi@gmail.com; campsite per 2 persons plus tent US$7, with power US$10, cabins US$40; P🏊) On a hill southwest of Cachi's plaza are grassy, tree-shaded campsites, some hedge-bordered and with barbecues. The municipal pool is here, along with a couple of cabins.

★El Cortijo BOUTIQUE HOTEL $$
(☎03868-491034; www.elcortijohotel.com; Av ACA s/n; d standard/superior from US$89/100; P❄📶🏊) This small hotel, owned by a Salta plastic surgeon, is stylish and comfortable. Rooms are decorated with finesse: ceramic tiled floors, beamed ceilings, marble-topped nightstands and washbasins. Some open onto the wonderful interior courtyard, others have fabulous views of the sierra. Superior rooms have space enough for a comfortable sitting area.

There's also a decent on-site restaurant and helpful staff.

Hostería Villa Cardón GUESTHOUSE $$
(☎03868-491701; www.facebook.com/hosteriavillacardon; Aranda s/n; d standard/superior from US$67/77; 📶) Friendly young owners bend over backward here to make your stay in Cachi a pleasant one, which it will be if you book one of their four white, minimalist, comfortable rooms with artistic flourishes that open onto a courtyard. Breakfast is a highlight, and the overall package is faultless. The teahouse out front is great too. Single rates are available off-season.

Sala de Payogasta BOUTIQUE HOTEL $$
(☎03868-496052; www.saladepayogasta.com; RN 40, Km4509, Payogasta; d/ste from US$55/73; P📶) This historic ranch has rustic rooms set around a beautiful courtyard. Suites

have hydromassage tubs and cute fireplaces; the best has a fine outlook over fields and mountains. The breakfast and dining room share the same vista. There's also a nearby winery where lunches are served. It's 10km from Cachi on the Salta road, just outside of Payogasta.

Miraluna CABAÑAS **$$**
(☎0387-432-0888; www.miraluna.com.ar; La Aguada; cabañas for 2 people US$106, 4 people US$185-195; P📶❄) Located 7km from Cachi in the hamlet of La Aguada, these romantic, rustic cabins come in three sizes and have a peaceful setting in a working vineyard surrounded by breathtaking mountain and valley views. Breakfast features tasty home-baked bread, but lunch or dinner isn't offered. It does have a small shop with pasta, sauces and oils.

In the summer you can also help yourself to vegetables from the organic garden. A winery visit is included.

La Merced del Alto HOTEL **$$$**
(☎03868-490030; www.lamerceddelalto.com; Fuerte Alto; d from US$149; P@📶❄) Built of traditional whitewashed adobe, with ceramic floors, marble washbasins and cane ceilings, this hotel across the river (2.5km from Cachi) is designed to resemble a historical monastery. It pairs excellent facilities with restrained, almost spare (for this price) rooms looking over either surrounding vineyards and the hills beyond or the interior patio.

Eating

Local eateries in the streets near the plaza do no-frills traditional plates, but there are some standouts.

★ **Ashpamanta** VEGETARIAN **$**
(☎03868-578-2244; Bustamante s/n; dishes AR$130-210; ⏲noon-3pm & 7-10pm; ✎) A tasty chef-driven vegetarian chalet set in the middle of adorable downtown Cachi, Ashpamanta does fresh pastas and pizzettas with local goat cheese, fresh tomato and pesto sauces, elaborate salads, veggie curry and much more. It's all served in an intimate historic adobe at candlelit tables under vaulted, beamed ceilings. There's a terrific atmosphere and the flavors deliver too.

El Molle de Maiz Pérez ARGENTINE **$**
(Suárez s/n; mains AR$90-150; ⏲noon-3pm & 7-11pm; 📶) This one-man show takes place in an attractive room, with cardón tables on upturned logs. There are a few quirks (just go with the flow), but the food – roast chicken, *locro* (a spicy stew of maize, beans, beef, pork and sausage), pizzas and *milanesas* (breaded cutlets) – is delicious.

Evening opening times are unreliable. In fact, some days it doesn't open at all.

Oliver PIZZA **$**
(☎03868-491903; Ruíz de los Llanos 160; mains AR$60-150; ⏲7am-midnight; 📶) This homey, multilevel restaurant and wine bar on the plaza is a reliable choice for tasty pizza, bruschetta, *picadas* (shared appetizer plates) and a couple of creative meaty mains. The setting, with its aged wood tables and fun-loving vibe, is a fine place for a sundowner. Or a nooner.

Information

Tourist Office (☎03868-491902; oficinadeturismo.cachi@gmail.com; Güemes s/n; ⏲9am-9pm) On the plaza.

Getting There & Away

Two to three daily buses run between Salta (AR$290, four hours) and Cachi: it's quite a ride!

From Cachi, Seclantás is serviced daily (AR$64), with the bus continuing four times weekly to Molinos (AR$70). There are no longer direct buses down the road to Angastaco and on to Cafayate – you'll have to divert all the way to Salta to get to either destination from Cachi. A tour from Cachi is also an option.

Buses run north as far as La Poma, the end of the line. The road beyond, to San Antonio de los Cobres, is an arduous ascent crisscrossing a river via lonely goat farms to a 4895m pass. It's only passable in a non-4WD at certain times (normally September to December); phone the **police** (☎03868-490-9051) for advice. Otherwise, approach San Antonio the long way round.

Seclantás

☎03868 / POP 600 / ELEV 2100M

Charming and peaceful Seclantás is the spiritual home of the Salta poncho. There are many weavers' workshops in town and along the eastern branch of the road to Cachi (dubbed the 'Ruta de los Artesanos'). Drop by their home studios and browse the wares. Most people who stop here are self-drivers, on their way between Cafayate or Angastaco and Cachi. Very few overnight, as there's not much to do here other than listen to the wind whistle through empty streets.

Sleeping

El Capricho GUESTHOUSE $
(☎03868-498069, 03868-498064; hosteriaelcapricho@gmail.com; Cornejo s/n; d US$53;) Set around a garden courtyard on a quaint plaza in little Seclantás, El Capricho makes a tranquil base for exploring the region. Rooms are cool and pleasant, with high ceilings. Staff can arrange meals upon request.

Getting There & Away

There's a daily morning bus from Cachi to Seclantás; it continues to Molinos four days a week.

Molinos

☎03868 / POP 1200 / ELEV 2020M

Molinos is a true backwater with a collection of striking colonial buildings and beautiful adobe houses surrounded by willowy mesquite trees that huddle on the windswept hills. It's even more laid-back than the nearby town of Cachi.

Still, there's no pressing reason to spend the night, which is why the vast majority of visitors hit and run as they're heading up or down the Valles Calchaquíes under their own steam.

Molinos takes its name from the still-operational flour mill on the Río Calchaquí.

Sights

Centro de Interpretación Molinos MUSEUM, WORKSHOP
(☎0387-15-459-2666; casaindaleciogomez@yahoo.com.ar; Cornejo s/n; donation AR$20; 8am-1pm & 2-6pm Mon-Sat, 8am-1pm Sun) This restored historic house has a good English and Spanish display on the region's culture and history, and tourist information. It's also a space for artisans – especially weavers – to work and sell their crafts, one of a number of inspiring sustainable projects around the area.

Iglesia San Pedro Nolasco CHURCH
(8am-8pm) The town church, built in the Cuzco style, dates from the 17th and 18th centuries, and features twin bell towers and a cactus-wood ceiling. The Stations of the Cross are tapestries by local artisans.

Sleeping

★**Hacienda de Molinos** BOUTIQUE HOTEL $$
(☎03868-494094; www.haciendademolinos.com.ar; Cornejo s/n; d from US$140;) Across from the church, this colonial adobe hacienda is also known as Casa de Isasmendi, after Salta's last colonial governor, who lived and died here. It's been well restored and offers handsome rooms with inviting beds, antique furniture and cane ceilings set around lovely patio spaces. It's on the edge of the village and utterly peaceful.

There's an overpriced but otherwise reasonable on-site restaurant (open from noon to 3pm and 7:30pm to 10:30pm).

Getting There & Away

There's a bus to Molinos from Salta (AR$305, six hours) via Cachi (AR$70, two hours) on Monday, Wednesday, Friday and Sunday. There are no longer any direct buses to Angastaco.

Local *remise* (taxi) operators run to Angastaco (around AR$700) on demand and can also take you to Colomé (AR$450 including waiting time) and other wineries.

Angastaco

☎03868 / POP 900 / ELEV 1955M

Talk about a special town waiting to be discovered – tiny Angastaco sits among some of the most dramatic rockscapes of the valley route. Located 40km south of Molinos and 54km north of San Carlos, it's an oasis with vineyards, fields of anise and cumin, and the ruins of an ancient *pucará* (walled city). Just south of town, back on RN 40 you'll navigate spectacular terrain, unofficially known as the **Angastaco Natural Monument**. Beauty is here in spades, the local population is inviting and warm, and there are some mom-and-pop bodegas too. One day the mass tourism dollar will discover her gifts, so get here soon.

Angastaco has an ATM and gas station, and the entire town is blessed with municipal wi-fi.

Sights

Bodega El Cese WINERY
(☎0387-15-032055; www.bodegaelcese.com.ar; RN 40, Km4421; hrs vary) This picturesque boutique winery sits in a lovely setting 7km north of the turnoff to Angastaco. The wines are uncomplicated but tasty, and free tastings are given. It's best to phone ahead.

Sleeping & Eating

There are only a few sleeping options in town. All are simple and none are sensational, but that's to be expected in still-to-be-discovered territory, so enjoy it. Campers should make their way south of town, into the Angastaco Natural Monument, where you'll find abundant free 'campsites' just off the highway.

WORTH A TRIP

COLOMÉ BODEGA

Fine wines are produced at this ecological **bodega** (03868-494200; www.bodegacolome.com; standard/old-vines tastings AR$100/300; 10:30am-6pm Tue-Sun), which is set (as they say hereabouts) 'where the devil lost his poncho,' 18km down a spectacular gravel road west from Molinos. The vineyards enjoy a stunning natural setting, surrounded by hills and mountains that seem to change color hourly. There's forward-thinking here on several fronts: the company generates its own energy, has funded substantial infrastructural improvements in the local community, and boasts a stunning museum featuring the work of artist James Turrell.

Both bodega and museum visits are combined into a single 90-minute tour and must be booked ahead by phone or email. Tours are offered between 10am and 4pm from Tuesday to Sunday. If you do just turn up, management may allow you to taste the goods or grab lunch, but don't expect a tour. The bodega serves delicious salads and sandwiches (AR$90 to AR$190) and a meat option (from 12:30pm to 2:30pm Tuesday to Sunday). A high-end hotel on-site was undergoing renovations at the time of research. It may be back up and running by the time you get here.

Some 9km beyond Colomé, **Bodegas Humanao** (0387-431-1058; www.humanao.com.ar; 10am-5pm Tue-Sun) is worth a visit for a delicious, balanced cabernet-malbec blend, among other wines.

Rincón Florido ARGENTINE $

(Castilla s/n; dishes AR$70-115; 11:30am-3pm) A curious and heartwarming lunch stop just beyond Angastaco's municipal building. Three courtyard tables in a family home are vine-shaded and watched over by a talking parrot and myriad curious objects, from farm implements to armadillo shells. There's no menu. Food is simple and good, with delicious empanadas, vegetables from the garden and their own sweetish red wine.

Getting There & Away

Buses head south to San Carlos and Cafayate Monday to Saturday mornings and Monday, Friday and Sunday afternoons (AR$81, two hours).

Buses arrive here from Salta (AR$295, eight hours) via Cafayate four days a week. At the time of research there were no bus lines making the run up RN 40 to Cachi. Ask around about shared *remises* or minivans that make the run to Molinos (about AR$600), where you can hop a bus to Cachi. Otherwise, it's a hitchhike, best done from the main road.

Given the attractions awaiting you on the outskirts of town, and the unpredictable transportation services, this area is best accessed with your own wheels.

San Carlos

03868 / POP 2200 / ELEV 1624M

A sizable village, San Carlos lies just north of Cafayate and is connected to the town by a paved road – a pleasant shock if you're arriving from the north. It's just a rest stop for weary road-trippers. There's not much of interest here.

Sleeping

La Casa de los Vientos GUESTHOUSE $

(03868-495075; www.casadelosvientos.com.ar; Alfareras s/n; d US$56; P @) This is a sweet spot, signposted off the main road at the Cachi end of town and built in the traditional adobe manner, with terra-cotta tiles and cane ceilings. It also incorporates some ingenious environmental innovations. The well-traveled owner is a potter, and the rooms (all different) are decorated with rustic flair and beauty.

Getting There & Away

San Carlos is set 22km north of Cafayate by a paved road. Several buses make the run from Cafayate (AR$23, 45 minutes) every day.

Cafayate

03868 / POP 13,700 / ELEV 1683M

Argentina's second center for quality wine production, Cafayate is a popular tourist destination but still has a tranquil small-town feel. It's good-looking territory, with the green of the vines backed by soaring mountains beyond, and is one of northwest Argentina's most seductive destinations. With a selection of excellent accommodations for every budget, and several wineries – from boutique upstarts to burly behemoths – to visit in and around town, it invites an extended stay.

Cafayate is famous for its torrontés, a grape producing aromatic white wines that can be a bit round when aged in oak. Thankfully there are progressive wineries in the area decoupling that traditional pairing, resulting in dry(-ish) torrontés. Bodegas hereabouts also produce fine reds from cabernet sauvignon, malbec and tannat, and some dry rosé too.

Sights

Museo de la Vid y El Vino MUSEUM

(www.museodelavidyelvino.gov.ar; Av General Güemes; foreigners/Argentines AR$40/20; 9am-7pm) This impressive museum gives a good introduction to the area's wine industry. The atmospheric first section, which deals with the viticultural side – the life of the vines – through a series of poems and images, is particularly appealing. The second part covers the winemaking side, and there's a cafe where you can try and buy. English translations appear throughout.

Museo Arqueológico MUSEUM

(cnr Colón & Calchaquí; entry by donation; 10:30am-9pm Mon-Fri, 11am-7:30pm Sat) This private museum's collection was left by enthusiastic archaeologist Rodolfo Bravo and merits a visit. Sourced mostly from grave sites within a 30km radius of Cafayate, the excellent array of ceramics, from the black and gray wares of the Candelaria and Aguada cultures to late Diaguita and Inca pottery, are well displayed across two rooms. While there's not much explanation, the material speaks for itself. It closes for an hour for lunch in summer.

Bodega El Transito WINERY

(www.facebook.com/bodega.eltransito; Belgrano 102; tastings AR$20; 9:30am-12:30pm & 3:30-7pm) A slick operation in Cafayate's center, where you can taste all seven of its wines in a room that feels like an upscale lounge.

Bodega Nanni WINERY

(03868-421527; www.bodegananni.com; Chavarría 151; tours free, tastings AR$50-80; 9:30am-1pm & 3-6:30pm Mon-Sat, 11am-1pm & 3-6pm Sun) Take the half-hour tour and taste four bright, young wines at this small, central winery with a lovely grass patio. The juice is organic, uncomplicated and drinkable. There's a good on-site restaurant.

Bodega Figueroa WINERY

(03868-421125; gualiama@gmail.com; Pasaje 20 de Junio 25; tastings per person AR$30; 9:30am-12:30pm & 3:30-6pm) This tiny family winery in Cafayate produces only 10,000 bottles of torrontés and malbec per year with small hand-operated equipment. Just one wine is poured for visitors. Ask for the malbec, which local chefs love. Its vineyards are 40km north of town.

El Porvenir WINERY

(03868-422007; www.elporvenirdecafayate.com; Córdoba 32; tours free, tastings from AR$100; 9am-1pm & 3-6pm Wed-Sat, 9am-1pm Sun & Mon) This well-run family bodega has recently been taken over by the 30-something daughter, who knows how to keep good torrontés from touching corrupting oak (you may have noticed that most torrontés is a bit oaky and round). Here, it's dry, as is the splendid rosé, and its reds have always been fantastic. The tour is free, but generous tastings cost from AR$100, depending on which wines you want to try. Reserve by phone.

★ **Finca las Nubes** WINERY

(03868-422129; www.bodegamounier.com.ar; tours incl tasting AR$75; 10am-5pm Mon-Sat, 11am-4pm Sun) Located 5km southwest of Cafayate along the road to Río Colorado (it's signposted 'Mounier'), this small, organic and friendly winery has a fabulous position at the foot of jagged hills. Tours depart hourly from 10am to 4:30pm. Tastings include four wines. The kitchen also serves empanadas (AR$18) and *picada* platters (AR$250). Grape-picking day in March – when volunteers are welcome – is lots of fun.

Piattelli WINERY

(03868-418214; www.piattellivineyards.com; RP 2; standard tours AR$115, with premium wines AR$170; 10am-6pm, tours 10am, 11am, noon, 1pm, 3pm & 4pm) Built as if money and space were no object, this upscale, over-the-top, US-owned winery is 3km from Cafayate. Tours show you three levels of relatively small-scale but state-of-the-art winemaking equipment and culminate in a long tasting of seven wines. There's an on-site restaurant that serves delicious lunches. Tours can be bilingual upon request.

Domingo Molino WINERY

(03868-452887; www.domingomolina.com.ar; tastings AR$100; 10am-5pm Wed-Sun, 10am to 1pm Mon) A small producer, perched on a gorgeous hillside overlooking the verdant valley,

Cafayate

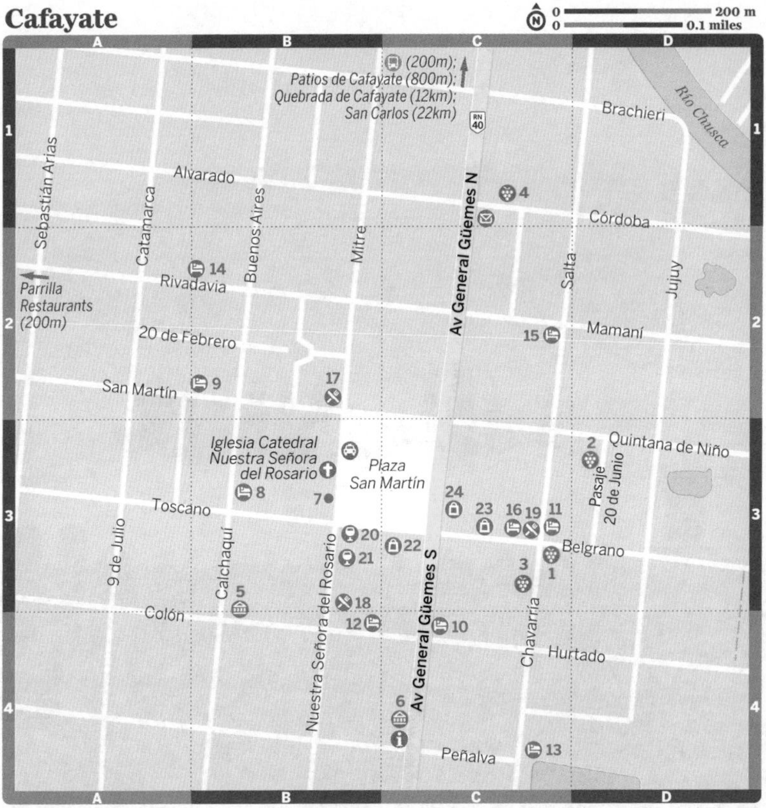

Cafayate

Sights

1 Bodega El Transito C3
2 Bodega Figueroa D3
3 Bodega Nanni C3
4 El Porvenir C1
5 Museo Arqueológico B3
6 Museo de la Vid y El Vino C4

Activities, Courses & Tours

7 Majo Viajes B3

Sleeping

8 Casa Árbol B3
9 Hostal del Valle B2
10 Hostel Ruta 40 .... C4
11 Hotel Munay C3
12 Killa B4
13 Portal del Santo C4
14 Rusty-K Hostal B2
15 Vieja Posada C2
16 Villa Vicuña C3

Eating

17 Casa de las Empanadas B2
18 Casa de las Empanadas II B3
19 Pacha C3
Retoño .... (see 3)

Drinking & Nightlife

20 Cafayateña B3
21 Chato's Wine Bar B3

Shopping

22 Cafayate Artesenal C3
23 El Colmado C3
24 Mercado Artesanal C3

backed by rugged mountains, with vineyards cascading down the slopes. It bottles 21 varieties of wine here, including some bubbles. You can't taste them all, but you can sip several by choosing one of five tasting options, each with a combination of reds and whites.

1

3

AG-CHAPELHILL/GETTY IMAGES ©

1. Vineyards
The Cafayate area is famous for its torrontés, a grape producing aromatic white wines.

2. Parque Nacional Los Cardones (p231)
This park takes its name from the cardón (candelabra cactus), the reserve's dominant plant species.

3. Parque Nacional Talampaya (p280)
This dusty desert boasts spectacular rock formations and canyons.

ECOPRINT/SHUTTERSTOCK ©

San Pedro Yacochuya WINERY
(www.yacochuya.com.ar; RP 2, Km6; ⏲10am-5pm Mon-Fri, 10am to 1pm Sat) An atmospheric boutique winery set at the end of a dusty desert road with cacti on one side and vineyards on the other. It makes 250,000 bottles of wine here each year, most stored in oak barrels in a wine cave cooled by running canals. The winery has been at it for a while: its malbec is picked from century-old vines, and it does a nice 80-20 blend of malbec and cabernet.

Try its dry malbec rosé, under the Coquena label. Tastings are always available, but service can be frosty.

Activities

★**Río Colorado** WALKING, SWIMMING
A picturesque walk 6km southwest from Cafayate leads you to Río Colorado. From here, follow the river upstream (the Diaguita community encourages taking a guide, around AR$300 per group) for about an hour to get to a 10m **waterfall**, where you can swim. A second waterfall and more cascades are further up.

Look out for **rock paintings** on the way. There's a car park at the trailhead, as well as a campground and a drinks and snacks stand. A visit here can be combined with the Finca las Nubes winery (p236).

Warning: if the river is high after rains in January and February, the route to the waterfall becomes strenuous and dangerous. Sudden torrents can come down quickly from the mountains at any time of year, so always keep an eye upstream while bathing.

Tours

A standard minibus tour of the Quebrada de Cafayate leaves in the afternoon, when colors are more vivid, and costs US$30. Three- to four-hour treks in the Quebrada and Río Colorado are also popular. Daylong trips to Cachi (US$100) are tiring, while trips to Quilmes (US$35) are faster and more comfortable in a taxi if you're two or more. Horseback rides start at two hours (US$85). Places around Cafayate's plaza hire out bikes (AR$250 for a full day).

Tour operators have offices on the plaza. Most are mediocre but the Quebrada scenery speaks for itself regardless.

Majo Viajes TOURS
(☎03868-422038; majoviajes@gmail.com; Nuestra Señora del Rosario 77) This reliable, straight-talking agency on Cafayate's plaza is better than most of the excursion operators in town, and offers tours to Quilmes, the Quebrada de Cafayate and Cachi, as well as horseback-riding trips through the surrounding countryside.

Festivals & Events

Serenata a Cafayate MUSIC
(www.serenata.todowebsalta.com.ar; Thu AR$250, weekend AR$600-AR$800; ⏲Feb) A worthwhile three-day *folklórico* festival.

Dia de la Cruz RELIGIOUS
(⏲May) A mass of devotees (what seems like the entire city – the young and old among them) makes a pilgrimage 1000m up San Isidro mountain – aka Cerro de la Cruz – to the white cross erected above town decades ago. It's quite a hike and unlike any other you're likely to have experienced.

Sleeping

Rusty-K Hostal HOSTEL $
(☎03868-422031; www.rustykhostal.todowebsalta.com.ar; Rivadavia 281; d with/without bathroom US$40/35; @📶) The peace of the vine-filled patio garden here is a real highlight, and the rooms are cozy too, with good quality terra-cotta floors, beamed ceilings and a colorful accent wall. The warm service makes it terrific value. Book ahead.

Hotel Munay HOTEL $
(☎03868-421189; www.munayhotel.com.ar; Chavarría 64; s/d US$41/71; P❄📶🏊) Expect elegant simplicity and unadorned, attractive and spotless rooms with clean lines and inviting bathrooms. Excellent value, helpful service and a hospitable atmosphere make this a sound choice.

Casa Árbol GUESTHOUSE, HOSTEL $
(☎03868-15-638434, 03868-422238; www.facebook.com/casaarbolcafayate; Calchaquí 84; dm US$12, d without bathroom US$28-30; 📶) 🍃 There's something pleasant about this intimate, charming hostel with pretty, spotless rooms and a four-bed dorm. Everyone shares two bathrooms. There's lounging room to spare in the patio, breakfast area and garden. It also rents bikes (AR$150 per half-day).

Hostal del Valle GUESTHOUSE $
(☎03868-421039; www.welcomeargentina.com/hostaldelvalle; San Martín 243; s/d US$54/60; ❄📶) An endearing old house festooned with potted plants, and blessed with pretty, yet aging, rooms. Upstairs rooms are

preferable, while smaller, darker rooms downstairs are a little cheaper and still worthwhile, though the wallpaper is peeling in spots. A simple breakfast is served in a rooftop conservatory with privileged views.

Hostel Ruta 40 HOSTEL $
(☎03868-421689; www.hostel-ruta40.com; Av General Güemes S 178; dm/d US$15/36; @ 📶) Doubles aren't huge but are well decorated and painted with pastels, and all have private baths, while the dorms are clean and airy, and outfitted with lockers. It's centrally located.

★**Portal del Santo** HOTEL $$
(☎03868-422400; www.portaldelsanto.com; Chavarría 250; d downstairs/upstairs US$106/124; P ❄ @ 📶 🏊) Cool white elegance is the stock-in-trade of this hospitable family-run hotel with arched arcades. Lower rooms open onto both the front porch and the inviting garden-pool-Jacuzzi area (reason enough to stay); top-floor chambers have mountain views and even more space. All have fridge and microwave; suites sleep four. The owners are helpful and put on a wonderful homemade breakfast.

Villa Vicuña BOUTIQUE HOTEL $$
(☎03868-422145; www.villavicuna.com.ar; Belgrano 76; standard/superior r from US$100/114; P ❄ @ 📶) Peacefully set around twin patios, Villa Vicuña offers an intimate retreat, with its spotless rooms with French doors, big beds and reproduction antique furniture. Rooms are in two styles: one is more colonial in feel, with dark wood and religious icons. There are numerous helpful little details, service and breakfast are good, and you can relax in the fine courtyard.

Vieja Posada HOTEL $$
(☎03868-422251; www.viejaposada.com.ar; Mamaní 87; s/d US$62/82; P 📶 🏊) This hotel has real character in its patio and garden spaces. A reformed historic building, it offers compact rooms and adobe ambience, antiques and solid wooden benches, perfect for contemplation. There's secure parking and a tiny plunge pool. Breakfast features homemade chayote jam.

Killa BOUTIQUE HOTEL $$
(☎03868-422254; www.killacafayate.com.ar; Colón 47; standard/superior r US$94/153; P ❄ 📶 🏊) Classy and comfortable, this handsome hotel has good-sized rooms (even in standard class) with creative timber accents, vaulted ceilings, a full tub and shower, a day bed and queen-sized beds. The superior rooms are even larger, the garden is gorgeous, and the colonial style is warmed by the hotel's creative use of natural wood, stone and local *artesanía*.

Patios de Cafayate ESTANCIA $$$
(☎03868-422229; www.patiosdecafayate.com; RN 40; r US$108-160, ste US$220-240; P ❄ @ 📶 🏊) North of town, and attached to the El Esteco winery, this is the only bodega with a lodging option. The hotel is set in a beautiful centenarian *estancia*, and rooms are decorated in classic colonial style, with noble dark-wood furniture, local *artesanía* and perspectives over either the surrounding vineyards or the garden area, which includes a swimming pool and Jacuzzi.

Grace Cafayate RESORT $$$
(La Estancia de Cafayate; ☎03868-427000; www.gracehotels.com; RN 40, Km4340; d/villas from US$196/245; P ❄ @ 📶 🏊) This huge gated development covers 7km of vines, golf course, and residential lots, most of them owned by *extranjeros* (foreigners) who come to golf and quaff wine. Rooms are spacious and well equipped, and the surrounding villas work well for family stays, with kitchens, barbecue areas and private patios. Bathrooms are romantic, with huge shower spaces and two-person tubs.

Eating & Drinking

Numerous plaza restaurants offer adequate if not inspiring local dishes backed by live *folklórica* music on weekends. Head to Calle Rivadavia, between San Lorenzo & 12 de Octubre, for a string of down-home parilla restaurants, where the grill-up is satisfying and prices quite low.

Parrilla Restaurants PARRILLA $
(Rivadavia, btwn San Lorenzo & 12 de Octubre; steaks AR$60-130; ⏲7pm-midnight Mon-Sat, 11am-3pm Sun) A long way from the mannered tourist scene around Cafayate's plaza, this string of no-frills grill houses makes a worthwhile dinner escape. The **Gallito** is locally renowned, but adjacent **Parrilla Santos** – just a concrete floor, a barbecue and a corrugated-metal roof – has equally tasty meat. Uncomplicated and great value.

Casa de las Empanadas EMPANADAS $
(Mitre 24; 12 empanadas AR$160; ⏲11am-3pm & 8pm-midnight Tue-Sun; 📶) Decorated with the scrawls of contented customers, this no-frills

place has a wide selection of empanadas that are all delicious. Local wine in ceramic jugs, and *humitas* and tamales can round out the meal. If it's closed, head to its other **branch** (Nuestra Señora del Rosario 156; 12 empanadas AR$160, mains AR$130-145; ⏲11am-3pm & 7-11pm).

Retoño ARGENTINE **$$**
(☎03868-638465; Chavarría 151; mains AR$140-210; ⏲11:30am-3:30pm & 7-11:30pm) With a lovely setting in the inner courtyard of Nanni winery, Retoño has a romantic, old-world interior. The menu is short, but features mains such as roast trout, and sweetbreads in a creamy torrontés sauce. As it's not owned by the bodega, the wines aren't especially good value.

★**Pacha** FUSION **$$$**
(☎03868-639002, 03868-480955; www.facebook.com/hostaldelapacha; Belgrano 92; mains AR$230-350; ⏲8pm-midnight Tue-Sat) A lovely new bistro, one block off Cafayate's main plaza. The Buenos Aires-trained chef sources ingredients (and wines) carefully and crafts a menu with welcome departures from traditional Argentine fare. Hits include seafood risotto, seared salmon, and pork ribs slathered with a whiskey barbecue sauce. He also bakes his own crusty sourdough bread with yeast he's been fermenting for years.

The kitchen will cater to vegetarian and vegan off-menu requests if you speak up.

★**Piattelli** ARGENTINE **$$$**
(☎03868-418214; www.piattellivineyards.com; RP 2; mains AR$175-450; ⏲12:30-4pm; 📶) The indoor-outdoor setting overlooking picture-perfect vineyards at this upmarket, yet slightly corny, winery 3km from Cafayate makes a fine lunch stop. The sophisticated food doesn't disappoint. A range of international influences spice up the menu, and on weekends (when booking is advisable) staff fire up the outdoor grill with some of the finest *parrilla* in the northwest.

★**Chato's Wine Bar** WINE BAR
(☎03868-418152; Nuestra Señora del Rosario 132; ⏲7pm-midnight) Run by a cordial English-speaker, the only proper wine bar in Cafayate serves a long list of dry whites, rosés and bold reds by the glass and bottle. Grab one of the round tables fashioned from wine barrels. It's a great spot for a flight (five-wine flights from AR$100) or a single glass in friendly surroundings.

Munch on a *picada* (shared appetizer plate) so it doesn't go to your head. A long-awaited change in location to San Martín 223 was still in the works when we visited.

Cafayateña CRAFT BEER
(☎03868-457983; Toscano 80; ⏲11am-midnight) This new craft brewery on Cafayate's plaza features their brew works behind the bar, and patio and streetside tables washed in music (a popular hangout at the time of research). It pours three brews a day: *roja*, *negra* and *rubia* – the lightest of all.

Shopping

Cafayate Artesenal ARTS & CRAFTS
(Toscano 58; ⏲10am-9pm) This is a mall of brick stalls piled with goods made from llama wool, leather and cactus wood. Here, handicrafts include artisanal journals, *mate* (a tea-like beverage) gourds, picture frames, candleholders, ceramic tableware, as well as jarred specialty food like mustard, pesto, olives and sweet spreads, all made in Cafayate.

El Colmado CLOTHING
(Belgrano 26; ⏲10am-12:30pm & 6-8:30pm Mon-Fri, 10:30am-12:30pm Sat) A stylish, casual clothing boutique steps from Cafayate's plaza with playsuits and dresses, scarves and jewelry, all of it well curated. The trick, as with all of Cafayate's stores, is popping by when it's actually open. No mean feat.

Mercado Artesanal ARTS & CRAFTS
(Av General Güemes; ⏲9am-10:30pm) 🍃 The Mercado Artesanal cooperative features quality local work at more-than-fair prices.

Information

Post Office (www.correoargentino.com.ar; Av General Güemes N 197; ⏲8:30am-1:30pm & 5-7pm Mon-Fri)

Tourist Office (☎03868-422442; Av General Güemes s/n; ⏲9am-7pm Tue-Sun) Attached to the Museo de la Vid y El Vino, it offers an invaluable printout of winery opening times.

Getting There & Away

Cafayate is at the center of most northwest Argentina road-trip itineraries as it's easily reached from Salta through the twisted, colorful and almost psychedelic rockscapes of the Quebrada de Cafayate, or via the equally spectacular and mostly unpaved RN 40, which snakes through the Valles Calchaquíes.

For those without wheels, the new **bus terminal** (RN 40) is at the northern entrance to town, where you can connect to Salta (AR$215, four hours, five to six daily) and Angastaco (AR$81, two hours) via San Carlos (AR$23, 45 minutes, one to four daily). Buses also leave two to four times daily for Tucumán (AR$385 to AR$430, five to 6½ hours) via Amaicha and Tafí del Valle (AR$230 to AR$275, 2½ to four hours); others go via Santa María (AR$120, two hours). Counterintuitively, quicker buses can be cheaper.

Getting Around

Taxis (☎03868-422128) congregate opposite the cathedral – call if there are none – and are useful for reaching bodegas and other destinations. Roundtrips to Quilmes with waiting time cost around AR$1200; to San Carlos one way it's AR$300.

Quebrada de Cafayate

North of Cafayate, the Salta road heads through barren, spectacular Quebrada de Cafayate, a wild landscape of multihued sandstone and unearthly rock formations. Carved out by the Río de las Conchas, the canyon's twisted sedimentary strata exhibit a stunning array of tones, from rich red ocher to ethereal green. While you get a visual feast from the road itself – it's one of the country's more memorable drives or rides – it's worth taking time to explore parts of the canyon. The best time to appreciate the Quebrada is in the late afternoon; low sun brings out the most vivid colors.

A short way north of Cafayate, **Los Médanos** is an extensive dune complex that gives way to the canyon proper, where a series of distinctive landforms are named and signposted from the road. Some, such as **El Sapo** (the Toad) are underwhelming, but at around Km46 to Km47, the adjacent **Garganta del Diablo** (Devil's Throat) and **Anfiteatro** (Amphitheater) are much more impressive. Gashes in the rock wall let you enter and appreciate the tortured stone, the visible layers of which have been twisted by tectonic upheavals into extraordinary configurations. These landmarks are heavily visited, and you may be followed by locals hoping for some pesos for a bit of 'guiding.' *Artesanía* sellers and musicians hover too. Though drinks are sometimes on sale, don't rely on it. Fill up your reusable water bottles before hitting the highway.

Getting There & Away

There are several ways to see and explore the canyon. Tours from Salta are brief; it's better to take a tour or taxi from closer Cafayate. Minibus tours stop at major sights; other longer tours add some hiking away from the road. Biking it from Cafayate is possible, but regular punctures make this an unreliable option. Obviously the best and easiest way to explore the area is via your own rental car.

You could also combine buses with some walking and/or hitchhiking. Carry food and plenty of water in this hot, dry environment. A good place to start is the Garganta del Diablo; several other attractions are within easy walking distance from there.

San Antonio de los Cobres

☎0387 / POP 4800 / ELEV 3775M

This dusty mining town is on the puna 168km west of Salta, and sits more than 2600m above it. It's suffered since the deterioration of the region's mining industry and associated railway, but is an example of a typical highland settlement, with adobe houses, near-deserted streets and a serious temperature drop after sundown. It's worth stopping in to experience this facet of Andean life. You can head north from here to the Quebrada de Humahuaca via the Salinas Grandes and Purmamarca, though most come for the day, direct from Salta, via the Tren a las Nubes tour (p221).

Sights

There's little to see in town (though sunsets are spectacular) but 16km to the west is the impressive viaduct at **La Polvorilla**, the last stop of the Tren a las Nubes rail trip. You can climb up a zigzag path to the top and walk across it. *Remises* in San Antonio charge about AR$300 for the return journey.

Tours

Turismo Responsable TOURS
(☎0387-431-4490; www.tures.tur.ar; 3-day tour per person from AR$3000) This tour operator runs enticing excursions from San Antonio to the remote far west of the province. Departures from Salta are also possible. See the website for upcoming dates.

Sleeping & Eating

Hotel de las Nubes HOTEL $$
(☎0387-490-9059; www.hoteldelasnubes.com; RN 51; d from US$77; P ᯤ) The town's best hotel has simple decorations in its sparsely furnished but toasty warm rooms. Book ahead. The restaurant (open noon to 2pm and 7pm to 9:30pm) serves a short menu of local dishes; it's overpriced (mains from

AR$125 to AR$200) but tasty enough. The long-serving barman is good for a chat.

★**Quinoa Real** ARGENTINE $
(☎0387-490-9270; Belgrano s/n; mains AR$90-240; ⏰10am-3pm & 8-11pm; 📶🌱) On the brushed-up central block, this tourist-oriented spot offers a menu of local ingredients. Llama features heavily, such as in tasty empanadas, plates of carpaccio and grilled fillets, but roast lamb with a chili-and-garlic kick is also popular. Vegetarians will be cheered by a range of savory tarts and quinoa options. There's also quinoa-flavored craft beer.

ℹ Information

Tourist Office (☎0387-15-578-7877; culturayturismoandino@gmail.com; RN 51; ⏰9am-9pm Mon-Sat, to 3pm Sun) Just by the bridge in the center of town, this complex includes a decent artisanal market and a cafe.

ℹ Getting There & Away

Two to three daily buses from Salta (AR$208, 5½ hours) and the Tren a las Nubes (p221) stop here. You can also join a shared *remise* for AR$225 per person. Ask at the main plaza. Precious little transportation crosses the Paso de Sico to Chile; ask around town for trucks. From San Antonio, a good *ripio* (gravel) road runs 97km north, skirting the Salinas Grandes to intersect with paved RP 52.

Salinas Grandes

Bring sunglasses for this spectacular **salt plain** in a remote part of the puna, some 3350m above sea level. A lake that dried up in the Holocene, this is now a 525-sq-km crust of salt up to 0.5m thick. On a clear day, the blinding contrast between bright blue sky and the cracked and crusty expanse of white is spellbinding. Over the course of a year, wind strips much of the salt away; it's most spectacular after summer rains replenish it.

The *salinas* are impressive, and make a terrific all-natural green screen if you care to stage hilarious photo shoots for your Instagram feed. However, the otherworldly *salares* of southwestern Bolivia are even better, and if you're heading that way (or have already been), you might prioritize other attractions.

Thanks to new tour operation **Ojo de Salar** (per vehicle AR$200; ⏰9am-4pm) a cooperative of indigenous guides, you can head out onto the salt pan to check out the *poquios* (ancestral carbonic chimneys) from which the salt is periodically dug out. Check in at the parking lot, where artisans sell stone carvings and llamas made from salt. Limited drinks and snacks are available from the same vendors.

COCA CHEWING

In the northwest, you'll see signs outside shops advertising *coca* and *bica*. The former refers to the leaves, mainly grown in Peru and Bolivia, which are traditionally chewed by Andean peoples. They have a mild stimulant effect and combat fatigue, altitude sickness and hunger (oh, and they're also used to produce cocaine). *Bica* refers to bicarbonate of soda, an alkaline that, when chewed along with the leaves, increases the effect. Chewing *coca* and possessing small amounts for personal use are legal, but only in the northwest. Taking it back down south or into Chile is illegal, and there are regular searches.

ℹ Getting There & Away

The *salinas* are in Salta province, but most easily reached by heading west along spectacular, mostly paved RP 52 from Purmamarca. Self-driving allows you to head onto the salt plains with a guide. There are plenty of hairpin turns, however, so be careful of truck drivers who tend to take up both(!) lanes as they wind their way up or down the mountain. Prepare to occupy the shoulder at a moment's notice.

The only way of reaching the *salinas* by public transportation is to jump off a Chile- or Susques-bound bus from Jujuy or Purmamarca. Check timetables carefully before doing this; on some days it's possible to catch a bus back to Purmamarca a couple of hours later, but on other days it's not, plus once you're there, you can't do a whole lot without your own wheels. This road does have enough traffic to hitchhike, however.

You could also grab a *remise* from Purmamarca, or take a tour from Purmamarca, Tilcara, Jujuy or Salta. From the last, it's a long day, unless you opt to overnight in the Quebrada de Humahuaca.

Jujuy

☎0388 / POP 258,000 / ELEV 1201M

Jujuy (pronounced hoo-hooey) has a livable feel, enticing restaurants and is the most culturally indigenous of any of Argentina's cities. However, it is often bypassed by travelers, as, among the trinity of northwestern cities, it lacks Salta's colonial sophistication and Tucumán's urban vibe.

The city of (San Salvador de) Jujuy was founded in 1593, after two previous incarnations were razed by angry indigenous groups who hadn't given planning permission.The province bore the brunt of conflict during the independence wars, with Spain launching repeated invasions down the Quebrada de Humahuaca from Bolivia; Jujuy was famously evacuated in what is known as the *éxodo jujeño*. Today the city and its politics still simmer with indigenous solidarity, as their communities remain marginalized. You may notice good roads and reliable government services available elsewhere evaporate in the indigenous north.

Sights

★Culturarte GALLERY

(www.facebook.com/culturarte.ccultural; cnr San Martín & Sarmiento; 8am-8pm Mon-Sat) FREE An attractive modern space, Culturarte showcases exhibitions by a collective of 26 well-established Argentine contemporary artists. There's often work of excellent quality here, and it makes a fun place to check out the Jujuy scene. The downstairs cafe has a nice little balcony terrace overlooking the center of town.

Iglesia Catedral CATHEDRAL

(museum hours 9:30am-12:30pm & 4-7pm Tue-Fri, 10am-1pm Sat) Jujuy's 18th-century cathedral replaced a predecessor destroyed by the Diaguita. The outstanding feature, salvaged from the original church, is the gold-laminated baroque pulpit, thought to be built by local artisans trained by a European master. The garden courtyard is a popular meeting place and venue for events. There's an attached museum (AR$20) that displays a nice collection of sacred art.

Museo Arqueológico MUSEUM

(0388-422-1343; Lavalle 434; 9am-noon & 3-8pm) FREE The central exhibit here is a vivid 3000-year-old fertility goddess figure, depicted with snakes for hair and in the act of giving birth. She's a product of the advanced San Francisco culture in Las Yungas from about 1400 BCE to 800 BCE. There's also a selection of skulls with cranial deformities (practiced for cosmetic reasons) and mummified bodies.

Museo Temático de Maquetas Tupac Amaru MUSEUM

(Alvear 1152; 8am-9pm) FREE Set up by and housed in the headquarters of an indigenous cultural center that also offers community yoga and Zumba classes, this charming museum tells the history, traditions and mythology of indigenous Argentina in a series of entertaining dioramas. If you read Spanish, you'll enjoy them all the more. There's lots of good information here.

Tours

Numerous Jujuy operators offer trips to the Quebrada de Humahuaca, Salinas Grandes, Parque Nacional Calilegua and other provincial destinations. The Provincial Tourist Office (p247) can give you a full listing.

Festivals & Events

Semana de Jujuy FIESTA

(Aug) Jujuy's biggest event, the weeklong Semana de Jujuy, commemorates Belgrano's evacuation of the city during the wars of independence.

Sleeping

Hostelina HOSTEL $

(0388-424-8522; www.hostelina.com.ar; Alvear 529; dm per person US$15;) A simple, tasteful and comfortable hostel set in a restored old building with original tile, and modern art on the walls. You'll snooze in one of four dorms, set up with four to six beds each. There's nothing smashing here, but the price works.

Hotel Alvear Jujuy HOTEL $

(0388-424-4580; www.hotelalvearjujuy.com.ar; Av Pérez 398; s/d US$47/65;) An aging three-star spot, blessed with views of the hills above town. Rooms have wood furnishings and crown moldings, plush carpeting, cable TV and rather nice bathrooms. A good deal at this price.

★Posada El Arribo BOUTIQUE HOTEL $$

(0388-422-2539; www.elarribo.com; Belgrano 1263; s/d from US$74/86;) An oasis in the heart of Jujuy, this impressive family-run place occupying a renovated 19th-century mansion is wonderful, with original floor tiles and high ceilings. There's plenty of patio space and a huge garden too, and the modern annex behind doesn't lose much by comparison. Still, go for an older room if you can.

Jujuy

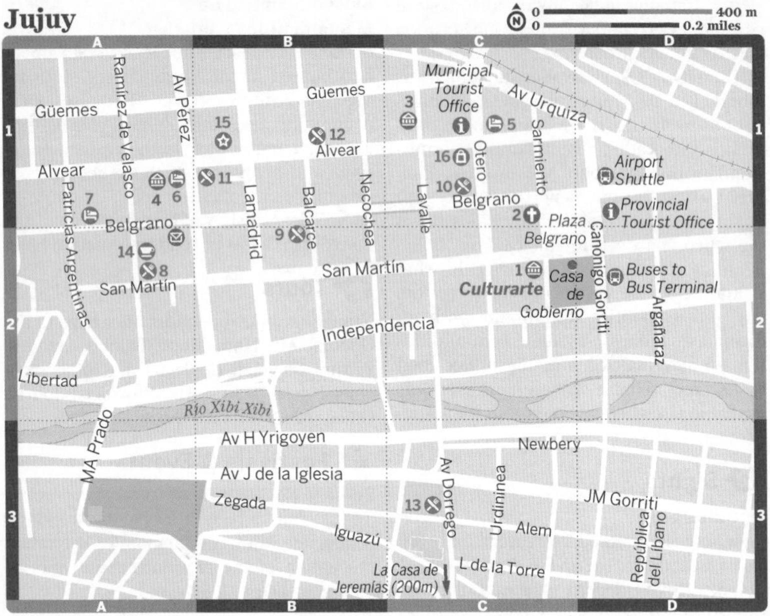

Jujuy

Top Sights

1 Culturarte C2

Sights

2 Iglesia Catedral C1
3 Museo Arqueológico C1
4 Museo Temático de Maquetas Tupac Amaru A1

Sleeping

5 Hostelina C1
6 Hotel Alvear Jujuy A1
7 Posada El Arribo A1

Eating

8 Africana A2
9 Krysys B2
10 Madre Tierra C1
11 Manos Jujeñas B1
12 Mercado Central 6 de Agosto B1
13 Mercado del Sur C3

Drinking & Nightlife

14 Casa Tomada A2

Entertainment

15 Plaza Ricardo Vilca B1

Shopping

16 Casa Garzon C1

Eating & Drinking

Jujuy's two lively markets, **Mercado del Sur** (Iglesia 1002-1060; meals AR$50-100; 8am-4pm) and **Mercado Central 6 de Agosto** (Alvear 885; 8am-6pm), are genuine trading posts where indigenous Argentines swig *mazamorra* (cold maize soup) and peddle *coca* leaves.

Madre Tierra BAKERY, CAFE $
(Belgrano 619; dishes AR$40-90; 7am-10pm Mon-Sat;) This place is a standout. The design is creative and inviting, the vegetarian food (there's a daily set menu) is excellent and the sandwiches and pizzas can be washed down with fresh juice or organic craft beer. There's lovely garden-patio seating, which is popular and fills up every evening, and the bakery up front does wholesome breads.

Manos Jujeñas ARGENTINE $
(0388-422-2366; Av Pérez 379; mains AR$90-210; 11am-3pm & 7-11pm Tue-Sun;) If you crave no-frills traditional slow-food cooking, make your way here for the *picante* – marinated chicken or tongue (or both) with onion, tomato, rice and Andean potatoes. That's the pride of the house. Take-out is also available.

Africana PIZZA **$**
(☎0388-424-3388; Ramírez de Velasco 203; pizzas AR$125-220; ⊙8pm-1am) A corner pizza parlor with a wood-burning brick oven, timber furniture, African masks on walls and an array of ingredients to lay atop your pie or stuff inside your calzone (you know, if that's your thing). Choose from traditional Neopolitan combinations or stretch out and opt for a pizza topped with the house special *trucha ahumada* (smoked trout).

★**Krysys** ARGENTINE **$$**
(☎0388-423-1126; Balcarce 272; mains AR$120-258; ⊙12:30-3pm & 8:30pm-12:30am Mon-Sat, 12:30-3:30pm Sun; 📶) The best *parrilla* option in Jujuy is this central, upscale place offering all your barbecued favorites in a relaxed atmosphere. But there's plenty more on the menu, with a range of tasty sauces to go with the chicken, pork or beef, plus octopus, stuffed trout and paella. Prices are fair, and you'll get the meat the way you want it cooked.

★**Casa Tomada** CAFE
(☎0388-424-4350; www.facebook.com/agustina.pachtman; Ramírez de Velasco 253; ⊙8:30am-3pm & 9pm-1am Mon-Thu, to 6am Fri & Sat) A funky art cafe that turns into Jujuy's bohemian playground after the sun drops. Expect a grab bag of offerings here, from tai chi and music classes to live music deep into the night. It serves food too, including a solid vegetarian menu.

☆ Entertainment

Plaza Ricardo Vilca ARTS CENTER
(Alvear 1015) Drop by this attractive enclosed plaza next to the city's major theater; there are often cultural events, handicraft shows or food stalls. There's also a likable bar, dance school and exhibition space.

Shopping

Casa Garzon ARTS & CRAFTS
(☎0388-422-3756; Alvear 636; ⊙9am-9pm) A leather workshop that also sells saddles, traditional cow-skin drums, boots, belts, wallets, bags and some cool hats. It can customize anything you like if you have the time to wait.

ℹ Information

Bolivian Consulate (☎0388-424-0501; www.consuladodebolivia.com.ar; Ramírez de Velasco 145, La Quiaca; ⊙7am-1pm Mon-Fri)

Hospital Pablo Soria (☎0388-422-1256; www.msaludjujuy.gov.ar; Güemes 1345)

Municipal Tourist Office (☎0388-402-0246; www.sansalvadordejujuy.gob.ar; cnr Alvear & Otero; ⊙7am-10pm) Friendly and central. Hours vary depending on staffing.

Post Office (www.correoargentino.com.ar; Belgrano 1136; ⊙8:30am-1pm & 5-8pm Mon-Fri)

Provincial Tourist Office (☎0388-422-1325; www.turismo.jujuy.gov.ar; Canónigo Gorriti 295; ⊙7am-10pm Mon-Fri, 8am-9pm Sat & Sun) Excellent office on the plaza, with helpful brochures and staff.

ℹ Getting There & Away

AIR

Aerolíneas Argentinas (☎0388-422-2575; www.aerolineas.com.ar; San Martín 96; ⊙8:30am-12:30pm & 4:30-8:30pm Mon-Fri, 8:30am-12:30pm Sat) services Buenos Aires and Córdoba from **Aeropuerto Horacio Guzmán** (☎0388-491-1102), 33km southeast of downtown Jujuy.

BUS

The new **bus terminal** is 6km southeast of the center. It's got great facilities, including showers and a **tourist office** (bus terminal; ⊙7:30am-9:30pm Mon-Fri, 8am-1pm & 3:30-9:30pm Sat & Sun).

Daily buses going from Salta to Chile stop here.

Buses from Jujuy

DESTINATION	COST (AR$)	TIME (HR)
Buenos Aires	2482	20-23
Córdoba	1275-1530	12-16
Humahuaca	105	2
La Quiaca	230	4-5
Mendoza	2074	21
Purmamarca	67	1¼
Salta	175	2
Salvador Mazza	612	7
Tilcara	70	1¾
Tucumán	578	5

ℹ Getting Around

An **airport shuttle** (☎0388-15-432-2482) leaves three times daily from the corner of Canónigo Gorriti and Belgrano to coincide with flights; alternatively it's AR$340 in a remise.

Several local buses head to the bus station (AR$5.50), including 8A and 9A from Canónigo Gorriti between San Martín and Independencia. From the bus terminal, several lines run regularly to the center.

Hertz (☎0388-422-9582; www.hertz.com; Balcarce 578; ⏰9am-1pm & 5-9pm Mon-Sat) is central for car rental; there are also airport operators.

Las Yungas

Eastern Jujuy province is a humid, fertile subtropical zone where the arid, barren altiplano gives way to montane forest and, in places, dense cloud forest. It's a spectacular, lush, vibrantly green region, and the center of it all is the stunning Parque Nacional Calilegua, where hiking trails and one of northwest Argentina's most scenic drives awaits.

Parque Nacional Calilegua

Parque Nacional Calilegua (☎03886-422046; www.parquesnacionales.gob.ar/areas-protegidas/region-noroeste/pn-calilegua; San Lorenzo; ⏰trails open 8am-3pm) FREE is an accessible, beautiful, biodiverse park that stretches up the Serranía de Calilegua range to peaks offering boundless views above the forest and across the Chaco to the east.

There's a spectacular 22km road that winds through the park, ascending from 550m to 1700m and taking you through the three types of forest that characterize the park's different altitude layers. Along this road are trailheads for 10 marked hikes, from 10-minute strolls to tough descents down to river level. The best places for bird- and mammal-watching are near the stream courses in the early morning or late afternoon. Most trailheads are within easy walking distance of the park entrance. Rangers offer guiding services on the longer trails.

Sleeping

Hostería Benítez HOTEL $

(☎03886-433119; benitezhosteria@gmail.com; 19 de Abril s/n, Calilegua; s/d US$45/60; ❄📶) On the parklike plaza in the heart of Calilegua, Hostería Benítez offers a warm family welcome and clean, comfortable, well-kept rooms of hotel standard. Good breakfasts and dinners are served in the appealing dining area, including a handful of vegetarian options. Try the tasty corn and lemon-juice concoction.

Jardín Colonial GUESTHOUSE $

(☎03886-430334; eljardincolonial@hotmail.com; San Lorenzo s/n, Calilegua; d US$30; P❄📶🏊) Jardín Colonial is a centenarian bungalow with attractive rooms and a verdant, sculpture-filled garden. It's cheap and very casual: there are no locks on the rooms and you're left to your own devices. Toucans roost in the trees opposite. Breakfast is US$3 extra.

Information

Ranger Station (calilegua@apn.gov.ar; ⏰9am-1pm & 2-6pm) Set at Aguas Negras, the park entrance, and the best source of information about trails and conditions. There's another outpost at Mesada de las Colmenas, halfway along the road through the park.

Getting There & Away

Regular buses between Jujuy or Salta and Salvador Mazza stop at Libertador General San Martín and Calilegua, and may let you off at the park junction, 3km north of Libertador's center and 2km south of Calilegua. It's 8km from here to the Aguas Negras ranger station; there's enough traffic to hitchhike. It's also easy to charter a taxi from either town.

Quebrada de Humahuaca

North of Jujuy, the memorable Quebrada de Humahuaca snakes north toward Bolivia. It's a harsh but vivid landscape, a network of dry yet river-scoured canyons overlooked by mountains with sedimentary strata that have been eroded into spectacular scalloped formations revealing a spectrum of colors in undulating waves. The palette of this World Heritage–listed valley changes constantly, from shades of creamy white to rich, deep reds; the rock formations in places recall a necklace of sharks' teeth, in others the knobby backbone of some unspeakable beast.

Dotting the valley are dusty, picturesque, indigenous towns offering a fine variety of places to stay, plus historic adobe churches, handicrafts and homey restaurants serving warming *locro* and llama fillets. It's no surprise that the region has experienced a tourism boom in recent years, but it remains an under-the-radar world-class destination. You won't be alone here, but with landscapes this magical, it will hardly matter.

Purmamarca

☎0388 / POP 900 / ELEV 2192M

Little Purmamarca, 3km west of the highway, sits under celebrated Cerro de los Siete Colores (Hill of Seven Colors), an otherworldly, jagged formation resembling the marzipan fantasy of a megalomaniac pastry chef. The village is postcard-pretty, with adobe houses and ancient algarrobo trees by the bijou 17th-century church. This, and its proximity to Jujuy, has made it very touristy; if you're looking for an authentic Andean village, move on. Nevertheless, Purmamarca is a glorious spot and an excellent place to shop for woven goods; a flourishing market sets up on the village plaza every day.

Make sure you take the easy but rewarding 3km walk around the *cerro* (hill), the striking colors of which are best appreciated in the morning or evening sunlight.

Sleeping

Given its heavy tourist traffic, in Purmamarca it's wise to book accommodations in advance, especially for weekends. The good news: the quality of lodging is high in this delightful town.

Hostal Inti Kay HOSTEL $
(☎0388-407-6204; Belgrano 205; d US$41; ❄📶) Just off the plaza, this place has five tiled rooms with beamed ceilings and wood furnishings, set around an interior courtyard where the mountains peek out above the rooftops. It's one of Purmamarca's few genuine budget options.

★Huaira Huasi LODGE $$
(☎0388-490-8070; www.huairahuasi.com.ar; RN 52, Km5; standard/superior r US$94/106; P❄@📶) One of a handful of charming nests above town, on the main road toward Salinas Grandes, this lodge stands out for its majestic valley views and handsome terra-cotta-tinted adobe buildings. Each room is unique and all are beautifully decorated with local fabrics and cardón wood. Superior rooms sleep three.

★Los Colorados APARTMENT $$
(☎0388-490-8182; www.loscoloradosjujuy.com.ar; Chapacal s/n; d/q from US$124/190; P❄📶) Looking like they're straight out of a science-fiction movie, these strange but inviting apartments will have you feeling like you've booked into a boutique sleep in Tatooine. They are tucked right into the *cerro*, and blend in with it. All of them are stylish, spacious and cozy; fine places to hole up for a while and a great option for families.

La Casa Del Abuelo LODGE $$
(☎0388-478-9164; Salta s/n; d from US$88; ❄📶) A sweet rambling lodge three blocks from Purmamarca's plaza. Rooms have ceramic tiled floors, beamed ceilings and pottery on the walls, and there are epic mountain views from the breakfast room. Considering the prices in Purmamarca, this is arguably the best value in town.

La Comarca BOUTIQUE HOTEL $$
(☎0388-490-8098, 0388-490-8001; www.lacomarcahotel.com.ar; RN 52, Km3.8; s/d US$114/145; P❄@📶🏊) On the main road but an easy stroll into town, this well-run place offers a variety of sweet mauve-colored accommodations that open onto a carefully tended lawn and garden. The main building offers a lounge area, a sauna, a pretty little pool and more. Houses and cabins sleep up to six. The staff are friendly and helpful. Views are fabulous.

Colores de Purmamarca CABAÑAS $$$
(☎0388-15-5598-6605; San Martín 600; cabañas US$182; P❄📶🏊) All rooms are split-level condo-like *cabañas*, with two bedrooms downstairs – including a master – and a living room and full kitchen upstairs along with a terrace overlooking the Siete Colores. There's a sliver of wi-fi by the lobby and a small pool area too. Each *cabaña* sleeps four, making it a great choice for families.

Eating

Purmamarca's kitchens all offer similar regional northwestern Argentine fare of good quality, though none of it is sensational.

La Posta ARGENTINE $
(Rivadavia; mains AR$130-260; ⏰noon-3pm & 8-10pm) A well-regarded restaurant on the main plaza. It roasts llama dishes, legs of lamb, steaks, trout and chicken, and offers

CARNAVAL IN THE QUEBRADA

Argentina's most intriguing Carnaval celebrations take place along the length of the Quebrada de Humahuaca in February and March. Indigenous traditions have melded with the customs of the Spanish conquerors to create this vibrant hybrid that kicks off on the Saturday that falls 50 days before Easter Sunday. In each town, a devil figure is dug up from where he was buried the previous year and paraded into town amid much noise, triggering an eight-day bender of dancing and copious drinking. The devil is then buried again, and sin symbolically put back in the closet for another year.

CHILE VIA SUSQUES

The paved road climbs doggedly from Purmamarca through spectacular bleak highland scenery to a 4150m pass, then crosses a plateau partly occupied by the Salinas Grandes before hitting civilization once again at Susques (130km from Purmamarca), which has gas and an ATM.

Susques is well worth a stop for its terrific village **church** (entry by donation; ⌚8am-6pm). Dating from 1598, it has a thatched roof, cactus-wood ceiling and beaten-earth floor, as well as charismatic, naïve paintings of saints on the whitewashed adobe walls. There's an occasionally open tourist office on the main road, and basic places to stay.

Beyond Susques, the road continues 154km to the Paso de Jama (4230m), a spectacular journey. This is the Chilean border, although Argentine immigration (open 8am to midnight) is some way before it. There's gas here. No fruit, vegetables or *coca* leaves are allowed into Chile – there are checks. The paved road continues toward San Pedro de Atacama.

Daily buses run from Jujuy to Susques (AR$194, four to five hours) via Purmamarca (AR$90). Services from Salta and Jujuy to Chile stop here.

but one vegetarian pasta dish to desperate herbivores. Nevertheless, it is an inviting room and a nice choice.

Kuntur ARGENTINE **$$**
(☎0388-403-4052; Lavalle 209; mains AR$150-190; ⌚11:30am-3:30pm & 8pm-late) An adorable and deservedly popular place where the hands-on chef prepares llama myriad ways, quinoa risotto, goat-meat *cazuelas* (stews), pizza, pasta and more. He'll even dream up some vegetarian dishes if you ask. The inviting back patio is a popular place for beers deep into the night.

La Diablada ARGENTINE **$$**
(☎0388-409-2777; Florida; mains AR$150-190; ⌚11am-11pm; 📶) A cute tiled dining room offering the northwest Argentine cookbook: beef, llama, a range of *cazuelas* and some trout dishes too. It has live music most nights during the tourist season.

ℹ Information

There's an ATM plaza-side.

Tourist Office (☎0388-490-8443; Florida s/n; ⌚7am-noon & 2-7pm year-round, extended hours Jan & Feb) Just off Purmamarca's plaza. Opening times are unreliable.

ℹ Getting There & Away

Buses run to Jujuy (AR$67, 1¼ hours) or Tilcara (from AR$17, 30 minutes) and Humahuaca (from AR$50, 1¼ hours). You can walk or get a cab (AR$30) to the main road junction where more buses pass.

Purmamarca has no gas station; the closest is 25km north, at Tilcara. Westward, the nearest is in Susques, a 130km climb away. South, the closest is Jujuy (62km).

Tilcara

☎0388 / POP 4700 / ELEV 2461M

Picturesque Tilcara is the people's choice as their Quebrada de Humahuaca base. The mixture of local farmers getting on with a centuries-old way of life and arty urban refugees looking for a quieter existence has created an interesting balance on the town's dusty streets. What emerges is a local scene that's both charming and accessible, and given the tourist traffic, the comforts of home are often within arm's reach. Yet, what captivates everyone here – locals and tourists alike – are the mountains that rise on all sides as if to remind all comers that no matter how comfortable they may feel, adventure awaits.

Sights & Activities

You'll see phone numbers for *cabalgatas* (horseback rides) everywhere; most accommodations can arrange these. Guides for walks around the area congregate at the tourist office (p253). There are two excellent trekking outfitters in town, as well.

Pucará RUINS
(☎0388-422-1325; entry incl Museo Arqueológico adult/student AR$100/25; ⌚9am-6pm) This reconstructed pre-Columbian fortification is 1km south of Tilcara's center, across an iron bridge. Its location is strategic, commanding the river valley both ways and, though the site was undoubtedly used earlier, the ruins date from the 11th to 15th centuries. There are great views and, seemingly, a cardón cactus for every soul that lived and died here.

For further succulent stimulation, there's a botanic garden by the entrance.

The 1950s reconstruction has taken liberties; worse yet is the earlier, ridiculous monument to pioneering archaeologists bang where the plaza would have been. Nevertheless, you can get a feel of what would've been a sizable fortified community. Most interesting is the 'church,' a building with a short paved walkway to an altar; note the niche in the wall alongside.

Museo Arqueológico MUSEUM
(Belgrano 445; entry incl Pucará adult/student AR$100/25; ⏲9am-6pm) This well-presented collection of regional artifacts in a striking colonial house has some pieces from the *pucará* just south of the center. Exhibits offer insight into the life of people living around the time of this fortification. The room dedicated to ceremonial masks is particularly impressive.

Garganta del Diablo HIKING
(entry AR$20) Of several interesting Tilcara walks, most popular is the 4km hike to Garganta del Diablo, a pretty canyon leading to a waterfall. Walk toward the *pucará,* 1km south of the center across an iron bridge, but turn left along the river before crossing the bridge. Swimming is best in the morning, when the sun is on the pool.

You can also reach it by road.

Tours

Operators in town run trips around the Quebrada and Salinas Grandes. A recommended guide for the spectacular multiday trek to Parque Nacional Calilegua is **Juan Pablo Maldonado** (☎0388-15-504-5322).

★**Caravana de Llamas** TREKKING
(☎0388-495-5326, 0388-15-408-8000; www.caravanadellamas.com; Huasamayo 976) A highly recommended llama-trekking operator running 90-minute (AR$425), half-day (AR$850), full-day (AR$1700) or multiday (from AR$4080) excursions of varying difficulty around Tilcara, Purmamarca and Salinas Grandes. Guides are personable and well informed about the area. Llamas are pack animals: you walk; they carry the bags. Drop by to meet them.

Tilcara Trekking TREKKING
(☎0388-505-4755, 0388-15-505-4755; www.tilcara-trekking.com) Offering overland trips, day hikes, multiday treks and mountaineering trips up snowcapped volcanoes including the 6739m summit of Volcán Llullaillaco. If you want to get out on the trails and into that thin Andean air, this is the outfitter for you.

Runa Tour CULTURAL
(☎0388-495-5388; www.runatour.tur.ar; Belgrano 481; 1-/2-/3-day excursions US$200/350/400) This operator offers interesting excursions to indigenous communities, where you learn about corn and quinoa cultivation and visit archaeological sites. You can combine this with a horseback ride or drive to the spectacular Serranía de Hornocal (p256), a jagged row of rock 'teeth.' Another option takes you over the mountains and down to the Yungas, combining riding and driving, or just riding.

Festivals & Events

Tilcara celebrates several festivals during the year, the most notable of which, apart from Carnaval, is **Enero Tilcareño** (⏲Jan), which features sports, music and cultural activities. **Pachamama** (⏲early Aug), an indigenous carnival in praise of Mother Earth, is alive with music, dance and evocative costumed processions through town.

Sleeping

La Calabaza CABAÑAS $
(☎0388-495-5169, WhatsApp 388-15-272442; www.calabazatilcara.com.ar; Sarahuaico s/n; d/q US$70/129; P ☎) Across the main road from Tilcara's center, this cute spot has a casual hippie vibe and friendly welcome. The view: just spectacular. There's a cabin with kitchen sleeping five, perfect for a family, and an adorable little double with views from the bed and tea/coffee facilities. There's a three-night minimum stay in summer. Breakfast is extra.

Malka GUESTHOUSE, HOSTEL $
(☎0388-495-5197; www.malkahostel.com.ar; San Martín 129; dm US$25, d US$59-88, cabañas US$82-165; P @ ☎) This rustic complex is both guesthouse and hostel. The secluded, shady location, thoughtfully different dorms, and smart stone-clad rooms with hammocks and deckchairs make it the sort of retreat where you end up staying longer than expected. A yoga and meditation room and courses are further reasons to linger.

Facing the church, head left for a block, then turn right and follow this road.

La Casa del Indio GUESTHOUSE $
(☎0388-495-5441; www.argentinaturismo.com.ar/casadelindio; Ambrosetti 100; d/tr from US$40/65;

BOLIVIA VIA SALVADOR MAZZA OR AGUAS BLANCAS

The RN 34 continues past Calilegua to Argentina's northernmost settlement, Salvador Mazza (aka Pocitos), a major frontier with Bolivia. Cross the border (open 24 hours), and take a shared taxi 5km to Yacuiba in Bolivia, which has buses to Tarija and Santa Cruz. There's no Bolivian consulate, so get your visa in Jujuy or Salta if you need one. Salvador Mazza is served by numerous buses from Jujuy, Salta and beyond.

Another crossing in this area is the international bridge between Aguas Blancas and Bermejo, from where there are good onward bus connections to Tarija. Aguas Blancas is served by bus from Salta, but there are more frequent connections to Orán, from where shared taxis leave for Aguas Blancas from opposite the bus station.

Pirate shared taxis outside Salta's bus terminal head direct for the Bolivian border and cost little more than the bus. They're faster but can be oddly less comfortable when full.

wi-fi) An appealing place, which consists of just two rooms off a sweet little courtyard beside the family home. Simple and traditional in style, with some attractive stonework, it offers tranquility, independence and comfort, as well as a wild garden. It can be tricky to find: go straight up the hill from the bus terminal and take the third right.

★Antigua Tilcara GUESTHOUSE, HOSTEL **$$**
(☎0388-527-3805; www.antiguatilcara.com.ar; Sorpresa 484; d US$71-92; @ wi-fi) A cute red adobe, adorned with flowers, and set up a dirt road from the town center, where the roads seemingly disappear into the hills. Rooms here are wonderful, with ceramic-tile floors, exposed stone, wood furnishings and artistic accents, such as cactus-wood lanterns. The service is charming, relaxed and conscientious.

★Cerro Chico CABAÑAS **$$**
(☎0388-495-5744; www.cerrochico.com; d from US$106; P wi-fi pool) Around 2km from town down a dirt road, this attractive, rustic complex is set on 4 hectares up a hill and has gorgeous Quebrada views and a remote, relaxing feel. The standard cabins are compact but handsome, and the front wall folds open so you can take in your majestic perch above the hillside garden, pool area and fledgling vineyard.

It's a great little spot. Turn left after the bridge into Tilcara and follow the signs. A three-night minimum stay usually applies.

Patio Alto HOTEL, HOSTEL **$$**
(☎0388-495-5792; www.patioalto.com.ar; Torrico 675; dm US$35, d from US$71; P @ wi-fi) Expect large modern rooms with chic industrial-design accents at this top-of-the-town hotel. A good breakfast, afternoon tea and other thoughtful details are included. There's also an upmarket dorm that is every bit as nice as the rooms, with four single beds, cane lockers and kitchen use. It's a unique sleep with a great vibe.

Posada de Luz LODGE **$$**
(☎0388-495-5017; www.posadadeluz.com.ar; Ambrosetti 661; r US$94-129; P @ wi-fi pool) With a nouveau-rustic charm, this little place is a fantastic spot to unwind for a few days. The pricier rooms have sitting areas, but all feature adobe walls, cane ceilings, pot-bellied stoves and individual terraces with deck chairs and views out over the valley. Pretty grounds include a barbecue area and children's playground; excellent personal service is a real highlight.

Al Sereno BOUTIQUE HOTEL **$$**
(☎0388-495-5568; Padilla 537; d from US$95; reception 9am-10pm; air-con wi-fi pool) A boutique hotel set on a dirt road just up from the center of Tilcara. Rooms in the new wing, set around a grassy courtyard and dipping pool, are recommended for polished concrete floors, pastel paint jobs, timber beamed ceilings and gorgeous bathrooms.

Cabañas Alas del Alma LODGE **$$**
(☎0388-525-0937; www.alasdelalmatilcara.com.ar; Padilla 437; d from US$74; P air-con wi-fi) A well-regarded midranger offering an exceptional deal on its five rooms with timber floors, beamed ceilings and cute tiled baths. Some rooms are split-level and sleep up to four adults. A great choice for families.

Gaia Habitaciones Boutique BOUTIQUE HOTEL **$$**
(☎0388-414-0833; www.gaiatilcara.com.ar; Belgrano 472; s/d/tr US$53/88/135; wi-fi) Right in the center, this hotel nevertheless offers seclusion in its upstairs rooms that overlook a court-

yard dominated by a spreading peppercorn tree. Sweet adobe-style chambers offer stylish, rustic decor, sizable showers and free tea and coffee (and no TV, for better relaxation).

Eating

Khuska ARGENTINE $
(☎0388-478-7356; Padilla 533; mains AR$80-100; ⏲6pm-midnight; 📶✍) Grab a table in this charming, rambling, creative dining room serving regional dishes including *humitas*, empanadas and *picadas Andinas*, along with some decent vegetarian options. Andean platters feature roasted local potatoes, sautéed quinoa and grilled goat cheese.

Ma'koka CAFE $
(☎0388-509-5617; Belgrano s/n; sandwiches AR$60-95; ⏲8:30am-9pm; 📶✍) 🍃 With an eclectic music mix and interesting texts on the area and the Andes in general, this excellent bookstore-cafe also has the best coffee in town, tasty cakes and top sandwiches using bread made from *coca* or local corn varieties. There are great choices for celiacs too, with manioc bread and other treats. The owner is knowledgeable about indigenous Argentina.

Arumi ARGENTINE $
(☎0388-414-6169; Lavalle 660; mains AR$85-170; ⏲7-11:30pm Tue-Sun; 📶) Art on the walls, regular live events and a comfortably attractive evening ambience are allied with highland ingredients of good quality here. Delicious tamales and pleasing stews take their place alongside tasty roast llama and beef, homemade pastas and pizzas.

Gugué EUROPEAN $
(☎0388-456-1555; Padilla 490; mains AR$80-180; ⏲11:30am-3pm & 8pm-midnight Thu-Tue; 📶) One of Tilcara's more sleek and urbanized restobars. It does a quinoa tabbouleh, five kinds of pizza, quiche, roast trout, a range of pastas and more in a cute, concrete-floor dining room.

★**El Nuevo Progreso** ARGENTINE $$
(☎0388-495-5237; www.facebook.com/elnuevoprogreso; Lavalle 351; mains AR$100-255; ⏲6-11:30pm Mon-Sat; 📶) An engaging, artsy ambience here is combined with delicious tourist-oriented cuisine. Think imaginatively prepared llama dishes, excellent meat plates, one interesting veggie option and great salads. The trout, steamed in spinach leaves and topped with roast pumpkin, is quite good. Service can be a bit standoffish. Book a table in advance on weekends.

El Patio ARGENTINE $$
(☎0388-495-5044; Lavalle 352; mains AR$120-250; ⏲11:30am-3:30pm & 7-11:30pm Wed-Mon; ✍) Tucked away between Tilcara's plaza and church, this place has a lovely shaded patio, garden seating and a cozy interior. It offers a wide range of salads, inventive llama dishes and a far-from-the-madding-crowd atmosphere. Presentation and quantity could be better, but quality is good.

Information

Tourist Office (Belgrano 366; ⏲8am-9pm Mon-Fri, 9am-1pm & 2-9pm Sat, 9am-1pm Sun) Has information on walks. Often open Sunday afternoons despite the official hours. Conversely, it's often not open when it's supposed to be.

Getting There & Away

The bus terminal is on the main street, Belgrano; further services stop on the highway nearby. There are buses roughly every 45 minutes to Jujuy (AR$70, 1½ hours) and north to Humahuaca (AR$36, 45 minutes) and La Quiaca (AR$164, three hours). Several daily buses hit Purmamarca (AR$17, 30 minutes) and Salta (AR$240, 3½ hours).

Around Tilcara

Maimará, 8km south of Tilcara, is a typical adobe valley settlement set beneath the spectacular and aptly named Paleta del Pintor (Painter's Palette) hill. Its hillside cemetery is a surprising sight with a picturesque backdrop, but the friendly village has more to offer, with decent accommodations and a bodega (winery).

Sights

La Posta de Hornillos MUSEUM
(Maimará; AR$50; ⏲9am-6pm) Part of a chain that ran from Lima to Buenos Aires during viceregal times, La Posta de Hornillos is a beautifully restored staging post 11km south of Tilcara. Founded in 1772, it was the scene of several important battles during the independence wars, and remained an important stop on the road to Bolivia until 1908, when the La Quiaca railway opened. The interesting exhibits here include some impressive and fierce 17th-century swords, 16th-century arrowheads and a fine 19th-century carriage.

It's set beside a working farm backed by mineral-streaked mountains.

Quebrada de Humahuaca

The tortured rockscapes and palette of mineral colors that changes through the day make this arid valley a highlight of the northwest. Exploring the indigenous villages and towns strung along it is a delight.

Iruya

A long, rickety drive over a spectacular mountain pass, this remote village preserves a traditional and indigenous feel. Surrounded by imposing cliffs and mountains, it's a place whose slow pace obliges you to step off the frenzied wheel for a day or three (p257).

Purmamarca

This small town is dominated by its surrounding crags, which feature some of the valley's most vibrant mineral colorings. The focus of things here is the great artisan market on the square (p248).

Tilcara

A range of excellent small hotels, stunning landscapes, excursions and the cactus-studded ruins of an indigenous fortress make this a favorite base in the Quebrada (p250).

Humahuaca

The valley's largest town has an authentic feel and makes a good base for the region. Picturesque cobbled streets, fair-trade handcrafts and typical northwestern dishes, such as *locro* or llama stew are highlights (p256).

Uquía

This village has the region's standout church, a beautiful 17th-century structure whose interior famously features paintings of the main angels packing muzzle-loading weaponry (p256).

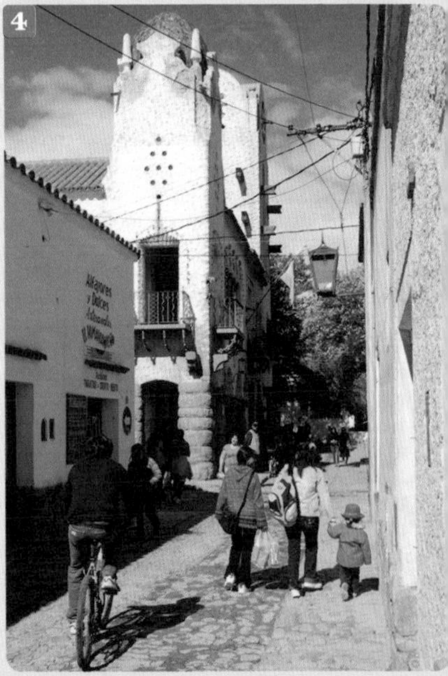

1. Iruya 2. Market, Purmamarca
3. Pucará (p250), Tilcara 4. Humahuaca

MATYAS REHAK/SHUTTERSTOCK ©

DABOOST/SHUTTERSTOCK ©

Getting There & Away

Maimará is around 11km south of Tilcara, signposted off the main highway. It can be accessed by a *remise* hired in Tilcara for about AR$250 roundtrip.

Uquía

03887 / POP 500 / ELEV 2818M

Uquía is a dusty, sleepy small town nestled just off RN 9, between Tilcara and Humahuaca. It's notable for its historic church blessed with armed angels. Yes, really. The angels have guns. There's some good home cooking at the top of the town, but otherwise it's just a quick stop.

Sights

Iglesia de Uquía CHURCH

(entry by donation; 10am-noon & 2-4pm) It's not often that you imagine the heavenly host armed with muzzle-loading weapons, but in this roadside village's picturesque 17th-century church that's just what you see. A restored collection of Cuzco School paintings – the *ángeles arcabuceros* (arquebus-wielding angels) – features Gabriel, Uriel et al putting their trust in God but keeping their powder dry. There's also a gilt altarpiece with fine painted panels.

Eating

Cerro la Señorita ARGENTINE $

(Viltipoco s/n; mains AR$85-140; 8am-8pm) For the best lunch option head three blocks uphill from Iglesia de Uquía and turn left. Cerro la Señorita has delicious home cooking and baking using fresh produce from the garden. You'll see it from the small dining area. The menu features quinoa burgers, vegetable tarts, llama steaks served with mushrooms and potatoes, and home-baked desserts.

Getting There & Away

Set roughly 33km north of Tilcara, and 12km south of Humahuaca, just off the highway, it's relatively easy to get here via buses that operate on RN 9. From Tilcara you'll have to pay the full fare to Humahuaca (AR$36), but the driver will let you out early if you ask. Ditto in reverse. A *remise* from Humahuaca is AR$200 roundtrip.

Humahuaca

03887 / POP 10,300 / ELEV 2989M

Quebrada de Humahuaca's largest settlement is handsome, dotted with adobe houses and a quaint plaza. However, the cobblestone streets buzz with traffic and an agenda that is not oriented toward tourism. But there are good handicrafts shops, local folk musicians strum and sing in the restaurants, and it's the most authentic, if least comfortable, of the three main Quebrada towns. Still, most visitors blow through on day trips to and from the spectacular Serranía de Hornocal. Nights get chilly – bring your poncho (or something similarly warm).

Sights

★ **Serranía de Hornocal** MOUNTAIN

Located 25km east of Humahuaca, this jagged row of rock 'teeth' offers utterly spectacular colors. Tours run here but it's drivable in a normal car with care. It's prettiest from 4pm onward, when the western sun brings out vivid hues. Turn left straight after crossing the bridge and follow the epic road (veer left 3km along for a short stretch of better road), which climbs to a 4000m pass. Here, head right for 1.7km to the viewpoint.

Cabildo NOTABLE BUILDING

(Plaza Gómez) The lovable *cabildo* (town hall building), built in the Spanish Moorish style in the 1940s, is famous for its clock tower, where a life-size figure of San Francisco Solano emerges at noon to deliver a benediction. Be sure to arrive early to see it; the clock is erratic. Fun fact: the inner mechanics of the clock weigh over 1800kg!

Sleeping

La Humahuacasa HOSTEL $

(03887-412-0868; www.humahuacasa.com.ar; Buenos Aires 740; dm/d US$11/40;) Artistic and personable, this hostel is central and offers cozy dorms around a small patio, with thick mattresses dressed in colorful blankets. It's a social place with a decent kitchen and a good vibe. Everything is very clean and well run. There's one private room – an en suite double.

Inti Sayana HOSTAL $

(03887-421917; www.intisayanahostal.com.ar; La Rioja 83; d from US$36; P) A central cheapie with spotless tiled rooms that sleep three, set around a courtyard and parking area. If you're toting a bag full of dirty clothes you'll want to take advantage of its inexpensive laundry service.

Hostería Naty GUESTHOUSE $

(03887-421022; www.hosterianaty.com.ar; Buenos Aires 488; s/d/tr US$31/35/45; P)

Friendly management offers dark, simple but comfortable rooms of varying shapes and sizes at a fair price in the center of town. The ones around the outside patio are quieter. There's parking round back. The owners are good sources of information on what to see and do around town.

Eating & Drinking

Humahuaca lacks the nightlife scene of nearby Tilcara, but you'll find cafes and restaurants with live music serving cold beer and decent wine on the main drag.

Aisito ARGENTINE $
(03887-488-6609; Buenos Aires 435; mains AR$80-150; 11am-3pm & 7-11pm;) Well decorated and blessed with caring service, this is a pleasing option for good-priced local cuisine. Tasty baked empanadas take their place alongside decent stir-fries and tender llama. There's live music on weekends, and nightly in summer.

Ser Andino CAFE $
(03887-421659; www.serandino.com.ar; Jujuy 393; mains AR$80-150; 9am-10pm) A homey cafe decked out with dried flowers and potted plants attached to a tour operator of the same name. Get coffee or tea, a hot meal or book a tour. You can do it all here. The cafe serves pasta, *cazuela de cabrito* (goat stew), breakfasts, tamales and more.

Mikunayoc ARGENTINE $
(03887-421442; cnr Corrientes & Tucumán; mains AR$50-110; 11am-3:30pm) The wide-ranging menu here includes several interesting llama dishes, cordial service and a range of empanadas with intriguing fillings. The salads are also a good bet. It's a pleasant, colorful place so you'll forgive the odd lapses in service. Lunch only.

Pacha Manka ARGENTINE $$
(Buenos Aires 457; mains AR$130-170; 7am-4pm & 7:30-10pm;) A century-old house has been converted to one of the town's better and most stylish restaurants. It trades in mostly traditional cuisine pepped up with a few innovations, and also does fajitas and a spicy chicken stew that comes highly recommended. It serves big breakfasts in the morning too.

Shopping

Near Humahuaca's plaza, **Manos Andinas** (Buenos Aires 401; 8am-noon & 3:30-8pm) sells fair-trade *artesanía*. The handicrafts market, near the defunct train station, has woolen goods, souvenirs and atmosphere.

Information

Tourist Office (Plaza Gómez s/n; 7am-9pm Mon-Fri, 9am-9pm Sat & Sun) Located in the *cabildo*.

Getting There & Away

The **bus terminal** (cnr Belgrano & Entre Ríos) is three blocks south of Humahuaca's plaza. There are regular buses to Salta (AR$175, 4½ hours), Jujuy (AR$105, 2¼ hours) and La Quiaca (AR$103, two to three hours). There are three to four daily buses to Iruya (AR$90, three hours).

Iruya

03887 / POP 5900 / ELEV 2780M

There's something magical about Iruya, a remote village just 46km from the main road but a world away. It makes a great destination for a few days to properly appreciate the Quebrada de Humahuaca region away from the highway. There's some epic hiking around town.

The journey is worthwhile in itself. Turning off RN 9, 26km north of Humahuaca, the *ripio* road ascends to a 4000m pass at the Jujuy–Salta provincial boundary. Here, there's a massive *apacheta* (travelers' cairn). Those discarded plastic bottles once carried liquid offerings to Pachamama.

You then wind down a spectacular valley and eventually reach Iruya, home to a pretty yellow-and-blue church, steep streets, adobe houses and breathtaking mountainscapes (with soaring condors). It's an indigenous community with traditional values, so tread lightly.

There's a bank with an ATM and a gas station.

Activities

Hiking and learning about local culture are two major attractions, and it's easy to combine them with walks to indigenous communities such as San Isidro (two hours) or San Juan (four hours). Both have appealing overnight possibilities with local families. Guides are available in Iruya for these and longer treks.

Sleeping & Eating

Locals offer cheap accommodations in their family homes, costing around US$15 per person in a private room.

Milmahuasi HOSTEL $
(☎03887-15-445-7994; www.milmahuasi.com; Salta s/n; s/d with view US$53/71, without view US$42/53; @ 📶) This guesthouse is brilliantly run by people with a real passion for Iruya. Management can explain anything from the best hikes to local geology. Rooms are spotless, rustic and attractive, a good breakfast is included, and evening vegetarian specials are offered.

Hotel Iruya HOTEL $$
(☎03887-15-509-4458; www.hoteliruya.com; San Martín 641; d with/without view US$124/109; P 📶) At the top of the town, this boutique nest offers simple rooms with wide beds, a spacious common area and a picturesque stone terrace with memorable views. It's worth the extra cash for the big-windowed rooms with valley vistas. There's a decent restaurant.

Comedor Tina ARGENTINE $
(Comedor Iruya; ☎03887-15-404-3606; mains AR$60-90; ⏰11am-4pm & 8pm-midnight Mon, Tue, Thu & Fri, 11am-4pm & 10:15pm-midnight Wed, Sat & Sun) By far the best place to eat in Iruya is this local favorite on the road into town just before the gas station. Tina serves delicious home-style meat and salad dishes in a cozy atmosphere. It's an absolute bargain. If they've just baked empanadas, grab as many as you can eat.

Getting There & Away

Buses from Humahuaca (AR$90, three hours) leave three to four times daily; there is also service from Tilcara (AR$100, four hours) and Jujuy (AR$180, five hours).

The *ripio* road is often impassable in summer due to rain. You'll see villagers hitchhiking – this is a good way to meet locals.

La Quiaca

☎03885 / POP 16,900 / ELEV 3442M

Truly the end of the line, La Quiaca is 5171km north of Ushuaia, and a major crossing point to Bolivia. It's a dry, windy place that can vacillate between frigid and blistering depending upon the month and the cloud cover. There are decent places to stay, but little to detain you, other than the indigenous travelers, who come from distant pueblos to trade in the open-air market in the town center, often dressed in vibrant traditional garb. If you're serious about photography and enjoy exploring oft-overlooked border towns, you may well do some time here.

La Quiaca is divided by its defunct train tracks; most services are west of them. North of town, a bridge crosses the river to Villazón, Bolivia.

Sleeping & Eating

Eating options are simple. Though the rooms aren't great, the restaurant in the **Hotel de Turismo** (☎03885-423390; cnr Árabe Siria & San Martín; mains AR$110 to AR$160; s/d US$24/35; piW) is best for grilled meats. The hospitable **Frontera** (cnr Belgrano & Árabe Siria; mains AR$60-100; ⏰10am-4pm & 7-11pm) also has meat plates, Spanish omelets and pasta.

★ **Copacabana Hostel** HOSTEL $
(☎03885-423875; www.hostelcopacabana.com.ar; Pellegrini 141; s/d US$18/30; @ 📶) Decked out in pinks, reds and ochers, this sweet hostel offers small, heated rooms serviced by amiable staff. Ongoing renovations are constantly improving the place. Staff can reserve Bolivian trains for you.

Hostería Munay HOTEL $
(☎03885-423924; www.munayhotel.com.ar; Belgrano 51; s/d US$35/57; P 📶) Set back from the pedestrian street (you can still drive in), this hotel is a decent option. Rooms are notched in a brick chalet off the parking area, and are superclean and decorated with *artesanía*. The service is lovely.

Information

Change money on the Bolivian side of the border or at the bus terminal.

Banco Macro (Árabe Siria 441) Has an ATM.

Information Kiosk (Av España s/n; ⏰10am-1pm & 4-8pm) Run by a hostel, it offers decent information. Opposite the bus terminal.

Tourist Office (☎03885-422644; turismo@laquiaca.com.ar; cnr Cabildo & La Madrid; ⏰7am-7pm) Branches at the border, and at the southern entrance to town. Often shut.

Getting There & Away

You'll earn your nomadic stripes at the rough and ready, old-school **bus terminal** (cnr Belgrano & España) where you'll step over sleeping dogs and humans to board connections to Jujuy (AR$230, four to five hours), Salta (AR$360, eight hours) and Buenos Aires (AR$1900, 27 hours). There is no transportation to Bolivia, but a few Argentine long-distance buses leave directly from the bus station over the border in Villazón.

After leaving the Quebrada de Humahuaca, paved RN 9 passes through Abra Pampa, a windy town 90km north of Humahuaca, and climbs through picturesque altiplano landscapes.

Yavi

☎03885 / POP 400 / ELEV 3440M

Picturesque, indigenous Yavi, 16km east of La Quiaca on a good road, is a border-town detour and a lazy little hideaway with tumbledown romanticism, thanks to its adobe-lined streets and two fascinating colonial-era buildings. It's so close to La Quiaca, but an utterly different world, and one sans phone signal, so disconnecting from the grid is mandatory.

Sights & Activities

Local walks can take you to **Yavi Chico**, which is even smaller than Yavi, or along the river to see cave paintings. A longer excursion heads to pretty **Laguna Colorada**.

★**Iglesia de San Francisco de Asís** CHURCH

(Marqués Campero s/n; entry by donation; ⏲9am-1pm & 2-6pm) Built by the local marquis in the late 17th century, Yavi's intriguing church – one of northern Argentina's most fascinating – preserves stunning altarpieces in sober baroque style, covered in gold leaf and adorned with excellent paintings and sculptures, mostly from the Cuzco School. The translucent onyx windows also stand out.

Sleeping & Eating

La Casona HOSTEL, GUESTHOUSE $

(☎03885-425148; mccalizaya@hotmail.com; cnr Pérez & San Martín; dm/d US$10/25; 📶) Simple but likable, this traveler favorite has rustic rooms (with stoves for winter nights) around the back courtyard, and offers a friendly welcome. It can whip up tasty meals (mains AR$60 to AR$150) at any time of day. A bar and handicrafts store with gnarled wooden floors is out front. This is also the most reliable spot for information.

Getting There & Away

Five buses run Monday to Saturday from La Quiaca (AR$30, 20 minutes), leaving from the school on Av Hipólito Yrigoyen. Shared *remises* (AR$35, 20 minutes) leave from the nearby Mercado Municipal once full.

BOLIVIA VIA LA QUIACA

From La Quiaca to Villazón, Bolivia, walk or take a taxi to the bridge, then clear immigration (open 24 hours). Bolivia is much nicer than Villazón promises, so head past the cut-price stalls and straight to the bus terminal or train station. Cheap but reliable accommodations are near the bus terminal and plaza if you need them. Buses and minibuses head to Tupiza (1½ hours), La Paz (20 hours) and elsewhere. The train station (see www.fca.com.bo for timetables) is 1.5km north of the border, and serves Tupiza (three hours), Uyuni (nine hours) and beyond. Bolivia is one hour behind northern Argentina. For a quick Villazón visit, clear Argentine immigration but don't get stamped into Bolivia (technically illegal but nobody minds). La Quiaca has a **Bolivian Consulate** (☎03885-422283; www.consuladoboliviano.com.ar; 9 de Julio 109; ⏲8am-4pm Mon-Fri).

TUCUMÁN & AROUND

Though the country's second-smallest province, Tucumán has played a significant role in Argentina's story. It was here that independence was first declared, and the massive sugar industry remains of great national economic importance. It makes sense then that Tucumán city is full of heat and energy, benefiting from a recent influx of young professionals, in complete contrast to the lung-cleansing air of Tafí del Valle up in the hills. Beyond, Argentina's most important pre-Columbian site is Quilmes, on the Cafayate road. South of Tucumán province, Santiago del Estero is an enjoyable backwater with music in the air and siesta time on the calendar.

Getting There & Away

The province is connected by bus, plane and train to Buenos Aires. It's bisected by RN 9, and there are frequent and easy bus connections to Salta and Catamarca. If you have the energy to walk, there is a gorgeous three- to four-day trail that links Tucumán city and Tafi del Valle.

Tucumán

☎0381 / POP 884,400 (URBAN AREA) / ELEV 420M

Baking hot, energetic and brash, (San Miguel de) Tucumán, the cradle of Argentine independence, is the nation's fifth-largest city and feels like it; the metropolitan bustle can come as quite a shock after visiting other more genteel northwestern capitals. You may prefer it at night, when the fumes and heat of the day have lulled, and cafes and bars come to life.

Tucumán's blue-collar feel and down-to-earth vibe around the main plaza is complemented by a lively cultural scene fueled by young professionals who have resettled here. The result is a range of comfortable rooms, tasty food, buzzy bars and a splashy shopping district. There's also world-class paragliding and hang gliding in the hills west of town.

History

Founded in 1565, Tucumán hosted the congress that declared Argentine independence in 1816. Unlike other northwestern colonial cities, it successfully reoriented its economy after independence. At the southern end of the sugarcane zone, it was close enough to Buenos Aires to take advantage of the capital's growing market. From 1874 the railway facilitated transportation and rapid growth. Economic crises have hit hard in the past, but sugarcane's increasing use as a fuel source keeps locals optimistic.

Sights

Casa de la Independencia MUSEUM
(Casa Histórica; ☎0381-431-0826; Congreso 151; ⊙10am-6pm) FREE Students and families descend from far and wide to visit this late-colonial mansion where a collection of Unitarist lawyers and clerics declared Argentina's independence from Spain on July 9, 1816. Portraits of the signatories line the walls of the room where the deed was done, and outside, in the courtyard, you'll find a bronze relief of the original *declaración*. There's plenty of information in Spanish on the lead-up to this seismic event, and free guided tours are available hourly.

There's a sound-and-light show nightly. Come to the museum between 11am and 6pm to get your free ticket, as there is limited space available.

Catedral Metropolitana CATHEDRAL
(Plaza Independencia s/n; ⊙9am-noon & 5:30-9:30pm) Tucumán's neoclassical cathedral is a handsome presence on Plaza Independencia, and has a Doric facade with a pediment depicting the Exodus. Curiously, Moses is receiving bunches of grapes in the desert; a reference to the fertility of Tucumán's surrounding area. The interior has a petite wooden choir, cheerily alive ceiling paintings and a canvas of the Annunciation behind the altar. Despite its glamour, it remains a hard-working church, with Mass held each morning (8am), at midday (noon) and at night (8:30pm).

Casa Padilla MUSEUM
(☎0381-431-9147; 25 de Mayo 36; ⊙9am-12:45pm & 4-9pm Mon-Fri, 9am-12:45pm & 5-9pm Sat & Sun) FREE Alongside the Casa de Gobierno, this partly restored mid-19th-century house belonged to provincial governor José Frías (1792–1874), then to his mayor son-in-law Ángel Padilla. European art, Chinese porcelain and period furniture make up the collection.

Casa de Gobierno ARCHITECTURE
(☎0381-484-4000; 25 de Mayo 90; ⊙9am-6pm) One of Tucumán's many magnificent structures, this neoclassic beauty has a Parisian quality, and you won't miss it as it's right on Plaza Independencia. While the exterior is rather majestic and the interior tiles are original, these days it's a behind-the-times, workaday government office complex. The interior halls are dank and dark, the wiring exposed and the lights fluorescent. But that facade is something!

Museo Folclórico Provincial MUSEUM
(☎0381-421-8250; Av 24 de Septiembre 565; ⊙9am-1pm & 5-9pm Tue-Fri, 5-9pm Sat & Sun) FREE Occupying a colonial house, this small but pleasant museum features a modest collection of traditional gaucho gear, indigenous musical instruments (check out the armadillo *charangos*), weavings and pottery. There was a room on local singer Mercedes Sosa, one of Argentina's finest vocalists, at the time of research.

Activities & Tours

Tour operators offer excursions ranging from sedate city strolls to canoeing, challenging hikes and paragliding; the city has hosted the Paragliding World Cup. Most paragliding operators are based in San Javier in the hills to the west. The tourist office (p264) can supply a full, up-to-date list of operators. One worthwhile hike is the beautiful 72km trek from Tucumán to Tafí del Valle. Many do it in three days,

Tucumán

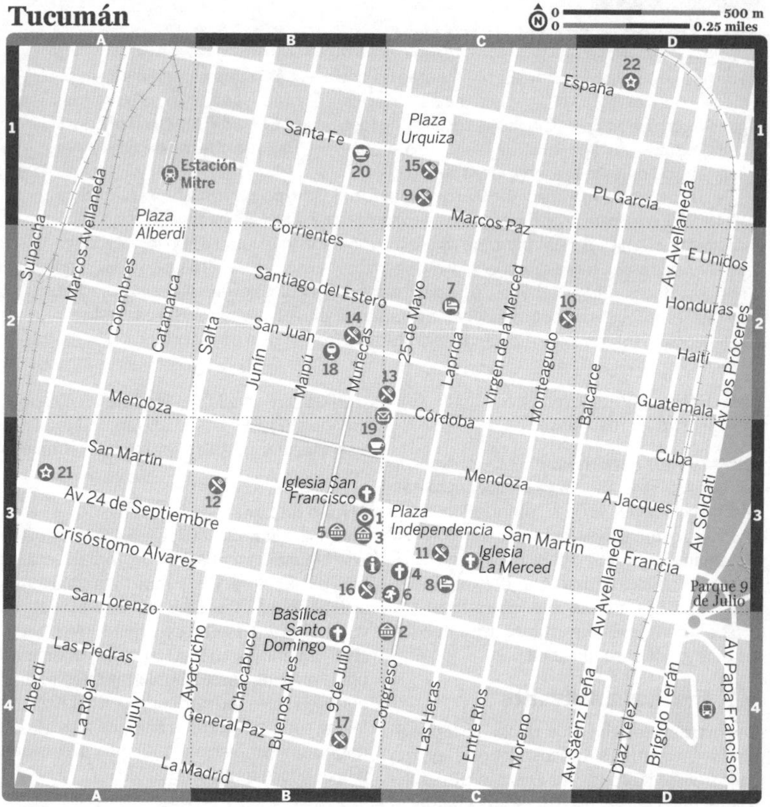

Tucumán

Sights

1 Casa de Gobierno B3
2 Casa de la Independencia C4
3 Casa Padilla B3
4 Catedral Metropolitana C3
5 Museo Folclórico Provincial B3

Activities, Courses & Tours

6 Antique Tour Experience C3

Sleeping

7 Amérian Tucumán C2
8 Hotel Bicentenario C3

Eating

9 Black Pan C1
10 Cilantro C2
11 El Portal C3
12 Il Postino B3
13 Il Postino 2 .... C2
14 La Leñita B2
15 Setimio C1
16 Shitake B3
17 Shitake 2 .... B4

Drinking & Nightlife

18 Costumbres Argentinas B2
19 Filipo B3
20 Plaza de Almas B1

Entertainment

21 Alto de la Lechuza A3
22 La Casa de Yamil D1

but it's mostly uphill, so four is more relaxed. Find waypoints on www.wikiloc.com (search for Yerba Buena–Tafí).

★ **Tucumán Parapente** PARAGLIDING
(WhatsApp 0381-15-444-7508; www.tucumanparapente.com.ar) Fantastic tandem

DAY-TRIPPING FROM TUCUMÁN

The fertile, hilly area northwest of Tucumán is known as **Las Yungas**, and it's an appealing day (or overnight) trip outside the hot, busy city. The tourist office (p264) provides good information on destinations such as the reservoir of **El Cadillal**, which offers camping, swimming, windsurfing and a 'ski lift,' and the **Parque Sierra de San Javier**, a university-operated reserve laced with trails.

To the south of Tucumán, the **Parque Nacional Campo de los Alisos** (☑ 03865-15-405985; www.parquesnacionales.gob.ar; ⏱ park office 7:30am-2:30pm) FREE is a tempting destination. A hilly park at the zone where the montane forest and cloud forest meets the Andes proper, there's enjoyable walking and climbing here. There's also free camping and a climbers' *refugio* (shelter). The park entrance is 12km beyond Alpachiri, reachable by bus from Tucumán, but more doable if you have your own wheels. The park office in Concepción, 18km before Alpachiri, might be able to help with transportation.

paragliding flights over the Yungas forests, as well as instruction.

Antique Tour Experience SCENIC DRIVE
(☑ 0381-430-5445; www.antiquetour.com.ar; Crisóstomo Álvarez 467) A unique operator offering scenic drives between the cities of Tucumán, Salta and Jujuy in vintage Ford Model A vehicles dating from 1928 and 1929. The route is slow but the views from the back seat of these convertibles are splendid, and the guides are top-shelf.

★ Festivals & Events

Celebrations of the **Día de la Independencia** (Argentina's Independence Day) on July 9 are vigorous. *Tucumanos* also celebrate the **Batalla de Tucumán** (Battle of Tucumán) on September 24.

🛏 Sleeping

Tucumán's hotels may seem pricey at first, but you can negotiate substantial discounts, particularly in low season and when paying cash.

Casa Calchaquí GUESTHOUSE $
(☑ 0381-425-6974; www.casacalchaqui.com; Lola Mora 92, Yerba Buena; d/q US$53/80, s/d without bathroom US$45/60; ⏱ Mar-Jan; P❋@🛜🏊) Located 8km west of the center in the upmarket Yerba Buena barrio, Casa Calchaquí is a welcome retreat. Comfortably rustic rooms surround a relaxing garden space with hammocks, bar service and a minipool. Yerba Buena has plenty of restaurants and nightlife, but isn't central. To get here grab a taxi (AR$150) or bus 102 or 118 from opposite the bus terminal.

The street is off Av Aconquija (at 1100): Banco Galicia is on the corner.

Bikes are available for hire. Ask about the guesthouse's rustic accommodations in a spectacular off-piste setting near Amaicha del Valle.

Arrullo de Luna B&B $
(Noemí Lizarraga; ☑ 0381-425-4852; arrullodelunayb@gmail.com; Bascary 36, Yerba Buena; d from US$40; P❋🛜🏊) Run by a charming, artistic couple, this B&B will appeal to those who value a personal experience over hotel-style amenities. It's a friendly, bohemian place offering three simple upstairs rooms; one is en suite with air-con, overlooking a relaxing suburban garden and pool. It's a good option for families, with kitchen access and whole-house rental available.

Posada Arcadia B&B $$
(☑ 0381-425-2214; www.posadaarcadia.com.ar; Güemes 480, Yerba Buena; d US$56-81; ❋🛜🏊) Posada Arcadia has four charming rooms in a gorgeous two-story home with a huge garden and pool in leafy Yerba Buena. The biggest of the bunch has a king-sized bed, walk-in closet, fireplace, flat-screen TV, tub and shower. The common room is cushy, and you'll snag a discount for stays of more than one night.

Hotel Bicentenario HOTEL $$
(☑ 0381-431-9119; www.hotelbicentenario.com.ar; Las Heras 21; s/d US$85/95; P❋@🛜🏊) Sometimes you're happy to give character a miss and just want a sparklingly clean, modern hotel where the showers work, the beds are comfortable and there's a rooftop pool, sundeck and gym. This is that place. Rooms have wood floors, built-in fixtures, flat-screen TVs and (usually) streamable internet.

Amérian Tucumán HOTEL $$
(☎0381-430-0100; www.amerian.com; Santiago del Estero 425; d from US$86; P ❄ @ ≋) Modern and efficient, this hotel offers good-sized, comfortable rooms with king-sized beds and large flat-screen TVs. Windows are double-glazed to help with the noise, and facilities include a pillow menu, e-books for borrowing and a small gym. The staff are excellent.

Eating

Tucumán is famous for its excellent eggy empanadas. The best are hand-cut: ask the tourist office for a *Ruta de la Empanada* leaflet to track down this specialty.

Black Pan BURGERS $
(www.facebook.com/blackpanburgers; 25 de Mayo 724; burgers AR$120-125; ⏲noon-1am) Black Pan is a hip spot, exceptionally well branded, and beloved by Tucumán's young and upwardly mobile. Its standard is a 120g burger with cheddar cheese, served on a brioche bun. But you can build yours as you like. In a nod to California's famous In-N-Out chain, it will even do your burger 'animal style' (with grilled onions, extra pickles and Thousand Island dressing).

El Portal ARGENTINE $
(☎0381-422-6024; Av 24 de Septiembre 351; empanadas AR$9, mains AR$80-140; ⏲noon-4pm & 8pm-midnight) Half a block east of Plaza Independencia, this rustic indoor-outdoor eatery is a true hole in the wall. It has a tiny but perfectly formed menu, based around empanadas, *locro* and wood-fired meat. Delicious and authentic.

Shitake VEGETARIAN $
(9 de Julio 94; all you can eat AR$125; ⏲11:30am-4pm & 7:30pm-midnight; ≋ ✎) With a tasty array of vegetarian dishes in its buffet (lentils, stir-fried vegetables and soy-based meats, roasted potatoes, quiches, pizzas and more), this small, well-run spot gives value for money. Drinks are extra, but dessert is part of the package. You can also take out, paying by weight. It has a **second location** (☎0381-422-1817; 9 de Julio 392; all you can eat AR$125, with juice AR$150; ⏲11:30am-4pm & 7:30pm-midnight; ≋ ✎) further down the street.

Il Postino ITALIAN $
(☎0381-421-7117; Junín 95; mains AR$135-260; ⏲9am-2am; ≋) Pizza and pasta are served in this atmospheric eatery. Dishes are decent and service is swift and professional. Ask for extra tomato sauce on your pizza – it's just better that way. There's another branch nearby at **Córdoba 501** (☎0381-421-0440; Córdoba 501; mains AR$35-260; ⏲9am-2am; ≋).

Setimio ARGENTINE $$
(Santa Fe 512; tapas AR$60-140, mains AR$110-350; ⏲meals 10am-4pm & 7:30pm-1:30am; ≋) Wall-to-wall bottles decorate this smart wineshop and restaurant, with a menu that features Spanish-style tapas, fine salads and well-prepared fish dishes among other gourmet delights. Wine is not offered by the glass, but you can pick any one of the hundreds of bottles from the shelves and uncork it for dinner.

La Leñita PARRILLA $$
(☎0381-422-0855; www.facebook.com/lalenita parrillada; San Juan 633; mains AR$153-235; ⏲coffee & snacks 7am-1am, meals 11am-3:30pm & 7:30pm-1am; ≋) The interior is charmless but locals flock here for the service and the good-quality meat. Try *picana* (rump steak) or the delicious *mollejitas* (sweetbreads). The empanadas – you'll get one as a welcome bite – are delicious. It does roast trout and chicken mains too. The staff often sing *folklórica* music halfway through the night.

Cilantro ARGENTINE $$$
(☎0381-430-6041; Monteagudo 541; mains AR$155-385; ⏲9pm-2am Mon-Sat; ≋) A sleek, well-lit dining room with some unique dishes for Argentina, including a stir-fried salmon and broccoli, a roast-pork curry and a range of wok-fried noodle offerings, along with the usual mixed grill and pastas you've come to expect.

Drinking & Entertainment

From Thursday to Saturday nights, the action is in the Abasto region, on Calle Lillo. Follow San Lorenzo west from the town center and you'll hit the middle of the zone. There are dozens of bars and nightclubs – take your pick. Other *boliches* (nightclubs) can be found in Yerba Buena, at least 6km west of the town center.

★ **Plaza de Almas** CAFE, BAR
(www.facebook.com/catorcealmas.argentina; Maipú 791; ⏲noon-1:30am Tue & Wed, to 2:30am Thu, to 3:30am Fri, 8:30pm-3:30am Sat, 8pm-3am Sun; ≋) This intimate, colorful and engaging multilevel place is popular with under-40 *tucumanos* and is one of the best of the city's many combination cafe/bar/restaurant/cultural centers. The short but

interesting menu (mains AR$60 to AR$140) offers a range of kebabs and salads, among other international choices. There's candle-lit outdoor seating, and an exhibition space on the top floor.

There's also a knot of bars around it, making it an appealing place to start or end your night.

Filipo CAFE
(☎0381-421-9687; Mendoza 301; ⏰7am-1am Mon-Thu, to 3am Fri & Sat, 8am-1am Sun; 📶) Glasses gleaming on the gantry, outdoor tables and bow-tied waiters make this a great cafe. Top espressos, beer served as if it were Bollinger and thirst-quenching *licuados* (blended fruit drinks; AR$60) are the highlights. Given the decor it would be cooler if the soundtrack veered closer to jazz than mindless pop, but that's just us.

Costumbres Argentinas BAR
(www.facebook.com/costumbresargentinas.bar; San Juan 666; ⏰11am-3pm & 8pm-3am Mon-Thu, to 4am Fri-Sun) Though the saintly devilish address seems like a contradiction in terms, this unusual, popular and welcoming bar has an arty bohemian vibe. The big two-level beer garden is the place to be on summer nights. Pub grub is also available. There's no sign, but you'll find it.

La Casa de Yamil LIVE MUSIC
(☎0381-422-8487; www.facebook.com/lacasa.deyamil; España 153; ⏰live music dinner Fri & Sat, lunch Sun; 📶) An untouristy *parrilla*, locally popular for its Friday and Saturday night live *folklórico* (folk music); there's also a Sunday lunchtime session. The food works too, and there are plenty of traditional northwestern dishes to try.

Alto de la Lechuza TRADITIONAL MUSIC
(☎0381-421-8940; www.facebook.com/alto.delalechuza; Av 24 de Septiembre 1199; ⏰9pm-1am Mon-Wed, to 5:30am Thu-Sat) This historic spot hosts traditional music on weekend nights. It starts soft and slow, but gets loud and burns late into the night.

ℹ Information

Hospital Padilla (☎0381-424-8012; Alberdi 550)

Post Office (www.correoargentino.com.ar; Córdoba 540; ⏰8am-1:30pm & 5-8pm Mon-Fri)

Tourist Office (☎0381-430-3644; www.tucumanturismo.gob.ar; Av 24 de Septiembre 484; ⏰8am-9pm Mon-Fri, 9am-9pm Sat & Sun) On Plaza Independencia; very helpful and knowledgeable. There's another office in the shopping center at the bus terminal with the same opening hours.

ℹ Getting There & Away

AIR

From **Aeropuerto Benjamín Matienzo** (☎0381-426-5072), **Aerolíneas Argentinas** (☎0381-431-1030; www.aerolineas.com.ar; 9 de Julio 110; ⏰8:30am-1pm & 5-8pm Mon-Fri, 9am-12:30pm Sat) and **LATAM** (☎0381-422-0606; www.latam.com; San Juan 426; ⏰9am-1pm & 5-8pm Mon-Fri) fly daily to Buenos Aires; Aerolíneas also flies to Córdoba five times weekly.

BUS

Tucumán's **bus terminal** (☎0381-430-0452; Brígido Terán 350; 📶) is a major affair, with 60 platforms and plenty of shops and services. The bus information booth is outside, by the supermarket.

Buses from Tucumán

DESTINATION	COST (AR$)	TIME (HR)
Buenos Aires	1958-2478	15-18
Cafayate	385-430	6½
Catamarca	300-350	3¼-3¾
Córdoba	750-976	7-9
Jujuy	456-660	4½-5½
La Quiaca	657-752	9-11
La Rioja	590	5½
Mendoza	1550-1783	13-15
Puerto Iguazú	1404-1886	21
Resistencia	1159-1242	11-12
Salta	415-548	4¼
Salvador Mazza	910-1050	10-13
Santiago del Estero	205	2
Tafí del Valle	156	2-3

TRAIN

Tucumán is connected to Buenos Aires (via La Banda/Santiago del Estero and Rosario) daily from beautiful **Estación Mitre** (☎0381-430-9220; www.sofse.gob.ar; Plaza Alberdi s/n). Expect long delays, poor visibility, ordinary food and questionable cleanliness. As the trip is so cheap it books up well in advance.

At the time of research, trains were leaving Buenos Aires' Retiro station seven times a day on the 15- to 18-hour journey. From Tucumán, trains leave twice daily for Buenos Aires. The trip costs AR$74/130 in 1st class/Pullman class (reclinable seats). There's a bar/restaurant on board.

Getting Around

The airport is 8km east of downtown; a remise costs around AR$250 from the town center.

Around the city, local buses have clearly marked major destinations on the front. Fares cost AR$8, using a prepurchased card; there's a sales point near the bus-terminal tourist office. Schedules are at www.tucubondi.com.ar.

There are several car-rental places, including **Avis** (0381-431-0025; www.avis.com.ar; 24 de Septiembre 364; 8am-8pm Mon-Sat, 9am-6pm Sun), **Hertz/Thrifty** (0381-452-4991; www.hertz.com.ar; Crisóstomo Álvarez 507; 9am-1pm & 5-9pm Mon-Fri, 9am-1pm & 5-8pm Sat) and **Móvil Renta** (0381-431-0550; www.movilrenta.com.ar; San Lorenzo 370; 9am-6pm).

Tafí del Valle

03867 / POP 3400 / ELEV 2100M

This lovely hill town, set in a green valley with fabulous vistas of the surrounding mountains, is where Tucumán folk traditionally head to take refuge from the summer heat. It's no wonder. Tafí makes a fine spot to hang out for a few days; it offers crisp mountain air, hiking options, budget accommodations, memorable *estancias*, and a laid-back scene.

The journey from Tucumán is spectacular: a narrow river gorge with dense subtropical forest on all sides opens onto the reservoir-filled valley beneath the snowy peaks of the Sierra del Aconquija. The precipitous mountain road merits a window seat.

Sights & Activities

Several people around town hire out horses (look for *'alquilo caballos'* or *'cabalgatas'*) for rides in the valley. The Casa del Turista (p267) can give you details of the Ruta del Artesano (p266), which features a number of handicraft workshops open to visitors in and around town.

Hiking in the mountains around Tafí is an attractive prospect. An easy, well-marked trail climbs **Cerro El Pelao** for views overlooking town. The path starts on the left as soon as you've crossed the bridge. From the same road you can walk a pleasant 10km to **El Mollar**, following the river and the reservoir, visit the Parque de los Menhires (p267) and take a bus back.

Trails also lead to the summits of 3000m **Matadero**, a four- to five-hour climb; 3600m **Pabellón** (six hours); and 4500m **El Negrito**, reached from the statue of Cristo Redentor on RN 307 to Acheral. These are badly marked, however, and no maps are available, but you can hire guides through the Casa del Turista.

You can also walk all the way to or from Tucumán, though it will likely take three to four days.

Capilla La Banda CHURCH, MUSEUM

(Av José Silva; AR$30; 8am-6pm) This is an 18th-century Jesuit chapel, built in 1708 and acquired by the Frías Silva family of Tucumán after the Jesuits' expulsion. It was expanded in the 1830s, but restored to its original configuration in the 1970s. Note the escape tunnel under the altar. A small collection of funerary urns, Cuzco School religious art, ecclesiastical vestments and period furniture is displayed.

The chapel is a short walk from downtown. Cross the river bridge and you'll see it on your left after 750m.

Sleeping

★**Estancia Los Cuartos** ESTANCIA $

(0381-15-587-4230; www.estancialoscuartos.com; Av Miguel Critto s/n; d US$53-62; P @) Oozing with character, this lovely spot with grazing llamas out front is two centuries old, and feels like a museum, with venerable books lining antique shelves and authentic rooms with aged wood and woolen blankets, but with great modern bathrooms. Newer rooms offer less history but remain true to the feel of the place.

Traditional cheeses are also made here. Don't confuse this place with nearby Hostería Los Cuartos.

Nomade Hostel HOSTEL $

(03867-307-5922; www.nomadehostel.com.ar; Los Castaños s/n; dm/d US$17/42; P @) Relaxed, colorful, enthusiastic and welcoming, this hostel is an easy 10-minute walk from the bus terminal (turn right, go round the bend, veer right). It's got a lovely location with great views from the spacious garden. Rates include breakfast and tasty home-cooked dinners, and the atmosphere here is excellent. It's best to book ahead in summer. Prices drop substantially in the low season.

OFF THE BEATEN TRACK

PARQUE NACIONAL BARITÚ

Parque Nacional Baritú (☎03878-15-511826, 03878-15-507-4432; www.parquesnacionales.gob.ar/areas-protegidas/region-noroeste/pn-baritu; San Ramón de la Nueva Orán) FREE is a remote 70-hectare slice of raw, subtropical wilderness, tucked up against the Bolivian border at elevations between 1800m and 2000m. The rivers run hard, the jungle is humid and it's spectacularly photogenic. Keep your eyes peeled for wildlife. Fauna includes puma, tapir and capybara (a guinea-pig-like rodent). The park has a ranger station and campground but no other services, though locals offer accommodations in their homes. There are various trails to tackle on foot or horseback. Speak to rangers or the National Parks Administration in Salta (p229) before coming. If only you could get there more easily. Remote Baritú can only be accessed by road through Bolivia.

★Descanso de las Piedras CABAÑAS $$
(☎0381-15-642-8100; www.descansodelaspiedras.com; Madre Teresa de Calcuta s/n; d US$53-71, q US$82-106; P 🛜 ≈) Welcoming and social, these cute orange riverside cabins and rooms, decked out with exquisite bathrooms and flat-screen TVs, surround a grassy area with a solar-heated pool, vegetable garden, a duck pen and a few wandering llamas. It's a relaxing retreat 20 minutes' walk from Tafí's center and a great option for families; cabins sleeping up to seven are available.

It's easy to pass weeks here, and if you're here to browse and buy along the Ruta del Artesano, the owners will clue you into the very best artisans in the area.

Cross the bridge and follow the signs.

Estancia Las Tacanas ESTANCIA $$
(☎03867-421821; www.estancialastacanas.com; Perón 372; d US$76; P @ 🛜) This historic complex in the center of town feels like a rural retreat. It was once a Jesuit *estancia* and its adobe buildings, more than three centuries old, house tasteful, rustic rooms. One is especially historic, with noble furniture and beamed ceilings. Others have more of a mix and match of furnishings.

Maintenance has gotten a bit loose here but it's still good value and a memorable place to stay. Don't expect modern luxury: it's the character and history that you're paying for.

Hostería Lunahuana HOTEL $$
(☎03867-421330; www.lunahuana.com.ar; Av Miguel Critto 540; s/d/ste US$75/120/135; P @ 🛜) This stylish and popular central hotel has rooms decorated with flair. Suites are huge, with gorgeous timber accents and furnishings, and are a worthy splurge. Standard rooms are a touch lived-in and worn, but it's still a choice spot with professional service.

Waynay Killa HOTEL $$$
(☎0381-15-589-8514; www.waynaykilla.com; Ubaldini s/n; d/tr US$141/158; P ❄ @ 🛜 ≈) Unobtrusively set on a hillside 2km north of Tafí's center, this sustainable hotel offers handsome public areas, and makes good use of natural light and local art. Rooms face the valley or the hills, either of which guarantees a great vista. Half have balconies (for the same rates).

Eating

★Restaurante El Museo ARGENTINE $
(Av José Silva s/n; dishes AR$30-130; ⏲noon-4pm) Set in the venerable adobe Jesuit chapel 1km from the center, this place makes an atmospheric venue for a lunch of traditional local specialties, such as *humitas,* tamales and empanadas. Just turn up and see what's cooking that day. It all smells divine!

Mi Abuela ARGENTINE $
(cnr Av Miguel Critto & Perón; empanadas AR$18, mains AR$65-170; ⏲8am-2pm & 5-8pm; 🛜) An endearing corner kitchen on the main drag, it does *humitas,* tamales, sandwiches and chicken and beef empanadas. Grab lunch for the road!

Rancho de Félix ARGENTINE $$
(cnr Belgrano & Perón; mains AR$90-210; ⏲11:30am-3pm & 8pm-midnight; 🛜) Rancho de Félix is an expansive and warm thatched barn that's incredibly popular for lunch. Regional specialties such as *locro* and *humitas* are served; *parrilla* and pasta are also on offer. The quality is reasonably good and prices are fair. It may not open evenings if the town is quiet.

Shopping

★Ruta del Artesano ART
(www.tucumanturismo.gob.ar/ruta-del-artesano/230/ruta-del-artesano-tafi-del-valle; ⏲hours vary)

Tafí's main diversion, aside from walks in the countryside, is this driving route to the home studios of area artisans, whose work includes ceramics, jewelry, musical instruments, art and more. The Casa de Turista (tourist office) will give you a map, or you can navigate an interactive Google map on the tourist office's website.

Information

Banco Macro (cnr Av Miguel Critto & Perón; 9am-4pm Mon-Fri) Has an ATM.

Casa del Turista (0381-15-594-1039; www.tafidelvalle.gob.ar; Los Faroles s/n; 8am-10pm) On the pedestrian street.

Getting There & Away

Tafí's **bus terminal** (03867-421025; Av Miguel Critto) is located in the town center.

Aconquija has six to nine buses a day to Tucumán (AR$156, two to three hours). There are also services to Santa María (AR$160, two hours, four to five daily) and Cafayate (AR$230 to AR$275, 3½ hours, two to five daily) via Amaicha del Valle (AR$125) and the Quilmes ruins turnoff (AR$150).

The road from Tucumán is beautiful, and the road to Santa María, Quilmes and Cafayate is even more magical, crossing the 3050m pass known as Abra del Infiernillo (Little Hell Pass).

Getting Around

Hourly in summer (every three hours in winter), local Aconquija buses do most of the circuit around Cerro El Pelado, in the middle of the valley. One goes on the north side, another on the south side, so it's possible to make a circuit of the valley by walking the link between them.

Around Tafí del Valle

The circuit of Tafí del Valle makes a beautiful drive or cycle (47km). Highlights include standout views, and the Jesuit *estancia,* hotel and cheese factory of Estancia Las Carreras (p268). Visit at 5pm to see the milking. At pretty **El Mollar**, at the other end of the valley from Tafí, you can visit the **Parque de los Menhires** (Plaza s/n, El Mollar; AR$50;

WORTH A TRIP

QUILMES

Dating from about 1000 CE, **Quilmes** (adult/child AR$50/free; 8am-6pm) was a complex indigenous urban settlement that occupied about 30 hectares and housed as many as 5000 people. The inhabitants survived contact with the Inca, which occurred from about 1480 CE onward, but could not outlast the seige of the Spanish, who in 1667 deported the remaining 2000 to Buenos Aires.

Quilmes' thick walls underscore its defensive purpose, but clearly this was more than just a *pucará* (walled city). Dense construction radiates from the central nucleus. For revealing views of the extent of the ruins, climb as high as you can; there are trails on either side up to the remains of the watchtower. Be prepared for intense sun with no shade, and, during the hot summer months, a large fly population keen on exploring your facial orifices. Guides at the entrance will offer an explanation and/or tour for a tip. Don't expect accurate archaeological analysis.

The long-defunct museum was finally under renovation at the time of research, and was due to reopen in 2018. This will be a good thing, as it's difficult to interpret the ruins without some solid reference at the site. Friendly folk selling local ceramics also have cold drinks to buy. There are no lodging options and no camping is allowed at the ruins, and nightlife at Quilmes belongs to the wildlife and the ghosts.

A trip to Quilmes can be combined with a visit to the ornate and unusual **Museo de Pachamama** (www.museopachamama.com; AR$70; 8:30am-6:30pm Mon-Sat, to 12:30pm Sun) in nearby Amaicha de Valle. The museum combines a picturesque collection of indigenous art and artifacts with the sculpture and tapestries of the artist who designed the striking indoor-outdoor building.

Buses between Cafayate and Santa María or Tafí will drop you off at the junction; from there it's a 5km walk or hitchhike to the ruins. Alternatively, get off at Amaicha del Valle, where a *remise* (taxi) will charge around AR$200 one way to the ruins: bargain to get a decent price, including waiting time. A *remise* from Cafayate or Santa María is also an option and tours run from Cafayate and Tafí.

WORTH A TRIP

TERMAS DE RÍO HONDO

Halfway between Santiago del Estero and Tucumán, and served by regular buses between them, this riverside resort area is renowned nationwide for its thermal water. Popular among Argentine families in winter, it has nearly 200 hotels that all have hot mineral baths. If you fancy a spa treatment (the quality of massage therapists in Argentina is high) it's a good stop, though there's little else of interest beyond its waters.

Buses passing between Tucumán (AR$125) and Santiago del Estero (AR$110) on RN 9 stop here.

The **Hotel Platino Termas** (☑ 03858-423246; www.hotelplatinotermas.com.ar; Caseros 126; d from US$165; P ❄ ⚡ ☒) has a swirly facade and thermal pools inside and out. Rooms aren't huge, but they are modern, clean and comfortable, with handsome wood furnishings. There's a games room for kids, a billiard room, and a restaurant and bar out by the pool.

⊙8am-noon & 5-8pm) on the plaza, where there is a collection of more than 100 carved standing stones produced by the Tafí culture some 2000 years ago.

🛏 Sleeping

⭐ **Estancia Las Carreras** ESTANCIA $$
(☑ 03867-421473; www.estancialascarreras.com; RP 325, Km13, Las Carreras; d US$141; P ⚡) In a visually striking location 13km from Tafí, surrounded by hills great for hiking and horseback riding, this *estancia* has only the lowing of cattle to disturb the tranquility. It offers superb accommodations in a 18th-century adobe complex. Public areas are wonderful; there are few better bases for relaxation hereabouts. The food is *ma-so-menos* (so-so). Guided visits are from 9am to 6pm for AR$30, including coffee.

🛈 Getting There & Away

Tour companies in Tafí run mediocre excursions around the valley circuit (costing from AR$400). If there's more than one of you, a *remise* will do it for less. Aconquija buses head to El Mollar (AR$17), and also to Las Carreras (AR$15). The final stop on the Las Carreras route is El Rincón, from where a 4km downhill walk will take you to El Mollar, allowing you to do the full valley circuit. Three daily buses also do the circuit (AR$55), but you can't get off.

Santiago del Estero

☑ 0385 / POP 392,000

Placid, hot Santiago del Estero enjoys the distinction of the title 'Madre de Ciudades' (Mother of Cities), for this city, founded in 1553, was the first Spanish urban colonisation in what is now Argentina. It boasts no architectural heritage from that period. Nevertheless, it makes a pleasant stop.

Santiagueños enjoy a nationwide reputation for folk music and, to put it politely, valuing rest and relaxation over work, but there's plenty of bustle around the town center, particularly in the evenings when life orbits around the pretty plaza and adjoining pedestrian streets.

⊙ Sights

⭐ **Centro Cultural del Bicentenario** MUSEUM, GALLERY
(CCB; www.ccbsantiago.com; Pellegrini 149 & Libertad s/n; adult/child 9-14yr AR$10/5; ⊙9am-2pm & 4-9pm Tue-Fri, 10am-1pm & 6-9pm Sat, 6-9pm Sun) This excellent cultural center is an airy, modern space housing three museums, all imaginatively displayed; the highlight is the **anthropological collection**, with an array of indigenous ceramics, jewelry and flutes. Fossils of mastodons and glyptodonts, extinct creatures that somewhat resembled large armadillos, also impress. The sparsely labeled **historical museum** is set around the attractive patio of Santiago's noblest building, and is focused on Argentina's independence movement. The top-floor **art gallery** features good temporary exhibitions. All information is in Spanish.

🎊 Festivals & Events

Marcha de los Bombos PARADE
(www.marchadelosbombos.com.ar; ⊙late Jul) During the last week of July, *santiagueños* celebrate the founding of their city. The main event is this boisterous procession into the center by thousands of locals banging all manner of drums.

Sleeping & Eating

There's free camping within Santiagio's vast, riverside **Parque Aguirre** (0385-422-9818; Olaechea s/n;), and plenty of hotels in the center.

★Hotel Avenida HOTEL $
(0385-421-5887; www.facebook.com/havenidasgo; Pedro León Gallo 403; s/d US$29/47;) You have to feel for management: they set up a welcoming little hotel, decorated with indigenous art and right opposite the bus terminal. Then the city moved the bus terminal to the other side of town. Spotless, renovated, friendly and always improving, it's well worth the short walk from the center.

Hotel Carlos V HOTEL $$
(0385-424-0303; www.carlosvhotel.com; Independencia 110; s/d US$81/115;) This hotel has a great central location and spacious rooms with business-class facilities and large comfortable beds. Some rooms have a balcony. Superiors are larger and have table and chairs. There's a gym, sauna and indoor pool.

★Aladdin LEBANESE $
(0385-422-0300; Belgrano Norte 228; dishes AR$45-100; noon-3pm & 9pm-midnight;) The marketing of this restaurant will look familiar to fans of the Disney film, but you've made the trek from the center of town for the authentic Lebanese fare. Think faithful hummus, baba ghanoush, falafel, kofta, kebabs, tabbouleh and a magnificent flakey, syrupy baklava. All of it well prepared in a family kitchen and served in an atmospheric arched dining room.

Mía Mamma ARGENTINE $
(0385-429-9715; 24 de Septiembre 15; mains AR$75-130; 8pm-1am;) Tucked away but on Plaza Libertad, this is a discreet and reliable restaurant with well-dressed waiters who see to your every need. There's a salad bar, and a wide-ranging menu that includes enormous *parrilla* options as well as *arroz a la valenciana* (paella).

Drinking & Entertainment

The nightlife buzzes along Av Roca into the wee hours – it's a barhopper's dream. In the early evening there's a fun scene at corner cafes up and down the same *avenida*.

★El Patio del Indio Froilán TRADITIONAL MUSIC
(www.elindiofroilan.com.ar; Av Libertador Norte s/n, Barrio Boca del Tigre; Sun) For more than 40 years, indigenous local hero Froilán González has been making drums from the trunks of the ceibo tree. They're used by some of the biggest names in Latin music. On Sundays, locals and visitors gather at this open space and workshop from early afternoon to eat empanadas, investigate drum-making and listen and dance to live music.

Information

Post Office (www.correoargentino.com.ar; Buenos Aires 252; 8:15am-1pm & 5-8pm Mon-Fri)

Tourist Office (0385-421-3253; www.turismosantiago.gob.ar; Libertad 417; 7am-9pm Mon-Fri, 10am-1pm & 5-8pm Sat, 10am-1pm Sun) On Plaza Libertad. There's also an **office** (8am-9pm Mon-Fri, 10am-1pm & 5-8pm Sat & Sun) at the bus terminal.

Getting There & Away

AIR

Aerolíneas Argentinas (0385-422-4333; www.aerolineas.com.ar; 24 de Septiembre 547; 8:30am-noon & 5-8pm Mon-Fri, 9am-noon Sat) flies daily to Buenos Aires from Santiago del Estero's **Aeropuerto Ángel de la Paz Aragonés** (0385-434-3654; Av Madre de Ciudades), 6km northwest of downtown. Buses 115 and 119 (AR$6) go to the airport. A taxi costs AR$80.

BUS

Santiago's swish **bus terminal** (0385-422-7091; www.tosde.com.ar; Chacabuco 550) is six blocks northwest of Plaza Libertad. For Salta and Catamarca, there are better connections via Tucumán. Bus 20 (AR$6) heads into town from here, but it's only AR$30 in a taxi.

TRAIN

Santiago del Estero's twin town La Banda is on the train line (p264) between Tucumán (four hours) and Buenos Aires' Retiro station (23 hours).

Getting Around

A new urban train links Santiago's bus terminal with La Banda.

Bus 117 does a circuit of Santiago's center before heading across the river to the train station.

CATAMARCA & LA RIOJA

Often overlooked by travelers, these provinces are an adventure, rich in scenery and tradition. Both were home to important pre-Columbian cultures and consequently the region contains many important archaeological sites. The provinces rise westward into the Andes, with some of the country's most spectacular highland scenery, punctuated by ice-crusted volcanoes soaring above 6000m, accessible by tour or 4WD. It's an utterly memorable landscape, and one you should not miss.

Catamarca

☎0383 / POP 159,100 / ELEV 530M

Youthful, vibrant, relatively affluent and abuzz with college students, San Fernando del Valle de Catamarca has a central plaza filled with robust jacaranda, araucaria, citrus and palm trees, and streets dotted with fine period buildings. A few blocks west, Parque Navarro's towering eucalypts scent the air and are backed by the spectacular sierra beyond.

Sights

Sights outside of town, easily accessible by bus, include the grotto where the town's Virgin was found, a reservoir, indigenous ruins and the picturesque foothills around Villa Las Pirquitas. The Municipal Tourist Office (p272) will explain them all and show you where to get the bus.

★Museo Arqueológico Adán Quiroga MUSEUM

(☎0383-443-7413; www.facebook.com/MuseoArqAdanQuiroga; Sarmiento 450; ⌚12:30-8:30pm Mon-Fri, 10am-7pm Sat & Sun) FREE This fine archaeological museum displays a superb collection of pre-Columbian ceramics from several different cultures and eras. Some pieces – particularly the black Aguada ceramics with their incised, stylized animal decoration – are of remarkable quality. There's also a colonial and religious section. Closed weekends in January.

★Catedral Basílica de Nuestra Señora del Valle CATHEDRAL

(☎0383-427779; Plaza 25 de Mayo; ⌚6am-9:30pm) This 19th-century cathedral shelters the Virgen del Valle, patron saint of Catamarca and one of northern Argentina's most venerated images. Her back is to the church: you can get a look at her face by ascending to the Camarín, a glorious mezzanine chapel with original tile and stained glass telling the virgin's story. It's accessed via a pedestrian lane and up a staircase decorated with more antiquated relics.

Museo de la Virgen del Valle MUSEUM

(☎0383-450-1765; República 449; ⌚9am-8pm Mon-Fri, 9am-2pm & 3-8pm Sat & Sun) FREE Quirky, strange and sanctimonious, this relatively new museum is free and stocked with sculpture, paintings and even digital and photographic art, all of it in praise of the renowned Virgen del Valle. It's also a historical reference to pioneering leaders of the Argentine Catholic church, which despite its spotty record (including postwar collusion with actual Nazis), has produced the most progressive pope in modern times.

Tours

Alta Catamarca DRIVING

(☎0383-443-0333; www.altacatamarca.tur.ar; Esquiú 433) A well-run agency offering tours of the sights close to the city, as well as longer excursions to the attractions in the west of the province, including Belén, the Ruta de Adobe, the Seismiles, Antofagasta de la Sierra and the surrounding puna.

Festivals & Events

Fiesta de Nuestra Señora del Valle RELIGIOUS

(⌚Apr) The Fiesta de Nuestra Señora del Valle takes place for two weeks after Easter, as hordes of pilgrims come to honor the Virgen del Valle and lead her on a procession through town. On her saint's day, December 8, she is similarly feted.

Fiesta Nacional del Poncho CULTURAL

(www.facebook.com/fiestadelponcho; ⌚mid-Jul) This celebration of handicrafts and traditional Catamarca culture brings a huge artisanal market, plenty of *folklórico* performers and an excellent atmosphere.

Sleeping

Residencial Tucumán GUESTHOUSE $

(☎0383-442-2209; Tucumán 1040; s/d US$30/36; P❄📶) This well-run, immaculate *residencial* (budget hotel) has simple yet comfortable rooms. It's nothing fancy but is excellent value and is about a one-minute walk from the bus terminal. It offers parking at a secure lot nearby for an additional charge.

Puna Hostel HOSTEL $

(☎0383-442-5296; www.facebook.com/punahostal; San Martín 152; dm/d US$12/35; 📶) It's

Catamarca

Catamarca

Top Sights
1 Catedral Basílica de Nuestra Señora del Valle C2
2 Museo Arqueológico Adán Quiroga C1

Sights
3 Museo de la Virgen del Valle B2

Activities, Courses & Tours
4 Alta Catamarca B1

Sleeping
5 Hotel Casino Catamarca A2
6 Puna Hostel A2
7 Residencial Tucumán D3

Eating
8 Bar Richmond C2
9 Sopra Tutto C1

Shopping
10 Mercado Artesanal y Fábrica de Alfombras A3
11 Santeria San Jose C2

a cheap sleep at this simple central hostel, but they sardine 'em into the fan-cooled dorms, with not much room to move between bunks. It's stuffy on hot days, but it's a friendly place with a back garden and kitchen.

★ **Hotel Casino Catamarca** HOTEL **$$**
(☎0383-443-2928; www.hotelcasinocatamarca.com; Esquiú 151; r standard US$107-126, superior US$168; P ❄ @ 📶 🏊) There's space to spare at this peaceful but central hotel, which features handsome modern design and bags of

facilities. Rooms are more than ample; some have balconies, while superiors add mini-bars, king-size beds and hydromassage tubs. There's a restaurant, decent gym, small spa complex and a cracking long pool and lawn. And a casino, of course.

Tour groups book out the place in high season. Reserve ahead.

✖ Eating

★ **Sopra Tutto** ITALIAN $
(☑ 0383-445-2114; Rivadavia 404; mains AR$80-160; ⊙ shop 9am-2pm, restaurant 11:30am-1:30pm; 🛜) Excellent homemade pasta plates, beautifully presented and flavorsome, are produced in this warm, cozy corner trattoria that doubles as a pasta shop. Family owned and operated, it stuffs delicate cannelloni with *choclo* (creamed corn) or spinach and fresh cheese, its bolognese is rich with red wine and gravy, and the house-made empanadas are special too.

Bar Richmond PIZZA $$
(☑ 0383-443-5695; República 534; pizzas AR$160-220, mains AR$120-350; ⊙ 8am-1am Sun-Thu, to 2am Fri & Sat; 🛜) The best choice on Plaza 25 de Mayo, this bright and tasteful place serves up delicious pizzas *à la parrilla*. Think wood-fired flatbreads layered with everything from *humitas* to prosciutto and *bandiola* to rocket and Parmesan. It serves other classic dishes, too.

La Cueva del Santo TAPAS $$
(☑ 0383-422-6249; www.facebook.com/lacueva. delsanto; Av República 1162; pintxos AR$16-70, dishes AR$60-160; ⊙ 9pm-1am Tue-Sat, coffee 8:30-11:30am Mon-Fri; 🛜) In a sweet spot opposite the striking 19th-century hospital, this place deals in authentic Spanish fare. The highlights are delicious Basque-style cold and hot *pintxos* (canapé-type tapas). There's a terrific atmosphere and it attracts a fun crowd.

🛍 Shopping

Catamarca enthusiastically promotes its fine natural products; the region is well known for wines, olive oil, walnuts, jams and conserves. There are several shops stocking these along Sarmiento and Rivadavia near the plaza.

Mercado Artesanal y Fábrica de Alfombras ARTS & CRAFTS
(www.artesaniascatamarca.gob.ar; Virgen del Valle 945; ⊙ 7am-1pm & 3-7pm Mon-Sat, 8am-2pm Sun)

 For Catamarca's characteristic hand-tied rugs, visit this artisans market, which also sells ponchos, blankets, jewelry, red onyx sculptures, musical instruments and basketry.

Adjacent is a carpet-weaving workshop, where staff will happily show you around for free (it's only open Monday to Friday morning).

Santeria San Jose GIFTS & SOUVENIRS
(San Martín 501 & Sarmiento; ⊙ 11am-9:30pm) A mystical art shop with a rocky altar encrusted on its rooftop, dealing in both new and vintage iconic Christian art. Peruse the shelves of Virgin sculpture and assorted miniatures for vintage gems hidden among the collection of sacred kitsch.

ℹ Information

Municipal Tourist Office (Sarmiento 620; ⊙ 8am-9:30pm) By the cathedral.

Post Office (www.correoargentino.com.ar; San Martín 761; ⊙ 8am-1pm & 5:30-8:30pm Mon-Fri)

Provincial Tourist Office (☑ 0383-443-7791; www.turismocatamarca.gob.ar; Virgen del Valle 945; ⊙ 7am-1pm & 3-7pm Mon-Fri, 8am-8pm Sat, 8am-2pm Sun) Adjacent to the Mercado Artesanal y Fábrica de Alfombras.

ℹ Getting There & Around

AIR

Aerolíneas Argentinas (☑ 0383-442-4460; www.aerolineas.com.ar; Sarmiento 589; ⊙ 8am-1pm & 6-9pm Mon-Fri, 9am-1pm Sat) has at least one daily flight from Buenos Aires to **Aeropuerto Felipe Varela** (☑ 0383-445-3684), 17km southeast of town on RP 33. It's AR$250 in a *remise* to the center.

BUS

Catamarca's spruce **bus terminal** (☑ 0383-442-3415; Av Güemes 850) includes a shopping complex and cinema. There are services around the province and across the country, including to Tucumán (AR$300 to AR$350, 3¾ hours), La Rioja (AR$240, two hours) and Buenos Aires (AR$1390 to AR$1650, 14 to 16 hours).

Belén

☑ 03835 / POP 12.300 / ELEV 1250M
Slow-paced Belén, a stop on RN 40, feels like, and is, a long way from anywhere, and will appeal to travelers who like things small-scale and friendly. It's one of the best places to buy woven goods, particularly ponchos. There are many *teleras* (textile workshops) around

OFF THE BEATEN TRACK

THE WILD NORTHWEST

If you like getting off the beaten track, you're sure to appreciate out-of-the-way Antofagasta de la Sierra in the far northwest of Catamarca province, 300km beyond Belén. This puna (Andean highlands) village sits at 3320m amid a spectacular landscape.

Driving yourself or by tour from Belén or Catamarca you can take in other sights in the area: the spectacular pumice fields of Campo de Piedra Pomez, remote volcanoes, the salt flats and hamlet of Antofalla, and flamingo-stocked lakes.

It's particularly worth visiting in early March for the Fiesta de la Puna, which is based on livestock and traditional culture. There are accommodations in family homes and a couple of guesthouses, including **Hostería Pueblo del Sol** (☎03837-431-2263; www.facebook.com/antofagastadelasierrahosteria; Antofagasta de la Sierra; d from US$67; P). It's freezing in winter. Buses run here from Catamarca via Belén twice weekly (AR$260, 12 to 15 hours).

town, turning out their handwoven wares made from llama, sheep and alpaca wool. The intriguing nearby ruins of El Shincal are another reason to visit. It's set smack in the middle of a red rock desert sprouting with cacti.

Sights

Museo Cóndor Huasi MUSEUM
(cnr Belgrano & San Martín; AR$10; 9am-1pm Mon-Fri) Upstairs at the end of a shopping arcade, this museum has a terrific collection of ceramics representing different eras of settlement in the region.

Arañitas Hilanderas ARTS CENTER
(☎03835-464487; www.facebook.com/aranitashilanderasok; Av Virgen de Belén s/n; 9am-7pm Mon-Fri, 9am to 6pm Sat) FREE This cooperative is a good place to watch weavers at work, and buy their goods. Follow Belgrano past the Hotel Belén to find it.

Rua Chaky ARTS CENTER
(☎03835-461068; ruachaky@hotmail.com; Casa 28, Barrio 17 de Agosto; 7am-10pm) FREE Drop by any time to this family home in a pretty barrio to watch shawls and ponchos being made on the loom in the traditional manner. They've been weaving for five generations and will explain their natural dyeing process. It's on the other side of the main road from town, just over 1km from the center.

Tours

★**Chaku Aventuras** TOURS
(☎03835-463976; www.chakuaventuras.com.ar; Belgrano 607; 2-/3-day tours from US$280/430) This well-run setup offers memorable excursions into the west and northwestern highlands of the province. A two-day trip takes in the Ruta del Adobe, the Termas de Fiambalá and the mighty mountains near the Chilean border; a three-day trip heads northwest to Antofagasta for some spectacular puna scenery. Other options and tailored trips are available.

Sleeping & Eating

Las Cardas Posada & Spa HOTEL $
(☎03835-463976; www.lascardas.com.ar; Belgrano 609; d US$71; P) To call it a 'spa' is generous and the pool is tiny, but the spotless, tiled rooms are bright, well laid-out and spacious, and it's at a quiet end of town. It's attached to Chaku Aventuras, Belén's best tour operator.

Hotel Belén HOTEL $
(☎03835-461501; www.belencat.com.ar; cnr Belgrano & Cubas; s/d US$50/77; P @) A surprising presence in town, this stylish hotel has dark, comfortable rooms featuring exposed rock bathrooms, indigenous art and an archaeological collection in the lobby. If you can ignore a few creaks and quirks – sound travels way too easily between bathrooms, service is patchy and not everything works all the time – it's a fun stay at a decent price.

★**1900** ARGENTINE $$
(☎03835-461100; Belgrano 391; mains AR$70-220; 12:30-3pm & 9pm-1:30am) Beyond-the-call service is the key to this wood-paneled local steak house, a block down from the plaza. It's very popular, but it hates to turn people away, so a Tetris-like reshuffling of tables is a constant feature. Prices are more than fair, and there are a number of large platters designed to be shared. Well-mixed salads and juicy brochettes are highlights.

Shopping

A marquee off the plaza is home to a number of *artesanía* stalls selling ponchos, camelid-wool clothing and foot-stomped local wine. For more-upmarket woven goods, head to the workshops around town or shops around the center. **Familia Avar Saracho** (03835-461091; www.facebook.com/AvarSaracho; Roca 144; 9:30am-11pm) has reasonable prices and arranges shipping.

Information

There's a bank with an ATM at the corner of General Paz and Lavalle, near the tourist office.

Tourist Office (03835-461304; turismobelencat@gmail.com; General Paz 168; 6am-1pm & 2-8pm) Also has a small mineral exhibition. There's a booth on the plaza, too.

Getting There & Away

Belén's **bus terminal** (cnr Sarmiento & Rivadavia) is one block south and one block west of the plaza. Catamarca (AR$310, four to five hours) is served several times daily. Night services run to La Rioja and Córdoba, and several weekly buses and minibuses go to Santa María (AR$170, four hours), which is a scenic journey. Three buses a week go to Tinogasta (AR$190, 3½ hours).

Londres & El Shincal

03835 / POP 2500 / ELEV 1170M

Lying 15km southwest of Belén, sleepy Londres does not hearken to its twin city across the pond. This is an age-old gaucho town, which today has been reduced to a collection of crumbling adobes and grazing horses hiding some important history. The town was founded in 1558, and its name (London) celebrated the marriage of the prince of Spain (later Philip II) to Mary Tudor, Queen of England, in 1554. It's just east of the Inca ruins at El Shincal, which is why most people pass through.

Sights

★El Shincal RUINS

(03835-491919; Enripiada s/n; AR$50; 9am-6pm) The Inca ruins of El Shincal are located 7km west of Londres. Founded in 1471, the town occupied a commanding position in the foothills of the mountains, surveying the vast valley to the south. The setting is spectacular, with fantastic views and great atmosphere. The renovated museum at the entrance has a scale model and good background on Inca and pre-Inca culture, while signs along the way explain local plants.

At the ruins, 500m beyond, the *ushnu* (ceremonial platform) is set in the middle of a central square and is flanked by two partially restored *kallankas* (buildings of unknown function). Two hilltop platforms aligned to the rising and setting sun probably served as both lookouts and altars. All information is in Spanish, including the guided tours, offered six times daily. There's a cafe-restaurant on-site.

Getting There & Away

Buses run Monday to Saturday from Belén to Londres (AR$60) and the ruins. Buses from further afield stop at Londres. A *remise* from Belén with waiting time is around AR$400.

Beyond Londres, Chilecito is 200km south in La Rioja province along RN 40, if you have your own transportation. The drive is a spectacular one, with the imposing Sierra de Famatina to the west and Sierra de Velasco to the east. The road is excellent.

Western Catamarca

03837

It takes some effort to reach western Catamarca, but your sweat will be rewarded. The area is home to historic adobe churches, vineyards, and stunning views from the hot springs above Fiambalá, an oasis town set in an arid valley among dunes. Its spectacular mountainscapes have been favorite terrain for the Dakar Rally since it moved from Africa. In the far west, a cluster of awe-inspiring 6000m-plus peaks form the planet's second-loftiest ensemble after the Himalaya range. The main settlements are Tinogasta, a forgettable dust-bowl town, and Fiambalá, a vibrant desert encampment, set 50km apart. If you don't have transportation, tours from Belén or Catamarca will get you here.

Sights

Ruta del Adobe HISTORIC BUILDING

(RN 60) FREE The road between Tinogasta and Fiambalá is designated the 'adobe route' for its ensemble of fantastic historic buildings. These are built with thick walls of mud, straw and dung and have cane roofs supported by algarrobo beams. Buildings are signposted off the road and include former inns and little museums. On public transportation you can check out the Iglesia de San Pedro, at the southern entrance to Fiambalá, and the adjacent Comandancia de Armas.

This was once an important trade route to Bolivia and Peru, hence the preponderance of old buildings.

Museo del Hombre MUSEUM
(☎03837-496250; Abaucan s/n, Fiambalá; AR$50; ⊙10am-6pm Mon-Sat) This interesting local museum has sections on geology and archaeology, including quality ceramics and two haunting Inca mummies with well-preserved funerary goods. Another room is dedicated to mountaineering, giving details about famous expeditions to the province's 14 6000m-plus peaks.

Termas de Fiambalá SPRING
(San Fernando del Valle de Catamarca; AR$150; ⊙7am-10pm) Lying 15km east into the mountains from Fiambalá, these thermal springs emerge from rock and cascade down the mountainside in a series of pools: the highest is around 104°F (40°C); the cooler ones are below. The views over the desert valley are epic. It's best after 5pm when there's more shade, and even better after dark, though weekends are rowdy. There's a campground and various simple accommodations options here. It's AR$250 in a *remise* from Fiambalá.

Duna Magicá DUNES
(Saují) A network of stunning, red and white sand dunes rises from the desert floor 15km north of Fiambalá. It's best to arrive in the early morning before the winds kick up, as they can turn a journey of mind-bending beauty into a sand-blasted nightmare. But if you do get here before the winds, you can spend hours trudging up and riding down the dunes on sand boards, which is both hilarious and exhilarating.

Check in with Hostel San Pedro which rents sand boards and can arrange transportation to and from the dunes for AR$500.

★Los Seismiles MOUNTAIN
West of Fiambalá, the paved road winds through the high desert, past picturesque red rock escarpments known as the Quebrada Angosturas, and into some serious altitude, topping out at the Chilean border. It's a stunning drive, with no services apart from a seasonal white-elephant hotel halfway between Fiambalá and the frontier. Los Seismiles are the peaks above 6000m, and you'll see several of them, including Ojos del Salado (6879m), the world's highest volcano.

The transition from desert into the high country is mind-boggling. You'll glimpse glacial streams and icy wetlands teeming with flamingos, yellow tundra home to grazing vicuñas, and then finally the spectacular Seismiles will appear from behind still other snowcapped peaks. During the summer the road is open all the way to the border, but at all other times of year, the road is closed at La Gruta, an Argentine border post 21km from Chile; a precaution against inclement weather on hazardous roads that can be icy and dangerous thanks to gusts of *viento blanco* (white wind) that may blow in at anytime.

Even more awe-inspiring scenery is accessed via a lonely (4WD-only) mining road that leads 90km to Monte Pissis (6793m), the Americas' third-highest peak. It's about five hours return (50km) to a viewpoint over this imposing mountain, with hauntingly beautiful blue, black and turquoise lakes in the foreground. Due to its isolation, this is best by tour; operators in Belén and Catamarca can make arrangements.

Sleeping

Casona del Pino BOUTIQUE HOTEL $
(☎03837-15-697429; www.casonadelpino.com; Fiambalá; d from US$70; P❄📶) The most attractive nest in Fiambalá is this converted house, sectioned off into a handful of tasteful rooms with parlor floors, pastel paint jobs and antique furnishings. It offers a wealth of excursions to Duna Magicá, Los Seismiles and the hot springs. Book ahead.

Hostel San Pedro HOSTEL $
(☎03837-453-3162; www.facebook.com/sanpedrohostelfiambala; Diego de Freites s/n, Fiambalá; dm US$12, d with/without bathroom US$35/30; 📶) This is a well-done, family-owned hostel, with tidy dorms and double rooms set around an attractive courtyard on Fiambalá's main drag. The owners are a wealth of local intel, and rent sand boards and can arrange excursions to the nearby sand dunes.

Information

Fiambalá Tourist Office (☎03837-496250; www.fiambala.gov.ar; Plaza Principal s/n, Fiambalá; ⊙7am-9pm Mon-Fri, 8am-9pm Sat & Sun) On the town's plaza.

Getting There & Away

There are three or more daily buses from Catamarca to Tinogasta and Fiambalá (AR$400, 5¾ hours). A few weekly reach La Rioja (AR$300 to AR$340) and Córdoba (AR$780 to AR$840). Five weekly buses link Belén and Tinogasta (AR$190, 3½ hours).

La Rioja

0380 / POP 179,000 / ELEV 500M

Encircled by the Sierra de Velasco's graceful peaks, La Rioja is quite a sight on a sunny day. And there are plenty of those: summer temperatures rise sky-high in this quiet, out-of-the-way, yet affluent provincial capital dotted with palm trees. It's an understated but quite charming place; even if you're on a short highlights tour, you might consider stopping off (it's halfway between Mendoza and Salta) to take a tour to Parque Nacional Talampaya and Parque Provincial Ischigualasto.

Sights & Activities

★Museo Folklórico MUSEUM

(Pelagio Luna 811; entry by donation; 9am-1pm & 5-9pm Tue-Fri, 9am-1pm Sat & Sun) This worthwhile museum is set in a wonderful early 17th-century adobe building, and has fine regional cultural displays. Themes include *chaya* (local La Rioja music), the Tinkunaco festival, weaving and winemaking. The guided tour is excellent if your Spanish is up to it.

Convento de Santo Domingo CHURCH

(cnr Pelagio Luna & Lamadrid; 9:30am-12:30pm & 6-8pm Mon-Fri) Built in 1623 by the Diaguita under the direction of Dominican friars, this is Argentina's oldest monastery. The date appears in the carved algarrobo door frame, also the work of Diaguita artists. There's a museum of religious art alongside.

Águila Blanca HANG GLIDING, PARAGLIDING

(Hugo Ávila; 0380-445-1635; www.turismoaguilablanca.com; Av Ramírez de Velasco Oeste 4900, Km7) Ever dreamt of flying without the assistance of jet propulsion? This gliding school offers instruction and tandem flights, as well as accommodations.

Tours

Several operators run excursions around the province, including visits to the Parque Nacional Talampaya, which normally include nearby Parque Provincial Ischigualasto ('Valle de la Luna') in San Juan province. These companies also offer excursions to remote corners of the Andes.

Corona del Inca TOURS

(0380-442-2142; www.coronadelinca.com.ar; Pelagio Luna 914) A rock-solid adventure-tour operator. Itineraries include 4WD tours through Parque Nacional Talampaya, mountain-biking trips around Laguna Brava and excursions to the Volcán Corona crater (5530m).

Festivals & Events

★La Chaya CARNIVAL

(Feb) The local variant of Carnaval. Its name, derived from a Quechua word meaning 'to get someone wet,' should give you an idea of what to expect. In other words, welcome to the biggest and most joyous water fight in South America! The musical style associated with the festival is also called *chaya*.

El Tinkunaco CULTURAL

(noon Dec 31) This December 31 ceremony reenacts friar Francisco Solano's mediation between the Diaguitas and the Spaniards in 1593. When accepting peace, the Diaguitas imposed two conditions: resignation of the Spanish mayor and his replacement by the Niño Jesús Alcalde (a Christ-child icon symbolically recognized as the city's mayor).

Sleeping

La Rioja's hotels are a mediocre bunch. That's the nicest way we can say it. Discounts are offered for cash, but unless you book into a hostel, you'll be hard-pressed to find good-value lodgings here.

Gute Nacht HOSTEL $

(0380-432-4325; www.facebook.com/GuteNachtHostel; Catamarca 43; dm/d without bathroom US$18/44;) A German-owned hostel with attached cafe and bar. It's rather well run, and well branded, with both shared and private rooms. All guests share spotless bathrooms. It's set in a restored row house, where rooms spill onto an attractive tiled courtyard with plenty of lounging space.

Hostel Apacheta HOSTEL $

(0380-15-444-5445; www.facebook.com/apachetahostel; San Nicolás de Bari 669; dm/d US$12/35;) This central hostel is a simple but

La Rioja

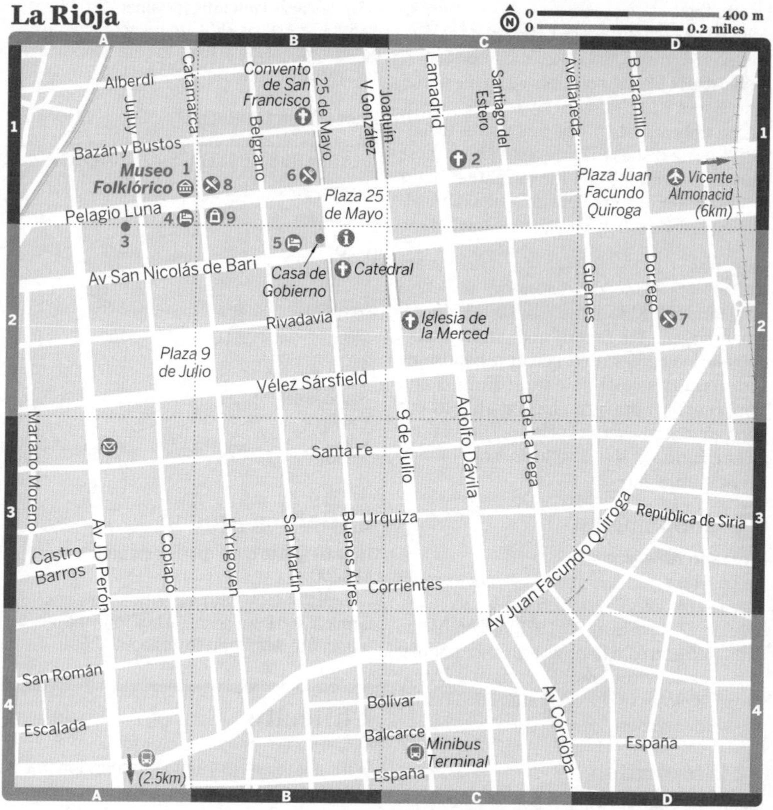

likable place in a great location, with air-con and room to move. It's clean, but a bit like when you told your parents you'd cleaned your room. Rental bikes and an inflatable paddle pool are on hand. Knock US$3 off if you don't want breakfast.

Eating

Regional dishes include *locro*, juicy empanadas, *chivito asado* (barbecued goat), *humitas*, *quesillo* (a cheese specialty) and olives. Area restaurants include some standouts if you're willing to splurge.

Café del Paseo CAFE $

(cnr Pelagio Luna & 25 de Mayo; light meals AR$60-140; 7:30am-3pm & 5:30pm-1am;) This is your spot on the corner of Plaza 25 de Mayo to observe local life. Executives with i-gadgets mingle with families, and tables of older men chew the fat, burning just another slow-paced La Rioja day.

La Rioja

Top Sights
1 Museo Folklórico A1

Sights
2 Convento de Santo Domingo C1

Activities, Courses & Tours
3 Corona del Inca A2

Sleeping
4 Gute Nacht A1
5 Hostel Apacheta B2

Eating
6 Café del Paseo B1
7 La Stanza D2
8 Orígenes B1

Shopping
9 Mercado Artesanal de La Rioja B1

La Stanza ITALIAN $$

(☎0380-443-0809; www.lastanzaresto.com.ar; Dorrego 164; mains AR$100-260; ⊙noon-3pm & 8pm-midnight Tue-Sat, noon-3pm Sun) One of the best places in town, this stylish restaurant has an upbeat, urban vibe and serves imaginative pasta dishes that are a cut above most places. Better still are the inventive main dishes, which feature delicious cuts of meat, accompanied by baked vegetable medleys.

Orígenes ARGENTINE $$$

(☎0380-442-8036; cnr Catamarca & Pelagio Luna; mains AR$180-300; ⊙11:30am-3:30pm & 8pm-midnight; 📶) Smart and enthusiastic, Orígenes occupies a corner of a handsome 19th-century school now turned into a cultural center. It draws on local traditions but adds a modern chef's expertise. The result is a refreshing jolt if you've had weeks of typical Argentine fare.

Shopping

Mercado Artesanal de La Rioja ARTS & CRAFTS

(Pelagio Luna 792; ⊙9am-12:50pm & 6-10pm Tue-Sat, 9am-12:50pm Sun) La Rioja crafts are exhibited and sold here, as are other popular artworks at prices lower than most souvenir shops. It closes in the early afternoon during the winter season.

Information

Municipal Tourist Office (Plaza 25 de Mayo; ⊙8am-1pm & 4-9pm Mon-Fri, 8am-9pm Sat & Sun) In a kiosk on Plaza 25 de Mayo.

Post Office (www.correoargentino.com.ar; Av JD Perón 258; ⊙8am-1pm & 5:30-8:30pm Mon-Fri)

Provincial Tourist Office (☎0380-442-6345; www.turismolarioja.gov.ar; ⊙8am-8pm) On the roundabout next to the bus terminal in the south of town.

Getting There & Away

AIR

Aerolíneas Argentinas (☎0380-442-6307; www.aerolineas.com.ar; Belgrano 63; ⊙8am-1pm & 5:30-8:30pm Mon-Fri, 8:30am-12:30pm Sat) flies six times weekly to and from Buenos Aires. **Aeropuerto Vicente Almonacid** (☎0380-446-2160) lies 7km east of town on RP 5.

BUS

La Rioja's **bus terminal** (Av Circunvalación s/n) is an interesting, modern building 3km south from the center of town, with services to various destinations.

There's also a **minibus terminal** (☎0380-446-8562; Artigas 750), from where you can board frequent departures to Catamarca and Tucumán.

Buses from La Rioja

DESTINATION	COST (AR$)	TIME (HR)
Buenos Aires	1950	14-17
Catamarca	240	2
Chilecito	150	3
Córdoba	590	6
Mendoza	965	8-9½
Salta	1056	10
San Juan	795	6
Santiago del Estero	825	7-8
Tucumán	590	5½-6½

Getting Around

The taxi fare to the airport costs around AR$200.

Local buses (AR$10) run between the bus terminal and town center. A taxi from the bus terminal to downtown costs about AR$90.

Chilecito

☎03825 / POP 33,700 / ELEV 1080M

With a gorgeous situation among low rocky hills, backed by the Sierra de Famantina (a range of mammoth, snowcapped peaks), Chilecito, a mere pit stop for most on RN 40, has several interesting things to see, including an abandoned cableway leading to a mine high in the sierra. With the intense heat, its mining heritage and the slopes around town dotted with cardón cacti, Chilecito has a Wild West feel and is an appealing place to spend a few quiet days. It's also a base for spectacular excursions into the sierra.

Sights

★**Museo del Cablecarril** MUSEUM, CABLE CAR

(Av Presidente Perón s/n; AR$25; ⊙8:30am-12:30pm & 2-6:30pm Mon-Fri, 8am-7pm Sat & Sun) This old cable-car station documents the extraordinary engineering and mining project that created modern Chilecito at the beginning of the 20th century. Yes, this town, like many in cowboy country the world over, was built on silver, gold and copper. The simple, picturesque museum preserves photos, tools (those mammoth wrenches are cool!)

WESTERN RIOJA TRIPS

The western portion of La Rioja province is fascinating, with plenty of intriguing destinations in the sierras. Parque Nacional Talampaya (p280) is one appealing trip, which also takes in the Parque Provincial Ischigualasto and (from Chilecito) crosses the picturesque Miranda pass. For some serious 4WD mountain action, head up to the abandoned mine at **La Mejicana** (4603m), an ascent blessed with amazing mountain scenery and a broad palette of colors, including a striking yellow river. Deeper into the sierras by the Chilean border is sizable **Laguna Brava**, a flamingo-freckled lake set among the Andes' beautiful desolation. Higher still, at 5600m, is the remote sapphire-blue crater lake of Corona del Inca (p276), only accessible in summer.

Operators in Chilecito such as **Salir del Cráter** and **Cuesta Vieja** run trips here, which cost from US$100 to US$400 for up to four people.

and documents, as well as communications equipment, including an early cell phone.

Peruse the museum on your own, then examine the cable-car terminus itself, where ore carts now wait fruitlessly in line. It's best in late afternoon when sun bathes the rusted metal and snowy sierras. With a car, you can investigate the second and third cable-car stations too. Guided tours visit the ninth and final stop of La Mejicana, high in the sierra.

The museum is on the main road at the southern entrance to town, a block south of the bus terminal.

Cristo del Portezuelo MONUMENT
(Maestro s/n; ⌚8am-10pm Mon-Fri, 8:30am-10pm Sat & Sun) FREE Head down Maestro from Chilecito's plaza to reach this relatively recent addition to the town: a huge statue of Christ on a platform accessed by a 203-step ascent flanked by terraced cactus gardens. Views from the top offer panoramic perspectives over town, while local couples canoodle, secure at the savior's feet. There are two cafes on street level as well as a painfully slow funicular (AR$20) for weary legs.

Molino de San Francisco MUSEUM
(Jamín Ocampo 63; AR$20; ⌚9am-noon & 2-7pm) Chilecito founder Don Domingo de Castro y Bazán owned this 300-year-old flour mill, which houses an eclectic assemblage of archaeological tools, antique arms, early colonial documents, minerals, traditional wood and leather crafts, banknotes, stuffed birds, woodcuts and paintings. It's four blocks west of Chilecito's plaza.

La Riojana WINERY
(☎03825-423150; www.lariojana.com.ar; La Plata 646; ⌚tours 11am, noon & 3pm Mon-Fri) FREE La Riojana is the area's main wine producer, and a sizable concern; some 30 million liters a year are produced here thanks to fruit sourced from vineyards owned by a multitude of local farmers. A good free tour shows you through the cooperative bodega – think large concrete fermentation tanks rather than gleaming rows of the state-of-the-art metallic variety – and culminate in a generous wine tasting. It's a block north and five west of Chilecito's plaza.

Tours

Cuesta Vieja TOURS
(☎03825-424874; www.cuestavieja.com.ar; González 467) This friendly, reliable Chilecito tour operator is an excellent choice for excursions into the sierra, to Parque Nacional Talampaya and Parque Provincial Ischigualasto, or for taking off on a scenic flight.

Salir del Cráter TOURS
(☎03825-15-679620; www.salirdelcrater.com.ar) A recommended Chilecito operator running 4WD excursions around western La Rioja province, including Parque Nacional Talampaya. Does hotel or guesthouse pick-ups.

Sleeping

★**El Viejo Molino** GUESTHOUSE $
(☎03825-429445, 03825-15-566040; nicorody@hotmail.com; Jamín Ocampo 64; d/q US$61/91; P❄☎) Run with a warm, personal touch, this attractive spot overlooks a small garden next to the Molino de San Francisco museum. Modern rooms are comfortable, stylish, spacious and well equipped. We love the exposed brick walls and beamed ceilings. There's an appealing restaurant on the ground floor serving pizzas and regional specialties. Management makes the extra effort for their guests.

Hotel Ruta 40 HOTEL $
(03825-422804; Libertad 68; s/d US$24/35;) A laid-back budget hotel a couple of blocks from Chilecito's plaza, this comfortable spot offers a variety of rooms with newish mattresses and clean, spacious bathrooms. Check out a few – some look over a vine-covered patio to the hills beyond.

Aparthotel Chilecito APARTMENT $
(03825-419035; Gordillo 300; s/d US$47/65;) Set against the boulder-strewn backdrop that is Los Colorados, these tiled apartments are bright and tidy with full kitchens, internet access and DirecTV. They are an especially good choice for families or self-caterers, and they're close to the center of town.

Posada Nocenta Pisetta GUESTHOUSE $
(03825-498108; claudiapisetta@hotmail.com; Finca la Cuadra, off RP 12; d US$50-60;) This historic country ranch, family owned for four generations, is a fun sleepover 4km from central Chilecito. The fine, thick-walled adobe house offers spare chambers with antique wooden furnishings and original floorboards and tiles. All are unique, and the service is relaxed and on point. There's no wi-fi.

Eating & Drinking

★El Rancho de Ferrito ARGENTINE $$
(www.elranchodeferrito.com; Av Pelagio Luna 647; mains AR$70-210; noon-3:30pm & 8pm-2am Tue-Sun) A block west and seven north of Chilecito's plaza, this inviting local restaurant is worth every step. You've seen the menu before – except for house specialties such as *cazuela de gallina* (chicken stew – yum) and local wines – but the quality, price and authentic atmosphere make it a nice find.

Borussia PUB FOOD $$
(03825-425413; 25 de Mayo 37; mains AR$70-190; 7am-3am) A cavernous and, dare we say, hip restobar on Chilecito's plaza that gets a crowd for big football games on their large screens. It serves pizza, burgers and *lomitos,* and a range of *milanesas* too. It also has some veggie options, but, beware, they come drenched in mayo and smothered in cheese. The kitchen is open all day.

★Yops BAR
(AE Dávila 70; 9:15am-2pm & 8:30pm-2am Mon-Sat) Simple but atmospheric, this bohemian spot is Chilecito's best cafe, serving fine coffee, cold beer and decent mixed drinks. Expect epic chess battles between locals by day, and live music some weekends, when the bar is often rented out for birthday parties and, well, divorce parties. True story. No matter what's on, you are always welcome.

Information

The plaza has banks with ATMs.

Tourist Office (03825-429665; www.emutur.com.ar; Castro y Bazán 52; 9am-10pm;) Half a block off the plaza. There's also a tourist booth at the bus terminal.

Getting There & Away

The **Chilecito Bus Terminal** (Av Presidente Perón s/n;) is 1.5km south of the center. It's a nice ride into Chilecito from La Rioja (AR$160, 2½ hours), passing the red rock formations of Los Colorados, with the snowcapped Sierra de Famatina in the background. There are direct services from Chilecito to further-flung destinations such as Buenos Aires, and daily services to Catamarca (AR$240, four hours).

There are also three daily **buses to Villa Unión** (03825-527178), from where you can access Parque Nacional Talampaya. It's a scenic ride that takes nearly three hours and traverses the spectacular Miranda Pass.

There are no buses north to Belén; to avoid the lengthy backtrack join a tour to El Shincal.

Parque Nacional Talampaya

03825 / ELEV 1300M

The spectacular rock formations and canyons of this dusty desert **national park** (03825-470356; www.parquesnacionales.gob.ar; foreigner/Argentine/child 6-12 yr AR$250/120/60; excursions 8am-5pm Oct-Feb, 8:30am-4:30pm Mar-Sep) are evidence of the erosive creativity of water; these days it's hard to believe that water and ice ever existed here. The sandstone cliffs are amazing, as are the distant surrounding mountains. Talampaya is relatively close to fossil-rich **Parque Provincial Ischigualasto** in San Juan province, and it's easy to combine the two if you have your own transportation or visit with a tour.

Sights & Activities

You must enter the Parque Nacional Talampaya by guided visit, arranged at the visitors center. The standard 2½-hour trip is included in your entrance fee. You'll spend much of the time in a comfortable minibus and there's little walking involved; nevertheless, take water and protection from the fierce sun. For a little extra, you can extend the visit to another nearby canyon or do the route on the roof of a truck. You may also visit further-flung valleys within the park.

Guided walks (AR$300 to AR$500) and trips on bicycles (AR$400) are also available; these are more appealing ways of exploring if the heat's not too intense, though you'll still likely have to pay for transportation into the park if you're on foot. There are often night excursions available when there's a full moon.

Cañón de Talampaya CANYON

The focus of a visit to Parque Nacional Talampaya is this spectacular, (usually) dry watercourse bounded by sheer sandstone cliffs. Condors soar on thermals, and guanacos, rheas and maras can be seen in the shade of algarrobo trees along the sandy canyon floor. A series of enigmatic petroglyphs carved into oxidized sandstone slabs are the first stop on the standard visit, followed by in-canyon highlights such as the Chimenea, the impressive echo of which is a guaranteed hit.

Ciudad Perdida & Cañón Arco Iris NATURAL FEATURE

In Parque Nacional Talampaya, accessed from the road 14km before reaching the main park entrance, these impressive formations are visited via guided 4WD tours, which wait to fill before departure (AR$300 to AR$500; three to four hours).

Sendero Triásico MUSEUM

(incl with entry to Parque Nacional Talampaya, foreigner/Argentine/child 6-12 yr AR$250/120/60; ⌚8am-5pm Oct-Feb, 8:30am-4:30pm Mar-Sep) This 'Triassic' path takes you past life-size replicas of dinosaurs whose fossilized remains have been found in the Talampaya area.

Tours

Runacay TOURS

(☎03825-470368; www.runacay.com) Provides tours around Parque Nacional Talampaya as well as good trips to Laguna Brava. It offers shuttle services between Catamarca destinations as well, including Villa Unión, and will pick you up at your accommodations.

Sleeping

There's shadeless camping at the visitors center, which has decent toilets and showers.

Simple accommodations are available in Pagancillo, 29km north. A further 29km up the road, larger Villa Unión has several cabin and hotel options, some quite stylish. It's also possible to visit in a long day trip from Chilecito.

Information

The visitors center is just off the RP 26. Here you pay the entrance fee and arrange guided visits. Entry is valid for two days and includes a free jaunt that introduces biological and cultural aspects of the park. Don't sweat if you miss it: you get most of this info on park tours.

Getting There & Away

Buses from La Rioja to Pagancillo and Villa Unión (AR$190, 3½ hours) will leave you at the park entrance, from where it's only a 500m walk to the visitors center. The earliest bus (Facundo) leaves La Rioja at 7am, giving you plenty of time to make a day trip. There are three buses per week between Villa Unión, 58km up the road, and Chilecito (AR$215, three hours) over the spectacular Miranda Pass.

If you want to see Talampaya and Ischigualasto in one day, tour operators such as Corona del Inca (p276) in La Rioja or Cuesta Vieja (p279) and Salir del Cráter (p279) in Chilecito will do it. It can be cheaper taking a *remise* from either of those or from closer Villa Unión.

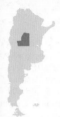

Córdoba & the Central Sierras

Includes ➡

Best Places to Eat

- ➡ La Tahua (p299)
- ➡ Sabía Que Venías y Preparé Un Pastel (p300)
- ➡ La Casona del Toboso (p297)
- ➡ El Bistro del Alquimista (p306)

Best Places to Stay

- ➡ Mousai Hotel Boutique (p300)
- ➡ Sacha Mistol (p289)
- ➡ 279 Boutique B&B (p303)
- ➡ Hotel Azur Real (p289)

Why Go?

Argentina's second city is bursting with life. Home to seven major universities, Córdoba has a young population that ensures an excellent nightlife and a vibrant cultural scene. Córdoba also has a complex history, with its architectural and cultural heritage rooted in the arrival of Jesuit missionaries from colonial Spain, who based themselves here when they first arrived in Argentina.

The rolling hill country outside of town is dotted with places that could grab your attention for a day or a month, including five Jesuit missions that each make for an easy day trip. Adventure buffs head to the hills for stellar paragliding and trekking in a couple of national parks nearby. The hippie towns of San Marcos Sierras and Capilla del Monte give a glimpse into Argentina's alternative lifestyles. Further southwest, the Valle de Conlara and the Sierras Puntanas offer a chance to get away from the crowds and into the heart of the countryside.

When to Go

Córdoba

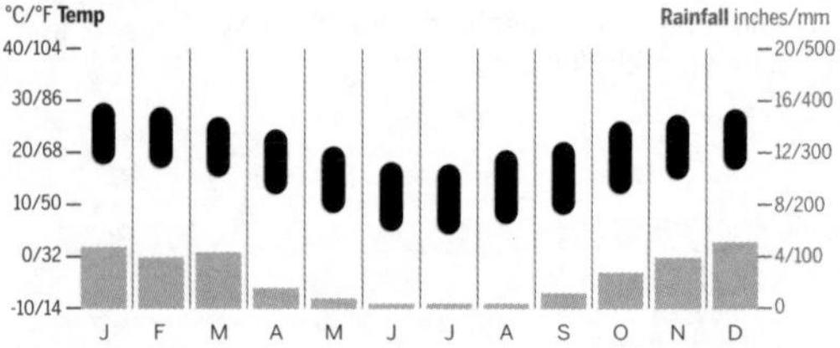

Nov–Feb During the day, cool off riverside in the Sierras. At night, hit Córdoba's bars.

Mar–Jun Clear, cool days with occasional rain – ideal for outdoor activities.

Jul–Sep Chances of snow at higher altitudes. Low rainfall makes for good trekking weather.

National Parks

In San Luis province, the rarely visited Parque Nacional Sierra de las Quijadas (p310) is an excellent alternative to the better-known Parque Provincial Ischigualasto in San Juan province: getting there is far easier, and you'll often have the desert canyons and rock formations all to yourself. Parque Nacional Quebrada del Condorito (p308) is well worth a day trip from Córdoba to see the impressive Andean condors the park protects.

Getting There & Around

Córdoba makes an excellent stop if you're heading south or southwest toward Mendoza. The city has bus connections throughout the country.

The towns throughout the Central Sierras are all easily accessible by public transportation, but many tiny remote towns and Jesuit s (ranches) can only be reached with your own wheels. The region's dense network of roads, many well paved but others only gravel, make them good candidates for bicycle touring; Argentine drivers here seem a bit less ruthless than elsewhere in the country. A mountain bike is still the best choice.

CÓRDOBA

☎0351 / POP 1.391 MILLION / ELEV 400M

It's an old guidebook cliché, but Córdoba really *is* a fascinating mix of old and new. Where else will you find DJs spinning electro-tango in crowded student bars next to 17th-century Jesuit ruins?

Despite being a whopping 715km away from Buenos Aires, Córdoba is anything but a provincial backwater – in 2006 the city was awarded the hefty designation of Cultural Capital of the Americas, and the title fit like a glove. Four excellent municipal galleries – dedicated to emerging, contemporary, classical and fine art respectively – are within easy walking distance of each other and the city center.

Sights

There's plenty to see, so allow yourself at least a couple of days for wandering around. Museum opening hours change regularly depending on the season and the administration.

Most colonial-era sights lie within a few blocks of Plaza San Martín, the city's urban nucleus. The commercial center is just northwest of the plaza, where the main pedestrian malls – 25 de Mayo and Rivera Indarte – intersect. Obispo Trejo, just west of the plaza, has the finest concentration of colonial buildings. Just southeast of downtown, Parque Sarmiento offers relief from the bustling, densely built downtown.

East–west streets change names at San Martín/Independencia and north–south streets change at Deán Funes/Rosario de Santa Fe.

Centro

Downtown Córdoba is a treasure trove of colonial buildings and other historical monuments.

Iglesia Catedral CATHEDRAL

(Independencia 80; ⏲8am-4pm & 5-8pm) The construction of Córdoba's cathedral began in 1577 and dragged on for more than two centuries under several architects, including Jesuits and Franciscans, and though it lacks any sense of architectural unity, it's a beautiful structure. Crowned by a Romanesque dome, it overlooks Plaza San Martín. The lavish interior was painted by renowned *cordobés* (Córdoban) painter Emilio Caraffa.

Museo de la Memoria MUSEUM

(Pje Santa Catalina 1; ⏲10am-6pm Tue-Fri) FREE A chilling testament to the excesses of Argentina's military dictatorship, this museum occupies a space formerly used as a clandestine center for detention and torture. It was operated by the dreaded Department of Intelligence (D2), a special division dedicated to the kidnapping and torture of suspected political agitators and the 'reassignment' of their children to less politically suspect families.

The space itself is stark and unembellished, and the walls are covered with enlarged photographs of people who are still 'missing' after 30 years. There's not much joy here, but the museum stands as a vital reminder of an era that human-rights groups hope will never be forgotten.

Museo Histórico Provincial Marqués de Sobremonte MUSEUM

(Rosario de Santa Fe 218; AR$15, Wed free; ⏲10am-5:30pm Tue-Sun) It's worth dropping into one of the most important historical museums in the country, if only to see the colonial house it occupies: an 18th-century home that once belonged to Rafael Núñez, the colonial governor of Córdoba and later viceroy

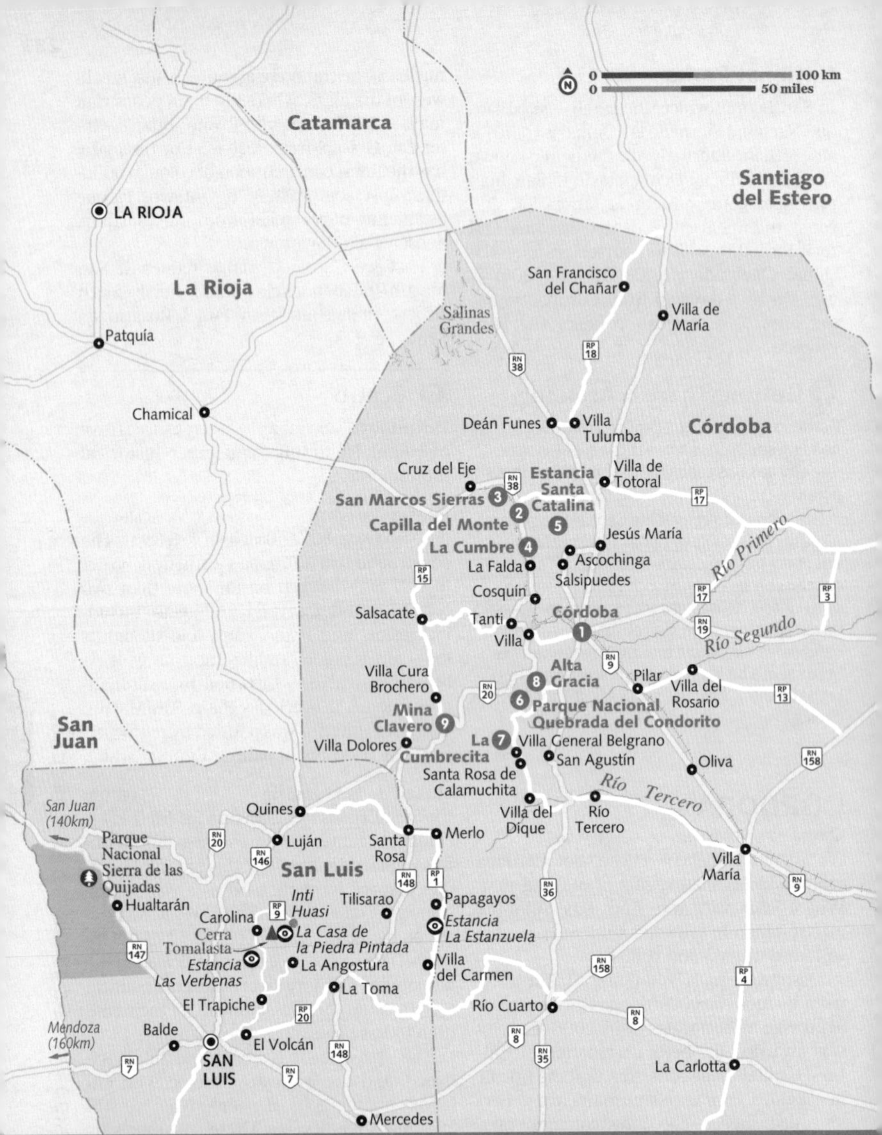

Córdoba & the Central Sierras Highlights

1. **Córdoba** (p283) Lapping up the culture and nightlife of Argentina's second-largest city.
2. **Capilla del Monte** (p300) Checking out the UFO-sighting hot spots.
3. **San Marcos Sierras** (p299) Soaking up the hippie vibe at this leafy dirt-road outpost.
4. **La Cumbre** (p296) Getting high with the paragliding fanatics at this mountain hideaway.
5. **Estancia Santa Catalina** (p301) Roaming this 17th-century Jesuit ranch.
6. **Parque Nacional Quebrada del Condorito** (p308) Looking out for condors at this national park.
7. **La Cumbrecita** (p306) Mellowing out in this mountain village.
8. **Alta Gracia** (p302) Visiting Che Guevara's house.
9. **Mina Clavero** (p308) Cooling off riverside in this quaint resort town in the Valle de Traslasierra.

of the Río de la Plata. The building has 26 rooms, seven interior patios, meter-thick walls and an impressive wrought-iron balcony supported by carved wooden brackets.

Cripta Jesuítica MUSEUM
(Av Colón 100; 9am-2pm Mon-Fri) FREE Built at the beginning of the 18th century by the Jesuits, the Cripta Jesuítica was originally designed as a novitiate and later converted to a crypt and crematorium. Abandoned after the Jesuit expulsion, it was demolished and buried around 1829 when the city, while expanding Av Colón, knocked the roof into the subterranean naves and built over the entire structure.

Museo Municipal de Bellas Artes Dr Genaro Pérez GALLERY
(Av General Paz 33; 10am-8pm Tue-Sun) FREE This art gallery is prized for its collection of paintings from the 19th and 20th centuries. Works, including those by Emilio Caraffa, Lucio Fontana, Lino Spilimbergo, Antonio Berni and Antonio Seguí, chronologically display the history of the *cordobés* school of painting, at the front of which stands Genaro Pérez himself. The museum is housed in Palacio Garzón, an unusual late 19th-century building named for its original owner. It also features outstanding contemporary-art exhibits that change on a regular basis.

Plaza San Martín PLAZA
Córdoba's lovely and lively central plaza dates from 1577. Its western side is dominated by the white arcade of the restored *cabildo* (town council) building, completed in 1785 and containing three interior patios, as well as basement cells. All are open to the public as part of the **Museo de la Ciudad** (Independencia 30; 9am-2pm Mon-Fri) FREE, a block to the south.

Iglesia de Santa Teresa y Convento de Carmelitas Descalzas de San José CHURCH
(Independencia 128; 6-8pm) Occupying nearly half a city block, the Iglesia de Santa Teresa y Convento de Carmelitas Descalzas de San José was completed in 1628 and has functioned ever since as a closed-order convent for Carmelite nuns. Only the church itself is open to visitors.

★**Manzana Jesuítica** NOTABLE BUILDING
(Obispo Trejo; 9am-1pm & 3-7pm Mon-Fri) Córdoba's beautiful Manzana Jesuítica (Jesuit Block), like its counterpart in Buenos Aires, is also known as the Manzana de las Luces (Block of Enlightenment), and was initially associated with the influential Jesuit order. The **Colegio Nacional de Monserrat** (Obispo Trejo 294; 9am-1pm & 2:30-4:30pm Mon-Fri, 10am-1pm Sat), which dates from 1782, is next door. In 2000 Unesco declared the Manzana Jesuítica a World Heritage site, along with five Jesuit *estancias* throughout the province.

Museo Histórico de la Universidad Nacional de Córdoba MUSEUM
(Obispo Trejo 242; AR$20, Wed free; 9:30am-6:30pm Mon-Sat; guided visits at 10am, 11am, 3pm & 5pm) In 1613 Fray Fernando de Trejo y Sanabria founded the Seminario Convictorio de San Javier, which, after being elevated to university status in 1622, became the Universidad Nacional de Córdoba, the country's oldest. Today the building contains, among other national treasures, part of the Jesuits' Grand Library and the Museo Histórico de la Universidad Nacional de Córdoba.

Guided visits are the only way to see the interior of the building and are well worth taking. The guides let you wander through the *colegio* and peek into the classrooms while students run around.

Iglesia de la Compañía de Jesús CHURCH
(Caseros 52; 7am-1pm & 5-8pm) FREE Designed by the Flemish Padre Philippe Lemaire, this church dates from 1645 but was not completed until 1671, with the successful execution of Lemaire's plan for a cedar roof in the form of an inverted ship's hull. (Lemaire, unsurprisingly, was once a boatbuilder.) Inside, the church's baroque altarpiece is made from carved Paraguayan cedar from Misiones province.

The Capilla Doméstica, completed in 1644, sits on Caseros, directly behind the church. Its ornate ceiling was made with cowhide stretched over a skeleton of thick taguaro cane and painted with pigments composed partially of boiled bones.

Nueva Córdoba & Güemes

Before the northwestern neighborhoods of Chateau Carreras and Cerro de las Rosas lured the city's elite to their peaceful hillsides, Nueva Córdoba to the south of Centro was the realm of the *cordobés* aristocracy. It's now popular with students, which explains the proliferation of brick high-rise apartment buildings. Still, a stroll past the stately

Córdoba

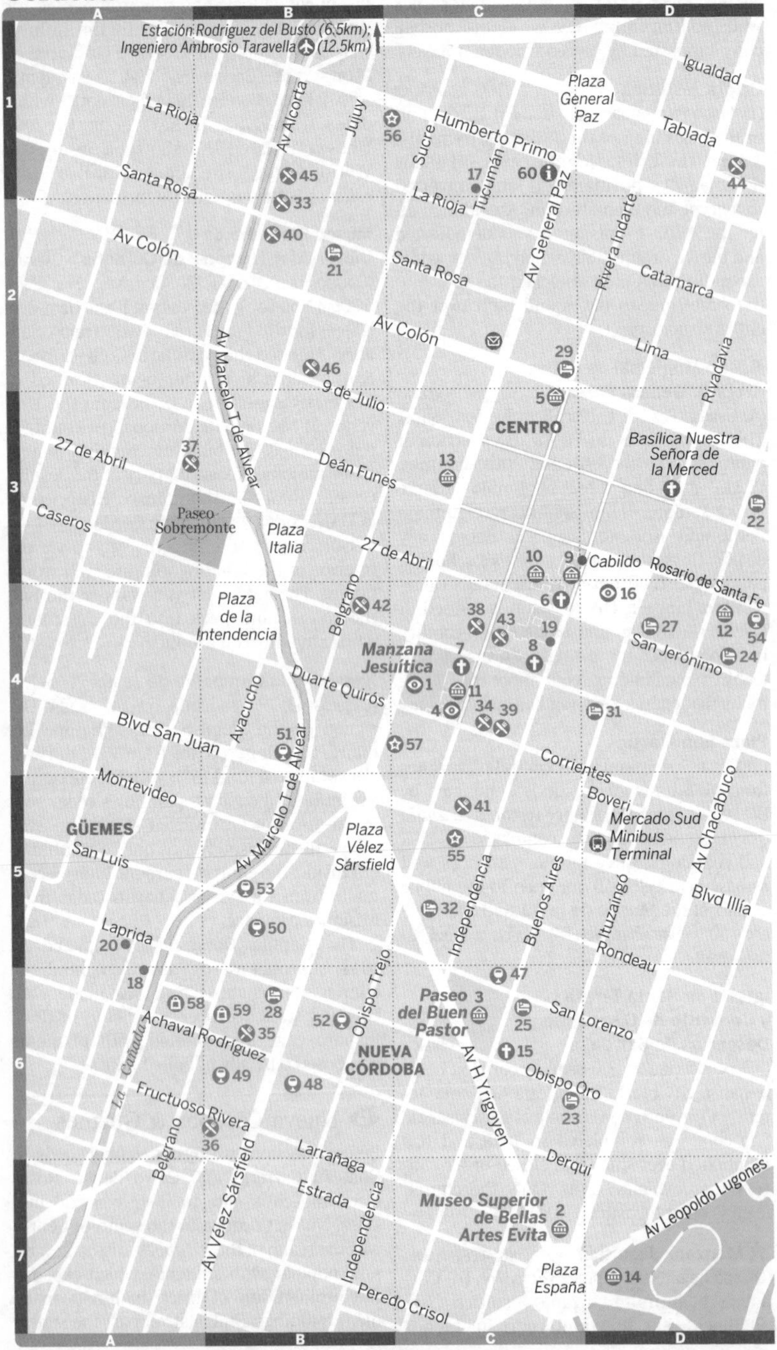

A
B
C
D
1
2
3
4
5
6
7
Estación Rodriguez del Busto (6.5km);
Ingeniero Ambrosio Taravella (12.5km)
La Rioja
Santa Rosa
Av Colón
Av Alcorta
Jujuy
Sucre
Humberto Primo
Tucumán
La Rioja
Santa Rosa
Av Colón
Av General Paz
Plaza General Paz
Igualdad
Tablada
Rivera Indarte
Catamarca
Lima
Rivadavia
9 de Julio
Av Marcelo T de Alvear
CENTRO
27 de Abril
Deán Funes
Basílica Nuestra Señora de la Merced
Caseros
Paseo Sobremonte
Plaza Italia
27 de Abril
Cabildo
Rosario de Santa Fe
Plaza de la Intendencia
Belgrano
San Jerónimo
Manzana Jesuítica
Duarte Quirós
Avacucho
Blvd San Juan
Corrientes
Boveri
Montevideo
Mercado Sud Minibus Terminal
GÜEMES
San Luis
Av Marcelo T de Alvear
Plaza Vélez Sársfield
Independencia
Buenos Aires
Ituzaingó
Av Chacabuco
Blvd Illía
Laprida
Rondeau
Obispo Trejo
Paseo del Buen Pastor
San Lorenzo
Achaval Rodríguez
La Cañada
NUEVA CÓRDOBA
Av H Yrigoyen
Obispo Oro
Fructuoso Rivera
Belgrano
Av Vélez Sársfield
Larrañaga
Derqui
Estrada
Independencia
Museo Superior de Bellas Artes Evita
Av Leopoldo Lugones
Plaza España
Peredo Crisol

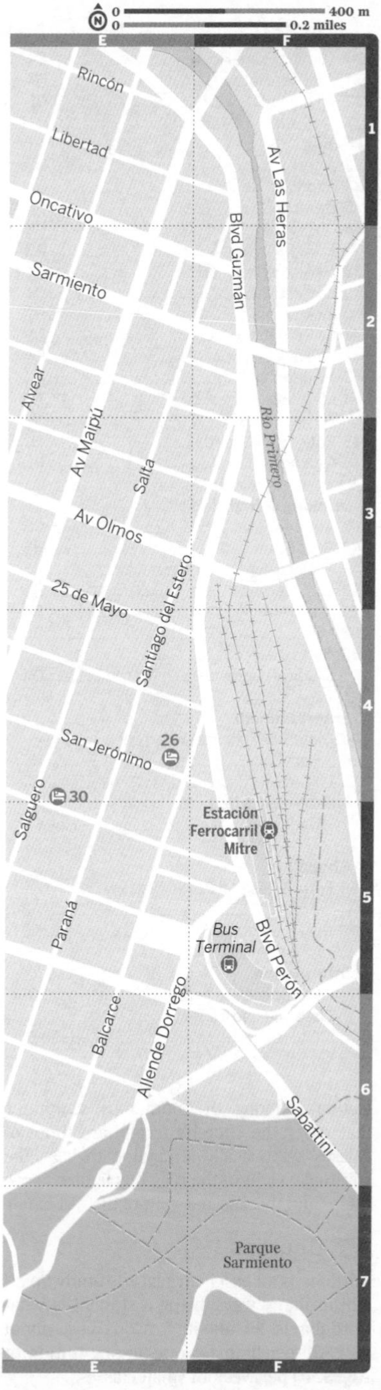

old residences that line the wide Av H Yrigoyen reveals the area's aristocratic past.

Once a strictly working-class neighborhood, Güemes to the southwest of Centro is now known for the hopping bar scene, eclectic antique stores and artisan shops that line the main drag of Belgrano, between Rodríguez and Laprida. Its weekend Feria Artesanal Paseo de las Artes (p295), one of the country's best, teems with antique vendors, arts and crafts and a healthy dose of Córdoba's hippies. It's within the same block as the **Museo Iberoamericano de Artesanías** (Belgrano 750; ⏲10am-5pm Tue-Fri, to 1pm & 4-8pm Sat & Sun) FREE, which houses beautiful crafts from throughout South America. A good route back to the city center is along La Cañada, an acacia-lined stone canal with arched bridges.

★Paseo del Buen Pastor GALLERY

(Av H Yrigoyen 325; ⏲10am-8pm) FREE This cultural center and performance space was built in 1901 as a combined chapel, monastery and women's prison. In mid-2007 it was re-inaugurated to showcase work by Córdoba's young and emerging artists. The central patio area houses a couple of hip cafe-bars where you can kick back with an Appletini or two. The attached chapel (now desanctified) hosts regular live-music performances; stop by for a program, or check Thursday's edition of the local newspaper *La Voz del Interior* for details.

★Museo Superior de Bellas Artes Evita GALLERY

(Av H Yrigoyen 551; AR$15, Wed free; ⏲10am-8pm Tue-Sun, 10am-1pm & 6-9pm in Jan) The Palacio Ferrerya – Nueva Córdoba's landmark building – was built in 1914 and designed by Ernest Sanson in the Louis XVI style. The building itself is amazing, and has now been converted into this fine-arts museum, featuring more than 400 works in 12 rooms spread over three floors. If you're into art or architecture, this place is a don't-miss.

Museo Provincial de Bellas Artes Emilio Caraffa MUSEUM

(www.museocaraffa.org.ar; Av Poeta Lugones 411; AR$15, Wed free; ⏲10am-8pm Tue-Sun) One of the city's best contemporary-art museums stands ostentatiously on the eastern side of Plaza España. Architect Juan Kronfuss designed the neoclassical building as a museum and it was inaugurated in 1916. Exhibits change monthly. South of the museum, the city unfolds

Córdoba

Top Sights
1 Manzana Jesuítica C4
2 Museo Superior de Bellas Artes Evita C7
3 Paseo del Buen Pastor C6

Sights
4 Colegio Nacional de Monserrat C4
5 Cripta Jesuítica C3
6 Iglesia Catedral C4
7 Iglesia de la Compañía de Jesús C4
8 Iglesia de Santa Teresa y Convento de Carmelitas Descalzas de San José C4
9 Museo de la Ciudad C3
10 Museo de la Memoria C3
11 Museo Histórico de la Universidad Nacional de Córdoba C4
12 Museo Histórico Provincial Marqués de Sobremonte D4
Museo Iberoamericano de Artesanías .... (see 58)
13 Museo Municipal de Bellas Artes Dr Genaro Pérez C3
14 Museo Provincial de Bellas Artes Emilio Caraffa D7
15 Parroquia Sagrado Corazón de Jesús de los Capuchinos C6
16 Plaza San Martín D4

Activities, Courses & Tours
17 Able Spanish School C1
18 ACXpanish A6
City Tours .... (see 9)
19 Nativo Viajes C4
20 Tsunami Tango A5

Sleeping
21 Aldea Hostel B2
22 Hostel Alvear D3
23 Hostel Rupestre C6
24 Hotel Azur Real D4
25 Hotel Buen Pastor Capuchinos C6
26 Hotel Quetzal E4
27 Hotel Sussex D4
28 Hotel Viena B6
29 Sacha Mistol C2
30 Turning Point Hostel E4
31 Windsor Hotel D4
32 Yrigoyen 111 .... C5

Eating
33 Alcorta B2
34 Alfonsina C4
35 Bruncheria B6
36 Chilli Street Food B6
37 El Papagayo A3
38 La Alameda C4
39 La Candela C4
40 La Mamma B2
41 La Parrilla de Raul C5
42 La Vieja Esquina B4
43 Mandarina C4
44 Mercado Norte D1
Novecento 900 .... (see 9)
45 Patio de la Cañada B1
46 Quadrata B2

Drinking & Nightlife
47 Antares C6
48 Beer Joint B6
49 El Mentidero de Güemes B6
50 Los Infernales B5
51 Maria Maria B4
52 Milk B6
53 Porto B5
54 Studio Theater D4

Entertainment
55 Cineclub Municipal Hugo del Carril C5
56 La Sala del Rey C1
57 Teatro del Libertador General San Martín C4

Shopping
58 Feria Artesanal Paseo de las Artes A6
59 Paseo Colonial B6

Information
60 Automóvil Club Argentino C1
Casa Cabildo Tourist Office .... (see 9)

into its largest open-space area, the Parque Sarmiento, designed by Charles Thays, the architect who designed Mendoza's Parque General San Martín.

Parroquia Sagrado Corazón de Jesús de los Capuchinos CHURCH
(Buenos Aires 600; ⏲10am-6pm Tue-Fri) FREE It's worth stopping by to check out this marvelous neo-Gothic church built between 1928 and 1934 – its glaring oddity is its missing steeple (omitted to symbolize human imperfection). Among the numerous sculptures that cover the church's facade are those of Atlases symbolically struggling to bear the spiritual weight of the religious figures above them (and the sins and guilt of the rest of us).

Courses

Córdoba is an excellent place to study Spanish; in many ways, being a student is what Córdoba is all about. Lessons cost about AR$360 per hour for one-on-one tuition or AR$3240 per week in small classes.

ACXpanish LANGUAGE
(☎ 0351-468-4805; www.acxpanish.com; Alvear 728, Local 2; ⏰ 9am-6pm Mon-Fri) Top-rated language school.

Able Spanish School LANGUAGE
(☎ 0351-422-4692; www.ablespanish.com; Tucumán 443; ⏰ 9am-4pm Mon-Fri) Offers accommodations and afternoon activities at extra cost and discounts for extended study.

Tsunami Tango DANCING
(☎ 0351-15-313-8746; Laprida 453) Tango classes and *milongas* (tango halls) on Monday (at 8pm), Tuesday (at 9pm), Wednesday (at 7:30pm) and Friday (at 10pm).

Tours

All of Córdoba's hostels and most of its hotels can arrange tours within the city and around the province. **Nativo Viajes** (☎ 0351-424-5341; www.nativoviajes.tur.ar; Independencia 174; ⏰ 8:30am-7:30pm Mon-Sat, to 2:30pm Sun) offers a range of day-trip excursions.

City Tours WALKING
(tour in English AR$200) Absorb Córdoba's rich history by taking one of the guided walking tours that depart from 9am till 5pm Monday to Friday from Casa Cabildo (p295). Reserve a day in advance if you want a tour in English. There are also free thematic tours on an irregular basis; ask at the tourist office (p295) to see the schedule.

Festivals & Events

During the first three weeks of April, the city puts on a large **crafts market** (locally called 'FICO') at the city fairgrounds, in the north near Chateau Carreras stadium. Buses 72 and 75 from Plaza San Martín go there. The **Feria del Libro** in mid-September is a regional book fair.

Sleeping

Hotels on and around Plaza San Martín make exploring the center a cinch, but you'll have to walk several blocks for dinner and nightlife. Staying in hotels along La Cañada and in Nueva Córdoba, on the other hand, means going out to dinner and hitting the bars is a simple matter of walking down the street.

Centro

Aldea Hostel HOSTEL $
(☎ 0351-426-1312; www.aldeahostelcordoba.com; Santa Rosa 447; dm/d US$12/47; 📶) Great location, a social vibe, a lovely terrace for hanging out over beers and BBQ, clean dorms and en suite doubles and triples make this hostel a great choice for budget overnights.

Hostel Alvear HOSTEL $
(☎ 0351-421-6502; www.hostelalvear.com; Alvear 158; dm/d from US$11.50/29; @📶) An excellent location and spacious dorms set in an atmospheric old building make this one of the better hostels in the downtown area.

Turning Point Hostel HOSTEL $
(☎ 0351-422-1264; www.turningpointhostel.com; Entre Ríos 435; dm/d US$13/44; 📶) A stone's throw from the bus terminal, this party hostel has courtyards for chilling out, two living rooms and a range of rooms from dorms to private doubles. Good amenities and fun vibes.

Hotel Quetzal HOTEL $
(☎ 0351-426-5117; www.hotelquetzal.com.ar; San Jerónimo 579; s/d US$43/58; ❄@📶) Spacious, minimalistic, modern rooms are on offer here. A tranquil choice in a busy neighborhood.

★ **Sacha Mistol** HOTEL $$
(☎ 0351-424-2646; www.sachamistol.com; Rivera Indarte 237; s/d US$65/78; ❄📶🏊) This stylish and original hotel is a favorite with the artsy crowd. Rooms are spacious and comfortable, decorated with eclectic art and well-chosen furnishings. It's set in a carefully renovated classic house and features art exhibitions and a small lap pool, all in a quiet, central location on the pedestrian mall.

Hotel Azur Real BOUTIQUE HOTEL $$
(☎ 0351-424-7133; www.azurrealhotelboutique-cordoba.com; San Jerónimo 243; r US$122-158; P❄@📶🏊) Surprisingly one of a kind here in Córdoba, the Azur mixes minimal chic with eclectic local and international furnishings to pull off a very stylish little boutique hotel. Rooms are all they should be and the common areas (including rooftop deck and pool area) are extremely inviting.

Windsor Hotel HOTEL $$
(☎ 0351-422-4012; www.windsortower.com; Buenos Aires 214; r from US$122; P❄📶🏊) In a great downtown location, the Windsor is one of the few classic hotels in town with any real style. The lobby's all dark wood and brass, and the rooms have been tastefully renovated with modern fittings.

Hotel Buen Pastor Capuchinos HOTEL $$
(☎ 0351-469-8390; www.hotelbuenpastor.com; San Lorenzo 110; s/d US$65/80; ❄📶) It's the location

right across from Buen Pastor (p287) – and its water fountains that perk up with music and lights each evening – that makes this hotel a good midrange choice. Rooms have all you need but lack a bit of soul. Breakfast is served at a cafe around the corner.

Hotel Sussex HOTEL **$$**
(0351-422-9070; www.hotelsussexcba.com.ar; San Jerónimo 125; s/d US$37/76;) A wonderful lobby sporting vaulted ceilings, a grand piano and fine art leads on to well-appointed rooms with a full range of amenities. Make sure you request a room with plaza views.

Nueva Córdoba & Güemes

Hostel Rupestre HOSTEL **$**
(0351-15-226-7412; Obispo Oro 242; dm US$10, r without bathroom US$25.50;) A very well-appointed, stylish hostel just on the edge of Nueva Córdoba's party zone. The location's great and the whole setup is well thought out, with an indoor climbing gym, spacious dorms and friendly, enthusiastic staff.

Yrigoyen 111 HOTEL **$$**
(0351-571-4000; www.y111hotel.com; Av H Yrigoyen 111; s/d US$88/110;) A swank hotel with an unbeatable location at the heart of Nueva Córdoba, showcasing all the bells and whistles in its spacious, tastefully decked-out rooms with great city views from the upper floors. There's a rooftop pool and gym facilities too, and a cozy lounge bar downstairs.

Hotel Viena HOTEL **$$**
(0351-460-0909; www.hotelviena.com.ar; Laprida 235; s/d US$45/77;) This modern hotel in the heart of Nueva Córdoba offers bright, clean rooms and an excellent breakfast buffet. There are lots of nooks for sitting in the lobby area, and there's a restaurant on the premises. A good choice.

Eating

Brunchería CAFE **$**
(Rodriguez 244; mains AR$90-175; 10am-9pm;) Down in the hipster sector of Güemes, the Brunchería offers a great mix of fresh decor, yummy food and cool music. It's a good spot for that second breakfast (in case the typical morning fare of coffee and croissant didn't fill you up), but the sandwiches are winners too.

Quadrata ITALIAN **$**
(9 de Julio 458; mains AR$30-60; 11:30am-10:30pm Mon-Fri, to 4pm Sat) Tiny spot that churns out top-notch Italian food at low prices. The pizzas, pastas and panini here are the real deal, made fresh daily. Great for a grab-n-go slice of pizza. Don't miss the tiramisu.

Mercado Norte MARKET **$**
(Oncativo 50; snacks & mains AR$20-250; 7am-7:30pm Mon-Fri, to 2:30pm Sat) Córdoba's indoor market has delicious and inexpensive food, such as pizza, empanadas (baked savory turnovers) and seafood. Browsing the clean stalls selling every imaginable cut of meat, including whole *chivitos* (goat) and pigs, is a must. Saturdays here are particularly lively.

Chilli Street Food GASTROPUB **$**
(Fructuoso Rivera 273; mains AR$90-135; noon-2am Tue-Sun) In a colorful storefront with exposed brick walls, this trendy Güemes gastropub does a great happy hour (a drink and a taco for just AR$100) and serves world-fusion bites. Think fried chicken, ramen, falafel and tikka masala.

Novecento 900 INTERNATIONAL **$$**
(0351-423-0660; Deán Funes 33; mains AR$195-380; 9am-3:30pm Mon-Fri;) There are few more atmospheric options for eating downtown than this cute little cafe-restaurant, set in the courtyard of the historic *cabildo* building. The menu ticks all the 'classic' boxes and throws in a few welcome surprises. The set lunch menu is a steal at AR$175.

La Mamma ITALIAN **$$**
(Av Alcorta 270; mains AR$190-260; noon-3:30pm & 8:30pm-12:30am;) Probably Córdoba's most famous pasta restaurant, with an excellent selection that goes far beyond the standard Argentine offerings. The Grande Mamma sauce (featuring caramelized onions, cream cheese, mushrooms and greens) comes highly recommended.

Mandarina ARGENTINE **$$**
(Obispo Trejo 171; mains AR$150-190; 7am-midnight Mon-Sat;) A cheerful, earthy spot on the pedestrian mall, with a good mix of typical mainstays, some Chinese dishes thrown in and excellent vegetarian options, such as amaranth *milanesas* (breaded cutlets). The sidewalk tables are a lovely spot for people watching.

Alfonsina ARGENTINE **$$**
(Duarte Quirós 66; mains AR$100-260; 8am-1am Mon-Fri, 8am-4pm & 6pm-2am Sat, 7pm-midnight Sun;) In a rambling colonial town house at the historic heart of Córdoba, this bric-a-brac-filled restaurant-bar has a huge menu of

LOCAL FLAVOR

Looking to chow down with Córdoba's student crowd? Pull up a stool at any of the following, where the empanadas, beer and *locro* (a spicy meat, beans and maize stew) flow freely.

La Alameda (Obispo Trejo 170; empanadas AR$15; ⏲11am-1:30am Mon-Fri) Sit on a bench and wash down your homemade empanadas with some ice-cold beer. Then write some graffiti on the wall.

La Candela (Duarte Quirós 67; empanadas AR$18, locro AR$100; ⏲noon-4:30pm & 7:30pm-1am) Rustic and wonderfully atmospheric, run by three cranky but adorable *señoras*.

La Vieja Esquina (Belgrano 193; empanadas AR$20, locro AR$105; ⏲11:30am-3pm & 7:30pm-1am Mon-Sat) A cozy little lunch spot with stools and window seating. Order at the bar.

favorites – pastas, pizzas, *locro* (a spicy meat, beans and maize stew), empanadas and steaks – and some regional mainstays such as *cabrito* (goat) stew. Though Alfonsina has a couple of other locations, this one wins on ambience. There's live music some nights.

La Parrilla de Raul PARRILLA **$$**
(Blvd San Juan 72; mains AR$190-270; ⏲noon-3pm & 8:30pm-12:30am; 📶) Of Córdoba's *parrillas* (steak restaurants), this is probably one of the most famous, known for its good-quality meats. *Parrillada* (mixed grill including steak) for two costs only AR$293, not including extras such as drinks or salad.

Patio de la Cañada PARRILLA **$$**
(☎0351-427-0628; Av Alcorta 360; mains AR$100-260; ⏲noon-4pm & 8:30pm-1am Tue-Sun, 8:30pm-1am Mon; 📶) One of the better-value *parrillas* around, offering top-quality meats at reasonable prices. The all-you-can-eat *parrilla* (AR$268) is especially good value.

El Papagayo ARGENTINE **$$$**
(☎0351-425-8689; Arturo M Bas 69; meals AR$400-500; ⏲noon-4pm Mon-Wed, noon-4pm & 9pm-midnight Thu-Sat; 📶) For a special dining experience, book a table inside this sleek two-floor restaurant, set in a narrow but light-flooded passageway. Chef Javier Rodriguez conjures up a gastronomic feast showcasing small plates that combine typical Argentine flavors with a Mediterranean touch, all prepared in wood-fired ovens or on a charcoal grill.

Alcorta PARRILLA **$$$**
(☎0351-424-7916; www.alcortacarnes.com.ar; Av Alcorta 330; mains AR$195-290; ⏲noon-3:30pm & 7:30pm-12:30am; 📶) This upmarket *parrilla* (steak restaurant) is esteemed for its grilled meats – many say they're the best in town – but also serves delicious pasta and fish. Try the *mollejitas al sauvignon blanc* (sweetbreads in a white-wine sauce).

Drinking & Nightlife

Córdoba's nightlife divides itself into distinct scenes. All the bright young things barhop in Nueva Córdoba – a walk along Rondeau between Avs H Yrigoyen and Chacabuco after midnight gives you a choice of dozens of bars, mostly playing laid-back (or ribcage-rattling) electronic music. Avenida Ambrosio Olmos, connected to Plaza España, also has a long strip of clubs for night owls.

Studio Theater CLUB
(Rosario de Santa Fe 272; cover AR$100-150; ⏲11pm-6am Fri-Sun) One of Córdoba's coolest spots, this three-floor revamped theater still has its original box seats, pillars and columns. It's known for DJs spinning reggaeton, cumbia and *cuarteto* (Argentina's original pop music, with an arresting rhythm and offbeat musical pattern, and working-class lyrics) but also hosts live-music performances on the main stage.

Antares BAR
(San Lorenzo 79; ⏲6pm-3am; 📶) Get here early to grab a seat at this tapas bar known for its craft beer, as Antares fills up fast and doesn't take reservations. Count on great happy-hour specials and front-row seats for the fountain light show outside Buen Pastor. Tapas cost AR$70 to AR$300.

Güemes

For a slightly older crowd and a more laid-back scene, check out the bars in Güemes, a barrio that has exploded in recent years

1

CHRISTIAN KOBER/SHUTTERSTOCK ©

SAIKO3P/SHUTTERSTOCK ©

Iglesia de la Compañía Jesús (p285)
e ornate ceiling of this church, which tes from 1645, was made with cowhide etched over a skeleton of taguaro cane.

2. Iglesia Catedral (p245)
Jujuy's 18th-century cathedral boasts a gold-laminated baroque pulpit.

3. Plaza San Martin (p285)
Córdoba's lovely and lively central plaza dates from 1577.

LOCAL KNOWLEDGE

FOND OF FERNET

Córdoba's drink of choice is fernet (a strong, medicinal-tasting herbed liquor from Italy), almost always mixed with Coca-Cola (*fernet con coca*). If you don't mind a rough morning, get into the stuff.

along its blocks, on its rooftops and inside its courtyards. A former working-class neighborhood, Güemes is now Córdoba's nexus for nightlife action with an edge.

Los Infernales BAR

(Belgrano 631; ⏲8pm-5am Tue-Sun) A Güemes classic, this laid-back bar in a historic townhouse plays an eclectic range of music and serves good food to boot. Live music Thursday to Sunday and a big *patio cervecero* (beer garden) make this a standout.

El Mentidero de Güemes PUB

(www.facebook.com/elmentiderodeguemes; Fructuoso Rivera 260; ⏲8pm-5am Tue, from 6pm Wed-Sun) In the back of Muy Güemes, one of the district's buzziest courtyards, this fun pub with outdoor seating has great craft beer, cocktails and plates for sharing. It also hosts a range of events, from live blues, jazz and rock to theater performances.

Milk COCKTAIL BAR

(Laprida 139; ⏲9pm-5am Thu-Sun) Plush red-velvet chairs, the soft glow of chandeliers and waitstaff in suspenders and cocktail dresses – the vibe at this swank cocktail bar screams speakeasy. Prices are a great deal for what you get. Live DJ acts liven it all up.

Maria Maria CLUB

(cnr Blvd San Juan & La Cañada; ⏲8pm-5am) An ever-popular spot for drinks and dancing, Maria Maria attracts a good range of locals, travelers and expats for its combo of live music and DJ acts. On weekdays, come for the beer happy hour (from 7pm to 9:30pm); on Sundays catch the karaoke. The bar usually gets going around 2am.

Beer Joint CRAFT BEER

(www.facebook.com/BeerJointGuemes; Achaval Rodríguez 183; ⏲6pm-2am) This chic hole-in-the-wall does the best happy hour (from 6pm to 9pm) in Güemes. Come for craft beer, free popcorn, cheap tacos and a local vibe.

Porto CLUB

(www.facebook.com/portocordoba; Alvear 595; ⏲11pm-5am Thu-Sat) Attracting a dress-to-impress party crowd in their late 20s/early 30s, this two-floor nightclub has DJs spinning on both levels and themed parties such as burlesque, black tie and spring fling.

Abasto

Across the river to the north on Blvd Las Heras between Roque Sáenz Peña and Juan B Justo (the area known locally as Abasto) are Córdoba's discos and nightclubs. Go for a walk along here and you'll probably pick up free passes to some, if not all, of them.

Zona Norte

The area around Tejeda street in Córdoba's Zona Norte has boomed in the last couple of years, attracting a well-heeled crowd to its chic bars and restaurants; you'll need to catch a taxi there and back as it's pretty far out.

☆ Entertainment

Cuarteto music (a Córdoba invention) is big here and played live in many venues. Unfortunately, it's also the gangsta rap of Argentine folk music and tends to attract undesirable crowds. **La Sala del Rey** (☎0351-422-0010; Humberto Primero 439; AR$100-150; ⏲depends on the show) is a respectable venue and the best place to catch a *cuarteto* show.

La Voz del Interior, Córdoba's main newspaper, has a reasonably comprehensive entertainment section every Thursday with show times and the like.

Cineclub Municipal Hugo del Carril CINEMA

(☎0351-434-1609; www.cineclubmunicipal.com; Blvd San Juan 49; Mon-Wed AR$45, Thu-Sun AR$80; ⏲1-11pm Mon-Fri, from 3pm Sat & Sun) For a great night (or day) at the movies, pop into this municipal film house, which screens everything from art flicks to Latin American award winners and local films. Stop by for a program. You can also catch live music and theatrical performances here.

Teatro del Libertador General San Martín THEATER

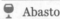

(☎0351-433-2612; Av Vélez Sársfield 365; AR$50-500; ⏲box office 9am-9pm Mon-Sat, 5-8pm Sun) It's well worth going to a performance here, if only to see the opulence of the country's most historic theater. The building was completed in 1891, and the floor was designed to be mechanically raised and leveled to the stage, so seats could be removed, allowing for grand parties for the aristocracy in the early 1900s.

Shopping

Antique stores line Calle Belgrano in Güemes. You'll find Argentine handicrafts at several stores downtown.

Feria Artesanal Paseo de las Artes MARKET
(Artisans Market; cnr Av Rodriguez & Belgrano; 5:30-11pm Sat & Sun) On weekends, the hip neighborhood of Güemes hosts this colorful artisans market, one of the country's best.

Paseo Colonial FASHION & ACCESSORIES
(Belgrano 773; 5-10pm Fri-Sun) To find out what the city's hip young designers have been working on, slip into this little arcade, featuring a variety of small shops selling clothes, homewares and jewelry.

Information

MEDICAL SERVICES

Emergency Hospital (0351-427-6200; Catamarca 44)

MONEY

Cambios (money-changers) and ATMs are on Rivadavia north of the plaza and at the main bus terminal and airport.

Cambio Barujel (Rivadavia 97; 9am-3pm Mon-Fri)

Maguitur (Alvear 84; 9am-5pm Mon-Fri)

POST

Main Post Office (Av Colón 210; 8am-7pm Mon-Fri)

TOURIST INFORMATION

Automóvil Club Argentino (0800-888-9888; Av General Paz 499; 10am-5pm Mon-Fri)

Casa Cabildo Tourist Office (0351-433-2758; Independencia 30; 9:30am-5pm Mon-Sat)

Getting There & Away

AIR

Córdoba's international airport, **Ingeniero Ambrosio Taravella** (0351-475-0881; www.aa2000.com.ar/cordoba; Av La Voz del Interior 8500), is about 15km north of the city center via Av Monseñor Pablo Cabrera.

Aerolíneas Argentinas (0810-2228-6527; www.aerolineas.com.ar; Av Colón 520; 10am-6pm Mon-Fri, 9:30am-12:30pm Sat) This airline has offices downtown and flies several times daily to Buenos Aires, Salta and Puerto Iguazú; there is also one daily flight to Neuquén.

Andes Líneas Aéreas (0810-777-2633; www.andesonline.com; 9am-7pm Mon-Fri) This is a reliable airline with cheap flights to Buenos Aires, Puerto Madryn, Bariloche and other destinations in Argentina.

Córdoba's international airport charges a departure tax on all international departures.

BUS

Córdoba's **bus terminal** (0351-434-1692; www.terminaldecordoba.com; Blvd Perón 380) is about a 15-minute walk from downtown.

In the new terminal (across the road, accessed by tunnel), several bus companies offer services to the same destinations as those offered at the minibus terminal. Be aware that services leaving from the minibus terminal stop everywhere, often adding an hour to the journey time.

Several firms offer service to Chilean destinations, including Santiago (AR$1880, 18 hours), although some involve changing buses in Mendoza.

Buses from Córdoba

DESTINATION	COST (AR$)	TIME (HR)
Bahía Blanca	1323	13
Bariloche	2189	23
Buenos Aires	950	9¼
Catamarca	580	6¼
Corrientes	1180	12¼
Esquel	2541	27¼
Jujuy	1351	14¼
La Rioja	590	6½
Mendoza	1080	11
Montevideo (Uruguay)	1975	14¼
Neuquén	1593	17
Paraná	780	6
Puerto Iguazú	2050	22
Puerto Madryn	2283	19¼
Resistencia	1180	12
Río Gallegos	4361	36¼
Rosario	600	7
Salta	1579	11
San Juan	800	10
San Luis	540	6
San Martín de los Andes (via Bariloche)	2500	27
Santiago del Estero	624	6
Tucumán	856	9

MINIBUS

Frequent minibuses leave from **Mercado Sud minibus terminal** (0351-424-6775; Blvd Illía 155). Most go direct, while some stop at every little town along the way. It's worth asking, as this can make an hour's difference to your travel time.

In summer there may be direct buses to La Cumbrecita, but it will probably be quicker to go first to Villa General Belgrano.

Minibuses from Córdoba

DESTINATION	COST (AR$)	TIME (HR)
Alta Gracia	63	1
Capilla del Monte	200	3
Cosquín	105	1¼
Jesús María	69	1
La Cumbre	170	3
Mina Clavero	220	3
Villa Carlos Paz	55	1
Villa General Belgrano	157	2

TRAIN

Trains leave Córdoba's **Estación Ferrocarril Mitre** (☎0351-426-3565; www.sofse.gob.ar; Blvd Perón 600) for Rosario (AR$90/110 in *primera*/Pullman class, 12 hours) and Buenos Aires' Retiro station (AR$300/360/525 in *primera*/Pullman/*camarote*, 20 hours) at 10:43am on Thursday and Sunday. There is a dining car and bar on board. Tickets often sell out weeks in advance, especially in the *camarote* (two-person sleeping cabin), so book as soon as possible.

Trains to Cosquín (AR$6.50, two hours) leave from **Estación Rodriguez del Busto** (☎0351-568-8979; cnr Cardeñosa & Rodríguez del Busto) on the northwest outskirts of town at 8:44am and 10:59am daily, with an extra noon service on weekends. Bus 26 stops at Plaza San Martín en route to the station or it's an AR$160 taxi ride.

Getting Around

Bus 25 runs between the airport and Plaza San Martín (AR$16) or you can take the airport bus (AR$50), also to/from the plaza. A taxi into town should cost around AR$230; a chauffeured ride (which you can book at the transfer desk) is AR$430.

The downtown area itself is quite walkable though you'll need transportation to get to some of the suburbs. Buses require rechargeable magnetic cards (AR$45), which are available from nearly every kiosk in town. A single ride costs AR$15.38.

A car is very useful for visiting some of the nearby Jesuit *estancias* that cannot be reached by bus. Depending on seasonal demand, economy cars cost around AR$950 per day with unlimited mileage. Try **Europcar** (☎0351-429-9640; www.europcar.com.ar; Av Colón 396; ⏲9:30am-6:30pm Mon-Fri).

Taxis can be hailed anywhere; rides rarely go above AR$150, even if you're going to the suburbs. The green taxis (remises) are more comfortable; you're supposed to call those ahead but they will stop if you hail one in the street.

THE CENTRAL SIERRAS

Nowhere near as visually spectacular as the nearby Andes, the Central Sierras more than make up for it by being way more hospitable. The area is dotted with little towns that are worth a quick visit or a longer stay, and is connected by an excellent road network with frequent bus services.

From the mountain chic of paragliding capital La Cumbre to the hippie vibe of quirky Capilla del Monte and San Marcos Sierras, you'd have to be one jaded traveler not to find something to your liking here. Kicking back is easily done – the riverside village of Mina Clavero is a favorite, as are the ex-Jesuit centers of Alta Gracia and Jesús María. Things get decidedly Germanic down south, and the pedestrian-only La Cumbrecita is not to be missed for *spaetzle* (German egg noodles), bush walks and swimming holes.

La Cumbre

☎03548 / POP 7540 / ELEV 1141M

A favorite getaway for Córdoba dwellers and foreigners alike, La Cumbre packs a lot of character into a small space. It's an agreeable little town due to its wide streets and mild mountain climate, and there are plenty of adventures to be had in the surrounding hills.

The town gained worldwide fame among paragliders when it hosted the 1994 World Paragliding Cup, and enthusiasts of the sport have made La Cumbre their home, giving the town an international feel. The launch site, 380m above the Río Pinto, provides a spectacular introduction to the sport and there are plenty of experienced instructors around, offering classes and tandem flights.

Activities

Renting bikes costs around AR$250 per day; ask at the tourist office (p297).

There are excellent views from the **Cristo Redentor**, a 7m statue of Christ on a 300m hilltop east of town; from Plaza 25 de Mayo,

WORTH A TRIP

FOLK FESTIVITIES

Cosquín is known throughout the country for its **Festival Nacional del Folklore** (www.aquicosquin.org; ⏲ late Jan), a nine-day national folk-music festival that's been held in the last week of January since 1961. The town gets packed for the festival, stays busy all summer and goes pleasantly dead the rest of the year.

There are many daily departures north to La Cumbre (AR$75, one hour); and south every 20 minutes to Villa Carlos Paz (AR$52, 40 minutes) and Córdoba (AR$94, 1¼ hours). There are a few departures daily for Buenos Aires (AR$930, 12 hours).

The scenic Tren de las Sierras departs for Córdoba's Estación Rodriguez del Busto (AR$6.50, 2½ hours) at 8am and 3pm daily, with an extra 4pm service on weekends.

cross the river and walk east on Córdoba toward the mountains – the trail begins after a quick leftward jut after crossing Cabrera.

Paragliding

Flying from the paragliding launch at Cuchi Corral (and hanging out by the Río Pinto afterward) is truly a memorable experience. The launch site (La Rampa) is about 10km west of town via a signed dirt road off the highway. **Pablo Jaraba** (☎03548-15-570951) offers tandem flights and lessons. Check at the tourist office for current operators and recommendations. Everyone charges about the same. Tandem flights cost around AR$1800 for a half-hour; full courses cost AR$9000.

At the **Aeroclub La Cumbre** (☎03548-639713; Camino a los Troncos s/n; ⏲9am-8pm) you can arrange everything from tandem flights to ultralights and parachute jumps.

Sleeping & Eating

Hostel La Cumbre HOSTEL $
(☎03548-451368; www.hostellacumbre.com; San Martín 186; dm/s/d US$18/30/60; @) A couple of blocks behind the bus terminal, this converted mansion is one of the most impressive hostels in the Sierras. The dorms and private rooms are tidy and cozy, and the views from the front balcony superb. Breakfast is included, and there's a kitchen for guest use.

Posada de la Montaña LODGE $$
(☎03548-451867; www.posadadelamontaña.com.ar; 9 de Julio 753; r US$80;) A short walk from downtown, this very comfortable hotel offers spacious, quaintly decorated rooms with great views and a leafy garden with a small pool. Breakfast is ample and the hotel is run by a friendly bunch of young locals.

Pan Tomate TAPAS $
(☎0351-736-3811; Carafa 270; tapas AR$80-160; ⏲noon-11pm Tue-Sun;) The best tapas in La Cumbre, with a fusion of Catalan and Argentine influences, featuring great seafood, handmade pastas and whatever the chef finds fresh at the market. The space is small and gets full fast at lunchtime so it's best to reserve ahead or be prepared to wait.

★ **La Casona del Toboso** ARGENTINE $$
(Belgrano 349; mains AR$155-300; ⏲noon-3pm & 8pm-midnight;) A La Cumbre classic and one of the town's oldest restaurants, La Casona del Toboso doesn't let you down when it comes to quality and warm family-style ambience. Inside a rambling town house with a lovely front lawn that has a clutch of tables set up, it serves up well-prepared Argentine mainstays, homemade pastas and specialties such as trout and rabbit.

Kasbah ASIAN $$
(Sarmiento 6; mains AR$150-180; ⏲8pm-midnight Mon-Fri, 12-3:30pm Sat & Sun;) You may not be expecting a good Thai curry out here, but this cute little triangular restaurant comes up with the goods. Also on offer is a range of Chinese and Indian dishes.

Shopping

Head to the south side of town to the 12km stretch of road known as **Camino de los Artesanos**, where residents of more than two dozen homes sell homemade goodies, from jams and chutneys to wool, leather and silver crafts. Most homes are open from 2pm to 10pm Thursday through Sunday.

Information

Banco de la Provincia de Córdoba (cnr López y Planes & 25 de Mayo; ⏲8:30am-1pm Mon-Fri) Has an ATM.

Tourist Office (☎03548-452966; www.lacumbre.gob.ar; Av Caraffa 300; ⏲8am-10pm) Across from the bus terminal in the old train station. Friendly staff will supply a handy map of the town and its surroundings.

Central Sierras

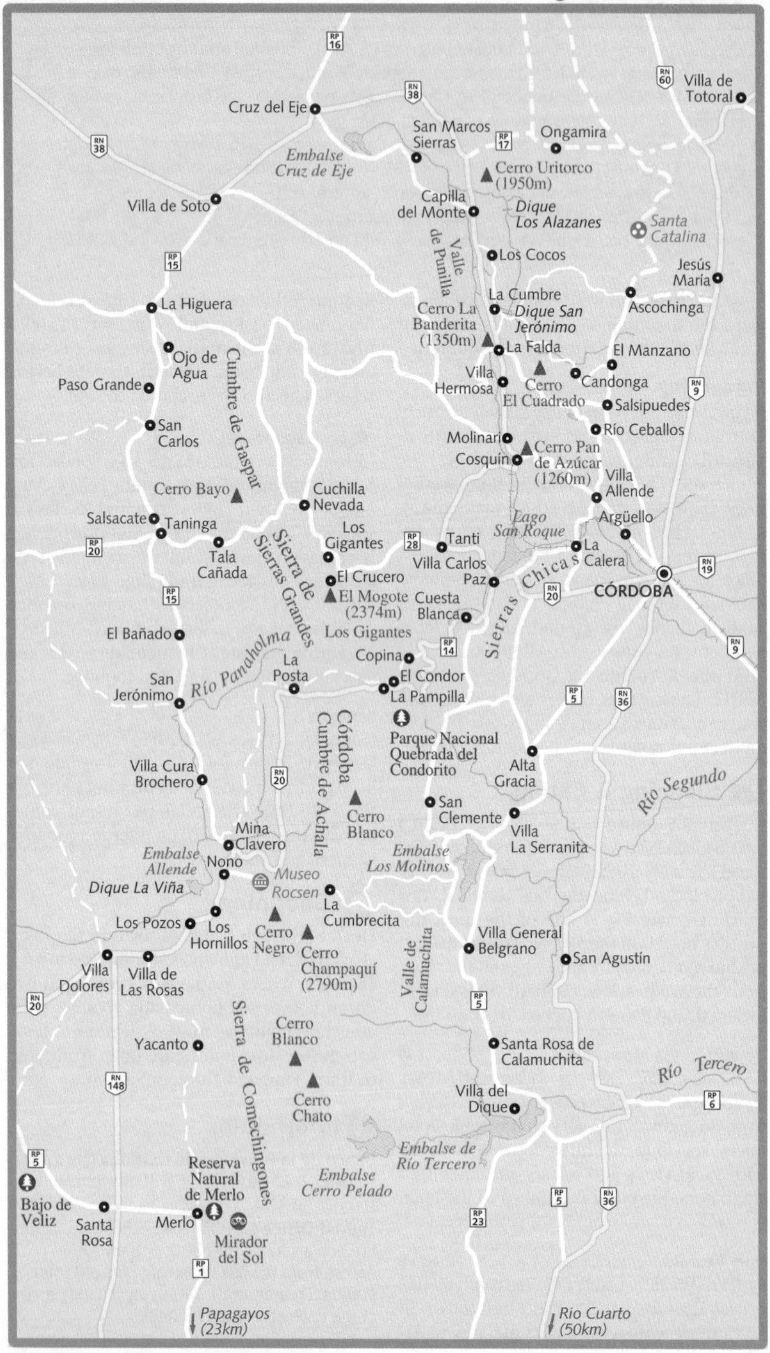

ℹ Getting There & Away

Buses depart regularly from La Cumbre's convenient **bus terminal** (cnr General Paz & Caraffa), heading north to Capilla del Monte (AR$52, one hour) and San Marcos Sierras (AR$75, 1½ hours) or south to Cosquín (AR$52, one hour), Villa Carlos Paz (AR$90, 1½ hours) and Córdoba (AR$122, two hours). Minibuses (which take about half an hour less) are the fastest way to Córdoba. There is also a direct service to Buenos Aires (AR$990, 12 hours).

San Marcos Sierras

☑ 03549 / POP 930 / ELEV 625M

San Marcos got an injection of life in the late 1960s when the hippies began flocking here for its mild climate, way-off-the-grid isolation and good farmland. Over the following decades, curious tourists began appearing, having heard about the hippie town in the Sierras, and eventually the town's emphasis shifted from agriculture and handicraft manufacture to tourism.

Taken aback by the swing toward capitalism, many of the old crew left and a younger crowd moved in. But San Marcos' hippie heritage remains – the community has successfully campaigned against the use of genetically modified crops in the valley as well as paved roads and even a gas station in town. These days San Marcos makes for a pleasant getaway and the riverside location in a pretty valley is as enticing as ever. Check out the hippie fair that sprouts along the river daily in the January and February high season.

◎ Sights & Activities

San Marcos enjoys a fabulous natural setting, and there are some excellent walks just out of town, including the riverside walk to El Viejo Molino, a 17th-century flour mill that was used to grind the town's grains until the 1950s.

El Árbol AGRICULTURAL CENTER
(Av Cacique Tulian; ⊙9am-1pm & 4-7pm) If you like honey and want to learn about the importance of bees to our planet's biodiversity, don't miss a 15-minute walk northwest of town to check out the artisanal honeys produced at El Árbol. The owner, Claudio, is passionate about beekeeping with minimal human intervention, and will tell you all about the indigenous trees that the local bees love.

Museo Hippie MUSEUM
(Callejon de las Loras s/n; AR$70; ⊙8am-8pm) Far more interesting for the stream-of-consciousness commentary on the evolution of the hippie movement in Argentina (dating back to the Greek philosophers) than the actual artifacts it holds, this small museum on the northern outskirts of town is worth a visit – if nothing else, it's a pleasant walk out there.

🛏 Sleeping

San Marcos Sierras Hostel HOSTEL $
(☑03549-496102; www.facebook.com/hostel.san marcossierras; Libertad 905; dm/d US$15/38; 🛜) Inside a rambling 19th-century house with a spacious front lawn, this great hostel is just one block from the plaza. It has two dorms that share a balcony, as well as several en suite rooms. There's a shared kitchen, a lovely veranda with hammocks, and swings set up in the garden.

Madre Tierra HOTEL $$
(☑03549-416950; secretosdemadretierra@hot mail.com; San Martín 650; r US$50; ❄🛜🏊) Probably the most formal setup in town, with stylish, modern rooms (a bit on the small side) arranged around a good-sized swimming pool. It's about 500m over the bridge north of the plaza.

🍴 Eating

Pastelería Saint Germain BAKERY $
(San Martín 898; pastries AR$15-20; ⊙9:30am-1pm & 4-7pm Tue-Sun) The baked goodies Ana sells in her home bakery on the road out of town toward the neighborhood of La Banda are downright delicious. If you ask, she'll make you tea or coffee to enjoy in her leafy front yard.

Piano Resto Bar INTERNATIONAL $
(Libertad 1098; mains AR$120-190; ⊙9am-midnight) A great little all-day cafe-restaurant on the plaza that serves up good mains and pizzas, and also has some vegetarian options.

★ La Tahua ARGENTINE $$
(San Martín 501; mains AR$160-230; ⊙8pm-midnight Fri-Sun) The food that comes out of the clay oven at this riverside restaurant is as delightful as the setting; think local trout, great steaks and a range of pizzas. Grab one of the outside tables to pair your meal with the sounds of the river.

> **OUTINGS FROM SAN MARCOS SIERRAS**
>
> In summertime don't miss an outing to Río Quilpo 4km southwest of town, an idyllic spot to spend a day; bring a picnic and find a shady spot by the riverside (admission AR$100). You can do horseback-riding jaunts from **La Posta del Gaucho** (☎03549-496272) and check out the artisanal honey production for which San Marcos Sierras is known at El Árbol (p299).

Information

There's an ATM in the municipal building on Sarmiento, but make sure to bring cash, as it often runs out of bills or simply doesn't work.

Tourist office (☎03549-496137; www.sanmarcossierras.gob.ar; cnr Libertad & Sarmiento; ⏰9am-8pm) Has a good map of the town and its surroundings, and decent info on walks and upcoming events.

Getting There & Away

The bus stop is eight long blocks from the main plaza. There are several buses daily from La Cumbre (AR$222, one hour). Buses also pass through here en route from Cruz del Eje to Córdoba (AR$250, four hours).

Capilla del Monte

☎03548 / POP 1200 / ELEV 983M

Capilla del Monte is the more mature alternative to San Marcos Sierras, where the hippie crowd that once settled San Marcos moved to when they 'grew up.' This otherwise sleepy town rose to fame in the 1930s when the first UFO sighting was reported. It has since been drawing UFO watchers from around the world who come here in the hope of communing with extraterrestrials from on top of the nearby Cerro Uritorco. The energy vortexes that are said to surround the town have been a magnet for spiritual seekers of all stripes.

Sights & Activities

Uritorco MOUNTAIN

(AR$250) The highest mountain of the Sierras Chicas, at 1950m, Uritorco is the main reason people come to Capilla del Monte. No matter what it is that draws them in – UFO sightings, energy vortexes or ancient vibes of the indigenous Comechingones tribe that once roamed these lands – Uritorco is a magnet for people from around the world. The 5km hike to the top affords spectacular views.

You must start the climb before noon, and begin your descent by 3pm. From Capilla del Monte, catch a taxi or walk the 3km to the base of the mountain. There are usually guides hanging around; you can hire one for AR$500.

Los Terrones HIKING

(AR$140) Hike amid towering sandstone rock formations as you take in waterfalls and lush foliage and look out for condors flying overhead. Choose between a couple of different trails inside this small nature park 14km northeast of town. Catch a taxi or one of the guided tours that run regularly from town. Wear proper hiking shoes or you won't be allowed in.

Sleeping & Eating

Hostel El Malecon HOSTEL $

(☎03548-482681; www.facebook.com/hostelelmalecon1; Diagonal Buenos Aires 173; dm/d US$18/59; @ 📶) A good budget choice in Capilla del Monte, with clean four-person dorms, triples and doubles, all with private bathrooms. There's a terrace with Uritorco vistas, a patio and a shared kitchen.

★**Mousai Hotel Boutique** BOUTIQUE HOTEL $$

(☎011-15-4140-0195; www.mousai.com.ar; Salta 235; s/d US$58/80; ❄📶🏊) Inside this gorgeously renovated 1920s house, each of the 12 rooms comes with heaps of character and amenities. Soak up the boho-chic vibe, lovely design touches, views of Uritorco from the rooftop terrace and complimentary classes of meditation, chi gong and tai chi.

★**Sabía Que Venías y Preparé Un Pastel** INTERNATIONAL $$

(www.sabiaquevenias.com.ar; Pueyrredón 681; mains AR$135-250; ⏰9am-11:30pm; 📶) The couple behind this amazing restaurant met while working as chefs in top Buenos Aires restaurants; now, at their own culinary playground, they experiment with creative recipes prepared with high-quality ingredients. The huge menu features regional specialties such as trout and goat, as well as great soups, sandwiches and baked goods.

La Tramontana ARGENTINE $$

(☎03548-15-635603; RN 38, Km 89.5; mains AR$145-250; ⏰by advance reservation only) If trout's your thing, don't miss a meal at La Tramontana, 10km out of Capilla del Monte along RN 38 (taxis charge AR$250 to take you there). Dining at this scenic 19th-century estate accessed along a dirt road is an experience not to miss. Choose between trout prepared in five different ways, from almond-crusted to smothered in Roquefort. Cash only.

Information

Tourist Office (Pueyrredón 550; 9am-8pm)

Getting There & Away

There is a frequent bus service south to Córdoba (AR$200, three hours), stopping at all towns on RN 38, and five long-distance services daily to Buenos Aires (AR$700, 13 hours).

Jesús María

03525 / POP 26,800

Sleepy little Jesús María earns its place on the map by being home to one of the most atmospheric Jesuit *estancias* in the region – the Unesco-listed **Museo Jesuítico Nacional de Jesús María** (Pedro de Oñate; 8am-6pm Tue-Fri, from 10am Sat & Sun) FREE. The church and convent were built in 1618 and are set on superbly landscaped grounds. The Jesuits, after losing their operating capital to pirates off the Brazilian coast, sold wine made here to support their university in colonial Córdoba. The museum has good archaeological pieces from indigenous groups, informative maps of the missionary trajectory and well-restored (though dubiously authentic) rooms.

Jesús María is also home to the annual **Fiesta Nacional de Doma y Folklore** (www.festival.org.ar; early Jan), a 10-day celebration of gaucho horsemanship and customs beginning the first weekend of January.

Most people visit Jesús María as a day trip from Córdoba. Frequent minibuses (AR$69, one hour) leave Córdoba's Mercado Sud terminal and the bus terminal daily.

Estancia Santa Catalina

One of the most beautiful of the Sierras' Unesco World Heritage sites, the

CLOSE ENCOUNTERS

It's not just the freaks and hippies. Even normal-looking people in Capilla del Monte have stories about strange lights appearing in formation in the night skies over nearby Cerro Uritorco. The stories go way back too. In 1935 Manuel Reina reported seeing a strange being dressed in a tight-fitting suit while he was out walking on a country road. In 1986 Gabriel and Esperanza Gómez apparently saw a spaceship so big that its lights illuminated the surrounding countryside. The next day a burn mark measuring 122m by 64m was found at the point where it had reportedly landed.

A couple of years later, 300 people were said to have witnessed another ship, which left a burn mark 42m in diameter. And in 1991, another burn mark was found. This one measured 12m in diameter, with an estimated temperature of 340°C (644°F). Geologists were called in and they claimed that nearby rocks had recently been heated to a temperature of 3000°C (5432°F).

Why all this activity around Capilla del Monte? This is where it gets really weird. One theory is that UFOs visit the area because Cerro Uritorco is where the knight Parsifal brought the Holy Grail and the Templar Cross at the end of the 12th century. He did this to lay them beside the Cane of Order, which had been made 8000 years before by Lord Voltán of the Comechingones, the indigenous tribe that inhabited this region.

Another theory is that they are drawn here because underneath Uritorco lies Erks, a subterranean city in which, according to 'hermetic scientists,' the future regeneration of the human species will take place. Inside you'll find the Esfera Temple and the three mirrors used to exchange data with other galaxies, and where you can see the details of the life of every human being.

The official explanation? Good ol' meteorological phenomena, caused by supercharged ion particles in the atmosphere, mixed in with a healthy touch of mass hysteria.

Whatever you believe, one thing's for sure – all this hype isn't hurting little Capilla del Monte's tourist industry one bit. Until recently, the only people climbing Uritorco were goatherds and a few interested townsfolk. These days, numbers can approach 1000 per day, all hoping to catch a glimpse of the mysterious lights.

WORTH A TRIP

LOS GIGANTES

This spectacular group of rock formations, 80km west of Córdoba, is fast becoming Argentina's rock-climbing capital. The two highest peaks are the granite giants of Cerro de La Cruz (2185m) and El Mogote (2374m). There are numerous Andean condors living here – the park is only 30km from Parque Nacional Quebrada del Condorito, and the birds have slowly taken to this area as well. The area is also home to the tabaquillo tree, with its papery peeling bark, which is endangered in Argentina and only found here and in Bolivia and Peru.

It's not a long hike to the top of Cerro de La Cruz, but there is some tricky rock scrambling involved. Guides are recommended because the maze of trails through the rocks can be hard to follow and if the fog comes down you can easily get lost.

Guides for hire at La Rotonda (the main settlement in the area) can take you around the cave complexes and atop Cerro de La Cruz.

Córdoba hostels such as Hostel Rupestre (p290) and tour operators such as Nativo Viajes (p289) offer trekking excursions and day trips to Los Gigantes. Córdoba's tourist office (p295) maintains a list of rock-climbing guides.

Getting here is complicated. **Sarmiento** (☎0810-5557-2764; ⏲8am-10pm Mon-Sat, from 10am Sun) buses leave Córdoba's main bus terminal at 7:45am daily (AR$479, four hours). The bus pretty much turns around and comes back again, meaning you have to spend the night. Schedules change frequently, so be sure to check.

Get off at El Crucero (tell the driver you're going to Los Gigantes). From there it's a 3km walk to La Rotonda.

Jesuit *estancia* of **Santa Catalina** (☎03525-421600; www.santacatalina.info; ⏲10am-1pm & 3-6pm Tue-Sun) FREE, some 20km northwest of Jesús María, is a quiet, tiny place, where the village store occupies part of the *estancia,* and old-timers sit on the benches outside and watch the occasional gaucho ride past on a horse. Much of the *estancia* is off-limits to visitors but travelers can take in the chapel, cloisters and novitiate, where unmarried slave girls were housed.

The grounds, although a fraction of their former selves, are lovely and well maintained and you can easily while away an hour or two wandering around. Outside the *estancia,* around the back, is the original reservoir built by the Jesuits, now slowly being overtaken by tall-stemmed lilies.

Sleeping & Eating

La Ranchería de Santa Catalina ESTANCIA $$
(☎03525-15-431558; r US$56; 📶) La Ranchería de Santa Catalina has a lovely inn, restaurant (mains AR$120 to AR$250) and crafts store in the *ranchería.* For accommodations, it has only two rooms with a shared bathroom, which occupy the atmospheric former slave quarters and, while small, are carefully decorated and retain their original stone walls.

Getting There & Away

It's best to have your own wheels. A taxi from Jesús María to Santa Catalina costs about AR$380.

Alta Gracia

☎03547 / POP 48,330 / ELEV 550M

Set around a 17th-century Jesuit-built reservoir, Alta Gracia is a tranquil little mountain town of winding streets and shady parks. The star attraction here is the 17th-century Jesuit *estancia*; its exquisite church, nighttime lighting and lovely location between a tiny reservoir and the central plaza make it one of the most impressive of Córdoba province's World Heritage sites. Revolutionary Che Guevara spent his adolescence in Alta Gracia and his former home is now a museum. Many people come on day trips from Córdoba, but the city is emerging as a destination in its own right and as a base for exploring the southern Sierras.

Sights

Museo Casa de Ernesto Che Guevara MUSEUM
(Avellaneda 501; AR$75; ⏲9am-7pm) In the 1930s, the family of young Ernesto (Che) Guevara moved here because a doctor recommended the dry climate for his asthma.

Though Che lived in several houses – including one in Rosario, where he was born – the family's primary residence was Villa Beatriz, which was purchased by the city and restored as this museum. Its cozy interior is now adorned with a photographic display of Che's life. Two huge photographs commemorate a visit from Fidel Castro and Hugo Chávez.

Jesuit Estancia NOTABLE BUILDING

The most impressive building on the *estancia* is the **Iglesia Parroquial Nuestra Señora de la Merced** (west side of Plaza Manuel Solares; 9am-8pm) FREE. Directly south of the church, the colonial Jesuit workshops of **El Obraje** (1643) are now a public school.

Museo Histórico Nacional del Virrey Liniers MUSEUM

(Padre Viera 41; AR$20; 9am-7pm Tue-Sun) Beside the Iglesia Parroquial Nuestra Señora de la Merced is this museum, named after the building's former resident Virrey Liniers, one of the last officials to occupy the post of Viceroy of the River Plate. On display are vestiges of the colonial era, from beds to musical instruments.

Sleeping & Eating

Alta Gracia Hostel HOSTEL $

(03547-428810; Paraguay 218; dm/r US$15/40;) Five short blocks downhill from the Jesuit museum, Alta Gracia's hostel offers a fair deal. Dorms are roomy enough and the kitchen should meet your needs.

279 Boutique B&B BOUTIQUE HOTEL $$

(03547-15-459493; www.279altagracia.com; Giorello 279; r US$77;) Alta Gracia's best accommodations by far. There's only two rooms, but that just adds to the charm. Run by an ex–New York photographer, it's a stylish, intimate place with just the right blend of old features rescued from the original house and slick modern styling. Breakfast is fantastic, the location's great and the attention to detail is superb.

WORTH A TRIP

ONGAMIRA VALLEY

Healing energy points, sightings of strange lights linked to extraterrestrial activity and ancient tales of indigenous tribes make Ongamira one of Argentina's most mysterious valleys. Though spiritual seekers from around the world flock to this enchanting spot in the north of Córdoba's Sierras Chicas, 25km from Capilla del Monte, it remains steeped in secrecy. Lack of cell-phone coverage adds to the otherworldly mystique.

From Capilla del Monte, follow RP 17 and you'll pass a number of spiritual communities that have set up home here, mostly in and around the Quebrada de la Luna. The spectrum of beliefs and faiths is wide, from Sierra del Cielo by the Uksim group to Centro Mariano del Espíritu Santo and the Community of Light inspired by Brazilian spiritual leader Trigueirinho. Many of these offer retreats, workshops and even brief visits for outside visitors, though it's always best to call ahead.

Dotted with red sandstone formations and verdant green pastures where horses roam free, the valley – named after chief Onga – was once home to Comechingones, an indigenous tribe who lived here about 200 BCE and used grottos carved out of sandstone as homes and ritual sites. Visiting the caves (AR$70) is one of the highlights of Ongamira; check out the mortars and the rock paintings of animals and humans.

When the Spanish invaded these lands in the 16th century, the Comechingones refused to give in and threw themselves to their deaths from the top of Cerro Colchiquí (1575m). Climbing to the top of the mountain makes for a great hike, which takes about three hours up and down. If you're lucky you'll catch sight of condors flying overhead; you may see some nests at the top but keep away so as not to disturb the young chicks and their mamas. There's a small welcome center at the bottom of the mountain, where you pay the AR$50 admission; you can also go up by horse (AR$400). The views are dazzling from the top, taking in the salt flats of Catamarca, the province to the north.

If you want to stay, the boutique *estancia* (ranch) of **Dos Lunas** (011-6091-2634; www.doslunas.com.ar; RP 17; r from US$39;) in Alto Ongamira is a top choice. Don't miss a meal at **A Orillas del Río** (0351-15-320-3150; mains AR$80-260; call ahead), a riverside teahouse smack out of a fairy tale, just off RP 17 en route to Ongamira.

The Legend of Che

One of Cuba's greatest revolutionary heroes, in some ways even eclipsing Fidel Castro himself, was an Argentine. Ernesto Guevara, known by the common Argentine interjection 'che,' was born in Rosario in 1928 and spent his first years in Buenos Aires. In 1932, after Guevara's doctor recommended a drier climate for his severe asthma, Guevara's parents moved to the mountain resort of Alta Gracia.

He later studied medicine in the capital and, in 1952, spent six months riding a motorcycle around South America, a journey that opened Guevara's eyes to the plight of South America's poor.

After his journey, Guevara traveled to Central America, finally landing in Mexico, where he met Fidel Castro and other exiles. The small group sailed to Cuba on a rickety old yacht and began the revolution that overthrew Cuban dictator Fulgencio Batista in 1959. Unfulfilled by the bureaucratic task of building Cuban socialism, Guevara tried, unsuccessfully, to spread revolution in the Congo, Argentina and finally Bolivia, where he was killed in 1967.

Today Che is known less for his eloquent writings and speeches than for the striking black-and-white portrait as the beret-wearing rebel – an image gracing everything from T-shirts to CD covers – taken by photojournalist Alberto Korda in 1960.

In 1997, on the 30th anniversary of Che's death, the Argentine government issued a postage stamp honoring Che's Argentine roots. You can take a look at the stamps and other Che memorabilia by visiting Alta Gracia's modest Museo Casa de Ernesto Che Guevara (p302).

1 & 2. Museo Casa de Ernesto Che Guevara (p302), Alta Gracia, Che's childhood home **3.** Guevara's image adorns a wall in Buenos Aires

2

TAESIK PARK/SHUTTERSTOCK ©

EITAN ABRAMOVICH/AFP/GETTY IMAGES ©

La Creación CAFE $
(Prudencio Bustos 99; pastries AR$25-80; ⏰8am-1pm & 5-9pm) Stellar French-style bakery and cafe that churns out the best bread you'll find in the entire province and delicious baked goodies too.

El Bistro del Alquimista FUSION $$
(Castellanos 351; mains AR$150-300; ⏰9pm-midnight Mon-Sat; 📶) This is the way the gourmet scene in Argentina *should* be heading – an open kitchen with chefs doubling as waitstaff and well-presented, innovative dishes served up in a casual atmosphere with superattentive service. The four-course menu changes daily and the wines all come from boutique winemakers.

Los Extremeños SEAFOOD $$
(☎03547-426772; Urquiza 90; mains AR$160-260; ⏰9am-9pm Mon-Sat) Family-run spot much loved by the locals for its for first-rate Spanish seafood. Must reserve ahead.

Information

Tourist Office (☎03547-428128; www.altagracia.gob.ar; cnr Padre Viera & Calle del Molino; ⏰7am-8pm Mon-Fri, from 8am Sat & Sun) Located inside the clock tower.

Getting There & Away

The **bus terminal** (cnr Costanera & Esperanza) near the river has departures for Córdoba and Buenos Aires (AR$800, 13 hours). Buses to Villa General Belgrano (AR$118, one hour) stop every hour on RP 5, about 2km along Av San Martín from the center. Minibuses depart regularly for Córdoba (AR$60, one hour) from a block uphill from the estancia.

Villa General Belgrano

☎03546 / POP 7800 / ELEV 720M

More a cultural oddity than a full-blown tourist attraction, Villa General Belgrano flaunts its origins as a settlement of unrepatriated survivors from the German battleship *Graf Spee,* which sank near Montevideo during WWII.

The annual Oktoberfest held here during the first two weeks of October draws beer lovers from all over the world. In summertime the village slowly fills with vacationers enjoying the tranquil streets and evergreen-dotted countryside. Unless you're really excited about microbrew beer, *torta selva negra* (Black Forest cake) and goulash, Villa General Belgrano makes a fine day trip from Córdoba or nearby La Cumbrecita. Despite its decidedly Germanic flavor, you'd be lucky to hear any of the modern-day inhabitants speaking the language of the old country.

Sleeping & Eating

Albergue El Rincón HOSTEL $
(☎03546-461323; www.hostelelrincon.com.ar; Fleming 347; campsites per person US$10, dm/d without bathroom US$15/45, s/d with bathroom US$41/53; 🏊) 🌿 This beautiful Dutch-owned hostel, surrounded by forest, has excellent, spacious dorm rooms, outdoor and indoor kitchens, a *parrilla* and its own biodynamic farm. The outstanding breakfasts cost AR$60. It's a good 900m walk from behind the bus terminal to the entrance gate; follow the signs.

Berna Hotel HOTEL $$
(☎03546-461097; www.bernahotel.com.ar; Sarfield 86; r from US$64; ❄📶🏊) Set on sprawling grounds in a great location between the bus terminal and town, the Berna offers spacious rooms with all the expected comforts. Some of the goodies here include an on-site spa, a children's play area and a huge pool.

Blumen INTERNATIONAL $$
(Roca 373; mains AR$170-300; ⏰noon-3pm & 8pm-midnight; 📶) With one of the widest menus in town, Blumen serves up tasty, if slightly expensive, dishes with German flair. It's a great spot for a few drinks – the huge, shady beer garden is all wooden tables and pagodas, with plenty of space in between and the microbrew beer flowing readily.

Information

Tourist Office (☎03546-461215; Roca 168; ⏰8:30am-8pm) On the main street, as are banks with ATMs.

Getting There & Away

The bus terminal is a few blocks uphill from the main street. Buses leave every hour for Córdoba (AR$164, two hours) and daily for Buenos Aires (AR$804, 12 hours). There are hourly departures for La Cumbrecita (AR$54, 30 minutes).

La Cumbrecita

☎03546 / POP 1000 / ELEV 1300M

The pace of life slows waaaay down in this alpine-style village, nestled in the forest in the Valle de Calamuchita. The tranquility is largely thanks to the town's pedestrian-only policy. It's a great place to kick back for a few days and wander the forest trails leading to swimming holes, waterfalls and scenic lookouts.

Visitors must park their cars in the dirt parking lot (AR$150) before crossing the bridge over Río del Medio by foot.

🏃 Activities

Hiking is the best reason to visit La Cumbrecita. Short trails are well marked and the tourist office can provide a crude but useful map of the area.

A 25-minute stroll will take you to **La Cascada**, a waterfall tucked into the mountainside. **La Olla** is the closest swimming hole, surrounded by granite rocks (people jump where it's deep enough). **Cerro La Cumbrecita** (1400m) is the highest point in town, about a 20-minute walk from the bridge. Outside town, the highest mountain is the poetically named **Cerro Wank** (1715m); a hike to the top takes about 40 minutes.

For guided hikes further into the mountains, as well as horseback riding (AR$400 for four hours), trout fishing and mountain biking, contact **Viviendo Montañas** (☑ 03546-481172; Cabiolsky s/n; ⊙ 9am-5pm Mon-Fri), which has an office on the main road in town. The company can also take you trekking to the top of **Cerro Champaquí** (2790m), the highest peak in the Sierras (a two-day trek).

La Peñon de Aguila ADVENTURE SPORTS
(www.penondelaguila.com.ar; day pass AR$800; ⊙ 11am-7pm Fri-Sun) Fun adventure park with hiking, archery, rock climbing, treetop courses and ziplining across canyons and waterfalls. There's a lovely riverside area where you can picnic, and cabins you can rent should you wish to stay.

🛏 Sleeping & Eating

La Cumbrecita has more than 20 hotels and *cabañas* (cabins) in the surrounding hills; the tourist office is a good resource. Make reservations in summer (January and February), during Easter and during Villa General Belgrano's Oktoberfest.

Hostel Planeta HOSTEL $
(☑ 03546-409847; planetacumbrecitahostel@gmail.com; Pública s/n; dm/r US$22/70; 🛜) The best hostel in town is reached via a steep path next to the Hotel Las Verbenas tennis court. It's set in a lovely traditional house

OKTOBERFEST IN VILLA GENERAL BELGRANO

If you're in the Sierras around the start of October, consider hitting Villa General Belgrano, which celebrates its German heritage with a 10-day, nationally recognized **Oktoberfest** (www.elsitiodelavilla.com/oktoberfest; ⊙ Oct). While the beer runs as freely as it does at Oktoberfests all over the world, there are also parades, endless concerts and other cultural presentations. The festival also features so much delicious street food that you'll be loosening a couple of buttons on your lederhosen, even if you're not a drinker.

and has a good dining area and kitchen, reasonable dorms and killer views.

Hostería El Ceibo HOTEL $$
(☑ 03546-481060; www.hosteriaelceibo.com; Pública s/n; s/d US$57/77; 🛜) It's the vistas that steal the show at this lovely hotel at the entrance to the village. The rooms are well appointed and the breakfast excellent.

Hotel La Cumbrecita HOTEL $$
(☑ 03546-481052; www.hotelcumbrecita.com.ar; Pública s/n; s/d US$72/90; ❄🛜♨) Built on the site of the first house in La Cumbrecita, this rambling hotel has some excellent views out over the valley. Rooms aren't huge, but most have fantastic balconies. The extensive grounds include a gym and tennis courts.

La Colina INTERNATIONAL $$
(☑ 03546-481063; Las Truchas s/n; ⊙ noon-3pm & 8:30-10:30pm; 🛜) Great views, superb food (try the trout) and attentive service make this restaurant a top choice in La Cumbrecita. Call ahead to arrange a pickup, as it's a little outside town and up a steep hill.

Bar Suizo EUROPEAN $$
(Pública s/n; mains AR$180-260; ⊙ noon-11pm; 🛜) Pull up a wooden bench under the pine tree and try some of the excellent Swiss-German options such as *spaetzle* (German egg noodles) with wild mushroom sauce.

ℹ️ Information

Tourist office (☑ 03546-481088; www.lacumbrecita.gob.ar; Cabiolsky s/n; ⊙ 9am-7pm) This place is on the left, just after you cross the bridge into town.

<div style="text-align:right">CÓRDOBA & THE CENTRAL SIERRAS LA CUMBRECITA</div>

❶ Getting There & Away

From Villa General Belgrano, **Transportes Pajaro Blanco** (☑03546-15-528213; ⊙7am-8pm) has many departures to La Cumbrecita (AR$54, 30 minutes) from 7am to 7:30pm. The last bus back from La Cumbrecita leaves at 7:30pm. In summer there may be occasional minibuses from Córdoba's Mercado Sud terminal (p295).

Parque Nacional Quebrada del Condorito

ELEV 1900-2300M

This national park protects 370 sq km of stunning rocky grasslands across the Pampa de Achala in the Sierras Grandes. The area, particularly the *quebrada* (gorge) itself, is an important condor nesting site and flight training ground for fledgling condors. A 9km hike (two to three hours) from the park entrance at **La Pampilla** leads to the Balcón Norte (North Balcony), a clifftop where you can view the massive birds circling on the thermals rising up the gorge. You can easily visit as a day trip from Córdoba or on your way to Mina Clavero.

For more information on the park, contact **Intendencia del PN Quebrada del Condorito** (☑03541-484511; Av JS Bach 504, Villa Carlos Paz; ⊙8am-3pm Mon-Fri).

Any bus from Córdoba to Mina Clavero will drop you at La Pampilla (AR$170, 2½ hours), where a trailhead leads to the gorge. To return to Córdoba (or on to Mina Clavero), flag a bus from the turnoff. Hostels and Nativo Viajes (p289) in Córdoba arrange day tours to the park. Note that the last bus going back to Córdoba departs at 6:30pm; you don't want to miss it.

Mina Clavero

🕿 03544 / POP 16,980 / ELEV 915M

Really jumping in summertime, Mina Clavero pretty much empties out for the rest of the year, leaving visitors to explore the limpid streams, rocky waterfalls, numerous swimming holes and idyllic mountain landscapes at their own pace.

Mina Clavero is 170km southwest of Córdoba via RN 20, the splendid Camino de las Altas Cumbres (Way of the High Peaks). It sits at the confluence of Río de los Sauces and Río Panaholma, in the Valle de Traslasierra.

☰ Sleeping

Many accommodations close around the end of March, when the town almost rolls up the sidewalks.

Andamundos Hostel HOSTEL $
(☑03544-470249; www.andamundoshostel.com.ar; San Martín 554; dm/s/d US$13/25/35; @ 🛜) A rustic little setup a couple of blocks from the center of town. The big yard backing onto the river is a bonus. Rooms are simple but clean, breakfast is included and there's a shared kitchen.

Costa Serrana HOTEL $$
(☑03544-471802; www.costaserrana.com.ar; Olmos 1303; apt US$80; ❄🛜☒) With a fantastic, central location, these apartments represent some of the best value for money in this price range. Furnishings are rustic-chic, the breakfast buffet is expansive and the grounds are lovely, featuring a generously sized swimming pool overlooking the river.

✖ Eating

Most of Mina Clavero's restaurants are along San Martín. Head south over the river for more upscale *parrillas* and other restaurants.

Rincón Suizo CAFE $
(Recalde 1200; mains AR$80-120; ⊙6-9pm Fri-Sun) This comfy teahouse on the river prides itself on its homemade ice creams, delicious Swiss food (including fondue, raclette and ratatouille) and *torta selva negra*.

❶ Orientation

The Río Mina Clavero splits the town in two. If you arrive at the **bus terminal**, take the pedestrian bridge across the river – it takes you straight into the downtown area. Otherwise, you have to go the long way around.

❶ Information

Tourist Office (☑03544-470171; Av San Martín 1464; ⊙8am-10pm)

❶ Getting There & Away

The **bus terminal** (☑03544-470171; Av Mitre) is across the Río Mina Clavero from the town center. There are several daily buses to Córdoba (AR$340, three hours) and at least four a day to Merlo (AR$200, 2½ to three hours). Minibuses to Córdoba are faster (AR$360, 2½ hours). A couple of buses per day depart for Buenos Aires (AR$990, 13 hours). For destinations in San Juan and Mendoza provinces, go to nearby Villa Dolores (AR$82, 30 minutes).

SAN LUIS & AROUND

The little-visited province of San Luis holds a surprising number of attractions, made all the better by the fact that you'll probably have them all to yourself.

The province is popularly known as La Puerta de Cuyo (The Door to Cuyo), referring to the combined provinces of Mendoza, San Luis, La Rioja and San Juan.

The regional superstar is without doubt the Parque Nacional Sierra de las Quijadas, but the mountain towns along the Valle de Conlara and the Sierras Puntanas are well worth a visit if you're looking to get further off the tourist trail.

Merlo

02656 / POP 1084 / ELEV 890M

At the top of the Valle de Conlara, the mountain town of Merlo is a growing resort known for its gentle microclimate (the local tourist-industry buzzword) in a relatively dry area. The town is located 200km northeast of San Luis, tucked into the northeast corner of San Luis province.

Sights & Activities

For a sweeping view of the town and valley, head up to the miradores (viewpoints) overlooking town. Taxis charge around AR$150 to take you to the **Mirador del Sol**, halfway up the mountain, and then another 12km to the **Mirador de los Condores**, which is on top of the mountain ridge, and gives views in both directions.

In Rincón del Este, 2km from the center, on the road to the miradores, the **Reserva Natural de Merlo** (daylight hours) FREE is a lovely spot for creekside walks up to a couple of swimming holes. Tour operators in the park offer a range of activities including guided walks, zip lines and rock climbing.

Serranias Tour (02656-474737; Av del Sol 186; 9:30am-12:30pm & 5:30-8:30pm Mon-Fri, to 12:30pm Sat) is one of the many established tour operators in town. It offers a variety of guided tours and activities.

Sleeping & Eating

Casa Grande Hostel HOSTEL $

(02656-474579; www.casagrandehostelmerlo.com; Av de los Venados 740; dm/d US$16/63;) A short walk from downtown, this is Merlo's hippest hostel by far, with splashes of color and a lovely vibe. There's plenty of party action, cozy rooms, a convivial kitchen for guest use and sprawling, leafy grounds with a small swimming pool.

Information

Tourist Office (02656-476079; cnr RP 1 & RP 5; 9am-9pm) This municipal office has maps and information on hotels and campgrounds.

Getting There & Away

Long-distance buses leave from the **new bus terminal** (02656-475441; cnr RP 1 & Independencia), about eight blocks south of the town center.

Buses from Merlo

DESTINATION	COST (AR$)	TIME (HR)
Buenos Aires	1020	11
Córdoba	415	5
Mendoza	650	7
Mina Clavero	130	2
San Luis	150	3

Getting Around

Local buses leave from the **old bus terminal** (02656-445-2000; cnr Avs del Fundador & Santos Ortiz) in the center of town. There are departures for Piedra Blanca (AR$170, three hours), Bajo de Veliz (AR$118, two hours), Papagayos (AR$50, 30 minutes) and the nearby artisan village of Cerro de Oro (AR$60, one hour).

San Luis

0266 / POP 204,000 / ELEV 700M

Even people from San Luis will tell you that the best the province has to offer lies outside of the capital. Still, it's not a bad little town – there are a few historic sights here and the central Plaza Pringles is one of the prettiest in the country. The town's main nightlife strip, Av Illia, with its concentration of bars, cafes and restaurants, makes for a fun night out.

The commercial center is along the parallel streets of San Martín and Rivadavia between Plaza Pringles in the north and Plaza Independencia in the south. Most services for travelers are within a few blocks of the plaza, with the exception of the bus terminal.

Sights

Cathedral CATHEDRAL

(Rivadavia 740; 7:30am-9:30pm) The center of town is the beautiful, tree-filled Plaza

WORTH A TRIP

EL VOLCÁN

A small village nestled in the hills east of San Luis, El Volcán (there is no volcano here, by the way) is a laid-back summer getaway spot. The star attraction is the river that runs through the middle of town, where Balneario La Hoya, a series of natural rock pools, offers shady swimming spots and picnic areas. El Volcán is close enough to San Luis to make it an easy day trip, but there are plenty of cabins for rent, especially during summer.

Regular buses run to and from San Luis' main bus terminal (AR$20, 30 minutes).

Pringles, anchored on its eastern side by San Luis' handsome 19th-century cathedral. Provincial hardwoods such as algarrobo (carob tree) were used for the cathedral's windows and frames, and local white marble for its steps and columns.

Mercado Artesanal MARKET
(cnr 25 de Mayo & Rivadavia; 8am-1pm Mon-Fri) Dominican friars at the mercado artesanal, next to **Iglesia de Santo Domingo** (25 de Mayo 912; 8am-10pm), sell gorgeous handmade wool rugs as well as ceramics, onyx crafts and weavings from elsewhere in the province.

Sleeping & Eating

San Luis' better hotels cater to a business crowd, filling up quickly on weekdays and offering discounts on weekends.

Hotel Regidor HOTEL $
(0266-442-4756; www.hotelregidorsanluis.com.ar; San Martín 848; s/d/apt US$28/43/73;) Don't let the shabby exterior fool you – the rooms here are lovingly cared for, the staff is great and the big garden and pool area out back is a welcome sight in summer months.

San Luis Hostel HOSTEL $
(0266-424188; www.sanluishostel.com.ar; Falucho 646; dm/d US$15/26; @) San Luis' best and most central hostel has it all, from pool table to DVD library, excellent kitchen and shady backyard with barbecue. The nine-person dorms (segregated for male and female) could be a bit more atmospheric, but apart from that it's pure gold.

Los Robles PARRILLA $$
(9 de Julio 745; mains AR$150-260; 12-3pm & 8-11pm;) This upmarket *parrilla* has great atmosphere, attentive service and a menu that goes way beyond the usual offerings.

Information

Several banks, mostly around Plaza Pringles, have ATMs.

Automóvil Club Argentino (0266-442-3188; Av Illia 401; 9am-5pm Mon-Fri) Auto club; good source for road maps of the province.

Post Office (San Martín 801; 8am-1pm & 5-8pm Mon-Fri)

Regional Hospital (0266-442-2627; Héroes de Malvinas 251)

Tourist Office (0266-442-3479; www.sanluis.gov.ar; Av Illia 35; 8am-8pm Mon-Fri, 9am-1pm Sat, 9am-9pm Sun) The helpful staff can supply a good map of the town and its attractions plus offer useful advice on things to see and do in the region.

Getting There & Away

On the north bank of the Río Chorrillos, San Luis is 260km from Mendoza via RN 7 and 456km from Córdoba via RN 148.

There's a **Hertz** (0266-15-454-9002; www.hertz.com.ar; Av Illia 305; 8am-noon & 4-8pm Mon-Fri, 8am-noon Sat) in town for car rentals.

Parque Nacional Sierra de las Quijadas

Fans of the *Road Runner* cartoons will feel oddly at home among the red sandstone rock formations in this rarely visited **national park** (0266-444-5141; www.parquesnacionales.gob.ar; AR$250). The park comprises 1500 sq km of canyons and dry lake beds among the Sierra de las Quijadas, the peaks of which reach 1200m at Cerro Portillo. Recent paleontological excavations by the Universidad Nacional de San Luis and New York's Museum of Natural History have unearthed dinosaur tracks and fossils from the Lower Cretaceous, 120 million years ago.

From the park entrance, a 6km dirt road leads west to a viewpoint overlooking the **Potrero de la Aguada**, a scenic depression beneath the peaks of the sierra that collects the runoff from much of the park and is a prime wildlife area.

Despite the shortage of visitors here, access to the park is excellent: buses from San Juan to San Luis pass every hour or so, though you might have to ask them to stop.

Buses drop visitors at the park entrance just beyond the village of Hualtarán, about 110km northwest of San Luis via RN 147 (San Juan is 210km to the northwest).

It's sometimes possible to catch a lift from the park entrance to the viewpoint overlooking the Potrero de la Aguada.

Valle de las Sierras Puntanas

From San Luis, RP 9 snakes its way northwards, following the course of the Río Grande. Along the way, small villages are slowly developing as tourist destinations while still retaining much of their original character. The picturesque mining town of Carolina and nearby Inti Huasi cave are highlights of the region, and the landscapes higher up in the valley, with their rolling meadows and stone fences, probably resemble the Scottish highlands more than anything you've seen in Argentina so far.

Sights

La Casa de la Piedra Pintada ARCHAEOLOGICAL SITE
(8am-8pm Dec-Mar, 10am-5pm Apr-Nov) FREE At La Casa de la Piedra Pintada, more than 50 rock carvings are easily visible in the rock face. Follow the road until you reach an open meadow at the base of Cerro Sololasta and you'll see the cable-and-wood walkway up the cliff face that alllows access to the site. Once you're finished looking at the rock art, continue up the hill for spectacular views out over the Sierras Puntanas.

Finding this place is a little tricky – you can ask directions at Inti Huasi, or pay someone to guide you for a nominal fee.

Inti Huasi Cave CAVE
(9am-7pm Dec-Mar, noon-5pm Apr-Nov) FREE This wide, shallow cave, the name of which means 'House of the Sun' in Quechua, makes an interesting stop, as much for the gorgeous surrounding countryside as the cave itself. Radiocarbon dating suggests that the cave was first inhabited by the Ayampitín some 8000 years ago. There are three regular buses here from Carolina (AR$70, 30 minutes).

Sleeping

Hostería Las Verbenas ESTANCIA $
(0266-443-0918; www.lasverbenas.com.ar; RP 9, Km 68; per person incl full board US$47;) Set in a gorgeous glade in the Valle de Pancanta, this *hostería* (lodging house) does rustic to the hilt, with plenty of hearty food served up amid animal-skin decoration and rough-hewn furniture. Rooms are basic but comfortable. Three-hour horseback-riding tours (AR$350 per person) to a nearby waterfall are bound to be a highlight of your stay here.

The signposted entrance to the property is just after the bridge on the highway, from where it's another 4km to the farmhouse. If you're coming by bus, call and staff will pick you up from the highway.

Carolina

02651 / POP 250 / ELEV 1610M

Nestled between the banks of the Río Grande and the foothills of Cerro Tomalasta (2020m), Carolina is a photogenic little village of stone houses and dirt roads. Take away the power lines and you could be stepping 100 years back in time. The region boomed in 1785 when the Spanish moved in to exploit local gold mines that had first been used by the Inca.

Sights & Activities

Across the creek and up the hill from the Museo de Poesia is a small stone labyrinth, set on the hilltop. It should provide an hour or so of entertainment (or, if your sense of direction is really bad, days of frustration).

Museo de Poesia MUSEUM
(8am-6pm Tue-Sun) FREE One of the quirkier museums in the country, Museo de Poesia honors San Luis' favorite son, poet Juan Crisóstomo Lafinur. The museum has a few artifacts from the poet's life, plus handwritten homages to the man penned by some of Argentina's leading poets.

Sleeping & Eating

Rincón del Oro Hostel HOSTEL $
(02651-490212; Pringles 800; dm US$22;) Set on a hilltop overlooking town, this great little hostel has a rustic, intimate feel despite its 57-bed capacity.

Huellas Cafe-Bar CAFE $
(cnr 16 de Julio & El Minero; mains AR$80-150; 11am-7pm;) Tasty sandwiches, pizzas and daily specials are served at the cafe-bar adjacent to the **Huellas Turismo** (02651-490224; www.huellasturismo.com.ar; 10:30am-7pm) agency, paired with nice views.

WORTH A TRIP

BEYOND THE MOUNTAINS, TO THE TRASLASIERRA VALLEY

Literally translated as 'beyond the mountains,' the Traslasierra is the least developed and most sparsely populated of the valleys surrounding Córdoba. It lies 150km west of the city along RP 20 across the Camino de las Altas Cumbres (Way of the High Peaks). In summertime, Argentine families come to this enchanting area to swim in its pretty rivers and go horseback riding, kayaking and gorge walking.

Mina Clavero is the center of the valley's tourist activity but it's worth heading off the beaten trail to explore other, more secluded spots. The sweet village of Nono is home to the quirky **Museo Rocsen** (www.museorocsen.org; Nono; AR$190; ⏲9am-7pm), a lovely riverfront with great swimming spots, and what many claim are the best *alfajores* (cookie-type sandwiches usually stuffed with dulce de leche) in the province, at **El Nazareno** (Av Libertad Sur 87, Nono; alfajores from AR$21; ⏲7:30am-10pm). Also check out the rose-filled town of Villa de las Rosas and the adorable adjacent villages of San Javier and Yacanto, leafy postcard-pretty hideaways backed by dramatic mountain views.

While the area is filled with lodging options of all kinds and for every budget, the gorgeous **Posada La Matilde** (☎03544-404512; www.posadalamatilde.com; RP 14, Km 4; r from US$135; ❄📶) is a standout; its farm-to-table restaurant (mains AR$210 to AR$280) serves delicious dishes prepared with ingredients from its own organic biodynamic farm. In the nearby village of Yacanto, don't miss a meal at **Hotel Yacanto** (☎03544-482002; Publica s/n, Yacanto; mains AR$175-325), an English-style hotel from 1922 which is known for its great golfing and homemade food.

ℹ Getting There & Away

Buses run from Carolina to San Luis (AR$70, 2½ hours), passing through El Volcán. Some continue on to Inti Huasi (p311; AR$10, 30 minutes).

Papagayos

☎02656 / POP 430

Possibly the last thing you're expecting to see in this part of the world is a valley full of palm trees, but that's exactly where this small town is situated. The town is located on the banks of the Arroyo Papagayos and has huge caranday palms surrounding it, giving the area a certain reputation for handicrafts made from their trunks and branches.

Small stores (mostly attached to workshops) selling these *artesanías en palma* are scattered around town. The tourist office can provide a map showing all the store locations, along with other local attractions.

The arroyo (creek) is a good place to cool off – its length is dotted with swimming holes. For a more formal swimming environment, the Balneario Municipal offers swimming pools, picnic and barbecue areas.

For horseback riding and trekking to local waterfalls and swimming spots out of town, ask at the **tourist office** (☎02656-481868; cnr San Pedro & RP 1; ⏲9am-8pm) or **Hostería Los Leños** (☎02656-481812; Av Comechingones 555; r US$58; P📶🏊).

From Papagayos' main plaza there are regular buses to Merlo (AR$50, 30 minutes).

Mendoza & the Central Andes

Includes ➡

Best Places to Eat

- Osadía de Crear (p332)
- Fuente y Fonda (p321)
- Siete Fuegos (p340)
- Azafrán (p321)
- Casa El Enemigo (p331)

Best Places to Stay

- Entre Cielos (p331)
- Lares de Chacras (p331)
- B&B Plaza Italia (p320)
- Gran Hotel Potrerillos (p334)
- Posta Huayra (p352)

Why Go?

A long, narrow sliver of desert landscape, the Mendoza region is home to two of Argentina's claims to fame – the Andes and wine. The city itself is lively and cosmopolitan and the surrounding area boasts hundreds of wineries offering tours – an educational (and occasionally intoxicating) way to spend an afternoon or a month.

If you can put your glass down for a minute, there's plenty more to keep you busy. Just down the road is Cerro Aconcagua, the Americas' highest peak and a favorite for mountain climbers the world over. A couple of ski resorts give you the chance to drop into fresh powder while Mendoza's tour operators offer up a bewildering array of rafting, mountain-biking and paragliding options.

To the north, often-overlooked San Juan province is worth visiting for its small but important selection of wineries, bucolic traditional villages and desert landscapes in Parque Nacional el Leoncito and Parque Provincial Ischigualasto.

When to Go

Mendoza

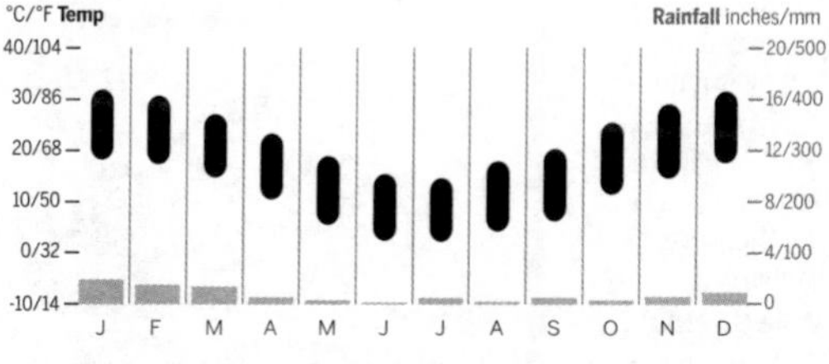

Dec–Mar Hot, dry weather makes this the perfect time to climb the region's highest peaks.

Apr–Jun Autumn is spectacular, thanks to the colors of Mendoza's trees and grapevines.

Jul–Sep Ski season paints the Andes white – a breathtaking sight, even for nonskiers.

Mendoza & the Central Andes Highlights

1. **Valle de Uco** (p338) Wining and dining over lunch at a rural bodega.
2. **Cacheuta** (p333) Soaking those aching bones in this mountainside thermal complex.
3. **Parque Nacional El Leoncito** (p350) Gazing up at an crystal clear nighttime sky sparkling with stars.
4. **Las Leñas** (p345) Carving tracks in fresh powder on the world-class slopes.
5. **Maipú** (p329) Grabbing some wheels and treating yourself to a tour of the wineries.
6. **Barreal** (p349) Getting away from the crowds and into the stunning Valle de Calingasta.
7. **Parque Provincial Ischigualasto** (p352) Discovering dinosaur fossils embedded in bizarre rock formations.
8. **Mendoza** (p322) Making the scene in any number of hip bars on Av Arístides.
9. **Cerro Aconcagua** (p338) Touching the roof of the highest peak in the western hemisphere.
10. **Valle Grande** (p342) Rafting or bodysurfing down this river shaped like a water-park chute.

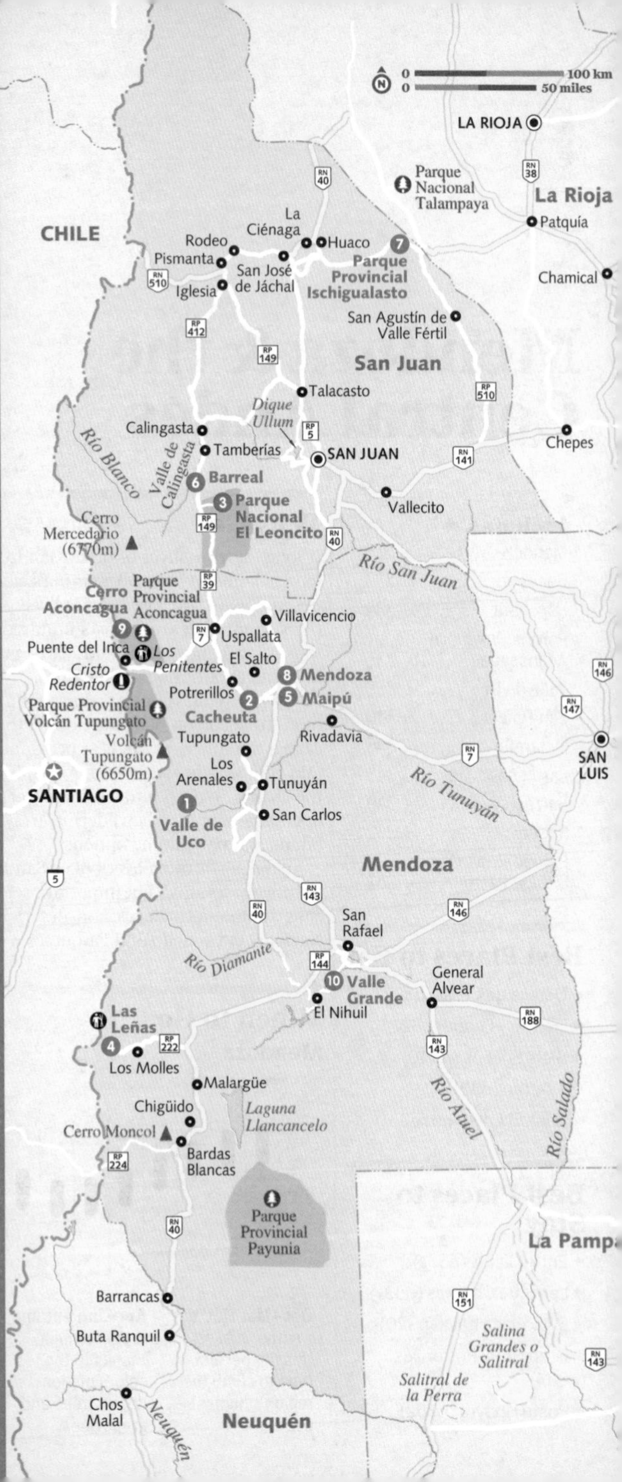

Mendoza

☎0261 / POP 1.2 MILLION / ELEV 769M

A bustling city of wide, leafy avenues, atmospheric plazas and cosmopolitan cafes, Mendoza is a trap. Even if you've (foolishly) only given it a day or two on your itinerary, you're likely to be captivated by the laid-back pace. Ostensibly it's a desert town, though you wouldn't know it – *acequias* (irrigation ditches) run beside the roads and glorious fountains adorn the plazas. Lively during the day, the city really comes into its own at night, when the bars and restaurants along Av Arístides overflow onto the sidewalks.

The name Mendoza is synonymous with wine, and this is the place to base yourself if you're up for touring the vineyards, taking a few dozen bottles home or just looking for a good vintage to accompany the evening's pizza. The city's wide range of tour operators also makes it a great place to organize rafting, skiing and other adventures in the nearby Andes.

Sights

★Parque General San Martín PARK

Walking along the lakeshore and snoozing in the shade of the rose garden in this beautiful 420-hectare park is a great way to enjoy one of the city's highlights. Walk along Sarmiento/Civit out to the park and admire some of Mendoza's finest houses on the way. Pick up a park map at the **Centro de Información** (☎0261-420-5052; cnr Avs Los Platanos & Libertador; ⏲9am-5pm), just inside the impressive entry gates, which were shipped over from England and originally forged for the Turkish Sultan Hamid II.

Iglesia, Convento y Basílica de San Francisco CHURCH

(Necochea 201; ⏲9am-1pm Mon-Sat) Many *mendocinos* (people from Mendoza) consider the image at this church of the Virgin of Cuyo, patron of San Martín's Ejército de los Andes, miraculous because it survived Mendoza's devastating 1968 earthquake. In the Virgin's semicircular chamber, visitors leave tributes to her and to José de San Martín, the general who liberated Argentina from the Spanish. A mausoleum within the building holds the remains of San Martín's daughter, son-in-law and granddaughter, which were repatriated from France in 1951.

Museo Fundacional MUSEUM

(museofundacional@ciudaddemendoza.gov.ar; cnr Alberdi & Videla Castillo; AR$27; ⏲9am-5pm Mon-Fri) Mendoza's recently renovated Museo Fundacional protects excavations of the colonial *cabildo* (town council), destroyed by an earthquake in 1861. At that time, the city's geographical focus shifted west and south to its present location. A series of small dioramas depicts Mendoza's history, working through all of human evolution as if the city of Mendoza were the climax (maybe it was). The **Ruinas de San Francisco**, across the Plaza Pedro del Castillo, are the sole remaining remnants of the city prequake.

Activities

Once you've sucked down enough fine wine and tramped around the city, get into the Andes, Mendoza's other claim to fame, for some of the most spectacular mountain scenery you'll ever see. Numerous agencies organize climbing and trekking expeditions, rafting trips, mule trips and cycling trips.

Climbing & Mountaineering

Mendoza is famous for Cerro Aconcagua (p338), the highest mountain in the Americas, but the majestic peak is only the tip of the iceberg when it comes to climbing and mountaineering here. The nearby Cordón del Plata boasts several peaks topping out between 5000m and 6000m, and there are three important rock-climbing areas in the province: Los Arenales (near Tunuyán), El Salto (near Mendoza) and Chigüido (near Malargüe). Get in touch with **Andes Vertical** (☎0261-476-0864; www.andes-vertical.com), recommended for beginning and experienced rock-climbers.

Pick up a copy of Maricio Fernandez' full-color route guide (Spanish only), *Escaladas en Mendoza,* at Inka Expediciones (p337). For up-to-date information and a list of recommended guides, contact the **Asociación Argentina de Guías de Montaña** (☎0294-443-2866; www.aagm.com.ar). **Trekking Travel Expediciones** (☎0261-421-0450; www.trekking-travel.com.ar) offers several multiday routes into the mountains, usually involving horseback riding.

For climbing and hiking equipment, both rental and purchase, visit **Chamonix** (☎0261-425-7572; www.chamonix-outdoor.com.ar; Barcala 267; ⏲9am-1pm & 3-6pm Mon-Sat).

Skiing & Snowboarding

When there's snow, Los Penitentes has the best skiing near Mendoza, although further south, Las Leñas has arguably the best skiing in South America. For standard ski

Mendoza

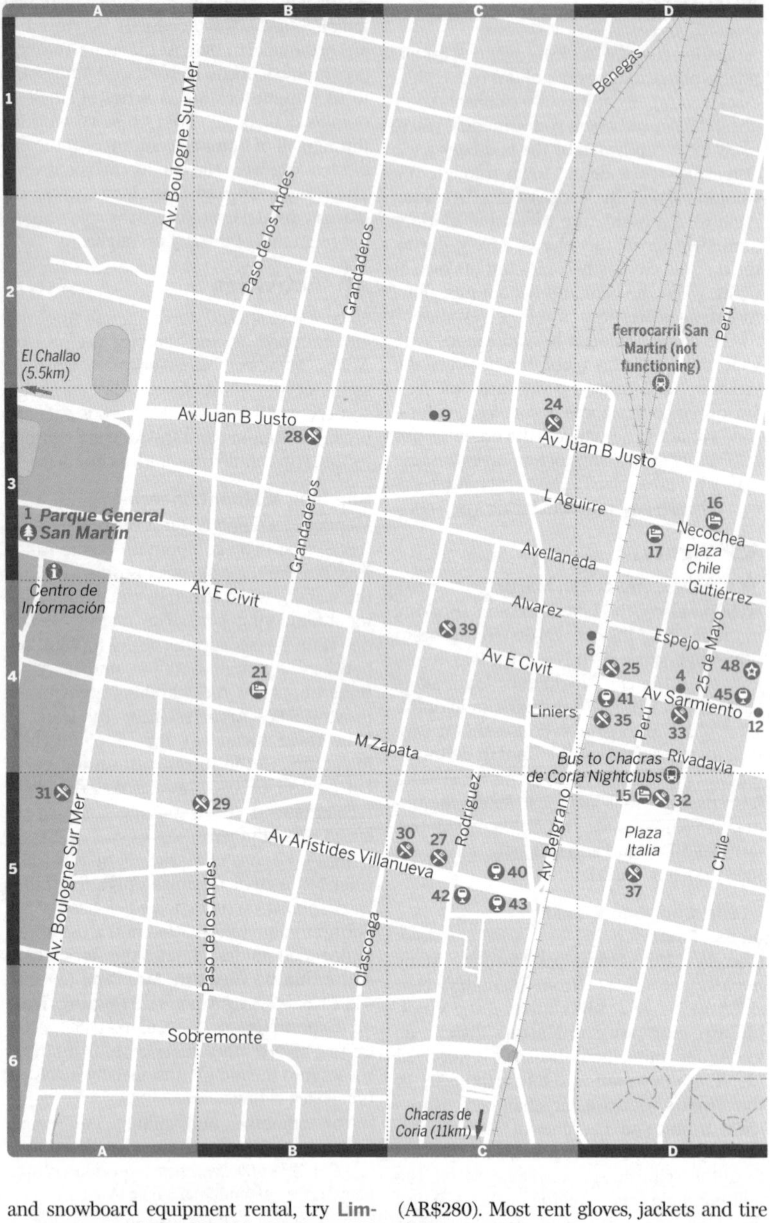

and snowboard equipment rental, try **Limite Vertical** (☎0261-423-1951; Sarmiento 675; ⏲9am-1pm & 4:30-9pm Mon-Sat) or any of the shops along Av Las Heras. In high season, all offer packages with either skis, boots and poles (AR$230), or snowboards and boots (AR$280). Most rent gloves, jackets and tire chains, as well.

White-Water Rafting

The major rivers are the Mendoza and the Diamante and Atuel, near San Rafael.

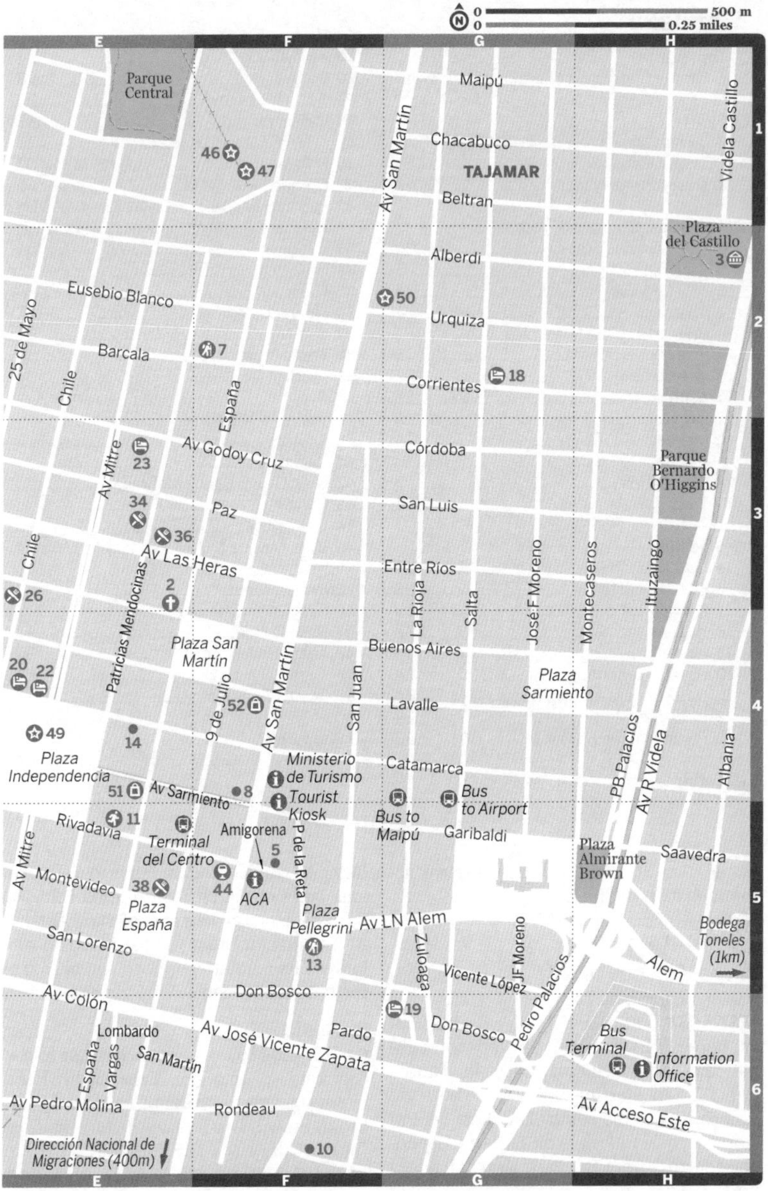

Most agencies offer half-day descents (from AR$420) and multiday expeditions. Transport is extra. Well-regarded **Argentina Rafting** (☎0261-429-6325; www.argentinarafting.com; Amigorena 86; ⏰9am-6pm Mon-Sat) operates a base in Potrerillos; book trips at its Mendoza office.

Courses

Intercultural LANGUAGE

(☎0261-429-0269; www.intercultural.com.ar/en/spanish-school; República de Siria 241; ⏰9am-8pm Mon-Sat) Offers group and private Spanish classes and internationally recognized

Mendoza

Top Sights
1 Parque General San Martín ... A3

Sights
2 Iglesia, Convento y Basílica de San Francisco ... E3
3 Museo Fundacional ... H2

Activities, Courses & Tours
4 Ampora Wine Tours ... D4
5 Argentina Rafting ... F5
6 Argentina Ski Tours ... D4
7 Chamonix ... F2
8 Huentata ... F4
9 Inka Expediciones ... C3
10 Intercultural ... F6
11 Kahuak ... E5
Limite Vertical ... (see 25)
12 Mendoza City Tour ... D4
Mendoza Wine Camp ... (see 6)
13 Tours4Tips ... F5
14 Trout & Wine ... E4

Sleeping
15 B&B Plaza Italia ... D5
16 El Portal Suites ... D3
17 Hostel Alamo ... D3
18 Hostel Lagares ... G2
19 Hostel Lao ... G6
20 Hotel Argentino ... E4
21 Hotel Bohemia ... B4
22 Hotel San Martín ... E4
23 Punto Urbano Hostel ... E3

Eating
24 Anna Bistro ... C3
25 Azafrán ... D4
26 Bröd ... E3
27 Cocina Poblana ... C5
28 El Asadito ... B3
29 El Mercadito ... B5
30 El Palenque ... C5
31 El Patio de Jesús María ... A5
32 Fuente y Fonda ... D5
Heladeria Famiglia Perin ... (see 25)
33 La Lucia ... D4
34 La Marchigiana ... E3
35 Maria Antioneta ... D4
36 Mercado Central ... E3
37 Silla 14 ... D5
38 Tasca de la Plaza ... E5
39 Via Civit ... C4

Drinking & Nightlife
40 Antares ... C5
41 Cachita's ... D4
42 Gran Ciervo Bar de Montaña ... C5
43 Hangar 52 ... C5
44 La Reserva ... F5
45 Uvas Lounge & Bar ... D4

Entertainment
46 Cine Universidad ... F1
47 Nave Cultural ... F1
48 Teatro Independencia ... D4
49 Teatro Quintanilla ... E4
50 Teatro Tajamar ... G2

Shopping
51 Raices ... E4
52 SBS ... F4

exams. Can also help find longer-term accommodation in Mendoza.

Tours

★Mendoza City Tour BUS TOUR
(www.mendozacitytour.com; adult/child AR$195/137; ⊙10am-8pm) Double-decker hop-on, hop-off bus tour with 20 stops throughout the city, including ones in Parque General San Martín and Godoy Cruz, the suburb just to the south. The most central stop and ticket kiosk is on Plaza Independencia, across from the Park Hyatt Mendoza hotel. Guides provide commentary in Spanish; more spare narration is provided in English and Portuguese via headphones.

Tours4Tips WALKING
(☎0261-642-8382; www.vivimza.com/free-walking-tour-mendoza-argentina; Plaza Pelligrini; ⊙11am & 3pm Mon-Sat, 11am Sun, 8pm Tue & Fri) Bilingual guides lead walking tours of various parts of the city; meet-up is Pelligrini Sq, a couple of blocks east of Plaza España. At the end of the tour you pay based on your budget. Its reputation is good, but of course, the tour quality depends on your guide.

Huentata TOURS
(☎0261-420-3863; www.huentata.com.ar; Sarmiento 45, Local 15; ⊙9am-8pm) Large travel agency that organizes trips in and around town. Possibilities include half-day tours of the city (AR$180), and day tours of the Cañon del Atuel (AR$570), Villavicencio (AR$280) or the high cordillera around Potrerillos, Vallecito and Uspallata (AR$480). Mostly Spanish-speaking.

Kahuak TOURS
(☎0261-423-8409; www.kahuak.com.ar; Rivadavia 234; ⊙8am-9pm Mon-Fri, to 1pm Sat) Big company offering full-day trips to Maipú win-

eries (AR$1990), Alta Montaña (AR$860), Aconcagua (AR$1890) and Cañón del Atuel (AR$990); half-day trips to Villavicencio (AR$500) and city wineries (AR$450). Valle de Uco trips on demand with a minimum of two people.

Wine Tours

For the casual sipper, a self-guided tour of Maipú or any of the bodega tours offered by various travel agencies around town will likely satisfy. There are also a few highly recommended companies operating out of Mendoza offering deluxe wine tours. They're not cheap, but benefits include small group sizes, knowledgeable and entertaining English-speaking guides and access to exclusive vineyards. Most also offer tours of the Valle de Uco, a beautiful, relatively new winegrowing region 150km south of Mendoza that's near impossible to explore by public transportation.

All of the operators can set you up customized trips, some with horseback tours of the vineyards; usually a full-day affair with gourmet lunch included (US$190).

Mendoza Wine Camp TOURS
(☎0261-423-6958; www.mendozawinecamp.com; Av Belgrano 1194B; per day US$150-185; ⏰11am-8:30pm Mon-Fri, from 5:30pm Sat) American expat Adam Stern runs this company offering small-group English- and Portuguese-speaking wine tours with an emphasis on interaction and education. Also offers a great *asado* (barbecue grill) cooking-class day trip held at a chef's house in Luján de Cuyo – you learn to build a fire and drink *mate* as well.

Evening wine tastings (US$45 to US$55) are held on demand on Tuesday and Thursday nights above the office.

Trout & Wine TOURS
(☎0261-425-5613; www.troutandwine.com; Espejo 266; ⏰8am-8pm Mon-Fri, noon-8pm Sat) Owned and operated by longtime Mendoza expat Charlie O'Malley, a fount of knowledge and insight about Mendoza area wineries and history. Organizes custom-designed, full-day tours of Luján de Cuyo (US$195) and the Valle de Uco (US$205) with maximum of eight people. From November to March they run fly-fishing tours in the Valle de Uco for US$190 to US$400, including all gear and an idyllic barbecue lunch in the highlands.

Ampora Wine Tours TOURS
(☎0261-429-2931; www.mendozawinetours.com; Av Sarmiento 647; ⏰9am-9pm Mon-Fri, 5-9pm Sat & Sun) Ampora is a well-established company with high standards run by a youngish German named Kai who has been in the Mendoza wine-tour biz for a dozen years. Groups max out at eight and focus on midrange and top-end wineries in Luján de Cuyo (US$175) and the Valle de Uco (US$185). Tastings (US$100) of six highly rated wines are held thrice weekly above the office.

Festivals & Events

Fiesta Nacional de la Vendimia WINE
(National Wine Harvest Festival; www.vendimia.mendoza.gov.ar; Teatro Griego Frank Romero Day; ⏰late Feb-early Mar) Mendoza's famous wine harvest festival lasts about a week. It draws tens of thousands of people to the Parque General San Martín amphitheater for music, dancing and a parade of beauty-pageant winners – it all culminates in the coronation of the festival's queen on the final day, which also usually ends in a massive fireworks display.

Classical Music by the Wine Roads MUSIC
(www.cultura.mendoza.gov.ar; ⏰early Apr) Classical music and wine seem to go together like malbec and aged cheddar. This festival, now in its 17th year, has nearly 50 concerts spread out over a wide range of venues in and around the city, including dramatic settings in picturesque wineries. Acquiring a ticket can be annoying – you have to stand in line at the **Cultural Ministry** (España and Gutierrez) on April 3 (10am–3pm and 4–7pm).

Sleeping

Several international chains have nice upscale outposts, including a downtown Sheraton and the colonial-style Park Hyatt. Any hotel on or within a block of Av Aristides Villanueva (these are mostly hostels) should only be considered by those not bothered by noise. Note that hotel prices rise from January to March. Home-sharing services are more and more popular. Luján de Cuyo and Chacras de Coria are less urban options, still close to the city.

Hostel Alamo HOSTEL $
(☎0261-429-5565; www.hostelalamo.com.ar; Necochea 740; dm US$14, d US$40-50; @☎⛆) Reliable, conveniently located hostel housed in a colonial-style family residence with roomy

four-bed dorms, great hangout areas and a wonderful backyard with a tiny plunge pool.

Hostel Lao HOSTEL $
(☎ 0261-438-0454; www.laohostel.com.ar; Rioja 771; dm US$14, r with/without bathroom US$45/34; ❄ 📶 🏊) English-owned converted family home, more of a B&B than hostel, with a variety of accommodations options, spacious lounge and outdoor garden (occasional communal *asados*) with hammocks and tiny plunge pool.

Hostel Lagares HOTEL $
(☎ 0261-423-4727; www.hostellagares.com.ar; Corrientes 213; dm/d US$12/45; ❄ 📶) With friendly, helpful owners, spotlessly clean Lagares is a good choice if you don't mind being a very long walk away from the nightlife on Aristedes Villanueva. The breakfast is generous and there are a couple of charming indoor and outdoor common areas.

Punto Urbano Hostel HOSTEL $
(☎ 0261-429-5281; www.puntourbanohostel.com; Av Godoy Cruz 326; dm US$11, d with/without bathroom US$34/25; @ 📶) Just north of the city center, this hostel maintains an air of intimacy despite its grand proportions. The dorms are basic, but the doubles are good value – roomy, with wide-screen TVs and tastefully decorated bathrooms. The large backyard – good for smoking, drinking, barbecuing and generally hanging out – is an added bonus, and the hostel schedules *asados,* happy hours and day trips.

★ **B&B Plaza Italia** B&B $$
(☎ 0261-615-2357; www.plazaitalia.net; Montevideo 685; d US$130; ❄ 📶) Comfortable and homey, a stay at this family-run B&B hits the right notes, combining personal intimacy and understated professionalism. Each of the five spacious rooms have comfy bedding and a delicious breakfast is served in an elegant downstairs dining room. The English-speaking owners, including Javier, who runs customized wine tours, are lovely and can give you the lowdown on all things Mendoza.

★ **Hotel Bohemia** BOUTIQUE HOTEL $$
(☎ 0261-420-0575; www.bohemiahotelboutique.com; Granaderos 954; d US$75-125; ❄ @ 📶 🏊) Located on a quiet residential street around eight blocks west of the Plaza Independencia, this refashioned family home features a few stylish and charming common areas and comfortable, if ordinary rooms. Dinners made to order can be enjoyed outside in the small patio area next to the pool.

El Portal Suites BOUTIQUE HOTEL $$
(☎ 0261-438-2038; www.elportalsuites.com.ar; Necochea 661; d from US$85; @ 📶) Conveniently located only a block or two from several restaurant-laden streets, El Portal has light and spacious rooms with laminated wood floors, some with their own balconies.

Hotel Argentino HOTEL $$
(☎ 0261-405-6300; www.argentino-hotel.com; Espejo 455; s/d from US$72/93; ❄ @ 📶 🏊) Fronting Plaza Independencia, this business-class hotel with Ikea-level furnishings offers attentive service and a good breakfast. Rooms vary in size: some can be quite small with little natural light so best to ask for an 'executive' or one with a balcony overlooking the plaza. A small pool is in an enclosed ground-floor back patio.

Hotel San Martín HOTEL $$
(☎ 0261-438-0677; www.hotelsanmartinmendoza.com; Espejo 435; s/d US$7/84; ❄ @ 📶) Fronting the plaza, this three-story brick hotel offers solid value. There's plenty of tasteful tile work and rooms are spacious and comfortable, with modern bathrooms and big windows.

Eating

Some of Mendoza's best restaurants, often with outdoor seating and lively young crowds, are along Av Arístides Villanueva, the western extension of Av Colón. West of Plaza Independencia, Av Sarmiento is lined with the city's most traditional, albeit touristy, *parrillas* (steak restaurants), while east of the plaza along the Sarmiento *peatonal* (pedestrian street), you'll find numerous sidewalk cafes with outdoor seating. Belgrano, between Gutirrez and Zapata, is another good stretch of restaurants.

★ **Bröd** CAFE $
(☎ 0261-425-2993; Chile 894; sandwiches AR$100-155; ⏰ 8am-9pm Mon-Sat, 9am-4pm Sun; 📶) There's no better spot in the city to pass a few hours on a sunny day than Bröd's whitewashed backyard patio. The pastries, sandwiches and egg dishes are done to exacting and delicious standards – unsurprising, since it's run by the former chef of an upscale wine lodge. There's even a *pétanque* court if you're looking for a little activity while enjoying brunch.

Heladeria Famiglia Perin
ICE CREAM $

(Sarmiento 799; ice creams AR$35; ⊘10am-2am; ☎) Traditional-looking ice-cream parlor serving up classic gelato since 1947. Wide range of flavors and good espresso drinks as well.

Via Civit
CAFE $

(Civit 277; mains AR$120-290; ⊘7am-10pm; ☎) An old-school place popular with locals in an upscale neighborhood, convenient as a stop on the way to or from Parque General San Martín. The coffee and bakery are the draw, but there's a small brunch menu, sandwiches, salads and a few basic pasta and meat dishes. The grand entrance is framed with Roman columns and an oversized clock.

★ Fuente y Fonda
ARGENTINE $$

(☑0261-429-8833; Montevideo 675; mains AR$450-588; ⊘noon-3pm & 8pm-midnight) Take the menu's suggestion with a grain of salt. Mains are good for two if you're overworked gauchos, but are more manageable for three healthy appetites, especially the meat dishes. Most come with bread, salad, a side and dessert, all served in farmhouse dishware. The large, wooden family table in back is often occupied by big groups.

Reservations recommended.

★ Silla 14
CAFE $$

(www.silla14cafe.com.ar; San Lorenzo 656; mains AR$195-250; ⊘8am-9pm Mon-Fri, from 9am Sat; ☎🍴) The priciest and finest coffee in the city is served at this elegant and sophisticated cafe. Silla 14 resembles the parlor of an upscale colonial-era home with contemporary touches, including suspendered waiters à la Brooklyn. Gourmet sandwiches and salads, healthy juices and pastries are on the menu.

El Patio de Jesús María
PARRILLA $$

(☑0261-429-6767; cnr Villanueva & Boulogne Sur Mer; mains AR$170-320; ⊘noon-3:30pm & 8pm-12:30am) Heaping slabs of top-quality meat cooked over flaming wood chips. That's what makes this simple, low-rills restaurant one of Mendoza's favorite *parrillas*. *Chivito* (goat), *bife de chorizo* (similar to New York Strip) and *costillitas de ternera* (veal ribs) are specialties.

El Palenque
ARGENTINE $$

(☑0261-429-1814; Av Arístides Villanueva 287; mains AR$150-250; ⊘noon-2am; ☎) Don't miss this superb, extremely popular restaurant styled after an old-time *pulpería* (tavern), where the house wine is served in traditional *pinguinos* (white ceramic penguin-shaped pitchers). The food, especially interesting pasta dishes, pizza and appetizers, is outstanding, and the outside tables are always full and fun.

El Mercadito
ARGENTINE $$

(☑0261-463-8847; www.elmercaditoar.com; Av Aristedes Villanueva 521; mains AR$145-220; ⊘11am-1am; ☎🍴) Charmingly rustic with a flowering outdoor patio and an equally discerning kitchen, it's no wonder El Mercadito is often packed with young locals. The menu runs the gamut from Thai pasta to vegetarian lasagna and lobster salad.

Tasca de la Plaza
SPANISH $$

(☑0261-423-1403; Montevideo 117; mains AR$170-270; ⊘11am-3pm & 8pm-12:30am Mon-Sat) With excellent Mediterranean and Spanish tapas (mostly seafood), good wines, a cozy atmosphere, rustic decor and friendly service, La Tasca is a excellent choice if you're looking for an alternative to other meat-heavy menus.

Cocina Poblana
MIDDLE EASTERN $$

(Av Arístides Villanueva 217; mains AR$170-230; ⊘noon-3pm & 7pm-1am Mon-Sat) The very tasty, inexpensive Middle Eastern food here (hummus, falafel, dolmas) comes as a welcome break from all that steak. The shish kebab served with tabouleh salad is a definite winner.

El Asadito
PARRILLA $$

(☑0261-205-8580; cnr Av Juan B Justo & Granaderos; mains AR$110-230; ⊘noon-3:30pm & 9pm-late) Deservedly popular cantina-style eatery that does juicy barbecue and meat sandwiches. Vegetarian options as well.

★ Azafrán
FUSION $$$

(☑0261-429-4200; Av Sarmiento 765; mains AR$210-450; ⊘noon-3pm & 7pm-midnight Mon-Sat) Classic gourmet Mendoza-style, Azafrán has a rustic-chic decor true to its roots as an ordinary deli. It serves innovative versions of classic Argentine meat dishes, enormous steaks (of course) and good fish dishes. Head to the restaurant's 500-label wine cellar with the sommelier to choose just the right bottle for your meal.

★ Anna Bistro
FUSION $$$

(www.annabistro.com; Av Juan B Justo 161; mains AR$195-368; ⊘8am-1am; ☎) Cool, loungy looking place with a wonderful garden area, relaxed vibe and carefully prepared dishes like lamb and ratatouille in malbec sauce and white fish filet with a vegetable soufflé.

★Maria Antioneta INTERNATIONAL **$$$**
(☎0261-420-4322; www.mariaantonietaresto.com.ar; Av Belgrano 1069; mains AR$250; ⏰8am-midnight Mon-Fri, from 9am Sat, 10am-4pm Sun; 📶) The wonderful, fresh blend of flavors on the menu here are echoed in the design of the dining room – a pleasing mix of retro and modern styling. Everything's good – well presented and flavorful – and accompanied by an excellent selection of wines and desserts.

La Marchigiana ITALIAN **$$$**
(☎0261-423-0751; www.marchigiana.com.ar; Patricias Mendocinas 1550; mains AR$207-260; ⏰noon-3pm & 7pm-1am) One of the city's frequently recommended Italian restaurants, this large and light-filled dining room is usually occupied by *mendocinos* enjoying simple and traditionally prepared Italian classics with a few Argentine dishes thrown into the mix.

La Lucia ARGENTINE **$$$**
(☎0261-425-0552; www.laluciagrillbar.com; Av Sarmiento 658; mains AR$200-400; ⏰noon-1am) Formally attired waitstaff and a black-and-white checkerboard floor give this top flight steak house a classic, old-school feel. Grab a seat at a sidewalk table for a more vibrant atmosphere. A few good pasta selections for those who've burned out on grilled meat.

Drinking & Nightlife

For a great night on the town, walk down Av Arístides Villanueva, where it's bar after bar; in summer entire blocks fill with tables and people enjoying the night. On the other side of town is the Alameda, which is less salubrious, though you might be able to catch some live music. Wine is available everywhere in Mendoza (right down to gas stations).

★Antares BAR
(Av Aristedes Villanueva 153; ⏰6pm-late) Nearly always packed, this hipster-like bar is the best place in the city for a wide selection of quality beer.

Gran Ciervo Bar de Montaña BAR
(Av Aristedes Villanueva 198; ⏰6pm-late) Large, two story space with an industry-meets-mountain aesthetic serving good beers, cocktails and a menu of innovative versions of regional specialties.

DON'T MISS

WINERIES NEAR MENDOZA

Thanks to a complex and very old system of river-fed aqueducts, land that was once desert now supports 70% of the country's wine production. Mendoza province is wine country, and many wineries near the capital offer tours and tasting. Countless tourist agencies offer day tours, hitting two or more wineries in a precisely planned day, but it's also easy enough to visit on your own. Hiring a *remise* (taxi) is also feasible. Some winery tours and tastings are free, though some push hard for sales at the end, and you never taste the *good* stuff without paying. Malbec, of course, is the definitive Argentine wine.

With a full day it's easy to hop on buses and hit several of the Mendoza area's most appealing wineries in the outskirts of neighboring Maipú (p329), only 16km away. For a look at what the cutting-edge wineries are doing, consider renting a car or going on a tour of the Valle de Uco (p338). Another option is the area of Luján de Cuyo, 19km south of Mendoza, which also has many important wineries.

There are several ways of getting to Maipú, including public buses leaving from La Rioja, between Garibaldi and Catamarca in central Mendoza; buses to wineries in Luján de Cuyo leave from Mendoza's bus terminal (p328).

Mendoza's tourist office (p328) on Garibaldi near Av San Martín provides a basic but helpful map of the area and its wineries. Also look for the useful three-map set *Wine Map: Wine and Tasting Tours*.

Bodega Toneles (☎0261-431-0403; www.bodegalostoneles.com; Acceso Este Lateral Norte 1360; tastings AR$150-470; ⏰9am-6pm), the closest bodega to downtown Mendoza, has been meticulously restored to its traditional 1920s-era classic architecture and declared a Cultural Heritage site. The winemaking facilities and techniques are very much *au courant*. **Abrasado** (lunch & dinner Tue-Sat), the winery's elegant and atmospheric restaurant, offers two to six course meals (AR$400–AR$1100).

Cachita's BAR
(☎0261-423-1702; Av Sarmiento 784; ⏰7pm-3am Tue-Sun) The best cocktails in the city are served up at Cachita's.

Hangar 52 BAR
(☎0261-694-6867; Av Aristides Villanueva 168; ⏰6pm-2am Mon-Thu & Sun, to 4am Fri & Sat) Argentine draft beers and a few house-made beers, totaling a selection of over 50, are on offer at this popular spot that feels a bit like a beer garden. The ticket system – pay at the cashier before ordering with the bartenders – doesn't exactly speed things up. DJs start spinning late.

Uvas Lounge & Bar WINE BAR
(Chile 1124; ⏰11am-midnight) Sleek and intimate wine bar, with cheese platter and tapas, in Mendoza's best-looking hotel, the Park Hyatt.

La Reserva GAY
(Rivadavia 34; ⏰from 9pm Tue-Sat) This small, nominally gay bar packs in a mixed crowd and has outrageous drag shows at midnight every night, with hard-core techno later. Some nights have a cover charge.

☆ Entertainment

Unfortunately, Mendoza is not the city for tango. But check tourist offices or museums for a copy of *La Guía,* a monthly publication with entertainment listings. *Los Andes,* the daily rag, also has a good entertainment section. For everything from live music to standup comedy, check the program at the **Centro Cultural Tajamar** (☎0261-425-6165; www.facebook.com/nuevotajamar; San Martín 1921; ⏰from 8pm). The main theater in town is **Teatro Independencia** (☎0261-438-0644; www.cultura.mendoza.gob.ar/teatroindependencia; Chile 1754; ⏰box office 6-9pm Tue-Sat), with **Teatro Quintanilla** (☎0261-423-2310; Plaza Independencia) a distant second; **Nave Cultural** (☎0261-449-5288; navecultural@ciudaddemendoza.gob.ar; cnr España & Maza, Parque Central), north of the center, also occasionally hosts performances.

★**Cine Universidad** CINEMA
(☎0261-429-7279; www.cine.uncuyo.edu.ar; Maza 240; tickets AR$100) Art-house films and docs, primarily Argentinian and South American, and the occasional Hollywood classic, are screened at this cinema on the campus of the Universidad Nacional de Cuyo.

Shopping

Av Las Heras is lined with souvenir shops, leather shops, chocolate stores and all sorts of places to pick up cheap Argentine trinkets. Items made of *carpincho* (spotted tanned hide of the capybara) are uniquely Argentine and sold in many of the stores.

Specialty wine stores stock fine wines, have staff who speak at least a little English and can pack your bottles for shipping. Locally produced olive oil is another fine souvenir.

Raices ARTS & CRAFTS
(Av Sarmiento 162; ⏰8am-7pm Mon-Fri, to 1pm Sat) High-quality weavings, jewelry and more.

SBS BOOKS
(Gutiérrez 54; ⏰9am-1pm & 4:30-8:30pm Mon-Fri, 9am-1pm Sat) A large range of novels in English, Lonely Planet guidebooks, maps and wine-related literature. Also textbooks for Spanish students.

LUJÁN PLAYA

Now Mendoza has everything, well, except the sea. But as of 2016 there's a **beach** (RP 82). Granted, this human-made one along the Río Mendoza 20km west of Chacras de Coria does have views of the Andes. All the trappings are there, including dozens of yellow umbrellas (free) and lifeguard stations. It gets extremely crowded on summer weekends and holidays.

ℹ Information

EMERGENCY

Ambulance ☎0261-428-0000

IMMIGRATION

Dirección Nacional de Migraciones (Immigration Office; ☎0261-424-3510; Av San Martín 211; ⏰9am-4pm Mon-Fri) South of the city center.

MEDIA

La Guía This free monthly events magazine is a must-have if you plan on keeping up with Mendoza's hectic cultural scene. Pick up a copy at any tourist office.

Wine Republic (www.wine-republic.com) Mostly written and edited by Charlie O'Malley of Trout & Wine, with the occasional guest columnist, this is an excellent English-language magazine focusing on wine but also featuring good reviews of up-and-coming restaurants, Mendoza gossip and a couple of entertaining articles. Pick up a copy at your hotel, cafes, Mendoza City Tour (p318) or Trout & Wine (p319).

(Continued on page 328)

Mendoza's Wine

Since the Jesuits first planted vines in northern Argentina more than 500 years ago, Argentine wine has gone from strength to strength, and the country is now recognized as one of the leading international wine producers. If you're at all interested in wine, make sure the Mendoza area is firmly on your itinerary.

From Humble Beginnings...

The first major improvement in Argentine wine came with the arrival of European immigrants in the 19th century. These folks brought varieties from their home countries, replacing the Jesuit's criollo vines with 'noble' varieties such as merlot and cabernet sauvignon. The new grapes brought a minimal increase in quality, but even so, Argentine wine remained a very domestic product, often to be enjoyed with a big blast of soda to take the edge off.

Then, as if from nowhere, Argentine wines hit the world stage with a vengeance, and these days a Mendoza merlot has just as much (if not more) cachet than a comparably priced Chilean red.

MENDOZA SHOPPING LIST

Looking for the *really* good stuff? Here are some of the top picks in the malbec category from the 2017 Argentine Wine Awards:

➡ Fabre Montmayou Reserva Malbec, 2016 – Bodegas Fabre S.A

➡ Santa Julia Reserva Malbec, 2016 – Bodega Santa Julia

➡ Rutini Apartado Gran Malbec, 2014 – La Rural Viñedos y Bodegas SA Ltda

➡ Colomé Malbec, 2015 – Bodega Colomé

Terroir & Technique

While the wineries have definitely improved their marketing, in the end it all comes down to quality – Argentine wines are good and they just keep getting better. One of the keys to successful wine making is controlled irrigation. A big rain before a harvest can spoil an entire crop, something winemakers in the desert-like Mendoza region don't have to worry about. Nearly every drop of water is piped in, and comes as beautiful fresh snowmelt from the Andes.

Desert vineyards have another advantage – the huge variation between daytime and nighttime temperatures. Warm days encourage sugar production and help the grapes grow a nice thick skin. Cool nights ensure good acidity levels and low humidity means bugs and fungus aren't a problem.

The techniques are improving, too – better hygiene standards; the further replacement of old criollo vines with noble varieties such as malbec, cabernet sauvignon, merlot and syrah; and the practice of aging wines in smaller oak barrels (with a lifespan of a few years) rather than large barrels (which would be used for up to 70 years) have all had positive effects.

And you can't talk about Argentine wines without talking price-to-quality ratio. The country's economic crash in

1. Bodega, Luján de Cuyo (p329)
2. Vineyards, Luján de Cuyo

1

2

1

2001 was a boon for exporters as prices plummeted and overnight Argentine wine became a highly competitive product. Land here is (relatively) cheap and labor so inexpensive that nearly every grape in the country is handpicked, a claim that only top-end wines in other countries can make.

Touring the Vineyards

As Mendoza's wine industry grows, so does its sister industry of wine tourism. These days it's not a matter of whether you can do a wine tour, but really which one and how.

There are options for every budget. If you're watching your pesos, biking around the Maipú region (p329) is an excellent-value option. Wineries here are close together and their tour prices are low, so you can visit several in a day and taste some decent wines without breaking the bank. Be aware that this is a very popular way to spend the day, and some wineries will herd you through like cattle to make space for the next group.

If you're not a cyclist but not ready to commit to a full-on wine tour either, a good middle option is the satellite town of Luján de Cuyo (p322), 19km south of Mendoza. You can bus and taxi around the area with a minimum of planning, hit three or four wineries and be back in Mendoza before nightfall.

Those who can afford a little more and are interested in learning about techniques in a relaxed setting should consider a tour (p318). You'll avoid the crowds and sometimes get to meet the winemakers. The gourmet lunch at one of the wineries and top-shelf tastings that come with these tours may tip the scales, too. Tour companies can organize custom tours for the serious connoisseur, designed to take in the specific wineries, regions or even wines that you are particularly interested in.

But if you have the time and money, the best way to tour the region is strictly DIY. Rent a car in Mendoza, buy one of the winery maps on sale at every newsstand and create your own itinerary. Make the most of your freedom by

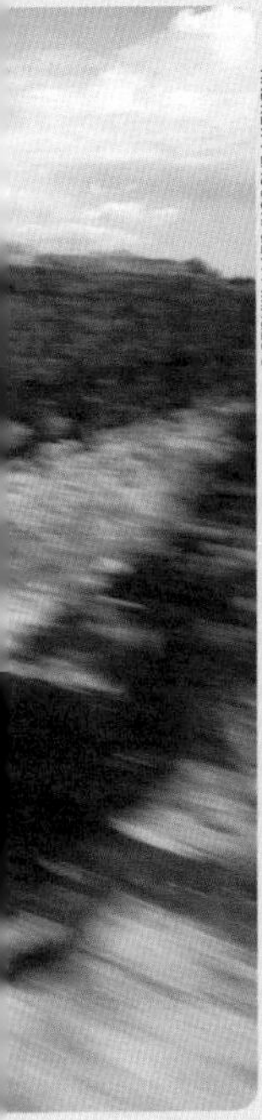

ANDREW PEACOCK/GETTY IMAGES ©

MATT MUNRO/LONELY PLANET ©

1. Cycling on a wine tour **2.** Wine grapes

visiting the Valle de Uco (p338) – home to some of the Mendoza region's most cutting-edge wineries. It's about 150km south of the city, but there are plenty of wineries offering accommodations and even specialty Wine Lodges – you can stay out there and tootle around to your heart's content. Be warned, though – Argentina has a zero-tolerance law for driving under the influence. If you get pulled over after a heavy day in the tasting room, you could be in big trouble.

SHIPPING WINE

While it's illegal to post wine from Argentina, countries such as the USA and Canada have no restriction on how much you can bring home in your luggage, provided you pay duty. And duty can be as low as US$5 for 40 bottles for the US.

If you are planning on transporting wine, it's best to stop in at a specialty wine store where they can pack bottles to avoid breakage (remember that many airlines have restrictions on bottles in hand luggage).

(*Continued from page 323*)

MEDICAL SERVICES

Hospital Central (☎0261-449-0570; cnr José F Moreno & Alem; ⊙24hr) The city's large, centrally located medical center.

SAFE TRAVEL

Mendoza is one of Argentina's safer destinations; however, like any large city, there is crime, and you should take common-sense precautions. Bag snatching and pickpocketing are things to watch out for. The areas around the bus terminal and on Cerro de la Gloria (in Parque General San Martín) have an increased police presence, but are considered dangerous at night. Increased caution is recommended during the early afternoon, too, as police tend to take the siesta along with everybody else. There have been reports of people picking locks on hostel lockers – leave valuables at your hostel's reception or in its safe.

TOURIST INFORMATION

ACA (Automóvil Club Argentina; ☎0261-420-2900; www.aca.org.ar; cnr Av San Martín & Amigorena; ⊙24hr) Argentina's auto club; good source for provincial road maps.

Ministerio de Turismo (☎0261-420-2800; www.turismo.mendoza.gob.ar; Av San Martín 1143; ⊙9am-9pm) Long counter with helpful staff, maps and regional information, housed in a grand building.

Tourist Kiosk (☎0261-420-1333; Garibaldi; ⊙8am-6pm) This helpful kiosk near Av San Martín is a convenient information source; there's another at the **bus terminal** (☎0261-431-5000; ⊙8am-8pm).

ℹ Getting There & Away

AIR

Francisco Gabrielli International Airport (El Plumerillo; ☎0261-520-6000; www.aa2000.com.ar; Acceso Norte s/n; 📶) is 6km north of downtown on RN 40. Newly renovated, it's an efficent and comfortable welcome to the city. Flights, especially from Santiago, afford spectacular views of the mountains. There's an ATM, but no exchange office; the gift shop sells – what else – wine.

Aerolíneas Argentinas (☎0261-420-4185; www.aerolineas.com.ar; Av Sarmiento 82; ⊙10am-6pm Mon-Fri, to 1pm Sat) Flies several times daily to Buenos Aires.

Andes Líneas Aéreas (www.andesonline.com) Regional airline with flights between Mendoza and Buenos Aires.

Gol (www.voegol.com.br/en) Brazilian airline with flights to Buenos Aires and onward connections to various cities in Brazil.

LATAM (☎0261-425-7900; www.latam.com; Rivadavia 256; ⊙10am-7pm Mon-Fri) Flies twice daily to Santiago (Chile) and several times weekly to Lima (Peru).

Sky (www.skyairline.cl) Chilean budget airline that began flying between Santiago and Mendoza in 2017.

BUS

Mendoza is a major transport hub, so you can travel to just about anywhere in the country. Mendoza's **bus terminal** (☎0261-431-3001; cnr Avs de Acceso Este & Costanera) has domestic and international departures. You can book tickets at no extra cost downtown at the **Terminal del Centro** (9 de Julio 1042; ⊙9am-1pm & 5-9pm).

Domestic

Several companies send buses daily to Uspallata (AR$106, two hours) and Los Penitentes (AR$128, 3¾ hours), the latter for Aconcagua.

During the ski season several companies go directly to Las Leñas (about AR$420, seven hours).

Empresa Vallecito offers a morning bus service to the Difunta Correa Shrine (AR$320 return, departs 8am Monday to Friday) in San Juan province; the journey is three hours each way and the bus waits three hours before returning.

Buses to Maipú leave from the stop on La Rioja between Garibaldi and Catamarca.

There are daily departures from Mendoza's bus terminal to most destinations in the following table, and sometimes upwards of 10 to 20 per day to major cities. Prices reflect midseason fares.

International

Numerous companies cross the Andes every day via RN 7 – Paso Internacional Los Libertadores (p332) – to Santiago, Chile (AR$700, seven hours), Viña del Mar (AR$700, eight hours) and

Buses from Mendoza

DESTINATION	COST (AR$)	TIME (HR)
Bariloche	1650	19
Buenos Aires	1395	14-17
Catamarca	964	11
Córdoba	985	11-12
Jujuy	1242	20
Malargüe	276	6¼
Mar del Plata	1312	20
Neuquén	1100	10½-12¾
Resistencia	2100	25
Rosario	1220	11
Salta	1400	18
San Juan	185	2¼
San Luis	380	3¾
San Rafael	138	3
Tucumán	1240	14

Valparaíso (AR$700, eight hours). The pass sometimes closes due to bad winter weather; be prepared to wait (sometimes days) if weather gets extreme.

Several carriers have connections to Lima, Peru (AR$3200, 57 hours), via Santiago, Chile.

International buses depart from the main bus terminal. Companies, including the recommended **Andesmar** (☎0810-122-1122; www.andesmar.com) and **Cata** (☎0800-122-2282; www.catainternacional.com), are at the eastern end of the terminal.

Getting Around

Mendoza is an eminently walkable city and wandering the wide avenues is one of the highlights of any stay.

TO/FROM THE AIRPORT

Bus 68 ('Aeropuerto') from **Calle Salta** (Salta, btwn Garibaldi & Catamarca) goes straight to the airport terminal. Taxis cost AR$175; drivers accept US dollars as well.

Mendoza's bus terminal is really just across the street from downtown. After arriving, walk under the Videla underpass and you'll be heading toward the center, about 15 minutes away. Otherwise, the 'Villa Nueva' trolley (actually a bus) connects the terminal with downtown.

BICYCLE

En La Bici (www.ciudaddemendoza.gov.ar/en-la-bici; ⏰8am-8pm Mon-Fri, 9am-3pm Sat) is Mendoza's bike-sharing system with nine stations throughout the city. Preregister online.

BUS

Local buses cost AR$5 – more for longer distances – and require a magnetic Redbus card, which can be bought at most kiosks in denominations of AR$5 and AR$10 (the card itself costs AR$10). Most *lineas* (bus lines) also have *internos* (internal route numbers) posted in the window; for example, *linea* 200 might post *interno* 204 or 206; watch for both numbers. *Internos* indicate more precisely where the bus will take you.

CAR

The following car-rental agencies are at the airport and in the city centre:

Avis (☎0261-447-0150; www.avis.com.ar; Primitivo de la Reta 914; ⏰8:30am-8:30pm Mon-Fri, 8:30am-1pm & 5:30-8pm Sat & Sun)

Hertz (www.hertz.com; Espejo 391) Also at the airport, but has surprisingly good rates at its convenient location in town, fronting Plaza Independencia.

Localiza (☎0261-448 5777; www.localiza.com/argentina/es-ar)

National/Alamo (www.alamoargentina.com.ar)

Try **Slowkar** (www.slowkar.com) to drive around wine country in high style in a classic Citroën.

For newbies, city driving can be challenging. There are lots of one-way streets, which means to make a left turn you often have to effect several rights. Even during the daytime, you need to have the car's headlights on. Be careful about where you park; some spaces require you to purchase a ticket (can be bought at small convenience shops) which you then place on the dashboard.

TRAM

Metrotranvía, the city's light-rail system runs for 12.5km (6am to 10pm) from the city center, along Belgrano, to Maipú (45 minutes). 'Redbus' cards can be purchased from most shops or the bus station.

Around Mendoza

The areas immediately surrounding Mendoza, once mostly agricultural, except for earlier incarnations of the semi-industrial wine industry in Maipú, are now a mix of commercial, residential and rural zones. Some feel quite suburban and are popular for weekending *mendocinos*. The further south you go the more rural it becomes until you reach Valle de Uco.

The small town of **Maipú**, just southeast of Mendoza, is the most urbanized and least picturesque of the regions. However, it's so packed with wineries, olive-oil farms and other gourmet businesses that it's easy to hit five or six in a day. All offer tours and most finish proceedings with at least a small sampling of their produce. The wine region of Chacras de Coria is due south of Mendoza. Further south from here is **Luján de Cuyo**. Agrelo, the southern part of Luján de Cuyo, has several well-known wineries.

Activities

A few companies in Maipú and Chacras de Coria rent bikes, making a day tour of either area an excellent outing, and a lot more fun than the often rushed half-day wine tours on offer from Mendoza tour agencies.

★**Carinae** WINE
(☎0261-499-0470; www.carinaevinos.com; Aranda 2899, Maipú; tours AR$50; ⏰10am-6pm) A small, French-owned winery producing a lovely rosé and some good reds located in the southern part of Maipú. Tour fees are deducted from any wine purchases you make.

CUYO

The provinces of Mendoza, San Juan, San Luis and La Rioja are traditionally known as the Cuyo, a term derived from the indigenous Huarpe word *cuyum*, meaning 'sandy earth.' The Huarpes were the original practitioners of irrigated agriculture in the region, a legacy still highly visible today. The term is one you'll encounter often, whether in the names of local bus companies, businesses and newspapers, or in everyday conversation.

Trapiche WINE
(☎ 0261-520-7666; www.trapiche.com.ar; Nueva Mayorga s/n, Maipú) This is the largest winery in Argentina.

Bodega la Rural WINE
(☎ 0261-497-2013; www.bodegalarural.com.ar; Montecaseros 2625, Maipú; tours AR$90; ⊙ 9am-1pm & 2-5pm Mon-Fri) Winery tours here are standard (the wine itself generally isn't considered top quality) but the **museum** is fascinating – there's a huge range of winemaking equipment on display, including a grape press made from an entire cowskin. Tours in Spanish leave on the hour. If you want one in English, call ahead – or you can simply walk around on your own for free.

Di Tomasso WINE
(☎ 0261-587-8900; www.familiaditommaso.com; Urquiza 8136, Maipú; tours AR$40; ⊙ 10am-6pm Mon-Sat) Di Tomasso is a beautiful, historical vineyard dating back to the 1830s, making it Argentina's oldest winery. The tour includes a quick pass through the original cellar section.

Tempus Alba WINE
(☎ 0261-4813501; www.tempusalba.com; Moreno 572, Maipú; ⊙ 10am-6pm Mon-Fri) A large, modern, family-run winery that offers a free, quick self-guided tour (including three wines AR$65) of the installations and a very tasty lunch menu in its restaurant overlooking the vines.

Viña del Cerno WINE
(☎ 0261-481-1567; www.elcerno.com.ar; Moreno 631, Maipú; ⊙ 10am-6pm Mon-Sat) The Viña del Cerno is a small, old-fashioned winery supervised by its two winemaker owners. The underground cellar complex is atmospheric and the winery's story, technique and philosophy are a nice counterpoint to the larger operations.

LAUR FOOD
(☎ 0261-499-0716; www.olvlaur.com; Aranda 2850, Maipú; ⊙ 10am-6pm Mon-Sat) LAUR is a 100-year-old olive farm. The 15-minute tour tells you everything you need to know about olive-oil production and is followed by a yummy tasting session.

★ **Alta Vista** WINE
(☎ 0261-496-4684; www.altavistawines.com; Álzaga 3972, Chaceras de Coria; ⊙ 9am-6pm) This is a medium-sized operation owned by a French family with over 350 years of winegrowing tradition and 350 hectares of vines spread over five farms. Architecturally, Alta Vista is a throwback, with the bones and bamboo roof of the original colonial era building circa 1899 and concrete storage tanks from the 1920s. Meanwhile, the tasting room resembles a high-tech chemistry lab.

Baccus Biking CYCLING
(www.baccusbiking.com; Mitre 1552, Chacras de Coria) Guided or self-guided tours of the wine region, just south of Mendoza city proper.

★ **Renacer** WINE
(☎ 0261-667-4523; www.bodegarenacer.com.ar; Brandsen 1863, Luján de Cuyo; ⊙ 9:30am-5:30pm Mon-Sat) Chilean-owned Reancer is designed to resemble a Tuscan tower, a nod to the family's Italian roots, with an irrigation pool doubling as a picturesque pond and a vine-covered pergola ideal for weddings. Virtual-reality glasses enhance visits since you can 'see' what goes on during other seasons, like the *appassimento* process used to dry out some of the grapes.

Pulenta Estate WINE
(☎ 0261-15-507-6426; www.pulentaestate.com; RP 86, Luján de Cuyo; ⊙ 9am-5pm Mon-Fri, to 1pm Sat) A boutique winery started by the ex-owners of the Trapiche label. Tours of the beautiful modern facility focus on tasting, not production.

Luigi Bosca WINE
(☎ 0261-498-1974; www.luigibosca.com.ar; San Martín 2044, Luján de Cuyo; tours AR$200; ⊙ by reservation Mon-Sat) Run by the Arizu family, Luigi Bosca, which also produces Finca La Linda, is one of Mendoza's premier wineries. If you're into wine, don't miss it. Tours in English and Spanish, however, are relatively lackluster.

Bodega Budeguer WINE

(☎0261-390-4291; www.budeguer.com; RP 15, Km 31.5, Agrelo, Luján de Cuyo; ⏰10am-5pm) One of the last remaining wholly Argentine-owned wineries in the area (the owners have been big in the sugarcane business in the north), Budeguer is a fairly small boutique player with young vines planted less than 10 years ago. The tasting room has only been open a year and paintings by Argentine artists hang on a gallery wall.

Catena Zapata WINE

(☎0261-413-1100; www.catenawines.com; Calle Cobos 5519, Agrelo, Luján de Cuyo; tours AR$200; ⏰by appointment 9am-6pm Mon-Fri) Catena Zapata is one of Argentina's most esteemed wineries. Tours, conducted in English, German or Spanish, are fairly mundane and you won't receive much personal attention. Get there by taxi (cheaper if you catch a bus to Luján de Cuyo and grab one from there).

Chandon WINE

(☎0261-490-9968; www.bodegaschandon.com.ar; RN 40, Km 29, Agrelo, Luján de Cuyo; tours AR$160; ⏰by reservation Mon-Sat) The modern Bodegas Chandon is popular with tour groups and known for its sparkling wines. Tours are available in Spanish and English.

Tours

Most hostels offer cheap minivan 'wine tours' of Maipú, including transfers, bike rental, helmets, insurance, wine tastings and visits to three wineries, lunch and transport, for around AR$800. Several recommended English-speaking tour companies, including Ampora (p319), Trout & Wine (p319) and Mendoza Wine Camp (p319), run wine-tasting and lunch tours to bodegas around Luján de Cuyo.

Sleeping

Chacras de Coria and Luján de Cuyo have a number of recommended boutique hotels, some set amid vineyards. These are nice compromises for those wishing to be within close range of the restaurants, cafes and amenities of Mendoza, but wanting a taste of the views and rural feel of Valle de Uco.

El Ecuentro Posada Boutique BOUTIQUE HOTEL $$

(☎0261-496-3828; www.posadaelecuentro.com; Capitán Candelaria 5413, Chacras de Coria; d US$140; 📶🏊) Homey, friendly family-run place with 10 simple, rustic rooms and a tiny plunge pool in the back.

★**Entre Cielos** BOUTIQUE HOTEL $$$

(☎0261-498-3377; www.entrecielos.com; Guardia Vleja 1998, Luján de Cuyo; d US$280-500; ❄@🏊) Mixing sophisticated contemporary style with playful, understated luxury, as well as a six-circuit hammam, Entre Cielos is one of the Mendoza area's best. All but one of the 16 rooms feature brushed concrete floors, mod furnishings and are named for an ingredient or quality of wine – the other is a unique pod-style structure on stilts built amidst the property's vineyard.

Weekly *asados* (barbecues) and afternoon teas are only for guests, while the hammam, housed in a modernist, bunker-like building, is open to all.

Lares de Chacras BOUTIQUE HOTEL $$$

(☎0261-496-1061; www.laresdechacras.com; Larrea 1266, Chacras de Coria; d US$180; ❄@📶🏊) Perfectly coiffed adobe-style brick boutique inn with only 11 spacious, ubercomfortable rooms and equally high-quality service. A basement cellar is visible through a clear glass floor near the doorway. There's a small resort-level pool area and cozy lounge with TV and DVDs, ideal for *Moana* and *Frozen*-loving toddlers. A nice restaurant, excellent breakfast and an *asado* for guests every Wednesday night.

Several bodegas and restaurants are within walking distance.

Eating & Drinking

Some of the region's, nay the country's finest restaurants are located in bodegas in Maipú, Chacras de Coria and Luján de Cuyo. These range from charmingly rustic affairs to polished and refined restaurants. Whatever the mise en scène, the quality, technique and creativity of the fare, usually including top cuts of juicy steak, is high. Pricier meals include wine pairings, especially popular at lunch. Many people experience these on organized tours from Mendoza.

★**Casa El Enemigo** ARGENTINE $$$

(☎0261-413-9178; www.elenemigowines.com; Aranda 7008, Maipú; 4-course lunch AR$760, 6-course dinner AR$2500; ⏰9:30am-5:30pm Mon-Sat) The passionate and philosophically inclined husband-and-wife team who created El Enemigo wines have also produced this similarly unique and inspired dining

CROSSING THE BORDER

There are two high mountain passes between Argentina and Chile. **Paso Internacional Los Libertadores** is a major, high-trafficked crossing reachable within a few hours from Mendoza, while **El Paso de Agua Negra**, in San Juan province, is an all-dirt track and sees relatively few travelers.

If driving a rental car, you'll need written permission and valid insurance to drive from one country to the other. Importantly, most rental-car companies require you to return the car to the country of origin, so you can't rent in Argentina and return it in Chile.

Paso Internacional Los Libertadores

The majestic and winding RN 7 leads from Uspallata to the Cristo Redentor Tunnel at the Chilean border, passing by the entrance to Parque Provincial Aconcagua (p336). It follows an old railway line, closed down in 1978 because of hostilities between the two countries, though there's perpetual talk of reopening the rail link.

Coming from Chile, the immigration and customs control post at **Horcones** is 16km from the border – Horcones is nothing more than this post. Each booth has a Chilean and Argentinian border officer who process passports. Cars are searched by other officers. Because of long lines, this can take several hours. Travelers in buses get to bypass the long line of cars.

Do not underestimate the potential complications of this border crossing, at 3200m one of the highest in the world. In good weather, things should proceed smoothly, if slowly, because of the immigration and customs stop on the Argentine side of the border (this is for travelers crossing into Argentina from Chile; if you are leaving Argentina you do not have to stop here). However, the crossing is often closed because of inclement weather and you don't want to be stuck up here at night without accommodations and warm clothing. Between June and September, the crossing is closed from 9pm to 9am. Check www.twitter.com/upfronterizos for the latest conditions and crossing times.

If entering Chile from Argentina, keep in mind that you'll need Chilean pesos to pay the four tolls between the border and Santiago.

Cata (p329) and Andesmar (p329) are recommended bus companies for making the trip.

El Paso de Agua Negra

At 4780m, **El Paso de Agua Negra** is the highest border crossing between Argentina and Chile, and is only used in the summer, from December to April. It involves white-knuckle turns and vertiginous switchbacks on dirt roads. There's roadwork, more paving and imminent plans to begin construction on a tunnel. The immigration post is open from 7am to 5pm.

experience. It combines a stunning setting, architecturally interesting bodega, warm and professional service and expertly conceived dishes elevated above the norm; the pea soup and lamb goulash are favorites. Dinner, served Monday to Friday, is by reservation only.

★ Osadía de Crear ARGENTINE **$$$**
(☎0261-498-9231; www.susanabalbowines.com.ar; Cochabamba 7801, Agrelo, Luján de Cuyo; 5-course lunch AR$1258) Osadia's five-course wine-paired lunch is one of the area's best, with beautifully presented dishes in portion sizes that won't bust your gut. Part of the Susana Balbo winery (whose namesake is the first female Argentine winemaker, and which is known for its torrontés whites), the restaurant is elegantly designed with rustic features and mountain views.

★ Casarena ARGENTINE **$$$**
(☎0261-696-7848; www.casarena.com; Brandsen 505, Luján de Cuyo; 6-course lunch incl wine AR$1180; ⏲noon-3pm) With wine glasses in the foreground and Cerro de la Plata framed by floor-length windows in the distance, the five-course meal seems almost a distraction. If you can tear yourself away from the views, you'll enjoy the meticulous presentation of dishes like mote wheat over carrot paste and pickled beets and spicy lamb gigot on mashed squash.

Clos de Chacras ARGENTINE **$$$**
(☎0261-496-1285; www.closdechacras.com.ar; Monte Líbano 125, Chacras de Coria; 3-course lunch AR$550, 7-course lunch incl wine AR$1100; ⊙12:30-3pm Mon-Sat, plus 8:30-11pm Fri & Sat) Housed in a family-owned, finely restored winery in a residential neighborhood, this restaurant serves three- and seven-course wine-paired menus, as well as an à la carte menu of European and Argentine dishes with seasonal, locally sourced ingredients. The outdoor patio fronting a pond with vineyard views is an idyllic spot on a sunny afternoon.

★**Taverna Beer Hall** BEER HALL
(☎0261-496-6161; Viamonte 4561, Chacras de Coria; ⊙7pm-3am Wed-Sat) Great vibe at this place with vaulted ceilings, communal tables and stained glass for a warm glow. Live music Thursday to Saturday nights.

Orientation

Maipú is just southeast of the Mendoza city center on the eastern side of RN 40; it's 17km from Plaza Independencia in Mendoza to Plaza 12 de Febrero in Maipú. Chacras de Coria is 18km due south of Mendoza on the western side of RN 40. Further south from here is Luján de Cuyo. RN 82 (Ruta Panamericana) marks its western border, before heading out along Río Mendoza and up into the mountains and Cacheuta.

Getting There & Away

To get to Maipú, catch the 10, 171, 172 or 173 bus from the bus stop on the corner of La Rioja and Catamarca in Mendoza and get off at the triangular roundabout. Or take the Metrotranvía (p329) from one of the stops along Belgrano in the Mendoza city center. A taxi should run around AR$75 to AR$100 – be sure to settle upon a fare in advance.

For Luján de Cuyo, a new hop-on, hop-off service, Bus Vitivinícola (p340), stops at a handful of wineries in Luján del Cuyo (three different itineraries) and Valle de Uco; the latter route is available only on Sundays. Buses begin the day with pickups from a variety of hotels in Mendoza.

Other areas like Chacras de Coria and Luján de Cuyo are reachable by public bus; however, they are more conveniently accessible in a rental car.

Many people visit Maipú and Luján de Cuyo as part of a guided tour from Mendoza.

Getting Around

Some people opt to tour Maipú on self-guided bicycle tours. Most bodegas are too spread out to make walking a convenient option.

A new hop-on, hop-off bus service, the **Maipú Wine Bus** (AR$200), operates around Maipú, an affordable compromise between cycling or taxiing around on your own and paying for a guided tour. Buses leave from the Estación Gutierrez in Maipú at 10:10am, 11:30am, 12:50pm, 2:10pm, 3:30pm and 4:50pm.

The center of Chacras de Coria has several good restaurants and bodegas within walking (and cycling) distance of one another.

Cacheuta

☎02624 / POP 640 / ELEV 1237M

About 40km southwest of Mendoza, in the mountains above the department of Luján de Cuyo, Cacheuta is rightfully renowned for its open-air medicinal thermal waters and agreeable microclimate. Two separate complexes – the more populous, larger and kid-friendly **Complejo Termal Cacheuta** (Parque de Agua; ☎02624-490-152; www.termascacheuta.com; RP 82, Km 41; adult/child under 10yr weekday AR$150/120, weekend AR$180/150; ⊙10am-6pm; 👪) and supremely tranquil and upscale **Spa Cacheuta** (☎0261-429-9133; www.termascachueta.com; RP 82, Km 38; AR$850; ⊙10am-6:30pm), owned by the same family – are near one another and share a similar bucolic cliffside setting.

Sleeping & Eating

Hotel Cacheuta HOTEL **$$$**
(☎02624-490-153; www.termascacheuta.com; RP 82, Km 38; s/d with full board from US$126/228; 📶🏊) There is lodging at the lovely and homey family-run hotel, where prices include access to the wonderful spa baths, swimming pool and massage. Eight of the 16 rooms have mountain and pool views. The ruins of an early 20th-century, larger and grander hotel, as well as a rail station are visible – old photos also attest to its former golden age.

Meals are as much a highlight as the views and spa, especially the gluttony-inducing buffet lunch. A small church, circa 1916, sits in the parking lot in front of the hotel.

Getting There & Away

Cacheuta is only 42km southwest of Mendoza, via RN 82, which is most easily accessible from Chacras de Coria or Vistalba, suburbs south of the city center.

Complejo Termal Cacheuta and Hotel Cacheuta run minivans from hotels in Mendoza to Cachueta and back daily.

Expreso Uspallata (in Mendoza 0261-438-1092) runs daily buses to Cacheuta (AR$33, 1¼ hours) from Mendoza.

Potrerillos

02624 / ELEV 1351M

Set above 12km-long Potrerillos reservoir in beautiful Andean *precordillera* (foothills), the small village of Potrerillos is one of Mendoza's white-water hot spots, usually visited during a day's rafting trip from the capital. Argentina Rafting (p317) and **Potrerillos Explorer Rafting** (in Mendoza 0261-653-8204; www.potrerillosexplorer.com.en) offer rafting and kayaking on the Río Mendoza. Trips range from a 5km, one-hour Class II float to a 50km, five-hour Class III–IV descent over two days.

Sleeping & Eating

★Gran Hotel Potrerillos RESORT $$
(0262-448-2001; www.granhotelpotrerillos.com; RN 7, Km 50; d US$138;) On a large hilltop property with commanding views and blending Spanish mission-style architecture with contemporary design, this is indeed one of the region's finest hotels. The 34 rooms with boutique features and colorful textiles are thoroughly modern and the common areas warm and inviting. Horseback riding, windsurfing, rafting and hiking are offered. The pool looks out onto a small vineyard.

La Escondida ARGENTINE $$
(0261-15-416-0246; Arroyo Pichueta; mains AR$220; 11am-5pm) Worth a stop when driving between Mendoza and the mountains, especially for Escondida's porch with views and charcuterie plate. Empanadas and steak are the main specialties and there's good if expensive beer, and of course a selection of malbec.

Getting There & Away

Most visitors to Portrerillos are on day trips from Mendoza (70km), on organized tours or in their own vehicles. Uspallata is only 50km to the north, along RN 7.

Uspallata

02624 / POP 3800 / ELEV 1751M

A humble little crossroads town on the way to the Chilean border, Uspallata is an oasis of poplar trees set in a desolate desert valley. The polychrome mountains surrounding the town so resemble highland Central Asia that director Jean-Jacques Annaud used it as the location for the epic film *Seven Years in Tibet*.

The town first gained fame as a low-budget base for the nearby ski fields at Los Penitentes, but has been coming into its own, with a few companies offering treks, horseback riding and fishing expeditions in the surrounding countryside.

Several places in the area retain their Incan names, a testament to the importance of their presence here prior to the arrival of the Spanish colonialists.

Sights & Activities

Fishing enthusiasts needn't be deterred by the high altitude. Río El Tigre, at 2600m, offers year-round trout fishing with the snow-capped Andean peaks in the near distance. There's also horseback riding and hiking in the nearby *precordilleras*. Ski and climbing shops rent equipment for those heading to Los Penitentes and Parque Provincial Aconcagua respectively.

Cerro Tunduqueral ARCHAEOLOGICAL SITE
(RP 52; 11am-6:30pm) FREE An easy 8km walk (or an easier drive) north of town brings you to Cerro Tunduqueral, where you'll find sweeping views and Inca rock carvings; *Seven Years in Tibet* scenes were shot here.

Tours

Desnivel Aventura OUTDOORS
(0261-15-554-8872; www.desnivelaventura.com; RN 7) Desnivel Aventura offers a range of outdoor activities, including horseback riding, mountain-bike tours, rock climbing, trekking and 4WD off-roading. It also rents mountain bikes (per hour/day AR$50/400). Friendly staff are a good source of general information about the area. Attached to the YPF gas station at main intersection.

Fototravesías 4x4 TOURS
(0261-15-511-9512; www.fototravesias4x4.com.ar) Fototravesías 4x4, near the main intersection, offers exciting 4WD tours and hiking in the surrounding mountains. The owner is a photographer and is especially amenable to ensuring travelers get good shots. Also, provides transfers to and from Los Penitentes for skiers in the winter.

Sleeping & Eating

Hostel Cerro de Cobre HOSTEL $
(0261-15-507-0883; www.hostelcerrodecobre.com; RN 7, Km 1143; dm US$30;) In a faux log cabin building 5km south of town, this

is good value, especially if you're the only one occupying one of the large dorm rooms. You make your own bed, and bath towels are provided. The cozy kitchen is available for guest use and a very basic breakfast is served in the attached TV room.

Hostel International Uspallata HOSTEL $
(☎0261-15-466-7240; www.hosteluspallata.com.ar; RN 7 s/n, Km 1141; dm/d US$11/45, cabins US$60-80;) Friendly hostel 7km east of town, with plain but comfortable rooms and a couple of sweet little cabins. Dinner (AR$120) is available. There's good hiking from the hostel and you can rent bikes and horses here. Ask the bus driver to drop you at the front before you hit Uspallata.

Hostería Los Cóndores HOTEL $$
(☎02624-420-002; www.loscondoreshotel.com.ar; Las Heras s/n; s/d US$63/92;) Close to the junction, this is the finest hotel in the center of town, which is faint praise since there's not much competition. The rooms could use an update, but there's a small indoor pool and gut-busting breakfast buffet.

Chocolates Cosita Suiza CAFE $
(Las Heras; sandwiches AR$80; 8:30am-1pm & 4-9pm;) Cozy little spot attached to the Hotel Los Cóndores with a crackling fire and old-timey skis on the ceiling. Real espresso drinks, hard to find elsewhere in Uspallata, as well as simple sandwiches, pies and cakes, make it a worthwhile stop.

El Rancho PARRILLA $$
(cnr RN 7 & Cerro Chacay; mains AR$140-360; noon-3pm & 7pm-1am Tue-Sun;) Uspallata's most upscale restaurant has an open barbecue grill carved out of a wall in the center of the dining room. Meat, especially a good roasted *chivo* (goat), is the way to go; trout and salmon also available, as well as very ordinary pasta dishes and sandwiches.

Information

Banco de la Nación The town's only bank with an ATM.

Tourist Office (☎02624-420009; RN 7 s/n; 8am-9pm) This tiny office is across from the YPF gas station. It has good information on local sights and activities and some very basic (but still useful) area maps.

Getting There & Away

Expreso Uspallata (☎0261-432-5055) and Buttini runs several buses daily to and from Mendoza (AR$107, 2½ hours). Buses continue from Uspallata along RN 7 to Las Cuevas (AR$76, two hours), near the Chilean border, and stop en route at Los Penitentes, Puente del Inca and the turnoff to Laguna Los Horcones for Parque Provincial Aconcagua. They can be flagged from all of these locations on their return to Uspallata from Las Cuevas.

RN 7 gets closed down suddenly and for extended periods during winter snowstorms.

Buses to Barreal in San Juan province (AR$200, 2½ hours) leave Sunday, Tuesday, Thursday and Friday. The road (RP 149) is a rough, rocky and scenic stretch for 38km and paved the remainder. There are two well-marked Incan archaeological sites along the way.

Andesmar has daily morning departures to Santiago (AR$650, six hours) and Valparaíso (AR$500, seven hours) in Chile. You'll also see loads of Ormeño (a Peruvian company) and TAS Choapa (a Chilean company) buses running through Uspallata on their way to the border.

All buses leave from the Expreso Uspallata office in the little strip mall near the junction.

Getting Around

Because of Upsallata's proximity to the border crossing with Chile there are frequent police roadside checkpoints. Be sure to have your ID handy. If driving your own vehicle, you'll likely be asked to pop your trunk and show your driver's license and insurance information.

Los Penitentes

☎02624 / ELEV 2581M

So named because the pinnacles resemble a line of monks, Los Penitentes has inspiring scenery and, depending on the year, often good snow cover for skiing in winter (these days, there is significantly less and less snow – the resort didn't open in 2017). Out of season, it's mostly shuttered, barren (far above the tree line) and abandoned, and somewhat resembles the hotel from the film *The Shining*. You can ride the lift to the peak in the summer. It's only 165km west of Mendoza via RN 7, and so primarily visited on day trips.

In high ski season (July and August) and during peak climbing season (December through to March), it's recommended to make reservations in advance.

Activities

Los Penitentes SKIING
(www.penitentesweb.com; RN 7; lifts pass per day AR$750; 9am-4pm) This ski resort, quiet for much of the year, comes alive with

day-trippers from Mendoza when there is snow. Skiing itself is more than serviceable, especially considering it's only 165km west of Mendoza via RN 7. The 'village' at the base is run-down and it's directly on the highway; however, it's situated amid Andean high peaks, including nearby Cerro Aconcagua.

Sleeping & Eating

Hostel Campo Base Los Penitentes HOSTEL $
(in Mendoza 0261-624-7900; www.penitentes.com.ar; RN 7; dm US$31) A cozy converted cabin, owned by Mendoza's HI Campo Base, accommodates 38 people in extremely close quarters, and has a kitchen, wood-burning stove and three shared bathrooms. It's good fun with the right crowd. Meals are available (AR$70 to AR$100).

Refugio Aconcagua HOTEL $$
(in Mendoza 0261-424-1565; RN 7, Km 1212; r with half board per person US$110) There's nothing fancy about the rooms at this place, easily identified by the Coca-Cola-emblazoned roof, but they're an OK size, and considering you're in the middle of the resort, with a private bathroom and two meals a day, they're not bad value. The restaurant here serves up hearty set meals (AR$150 to AR$220).

Getting There & Away

Buttini buses connect Mendoza and Los Penitentes (AR$130, 3¾ hours), with stops along the way in Potrerillos and Uspallata.

Several ski shops in Mendoza, as well as Uspallata, also run shuttle services to the mountain in the high season.

Winter storms can close RN 7 with little notice and for days at a time.

Parque Provincial Aconcagua

North of RN 7, nearly hugging the Chilean border, **Parque Provincial Aconcagua** (10am-6pm) protects 710 sq km of the wild high country surrounding the western hemisphere's highest summit, 6962m (922,841ft) Cerro Aconcagua. Passing motorists (and those who time their buses correctly) can stop to enjoy the view of the peak from **Laguna Los Horcones**, a 2km walk from the parking lot just north of the highway.

Only highly experienced climbers should consider climbing Aconcagua without the relative safety of an organized tour – even then, it's a serious climb that requires training and preparation.

Activities

Even if you're not here to summit – and most visitors aren't – you can experience the majestic scenery on short hikes in the park. Highly recommended is the 16km roundtrip to **Confluencia** (3400m), the first base camp for climbers on the Northwest Route. It's best to budget four to six hours – obviously, you can stop at any time to shorten the distance (at only 2km oneway, the small glacier lake, **Laguna Horcones** is a good turnaround point). It's at high altitude and involves 400m of elevation gain, so the non-acclimatized should expect some aerobic challenges. The trail begins at the parking lot 1km past the ticket office of the park's

WORTH A TRIP

CRISTO REDENTOR

Pounded by chilly but exhilarating winds, the rugged high Andes make a fitting backdrop for 3832m **Cristo Redentor** (Christ the Redeemer), the famous monument erected at El Cumbre pass after a territorial dispute between Argentina and Chile was settled in 1902. The view, a must-see, either with a tour or by private car, is reached via a narrow dirt and gravel road with no guardrails, steep drop-offs and hairpin turns. (Confident drivers only.) If you have even a hint of vertigo, you'll be miserable. The first autumn snowfall closes the route. You can hike the very steep 8km up to El Cristo via trails from the roadside if you don't have a car – only possible from December to February; otherwise, ice renders it too dangerous.

It's also possible to bypass the main Paso Internacional Los Libertadores (p332) border crossing into Chile by driving over the pass, down an equally intimidating road, before meeting the highway (Rte 60) 6km before the immigration and customs post. This is a potentially dangerous drive, never to be attempted in rainy or inclement weather.

Laguna Horcones entrance. Permits are AR$200 (to Laguna Horcones AR$20) and you'll need your passport. Some tour and climbing companies in Mendoza offer this trip as well.

Trekking companies also offer three-day trips to **Plaza Francia** (4200m), at the South Face, the next base camp after Confluencia.

Tours

Many of the adventure-travel agencies in and around Mendoza arrange excursions into the high mountains. It is also possible to arrange trips with some overseas-based operators.

Several guides from the Asociación Argentina de Guías de Montaña (www.aagm.com.ar) lead two-week trips to Aconcagua, including **Pablo Reguera** (0249-15-448-1074; www.pabloreguera.com.ar) and **Mauricio Fernández** (www.summit-mza.com.ar).

All guides and organized trips are best set up online or by telephone *at least* a month in advance. Everything – guides, mules, hotels etc – must be booked far in advance during peak climbing months.

Prices vary between operators and depend very much on what is included in the expedition, but US$3500 is a ballpark figure for the basic Aconcagua ascent.

Fernando Grajale HIKING
(0261-658-8855; www.grajales.net) A well-established and highly recommended operator with experience on the main and less-traveled routes. Its base camps are served by professional chefs and internet access.

Inka Expediciones HIKING
(0261-425-0871; www.inka.com.ar; Av Juan B Justo 345, Mendoza; 9am-6pm Mon-Fri, to 1pm Sat) Company with more than 1000 expeditions in the bank offering fixed and tailor-made expeditions.

Sleeping

Portezuelo del Viento HOSTEL $
(0261-651-1466; www.portezuelodelviento.com; RN 7, Km 1233, Las Cuevas; dm from US$25) One of the last lodging options on the Argentine side of the border and one of the few truly open year-round. Basic dorm rooms with a cozy, log-cabin feel to the lounge.

Hostel El Nico HOSTEL $
(0261-592-0736; elnicohostel@gmail.com; RN 7, KM 1221, Puente del Inca; dm/d US$25/55) A cozy little hostel sleeping 14 people, only 50m from Puente del Inca stone bridge. Can organize treks in summer and snowshoe and skiing expeditions in winter.

OFF THE BEATEN TRACK

PARQUE PROVINCIAL VOLCÁN TUPUNGATO

Tupungato (6650m) is an impressive volcano, partly covered by snowfields and glaciers, and serious climbers consider the mountain a far more challenging, interesting and technical climb than Aconcagua. The main approach is from the town of Tunuyán, 82km south of Mendoza via RN40, where the tourism office (p340) can provide info. Many of the outfitters who arrange Parque Provincial Aconcagua treks can also deal with Tupungato.

Information

During trekking season there are rangers stationed at Laguna Los Horcones; the Confluencia camp; at Plaza de Mulas and Nido de Cóndores on the main route to the peak; at Quebrada de Vacas; Pampa de Leñas; and Casa de Piedra and Plaza Argentina, along the Polish Glacier Route.

Check out the Mendoza-based journal *Cumbres* (www.revistacumbres.com.ar) for stories, photos, history and services for trekking here and in other nearby Andean peaks.

The website www.aconcagua.com.ar and Mendoza government's website, www.aconcagua.mendoza.gob.ar, are also helpful.

Getting There & Away

The two park entrances – Laguna Los Horcones and Punta de Vacas – are directly off RN 7 and are well signed. The Los Horcones turnoff is only 4km past Puente del Inca. If you're part of an organized tour, transport will be provided. To get here by bus, take an early morning Expreso Uspallata bus from Mendoza. Buses bound for Chile will stop at Puente del Inca, but often fill up with passengers going all the way through.

If only visiting the park for a day hike, you can grab a Buttini bus in Mendoza or Uspallata and ask to be dropped at the park's entrance at Los Horcones. When returning, walk back along the RN 7 to Puente del Inca to grab a Mendoza-bound bus back down. Check schedules, which change depending on season, in advance.

If driving your own vehicle, there's parking at the Los Horcones entrance.

CLIMBING CERRO ACONCAGUA

Often called the 'roof of the Americas,' the volcanic summit of Aconcagua covers a base of uplifted marine sediments of relatively young age, in geologic terms. In fact, the mountains are growing around 1cm a year. The origin of the name is unclear; one possibility is the Quechua term *ackon-cahuac*, meaning 'stone sentinel,' while another is the Mapuche phrase *acon-hue*, signifying 'that which comes from the other side.'

Italian-Swiss climber Matthias Zurbriggen made the first recorded ascent in 1897. Since then, the peak has become a favorite destination for climbers from around the world, even though it is technically less challenging than other nearby peaks. In 1985 the Club Andinista Mendoza's discovery of an Incan mummy at 5300m on the mountain's southwest face proved that the high peaks were a pre-Columbian funerary site.

Reaching the summit requires a commitment of at least 13 to 15 days, including acclimatization time.

Technical climbing skills aren't at a premium, except on the Polish Glacier Route, whereas aerobic endurance and overall fitness and strength are. The climbing season is from mid-November to the end of March.

The cost of renting cargo mules, which can carry about 60kg each, has gone through the roof. If you're going up on an organized tour, mules are, of course, included in the overall cost of the trip.

Potential climbers should acquire RJ Secor's climbing guide *Aconcagua* (1999).

Permits

From December to March permits are obligatory for both trekking and climbing in Parque Provincial Aconcagua; park rangers at Laguna Los Horcones will not permit visitors to proceed up the Quebrada de los Horcones without one. Fees vary according to the complex park-use seasons: a high-season ascent with assistance via Horcones/Vacas costs US$944/1133; a low-season trek of seven days via either route with assistance costs US$261. Check www.aconcagua.mendoza.gob.ar for the latest information.

Organized tours rarely, if ever, include the park entrance fee. Fees should be paid in Argentine pesos but can be paid in US dollars, and you must bring your original passport with you when you pay the fee. The permit begins from when you enter the park.

All permits are available only in Mendoza at the Ministerio de Turismo (p328).

Routes

There are three main routes up Cerro Aconcagua. The most popular one, approached by a 40km trail from Los Horcones, is the **Northwest Route** (Ruta Noroeste, also called the 'Normal Route') from Plaza de Mulas, 4230m above sea level. The **South Face** (Pared Sur), approached from the base camp at Plaza Francia via a 36km trail from Los Horcones, is a demanding technical climb.

From Punta de Vacas, 15km southeast of Puente del Inca, the longer but more scenic **Polish Glacier Route** (Ruta Glaciar de los Polacos) first ascends the Río de las Vacas to the base camp at Plaza Argentina, a distance of 76km. Climbers on this route must carry ropes, screws and ice axes, in addition to the usual tent, warm sleeping bag and clothing, and plastic boots. This route is more expensive because it requires the use of mules for a longer period.

Valle de Uco

Pear, potato, walnut, almond and garlic fields are interspersed with the picturesque vineyards that run up to the foothills of the Andes. Pumas come out at night and condors soar from cliff faces. Remote and poorly signposted, the Valle de Uco is nonetheless home to some of Mendoza's top wineries. Its versatile terroir (*terruño* in Spanish) and dry climate mean it's suitable for varietals that suffer from humidity. **Cerro Tupungato** (6570m), a semi-active volcano, looms majestically in the near distance with a solitary cloud almost perpetually hovering above its cone. **Tunuyán**, a fairly ordinary town built on and around RN 40, is the largest municipality in the valley.

The area is best visited on a guided tour, but if you've got the time and patience you can easily rent a car in Mendoza to make the trip.

Activities

Spectacular vineyards and wine tasting have put Valle de Uco on the map. Reservations are essential for touring any of the 'must-see' wineries in the region.

Wineries

★Monteviejo WINE
(www.monteviejo.com.ar; Clodomiro Silva s/n, Vista Flores; 4-course lunch incl wine AR$850; noon-3pm Mon-Sat) With a front facade of geometric cut outs and a back side featuring a sloping lawn of vines, Monteviejo is one of Valle de Uco's more architecturally impressive wineries, along with one of its best restaurants. It's part of the Clos de los Siete communal project of five wineries, all with owners of French ancestry. Monteviejo didn't produce its first vintage until 2002.

O. Fournier WINE
(02622-451 088; www.ofournier.com; Calle los Indios s/n; 9am-6pm) Possibly the valley's most architecturally stunning complex, O. Fournier is a modernist masterpiece set against a backdrop of nature's own sublime architecture. The 283-hectare estate has a similarly massive barrel room that doubles as an art gallery and restaurant, Urban at O. Fournier is run by co-owner and celebrity chef Nadia Harón.

Masi Tumpungato WINE
(0261-15-653-9573; www.masitupungato.com; Luis Pizarro, Km 3; tastings & tours 9:30am, 11:30am, 2pm & 3:30pm) Masi, owned by the seventh generation of an Italian winemaking family, is a fully organic operation built on the site of a former Coca Cola mint farm. It's one of the few wineries in the region to employ the *appassimiento* method, essentially a technique to dry out grapes even more after harvesting and before fermenting in tanks. Tours and tastings are extremely informative.

Vines of Mendoza WINE
(0261-461-3900; www.vinesofmendoza.com; RP 94; 11:30am-4pm Mon-Sat) A sort of gated community or cooperative of 190 winegrowers, from small hobbyists to small exporters. Vines provides the production facilities, staff and expertise. Vines itself produces around 25% of the total wine made here, and sells only in the resort and tastings. The Vines Resort & Spa (p340) and the restaurant Siete Fuegos, both highly recommended, are part of the development.

Salentein WINE
(0262-242-9000; www.bodegasalentein.com; RP 89 s/n; 9am-5pm Mon-Sat) A state-of-the-art, Dutch-owned winery that's distinctive for its architecturally cutting-edge design – appropriate as the lair of a James Bond villain – and museum-quality, on-site, contemporary-art gallery. Wine-wise, it also employs a unique method of moving grapes and juice by hand and gravity, rather than by machine. English-language tours take place at 11am and 3pm.

Andeluna Estate WINE
(0261-15-508-9525; www.andeluna.com.ar; RP 89, Km 11; 10am-5pm) Tastings of the wonderful wines produced here take place in a charming old-world, style tasting room. There are also great views of Cerro Tupungato from the patio and **restaurant**, which features delicious dishes like chard pastry, Paraguayan soup, veal casserole and homemade flan with *dulce de leche* (milk caramel).

Francois Lurton WINE
(Bodega Piedra Negra; 0261-441-1100; www.francoislurton.com; RP 94, Km 21) An ultramodern facility run by two French brothers from a famous winemaking family, producing one of the best Mendoza torrontés on the market. Excellent tours with impressive tasting areas and barrel room.

Fishing

Estancia San Pablo (0261-572-4486; www.sanpabloestancia.com; Tupungato; d US$200), a working ranch nearly the size of Bordeaux, France that stretches from dry foothills to snowcapped Andean peaks, has a narrow, gurgling brook ideal for trout fishing. Other rivers in the area include Manzanao Historico and El Manzanito. The season runs roughly from October to April. Contact Trout & Wine (p319) in Mendoza for guided trips.

Sleeping & Eating

Postales Hotel BOUTIQUE HOTEL $$
(0261-545-7624; www.postalesarg.com/home-en; Colonia las Rosas; d US$125;) The small, low-slung adobe building offers low-key valley digs with a backyard pool, vineyard and unobstructed views of the Andes. Rooms have high ceilings, comfy beds and

WORTH A TRIP

PUENTE DEL INCA

One of Argentina's most striking natural wonders, this **stone bridge** over the Río de las Cuevas was used by Inca traveling in the area. It glows a dazzling orange from the sediment deposited by the warm sulfuric waters. The brick ruins of an old spa, built as part of a resort and later destroyed by flood, sit beneath the bridge, slowly yielding their form to the sulfuric buildup from the thermal water that trickles over, around and through it. Due to the unstable nature of the structure, the area has been closed off and you can't cross the bridge or enter the hot baths, but you can still get some fairly wild photos.

Puente del Inca enjoys a spectacular setting, and whether or not you climb (those tackling Cerro Aconcagua usually overnight here), it's a good base for exploring the area. Trekkers and climbers can head north to the base of Aconcagua, south to the pinnacles of Los Penitentes, or even further south to 6650m Tupungato (p337).

About 1km before Puente del Inca (directly across from Los Puquios), the small **Cementerio Andinista** is a cemetery for climbers who died on Aconcagua.

Buses from Chile pass through (it's only 1km from the immigration and customs post at **Horcones**) but are often full and won't stop to pick you up. Nearly every Mendoza tour operator offers day tours to Puente del Inca in the summer months.

large bathrooms, but it's the lodge-cum-dining room that is truly special, especially on cool nights with the fireplace blazing while you enjoy the talented chef's inventive dishes and a glass of wine.

Tupungato Divino INN **$$**
(☎0262-244-8948; www.tupungatodivino.com.ar; cnr RP 89 & Calle los Europeos; r from US$125; ❄@📶) A wonderfully atmospheric and tranquil place with friendly hosts and inspiring views.

★**Casa Antucura** GUESTHOUSE **$$$**
(☎0261-15-339-0491; Barandica s/n, Tunuyán; r from US$320; ❄@🏊) Set in the middle of 94 hectares of vineyard, Casa Antucura is one of the more intimate wine lodges. Of the eight rooms, only two have mountain views – try to get one if you can.

Vines Resort & Spa RESORT **$$$**
(☎0261-461-3900; www.vinesresortandspa.com; RP 94, Km 11; d US$750; ❄@📶🏊) One of the valley's most luxurious resorts looks fit for a magazine shoot or as the lair of a Bond villain. Even the gym, a modernist structure perched over the vineyard, is architecturally stunning. Only four years old and with 21 rooms varying in size from 90 to 240 sq m. The resort's restaurant **Siete Fuegos** (7fuegos@vinesresortandspa.com; mains AR$480-920; ⏰12:30pm-4pm & 8:30-11pm) is a destination in itself.

Ilo Tupungato SEAFOOD **$$**
(☎0262-248-8323; Belgrano 703, Tupungato; mains AR$110-250; ⏰noon-3pm & 8pm-midnight Mon-Sat) Ilo is generally considered the best place to eat in Tupungato – the good range of seafood dishes, especially shellfish, makes it a local winemakers' favorite.

ℹ Information

Tourism Office (Centro de Informes; www.valledeuco.tur.ar; Belgrano 1060, Hotel Turismo Tupungato) Has an excellent website with suggested itineraries in the valley.

ℹ Getting There & Away

The majority of travelers visit Valle de Uco on a guided wine-tasting tour from Mendoza. You can take a taxi from Mendoza, but it's challenging to get around on your own once in the area.

The most convenient way is to rent a car in Mendoza. Many of the old roads in the area are former cattle crossings, some in poor conditions and best navigated cautiously.

The hop-on, hop-off **Bus Vitivinícola** (☎0800-122-2282, 0261-596-5308; www.busvitivinicola.com; AR$550-850) tours Valle de Uco on Sundays with stops at Monteviejo, Salentein and Andeluna.

San Rafael

☎0260 / POP 130,000 / ELEV 690M

A busy, modern town, originally founded in 1895, whose streets are lined with majestic old sycamores and open irrigation channels. San Rafael reveals its charms slowly – if you have a few days, it's worth giving it a chance. There is nothing to do in town – part of its allure, really – except wander the shady streets and plazas or while the day away in a cafe. There are, however, several esteemed wineries within biking distance that are well worth a visit; dozens more are little, family-run bodegas. The town is best thought of as a base for exploring nearby regions, especially Cañon del Atuel and Valle Grande.

Activities

Serious oenophiles come here to check out quality vinos at the city's esteemed bodegas. Wine tourism is relatively undeveloped, but most wineries offer free tours and tastings and are just outside downtown, easily visited by taxi or bicycle.

There's no shortage of outdoor activities available nearby, including rafting on level IV and V rapids on Río Diamante, and a smorgasbord of river and land activities available in Valle Grande.

★Bodega La Abeja WINE
(0260-443-9804; www.bodegalaabeja.com.ar; Av H Yrigoyen 1900; 9am-5pm Mon-Sat) FREE San Rafael's first winery, established in 1885 by the Iselin family (also founders of the city) is worth a visit to check out the original machinery and learn how the process of making sparkling wines developed from the old ancestral method. Tours in English with reservations.

Casa Bianchi WINE
(0260-444-9661; www.vbianchi.com; cnr RN 143 & Valentín Bianchi; tasting & tours AR$35; 9am-noon & 2:30-5pm Mon-Sat) Entering San Rafael, you can't miss the large, modern and highly regarded Bianchi Champañera perched on a small hill just before the airport on RN 143. Tours are friendly, offering visitors a glimpse into the making of sparkling wine; English is spoken.

Suter WINE
(0260-442-1076; www.sutersa.com.ar; Av H Yrigoyen 2850; 9:30am-1pm & 2-6pm Mon-Fri, 9:30am-1pm & 2-5pm Sat) FREE Situated halfway between Fincas Andinas and San Rafael, Suter is a rather unromantic, modern affair, but makes for a worthwhile stop if you want some discounted wine. You can organize a half-day tour, visiting the vineyards with an agronomist, tasting specialty wines and eating a big lunch in the vineyard.

Ciclos Adelcor CYCLING
(0260-442-0102; Av H Yrigoyen 703; per hour AR$20; 9am-1pm & 4-8pm Mon-Sat) Several places around town rent out clunkers, but if you're looking for a smooth ride, try Ciclos Adelcor.

Sleeping

★Hotel Francia HOTEL $
(0260-442-9351; www.alojamientofrancia.com.ar; Francia 248; d from US$45;) Lovely, spacious rooms set around a leafy garden a couple of blocks from the main drag. The young couple (ask for Micaela) who run the place are charming and have loads of info on things to do in town and around.

San Martín Hotel & Spa HOTEL $$
(0260-442-0400; www.sanmartinhotelspa.com; San Martín 435; d US$81; P@) Small, relatively snazzy hotel and surprisingly good deal, with large, bright rooms, spacious and modern bathrooms and a full-service on-site day spa.

Hotel Regine HOTEL $$
(0260-442-1470; www.hotelregine.com.ar; Independencia 623; d from US$55;) Nothing out of the ordinary in terms of its simple, if good-sized rooms with aging furniture, this hotel's highlight is the beautiful backyard pool and garden area.

★Algodon Wine Estates Wellness Resort RESORT $$$
(www.algodonhotels.com; RN 144, Km 674; ste US$180-260; @) Luxurious bodega owned by a former professional golfer with spacious and sophisticated rooms in a classic finca-style lodge. Guests can play on the estate's golf course (Wednesday to Sunday), play tennis, and, of course, tour and taste Algodon's wines. **Chez Gaston**, the resort's restaurant, does haute *asado* and other gourmet dishes with seasonal and local ingredients.

Eating & Drinking

San Rafael's nightlife zone is spread out along eight blocks west of the casino at the corner of Yrigoyen and Pueyrredón. There are a handful of bars and clubs, but many of the latter don't survive for long. Otherwise, most restaurants are open late and make good places for drinks.

★Lupe Taqueria MEXICAN $$
(Av Chile 502; mains AR$150-175; 7pm-4am Tue-Sun;) A chance for a little variety, a welcome rarity in these parts, might make this taqueria's tacos and quesadillas seem exceptionally good. It's a cool and contemporary place with pastel-colored walls, Corona and Sol, as well as artisanal beers on offer, and live music weekend nights at 11pm.

La Máquina ARGENTINE **$$**
(Av Rivadavia 18; mains AR$230-400; ⏰8am-3pm & 8pm-midnight) Housed in a stately brick building with a sort of bland contemporary interior and appealing sidewalk seating, great for a sunny day, La Máquina is located across from the former train station. The varied menu runs the gamut from pizza to steak and potatoes. Service can be slow and sauces on the heavy side.

Diablo's SEAFOOD **$$**
(cnr Av H Yrigoyen & Castelli; mains AR$75-215; ⏰noon-1am Tue-Sun; 📶) This cozy little corner eatery features a great range of tapas, surprisingly fresh seafood dishes, some good local wines and an impressive range of imported and microbrew beers.

ℹ Information

Banco de Galicia (Av H Yrigoyen 28; ⏰9am-1pm Mon-Fri) Several banks along Av H Yrigoyen have ATMs, including Banco de Galicia.

Cambio Santiago (Almafuerte 64; ⏰9am-1pm & 4-9pm Mon-Fri, 9am-1pm Sat) Speedy service and good rates.

Hospital Teodoro J Schestakow (☎0260-442-4490; Emilio Civit 151; ⏰24hr) Recommended hospital.

Municipal Tourist Office (☎0260-442-4217; www.sanrafaelturismo.gov.ar; Av H Yrigoyen 1530; ⏰8am-8:30pm; 📶) A large, modern office lined with helpful staff supplying useful brochures and maps. Some English spoken.

ℹ Getting There & Away

San Rafael is 230km southeast of the city of Mendoza via RN 40 and RN 143, and 189km northeast of Malargüe via RN 40.

AIR

Aeropuerto Las Paredes (www.aa2000.com.ar; RN 143) is only 3km west of downtown.

Aerolíneas Argentinas (☎0260-443-8808; www.aerolineas.com.ar; Av H Yrigoyen 395; ⏰10am-6pm Mon-Fri, to 1pm Sat) Flies to and from Buenos Aires daily except Sunday.

BUS

San Rafael's **bus terminal** (☎0260-442-7720; General Paz 800) is an AR$40 taxi ride from downtown. If you're headed to Patagonia, there's one Transportes Leader minibus per day that leaves from the bus terminal for Buta Ranquil (AR$535, eight hours) in Neuquén province via Malargüe. It leaves at 7:30pm daily except on Saturday and seats sell out very quickly. Book (and pay) a couple of days in advance to ensure a seat.

There are regular daily departures to the following destinations.

Buses from San Rafael

DESTINATION	COST (AR$)	TIME (HR)
Bariloche	1375	14
Buenos Aires	1021	14
Córdoba	750	11
Las Leñas	150	3
Malargüe	147	2¼
Mendoza	160	3
Neuquén	920	9
San Luis	360	4

CAR

Renta Car (☎0260-442-4623; www.rentacarsur.com.ar; Av H Yrigoyen 797; ⏰9am-6pm Mon-Fri, 9am-1pm & 5-8pm Sat & Sun) offers the best deals on car rentals in town.

Cañon del Atuel & Valle Grande

South of San Rafael, along the Río Atuel, RP 173 passes through a multicolored ravine that locals compare to Arizona's Grand Canyon, though much of the 67km Cañon del Atuel has been submerged by four hydroelectric dams. Nevertheless, there is white-water rafting on its lower reaches, and several operators at the tourist complex of Valle Grande, midway down the canyon, do short but scenic floats down the river, and other water-based trips. Horseback riding, trekking, rappelling and canyoning are also offered.

Coming from San Rafael, you have two options for visiting the canyon. You can travel via RP 173 to Valle Grande to explore the lower reaches of the canyon and go rafting on the Río Atuel, returning the same way at the end of the day. This is easy to do in your own vehicle or via public bus.

Or you can make a full loop. To do this, you'll need a private vehicle, preferably a 4WD, or to join a tour group.You can travel in either direction, but the most sensible thing is to leave San Rafael on RP 144, and then take RP 180 to the Podunk village of El Nihuil, 79km from the city. RP 173 then turns into a dirt road through the scenic Cañon del Atuel all the way to the dam at Valle Grande. It's then paved all the way back to San Rafael. You'll have to start early in the morning to make this full loop.

Activities

There are loads of operators, but two especially good all-service ones offering water and land activities are **Raffeish** (www.raffeish.com.ar; RP 173, Km 29) and **Sport Star** (0260-15-458-1068; www.sportstaraventuras.com.ar; RP 173, Km 35). Big groups and families book things out in advance, so if visiting during the height of the summer, it's best to reserve ahead.

Sleeping

Hotel Valle Grande HOTEL $$
(0260-15-458-0660; www.hotelvallegrande.com; RP 173, Km 35; d from US$110;) One of the larger complexes, this ostensibly three-star hotel offers some of the better accommodations around, even if things are dated in terms of design and furnishings. The setting and grounds are lovely, and it has a good restaurant, too.

Cabañas Río Azul CABIN $$
(0260-442-3663; www.complejorioazul.com.ar; RP 173, Km 33; 2-/4-person cabins US$111/120;) Comfortable blue-roofed *cabañas* (cabins) with a lovely grassy area over the river – a great spot to while away a day or two in the sun, especially in the off-season.

Getting There & Away

Numerous San Rafael tour companies run day trips to Valle Grande, starting at AR$630. Three daily Iselin buses run from San Rafael's bus terminal to Valle Grande (AR$57, one hour). Several daily Buttini buses to El Nihuil (AR$57) take the alternative RP 144, which doesn't go through the canyon. Check schedules, which vary by season, in advance so you don't miss the last bus of the day back to town.

Malargüe

0260 / POP 25,000 / ELEV 1400M

Despite serving as a base for Las Leñas (one of Argentina's snazzier ski resorts), Malargüe is a mellow little town and popular as a cheaper alternative to the luxury hotels on the mountain.

Geologically distinct from the Andean mountains to the west, the volcanically formed landscapes surrounding Malargüe are some of the most mind-altering in Argentina, and have only recently begun to receive tourist attention. Visiting these places is impossible without your own transportation, though Malargüe's excellent travel agencies can arrange excursions to all of them.

Sights

★ **Parque Provincial Payunia** NATURE RESERVE
Just over 200km south of Malargüe on the RN 40, the spectacular Parque Provincial Payunia is a 4500-sq-km reserve with a higher concentration of volcanic cones (over 800 of them) than anywhere else in the world. The scenery is breathtaking and shouldn't be missed. The 12-hour 4WD tours or three-day horseback trips offered by most of the agencies in Malargüe are well worth taking. Be sure your tour stops at all the sites – those combining the visit with Laguna Llancancelo only visit half.

Laguna Llancancelo LAKE
Lying within its namesake fauna reserve about 60km southeast of Malargüe, Laguna Llancancelo is a high mountain lake visited by more than 100 bird species, including flamingos.

Planetarium PLANETARIUM
(0260-447-2116; www.planetariomalargue.com.ar; cnr Villegas & Aldeo; over/under 12yr AR$70/50; 5-9pm Mon-Fri, from 3pm Sat & Sun) Malargüe's remote location makes it a great spot for stargazing, and this Planetarium is an excellent, state-of-the-art complex featuring some freaky architecture and some reasonably entertaining audiovisual presentations.

Caverna de Las Brujas CAVE
(AR$380; sunrise-sunset) Caverna de Las Brujas is a magical limestone cave on Cerro Moncol, 72km south of Malargüe and 8km north of Bardas Blancas along RN 40. Its name means 'Cave of the Witches.' The cave complex stretches for 5km. Guided tours (admission and flashlights included in the price) take two to three hours. Tours depart with a minimum group size of two, although getting more people together will bring down the per-person cost. Check with tour operators in Malargüe for details.

Tours

Several companies offer excellent 4WD and horseback-riding excursions, and if you don't have a car, these are generally the best way to get into the surrounding mountains. One of the most exciting drives you may ever undertake is the 12-hour 4WD tour through Parque Provincial Payunia, a 4500-sq-km reserve with the highest concentration of volcanic cones in the world.

Caving is possible at Caverna de Las Brujas and Pozo de las Animas.

Karen Travel TOURS
(☎0260-447-2226; www.karentravel.com.ar; Av San Martín 54) With more than 20 years guiding experience, the English-speaking owner of Karen Travel runs a well-respected operation. It specializes in tours to Payunia (AR$1300), Cueva de las Brujas (AR$980) and Llancanelo Lagoon (AR$700). Customized multiday itineraries, including accommodations in Malargüe, are also available.

Payunia Travel TOURS
(☎0260-447-2701; www.payuniatravel.com; Av San Martín 13) Well-established agency in town offering 4WD, horseback and trekking tours in the surrounding countryside.

Festivals & Events

Fiesta Nacional del Chivo FOOD & DRINK
(eventos@malargue.gob.ar) All things *chivo* (goat), as well as the typical beauty-queen coronation, and music and dance performances, are celebrated the first weekend in January. Vegetarians may want to skip. If you love *asado*, this is the fiesta for you.

Sleeping & Eating

Malargüe has reasonably priced, if purely functional, accommodations, most lining Av San Martín, the city's main thoroughfare. Prices drop by up to 40% outside the ski season (mid-June to mid-September). Singles are nonexistent during ski season, when you'll likely be charged for however many beds are in the room.

★**Eco Hostel Malargüe** HOSTEL $
(☎0260-447-0391; www.hostelmalargue.net; Finca 65, Colonia Pehuenche; dm US$13, d with/without bathroom US$72/56;) Six kilometers south of town, this whimsically designed hostel and B&B is set on an organic farm and built using sustainable practices. Rooms are rustically simple but comfortable, the surrounds are beautiful, and breakfast (featuring farm produce) is a winner too.

★**Hotel Malargüe Suite** BOUTIQUE HOTEL $$
(☎0260-4472-3001; www.hotelmalarguesuite.com; RN 40 s/n; s/d from US$88/100; P@) At the northern edge of town, the most luxurious hotel for kilometers around lays it all on – buffet breakfast, art gallery, indoor pool... Rooms are spacious and modern and come with hydromassage tubs, which are a welcome sight after a hard day on the slopes.

El Quincho de María ARGENTINE $
(Av San Martín 440; mains AR$100-190; noon-3:30pm & 8-11pm) Centrally located, cozy little *parrilla*, where everything from the gnocchi to the empanadas is handmade. Don't miss the mouthwatering shish kebabs.

★**La Cima Restaurant & Parrilla** ARGENTINE $$
(☎0260-429-0671; San Martín 886; mains AR$150-255; noon-3pm & 8:30-11:30pm Mon-Sat;) The name, a holdover from when the restaurant was located at high altitude in Las Leñas, could refer to its status in the Malargüe dining scene, such as it is. It's at the top of the heap. Besides good-quality *asado*, there's rare variety on the menu, including salmon, trout, lasagna and a version of chop suey.

Information

Tourist Office (☎0260-447-1659; www.malargue.gob.ar; RN 40, Parque del Ayer; 8am-8pm) Helpful tourist office with facilities at the northern end of town, on the highway. A small **kiosk** (9am-9pm) also operates out of the bus terminal.

Getting There & Away

From Malargüe's **bus terminal** (cnr Av General Roca & Aldao) there are several direct buses to Mendoza daily (AR$276, five hours), plus others requiring a change in San Rafael (AR$138, three hours). Outside of winter, there's one bus per day to Los Molles and Las Leñas (AR$76, 1½ hours), leaving at 8:30am and returning from Las Leñas at 5:30pm.

From Malargüe the RN 40 winds its way south through rugged desert landscapes and into Neuquén province. Despite what many will tell you, there is public transportation along this route. Transportes Leader (www.leader.com.ar) has one minibus a day between San Rafael and Buta Ranquil Sunday to Friday, stopping in Malargüe (it operates out of Club Los Amigos pool hall). It's recommended that you book (and pay) at least two days in advance; it leaves Malargüe around 9pm (AR$271, five hours). From Buta Ranquil there are connections to Neuquén and Chos Malal, but you may get stuck for the night.

For winter transportation to Los Molles and Las Leñas ski resorts, Malargüe travel agencies offer a round-trip shuttle service, including ski rentals.

Las Leñas

0260 / ELEV 2240M

This is a big mountain, with some of the best off-piste skiing on the continent. However, its remoteness and high accommodations costs are obstacles to those without very deep pockets. Think of it as the Aspen of Argentina. Despite its old, rickety lifts, **Las Leñas** (0260-447-1281; www.laslenas.com; 1-day ticket AR$1270; 8:30am-5pm mid-Jun–late Sep) is the country's most self-consciously prestigious ski resort. Since its opening in 1983 it has attracted an international clientele, who spend their days on the slopes and nights partying until the sun comes up. Because of the dry climate, Las Leñas has incredibly dry powder.

Las Leñas is 445km south of Mendoza and 70km from Malargüe, all via RN 40 and RP 222.

Activities

On the map for world-class skiing, Las Leñas won't disappoint travelers who haul their way out here in the summertime – there's horseback riding, hiking, fishing, rappelling and mountain biking on offer. Keep in mind that many of the hotels shut down, however.

Sleeping

Las Leñas has five luxury hotels and a group of 'apart hotels' (Apart Hotel Delphos is a good one) all under the same management; make reservations through www.laslenas.com or **Ski Leñas** (in Buenos Aires 011-4819-6000; www.laslenasski.com; Cerrito 1186, 8th fl, Buenos Aires). Most are booked as part of a weeklong package, which includes lodging, unlimited skiing and two meals per day.

There are also small apartments with two to six beds and shared bathrooms, equipped with small kitchens; try **Manlio DeMartis** (0260-442-6665; www.demartis.com.ar). More economical accommodations are available at Los Molles, 20km down the road, or at Malargüe, 70km away.

★Hotel Piscis HOTEL $$$

(s/d per week from US$3864/4300;) The most extravagant of Las Leñas' lodgings is the nominally five-star, 99-room Hotel Piscis, with great valley views. Repairs and improvements are needed throughout, however it has wood-burning stoves, a gymnasium, sauna, an indoor swimming pool, the elegant **Las Cuatro Estaciones** restaurant, a bar, a casino and shops. Rates depend on the season.

★Virgo Hotel & Spa HOTEL $$$

(s/d per week from US$1400/2800;) The valley's largest and most modern hotel is ideally located at the resort's base. It has a heated outdoor swimming pool, sushi bar, whirlpool bath, wine bar, spa and cinema; it's also developed something of a reputation as a party spot so families with young'uns might need to look closely before booking.

Hotel Acuario HOTEL $$$

(s/d per week from US$1400/2800;) This small, recently refurbished ski-in/ski-out hotel at the base of the mountain has a good restaurant, bar and après-ski lounges.

Getting There & Away

Las Leñas is 445km south of Mendoza and 70km from Malargüe (the closest airport, with daily flights to Buenos Aires in ski season), all via RN 40 and RP 222. San Rafael, 200km away, is another option for flights.

There is a bus service operating in season from Mendoza (AR$300, 6½ hours), San Rafael (AR$160, three hours) and Malargüe (AR$85, 1½ hours).

If you're driving, tire chains are required in winter.

Los Molles

This dusty, windswept village would be slowly sinking into obscurity if not for its reasonably priced accommodations alternatives for those wishing to be near, but not in, the famed ski resort of Las Leñas. It also draws rock climbers, hikers and other rugged outdoor types, and there are thermal baths in the area. The village straddles RP 222, 55km northwest of Malargüe.

Sleeping

★Hostel Pehuenche HOSTEL $

(0260-15-436-4423; www.pehuenchehostel.com; dm US$24;) Hostel Pehuenche is one of the best set-up hostels in the country, offering a bar, 'digital playroom,' transfers to Las Leñas and snuggly duck-down comforters in cozy and functional rooms. Dinner (AR$250) is available for guests.

Hualum Hotel HOTEL $$
(☎0261-476-0409; www.hotelhualum.com.ar; RN 222, Km 30; d US$) Mountain lodge open year-round with small rooms, spacious lounge area and good restaurant.

Getting There & Away

Buses heading between Malargüe (AR$100, one hour) and Las Leñas (AR$30, 30 minutes) pass through the village. All hotels in Los Molles offer shuttle services to the ski resort.

San Juan

☎0264 / POP 503,000 / ELEV 650M

Life in this provincial capital with long, shaded avenues moves at its own pace, and the locals are humbly proud of their little town. In 1944 a massive earthquake destroyed the city center, killing more than 10,000 people – Juan Perón's subsequent relief efforts are what first made him a national figure.

No slouch on the wine-production front, San Juan's wineries are refreshingly low-key compared to the Mendoza bustle, and the province's other attractions are all within easy reach of the capital. Most come here en route to Parque Provincial Ischigualasto. Driving only a short distance north of town, you'll notice the dusty clouds produced by large-scale mining. To the south, just off RN 40, there are six olive-oil producers.

The city goes dead in summer, especially on Sunday, when all of San Juan heads to the nearby shores of Dique Ullum for relief from the sun.

Sights & Activities

Museo de Vino Santiago Graffigna MUSEUM
(☎0264-421-4227; www.graffignawines.com; Colón 1342 Norte; ⏲tours hourly 11:15am-4:15pm Thu-Sat) FREE Museo de Vino Santiago Graffigna is a wine museum housed in a handsome brick building, a reconstruction of what the winery looked like before the 1944 quake. It also has a wine bar where you can taste many of San Juan's best wines. The bodega produces both reds and whites; it's now owned by French beverage company, Pernod Ricard. Take bus 12A from in front of the tourist office on Sarmiento (AR$3, 15 minutes) and ask the driver to tell you when to get off.

Casa Natal de Sarmiento MUSEUM
(Sarmiento 21 Sur; ⏲9am-7pm Mon-Fri, to 2pm Sat, 11am-6pm Sun) FREE Casa Natal de Sarmiento is named for Domingo Faustino Sarmiento, whose prolific writing as a politician, diplomat, educator and journalist made him a public figure within and beyond Argentina. Sarmiento's *Recuerdos de Provincia* recounted his childhood in this house and his memories of his mother. It's now a museum and was the country's first national historic monument.

Dique Ullum WATER SPORTS
Only 18km west of San Juan, the 32-sq-km Dique Ullum is a center for nautical sports: swimming, fishing, kayaking, waterskiing and windsurfing (though no rental equipment is available). *Balnearios* (beach clubs) line its shores, and hanging out for a day in the sun is part of being in San Juan. At night, many of the *balnearios* function as dance clubs.

Bus 23 from Av Salta and bus 29 from the San Juan bus terminal via Av Córdoba both go hourly to the dam outlet.

Tours

Mario Agüero Turismo TOURS
(☎0264-422-5320; www.marioagueroturismo.tur.ar; General Acha 17 Norte; ⏲9am-1pm & 4-8pm Mon-Fri, 9am-1pm Sat) Recommended company offering organized tours of the area, most importantly to including Parque Provincial Ischigualasto.

Festivals & Events

Fiesta Nacional del Sol CULTURAL
(www.fiestanacionaldelsol.com) San Juan comes alive the last weekend in February with four nights of singing and dancing exhibitions and parading beauty queens elected from surrounding provinces. The final-night *espectáculo* (show) involving the selection of a fiesta queen takes place in the Autódromo Eduardo Copello.

Sleeping

San Juan Hostel HOSTEL $
(☎0264-420-1835; www.sanjuanhostel.net; Av Córdoba 317 Este; dm US$12, s/d US$25/32, without bathroom US$23/28; ❄@🛜) A basic hostel with a variety of aging rooms in a residential neighborhood placed conveniently between the bus terminal and downtown. Good info on tours and local attractions, and a rooftop patio.

RUTA DEL VINO DE SAN JUAN

San Juan's winery tourism industry isn't quite as developed as that of Mendoza, but in a lot of ways that's a good thing. There are no crowds for a start, and tours are occasionally conducted by the winemakers themselves. A few wineries have gotten together to promote the Ruta del Vino de San Juan (the San Juan Wine Route; www.rutadelvinosanjuan. com.ar). The best way to do it, if you want to hit them all in one day, is to hire a car. Starting from downtown San Juan, it's about a 40km roundtrip. It is feasible to do it by public transportation and taxi too.

The first stop on the route should be **Las Marianas** (✆0264-463-9136; www.bodega-lasmarianas.com.ar; Calle Nuevo s/n; ⊙10am-5pm Tue-Sat) **FREE**. One of the prettiest wineries in the region, this one was built in 1922, abandoned in 1950 and reinstated in 1999. The main building is gorgeous, with thick adobe walls and a few examples of the original winemaking equipment lying around. The mountain views out over the vineyard are superb. If you're coming by bus, catch the 16 (40 minutes) near the corner of Santa Fe and Mendoza in San Juan. Get off at the corner of Calle Aberastain and Calle Nuevo, where you'll see a signpost to the winery (an 800m walk).

Making your way back to Calle Aberastain, turn right and follow the road south for 500m to **Viñas de Segisa** (✆0264-492-2000; www.saxsegisa.com.ar; cnr Aberastain & Calle 15, Pocito; ⊙10am-7pm Mon-Sat, to 2pm Sun) **FREE**. This stately old winery has more of a museum feel than others. The tour of the underground cellar complex is excellent and tastings are generous.

If you're not up for a walk, now's the time to call a *remise* (shared taxi). If you are, make your way back north to Calle 14, turn right and continue for 5km until you hit RN 40. Turning left, after about 1km you'll come to **Fabril Alto Verde** (✆0264-421-2683; www.fabril-altoverde.com.ar; RN40, btwn Calle 13 & 14; AR$75; ⊙9am-1pm & 2:30-6:30pm Mon-Fri), a big, state-of-the-art winery that sells 90% of its wine for export; tours are in English or Spanish and come accompanied by a rather dreary promotional video. The award-winning organic brands Buenas Hondas and Touchstone are produced here.

Next, catch a 24 bus heading north on RN 40 up to Calle 11. Turning right down Calle 11 for 300m brings you to **Champañera Miguel Mas** (✆0264-422-5807; miguelmas@infovia.com.ar; RP 215, Villa Alberastain; ⊙9am-5pm Mon-Fri) ✔ **FREE**. This small winery makes some of the country's only organic sparkling wine, as well as other varieties. The whole process – apart from inserting the cork in bottles – is done by hand. Tours (in Spanish only) take you through every step of the process.

Make your way back out to RN 40, and flag down a 24 bus, which will take you back to the bus terminal in San Juan.

Hotel Selby　　　　　　　　HOTEL **$**

(✆0264-422-4766; www.hotelselby.com.ar; Rioja 183 Sur; s/d US$45/50; ❉🛜) There's nothing really flash going on here, but the rooms are a decent size and the downtown location can't be beat. Good value for the price.

Del Bono Suites Art Hotel　　　HOTEL **$$**

(✆0264-421-7600; www.delbonohotels.com/suites.html; Mitre 75 Oeste; d/ste US$96/110; ❉🛜🏊) Downtown's most contemporary hotel with design features taking the edge off the corporate blandness, this is a good deal for the price, and the well-stocked kitchenettes and rooftop pool are added bonuses.

🍴 Eating & Drinking

Tres Cumbres　　　　　　　　CAFE **$**

(Rivadavia 2; sandwiches AR$90; ⊙7:30am-10:30pm; ❉🛜) Centrally located modern coffee shop with windows looking out onto the city's main downtown plaza. Simple sandwiches, cookies, muffins, croissants and pies make it a good place to spend an afternoon.

Soychú　　　　　　　　VEGETARIAN **$**

(✆0264-422-1939; Av José Ignacio de la Roza 223 Oeste; mains AR$95; ⊙noon-3pm & 8pm-midnight Mon-Sat, noon-3pm Sun; ✔) Vegetarians rejoice! This simple restaurant – attached to a health-food store selling all sorts of groceries and a range of teas – has an

San Juan

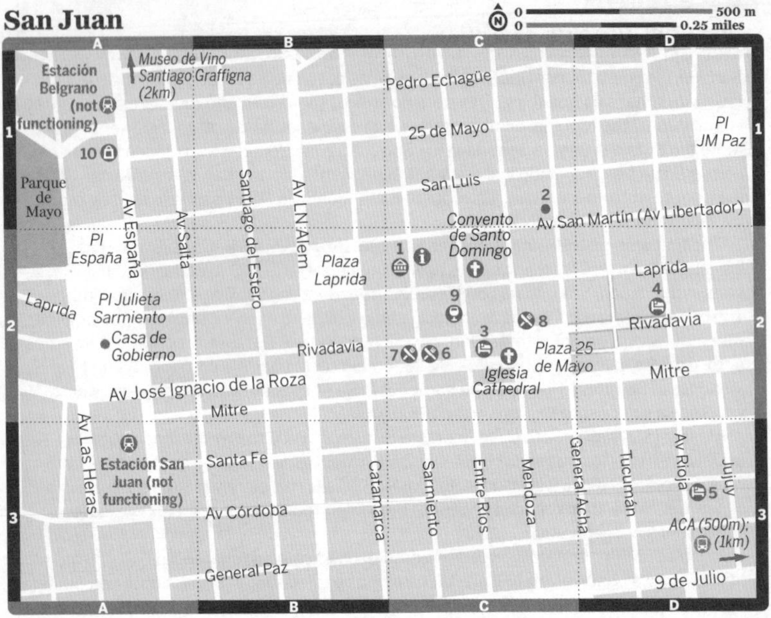

San Juan

Sights

1 Casa Natal de Sarmiento........C2

Activities, Courses & Tours

2 Mario Agüero Turismo........C1

Sleeping

3 Del Bono Suites Art Hotel........C2
4 Hotel Selby........D2
5 San Juan Hostel........D3

Eating

6 Remolacha........C2
7 Soychú........C2
8 Tres Cumbres........C2

Drinking & Nightlife

9 Flores Art Bar........C2

Shopping

10 Mercado Artesanal Tradicional........A1

excellent buffet with a wide range of tasty fare. Arrive early for the best selection since it's very popular with locals ordering take-out for the office.

Remolacha PARRILLA **$$**
(cnr Av José Ignacio de la Roza & Sarmiento; mains AR$118-350; ⏲noon-3pm & 8pm-1am) This place is one of the biggest *parrillas* in town. The dining room is a bit ordinary, but eating in the garden is a lush experience. Get a table by the picture windows looking into the kitchen and you'll be able to see your meal being hacked off the carcass before getting thrown on the flames. Excellent salads too.

★ **Flores Art Bar** BAR
(Entre Rios 145; ⏲7pm-3am) Granted, there's little to no competition, but this labyrinthine bar would qualify as cool in Buenos Aires or Mexico City – it is evocative of the latter with its tile work and pastel colors. Old American rock memorabilia hangs on the walls and small groups colonize the various rooms enjoying excellent cocktails and bar food. Fresh air is available in the upstairs outdoor patio.

Shopping

Mercado Artesanal Tradicional MARKET
(Traditional Artisans Market; Centro de Difusión Cultural Eva Perón, Av España; ⏲8:30am-8pm Mon-Fri,

9:30am-1:30pm Sat) The Mercado Artesanal Tradicional is an excellent local handicrafts market with an assortment of items for sale, including ponchos and the brightly colored *mantas* (shawls) of Jáchal.

ℹ Information

ACA (Automóvil Club Argentina; ☑ 0264-422-3781; 9 de Julio 802) Argentina's auto club; good source for provincial road maps.

Banco de San Juan (cnr Rivadavia & Entre Ríos; ⊙ 8:30am-12:30pm & 5-9pm Mon-Fri, 9am-1pm Sat) Has an ATM. There are plenty of other banks along the eastern edge of Plaza 25 de Mayo.

Cambio Santiago (General Acha 52 Sur; ⊙ 8am-1pm & 5-8:30pm Mon-Fri, 9am-1pm Sat) Money exchange with good rates and quick service.

Hospital Rawson (☑ 0264-422-2272; cnr General Paz & Estados Unidos) Recommended hospital.

Tourist Office (☑ 0264-421-0004; www. turismo.sanjuan.gob.ar; Sarmiento 24 Sur; ⊙ 8am-8pm) Has good city, wine-touring and regional maps, plus useful information on the rest of the province, particularly Parque Provincial Ischigualasto. Usually at least one English-speaking staff member.

ℹ Getting There & Away

San Juan is 170km north of Mendoza via RN 40 and 1140km from Buenos Aires.

AIR

Domingo Faustino Sarmiento Airport (Las Chacritas; ☑ 0264-425-4133; www.aa2000. com.ar) is 13km southeast of town on RN 20. A taxi or remise (radio taxi) costs AR$110.

Aerolíneas Argentinas (☑ 0264-421-4158; www.aerolineas.com.ar; Av San Martín 215 Oeste; ⊙ 10am-6pm Mon-Fri, to 1pm Sat) Three daily flights to Buenos Aires except Sunday (once only).

LATAM (www.latam.com) Flights to Santiago (Chile) on Tuesday, Thursday and Friday.

BUS

From San Juan's **bus terminal** (☑ 0264-422-1604; Estados Unidos 492 Sur) you can book tickets to Santiago, Viña del Mar and Valparaíso in Chile but you'll have to change buses in Mendoza, 167km to the south.

Except in summer, when there may be direct buses, travel to Patagonian destinations south of Neuquén requires a change of bus in Mendoza, though through-tickets can be purchased in San Juan. Various companies serve the following destinations daily.

Buses from San Juan

DESTINATION	COST (AR$)	HOUR (HR)
Barreal	125	4
Buenos Aires	1300	14
Calingasta	210	3½
Catamarca	1100	8
Córdoba	730	8½
Huaco	174	3
La Rioja	500	6
Mendoza	220	2½
Rodeo	180	3½
San Agustín de Valle Fértil	202	4
San José de Jáchal	130	2
San Luis	410	4
Tucumán	1026	13
Vallecito	72	1

ℹ Getting Around

If there's two or more of you, hiring a car to get to Ischigualasto can work out a better deal than taking a tour. The tourist office keeps a list of rental operators, including **Classic** (☑ 0264-422-4622; www.classicrentacar.com.ar; Av San Martín 163 Oeste; ⊙ 9am-7pm), across from the tourist office and **Trebol** (☑ 0264-670-2783; www.trebolrentacar.com.ar; Laprida 82 Este; ⊙ 9am-1pm & 5-9pm Mon-Fri), inside the Alkazar Hotel.

Barreal

☑ 02648 / POP 3500 / ELEV 1650M

Barreal's divine location makes it one of the most beautifully situated towns you'll likely ever come across. Sauces (weeping willows), álamos and eucalyptus trees drape lazily over the dirt roads that meander through town, and views of the Cordillera de Ansilta – a stretch of the Andes with seven majestic peaks ranging from 5130m to 5885m – are simply astonishing. Wandering along Barreal's back roads and down to the Río de los Patos is an exercise in dreamy laziness. To the south, Aconcagua and Tupungato are both visible, as is the peak of Cerro Mercedario (6770m).

Presidente Roca is the main drag through town, a continuation of RP 149 that leads from Calingasta to Barreal and on to Parque Nacional El Leoncito. Only a few streets

ENVIRONMENTAL ISSUES

Standing in a vineyard, surrounded by ripening grapes with the snowcapped Andes in the distance, the landscape appears as a picturesque mix of well-ordered agriculture and awe-inspiring nature. And because the wine industry is such an important pillar of the region's and country's economy, there's little doubt that its well-being is a priority. There are threats, of course.

Enormous copper and shale deposits have been discovered in the Mendoza region. Oil derricks dot the flat plains on the eastern side of the highway from San Rafael to San Juan. Large-scale gold mining and its concomitant environmental risks, namely cyanide leaking into rivers, has been going on just outside San Juan for more than a decade.

And of course, this desert region is dependent on snowmelt from the Andes to supply water to the dams which control irrigation to the vineyards and other farms. If the mountain glaciers disappear or the snow decreases due to global climate change, then Mendoza's future is imperiled.

have names; locals will be able to give you directions.

Sights & Activities

Only 22km south of town is Parque Nacional El Leoncito, worth visiting for short walks amidst stunning desert landscapes and nighttime stargazing. White-water rafting is excellent – more for the scenery than for the rapids themselves – and most trips start 50km upriver at **Las Hornillas**. Contact **Hostel Barreal** (☎0264-415-7147; www.hostelbarreal.com; San Martín s/n; dm/r per person US$10/14; 📶) for organized rafting adventures.

Parque Nacional El Leoncito PARK
(☎0264-844-1240) The 76-sq-km Parque Nacional El Leoncito occupies a former *estancia* (ranch) 22km south of Barreal. The landscape is typical of the Andean *precordillera*. The high, dry and wide-open valley rarely sees a cloud, making for superb stargazing. Hence, the park is home to the **Complejo Astronómico El Leoncito** (☎0264-421-3653; www.casleo.gob.ar; ⏰10am-noon & 2:30-5pm Apr-Sep, 10am-noon & 3-5:30pm Oct-Mar), which contains two important observatories, the Observatorio El Leoncito (C.AS.LEO) and Observatorio Cesco. Night visits are also possible, but must be scheduled ahead of time by contacting the Complejo's San Juan office.

Entre Tapias WINE
(☎0264-423-9070; www.entretapias.com; Presidente Roca s/n; ⏰10am-1pm & 5-8pm) The family-run high-altitude Entre Tapias (1650m) is the Valle de Calingasta's only boutique winery. It's a bucolic, low-key place with casual tastings and lunch and dinner available (reserve ahead).

Climbing

Las Hornillas (site of two *refugios* – rustic shelters – and a military outpost) also provides climbing access to the Cordón de la Ramada, which boasts five peaks over 6000m, including Cerro Mercedario. Climbing here is more technical than Aconcagua and many mountaineers prefer the area. Ramon Ossa, a Barreal native, is a highly recommended mountain guide and excursion operator who knows the cordillera intimately; contact him at **Posada Don Ramon** (☎0264-844-1004; www.fortunaviajes.com.ar; Presidente Roca s/n). He can arrange trips to Cerro Mercedario and expeditions across the Andes in the footsteps of San Martín, including mules and equipment.

For access to the *refugio* at Las Hornillas, climbing information, guide services and mountain-bike rental, visit Maxi at **Cabañas Kummel** (☎0264-404-0913; wm kummel@hotmail.com; Presidente Roca s/n).

Mauro Olivera, an experienced guide, can organize climbing trips including three days in the mountains and two nights at Posada Don Lisandro (per person AR$5000, minimum four people).

Hiking

At the south end of Presidente Roca is a sort of triangular roundabout. Follow the road east (away from the Andes) until it leads into the hills; you'll see a small **shrine** and you can hike into the foothills for more stunning views. Follow this road for 3km and you'll come to a mining site (the gate should be open). Enter and continue for 1km to reach a **petrified forest**.

Land Sailing

Barreal is best known for *carrovelismo* (land sailing), an exhilarating sport practiced on a small cart with a sail attached. Fanatics come from kilometers away to whizz around out on the gusty, cracked lake bed at **Pampa del Leoncito** (☎0264-622-2474; www.pampaelleoncito.com), about 20km from town and adjacent to the national park. Adventurers who want to give it a spin can try Mauro Olivera, who can provide the necessary equipment and also give lessons.

The high season, when winds reach near gale force every afternoon around 5pm, is from mid-October to mid-March.

Sleeping & Eating

During siesta time, when everything shuts down and Barreal feels like a ghost town, **Servicompras** (Presidente Roca s/n; ⏲24hr; 📶), the gas station, is your only option for scoring basic food and snacks. Otherwise, there are a few restaurants strung out along Presidente Roca (RN 149), Barreal's main thoroughfare.

★ Posada Don Lisandro HOSTEL **$**
(☎0264-505-9122; www.donlisandro.com.ar; San Martín s/n, RN 149; dm US$11, d with/without bathroom US$29/23; 📶) Mauro Olivera, an experienced land-sailer and climbing guide, runs this tiny posada (inn), housed in a building that's over 100 years old and has its original cane-and-mud ceilings, and a few sticks of antique furniture. The bed in the cozy room without a bathroom is especially comfortable. There's a well-stocked kitchen for guest use and a small bar for lounging.

Eco Posada El Mercedario POUSADA **$$**
(☎0264-15-509-0907; www.elmercedario.com.ar; Presidente Roca, cnr de los Enamorados; d US$57; ❄📶) Housed in Barreal's oldest building at the northern end of town, El Mercedario's rooms have a cozy, colonial-era vibe with antique furnishings that open up in back to a tranquil patio area and small farm. The restaurant serves breakfast and dinner for guests.

Restaurante Isidro ARGENTINE **$**
(Presidente Roca s/n; mains AR$100-200; ⏲8am-3pm & 8pm-11:30pm; 📶) Offers a fairly standard range of meats and pastas, and some good meat empanadas. Also a good selection of wines from the San Juan region.

Information

Banco de la Nación (Presidente Roca s/n; ⏲9am-1pm Mon-Fri) Has an ATM.

Tourist Office (☎02648-441066; Presidente Roca s/n; ⏲9am-midnight) Located beside the main plaza; offers a list of excursion operators and accommodations. Only Spanish spoken.

Getting There & Away

There are two bus departures per day for San Juan (AR$200, four hours), which pass through Calingasta (AR$35, 30 minutes). The stop is at the Servicompras.

The road between Barreal and Uspallata in Mendoza province takes you through some stunning scenery. A 38km stretch is unpaved, and likely will remain that way for some time. In a compact vehicle it is best handled cautiously; it's a dirt and rocky roadway with nothing, and likely no one around in case you need assistance.

DIFUNTA CORREA

Since the 1940s, the shrine of Difunta Correa, once a simple cross, has metastasized into a village with basic hotels, restaurants and shops, all dedicated to the legend of Difunta Correa. The story goes that during the civil wars of the 1840s, a woman named Deolinda Correa followed her conscript husband's battalion through the deserts of San Juan, carrying their baby son in her arms. She died when supplies ran out, but the infant was later found still nursing at the dead woman's breast.

The shrine at Vallecito commemorates what is widely believed to be the site of her death. Difunta literally means 'defunct,' and Correa is her surname. People visit year-round, but at Easter, May 1 and Christmas, up to 200,000 make pilgrimages here. Weekends are busier than weekdays. There are regular departures to Vallecito from San Juan and Mendoza.

Rodeo

☎0264 / POP 2600 / ELEV 2010M

Rodeo, 42km west of San José de Jáchal, is a small, ramshackle town with picturesque adobe houses typical of the region. It's on the map, and in fact, is world-famous, for **windsurfing** and **kitesurfing** on **Dique Cuesta del Viento**, a reservoir surrounded by spectacular scenery only 3km away. Between mid-October and early May, wind speeds reach 120km/h nearly every afternoon, drawing surfers from around the globe. Even if you don't take to the wind, it's worth spending a day or two wandering around Rodeo and hanging out on the beach, absorbing the views and watching the insanity of airborne windsurfers.

West of town on RN 510 is the department of Iglesia, home of the *precordillera* thermal baths of **Pismanta**. RN 510 continues west to Chile via the lung-busting 4765m **Paso del Agua Negra** (open summer only).

Sleeping & Eating

Rancho Lamaral HOSTEL $

(☎0264-15-660-1197; www.rancholamaral.com; Cuesta del Viento; campsites per person US$12, dm/d US$20/35) You'll find this peaceful, laid-back refuge down a sandy road, around 500m from the shore of the Dique Cuesta del Viento. Rooms located in the adobe house are simple and cozy, and the small, charming courtyard, if unkempt, is a great place to hang out along with the many dogs on hand. Windsurfing and kitesurfing courses and rental equipment offered.

★**Posta Huayra** HOTEL $$

(☎0264-15-451-6179; www.postahuayra.com.ar; Zeballos s/n; s/d US$45/75;) Nestled amongst the poplars below town, this atmospheric little option offers supremely comfortable rooms in a hippy-chic style with plenty of indigenous motifs. The recommended on-site restaurant is open to nonguests.

La Surfera INTERNATIONAL $

(Santo Domingo s/n; mains AR$110-200; ⌚noon-1am;) La Surfera is on the main street in the center of town. This laid-back restaurant-cafe-reggae-bar is headquarters for Rodeo's surprisingly large hippy community. Vegetarian meals are predictably good; meat dishes could be better.

Information

Tourist Office (☎0264-493068; Plaza de la Fundción; ⌚8am-9pm) Inside the town hall, this office provides a list of places to stay and information on local attractions.

Getting There & Away

From San Juan's bus terminal, there are two departures daily for Rodeo (AR$180, 3½ hours).

The way to San José de Jáchal, 46km to the east, is along the beautifully scenic, narrow and twisty RP 150, carved into a mountain above Río Jáchal.

As the crow flies, the most direct route between Rodeo and Barreal is via RP 412. But unless you're a crow or you're in a 4WD with high clearance, do not be tempted. It's very rough and rocky for some ways south of Bella Vista. To travel between the two, you can take RP 149, an incredibly scenic route passing through dramatic desert mountain landscapes.

Parque Provincial Ischigualasto

Also known fittingly as Valle de la Luna, this **park** (Valley of the Moon; ☎0264-422-5778; www.ischgualasto.gob.ar; AR$250; ⌚8am-5pm) takes its name from the Diaguita word for 'land without life'. Visits here are a spectacular descent into a world of surreal rock formations, dinosaur remains and glowing red sunsets. The 630-sq-km park is in a desert valley between two sedimentary mountain ranges, the Cerros Colorados in the east and Cerro Los Rastros in the west. Over millennia, the waters of the nearly dry Río Ischigualasto have carved distinctive shapes in the malleable red sandstone, monochrome clay and volcanic ash. Predictably, some of these forms have acquired popular names, including **Cancha de Bochas** (the Ball Court), **El Submarino** (The Submarine) and **El Gusano** (The Worm), among others. Time and water have also exposed a wealth of fossils, some up to 180 million years old, from the Triassic period.The desert flora of algarrobo trees, shrubs and cacti complement the eerie land forms.

Sights

The park's **museum** displays a variety of fossils, including the carnivorous dinosaur *Herrerasaurus* (not unlike *Tyrannosaurus rex*), the *Eoraptor lunensis* (the oldest-known predatory dinosaur) and good dioramas of the park's paleoenvironments.

From the **visitor center**, isolated 1748m **Cerro Morado** is a three- to four-hour walk, gaining nearly 800m in elevation and yielding outstanding views of the surrounding area. Take plenty of drinking water and high-energy snacks.

Tours

All visitors to the park must go accompanied by a ranger. The most popular tours run for three hours and leave on the hour (more or less), with cars forming a convoy and stopping at noteworthy points along the way, where the ranger explains (in Spanish only) exactly what you're looking at.

If you have no private vehicle, an organized tour is the only feasible way to visit the park. These are easily arranged in San Agustín de Valle Fertil or San Juan. Tour rates (not including entry fees) start from AR$1600 per person from San Juan (the city's tourism office can provide advice), or AR$800 per person from San Agustín. Tours from San Juan are exhausting and involve nearly eight hours of driving; they depart at 5am and return well after dark.

A variety of other tours are available from the visitor center in the park. Options include spectacular full-moon tours (AR$250, 2½ hours) in the five days around the full moon, treks to the summit of Cerro Morado (three to four hours), and a 12km circuit of the park on mountain bikes (AR$150).

Getting There & Away

Ischigualasto is about 72km north of San Agustín via RP 510 and 125km east of Huaco via RP 150. Given its size and isolation, the only practical way to visit the park is by private vehicle or organized tour. Note that the park roads are unpaved and some can be impassable after rain.

Bariloche & the Lake District

Includes ➡

Best Places to Eat

- Butterfly (p362)
- Alto El Fuego (p362)
- Morphen (p383)
- Il Gabbiano (p370)
- Pistach' (p378)

Best Places to Stay

- Estancia Peuma Hue (p361)
- El Casco Art Hotel (p361)
- Earthship Patagonia (p373)
- La Casona de Odile (p373)
- Hotel Llao Llao (p369)

Why Go?

Home to some of the country's most spectacular scenery, the Lake District is one of Argentina's prime tourist destinations. People come to ski, fish, climb, trek and generally bask in the cool, fresh landscapes created by the huge forests and glacier-fed lakes of Argentina's largest national park.

The paleontological sites and outstanding wineries just out of the city of Neuquén are well worth stopping off for en route; and way, way south is the resort town of Bariloche, with its picture-postcard location on the banks of the Lago Nahuel Huapi.

Getting away from the crowds is easily done. The lakeside villages of Villa Traful and San Martín de los Andes fill up for a short time in summer and are blissfully quiet the rest of the year. To the north, Chos Malal makes an excellent base for exploring nearby volcanoes, lagoons and hot springs.

When to Go

Bariloche

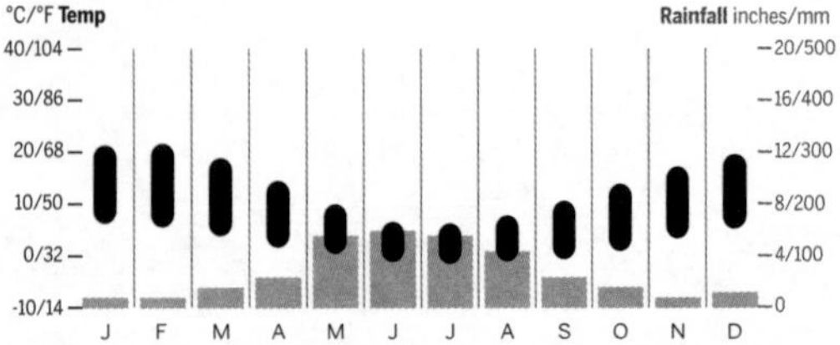

Mar–May Warm days and cool nights make this a great time to visit.

Jun–Sep Snow season means spectacular mountain vistas and powder under your skis

Nov–Jan Moderate temperatures and blooming wildflowers; put your trekking boots on.

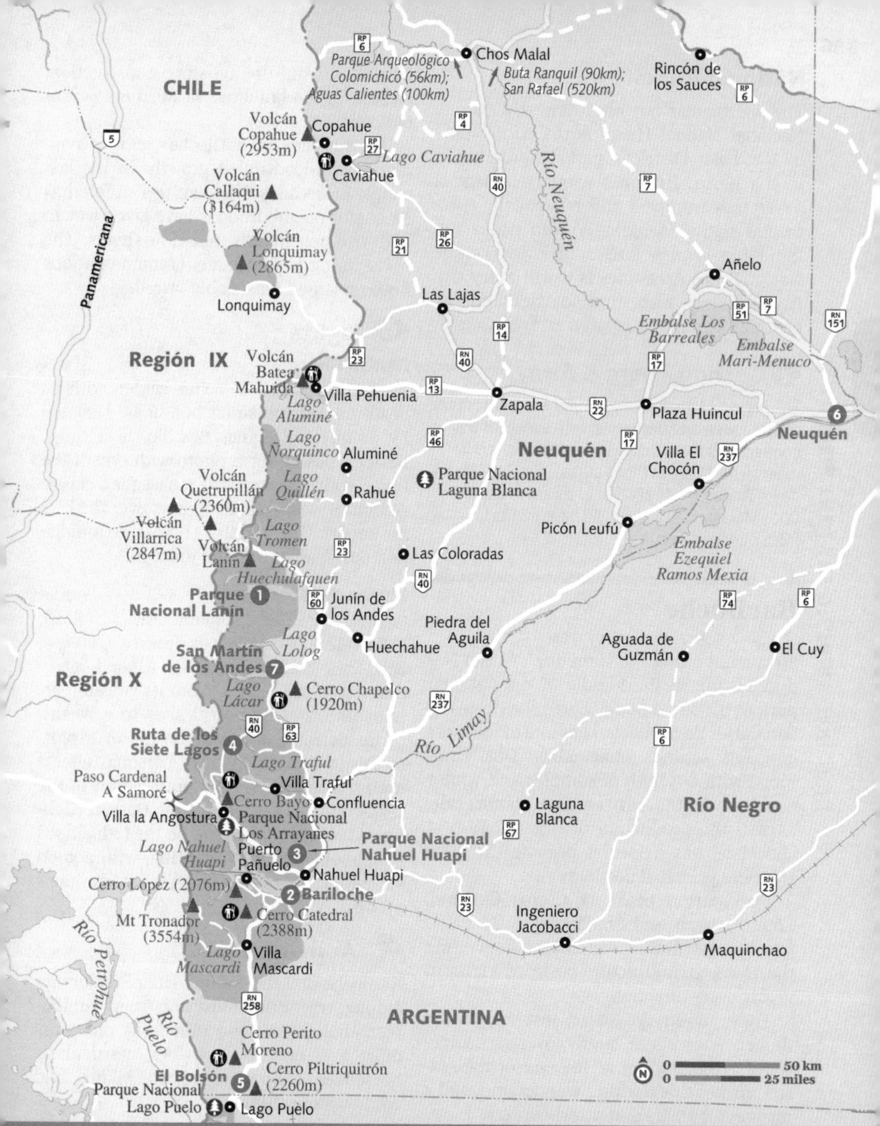

Bariloche & the Lake District Highlights

1 **Parque Nacional Lanín** (p386) Climbing the Lake District's most picturesque volcano or hiking amid pristine lakes and araucaria pine forests.

2 **Bariloche** (p356) Sampling some of the region's best gastronomy and sailing on the spectacular Lago Nahuel Huapi.

3 **Parque Nacional Nahuel Huapi** (p367) Tackling some of the region's best trekking.

4 **Ruta de los Siete Lagos** (p385) Driving the legendary RN 40, which winds between lakes and *pehuén* forests.

5 **El Bolsón** (p372) Hiking, biking and sampling great beer in this former hippie capital.

6 **Neuquén** (p396) Following in the footsteps of dinosaurs and sampling the region's best wines.

7 **San Martín de los Andes** (p380) Combining beautiful lakefront scenery with outdoor adventures and good food.

National Parks

The spectacular but often crowded Parque Nacional Nahuel Huapi is the cornerstone of the Lake District's parks. Bordering it to the north, Parque Nacional Lanín gets fewer trail trampers and has equally spectacular sights, including Volcán Lanín and humbling *pehuén* forests. The tiny Parque Nacional Los Arrayanes is worth a day trip from Villa la Angostura to check out its beautiful cinnamon-colored arrayán trees.

Getting There & Away

The region's two primary ground-transport hubs are Neuquén and Bariloche, with excellent bus connections to countrywide destinations. The main airports are in these cities, plus San Martín de los Andes, while smaller ones are in Zapala, Chos Malal and El Bolsón. All have flights to/from Buenos Aires.

Bariloche

☎0294 / POP 127,300 / ELEV 770M

Strung out along the shoreline of Lago Nahuel Huapi, in the middle of the national park of the same name, Bariloche (formally San Carlos de Bariloche) has one of the most gorgeous settings imaginable. This, combined with a wealth of summer and winter activities in the surrounding countryside, as well the production of Argentina's best chocolate, has helped it become the Lake District's principal destination.

The soaring peaks of Cerros Catedral, López, Nireco and Shaihuenque (to name just a few) – all well over 2000m high – ring the town, giving picture-postcard views in nearly every direction.

These mountains aren't just for gazing, though – excellent snow coverage (sometimes exceeding 2m at the *end* of the season) makes this a winter wonderland, and a magnet for skiers and snowboarders.

In summertime the nature buffs take over, hitting the hills to climb, hike trails, fish for trout and ride mountain bikes and horses.

History

Officially founded in 1902, the city really began to attract visitors after the southern branch of the Ferrocarril Roca train line arrived in 1934 and architect Ezequiel Bustillo adapted Central European styles into a tasteful urban plan. Bariloche is now known for its alpine architecture, which is given a Patagonian twist through the use of local hardwoods and unique stone construction, as seen in the buildings of Bustillo's *centro cívico* (civic center).

The flip side of Bariloche's gain in popularity is uncontrolled growth: in the last couple of decades the town has suffered as its quaint neighborhoods have given way to high-rise apartments and time-shares. The silver lining is that many accommodations have remained reasonably priced.

Sights

Centro Cívico AREA

A stroll through Bariloche's center, with its beautiful log-and-stone buildings designed by architect Ezequiel Bustillo, is a must. Besides, posing for a photo with one of the barrel-toting St Bernards makes for a classic Argentine snapshot, and views over the lake are superb. The buildings house the municipal tourist office and the museum.

Museo de la Patagonia MUSEUM

(☎0294-442-2309; Centro Cívico; AR$50; ⏲10am-12:30pm & 2-5pm Tue-Fri, 10am-5pm Sat) This small museum is a good introduction to the region, from its volcanic origins and archaeological sites to a wealth of taxidermied wildlife, the life of explorer Perito Moreno (whose personal effects are on display here) and an account of the 19th-century Conquest of the Desert. Highlights include the section on the indigenous people of southern Argentina, with a good selection of Mapuche and Yamaná artifacts on display.

Activities

Bariloche and the Nahuel Huapi region are among Argentina's most important outdoor recreation areas, and numerous operators offer a variety of activities, particularly horseback riding, mountain biking and white-water rafting.

Mountaineering & Trekking

The Nahuel Huapi national park office distributes a brochure with a simple map, adequate for initial planning, that rates hikes as easy, medium or difficult and suggests possible loops.

Skiing

Nahuel Huapi's ski resort, Cerro Catedral (p370), was once South America's trendiest, and has been superseded only by Las Leñas (near Mendoza) and resorts in Chile. Las Leñas has far superior snow (dry powder), but it lacks Catedral's strong point: views. There's nothing like looking over the shimmering lakes of Nahuel Huapi from its snowy slopes.

Day passes run between AR$750 and AR$980, depending on the season. If you need lessons, stop into the ski schools at Cerro Catedral or Club Andino Bariloche. Two-hour private lessons are about AR$2000. For rental equipment, try **Martín Pescador** (☎0294-442-2275; Rolando 257; ⏲9am-1pm & 4:30-9pm Mon-Fri, 10am-1pm & 6-9pm Sat). Equipment is also available on-site. Sets of skis, boots and poles rent for around AR$350, and snowboarding gear about AR$400 per day.

Mountain Biking

Bicycles are ideal for the Circuito Chico (though this 60km loop demands endurance) and other trips near Bariloche; most roads are paved and even the gravel roads are good.

Bikeway MOUNTAIN BIKING
(☎0294-461-7686; www.bikeway.com.ar; Av Bustillo, Km12.5) Mountain-bike rental, including gloves and helmet, costing around AR$250 per day. A number of similar rental places offer the same rates.

Fishing

Fly fishing draws visitors from around the world to Argentina's accessible Andean-Patagonian parks, from Lago Puelo and Los Alerces in the south to Lanín in the north.

On larger lakes, such as Nahuel Huapi, trolling is the preferred method, while fly fishing is the rule on most rivers. The season runs from mid-November to mid-April. For more information, contact the **Asociación de Pesca y Caza Nahuel Huapi** (Hunting & Fishing Club; ☎0294-442-1515; www.facebook.com/PescaYCazaNahuelHuapi; cnr Av 12 de Octubre & Onelli; ⏲9am-6pm Mon-Sat). For rental equipment and guide hire, try Martín Pescador. It offers guided fishing trips for about AR$7500 per day for one or two people (price is the same either way and includes all equipment, lunch, transportation and guide). Fishing licenses (AR$480/1280/1670 per day/week/season) are required and are available at this shop.

Horseback Riding

Most travel agencies along Av Bartolomé Mitre offer horseback-riding trips.

Cabalgatas Carol Jones HORSEBACK RIDING
(☎0294-442-6508; www.caroljones.com.ar) For something special, contact the amiable Carol Jones, who offers half-day horseback riding from her family *estancia* (ranch) outside of Bariloche for AR$1500 per person. Includes transportation to/from town and an excellent *asado* (barbecue grill) outside. She also offers multiday pack trips by horse for AR$3500 per person per day.

Cabalgatas Tom Wesley HORSEBACK RIDING
(☎0294-444-8193; http://cabalgatastomwesley.com; Av Bustillo, Km15.5) This horseback-riding specialist has been in the business since 1980 and has an excellent reputation. Horseback-riding outings range from 1½-hour Cerro Campanario rides to three-day crossings of the Valle del Río Pichi Leufú.

Rafting & Kayaking

Rafting and kayaking on the Río Limay and the Río Manso have become increasingly popular in recent years. The best time to be on the rivers is November through February, though you can raft October through Easter.

★**EXtremo Sur** RAFTING
(☎0294-442-7301; www.extremosur.com; Morales 765; ⏲9am-6pm) In business since 1991, this outfit offers trips on the Río Manso, from Class II to III (AR$1490 per person), suitable for all ages, to Manso a la Frontera (Class III to IV, AR$1900 per person, ages 14 and up). It also has gentle rafting on Río Limay and adrenalin-packed stand-up rafting and ducky excursions.

There's also a three-day Expedición Río Manso (Class III to IV), in which you camp riverside at excellent facilities.

★**Aguas Blancas** RAFTING
(☎0294-469-0426; www.aguasblancas.com.ar; Morales 564; ⏲9am-1pm & 3-7pm) This business has an excellent reputation and offers trips on the Río Manso, from gentle paddles for beginners (Class II) to demanding whitewater rapids (Class IV).

Pura Vida Patagonia KAYAKING
(☎0294-441-4053; www.puravidapatagonia.com.ar) Offers kayaking trips on the Lago Nahuel Huapi, ranging from half-day stints to 12-day camp-'n'-kayak explorations of the lake, custom designed to match your skill level.

Paragliding

Parapente Bariloche PARAGLIDING
(☎0294-15-480-3050; www.bariloche-paragliding.com; Cerro Otto base) The mountains around Bariloche make for spectacular paragliding. If you wish to take to the sky, it

Bariloche

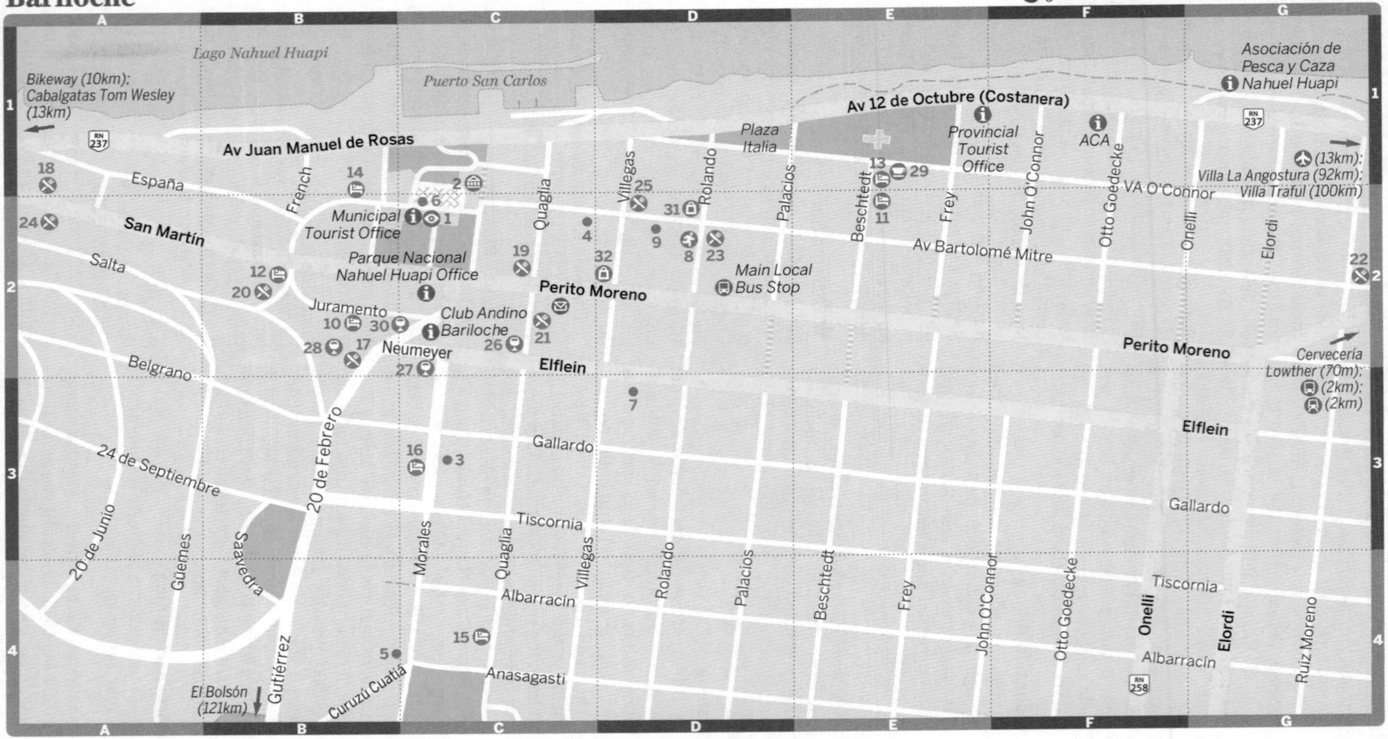
400 m
0.2 miles
Lago Nahuel Huapi
Puerto San Carlos
Bikeway (10km); Cabalgatas Tom Wesley (13km)
Asociación de Pesca y Caza Nahuel Huapi
Av 12 de Octubre (Costanera)
Av Juan Manuel de Rosas
Plaza Italia
Provincial Tourist Office
ACA
(13km); Villa La Angostura (92km); Villa Traful (100km)
VA O'Connor
España
French
San Martín
Salta
Municipal Tourist Office
Parque Nacional Nahuel Huapi Office
Juramento
Club Andino Bariloche
Neumeyer
Belgrano
Perito Moreno
Elflein
Main Local Bus Stop
Av Bartolomé Mitre
Cervecería Lowther (70m); (2km); (2km)
Quaglia
Villegas
Rolando
Palacios
Beschtedt
Frey
John O'Connor
Otto Goedecke
Onelli
Elordi
Ruiz Moreno
Gallardo
Tiscornia
Albarracín
Anasagasti
Morales
20 de Febrero
24 de Septiembre
20 de Junio
Güemes
Saavedra
Gutiérrez
Curuzú Cuatiá
El Bolsón (121km)

Bariloche

Sights

1	Centro Cívico	C2
2	Museo de la Patagonia	C1

Activities, Courses & Tours

3	Aguas Blancas	C3
4	Espacio	C2
5	EXtremo Sur	B4
6	Historias de Bariloche	C2
7	La Montaña	D3
8	Martín Pescador	D2
9	Turisur	D2

Sleeping

10	Hostel 41 Below	B2
11	Hostería Piuke	E2
12	Hotel Edelweiss	B2
13	Hotel Milan	E1
14	Hotel Tirol	B1
15	La Justina Hostel	C4
16	Periko's	C3

Eating

17	Alto El Fuego	B2
18	Don Molina	A1
19	Helados Jauja	C2
20	Huacho	B2
21	La Casita	C2
22	La Fonda del Tio	G2
23	La Marmite	D2
24	La Parilla de Julián	A2
25	Rapa Nui	D2

Drinking & Nightlife

26	Cerveceria Bachmann	C2
27	Cervecería Manush	C2
28	Cervecería Wesley	B2
29	La Estepa Cafe	E1
30	Los Vikingos	C2

Shopping

31	Mamuschka	D2
32	Paseo de los Artesanos	D2

will cost you around AR$1800 for a tandem flight (20 to 30 minutes). There are a number of other operators with similar rates.

Courses

La Montaña LANGUAGE
(0294-452-4212; www.lamontana.com; Elflein 251, 2nd fl; 9am-4pm Mon-Fri) This is a recommended Spanish-language school. A Spanish crash course costs US$210 per week.

Tours

Countless tourist agencies along and near Av Bartolomé Mitre, such as Turisur, run minibus tours to Parque Nacional Nahuel Huapi and as far south as El Bolsón. Prices range from AR$240 for a half-day trip along the Circuito Chico to AR$450 to San Martín de los Andes via the scenic Ruta de los Siete Lagos (p385).

★ **Historias de Bariloche** WALKING
(0294-460392; www.historiasdebariloche.com.ar; Centro Cívico; 2hr tours AR$280) These excellent themed walking tours shed light on Bariloche's history. Tours, such as the German Footprint: German Immigration and Nazi Presence, and European Legacy: Pioneer Imprint, depart from in front of the tourist office and typically last two hours. Check the website for the exact schedule.

Bariloche Moto Tours MOTORCYCLING
(0294-446-2687; www.barilochemototours.com) Recommended operator organizing custom motorcycling tours to everywhere between southern Patagonia and northern Chile, and beyond. Fifteen-day tours, such as Bariloche to Ushuaia, use Kawasaki KLR650s.

Turisur BOATING
(0294-442-6109; www.cruceandino.com; Av Bartolomé Mitre 219; per person from US$280) This long-standing operator arranges the bus-boat-bus-boat day-long crossing into Chile. Bicycle-boat options are available.

Espacio BOATING
(0294-443-1372; www.islavictoriayarrayanes.com; Av Bartolomé Mitre 139; adult/5-11yr AR$1060/530) Espacio offers cruises on Lago Nahuel Huapi in its 40ft catamaran *Cau Cau* during summer. Reserve your place two days in advance.

Festivals & Events

Bariloche hosts numerous festivals throughout the year, from cultural to food-related events.

Festival de Música de Verano MUSIC
(Jan & Feb) In January and February the Festival de Música de Verano (Summer Music Festival) puts on several different events, including the Festival de Música de Cámara (Chamber Music Festival), the Festival de Bronces (Brass Festival) and the Festival de Música Antigua (Ancient Music Festival).

★ **Bariloche a La Carta** FOOD & DRINK
(www.barilochealacarta.com; Oct) Held in the first half of October, this week-long food fest

THE CRUCE DE LAGOS

One of Argentina's classic journeys is the Cruce de Lagos, a scenic 12-hour bus-and-boat trip over the Andes to Puerto Montt, Chile. Operated exclusively by Turisur (p359), the trip begins around 8am in Bariloche (departure times vary) with a shuttle from Turisur's office to Puerto Pañuelo near Hotel Llao Llao. The passenger ferry from Puerto Pañuelo leaves immediately after the shuttle arrives, so if you want to have tea at Llao Llao, get there ahead of time on your own (but make sure to buy your ticket in advance). Service is daily in the summer, Monday to Friday the rest of the year. In winter (mid-April to September), and in summer by request, the trip takes two days and passengers are required to stay the night in Peulla, Chile, where you have the choice of the **Hotel Natura Patagonica** (☑in Chile 065-297-2289; www.hotelnatura.cl; s & d US$140, tr US$183; ☎) or the **Hotel Peulla** (☑in Chile 065-297-2288; www.hotelpeulla.cl; s & d US$97, tr US$132; ☎). The more economical option is to stay at the beautifully situated **Hotel Puerto Blest** (☑0294-442-6109; www.hotelpuertoblest.com.ar; s/d from US$151/182; ☎) in Puerto Blest instead.

As of 2017, Turisur offers a cheaper boat-and-bike option alongside the standard boat-and-bus trip, both as a day trip and with an overnight stay in either Peulla or Puerto Blest. Cyclists need to make sure that they're at the departure point on time. They then get to ride the picturesque stretches between Bariloche and Pañuelo (25km), Puerto Blest and Puerto Alegre (15km), Puerto Frías and Peulla (27km), and Petrohué and Puerto Montt (76km); the Municipal Tourist Office (p366) in Bariloche may have info about alternative transportation between Petrohué and Puerto Montt for cyclists hoping to avoid this ride.

A day trip for cyclists costs US$280, whereas a bus–boat–bus day trip costs US$392. Though the trip rarely sells out, it's best to book it at least a day or two in advance.

celebrates the best of Bariloche's culinary offerings. Dozens of restaurants offer special menus and the city's microbreweries and food stalls set up shop in the main square.

🛏 Sleeping

From camping, hostels and guesthouses to five-star hotels, Bariloche's abundant accommodations make it possible to find good value even in high season, when reservations are best. Prices peak during ski season (July and August), drop slightly during high season (January and February) and are lowest the rest of the year.

★**Bonita Lake House** HOSTEL $

(☑0294-446-2561; www.bonitalakehouse.com.ar; Av Bustillo, Km 7.8; r with/without bathroom US$67/50, bungalow US$106; P◉☎) With its gorgeous lakefront setting, close to Playa Bonita, this friendly hostel is where international travelers mingle with locals looking for some R&R. There are common spaces and nooks for more privacy. The fully equipped apartments are a boon for groups, and there's easy bus access.

★**Periko's** HOSTEL $

(☑0294-452-2326; www.perikos.com; Morales 555; dm from US$14, d with/without bathroom

US$49/40; @☎) An atmospheric little hostel set up on the hill overlooking Bariloche. The rooms are nicely situated around the kitchen, the social hub of the place, staff organize all manner of activities, and impromptu barbecues are frequent happenings. The DVD library and laundry service for your dirty togs are nice touches.

La Justina Hostel HOSTEL $

(☑0294-452-4064; www.lajustinahostel.com.ar; Quaglia 726; dm US$12, d with/without bathroom US$95/79; ☎) An intimate, colorful hostel with a roaring hearth in colder months and a garden in which to chill out in summer. A homey atmosphere reigns and owner Leo is very informative and helpful.

Hostel 41 Below HOSTEL $

(☑0294-443-6433; www.hostel41below.com; Juramento 94; dm US$18-22, d without bathroom US$63; @☎) An intimate hostel with clean dorms, fine doubles (with good views) and a mellow vibe. The staff make guests feel like family, there are communal vegan dinners and breakfasts, and the common room is a cozy space for mingling with like-minded souls.

La Selva Negra CAMPGROUND $

(☑0294-444-1013; www.campingselvanegra.com.ar; Av Bustillo, Km2.95; campsite per person from

US$13) Located 3km west of Bariloche on the road to Llao Llao, this is the nearest organized camping area to town. It has good facilities and, in the fall, you can step outside your tent to pick apples. The backpacker section gets an AR$30 discount.

★**Posada Los Juncos** GUESTHOUSE $$
(☎0294-495-7871; www.posadalosjuncos.com; Av Bustillo, Km20.1; ste US$115-145; P ☎) Sitting on a tranquil piece of land, surrounded by ancient araucaria pines, this homey, luxurious guesthouse gets pretty much everything right. The personalized service is friendly yet unobtrusive, the suites are individually decorated to represent one of the four elements, the lake views are gorgeous and breakfast is ample.

Hotel Tirol HOTEL $$
(☎0294-442-6152; www.hoteltirol.com.ar; Libertad 175; r with city/lake view US$100/124; @ ☎) Right in the middle of Bariloche, this charming little lodge offers comfortable, spacious rooms. Those out the back have spectacular views out over the lake and to the mountain range beyond, as does the bright sitting/breakfast area.

Hotel Milan BUSINESS HOTEL $$
(☎0294-442-2624; www.hotelmilan.com.ar; Beschtedt 128; r US$80; P ☎) A block from the lakeshore and a short walk from the heart of Bariloche, this smart hotel features spotless rooms in tranquil creams and beiges that come in a variety of shapes and sizes. Have a look at a few (the price is the same) and try to snag a lake view.

Hostería Piuke HOTEL $$
(☎0294-442-3044; res.piuke@gmail.com; Beschtedt 136; r/tr US$97/108; ☎) One of the better-value hotels down near the lakefront in Bariloche, Hostería Piuke has good-sized, comfortable rooms and some very hip retro '70s furnishings. Rooms are well heated in the colder months.

★**Estancia Peuma Hue** LODGE $$$
(☎0294-450-1030; www.peuma-hue.com; Cabecera Sur del Lago Gutiérrez; r US$265; ☎) Sitting amid pristine forests and waterfalls on the banks of Lago Gutiérrez, off RN 40, this wonderful ecolodge retreat is ideal for outdoor adventurers. Kayaking, horseback riding and hiking are on offer, with yoga classes and massages for winding down. Rooms are simple but luxurious and dining is enhanced with organic produce from the lodge's garden and an excellent wine selection.

★**El Casco Art Hotel** BOUTIQUE HOTEL $$$
(☎0294-446-3131; www.hotelelcasco.com; Av Bustillo, Km 11.5; r US$240; P ☎) Nestling on a land spur overlooking Lago Nahuel Huapi, this intimate boutique hotel is both for art lovers (the place is decorated with over 500 pieces of contemporary Argentine art) and those that appreciate the finer things in life: hot tubs overlooking the water, a luxury spa, a fine restaurant, and mod cons in the spacious, bright rooms.

Hotel Edelweiss BUSINESS HOTEL $$$
(☎0294-444-5500; www.edelweiss.com.ar; San Martín 202; r from US$172; P @ ☎) One of the better business-class hotels in Bariloche, the Edelweiss manages to retain a warmth despite its size. All the facilities are here, including a fantastic 7th-floor day spa and swimming pool, and the service is both pleasant and efficient.

Eating

Bariloche has some of Argentina's best food, and it would take several wallet-breaking and belt-bursting weeks to sample all of the worthwhile restaurants. Regional specialties, including *cordero* (lamb, cooked over an open flame), *jabalí* (wild boar), *ciervo* (venison) and *trucha* (trout), are especially worth trying, and there are several fine-dining venues worth your time.

★**Helados Jauja** ICE CREAM $
(☎0294-443-7888; www.heladosjauja.com; Perito Moreno 48; ice cream from AR$50; ⊙10am-midnight) Ask Bariloche residents who serves the best ice cream in Bariloche and most will reply with one word: 'Jauja.' Of the 60 or so flavors, there are usually a couple dozen in rotation at any given time.

Rapa Nui ICE CREAM $
(☎0294-443-3999; https://chocolatesrapanui.com.ar; Av Bartolomé Mitre 202; ice cream from AR$60; ⊙8:30am-11:30pm Mon-Thu, 9am-midnight Sat, 9am-11:30pm Sun) Rapa Nui wears many hats and we love all of them. It's simultaneously a chocolate shop, an ice-cream parlor (with some of the best ice cream in Bariloche) and a bright and airy cafe. And if that weren't enough, there's a small ice rink in the back (open 2pm to 10pm) for you to practice your toe loops and triple axels.

BARILOCHE'S BEER TRAIL

Chocolate isn't Bariloche's only claim to culinary fame: the town is central to the region's craft-beer movement that has really taken off in recent times. There are excellent breweries and brewpubs to be found both in the town itself and dotted along the Circuito Chico. Here are some stops that a beer lover shouldn't miss:

Cervecería Manush The most popular microbrewery in town, where the gourmet snacks are as good as the stout and porter.

Cervecería La Cruz Beer garden on the outskirts of Bariloche, with excellent porter and IPAs and live music on weekends.

Cervecería Lowther Formerly a one-man show, this brewery is very highly rated for its darker brews – the stouts and the porter.

Cervecería Blest (☑0294-489-1894; www.cervezablest.com.ar; Av Bustillo, Km11.5; ⊙noon-midnight; 🔊) Argentina's original brewpub where the *picadas* (cold-cut platters) go extremely well with the Scotch ale, amber ale and bock.

Cervecería Patagonia (p370) Microbrewery/beer hall with an excellent ambience, delightful terrace overlooking the lake and slow-cooked food to go with your Bohemian pilsner or golden ale.

Cervecería Berlina (☑0294-452-3336; https://cervezaberlina.com; Av Bustillo, Km12; ⊙noon-1am; 🔊) Award-winning brewery known for its 15 beers, with the smoked Rauch Bier and the Colonia Suiza blond ale particularly popular with connoisseurs.

La Fonda del Tio
ARGENTINE $

(☑0294-443-5011; www.lafondadeltio.com. ar; Av Bartolomé Mitre 1130; mains AR$120-180; ⊙noon-3:30pm & 8pm-midnight; 🔊) No nonsense here – just big servings of homemade pastas and raviolis, along with a carefully chosen wine list.

★ Alto El Fuego
PARRILLA $$

(☑0294-443-7015; www.facebook.com/altoelfue gopatagonia; 20 de Febrero 445; mains AR$190-320; ⊙noon-3pm & 8pm-midnight; 🔊) The most frequently recommended *parrilla* (steak restaurant) in town, featuring the killer combination of great cuts of expertly seared meat and a well-chosen wine list. It's a small place – if you're coming for dinner, make a reservation. Or (if weather permits) go for lunch and take advantage of the breezy deck area.

★ La Parilla de Julián
PARRILLA $$

(☑0294-443-3252; www.laparrilladejulian.com; San Martín 590; mains AR$175-430; ⊙noon-4pm & 8pm-midnight) This friendly, family-run *parilla* is a long-standing local favorite and one of the few places open on Sunday. Waiters bustle about, bearing beautifully grilled cuts of beef, *cordero patagónico* (spit-roasted lamb), *morcilla* (blood sausage) and grilled provolone cheese. Portions are ample and reservations are a good idea, particularly on weekends.

La Casita
GERMAN $$

(☑0294-442-3775; www.hosterialacasita.com. ar; Quaglia 342; mains AR$135-320; ⊙noon-3pm & 8-11:30pm Wed-Mon; 🔊) This snug restaurant puts a German spin on dishes crafted from local ingredients, so expect the likes of smoked pork chop with *chukrut* (sauerkraut), hearty goulash with spätzle and venison casserole. Bring a friend to order *arróz de montaña* (mountain paella with wild mushrooms) and *morcilla* (blood sausage).

La Marmite
ARGENTINE $$

(☑0294-442-3685; http://lamarmite.com.ar; Av Bartolomé Mitre 329; mains AR$220-398; ⊙noon-1am; 🔊) A trusty choice for Patagonian standards such as trout and venison. But it's the fondues that set La Marmite apart from the other places in Bariloche, including the decadent chocolate fondue (AR$620 for two), just in case you haven't eaten enough of the stuff cold.

★ Butterfly
FUSION $$$

(☑0294-446-1441; www.butterflypatagonia.com. ar; Hua Huan 7831, off Av Bustillo, Km7.8; tasting menu AR$1500; ⊙seatings 7.45pm & 9.30pm Mon-Sat; 🔊) A chandelier gently spins, casting soft shadows on the rough stone walls. A fire gently crackles in the fireplace and an almost reverential hush reigns as diners tuck into the seven-course tasting menu that changes frequently but may comprise the likes of red cabbage, goat's cheese and almond salad, panko-coated shrimp and a beautifully seared sirloin with mango emulsion.

Huacho PARRILLA **$$$**
(☎0294-452-6525; www.facebook.com/Huachobariloche; Salta 217; mains AR$290-380; ⏰8pm-midnight Mon-Sat; 📶) The tantalizing aromas of a wood fire and grilled meat waft down the street, enticing you into this diminutive *parrilla* – one of Bariloche's best. Choose from spit-roasted lamb, three types of steak, trout or homemade pasta, and wash it down with a Patagonia beer or one of the carefully chosen wines. Perfection. At time of research it was preparing to move to a new location.

Don Molina STEAK **$$$**
(☎0294-443-6616; San Martín 609; mains AR$260-370; ⏰11:30am-midnight) Upholstered in cow hide, this large brick hall is the favorite gathering place of the carnivorously inclined. Opt for the house specialty of *cordero al palo* (spit-roasted lamb) or a slab of juicy steak (half-portions are available for those not wishing to eat their body weight in meat). Extensive wine list too, from mostly small, independent bodegas.

Drinking & Nightlife

Bariloche is at the epicenter of the region's craft-beer movement, and breweries and brewpubs are both numerous and excellent quality.

★**Cervecería Manush** MICROBREWERY
(☎0294-442-8905; www.cervezamanush.com.ar; Neumeyer 20; ⏰5:30pm-3am; 📶) Going strong since 2011, not only is Manush responsible for some of the region's best stout, brown porter, pale ale and kölsch, this is the only brewpub where the quality of the tapas and *picadas* matches the beer, courtesy of the husband-and-wife-professional chef team. Go early or be prepared to wait; this place is super popular!

Cervecería La Cruz BEER GARDEN
(☎0294-444-2634; http://cervecerialacruz.com.ar; Nilpi 789; ⏰6pm-1am Tue-Sun; 📶) This microbrewery/beer garden is almost a place of pilgrimage for local beer aficionados, who make their way nightly to Bariloche's suburbs for the world-class Workingman porter, the IPAs and the live music (on weekends).

Cervecería Lowther BREWERY
(☎0294-441-3435; www.facebook.com/CervezaLowther; Av Bartolomé Mitre 1160; ⏰6pm-2am; 📶) Originally a one-man enterprise, this award-winning brewery is locally revered for its dozen or so beers, particularly the darker varieties – the porter, cream stout and milk stout. The food is less exciting, but *la buena onda* (good vibes) and good music more than make up for it.

La Estepa Cafe COFFEE
(VA ÓConnor 511; ⏰8am-8pm Mon-Sat; 📶👪) The lattes, ristrettos and cappuccinos at this cafe are brought to you by a couple from Buenos Aires, bringing some big-city coffee-culture sophistication to the Lake District. The place is equally popular with the iPad-toting young crowd and with families (there's a creative corner for kids), and, aside from breakfast, you can also grab an empanada or cookie.

Cerveceria Bachmann CRAFT BEER
(☎0294-442-2249; www.cerveceriabachmann.com.ar; Elflein 90; ⏰noon-1am Mon-Sat, 6pm-midnight Sun; 📶) Particularly popular for its Munich-style *negra schwarzbier*, Scottish amber ale, cream stout and kölsch, this cheerful brewpub pairs its beers with gourmet burgers, *picadas* (platters of cold cuts) and pizzas.

Cervecería Wesley CRAFT BEER
(☎0294-428-3664; www.cervezawesley.com; 20 de Febrero 451; ⏰7pm-midnight Mon-Sat) In a mini-forest of the Paseo de la Colina, in the heart of Bariloche, the Wesley brothers' brewpub is very much part of the city's craft-beer circuit. Take your golden ale, the special bitter or a pint of one of the two IPAs and sit on the deck overlooking the lake.

Los Vikingos BAR
(www.facebook.com/losvikingosbar; cnr Juramento & 20 de Febrero; ⏰7pm-3am Mon-Sat) A laid-back little corner bar serving a good range of local microbrewery beers at excellent prices. The music's cool and the decor eclectic. DJs play on weekends.

Shopping

Bariloche is renowned for its chocolates, and dozens of stores downtown, from national chains to mom-and-pop shops, sell chocolates of every style imaginable. Quality, of

1

3

1. Lago Nahuel Huapi (p367)
This spectacular lake is a glacial remnant over 100km long that covers more than 500 sq km.

2. Cerro Catedral (p370)
This 2388m peak is the area's most important snow-sports center.

3. Parque Nacional Los Arrayanes (p377)
This small, enchanting national park protects remaining stands of the cinnamon-barked *arrayán*.

BARILOCHE BUS CARDS

Bariloche's local buses work with either Santa Fé or Sube magnetic cards, available from kiosks at Av Bartolomé Mitre 91 and Moreno 480, and Moreno 69 and Morales 501, respectively. You can also pick up handy *horarios* (schedules) for all destinations from the bus terminal. Cards cost AR$20 (recharged with as much credit as you want). For most routes a ride will cost AR$10, with AR$25 being the highest fare (for bus 55). Some hostels loan cards to guests on payment of a deposit.

course, varies: don't get sick on the cheap stuff.

★Mamuschka CHOCOLATE
(0294-442-3294; Av Bartolomé Mitre 298; 8:30am-11pm) Quite simply, the best chocolate in Bariloche. Don't skip it. Seriously.

Paseo de los Artesanos ARTS & CRAFTS
(cnr Villegas & Perito Moreno; 10am-7pm Mon-Sat) Local craftspeople display wares of wool, wood, leather, silver and other media here.

Orientation

The principal commercial area is along Av Bartolomé Mitre. Do not confuse VA O'Connor (also known as Vicealmirante O'Connor or Eduardo O'Connor) with similarly named John O'Connor, which cross each other near the lakefront. Similarly, Perito Moreno and Ruiz Moreno intersect near Diagonal Capraro, at the east end of the downtown area.

Information

Banks with ATMs are ubiquitous in the downtown area, with several along Perito Moreno.

Cambio Sudamérica (Av Bartolomé Mitre 63; 9am-8pm Mon-Fri, to 1pm Sat) Change foreign cash and traveler's checks here.

Chilean Consulate (0294-443-1680; Juan Manuel de Rosas 180; 9am-2pm Mon-Fri) In case you need to apply for a Chilean visa.

Hospital Ramón Carrillo (0294-442-6100; Perito Moreno 601) *Long* waits; no charge.

Post Office (Perito Moreno 175; 8am-6pm Mon-Fri, 9am-1pm Sat)

TOURIST INFORMATION

ACA (Automóvil Club Argentino; 0294-442-3001; Av 12 de Octubre 785; 9am-4pm Mon-Fri, to 1pm Sat) Argentina's auto club has provincial road maps.

Asociación de Pesca y Caza Nahuel Huapi (p357) Fishing permits and information.

Club Andino Bariloche (0294-442-2266; www.clubandino.org; 20 de Febrero 30; 9am-1:30pm & 3-7pm) Excellent, in-depth information on trekking routes and *refugios* in Parque Nacional Nahuel Huapi. Also sells excellent hiking maps.

Municipal Tourist Office (0294-442-3022; Centro Cívico; 8am-9pm) Has many giveaways, including useful maps and the blatantly commercial but still useful *Guía Busch*, updated biannually and loaded with basic tourist information about Bariloche and the Lake District.

Parque Nacional Nahuel Huapi Office (0294-442-3111; San Martín 24; 8am-6pm Mon-Fri year-round, plus 9am-3pm Sat & Sun Jan & Feb) Office for the nearby national park.

Provincial Tourist Office (0294-442-3188, 0294-442-3189; secturrn@bariloche.com.ar; cnr Av 12 de Octubre & Emilio Frey; 9am-7pm) Has information on the province, including an excellent provincial map and useful brochures in English and Spanish.

Getting There & Away

AIR

From **San Carlos de Bariloche International Airport** (0294-440-5016) there are at least a dozen flights daily to Buenos Aires with Aerolíneas Argentinas, GOL and LATAM. LADE serves Esquel, Mar de Plata, Comodoro Rivadavia, El Calafate and Puerto Madryn. There are also seasonal flights to Sao Paulo with LATAM, and to Salta, Mendoza, Ushuaia and Puerto Iguazú with Aerolíneas Argentinas.

BOAT

It's possible to travel by boat and bus to Chile aboard the Cruce de Lagos tour (p360).

BUS

Bariloche's **bus terminal** (0294-443-2860) and train station are east of town across the Río Ñireco on RN 237. During high season it's wise to buy tickets at least a day in advance.

The principal route to Chile is over the Cardenal A Samoré (Puyehue) pass to Osorno (AR$600 to AR$720, 5¼ hours) and Puerto Montt (AR$600 to AR$720, eight hours), which has onward connections to northern and southern Chilean destinations. Companies such as Andesmar make the run.

To San Martín de los Andes and Junín de los Andes, Albus, Transportes Ko-Ko and **Turismo Algarrobal** (0294-442-7698; www.turismoalgarrobal.com; Terminal de Ómnibus Bariloche) take the scenic (though possibly chokingly dusty) Ruta de los Siete Lagos (RN 40) during summer, and the longer, paved La Rinconada route (RN 237) during the rest of the year.

During the peak months of December to February, **Chaltén Travel** (☎0294-442-3809; www.chaltentravel.com; Av Bartolomé Mitre 442; ⏲9am-1pm & 5-9pm Mon-Sat) runs buses along the legendary RN 40 as far south as El Calafate. There are a couple of weekly departures from Bariloche.

Buses from Bariloche

TO	COST (AR$)	TIME (HR)	SERVICE
Bahía Blanca	1175	12¾-14	4 daily
Buenos Aires	851-1905	20½-24½	5 daily
Córdoba	1912	22¼	daily at 2pm
El Bolsón	95	2¼	14 daily
Esquel	232-380	4½-5½	6 daily
Junín de los Andes	227	3	2 daily
Mendoza	1650-1800	19½	2 daily
Neuquén	523-613	5½	7 daily
San Martín de los Andes	265	4	2 daily
San Rafael	1375-1580	15¾	2 daily
Villa la Angostura	90	1¼	8 daily

TRAIN

When it's running, the **Tren Patagonico** (☎0294-442-3172; www.trenpatagonico-sa.com.ar) leaves the **train station** (☎0294-442-3172), across the Río Ñireco, next to the bus terminal. It generally leaves Bariloche for Viedma (16 hours) at 5pm on most Sundays (and the occasional Monday); fares range from AR$930 in *primera* (1st-class seated) to AR$1560 in *camarote* (1st-class sleeper). Check departures with the tourist office beforehand.

ℹ Getting Around

TO/FROM THE AIRPORT

Bariloche's airport is 15km east of town via RN 237 and RP 80. A *remise* (taxi) costs around AR$280 to RP$300. Bus 72 (AR$20) leaves from the main bus stop on Perito Moreno.

BUS

At the **main local bus stop** (Perito Moreno, btwn Rolando & Palacios), Codao del Sur and Ómnibus 3 de Mayo run hourly buses to Cerro Catedral. Codao uses Av de los Pioneros, while 3 de Mayo takes Av Bustillo.

From 6am to midnight, municipal bus 20 leaves the main bus stop every 20 minutes for the attractive lakeside settlements of Llao Llao and Puerto Pañuelo. Bus 10 goes to Colonia Suiza 14 times daily. During summer three of these, at 8:05am, noon and 5:40pm, continue to Puerto Pañuelo, allowing you to do most of the Circuito Chico using public transportation. Departure times from Puerto Pañuelo back to Bariloche via Colonia Suiza are 9:40am, 1:40pm and 6:40pm. You can also walk any section and flag down buses en route.

Ómnibus 3 de Mayo buses 50 and 51 go to Lago Gutiérrez every 30 minutes, while in summer the company's Línea Mascardi goes to Villa Mascardi/Los Rápidos three times daily. Ómnibus 3 de Mayo's Línea El Manso goes twice on Friday to Río Villegas and El Manso, on the southwestern border of Parque Nacional Nahuel Huapi.

Buses 70, 71 and 83 stop at the main bus stop, connecting downtown with the bus terminal.

CAR

Bariloche is loaded with the standard car-rental agencies and is one of the cheapest places to rent vehicles in the country. Prices vary greatly depending on season and demand, but usually come in around AR$700 per day, with unlimited mileage.

Andes (☎0294-443-1648; www.andesrentacar.com.ar; San Martín 162; ⏲9am-6pm)

Budget (☎0294-444-2482; www.budgetbariloche.com; Av Bartolomé Mitre 717; ⏲9am-7pm)

Hertz (☎0294-442-3457; www.hertz.com.ar; Elflein 190; ⏲9am-9pm)

TAXI

A taxi from the bus terminal to the center of town costs around AR$90. Taxis to the airport cost around AR$280 to AR$300 and within town generally don't go over the AR$50 mark.

Parque Nacional Nahuel Huapi

☎0294

One of Argentina's most-visited national parks, **Nahuel Huapi** (☎0294-442-3111; adult/student AR$250/130) occupies 7500 sq km in the mountainous southwestern Neuquén and western Río Negro provinces. The park's centerpiece is Lago Nahuel Huapi, a glacial remnant over 100km long that covers more than 500 sq km. To the west, a ridge of high peaks separates Argentina from Chile; the tallest is 3554m Monte Tronador, an

Parque Nacional Nahuel Huapi

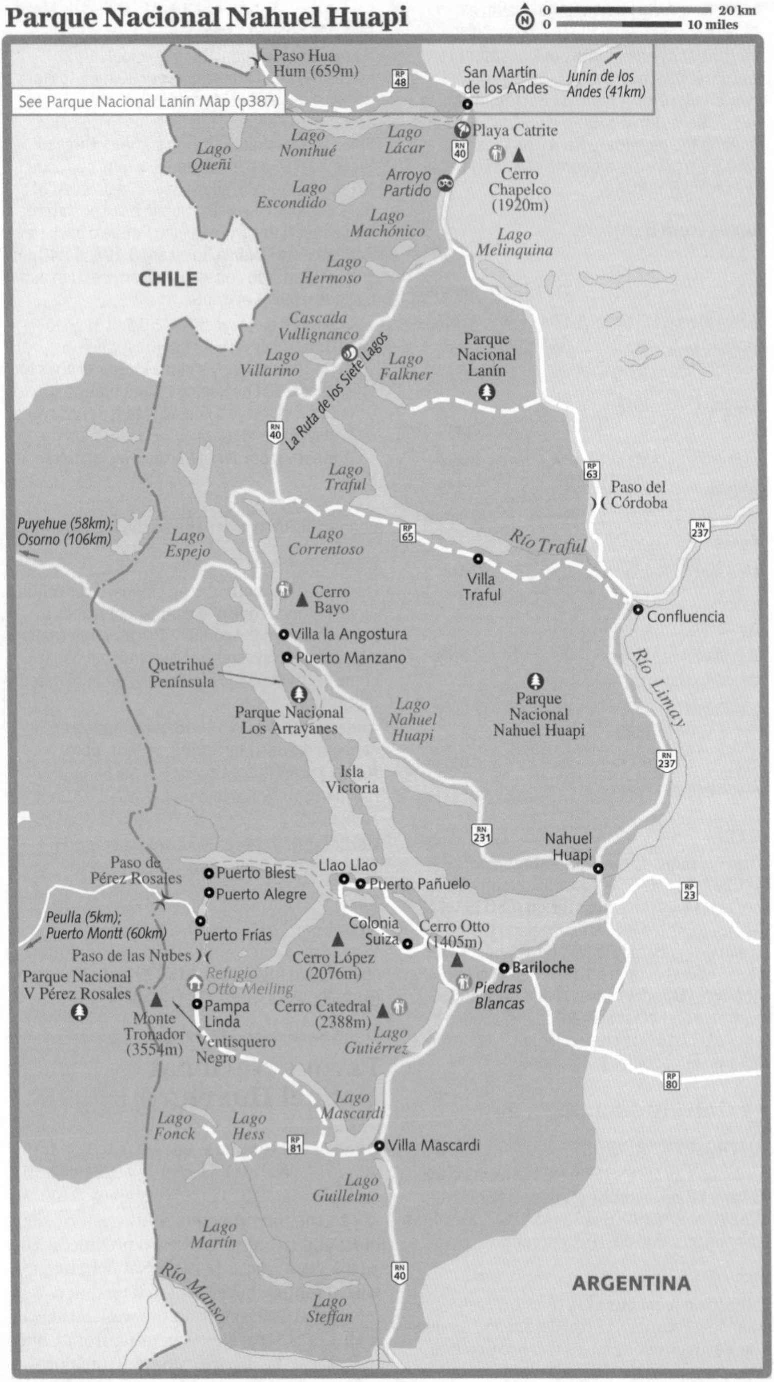

extinct volcano that still lives up to its name (meaning 'Thunderer') when blocks of ice tumble from its glaciers. During the summer months, wildflowers blanket the alpine meadows.

Parque Nacional Nahuel Huapi was created to preserve local flora and fauna, including its AndeanPatagonian forests and rare animals. Important animal species include the huemul (Andean deer) and the miniature deer known as pudú. Most visitors are unlikely to see either of these, but several species of introduced deer are common, as are native birds.

Information

A good source of information about the park is the Parque Nacional Nahuel Huapi Office (p366) in Bariloche. For permits, trail info, *refugio* bookings and more, seek out Club Andino Bariloche (p366); it also sells detailed maps of the park.

For trekking maps and information about hiking in the region, if you read Spanish, the locally published *Las Montañas de Bariloche*, by Toncek Arko and Raúl Izaguirre.

Getting There & Away

Cerro Catedral, Cerro Otto and parts of the Circuito Chico are reachable by bus from Bariloche. To explore Monte Tronador and Pampa Linda you'll need your own wheels, though it's also possible to take a day tour from Bariloche.

Getting Around

For road conditions in and around the national parks, call **Parque Nacional Estado de Rutas** (www.vialidad.gov.ar) at 105, toll free, or consult its offices. Cycling is a good way of getting around the Circuito Chico.

Circuito Chico

0294

One of the area's most popular and scenic driving excursions, the 65km-long Circuito Chico begins on Av Bustillo, on Bariloche's outskirts, and continues to the tranquil resort of **Llao Llao**. At Cerro Campanario the **Aerosilla Campanario** (0294-442-7274; Av Bustillo, Km18; return AR$220; 9am-5:30pm) lifts passengers to a panoramic view of Lago Nahuel Huapi.

Llao Llao's **Puerto Pañuelo** is the point of departure for the boat-and-bus excursion across the Andes to Chile, as well as for day trips to Parque Nacional Los Arrayanes on Península Quetrihué, Isla Victoria and Puerto Blest.

From Llao Llao you can head across to **Colonia Suiza**, named for its early Swiss colonists.

The road passes the trailhead to 2076m **Cerro López**, topped with the **Refugio López** (0294-15-458-4459; dm US$26; mid-Dec–mid-Apr), the starting point for several long treks.

As you make your way around the forested, mountainous circuit, you can pay homage to Bariloche's many craft-beer breweries and linger at numerous excellent restaurants.

Tours

Puerto Pañuelo Boat Trips BOATING
(Av Bustillo, Km25) Several boat companies run enjoyable outings on Lago Nahuel Huapi. Destinations include Isla Victoria, Puerto Blest (where you can stay overnight in a wonderful hotel) and Peulla in Chile. Purchase tickets from the booths or inside the information center.

Sleeping

Hostería Katy GUESTHOUSE $
(0294-444-8023; www.hosteriakaty.com; Av Bustillo, Km24.3; s/d US$44/76;) Multilingual Dirk and Adrianna welcome guests as if they were family, and there's a lot to love about this guesthouse: spotless, carpeted rooms with down comforters, excellent breakfasts to fuel you for the day's adventures, mountain bikes for guest use and proximity to many of Circuito Chico's attractions.

★ **Aldebaran Hotel & Spa** BOUTIQUE HOTEL $$
(0294-444-8678; http://aldebaranpatagonia.com; Av Bustillo, Km20.4; r/ste US$141/197;) Picture yourself sitting by a roaring fire in a cozy lounge with rough-hewn stone walls, or stargazing with your sweetie in a hot tub overlooking an artery of Lago Nahuel Huapi. Intimate Aldebaran has all that, and more: custom-cooked breakfasts, unobtrusive, professional service, elegant rooms and blissful silence at night.

★ **Hotel Llao Llao** HOTEL $$$
(0294-444-8530; www.llaollao.com.ar; Av Bustillo, Km25; d from US$374;) Arguably Argentina's most famous hotel, Llao Llao sits on a bluff overlooking Lago

Moreno. It has everything you'd expect it to have: beautifully appointed rooms, attentive service and lots of wonderful extras, such as the heated infinity pool, terrific dining and outdoor equipment (mountain bikes, skis) for any time of year. It's very popular with honeymooners.

Eating & Drinking

Circuito Chico boasts some of the region's best microbreweries and brewpubs, including Cervecería Blest (p362) and Cervecería Berlina (p362).

★**Il Gabbiano** ITALIAN **$$**
(☎0294-444-8346; Av Bustillo, Km24; mains AR$180-250; ⌚7:30-11:30pm Wed-Mon; 📶🍷) At the best Italian restaurant in the region, chef Mimi Barchetta imbues each dish with plenty of *amore,* and it shows. Standout dishes include gnocchi with octopus ragout, *tagliatelle alla boscaiola* (with mushrooms and tomatoes), rigatoni with lamb ragout and beautifully seared meats. A convivial, easy vibe reigns and it's a great place for a romantic tête-à-tête.

Rincón Patagónico PARRILLA **$$**
(☎0294-446-3063; www.rinconpatagonico.com.ar; Av Bustillo, Km14.2; mains AR$180-260; ⌚noon-midnight; 📶) This log-cabin-style restaurant has been thrilling the palates of the carnivorously inclined for years. Specialties include Patagonian-style, spit-roasted lamb, slow-cooked venison in red wine and steak with wild-mushroom sauce. Portions are ample, and beer and wine flow freely.

★**Cervecería Patagonia** BEER HALL
(☎0294-445-0124; www.cervezapatagonia.com.ar; Av Bustillo, Km24.7; ⌚noon-midnight; 📶) Overlooking Lago Moreno, this delightful beer hall with hanging lanterns and copper taps is as known for its food – slow-cooked lamb, mammoth sandwiches – as it is for its brews. When the weather is warm, it's hard to resist taking your pint of porter, Bohemian pilsner or golden ale out on to the waterfront patio.

Getting There & Away

From Bariloche, bus 20 runs every 20 minutes to Llao Llao and Puerto Pañuelo, while bus 10 serves Colonia Suiza 14 times daily. Having your own wheels gives you greater flexibility, and it's best to either drive the circuit or cycle it. To cut out the less scenic sections, hop a bus to Km18.6 and rent a bike at **Bike Cordillera** (☎0294-452-4828; www.cordillerabike.com; Av Bustillo, Km18.6; per hour/day AR$150/420; ⌚9am-6pm). Call ahead to reserve a bike.

Cerro Otto

☎0294

Cerro Otto (1405m) is an 8km hike on a gravel road west from Bariloche. There's enough traffic to make hitchhiking feasible, and it's also a steep and tiring but rewarding bicycle route. The **Teleférico Cerro Otto** (☎0294-444-1035; www.telefericobariloche.com.ar; Av de Los Pioneros, Km5; adult/6-11yr AR$400/250; ⌚10am-5:30pm) carries passengers to the summit, from where you get sweeping views of Lago Nahuel Huapi.

A 1.3km trail leads from the top of Cerro Otto to Club Andino's **Refugio Berghof** (☎0294-414-6018; www.facebook.com/BerghofRefugio; dm US$20) (1240m), which hosts events and accepts overnight guests, though not always. The *refugio* also contains the **Museo de Montaña Otto Meiling** (☎0294-414-6018; www.facebook.com/BerghofRefugio; guided visit AR$50; ⌚hours vary), named for a pioneering climber.

Getting There & Away

A free bus connects Bariloche (from the corners of Bartolomé Mitre and Villegas or Perito Moreno and Independencia) with the chairlift base a dozen or so times daily.

Cerro Catedral

☎0294

This 2388m peak, 20km southwest of Bariloche, is the area's most important snow-sports center. Several chairlifts and the **Aerosilla Cerro Bellavista cable car** (☎0294-440-9000; AR$480; ⌚9am-5pm) carry passengers up to 2000m, where there's a restaurant-*confitería* offering excellent panoramas.

Four excellent **hiking** trails traverse the mountain, two of which are open year-round.

Activities

★**Cerro Catedral** SKIING
(☎0294-440-9000; www.catedralaltapatagonia.com; ⌚mid-Jun–mid-Oct) This 2388m peak, 20km southwest of Bariloche, is the area's most important snow-sports center, served by over a dozen chairlifts, three pomas and two cable cars. There are 120km worth of intermediate and advanced ski runs, with a few steep black runs at the top and some

tree runs near the base, and a single beginners' run at the base.

The rates for lift passes vary from low to mid to high season. Basic rental equipment is cheap, but quality gear is more expensive. There are several on-site ski schools.

Hiking

Four hiking trails traverse Cerro Catedral. The last two trails listed are closed May to October, and in April and November you have to be prepared to navigate difficult, snowy conditions.

Gutiérrez–Frey Starting at the Lago Gutiérrez campground, this fairly straightforward trail (around five to six hours) climbs through coihue forest up to the Refugio Emilio Frey.

Villa Catedral–Frey This easy, well-signposted four-hour hike begins near the top of the Cerro Catedral lift and crosses a river before leading to the Refugio Emilio Frey.

Lynch–Frey Beginning at Refugio Lynch near the top of Cerro Catedral, this steeper, more direct route to Refugio Emilio Frey (four hours) climbs a scree slope before descending steeply toward Laguna Schmoll.

Frey–Jacob This six-hour trek climbs steeply from Refugio Emilio Frey to Laguna Schmoll, traverses the rocky 'football field' and climbs the side of Cerro Brecha Negra before descending toward Laguna Jacob and Refugio San Martín.

Rock Climbing

Refugio Emilio Frey is located in Argentina's prime rock-climbing area. For more on rock climbing in the area, including guided trips and equipment hire, contact Club Andino Bariloche (p366) in Bariloche.

Sleeping

Refugio Emilio Frey HOSTEL $

(☎0294-15-431-1112; http://refugiofreybariloche.com; dm US$20, full board US$39) An easy, four-hour trail starts near the top of the Cerro Catedral lift, leading to Club Andino's Refugio Emilio Frey, on the banks of picturesque Laguna Tonchek. There, 40 beds and simple meals are available, as are kitchen facilities (AR$70). This *refugio* itself is exposed, but there are free sheltered tent sites.

Getting There & Away

Public transportation from Bariloche to the base of the lifts is excellent, consisting of hourly buses marked 'Catedral' from downtown with Ómnibus 3 de Mayo.

Monte Tronador & Pampa Linda

☎0294

Two dusty, single-lane roads lead into the heart of Parque Nacional Nahuel Huapi. Worth at least a day of your time, Pampa Linda is reachable via a particularly scenic stretch of road that skirts the shores of Lago Mascardi and leads on to the spectacular Ventisquero Negro and the base of Monte Tronador (3554m). Visitors are rewarded with views of dozens of waterfalls plunging over the flanks of extinct volcanoes en route. Pampa Linda is the starting point for nine hikes of varying length and difficulty.

Sights

★Ventisquero Negro GLACIER

(Black Glacier; RP 82; 24hr) From Pampa Linda, it's a 6km drive (or over an hour's walk) along a severely potholed dirt road to the Ventisquero Negro lookout. It's a spectacular sight: a gray glacial lake surrounded by spiky, snow-streaked peaks, with house-sized chunks of ice calving from the gently sloping glacier.

Cascada de Los Alerces WATERFALL

(RP 81) This 20m waterfall is worth the drive for the spectacular setting. If you use your imagination, you may see the resemblance between the falls and the spread skirts of a sitting 19th-century lady.

Activities

Pampa Linda is the starting point for a number of superb hikes, which include:

Saltillo de las Nalcas A gentle, 800m (half-hour) walk each way, with a small waterfall at the end.

Glaciar Castaño Overo This fairly straightforward hike (9.5km) takes around 2½ hours, crossing the Río Castaño Overo along a pedestrian bridge and leading to a viewpoint overlooking the glacier.

Laguna Ilón A moderately strenuous hike (14km) that involves fording Río Alerce and a steep, tough section that leads to the gorgeous namesake lake. Four hours each way.

Refugio Otto Meiling A dirt-and-gravel road leads to a pedestrian bridge over the Río Castaño Overo, after which a footpath climbs through coihue forest and over exposed rock to the *refugio*. The 18km hike takes five hours.

Refugio Viejo del Tronador This moderately tough 25km trek (eight hours each way) is permitted only with a mountain guide. Part of the trek crosses the Chilean border. Take all supplies with you for the overnight shelter stay.

Paso de Las Nubes This straightforward two-day trek involves two river crossings on pedestrian bridges, a steep slog up to the meadow where you stay overnight at the Refugio Agostino Rocca and a beautiful descent through lenga forest to Lago Frías. Buy your boat ticket at the *refugio* to Puerto Pañuelo, where you can catch a bus back to Bariloche.

Climbers intending to scale **Monte Tronador** should anticipate a three- to four-day technical climb requiring experience on rock, snow and ice.

Sleeping & Eating

★Refugio Agostino Rocca HOSTEL $
(☎0294-15-465-5903; www.facebook.com/refugioagostinorocca; dm US$33, full-board US$127; ⏲Nov-late Apr) This cozy mountain lodge has room for 80 guests, made welcome in eight co-ed dorms. Hot meals are available at extra cost, though guests are welcome to use the kitchen. The *refugio* is in an excellent location for several treks of varying length, from a three-hour jaunt to Glaciar Frias to a two-day crossing of the Paso de las Nubes.

★Refugio Otto Meiling HUT $
(☎0294-15-421-3921; http://refugiomeiling.com; dm US$20) This snow-line Club Andino *refugio* can be reached via a five-hour hike from Pampa Linda. There's room for 60 people (it can get rather cozy!); bring your own sleeping bag. Meals, beer and wine are available on request. In high season, there's daily transport to Pampa Linda from Bariloche. Mountain guides can be hired here for numerous trekking excursions.

Hotel Tronador HOTEL $$
(☎0294-449-0556; www.hoteltronador.com; RP 82; s/d from US$107/121; ⏲Nov–mid-Apr; 📶) For a real treat, stay at the secluded Hotel Tronador, at the northwest end of Lago Mascardi on the Pampa Linda road. Expect bright, wood-paneled rooms, plenty of outdoor adventure, from horseback riding to white-water rafting, and a good restaurant specializing in Argentine and Central European cuisine.

Hostería Pampa Linda HOTEL $$$
(☎0294-449-0517; www.hosteriapampalinda.com.ar; RP 82; s/d incl half-board US$180/250; 📶) In the heart of Parque Nacional Nahuel Huapi, in the southern foothills of Cerro Tronador, this hotel is in an ideal location for hikers. The snug, well-heated rooms are a pleasure to retreat to after a hearty meal at the onsite restaurant, which is a favorite stop for day-trippers.

Information

Park entry fees (adult/student AR$250/130) must be paid en route at the **ranger station** (⏲8am-6pm) at Villa Mascardi (the bus stops so you can do this). There's another ranger post at Pampa Linda.

Getting There & Away

The potholed dirt-and-gravel road from the Parque Nacional Nahuel Huapi entrance forks after 9km at Los Rápidos. The left branch continues for 17km to the Cascada de Los Alerces, while the right fork presses on for 29km to Pampa Linda.

Both roads are very narrow, necessitating a special timetable. Traffic is therefore allowed up to Pampa Linda until 2pm. At 4pm cars are allowed to leave Pampa Linda for the return trip. Entry only to Los Alerces is between 2pm and 5pm and exit only between 11am and 1pm. Outside the set hours, it's two-way traffic along both roads. It takes around an hour to drive from the RN 40 turnoff to the Pampa Linda area, and around 45 minutes to Cascada de Los Alerces.

For AR$200 one way, Club Andino Bariloche has summer transportation (from the end of November to April) to Pampa Linda at 8:30am daily, returning around 5pm. Buses depart from in front of Club Andino, and the 90km ride takes about 2½ hours. Several tour companies in Bariloche run day trips to Pampa Linda.

El Bolsón

☎0294 / POP 17,061 / ELEV 304M

It's not hard to see why the hippies started flocking to El Bolsón back in the '70s. It's a mellow little village for most of the year, nestled in between two mountain ranges. When summer comes, it packs out with

Argentine tourists who drop big wads of cash and disappear quietly to whence they came.

In the last 30-odd years El Bolsón has been declared both a non-nuclear zone and an 'ecological municipality' (are you getting the picture yet?). What's indisputable is that just out of town are some excellent, easily accessible hikes and mountain-bike rides that take in some of the country's most gorgeous landscapes.

The town welcomes backpackers, who find themselves stuffing their bellies with natural and vegetarian foods, as well the excellent beer, sweets, jams and honey made from the local harvest.

◉ Sights & Activities

★ Feria Artesanal MARKET
(Plaza Pagano; ⊙10am-4pm Tue, Thu, Sat & Sun) 🥐 Local craftspeople sell their wares at this market, along the eastern edge of Plaza Pagano, which boasts over 300 artists, who make and sell everything from wooden cutting boards and handcrafted *mate* (a bitter ritual tea) gourds to jewelry, flutes and marionettes. With numerous food vendors (adhering to the regulation that everything sold in the market must be handmade), it's also a chance to sample local delicacies. On sunny Sundays the *feria* (market) operates about half-tilt.

Grado 42 OUTDOORS
(☑0294-449-3124; www.grado42.com; Av Belgrano 406; ⊙8:30am-8:30pm Mon-Sat, 10:30am-1pm & 5-7pm Sun) For adventures in the surrounding countryside, this travel agency arranges trekking, paragliding, horseback riding, mountain biking and other tours around El Bolsón, and rafting on the Río Manso. Trips on the Manso a la Frontera (Class II to IV) cost AR$2200 (including breakfast).

⚒ Festivals & Events

★ El Lúpulo al Palo BEER
(⊙mid-Feb) Award-winning local beer gets headlines during the National Hops Festival over four days in mid-February.

🛏 Sleeping

Budget travelers are more than welcome in El Bolsón, where there are several hostels and campgrounds. Otherwise, midrange hotels and *cabañas* abound.

★ La Casona de Odile HOSTEL $
(☑0294-449-2753; www.odile.com.ar; dm/d AR$170/600; @🛜) 🥐 Five kilometers north of the center, off Av San Martín, is one of the best hostels in Argentina. Traveler-run and sitting on two hectares of park-like riverside land, it's got all you could possibly want – good amenities, comfy dorms and rooms, an on-site microbrewery, yoga classes, massage, bike hire and cheap, hearty dinners. Many come for days and stay for weeks.

★ Earthship Patagonia BOUTIQUE HOTEL $
(☑0294-448-3656; www.earthshippatagonia. com; Azcuénaga 754; d US$35; P🍴🛜) 🥐 Its construction having involved earth-packed tires, recycled glass bottles, tin cans and solar panels, Earthship Patagonia is a labor of love. Brought to you by American transplants Trent and Natalie, it houses guests in stylishly decorated Mongolian yurts, with optional communal dinners including organic vegetables from the garden, mountain biking and yoga retreats on offer.

Hostel Kaly Do Sur HOSTEL $
(☑0299-404-1692; www.facebook.com/kalydosur hostel; 25 de Mayo 2731; dm/d US$16/45; 🍴🛜) *La buena onda* (good vibes) permeates this cozy, couldn't-be-more-central hostel in the heart of El Bolsón. Lila and Juan take great care of their guests and the ample breakfast provides fuel for hiking, biking and other outdoor adventures.

Cabañas Tulquelen CABAÑAS $
(☑0294-448-3251; www.cabanastunquelen.com; Feliciano 771; 2-person cabañas US$40; P🍴🛜) Friendly owners preside over this clutch of cozy *cabañas*, just a couple of blocks from El Bolsón's main square. All come with kitchenettes and dining areas on the ground floor and snug sleeping lofts upstairs.

La Posada de Hamelin GUESTHOUSE $$
(☑0294-449-2030; Granollers 2179; s/d US$77/100; 🛜) This creeper-clad house sitting in an overgrown garden resembles something out of a fairy tale. There are only four rooms, but they're all gorgeous, with exposed beams and rough-hewn walls. The sunny upstairs dining area is a great place to munch on an empanada (baked savory turnover).

Hostería La Escampada BOUTIQUE HOTEL $$
(☑0294-448-3905; www.laescampada.com; Azcuénaga 561; s/d from US$69/103; 🛜) Comprising just 10 rooms behind a salmon-colored facade, Hostería La Escampada

El Bolsón

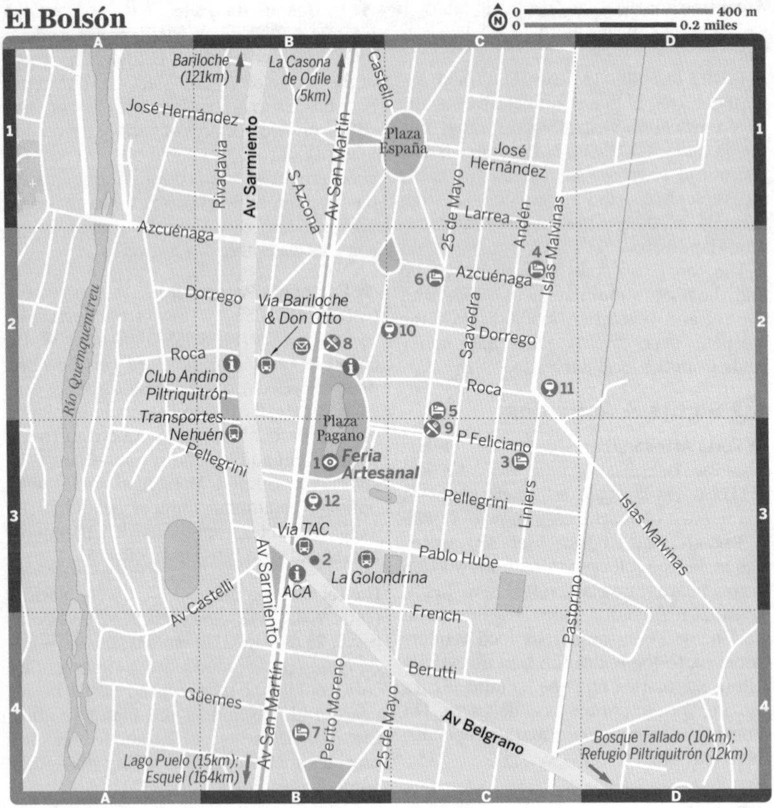

El Bolsón

Top Sights
1 Feria Artesanal B3

Activities, Courses & Tours
2 Grado 42 .... B3

Sleeping
3 Cabañas Tulquelen C3
4 Earthship Patagonia C2
5 Hostel Kaly Do Sur C2
6 Hostería La Escampada C2
7 La Posada de Hamelin B4

Eating
Feria Artesanal .... (see 1)
8 Jauja B2
9 La Gorda C3

Drinking & Nightlife
10 Awka Cervecería C2
11 Otto Tipp C2
12 Patio Cervecero El Bolsón B3

Shopping
Monte Viejo .... (see 2)

delights with warm service and attention to detail. The beds are properly comfortable, the breakfast spread is excellent and the superior rooms come complete with whirlpool tubs.

Eating

El Bolsón's restaurants lack Bariloche's variety, but food is consistently good value and often outstanding, thanks to fresh local ingredients and careful preparation. *Trucha arco iris* (rainbow trout) is the local specialty.

Jauja
CAFE, ICE CREAM **$**

(☑0294-449-2448; www.heladosjauja.com; Av San Martín 2867; cones from AR$35; ⊙8am-11pm; ☎) The most dependable *confitería* (cafe offering light meals) in town serves up all your faves with some El Bolsón touches (such as homemade bread and strawberry juice) thrown in. The daily specials are worth checking out – the risotto with lamb and wild mushrooms is divine. The attached ice creamery is legendary – make sure you leave room for a kilo or two.

Feria Artesanal
MARKET **$**

(Plaza Pagano; snacks from AR$35; ⊙10am-4pm Tue, Thu, Sat & Sun) ✐ The market is the best and most economical place to snack in El Bolsón. Goodies here include fresh fruit, Belgian waffles with berries and cream, huge empanadas for AR$35, sandwiches, frittatas, *milanesa de soja* (soy patties), locally brewed beer and regional desserts.

★La Gorda
INTERNATIONAL **$$**

(☑0294-472-0559; 25 de Mayo 2709; mains AR$150-345; ⊙7-11:30pm Tue-Sun; ☎✐) This is El Bolsón's don't-miss eating spot, with large portions of delicious, well-prepared food in relaxed, stylish surrounds. There are good vegetarian options, a couple of Asian dishes, beautifully cooked cuts of meat and some interesting sides. If it's a warm night, try for a garden table. Bookings are highly recommended.

🍷 Drinking & Nightlife

Otto Tipp
BREWERY

(☑0294-449-3700; cnr Roca & Islas Malvinas; ⊙noon-1am Dec-Feb, from 8pm Wed-Sat Mar-Nov; ☎) After a hard day of doing anything (or nothing) there are few better ways to unwind than by working your way through the selection of microbrews at El Bolsón's original microbrewery. Guests are invited to a free sampling of the six varieties, including a smoky stout, wheat ale and blond ale. The food takes a back seat to the beer.

Patio Cervecero El Bolsón
BEER GARDEN

(www.facebook.com/PatioCerveceroElBolson-Centro; Av San Martín 2400; ⊙noon-1am; ☎) If you're a beer drinker, make for the patio here on a warm day and kick back with an IPA, a smoky *negra ahumada* (extra-dark bock), a pilsner-style *rubia* or one of the seasonal flavored beers. Inside, it's soccer on TV, a grungy rock soundtrack and half-decent pizzas and burgers to line your stomach.

Awka Cervecería
CRAFT BEER

(www.facebook.com/awka.cerveceria.5; cnr Perito Moreno & Dorrego; ⊙6pm-3am; ☎) Packed in the evenings with young locals and visitors alike, this is the place to enjoy locally brewed oatmeal stout, Belgian Tripel-style beer, a hoppy IPA or a skull-crushing barley wine.

🛍 Shopping

El Bolsón is a craft-hunter's paradise. Besides the regular *feria artesanal* (p373) there are several other outlets for local arts and crafts.

Monte Viejo
ARTS & CRAFTS

(cnr Pablo Hube & Av San Martín; ⊙9am-6pm) Quality ceramics, woodcrafts, silver and Mapuche textiles.

ℹ Information

ACA (Automóvil Club Argentino; ☑0294-449-2260; cnr Avs Belgrano & San Martín; ⊙8:30am-8pm Mon-Sat, 9am-8pm Sun) Auto club stocking provincial road maps.

Banco de la Nación (cnr Av San Martín & Pellegrini) and **Banco Patagonia** (Av San Martín 2821) have ATMs.

Club Andino Piltriquitrón (CAP; ☑0294-449-2600; www.facebook.com/capbolson; Av Sarmiento, btwn Roca & Feliciano; ⊙6-8pm) Has information on exploring the surrounding mountains, such as hiking conditions, which *refugios* are open and general trail queries. Keeps a desk in the tourist office during hiking season.

Post Office (Av San Martín 2806; ⊙8am-6pm Mon-Fri, 9am-1pm Sat)

Tourist Office (☑0294-449-2604; www.elbolson.gov.ar; off Plaza Pagano; ⊙8am-8pm) Helpful, with plenty of information on accommodations, tours and more. Provides maps of the area.

ℹ Getting There & Away

El Bolsón has no central bus terminal; **Via Bariloche** (☑0294-445-5554; www.viabariloche.com.ar; cnr Onelli & Roca) and **Don Otto** (☑0294-449-3910; http://donotto.com.ar; cnr Onelli & Roca) buses depart from the corner of Onelli and Roca, while **Via TAC** (☑0294-449-3124; www.viatac.com.ar; cnr Avs Belgrano & San Martín) leaves from the corner of Belgrano and San Martín. All three serve similar destinations; Don Otto is the only company to serve

Comodoro Rivadavia. Change in Esquel for Trelew and Puerto Madryn and in Neuquén for destinations further north.

Buses from El Bolsón

TO	COST (AR$)	TIME (HR)	SERVICE
Bariloche	95-115	2	14 daily
Comodoro Rivadavia	875-1000	12½	5.15pm daily
Esquel	138-220	2¼-3½	6 daily
Neuquén	618-749	8½	11.15am daily

Getting Around

BICYCLE

Maputur (0294-449-1440; Perito Moreno 2331; 9am-6pm Mon-Sat, 10am-4pm Sun) rents mountain bikes for AR$100/180 per half-/full day.

BUS

Local bus service to nearby sights is extensive during the busy summer months, but sporadic in fall and winter, when you'll have to hire a taxi or take a tour. The tourist office provides up-to-date information. Local buses cost AR$10.

Transportes Nehuén (0294-449-1831; cnr Av Sarmiento & Feliciano) has summer bus services to many local destinations.

La Golondrina (0294-449-2557; cnr Pablo Hube & Perito Moreno) goes to Cascada Mallín Ahogado, leaving from the south end of Plaza Pagano; and to Lago Puelo, leaving from the corner of Av San Martín and Dorrego.

TAXI

Remises (taxis) are a reasonable mode of transportation to nearby trailheads and campgrounds. Companies include **La Unión** (0294-449-2858).

Around El Bolsón

0294

The outskirts of El Bolsón offer numerous ridges, waterfalls and forests for hikers and cyclists to explore.

Popular destinations include **Cabeza del Indio**, a lookout 7km from town, and **Cascada Mallín Ahogado**, a small waterfall 10km north of town that provides access to the Club Andino Piltriquitrón's Refugio Perito Moreno, a great hiking base.

In Chubut province, 15km south of El Bolsón, the **Parque Nacional Lago Puelo** protects a windy, azure lake suitable for swimming, fishing, boating, hiking and camping. By the waterfront the launch **Juana de Arco** (0294-449-8946; www.interpatagonia.com/lagopuelo/sailing-lake-puelo.html; RP 16; 2pm departure) does three-hour lake tours as far as Argentina's Pacific Ocean outlet at the Chilean border. Hiking into Chile may be possible from there.

Sights & Activities

Bosque Tallado FOREST

(Sculpted Forest; Jan, Feb & Easter AR$100) A signposted road leads from RN 40 up the wooded slopes of Cerro Piltriquitrón. From the end of the road, it's a 40-minute hike to the Sculpted Forest, where local artisans have transformed tree stumps into mythological and grotesque carvings.

Hiking

From the Refugio Perito Moreno it's 2½ hours to the 2206m summit of Cerro Perito Moreno, a small ski resort with a base elevation of 1000m.

Serious hikers head for the 2260m Cerro Piltriquitrón, a granite ridge yielding panoramic views across the valley of the Río Azul to the Andean crest along the Chilean border. Midway up is the Bosque Tallado and the Club Andino's Refugio Piltriquitrón. From the *refugio* it's another two hours to the summit. Water is abundant along most of the summit route, but hikers should carry a canteen and bring lunch to enjoy at the top.

Another popular hike in the area is the Cerro Hielo Azul Circuit, which takes in gorgeous glacier views.

For more information on these and other hikes and the various hikers' *refugios*, contact the Club Andino Piltriquitrón (p375) in El Bolsón.

Sleeping

There are numerous campgrounds in the Lago Puelo area, as well as some *cabañas*. Club Andino Piltriquitrón runs two mountain *refugios*, which are best booked in advance.

Refugio Perito Moreno HUT $

(in El Bolsón 0294-448-3433; dm US$16;) Cascada Mallín Ahogado, a small waterfall on the Arroyo del Medio, is 10km north of El Bolsón, off RN 40, west of RN 258. Beyond the falls, a gravel road leads to Club Andino Piltriquitrón's Refugio Perito Moreno, a great base for several outstanding hikes in summer and skiing in winter. The *refugio* has capacity for 80 people; meals are an additional AR$80.

Refugio Piltriquitrón HUT $

(☎in El Bolsón 0294-448-3433; dm US$14, camping free) Beds in the Club Andino's Refugio Piltriquitrón are outstanding value, but bring your own sleeping bag. Moderately priced meals are available and the *refugio* makes a terrific base for hikes. Take the signposted road from RN 40. An hour's hike from the end of the road takes you here.

Getting There & Away

Regular buses go to Lago Puelo from El Bolsón in summer, but there's reduced service on Sunday and in low season. Mountain biking is an excellent way to get out on your own; for rentals try **Maputur** in El Bolsón.

Villa la Angostura

☎0294 / POP 11,063 / ELEV 850M

An upmarket resort town on the northwestern shore of Lago Nahuel Huapi, Villa la Angostura provides accommodations and services for nearby Cerro Bayo, a small but popular winter-sports center. The proliferation of chocolate shops on the main street makes it feel like a smaller version of Bariloche.

It's worthwhile stopping by in summer for lake cruises and walks in the small but incredibly diverse Parque Nacional Los Arrayanes, and because this is the southern starting point for the breathtaking trip along the Ruta de los Siete Lagos.

The village consists of two distinct areas: El Cruce, which is the commercial center along the highway, and La Villa, nestled against the lakeshore, 3km to the south. Though La Villa is more residential, it still has hotels, shops, services and, unlike El Cruce, lake access. Puerto Manzano, in La Villa, is where boats leave for tours to the Parque Nacional Los Arrayanes.

Sights & Activities

Several outfitters in town offer trekking, horseback riding and guided mountain-bike rides, and the tourist office provides information on each. Mountain biking is a great way to explore the surrounding area. The local ski resort is the big draw between late June and late September.

★Parque Nacional Los Arrayanes NATIONAL PARK

(www.parquesnacionales.gob.ar; adult/student AR$250/130; ⏲8am-7pm) This small national park, encompassing the entire Quetrihué Peninsula that juts out into the waters of Lago Nahuel Huapi, protects remaining stands of the cinnamon-barked *arrayán*, a member of the myrtle family. In Mapudungun (language of the Mapuche) the peninsula's name means 'place of the *arrayánes*.' Regulations require hikers to enter the park before noon and leave by 4pm in winter, and around 6pm to 7pm in summer. It's off Blvd Nahuel Huapi, a 12km drive or bike ride from Villa la Angostura.

The park headquarters is at the southern end of the peninsula, near the largest concentration of *arrayánes*, in an area known as **El Bosque**. There's an enchanted-wood feel to the place, with some of the slow-growing trees at least 600 years old. It's a three-hour, 12km hike to the tip of the peninsula, on an excellent **interpretive nature trail** that passes by two lakes. Several sightseeing boats per day run to the tip of the peninsula from the two small bays to either side of the park entrance; you can take a boat out and hike back.

From the park's northern entrance at La Villa, a very steep 20-minute hike leads to two **panoramic overlooks** of Lago Nahuel Huapi.

Cerro Belvedere HIKING

(Av Siete Lagos) A 4km hiking trail starts from Av Siete Lagos, northwest of the tourist office, and leads to an **overlook** with good views of Lago Correntoso, Nahuel Huapi and the surrounding mountains. It then continues another 3km to the 1992m summit. After visiting the overlook, retrace your steps to a nearby junction that leads to **Cascada Inayacal**, a 50m waterfall.

If you're coming out here, get a map at the tourist office, as the trails can be confusing.

Centro de Ski Cerro Bayo SKIING

(☎0810-345-0168; www.cerrobayo.com.ar; full-day pass AR$570-940) From late June to late September, lifts carry skiers from the 1050m base up to 1700m at this 'boutique' (read: small but expensive) winter resort, 9km northeast of El Cruce via RP 66. There are 24 runs (no black ones) and a snow park for freestyling. All facilities, including rental equipment (around AR$380), are available on-site.

The main cable car is open to hikers outside ski season (from 9am to 5pm; adult/child AR$420/360).

Cabalgatas Correntoso HORSEBACK RIDING
(☎ 0294-15-451-0559; www.facebook.com/cabalgatacorrentoso.com.ar; Cacique Antriao 1850) For horseback riding (half-days to multiday trips), contact Tero Bogani, who brings the gaucho side of things to his trips. Prices start at AR$800 for a two-hour outing to Nahuel Huapi and Río Bonito.

Sleeping

Except for camping and Angostura's growing hostel scene, accommodations are pricey. In summer, single rooms are almost impossible to find – expect to pay for two people. *Hosterías* and hotels abound.

★ **Hostal Bajo Cero** HOSTEL $
(☎ 0294-449-5454; www.bajocerohostel.com; Río Caleufu 88; dm/d US$29/68; @ 📶) A little over 1km northwest of the bus terminal is this gorgeous hostel, with large, well-designed dorms and lovely doubles with down comforters. It has a nice garden and kitchen, plus airy common spaces. Bicycles are available for rent.

La Roca de la Patagonia BOUTIQUE HOTEL $$
(☎ 0294-449-4497; www.larocadelapatagonia.com.ar; Pascotto 155; s/d US$65/94; ❄ 📶) A cute little place off the main drag, with just six rooms. It's set in a large converted house, so there are some great dimensions here. Decor is very Patagonian – lots of wood and stone, and there are fantastic mountain views from the deck.

Hotel Angostura HOTEL $$
(☎ 0294-449-4224; www.hotelangostura.com; Blvd Nahuel Huapi 1911, La Villa; s/d from US$72/83; 📶) Ignore the squishy rooms and the deer-antler light fittings – this place is in an awesome location. It's perched on a clifftop overlooking the bay and Parque Nacional Los Arrayanes; your biggest problem here is going to be neck crick from checking out the view – no matter which way you're walking. Bicycle rental is available for guests.

Verena's Haus BOUTIQUE HOTEL $$
(☎ 0294-449-4467; www.verenas-haus.com.ar; Los Taiques 268, El Cruce; s/d US$85/101; 📶) With all the heart-shaped motifs and floral wallpaper, this place probably doesn't qualify as a hunting lodge, but it is a good deal for couples looking for a quiet, romantic spot. Rooms are big, spotless and packed with comfy features, and the homemade bread and jam are excellent.

Encanto del Rio HOTEL $$$
(☎ 0294-447-5357; www.encantodelrio.com.ar; RN 40, Km1110; r/cabins/apt US$151/159/223; ❄ 📶 🏊) Located halfway between downtown and Puerto Manzano, this supremely comfortable set-up has a great range of options. The rooms are well equipped and spacious, with views of the mountains or river. The cabins add a touch of privacy and include a full kitchen. The apartments are good, too, although a little overpriced.

Eating

Gran Nevada ARGENTINE $
(☎ 0294-449-4512; Av Arrayanes 106; mains AR$130-210; ⏲ noon-11:30pm) With its big-screen TV (quite possibly showing a soccer game) and big, cheap set meals (stews, grilled fish), this is a local favorite. Come hungry, leave happy.

★ **Pistach'** FUSION $$
(☎ 0294-449-5203; Cerro Inacayal 44; mains AR$210-350; ⏲ 8-11:30pm Tue, noon-3pm & 8-11:30pm Wed-Sun; 📶 🍷) A feisty newcomer on a dining scene dominated by *parillas* and pizzerias, Pistach' blends elegant surroundings with dishes inspired by the chef's heritage and travels and conjured from fresh market ingredients. Feast on shrimp and fish curry, homemade hamburgers, pad thai and lamb slow-cooked in malbec.

Nicoletto ITALIAN $$
(☎ 0294-449-5619; Pascotto 165; mains AR$140-230; ⏲ noon-3pm & 8:30-11:30pm) The best pasta for miles around is to be found at this unassuming family-run joint just off the main street. It's all good – freshly made and with a fine selection of sauces – but the trout *sorrentino* with leek sauce comes highly recommended.

Tinto Bistro INTERNATIONAL $$
(☎ 0294-449-4924; Av Arrayanes 256; mains AR$200-450; ⏲ noon-11:30pm Mon-Sat; 📶) Besides the fact that the food (regional cuisine prepared with European flair) is excellent, the owner, Martín Zorreguieta, is the brother of Máxima, Queen of the Netherlands. Inspired dishes include the likes of trout with grilled endive and deer carpaccio.

La Luna Encantada ARGENTINE $$$
(☎0294-449-5515; Cerro Belvedere 69, El Cruce; mains AR$200-500; ⏰noon-4pm & 8pm-midnight; 📶) A cute little cottage offering all of your Patagonian and Argentine favorites. The food is carefully prepared and nicely presented, and the atmosphere is warm and inviting. The pizzas and fondues are some of the best in town and there's a good selection of local beers and wines.

Information

Banco de la Provincia (cnr Las Frambuesas & Av Nahuel Huapi; ⏰9am-1pm Mon-Fri) Has an ATM.

Post Office (Las Fuschias 121; ⏰8am-6pm Mon-Fri, 9am-1pm Sat) In a shopping gallery behind the bus terminal.

Tourist Office (☎0294-449-4124; www.villanagostura.gov.ar; cnr Avs Siete Lagos & Arrayanes; ⏰8am-9pm) Info on the town and surrounds.

Getting There & Away

The **Terminal de Omnibus Villa la Angostura** (☎0294-449-5104; cnr Av Siete Lagos & Av Arrayanes) is across the street from the tourist office. Some buses stop in El Cruce on runs between Bariloche and San Martín de los Andes.

For Chile, **Andesmar** (www.andesmarchile.cl) goes over Paso Cardenal Samoré to Osorno (AR$555, four hours, two daily).

Buses from Villa la Angostura

TO	COST (AR$)	TIME (HR)	SERVICE
Bariloche	90	1¼	8 daily
Neuquén	855-1084	6¾	2 daily
San Martín de los Andes	177	2¼	2 daily
Villa Traful	102	2	daily

Getting Around

BICYCLE

Aquiles (☎0294-448 8345; www.facebook.com/aquiles.rental; Av Arrayanes 150; ⏰9am-1pm & 4-8pm) rents out quality mountain bikes for AR$150 per day.

BOAT

Five companies run daily ferries from the dock (next to Hotel Angostura in La Villa) to the tip of Quetrihué Peninsula in Parque Nacional Los Arrayanes (around AR$495/650 one way/return, plus AR$250 national-park entrance). Departures are typically at 11am and 2:30pm. Purchase tickets at the dock before hiking out, to secure a space on the return. The ride takes around 45 minutes and you can put a bicycle on the boat.

BUS

Local buses cost AR$10 to go anywhere in town. Transportes 15 de Mayo runs hourly buses from the bus terminal to La Villa (15 minutes), up Av Siete Lagos to Lago Correntoso (15 minutes), and south down Av Arrayanes to Puerto Manzano on Lago Nahuel Huapi (15 minutes). From July through September, and December through March, 15 de Mayo runs six or seven daily buses to the ski resort at Cerro Bayo (AR$80, one hour).

TAXI

Taxis (or your own wheels) are the best means of getting to the trailheads, although some are served by local buses. Taxis and buses leave from the **Terminal de Omnibus Villa La Angostura** on Av Siete Lagos, just north of Av Arrayanes.

Villa Traful

☎0294 / POP 360 / ELEV 720M

This little village enjoys an almost achingly beautiful location surrounded by mountains on the southern banks of Lago Traful. The place really packs out in January, February and Easter, for which it's advisable to have booked accommodations three months in advance. The rest of the year, you may just have it to yourself. Depending on what you're into, November, December, March and April are great times to be here.

Sights & Activities

Cascada Coa Có WATERFALL
This waterfall is a moderately easy, two-hour roundtrip walk from Villa Traful that can be done without a guide. Walk uphill on the street running beside the *guardaparque* (park ranger) office and follow the signs. From where the path forks at the open field it's 500m on the left to the 30m-high Coa Có. Return and take the other fork for 1km to the smaller Cascadas de los Arroyos Blanco.

Lagunas las Mellizas HIKING
Starting with a boat ride across the lake, this trek of moderate difficulty begins with a 2½-hour climb through cypress forests, before reaching a lookout with views of the Lagunas Azul and Verde (Blue and Green Lagoons).

If you've still got the legs for it, fording a stream gets you to an area with a variety of well-preserved Tehuelche rock paintings, dated at around 600 years old. It helps to have a local guide for this, as there are multiple tracks.

Sleeping & Eating

Albergue & Camping Vulcanche HOSTEL, CAMPGROUND $
(☎0294-447-9028; www.vulcanche.com; camping per person US$7, dm US$15; 📶) In a beautiful wooded area on the eastern edge of Villa Traful, this grassy campground and hostel has decent dorms and a good kitchen. There are also cozy, fully equipped *dormis* (wooden huts) for up to four people.

Hostería Villa Traful HOTEL $$
(☎0294-447-9005; www.hosteriavillatraful.com; RP 65; s/d from US$96/114; 📶) A pleasant little mom-and-pop-run operation on the western edge of Villa Traful. Rooms are aging but comfortable, there's a good restaurant on the premises, and the owners organize boating and fishing trips. *Cabañas* are available for groups.

Ñancú Lahuén ARGENTINE $$
(☎0294-447-9017; mains AR$190-260; ⏲11:30am-11pm; 📶) A cute little log cabin set up in the center of the village, where trout dishes are the specialty (try 'em with the almond sauce), although the menu stretches to *parrilla* and a good range of salads as well.

Information

Banco de la Provincia de Neuquén, in the middle of the village, has an ATM that accepts Visa and MasterCard.

Tourist Office (☎0294-447-9099; ⏲9am-8pm daily Dec-Feb, Sat-Wed Mar-Nov) Shares an office with the *guardaparque* (park ranger) in the middle of the village.

Getting There & Away

Villa Traful has better bus connections in summertime (December to February) than the rest of the year. La Araucana has daily services to Villa la Angostura (AR$102, two hours) and summer services to San Martín de los Andes (AR$165, 2½ hours). There are services from Bariloche (AR$86, two hours) daily in summer.

If you're driving, getting here is half the fun – Villa Traful is 80km north of Bariloche via unpaved RP 65.

San Martín de los Andes

☎02972 / POP 33,600 / ELEV 645M

Like a mellower version of Bariloche, San Martín has two peak periods: winter for skiing at Cerro Chapelco and summer for trekking, climbing etc, in nearby Parque Nacional Lanín. Brave souls also swim in the chilly waters of Lago Lácar on the western edge of town. Between these times it's a quiet little town with a spectacular setting that retains much of the charm and architectural unity that once attracted people to Bariloche. A boat ride on the lake is pretty much a must if you're passing through, and if the snow's cleared (anytime from November onward) and you're heading south, you should seriously think about leaving town via the scenically neck-straining Ruta de los Siete Lagos (RN 40), which runs south to Villa la Angostura, Lago Nahuel Huapi and Bariloche.

Sights

Almost everything in San Martín de los Andes is within walking distance of the *centro cívico,* and the shady lakefront park and pier are delightful places to spend an afternoon.

Museo Primeros Pobladores MUSEUM
(☎02972-427347; M Rosas s/n; AR$50; ⏲8am-5pm Mon-Fri, 4-6pm Sat) Regional archaeological and ethnographic items such as arrowheads, spear points, pottery and musical instruments are the focus of this museum. Good temporary exhibitions are sometimes held.

La Pastera Museo del Che MUSEUM
(☎02972-411994; cnr Sarmiento & Roca; ⏲9:30am-2pm & 5-8pm Mon-Sat) FREE This small museum is located in a former barn, where Che Guevara spent a couple of nights in late January 1952 during the motorcycle trip immortalized in *The Motorcycle Diaries*. You can watch a short film, dedicated to Che, and see the bale of hay on which the man himself allegedly slept.

Activities

★ **Ruta de los Siete Lagos** SCENIC DRIVE
(Seven Lakes Route) From San Martín de los Andes, RN 40 follows an eminently scenic but rough, narrow and sometimes dusty route past numerous alpine lakes to Villa la Angostura. It's known as the Ruta de los Siete Lagos (p385) and its spectacular scenery

SKIING IN CERRO CHAPELCO

Located 20km southeast of San Martín, **Cerro Chapelco** (☎02972-427845; www.chapelco.com; RP 19; ski day passes adult AR$930-1330, child AR$750-1070; ⏰mid-Jun–early Oct) is one of Argentina's principal winter-sports centers, with a mix of 28 runs for beginners and experts, and a maximum elevation of 1920m. Full ski-equipment rental is available (AR$780 per day). Transportes Ko-Ko (p386) runs three buses daily (AR$90 return) during ski season to the mountain from San Martín's bus terminal.

The **Fiesta Nacional del Montañés**, the annual ski festival, is held during the first half of August. The slopes are open from mid-June to early October. The low season is mid-June to early July and from August 28 to mid-October; high season is around the last two weeks of July. Rental equipment is cheaper in San Martín. Travel agencies in San Martín also offer packages with shuttle service, or shuttle service alone (AR$150); they pick you up at your hotel.

has made the drive famous. Sections of the 110km route close every year due to heavy snowfalls.

December to May is the best time to schedule this trip, but ask around for current conditions.

Full-day tours from San Martín, Villa la Angostura and Bariloche regularly do this route, but there's also a scheduled bus service and, with a little forward planning, it's possible to drive/cycle it yourself.

Mirador Bandurrias HIKING
A 2.5km steep, dusty hike ends with awesome views of Lago Lácar; be sure to take a snack or lunch. Tough cyclists can reach the mirador (viewpoint) in about an hour via dirt roads.

Lanín Turismo OUTDOORS
(☎02972-425808; www.laninturismo.com; Av San Martín 437; ⏰9am-1pm & 5-9pm Mon-Sat) This outfit arranges numerous outdoor outings, including rafting on the Río Chimehuin or Río Aluminé. Ascents of Volcán Lanín and multiday treks are also organized.

Andestrack OUTDOORS
(☎02972-420588; www.andestrack.com.ar; Coronel Rohde 782; ⏰9am-1pm & 3-8pm Mon-Sat) There are excellent opportunities for trekking and climbing in Parque Nacional Lanín. This young, enthusiastic company is highly recommended for mountain biking and ascents of the Lanín, Domuyo and Tromen volcanoes as well as adventures further afield.

Tours

Naviera BOATING
(☎02972-427380; https://lagolacarynonthue.com; Costanera MA Camino s/n; ⏰9:30am-7:30pm Mon-Sat, 10:30am-7:30pm Sun) Naviera runs worthwhile seven-hour boat excursions to Hua Hum (AR$1100 per person) and 30-minute jaunts to Quila Quina (AR$380 per person).

Festivals & Events

Fiesta de Fundación CULTURAL
(⏰Feb 4) San Martín de los Andes celebrates its founding on February 4, with speeches, parades and other festivities; the parade itself is an entertainingly incongruous mix of military folks, firefighters, gauchos, polo players and fox hunters.

Sleeping

San Martín is loaded with accommodations, but they're relatively costly in all price ranges, especially in summer high season (January to March) and peak ski season (mid-July and August), when reservations are a must. Quality, however, is mostly high. In low season, prices can drop by 40%.

★ **Adventure Bed & Bike** HOSTEL $
(☎02972-413236; http://adventurebedandbike.com-losandes.info; Atahualpa Yupanqui 289; dm US$20, d with/without bathroom US$61/56; 📶) On most days here, you'll find gregarious owner Indiana chatting with (predominantly cyclist) guests over ample breakfasts or in the chillout areas, advising them on the area's best routes. The wood-paneled rooms are cozy and you don't have to be a cyclist to stay here. Roughly halfway between San Martín and Lago Lolog, it's connected to town by shuttle buses.

Hotel Antiguos HOTEL $
(☎02972-411876; www.hotelantiguos.com.ar; Diaz 751; d/tr from US$67/92; ❄📶) Set just off the main drag, the Antiguos indulges in San

San Martín de Los Andes

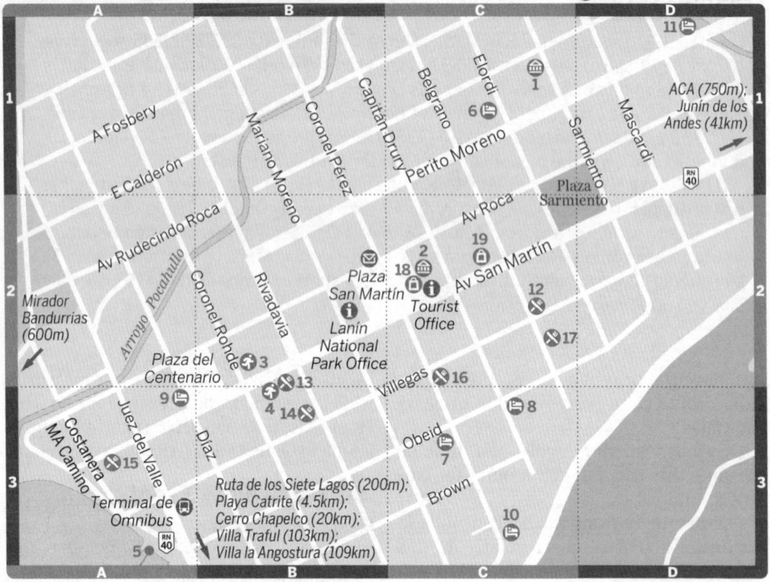

San Martín de Los Andes

Sights
1 La Pastera Museo del Che ... C1
2 Museo Primeros Pobladores ... C2

Activities, Courses & Tours
3 Andestrack ... B2
4 Lanín Turismo ... B3
5 Naviera ... A3

Sleeping
6 El Oso Andaluz Hostel ... C1
7 Hostería Hueney Ruca ... C3
8 Hostería La Masía ... C3
9 Hotel Antiguos ... A3
10 La Raclette ... C3
11 Rotui Apart Hotel ... D1

Eating
12 Bamboo Brasas ... C2
13 Corazón Contento ... B2
14 El Mesón de la Patagonia ... B3
15 Morphen ... A3
16 Nobuko Restoran & Sushi Bar ... C2
17 Ulises ... C2

Shopping
18 Artesanías Neuquinas ... C2
19 Patalibro ... C2

Martín's heavy-wood-and-stone fetish, and does it well. Some rooms have sweeping garden/mountain views; all are spacious and luxuriously appointed. The roaring fireplace in the lounge area makes for a welcome sight in winter.

El Oso Andaluz Hostel HOSTEL $
(☎02972-413010; www.elosoandaluz.com.ar; Elordi 569; dm/d from US$15/46; ❄@🛜) San Martín's coziest little downtown hostel has a good bed-to-bathroom ratio, atmospheric common areas and good-value private rooms.

★**La Raclette** HOTEL $$
(☎02972-427664; www.laraclette.com.ar; Coronel Pérez s/n; r US$96; @🛜) Inside this turreted residence, the narrow, low-ceilinged hallways lead on to spacious, comfortable rooms. What really tips the scales are the downstairs common areas – a lounge-bar area and cozy little conversation pit centered on a big open fireplace.

★ **Hostería La Masía** HOTEL $$
(☎ 02972-427688; www.hosterialamasia.com.ar; Obeid 811; s & d US$99, tr US$142; 📶) Taking the whole Edelweiss thing to the next level, La Masía offers plenty of dark-wood paneling, heavy wooden beams, arched doorways and cast-iron light fittings. Rooms are big and comfortable and most have mountain views. Fireplaces warm the lobby, and the owners are usually around to make sure everyone feels at home. Superb.

Hostería Hueney Ruca HOTEL $$
(☎ 02972-421499; www.hosteriahueneyruca.com.ar; cnr Obeid & Coronel Pérez; s/d US$74/86; 📶) The big terra-cotta-tiled rooms at this araucaria-shaded property look onto a cute, well-kept little backyard. Beds are big and firm and bathrooms spacious, with glass-walled showers. The fireplace in the common area is a boon in colder months.

Rotui Apart Hotel HOTEL $$$
(☎ 02972-429539; www.rotui.com.ar; Perito Moreno 1378; apt from US$228; ❄📶) A lovely wood-and-stone lodge set on immaculately manicured grounds overlooking the Arroyo Pochulla creek. Apartments for up to five people are sumptuously appointed, with king-size beds, polished floorboards and duck-down quilts.

Eating

Corazón Contento CAFE $
(☎ 02972-412750; Av San Martín 467; mains AR$100; ⌚ 9am-11pm; 📶) A cute little bakery-cafe serving up an excellent range of snacks, such as empanadas and quiches, as well as inexpensive daily specials. The salads are great and the freshly baked scones and muffins hit the spot.

★ **El Mesón de la Patagonia** INTERNATIONAL $$
(☎ 02972-424970; Rivadavia 885; mains AR$190-280; ⌚ noon-3pm & 8-11:30pm) This cute little place has one of the most creative menus in town, with plenty of trout dishes, homemade pastas and meaty mains, such as lamb with mint sauce. Little touches, such as amuse-bouches and a taste of after-dinner homemade liquor, are most welcome.

★ **Morphen** FUSION $$
(☎ 02972-422545; www.morphen.com.ar; Av San Martín 151; mains AR$225-340; ⌚ 8-11:30pm; 📶🖉) Enter Morphen, and you enter a wonderland of Banksy graffiti, surreal sculpture, swirling murals and strange mobiles suspended from the ceiling. The food is a pleasant deviation from the meaty standards touted by most of the town's restaurants. Feast on vegan 'hamburgers,' pizza-caccia with pesto, and pumpkin ravioli with shrimp in curry sauce, and wash it all down with craft beer.

Ulises ARGENTINE $$
(☎ 02972-428734; www.facebook.com/ulisesrestaurante; Belgrano 940; mains AR$170-450; ⌚ noon-3pm & 7:30-11:30pm Tue-Sun; 📶) This small, refined, family-run restaurant's strengths lie in its attention to detail: friendly service, a succinct, well-executed menu of homemade pastas, *bife de chorizo* cooked several different ways and a couple of trout dishes, and a well-chosen wine selection. The *sorrentinos* (large ravioli) with multiple fillings are particularly good.

Nobuko Restoran & Sushi Bar JAPANESE $$
(☎ 02972-414910; www.facebook.com/NobukoRestaurantSmandes; Coronel Pérez 910; mains AR$180-320; ⌚ 8-11:45pm Tue-Sat; 📶) Minimalist, Japanese-style decor and creative use of local ingredients in its Japanese and fusion dishes distinguish this restaurant from San Martín's more standard offerings. There's an extensive sushi list and sakes as well as Argentine wines.

★ **Bamboo Brasas** PARRILLA $$$
(☎ 02972-420042; cnr Belgrano & Villegas; mains AR$210-350; ⌚ noon-3:30pm & 8pm-midnight; 📶) As you'd expect, this upmarket *parrilla* does wonderful things with meat, from steaks to *morcilla* and chorizo. Some even claim that it serves the best meat in all of Argentina. We haven't tried all the meat in Argentina (yet), but judging from the way they cooked our sweetbreads, they know what they're doing.

Shopping

Artesanías Neuquinas ARTS & CRAFTS
(☎ 02972-428396; M Rosas 790; ⌚ 9am-6pm Mon-Sat) A Mapuche cooperative with high-quality weavings and wood crafts on offer.

Patalibro BOOKS
(☎ 02972-421532; Av San Martín 866; ⌚ 9am-8pm) Has a good selection of books on Patagonia in Spanish and some Lonely Planet titles and novels in English. Carries the excellent *Sendas y Bosques* guide and park trail maps.

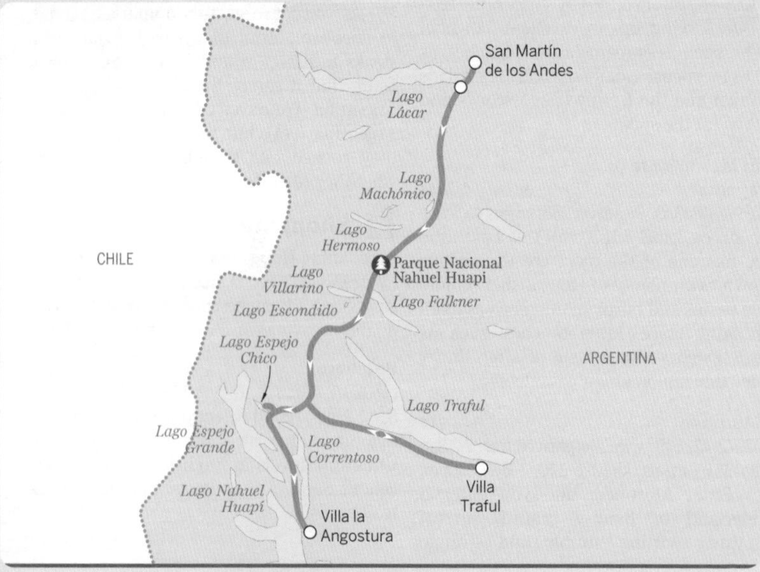

San Martín de los Andes
Lago Lácar
Lago Machónico
Lago Hermoso
Parque Nacional Nahuel Huapi
Lago Villarino
Lago Falkner
Lago Escondido
Lago Espejo Chico
CHILE
ARGENTINA
Lago Traful
Lago Espejo Grande
Lago Correntoso
Lago Nahuel Huapí
Villa Traful
Villa la Angostura

GUAXINIM/SHUTTERSTOCK ©

KOVGABOR/SHUTTERSTOCK ©

Top: Cycling alongside Lago Traful
Bottom: La Ruta de los Siete Lagos

1 DAY La Ruta de los Siete Lagos

A spectacular road between towering, snow-capped mountains, crystal-clear lakes and dense pine forests, this is a 110km Lake District classic. Bike it in a few days, drive it in one, tour it or bus it – just don't miss it.

Starting at **San Martín de los Andes** (p380), head out of town on the RN 40, skirting the banks of **Lago Lácar** (p388) and passing the Mapuche town of Curruhuinca. After 20km you'll come to the lookout at Arroyo Partido.

From here it's a 5km downhill coast to a bridge over the Río Hermoso. Two short climbs and 5km later, you'll reach the dark-blue Lago Machónico. A further 5km brings you to a turnoff to the right, where it's 2km of dirt road to Lago Hermoso, surrounded by mixed ñire and radale forests. Colored deer are common in this area, as are hunters, so be on the lookout (for both) when walking in the woods.

Entering the **Parque Nacional Nahuel Huapi** (p367), it's 15km to the Cascada Vullignanco, a 20m waterfall made by the Río Filuco. Two kilometers on, the road runs between Lago Villarino and Lago Falkner, which has a wide sandy beach.

Two kilometers further on is Lago Escondido, from where it's 8km of downhill zigzag to a turnoff to the left. Follow this side (dirt) road for 2km to get to the north end of Lago Traful.

After 30km look for the turnoff for **Villa Traful** (p379) – it's 27km from here to the villa, down a good dirt road, passing scenic lakeside bush campgrounds.

Sticking to the main road, though, you'll skirt the banks of Lago Correntoso and after 20km you'll come to a bridge and a disused *hostería* (lodging house). If you're looking for a side trip, just before the bridge, turn right and take the uphill road that ends at Lago Espejo Chico after 2km.

Continuing south, you'll catch glimpses of Lago Espejo Grande on the right through the trees. There are several lookouts along the road.

From here it's another 15km to a crossroads where you turn left, and 10km on asphalt to **Villa la Angostura** (p377).

Information

ACA (Automóvil Club Argentino; 02972-429194; Av Koessler 2175; 24hr) Good source for provincial road maps.

Andina Internacional (02972-427871; Capitán Drury 876; 9am-6pm) Money exchange, including traveler's checks.

Banco de la Nación (Av San Martín 687; 9am-1pm Mon-Fri) Has an ATM.

Lanín National Park Office (Intendencia del Parque Nacional Lanín; 02972-427233; www.pnlanin.org; Plaza San Martín; 8am-3pm Mon-Fri) Has limited maps as well as brochures and information on road conditions on the Ruta de los Siete Lagos.

Post Office (cnr Coronel Pérez & Roca; 8am-6pm Mon-Fri, 9am-1pm Sat)

Ramón Carrillo Hospital (02972-427211; cnr Coronel Rohde & Av San Martín) Basic medical care.

Tourist Office (02972-427347; www.sanmartindelosandes.gov.ar; cnr Av San Martín & M Rosas; 8am-8:30pm) Provides surprisingly candid information on hotels and restaurants, plus excellent brochures and maps.

Getting There & Away

AIR

There are regular flights from **Chapelco Airport** (02972-428388; RN 40) to Buenos Aires with Aerolíneas Argentinas. The airport is between San Martín and Junín. Any bus heading north out of San Martín can drop you at the entrance.

BOAT

Naviera (p381) sails from the **passenger pier** (Muelle de Pasajeros; Costanera MA Camino) at noon on a sightseeing trip of Lago Lácar's lakeside villages. Eventually it reaches Paso Hua Hum on the Chilean border, where Chile-bound passengers can disembark and continue on foot. Departure times change; call the ferry company or check with the tourist office. The seven-hour return trip costs AR$1100.

BUS

The **Terminal de Omnibus** (02972-427044; cnr Villegas & Juez del Valle) is a block south of RN 40 and 3½ blocks southwest of Plaza San Martín.

La Araucana (02972-420285; Terminal de Omnibus) goes to Villa Traful daily during summer (AR$165, 2½ hours). If you're heading to Villa la Angostura or Bariloche in summer, Albus regularly takes the scenic Ruta de los Siete Lagos (RN 40) instead of the longer but smoother Rinconada route.

To get to Aluminé you must first change buses in Zapala or Junín de los Andes (where there are three departures per week).

Igi-Llaima (02972-428878; www.igillaima.cl; Terminal de Omnibus) takes RP 60 over Paso Tromen (AKA Mamuil Malal) to Pucón, Chile (AR$360, five hours, daily at 6am), passing the Volcán Lanín en route; sit on the left for views.

From San Martín there is direct service in summer via RN 231 over Paso Cardenal A Samoré (Puyehue) to Osorno and Puerto Montt in Chile.

There are frequent daily departures to these destinations.

Buses from San Martín de los Andes

TO	COST (AR$)	TIME (HR)	SERVICE
Bariloche	177	3½-4	2 daily
Buenos Aires	842-1886	20¼-23	3 daily
Junín de los Andes	53-95	¾	7 daily
Neuquén	570-950	6¾	4 daily
Villa la Angostura	216	2¼	2 daily
Zapala	391-495	3¾	3 daily

Getting Around

Transportation options slim down during low season. In summer **Transportes Ko-Ko** (02972-427422; Terminal de Omnibus) goes twice daily to Puerto Canoa on Lago Huechulafquen (AR$80) and will stop at campgrounds en route. **Albus** (02972-428100; www.albus.com.ar; Terminal de Omnibus) goes to the beach at Playa Catrite on Lago Lácar (AR$55) several times daily, while Transportes Ko-Ko runs four buses daily to Lago Lolog (AR$46) in summer only.

San Martín has no lack of car-rental agencies, including **Alamo** (02972-410811; Av San Martín 836, 2nd fl; 9am-6pm) and **Sur** (02972-429028; Villegas 830; 9am-6pm Mon-Fri, to 2pm Sat & Sun).

Mountain biking is an excellent way to explore the surrounding area (and a good way to travel the Ruta de los Siete Lagos). Rent bikes at **HG Rodados** (02972-427345; Av San Martín 1061; 9am-1pm & 4-8pm Mon-Fri, 9am-8pm Sat) for around AR$70/200 per hour/day.

Parque Nacional Lanín

02972

Dominating the view in all directions along the Chilean border, the snowcapped cone of 3776m Volcán Lanín is the centerpiece of this **national park** (www.pnlanin.org; adult/student AR$250/130), which extends 150km from

Parque Nacional Lanín

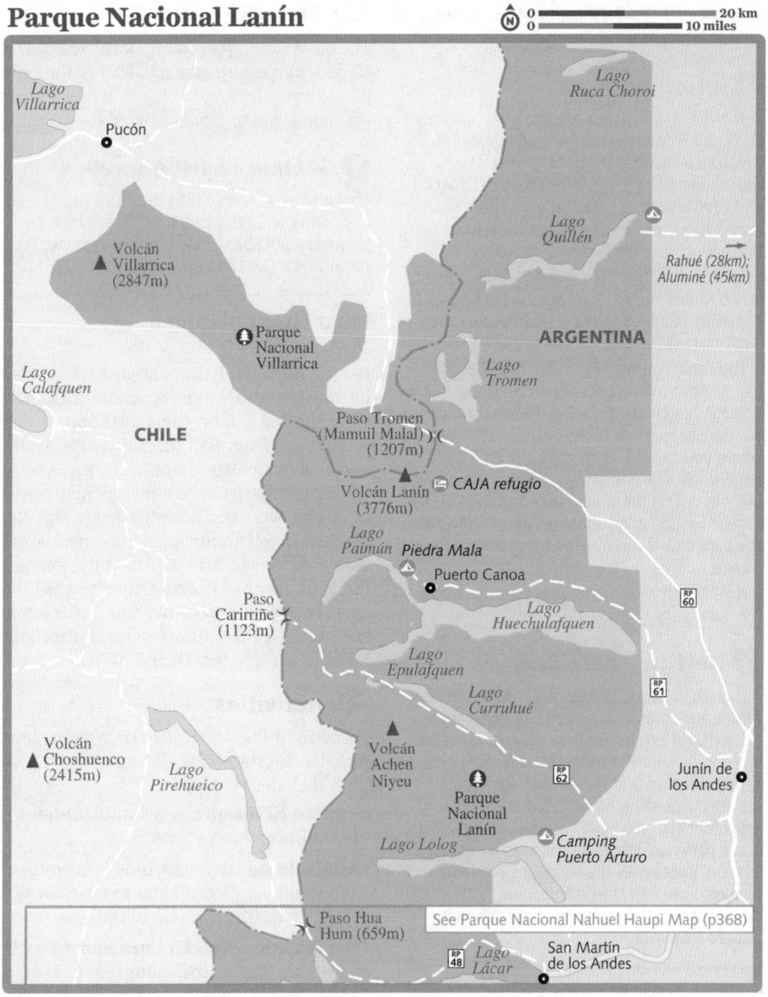

Parque Nacional Nahuel Huapi in the south to Lago Ñorquinco in the north.

Protecting 3790 sq km of native Patagonian forest, Parque Nacional Lanín is home to many of the same species that characterize more southerly Patagonian forests, such as the southern beeches – lenga, ñire and coihue. The area does host some unique specimens, though, such as the extensive stands of the broadleaf, deciduous southern beech, raulí, and the curious *pehuén* (monkey puzzle tree; *Araucaria araucana*), a pinelike conifer whose nuts have long been a dietary staple for the Pehuenches and Mapuches.

Trekking up Volcán Lanín is the park's most popular challenge, though there are great hikes around each of the park's lakes.

Activities

Most national park trails are accessible from December to April, though it can snow at any time of year. Some trails are open year-round but require you to possess the necessary backcountry hiking skills, while others are off-limits outside the peak months. For most trails, you are supposed to register with the nearest ranger station. For the ascent of Volcán Lanín, registration is mandatory and it's best to trek with a reliable mountain guide.

Information

Volcán Lanín sits between Lago Huechulafquen and Lago Tromen, in the park's central sector, which also includes the hard-to-reach Lago Curruhue and Lago Epulafquen. Lago Lácar and Lago Lolog are part of the southern sector, while Lago Quillén, Lago Ruca Choroi and Lago Ñorquinco form the northern sector.

The towns of San Martín de los Andes, Junín de los Andes and Aluminé are the best bases for exploring Lanín's southern, middle and northern sectors, respectively.

The Lanín National Park Office (p386) in San Martín produces brochures on camping, hiking and climbing in the park. Scattered throughout the park proper are several ranger stations where you can get up-to-date info on trail conditions. The national park's website (www.pnlanin.org) is full of useful information. At the time of writing admission was charged to enter the park only if you were heading toward Puerta Canoa.

Note that there is no phone reception inside the park.

Getting There & Away

Although the park is close to San Martín de los Andes and Junín de los Andes, public transportation is not extensive. Two or three buses per day connect Junín and San Martín with Lago Huechulafquen and Junín with Lago Tromen during the peak months of January and February; otherwise you need your own wheels. With some patience, hitchhiking is feasible in high season. Buses over the Hua Hum and Tromen passes, from San Martín and Junín to Chile, will carry passengers to intermediate destinations but are often full.

Lago Lácar & Lago Lolog

☎02972

From San Martín de los Andes, at the east end of Lago Lácar, there is a bus service on RP 48 that runs along the lake to the Chilean border at Paso Hua Hum. You can get off the bus anywhere along the lake or get off at Hua Hum and hike to **Cascada Chachín** (24hr) FREE; bus drivers know the stop. From the highway it's 3km down a dirt road and then another 20 minutes' walk along a trail to the waterfall. It's a great spot for a picnic.

About 15km north of San Martín de los Andes, Lago Lolog offers good fishing in a largely undeveloped area.

Sleeping

The basic **Camping Puerto Arturo** (☎02972-426353; camping per person US$10) is the only place to stay by Lago Lolog. Nearest accommodations are in San Martín de los Andes.

Getting There & Away

Transportes Ko-Ko (p386) runs four buses daily in summer to Lago Lolog from San Martín de los Andes (AR$58). Chile-bound buses can let you off near Cascada Chachín.

Lago Huechulafquen

☎02972

Parque Nacional Lanín's largest lake is also its most central and accessible area. Despite limited public transportation, it can be reached from San Martín de los Andes and – more easily – Junín de los Andes. RP 61 climbs from a junction just north of Junín, west to Huechulafquen and the smaller Lago Paimún, offering outstanding views of Volcán Lanín. The tiny, spread-out settlement of Puerto Canoa toward the western end of Lago Huechulafquen offers access to trailheads of several excellent hikes of varying length and difficulty.

Activities

Hikes from Puerto Canoa range from short rambles to strenuous day-long treks. Options include:

Sendero El Bosque A beautiful 20-minute trail near Lago Paimún.

El Saltillo An easy walk (one-hour return) from Camping Piedra Mala to Cascada El Saltillo, a nearby forest waterfall.

Puerto Canoa–Volcán Cara Sur A tough eight-hour hike to the south face of Volcán Lanín. Park rangers require you to set out between 8am and 11am.

Another good backcountry hike circles Lago Paimún. This requires about two days from Puerto Canoa; you return to the north side of the lake by crossing a cable platform strung across the narrows between Huechulafquen and Paimún.

With a guide, it's also possible to hike across to Paso Tromen or continue climbing to the Nuevo Refugio Militar, halfway up Volcán Lanín, and make an attempt on the summit from there. The initial segment follows an abandoned road, but after about 40 minutes it becomes a pleasant woodsy trail along the Arroyo Rucu Leufu, an attractive mountain stream. Halfway to the *refugio* is an extensive *pehuén* forest, the southernmost in the park, which makes the walk worthwhile if you lack time for the entire route. The route to the *refugio* takes about seven hours one way.

Tours

Jose Julian BOATING
(☎02972-428029; www.catamaranjosejulian.com.ar; boat trips adult/4-11yr AR$550/420) From Puerto Canoa, the *Jose Julian* offers enjoyable boat trips on Lago Huechulafquen.

Sleeping

Campsites are abundant along RP 61; travelers camping in the free sites in the narrow area between the lakes and the highway must dig a latrine and remove their own trash. If you camp at the maintained sites, you'll support local Mapuche concessionaires. There are several appealing midrange fishing lodges around Puerto Canoa.

Refugio del Pescadór HOTEL $$
(☎in Buenos Aires 011-5254-2392; www.refugiodelpescador.com; RP 61, Km56; r per person incl full board US$91) Popular with fishing parties, this lodge has can't-swing-a-cat cozy, wood-paneled rooms, some with views of Volcán Lanín. Horseback-riding, fishing and boating outings are among the activities offered.

Hostería Paimún LODGE $$$
(☎02972-491758; www.hosteriapaimun.com.ar; RP 61, Km58; r per person incl full board US$137; ⊙Nov–mid-Apr) This rough-hewn stone lodge makes an ideal base for fresh-air fiends into trekking, horseback riding and fishing. Rooms are on the compact side but benefit from lake views.

Information

Pay your entry fee at the ranger station, **Guardaparque Lago Huechulafquen** (RP 61, Km22; adult/child AR$250/130; ⊙8am-6pm), at the east end of Lago Huechulafquen. At Lago Paimún there's another ranger station, **Guardaparque Lago Paimún** (RP 61, Km58; ⊙8am-6pm), where you can consult about trail conditions; register here before setting off on hikes.

Getting There & Away

Junín de los Andes–based **Transporte Castelli** (☎02972-491557; http://transportecastelli.com.ar) runs three buses daily as far as Hostería Paimún in January and February. Transportes Ko-Ko (p386) runs buses to Piedra Mala daily in summer from the San Martín de los Andes bus terminal. The rest of the year you'll have to rely on your own wheels; it's a 56km drive from Junín along the mostly unpaved, scenic and winding RP 61 to Puerto Canoa.

Lago Tromen & Volcán Lanín

☎02972

The Lago Tromen section of Parque Nacional Lanín is primarily of interest to trekkers wishing to tackle the region's most spectacular hike. The northern approach to Volcán Lanín, which straddles the Argentina–Chile border, is the shortest and usually the earliest in the season to open for hikers and climbers.

Activities

Besides the challenging Lanín ascent, there are two excellent short walks from the ranger station. One is a 10km loop that takes you down to Lago Tromen, passing through a beautiful araucaria forest and a stretch of ñire forest. Alternatively, you can do the 2.5km walk to the base of Volcán Lanín's north face (around 40 minutes each way).

★**Volcán Lanín** TREKKING
This magnificent, snow-peaked volcano (3776m) is the star attraction of both Parque Nacional Lanín and the Lake District. Its perfect cone entices scores of hikers and climbers and its accessibility is part of its appeal. The ascent of the volcano's north face, typically done over two days, is a tough physical challenge but within reach of reasonably fit hikers.

Unless you're an experienced mountaineer, it's foolhardy to attempt the ascent without a mountain guide. Andestrack (p381) arranges group hikes and the park offices in San Martín and Junín have lists of authorized mountain guides. Before the trek, you need to register with the ranger station at Lago Tromen. To prove that you are adequately equipped, it's obligatory to show equipment, such as cooker, helmet, crampons and ice axe, and other items, including sunglasses, sunblock, gloves, hat and waterproof padded jacket.

You have to register and start the hike before 11am. From the trailhead at the ranger station, it's around an hour's walk to the base of the volcano, then an hour along the moderately inclined Espina de Pescado ('Fish Bone') before you tackle the steeper

Camino de Mulas ('Mule Track') that takes around three hours. It brings you to the Nuevo Refugio Militar (2450m; capacity 20 people), where you roll out your sleeping bag until 2am the following morning, when you commence your ascent. It takes around 40 minutes to reach the old CAJA *refugio* (now a mere shelter) at 2600m; above that point, snow equipment is necessary. The last section is steep and tough going, and it takes around six hours to reach the summit. After admiring the tremendous view, you descend all the way back down.

If you want to go up in winter, Andestrack can set you up with guides to hike up and ski or board down.

Sleeping

There's a basic Mapuche-run campground near the ranger station, and a *refugio* en route to the peak of Volcán Lanín.

Information

Contact Andestrack (p381) or the Lanín National Park Office (p386) in San Martín de los Andes to organize guides for climbing Lanín.

If doing a shorter hike in the Lago Tromen area, ask about trail conditions at **Guaradaparque Lago Tromen** (RP 60, Km67; 8am-6pm), the helpful ranger station, and register here before doing any walking.

Getting There & Away

Buses depart Junín de los Andes twice daily for Lago Tromen. Lago Tromen can also be reached by taking any bus that goes to Chile and getting off at Tromen.

The RP 60 is a beautifully paved road, apart from the last 10km to the Chilean border, which is gravel.

Northern Lakes

02972

Situated in the park's densest *pehuén* forests, isolated **Lago Quillén** is accessible by dirt road from Rahué, 17km south of Aluminé. Other nearby lakes include **Lago Ruca Choroi**, directly west of Aluminé, and **Lago Ñorquinco** on the park's northern border. There are Mapuche reservations at Ruca Choroi and Quillén. The appeal of the three lakes lies in their lack of crowds and their beautiful scenery.

There are hiking trails of varying difficulty around all the lakes, none of them particularly strenuous, and the longest taking around six hours each way. It's possible to hike between Lago Quillén and Lago Ruca Charoi.

There is a ranger station at each of the three lakes.

Getting There & Away

You'll need your own vehicle to get out to the three lakes. Lago Ñorquinco is part of the Circuito Pehuenia scenic drive that passes through Villa Pehuenia. The unpaved roads to Lago Quillén and Lago Ruca Choroi are fairly rough and bumpy.

Junín de los Andes

02972 / POP 12,621 / ELEV 800M

A much more humble affair than other Lake District towns, Junín's a favorite for fly fishers – the town deems itself the trout capital of Neuquén province and, to drive the point home, uses trout-shaped street signs. A couple of circuits leading out of town take in the scenic banks of the Lago Huechulafquen, where Mapuche settlements welcome visitors. Outside of peak season, these circuits are best done by private vehicle (or by bicycle, if you're incredibly enthusiastic), but travel agents based here offer reasonably priced tours. Junín is also a good base for exploring the main sections of Parque Nacional Lanín.

Sights

Museo Mapuche MUSEUM

(Domingo Milanesio 751; entry by donation; 8:30am-12:30pm & 2-7pm Mon-Fri, 9am-12:30pm Sat) This small but interesting museum showcases Mapuche pottery, pipes, *piñon* (araucaria tree nut) grinders and musical instruments. Another display features dinosaur bones.

Vía Cristi LANDMARK

(24hr) Situated about 2km from the center of Junín de los Andes, near the end of Av Antártida Argentina, Vía Cristi contains a collection of 22 sculptures, bas-reliefs and mosaics winding its way up Cerro de la Cruz and vividly depicting the Conquest of the Desert, Mapuche legends, Christian themes and indigenous history.

Sleeping & Eating

There are several local restaurants to choose from. Local specialties such as trout, wild boar and venison may be available.

Hostería Chimehuín HOTEL $

(☎ 02972-491132; www.interpatagonia.com/hosteriachimehuin; cnr Coronel Suárez & 25 de Mayo; s & d US$71, tr US$77; wifi) This is a beautiful spot a few minutes from the center of town. Book early and you'll have a good chance of snagging a room with a balcony overlooking the creek. Either way, rooms are big, warm and comfortable and the whole place has a tranquil air about it.

Sigmund ARGENTINE $$

(☎ 02972-492189; www.facebook.com/sigmund.restaurante.3; Juan M de Rosas 690; mains AR$130-230; ⊙noon-3pm & 8pm-midnight; wifi) A fabulous trendy eatery with colorful artsy decor, healthy food and a great *onda* (vibe). Choose from dozens of pizzas, pastas, sandwiches and salads, all delivered with friendly service.

Shopping

Paseo Artesanal ARTS & CRAFTS

(Domingo Milanesio s/n; ⊙9am-5pm Mon-Sat) Various Mapuche crafts for sale, including some beautiful polished woodwork and intricate weavings.

Information

Banco de la Provincia de Neuquén (Av San Martín, btwn Coronel Suárez & General Lamadrid; ⊙9am-1pm Mon-Fri) Opposite Plaza San Martín.

Club Andino Junín de los Andes (Domingo Milanesio 362; ⊙4-6pm Tue-Fri, 11am-1pm Sat) Come here for info on the Volcán Tromen climb and other Parque Nacional Lanín outings.

Lanín National Park Office (☎ 02972-491160; cnr Domingo Milanesio & Coronel Suárez; ⊙8am-9pm) Inside the tourist office. Has information on Parque Nacional Lanín.

Tourist Office (☎ 02792-491160; www.junindelosandes.gov.ar; cnr Domingo Milanesio & Coronel Suárez; ⊙8am-9pm) Helpful office providing maps, fishing permits and a list of licensed fishing guides.

Getting There & Away

AIR

Junín and San Martín de los Andes share Chapelco Airport (p386), which lies between the two towns. There are regularly scheduled flights to Buenos Aires and Neuquén. A *remise* (taxi) into town should run you about AR$150. Another option is walking the 1km out to the highway and flagging down a passing bus (AR$45, 25 minutes).

BUS

The **Terminal de Omnibus** (☎ 02792-492038; cnr Olavarría & Félix San Martín) is three blocks from the main plaza.

Transporte Castelli (p389) runs twice-daily services to Lago Tromen and to Lago Huechulafquen three times daily in January and February.

Aluminé

☎ 02942 / POP 4600 / ELEV 400M

Time seems to have stopped for Aluminé and, although it's an important tourist destination, it is less visited than destinations to the south. Situated 103km north of Junín de los Andes via RP 23, it's a popular fly-fishing destination and offers access to the less-visited northern sector of Parque Nacional Lanín. The Río Aluminé also offers excellent white-water rafting and kayaking.

Sights & Activities

The Aluminé tourist office keeps a list of available **fishing** guides and sells licenses (AR$630/1890/2520 per day/week/season).

Mali Viajes (☎ 02942-496310; Christian Jouvert s/n; ⊙9am-6pm Mon-Sat) offers scenic back-road tours along the Circuito Pehuenia (p392) in summer.

Salazar VILLAGE

(RP 16) This Mapuche community on the 26km dirt road to Lago Ruca Choroi (in Parque Nacional Lanín) sells traditional weavings, araucaria pine nuts and, in summer, *comidas tipicas* (traditional dishes). Salazar is an easy, signposted 12km bike ride out of Aluminé – just follow the river.

Aluminé Rafting OUTDOORS

(☎ 02942-496322; www.interpatagonia.com/aluminerafting; Conrado Villegas 610; ⊙9am-6pm Mon-Sat) For rafting on the Río Aluminé (best in November and December), as well as kayaking, fly fishing, trekking and rock climbing.

Sleeping & Eating

★ **El Hostal del Río** HOTEL $$

(☎ 02942-15-696808; www.elhostaldelrio.com.ar; RP 23 s/n; s & d US$57, tr US$80; wifi) A couple of kilometers north of town, this charming stone-and-wood fishing lodge offers supreme comforts with fantastic views of the Río Aluminé from the deck. Rooms are spacious and spotless and the shady grounds and other common areas are lovingly maintained.

La Posta del Rey ARGENTINE $$
(☎ 02942-496347; Christian Jouvert 336; mains AR$100-250; ⊙ noon-3:30pm & 8:30-11:30pm; 📶) Inside the Hostería Aluminé, this is the best eating option in Aluminé, serving up all the Argentine standards, plus Patagonian favorites such as lamb, venison and trout. Try the signature homemade *pastas patagónicas* in wild-mushroom and *piñon* (araucaria tree nut) sauce.

Information

Banco del Provincia del Neuquén (cnr Villegas & Mordarelli; ⊙ 9am-1pm Mon-Fri) Bank and ATM.

Tourist Office (☎ 02942-496001; info@alumine.gov.ar; Plaza San Martín; ⊙ 8am-9pm) Has lists of local accommodations, maps, fishing permits and road-condition info.

Getting There & Away

Aluminé's **bus terminal** (☎ 02941-496048; Av 4 de Caballeria s/n) is just downhill from the plaza, an easy walk to hotels. Campana Dos and Albus go at least once daily to/from Neuquén (AR$627, 5½ hours), Zapala (AR$321, 2¾ hours), San Martín de los Andes (AR$283, three hours) and Villa Pehuenia (AR$198, 1¾ hours).

Heading south, RP 23 is a gravel road in good condition, though it's narrow and winding in parts.

Villa Pehuenia

☎ 02942 / POP 700 / ELEV 1200M

Villa Pehuenia is an idyllic little lakeside village situated on the shores of Lago Aluminé, 102km north of Junín de los Andes (via RP 23 and Aluminé) and 120km west of Zapala (via RP 13). There are several Mapuche communities nearby, including Puel, located between Lago Aluminé and Lago Moquehue. The main attractions here are hiking in summer and skiing in winter, and it's part of the Circuito Pehuenia, a gorgeous scenic loop drive along a good gravel road.

The village lies at the heart of the Pehuen region, named of course after the *pehuén* (araucaria) trees that are so marvelously present.

Activities

★ **Circuito Pehuenia** SCENIC DRIVE
If you have a car, the Circuito Pehuenia is a great drive; it's a four- to six-hour loop from Villa Pehuenia past Lago Moquehue, Lago Ñorquinco, Lago Pulmarí and back around Lago Aluminé. It takes in the beautiful mountain lakes and araucaria forests of one of the least well-trodden parts of the Lake District.

Volcán Batea Mahuida HIKING
(off RP 13; ⊙ Dec-Mar) From the top of this volcano you can see eight others (from Lanín to the south to Copahue to the north) in both Argentina and Chile. Inside Batea Mahuida is a small crater lake. To get here you drive nearly to the top (in summer only) and then it's an easy two-hour walk to the summit (1948m).

Sleeping

Hostel Andino HOSTEL $
(☎ 02942-524420; www.hostelandino.com.ar; Arroyo Pehuen-co & Arroyo Chañy; dm US$23; 📶) An easy 3km bike ride from the heart of the village, this delightful hostel takes great care of backpacker needs. Owners Claudia and Javier are treasure troves of local info, the three dorms are all en suite and come with lockers, and there are lots of thoughtful extras – a barbecue area, fully equipped kitchen, DVDs, games, Wii and pool table.

★ **La Escondida** BOUTIQUE HOTEL $$$
(☎ 02942-15-691166; www.posadalaescondida.com; r/cottages from US$234/265; 📶) A small posada (inn) tucked away down by the lakefront. There are just six rooms, all fitted out in fine detail and with decks overlooking the water. Sitting areas are sumptuous, the restaurant is one of the best in the village, and there are good-value cabins (without water views) on offer if you're traveling in a group.

Eating & Drinking

Sorrento's ARGENTINE $$
(☎ 02942-551166; www.facebook.com/SorrentosVillaPehuenia; Manzana C III Lote 13; mains AR$198-265; ⊙ 7:30-11pm; 📶) Hearty local-fare options, such as trout-filled *sorrentinos* (ravioli) and lamb goulash with spaetzle, are menu staples here, as well as the surprising Dublin coddle (hot pot). Portions are generous and there's a particularly solid list of Argentine reds to help the food on its way.

Estacíon de la Montaña ARGENTINE $$
(☎ 02942-410678; off RP 13, Centro Comercial; mains AR$170-240; ⊙ noon-11pm; 📶) Step back in time by dining inside this atmospheric, wood-paneled carriage, decorated with early-20th-century posters and ads. The menu has solid Argentine standards, the friendly owner likes to practice his English and the decor deserves full marks.

Borravino WINE BAR
(☎02942-598701; www.facebook.com/borravinowine; Los Maitenes s/n; ⏲12:30-3pm & 7:30-11:30pm; 📶) An excellent wine list and a succinct menu of imaginative salads and meaty light bites dominate at this buzzy lakefront wine bar.

Information

Banco de la Provincia del Neuquén (Los Condores; ⏲9am-1pm Mon-Fri) Next to the police station; has an ATM.

Oficina de Turismo (☎02942-498044; www.villapehuenia.gov.ar; RP 13 s/n; ⏲8am-8pm) Stop by the entrance to town for good maps of the region and plenty of local info.

Getting There & Away

Exploring the area is tough without your own vehicle, though hitchhiking is feasible in summer. **Destinos Patagónicos** (☎02942-498067; Centro Comercial) is the representative for Albus, the only bus company serving the village. There is a single daily bus at the awkward time of 11pm to Neuquén (AR$815, seven hours), via Aluminé (AR$198, 1½ hours) and Zapala (AR$510, 4¼ hours).

Caviahue

☎02948 / POP 610 / ELEV 1600M

On the western shore of Lago Caviahue, the ski village of Caviahue lies at the southeast foot of the smokin' Volcán Copahue. Backed against snow-tipped mountains and dotted with umbrella-like araucaria pines, Caviahue could hardly be more picturesquely situated, and it's growing rapidly, too, with ski chalets popping up like mushrooms after rain. In the stretch between ski season and summer (October and November) the place is dead as heaven on a Saturday night.

Activities

Between mid-June and mid-September, Caviahue is all about skiing, snowshoeing, snowmobiling and even dog-sledding. In the summer months (December to March), Caviahue acts as a gateway to the Copahue hot springs, and there's some excellent hiking to be done in the area as well when the snow melts.

Cascadas Agrio HIKING
A straightforward walk running along a succession of six waterfalls known as Cascadas Agrio starts off RP 26, from across the bridge at the entrance to Caviahue, and meanders between araucaria trees. Allow a couple of hours or more for the roundtrip, depending on how many falls you decide to see.

Laguna Escondida HIKING
Reflecting the smoking resident Volcán Copahue and surrounded by umbrella-like araucaria pines, this beautiful lake lies an easy 4km hike from Caviahue. The trailhead is at the top of Calle Volcán Copahue.

Centro de Ski Cerro Caviahue SKIING
(☎02948-495043; www.caviahue.com; adult day pass AR$705-1130; ⏲mid-Jun–mid-Sep) A little under 2km west of Caviahue, this ski resort has four chairlifts, nine drag lifts, and 22 ski runs, some of which take skiers all the way up to the peak of active Volcán Copahue (2953m). The ski season runs from mid-June to mid-September and day-pass costs vary depending on the season.

Sleeping

Hebe's House Hostel HOSTEL $
(☎02948-495138; www.hebeshouse.com.ar; cnr Mapuche & Puesta del Sol; dm/d US$17/40; ⏲Dec-Sep; 📶) Hebe crams travelers into cozy but cramped dorms. It's set in a cute alpine building and offers kitchen access, laundry facilities and plenty of tourist information. If you're coming in winter, book well ahead.

Grand Hotel Caviahue HOTEL $$
(☎02948-495044; www.grandhotelcaviahue.com; 8 de Abril s/n; s/d US$57/77; 📶) A rambling, older-style hotel at the base of the ski slopes, with views out over the village, lake and mountains. The hotel was closed for renovation at the time of research, and due to reopen sometime in 2018.

Eating & Drinking

Trois TAPAS $$
(☎0299-15-411-0720; Los Ñires s/n; mains AR$180-290; ⏲8pm-1am; 📶) The menu at the most ambitious eatery in Caviahue changes daily, so it can be fondue one evening, tacos the next, and sushi the day after. Local craft beers and a convivial atmosphere keep the party hopping late into the night. Reservations advisable.

Gringa Cervecería Artesanal de Montaña BREWERY
(☎02948-495149; Los Ñires s/n; ⏲5-11:30pm; 📶) Apart from its celebrated smoked porter, German-style wheat beer, stout and a couple of other locally produced beers, this brewery-pizzeria pairs potent barley wine with platters of smoked meats. It's particularly lively during the ski season.

Cervecería Las Bruscas CRAFT BEER
(☎02942-15-554179; Los Ñires s/n; ⊙4pm-late;) This friendly little bar serves five locally made brews, including a stout, an amber ale involving the toasted nuts of an araucaria pine and the wonderfully smoky *ahumada*. The place gets hopping in the evenings as part of the après-ski scene.

Information

Oficina de Turismo (☎02948-495408; www.caviahue-copahue.gov.ar; RP 26; ⊙8am-8pm) Pick up your maps of Caviahue and the surrounding area at the entrance to town.

Getting There & Away

BUS

Cono Sur (☎02942-432607; Los Pehuenches) Three buses run daily at 5am, 10am and 4pm to Neuquén (AR$632, six hours) via Zapala (AR$376, three hours). If you're headed for Chos Malal, take one of the two morning buses and change in Las Lajas (AR$276, 2½ hours).

In summer (December through February) several daily buses run to and from Copahue.

CAR

If driving to Chos Malal, you'll have to take the unsealed, wonderfully scenic RP 21 – the road less travelled. After emerging on RN 21, take the RN 6 rather than the RN 4.

Copahue

☎02948 / ELEV 2030M

This small thermal-springs resort stands on the northeastern side of its namesake volcano among steaming, sulfurous pools, including a bubbling hot-mud pool, the popular Laguna del Chancho. The setting of this hamlet, in a natural amphitheater formed by the mountain range, is spectacular.

Copahue is very popular, mainly with Argentine visitors, as the growth in tourist infrastructure shows. Due to snow cover, the village is only open from the start of December to the end of April.

The village centers on the large, modern **Termas de Copahue** (☎0299-442-4140; www.termasdecopahue.com.ar; Ortiz Velez; baths AR$180, spa treatments from AR$280), which offers a wide range of curative bathing programs.

Activities

★**Laguna Termal** HIKING
This beautiful day trek, which should be possible in around eight hours, is easy enough to do on your own, leaving from Copahue. Due to snow conditions, it's only possible from December to April unless you bring special equipment. **Caviahue Tours** (☎02948-495138; www.caviahuetours.com; Los Pehuenches s/n; ⊙9am-1pm & 4-8pm) is among the many operators offering guides on this route.

Sleeping & Eating

Hotel Termas de Copahue HOTEL $$
(☎02948-495525; www.hoteltermascopahue.com.ar; Doucloux s/n; s/d from US$86/120; ⊙Dec-Apr;) One of Copahue's most convenient lodgings, a minute's walk from the hot-spring complex, Hotel Termas features modern rooms, atmospheric common areas and an excellent restaurant serving traditional Argentine and regional foods.

Parrilla Nito PARRILLA $$
(☎02948-495040; Jara s/n; mains AR$190-280; ⊙noon-3pm & 8-11pm Dec-Apr;) This place is the most reliable *parrilla* in town.

Getting There & Away

Several buses daily run between Caviahue and Copahue during high season. Change in Caviahue for long-distance departures to Neuquén via Zapala.

Chos Malal

☎02948 / POP 13,100 / ELEV 842M

Cruising through the stark, desertlike landscape north of Zapala doesn't really prepare you for arrival at this pretty little oasis town, named by the Mapuche for the yellow rock in the surrounding hills. Set at the convergence of Río Neuquén and Río Curi Leuvú, the town boasts two main plazas, bearing the names of the two superheroes of Argentina – San Martín and Sarmiento. Around the former is the majority of the historic buildings, including the Fuerte IV Division fort (go around the back for sweeping views out over the river valley). Five blocks south is Plaza Sarmiento, where you'll find banks and businesses.

Sleeping & Eating

Hosteria La Farfalla HOTEL $$
(☎02948-421349; www.farfalla.com.ar; cnr Salta & Islas Malvinas; s/d US$85/114;) Chos Malal's most comfortable accommodations can be found at this charming little lodge a few blocks south of Plaza Sarmiento. Rooms are spacious and comfortable, but it's the grounds and lovely garden that make the place.

OFF THE BEATEN TRACK

NORTH OF CHOS MALAL

Heading north from Chos Malal brings you to a couple of wonderful, rarely visited attractions: some hot springs and geysers, and an archaeological site featuring Pehuenche rock art, both near the village of Varvarco. Public transportation is rare and often nonexistent, but if you have the time and patience to get here you'll be well rewarded.

Parque Arqueológico Colomichicó (⏲24hr) This small archaeological site features one of the most important collections of Pehuenche rock art in Patagonia. There are over 600 examples here, carved with symbolic figures and abstract designs. The site is 8km along a dirt road off RP 39; the signposted turnoff is 9km south of Varvarco, at the Escuela Colo Michi-Co. You're supposed to visit the site only with a guide; contact the **tourist office** (✆02948-421329; RP 43; ⏲8am-2pm Mon-Fri) in advance to arrange one.

Aguas Calientes (RP 43) These excellent natural hot springs located at the foot of the Volcán Domuyo are spread over 20 sq km, and feature principal main sites. The main one, **Villa Aguas Calientes**, is suitable for swimming; **Las Olletas** is a collection of bubbling mud pits and **Los Tachos** are geysers, spurting up to heights of 2m. The site is 40km north of Varvarco.

If you don't have your own wheels, ask about hiring a driver with **Señora La Gallega** (✆02948-421329).

Restaurant Petit ARGENTINE **$$**
(✆02948-421718; 25 de Mayo 1251; mains AR$170-250; ⏲8pm-midnight Mon-Sat) This cozy little place is run by a friendly local lady who whips up traditional Argentine dishes and inspired desserts like some kind of culinary magician.

Information

Banco de la Nación (cnr Sarmiento & Urquiza; ⏲9am-1pm Mon-Fri) Has an ATM.

Hospital Zonal Gregorio Avárez (✆02948-421400; Flores 650; ⏲24hr) Basic medical care, with an on-site English speaker.

Oficina de Turismo Municipal (✆02948-421425; turnorte@neuquen.gov.ar; 25 de Mayo 89; ⏲8am-9pm) Has good maps of the town and surrounds.

Oficina de Turismo Provincial (✆02948-421991; RN 40 s/n; ⏲8am-9pm) Lots of useful regional info, as well as maps.

Getting There & Away

BUS

From the **bus terminal** (✆02948-422676; cnr Neuquén & Paz) there are departures for Neuquén (AR$719, six hours, at least nine daily) via Zapala (AR$412, 3½ hours). One Cono Sur bus runs to Varvarco (AR$243, three hours) at 2:30pm on weekdays. One or two Norte Neuquino minibuses a day leave for Buta Ranquil (AR$143, two hours), where you can connect to a Mendoza-bound bus.

CAR

If driving to Varvarco, take the gravel RP 43 rather than RP 39, as it's in better condition.

Parque Nacional Laguna Blanca

At 1275m above sea level and surrounded by striking volcanic deserts, Laguna Blanca is only 10m deep, an interior drainage lake that formed when lava flows dammed two small streams. Only 30km southwest of Zapala, the lake is too alkaline for fish, but hosts many bird species, including coots, ducks, grebes, upland geese, gulls and even a few flamingos. The 112.5-sq-km park primarily protects the habitat of the black-necked swan, a permanent resident. Birdlife is most abundant between November and March, and a short nature trail takes you across the steppe to the lakeshore from the visitors center.

Information

Centro de Visitantes Laguna Blanca (⏲9am-7pm daily mid-Dec–Mar, 9am-7pm Sat & Sun Apr–mid-Dec) A good visitors center with information displays and maps of walking trails.

Getting There & Away

Starting 10km south of Zapala, paved and well-marked RP 46 leads through the park toward the town of Aluminé. A couple of buses pass by the park in the afternoons; ask the driver to drop you off at the visitors center. This does, however, leave you stranded until the following day.Ask at the national park office in Zapala if you can get a ride out with the rangers in the morning. A taxi to the park should charge around AR$650, including two hours' waiting time.

THE LAND OF THE DINOSAURS

Neuquén is one of the planet's dinosaur hot spots, with numerous important fossils found in the area since 1988, including those of the world's second-largest herbivore and the largest predator ever to have walked the earth. Here, three important paleontology sites – Plaza Huincul, Villa El Chocón and Centro Paleontológico Lago Barreales – lie within a couple of hours' drive of Neuquén city and will delight anyone even slightly interested in dinosaurs.

In 1989 a local Neuquénian named Guillermo Heredia discovered a dinosaur bone on his property 7km east of the town of **Plaza Huincul**. Paleontologists later unearthed a dozen bones belonging to what they named *Argentinosaurus huinculensis* – the largest known dinosaur in the world at the time. The gargantuan herbivore, dating from the mid-Cretaceous period, measured an incredible 40m long and 18m high. The sheer size of the *Argentinosaurus huinculensis* is difficult to fathom, which is why stopping to gawk at the replica skeleton at the **Museo Municipal Carmen Funes** (☑0299-496-5486; Córdoba 55, Plaza Huincul; AR$40; ⊙9:30am-7:30pm Mon-Fri, 10am-8pm Sat & Sun) is a humbling lesson in size.

About 80km southwest of Neuquén city, the **Museo Municipal Ernesto Bachmann** (☑0299-490-1230; Natali s/n, Villa El Chocón; AR$50; ⊙8am-8pm) boasts the remains of the 100-million-year-old, 13m-long, 8-tonne, meat-eating *Gigantosaurus carolinii*, the world's largest known carnivore. Discovered in 1993 by fossil hunter Rubén D Carolini, the dinosaur is even bigger than North America's better-known *Tyrannosaurus rex*. El Chocón is also home to giant dinosaur footprints along the shore of Ezequiel Ramos Mexía reservoir. Those with a serious interest in paleontology can arrange a visit or a multiday stay at the **Centro Paleontológico Lago Barreales** (Proyecto Dino; ☑0299-420-9875; www.proyectodino.com; Costa Dinosaurio; ⊙open on request), located 90km northwest of Neuquén. While its lack of funding means that it's not in a position to receive casual visitors, it's open to researchers and students of paleontology, and it's well worth getting in touch with renowned paleontologist and bilingual project director Jorge Calvo to see if your visit can be accommodated. This is a working paleontology site where volunteers can get their hands dirty, dusting off Cretaceous-period bones and picking at fossils, and spending their nights in the silence of the desert. The on-site museum contains some wonderful finds, including part of a jaw bone of the *Gigantosaurus carolinii*, dinosaur eggs and much, much more.

If driving between Chos Malal and Neuquén, for hardcore dinosaur fans it's worth going the long way and swinging by the **Museo Municipal Argentino Urquiza** (☑0299-532-4970; Juluy s/n, Rincón de Los Sauces; AR$40; ⊙8am-noon & 4-8pm Mon-Sat, 4-8pm Sun) to have a look at the only known fossils of a *Titanosaurus*, as well as fossilized *Titanosaurus* eggs.

From Neuquén's bus terminal, there are regular buses to Plaza Huincul (AR$138, 1½ hours, five daily), Villa El Chocón (AR$107, 1¼ hours, three daily) and Rincón de Los Sauces (AR$290, four hours, five to seven daily). To reach the Centro Paleontológico Lago Barreales you need your own wheels; take RP 51, not RN 7.

Neuquén

☑0299 / POP 231,200 / ELEV 265M

There are two reasons to stop in Neuquén – the wealth of paleontological sites in the surrounding area, and the excellent wineries just out of town. The town itself is a pleasant one, with its wide, tree-lined boulevards, liberal smattering of leafy, green plazas, good dining scene and worthwhile art museum.

At the confluence of the Río Neuquén and the Río Limay, Neuquén is the province's easternmost city. Most travelers hit Neuquén en route to more glamorous destinations in Patagonia and the Lake District – the town is the area's principal transport hub, with good connections to Bariloche and other Lake District destinations, to the far south and to Chile. Paved highways go east to the Río Negro valley, west toward Zapala and southwest toward Bariloche.

⊙ Sights

Museo Nacional de Bellas Artes MUSEUM
(☑0299-443-6268; www.mnbaneuquen.gov.ar; cnr Bartolomé Mitre & Santa Cruz; ⊙9:30am-8pm Mon-Fri, 9:30am-2pm & 5-9pm Sat, 5-9pm Sun) FREE An offshoot of the fine arts museum in Buenos Aires, MNBA showcases fine arts from the

region, as well as paintings representative of major European art movements and an excellent contemporary art section. It frequently hosts worthwhile temporary exhibitions.

Sleeping & Eating

The many *confiterías* along Av Argentina are all pleasant spots for breakfast and morning coffee. The dining scene is the most varied in the region, aside from Bariloche.

Punto Patagonico Hostel HOSTEL $
(☎0299-447-9940; www.puntopatagonico.com; Periodistas Neuquinas 94; dm/s/d US$26/57/69; @📶) Neuquén's best hostel is a good deal – comfy dorms, a spacious lounge and a good garden area, with several restaurants and microbreweries just minutes away on foot.

Hotel Neu HOTEL $$
(☎0299-443-0084; www.hotelneu354.com; Rivadavia 354; s/d US$110/120; ❄📶) One of the better business-class hotels in town, the Neu keeps it simple with modern decor in medium-sized rooms. The location is central and there's an on-site gym; wi-fi signal comes and goes.

La Nonna Francesa INTERNATIONAL $$
(☎0299-430-0930; www.lanonnafrancescanqn.com; 9 de Julio 56; mains AR$160-270; ⏰11am-3pm & 8:30pm-midnight Mon-Sat; 📶) Some of Neuquén's finest dining can be found at this French-Italian trattoria – the pastas are all extremely good, and dishes such as *fusilli al proscuito* and lasagna are standouts. Service could be a tad more gracious, though.

DON'T MISS

NEUQUÉN'S WINERIES

Neuquén lies at the heart of one of Argentina's southernmost wine regions, with a string of superb wineries along northbound RP 7 fed by artificial oases that make grape cultivation possible in semi-desert conditions. The region is known best for its cool-climate varietals, such as malbec, semillon and chardonnay, as well as some of Argentina's most prominent pinot noirs and most of the country's sparkling wines. The wineries are open year-round, but the best time to visit is during the harvesting season from February to April, when you can witness the different stages of wine production in action.

The five wineries known as the Bodegas de Neuquén lie between 40km and 60km north of the city, just north of the tiny town of San Patricio del Chañar. Of the five, **Bodega Patritti** (www.bodegaspatritti.com.ar) and **Bodega Secreto Patagónico** (www.secretopatagonico) have wine shops where you can purchase their vintages, whereas the other three run guided tours. Winery tour costs are typically waived if you purchase some wine or dine at the on-site restaurants.

Bodega Familia Schroeder (☎0299-489-9600; www.familiaschroeder.com; Calle 7 Nte, San Patricio del Chañar; tours AR$50; ⏰10am-5pm) An award-winning winery that produces nine wine ranges, two of which are named after the fossil of the dinosaur *Panamericansaurus schroederi* found on-site. The excellent restaurant serves three-course lunches (AR$500).

Bodega Malma (☎0299-489-7500; www.bodeganqn.com.ar; RP 7, Picada 15; tours AR$70; ⏰10am-4pm Tue-Sun) A delightful winery where you can sample from its five wine ranges during hourly tours. Stay for lunch at their excellent on-site restaurant, known for its steaks and pastas.

Bodega del Fin del Mundo (☎0299-580-0414; www.bodegadelfindelmundo.com; RP 8, Km9, San Patricio del Chañar; tours AR$50; ⏰10am-4pm Tue-Sun) Patagonia's largest winery runs 45-minute tours that conclude with wine tasting from its 12 wine ranges.

East of Neuquén lie three more wineries, collectively referred to as the Bodegas de Río Negro. Of the three, **Bodega Humberto Canale** (☎0294-143-3879; www.bodegahcanale.com; Humberto Canale s/n; tours AR$40; ⏰10am-4pm Tue-Sat), off RN 22, is the only one that conducts in-depth tours that take you through each stage of the wine-making process, before culminating in wine tasting at the on-site museum (book ahead).

You'll need your own wheels to get to the vineyards, though **Turismo Arauquen** (☎0299-442-6476; www.arauquen.com; Yrigoyen 720; ⏰9am-7pm Mon-Fri, to 1pm Sat) can get you out here, often in combination with a paleontological tour.

★**Casa Tinta** FUSION $$$
(☎0299-517-6304; Fotheringham 166; set menu AR$400; ⊙8:30-11:30pm; 📶) This intimate little restaurant offers a nightly three-course set menu, accompanied by a number of vintage wines from nearby bodegas. The menu changes nightly, but you can expect the likes of trout tartar, shrimp risotto and pears in wine.

Shopping

Artesanías Neuquinas ARTS & CRAFTS
(www.facebook.com/artesanias.neuquinas; Brown 280; ⊙8am-1pm & 5-9pm Mon-Fri, 9am-1pm Sat) This provincially sponsored store offers a wide variety of high-quality Mapuche textiles, silver jewelry and wood crafts.

Paseo de los Artesanos ARTS & CRAFTS
(Av Independencia, Parque Central; ⊙10am-9pm Wed-Sun) Neuquén's largest selection of regional handicrafts is at this outlet, north of the old train station.

Information

Several banks around the corner of Av Argentina and Juan B Justo have ATMs.

ACA (Automóvil Club Argentino; ☎0299-442-2325; cnr Diagonal 25 de Mayo & Rivadavia; ⊙8am-8pm Mon-Fri, to 2pm Sat) Argentina's auto club; a good source for local road maps.

Cambio Pullman (Ministro Alcorta 144; ⊙9am-7pm Mon-Sat) Money exchange.

Hospital Provincial Neuquén (☎0299-449-0800; www.hospitalneuquen.org.ar; Buenos Aires 450; ⊙24hr) Emergency medical services.

Post Office (cnr Rivadavia & Santa Fe; ⊙8am-6pm Mon-Fri, 9am-1pm Sat)

Provincial Tourist Office (☎0299-442-4089; www.neuquentur.gov.ar; San Martín 182; ⊙7am-9pm) Great maps and brochures. There's a more centrally located **kiosk** (⊙8am-8pm) in Parque Central.

Getting There & Away

AIR

Aeropuerto Internacional de Neuquén (☎0299-444-0525; www.anqn.com.ar) is west of town off RN 22. There are at least six flights per day with **Aerolíneas Argentinas** (www.aerolineas.com.ar) to Buenos Aires, as well as several more with **LATAM** (www.latam.com). **Austral** (www.austral.com.ar) serves Mendoza, Bahía Blanca, Córdoba and Comodoro Rivadavia daily, and there are frequent international flights to Santiago de Chile with LATAM.

BUS

Neuquén is a major hub for domestic and international bus services. Accordingly, the **Terminal de Omnibus Neuquén** (☎0299-445-2300; www.terminalneuquen.com.ar; cnr Solalique & RN 22), about 3.5km west of Parque Central, is well decked out, with restaurants, gift stores and even a luggage carousel. To get downtown take either a Pehueche bus (AR$10; buy a ticket at local 41) or a taxi (AR$90).

Several carriers offer service to Chile: **Via Bariloche** (www.viabariloche.com.ar) goes to Temuco (AR$510, 11 hours, 9am daily).

Neuquén is a jumping-off point for deep-south Patagonian destinations. Northern destinations such as Catamarca, San Juan, Tucumán, Salta and Jujuy may require a bus change in Mendoza, though the entire ticket can be bought in Neuquén.

Buses from Neuquén

TO	COST (AR$)	TIME (HR)	SERVICE
Aluminé	627	6	7:20pm daily
Bahía Blanca	629	7-8½	8 daily
Buenos Aires	632-1414	15-18¾	10 daily
Chos Malal	567-719	6	11:20pm daily
Córdoba	1395-1593	16½	12:15pm daily
El Bolsón	618-749	8	5:40pm daily
Esquel	815-978	10¼	7:50pm daily
Junín de los Andes	565-837	6	4 daily
Mendoza	1100-1505	11¼-12¾	2 daily
Puerto Madryn	760-1075	11	7 daily
San Martín de los Andes	570-950	6½-8	4 daily
San Rafael	800-1125	7¾-9½	5 daily
Viedma	780	8¼-9	2 daily
Villa la Angostura	855-1084	6¼	2 daily
Zapala	249-316	3	5 daily

Getting Around

Central Neuquén is perfectly walkable, but ideally you'll have your own wheels for exploring the surrounding area. Drivers should be aware that RN 22, both east along the Río Negro valley and west toward Zapala, suffers from heavy truck traffic. The airport has branches of the main international car-rental firms.

Patagonia

Includes ➜

Best Places to Eat

- En Mis Fuegos (p406)
- Maffía (p449)
- Pura Vida (p461)

Best Places to Stay

- Aguas Arriba (p461)
- Oceano Patagonia (p414)
- Puesto Cagliero (p467)

Why Go?

On South America's southern frontier, nature grows wild, barren and beautiful. Spaces are large, as are the silences that fill them. For the newly arrived, such emptiness can be as impressive as the sight of Patagonia's jagged peaks, pristine rivers and dusty backwater oases. In its enormous scale, Patagonia offers a wealth of potential experiences and landscapes.

Though now mostly paved, lonely RN 40 remains the iconic highway that stirred affection in personalities as disparate as Butch Cassidy and Bruce Chatwin. On the eastern seaboard, paved RN 3 shoots south, connecting oil boomtowns with ancient petrified forests, Welsh settlements and the incredible Península Valdés. Then there is the other, trendy Patagonia where faux-fur hoodies outnumber the guanacos. Don't miss the spectacular sights of El Calafate and El Chaltén, but remember that they're a world apart from the whistling solitude of the steppe.

When to Go

El Calafate

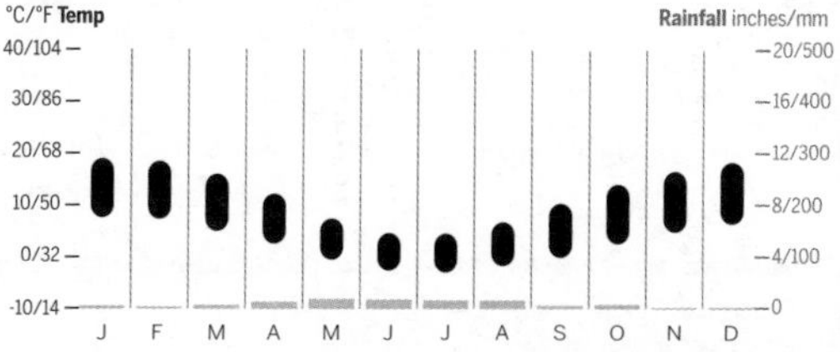

Nov–Mar Warmest months, ideal for *estancia* visits and driving RN 40.

Jun–mid-Dec Right whales migrate to Península Valdés.

Mid-Sep–early Mar Coastal fauna, including penguins, marine birds and sea lions, abounds.

Patagonia Highlights

1 Glaciar Perito Moreno (p464) Gazing upon the blue-hued glacier as icebergs fall in thunderous booms.

2 Parque Nacional Los Alerces (p436) Getting immersed in the millennial forests and clear lakes of this lush national park.

3 Cerro Fitz Roy (p451) Hiking under the toothy summit near El Chaltén, Argentina's trekking capital.

4 Reserva Faunística Península Valdés (p408) Seeing southern right whales cavort in this wildlife reserve's waters.

5 Estancias (p446) Riding the wide-open range and feasting on slow-roasted lamb at one of Patagonia's ranches.

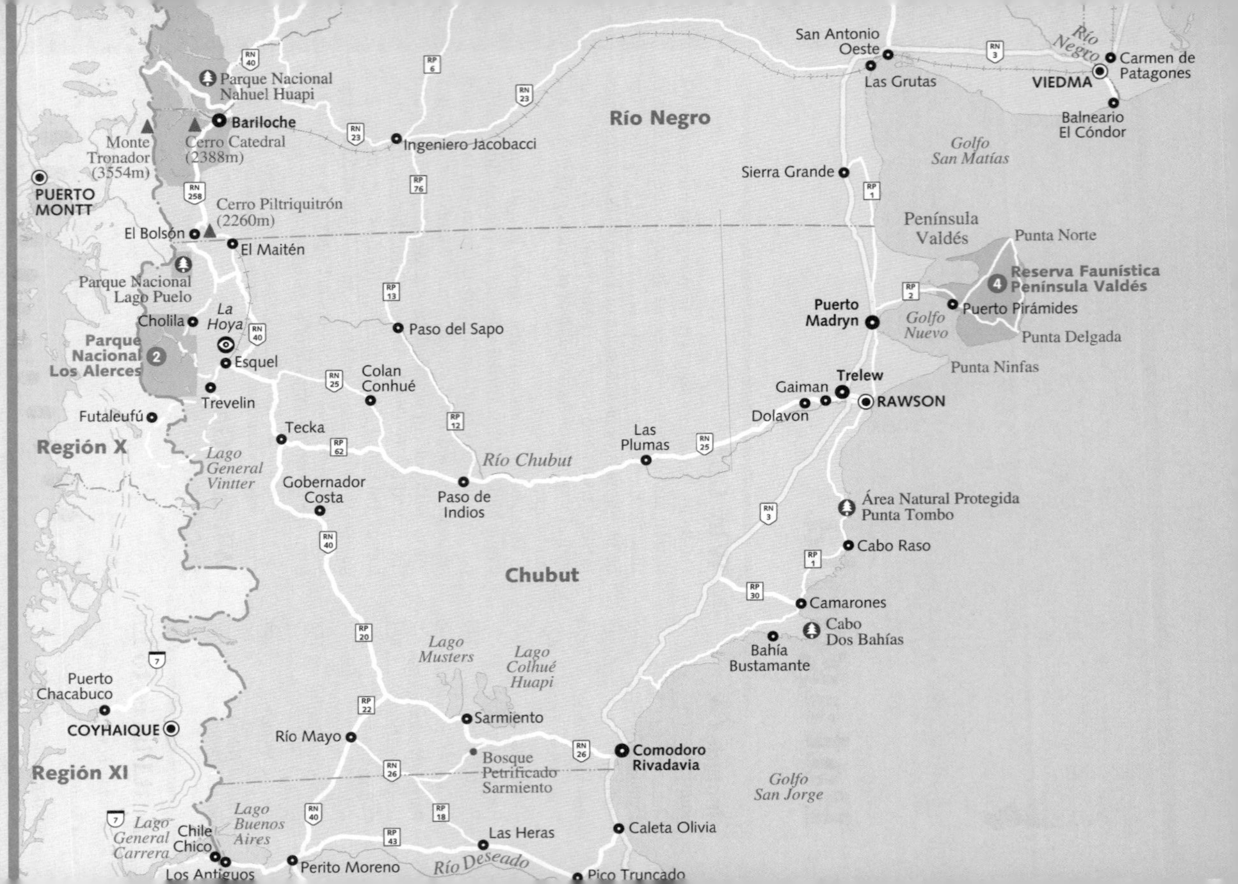

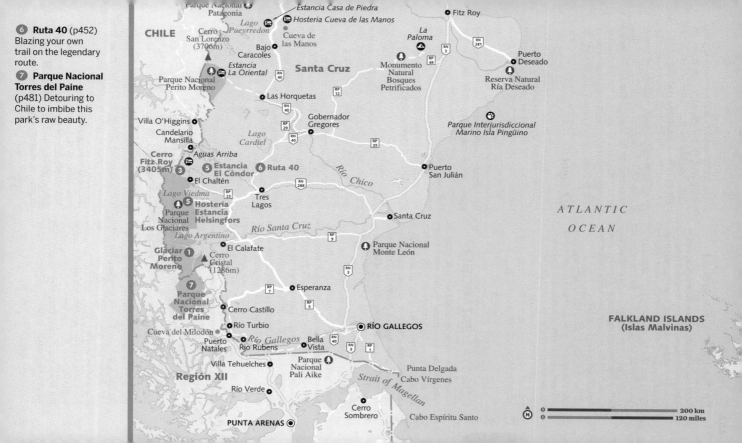

6 **Ruta 40** (p452) Blazing your own trail on the legendary route.

7 **Parque Nacional Torres del Paine** (p481) Detouring to Chile to imbibe this park's raw beauty.

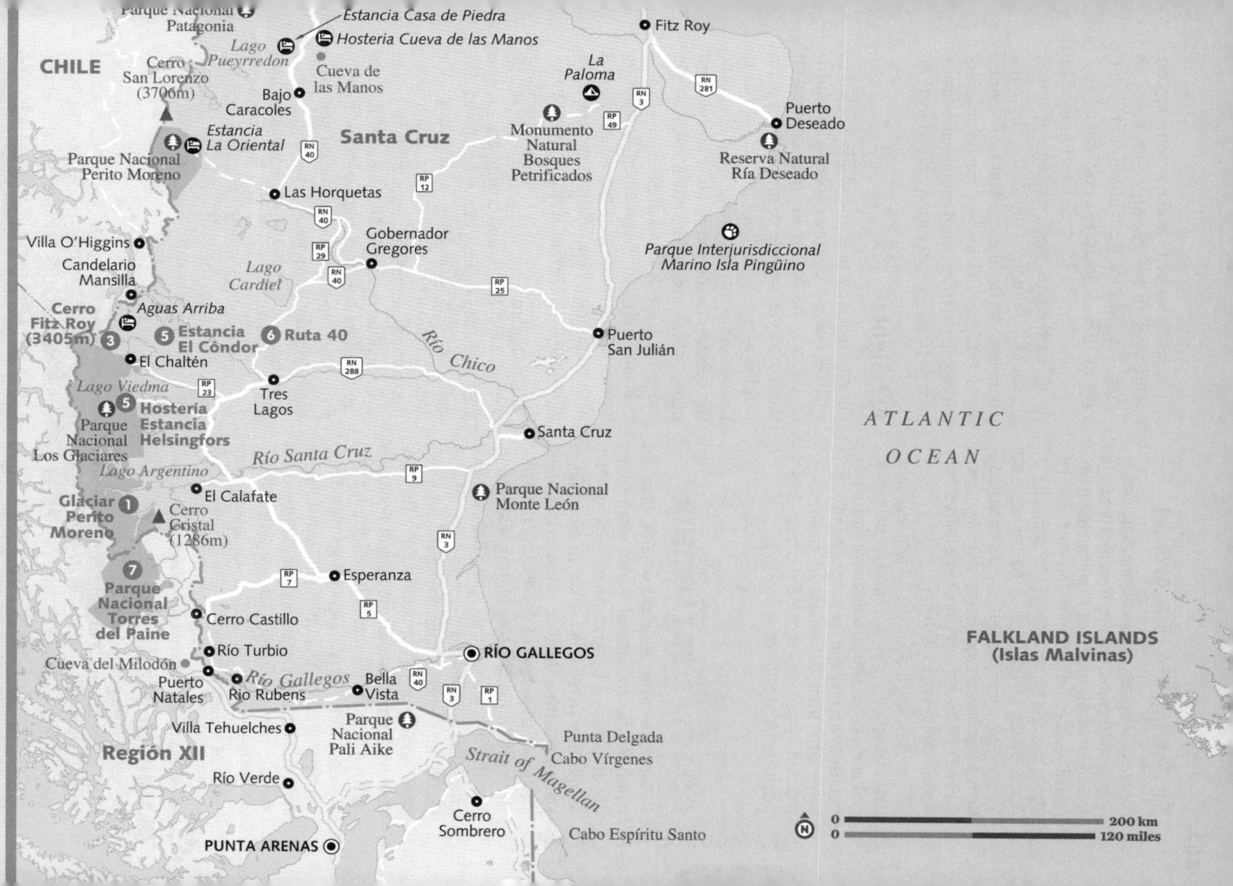

Getting There & Around

Patagonia is synonymous with unmaintained *ripio* (gravel) roads, missing transport links and interminable bus rides. Flight options have recently expanded, with more low-cost regional flights and new flights linking El Calafate with Punta Arenas, Chile. Flying can be expensive, but it's an efficient way to see the area's highlights. Before skimping on your transport budget, bear in mind that the region comprises a third of the world's eighth-largest country.

If you're busing it along the eastern seaboard, note that schedules are based on the demands of Buenos Aires, with arrivals and departures frequently occurring in the dead of night. Low-season transport options are greatly reduced. In high season demand is high – buy tickets as far in advance as possible.

COASTAL PATAGONIA

Patagonia's cavorting right whales, penguin colonies and traditional Welsh settlements are all accessed by Argentina's coastal RN 3. While this paved road takes in some fascinating maritime history, it also travels long yawning stretches of landscape that blur the horizon like a never-ending blank slate. It's also a favored travel route for oversized trucks on long-haul trips.

Wildlife enthusiasts shouldn't miss the world-renowned Península Valdés, the continent's largest Magellanic penguin colonies at Área Natural Protegida Punta Tombo, and Reserva Natural Ría Deseado's diverse seabird population. The quiet villages of Puerto San Julián and Camarones make for quiet seaside retreats, while Gaiman tells the story of Welsh settlement through a lazy afternoon of tea and cakes.

Puerto Madryn

0280 / POP 94,000

The gateway to Península Valdés, Puerto Madryn is Patagonia's star destination for marine wildlife watching. With a beachfront location, it's also a pleasant place in itself. While the city bustles with tourism and industry, it retains a few small-town touches: the radio announces lost dogs, and locals are welcoming and unhurried. With summer temperatures matching those of Buenos Aires, Madryn holds its own as a modest beach destination, but from June to mid-December visiting right whales take center stage.

The sprawling city is the second-largest fishing port in the country and home to Aluar, Argentina's first aluminum plant, built in 1974. A sheltered port facing Golfo Nuevo, Puerto Madryn was founded by Welsh settlers in 1886. Statues of immigrants and Tehuelche along the shoreline pay tribute to its history. The Universidad de la Patagonia is known for its marine-biology department, and ecological centers here promote conservation and education.

Sights

Puerto Madryn is just east of RN 3, 1371km south of Buenos Aires and about 65km north of Trelew. The action in town centers on the *costanera* (seaside road) and two main parallel avenues, Av Roca and 25 de Mayo. Bulevar Brown is the main drag alongside the beaches to the south. Most hostels rent bikes, which are a convenient way to get around and see area beaches.

From July to September, migrating whales come so close they can be viewed without taking a tour – either from the coast 20km north of town or from the town pier.

★EcoCentro MUSEUM
(0280-445-7470; www.ecocentro.org.ar; J Verne 3784; adult/child AR$250/180; 5-9pm Wed-Mon, cruise-ship days 10am-1pm) Celebrating the area's unique marine ecosystem, this masterpiece brings an artistic sensitivity to extensive scientific research. There are exhibits on the breeding habits of right whales, dolphin sounds and southern-elephant-seal harems, a touch-friendly tide pool and more.

Bring your binoculars: whales may be spotted from here. It's an enjoyable 40-minute walk or 15-minute bike ride along the *costanera* to the EcoCentro. Shuttles run three times daily from the tourist office on Av Roca, or you can catch a Línea 2 bus to the last stop and walk 1km.

Observatorio Punta Flecha WILDLIFE RESERVE
(high tide) FREE Run by Fundación Patagonia Natural, this whale-watching observatory sits 17km north of Puerto Madryn on Playa el Doradillo. It offers tourist information and opens at high tide, when there are more whales and visitors at the beach.

Museo Oceanográfico y de Ciencias Naturales MUSEUM
(0280-445-1139; cnr Domecq García & Menéndez; 9am-7pm Mon-Fri, 3-7pm Sat) FREE Feeling strands of seaweed and ogling a preserved

Puerto Madryn

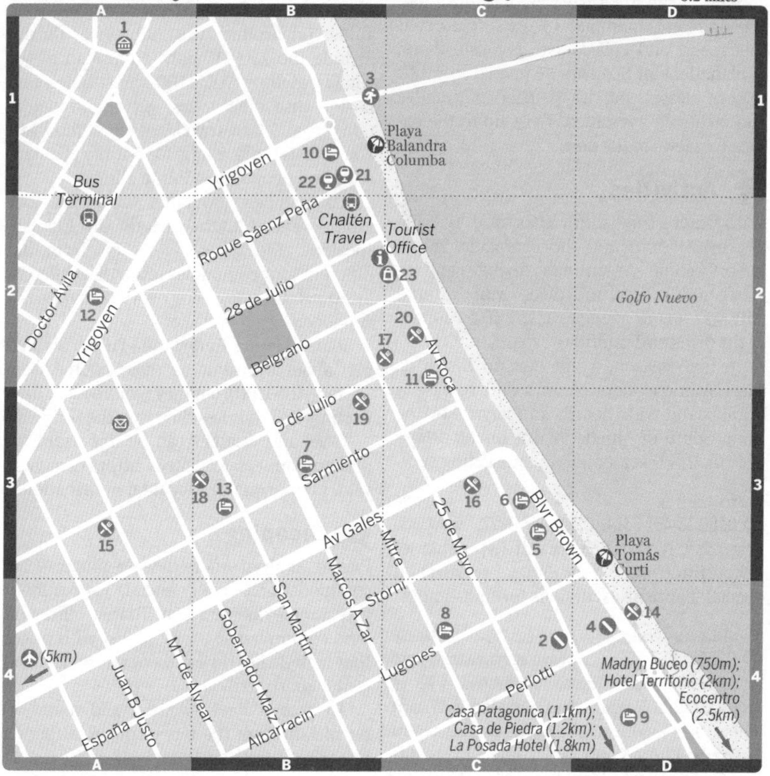

Puerto Madryn

Sights

1 Museo Oceanográfico y de Ciencias Naturales........A1

Activities, Courses & Tours

2 Lobo Larsen........C4
Napra Club........(see 14)
3 Regina Australe........B1
4 Scuba Duba........D4

Sleeping

5 Chepatagonia Hostel........C3
6 Dazzler........C3
7 El Gualicho........B3
8 El Retorno........C4
9 Hi Patagonia Hostel........D4
10 Hotel Bahía Nueva........B1
11 Hotel Piren........C2
12 La Casa de Tounens........A2
13 La Tosca........B3

Eating

14 Bistro de Mar Nautico........D4
Coiron........(see 6)
15 El Almendro........A3
16 En Mis Fuegos........C3
17 Guiseppe........C2
18 La Milonga........B3
19 Mr Jones........B3
20 Olinda........C2

Drinking & Nightlife

21 James Beer........B1
22 Margarita Bar........B1

Shopping

23 Boutique del Libro........C2

octopus gives a hands-on museum experience here. The 1917 Chalet Pujol features marine-and-land mammal exhibits, preserved specimens, and collections of Welsh wares. Explanations in Spanish are geared to youth science classes, but it's visually informative and creatively presented. Twist up to the cupola for views of the port.

Activities

With interesting shipwrecks and sea life nearby, Madryn and the Península Valdés have become Argentina's diving capitals. Newcomer 'baptism' dives run around AR$800; some agencies also offer courses, night dives and multiday excursions.

In high season, a hut next to Bistro de Mar Nautico offers lessons and rents out regular and wide boards and kayaks by the hour. South of Muelle Piedra Buena, **Playa Tomás Curti** is a popular windsurfing spot.

Lobo Larsen DIVING
(☎0280-15-451-6314, 0280-447-0277; www.lobolarsen.com; Av Roca 885, Local 2) Reputable local outfitter; offers multilingual service and special 'baptism' excursions for first-timers.

Regina Australe CRUISE
(☎0280-445-6447; www.reginaaustrale.com.ar; Muelle Piedra Buena; adult/child 4-12 yr AR$600/500; ⏲ticket office 10am-1pm & 2-7pm) This 300-passenger ship cruises the Golfo Nuevo to Punta Lobo, departing conveniently from the town pier, where tickets are sold. The three-hour tour leaves at 1pm on Saturday, Sunday, Wednesday and holidays. The ship has three decks, a bar and fast food.

Napra Club WATER SPORTS
(☎0280-445-5633; www.napraclub.com; Bulevar Brown 860; ⏲9am-8pm) This rental shack offers bicycles (per day AR$300), stand-up paddle boards (per hour AR$450) and guided sea kayaking (per two hours AR$550) in sit-on-tops. If need be, you can also rent a wet suit. Located next to Bistro de Mar Nautico.

Madryn Buceo DIVING
(☎0280-15-456-4422; www.madrynbuceo.com; Bulevar Brown 1900) Offers dive 'baptisms' for newcomers, snorkeling with sea lions and regular outings, with hostel-pickup service.

Scuba Duba DIVING
(☎0280-445-2699; www.scubaduba.com.ar; Bulevar Brown 893) Quality scuba-diving operator.

Tours

Countless agencies sell tours to Península Valdés for around AR$1200; prices do not include the AR$415 park admission fee or whale watching (AR$1400). Most hotels and hostels also offer tours; get recommendations from fellow travelers before choosing. You can also take a tour to visit the elephant seals and penguins at Punta Ninfas.

Ask agencies about the size of the tour group, and if tours include an English-speaking guide, meals and stops. Note that different tour companies often visit different locations. Bringing your own binoculars is a good idea.

Tours to Punta Tombo from Puerto Madryn cost about the same as those offered from Trelew (AR$1200), but they require more driving time and thus less time with the penguins.

Tides and weather can be important for planning tour dates; check http://peninsulavaldes.org.ar/mareas for tidal information.

Sleeping

Puerto Madryn offers a wide range of accommodations. Book ahead, especially if you want a double room. Tourist offices offer a comprehensive lodging list with prices that include nearby *estancias* (ranches) and rental apartments.

All hostels have kitchens and many offer pickup from the bus terminal, although most are only a short, flat walk away.

★**Hi Patagonia Hostel** HOSTEL $
(☎0280-445-0155; http://hipatagonia.com; Av Roca 1040; dm US$19, d with/without bathroom US$65/53; 📶) With wonderful service, this central hostel provides a congenial adventure base. Double-glazed windows ensure your rest, while a grassy backyard and barbecue area create a social atmosphere. There are also bikes and cars for rent on-site, tour information, plus precise weather forecasts and tidal details from host Gaston.

La Tosca HOSTEL $
(☎0280-445-6133; www.latoscahostel.com; Sarmiento 437; dm US$18, d with/without bathroom US$71/44; @📶) A cozy guesthouse where the owners and staff greet you by name. The creation of a well-traveled couple, La Tosca is modern and comfy, with a grassy courtyard, good mattresses, and varied breakfasts with homemade cakes, yogurt and fruit. Double suites and a post-checkout bathroom with showers are wonderful additions. There's also bike rental.

Casa Patagonica B&B $
(☎ 0280-445-1540; www.casa-patagonica.com.ar; Av Roca 2210; d/tr US$53/82; @ 📶) Warm and relaxed, with homemade cakes for breakfast and a *quincho* (thatched-roof building) for cooking or barbecues. Lodgings are in a brick home with vaulted ceilings and impeccably kept rooms, five blocks from the beach and 1km south of the town center.

El Retorno HOSTEL $
(☎ 0280-445-6044; www.elretornohostel.com.ar; Mitre 798; dm/s/tw incl breakfast US$21/35/41; @ 📶) Run by the indefatigable Gladys, a den mother to travelers from all over. Besides dorms and snug doubles, there is a solarium and a barbecue area, and bike rental. Also available for rent are nice, centrally located apartments.

Chepatagonia Hostel HOSTEL $
(☎ 0280-445-5783; www.chepatagoniahostel.com.ar; Storni 16; dm US$18, d with/without bathroom US$59/53; @ 📶) This stylish and cheerful hostel is owned by a friendly couple who book tours for guests and fire up the grill for barbecues twice a week. Adding to the appeal are comfortable beds and the possibility of glimpsing whales from the hostel balcony. Guests can wash clothes and cook. There are also bikes for rent (AR$350 per day).

La Casa de Tounens HOSTEL $
(☎ 0280-447-2681; www.lacasadetounens.com; Passaje 1 de Marzo 432; s/d with bathroom US$45/60, dm/s/d without bathroom US$15/40/50; @ 📶) A congenial nook near the bus station, run by a friendly Parisian-Argentine couple. With few rooms, personal attention is assured. There's a cozy stone patio strewn with hammocks, a living area with pool table, barbecue grill, and homemade bread for breakfast.

El Gualicho HOSTEL $
(☎ 0280-445-4163; www.elgualicho.com.ar; Marcos A Zar 480; dm US$17, d with/without bathroom US$65/53; P @ 📶) This sleek, contemporary hostel provides very stylish digs, though mattresses are mysteriously cheap quality. We love the immense kitchen and ample common spaces, with billiards and hammocks, but being truly massive (with 120 beds) makes it somewhat impersonal. Doubles have TVs. Bikes are available for rent and a massive activity board keeps you posted.

★ **Casa de Piedra** B&B $$
(☎ 0280-447-3521, 0280-15-499-1611; www.laspiedrashosteria.com; Arenales 82; d/tr incl breakfast US$88/110; @ 📶) 🍃 This wonderful B&B shines with warm and attentive service. The artisan owners have thoughtfully crafted every detail, from stone patterns in the walkway to wood details and an oversized rocking horse. Immaculate rooms with private entrances off a cement courtyard feature coffee-and-tea service, flat-screen TVs, lock boxes and mini-fridges.

Hotel Piren HOTEL $$
(☎ 0280-445-6272; www.hotelpiren.com.ar; Av Roca 439; d US$88-182; 📶) This decent-value high-rise on the waterfront shares space with time-share condominum apartments. Staff could not be prouder of the *Charlie and the Chocolate Factory*–style glass elevator, which climbs 10 floors to dizzying views. Public spaces sport sleek design, though there's considerable difference in quality between the old and new sections.

La Posada Hotel INN $$
(☎ 0280-447-4087; www.la-posada.com.ar; Mathews 2951; d US$100-120; @ 📶 🏊) This modern inn amid rolling green lawns offers a quiet alternative to lodging in town. Its tidy, light-filled rooms with bright accents come with cable TV; in the garden there's a pool and barbecue grill. It's 2km south of the town center.

Hotel Bahía Nueva HOTEL $$
(☎ 0280-445-0045, 0280-445-0145; www.bahianueva.com.ar; Av Roca 67; s/d/tr incl breakfast US$92/108/134; P @ 📶) Stretching to resemble an English countryside retreat, the Bahía Nueva includes a foyer library and flouncy touches. Its 40 rooms are well groomed, but only a few have ocean views. Highlights include a bar with billiards and a TV (mostly to view movies and documentaries), and tour information.

★ **Hotel Territorio** BOUTIQUE HOTEL $$$
(☎ 0280-447-1496; www.hotelterritorio.com.ar; Bulevar Brown 3251; ste US$200; @ 📶) Set behind beautiful dunes with ocean views, this 36-room hotel is minimalist chic, with polished concrete, plush modern furniture and an entire whale vertebrae gracing a yawning hall. Kids can use a spacious play room. The Punta Cuevas location is a trek from the town center, but there's a cool cocktail bar and a contemporary spa.

Dazzler HOTEL $$$

(☎0280-447-5758; Bulevar Brown 637; d with city/sea views US$150/190; 📶) This upscale newcomer sports 95 oversized rooms with great ocean views, king-sized beds and all the amenities in a modern, minimalist style. The rooftop solarium, Jacuzzi and spa are welcome extras. The on-site restobar has had some acclaim, but its lobby location lacks privacy.

Eating

La Milonga PIZZA $

(☎0280-447-0363; 9 de Julio 534; pizzas AR$200; ⏲7pm-12:30am Tue-Sun) Locals flock to this retro pizzeria for its huge variety of clay-oven pizzas, with toppings like tapenade (marinated-olive spread) and arugula.

Mr Jones INTERNATIONAL $

(☎0280-447-5368; 9 de Julio 116; mains AR$100-200; ⏲8pm-late) Serving a wealth of yummy stouts and reds, homemade pot pie, and fish and chips, this favorite local pub always delivers. Service is friendly but tends to be slow.

Bistro de Mar Nautico SEAFOOD $$

(☎0280-447-4289; Bulevar Brown 860; mains AR$110-450; ⏲8am-midnight) With unbeatable beachfront atmosphere and bustling old-school waiters, this busy cafe does the job. Seafood lovers can get grilled fish or crisp calamari. There are also burgers, pizzas and even breakfast with gorgeous water views that few Madryn restaurants can boast. After 8pm there's a limited menu.

El Almendro INTERNATIONAL $$

(☎0280-447-0525; MT de Alvear 409; mains AR$110-240; ⏲8pm-late Tue-Sun) With guests often treated to an aperitif, it isn't hard to love this family-run restaurant with its tantalizing menu, attentive service and reasonable wine list. Dine on gnocchi with pumpkin seeds or balsamic glazed steaks in this cozy and elegant house.

Guiseppe ITALIAN $$

(☎0280-445-6891; 25 de Mayo 381; mains AR$100-220; ⏲noon-4pm & 8pm-1am) This Italian bistro hits just the right note with fresh pastas, gnocchi and pizza *a la piedra*, served up on classic red-checkered tablecloths. If you want something a little more exotic, go for the *risotto de langostinos* (with crawfish).

Coiron ARGENTINE $$

(☎0280-447-5758; Bulevar Brown 637; mains AR$230-300; ⏲7am-11:30pm) In the hotel Dazzler, this upscale restaurant doesn't quite live up to that name's expectation, but it does serve decent gourmet meals that come nicely plated. Steak medallions wrapped in bacon are a winner, as are salads, though pastas fail to excite.

Olinda ARGENTINE $$

(☎0280-447-0304; Av Roca 385; mains AR$130-255; ⏲noon-4pm & 7:30pm-1am) With deck seating and a cool candlelit atmosphere, this contemporary cafe serves a range of tasty blackboard specials that go down easy with pitchers of lemonade or gin and tonic. Dishes like Patagonian lamb, local shrimp grilled with sea salt and homemade bread come fresh. Set menus are a good deal and the elaborate desserts easily serve two.

★**En Mis Fuegos** PATAGONIAN $$$

(☎0280-445-8740; Av Gales 32; 4-course meal AR$400; ⏲8:30pm-midnight Tue-Sun) It's rare to get a taste of Patagonia beyond roast lamb. Splash out for a four-course dinner here and you'll be pleasantly enticed by the regularly changing menu that emphasizes local ingredients. Items like broth of wakame seaweed, exquisite trout with homemade pickles, melt-in-your-mouth pork and outstanding rabbit confit offer a broader vision of the region. It's upscale, with low-key service.

Drinking & Nightlife

James Beer CRAFT BEER

(☎0280-15-483-4428; cnr Av Roca & Roque Sáenz Peña; ⏲7pm-2am Sun-Thu, to 4am Fri & Sat) With modern ambience and 12 microbrews from all over Argentina on tap, this hipster bar is the latest addition to Madryn's nightlife. It also serves pub food like burgers and sausages (mains AR$105 to AR$165). Soon it will add its own craft beer to the mix.

Margarita Bar PUB

(☎0280-447-2659; Roque Sáenz Peña 15; ⏲11am-4am) With a trendy edge, this low-lit brick haunt has a laundry list of cocktails, friendly bar staff and decent food, with popular sushi Wednesdays. On Friday and Saturday there's dancing after 1:30am.

Shopping

Boutique del Libro BOOKS

(☎0280-445-7987; cnr 28 de Julio & Av Roca, Portal de Madryn 208; ⏲9:30am-1:30pm & 3:30-9pm Mon-Fri, 9:30am-9:30pm Sat, 11am-9pm Sun) Stocks a good selection of regional Patagonia books, maps, and a few English-language novels and guidebooks. It's on the 2nd floor of a mall next to the tourist information center.

Information

Argentina Vision (0280-445-5888; http://argentinavision.com; Av Roca 536; 8am-8:30pm Mon-Fri, 9am-12:30pm & 5-8:30pm Sat) The only tour agency in Puerto Madryn that handles visits to Estancia San Lorenzo and its penguin colony on Península Valdés.

Banco de la Nación (0280-445-0465; 9 de Julio 117; 8am-1pm Mon-Fri) Has an ATM and changes traveler's checks.

Flamenco Tour (0280-445-5505; www.flamencotour.com; Belgrano 25; 9am-1pm & 4:30-8:30pm Mon-Fri, 9am-1pm Sat) Offerings range from the standard whale-watching and snorkeling trips to stargazing 4WD journeys along the coast (telescopes and bilingual instruction included).

Hospital Subzonal (0280-445-1999; R Gómez 383)

Post Office (cnr Belgrano & Gobernador Maíz; 8am-1pm & 4-7pm Mon-Fri)

Tourist Office (0280-445-3504; https://madryn.travel; Av Roca 223; 8am-9pm Dec-Feb, limited hours Apr-Nov) Has helpful and efficient staff, and there's usually an English or French speaker on duty. Check the *libro de reclamos* (complaint book) for traveler tips. There's another helpful desk at the bus terminal (open 7am to 9pm in high season).

Getting There & Away

Due to limited connections, it pays to book in advance, especially for travel to the Andes.

AIR

Though Puerto Madryn has its own modern airport, **Aeropuerto El Tehuelche** (0280-445-6774), 5km west of town, most commercial flights still arrive in Trelew's **Airport Almirante Marcos A Zar** (0280-443-3443; RN 3, Km1450), 65km south.

Regional airline **Andes** (0280-447-5877; www.andesonline.com; Belgrano 41; 7am-7pm Mon-Sat, noon-8pm Sun) has flights to Buenos Aires' Aeroparque (AR$1800) several times a week. **Aerolíneas Argentinas** (0280-445-1998; Av Roca 427; 4-8pm Mon-Fri, 9:30am-1pm Sat) and **LADE** (0280-445-1256; Av Roca 119; 9am-4pm Mon-Fri) fly from Trelew, but each has a ticketing representative here.

Starting in 2018, **Alas del Sur** (www.alasdelsurla.com) will have regional flights. For other new regional flight services, check out the website of **Aviación Civil Argentina** (ANAC; www.anac.gob.ar), which has a map with new routes and airlines.

BUS

Puerto Madryn's full-service **bus terminal** (0280-445-1789; www.terminalmadryn.com; cnr Ciudad de Nefyn & Dr Ávila), behind the historic 1889 Estación del Ferrocarril Patagónico, has an ATM, a cafe and a helpful tourist information desk. Bus timetables are clearly posted and luggage storage is available.

Bus companies include **Andesmar** (0280-447-3764), **Don Otto** (0280-445-1675), **Mar y Valle** (0280-445-0600), **Que Bus** (0280-445-5805), **Via TAC** (0280-445-5805) and **TUS** (0280-445-1962). **Chaltén Travel** (0280-445-4906; Av Roca 115) has buses to Esquel and offers connecting service north on RN 40 (to Bariloche) or south (to Perito Moreno and El Chaltén).

The bus to Puerto Pirámides, operated by Mar y Valle (AR$114, 1½ hours), leaves at 9:45am and 5pm, returning to Madryn at 11am and 6pm. Monday through Friday there are 6:30am and 4pm departures. Times may change seasonally, so consult ahead.

Buses from Puerto Madryn

DESTINATION	COST (AR$)	TIME (HR)
Bariloche	1200-1600	15
Buenos Aires	1650-1900	18-20
Comodoro Rivadavia	800	6-8
Córdoba	1600-2300	18
Esquel	1000	9
Mendoza	1900-2900	23-24
Neuquén	1100	12
Río Gallegos	2000	15-20
Trelew	67	1
Viedma	650	5-6

Getting Around

Rent a bicycle for travel in and around town, including at **Na Praia** (0280-455-633; Bulevar Brown 860; 9am-7pm).

Taxis can be hired to Puerto Pirámides (AR$2000) and Punta Loma/Doradillo (AR$900).

TO/FROM THE AIRPORT

Airport Almirante Marcos A Zar Southbound 28 de Julio buses to Trelew, which run hourly Monday through Saturday between 6am and 10pm, will stop at Trelew's airport on request. **Transfer Aeropuerto** (0280-15-487-3000, 0280-443-3443; to Trelew airport AR$300) runs shuttle services to Trelew's airport.

Aeropuerto El Tehuelche Radio taxis, including **La Nueva Patagonia** (0280-447-6000), take travelers to and from Madryn's airport for about AR$900.

CAR

A roundtrip to Península Valdés is a little over 300km. A group sharing expenses can make car rental a relatively reasonable and more flexible alternative to taking a bus tour, if you don't have to pay for extra kilometers – ensure that the terms of rental are clear.

Rates vary, depending on the mileage allowance and age and condition of the vehicle. The best bet for competitive rates and friendly and comprehensive service is **Hi Patagonia Rent-a-Car** (☎0280-445-0155; www.hipatagonia.com; Rawson 419; ⏲by reservation). The family-owned agency **Centauro** (☎0280-15-340400; www.centaurorentacar.com.ar; Av Roca 733; ⏲9am-8pm Mon-Sat) also gets high marks. Basic vehicles run AR$1600 per day, with insurance and 200km included.

Around Puerto Madryn

Exploring the coast around Puerto Madryn is a good way to take in the rugged solitude and some marine wildlife. Home to a permanent sea-lion colony and cormorant rookery, the **Reserva Faunística Punta Loma** (AR$185) is 17km southeast of Puerto Madryn via a good but winding gravel road. The overlook is about 15m from the animals, best seen during low tides. Many travel agencies organize two-hour tours according to the tide schedules; otherwise, check tide tables and hire a car or taxi, or make the trek via bicycle.

Continue on this road for Unesco-protected **Punta Ninfas**, a cliffside marked by a lighthouse, to see elephant seals on the beach. There's also a penguin colony. Please exercise self-restraint and snap photos at a nonthreatening distance. It's 78km from Puerto Madryn on a dusty dirt road.

> **THE ANCIENT ALERCE**
>
> Resembling California's giant sequoia, the alerce flourishes in middle Patagonia's temperate forests, growing only about 1cm every 20 years. As one of the planet's longest-living species, it can live for thousands of years. Individual specimens of this beautiful tree can reach over 4m in diameter and exceed 60m in height. Like the giant sequoia, it has suffered overexploitation because of its valuable timber.

Punta Flecha observatory is a recommended whale-watching spot 20km north of Puerto Madryn via RP 1.

Sleeping

★**El Pedral** ESTANCIA **$$$**
(☎0280-447-3043; www.reservaelpedral.com; camino a Punta Ninfas; s/d incl meals & transfer US$400/550; ⏲mid-Sep–mid-Apr; 🅿) El Pedral is a private *estancia* and nature reserve with a growing Magellanic penguin colony and beautiful coastal digs in a historic home. Accommodations are in farmhouse rooms with en suite bathrooms and elegant wooden furnishings. The *casco* (main house) has a turret with top stargazing possibilities. There's also a cozy living room with a fireplace. Meals, crafted by a local chef, are outstanding.

Getting There & Away

These areas are usually accessed via organized tour, but if you have a rental car (preferably 4WD) you can visit on your own schedule. Always ask locals about the state of roads before going, since rain and deteriorating conditions can make some areas impassable.

Reserva Faunística Península Valdés

Home to sea lions, elephant seals, guanacos, rheas, Magellanic penguins and numerous seabirds, Unesco World Heritage site Península Valdés is one of South America's finest wildlife reserves. More than 80,000 visitors per year come to this 3600-sq-km sanctuary, which has more than 400km of coastline.

The wildlife viewing is truly exceptional, the undisputed main attraction being the endangered *ballena franca austral* (southern right whale). The warmer, more enclosed waters along the Golfo Nuevo, Golfo San José and the coastline near Caleta Valdés from Punta Norte to Punta Hércules become prime breeding zones for right whales between June and mid-December.

Sheep *estancias* occupy the peninsula's interior, which includes one of the world's lowest continental depressions, the salt flats of Salina Grande and Salina Chica, 42m below sea level. At the turn of the 20th century, Puerto Pirámides, the peninsula's only village, was the shipping port for the salt extracted from Salina Grande.

Reserva Faunística Península Valdés

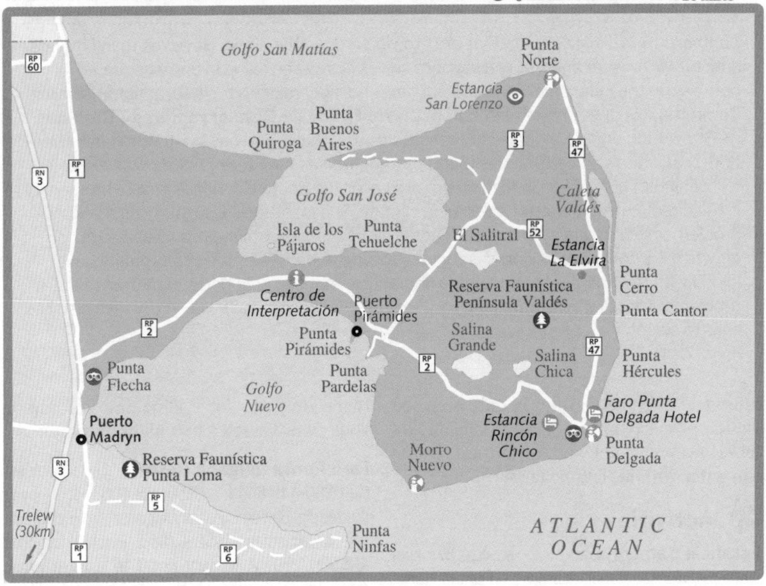

Sights

In spring, elephant seals haul themselves onto the long gravel spit at **Punta Cantor**, the sheltered bay 43km north of Punta Delgada. September sees females giving birth to pups, while males fight it out defending their harem – a dramatic sight from the trails that wind down the hill. You may even see guanacos strolling the beach.

A few kilometers north of the private Estancia La Elvira there's a sizable colony of burrowing Magellanic penguins.

Reserva Faunística Península Valdés WILDLIFE RESERVE
(☎0280-445-0489; http://peninsulavaldes.org.ar; adult/child 5-12 yr AR$415/210; ⏲8am-8pm) Lying on Argentina's barren eastern Patagonian coast, this oddly shaped peninsula is home to some of the country's richest wildlife. Elephant seals, Magellanic penguins, southern right whales, guanacos, armadillos and foxes are almost guaranteed sightings during their high seasons. Whale watching is also big. From February to April, orcas can be seen at high tide. They have been filmed snatching pinnipeds (the genus including seals and sea lions) off the beach here. Elephant seals, sea lions and dolphins are present year-round.

Punta Norte WILDLIFE RESERVE
At the far end of Península Valdés, solitary Punta Norte boasts an enormous mixed colony of sea lions and elephant seals. Its remote location means it is rarely visited by tour groups. But the real thrill here is the sight of orcas: from mid-February through mid-April these killer whales come to feast on the unsuspecting colonies of sea lions. Chances are you won't see a high-tide attack, but watching the dorsal fins carving through the water is enough to raise goose bumps.

Centro de Visitantes Istmo Carlos Ameghino CULTURAL CENTER
(⏲8am-8pm) FREE This cultural center, 22km beyond the reserve's entrance, focuses on natural history, displays a full right-whale skeleton and has material on the peninsula's colonization, from the area's first Spanish settlement at Fuerte San José to later mineral exploration. Don't miss the stunning panoramic view from the observation tower.

Punta Delgada WILDLIFE RESERVE
(guided visit adult/child AR$120/60) In Península Valdés' southeast corner, 76km southeast of Puerto Pirámides, sea lions and, in spring, a huge colony of elephant seals are visible from the cliffs of Punta Delgada. Visitors

WHALE TROUBLES

Southern-right-whale populations are growing around the world. However, many threats affect their present and future. Newborn calves have been dying in unprecedented numbers in the Península Valdés nursery ground, according to the International Whaling Commission. Long-term research from the **Instituto de Conservación de Ballenas** (ICB; www.icb.org.ar), a nonprofit that studies the whales and has photo-identified over 3000 individuals since 1971, has found that the whales have fewer calves than expected following diminished krill in feeding grounds near the South Georgia Islands. The scarcity is the direct consequence of a warming climate. The institute is also studying a vexing problem on Península Valdés: gulls feeding off live whales, which produces lesions and affects their normal behavior. Members of the local whale-watching community have joined with the ICB, contributing data and photographs to help better understand the problems. Those who want to help can Adopt a Whale via the ICB website, which also has links to scientific publications.

must pay a fee as viewing is only accessed via the property of Faro Punta Delgada Hotel. However, hotel and restaurant guests can enter without extra charge.

Activities

Estancia San Lorenzo WILDLIFE WATCHING
(www.pinguinospuntanorte.com.ar; Punta Norte; adult/child 5-12 yr AR$900/450; ⏲10am-6pm Sep-Mar) An *estancia* on Península Valdés with excellent wildlife watching. Book visits through Argentina Vision (p407) in Puerto Madryn.

Tours

Zonotrikia OUTDOORS
(☎0280-445-5888; www.zonotrikia.com.ar; all-day tour per person AR$3500; ⏲Sep-Nov) Active travelers can tour Península Valdés in a Mercedes overland van with a bilingual guide, sea kayaking with whales in San José bay and mountain biking on gentle sandy roads. Tours include an open-air barbecue lunch. It also offers combo trekking-4WD tours. Make reservations online. It's affiliated with the Puerto Madryn–based agency Argentina Vision.

Sleeping & Eating

★**Estancia Rincón Chico** ESTANCIA $$$
(☎0280-447-1733; www.rinconchico.com.ar; Punta Delgada; d per person incl full board US$475; ⏲mid-Sep–Mar) With a prime location for wildlife watching, this refined inn hosts university marine biologists, student researchers and tourists. Lodging is in a modern, corrugated-tin ranch house with eight well-appointed doubles and a *quincho* for barbecues. In addition to guided excursions there are paths for cycling and walking on your own. There's a two-night minimum.

Faro Punta Delgada Hotel HOTEL $$$
(☎0280-445-8444, 02965-15-406304; www.puntadelgada.com; Punta Delgada; s/d incl breakfast & excursion US$236/280, lunch adult/child AR$500/250) A luxury hotel in a lighthouse complex that once belonged to the Argentine postal service. Horseback riding, 4WD tours and other activities are available. Nonguests can dine at the upscale restaurant serving *estancia* fare. Guided naturalist walks down to the beach leave frequently in high season.

Parador La Elvira ARGENTINE $
(☎0280-494-5011; Punta Cantor; mains AR$80-150; ⏲9:30am-8pm) This simple cafe provides shelter from the blasting wind and some Argentine-style fast food like *milanesas* (breaded cutlets), burgers or a full set lunch of barbecued lamb.

Getting There & Away

About 17km north of Puerto Madryn, paved RP 2 branches off RN 3 across the Istmo Carlos Ameghino to the entrance of the reserve. There's a bus service to Puerto Pirámides from Puerto Madryn, but most visitors arrive via tours or rented vehicles.

Getting Around

Since the peninsula is so large, it's best for visitors to come by tour or use their own transportation.

If you're driving around the peninsula, take it easy. Roads are *ripio* (gravel) and washboard, with sandy spots that grab the wheels. If you're in a rental car, make sure you get all the details of the insurance policy. Hitchhiking here is nearly impossible and bike travel is a long and unnervingly windy experience.

Puerto Pirámides

0280 / POP HUMANS 565, WHALES 400–2700

Set amid sandy cliffs by a bright blue sea, this sleepy old salt port now bustles with tour buses and visitors clad in orange life jackets. Whales bring whopping and ever-growing tourism. But at the end of the day the tour buses split and life in this two-street town regains its cherished snail's pace. Av de las Ballenas is the main drag, which runs perpendicular to Primera (1era) Bajada, the first road to the beach, stuffed with tour outfitters.

While most visitors focus on whale watching, adventure offerings continue to grow. If planning whale watching from Puerto Madryn, it's helpful to look at the forecast, as high winds and storms can close the port.

Activities

Bicycles or kayaks can be rented and area *estancias* offer **horseback riding**. There's also **mountain biking** aplenty. Or visitors can go **walking** uphill to the sea-lion colony less than 5km from town. It's a magnificent spot for catching the sunset and occasional whale sightings. Time your visit with the tides: sea lions swim out to sea at high tide.

Traccion a Sangre MOUNTAIN BIKING
(0296-549-5047, WhatsApp +54 9280-434-3512; www.traccion-asangre.com.ar; Av de las Ballenas s/n; guided half-day AR$1100) Rents mountain bikes (AR$500 per day) and offers guided mountain-biking tours on Península Valdés. The office is shared with Patagonia Scuba.

Tours

This is the place to glimpse spy-hopping, breaching and tailing cetaceans on a **whale-watching excursion** (adult/child AR$1400/700), arranged in Puerto Madryn or Puerto Pirámides. The standard trip lasts 1½ hours, but longer excursions are available.

When choosing a tour, check what kind of boat will be used: smaller, Zodiac-style inflatable rafts offer more intimacy but may be less comfortable. By law, outfitters are not allowed within 100m of whales without cutting the motor, nor are they allowed to pursue them.

Check your outfitter's policies. When the port is closed due to bad weather, tour bookings are usually honored the following day (although these days are more crowded). Outside of whale-watching season (June to December), boat trips aren't worthwhile unless you adore sea lions and shorebirds.

★ **Patagonia Explorers** KAYAKING
(0280-15-434-0618; www.patagoniaexplorers.com; Av de las Ballenas; kayak day trip US$120) This band of brothers – and sister – offers top-notch guided hikes and sea-kayaking trips. A three-day excursion on the Golfo San José includes paddling with sea lions and lots of wildlife watching and wilderness camping. There are also full-moon and sunset options. Check the website or visit the office (shared with Hydrosport) for details.

Southern Spirit WHALE WATCHING
(0280-449-5094; www.southernspirit.com.ar; 1era Bajada; sub adult/child AR$2800/1400) This reputable outfitter offers both conventional and underwater viewing via the semi-submersible, custom-built *Yellow Submarine*. Though not an actual sub, its narrow underwater chamber lined with stools and windows provides full views of cavorting whales when there's good visibility. The boat holds 35 to 40 passengers. Also offers a coastal overnight trek to spend an evening with whale song.

Bottazzi WHALE WATCHING
(0280-449-5050; www.titobottazzi.com; 1era Bajada) A recommended second-generation family business with its own agency in Puerto Madryn. Popular and more personalized sunset cruises feature a smaller boat; it's a great option for wildlife photography.

Patagonia Scuba DIVING
(0280-15-457-8779; http://patagonia-scuba.negocio.site; Av de las Ballenas s/n) A reputable PADI-certified outfitter offering diving trips and snorkeling with sea lions; the best water visibility is in August. It rents kayaks, too. Also check its Facebook page.

Hydrosport WHALE WATCHING
(0280-449-5065; www.hydrosport.com.ar; 1era Bajada) In addition to whale watching, Hydrosport runs dolphin-watching tours and has naturalists and submarine audio systems on board.

Whales Argentina WHALE WATCHING
(0280-449-5015; www.whalesargentina.com.ar; 1era Bajada) Offers quality trips with a bilingual guide; also runs personalized excursions on a four-seater semi-rigid boat.

Patagonian Wildlife

Thanks to deep ocean currents that bring nutrients and abundant food, the coast of southern Argentina plays host to bountiful marine life. To see them hunt, court, nest and raise their young renews one's sense of wonder along these lonely Atlantic shores.

Magellanic Penguins

Adorable and thoroughly modern, penguins co-parent after chicks hatch in mid-November. See the action at Punta Tombo (p420), Ría Deseado (p424) and Bahía Bustamante (p422).

Southern Sea Lions

Found year-round along the southern coast of Argentina, these burly swimmers feed on squid and the odd penguin.

Commerson's Dolphins

These small dolphins often join boaters in play. See them all year at Playa Unión (p415), in Ría Deseado (p424) and at Puerto San Julián (p427).

Southern Right Whales

In spring, the shallow waters of Península Valdés (p408) attract thousands of these creatures to breed and bear young.

Orcas

To witness raw nature at work, visitors flock to Punta Norte (p409) on Península Valdés, where these powerful creatures almost beach themselves in the hunt for sea lions, from mid-February to mid-April.

Southern Elephant Seals

Consummate divers, these monsters spend most of the year at sea. In austral spring, spy on their breeding colony at Punta Delgada (p409) on Península Valdés. Watch for beachmasters – dominant males controlling harems of up to 100 females.

1. Magellanic penguins, Punta Tombo 2. Southern sea lions 3. Commerson's dolphins 4. Southern right whale, Península Valdés

ANDREA IZZOTTI/SHUTTERSTOCK ©

JOHNNY GIESE/SHUTTERSTOCK ©

Sleeping

Staying over at Puerto Pirámides allows more wildlife watching, though lodgings are few and there's little happening at night. Still, campers gloat about hearing whales' eerie cries and huffing blowholes at night – an extraordinary experience.

You'll have to get a voucher from your hotel to exit and reenter the reserve, to avoid paying the park entry fee twice. Signs advertise lodgings for rent along the main drag. Wi-fi is slow no matter where you stay.

Hidden House GUESTHOUSE **$**
(0280-15-464-4380, 0280-449-5078; hiddenhouse@gmail.com; Segunda Bajada; d/tr US$71/88;) Partially tucked behind the dunes, this lovely, airy home is a fun destination, with flower boxes, friendly dogs and chair loungers in the dunes. Very personal service is provided by chef host Mumo, who can cook up meals and put on a great barbecue, though breakfast is not included.

The street is unmarked; it's the second sea-access road. They're on Facebook.

De Luna GUESTHOUSE **$**
(0280-449-5083; www.deluna.com.ar; Av de las Ballenas s/n; d/cabins incl breakfast US$65/90) A bright and cheerful option. Choose from spacious and inviting rooms in the main house, or a crunched but lovely guest cabin, perched above the house with excellent views. There's no sign; check-in is at Del Nomade next door.

La Casa de la Tía Alicia GUESTHOUSE **$**
(0280-449-5046; info@hosteriatiaalicia.com.ar; Av de las Ballenas s/n; d incl breakfast US$71;) A cozy spot for couples, this petal-pink house has just three cabin-style rooms in bright crayon-box colors around a cute garden area. There's in-room tea service, and management has a conscientious approach to recycling water and composting.

La Reserva CABIN **$$**
(0280-449-5049, 0280-15-466-1629; www.cabañasenelmar.com; Av de las Ballenas; 4-/5-person cabins US$132/165;) La Reserva is smack in the center of all the action (it's right where the road splits to the waterfront); its comfortable, newish cabins are spotless, cool and well equipped. Bedrooms have TVs, and kitchens have full-size refrigerators and stoves.

★Oceano Patagonia CONDO **$$$**
(0280-11-5258-8767; http://oceanopatagonia.com; 1era Bajada; d US$180-370;) These luxury oceanfront condos bring a dose of Miami to sleepy Pirámides. Eleven condos have private terraces, kitchenettes, TVs and concierges on 24-hour call. It's all-in, curated minimalist chic, with artfully worn wooden details, cozy woven throws and chipped paint to telegraph an oh-so-carefree vibe. At the time of research it was in the process of LEED certification.

★Del Nomade Hostería Ecologica LODGE **$$$**
(0280-449-5044; www.ecohosteria.com.ar; Av de las Ballenas s/n; d incl breakfast US$150;) Owned by a renowned Argentine nature photographer, these eight stylish ecolodge rooms have a homey, minimalist style. There are homemade breakfasts, and maximum effort has been put into making it green – using wood from fallen trees, enzymatic water treatment, solar panels, composting and natural cleaning agents. Get in the wildlife mood by browsing the photo displays and stacks of *National Geographic* magazines.

BA Haus & Finnis Terrae APARTMENT **$$$**
(0280-456-2855; www.bahouse.com.ar; Av de las Ballenas s/n; q apt US$200;) These adorable two-story apartments offer a comfortable and stylish crash pad for traveling groups or those who want room to spread out a bit. There's a spacious living room and large LCD-screen TV, a fully equipped kitchen, a small terrace and off-street parking.

Eating & Drinking

El Viento Viene CAFE **$**
(0280-449-5047; 1era Bajada; mains AR$110-175; 9am-8pm;) This little nook is a charming spot for coffee, sandwiches and homemade pie, and also sells innovative arts and crafts.

★Guanaco PUB FOOD **$$**
(0280-449-5046; Av de las Ballenas s/n; mains AR$140-200; 7-11:30pm Mon, Tue, Thu & Fri, noon-3:30pm & 7-11:30pm Sat & Sun) Art installations on a covered porch announce this funky *cervecería* serving Hernan's artisan brews and other regional offerings. Dishes like lamb ravioli, fish with butter and herbs and huge salads are satisfying. Service might be slow; it's a small operation. A sure sign things are going well is that it's been known to close for lack of inventory.

El Origen CAFE $$
(☎0280-449-5049; Av de las Ballenas s/n; mains AR$150-200; ⊙8:30am-7pm) If you're looking for a quick bite, this cute cafe does homemade sandwiches, salads and pizza. Organic coffee, loose-leaf tea or organic juice will satisfy your thirst. There's attention to health-conscious items too (check out the dairy-free chia and coconut-milk dessert).

Information

Banco del Chubut (Av de las Ballenas; ⊙10am-3pm Mon-Fri) Has an ATM.
Tourist Office (☎0280-449-5048; www.puertopiramides.gov.ar; 1era Bajada; ⊙8am-8pm) This small office helps with travelers' needs.

Getting There & Away

Buses stop behind the YPF gas station, the site of the future bus station. The Mar y Valle bus service travels from Puerto Pirámides to Puerto Madryn (AR$114, 1½ hours) Monday through Friday at 8:10am and 6pm. On weekends there are 6pm departures. Bus tours from Puerto Madryn may allow passengers to get off here.

Trelew

☎0280 / POP 98,600

Steeped in Welsh heritage, this uneventful midsize hub is convenient to many attractions. However, it's home to few itself, and isn't a postcard city. The region's commercial center, it's a handy base for visiting the Welsh villages of Gaiman and Dolavon. Also worthwhile is the top-notch dinosaur museum.

Founded in 1886 as a railway junction, Trelew (tre-*ley*-ooh) owes its easily mispronounced name to the Welsh contraction of *tre* (town) and *lew* (after Lewis Jones, who promoted railway expansion). During the following 30 years, the railway reached Gaiman, the Welsh built their Salón San David (a replica of St David's Cathedral, Pembrokeshire), and Spanish and Italian immigrants settled in the area. In 1956 the federal government promoted Patagonian industrial development and Trelew's population skyrocketed.

Sights

The tourist office sometimes has an informative walking-tour brochure, in Spanish and English, describing most of the city's historic buildings.

★Museo Paleontológico Egidio Feruglio MUSEUM
(☎0280-443-2100; www.mef.org.ar; Av Fontana 140; adult/child AR$120/85; ⊙9am-6pm Mon-Fri, 10am-6pm Sat & Sun) Showcasing the most important fossil finds in Patagonia, this natural-history museum offers outstanding life-size dinosaur exhibits and more than 1700 fossil remains of plant and marine life. Nature sounds and a video accent the informative plaques, and tours are available in a number of languages. The collection's most exciting addition is the recently discovered Patagotitan, possibly the largest animal to ever walk the earth. In order to display it, a whole new structure will need to to be built.

Other local dinosaurs here include the tehuelchesaurus, patagosaurus and titanosaurus. With an international team, museum researchers helped discover a new and unusual species called *Brachytrachelopan mesai,* a short-necked sauropod. Egidio Feruglio, after whom the museum is named, was an Italian paleontologist who came to Argentina in 1925 as a petroleum geologist for YPF.

Kids aged eight to 12 can check out the 'Explorers in Pyjamas' program, which invites kids to sleep over and explore the museum by flashlight. The museum also sponsors interesting group tours to Geoparque Paleontológico Bryn Gwyn, in the badlands along the Río Chubut (25km from Trelew, or 8km south of Gaiman via RP 5). The three-hour guided visits are a walk through time, visiting exposed fossils dating as far back as the Tertiary period, some 40 million years ago.

Playa Unión BEACH
(Puerto Rawson) The region's principal playground, Playa Unión is a long stretch of white-sand beach with blocks of summer homes and restaurants serving crisp, fresh *rabas* (calamari). The capital attraction are *toninas overas* (Commerson's dolphins) from April to December.

Museo de Artes Visuales MUSEUM
(☎0280-443-3774; Mitre 351; AR$35; ⊙9am-7pm Mon-Fri, 2-8pm Sat & Sun) Adjoining the tourist office, this small visual-arts museum features works on loan from the Museo Nacional de Bellas Artes in Buenos Aires, as well as polished relics from Welsh colonization.

Trelew

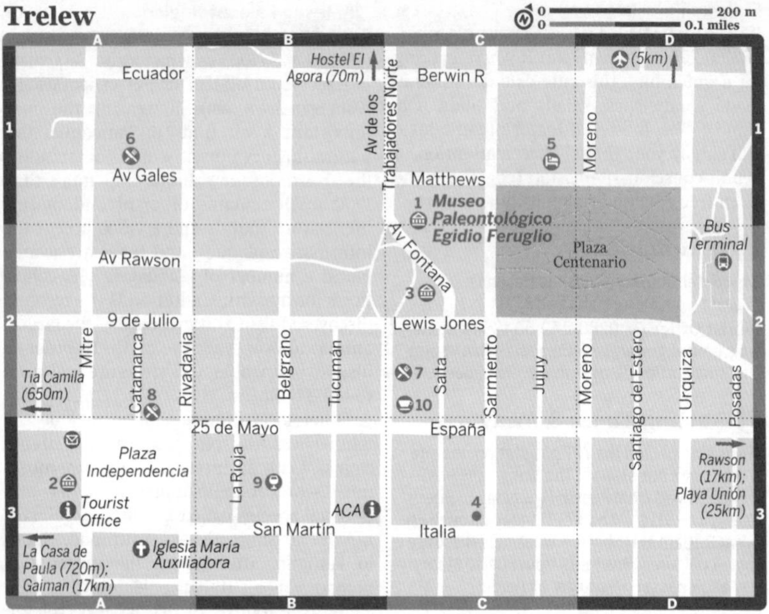

Trelew

Top Sights
1 Museo Paleontológico Egidio Feruglio ... C1

Sights
2 Museo de Artes Visuales ... A3
3 Museo Regional Pueblo de Luis ... C2

Activities, Courses & Tours
4 Nievemar ... C3

Sleeping
5 Patagonia Suites & Apart ... C1

Eating
6 Majadero ... A1
7 Miguel Angel ... C2
8 Sugar ... A2

Drinking & Nightlife
9 Boru Irish Pub & Restobar ... B3
10 Touring Club ... C2

Museo Regional Pueblo de Luis MUSEUM
(0280-442-4062; cnr Av Fontana & Lewis Jones; AR$35; 8am-8pm) In a former train station, this small museum displays historical photographs, clothing and period furnishings of Welsh settlers, along with relics from the area's indigenous peoples.

Tours

Several travel agencies run excursions to Área Natural Protegida Punta Tombo (AR$1200, plus admission), some passing by Puerto Rawson on the way back to see *toninas overas* (Commerson's dolphins) when conditions are agreeable. The actual time at Punta Tombo is only about 1½ hours.

Full-day trips to Península Valdés (AR$1200, plus admission) are also on offer, but going to Puerto Madryn first is a better bet: there are more options, prices are similar and there's less driving time.

Local agencies worth checking out are Amex representative **Nievemar** (0280-443-4114; www.nievemartours.com.ar; Italia 20; 8:30am-12:30pm & 3:30pm-8:30pm Mon-Fri, 9am-1pm Sat), which accepts traveler's checks, and **Explore Patagonia** (0280-443-7860; Roca 94; 10am-1pm & 3-7pm Mon-Fri, 10am-1pm Sat).

Estacion Maritima BOATING
(estacionmaritima@gmail.com; Rawson; adult/child AR$1000/500) Reputable dolphin-watching tours from Rawson. Contact by email only.

Toninas Adventure BOATING
(0280-449-8372, 0280-15-467-5741; www.facebook.com/ToninasAdventure; Rawson; adult/child AR$1000/500) Dolphin tours departing Puerto Rawson from April to December.

Festivals & Events

Gwyl y Glaniad CULTURAL
(Jul 28) The landing of the first Welsh here is celebrated by taking tea in one of the many chapels.

Eisteddfod de Chubut CULTURAL
(late Oct) A Welsh literary and musical festival. The tradition started in 1875.

Sleeping

La Casona del Río B&B $
(0280-443-8343; www.lacasonadelrio.com.ar; Chacra 105; d/tr US$71/88; @) Located 5km outside the city center, on the bank of the Río Chubut, this English-style B&B is a thoroughly charming refuge. Guest rooms are smart and bright; other features include library, tennis court, gazebo and rental bikes. It's off Capitan Murga.

Hostel El Agora HOSTEL $
(0280-442-6899; www.hostelagora.com.ar; Edwin Roberts 33; dm/d US$19/50; @) This cute brick house is a backpacker haven. Features include a tiny patio, a book exchange and laundry. It also does guided bicycle tours. It's two blocks from Plaza Centenario and four blocks from the bus terminal.

★**La Casa de Paula** B&B $$
(0280-15-435-2240; www.casadepaula.com.ar; Marconi 573; d/tr/q incl breakfast US$94/106/115; P) A haven after a day of sun and wind, artist Paula's house beckons with huge king beds covered in down duvets and woven throws. An eclectic and warm decor fills this modern home, with jazz on the radio and cozy living areas stacked with fashion mags. There's also a lush garden and an outstanding breakfast with homemade jam.

The newer suites with balcony or patio are ideal for families.

Patagonia Suites & Apart APARTMENT $$
(0280-442-1345, 0280-453-7399; www.patagoniansuites.com; Matthews 186; d from US$65;) A foxy addition to town, these 13 modern apartments (from studios to multiple bedrooms) feature wood details, hairdryers and corduroy bedspreads. They also come with fully equipped kitchens and cable TV. The complex faces Plaza Centenario.

Eating

Tia Camila ARGENTINE $
(0280-443-2950; 25 de Mayo 951; mains AR$90-180; 12:30-3pm & 8:30-11:45pm Thu-Mon) A humble neighborhood restaurant, Tia Camila does a brisk business in simple and filling fare, ranging from homemade pastas to delectable *costellitas* (ribs) served with mashed potatoes and salad. There's also take-out.

Miguel Angel ITALIAN $$
(0280-443-0403; Av Fontana 246; mains AR$110-230; noon-3pm & 8pm-midnight Tue-Sun) This chic eatery, outfitted with sleek white booths, departs from the everyday with savory dishes such as gnocchi and wild mushrooms, and pizza with bacon and basil on a crisp, thin crust.

Sugar ARGENTINE $$
(0280-442-1210; 25 de Mayo 247; mains AR$130-230; 7am-1am;) Facing Plaza Independencia, this modern restaurant spices up a basic menu of classic Argentine fare with options like quinoa *milanesas,* stir-fried beef, grilled vegetables and herbed fish. There are salads and fresh juice on offer too. While it isn't gourmet, it's still a welcome change from the Argentine same-old, same-old.

Majadero ARGENTINE $$$
(0280-443-0548; Av Gales 250; mains AR$130-340; 8pm-midnight Mon-Sat, noon-6pm Sun) Iron lamps and brickwork restore the romance to this 1914 flour mill – undoubtedly the nicest restaurant setting in town. On weekends it's busy, with the wood-fired *parrilla* grilling steaks and even vegetables.

Drinking & Nightlife

Touring Club CAFE
(Av Fontana 240; 6:30am-2am) Old lore exudes from the pores of this historic *confitería* (cafe offering light meals), from the Butch Cassidy 'Wanted' poster to the embossed tile ceiling and antique bar back. Even the tuxedoed waitstaff appear to be plucked from another era. Service is weak and the sandwiches are only so-so, but the ambience is one of a kind.

Boru Irish Pub & Restobar PUB
(0280-442-3755; Belgrano 341; 8pm-4am) Hip and attractive, featuring a beautiful wood bar and a row of cozy red booths, Boru serves up icy beer and plates piled high with french fries.

Orientation

The city center surrounds Plaza Independencia, with most services located on Calles 25 de Mayo and San Martín, and along renovated Av Fontana. East–west streets change names either side of Av Fontana.

WELSH LEGACY

The Welsh opened the door to settling Patagonia in 1865, though the newfound freedom cost them dearly. Few had farmed before and the arid steppe bore little resemblance to their verdant homeland. After nearly starving they survived with the help of the Tehuelche, and eventually occupied the entire lower Chubut valley, founding the towns and teahouses of Rawson, Trelew, Puerto Madryn and Gaiman. Today about 20% of Chubut's inhabitants have Welsh blood, but a revival of Welsh culture is dragging it back from the grave. The renewed bond means yearly British Council appointments of Welsh teachers and exchanges for Patagonian students, though with the passage of Brexit, funding for many of these programs has disappeared. Curious Welsh tourists visit to time travel in their own culture, thanks to Patagonia's longtime isolation.

Information

ATMs are plentiful downtown and around Plaza Independencia.

ACA (Automóvil Club Argentino; ☎0280-435197; cnr Av Fontana & San Martín; ⏲9am-6pm Mon-Fri) Argentina's auto club; a good source for provincial road maps.

Post Office (cnr 25 de Mayo & Mitre; ⏲8am-1pm & 4-6pm)

Tourist Office (☎0280-442-0139; www.trelew.gov.ar; cnr San Martín & Mitre; ⏲8am-8pm Mon-Fri, 9am-9pm Sat & Sun; 📶) Helpful and well stocked, with some English-speaking staff.

Getting There & Away

AIR

Trelew's Airport Almirante Marcos A Zar (p407) is 5km north of town off RN 3. The **Transfer Aeropuerto** (☎0280-487-7300; AR$300) service goes to Puerto Madryn. From the airport, a **taxi** (☎0280-442-0404) to downtown is AR$130 (AR$1100 to Puerto Madryn).

Aerolíneas Argentinas (☎0280-442-0222; Rivadavia 548; ⏲9am-5pm Mon-Fri) flies direct daily to Buenos Aires (AR$4160), and several times a week to Ushuaia (AR$2500) and El Calafate (AR$3590).

LADE (☎0280-443-5740; Italia 170; ⏲8am-3pm Mon-Fri) flies to Comodoro Rivadavia weekly. Starting in mid-2018, additional low-cost carriers are expected to serve Trelew, linking it with more provincial destinations. **Aviación Civil Argentina** (ANAC; www.anac.gob.ar) has a map with new routes and airlines.

BUS

Trelew's full-service **bus terminal** (☎0280-442-0121; Urquiza 150) is six blocks northeast of downtown.

For Gaiman (AR$23), **28 de Julio** (☎0280-443-2429) has 18 services daily between 7am and 11pm (less on weekends), with most continuing to Dolavon (AR$45, 30 minutes). Buses to Playa Unión (AR$35) leave hourly.

Mar y Valle (☎0280-442-4119) and 28 de Julio run hourly buses to Puerto Madryn. Mar y Valle goes to Puerto Pirámides (AR$70, 2½ hours) at 8:15am daily, with additional services in summer. **El Ñandú** (☎0280-442-7499) goes to Camarones (AR$250, four hours) at 8am on Monday, Wednesday and Friday.

Long-distance bus companies include **El Cóndor** (☎0280-443-1675), **Que Bus** (☎0280-442-2760), **Andesmar** (☎0280-442-2402), **TAC** (☎0280-443-9207), **TUS** (☎0280-442-1343) and **Don Otto/Transportes Patagonia** (☎0280-442-9496). Don Otto has the most comfortable and direct service to Buenos Aires. Only Don Otto goes to Mar del Plata, while TAC goes to La Plata. There are a few daily departures with TAC, Don Otto or Andesmar to Comodoro Rivadavia, continuing to Río Gallegos.

Buses from Trelew

DESTINATION	COST (AR$)	TIME (HR)
Bahía Blanca	1150	12
Bariloche	1500	13-16
Buenos Aires	850	18-21
Comodoro Rivadavia	680	5-6
Córdoba	800	19
Esquel	872	8-9
Mar del Plata	1940	17-21
Mendoza	2000	24
Neuquén	1200	10
Puerto Madryn	70	1
Río Gallegos	1300	14-17
Viedma	700	8

Getting Around

Local buses (AR$9) cross the city. Car-rental agencies at the airport include **Hertz** (☎0280-447-5247) and **Rent a Car Patagonia** (☎0280-442-0898; www.rentacarpatagonia.com.ar).

Gaiman

☎0280 / POP 9600

Cream pie, dainty tea cakes, *torta negra* (a rich, dense fruitcake) and a hot pot of black tea – most visitors eat their dose of culture when visiting this quintessential Welsh river-valley village. Locals proudly recount the day in 1995 when the late Diana, Princess of Wales, visited Gaiman to take tea. Today one-third of the residents claim Welsh ancestry and teahouse traditions persist.

The town's name, meaning Stony Point or Arrow Point, originated from the Tehuelche who once wintered in this valley. After the Welsh constructed their first house in 1874, the two groups peacefully coexisted for a time. Later, immigrant groups of criollos, Germans and Anglos joined them. The town offers little diversion beyond quiet strolls past stone houses and rose gardens after a teahouse visit.

Sights

Gaiman is ideal for an informal walking tour, past homes with ivy trellises and drooping, oversize roses. Architecturally distinctive churches and chapels dot the town. **Primera Casa** (cnr Av Eugenio Tello & Evans; AR$30; 11am-6pm) was its first house, built in 1874 by David Roberts. Dating from 1906, the **Colegio Camwy** (MD Jones 490) is considered the first secondary school in Patagonia.

Museo Histórico Regional Gales MUSEUM
(☎0280-449-1007; cnr Sarmiento & 28 de Julio; AR$20; 3-8pm daily Dec-Mar, 3-7pm Tue-Sun Apr-Nov) The old train station houses this fine small museum holding the belongings and photographs of Gaiman pioneers.

Sleeping

Hostería Gwesty Tywi B&B $
(☎0280-449-1292; www.hosteria-gwestytywi.com.ar; Chacra 202; s/d/tr US$55/70/85; @) Diego and Brenda run this wonderful Welsh B&B with large gardens and snug, frilly rooms. They are glad to help with travel planning and occasionally fire up the barbecue, to the delight of guests. Breakfast includes a selection of jams, cold meats and bread. The location is a bit far from the town center.

Camping Bomberos Voluntarios CAMPGROUND $
(☎0280-449-1117; cnr Av Yrigoyen & Moreno; camping per person US$3) An agreeable campground with hot-water showers and fire pits.

Eating & Drinking

Tarten afal, tarten gwstard, cacen ffrwythau, spwnj jam and *bara brith* and a bottomless pot of tea – hungry yet? Afternoon tea is taken as a sacrament in Gaiman – though busloads of tourists get dump-trucked into teahouses without warning. The best bet is to look for places without buses in front. Tea services usually run from 2pm to 7pm. There are just a few restaurants and opening hours can be short.

Siop Bara BAKERY $
(☎0280-449-1082; Av Eugenio Tello 505; snacks AR$80; 8am-1pm & 3-9pm) This Welsh bakery is the perfect quick, no-fuss stop for pastries, gelato and excellent sandwiches.

Gwalia Lan ARGENTINE $$
(☎0280-436-5840; cnr Av Eugenio Tello & MD Jones; mains AR$180-250; 12:30-3pm & 7:30pm-midnight Tue-Sat, 12:30-3pm Sun) Considered Gaiman's best restaurant, Gwalia Lan is a fine alternative to teatime if you've already done that. Excellent homemade pasta and well-seasoned meat dishes are consistently good. Service is attentive.

★ **Ty Gwyn** TEAHOUSE
(☎0280-499-1009; 9 de Julio 111; 2-7:30pm) A favorite of locals, this white house serves cakes, jams and breads that are all homemade and fresh, *always* (tea adult/child AR$350/200).

Plas y Coed TEAHOUSE
(☎0280-449-1133; www.plasycoed.com.ar; MD Jones 123; 2-7:30pm) Run by the original owner's great-granddaughter in a gorgeous brick mansion, Plas y Coed pleases the palate and senses, with friendly service, fresh cakes and serious crochet cozies for that steaming-hot pot (tea adult/child $300/150). Rooms are also available for rent.

Information

There's one ATM on Plaza Roca at Banco del Chubut, but it does not always work, so bring cash.

Post Office (cnr Evans & Yrigoyen; 8am-4pm Mon-Fri) Just north of the river bridge.

Tourist Office (☎0280-449-1571; www.gaiman.gov.ar; cnr Rivadavia & Belgrano; 9am-8pm Dec-Mar, 9am-6pm Apr-Nov;) Very helpful with information.

Getting There & Away

Tiny Gaiman is 17km west of Trelew via RN 25. During the week, 28 de Julio buses depart for

Trelew frequently from Plaza Roca (AR$23, from 7am to 11pm, fewer services on weekends). Most buses to Dolavon (AR$23) use the highway, but some take the much longer gravel 'valley' route.

Tours from Trelew and Puerto Madryn also stop in here.

Área Natural Protegida Punta Tombo

Continental South America's largest penguin nesting ground, **Área Natural Protegida Punta Tombo** (adult/child AR$320/165; 8am-6pm Sep-Apr) has a colony of up to a million Magellanic penguins and attracts many other birds, most notably king and rock cormorants, giant petrels, kelp gulls, flightless steamer ducks and black oystercatchers. A strict management plan requires rangers to accompany visitors on rookery visits.

Trelew-based travel agencies run day-long tours. If possible, come in the early morning to beat the crowds. Most of the nesting areas in the 200-hectare reserve are fenced off: respect the limits and remember that penguins can inflict serious bites.

Information

Centro Tombo (8am-6pm) An interpretative visitor center with cafe service; it's the departure point for shuttles to the rookery.

Getting There & Away

Punta Tombo is 110km south of Trelew and 180km south of Puerto Madryn via well-maintained gravel RP 1 and a short southeast lateral. Motorists can proceed south to Camarones via scenic but desolate Cabo Raso.

Tours from Puerto Madryn and Trelew are frequent. If you can get a group together, it may be worth renting a car in Puerto Madryn or Trelew to visit.

Guests park at the Centro Tombo and shuttle to the rookery. Shuttle frequency depends on demand, but it's greater in the morning.

Camarones

0297 / POP 1300

In the stiff competition for Patagonia's sleepiest coastal village, Camarones takes home the gold. But don't diss its languorous state: if you've ever needed to run away, this is a good option. Its empty beaches invite strolling and the townsfolk are masters at shooting the breeze. From here, visit the lesser-known nature reserve Cabo Dos Bahías.

Spanish colonial explorer Don Simón de Alcazaba y Sotomayor anchored here in 1545, proclaiming it part of his attempted Provincia de Nueva León. When the wool industry took off, Camarones became the area's main port. The high quality of the local wool didn't go unnoticed by justice of the peace Don Mario Tomás Perón, who operated the area's largest *estancia*, Porvenir, on which his son (and future president) Juanito would romp about. The port flourished, but after Comodoro Rivadavia finished its massive port, Camarones was all but deserted.

Sights

Museo Perón MUSEUM
(0297-496-3014; JM Estrada s/n; 11am-6pm Tue-Sat) FREE This newish multistory museum documents the life of ex-president Juan Domingo Perón.

Festivals & Events

Fiesta Nacional del Salmón CULTURAL
(Feb) A weekend of deep-sea-fishing competitions featuring a free Sunday seafood lunch and the crowning of Miss Salmoncito.

Sleeping & Eating

Las Cabañas CABIN $
(0297-15-422-2270, 0280-487-6980; almapatagonicacamarones@gmail.com; cnr Roca & Estrada; d US$56) Located opposite Camarones' plaza, these pastel shoebox cabins are good value. Like new, they feature small, clean bedrooms with a bathroom and kitchenette. There's also the option to stay in the two-story main house next door for the same rate. If no one is here, ask at Alma Patagonica, the restaurant that runs the cabins.

Camping Camarones CAMPGROUND $
(0297-15-436-9174; San Martín; campsite per person/vehicle US$8/6, cabin s/d US$28/54;) At the waterfront port, this peaceful campground with hot showers and electricity is run by a friendly older couple. A basic store sells provisions and ice cream.

★**El Faro Casas de Mar** APARTMENT $$
(0297-414-5510; www.elfaro-patagonia.com.ar; d US$65, 2-/4-person houses US$94/112) A great option, these shiny corrugated-tin houses are trimmed with varnished wood and offer sea views. Guests can rent a comfortable house with kitchen, grill and terrace or a

OFF THE BEATEN TRACK

DOLAVON

To experience an authentic historic Welsh agricultural town, head to the distinctly non-touristy **Dolavon** (population 2800; www.dolavon.com.ar), 19km west of Gaiman via paved RN 25.

Its name is Welsh for 'river meadow,' and the town offers pastoral appeal, with wooden waterwheels lining the irrigation canal framed by rows of swaying poplars. The historic center of Dolavon is full of brick buildings, including the 1880 **Molino Harinero** (0280-449-2290; romanogi@infovia.com.ar; Maipú 61; hours vary), with still-functioning flour-mill machinery. Its cafe-restaurant, **La Molienda** (0280-449-2290; mains AR$130-200), serves handmade breads and pasta with local wines and cheeses. Call owner Romano Giallatini for opening hours.

Frequent buses from Trelew pass through Gaiman before reaching Dolavon (AR$45, 30 minutes).

room for two, both with satellite TV. There's no street address. It's in front of the historic Casa Rabal near the port.

Alma Patagonica CAFE $$
(0297-422-2270; cnr Sarmiento & Roca; mains AR$165-255; 10am-2pm & 7:30-11pm Mon-Sat) This restored century-old frontier bar is run with an eye to preserving local tradition. The homemade fish empanadas (baked savory turnovers) are excellent, washed back with a massive cold beer. It also runs Las Cabañas, located one block away.

Information

Tourist Office (0297-496-3013; www.camarones.gob.ar; San Martín 570; 8am-8pm Dec-May) Very helpful, with maps, good tips on scenic outings and lodging information.

Getting There & Away

At a gas-station junction 180km south of Trelew, RP 30 splits off from RN 3 and heads 72km east to Camarones.

In Camarones, buses leave from the **bus terminal** (cnr 9 de Julio & Rivadavia). El Ñandú buses go to Trelew (AR$250, four hours) at 4pm on Monday, Wednesday and Friday. Etap goes to Comodoro Rivadavia (AR$230, 3½ hours) at 1pm on Tuesday and Thursday.

Local taxis make the 30-minute ride to Cabo Dos Bahías.

Cabo Dos Bahías

A rough 30km southeast of Camarones, the isolated rookery **Cabo Dos Bahías** (AR$185; year-round) attracts far fewer visitors than Punta Tombo, making it an excellent alternative. You'll be rewarded with orcas, a huge colony of 9000 nesting penguin couples in spring and summer, whales in winter, and a large concentration of guanacos and rheas. Seabirds, sea lions, foxes and fur seals are year-round residents.

You can pitch a tent for free at Cabo Dos Bahías Club Naútico or on any of the beaches en route from Camarones. Otherwise, Camarones has the closest lodgings.

Comodoro Rivadavia

0297 / POP 177,000

Comodoro (as it's commonly known) sits at the eastern end of the Corredor Bioceánico, which leads to Coyhaique, Chile. It's surrounded by dry hills of drilling rigs, oil tanks and wind-energy farms. Tourism in this dusty port usually means little more than a bus transfer. This modern, hardworking city does provide a gateway to nearby attractions with decent services (cue the Walmart).

Founded in 1901, Comodoro was once a transport hub linking ranches in nearby Sarmiento. In 1907 the town struck it rich when workers drilling for water found oil instead. With the country's first major gusher, Comodoro became a state pet, gaining a large port, an airport and paved roads. Today it is a powerhouse in the oil industry, with the dubious status of the largest consumer of being plasma TVs in Argentina. Although the oil-industry downswing looks gloomy, there's still a casino and hot rods racing in the streets.

Sights

Museo Nacional del Petróleo MUSEUM
(0297-455-9558; AR$120; 9am-5pm Tue-Fri, 3-6pm Sat) This museum provides an insider look at the social and historical aspects of petroleum development. Don't expect balanced

DON'T MISS

BAHÍA BUSTAMANTE

A number of coastal reserves feature Patagonia's diverse marine life, but few illuminate the exuberance of this ecosystem like this historic 80-hectare **estancia** (0297-480-1000, in Buenos Aires 011-4778-0125; www.bahiabustamante.com; s/d/tr sea cottages incl full board & activities US$450/590/720, basic 3-person cottage US$135;) located between Trelew and Comodoro Rivadavia. The sprawling steppe, rolling grass dunes and pebble beaches beg you to bask in the slow rhythms of life on this deserted coast. Excursions are thoughtfully guided by bilingual naturalists, and include sea kayaking, trekking the on-site 65-million-year-old petrified forest and boat trips to see Magellanic penguins, sea lions and marine birds.

Another quirky footnote in Patagonian history, Bahía Bustamante was founded by an entrepreneurial Andalucian immigrant who used the abundant algae in the bay to manufacture agar-agar, a natural food thickener. At one point hundreds of workers lived on the *estancia*, which became a kind of Wild West, complete with a police station and jail cell. In pre-settlement times, Tehuelches traveled the area, leaving behind their small tools and middens.

The time to see fauna is between mid-September and early March, with January and February ideal for swimming. Bird watching is best during November hatching, but it's also cool to watch sea lions nurse new pups in January.

Check out 'Mysteries,' a wind-song installation consisting of animal bones. The on-site land art was created by French sculptor Christian Boltanski for Bienalsur, the South American branch of a lauded worldwide art exposition.

Access is by private vehicle only. Most visitors fly into Comodoro, but if you have a car, it's worth taking the scenic coastal route (all gravel roads) from nearby Camarones.

treatment of oil issues – it was built by the former state oil agency YPF (and is now managed by the Universidad Nacional de Patagonia). While its historical photos are interesting, the detailed models of tankers, refineries and the entire zone of exploitation are best left to die-hards. Guided tours are available.

The museum is in the suburb of General Mosconi, 3km north of downtown. Take a *remise* from downtown or bus 7 'Laprida' or 8 'Palazzo;' get off at La Anónima supermarket.

Tours

Several agencies arrange trips to Bosque Petrificado Sarmiento and Cueva de las Manos.

Ruta 40 TOURS
(0294-452-3378; www.ruta-40.com) If you're really up for a road trip, contact Ruta 40. The small, multilingual outfitter is based in Bariloche, but some tours start in Comodoro, like the eight-day Ruta 40 tour, with stops at Puerto Deseado, Cueva de las Manos and several lovely *estancias* before ending up in El Calafate. Contact it for current rates and departure dates.

Circuito Ferroportuario TOURS
The free urban train tour Circuito Ferroportuario takes visitors on a circuit from the tourism office to visit containers, warehouses and workshops on the port.

Sleeping

Catering mainly to business travelers and long-term laborers, accommodations here fit two categories: the ritzy and the rundown. Brisk business means lodgings are overpriced and often full – book ahead.

WAM BOUTIQUE HOTEL $$
(0297-406-8020; www.wamhotel.com.ar; Av Hipólito Yrigoyen 2196; d US$112; P) Think industrial boutique, with an unfortunate office-building-like exterior. The contemporary rooms have crisp white linens, neutral tones and glass-walled tubs. There's restaurant service and a gym. Guests have access to a spa, Jacuzzi and pool. It's located just off the *costanera*, south of downtown.

Hotel Victoria HOTEL $$
(0297-446-0725; www.hotelvictoriacrd.com.ar; Belgrano 585; s/d/tr incl breakfast US$68/87/100; P) The friendliest hotel on the block, with soothing, good-sized rooms with firm twin beds, desks and cable TV. If the aroma of baking pastries is any indication, it's worth taking breakfast. Parking is extra.

Lucania Palazzo Hotel HOTEL $$$
(☎0297-449-9300; www.lucania-palazzo.com; Moreno 676; d incl breakfast US$185; @🛜) Comodoro's answer to the Trump Towers, the sparkling Palazzo offers ocean views from every room and tasteful modern decor, although ventilation could be better. While its features only add up to those of a solid chain hotel, there's a decent restaurant and the eager staff offers helpful recommendations.

Eating

The oil industry has bankrolled a taste for fine dining, with decent options in upscale hotels. Look for the free *Sabores del Sur* restaurant directory in hotels.

Hilario CAFE $$
(☎0297-444-2516; Belgrano 694; mains AR$180-260; ⏱10am-midnight Tue-Sat, from 5pm Sun) A modern cafe with brickwork and bare lightbulbs, it draws locals for stews served as pot pies with seeded crusts, pizza and mint-ginger lemonade. It's a good alternative to the traditional Argentine palate, with even quinoa on the menu.

Bajo Belgrano Resto Bar ARGENTINE $$
(☎0297-444-2116; Belgrano 556; mains AR$200-300; ⏱11:30am-2pm & 8-11pm) Tuck into this cute restaurant's offerings of pastas, *milanesa* or stuffed roasted squash.

Information

ACA (Automóvil Club Argentino; ☎0297-446-0876; cnr Dorrego & Alvear; ⏱8am-2pm) Maps and road info.

Banco de la Nación (cnr Av San Martín & Güemes; ⏱10am-3pm) Most of Comodoro's banks and ATMs, including this one, are along Avs San Martín or Rivadavia.

Hospital Regional (☎0297-444-2287; Av Hipólito Yrigoyen 950)

Post Office (cnr Av San Martín & Moreno; ⏱8am-4:30pm Mon-Fri)

Tourist Office (☎0297-444-0664; www.comodoroturismo.gob.ar; Parque Soberania; ⏱8am-8pm Mon-Fri, 9am-3pm Sat & Sun) Friendly, well stocked and well organized.

Getting There & Away

The Corredor Bioceánico – RN 26, RP 20 and RP 55 – is a straight highway link to Coyhaique, Chile, and its Pacific port, Puerto Chacabuco. Developers are promoting this commercial transport route as an alternative to the Panama Canal, since it is open year-round and it is the continent's shortest distance between ports on both oceans. Paved RN 26, RP 20 and RN 40 lead to Esquel and Bariloche.

AIR

Aeropuerto General Mosconi (☎0297-454-8190) is 9km north of town. New low-cost airlines plan to offer flights to Buenos Aires, Río Gallegos and Trelew. **Aviación Civil Argentina** (ANAC; www.anac.gob.ar) has a map with new routes and airlines.

Aerolíneas Argentinas (☎0297-444-0050; www.aerolineas.com.ar; Av Rivadavia 156; ⏱8am-noon & 3-7pm Mon-Fri) and **LATAM** (☎0297-454-8160; www.latam.com) fly a couple of times daily to Buenos Aires (one way from AR$4328).

Comodoro is the hub for **LADE** (☎0297-447-0585; www.lade.com.ar; Av Rivadavia 360; ⏱8am-8pm Mon-Fri, 10am-5pm Sat), which goes at least once a week to El Calafate, Río Gallegos, Trelew, Ushuaia, Buenos Aires and points in between.

BUS

The chaotic **bus terminal** (Pellegrini 730) receives all buses plying RN 3.

Most bus schedules are divided into northbound and southbound departures. **Andesmar** (☎0297-446-8894) departs five times daily (between 1:15am and 3pm) for points north, including Trelew, Rawson and Puerto Madryn. **TAC** (☎0297-444-3376) follows the same route and continues to Buenos Aires. **Etap** (☎0297-447-4841) runs to Esquel and Río Mayo daily, to Sarmiento four times daily and to Coyhaique, Chile, at 8am on Wednesday and Saturday.

Sportman (☎0297-444-2988) has services to Los Antiguos and connections to Chile Chico, via the town of Perito Moreno. **Taqsa/Marga** (☎0297-447-0564) goes to Bariloche and El Calafate in the evening.

Buses from Comodoro Rivadavia

DESTINATION	COST (AR$)	TIME (HR)
Bariloche	1015-1200	12
Buenos Aires	2375	24
Coyhaique (Chile)	1060	11
El Calafate	1415	14
Esquel	960	10
Los Antiguos	550	5
Puerto Deseado	400	4
Puerto Madryn	782	6
Río Gallegos	1150	10-12
Río Mayo	390	3½
Sarmiento	230	2
Trelew	679	5

OFF THE BEATEN TRACK

CABO RASO

Old Patagonia still lives, breathes and gusts on this rocky, arid coast replete with a reviving ghost town and near-secret surf spots.

Formerly a booming sheep-ranching settlement, founded in the late 1800s, the cape was abandoned by the 1950s. Now a wonderful Argentine family is attempting a slow revival through sustainable tourism. They labored for eight years to restore the coast; once littered with decades of garbage, it now sparkles with the powerful, spare beauty nature intended. There's plenty of coastal walking, DIY bird watching, kayaking and fishing. Surfing's at its best here when the north wind blows in August.

Access is via private vehicle, though it's possible to arrange pickups from Punta Tombo with advance notice. Cabo Raso is 55km south of Punta Tombo, and 80km north of Camarones via gravel roads.

Want to really get away? Stay at offbeat guesthouse **El Cabo** (☎0280-15-467-3049, 0280-442-0354; www.caboraso.com.ar; RP 1, Km294; per person campsites US$6, per person hosterías/buses with shared bathroom US$47/41, cabins for 2-6 people US$88-106) or rent simple stone cottages from the original settlement, artfully restored with recycled and repurposed materials. Budget travelers can stay in cool retro-style buses, or camp alongside a former military bunker, now a *quincho*, with sheltered cooking facilities for campers.

Reservations can be slow to arrange as there's no on-site cell-phone service or wi-fi.

Schedules are in constant flux; upon arrival at the bus terminal, ask at each bus line's desk for the latest information on departure times.

Getting Around

Bus 8 'Directo Palazzo' goes directly to the airport from outside Comodoro's bus terminal. A taxi to the airport costs AR$160 from downtown.

Expreso Rada Tilly links the bus terminal to the nearby beach resort (AR$9) every 20 minutes on weekdays and every 30 minutes on weekends.

Rental cars are available from **Avis** (☎0297-454-9471; Airport) and **Localiza** (☎0297-446-1400; Airport). **Dubrovnik** (☎0297-444-1844; www.rentacardubrovnik.com; Moreno 941; ⏱8am-noon & 3-7:30pm) rents 4WD vehicles.

Puerto Deseado

☎0297 / POP 14,200

The draw of the serene and attractive deep-sea-fishing town of Puerto Deseado is the submerged estuary of Ría Deseado, brimming with seabirds and marine wildlife, including dolphins and the punked-out rockhopper penguin. With a lovely historic center, the town is ripe for revitalization, though change happens at a glacial pace here: witness the vintage trucks rusting on the streets like beached cetaceans. History looms large. Hernando de Magallanes sought shelter here in 1520. The town later became a port for whaling and seal hunting. Charles Darwin left his indelible stamp here too.

Puerto Deseado is two hours southeast of the RN 3 junction at Fitz Roy via dead-end RN 281. The center of activity is the axis formed by main streets San Martín and Almirante Brown.

History

In 1520 the estuary provided shelter to Hernando de Magallanes after a crippling storm waylaid his fleet; he dubbed the area 'Río de los Trabajos' (River of Labors).

In 1586 English privateer Thomas Cavendish explored the estuary and named it after his ship *Desire*, its name today. The port attracted fleets from around the world for whaling and seal hunting, compelling the Spanish crown to send a squadron of colonists under the command of Antonio de Viedma. After a harsh winter, more than 30 of them died of scurvy. Those who survived moved inland to form the short-lived colony of Floridablanca. In 1834 Darwin surveyed the estuary.

Sights & Activities

A self-guided tour is a good start if you want to catch the vibes of Deseado. Pick up a *Guía Historica* map (in Spanish) from the Dirección Municipal de Turismo offices (p426).

Estación del Ferrocarril Patagónico HISTORIC SITE

(entry by donation; ⏱4-7pm Mon-Sat) Train fans can check out the imposing English-designed train station off Av Oneto, built by

Yugoslav stonecutters in 1908. Puerto Deseado was once the coastal terminus for a cargo and passenger route that hauled wool and lead from Chilean mines at Pico Truncado and Las Heras, located 280km northwest.

Vagón Histórico LANDMARK
(cnr San Martín & Almirante Brown; ⏲5-8pm) This restored 1898 wagon is famous as the car from which rebel leader Facón Grande prepared the 'Patagonia Rebellion.' In 1979 the car was almost sold for scrap, but townspeople blocked the roads to stop the sale.

A few blocks west is the attractive **Sociedad Española** (San Martín 1176), c 1915.

Museo Municipal Mario Brozoski MUSEUM
(☎0297-487-1358; cnr Colón & Belgrano; ⏲8am-5pm Mon-Fri, 3-6pm Sat) FREE Displays relics of the English corvette *Swift*, sunk off the coast of Deseado in 1776. Divers continue to recover artifacts from the wreck, which was discovered in 1982.

Tours

Darwin Expediciones ADVENTURE
(☎0297-15-624-7554; www.darwin-expeditions.com; Av España 2601; Isla Pingüinos excursion US$120) Offers sea-kayaking trips, wildlife observation, and multiday nature and archaeology tours with knowledgeable guides. Its best seller is the EcoSafari tour of Reserva Natural Ría Deseado (US$60), the agency's prime wildlife-watching tour, offering sightings of dolphins, sea lions, Magellanic penguins and marine birdlife.

Los Vikingos ADVENTURE
(☎0297-487-0020, 0297-15-624-4283, 0297-15-624-5141; www.losvikingos.com.ar; Moreno & Prefectura Naval) Trips on land and sea. Tours, some led by marine biologists, include the Reserva Natural Ría Deseado. Contact via the website or by phone.

Sleeping & Eating

Ask at the tourist office about (relatively) nearby *estancias*.

Tower Rock APARTMENT $$
(☎011-3935-0150, in Buenos Aires 011-3935-0188; www.tower-rock.com; Pueyrredón 385 or Almirante Zar 305; apt US$85-165; ❄📶) With studios and multiple-bedroom apartments, this comfortable option offers peace and privacy. Apartments come fully equipped with outfitted kitchen, flat-screen TV, lock box and daily maid service. Hosts Patricia and Jorge are happy to answer questions.

Hotel Los Acantilados HOTEL $$
(☎0297-475-2539; losacantiladoshotel@speedy.com.ar; cnr Pueyrredón & Av España; superior d US$97; P@📶) More inspiring from outside than in, these cliff-top digs boast an extensive lounge with fireplace: the perfect chill spot. Mattresses are firm and comfortable. The dining room looks out on the waterfront; the few rooms with views go fast.

Lo de Piola CAFE $$
(☎0297-487-2644; San Martín 1280; mains AR$120-220; ⏲11:30am-10pm Mon-Sat) Recommended by locals, this unassuming *confitería* serves satisfying meals and snacks, with grilled meats, beer and wine.

Puerto Cristal SEAFOOD $$
(☎0297-487-0387; Av España 1698; mains AR$110-260; ⏲noon-3pm & 8pm-midnight Thu-Tue) This

WORTH A TRIP

BOSQUE PETRIFICADO SARMIENTO

Fallen giants scatter the pale sandstone landscape at this **petrified forest** (⏲10am-6pm) FREE, 30km southeast of Sarmiento. The forest, brought here by strong river currents from the mountainous regions about 65 million years ago, has logs 100m in length and 1m wide. For travelers, this area is much more accessible than the Monumento Natural Bosques Petrificados further south.

Go with your own rental car, or ask at the tourist office in Sarmiento for *remise* (taxi) rates for the 1½-hour roundtrip. Try to stay through sunset, when the striped bluffs of Cerro Abigarrado and the multihued hills turn brilliantly vivid.

The eager staff at Sarmiento's tourist office can provide maps and lodging information.

Sarmiento is 148km west of Comodoro along RN 26 and RP 20. **Etap** (☎0297-489-3058; cnr Av San Martin & 12 de Octubre, Sarmiento) has buses running daily to Comodoro Rivadavia (AR$230, two hours); its buses to Río Mayo (AR$230, 1½ hours) go at 9:30pm daily. To access the petrified forest, visitors go by private vehicle or regional tour.

popular seafood haunt satisfies with sturdy portions of grilled fish, fried calamari and an extensive wine selection.

Information

Banks and ATMs, including **Banco de la Patagonia** (San Martín & Almirante Brown; ⏲10am-3pm Mon-Fri) (as well as *locutorios* and internet options), can be found along San Martín.

CIS Tours (☎0297-487-2864; www.cistours.com.ar; San Martín 916; ⏲10am-8pm Mon-Fri) Handles local tours and flight reservations.

Dirección Municipal de Turismo (☎0297-487-0220; http://deseado.gob.ar/turismo/lugares-turisticos; San Martín 1137; ⏲8am-8pm) Helpful with maps; there's another English-speaking desk at the **bus terminal**, but its hours are limited. See the Facebook page for events.

Hospital Distrital (☎0297-487-0200; España 991)

Post Office (San Martín 1075; ⏲8am-4:30pm Mon-Fri)

Getting There & Away

The **bus terminal** (Sargento Cabral 1302) is on the northeast side of town, nine long blocks and slightly uphill from San Martín and Av Oneto. **Taxis** (☎0297-487-2288, 0297-487-0645) are metered.

There are five daily departures to Comodoro Rivadavia (AR$400, four hours) with **La Unión** (☎0297-487-0188) and **Sportman** (☎0297-487-0013). Sportman also goes to Río Gallegos (AR$1223, 13 hours) twice daily. Schedules change frequently;check at the bus terminal.

Some 125km southeast of the RN 3 junction, RN 281 weaves through valleys of rippling pink rock, past guanacos in tufted grassland, to end at Puerto Deseado. If you're thinking of getting off at godforsaken Fitz Roy to make progress toward Comodoro or Río Gallegos, think again: buses arrive at a demonic hour and the only place to crash is the campground behind Multirubro La Illusion.

Reserva Natural Ría Deseado & Parque Interjurisdiccional Marino Isla Pingüino

Flanked by sandy cliffs, these aquamarine waters create sculpted seascapes you won't forget. Considered one of South America's most important marine preserves, Ría Deseado is the unique result of a river abandoning its bed, allowing the Atlantic to invade 40km inland and create a perfect shelter for marine life. The designation of Parque Interjurisdiccional Marino Isla Pingüino will likely expand offerings.

Marine life is abundant. Several islands and other sites provide nesting habitats for seabirds, including Magellanic penguins, petrels, oystercatchers, herons, terns and five species of cormorant. Isla Chaffers is the main spot for the penguins, while Banco Cormorán offers protection to rock cormorants and the striking gray cormorant. Isla Pingüino has nesting rockhoppers (arriving mid-October) and elephant seals. Commerson's dolphins, sea lions, guanacos and ñandús (ostrich-like rheas) can also be seen while touring the estuary.

The best time to visit is December to April.

Activities

Darwin Expediciones (p425) runs circuits that include Commerson's dolphins, Isla Chaffers, Banco Cormorán and a walk to a penguin colony. Rockhopper penguins are the main attraction of all-day Isla Pingüinos excursions, but the tour also has other wildlife watching, sailing and hiking (four-person minimum). Los Vikingos (p425) makes similar excursions with bilingual guides and organizes overland trips.

Getting There & Away

Reserva Natural Ría Deseado is adjacent to Puerto Deseado. Take a tour from there to visit the sites; many require boat access.

Monumento Natural Bosques Petrificados

During Jurassic times, 150 million years ago, this area enjoyed a humid, temperate climate with flourishing forests, but intense volcanic activity buried them in ash. Erosion later exposed the mineralized Proaraucaria trees (ancestors of the modern araucaria, unique to the southern hemisphere), up to 3m in diameter and 35m in length. Today the 150-sq-km **Monumento Natural Bosques Petrificados** (Petrified Forests Natural Monument; AR$185; ⏲9am-9pm) has a small visitor center, English-language brochure and short interpretative trail, leading from park headquarters to the largest concentration of petrified trees.

Until its legal protection in 1954, the area was plundered for specimens; please don't perpetuate this unsavory tradition.

The park is 157km southwest of Caleta Olivia, accessed from the good gravel RP 49, leading 50km west from a turnoff at Km2074 on RN 3. There's no public transportation. Buses from Caleta Olivia leave visitors at the junction, but you may have to wait several hours for a lift into the park. Los Vikingos runs tours from Puerto Deseado.

There's basic camping and provisions at La Paloma, 20km before park headquarters. Camping in the park is prohibited.

Puerto San Julián

☎02962 / POP 7900

The perfect desolate-yet-charismatic locale for an art film, this small town bakes in bright light and dust, in contrast to the startling blue of the bay. Considered the cradle of Patagonian history, the port of San Julián was first landed in 1520 by Ferdinand Magellan, whose encounter with local Tehuelches provided the region's mythical moniker. Francisco de Viedma, Francis Drake and Darwin followed. While its human history is proudly put forth, the landscape speaks of geologic revolutions, with its exposed, striated layers, rolling hills and golden cliffs.

Puerto San Julián's first non-native settlers came from the Falkland Islands (Islas Malvinas) with the late-19th-century wool boom. Scots followed with the San Julián Sheep Farming Company, the region's economic engine for nearly a century. Today the city is developing like never before, with mining and seafood-processing industries plus a local university. For travelers, it's a relaxing stop and a great place to see Commerson's dolphins.

Sights & Activities

Puerto San Julián's most popular attractions are the Museo Nao Victoria and the penguin colony. You can also trek the coastline and check out the abundant birdlife. For more information, consult the tourist information booth in the bus terminal, or the branch on the highway.

Museo Nao Victoria MUSEUM
(AR$50; ⏲8am-9:30pm) Relive Magellan's landing at this museum and theme park with life-size figures cloaked in armor and shown celebrating Mass and battling mutiny. Located at the port on a reproduction of the original ship.

Circuito Costero DRIVING
Take a *remise* or your own poor, abused rental car on the incredibly scenic 30km drive following Bahía San Julián on a dirt road. A series of golden bluffs divides beautiful beaches with drastic tides. The area includes a sea-lion colony and the penitent attraction of Monte Cristo (with its stations of the cross).

Tours

Banco Cormorán WILDLIFE
(per person AR$150; ⏲Oct-Apr) The last census found 130,000 penguins inhabiting this stretch of Bahía San Julián, which you can visit by boat. When conditions permit, you'll be able to step off the boat and walk around an island where penguins swim, doze and guard their eggs. From December to March there's a good chance you'll see Commerson's dolphins, the world's smallest dolphins.

The tour also stops at Banco Justicia's cormorant rookeries.

Expediciones Pinocho TOURS
(☎02962-454600; www.pinochoexcursiones.com.ar; Costanera s/n; ⏲9am-9pm Jan & Feb) Expediciones Pinocho's two-hour excursions on Bahía San Julián are run by a marine-biologist-led team. The office is in a small cabin on the waterfront.

Sleeping & Eating

Hostería Miramar GUESTHOUSE $
(☎02962-454626; hosteriamiramar@uvc.com.ar; San Martín 210; d incl breakfast US$50-71; @📶) Natural light fills this cheerful waterfront option run by a local family. The 11 rooms, including those in a family-sized apartment, are super clean, with TV, decent beds and carpeted floors. Showers spray in powerful torrents.

Hotel Bahía HOTEL $$
(☎02962-453145; hotelbahiasanjulian@gmail.com; San Martín 1075; s/d/tr incl breakfast US$68/86/94; @📶) This glass-front hotel feels decadent in a place like San Julián. Rooms are modern and beds firm, while TV and laundry service are perks. The cafe-bar is open to the public.

★**Naos** SEAFOOD $$
(☎02962-452714; Costanera s/n; mains AR$100-220; ⏲8-11pm) The best restaurant in town

sits on the waterfront but doesn't have ocean views. Still, you will be entertained enough with the excellent wine recommendations, fresh fish and salads. Local seafood and game offerings, like guanaco empanadas and breaded jumbo shrimp, are outstanding, and the service is good. Go early as the tables fill up.

Shopping

Centro Artesenal Municipal ARTS & CRAFTS
(02962-414882; Costanera s/n; 9am-7pm Mon-Fri) A cool cooperative selling handmade ceramics, woven goods and an excellent but powerful homemade cherry liqueur.

Information

Banco Santa Cruz (02962-452460; cnr San Martín & Moreno; 10am-3pm) Has a Link ATM.

Dirección de Turismo (02962-454396; www.sanjulian.gov.ar; San Martín 1552; 8am-10pm Mon-Fri, 11am-8pm Sat & Sun) The main office is located in the bus terminal and has friendly service.

Post Office (cnr San Martín & Belgrano; 9am-4:30pm Mon-Fri)

Getting There & Away

Most RN 3 buses visit Puerto San Julián's **bus terminal** (San Martín 1552) at insane hours. Before settling for a bus that will drop you off at the port at 4am, try **Don Otto** (02962-452072), which delivers southbound travelers to San Julián at civilized evening hours. **Via Tac** (02962-454049) goes to Puerto Madryn (AR$990, 12 hours). **Andesmar** (02962-454403) goes to Comodoro Rivadavia (AR$337, six hours). **Taqsa/Marga** (02962-454667) goes to Bariloche (AR$1250, 14 hours) and Río Gallegos (AR$317, 4½ hours) at 4am, where travelers can make connections south.

There are slightly more expensive door-to-door options, all operating Monday to Saturday in the early morning hours.

Bus schedules may change, so always confirm departures ahead of time.

Parque Nacional Monte León

Inaugurated in 2004, this fine coastal national park protects over 600 sq km of striking headlands and archetypal Patagonian steppe, and 40km of dramatic coastline with bays, beaches and tidal flats. Once a hunting ground for nomads, and later frequented by the Tehuelche, this former *estancia* is home to abundant Magellanic penguins, sea lions, guanacos and pumas. Bring binoculars: the wildlife watching is prime.

Nature trails split off from the main road, leading to the coast. The **penguin trail** crosses the steppe, leading to an overlook of the rookery. It's forbidden to leave the trail, but seeing these 75,000 couples shouldn't be difficult. The roundtrip takes 1½ hours. Cars can reach the prominent cliff **Cabeza de León** (Lion's Head), where a 20-minute trail leads to the sea-lion colony.

For boat excursions or fly fishing for steelhead, consult with the **park office** (0296-249-8184; www.parquesnacionales.gob.ar/areas-protegidas/region-patagonia-austral/pn-monte-leon; 9am-8pm).

Sights & Activities

Hiking along the coastline, with its unusual geographic features, is best when low tide exposes stretches of sandy and rocky beach. In October 2006 the park lost its signature landscape attraction, **La Olla** (a huge cavelike structure eroded by the ocean), when it collapsed from repeated tidal action.

Accessible at low tide, **Isla Monte León** is a high offshore sea stack that was heavily mined for guano between 1933 and 1960. Now it has been recolonized by cormorants, Dominican gulls, skuas and other seabirds. Use caution and know the tide tables before setting out: the tidal range is great, exposed rocks are slippery and the water returns quickly.

Sleeping

Doraike ESTANCIA **$$**
(Hostería Monte León; in Buenos Aires 011-6155-1360; d US$97, without bathroom from US$74; Nov-Apr) A refurbished century-old *casco* (ranch house) of an 1895 *estancia*. The four-bedroom house retains the spartan yet elegant style of the Patagonian farmhouse, with rod-iron beds, fireplaces with handpainted tiles and tasteful original furnishings. There's restaurant service, and a wonderful collection of fossils, bones and photography books.

Getting There & Away

There's no public transportation to the park, though buses plying RN 3 could drop you off within walking distance.

The park entrance is 30km south of Comandante Luis Piedrabuena or 205km north of Río Gallegos, directly off RN 3. Watch for it carefully as signage is poor. Note that beach access is impossible after heavy rains, when the clay roads become impassable.

Río Gallegos

02966 / POP 95,800

This coal shipping, oil-refining and wool-raising hub is a busy port with a few merits for travelers. Since the reign of the Kirchners, the capital city of their home province has been spruced up and spit polished. It is more of a stopover than a tourist destination, however. Outside of town, visitors can find some of the continent's best fly fishing, traditional *estancias* and amazingly low tides (retreating 14m). Traveler services are good here, but most zip through en route to El Calafate, Puerto Natales or Ushuaia.

Gallegos' economy revolves around the nearby oilfields, with coal deposits shipped to ocean-going vessels at Punta Loyola. Home to a large military base, the city played an active role during the Falklands War. The main street, formerly Roca, was renamed Kirchner in honor of the former president.

Sights

Museo Provincial Padre Jesús Molina MUSEUM
(02966-426427; cnr Av San Martín & Ramón y Cajal; 9am-7pm Mon-Fri, 11am-7pm Sat & Sun) FREE Satiate your appetite for dinosaur dioramas and modern art at this museum offering exhibits on anthropology, paleontology, geology and fine arts. The Tehuelche ethnology exhibit includes fascinating photographs and local history.

Museo Malvinas Argentinas MUSEUM
(02966-437618; cnr Pasteur & Av San Martín; 11am-6pm Mon-Fri, 10am-5pm Sat & Sun) FREE Perhaps a must-see for Brits, this museum gets inside the Argentine claim to the Islas Malvinas. New exhibits include signs made by ex-combatants and a video on the subject in English.

Plaza San Martín PLAZA
A pretty plaza, with quiet benches in the shade of poplars and purple-blossom jacarandas.

Museo de los Pioneros MUSEUM
(02966-437763; cnr Elcano & Alberdi; 10am-5pm) FREE In a prefabricated 1890s metal-clad house shipped from England, this museum has good displays on early immigrant life.

Funda Cruz CULTURAL CENTER
(02966-424812; G Lista 60; 4-8pm Fri-Sun) An attractive, imported, prefabricated wooden house. Once a customs office, it now hosts cultural activities as well as a *salón de té* (teahouse).

Reserva Provincial Cabo Vírgenes WILDLIFE RESERVE
(02966-457829) Magellanic penguins nest September through March at Argentina's second-largest penguin rookery in this provincial reserve. There's also a lighthouse and snack bar open seasonally. It's 140km from Río Gallegos on slow gravel roads; the drive can take three hours each way.

Travel agencies in Río Gallegos offer day trips to both the *estancia* and the reserve starting in mid-November.

Tours

The large penguin rookery at Cabo Vírgenes, 140km southeast of Río Gallegos, can be visited from October to March. Excursions can be booked through **Al Sur Turismo** (02966-436743; www.alsurturismo.com.ar; Errázuriz 194); an eight-hour trip costs AR$3250 per person, with a minimum of three travelers. Prices go up for smaller groups.

Sleeping & Eating

Since hotels cater mainly to business travelers, good-value budget accommodations are scarce.

Hostel Elcira HOSTEL $
(02966-429856; Zuccarino 431; dm/d US$15/32;) An impeccable yet kitschy family home with friendly hosts. It's far from the town center but just a 10-minute walk from the bus terminal.

Hotel Aire de Patagonia BOUTIQUE HOTEL $$
(02966-444950; www.hotelairepatagonia.com.ar; Vélez Sársfield 58; d incl breakfast US$95;) Modern but showing a little wear and tear,

Río Gallegos

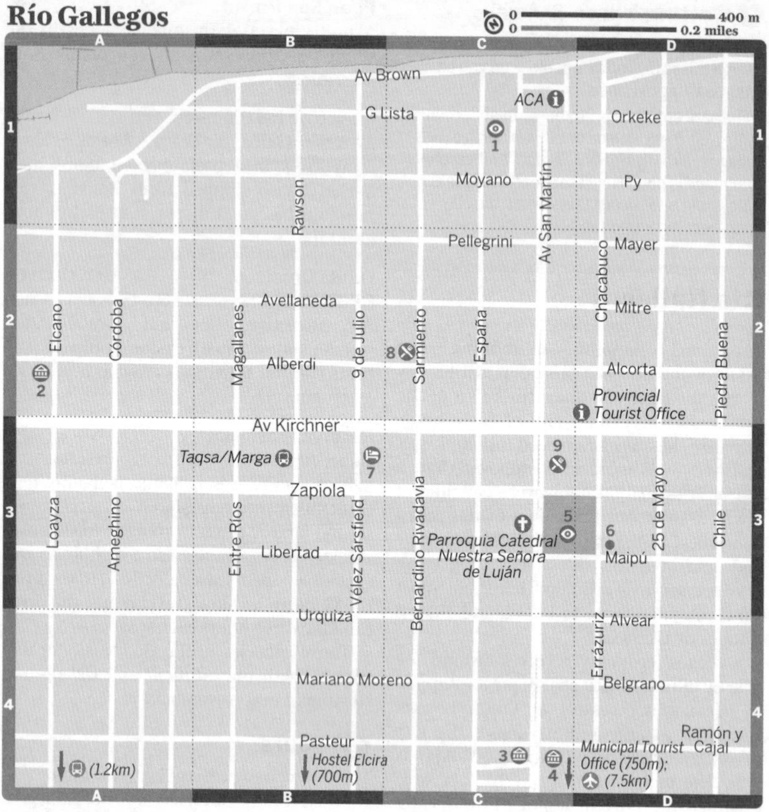

PATAGONIA RÍO GALLEGOS

Río Gallegos

Sights
1 Funda Cruz C1
2 Museo de los Pioneros A2
3 Museo Malvinas Argentinas C4
4 Museo Provincial Padre Jesús Molina C4
5 Plaza San Martín C3

Activities, Courses & Tours
6 Al Sur Turismo D3

Sleeping
7 Hotel Aire de Patagonia B3

Eating
8 La Lechuza C2
9 Pizza Express C3

this welcoming boutique hotel has rooms with soft Egyptian-cotton sheets, radiant floors and flat-screen TVs. The cute *confit-ería* is a good spot for a quiet espresso or board game.

Pizza Express PIZZA $
(☎02966-434400; Av San Martín 650; pizzas AR$75-210; ⏲11am-late) Cheap and casual, with service that's friendlier than you'll find elsewhere in Río Gallegos, this is where students and families dine on burgers, gnocchi and salads, and older gents share big bottles of cold Quilmes beer.

★ **La Lechuza** ARGENTINE $$
(☎02966-425421; Sarmiento 134; mains AR$165-250; ⏲11:30am-4pm & 8pm-midnight) This chic pizzeria and restaurant that first found success in El Calafate is hands down the most ambient eatery in Río Gallegos. The room is low lit, with walls sheathed in old newspapers and wine crates. There's an encyclopedic list of pizzas, including spinach, caprese and Patagonian lamb and mushroom. It also offers wines and other liquor.

Information

Banks on Av Kirchner have ATMs.

ACA (Automóvil Club Argentino; 02966-420477; Orkeke 10; 10am-2pm Mon-Fri) Gas station, maps and traveler services.

Chilean Consulate (02966-422364; Moreno 148; 9am-1pm Mon-Fri) For visas to Chile.

Hospital Regional (02966-420289; José Ingenieros 98)

Immigration Office (02966-420205; Urquiza 144; 9am-3pm Mon-Fri)

Municipal Tourist Office (02966-436920; www.turismo.riogallegos.gov.ar; Av Beccar 126; 7am-9pm Mon-Fri, 8am-2pm & 4-8pm Sat & Sun) Helpful tourist office outside the downtown area. A desk at the bus terminal keeps sporadic hours.

Post Office (cnr Avs Kirchner & San Martín; 9am-4:30pm Mon-Fri)

Provincial Tourist Office (02966-437412; www.santacruzpatagonia.gob.ar; Av Kirchner 863; 9am-3pm Mon-Fri) Most helpful, with maps, bilingual staff and detailed info.

Getting There & Away

AIR

Río Gallegos' **Piloto Civil Norberto Fernández International Airport** (02966-442340; RN 3, Km8) is 7km northwest of town. New low-cost airlines plan to offer routes to Buenos Aires, El Calafate and Comodoro Rivadavia. **Aviación Civil Argentina** (ANAC; www.anac.gob.ar) has a map with new routes and airlines.

Aerolíneas Argentinas (0810-2228-6527; Av San Martín 545; 9:30am-5pm Mon-Fri, to noon Sat) flies daily to Buenos Aires (AR$2900 oneway) and frequently to Ushuaia (AR$7027). **LADE** (02966-422316; Fagnano 53; 8am-3pm Mon-Fri) flies several times a week to Buenos Aires, Río Grande, El Calafate, Comodoro Rivadavia and Ushuaia.

LATAM (02966-457189; www.latam.com) has a ticket counter at the airport.

BUS

Río Gallegos' **bus terminal** (cnr RN 3 & Av Eva Perón) is located about 3km southwest of the city center. Companies include **El Pingüino** (02966-442169), **Don Otto** (02966-442160), **Bus Sur** (02966-442687), **Andesmar** (02966-442195), **Sportman** (02966-442595) and **TAC** (02966-442042). Companies going to Chile include **Ghisoni** (02966-457047), **Pacheco** (02966-442765) and **Tecni-Austral** (02966-442427). **Taqsa/Marga** (02966-442003; www.taqsa.com.ar; Estrada 71) beelines straight from the airport to Puerto Natales and El Calafate.

Buses from Río Gallegos

DESTINATION	COST (AR$)	TIME (HR)
Buenos Aires	2750	36-40
Comodoro Rivadavia	725	9-11
El Calafate	400	4
El Chaltén	440	9
Esquel	1930	18
Puerto Madryn	1157	15-20
Puerto San Julián	337	4½
Punta Arenas (Chile)	540	5-6
Río Grande	850	8-10
Trelew	1270	14-17
Ushuaia	920	12

Getting Around

It's easy to share metered taxis (AR$100) between the city center, the bus terminal and the airport. From Av Kirchner, buses marked 'B' or 'Terminal' link the city center and the bus terminal (AR$14).

Car rental is expensive due to the poor conditions of the roads to most places of interest. Despite exchange rates, rental deals are often better in Punta Arenas, Chile. For local rentals, try **Riestra Rent A Car** (02966-421321; www.riestrarentacar.com; Av San Martín 1508; 9am-1pm & 3-7pm Mon-Fri, 10am-1pm Sat).

INLAND PATAGONIA

Save for the travel hubs of El Calafate and El Chaltén, RN 40 and its offshoots take you deep into the Patagonian backwater. The ultimate road trip, RN 40 parallels the backbone of the Andes, where ñandús doodle through sagebrush and trucks kick up whirling dust.

RN 40 parallels the Andes from north of Bariloche to the border with Chile near Puerto Natales, then cuts east to the Atlantic Coast. Highlights include the Perito Moreno and Los Glaciares national parks and the rock art of Cueva de las Manos.

Esquel

02945 / POP 32,400 / ELEV 570M

If you tire of the gnome-in-the-chocolate-shop ambience of Bariloche and other cutesy Lake District destinations, regular old

Esquel is a breath of fresh air. Set in western Chubut's dramatic, hikeable foothills, Esquel is a hub for Parque Nacional Los Alerces and an easygoing, friendly base camp for abundant adventure activities – the perfect place to chill after hard travel on RN 40.

Founded at the turn of the 20th century, Esquel is the region's main livestock and commercial center. It's also the historical southern end of the line for *La Trochita,* the narrow-gauge steam train. The town takes its name from the Mapudungun, and means either 'bog' or 'place of the thistles.'

RN 259 zigzags through town to the junction with RN 40, which heads north to El Bolsón and south to Comodoro Rivadavia. South of town, RN 259 passes a junction for Parque Nacional Los Alerces en route to Trevelin.

Sights & Activities

Esquel's best attractions are of the outdoor variety, notably Parque Nacional Los Alerces and La Hoya. Esquel's nearby lakes and rivers offer excellent **fly-fishing**, with the season running from November to April. You can purchase a license at the ACA (p434) inside the YPF gas station. **Mountain biking** is a good way to explore the surrounding hills and trails.

Museo del Tren MUSEUM
(☎02945-451403; cnr Roggero & Urquiza; ⊙9:30am-noon Mon, Wed & Fri) FREE Just outside town, this train museum is in the Roca train station where *La Trochita,* Argentina's famous narrow-gauge steam train, stops. In summer several tour agencies sell tickets for roundtrip rides on the antique train.

Cerro La Hoya SNOW SPORTS
(☎02945-453018; www.cerrolahoya.com; lift ticket adult/child AR$600/450; ⊙skiing Jun-Oct) Despite wide open bowls and some of Argentina's best powder skiing, this 1350m resort is just starting to become well known. While cheaper and less crowded than Bariloche, it is smaller and comparatively tame, ideal for families. Equipment can be rented on-site or at sport shops in Esquel. There are minibus transfers and a taxi service. It's 13km north of Esquel.

Coyote Bikes CYCLING
(☎02945-455505; www.coyotebikes.com.ar; Rivadavia 887; all-day rental AR$180; ⊙9am-1pm & 4-8:30pm Mon-Fri, 9am-1pm Sat) Coyote Bikes has mountain-bike rentals and trail details in summer.

Tours

Circuito Lacustre BOATING
Numerous travel agencies sell tickets for the Circuito Lacustre boat excursion in Parque Nacional Los Alerces; buying a ticket in Esquel assures a place on the often-crowded trip. Full-day excursions, including the lake cruise, visit the alerce-viewing area (AR$1800) or Glacier Torre Sillas (AR$2400), and include transfers to and from the park.

EPA ADVENTURE
(Expediciones Patagonia Aventura; ☎02945-457015; www.epaexpediciones.com; Av Fontana 484; ⊙9am-1pm & 5-8:30pm) EPA offers rafting, canyoning, horseback riding and trekking. Those whitewater rafting (half-day AR$1500 with transportation) on Río Corcovado (90km away) can overnight at the recommended riverside hostel. Canopy tours, horseback riding and trekking use the mountain center, an attractive wooden lodge in Parque Nacional Los Alerces. Guests have access to kayaks, and camping is also available.

Festivals & Events

Semana de Esquel CULTURAL
(⊙Feb) A week-long event that celebrates the city's 1906 founding.

Fiesta Nacional de Esquí SPORTS
(National Skiing Festival; ⊙mid-Sep) Takes place at La Hoya, with snow-sports events at Cerro La Hoya, gourmet encounters and even a fashion show.

Sleeping

Esquel has many accommodations; check with the tourist office (p434) for complete listings, including cabins and apartments geared for ski vacations.

Planeta Hostel HOSTEL $
(☎02945-456846; www.planetahostel.com; Av Alvear 1021; dm/d incl breakfast US$24/82; 📶) This old but boldly painted downtown house features friendly service but cramped rooms. Down comforters, a spotless communal kitchen and a TV lounge are a cut above the usual.

Hostería Canela B&B B&B $$
(☎02945-453890; www.canelaesquel.com; cnr Los Notros & Los Radales, Villa Ayelén; d/tr incl

breakfast US$135/170, q apt US$244;) Veronica and Jorge's refined B&B, tucked away in a pine forest 2km outside Esquel's town center, feels elegant and comfortable, an ideal match for mature guests. The English-speaking owners offer in-room tea service and the comfortable beds are topped with pristine white linens.

Hostería La Chacra B&B $$
(02945-452802; www.lachacrapatagonia.com; RN 259, Km5; d/tr incl breakfast US$85/100;) If you want a shot of local culture, nothing is better than this country lodging in a 1970s home with ample bright rooms, generous gringo breakfasts and thick down bedding. Owner Rini is a consummate host and expert on local Welsh history. Get here via shuttle, taxi or Trevelin bus – they pass hourly.

Sur Sur HOTEL $$
(02945-453858; www.hotelsursur.com; Av Fontana 282; d/tr incl breakfast US$88/118;) A popular option, this family enterprise delivers warmth and comfort. Small tiled rooms feature TV, fan and hairdryers, and the hallways are decked out with regional photos taken by former guests. Breakfast is served buffet style.

Hostería Angelina INN $$
(02945-452763; www.hosteriaangelina.com.ar; Av Alvear 758; d/apt from US$76/107;) Hospitable and polished, with a courtyard fountain, Angelina follows international standards with professional service and a good breakfast buffet.

★**Las Bayas Hotel** BOUTIQUE HOTEL $$$
(02945-455800; www.lasbayashotel.com; Av Alvear 985; d/tr incl breakfast from US$186/204;) Simply lovely, this elegant boutique lodging sits head and shoulders above other hotels. Tasteful decor includes wood accents, warm woolen throws and modern touches. Spacious rooms feature LCD screens and DVD libraries, kitchenettes, and tubs with massage jets. There are also spa services available. The gourmet restaurant offers an interesting menu (mains AR$195 to AR$300) emphasizing local ingredients, game and trout.

Eating

Quillen VEGETARIAN $
(02945-400212; Av Fontana 769; mains AR$120-200; 9am-3pm Tue, 9am-3pm & 8pm-1am Thu-Sat;) Serving organic pizza, pastas, fresh lemonade and artisan beer, Quillen might be more at home in Palermo, Buenos Aires, than the Andean foothills, but here it is. The light vegan and vegetarian options are a godsend for those fresh from the RN 40.

Dimitri BAKERY $
(02945-15-584410; Rivadavia 805; mains AR$45-80; 9am-8pm Mon-Sat) Overboard adorable, this pastel cafe serves big salads, baked goods and sandwiches with three kinds of homemade bread on mismatched

LA TROCHITA: THE OLD PATAGONIAN EXPRESS

Clearly an anachronism in the jet age, Ferrocarril Roca's **La Trochita** (02945-451403; www.latrochita.org.ar; AR$750), Argentina's famous narrow-gauge steam train, averages less than 30km/h on its meandering journey between Esquel and Nahuel Pan – if it runs at full speed. The train Paul Theroux facetiously called the *Old Patagonian Express* is more tourist attraction than public transportation. It departs weekly in low season but almost daily in January and February.

Like many state projects, its completion seemed an interminable process, beginning in 1906 and finishing in 1945. It has suffered some of the oddest mishaps in railroad history. In the late 1950s and early 1960s, the train was derailed three times by high winds, and ice has caused other derailments. In 1979 a collision with a cow derailed the train at Km 243 south of El Maitén; the engine driver was the appropriately named Señor Bovino.

La Trochita's original 402km route between Esquel and Ingeniero Jacobacci was probably the world's longest remaining steam-train line, in full operation until 1993, with half a dozen stations and another nine *apeaderos* (whistle-stops). Belgian Baldwin and German Henschel engines refilled their 4000L water tanks at strategically placed *parajes* (pumps) every 40km to 45km. Most of the passenger cars, heated by wood stoves, date from 1922, as do the freight cars.

Nahuel Pan is the first station down the line, 20km east. The trip takes 45 minutes. It's popular with groups, so book ahead. For a small additional charge, you can organize with one of the Esquel travel agencies to return by minibus.

china. There's both beer and barista drinks in a cheerful, casual atmosphere.

Don Chiquino ITALIAN **$$**

(☎02945-450035; Av Ameghino 1641; mains AR$190; ⊙noon-3:30pm & 8pm-midnight) Of course, pasta is no novelty in Argentina, but the owner-magician performing tricks while you wait for your meal here is. The ambience is happy-cluttered and dishes such as *sorrentinos* with arugula prove satisfying.

La Esquina ARGENTINE **$$**

(☎02945-455362; 25 de Mayo 602; mains AR$140-270; ⊙7:30am-2am; 📶) This busy restobar with leather banquettes and checkered tile has all the airs of a Buenos Aires cafe, serving everything from beer on tap to *cafe con leche* with *medialunas*, salads and heartier fare. It's also a good spot to grab bacon-and-eggs breakfasts if you've been missing them.

★**Legua 50** INTERNATIONAL **$$$**

(☎02945-452875; cnr Belgrano & San Martín; mains AR$220-300; ⊙11am-3pm & 8pm-midnight Mon-Sat, 11am-3pm Sun) Considered Esquel's best restaurant, Legua 50 is certainly the city's most elegant address, with ivory leather booths, cascading lights and stained glass in the bar. Extraordinary rib-eye steak, green salads and moist trout in black butter are artfully presented. There's an excellent wine list and service is top notch. Cocktails are also notable.

Drinking & Nightlife

Heiskel MICROBREWERY

(☎02945-15-507177; Chacabuco 2311; ⊙7-11:30pm Tue-Sat) This tiny home bar can get pretty crowded. Simplicity is the name of the game – it serves a variety of decent beers made on-site (we liked the IPA), with meat and cheese boards. Large picture windows give views into the brewing room.

Charla Cafe CAFE

(☎02945-400714; 25 de Mayo 602; ⊙8am-9pm) This stylish cafe does real coffee with scones, homemade cakes and *alfajores* (cookie-type sandwiches usually stuffed with milk caramel) for those in the mood for a pick-me-up. There are outdoor tables, too.

Entertainment

Dirección Municipal de Cultura LIVE PERFORMANCE, CINEMA

(☎02945-451929; https://es-la.facebook.com/CulturaEsquel; Belgrano 330) Dirección Municipal de Cultura sponsors regular music, cinema, theater and dance.

Information

ACA (Automóvil Club Argentino; ☎02945-452382; cnr 25 de Mayo & Av Ameghino; ⊙daylight hours) Inside the YPF gas station; sells fishing licenses.

Banco de la Nación (☎02945-450005; Av Alvear 866; ⊙8am-1pm) Has an ATM and changes traveler's checks.

Banco del Chubut (Av Alvear 1147; ⊙8am-1pm) Has an ATM.

Chilean Consulate (☎02945-451189; Molinari 754; ⊙by appointment)

Hospital Regional (☎02945-450009; 25 de Mayo 150)

Post Office (☎02945-451865; Av Alvear 1192; ⊙8am-1pm & 4-7pm Mon-Fri) Next to the tourist office.

Tourist Office (☎02945-451927; www.esquel.tur.ar; cnr Av Alvear & Sarmiento; ⊙8am-8pm Mon-Fri, 9am-8pm Sat & Sun) Well organized, helpful and multilingual, with an impressive variety of detailed maps and brochures.

Getting There & Away

AIR

Esquel's **airport** (☎02945-451676) is 20km east of town off RN 40. Taxis (AR$400) shuttle visitors to town. New low-cost airlines, including **Norwegian Air** (www.norwegian.com/ar) plan to offer flights to Buenos Aires starting in mid-2018.

Aerolíneas Argentinas (☎02945-453614; Av Fontana 406; ⊙9am-5pm Mon-Fri) flies to Buenos Aires (oneway from AR$3490) several times a week.

BUS

Esquel's full-service **bus terminal** (cnr Av Alvear & Brun) is close to the town center.

Transportes Jacobsen (☎02945-454676) goes to Futaleufú, Chile (AR$105, 1½ hours), at 8am and 6pm Monday and Friday. Buses go hourly to Trevelin (AR$30, 30 minutes), stopping near the corner of Av Alvear and 25 de Mayo on the way out of town.

In summer **Transportes Esquel** (☎02945-453529; www.transportesesquel.com.ar) goes through Parque Nacional Los Alerces (1¼ hours) to Lago Futalaufquen at 8am daily (and also at 2pm and 6pm in January). The first bus goes all the way to Lago Puelo (six hours), stopping in Lago Verde at 10:30am and Cholila (AR$150) at noon. An open ticket allows passengers to make stops along the way between Esquel and Lago Puelo or vice versa. Note that the service is reduced in low season.

From December through April, tourism bus service **Chaltén Travel** (www.chaltentravel.com) picks up passengers from the rotunda at the junction of RN 40 on odd-numbered days to go to El Chaltén, El Calafate (AR$2140) and destinations in between via RN 40.

Buses from Esquel

DESTINATION	COST (AR$)	TIME (HR)
Bariloche	330	4¼
Buenos Aires	2300	25
Comodoro Rivadavia	830	8
El Bolsón	190	2½
Neuquén	815	10
Puerto Madryn	882	7-9
Río Gallegos	1930	18
Trelew	871	8-9

CAR

Compact rentals start at around AR$1600 per day, including 100km and insurance. Try **Los Alerces Rent A Car** (02945-456008; http://losalercesrentacar.com.ar; Sarmiento 765; 9:30am-1:30pm & 4:30-8:30pm Mon-Fri, 9:30am-1:30pm Sat), which has a good range of vehicles.

TRAIN

The narrow-gauge steam train La Trochita (p432) departs from the diminutive **Roca train station** (cnr Roggero & Urquiza; 8am-2pm Mon-Sat). There's a frequent tourist-oriented service to Nahuel Pan. Confirm schedules online or via the tourist office.

Trevelin

02945 / POP 7900 / ELEV 735M

Historic Trevelin (treh-*veh*-lean), from the Welsh for town *(tre)* and mill *(velin)*, is the only community in interior Chubut with a notable Welsh character. Easygoing and postcard pretty, this pastoral village makes a tranquil lodging alternative to the much busier Esquel (remember, everything is relative here), or an enjoyable day trip for tea. The surrounding countryside is ripe for exploration.

Just 22km south of Esquel via paved RN 259, Trevelin centers around the octagonal Plaza Coronel Fontana. Eight streets radiate from it, including the principal thoroughfare, Av San Martín (also the southward extension of RN 259). RN 259 forks west 50km to the Chilean border and to Futaleufú, 12km beyond.

Festivals & Events

Eisteddfod CULTURAL

(end Oct) The biggest Welsh celebration of the year, this multilingual festival sees bards compete in song and poetry.

Sleeping

Hostería Casa de Piedra LODGE $$

(02945-480357; www.casadepiedratrevelin.com; Brown 244; d incl breakfast US$100;) A haven for anglers and 4WD enthusiasts, this elegant stone lodge boasts a huge fireplace and rustic touches. There are spinning bikes in rooms and the buffet breakfast includes yogurt, homemade bread, cakes and fruit. Credit cards are accepted.

Cabañas Wilson CABIN $$

(02945-480803; www.wilsonpatagonia.com.ar; RN 259 at RP 71; 4-/6-person cabins US$147/190;) Savor the serenity surrounding these wood-and-brick cabins on the edge of town. They include a daily cleaning service, extra covers, log furniture and a barbecue deck. An abundant breakfast is optional.

Cabañas Oregon CABIN $$

(02945-480408; www.oregontrevelin.com.ar; cnr Av San Martín & JM Thomas; 4-person cabins US$94;) Scattered around an apple orchard on the south side of town, these appealing log cabins come with handmade wooden furniture, kitchen and TV. It's kid friendly and there's also a swing set. The on-site grill restaurant (buffet grill AR$250 to AR$350, closed Tuesday) is reputed to be the best spot in town to eat meat, and has good service.

Eating & Drinking

There are several decent restaurants in Trevelin. Also, just as visitors to Trelew flock to Gaiman, so visitors to Esquel head to Trevelin for Welsh tea. Teahouses are typically open from around 3pm to 8pm. Often the portions are big enough to share – ask first if it's OK to do so.

★**Nikanor** ARGENTINE $$

(02945-480400; Libertad 56; mains AR$190-280; 12:30-2:30pm & 8:30-11pm) A welcoming husband-and-wife team serve up excellent home-cooked meals at this historic 20th-century house. Think ravioli stuffed with local lamb, homemade pickled vegetables and pâté, and flambé crepes for dessert. Choose from the Argentine wine list. It's in a lovely renovated space with exposed brick and beams, with a window showing the original adobe and bamboo construction.

La Mutisia TEAHOUSE
(☎02945-480165; www.casadetelamutisia.com.ar; Av San Martín 170; ⏲3:30-8:30pm) Everything is reliably homemade at this teahouse (tea service per person AR$280). Those with smaller appetites can split the tea service and just order an extra cup (AR$50).

Nain Maggie TEAHOUSE
(☎02945-480232; www.nainmaggie.com; Perito Moreno 179; ⏲3:30-8pm) Trevelin's oldest teahouse occupies a modern building but has high traditional standards. Along with a bottomless pot, there's cream pie, *torta negra* and scones (tea service AR$310).

Shopping

Mercado de Artisanos MARKET
(⏲9am-3pm) This artisans market fills Plaza Coronel Fontana on Sundays in summer and on alternate Sundays the rest of the year.

Information

Banco del Chubut (cnr Av San Martín & Brown; ⏲8am-1pm Mon-Fri) Just south of Trevelin's plaza, with an ATM.

Gales al Sur (☎02945-480427; www.galesalsur.com.ar; Patagonia 186; ⏲9am-noon & 3:30-8:30pm Mon-Sat) Arranges regional tours.

Post Office (Av San Martín; ⏲8:30am-3pm Mon-Fri) Just south of Trevelin's plaza.

Tourist Office (☎02945-480120; www.trevelin.gov.ar; ⏲8am-8pm) Helpful, with a free town map, information on local hikes and English-speaking staff.

Getting There & Away

Having a car makes it possible to explore the lovely surrounding countryside. Near **Gales del Sur** (☎02945-480427; RN 259) there's a **bus stop** (RN 259) with hourly departures to Esquel (AR$19, 30 minutes) and buses to Futaleufú and Comodoro Rivadavia.

Buses cross the border to Chile's Futaleufú (AR$84, one hour) on Monday and Friday at 8:30am and 6pm, plus Wednesday in summer.

Parque Nacional Los Alerces

This collection of spry creeks, verdant mountains and mirror lakes resonates as unadulterated Andes. West of Esquel, this 2630-sq-km **park** (www.parquesnacionales.gob.ar/areas-protegidas/region-patagonia/pn-los-alerces; adult/child AR$250/60) protects some of the largest forests of ancient alerce *(Fitzroya cupressoides)* that still remain. In 2017 it was declared a Unesco World Heritage site thanks to these specimens, which have survived up to 4000 years. While its wild backcountry supports the seldom-seen huemul (Andean deer) and other wildlife, Los Alerces functions primarily as a trove of botanical riches that characterize the dense Valdivian forest.

Lured by well-known parks to the north and south, most hikers miss this gem, which makes it all the more enjoyable for those who do visit. Since the Andes are relatively low here, westerly storms deposit nearly 3m of rain annually. The park's eastern sector is much drier. Winter temperatures average 2°C, but it can be much colder. The summer average high reaches 24°C, but evenings are usually cool.

Activities

As well as sailing and hiking, travel agencies in Esquel have fishing, canoeing, mountain biking, snorkeling and horseback riding.

Sailing

Traditionally, **Circuito Lacustre** is Los Alerces' most popular excursion. Launches from Puerto Chucao (1½ hours) go to the nature trail **El Alerzal**, the most accessible stand of alerces. Visitors can also arrive at Puerto Chucao via a very scenic 1500m trail that crosses the bridge over Río Arrayanes.

The launch remains docked for over an hour at El Alerzal trailhead, sufficient for an unhurried hike around the loop trail that passes **Lago Cisne** and an attractive waterfall to end up at **El Abuelo** (Grandfather), a 57m-tall, 2600-year-old alerce.

Excursions leave from Puerto Chucao (AR$1200), departing at 11:30am and returning around 5pm. In summer, purchase tickets in Esquel to ensure a seat.

There are also kayak excursions on many of the park's lakes. Motorboats are no longer allowed in Lago Futalaufquen or Río Arrayanes.

Kayak Soul Aventuras KAYAKING
(☎02945-15-415669; www.kayaksoul.com.ar; tours from AR$840; ⏲Nov-Mar) Offers guided kayak excursions and longer expeditions on different lakes in Parque Nacional Los Alerces.

Hiking

Hikers must sign in at one of the ranger stations before heading out.

Parque Nacional Los Alerces

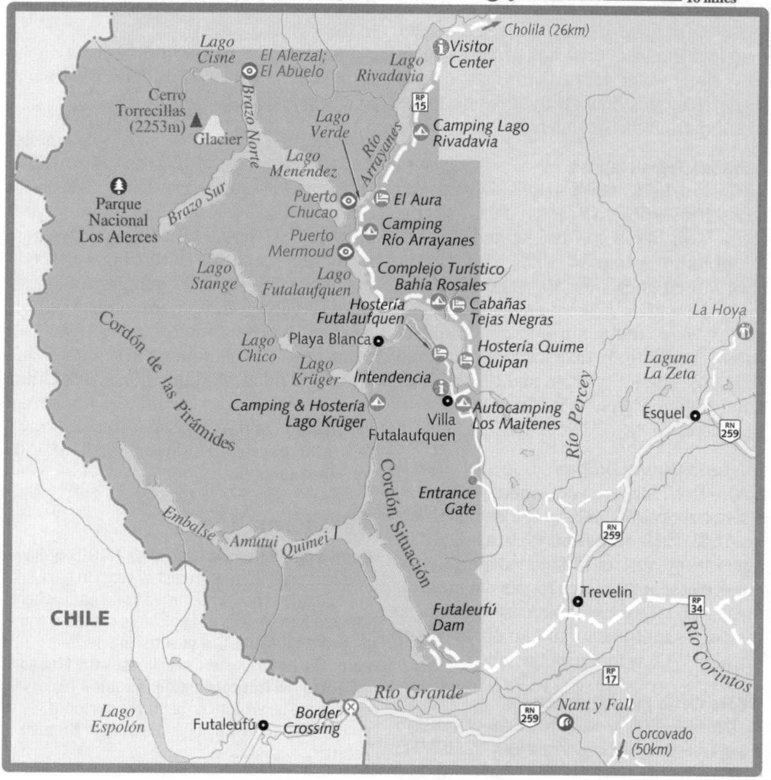

Day hikes can be undertaken from several interpretative trails located near **Lago Futalaufquen**. There is also a 25km trail from **Puerto Limonao** along the south shore of Futalaufquen to **Hostería Lago Krüger**, which can be done in a long day, or broken up by camping at **Playa Blanca**.

Sleeping & Eating

En route to the park watch for roadside signs advertising ideal picnic goods: homemade bread, delicious Chubut cheese, fresh fruit and Welsh sweets. In Villa Futalaufquen there are a couple of basic grocery stores and a summer-only restaurant, but it's best to bring your own provisions.

Los Alerces has several full-service campgrounds (per person US$13), all of which have showers, grocery stores and restaurants on-site or nearby. Free (no services) and semi-organized campgrounds exist near most of these fee sites.

There are inns and high-end lodgings open seasonally. With a group, *cabañas* can be an affordable option.

Complejo Turístico Bahía Rosales CAMPGROUND $
(☎02945-15-403413, 02945-471044; http://bahiarosales.com; campsites per adult/child US$12/6, 4-/6-person cabins US$100/129; ⏲Dec-Mar) This sprawling complex with sporting facilities sits at the north end of Lago Futalaufquen, 1.5km from the main road via a dirt path. Campsites include fire pits and picnic tables; they will soon be adding *domos* (luxury tents/yurts).

Camping Lago Rivadavia CAMPGROUND $
(☎02945-454381; campsites per adult/child US$6/4) These idyllic spots at Lago Rivadavia's south end are sheltered in the trees, with picnic tables and a boat launch. There's electricity hookup, too. It's 42km north of Villa Futalaufquen.

Autocamping Los Maitenes CAMPGROUND $
(☎02945-471006; campsites per adult/child US$13/8) On a slip of grass between the main road and the lake, this campground's spots have lovely water views. Campsites include shade, electricity hookup and fire pits, located 200m from the Intendencia.

Cabañas Tejas Negras CABIN $$
(☎02945-471046, 02945-471012; 4-/5-person cabins US$129/165) Cabañas Tejas Negras has a lawn like a golf course and a handful of prim A-frames; Nilda and Hector have hosted guests for 40 years. Think retreat: there are no *fútbol* matches on these greens, where tranquility is savored. Note to parents – they only take kids who are well behaved! There's a three-night minimum. Contact them via phone as the internet runs slow here.

Hostería Quime Quipan INN $$
(☎02945-471021; www.quimequipan.com.ar; 5-person apt/cabins US$159/171, d with forest/lake view US$147/159; ⏲Nov-Apr; 📶) In a breathtaking setting, this old-fashioned guesthouse offers pleasant but dated rooms – splurge for those with lake views. Nonguests can dine at the cozy, sunlit restaurant, an après-fishing pit stop. Wi-fi is in the lobby only.

★**Hostería Futalaufquen** INN $$$
(☎02945-471008; www.hosteriafutalaufquen.com; d incl breakfast with lake/forest view US$185/145, 3-person cabins US$240; 📶) Exclusive and elegant, this country inn is on the quieter western shore of Lago Futalaufquen, 4.5km north of Villa Futalaufquen at the end of the road. It offers well-appointed doubles and log cabins (without kitchens). Activities ranging from kayaking to rappelling can be arranged from here. Afterwards, collapse by the fire with a plate of dessert. There's wi-fi in the lobby.

Cabins come in varying sizes for up to eight guests. Make reservations at Sarmiento 635 in Esquel.

El Aura CABIN $$$
(Lago Verde Lodge; ☎in Buenos Aires 011-5512-2611; www.elaurapatagonia.com; 2-/4-person cabins US$294/447, 2-/4-person yurts US$94/124; ⏲Nov-Apr) Rustic yet ritzy, these raspy stone *cabañas* feature big, cozy beds, panoramic forest views and earthy motifs. *Domos* (yurts) offer an economical option. Anglers can rent motorized rafts to cast from Lago Futalaufquen's every nook and cranny. Guided trekking, horseback riding and fly-fishing are also offered. A gourmet restaurant and teahouse cater to travelers and guests. It's 35km north of Villa Futalaufquen.

ℹ Information

Centro de Visitantes (☎02945-471015; ⏲8am-9pm summer, 9am-4pm rest of year) In Villa Futalaufquen you'll find this visitor center, where rangers have details about hiking, camping and guided excursions. Get your fishing permits here. The headquarters also houses the **Museo y Centro del Interpretación**, a natural-history museum. The visitor center at the northern end of the park is only open December through February.

ℹ Getting There & Away

Most visitors come by car, but there are buses between Cholila and Esquel (AR$150) with stops in the park with Transportes Esquel (p434). Buses run Wednesday, Saturday and Sunday, and daily in the January–February high season. Northbound

DON'T MISS

THRU TREKKING PATAGONIA

The US has the Appalachian Trail, New Zealand has the Te Araroa Trail, and now Argentina has **Huella Andina** (http://trekbariloche.com/huella-andina-trek.php), the country's first long-distance trail. Huella, literally 'footprint,' is the local term for footpaths.

The project was the brainchild of Estefanía Chereguini and Walter Oszust, two young mountaineers in Esquel. It took them three years to mark 430km of trails through the Andes with 31 stages. Huella Andina crosses from Neuquén to Chubut, passing through five national parks, including Parque Nacional Los Alerces, and private lands. Scenery shifts from araucaria to alerce forest, from mountain heights to river valleys and pristine lakes. It's marked by a couple of blue and white parallel bands.

Now managed by the Ministerio Nacional de Turismo, the project is expected to eventually feature over 600km of linked trails. Visit the website for details on trail stages and a map.

buses stop in Villa Futalaufquen at 9:15am and southbound buses stop there at 7:45pm.

Gobernador Costa

☎02945 / POP 2400

When you find a town where a child snaps the tourist's picture (and not the reverse), it's something of an anomaly. This rusted little cattle town abuts the yawning stretch of RN 40 between Esquel and Río Mayo, at the intersection of RP 20 for Sarmiento and Comodoro Rivadavia. Traveler services are few but reasonable.

Some 20km west of town, RP 19 leads to Lago General Vintter and several smaller blue-ribbon lakes near the Chilean border; camping is possible along the shores.

Getting There & Away

From the **bus terminal** (Av Roca s/n), buses go to Esquel (two hours) and continue to Bariloche at 3:45am every day but Saturday. For Comodoro Rivadavia (eight hours), buses leave at 11:30pm every day except Sunday.

Río Mayo

☎02903 / POP HUMANS 2800, SHEEP 800,000

This little town in the middle of nowhere provides a few services for those who are road weary. The national capital of sheep shearing is a surprisingly humdrum place, save for the petroleum workers and waylaid gauchos practicing their wolf whistles on female *turistas*. This barren pit stop is 200km south of Gobernador Costa and 135km north of Perito Moreno.

Sleeping & Eating

Dining options are slim. The YPF is a good bet for a quick sandwich and coffee.

Estancia Don José ESTANCIA **$$$**
(GuenGuel; ☎0297-15-624-9155, 02903-420015; www.turismoguenguel.com.ar; per person US$200; ⏲Oct-Apr; 📶) A welcoming alternative to barren Río Mayo is this friendly *estancia* with horseback riding, fishing and walks to cave paintings. But the real attraction is that it might be the only place to see guanaco-shearing demonstrations: guanaco and ñandú are raised here. Activities and home-cooked meals with organic meat are included. It's 2.5km west of Río Mayo.

Getting There & Away

There are daily morning services from the **bus terminal** (☎02903-420174; cnr Fontana & Yrigoyen) to Comodoro Rivadavia (AR$430, 4½ hours) and Sarmiento (AR$230, two hours). Services go twice weekly to Coyhaique in Chile (six hours) on Wednesday and Saturday. Schedules change regularly, so check details at the bus terminal. Heading north, there's service to Esquel (AR$610, six hours). At the time of research there was 43km of unpaved road heading south to Perito Moreno. The only regularly scheduled services on this rugged stretch of RN 40 are summer-only backpacker shuttles.

Perito Moreno

☎02963 / POP 4620

Perito Moreno has a good range of services for a town on RN 40. However, don't confuse this dull town with the jaw-dropping national park of the same name or the glacier near El Calafate – the only tourist attraction here is cruising the strip on Saturday night. It's a brief stopover en route to the more inviting Andean oasis of Los Antiguos, though area mining means hotels are often booked. Attractions Cueva de las Manos and Parque Nacional Perito Moreno are not far away. A dedicated archaeological museum, Museo Gradin, exhibiting discoveries from the Río de las Pinturas, was in the works at the time of research and promises to be a useful companion stop.

The town's glory came in 1898, when explorer Perito Moreno challenged Chile's border definition of *'divortum aquarum continental'* (which claimed the headwaters of Pacific-flowing rivers as Chilean territory) by rerouting Río Fénix, which flows through town, to Atlantic-bound Río Deseado. The river and the area remained Argentine, and the town took his name.

Tours

Zoyen TOURS
(☎02963-432207; www.zoyenturismo.com.ar; San Martín 1055; ⏲9am-1pm & 5-9pm) This good local travel agency offers day trips to Cueva de las Manos (p442; AR$1100) and manages Hostería Cueva de las Manos.

GuanaCondor Tours TOURS
(☎02963-432303; jarinauta@yahoo.com.ar; Perito Moreno 1087; ⏲10am-noon & 4-8pm Mon-Wed & Sat, 5-8pm Sun) An experienced operator with summer trips to Cueva de las Manos, accessing the park via a challenging hike that adds

ON BUTCH CASSIDY'S TRAIL IN CHOLILA

Tiny Cholila is a scenic blip just off RN 40 that holds a curious piece of frontier history. Butch Cassidy, the Sundance Kid and Etta Place tried settling down and making an honest living near this quiet farming community outside the northeast entrance to Parque Nacional Los Alerces. The bandits' tale is recounted by Bruce Chatwin in the travel classic *In Patagonia*. Though the threesome's idyll only lasted a few years, their partially restored homestead still stands, just off RP 71 at Km21, 8km north of Cholila. Cholila's enthusiastic **Casa de Informes** (☎02945-498040, 02945-498208; www.turismocholila.gov.ar; RP 71 at RP 15; ⊙sporadic hours Dec-Mar) has a helpful regional map and will gladly point you in the right direction.

The mountain location is ideal for exploration. Cholila and the Río Pico area are also world-renowned fly-fishing destinations, and guided trips are available through **Trekking for Trout** (☎02945-553545; www.facebook.com/trekandtrout).

Transportes Esquel stops here at 5:10pm on its way between Lago Puelo and Esquel (AR$150, four hours), driving the slower route through Parque Nacional Los Alerces. Northbound buses stop at noon.

considerably to the experience. Also ask about trips to Monte Zeballos, a high mesa with excellent views, and the overnight trip to Paso Tehuelche.

Sleeping & Eating

In addition to a few eateries, there are a couple of well-stocked *panaderías* (bakeries) and supermarkets along San Martín.

Hotel Americano HOTEL $
(☎02963-432074; www.hotelamericanoweb.com.ar; San Martín 1327; incl breakfast s/d US$41/59, superior d US$82; P) The rooms at the thriving Americano vary widely – some lack windows, others can be quite cozy – so ask to see a few before deciding. There's also a decent grill and cafe that's busy in the evenings.

Camping Municipal CAMPGROUND $
(Laguna de los Cisnes; per tent US$4, plus per vehicle from US$4, 4-person cabañas US$36) The cheapest sleeping option for backpackers is this campground with rustic cabins on the south side of town, off Mariano Moreno. It's shaded by breezy poplars and has hot showers. Renovations already under way at the time of research might bring prices up.

★**Chacra Kaiken Lodge** B&B $$
(☎0297-15-408-6996, 02963-432079; www.chacrakaiken.com.ar; Yrigoyen 2012; s/d/tr incl breakfast US$97/130/162; ⊙Oct-Mar;) A solid newer option, this four-room B&B is run by Petty and Coco, lifelong area residents who used to run a well-known *estancia*. So in addition to a snug sleep, they offer a lovely setting and a fresh taste of the real Patagonia.

Salón Iturrioz CAFE $
(cnr Rivadavia & San Martín; sandwiches AR$40-150; ⊙8am-11pm;) With cappuccinos, snacks and wi-fi, this charming brick corner cafe is a godsend to RN 40. It's also a social hub, and the best place to get information on Museo Gradin across the street.

Information

Banco de Santa Cruz (cnr San Martín & Rivadavia; ⊙9am-3pm Mon-Fri) Has an ATM and changes traveler's checks.

Hospital Distrital (☎02963-432040; Colón 1237)

Post Office (cnr JD Perón & Belgrano; ⊙8am-4:30pm Mon-Fri)

Tourist Office (☎02963-432732; peritomoreno@santacruzpatagonia.gob.ar; San Martín s/n; ⊙7am-11:30pm Mon-Fri, 8am-3pm Sat & Sun) Helpful, with a surprising number of pamphlets and brochures, and information on homestay lodgings. There is also a desk at the bus terminal (on the access road to RN 43).

Getting There & Away

LADE (☎02963-432055; San Martín 1065; ⊙9am-5pm Mon-Fri) flies to El Calafate, Río Gallegos, Río Grande and Ushuaia.

The main drag, San Martín, leads north to RP 43 and south to RN 40; it's 128km south to Bajo Caracoles and 135km north to Río Mayo.

The **bus terminal** (access road to RN 43) sits behind the YPF rotunda at the northern entrance to town. Taxis provide the only transport between here and the town center; other than that it's a flat 15-minute walk. Buses leave a few times daily for Los Antiguos (AR$118, 40 minutes), though departure times aren't reliable as they're usually scheduled to connect with incoming buses from RN 40, which are often delayed. In the afternoon, starting at 3:50pm, multiple buses also head for Comodoro Rivadavia (AR$500, six hours) and Río Gallegos (AR$1240, 14 hours) via RN 3.

Several shuttle services also offering excursions serve travelers on RN 40. From November to April, **Chaltén Travel** (☎ 02902-492212; www.chaltentravel.com) goes north to Bariloche (11 hours), departing from Hotel Belgrano in Perito Moreno at 8pm on even-numbered days. Shuttles leave Hotel Belgrano at 8am to head south to El Chaltén (11 hours) on odd-numbered days.

The bus company **Taqsa/Marga** (☎ 02963-432675) now runs the entire stretch of RN 40 between El Calafate and Bariloche, several times a week starting at the end of October, stopping at El Chaltén, Bajo Caracoles, Perito Moreno (AR$1260) and Esquel along the way. The route between Perito Moreno and El Calafate costs AR$1300 (12 hours).

Los Antiguos

☎ 02963 / POP 3360

Situated on the windy shores of Lago Buenos Aires, the agricultural oasis of Los Antiguos is home to orchards of cherries, strawberries, apples, apricots and peaches. To the indigenous Tehuelches, it was known as I-Keu-khon (Place of the Elders). It makes an attractive crossing into Chile, with great outdoors access on both sides of the border, including to the new Parque Nacional Patagonia, with a trail to the mesa top that starts right outside town.

In 1991 the eruption of Volcán Hudson in Chile covered the town in ash, but the orchards have bounced back. In summer, Lago Buenos Aires, South America's second-biggest lake, is warm enough for a brisk swim. The stunning Río Jeinemeni is a favored spot for trout and salmon fishing. The stretch of road between Perito Moreno and Los Antiguos affords spectacular lake views.

Sights & Activities

Parque Nacional Patagonia NATURE RESERVE
(☎ 02966-1562-2852; www.parquesnacionales.gob.ar/areas-protegidas/region-patagonia-austral/parque-nacional-patagonia; RN 41) Out on the steppe, this 530-sq-km park was created in 2015 primarily to protect the *maca tobiano,* an endangered grebe brought to the brink of extinction principally by non-native mink. It's also a hiking and bird-watching destination. Park infrastructure is still developing. Visitors can stay at the El Sauco campground, which has wild camping on Río Blanco, located 190km from Los Antiguos via RN 40 and RN 41 (Paso Zeballos). There's also camping and trails from Portal La Ascensión.

It's part of a much larger project to create a binational park between Chile and Argentina, spread in points throughout the region and designed to protect many native species, environments and heritage areas, including the canyon area surrounding Cueva de las Manos.

★ **Portal La Ascensión** NATURE RESERVE
(☎ 02966-652577; www.florayfaunaargentina.org; ⌚ 9am-7pm Oct-Apr) An outstanding addition to Parque Nacional Patagonia, this historic *estancia* on Lago Buenos Aires has an information center, lakeside car camping and a 25km trail circuit that ascends the *meseta* following the course of a mountain stream. It's apt for backpacking too: there are two campgrounds and a dome shelter on the circuit with water, a cooking area and latrines.

Maca Tobiano CYCLING, KAYAKING
(☎ 0297-15-5014-4444; kayakmacatobiano@hotmail.com.ar; Costanera s/n) On the lakefront, this kayak- and bike-rental agency also offers adrenaline-soaked mountain-biking descents from Monte Zeballos. It has wet suits for lake activities. See their Facebook page for information.

Tours

Chelenco Tours TOURS
(☎ 02963-491198; www.chelencotours.tur.ar; Av 11 de Julio Este 584; ⌚ 10am-1pm & 4:30-9:30pm) In a log-cabin office, this savvy tour operator offers trekking to Cueva de Las Manos (US$80), hiking and wildlife-watching trips to the scenic road to Monte Zeballos (US$90), in addition to worthwhile longer excursions to Parque Nacional Perito Moreno and Lago Posadas. It also offers airport transfers from Comodoro Rivadavia with a visit to Bosque Petrificado Sarmiento.

Festivals & Events

Fiesta de la Cereza CULTURAL
(⌚ Jan) Fiesta de la Cereza has rodeos, live music and the crowning of the national Cherry Queen during the second weekend of January. Artisan goods are sold and *peñas folklóricas* (Argentine folk-music concerts) at private farms go on all night long – visit

the tourist information office to find out more.

Sleeping & Eating

Cabañas Rincon de los Poetas CABIN $
(☎02963-491051; Patagonia Argentina 226; d/tr/q US$60/71/82;) These snug and kitschy wooden cabins equipped with kitchenettes are nothing fancy, but they prove good value for groups and families. Located two blocks from the town center.

Hostería Antigua Patagonia HOTEL $$
(☎02963-491038; www.antiguapatagonia.com.ar; RP 43 Acceso Este; s/d incl breakfast US$107/128;) In a stunning setting, this lakefront complex is comfortably rustic, with sturdy four-poster beds, wooden trunks and a stone fireplace that begs you to curl up in front of it like a cat. Avoid the ground floor, with its flimsy patio door locks. Service is good, and there's a pool and sauna, plus bikes and kayaks for guests. It's 2km east of town, by the police checkpoint.

Hotel Mora HOTEL $$
(☎0297-15-420-7472; www.hotelmorapatagonia.com; Av Costanera 1064; s/d incl breakfast US$76/106;) With its corrugated-tin facade and lovely deck, Hotel Mora holds promise. The best rooms are doubles with lake views. Others run toward the basic end with fatigued mattresses and showerheads without stalls. Still, the deck overlooking a waterfront promenade is ideal for a sunset beer.

Viva El Viento CAFE $$
(☎02963-491109; www.vivaelviento.com; Av 11 de Julio 477; mains AR$90-270; 9am-9pm;) This stylish cafe and restaurant is the go-to spot for strong coffee and warm service. The menu offers fresh juices and salads, good gnocchi and steak. Avoid the trout – it's a little too fishy and very dry. The kitchen is willing to make adaptations for vegetarians.

Information

Banco de Santa Cruz (Av 11 de Julio 531; 9am-5pm Mon-Fri) Has a 24-hour LINK-access ATM.

Parques Nacionales (☎02966-622852; www.sib.gob.ar; Av Tehuelches s/n; 9am-4pm Mon-Fri) This administrative office of National Parks handles the Parque Nacional Patagonia, with information on camping and directions.

Tourist Information Office (☎02963-491261; turismolosantiguos@gmail.com; Av 11 de Julio 446; 8am-8pm) Helpful, with a map of town and farms selling fresh produce. Check the Facebook page Los Antiguos Santa Cruz Patagonia for news.

Post Office (☎02963-491355; Gregores 19; 8am-4:30pm Mon-Fri)

Getting There & Away

Most services in town are on or near east–west Av 11 de Julio, which heads west to the Chilean frontier at Chile Chico, the region's most convenient border crossing. Perito Moreno and RN 40 are 60km east.

Chelenco Tours (p441) offers airport transfers to Comodoro Rivadavia, site of the nearest major airport, combined with a visit to Bosque Petrificado Sarmiento (US$150).

From the **bus terminal** (Av Tehuelches s/n), there are services several times daily to nearby Perito Moreno (AR$118, 40 minutes). Those in a rush to move on will find more transport links in Perito Moreno to other parts of Patagonia.

From mid-November to March, **Chaltén Travel** (☎0297-623-4882; www.chaltentravel.com; Av Tehuelches s/n) goes to El Chaltén on even-numbered days at 9am, stopping first in Perito Moreno.

Chile-based **Martín Pescador** (☎in Chile +56-997865285; Chile Chico) provides service between Los Antiguos and Chile Chico once daily.

Sportman (☎02963-491175; Av Tehuelches s/n) has daily buses to Río Gallegos, El Calafate and Comodoro Rivadavia.

BORDER CROSSING

For Chile, there is a border crossing to Chile Chico. At the time of research, public transportation across the border was suspended. Inquire locally, as this situation could likely change. It's 1.5km from Los Antiguos to the Argentine border, then 1km further to the Chilean border, with Chile Chico 5km beyond.

A Chilean ferry run by **Somarco** (☎67-241-1093; www.barcazas.cl/barcazas/wp/region-de-aysen/lago-general-carrera; Muelle Chile Chico; passenger/automobile CH$2250/19,500) crosses Lago General Carrera daily from Chile Chico to Puerto Ingeniero Ibañez almost daily, a big shortcut to Coyhaique.

Getting Around

Sur de Oro (☎0297-15-6249150, 02963-491210) is a taxi service that's useful when it's pouring rain and you need a ride to your hotel.

Cueva de Las Manos

Unesco World Heritage site **Cueva de las Manos** (Cave of the Hands; www.cuevadelasmanos.org; AR$200; 9am-7pm) features incredible rock art, a must-see if you pass through. Dating from about 7370 BCE, these polychrome paintings cover recesses in the near-vertical walls with imprints of human hands, drawings of guanacos and, from a later period, abstract designs. Of around 800 images, more than 90% are of left hands; one has six fingers.

Fundación Flora y Fauna donated an additional 600 hectares to the expansion of Patagonia National Park surrounding it, and will eventually add three new trekking circuits, one with a *condorera* (condor nesting area), and possibly a campground.

Guides in Perito Moreno and Los Antiguos organize day trips. The trip from Perito Moreno is about 3½ hours (one way) over rocky roads. Once you arrive at the caves, free 45-minute guided walks are given every hour by knowledgeable staff.

Activities

Cañon de las Pinturas HIKING

Hikers can access a beautiful day-long hike to the Cueva de las Manos via Cañon de las Pinturas, with gorges and excellent scenery. There's access from the north (via Hostería Cueva de las Manos) and from the west (via Estancia Casa de Piedra; nonguests pay AR$60 for access). Get an early start and bring your own food.

Guides can be contracted, but the trail is clear enough to go without one.

From Estancia Casa de Piedra, it's 12km to the canyon, then another 6km to the cave – it's about 10 hours for the roundtrip.

Sleeping & Eating

There's a basic *confitería* with sporadic offerings at the reception house near the southern entrance, but it's best to bring your own food.

Hostería Cueva de las Manos ESTANCIA $

(☎02963-432207; www.cuevadelasmanos.net; dm/s/d/tr incl breakfast US$25/80/100/130, 4-6 person cabins from US$180; ⊙Nov-Apr) On the doorstep of Argentina's best deposit of rock art, Hostería Cueva de las Manos sits 60km south of Perito Moreno via RN 40, the last 4km on gravel roads. At this former *estancia* guests stay in cabins with hardwood details, in the *hostería* or dorm bunks. Open to the public, the restaurant serves a fixed menu (AR$300) of country classics.

Independent and guided hikers can approach Cueva de las Manos via a scenic but challenging trail (summer only) that descends the canyon and crosses Río de las Pinturas. From the *hostería*, drive 18km on a gravel road. The last 2.5km is a trail for hikers only.

Getting There & Away

Visitors arrive by private vehicle or tour group. The approach is via rough but scenic provincial roads off RN 40, abutting Río de las Pinturas. Drive with caution: bounding guanacos are abundant. There are three points of access: a 28km unpaved road from RN 40, direct but with loose gravel; a route via Bajo Caracoles, with 46km of gravel roads; and another from the north side and Hostería Cueva de las Manos (closed in low season), with 22km of gravel and 4km on foot via a footbridge.

Bajo Caracoles

Little has changed since Bruce Chatwin dubbed Bajo Caracoles 'a crossroads of insignificant importance with roads leading all directions apparently to nowhere' in *In Patagonia* in 1975. Blink and you'll miss this dusty gas stop, but if you're headed south, do fill the tank, as it's the only reliable gas pump between Perito Moreno (128km north) and Tres Lagos (409km south). From here RP 39 heads west to Lago Posadas and the Paso Roballos to Chile.

Sleeping & Eating

There are no attractions in Bajo Caracoles, but people sleep here because it's the only stop for miles. There are a couple of lodging options, but the only one that's consistently open is **Hotel Bajo Caracoles** (☎02963-490100; RN 40 s/n; d with/without bathroom US$59/47; 🛜).

There are provisions in a general store fronting Hotel Bajo Caracoles.

Getting There & Away

Some buses ply this route along RN 40, with more frequency in summer, but there is no reason to stop here besides fueling up your vehicle. Heading south, it's 128km to Gobernador Gregores.

Parque Nacional Perito Moreno

Wild and windblown, **Parque Nacional Perito Moreno** (⊙visitor registration 9am-9pm, park open Oct-Apr) is an adventurer's dream. Approaching from the steppe, the massive snowcapped peaks of the Sierra Colorada rise like sentinels. Guanacos graze the tufted grasses, condors circle above, and wind blurs the surface of aquamarine and cobalt lakes. If you come here, you will be among 1000 yearly visitors – that is, mostly alone. Solitude reigns and, save for services offered by local *estancias,* you are on your own.

Honoring the park system's founder, this remote but increasingly popular park encompasses 1150 sq km, 310km southwest of Perito Moreno town. Don't confuse this gem with Parque Nacional Los Glaciares (home to the Glaciar Perito Moreno) further south.

Sights & Activities

The sedimentary Sierra Colorada is a palette of rusty hues. Beyond the park boundary, glacier-topped summits such as 3706m **Cerro San Lorenzo** (the highest peak in the area) tower over the landscape. The highest peak within the park is Cerro Mié (2254m).

As precipitation increases toward the west, the Patagonian steppe grasslands along the park's eastern border become sub-Antarctic forests of southern beech, lenga and coihue. Because the base altitude exceeds 900m, weather can be severe. Summer is usually comfortable, but warm clothing and proper gear are imperative in any season.

Hiking

Behind the information center, a one-hour trail leads to **Pinturas Rupestres**, somewhat denigrated cave paintings with interpretative signs in English. Consult park rangers for backpacking options and guided walks to the pictographs at **Casa de Piedra** on Lago Burmeister, and to **Playa de los Amonites** on Lago Belgrano, where there are fossils.

Lago Burmeister is an eight-hour roundtrip walk. The peninsula of **Lago Belgrano** has two hikes: an all-day walk around the perimeter or a four-hour roundtrip to an interior lake. When conditions are very windy, the above options, and El Rincón, are the best: stay off the peaks!

From Estancia La Oriental, it's a 3½-hour hike to the summit of 1434m **Cerro León** for a dazzling panorama. Immediately east of the summit, the volcanic outcrop of **Cerro de los Cóndores** is a nesting site, with condors circling a 300m cliff. Pumas have also been spotted here and guanacos down below.

Sleeping & Eating

There are free campgrounds on the steppe at Lago Burmeister, 16km north of the information center (more scenic and well sheltered among dense lenga forest); and at El Rincón, 15km south. Fires are not allowed. Campgrounds have pit toilets, picnic tables and potable water. Pack trash out.

A nearby *estancia* has lodgings for limited numbers of guests.

The water is pure, but you must bring all food and supplies. If coming from the north, the last chance to stock up is in Perito Moreno. From the south it's Gobernador Gregores.

Refugio Río Lacteo CABIN $

(free) Accessed via a scenic 12km trail (four to five hours one way) along the north side of Río Lacteo with views of the San Lorenzo massif, this rustic hut sleeps six to eight people. There's a nearby hut for cooking – bring your own provisions. To stay, register first at the ranger station.

Estancia La Oriental ESTANCIA $

(☎011-15-407197, in Buenos Aires 011-4152-6901; laorientalpatagonia@yahoo.com.ar; 3-person tents US$30, 4-person dm US$70, s/d/tr/q US$140/175/230/260; ⊙Nov-Mar; 🅿) At the foot of Cerro León at the end of the road on Lago Belgrano's north shore, La Oriental is the ideal base camp for exploring Parque Nacional Perito Moreno's varied backcountry. The ranch mostly caters to groups, and does a good job with food and 4WD and horseback-riding trips. Two-night stays are required.

Information

Visitors must register at the park's information center on the eastern boundary upon arrival. It's stocked with informative maps and brochures. Information can also be obtained at the **National Parks Administration Office** (Intendencia del Parque Nacional Perito Moreno; ☎02962-491477; Paseo 9 de Julio 610; ⊙9am-4pm Mon-Fri) in Gobernador Gregores.

Getting There & Away

Access road RN 37 is not transitable in winter, and the park is closed then anyway. In shoulder seasons the road may be impassable – check with the National Parks Administration Office in Gobernador Gregores before heading out.

Public transportation only goes to the junction of RN 37 and RN 40, and hitchhiking is a poor option (trailheads are far from the information center). It's best to come with a 4WD as roads can be poor. If you're driving, carry spare gas and tires.

Gobernador Gregores

☎02962 / POP 4500

Sleepy Gobernador Gregores is one of the better stops on RN 40, with hotels and shops offering a cheerful demeanor.

Gregores is 60km east of RN 40 on RP 25. It's the nearest town to Parque Nacional Perito Moreno (still 200km west) and an ideal spot to get supplies and arrange transportation.

Around 70km west of town via RP 29, the waters of **Lago Cardiel** are well loved by anglers for blue-ribbon salmon and rainbow-trout fishing. From the junction to the lake it's another 116km to **Tres Lagos**, where a jovial couple runs a 24-hour YPF gas station, then a further 123km west to El Chaltén.

Sleeping

Cañadón León HOTEL $

(☎02962-491082; Roca 397; s/d/tr incl breakfast US$35/59/77;) Cañadón León has 25 tidy rooms, with firm beds, that are ample and spotless. There are hot meals, including excellent homemade pasta. Reserve ahead. It also rents cars and provides regional transfers.

Information

Gobernador Gregores has a very enthusiastic **tourist office** (☎02962-491024; www.santacruz.tur.ar/corredores/localidades/Gregores/index.html; San Martin 514; 8am-2pm Mon-Fri) with comprehensive information on lodgings. The **National Parks Administration Office** can be helpful if you have plans to go to Parque Nacional Perito Moreno.

Getting There & Away

Heading south on RN 40, there is still a short stretch of unpaved road between Gobernador Gregores and the useful gas stop Tres Lagos, though paving is ongoing.

A new bus terminal is promised for the future. **Taqsa/Marga** (☎ in Río Gallegos 02966-442003; Paradelo 956) goes to Río Gallegos daily (AR$670, six hours) and Esquel with varying frequency (AR$1130, 13½ hours).

El Chaltén

☎02962 / POP 1630

This colorful village overlooks the stunning northern sector of Parque Nacional Los Glaciares. Every summer thousands of trekkers explore the world-class trails that start right here. Founded in 1985, in a rush to beat Chile to the land claim, El Chaltén is still a frontier town, albeit an offbeat one, featuring constant construction, hippie values and packs of roaming dogs. Every year more mainstream tourists come to see what the fuss is about, but in winter (May–September) most hotels and services board up and transportation links are few.

El Chaltén is named for Cerro Fitz Roy's Tehuelche name, meaning 'peak of fire' or 'smoking mountain' – an apt description of the cloud-enshrouded summit. Perito Moreno and Carlos Moyano later named it after the *Beagle's* Captain FitzRoy, who navigated Darwin's expedition up the Río Santa Cruz in 1834, coming within 50km of the cordillera.

Visit www.elchalten.com for a good overview of the town.

Sights & Activities

The surrounding Parque Nacional Los Glaciares is the playground of El Chaltén; various adventure options are available in the northern part of the park (p451).

Capilla de los Escaladores CHAPEL

A simple chapel of Austrian design memorializes the many climbers who have lost their lives to the precarious peaks since 1953.

Spa Yaten HEALTH & FITNESS

(☎02962-493394; spayaten@gmail.com; Av San Martín 36; 1hr massage AR$1300; 10am-10pm) Spa Yaten has showers, robes and slippers, so sore hikers can come straight here off the trail. There are various therapies, massage, dry sauna and Jacuzzi tubs in a communal room. Reserve massages ahead.

Tours

Zona Austral TOURS

(☎02902-489755; http://zonaaustralturismo.com; Av MM de Güemes 173; tour US$60) Offers sea kayaking and the Glaciar Vespignani tour at Lago del Desierto.

El Relincho HORSEBACK RIDING

(☎02962-493007, in El Calafate 02902-491961; www.elrelinchopatagonia.com.ar; Av San Martín

ESTANCIAS IN PATAGONIA

Most assume *estancias* (ranches) are all about livestock, but these offbeat offerings prove otherwise.

A Wealth of Wildlife

➡ Meet the neighbors – that would be the penguins, seabirds and elephant seals – around Península Valdés' Estancia Rincón Chico (p410).

➡ Spot dozens of the namesake species of Estancia El Cóndor (p463) at this rugged mountain ranch north of El Chaltén.

➡ View the diverse fauna of Magellanic penguins, sea lions, guanacos and pumas at Doraike (Hostería Monte León, p428).

Breathtaking Beauty

➡ Luxuriate among glaciers, lakes and the ragged Cerro Fitz Roy in the exclusive Hostería Estancia Helsingfors (p466).

➡ Explore the wonders of a petrified forest and sea islands inhabited solely by birds, penguins and sea lions at the magical Bahía Bustamante (p422).

Just like Indiana Jones

➡ Trek to Unesco World Heritage site Cueva de las Manos from Hostería Cueva de las Manos (p443), via the serpentine red-rock canyon of Río de las Pinturas.

The Bargain Bin

➡ Grab your zzzs in a bunk bed and save some bucks: Estancia El Cóndor, Hostería Cueva de las Manos, and **Estancia Casa de Piedra** (☎02963-432207, 0297-504-6785; off RN 40; campsites per person US$8; ⏲Jan & Feb) all offer affordable *refugio* (rustic shelter) lodgings. Those with higher price tags can include all meals and excursions, delivering a lot for your money.

505) Outfitter El Relincho takes riders to the pretty valley of Río de las Vueltas (three hours) and also offers more challenging rides up the Vizcacha hill followed by a barbecue on a traditional ranch. Cabin-style accommodations are also available through the company.

Camino Abierto TOURS
(☎02962-493043; www.caminoabierto.com) An operator offering trekking throughout Patagonia and guided crossing to Villa O'Higgins. It's off Av San Martín.

Patagonia Mágica OUTDOORS
(☎02962-486261; www.patagoniamagica.com; Fonrouge s/n) The friendly Patagonia Mágica runs one-day rock-climbing workshops for beginners on the natural rock-climbing walls near El Chaltén. Experienced climbers can go on expeditions with certified guides.

Festivals & Events

Fiesta Nacional de Trekking SPORTS
(⏲Mar) This multiple-location event brings a circus of outdoor freaks for rock-climbing, bouldering and woodcutting competitions, as well as running and mountain-bike races.

Sleeping

Lodgings range from budget to high end. Reservations should be made at least one month in advance for the January–February high season – demand here is that great. Dorm beds fill up fast in summer. If you bring a sturdy tent, however, there's always space in the campgrounds.

Albergue Patagonia HOSTEL $
(Patagonia Travellers' Hostel; ☎02962-493019; www.patagoniahostel.com.ar; Av San Martín 376; incl breakfast d/tr US$105/130, dm/s/d without bathroom US$25/60/75; ⏲Sep-May; @📶) A gorgeous and welcoming wooden farmhouse with helpful staff. Dorms in a separate building are spacious and modern, with good service and a humming atmosphere. A B&B option features rooms with private bathrooms, kitchen use and a sumptuous buffet breakfast at Fuegia Bistro.

Also rents bikes and offers a unique bike tour to Lago del Desierto (AR$1100) with shuttle options.

Condor de Los Andes HOSTEL $
(☎02962-493101; www.condordelosandes.com; cnr Río de las Vueltas & Halvor Halvorsen; dm/d US$28/91; @📶) This homey hostel has the feel of a ski lodge, with worn bunks, warm rooms and a roaring fire. Prices take a leap to stylish private doubles, though it's an unlikely choice for couples. The guest kitchen is immaculate and there are comfortable lounge spaces.

Lo de Trivi HOSTEL $
(☎02962-493255; www.lodetrivi.com; Av San Martín 675; d US$80, dm/d without bathroom US$19/76; 📶) A good budget option, this converted house has added shipping containers and decks with antique beds as porch seating. It's a bit hodgepodge but it works. There are various tidy shared spaces with and without TV; best is the huge industrial kitchen for guests. Doubles in snug containers can barely fit a bed.

Rancho Grande Hostel HOSTEL $
(☎02962-493005; www.ranchograndehostel.com; Av San Martín 724; dm/d/tr/q US$35/147/170/194; @📶) Serving as Chaltén's Grand Central Station (Chaltén Travel buses stop here), this bustling backpacker factory has something for everyone, from bus reservations to internet (extra) and 24-hour cafe service. Clean four-bed rooms are stacked with blankets, and bathrooms sport rows of shower stalls. Private rooms have their own bathroom and free breakfast.

Camping El Relincho CAMPGROUND $
(☎02962-493007; www.elrelinchopatagonia.com.ar; Av San Martín 545; campsites per person/vehicle/motorhome US$9/3/5, 4-person cabins US$118; 📶) A private campground with wind-whipped and exposed sites, and an enclosed cooking area.

★ **Nothofagus B&B** B&B $$
(☎02962-493087; www.nothofagusbb.com.ar; cnr Hensen & Riquelme; s/d/tr US$74/94/106, without bathroom US$59/71/99; ⊙Oct-Apr; @📶) 🍃 Attentive and adorable, this chalet-style inn offers a toasty retreat with hearty breakfast options. Practices that earn them the Sello Verde (Green Seal) include separating organic waste and replacing towels only when asked. Wooden-beam rooms have carpet and some views. Those with hallway bathrooms share with one other room. The owners, former guides, are helpful with hiking information.

Anita's House CABIN $$
(☎02962-493288; www.anitashouse.com.ar; Av San Martín 249; 2-/3-/4-person cabins US$118/129/141, 6-person cabins US$188; 📶) When the wind howls, these few modern cabins are a snug spot for groups, couples or families, smack in the center of town. Owner run and with impeccable service. Kitchens come fully equipped and there's room service and cable TV. The larger two-story cabins are downright spacious.

El Barranco INN $$
(☎02962-493006; www.posadaelbarranco.com; Calle 2, No 45; d/tr/q incl breakfast US$150/165/175; 📶) This 10-room inn hits just the right note, with sleek rooms and their glass showers, LED TVs and lock boxes. The double water-heater system ensures you won't go without a hot shower. There are also three high-ceiling cabins with kitchenettes set in the grassy yard. With 24-hour reception.

Pudu Lodge HOTEL $$
(☎02962-493365; www.pudulodge.com; Calle Las Loicas 97; d incl breakfast US$90; P@📶) This comfy lodging with modern style and congenial service has 20 spacious rooms with good mattresses. It's great value for El Chaltén. Buffet breakfasts are served in the cathedral-ceilinged great room.

Inlandsis GUESTHOUSE $$
(☎02962-493276; www.inlandsis.com.ar; Lago del Desierto 480; d US$84-99; ⊙Oct-Apr; 📶) This small, relaxed brick house offers economical rooms with bunk beds (some are airless; check before booking) or larger, pricier doubles with two twin beds or a queen-size bed. It also has bi-level cabins with bathtubs, kitchens and DVD players. There are great extras, like afternoon cakes or wine, bag lunches for the trail and transport in and out of town.

Posada Lunajuim INN $$
(☎02962-493047; www.lunajuim.com; Trevisán 45; s/d/tr incl breakfast from US$112/136/163; 📶) 🍃 This offbeat, modern inn displaying the owner's art lost some of its intimacy when it doubled its size, but it's still a decent spot to overnight. The 26 rooms vary in size (and category). A stone fireplace and library provide a rainy-day escape. Nice touches include DIY box lunches and a buffet breakfast.

El Chaltén

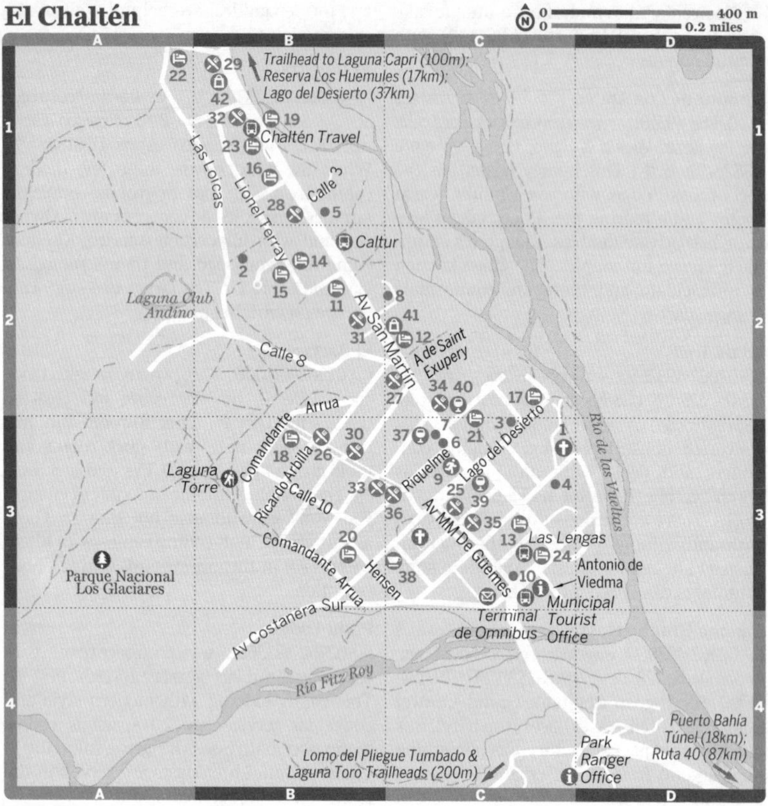

★ **Senderos Hostería** B&B $$$
(☎ 02962-493336; www.senderoshosteria.com.ar; Perito Moreno 35; s/d incl breakfast from US$125/150) This contemporary, corrugated-tin home offers wonderful amenities for trekkers seeking creature comforts. The on-site restaurant serves exquisite gourmet meals with excellent wines and attentive service – a real perk when you've spent a day outdoors. Smart rooms have soft white sheets, firm beds, lock boxes and occasional Fitz Roy views.

Kaulem BOUTIQUE HOTEL $$$
(☎ 02962-493251; www.kaulem.com.ar; cnr Av Antonio Rojo & Comandante Arrua; d incl breakfast US$155, cabin d US$135; 📶) 🍃 With a cozy lodge atmosphere, cafe and public art gallery, this boutique hotel is rustic and stylish, with just four rooms, all with Fitz Roy views, and an adjacent cabin with kitchen. The buffet breakfast includes yogurt, homemade bread, and fruit. Guests share a huge open dining and living area piped with good music and stocked with books and chess.

Hostería El Puma LODGE $$$
(☎ 02962-493095; www.hosteriaelpuma.com.ar; Lionel Terray 212; s/d/tr US$146/164/191; P 📶) This luxury lodge with 12 comfortable rooms offers intimacy without pretension, as well as huge buffet breakfasts. The rock-climbing and summit photographs and maps lining the hall may inspire your next expedition, but lounging by the fireplace is the most savory way to end the day.

Hotel Poincenot HOTEL $$$
(☎ 02962-493252; www.hotelpoincenot.com; Av San Martín 668; d US$175-200; ⏲ Oct-Apr; 📶) Popular with groups, this busy, modern hotel has 20 rooms with flat-screen TVs, and comfortable beds with down bedding and colorful throws. Spacious rooms include a cathedral-ceilinged living room, dining area and bar. Service is professional and attentive.

El Chaltén

Sights

1 Capilla de los Escaladores C3

Activities, Courses & Tours

2 Camino Abierto B2
3 Casa de Guias C3
4 Chaltén Mountain Guides C3
5 El Relincho B1
6 Fitzroy Expediciones C3
7 Patagonia Aventura C3
8 Patagonia Mágica C2
9 Spa Yaten C3
10 Zona Austral C3

Sleeping

11 Albergue Patagonia B2
12 Anita's House C2
Camping El Relincho .... (see 5)
13 Condor de Los Andes C3
14 El Barranco B2
15 Hostería El Puma B2
16 Hotel Poincenot B1
17 Inlandsis C2
18 Kaulem B3
19 Lo de Trivi B1
20 Nothofagus B&B B3
21 Posada Lunajuim C3
22 Pudu Lodge A1
23 Rancho Grande Hostel B1
24 Senderos Hostería C3

Eating

25 Ahonikenk C3
26 Cúrcuma B3
27 Domo Blanco C2
28 Don Guerra B1
29 El Muro B1
30 Estepa B3
31 La Cervecería B2
32 La Oveja Negra B1
33 La Tapera B3
34 Maffía C2
35 Patagonicus C3
36 Techado Negro C3

Drinking & Nightlife

37 Fresco C3
38 La Chocolatería C3
39 La Vinería C3
40 Laguna los Tres C2

Shopping

41 Chalteños C2
42 Viento Oeste B1

Eating

Techado Negro CAFE $

(02962-493268; Av Antonio Rojo; mains AR$90-180; noon-midnight;) With local paintings on the wall, bright colors and a raucous, unkempt atmosphere in keeping with El Chaltén, this homespun cafe serves up abundant, good-value and sometimes healthy Argentine fare. Think homemade empanadas, squash stuffed with *humitas* (sweet tamale), brown rice vegetarian dishes, soups and pastas. It also offers box lunches.

Cúrcuma VEGAN $

(02902-485656; Av Rojo 219; mains AR$160; 10am-10pm;) With an avid following, this vegan, gluten-free cafe does mostly take-out, from adzuki-bean burgers to whole-wheat pizzas, stuffed eggplant with couscous and arugula. Salads, coconut-milk risottos and smoothies are rare as endangered species in Patagonia – take advantage. Hikers can reserve a lunch box a day in advance.

Patagonicus PIZZA $

(02962-493025; Av MM de Güemes 57; pizza AR$100-160; 11am-midnight Nov-Apr) Serving 20 kinds of pizza, salads and wine at sturdy wood tables surrounded by huge picture windows, Patagonicus is a local favorite. Cakes and coffee are also worth trying.

Domo Blanco ICE CREAM $

(Av San Martín 164; snacks AR$90; 2pm-midnight) Excellent homemade ice cream made with flavors like lemon ginger and berry marscarpone, with fruit harvested from a local *estancia* and calafate bushes in town.

★**Maffía** ITALIAN $$

(02966-449574; Av San Martín 107; mains AR$180-360; 11am-11pm) Bring your appetite. In a gingerbread house, this pasta specialist makes delicious stuffed *panzottis* and *sorrentinos*, with creative fillings like trout, eggplant and basil or fondue. There are also homemade soups and garden salads. Service is professional and friendly. For dessert, the oversize homemade flan delivers.

Estepa ARGENTINE $$

(02962-493069; cnr Cerro Solo & Av Antonio Rojo; mains AR$100-300; 11:30am-2pm & 6-11pm) Local favorite Estepa cooks up consistent, flavorful dishes such as lamb with calafate sauce, trout ravioli or spinach crepes. Portions are small but artfully presented, with veggies that hail from the on-site greenhouse. For a shoestring dinner, consider its rotisserie take-out service.

Don Guerra INTERNATIONAL **$$**
(☎011-15-6653-5746; Av San Martín s/n; mains AR$190-230; ⏰noon-11pm) Patagonian to its wooden bones, with sheepskin stools that wrap around an island bar and cozy booths. There are Esquel microbrews on tap and a variety of worthwhile dishes, from *milanesas* to stir-fries and fajitas.

La Oveja Negra GRILL **$$**
(☎02962-271437; Av San Martin 226; mains AR$180-240; ⏰noon-11:30pm) In a pleasant wooden house, a classic Argentine grill cooks up butterflied lamb over wood fires, plus beef and sausages. Vegetarians will have to satisfy themselves with grilled vegetables. There's artisan beer on tap and wines.

La Cervecería PUB FOOD **$$**
(☎02962-493109; Av San Martín 320; mains AR$100-190; ⏰noon-midnight) That après-hike pint usually evolves into a night out at this humming pub with *simpatico* staff and a feisty female beer master. Savor a stein of unfiltered blond pilsner or turbid bock with pasta or *locro* (a spicy stew of maize, beans, beef, pork and sausage).

El Muro ARGENTINE **$$**
(☎02962-493248; Av San Martín 912; mains AR$90-210; ⏰noon-3pm & 7-11pm) For rib-sticking mountain food (think massive stir-fries, tenderloin stroganoff or trout with crisp, grilled veggies), head to this tiny outpost at the end of the road.

Ahonikenk ARGENTINE **$$**
(☎02962-493070; Av MM de Güemes 23; mains AR$130-240; ⏰noon-3pm & 7-11pm) This pint-sized log restaurant is known for its good price-to-quality ratio. Bus drivers feed on oversized *milanesas* that could feed a family of four, particularly if ordered with fried eggs on top. There's also good trout, pasta, pizza and salads.

★ **La Tapera** ARGENTINE **$$$**
(☎02962-493195; Antonio Rojo 74; mains AR$260-330; ⏰noon-3pm & 6:30-11pm Oct-Apr) With tender steak in balsamic-reduction sauce, ultra-fresh trout from Lago del Desierto and red-wine glasses as big as your head, it's hard to go wrong at Chipo's place, reminiscent of a log cabin with an open fireplace. Vegetarian options invite less enthusiasm – best to try elsewhere. Otherwise, service is snappy, portions generous and there are wonderful wine options.

Drinking & Nightlife

La Vinería WINE BAR
(☎02962-493301; Lago del Desierto 265; ⏰2:30pm-3am Oct-Apr) Transplanted from Alaska, this tiny, congenial wine bar offers a long Argentine wine list accompanied by 70 craft-beer options and standout appetizers. With 50 wines sold by the glass, and an entire gin menu, enthusiasts might be tempted to sabotage their next day on the trail.

La Chocolatería CAFE
(☎02962-493008; Lago del Desierto 105; ⏰11am-9pm Mon-Fri, 9am-9pm Sat & Sun Nov-Mar) This irresistible chocolate factory tells the story of local climbing legends on the walls. It makes for an intimate evening out, with options ranging from spirit-spiked hot cocoa to wine and fondue. Chocolate and coffee drinks are AR$90.

Laguna los Tres BAR
(Trevisán 42; ⏰6pm-2am) For a dose of rock or reggae with ping-pong on the side, this disheveled bar will do nicely. There's live music on weekends; check the Facebook page for events.

Fresco BAR
(Cabo García 38; ⏰5pm-midnight Mon-Sat) In a corrugated-tin house, this bare-bones bar gets lively when there's live music. There's also La Zorra beer on tap, one of Patagonia's finest.

Shopping

Chalteños CHOCOLATE
(Av San Martín 249; ⏰10am-1pm & 4-9pm) Bring home Chalteños' handmade *alfajores* filled with *dulce de leche* or homemade jams and your loved ones will forgive all your wanderings.

Viento Oeste BOOKS
(☎02962-493200; Av San Martín 898; ⏰10am-11pm) Sells books, maps and souvenirs and also rents a wide range of camping equipment, as do several other sundries shops around town.

Information

El Chaltén has been slow to catch up to modern times but now boasts two Link ATMs (as well as cell-phone service and slow internet).

Those coming from El Calafate should bring extra cash in case ATMs are out of money or service.

Banco de Santa Cruz (⊗24hr) has a LINK-access ATM in the bus terminal. There's another one outside the terminal.

New regulations require lodgings and restaurants to accept credit cards, but it may take some time for local businesses to implement them. There's one gas station at the entrance to town that accepts cash only. Euros and US dollars are widely accepted.

Chaltén Travel (☑02962-493092; www. chaltentravel.com; Av MM de Güemes 7; ⊗7am-noon & 5-9pm) Books airline tickets (flights out of Calafate) and bus travel on RN 40.

Municipal Tourist Office (☑02962-493370; www.elchalten.tur.ar; Bus Terminal; ⊗8am-10pm) Friendly and extremely helpful, with lodging lists and good information on the town and tours. English is spoken.

Park Ranger Office (☑02962-493024, 02962-493004; pnlgzonanorte@apn.gob.ar; ⊗9am-5pm Sep-Apr, 10am-5pm May-Aug) Many daytime buses stop for a short bilingual orientation at this visitor center, just before the bridge over the Río Fitz Roy. Park rangers distribute a map and town directory and do a good job of explaining Parque Nacional Los Glaciares' ecological issues. Climbing documentaries are shown at 2pm daily – great for rainy days.

Post Office (⊗8am-4:30pm Mon-Fri)

Puesto Sanitario (☑02962-493033; AM De Agostini 70) Provides basic health services.

❶ Getting There & Away

El Chaltén is 220km from El Calafate via smooth paved roads. A bicycle path heads from town to Hostería El Pilar, in Parque Nacional Los Glaciares. Bike rentals are available in various locations.

All buses go to the **Terminal de Omnibus** (☑02962-493370), located near the entrance to town. Outbound passengers must pay a separate departure tax (AR$20).

For El Calafate (AR$600, 3½ hours), **Chaltén Travel** (p452) has daily departures at 7:30am, 1pm and 6pm in summer. **Caltur** (☑02962-493150; Av San Martín 520) and **Taqsa/Marga** (☑02962-493130; Bus Terminal) also make the trip. Service is less frequent in low season.

Las Lengas (☑02962-493023; Antonio de Viedma 95) has shuttle service directly to El Calafate's airport (AR$600) in high season. It also has minivans to Lago del Desierto (AR$450 roundtrip), stopping at Hostería El Pilar and Río Eléctrico.

Chaltén Travel also goes to Bariloche on odd days of the month in high season (AR$2425, two days), with an overnight stop (meals and accommodations extra). Taqsa also goes to Bariloche (AR$2020), to points on RN 40 in between, and to Ushuaia (AR$2150).

Parque Nacional Los Glaciares (North)

This surreal and stunning mountain landscape defies all logic. In the northern part of the park, the **Fitz Roy Range** – with its rugged wilderness and shark-tooth summits – is the de facto trekking capital of Argentina. It also draws world-class climbers for whom **Cerro Torre** and **Cerro Fitz Roy** are milestone ascents notorious for brutal weather conditions. But you don't have to be extreme to enjoy the numerous well-marked trails for hiking and jaw-dropping scenery – that is, when the clouds clear.

Parque Nacional Los Glaciares is divided into geographically separate northern and southern sectors. El Chaltén is the gateway town for the northern part of the park. El Calafate is the gateway town for the southern section, which features the Glaciar Perito Moreno. They are not connected by trails and are essentially seen as separate parks.

🏃 Activities

Before heading out on hikes, stop by El Chaltén's Park Ranger Office for updated trail conditions. The most stable weather for hiking comes not in summer but in March and April, when there is less wind (and fewer people). From May to September hikers must register pre- and post-hike at the office. During the winter months of June and July trails may be closed or high water may flood bridges – check first with the Park Ranger Office.

Experienced backpackers can register to hike in the remote areas, which require some route finding. A first-person ranger update is necessary for these hikes.

★ Laguna de Los Tres HIKING

This hike to a high alpine tarn provides one of the most photogenic spots in Parque Nacional Los Glaciares. It's somewhat strenuous (10km and four hours one way) and best for those already in good physical shape. Exercise extra caution in foul weather as trails are very steep.

The trail starts from a yellow-roofed pack station. After about an hour there's a

THE EPIC RUTA NACIONAL 40

Patagonia's RN 40 is the quintessential road trip. It's not for rushing – the weather can be wily, winds overpowering and it can seem to go on forever. But it is also magical when the interminable flat line of steppe bursts open with views of glacial peaks and gem-colored lakes. As it is now mostly paved, travel here is becoming easier, though if you explore the road's offshoots, expect loose gravel.

Be Prepared

There is no cell-phone coverage outside of towns, so drivers must be self-sufficient. Travel with necessary repair equipment. If renting a car, check that the headlights work and that the suspension, tires, spare tire and brakes are all in good shape. Gas stations are few, so fill up at every chance, and bring generous supplies of food and water.

Road Rules

The law requires seatbelts and headlights during daylight hours. Respect speed limits: on gravel 65km/h to 80km/h is a safe maximum speed. Sheep *always* have the right of way. Guanacos and ñandús are other potential hazards. Slow down, give them space and watch out for unsigned *guardaganados* (cattle guards).

Take the Backseat

Several travel agencies coordinate two- to five-day minivan transport along RN 40 from El Calafate to Bariloche, via El Chaltén, Perito Moreno and Los Antiguos. Service follows fair weather, from mid-October/November to early April, depending on demand and road conditions. Pricier guided tours stretch the trip over four or five days.

If you're really up for a road trip, contact Ruta 40 (p422). This small, multilingual outfitter takes travelers on 10-day journeys on RN 40 from Bariloche to El Calafate, with stops at Cueva de las Manos and *estancias* El Cóndor and La Oriental. Consult for rates and departure dates.

Quicker, more straightforward travel along RN 40 can be arranged through **Chaltén Travel**, which has branches in El Calafate (p457), **El Chaltén** (☎02962-493092, 02962-493005; Av San Martín 635), Puerto Madryn (p407) and Bariloche (p356). It runs northbound two-day shuttles, leaving at 8am from El Calafate, with accommodation in Perito Moreno. Southbound three-day shuttles leave Bariloche at 6:45am on odd-numbered days, with accommodations in Perito Moreno and El Chaltén. Buses stop in Los Antiguos as well. The trip is usually available from November to March. The one-way trip between El Calafate and Bariloche (AR$2425 per person) does not include accommodation or food. It's possible to hop on and off along the route, but space on the next shuttle cannot be reserved. Combinations to Puerto Madryn are also available for northbound travelers.

Some travelers have had good experiences with bus line Taqsa/Marga (p441), which offers slightly cheaper high-season service north and south between El Calafate and Bariloche (28 hours, October to April), with stops in El Chaltén, Perito Moreno and Esquel.

signed lateral to excellent free backcountry **campsites** at Laguna Capri. The main trail continues gently through windswept forests and past small lakes, meeting the Lagunas Madre and Hija trail. Carry on through wind-worn ñire (a small, deciduous southern beech species) forest and along boggy terrain to **Río Blanco** (three hours) and the woodsy, mouse-plagued **Campamento Poincenot**. The trail splits before Río Blanco to Río Eléctrico. Stay left to reach a climbers' base camp. Here the trail zigzags steeply up the tarn to the eerily still, glacial **Laguna de los Tres**, in close view of 3405m Cerro Fitz Roy. Be prepared for high, potentially hazardous winds and allow extra time.

Laguna Torre HIKING

Views of the stunning rock needle of Cerro Torre are the highlight of this 18km roundtrip hike. If you have good weather – ie little wind – and clear skies, make this hike (three hours one way) a priority, since the toothy Cerro Torre is the most difficult local peak to see on normal blustery days.

There are two trail options that later merge. One starts at the northwestern edge of El Chaltén. From a signpost on Av San Martín, head west on Eduardo Brenner and then right to find the signposted start of the track. The Laguna Torre track winds up westward around large boulders on slopes covered with typical Patagonian dry-land plants, then leads southwest past a wet meadow to a junction with a trail coming in from the left after 35 to 45 minutes.

Starting from the southern end of El Chaltén, follow Lago del Desierto west past the edge of town, then drop to the riverbed, passing a tiny hydroelectric installation. At a signpost the route climbs away from the river and leads on through scattered lenga and ñire woodland, with the odd wire fence to step over, before merging with a more prominent (signposted) path coming in from the right.

Continue up past a rounded bluff to the **Mirador Laguna Torre**, a crest with the first clear view up the valley to the extraordinary 3128m rock spire of Cerro Torre, above a sprawling mass of intersecting glaciers.

The trail dips gently through stands of lenga, before cutting across open scrubby river flats and old revegetated moraines to reach a signposted junction with the Sendero Madre e Hija, a shortcut to Campamento Poincenot, 50 to 90 minutes on. Continuing upvalley, bear left at another signposted fork and climb over a forested embankment to cross a small alluvial plain, following the fast-flowing glacial waters of the Río Fitz Roy. You'll arrive at **Campamento De Agostini** (formerly Bridwell) after a further 30 to 40 minutes. This free campground (with pit toilet) gets busy; it serves as a base camp for Cerro Torre climbers. The only other nearby camping is in a pleasant grove of riverside lengas below Cerro Solo.

Follow the trail along the lake's north side for about an hour to **Mirador Maestri** (no camping).

Piedra del Fraile HIKING

This 16km roundtrip (three hours one way) follows the Valle Eléctrico. There are some stream crossings with sturdy tree trunks to cross on and one bridge crossing; all are well-marked. From **Hostería El Pilar** walk 1km northeast on the main road to hit the signposted trailhead for Piedra del Fraile, near a big iron bridge.

Pass through pastures and branches left up the valley along **Río Eléctrico**, enclosed by sheer cliffs, before reaching the private Lodge Los Troncos (p454). There's a restaurant but no guest kitchen. Dorm rates are cheapest with your own sleeping bag. Reservations are not possible since there are no phones – simply show up. Visitors must pay a trail fee (AR$300). The campground has a kiosk, a restaurant and excellent services, and the owners can recommend trails.

Buses to Lago del Desierto drop hikers at the Río Eléctrico bridge.

Lago del Desierto–Chile Trail HIKING

Some 37km north of El Chaltén (a one-hour drive on a gravel road), Lago del Desierto sits near the Chilean border. At the lake a 500m trail leads to an overlook with fine lake and glacier views. A lake trail along the eastern side extends to Candelario Mansilla in Chile.

An increasingly popular way to get to Chile is by crossing the border here with a one- to three-day trekking/ferry combination to Villa O'Higgins, the last stop on the Carretera Austral. The route is also popular with cyclists, though much of their time is spent shouldering their bike and gear through steep sections too narrow for panniers. Plans have started to put a road in here, but it may take decades.

Lomo del Pliegue Tumbado & Laguna Toro HIKING

Heading southwest from El Chaltén's Park Ranger Office, this trail (10km and four to five hours one way) skirts the eastern face of Loma del Pliegue Tumbado going toward Río Túnel, then cuts west and heads to Laguna Toro. It's less crowded than the main routes. The hike is gentle, but prepare for strong winds and carry extra water.

It's the only hike that allows views of both Cerros Torre and Fitz Roy at once.

Tours

Ice Climbing & Trekking

Many companies offer ice-climbing courses and ice treks, some including sleds pulled by Siberian huskies. Multiday guided hikes over the Hielo Patagónico Continental (Continental Ice Field) have the feel of polar expeditions. Catering to serious trekkers, this route involves technical climbing, including use of crampons, and strenuous river crossings.

Fitzroy Expediciones OUTDOORS
(Adventure Patagonia; ☎02962-436110; www.fitzroyexpediciones.com.ar; Av San Martín 56, El Chaltén; ⊗9am-1pm & 2-8pm) Runs trekking excursions, ice trekking on Glaciar Cagliero, kayaking and a five-day itinerary that includes trekking in the Fitz Roy and Cerro Torre area. Note that Fitzroy Expediciones does accept credit cards, unlike most businesses in town.

Casa de Guias OUTDOORS
(☎02962-493118; www.casadeguias.com.ar; Lago del Desierto 470, El Chaltén; ⊗10am-1pm & 4:30-9pm) Friendly and professional, with English-speaking guides certified by the Argentine Association of Mountain Guides (AAGM). It specializes in small groups. Offerings include mountain traverses, ascents for the very fit and rock-climbing classes.

Patagonia Aventura ADVENTURE
(☎02962-493110; www.patagonia-aventura.com; Av San Martín 56, El Chaltén) Offers cruises (AR$1100) on Lago Viedma to view Glaciar Viedma, and trekking (AR$2100) on the peninsula overlooking the glacier, or the option of doing both as part of a package (AR$2400). There used to be an option to trek on the glacier, but its recession has now made this impossible. Departs from Puerto Bahía Túnel.

Chaltén Mountain Guides OUTDOORS
(☎02962-493329; www.chaltenmountainguides.com; Rio de las Vueltas 212, El Chaltén) Licensed guides do ice-field traversing, trekking and mountaineering. Rates decrease significantly with group size. The office is in the Kaulem hotel.

Fly Fishing

Commercial trips go to Lago del Desierto; some are full-day excursions that include a few hours at Laguna Larga. Equipment is provided.

Horseback Riding

Horses can be used to trot round town and to carry equipment with a guide (prices negotiable), but are not allowed unguided on national-park trails. Outfitter El Relincho (p445) takes riders to the pretty valley of Río de las Vueltas and also offers more challenging rides, combined with a ranch barbecue. Cabin-style accommodations are also available.

Water Activities

As El Chaltén grows, so do the aquatic offerings. Fitzroy Expediciones has half-day guided kayaking trips on the Río de las Vueltas that stop for lunch at the company's adventure camp. (Overnight stays are also available in the timber lodge and eight cabins, 17km north of town – ask at the office in El Chaltén for more info.) You can also book two-day canoe and camping trips to Río La Leona.

All-day kayak trips on Lago del Desierto (AR$1075) are offered through Zona Austral (p445); rates include transport from El Chaltén. **Anfibio Chaltén** (☎02966-15-499375) offers snorkeling trips on the same lake, with ethereal hues and cool underwater vegetation like fallen hardwoods.

Lake Cruises

Patagonia Aventura offers cruises on Lago Viedma with impressive views of the 40m Glaciar Viedma, with a hiking option. Boat trips leave from Puerto Bahía Túnel and last 2½ hours.

Exploradores Lago del Desierto (☎02962-493081; www.receptivochalten.com; glacier tour incl bus transfer AR$1450) offers trips to see Glaciar Vespignani and crossings of Lago del Desierto for hikers headed to Chile.

Rock Climbing

Outfitters around El Chaltén rent equipment; Patagonia Mágica (p446) runs one-day rock-climbing workshops for beginners. Experienced climbers can go on the Glaciar Laguna Torre with certified guides.

Sleeping

Free backcountry campgrounds have a pit toilet. Some sites have dead wood for windbreaks, but fires are prohibited. Water is as pure as glacial melt; only wash downstream from campgrounds and pack out all trash.

Lodge Los Troncos HUT $
(campsites per person US$20, dm US$50) Reservations are not possible at Lodge Los Troncos since there are no phones – simply show up. The campground has a kiosk, a restaurant and excellent services.

Hostería El Pilar ESTANCIA $$$
(☎02962-493002; www.hosteriaelpilar.com.ar; RP 23, Km 17; s/d incl breakfast US$160/180; ⊗with advance reservation only Nov-Mar) At the south end of the Lago del Desierto, travelers can stay in one of 10 cozy *estancia* rooms or dine in the inviting restaurant serving excellent *cocina de autor* (gourmet cuisine). There are trails here that lead into the park or up Valle Río Eléctrico. It's 17km from El Chaltén.

Parque Nacional Los Glaciares (North)

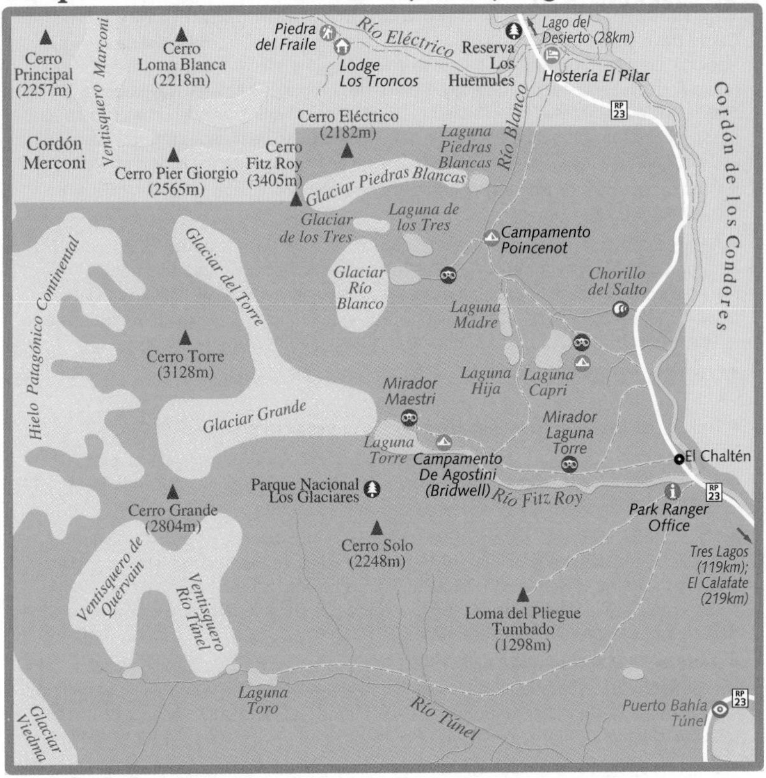

Getting There & Away

Parque Nacional Los Glaciares is just outside El Chaltén. Most trails start on the outskirts of town and require no transportation. Otherwise, excursions and taxis offer transfers to more distant trailheads, though costs tend to be exorbitant.

Las Lengas (02962-493023; Antonio de Viedma 95, El Chaltén) has a minibus service to Lago del Desierto (AR$450 roundtrip, two hours), leaving El Chaltén at 8am, noon and 3pm daily.

From Candelario Mansilla, Chile, the catamaran **Hielo Sur** (in Chile +56-0672-431821; www.villaohiggins.com) makes border crossings.

El Calafate

02902 / POP 21,130

Named for the berry that, once eaten, guarantees your return to Patagonia, El Calafate hooks you with another irresistible attraction: Glaciar Perito Moreno, 80km away in Parque Nacional Los Glaciares. This magnificent must-see has converted once-quaint El Calafate into a chic fur-trimmed destination. With a range of traveler services, it's still a fun place to be. Its strategic location between El Chaltén and Torres del Paine (Chile) makes it an inevitable stop for those in transit.

Located 320km northwest of Río Gallegos, and 32km west of RP 11's junction with northbound RN 40, El Calafate flanks the southern shore of Lago Argentino. Its main strip is dotted with souvenir and chocolate shops, restaurants and tour offices. Beyond here, pretensions melt away quickly: muddy roads lead to ad hoc developments and open pastures.

January and February are the most popular (and costly) months to visit, but shoulder-season visits are growing steadily.

TREKKING INTO CHILE

Gonzo travelers can skirt the Southern Ice Field on foot to get from Argentina's Parque Nacional Los Glaciares and El Chaltén to Villa O'Higgins, the last stop on Chile's Carretera Austral. This one- to three-day trip can be completed between November and March (the border closes in low season). Bring all provisions, Chilean currency, plus your passport and rain gear. Boat delays are not unheard of, so be prepared to stay overnight and pack enough food and extra cash in Chilean pesos. Here are the nuts and bolts:

- Grab the shuttle bus from El Chaltén to the south shore of Lago del Desierto, 37km away (AR$450, one hour).
- A ferry/tour boat travels to the north shore of Lago del Desierto (AR$1025, one-hour ferry or 4½-hour tour). Another option is to hike the demanding mountain trail (15km, five hours) that follows the coast at a distance. Warning: cyclists will have to carry their bikes in many places on narrow trails thick with vegetation. Pass through Argentine customs and immigration here. Camping is allowed at the border post only.
- From the north shore of Lago del Desierto, trek or ride to Laguna Larga (1½ hours). Camping is not allowed.
- Trek or ride to Laguna Redonda (1½ hours). Camping is not allowed.
- Trek or ride to Candelario Mansilla (two hours). Candelario Mansilla has lodging in a family farmhouse, guided treks and horse rental (riding or pack horse per day CH$30,000). Pass through Chilean customs and immigration here.
- Take the Hielo Sur catamaran *El Quetru* (CH$36,000, four hours) from Candelario Mansilla, on the south edge of Lago O'Higgins, to Puerto Bahamondez, with an optional side trip to Glaciar O'Higgins (CH$40,000). Trips go one to three times a week, usually on Saturday, with some departures on Monday or Wednesday. A bus goes from Puerto Bahamondez to Villa O'Higgins (CH$2500).
- **Ruedas de la Patagonia** (☎ cell 9-7604-2400; www.turismoruedasdelapatagonia.cl; Padre Antonio Ronchi 28; ⏲ 9am-9pm) uses a smaller, faster boat to shuttle between Candelario Mansilla and Puerto Bahamondez (1 hour 40 minutes, CH$35,000), including transfer to Villa O'Higgins.

In Villa O'Higgins, **El Mosco** (☎ 67-243-1819, cell 9-7658-3017; www.patagoniaelmosco.blogspot.com; Carretera Austral, Km 1240; campsites per person CH$6000, dm CH$9000, incl breakfast d CH$45,000, s/d without bathroom CH$18,000/30,000, 4-person cabins CH$50,000) has good lodging options. For Chilean ferry information, consult **Robinson Crusoe** (☎ 67-243-1811; www.robinsoncrusoe.com; Carretera Austral s/n; glacier tour CH$99,000; ⏲ 9am-1pm & 3-7pm Mon-Sat Nov-Mar) in Villa O'Higgins.

Sights & Activities

★Glaciarium MUSEUM
(☎ 02902-497912; www.glaciarium.com; adult/child AR$300/120; ⏲ 9am-8pm Sep-May, 11am-8pm Jun-Aug) Unique and exciting, this gorgeous museum illuminates the world of ice. Displays and bilingual films show how glaciers form, along with documentaries on continental ice expeditions and stark meditations on climate change. Adults suit up in furry capes for the *bar de hielo* (AR$240 including drink), a blue-lit below-zero club serving vodka or fernet and Coke in ice glasses.

The gift shop sells handmade and sustainable gifts crafted by Argentine artisans. Glaciarium also hosts international cinema events. It's 6km from Calafate toward Parque Nacional Los Glaciares. To get here, take the free hourly shuttle from 1 de Mayo between Av Libertador and Roca.

Reserva Natural Laguna Nimez WILDLIFE RESERVE
(AR$150; ⏲ daylight hours) Reserva Natural Laguna Nimez is a prime avian habitat alongside the lakeshore north of El Calafate, with a self-guided trail and staffed Casa Verde information hut with binoculars rental. It's a great place to spot flamingos – but watching birds from El Calafate's shoreline on Lago Argentino can be just as good.

Centro de Interpretacíon Historico MUSEUM
(☎02902-497799; www.museocalafate.com.ar; Brown & Bonarelli; AR$170; ⏲10am-8pm Sep-May, 11am-5pm Jun-Aug) Small but informative, with a skeleton mold of *Austroraptor cabazai* (found nearby) and Patagonian history displays. The friendly host invites museum-goers for a post-tour *mate* (a bitter ritual tea).

Hielo y Aventura OUTDOORS, CRUISE
(☎02902-492205, 02902-492094; www.hieloyaventura.com; Libertador 935) Hielo y Aventura's conventional cruise Safari Nautico (AR$500, one hour) tours Brazo Rico, Lago Argentino and the south side of Canal de los Témpanos. Catamarans crammed with up to 130 passengers leave hourly between 10:30am and 4:30pm from Puerto Bajo de las Sombras. During busy periods buy tickets in advance for afternoon departures.

To hike on Glaciar Perito Moreno, try minitrekking (AR$2700, under two hours on ice), or the longer and more demanding Big Ice (AR$5200, four hours on ice). Both involve a quick boat ride from Puerto Bajo de las Sombras, a walk through lenga forests, a chat on glaciology and then an ice walk using crampons. Children under eight are not allowed; reserve ahead and bring your own food. Don't forget rain gear: it's often snowing around the glacier and you might get wet and cold quickly on the boat deck. Transfers cost extra (AR$1000).

Tours

Some 40 travel agencies arrange excursions to Glaciar Perito Moreno and other local attractions, including fossil beds and stays at regional *estancias,* where you can hike, ride horses and relax. Tour prices for Glaciar Perito Moreno don't include the park entrance fee. Ask agents and other travelers about added benefits, such as extra stops, boat trips, binoculars or multilingual guides.

★**Glaciares Sur** ADVENTURE
(☎02902-495050; www.glaciarsur.com; 9 de Julio 57; per person US$250; ⏲10am-8pm) Get glacier stunned *and* skip the crowds with these recommended day tours to the unexplored end of Parque Nacional Los Glaciares. Small groups drive to Lago Roca with an expert multilingual guide to view Glaciar Frias. The adventure option features a four-hour hike; the culture option includes a traditional *estancia asado* (barbecue grill) and off-hour visits to Glaciar Perito Moreno.

Trips run October through April, weather permitting.

Chaltén Travel TOURS
(☎02902-492212; www.chaltentravel.com; Libertador 1174; ⏲9am-9pm) Recommended tours to Glaciar Perito Moreno, stopping for wildlife viewing (binoculars provided); also specializes in RN 40 trips. It outsources some excursions to **Always Glaciers** (☎02902-493861; www.alwaysglaciers.com; Libertador 924).

Calafate Fishing FISHING
(☎02902-496545; www.calafatefishing.com; Libertador 1826; ⏲10am-7pm Mon-Sat) Offers fun fly-fishing trips to Lago Roca (half-day US$170) and Lago Strobel, where you can test rumors that the biggest rainbow trout in the world lives here. There are also multiday excursions that go further afield.

Overland Patagonia TOURS
(☎02902-492243, 02902-491243; www.glaciar.com; glacier tour US$52) Overland Patagonia operates out of both Hostel del Glaciar Libertador (p459) and Hostel del Glaciar Pioneros (p459), and organizes an alternative trip to Glaciar Perito Moreno, which consists of an *estancia* visit, a one-hour hike in the park and optional lake navigation (AR$500 extra).

Caltur TOURS
(☎02902-491368; www.caltur.com.ar; Libertador 1080) Specializes in El Chaltén tours and lodging packages.

Festivals & Events

Fiesta del Pueblo CULTURAL
(⏲Oct 12) On the wet heels of winter, while streets are still mired in mud, El Chaltén celebrates the town anniversary with dancing in the school gym, barbecues and live music.

Sleeping

Though lodgings are abundant, popular offerings may book out well in advance. The core high season is January–February, although some places extend it from mid-October until April. Luxury hotels are being added at a quick clip, though standards vary. Look for deep discounts in low season.

The Municipal Tourist Office has a list of *cabañas* and apartment hotels – the best deals for groups and families. Most hostels offer pickups from the bus terminal.

El Calafate

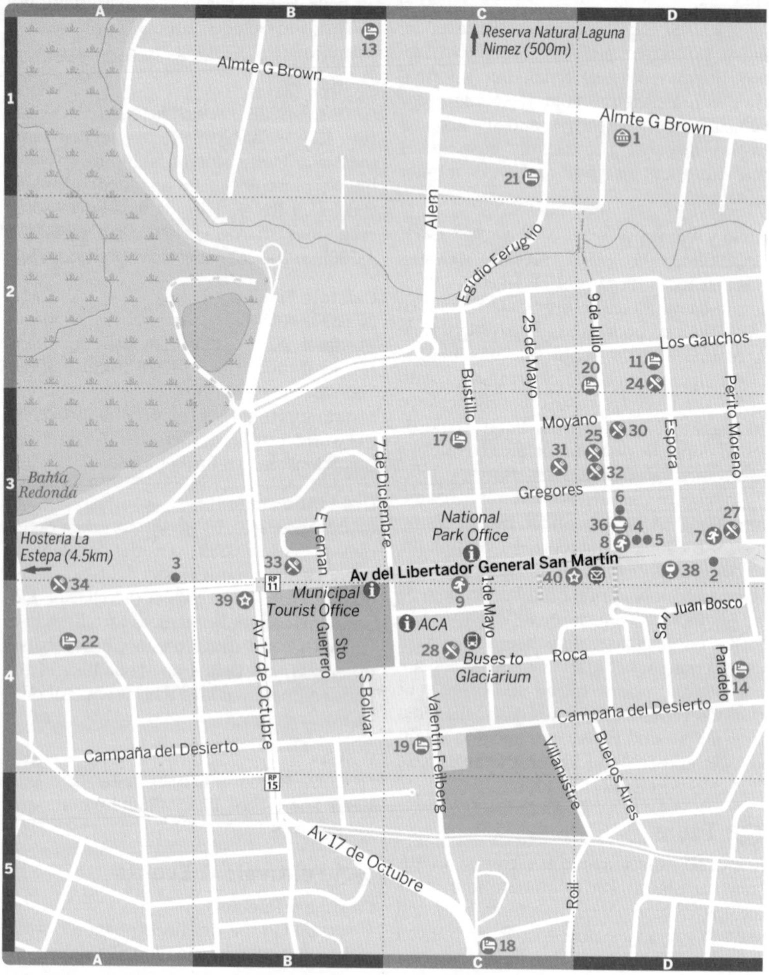

Hostal Schilling GUESTHOUSE $
(☎02902-491453; http://hostalschilling.com; Paradelo 141; dm US$26, d without bathroom US$65, s/d/tr with bathroom US$65/82/106; ☎) Good value and centrally located, this friendly guesthouse is a top choice for travelers who value service. Much is due to the family owners, who look after guests with a cup of tea or help with logistical planning. Breakfast includes scrambled eggs, yogurt and cakes. There are also multiple living rooms, adult coloring books and games.

Staff can also help with reservations for Estancia El Cóndor (p463).

America del Sur HOSTEL $
(☎02902-493525; www.americahostel.com.ar; Puerto Deseado 151; dm US$30, d & q US$140; @☎) This backpacker favorite has a stylish lodge setting with views and heated floors. Hip, modern doubles with artwork make you rethink the limitations of a hostel. There's a well-staffed and fun social scene, including affordable nightly barbecues with salad buffet in high season. It also offers electric-bike rentals.

Posada Karut Josh B&B $
(☎02902-496444; www.posadakarutjosh.com.ar; Calle 12, No 1882, Barrio Bahía Redonda; d US$71;

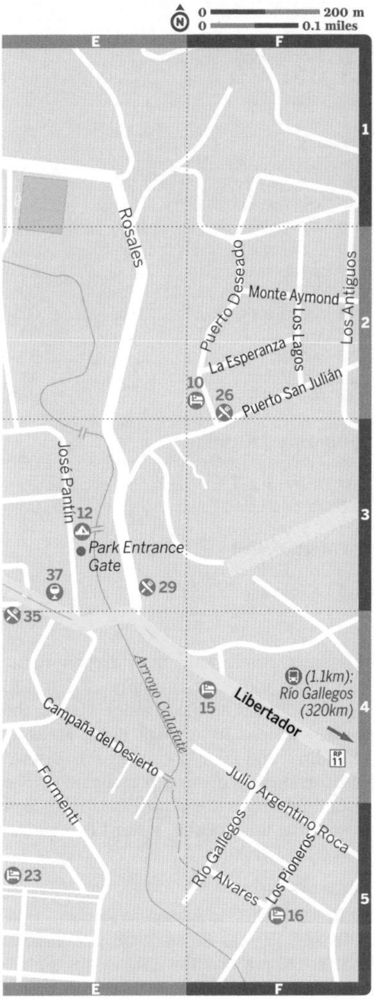

) Run by an Italian-Argentine couple, this peaceful aluminum-sided B&B features big, bright rooms and a lovely garden with lake views. Breakfast is abundant and satisfying meals (AR$280) are also available.

Las Cabañitas CABIN $
(02902-491118; www.lascabanitascalafate.com; Valentín Feilberg 218; incl breakfast 2-/3-person cabins US$60/70, 4-person apt US$80; Sep-May;) A restful spot that has snug storybook A-frames with spiral staircases leading to loft beds and apartments, all with LED TVs. It's run by Eugenia, the helpful daughter of the original owner. Touches include a barbecue area, guest cooking facilities, and English lavender in the garden.

Hostel del Glaciar Libertador HOSTEL $
(02902-492492; www.glaciar.com; Libertador 587; dm/s/d US$25/77/88;) The best deals here are dorm bunk beds with thick covers. Behind a Victorian facade, the modern facilities include a top-floor kitchen, radiant floor heating, computers and a spacious common area with a plasma TV glued to sports channels. Breakfast is extra for dorm users (AR$84).

I Keu Ken Hostel HOSTEL $
(02902-495175; www.patagoniaikeuken.com.ar; FM Pontoriero 171; dm US$24, cabins per person incl breakfast US$70;) With helpful staff, artisan beer and deck chairs on industrial springs, this quirky hostel has proven popular with travelers. Features include inviting common areas, a terrace for lounging and first-rate barbecues. Its location, near the top of a steep hill, offers views (and a workout); it's an AR$80 taxi ride to the bus terminal.

Bla! Guesthouse HOSTEL $
(02902-492220; www.blahostel.com; Espora 257; dm US$21, d/tr US$88/106;) If you're wondering where all the hipsters are, check out this tiny, mellow design hostel. While dorms are cramped, private rooms are comfortable, although walls are on the thin side.

Hostel del Glaciar Pioneros HOSTEL $
(02902-491243; www.glaciar.com; Los Pioneros 251; dm/s/d US$20/53/59; Nov-Mar;) A 15-minute walk from town, this sprawling, renovated red house is one of El Calafate's most long-standing hostels. A sociable place, it includes comfortable common areas, snug dorms and a small restaurant with homemade meals.

Camping El Ovejero CAMPGROUND $
(02902-493422; www.campingelovejero.com.ar; José Pantín 64; campsites per person US$7;) El Ovejero has woodsy, well-kept (and slightly noisy) campsites with spotless showers that have 24-hour hot water. Locals boast that the on-site restaurant is one of the best deals in town for grill food. Extras include private tables, electricity and grills. It's located by the creek just north of the bridge into town. Make reservations online.

El Calafate

Sights
1 Centro de Interpretacíon Historico....... D1

Activities, Courses & Tours
2 Always Glaciers....... D3
3 Calafate Fishing....... A3
4 Caltur....... D3
5 Chaltén Travel....... D3
6 Glaciares Sur....... D3
7 Hielo y Aventura....... D3
Mar Patag....... (see 9)
8 Solo Patagonia SA....... D3
9 Southern Spirit....... C4

Sleeping
10 America del Sur....... F2
11 Bla! Guesthouse....... D2
12 Camping El Ovejero....... E3
13 Cauquenes de Nimez....... B1
14 Hostal Schilling....... D4
15 Hostel del Glaciar Libertador....... F4
16 Hostel del Glaciar Pioneros....... F5
17 Hotel Posada Los Álamos....... C3
18 I Keu Ken Hostel....... C5
19 Las Cabañitas....... C4
20 Madre Tierra....... D2
21 Miyazato Inn....... C1
22 Posada Karut Josh....... A4
23 South B&B....... E5

Eating
24 Buenos Cruces....... D2
25 El Cucharón....... D3
26 Esquina Varela....... F2
27 La Anónima....... D3
28 La Cantina....... C4
29 La Tablita....... E3
30 Mi Rancho....... D3
31 Morphi al Paso....... C3
32 Olivia....... D3
33 Panaderia Don Luis....... B3
34 Pura Vida....... A4
35 Viva la Pepa....... E4

Drinking & Nightlife
36 el ba'r....... D3
37 La Zorra....... E3
38 Librobar....... D3

Entertainment
39 Don Diego de la Noche....... B4
40 La Toldería....... C3

Cauquenes de Nimez B&B **$$**
(02902-492306; www.cauquenesdenimez.com.ar; Calle 303, No 79; d/tr incl breakfast US$100/124;) Both modern and rustic, Gabriel's welcoming two-story lodge offers views of flamingos on the lake (from November through summer). Smart rooms decorated with corduroy duvets and nature photography also feature lock boxes and TVs. Personalized attention is a plus, as is the complimentary tea time with lavender muffins, and free bikes (donations support the nature reserve).

South B&B B&B **$$**
(02902-489555; www.southbb.com.ar; Av Juan Domingo Perón 1016; d/tr/q incl breakfast US$85/120/150; Oct-Apr;) You would need a drone to get views of Lago Argentino to beat those from this enormous hillside hotel converted to a large B&B. Rooms are spacious, colorful and bright, though wi-fi reaches only some. It's attentive and family run, with a trio of toy poodles standing guard. It also offers box lunches (US$15).

Hosteria La Estepa BOUTIQUE HOTEL **$$**
(02902-496592; www.hosterialaestepa.com; Libertador 5310; s/d incl breakfast from US$130/150;) Guests happily tuck into this snug, rustic lodging with panoramic lake views and farm antiquities. Of the 26 rooms, a handful have water views; the deluxe versions have small living areas. A sprawling 2nd-floor social area is strewn with regional maps and board games. The restaurant serves homemade meals. It's 5km west of the town center, toward Parque Nacional Los Glaciares.

Miyazato Inn B&B **$$**
(02902-491953; www.miyazatoinn.com; Egidio Feruglio 150, Las Chacras; s/d incl breakfast US$100/120;) Resembling a simple Japanese inn, this elegant B&B wins points for personalized service. Breakfast include sweets and *medialunas* (pastries), and excursionists get a hot thermos of coffee or tea to go. It's a five-minute walk away from the center of town.

Madre Tierra BOUTIQUE HOTEL **$$$**
(02902-489880; www.madretierrapatagonia.com; 9 de Julio 239; d incl breakfast US$165) A beaut wrapped in Andean textiles and rustic simplicity. The biggest draw is the 2nd-floor living room, with comfy sofas and a blazing woodstove on chilly days. The house has just seven rooms, outfitted with oversized dressers and a clean, modern sensibility. It's run by longtime area guides Natacha and Mari-

ano, who also offer 4WD tours and transfers. Reservations required.

Hotel Posada Los Álamos RESORT **$$$**
(☎02902-491144; www.posadalosalamos.com; Moyano 1355; s/d incl breakfast US$248/270; @☎) Considering the amenities, prices are pretty reasonable at Calafate's original resort. There are lush rooms, overstuffed sofas, spectacular gardens, tennis courts, putting greens and a spa. It's enough to make you almost forget about seeing Glaciar Perito Moreno.

Eating

There's a range of eating establishments for all budgets. Small shops selling picnic provisions such as fresh bread, fine cheeses, sweets and wine are found on the side streets perpendicular to Libertador. Head to **La Anónima** (cnr Libertador & Perito Moreno; take-out AR$120; ⏰9am-10pm) for cheap take-out and groceries.

Olivia CAFE **$**
(☎02902-488038; 9 de Julio 187; snacks AR$40-120; ⏰10am-8pm; ☎) This adorable coffee shop does *croque monsieurs* (grilled ham and cheese), fresh donuts and espresso drinks in a loungy pastel setting. It also uses whole-bean Colombian coffee. Want to take the chill off? Try the cheese scones served hot with cream.

Viva la Pepa CAFE **$**
(☎02902-491880; Amado 833; mains AR$85-200; ⏰noon-9pm Mon-Sat) Decked out in children's drawings, this cheerful cafe specializes in crepes but also offers great sandwiches with homemade bread (try the chicken with apple and blue cheese), fresh juice and gourds of *mate*.

Morphi al Paso FAST FOOD **$**
(☎911-3143-6005; 25 de Mayo 130; mains AR$50-150; ⏰noon-1am Mon-Sat) For fresh *milanesas*, hot dogs and burgers in the off hours, this clean come-and-go counter flanked with bar stools is the way to go. *Morphi* means to chow down in Lunfardo, an Argentine slang derived from a dialect in Lombardy, Italy.

Panaderia Don Luis BAKERY **$**
(Libertador 2421; snacks AR$70; ⏰7am-9pm) *Medialunas* (pastries) and much more are available at this enormous bakery.

★ **Buenos Cruces** ARGENTINE **$$**
(☎02902-492698; Espora 237; mains AR$130-280; ⏰7-11pm Mon-Sat; 🚸) This dynamic family-run enterprise brings a twist to Argentine classics. Start with a warm beet salad with balsamic reduction. The nut-crusted trout is both enormous and satisfying, as is the guanaco meatloaf or the baked ravioli crisped at the edge and bubbling with Roquefort cheese. The service is excellent and there's a play area for children.

★ **Pura Vida** ARGENTINE **$$**
(☎02902-493356; Libertador 1876; mains AR$130-240; ⏰7:30-11:30pm Thu-Tue; 🖊) Featuring the rare treat of Argentine home cooking, this offbeat, low-lit eatery is a must. Its longtime owners are found cooking up buttery spiced chicken pot pies and filling wine glasses. For vegetarians, brown rice and wok veggies or salads are satisfying. Servings are huge. Don't skip the decadent chocolate brownie with ice cream and warm berry sauce. Reserve ahead.

WORTH A TRIP

AGUAS ARRIBA

Set on the remote Lago del Desierto by the Chilean border, this exclusive **nature lodge** (☎in Buenos Aires 11-15-6134-8452; www.aguasarribalodge.com; Lago del Desierto; s/d incl meals & activities US$700/1020) provides a wondrous retreat into a silent lenga forest frequented by endangered huemul (Andean deer). The lodge itself has only five guest rooms and decks facing the massive Glacier Vespignani, with distant views of Cerro Fitz Roy on a clear day. There's guided fly fishing and hiking on an extensive trail system with waterfalls, lookouts and secluded benches. Green practices include composting, recycling and sustainable building, but it's made a true haven by the warm welcome from owners Pato and Ivor. Just getting here takes a while; guests arrive by private transfer and boat. A three-night stay is ideal. For ages 12 and up.

Esquina Varela ARGENTINE $$
(☎02902-490666; Puerto Deseado 22; mains AR$190-245; ⊙7pm-late Thu-Tue; ☑) Start with some fried calamari and beer at this corrugated-tin eatery. Filling lamb stew, steak and homemade pasta grace a short menu that also has vegetarian options. There's live music, too.

La Tablita PARRILLA $$
(☎02902-491065; www.la-tablita.com.ar; Rosales 24; mains AR$130-300; ⊙noon-3:30pm & 7pm-midnight) Steak and spit-roasted lamb are the stars at this satisfying *parrilla* that's popular beyond measure for good reason. For average appetites a half-steak will do, rounded out with a good malbec, fresh salad or garlic fries.

La Cantina ITALIAN $$
(☎02902-491151; Roca 1299; mains AR$140-180; ⊙noon-3pm & 7-11:30pm Mon-Sat) This friendly, family-run eatery specializes in *piadinas*, an Italian bread topped with cheese and fillings, taco style. They're enormously filling, but you can order the smaller size. There's also worthwhile vegetarian *humitas* (corn tamales). The setting is casual bohemian, with vinyl on the record player and live blues on Thursdays and weekends.

Mi Rancho ARGENTINE $$$
(☎02902-490540; Moyano 1089; mains AR$180-310; ⊙noon-3:30pm & 8pm-midnight) Inspired and intimate, Mi Rancho serves up oversized osso buco, delicious braided pastas stuffed with king crab, divine salads and sweetbreads with wilted spinach on toast. For dessert, chocolate fondant or passion-fruit semifreddo are both worth the calorie hit, and more. Located in a tiny brick pioneer house with space for few.

There's a second address, but we like the ambience of the original. Reserve ahead.

El Cucharón ARGENTINE $$$
(☎02902-495315; 9 de Julio 145; mains AR$180-290; ⊙noon-3pm & 8-11pm) This sophisticated eatery, tucked away in a small space a few blocks off El Calafate's main street, is a relatively undiscovered gem and an excellent place to try the regional classic *cazuela de cordero* (lamb stew). The trout with lemon sauce and grilled vegetables is delicious, too.

Drinking & Nightlife

★La Zorra MICROBREWERY
(☎02902-490444; Av San Martin s/n; ⊙6pm-2am Tue-Sun) Long, skinny tables fill with both locals and travelers to quaff what we consider to be the best artisan beer in Patagonia, La Zorra. The smoked porter and double IPA do not disappoint. There's also pub fare such as fries and sausages.

Librobar BAR
(Libertador 1015; ⊙11am-3am; ☎) Upstairs in the gnome village, this hip bookshop-bar serves coffee, artisan beers and pricey cocktails. Peruse the oversized photography books on Patagonian wildlife or bring your laptop and take advantage of the free wi-fi. There's also 2nd-story deck seating.

el ba'r CAFE
(9 de Julio s/n; ⊙11am-10pm Thu-Tue) This patio cafe is the hot spot for you and your sweater-clad puppy to order espresso, *submarinos* (hot milk with melted chocolate bar), green tea, gluten-free snacks or sandwiches (mains AR$80 to AR$180).

☆ Entertainment

La Toldería LIVE MUSIC
(☎02902-491443; www.facebook.com/LaTolderia; Libertador 1177; ⊙noon-4am Mon-Thu, to 6am Fri-Sun) This petite storefront opens its doors to dancing and live acts at night; it's probably the best spot to try if you're feeling boisterous.

Don Diego de la Noche LIVE MUSIC
(Libertador 1603; ⊙8pm-late) This perennial favorite serves dinner and features live music such as tango, guitar and *folklórica* (folk music).

Information

MEDICAL SERVICES

Hospital de Alta Complejidad SAMIC
(☎02902-491889; www.hospitalelcalafate.org; Jorge Newbury 453) Located in El Calafate's upper neighborhood, a taxi ride from downtown.

MONEY

Withdraw your cash before the weekend rush – it isn't uncommon for ATMs to run out on Sundays. If you are headed to El Chaltén, consider getting extra cash here.

Banco Santa Cruz (Libertador 1285; ⊙8am-1pm Mon-Fri) Changes traveler's checks and has an ATM.

POST

Post Office (Libertador 1133; ⊙8am-4:30pm Mon-Fri)

TOURIST INFORMATION

ACA (Automóvil Club Argentino; 02902-491004; Valentin Feilberg 51; 24hr) Argentina's auto club; a good source for provincial road maps.

Municipal Tourist Office (02902-491090, 02902-491466; www.elcalafate.tur.ar; Libertador 1411; 8am-8pm) Has town maps and general information. There's also a kiosk at the bus terminal; both have some English-speaking staff.

National Park Office (02902-491545; Libertador 1302; 8am-8pm Dec-Apr, to 6pm May-Nov) Offers brochures and a decent map of Parque Nacional Los Glaciares. It's best to get information here before reaching the park.

TRAVEL AGENCIES

Most agents deal exclusively with nearby excursions and are unhelpful for other areas.

Tiempo Libre (02902-492203; www.tiempolibreviajes.com.ar; Gregores 1294; 10am-1pm & 4-8pm Mon-Fri) Books flights.

Getting There & Away

AIR

The modern **Aeropuerto El Calafate** (02902-491220) is 23km east of town off RP 11. New low-cost airlines plan to offer flights to Buenos Aires, Ushuaia and Río Grande. **Aviación Civil Argentina** (ANAC; www.anac.gob.ar) has a map with new routes and airlines.

The following rates are one way. **Aerolíneas Argentinas** (02902-492814, 02902-492816; Libertador 1361; 9:30am-5pm Mon-Fri, 10am-1pm Sat) flies daily to Bariloche (from AR$1860), Ushuaia (AR$1800), Trelew (AR$4000), and Aeroparque and Ezeiza in Buenos Aires (from AR$4400).

LADE (02902-491262; Jean Mermoz 160) flies a few times a week to Río Gallegos, Comodoro Rivadavia, Ushuaia, Esquel, Puerto Madryn, Buenos Aires and other smaller regional airports.. **LATAM** (02902-495548; 9 de Julio 81; 9am-8pm Mon-Fri) flies to Ushuaia weekly. **Aerovías DAP** (61-261-6100; www.aeroviasdap.cl; O'Higgins 891) flies to Punta Arenas in high season (December through March).

OFF THE BEATEN TRACK

ESTANCIA EL CÓNDOR

A burly slice of heaven, this remote **estancia** (in Buenos Aires 011-4735-7704, satellite phone 011-4152-5400; www.cielospatagonicos.com; Lago San Martín; s/d incl meals & excursions US$290/440; Oct-Mar) sits tucked into the shores of Lago San Martín. A private nature reserve, tawny steppe, mossy beech forest and frozen mountaintops make up its 400 sq km.

Even for Patagonia this landscape seems oversize – from the massive turquoise lake (known as O'Higgins on its Chilean side), to the 13 kinds of orchids and the craggy cliffs where condors wheel on the wind.

The *estancia* occupies a curious footnote in Patagonian history. Its *puesto* (homestead) La Nana was home to an infamous Brit named Jimmy Radburn, who kidnapped a Tehuelche woman named Juana (with her consent – she had already been sold off by her father to pay a gambling debt) and came to this ultra-remote spot at the turn of the 20th century to raise a family. At the time of research La Nana was only accessible by a day-long hike or ride from the main *casco* (ranch house).

The lodgings at Estancia El Cóndor are comfortable but not luxurious. Rates include all meals and excursions. The *casco* has six rooms, each with a private bathroom, a large stone fireplace and a small collection of literature on the region. Cheaper accommodations are available at a more rustic bunkhouse; email for options.

Riding enthusiasts could do a week on horseback without running out of fresh terrain, and the mountain refuge of La Nana provides a base camp deeper in the wilderness. Trails are suitable for hiking (river crossings should always be made with a guide). A day trip to the *condorera* (where condors nest) is a highlight.

Visitors can drive on their own or take a five-hour transfer from El Calafate (US$140 per person), with set departures on Tuesday and Friday at 8am, returning at 3pm. El Cóndor is located three hours from Tres Lagos, 118km off RN 40, on the way to El Chaltén. At the time of research there was no legal border crossing here.

BUS

El Calafate's hilltop **bus terminal** (☎02902-491476; Jean Mermoz 104; ⏰24hr) is easily reached by a pedestrian staircase from the corner of Libertador and 9 de Julio. Book ahead in high season, as outbound seats can be in short supply.

For Río Gallegos, buses go four times daily; contact **Taqsa/Marga** (☎02902-491843; Jean Mermoz 104) or **Andesmar** (☎02902-494250; Jean Mermoz 104). Connections to Bariloche and Ushuaia may require leaving in the middle of the night and a change of buses in Río Gallegos. **Sportman** (☎02902-492680; Jean Mermoz 104) serves various destinations in Patagonia.

For El Chaltén, buses leave daily at 8am, 2pm and 6pm. Both **Caltur** (☎02902-491368; www.caltur.com.ar; Jean Mermoz 104) and Chaltén Travel (p457) go to El Chaltén and also drive the RN 40 to Bariloche (AR$2425, two days) in summer. General buses to Bariloche take longer in winter as they take the coastal route.

For Puerto Natales (Chile), **Cootra** (☎02902-491444; Jean Mermoz 104) and **Turismo Zahhj** (☎02902-491631; Jean Mermoz 104) depart at 8am and 8:30am daily (three times weekly in low season), crossing the border at Cerro Castillo, where it may be possible to connect to Torres del Paine.

Getting Around

Airport shuttle **Ves Patagonia** (☎02902-494355; www.vespatagonia.com.ar; airport transfer AR$160) offers door-to-door service, or you can take a taxi (AR$480). There are several car-rental agencies at the airport. **Localiza** (☎02902-491398; www.localiza.com.ar; Libertador 687; ⏰9am-8pm) and **Servi Car** (☎02902-492541; www.servi4x4.com.ar; Libertador 695; ⏰9:30am-noon & 4-8pm Mon-Sat) offer car rentals from convenient downtown offices.

Renting a bike is an excellent way to get a feel for the area and cruise the dirt roads by the lake. Many lodgings and some downtown shops offer rentals.

Parque Nacional Los Glaciares (South)

Among the Earth's most dynamic and accessible ice fields, **Glaciar Perito Moreno** is the stunning centerpiece of the southern sector of Parque Nacional Los Glaciares. It's 30km long, 5km wide and 60m high, but what makes it exceptional in the world of ice is its constant advance – it creeps forward up to 2m per day, causing building-sized icebergs to calve from its face. Watching the glacier is a sedentary park experience that manages to be thrilling.

The glacier formed as a low gap in the Andes allowed moisture-laden Pacific storms to drop their loads east of the divide, where they accumulate as snow. Over millennia, under tremendous weight, this snow recrystallized into ice and flowed slowly eastward. The 1600-sq-km trough of **Lago Argentino**, the country's largest body of water, shows that glaciers were once far more extensive here. While most of the world's glaciers are receding, Glaciar Perito Moreno is considered 'stable.'

Activities

Glaciar Perito Moreno Boardwalks

Beyond a short walk that parallels the shoreline at the boat dock and climbs to the lookout area, there are no trails in this sector of Parque Nacional Los Glaciares accessible without boat transportation. These nautical excursions allow you to sense the magnitude of Glaciar Perito Moreno, still from a safe distance. Tours do not include transfers to Parque Nacional Los Glaciares or the park entry fee.

Southern Spirit CRUISE
(☎02902-491582; www.southernspiritfte.com.ar; Libertador 1319, El Calafate; 1hr cruise AR$1800; ⏰9am-1pm & 4-8pm) Southern Spirit has one- to three-hour cruises on Lago Argentino in southern Parque Nacional los Glaciares to see the Perito Moreno Glacier. An active alternative includes hiking.

Glaciar Upsala & Lago Onelli

Glaciar Upsala – a huge 595 sq km, 60km long and 4km wide in parts – can be admired for its monumental dimensions alongside the strange and graceful forms of the nearby icebergs. The downside is that it can only be enjoyed from the crowded deck of a massive catamaran: just nature, you and 300 of your closest friends.

On an extension of the Brazo Norte (North Arm) of Lago Argentino, it's accessible by launch from Puerto Punta Bandera, 45km west of El Calafate by RP 11 and RP 8. Not included in cruise prices is the bus transfer from El Calafate.

Mar Patag CRUISE
(☎02902-492118; www.crucerosmarpatag.com; Libertador 1319, El Calafate; day cruise AR$2550; ⏰7am-9pm) Mar Patag has luxury cruises with a chef serving gourmet meals. The

day trip leaves from the private port of La Soledad and visits Glaciar Upsala, with a four-course meal served on board. The two-day cruise (from US$1050 per person) leaves five times a month and also visits the Mayo and Perito Moreno glaciers. Transfers from El Calafate are not included (AR$550).

Solo Patagonia SA CRUISE
(☎02902-491115; www.solopatagonia.com; Libertador 867, El Calafate; ⏲9am-12:30pm & 4-8pm) Solo Patagonia offers the Rios de Hielo Express (AR$1350) from Puerto Punta Bandera, visiting Glaciar Upsala, Glaciar Spegazzini and Glaciar Perito Moreno. Weather may alter the route. Transfers from El Calafate cost extra (AR$450).

Lago Roca

The serene south arm of Lago Argentino, with lakeshore forests and mountains, features good hikes and pleasant camping. *Estancia* accommodations occupy this section of Parque Nacional Los Glaciares, where most visitors rarely travel. No entrance fee is charged. For transportation, contact Caltur (p457).

Cabalgatas del Glaciar HORSEBACK RIDING
(☎02902-495447; www.cabalgatasdelglaciar.com; full day AR$2250) Cabalgatas del Glaciar runs one-day and multiday riding or trekking trips with glacier panoramas to Lago Roca and Paso Zamora on the Chilean border. Tours include transfer from El Calafate and a steak lunch. There's no office in El Calafate; the tour is sold online and via the Caltur office.

Cerro Cristal HIKING
A rugged but rewarding 3½-hour DIY hike, with views of Glaciar Perito Moreno and the Torres del Paine on clear days. The trail begins at the education camp at La Jerónima, just before the Camping Lago Roca entrance, 55km southwest of El Calafate along RP 15.

Around El Calafate & PN Los Glaciares (South)

Sleeping & Eating

★Camping Lago Roca CAMPGROUND $
(☎02902-499500; www.losglaciares.com/camping lagoroca; per person US$14, cabin dm per 2/4 people US$88/59) This full-service campground with restaurant-bar, located a few kilometers past the education camp, makes an excellent adventure base. The clean concrete-walled dorms provide a snug alternative to camping. Hiking trails abound, and the center rents fishing equipment and bikes, and coordinates horseback riding at the nearby Estancia Nibepo Aike.

★Estancia Cristina ESTANCIA $$$
(☎02902-491133, in Buenos Aires 011-4803-7352; www.estanciacristina.com; d 2 nights incl full board & activities US$1738; ⊙Oct-Apr) Locals in the know say the most outstanding trekking in the region is right here. Lodgings are in bright, modern cabins with expansive views. A visit includes guided activities and boating to Glaciar Upsala. Accessible by boat from Puerto Punta Bandera, off the northern arm of Lago Argentino.

Hostería Estancia Helsingfors ESTANCIA $$$
(☎satellite phone 011-5277-0195; www.helsingfors.com.ar; per person incl full board, transfer & activities US$395; ⊙Oct-Apr) The simply stunning location ogling Cerro Fitz Roy from Lago Viedma makes for lots of love-at-first-sight impressions. Intimate and welcoming, this former Finnish pioneer ranch is a highly regarded luxury destination, though it cultivates a relaxed, unpretentious ambience. Guests pass the time on scenic but demanding mountain treks, rides and visits to Glaciar Viedma.

Transfers are made on Tuesday, Thursday and Sunday, otherwise you can order a chartered van. It's on Lago Viedma's southern shore, 170km from El Chaltén and 180km from El Calafate.

Eolo HOTEL $$$
(☎in Buenos Aires 011-4700-0075; www.eolopatagonia.com; RP 11; d all-inclusive from US$823; 🏊) Ringed by sprawling Patagonian steppe, this luxury Relais & Châeaux property leaves the rustic life outside the double-glazed windows. Guests first see an interior courtyard filled with lavender. There are 17 tasteful guest rooms, a sauna, a small pool and spa services. Beautiful antique *estancia* furniture and a collection of old regional maps and publications set the mood. Prices include transfers, meals and activities.

Estancia Nibepo Aike ESTANCIA $$$
(☎02902-492797, in Buenos Aires 011-5272-0341; www.nibepoaike.com.ar; RP 15, Km60; d per person incl full board & activities from US$152; ⊙Oct-Apr; 📶) This Croatian pioneer ranch, still a working cattle ranch, offers the usual assortment of *estancia* highlights, including demonstrations and horseback riding with bilingual guides. Rooms are simply lovely and high-quality photos give a sense of the regional history. Guests can also explore the surroundings on two wheels from the bicycle stash. Transfers to and from El Calafate are included.

The *estancia* also offers a day-trip excursion (AR$1300) that includes a sheep-shearing demonstration and barbecue, with transfers from El Calafate extra (AR$450 roundtrip).

Adventure Domes CAMPGROUND $$$
(☎02962-493185; http://adventure-domes.com; 2-night all-inclusive d US$360-740) Reviews have been mixed for this all-inclusive nature camp, which features hikes, a glacier cruise and overnights in domes that have comfortable beds, hot-water showers and all meals (lunch boxes for day trips). Provides transfers.

Getting There & Away

The main gateway town to Parque Nacional Los Glaciares' southern sector, El Calafate, is where you'll find most operators for tours and activities. Glaciar Perito Moreno is 80km west of El Calafate via paved RP 11, which passes through the breathtaking scenery around Lago Argentino. Bus tours (AR$650 roundtrip) are frequent in summer. Buses leave El Calafate in the early morning and afternoon, returning around noon and 7pm.

In the park, there is a free shuttle from the parking area to the boardwalks.

Reserva Los Huemules

The private 56-sq-km Reserva Los Huemules has 25km of marked trails, and offers a quiet alternative adjacent to Parque Nacional Los Glaciares. It's an original concept combining a few private residences in an area of conservation with an emphasis on sustainable practices. Guests must stop by the visitor center to check in. Fauna includes the torrent duck, Magellanic woodpecker, condor, red fox and puma. The most notable resident is the endangered huemul deer, which the reserve endeavors to protect through scientific studies and habitat preservation, with breeding areas off-limits to visitors. The addition of Puesto Cagliero, a mountain refuge, opens up overnight treks to see Glaciar Cagliero. A *via ferrata* and glacier treks are slated to follow.

Activities

A moderate trail to **Laguna Diablo** (7km, three hours one way) ends at the alpine lake overlooking Glaciar Cagliero. The mountain refuge is here and there are ice-trekking activities (available through El Chaltén outfitters).

There's a shorter circuit hike to **Laguna Azul**. You can also hike to **Lago Eléctrico**, where trails link to Parque Nacional Los Glaciares.

Sleeping

★**Puesto Cagliero** CABIN $$$
(WhatsApp +54 911-4152-5300; www.puestocagliero.com; s/d/tr/q incl full board US$90/170/250/330) This stylish mountain hut borders an alpine lake facing Glaciar Cagliero, a privileged spot only available to those who make the 7km trek from the information center. The on-site kitchen serves home-cooked meals to guests and some day visitors (by reservation). Shared bunk rooms come with linens and blankets. There are also showers and a wood stove in the living room.It's essential to reserve ahead.

Information

Visitor Center & Museum (9am-6pm) Visitors must register here and pay the park entry fee in order to access trails. There's a great on-site museum with information on the ecosystem and local fauna. It also covers indigenous and pioneer history in the immediate area and the greater region. If no one is here, use the radio to contact a ranger.

Getting There & Away

The reserve is 17km beyond El Chaltén, just after Río Eléctrico. Transporte Las Lengas has vans to Lago del Desierto that can stop here.

CHILEAN PATAGONIA

Rugged seascapes rimmed with glacial peaks, the stunning massifs of Torres del Paine and howling steppe characterize the other side of the Andes. Once you come this far, it is well worth crossing the border. Chilean Patagonia consists of the isolated Aisén and Magallanes regions, separated by the southern continental ice field. This area covers Punta Arenas, Puerto Natales and Parque Nacional Torres del Paine. For in-depth coverage of Chile, pick up Lonely Planet's *Chile & Easter Island*.

Most nationals of countries that have diplomatic relations with Chile don't need a visa. Upon entering, customs officials issue a tourist card, valid for 90 days and renewable for another 90; authorities take it seriously, so guard your card closely to avoid the hassle of replacing it.

Temperature-sensitive travelers will quickly notice a difference after leaving energy-rich Argentina: in public areas and budget accommodations central heating is rare; warmer clothing is the norm indoors.

US cash is not widely accepted. Prices here are given in Chilean pesos (CH$), except where hotels and tour companies list their prices in US dollars.

Punta Arenas

061 / POP 124,500

A sprawling metropolis on the edge of the Strait of Magellan, Punta Arenas defies easy definition. It's a strange combination of the ruddy and the grand, with elaborate wool-boom mansions and port renovations alongside urban sprawl. Magellanic hospitality still pervades local culture, undeterred and even nurtured by nature's inhospitality. Recent prosperity, fed by a petrochemical-industry boom and a growing population, has sanded down the city's former roughneck reputation. Visitors will find it the most convenient base for traveling around the remote Magallanes region, with good traveler services.

Founded in 1848 as a penal settlement and military garrison, Punta Arenas was conveniently situated for ships headed to Alta California during the gold rush. The economy took off in the late 19th century, after the territorial governor authorized the purchase of 300 pure-bred sheep from the Falkland Islands (Islas Malvinas). This experiment encouraged sheep farming and, by the turn of the century, nearly two million grazed the territory.

Sights & Activities

★**Cementerio Municipal** CEMETERY
(main entrance at Av Bulnes 949; 7:30am-8pm) FREE Among South America's most fascinating cemeteries, with both humble

Punta Arenas

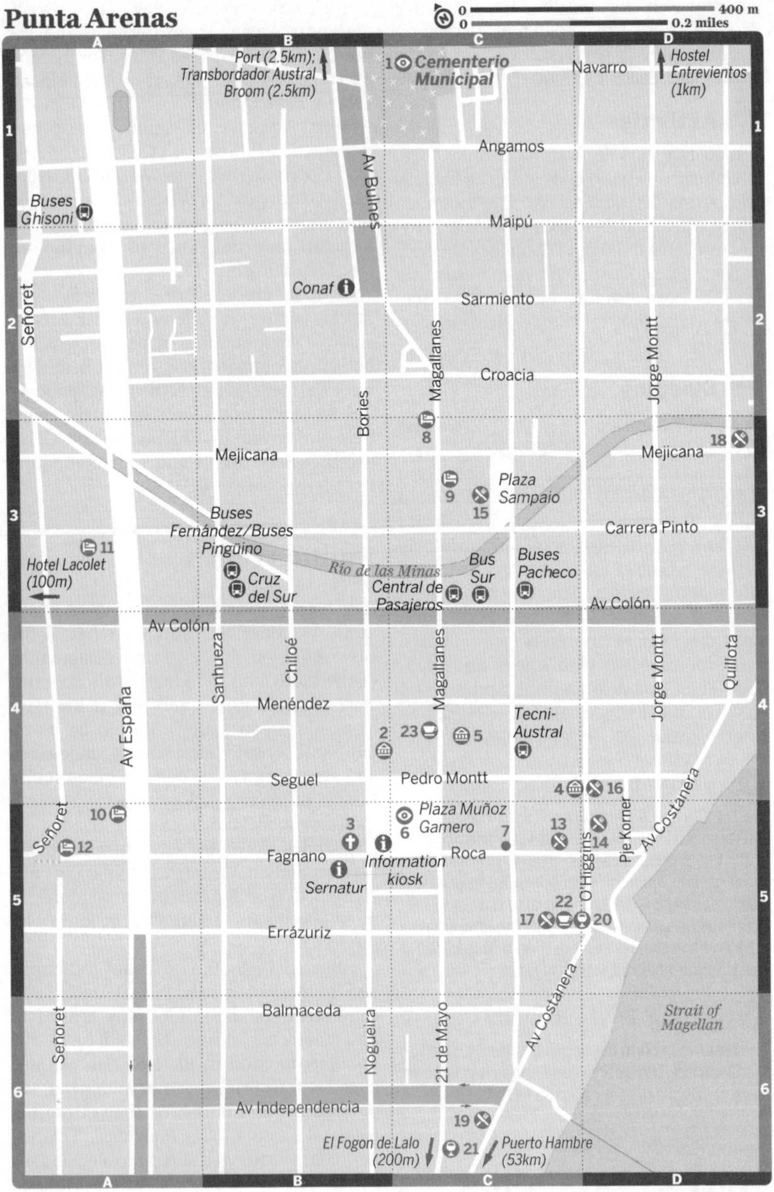

immigrant graves and flashy tombs, like that of wool baron José Menéndez, a scale replica of Rome's Vittorio Emanuele monument, according to author Bruce Chatwin. See the map inside the main entrance gate.

It's an easy 15-minute stroll northeast of the plaza, or catch any taxi *colectivo* (shared taxi with specific route) in front of the Museo Regional Braun-Menéndez on Magallanes.

Museo Regional de Magallanes MUSEUM
(Museo Regional Braun-Menéndez; ☎61-224-4216; www.museodemagallanes.cl; Magallanes 949; ⏲10:30am-5pm Wed-Mon, to 2pm May-Dec) **FREE**

Punta Arenas

This opulent mansion testifies to the wealth and power of pioneer sheep farmers in the late 19th century. The well-maintained interior houses a regional historical museum (ask for booklets in English) and original exquisite French-nouveau family furnishings, from intricate wooden inlaid floors to Chinese vases. In former servants' quarters, a downstairs cafe is perfect for a pisco sour while soaking up the grandeur.

Museo Naval y Marítimo MUSEUM
(61-220-5479; www.museonaval.cl; Pedro Montt 981; adult/child CH$1000/300; 9:30am-12:30pm & 2-5pm Tue-Sat) A naval and maritime museum with historical exhibits that include a fine account of the Chilean mission that rescued Sir Ernest Shackleton's crew from Antarctica. The most imaginative display is a replica ship complete with bridge, maps, charts and radio room.

Plaza Muñoz Gamero PLAZA
A central plaza of magnificent conifers surrounded by opulent mansions. Facing the plaza's north side, **Casa Braun-Menéndez** (61-224-1489; 10:30am-1pm & 5-8:30pm Tue-Fri, 10:30am-1pm & 8-10pm Sat, 11am-2pm Sun) FREE houses the private Club de la Unión, which also uses the tavern downstairs (open to the public). The nearby **monument** commemorating the 400th anniversary of Magellan's voyage was donated by wool baron José Menéndez in 1920. Just east is the former **Sociedad Menéndez Behety**, which now houses Turismo Comapa. The **cathedral** sits west.

Museo Rio Seco MUSEUM
(cell 9-5335-0707; www.museodehistorianaturalrioseco.org; Rio Seco; 3-6pm Mon-Fri, 10am-noon & 3pm-6pm Sat & Sun) FREE The pet project of the Caceres brothers, this funky homespun museum is a delightful detour for fans of natural history. Imaginative displays use fine naturalist drawings and painstakingly restored skeletons of seabirds, sea lions and whales to give a picture of life on the strait. Call ahead before visiting, as they might be cleaning whale bones out back.

Volunteers are welcome with a one-week minimum.

Reserva Forestal Magallanes PARK
(daylight hours) FREE Great hiking and mountain biking through dense lenga and coihue, 8km from town.

Tours

Torres del Paine tours are abundant from Punta Arenas, but the distance makes for a very long day; it's best to organize transport from Puerto Natales.

Worthwhile day trips include visits to **Parque del Estrecho de Magallanes** (61-272-3195; www.phipa.cl; Km56 Sur; adult/child CH$14,000/6000; 9:30am-5:15pm), with the town's first settlements at Fuerte Bulnes and Puerto Hambre. Most lodgings will help arrange tours – if they don't run their own.

If you have the time, a more atmospheric alternative to Seno Otway is the Magellanic-penguin colonies of Monumento Natural Los Pingüinos (p475) on Isla Magdalena.

1

2

BLUESNAPS/SHUTTERSTOCK ©

Trekking on the Glacier Perito Moreno (p464) **2.** Ruta
acional 40 **3.** Ice climbers on the Glaciar Perito Moreno

Extreme Patagonia

More than 130 years ago, Lady Florence Dixie ditched high society to ride horses across the Patagonian steppe. Today, you can still fulfill a dream of scaling unnamed peaks, paddling alongside sea lions or tracing a glacier's edge.

Horseback Riding

Estancias (ranches) remind us how good it is to ride without fences, to feel the heat of a campfire and to sleep under the stars.

Ice Climbing

Adrenaline, check. Thrill seekers can ice climb or ice trek on Glaciar Perito Moreno, in the northern part of Parque Nacional Los Glaciares (p451).

Glacier Trekking

More than a hike, it's a full-immersion aesthetic experience. Strap on crampons and explore these living sculptures in Torres del Paine or Parque Nacional Los Glaciares. Another option for ice trekking is at Reserva Los Huemules (p466), near El Chaltén, with the activity newly available on Glaciar Cagliero.

Diving

Clear waters, nearby shipwrecks and cool marine life make Península Valdés (p408) the diving capital of Argentina, with the best visibility in August.

Sea Kayaking

Paddle with penguins and Commerson's dolphins in Ría Deseado (p426) and Bahía Bustamante (p422), or play alongside sea lions near Península Valdés (p408).

Driving Ruta Nacional 40

Watch herds of dusky guanaco, or the slow approach of shimmering peaks; the sky was never bluer or bigger than on this remote road, an icon of slow travel that flanks the Andes.

THE STORY OF THE GLACIERS

Ribbons of ice, stretched flat in sheets or sculpted by weather and fissured by pressure, glaciers have a raw magnificence that is mind-boggling to behold.

As snow falls on the accumulation area, it compacts to ice. The river of ice is slugged forward by gravity, which deforms its layers as it moves. When the glacier surges downhill, melted ice mixes with rock and soil on the bottom, grinding it into a lubricant that keeps pushing the glacier along. At the same time, debris from the crushed rock is forced to the sides of the glacier, creating features called moraines. Movement also causes cracks and deformities called crevasses.

The ablation area is where the glacier melts. When accumulation outpaces melting at the ablation area, the glacier advances; when there's more melting or evaporation, the glacier recedes. Since 1980 global warming has contributed greatly to widespread glacial retreat.

Another marvel of glaciers is their hue. What makes some blue? Wavelengths and air bubbles. The more compact the ice, the longer the path that light has to travel and the bluer the ice appears. Air bubbles in uncompacted areas absorb long wavelengths of white light so we see white. When glaciers calve into lakes, they dump a 'glacial flour' composed of ground-up rock that gives the water a milky, grayish color. This same sediment remains unsettled in some lakes and diffracts the sun's light, creating a stunning palette of turquoise, pale mint and azure.

Kayak Agua Fresca KAYAKING
(☎ cell 9-9655-5073; www.kayakaguafresca.com; 4½hr tour CH$70,000) On the rare day in Punta Arenas when winds are calm and the sea is glass, the sea kayaking can be spectacular. This company also does zodiac boat excursions. There's no office; see the website for information.

Turismo Aonikenk TOURS
(☎ 61-222-8616; Magallanes 570) Now only organizing trips with visitors in person, this recommended agency offers Cabo Froward treks, visits to the king-penguin colony in Tierra del Fuego, and cheaper open expeditions geared at experienced participants. With English-, German- and French-speaking guides.

Sleeping

Hostel Entrevientos HOSTEL $
(☎ 61-237-1171; www.hostelentrevientos.cl; Jorge Montt 0690; incl breakfast dm US$21, d/tr US$56/80; wi-fi) Near the sparkling waterfront, this spacious A-frame has commanding sea views from an ultra-cozy 2nd-floor living room. There's an ample guest kitchen, and dorm rooms and snug private rooms downstairs. It's warmly attended by the owners, who also rent bikes (CH$7000 per day). The downside: it's a 25-minute walk to the center, but buses also go.

Hotel Lacolet BOUTIQUE HOTEL $$
(☎ 61-222-2045; www.lacolet.cl; Arauco 786; d incl breakfast US$125-145; P wi-fi) On the foothills of the Cerro de la Cruz lookout, this gorgeous brick heritage house has parquet floors and five comfortable rooms with TVs, and hairdryers in the tiled bathrooms. Service is good and the buffet breakfast easily stands among Patagonia's best, serving four types of homemade bread, local rhubarb jam, eggs, fruit and deli meats and cheeses.

On the cruise-ship circuit, Punta Arenas has a plethora of hotels but few bargains. Foreigners are not required to pay the additional 18% IVA charge if paying with US cash or credit card. Low season (mid-April to mid-October), prices drop. Rates include breakfast.

Hospedaje Magallanes B&B $$
(☎ 61-222-8616; www.hospedaje-magallanes.com; Magallanes 570; d CH$60,000, dm/d without bathroom CH$20,000/45,000; @ wi-fi) A great inexpensive option run by a German-Chilean couple who are also Torres del Paine guides with an on-site travel agency. With just a few quiet rooms, there are often communal dinners or backyard barbecues by the climbing wall. Breakfast includes brown bread and strong coffee.

Hotel Patagonia HOTEL $$
(☎ 61-222-7243; www.patagoniabb.cl; Av España 1048; d incl breakfast US$85-125; P wi-fi) A solid midrange option offering no-nonsense rooms with crisp white linens and simple style. Service could be a few degrees warmer.

It's accessed via a long driveway behind the main building.

★Ilaia Hotel BOUTIQUE HOTEL **$$$**
(61-272-3100; www.ilaia.cl; Carrera Pinto 351; s/d/tr incl breakfast US$110/150/200; Sep-Apr; P) Playful and modern, this high-concept boutique hotel is run with family warmth. Sly messages are written to be read in mirrors, rooms are simple and chic and an incredible glass study gazes out on the strait. Offers massage and healthy breakfasts with chapati bread, homemade jam, avocados, yogurt and more. But you won't find a television. Recycles and composts.

★La Yegua Loca BOUTIQUE HOTEL **$$$**
(61-237-1734; www.yegualoca.com; Fagnano 310; r US$200-220) Immerse yourself in regional lore at this gorgeous boutique hotel with relics from ranching life repurposed as clever fixtures and decor. Ample rooms play with themes such as shearing sheds, carpentry workshops and milking halls, all with comfortable beds and central heating. The service is attentive. It sits on a hillside with great views of the city; there's an on-site restaurant.

Hostal Innata GUESTHOUSE **$$$**
(cell 9-6279-4254; www.innatapatagonia.com; Magallanes 631; d/apt CH$97,000/120,000; P) This pleasant and central guesthouse consists of a stylish home with 11 guest rooms with down duvets and LED TVs, and a new block of apartments out back. Breakfast is available at the hour you request it and there are box-breakfasts for early tours. Reserve ahead.

Eating

Punta Arenas has a wide range of eating options, from budget to gourmet. Local seafood is an exquisite treat: go for *centolla* (king crab) between July and November or *erizos* (sea urchins) between November and July.

La Vianda MARKET **$**
(Errázuriz 928; snacks CH$4000; 10:30am-6:30pm Mon-Fri) The first stop for picnickers or those soon to climb aboard a long-distance bus, this market does a variety of excellent breads, including sweet varieties and sourdough, all-natural soups and fresh rhubarb juice and jams. Decent pre-made sandwiches are on offer too.

Mercado Municipal MARKET **$**
(21 de Mayo 1465; mains CH$3000-6000; 8am-3pm) Fish and vegetable market with cheap 2nd-floor *cocinerías* (eateries), a great place for inexpensive seafood dishes.

La Mesita Grande PIZZA **$**
(61-224-4312; O'Higgins 1001; mains CH$4000-9000; noon-11pm Mon-Sat, 1pm-8pm Sun) If you're homesick for Brooklyn, La Mesita Grande might do the trick. This mod exposed-brick pizzeria serves them up thin and chewy, with organic toppings and pints of local brew. Also has awesome Caesar salads. Save room for its homemade ice cream. The original outlet is in **Puerto Natales** (cell 9-6141-1571; www.mesitagrande.cl; Arturo Prat 196; pizza CH$4000-9000; 12:30-3pm & 7-11:30pm Mon-Sat, 1-3pm & 7-11:30pm Sun).

Los Inmigrantes CAFE **$**
(61-222-2205; www.inmigrante.cl; Quillota 559; mains CH$5000; 2:30-9pm) In the historic Croatian neighborhood, this cafe serves decadent cakes in a room full of interesting relics from Dalmatian immigrants.

Café Almacen Tapiz CAFE **$**
(cell 9-8730-3481; www.cafetapiz.cl; Roca 912; mains CH$5000; 9am-9:30pm;) Cloaked in alerce shingles, this lively cafe makes for an ambient tea break. In addition to gorgeous layer cakes, there are salads and pita sandwiches with goat cheese, meats or roasted veggies.

La Marmita CHILEAN **$$**
(61-222-2056; www.marmitamaga.cl; Plaza Sampaio 678; mains CH$8000-12,000; 12:30-3pm & 6:30-11:30pm Mon-Sat;) This classic bistro enjoys wild popularity for its playful ambience and tasty fare. Besides fresh salads and hot bread, hearty dishes such as casseroles or seafood hark back to grandma's cooking, Chilean style. With good vegetarian options and take-out service.

La Cuisine FRENCH **$$**
(61-222-8641; O'Higgins 1037; mains CH$8000-13,000; 12:30-2:45pm & 7:30-11pm Mon-Sat) If you're craving veggies beyond the trusted potato, this plain-Jane French restaurant is a good bet. Seafood dishes come with sautéed vegetables, green salad or ratatouille. There's also homemade pâté, and wine by the glass is cheap.

Drinking & Nightlife

★Bodega 87 BAR
(☎61-237-1357; 21 de Mayo 1469; ⊙8:30pm-1:30am Sun-Thu, to 2:30am Fri & Sat) A fine addition to the city, this neighborhood bar is friendly and bubbling with life. There are memorable craft cocktails and local beer. Try a not-too-sweet calafate mojito.

Bar Clinic PUB
(☎61-237-1250; Errázuriz 970; ⊙6pm-2:30am Mon-Sat) This gorgeous corner pub with leather details and polished floors has had nine lives: in its current incarnation it is a franchise outlet of the Santiago bar named for the humorous political newspaper. However, the intriguing backstory isn't evident to a casual visitor, but the drinks are OK, and half-price from 6pm to 9pm Monday through Thursday.

Meraki Cafe COFFEE
(☎61-224-4097; Magallanes 922; ⊙9am-8pm Mon-Sat) If you're picky about espresso, beeline to this unassuming cafe and roaster also serving sandwiches and cakes. For those traveling on to bleaker coffee pastures, it's well worth nabbing a bag of its single-origin beans (ground, if you wish) for the road.

Cafe Wake Up COFFEE
(☎61-237-1641; Errázuriz 944; ⊙7am-8pm Mon-Fri, 9am-4pm Sat, 10am-4pm Sun) If you've lost your hipster in Magallanes, he's probably hanging out at this industrial-chic cafe with a double latte in hand. There's also some light fare that's reasonably priced.

Information

Banks with ATMs dot the city center. **Sur Cambios** (☎61-271-0317; Navarro 1001; ⊙9am-7pm Mon-Fri, 9:30am-1pm Sat) exchanges money, as do some travel agencies.

Sernatur has a list of recommended doctors. Get medical care at the **Hospital Regional** (☎61-220-5000; cnr Arauco & Angamos).

Police (☎61-224-1714; Errázuriz 977)

Sernatur (☎61-224-1330; www.sernatur.cl; Fagnano 643; ⊙8:30am-6pm Mon-Fri, 10am-4pm Sat) With friendly, well-informed, multilingual staff and lists of accommodations and transportation. Reduced hours in low season.

Information kiosk (☎61-220-0610; Plaza Muñoz Gamero; ⊙8am-7pm Mon-Sat, 9am-7pm Sun Dec-Feb) Tourist information on the south side of the plaza.

Conaf (☎61-223-0681; Av Bulnes 0309; ⊙9am-5pm Mon-Fri) Has details on nearby parks.

Getting There & Away

The tourist offices distribute a useful brochure that details all forms of transport available.

AIR

Punta Arenas' airport (PUQ) is 21km north of town.

Aerovías DAP (p463) offers Antarctica tours (full day US$5500), charter flights over Cabo de Hornos and to other Patagonian destinations, including Ushuaia and Calafate, Argentina. From November to March, flights run to Porvenir (CH$55,000 round-trip) Monday through Saturday several times daily, to Pampa Guanaco in Tierra del Fuego, and to Puerto Williams (CH$143,000 round-trip) Monday through Saturday at 10am. Luggage is limited to 10kg per person.

Sky Airline (☎61-271-0645; www.skyairline.cl; Roca 935) and **LATAM** (☎61-224-1100; www.latam.com; Bories 884) serve Puerto Montt and Santiago. At the time of writing, LATAM was expected to add flights to Ushuaia. Aerolineas Argentinas has flights within and sometimes to Argentina.

BOAT

Transbordador Austral Broom (☎61-272-8100; www.tabsa.cl; Av Bulnes 05075) operates three ferries to Tierra del Fuego. The car and passenger ferry to/from Porvenir (CH$6200/39,800 per person/vehicle, 2½ to four hours) usually leaves at 9am but has some afternoon departures; check the current online schedule. From Punta Arenas, it's faster to do the Primera Angostura crossing (CH$1700/15,000 per person/vehicle, 20 minutes), northeast of Punta Arenas, which sails every 90 minutes between 8:30am and 11:45pm. Broom sets sail for Isla Navarino's Puerto Williams (reclining seat/bunk CH$108,000/151,000 including meals, 30 hours) three or four times per month on Thursday only, returning Saturday.

Cruceros Australis (☎in Santiago 2-442-3110; www.australis.com; ⊙Sep-May) runs luxurious four-day and five-day sightseeing cruises to Ushuaia and back. **Turismo Comapa** (☎61-220-0200; www.comapa.com; Lautaro Navarro 1112; ⊙9am-1pm & 2:30-6:30pm Mon-Fri) handles local bookings.

BUS

Buses depart from company offices, most within a block or two of Av Colón. Buy tickets several hours (if not days) in advance. The **Central de Pasajeros** (☎61-224-5811; cnr Magallanes & Av Colón) is the closest thing to a central booking office.

For Puerto Natales, try **Buses Fernandez** (☎61-224-2313; www.busesfernandez.com;

Sanhueza 745) or **Bus Sur** (☎61-261-4224; www.bus-sur.cl; Av Colón 842).

For Argentina, try **Buses Ghisoni** (☎61-224-0646; www.busesbarria.cl; Av España 264), **Buses Pacheco** (☎61-224-2174; www.busespacheco.com; Av Colón 900) and **Tecni-Austral** (☎61-222-2078; Navarro 975).

For Chile's Lake District, try **Cruz del Sur** (☎61-222-7970; www.busescruzdelsur.cl; Sanhueza 745).

Buses from Punta Arenas

DESTINATION	COST (CH$)	TIME (HR)
Osorno	35,000	30
Puerto Natales	7000	3
Río Gallegos	20,000	5-8
Río Grande	30,000	7
Ushuaia	35,000	10

Getting Around

TO/FROM THE AIRPORT

Buses depart directly from the airport to Puerto Natales. Buses Fernández does regular airport transfers (CH$4000).

BUS & TAXI COLECTIVO

Taxi colectivos, with numbered routes, are only slightly more expensive than buses (about CH$500, or a bit more late at night and on Sundays), but more comfortable and much quicker.

CAR

Cars are a good option for exploring Torres del Paine, but renting one in Chile to cross the border into Argentina gets expensive due to international insurance requirements. If heading to El Calafate, rent your vehicle in Argentina.

Punta Arenas has Chilean Patagonia's most economical rental rates, and locally owned agencies tend to provide better service. Recommended **Adel Rent a Car** (☎61-222-4819; www.adelrentacar.cl; Pedro Montt 962; ⏰9:30am-1pm & 3:30-6pm Mon-Fri, 9:30am-1pm Sat) provides attentive service, competitive rates, airport pickup and good travel tips. Other choices include **Hertz** (☎61-224-8742; O'Higgins 987) and **Lubag** (☎61-271-0484; www.lubag.cl; Magallanes 970).

Monumento Natural Los Pingüinos

The thriving Magellanic penguin colonies of **Monumento Natural Los Pingüinos** (www.conaf.cl/parques/monumento-natural-los-pinguinos; adult/child CH$7000/3500; ⏰Nov-Mar) on Isla Magdalena and Isla Marta are well worth visiting, particularly if you have never seen penguins before. The islands are 35km northeast of Punta Arenas. Five-hour ferry tours (adult/child CH$50,000/25,000) take 1.5 hours and land for an hour at the island; they depart the port on Tuesday, Thursday and Saturday, December through February. Confirm times in advance. Book tickets through Turismo Comapa and bring a picnic.

Parque Nacional Pali Aike

Rugged volcanic steppe pocked with craters, caves and twisted formations, Pali Aike means 'devil's country' in Tehuelche. This desolate landscape is a 50-sq-km **park** (www.conaf.cl/parques/parque-nacional-pali-aike; adult/child under 12yr CH$3000/1000) along the Argentine border. Mineral content made lava rocks red, yellow or green-gray. Fauna includes abundant guanaco, ñandú, gray fox and armadillo. In the 1930s Junius Bird's excavations at 17m-deep **Pali Aike Cave** yielded the first artifacts associated with extinct New World fauna such as the milodón and the native horse *Onohippidium*.

The park has several trails, including a 1.7km path through the rugged lava beds of the **Escorial del Diablo** to the impressive **Crater Morada del Diablo**; wear sturdy shoes or your feet could be shredded. There are hundreds of craters, some four stories high. A 9km trail from Cueva Pali Aike to **Laguna Ana** links a shorter trail to a site on the main road, 5km from the park entrance.

Parque Nacional Pali Aike is 200km northeast of Punta Arenas via RN 9, Ch 255 and a graveled secondary road from Cooperativa Villa O'Higgins, 11km north of Estancia Kimiri Aike. There's also access from the Chilean border post at Monte Aymond. There is no public transport, but Punta Arenas travel agencies offer full-day tours.

Puerto Natales

☎61 / POP 18,000

A formerly modest fishing port on Seno Ùltima Esperanza, Puerto Natales has blossomed into a Gore-Tex mecca. The gateway to Parque Nacional Torres del Paine, this town feeds off tourism, an all-you-can-eat feast with unwavering demand. Boutique beers and wine tastings have overtaken tea time, and gear shops have replaced the yarn sellers. While there are growing services that cater to international tastes, there's appeal in Natales' corrugated-tin houses strung shoulder to shoulder and cozy granny-style lodgings. Most notably, in spite of a near-constant swarm of visitors, the town still maintains the glacial pace of living endemic to Patagonia.

Puerto Natales sits on the shores of Seno Última Esperanza, 250km northwest of Punta Arenas via Ruta 9, and has some striking views out over the mountains. It is the capital of the province of Última Esperanza and the southern terminus of the ferry trip through the Chilean fjords.

Sights & Activities

Museo Histórico MUSEUM
(☎61-241-1263; Bulnes 28; CH$1000; ⊙8am-7pm Mon-Fri, 10am-1pm & 3-7pm Sat & Sun) Worth a quick visit, this is a crash course in local history, with archaeological artifacts, a Yaghan canoe, Tehuelche bolas and historical photos.

Estancia La Peninsula OUTDOORS
(☎cell 9-6303-6497; www.estanciaspatagonia.com; Peninsula Antonio Varas; day tour CH$130,000) Run by a family with pioneer roots in the region, this classic *estancia* across the water offers day visits that include hiking or riding, herding-dog and sheep-shearing demonstrations and an awesome barbecue lunch of spit-roasted lamb. There are also excellent multiday hiking options with a remote feel. The meeting place is the dock at Singular Hotel.

Mandala Andino SPA
(☎cell 9-9930-2997; mandalaandino@yahoo.com; Bulnes 301; massages from CH$25,000; ⊙10am-9pm Nov-Mar) A recommended full-service wellness center with spot-on massages, tub soaks and various pampering treatments, including cannabis-oil massages. Also sells interesting gifts and local crafts.

Tours

Antares/Bigfoot Patagonia ADVENTURE
(☎61-241-4611; www.antarespatagonia.com; Costanera 161, Av Pedro Montt; Lago Grey kayaking CH$66,000) Specializing in Torres del Paine, Antares can facilitate climbing permits and made-to-order trips. Its sister company Big Foot has the park concession for Lago Grey activities, including Glacier Grey ice-trekking and kayak trips, with a base in the park.

Baqueano Zamora HORSE RIDING
(☎61-261-3530; www.baqueanozamora.cl; Baquedano 534; ⊙10am-1pm & 3-7pm) Runs recommended horseback-riding trips and wild-horse viewing in Torres del Paine.

Pingo Salvaje HORSE RIDING
(☎cell 9-6236-0371; www.pingosalvaje.com; Estancia Laguna Sofia; half-day horse ride CH$40,000; ⊙Oct-Apr) This lovely *estancia* getaway offers horseback riding and condor spotting. You can stay over in a comfortable shared cabin (CH$22,000 per person; bring a sleeping bag) or campsite (CH$8000 per person) under a stand of trees, outfitted with grills, tables and hot showers. It's 30km from Puerto Natales; transport costs CH$12,000 per person.

Chile Nativo ADVENTURE
(☎61-241-1835, cell 9-9078-9168; www.chilenativo.cl; Eberhard 230, 2nd fl) Links visitors with local gauchos, organizes photo safaris and can competently plan your tailor-made dream adventures.

Turismo 21 de Mayo TOURS
(☎61-261-4420; www.turismo21demayo.com; Eberhard 560; ⊙8am-10pm Oct-Mar) Organizes day-trip cruises and treks to the Balmaceda and Serrano glaciers (CH$90,000) and horseback riding on Cerro Dorotea (CH$30,000), just outside Puerto Natales.

Sleeping

Options abound, most with breakfast, laundry, and discounted rates in the low season. Reserve ahead from November through March. Hostels often rent equipment and help arrange park transport.

★**Wild Patagonia** HOSTEL $
(☎cell 9-7715-2423; www.wildhostel.com; Bulnes 555; incl breakfast d US$85, dm/d without bathroom US$24/70; ⊙Sep-Apr; 📶) Emanating happy vibes, this hostel has pleasant rooms, with tin-clad cabins around a courtyard with a fire pit. Breakfast includes fresh bread, yogurt and jam. Open to the public from 3pm on, the cafe serves great local beef burgers and often features live music at night. The polyglot owners speak a heap of languages and orient guests on park services.

With equipment rental.

★**Vinn Haus** BOUTIQUE HOTEL $
(☎cell 9-8269-2510; http://vinnhaus.com; Bulnes 499; dm/d incl breakfast US$24/80; ⊙Sep-May; 📶) Taking dormitory living to a new level, this Chilean-Finnish enterprise employs a gorgeous vintage concept with old suitcases, antique tiles and pleated leather. Each

bunk has its own USB outlet, and outlets for various plug designs. The wine bar and cafe serves some of the best coffee this side of Colombia. With buffet breakfast and a cute courtyard for lounging.

Singing Lamb HOSTEL $
(☎61-241-0958; www.thesinginglamb.com; Arauco 779; incl breakfast dm US$23-28, d US$80; @📶) 🍃 A clean and green hostel with compost, recycling, rainwater collection and linen shopping bags. Dorm rooms are priced by the number of beds (maximum nine) and shared spaces are ample. Nice touches include central heating and homemade breakfasts. To get here, follow Raimírez one block past Plaza O'Higgins.

Hostal Dos Lagunas GUESTHOUSE $
(☎cell 9-8162-7755; hostaldoslagunas@gmail.com; cnr Barros Arana & Bories; dm/d without bathroom & incl breakfast CH$13,000/$35,000; 📶) Natales natives Alejandro and Andrea are attentive hosts, spoiling guests with filling breakfasts, steady water pressure and travel tips. Among the town's most longstanding lodgings, the place is spotless.

We Are Patagonia B&B $
(☎cell 9-7389-4802; www.wearepatagonia.com; Barros Arana 155; dm incl breakfast US$25; 📶) A lovely art hostel with minimalist Nordic charm and a grassy backyard. The small house has mixed dorms with 30 beds with down duvet covers, four bathrooms and a small open kitchen. Reception is 24-hours and it rents bikes (CH$2000 per hour).

Hotel Vendaval BOUTIQUE HOTEL $$
(☎61-269-1760; http://hotelvendaval.com; Eberhard 333; d incl breakfast US$125; 📶) Ushering in a new generation of lodgings in Puerto Natales, Vendaval is a Natalino-owned metal-clad beauty, with polished-concrete floors, folkloric Chilean etchings and art with maritime themes. Its 23 rooms are spread over four floors, with central heating, glass showers and cozy down bedding. There are panoramic views from the roof terrace, and a restaurant was in the works at the time of research.

Kau B&B $$
(☎61-241-4611; www.kaulodge.com; Costanera 161, Av Pedro Montt; d incl breakfast CH$72,000-88,500; 📶❄) 🍃 With a mantra of simplicity, this aesthetic remake of a box hotel is cozy and cool. Thick woolen throws, picnic-table breakfast seating and well-worn, recycled wood lend casual intimacy. Rooms boast fjord views, central heating, bulk toiletries, and safe boxes. The **Coffee Maker** espresso bar boasts killer lattes and staff have tons of adventure information on tap.

★ **Singular Hotel** BOUTIQUE HOTEL $$$
(☎61-241-4040, bookings in Santiago 22-387-1500; www.thesingular.com; RN 9, Km1.5; d incl breakfast US$530, d incl full board & excursions US$1630; P@📶❄) A regional landmark reimagined, the Singular is a former meat-packing and shipping facility on the sound. Heightened industrial design, like chairs fashioned from old radiators in the lobby, mixes with vintage photos and antiques. The snug glass-walled rooms have water views, and a well-respected bar-restaurant (alongside the museum; open to the public) serves fresh local game.

Guests can use the spa with pool and explore the surroundings by bike or kayak. It's located in Puerto Bories, 6km from the center.

Simple Patagonia BOUTIQUE HOTEL $$$
(☎cell 9-9640-0512; www.simplepatagonia.cl; Puerto Bories; d incl breakfast US$250-290; 📶) 🍃 Emanating tranquility, this modern lodge employs recycled light posts, polished concrete and raw lenga details with lovely results. It's family run by warm Chileans, with 11 rooms with safes, hairdryers, radiant heat and sea views. The on-site restaurant offers gourmet dinners and breakfast when you want it. There are also bicycles for use. It's 4.5km from Puerto Natales. These rates allow a free change of date.

Hotel IF Patagonia BOUTIQUE HOTEL $$$
(☎61-241-0312; www.hotelifpatagonia.com; Magallanes 73; s/d incl breakfast US$150/160; P📶) 🍃 Brimming with hospitality, IF (for Isabel and Fernando) is minimalist and lovely. Its bright, modern interior includes wool throws, down duvets and deck views of the fjord. There are also a garden sauna and a wooden hot tub.

Eating

Cafe Kaiken CHILEAN $
(☎cell 9-8295-2036; Baquedano 699; mains CH$7800-11,000; ⏰1-3:30pm & 6:30-11pm Mon-Sat) With just five tables and one couple cooking, serving and chatting up customers, this is as intimate as it gets. The owners moved here to get out of the Santiago fast lane, so you'd best follow their lead. Dishes

Puerto Natales

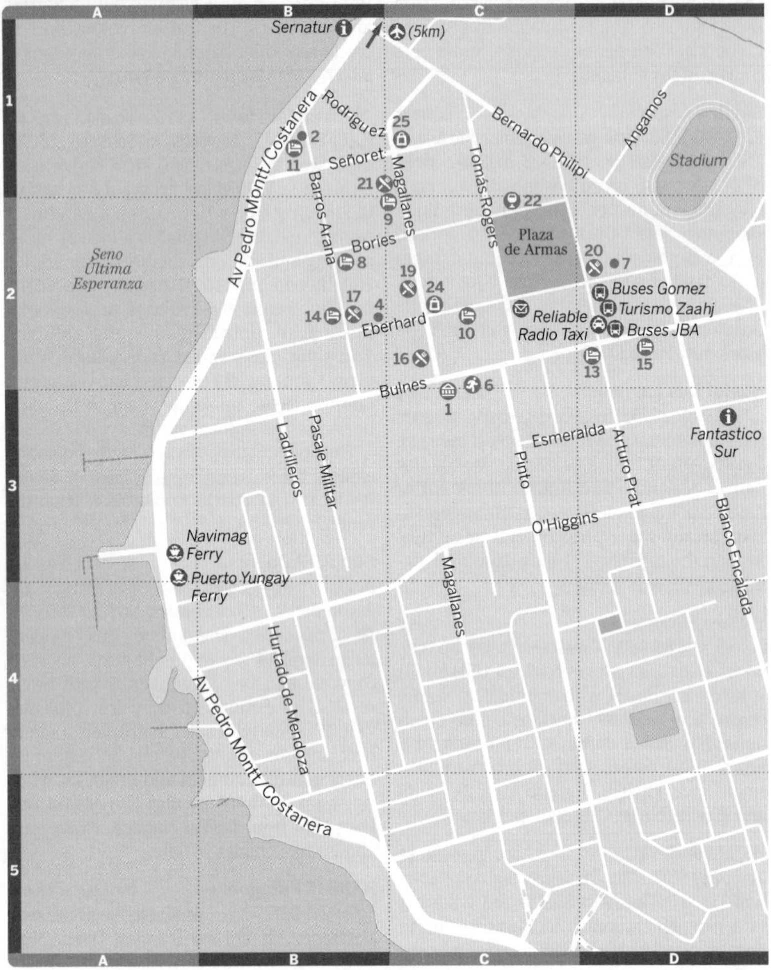

such as mushroom ceviche, slow-roasted lamb or homemade ravioli are well worth the wait. Arrive early to claim a spot.

La Forestera BURGERS $

(cell 9-7389-4802; Barros Arana 155; mains CH$6900; 1-3pm & 7:30-11pm Tue-Sun) These gorgeous gourmet burgers do disappear fast. Tasty regular and lamb burgers or lentil and beet alternatives are served on airy brioche buns. It also does super-spicy wings and crisp onion rings, well matched with a local brew. There are just a few tables but also takeout service.

Aluen ICE CREAM $

(Barros Arana 160; ice cream CH$2000; 2-7:30pm Tue-Sun) Delicious flavors like tart natural yogurt, *arroz con leche* (rice pudding) and calafate berry are made on-site.

La Guanaca PIZZA $$

(61-241-3245; Magallanes 167; mains CH$5000-16,000;) From crisp oven-fired pizzas to crepes and marinated mushroom appetizers, this homespun restaurant delivers warming and satisfying meals. Oversized salads, like the quinoa with roasted vegetables, are abundant and varied. There's craft beer and several wines to choose from.

Puerto Natales

Sights
1 Museo Histórico.......C3

Activities, Courses & Tours
2 Antares/Bigfoot Patagonia.......B1
3 Baqueano Zamora.......E3
4 Chile Nativo.......B2
5 Erratic Rock.......E5
6 Mandala Andino.......C2
7 Turismo 21 de Mayo.......D2

Sleeping
8 Hostal Dos Lagunas.......B2
9 Hotel IF Patagonia.......C2
10 Hotel Vendaval.......C2
11 Kau.......B1
12 Singing Lamb.......E5
13 Vinn Haus.......D2
14 We Are Patagonia.......B2
15 Wild Patagonia.......D2

Eating
16 Afrigonia.......C2
17 Aluen.......B2
18 Cafe Kaiken.......E4
La Forestera.......(see 14)
19 La Guanaca.......C2
20 La Mesita Grande.......D2
21 Santolla.......B1

Drinking & Nightlife
22 Baguales.......C2
23 Last Hope.......E2

Shopping
24 Oneaco.......C2
25 Wine & Market.......C1

Afrigonia FUSION **$$**
(☎61-241-2877; Magallanes 247; mains CH$12,000-14,000; ⌚1-3pm & 6:30-11pm) Outstanding and wholly original, you won't find Afro-Chilean cuisine on any NYC menu. This romantic gem serves up fragrant rice, fresh ceviche and mint roasted lamb prepared with succulent precision. Desserts also hit the mark. Make reservations.

★ **Singular Restaurant** CHILEAN **$$$**
(☎61-272-2030; Puerto Bories; mains CH$12,000-18,000; ⌚8am-11pm) The perfect port in a storm, part supper club of yore, part modern bistro, with exquisite food and attentive service. Leather sofas and polished wood meet bare beams and stark views of the sound. Chef Hernan Vaso reinvigorates local ingredients: the freshest ceviche, tender lamb medallions and lovely salads come with original sides and fine Chilean wines. Vegetarian options excel.

★ **Santolla** SEAFOOD **$$$**
(☎61-241-3493; Magallanes 77; mains CH$15,000-22,000; ⌚7-11pm Mon-Sat) For worthwhile upscale seafood, look no further than this cozy container restaurant attended by the owner. Feast on gorgeous salads and local king crab prepared several ways; we liked it with *merken* (smoked chilli), white wine and parsley. Non-seafood eaters have options such as steak or rabbit in black-truffle sauce.

Drinking & Nightlife

★Last Hope DISTILLERY

(☎cell 9-7201-8585; www.lasthopedistillery.com; Esmeralda 882; ⏲5pm-2am Wed-Sun) Two Australians on vacation tossed their day jobs to distill whiskey and gin at the end of the world. With bonhomie to spare, their bar caters to locals and travelers alike with a rotating menu of gorgeous cocktails. The signature drink is a calafate berry gin and tonic. It's tiny and the overflow waits outside – wear your down jacket.

Baguales MICROBREWERY

(www.cervezabaguales.cl; Bories 430; ⏲6pm-2:30am Mon-Sat; 📶) Climber friends started this microbrewery as a noble quest for quality suds and the beer (crafted on-site) does not disappoint. A 2nd-floor addition seeks to meet the heavy demand. The gringo-style bar food is just so-so.

Shopping

Wine & Market WINE

(☎61-269-1138; www.wmpatagonia.cl; Magallanes 46; tasting CH$20,000; ⏲10am-10pm Mon-Sat) Picnickers should pop in here for a range of tasty gourmet products from all over Chile, and a great wine and craft-beer selection. If your trip doesn't take you to wine country, it's well worth attending one of its daily tastings, with a sommelier presenting four classic wines.

Oneaco SPORTS & OUTDOORS

(cnr Eberhard & Magellanes; ⏲10am-9pm Mon-Sat, 11am-2pm & 4-8:30pm Sun) Down jackets, hiking boots and mountain equipment from international brands are sold here. Ticket prices may be double those back home, but for those waiting on lost luggage it's a life-saver.

Information

Most banks in town are equipped with ATMs. **La Hermandad** (Bulnes 692; ⏲10am-7pm Mon-Fri) has decent exchange rates on cash and traveler's checks.

The best bilingual portal for the region is www.torresdelpaine.cl.

Conaf (☎61-241-1438; www.parquetorresdelpaine.cl; Baquedano 847; ⏲8:30am-12:45pm & 2:30-5:30pm Mon-Fri) National parks service administrative office. Contact online to book Torres del Paine campgrounds under park administration; advance reservations are required.

Fantastico Sur (p484) Runs Refugios Torres, El Chileno and Los Cuernos in Torres del Paine and offers park tours, guiding and trek-planning services, including a popular self-guided option.

Municipal tourist office (☎61-261-4808; Bus Terminal; ⏲8:30am-12:30pm & 2:30-6pm Tue-Sun) With region-wide lodgings listings.

Sernatur (☎61-241-2125; infonatales@sernatur.cl; Costanera 19, Av Pedro Montt; ⏲9am-7pm Mon-Fri, 9:30am-6pm Sat & Sun) With useful city and regional maps and a second plaza location in high season.

Turismo Comapa (☎61-241-4300; www.comapa.com; Bulnes 541; ⏲9am-1pm & 3-7pm Mon-Fri, 10am-2pm Sat) Navimag ferry and airline bookings; also books packages in Torres del Paine.

Vertice Patagonia (☎61-241-2742; www.verticepatagonia.com; Bulnes 100; ⏲9am-1pm & 2:30-6pm Mon-Fri, 9:30am-noon Sat) Runs Refugios Grey, Dickson and Paine Grande, as well as Camping Perros, in Torres del Paine. Advance booking essential.

Hospital (☎61-241-1582; Pinto 537) For emergency services.

Post office (Eberhard 429; ⏲9am-1pm & 3-6pm Mon-Fri)

Getting There & Away

AIR

Puerto Natales' small **airport** (Aeropuerto Teniente Julio Gallardo; Ruta 9) has irregular service to Punta Arenas, with connections beyond. LATAM (p474) offers direct flights to Santiago two times per week in high season only. **Sky Airline** (☎toll-free in Chile 600-600-2828; www.skyairline.cl; Bulnes 682) offers service to Santiago with a stop in Puerto Montt.

BOAT

Navimag Ferry

For many travelers, a journey through Chile's spectacular fjords aboard the **Navimag Ferry** (☎61-241-1421, Rodoviario 61-241-1642; www.navimag.com; Costanera 308, Av Pedro Montt; ⏲9am-1pm & 2:30-6:30pm Mon-Fri) becomes a highlight of their trip. This four-day and three-night northbound voyage has become so popular it should be booked well in advance. To confirm when the ferry is due, contact Turismo Comapa or Navimag a couple of days before your estimated arrival date. There is a second office in the **Rodoviario** (Bus Terminal; ☎61-241-2554; Av España 1455; ⏲6:30am-midnight).

The ferry leaves Natales at 8am on Tuesdays and stops in Puerto Edén (or Glaciar Pía XI on southbound sailings) en route to Puerto Montt. It usually arrives in Puerto Montt on Friday at

8am, but schedules vary according to weather conditions and tides. Disembarking passengers must stay on board while cargo is transported; those embarking have to spend the night on board.

High season is November to March, mid-season is October and April and low season is May to September. Fares vary according to view, cabin size and private or shared bathroom, and include all meals (request vegetarian meals when booking) and interpretative talks. Bring water, snacks and drinks anyway. Per-person high-season fares range from US$450 for a bunk berth to US$2100 for a triple-A cabin; students and seniors receive a 10% to 15% discount. Check online for current schedules and rates.

Puerto Yungay Ferry

This new ferry option between Puerto Natales and Puerto Yungay links two areas of Patagonia with no road connections. Transbordador Austral Broom (TABSA) runs the 41-hour **Puerto Yungay Ferry** (Cruz Australis; ☎61-241-5966; www.tabsa.cl; Costanera s/n; passenger/bicycle CH$120,000/10,000) with a stop in Puerto Eden. Frequency varies month to month, but high season offers around 10 departures per month.

Travelers should note that under the current schedule it usually arrives in Puerto Eden and Puerto Yungay (where there are no services) late at night, so reserve Puerto Eden hotels in advance and bring a headlamp to get around.

BUS

Buses arrive at the **Rodoviario**, a bus terminal on the town outskirts, though companies also sell tickets at their downtown offices. Book at least a day ahead, especially for early-morning departures. Services are greatly reduced in the low season. Several lines go to Punta Arenas. For Argentina, try **Turismo Zaahj** (☎61-241-2260; www.turismozaahj.co.cl; Arturo Prat 236/270), **Cootra** (☎61-241-2785; Baquedano 244), **Bus Sur** (☎61-242-6011; www.bus-sur.cl; Baquedano 668) or **Buses Pacheco** (☎61-241-4800; www.busespacheco.com; Ramírez 224).

Torres del Paine–bound buses include **Buses Fernandez** (☎61-241-1111; www.busesfernandez.com; cnr Esmeralda & Ramírez), **Buses Gomez** (☎61-241-5700; www.busesgomez.com; Arturo Prat 234), **Buses JBA** (☎61-241-0242; Arturo Prat 258), and Turismo Zaahj. Buses leave for Torres del Paine two to three times daily at around 7am, 8am and 2:30pm. If you are headed to Mountain Lodge Paine Grande in the low season, take the morning bus to meet the catamaran. Tickets may also be used for transfers within the park, so save your stub. Schedules change, so double-check them before heading out.

Buses from Puerto Natales

DESTINATION	COST (CH$)	TIME (HR)
El Calafate	17,000	5
Punta Arenas	7000	3
Torres del Paine	8000	2
Ushuaia	38,000	13

Getting Around

Many hostels rent bikes. Car-rental rates are generally better in Punta Arenas. Try **Emsa/Avis** (☎61-261-4388; Barros Arana 118; ⏲9am-1pm & 2:30-7pm). Drivers should know that there are two routes into Torres del Paine; the more direct gravel one goes via Lago Toro.

Reliable Radio Taxi (☎61-241-2805; cnr Arturo Prat & Bulnes) can even be counted on for after-hours deliveries.

Parque Nacional Bernardo O'Higgins

Virtually inaccessible, **Parque Nacional Bernardo O'Higgins** (www.conaf.cl/parques/parque-nacional-bernardo-ohiggins) remains an elusive cache of glaciers. It can be entered only by boat. From Puerto Natales, full-day excursions (CH$90,000, lunch included) to the base of Glaciar Serrano are run by Turismo 21 de Mayo (p476).

The same outfitter also offers Glacier Serrano tours that access Torres del Paine by boat. After the glacier visit, passengers transfer to a Zodiac (a motorized raft), stop for lunch at Estancia Balmaceda and continue up Río Serrano, arriving at the southern border of the park by 5pm. The same tour can be done leaving the park but may require camping near Río Serrano to catch the Zodiac at 9am.

Parque Nacional Torres del Paine

Soaring almost vertically above the Patagonian steppe, the granite pillars of Torres del Paine (Towers of Paine) dominate the landscape of South America's finest **national park** (www.parquetorresdelpaine.cl; 3-day admission high/low season CH$21,000/11,000). Part of Unesco's Biosphere Reserve system since 1978, this 1810-sq-km park is, however, much more than its one greatest hit. Its diversity of landscapes range from teal and

WORTH A TRIP

CUEVA DEL MILODÓN

In the 1890s, German pioneer Hermann Eberhard discovered the partial remains of an enormous ground sloth in a cave 25km northwest of Puerto Natales. The slow-moving, herbivorous *milodón*, which stood nearly 4m tall, was supposedly the motivating factor behind Bruce Chatwin's book *In Patagonia*. The 30m-high **Cueva del Milodón** (www.cuevadelmilodon.cl; adult/12yr & under CH$4000/500; ⏲8am-7pm Oct-Apr, 8:30am-6pm May-Sep) pays homage to its former inhabitant with a life-size plastic replica of the animal. It's not exactly tasteful, but it's still worth a stop to appreciate the grand setting and ruminate over its wild past. An easy walk leads up to a lookout point.

There's no overnighting here, but it's easy enough to make a day trip from Puerto Natales. Bring your own provisions to take advantage of the picnic area. Drinking water is available on-site.

Some Torres del Paine–bound buses pass the entrance, which is 8km from the cave proper. There are infrequent tours from Puerto Natales; alternatively, you can hitch or share a taxi *colectivo* (CH$20,000). Outside of high season, bus services are infrequent.

azure lakes to emerald forests, roaring rivers and that one big, radiant blue glacier. Guanacos roam the vast open steppe, while Andean condors soar alongside looming peaks.

Forget roughing it. You can hike the whole 'W' while sleeping in beds, eating hot meals, taking showers and toasting your day with a pisco sour. Yet it isn't fully tamed. Weather can present four seasons in a day, with sudden rainstorms and knock-down gusts like a hearty Patagonian handshake.

The park's wild popularity has been taxing on infrastructure, an issue now being addressed by a strict reservations system for overnighters.

Activities

Torres del Paine's 2800m granite peaks inspire a mass pilgrimage of hikers from around the world. Most go for the **Paine Circuit** or **the 'W'** to soak in these classic panoramas. The Paine Circuit (the 'W' plus the backside of the peaks) requires seven to nine days, while the 'W' (named for the rough approximation to the letter that it traces out on the map) takes four to five. Add another day or two for transportation connections.

Trekkers either start from **Laguna Amarga** or take the catamaran from Pudeto to Lago Pehoé and start from there; hiking roughly southwest to northeast along the 'W' presents more views of the black sedimentary peaks known as Los Cuernos (2200m to 2600m).

For trekkers who arrive in the shoulder season, be aware of early-season and foul-weather route closures. Trekking alone, especially on the backside of the circuit, is unadvisable, and may be regulated by Conaf (Corporación Nacional Forestal; National Forest Corporation).

In a move to emphasize safety, Conaf requires all visitors to sign a contract upon entering. The document details park regulations and explains the penalties for breaking them.

Hiking the 'W'

Hiking west to east provides superior views of Los Cuernos, especially between Lago Pehoé and Valle Francés. Most hikers take the catamaran across Lago Pehoé and head to Mountain Lodge Paine Grande. Going in this direction, the hike is roughly 71km in total. It's also possible to take a cruise from Hotel Lago Grey to Refugio Grey to avoid some backtracking.

The following distances are one way:

Guardería Paine Grande to Refugio Lago Grey (10km, four hours one way from Guardería Paine Grande) This relatively easy trail from Lago Pehoé has a few challenging uphills and camping and *refugios* at both ends. The glacier lookout is another half-hour's hike beyond. Still in recovery, this route burned in 2011. Return via the same route.

Guardería Paine Grande to Valle Francés (13km, five hours) From Mountain Lodge Paine Grande, the ferry dock is ahead to the right. The spectacular Cuernos loom overhead on the left, and Lago Skottsberg is passed on the right. Ascend beyond it to Valle Francés, reaching a hanging bridge before Campamento Británico.

Valle Francés to Los Cuernos/Lago Pehoé (10km, five hours) In clear weather, this hike is the most beautiful stretch between 3050m Cerro Paine Grande to the west and the lower but still spectacular Torres del Paine and Los Cuernos to the east, with glaciers hugging the trail. Camp at Italiano and at Británico, or at the valley entrance at Camping Francés.

Los Cuernos to Refugio Las Torres (12km, seven hours) Hikers should keep to the lower trail as many get lost on the upper trail (unmarked on maps). There's a hotel, camping and a *refugio*. Summer winds can be fierce.

Refugio Las Torres to Mirador Las Torres (8km, four hours) A moderate hike up Río Ascencio to a treeless tarn beneath the eastern face of the Torres del Paine for the closest view of the towers. The last hour follows a scree field of huge boulders (covered with knee- and waist-high snow in winter). There are camping and *refugios* at Las Torres and Chileno. Return via the same route.

Guardería Paine Grande to Administración (16km, five hours) Only open between May 1 and September 30, this trail is an alternative to the Pudeto ferry. It goes around Lago Pehoé, then through extensive grassland along Río Grey. Mountain Lodge Paine Grande can radio in and make sure that you can catch a bus from the Administración back to Puerto Natales. You can also enter the 'W' this way to hike it east to west.

Hiking the Paine Circuit

For solitude, stellar views and bragging rights over your compadres doing the 'W,' this longer trek is the way to go. This loop takes in the 'W', plus the backside between Refugio Grey and Refugio Las Torres; the total distance is roughly 112km. The landscape is desolate yet beautiful. **Paso John Gardner** (the most extreme part of the trek) sometimes offers knee-deep mud and snow.

Conaf prefers that hikers do the route counterclockwise. Enter the park (by bus) at Laguna Amarga and finish the circuit in Valle Francés and Los Cuernos, hiking out to Refugio Las Torres bus stop. The Paine Circuit is closed during winter.

Distances are one way:

Laguna Amarga to Campamento Serón (15km, four to five hours) A gentle start to the trek, with fairly open terrain. You can also start from Refugio Las Torres.

Campamento Serón to Campamento Lago Dickson (19km, six hours) As the trail wraps around Lago Paine, winds can get fierce and the trails vague; stay along the trail furthest away from the lake.

Campamento Dickson to Campamento Los Perros (9km, around 4½ hours) A relatively easy but windy stretch.

Campamento Los Perros to Campamento Paso (12km, four hours) This route has plenty of mud and sometimes snow; its physical and psychological high point is Paso John Gardner (1241m). Don't be confused by what appears to be a campsite right after crossing the pass; keep going until you see a shack.

Campamento Paso to Refugio Lago Grey (10km, two hours going south) This steep downhill section offers great glacier views. Trekking poles can save your knees here. The route has three hanging bridges (formerly staircases) over narrow gullies.

Day Hikes

Walk from Guardería Pudeto, on the main park highway, to **Salto Grande**, a powerful waterfall between Lago Nordenskjöld and Lago Pehoé. Another easy hour's walk leads to **Mirador Nordenskjöld**, an overlook with superb views of the lake and mountains.

For a more challenging day hike with tranquility and gorgeous scenery, try the four-hour trek to **Lago Paine**; its northern shore is only accessible from Laguna Azul.

Kayaking & Boating

Bigfoot Patagonia (☎61-241-4611; www.bigfootpatagonia.com; kayaking CH$66,000, ice hike CH$105,000; ⏲Oct-Apr) leads 2½-hour tours of the iceberg-strewn Lago Grey several times daily in summer; this is a great way to get up close to glaciers. A more demanding five-hour tour (CH$160,000) starts at Río Pingo to paddle the river toward Glacier Grey, surrounded by icebergs, ending at Río Serrano.

From October through April, catamaran *Grey III* does **Navegación Glaciar Grey** (Glacier Grey Cruise; ☎61-271-2100; www.lagogrey.com; adult/child roundtrip CH$75,000/37,500, 1 way CH$65,000; ⏲Oct-Apr), a three-hour cruise to take in the massive glacier up close,

The 'W'

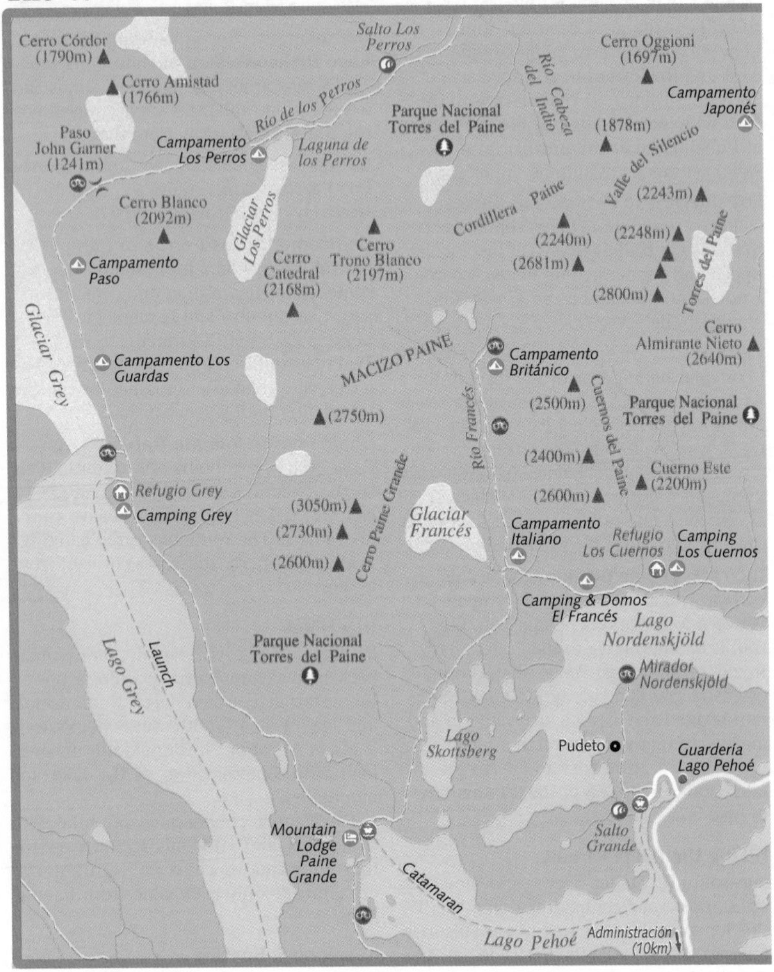

with a stop to let hikers on and off. In high season there are four daily departures; the last two do glacier viewing before stopping at the trail for passengers.

Family-oriented floating trips that take rafts down the mild Río Serrano are run by **Fantastico Sur** (☎61-261-4184; www.fantasticosur.com; Esmeralda 661; ⊙9am-1pm & 3-6pm Mon-Fri).

Horseback Riding

Due to property divisions within the park, horses cannot cross between the western sections (Lagos Grey and Pehoé, Río Serrano) and the private eastern sector known as Reserva Cerro Paine (Camping Francés is the approximate cutoff).

Baqueano Zamora (p476) runs excursions to Laguna Azul, Valle Frances, Dickson glacier and more remote locations, with one-day and multiday options.

Hotel Las Torres (p489) offers full-day horseback-riding trips around Lago Nordenskjöld and beyond.

Ice Trekking

A fun walk through a sculpted landscape of ice, and you don't need experience to go. Antares' Bigfoot Patagonia is the sole company with a park concession for ice

0 —————— 4 km
0 —————— 2 miles

Campamento Torres
Cerro Paine ▲ (1508m)
Río Ascensio
Mirador las Torres
Camping Chileno
Refugio Chileno
Refugio Las Torres
Laguna Amarga (5km)
Hotel Las Torres
Camping Las Torres
Cerro Paine
Estancia
Río Paine
Laguna Larga
Lago Sarmiento de Gamboa
Parque Nacional Torres del Paine

hikes on Glacier Grey, using the Conaf house (former Refugio Grey) as a starting point. The five-hour excursion is available from October to April, in high season three times per day.

🛏 Sleeping

Regulations implemented in 2017 require hikers doing the Circuit or the 'W' to reserve all lodgings ahead, both *refugios* and camping (yes, even free campsites). This requires some tedious logistics work, as there's no central booking website. Visitors (or travel agencies) book with the two park concession

companies and Conaf. Reservations require passport information that park staff may scan and verify.

Phone numbers listed are for Puerto Natales offices.

Refugios & Domos

If you are hiking the 'W' or the Paine Circuit, you will be staying in *refugios*, *domos* ('domes,' also known as yurts) or campsites along the way. It is essential to reserve your spot and specify vegetarian meals in advance. Try to do this as soon as you book your trip.

Refugio rooms have four to eight bunk beds each, kitchen privileges (for lodgers and during specific hours only), hot showers and meals. To prevent bedbugs, lodgings generally include bedding or sleeping bags. Meals are extra. Should a *refugio* be overbooked, staff provide all necessary camping equipment. Most *refugios* close by the end of April. *Domos* are either cloth or plastic permanent camp structures with bunks or cots. Their operating season may be shorter.

Guests should use resources wisely and conserve water and electricity. There are no plugs in rooms, so bring a solar charger or extra batteries to charge electronics.

Accommodations require photo ID (ie a passport) upon check-in. Photocopy your tourist card and passport for all lodgings in advance to expedite check-in. Staff can radio ahead to confirm your next reservation. Given the huge volume of trekkers, snags are inevitable, so practice your Zen composure.

Wireless internet connections, where available, usually cost extra.

Mountain Lodge Paine Grande CABIN **$**
(☎61-241-2742; www.verticepatagonia.cl; dm from US$50, incl full board US$100; 🛜) Though gangly, it's nicer than most dorms, with sublime Los Cuernos views in all rooms. Its year-round presence is a godsend to cold, wet winter hikers, though meals are not available in winter (May to September). There's on-site camping, a kiosk with basic kitchen provisions and a more deluxe version of camping in domes.

Between Lago Grey and Valle Francés, it's a day hike from either and also accessible by ferry across Lago Pehoé. Advance reservations required.

Refugio Grey HUT **$**
(☎61-241-2742; www.verticepatagonia.cl; dm from US$32, incl full board US$82; ☺year-round) Inland from the lake, this deluxe trekkers'

Parque Nacional Torres del Paine

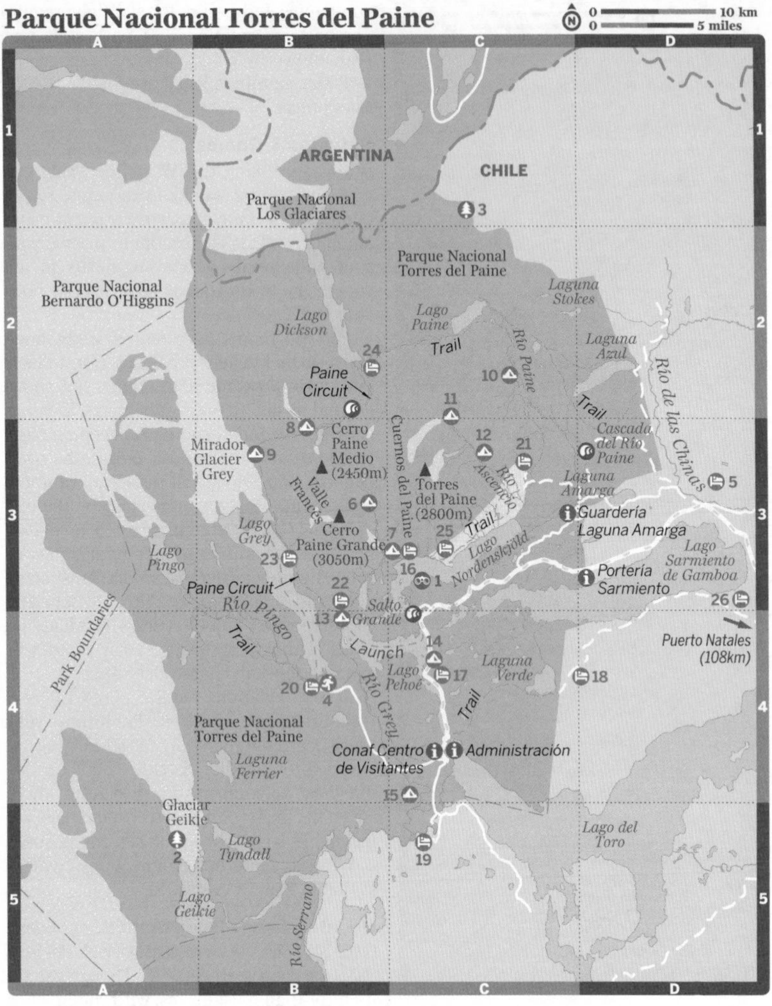

lodge features a decked-out living area with leather sofas and bar, a restaurant-grade kitchen and snug bunk rooms that house 60, with plenty of room for backpacks. There's also a general store, and covered cooking space for campers.

It runs in winter without meal service (May to September). You can also arrive here via catamaran *Grey III*. Advance reservations required.

Refugio Lago Dickson CABIN **$**
(☎61-241-2742; dm from US$32, incl full board US$82; ⏲Nov-Mar) One of the oldest *refugios* and smallest, with 30 beds, in a stunning setting on the Paine circuit, near Glaciar Dickson.

Advance reservations required.

Refugio Las Torres LODGE **$$**
(☎61-261-4184; www.fantasticosur.com; dm US$120, incl full board US$200; ⏲year-round; 📶) This is an ample, attractive base camp with 60 beds and the added feature of a comfortable lounge, restaurant and bar. In high season a nearby older building is put into use to handle the overflow, at discounted rates.

Parque Nacional Torres del Paine

Sights
1 Mirador Nordenskjöld C3
2 Parque Nacional Bernardo O'Higgins A5
3 Parque Nacional Torres del Paine C1

Activities, Courses & Tours
4 Navegación Glaciar Grey B4

Sleeping
5 Awasi D3
6 Campamento Británico B3
7 Campamento Italiano C3
Campamento Lago Dickson ..... (see 24)
8 Campamento Los Perros B3
9 Campamento Paso B3
10 Campamento Serón C2
11 Campamento Torres C2
12 Camping Chileno C3
Camping Francés ..... (see 16)
Camping Grey ..... (see 23)
Camping Las Torres ..... (see 21)
Camping Los Cuernos ..... (see 25)
13 Camping Paine Grande B4
14 Camping Pehoé C4
15 Camping Río Serrano C4
16 Domos El Francés C3
17 Explora C4
18 Hostería Mirador del Payne D4
19 Hotel Cabañas del Paine C5
20 Hotel Lago Grey B4
21 Hotel Las Torres C3
22 Mountain Lodge Paine Grande B3
23 Refugio Grey B3
24 Refugio Lago Dickson B2
Refugio Las Torres ..... (see 21)
25 Refugio Los Cuernos C3
26 Tierra Patagonia D3

Refugio Los Cuernos CABIN **$$$**
(☎61-261-4184; www.fantasticosur.com; dm incl full board US$170, 2-person cabins US$310, incl full board $470; ⊙year-round) This mid-'W' location tends to bottleneck with hikers going in either location. But with eight beds per room, this small lodge is more than cozy. Separate showers and bathrooms for campers relieve some of the stress. For a deluxe option, cabins with shared bathroom offer privacy, with access to a piping-hot wooden hot tub.

Domos El Francés DOME **$$$**
(☎61-261-4184; www.fantasticosur.com; dm US$130, incl full board US$210; ⊙Oct-Apr) Newish domes with dining hall located at Camping Francés, a 40-minute walk from Los Cuernos. Each has four bunks, central heating and individual bathrooms with showers.

Advance reservations required.

Camping

The park has both fee camping, with some services, and free camping. Conaf allows visitors to stay just one night in free campsites. According to new regulations, all must be reserved in advance or hikers will not be permitted to hike sections of the trail that are not day hikes.

Refugios and some *domos* rent equipment – tent (US$25 per night), sleeping bag (US$17) and mat/pad (US$7) – but quality may be inferior to your own gear. Small kiosks sell expensive pasta, soup packets and butane gas, and cooking shelters (at some campgrounds) prove useful in foul weather.

Campgrounds generally operate from mid-October to mid-March, though those on the backside of the Paine Circuit may not open until November due to harsher weather. The decision is made by Conaf.

For bookings, Vertice Patagonia (www.verticepatagonia.com) looks after **Camping Paine Grande** (campsites per person US$10, incl full board US$60), **Camping Grey** (campsites per person US$8, incl full board US$58), **Campamento Lago Dickson** (campsites per person US$8; ⊙around Nov-Mar), **Campamento Los Perros** (campsites per person US$8; ⊙around Nov-Mar) and **Paine Grande**. Fantastico Sur (www.fantasticosur.com) owns **Camping Las Torres** (campsites per person from CH$13,000, s/d deluxe platform camping US$50/80, incl full board US$130/240), **Camping Chileno** (s/d deluxe platform camping incl full board US$130/240), **Camping Francés** (campsites per person CH$13,000, s/d deluxe platform camping US$50/80, incl full board US$130/240; ⊙Oct-Apr), **Camping Los Cuernos** (campsites per person incl full board from CH$70,000) and **Campamento Serón** (campsites per person from CH$13,000; ⊙Oct-Apr).

Sites on the trekking routes which are administered by Conaf (www.parquetorresdelpaine.cl) are free but very basic. They do not rent equipment or offer showers. These include: **Campamento Británico**, **Campamento Italiano**, **Campamento Paso**, **Campamento Torres** and **Camping Guardas**. Other private campgrounds

THE LITTLE PRINCE

From an apartment in Manhattan in 1941, a French pilot and writer, in exile from the battlefields of Europe, scripted what would become one of the most-read children's fables, *The Little Prince*. Antoine de Saint-Exupéry, then 40 years old, had spent the previous 20 years flying in the Sahara, the Pyrenees, Egypt and Patagonia – where he was director of Aeropostal Argentina from 1929 to 1931. Intertwined in the lines of *The Little Prince* and Asteroid B612 are images of Patagonia ingrained from flights over the windy, barren landscape.

Legend has it that the shape of Isla de los Pájaros, off the coast of Península Valdés, inspired the elephant-eating boa constrictor (or hat, as you may see it), while the perfectly conical volcanoes on the asteroid are modeled on those seen en route to Punta Arenas, Chile.

Sadly, Antoine de Saint-Exupéry never witnessed the influence his book would enjoy. In 1944, just after the first publication of *The Little Prince*, he disappeared during a flight to join French forces-in-exile stationed in Algiers.

include **Camping Pehoé** (in Punta Arenas 61-224-9581; http://campingpehoe.com; campsites per person CH$11,000, s/d dome incl breakfast CH$60,000/90,000) and **Camping Río Serrano** (toll free 600-510-0000; www.cajalosandes.cl/turismo-y-recreacion/centros-turisticos/rio-serrano; 6-person campsites from CH$3000, motorhomes CH$50,000).

Rodents lurk around campsites, so don't leave food in packs or in tents – hang it from a tree instead.

★Patagonia Camp YURT **$$$**
(in Puerto Natales 61-241-5149; www.patagoniacamp.com; d all-inclusive incl tours & transfers 3 nights US$3800; Sep–mid-May;) This deluxe camp delivers full wilderness immersion far away from the park crowds. Raised boardwalks connect a series of spacious and comfortable yurts overlooking Lago del Toro. It's tucked into a 100,000-acre private *estancia* with on-site kayaking, stand-up paddling, hiking and fly fishing. Both the service and the dining are top notch. Eco credentials include an independent water-treatment plant.

It's at Km74 on the unpaved road to the park that passes Cueva del Milodon.

Hotels

When choosing lodgings, pay particular attention to location. Lodgings that adjoin the 'W' offer more independence and flexibility for hikers. Most offer multiday packages.

Cheaper hotels occupy the sector of **Pueblito Río Serrano**, just outside the park on the gravel road from Puerto Natales. Banked on the S-curves of Río Serrano, there are stunning views of the entire Paine massif, though reaching the principal trailheads requires transport.

★Tierra Patagonia LODGE **$$$**
(in Santiago 22-207-8861; www.tierrapatagonia.com; d 3 nights incl full board & transfers from US$5267; Oct-May;) Sculpted into the sprawling steppe, this sleek luxury lodge is nothing if not inviting, with a lively living room and circular bar focused on a grand fire pit and a beautiful oversize artist's rendition of a park map. Large, understated rooms enjoy panoramas of the Paine massif. All-inclusive rates include airport transfer, daily excursions, use of spa, meals and drinks.

Located on Cerro Guido *estancia*, the hotel's ranch-focused activities are a strong asset. It's on Lago Sarmiento, just outside the national park about 20km from Laguna Amarga.

★Awasi LODGE **$$$**
(in Santiago 22-233-9641; www.awasipatagonia.com; 3-night all-inclusive per person US$3200;) Awasi dazzles with its modern, understated style and a remote location that drinks in the wild surroundings. Villas with individual hot tubs surround a main lodge offering fine dining, lounge areas and wi-fi. Each lodging is connected by radio. It's sheepskin chic and well attended, with quality individually tailored tours included. Rates are based on double occupancy.

It's located outside the park, on the northeast side of Lago Sarmiento in the private reserve of Tercera Barranca. Travel time might require a little patience: it's a good distance by gravel road from the main attractions, though transfers are provided.

Explora HOTEL **$$$**
(in Santiago 2-2395-2800; www.explora.com; d 3 nights incl full board & transfers from

US$5736; @) These upscale digs sit perched above the Salto Chico waterfall at the outlet of Lago Pehoé. Views of the entire Paine massif pour forth from every inch of the hotel. The spa features a heated lap pool, a sauna and an open-air Jacuzzi. Rates include airport transfers, full gourmet meals and a wide variety of excursions led by young, affable, bilingual guides.

Hotel Lago Grey HOTEL **$$$**
(61-271-2100; www.lagogrey.cl; booking address Lautaro Navarro 1061, Punta Arenas; s/d incl breakfast from US$305/360; @) Open year-round, this tasteful hotel has snug white cottages linked by raised boardwalks. Deluxe rooms are lovely, featuring lake views and sleek modern style. The cafe (open to the public) overlooks the grandeur. Also offers guided excursions and transfers within the park. Glacier cruises stop on the other side of Lago Grey to pick up and drop off hikers.

Hotel Las Torres HOTEL **$$$**
(61-261-7450; www.lastorres.com; booking address Magallanes 960, Punta Arenas; s/d incl breakfast from US$382/437; Jul-May;) A hospitable and well-run hotel with international standards, a spa with Jacuzzi and good guided excursions. Most noteworthy, the hotel donates a portion of fees to nonprofit park-based environmental group AMA. The buffet serves organic vegetables from the greenhouse and organic meat raised on nearby ranches. High-season rates reflect the demand for sleeping trailside.

Hostería Mirador del Payne INN **$$$**
(61-222-8712; www.miradordelpayne.cl; Laguna Verde; s/d/tr US$200/245/265) On the Estancia El Lazo in the seldom-seen Laguna Verde sector, this comfortable inn is known for its serenity, proximity to spectacular viewpoints and top-rate service – but not for easy access to the most popular trails. Activities include bird watching, horseback riding and sport fishing. Call to arrange a ride from the road junction.

Hotel Cabañas del Paine CABIN **$$$**
(61-273-0177; www.hoteldelpaine.cl; Pueblito Río Serrano; d incl breakfast US$200) On the banks of the Río Serrano, these cabin-style rooms stand apart as tasteful and well integrated into the landscape with great views. There's

FALKLAND ISLANDS (ISLAS MALVINAS)

The Falkland Islands are a popular addition to many Antarctic voyages, but they're well worth seeing on their own for their spectacular penguin, seal and albatross populations. Surrounded by the South Atlantic, the islands lie 490km east of Patagonia. Two main islands, East Falkland and West Falkland, and more than 700 smaller ones cover 12,173 sq km. Alternately settled and claimed by France, Spain, Britain and Argentina, the Falklands (known as the Islas Malvinas in Argentina) have been an overseas territory of the UK since 1833, a status the Argentines have fought and still contest.

Since the advent of large sheep stations in the late 19th century, rural settlement in the Falklands has consisted of tiny hamlets built near sheltered harbors where coastal shipping could collect the wool clip. The Falklands retain their rural character: the islands are laced with 400km of roads, but there's not one traffic light. Interesting 'stone runs' of quartzite boulders descend from many of the ridges and peaks on both East and West Falkland.

Besides the five types of penguin (gentoo, king, macaroni, Magellanic and rockhopper) that breed here, there are many other birds equally interesting and uncommon.

Among the 13 endemic plants are several unusual species, including snake plant (*Nassauvia serpens*), with its long stalks and tiny leaves, and Felton's flower (*Calandrinia feltonii*), a caramel-scented, magenta-blossomed annual until recently thought to be extinct in the wild. Vanilla daisy (*Leuceria suaveolens*), while not endemic, is still interesting – its flowers smell remarkably like chocolate. There are no remaining native land animals.

The vast majority of visitors arrive by ship, often on cruises that also visit South Georgia and the Antarctic Peninsula, but LATAM Airways (p474) operates one weekly flight (Saturday; round trip CH$530,000) from Punta Arenas, Chile, to Mt Pleasant International Airport (MPN), occasionally stopping in Rio Gallegos, Argentina, en route.

a bar and restaurant and bicycle rentals are available. With shuttle service.

Information

Parque Nacional Torres del Paine (p481) is open year-round, subject to your ability to get there. Unfortunately, Conaf's National Parks Pass does not include entrance here. Entry is good for three days. If you plan to sleep outside the park during your visit, collect an exit stamp so you can return on the same ticket.

Transportation connections are less frequent in low season, and lodging and services are more limited. Yet the months of November and March are some of the best times for trekking, with fewer crowds and windy conditions usually abating in March. Check the opening dates of all the services you will require in advance (they change based on the weather in any given year). The website www.parquetorresdelpaine.cl also has useful information.

The main entrance where fees are collected is **Portería Sarmiento** (daylight hours). **Conaf Centro de Visitantes** (9am-8pm Dec-Feb), located 37km from Portería Sarmiento, has good information on park ecology and trail status. **Administración** (61-236-0496; Villa Monzino; 8:30am-8pm) is also here. There is a small cafeteria at **Pudeto** and another at the southern tip of Lago Grey. **Portería & Guardería Río Serrano** is located at the access point to Río Serrano.

Erratic Rock (61-241-4317; www.erraticrock.com; Baquedano 955; 10am-1pm & 2-11pm) features a good backpacker equipment list on its website. It also holds an excellent information session every day at 3pm at its Puerto Natales Base Camp location; go for solid advice on everything from trail conditions to camping. **Fantastico Sur** (p484) also provides information sessions at 10am and 3pm daily in its Puerto Natales office.

Trekking maps, by JLM and Luis Bertea Rojas, are widely available in Puerto Natales.

Getting There & Away

Parque Nacional Torres del Paine is 112km north of Puerto Natales. An unpaved alternative road from Puerto Natales to the Administración provides a shorter, more direct southern approach via Pueblito Río Serrano.

Argentina is nearby, but there is no direct transportation from the park. About 40km south of the main park entrance, the seasonal border crossing of Cancha Carrera accesses Argentina at Cerro Castillo. Going to El Calafate from the park on the same day requires joining a tour or careful advance planning, since there is no direct service. Your best bet is to return to Puerto Natales.

Getting Around

Shuttles (CH$4000) within the park drop off and pick up passengers at Laguna Amarga, at the catamaran launch at Pudeto, and at Administración.

Catamaran **Hielos Patagónicos** (61-241-1133; www.hipsur.com; Pudeto; 1 way/roundtrip CH$18,000/28,000; Sep-Apr) connects Pudeto with Mountain Lodge Paine Grande.

Hikers can take advantage of **Navegación Glaciar Grey** (p483), a cruise that links Refugio Grey to Hotel Lago Grey with glacier viewing.

Tierra del Fuego

Includes ➡

Best Places to Eat

- ➡ Kalma Resto (p503)
- ➡ Kaupé (p506)
- ➡ María Lola Restó (p506)
- ➡ Chiko (p503)
- ➡ Don Peppone (p512)

Best Places to Stay

- ➡ Galeazzi-Basily B&B (p500)
- ➡ Antarctica Hostel (p499)
- ➡ Estancia Las Hijas (p513)
- ➡ Yendegaia House (p515)
- ➡ Los Cauquenes Resort & Spa (p501)

Why Go?

The southernmost extreme of the Americas, this windswept archipelago is as alluring as it is moody – by turns beautiful, ancient and strange. Travelers who first came for the ends-of-the-earth novelty discover a destination that's far more complex than a mere source of bragging rights. Intrigue remains in a past storied with shipwrecks, native peoples and failed missions. In Tierra del Fuego, nature is writ bold and reckless, from the scoured plains, rusted peat bogs and mossy lenga forests to the snowy ranges above the Beagle Channel.

While distant and isolated, Tierra del Fuego is by no means cut off from the mainland, though the Argentine half is far more developed. Ports buzz with commerce and oil refineries prosper, while adventure seekers descend in droves to fly fish, hike and begin Antarctic cruises. Shared with Chile, this archipelago features one large island, Isla Grande, Chile's Isla Navarino and many smaller uninhabited isles.

When to Go

Ushuaia

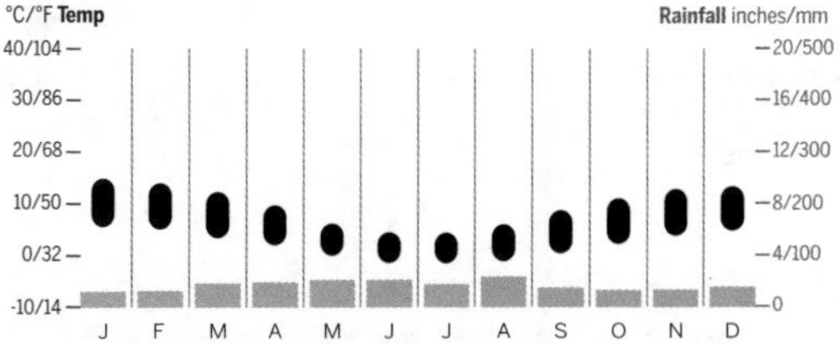

Nov–Mar Warmest months, best for hiking, penguin-watching and *estancia* (ranch) visits.

Mid-Nov–mid-Apr Fly-fishing season.

Jul–Sep Optimal for skiing, snowboarding and dogsledding.

Tierra del Fuego Highlights

1 **Parque Nacional Tierra del Fuego** (p508) Exploring the ancient Fuegian forests of this coastal national park.

2 **Dogsledding Tour** (p499) Speeding through frozen valleys on a memorable adventure near Ushuaia.

3 **Estancias** (p512) Landing the big one while fly fishing at a ranch near Río Grande.

4 **Museo Marítimo & Museo del Presidio** (p494) Reliving grim times in Ushuaia's infamous prison-turned-museum.

5 **Cerro Castor** (p497) Skiing and snowboarding with sublime views at the world's southernmost resort.

6 **Porvenir** (p515) Browsing back in time in this quiet seaside village in Chilean Tierra del Fuego.

7 **Dientes de Navarino** (p513) Trekking around the jagged peaks and sculpted landscapes on this spectacular five-day circuit near Puerto Williams.

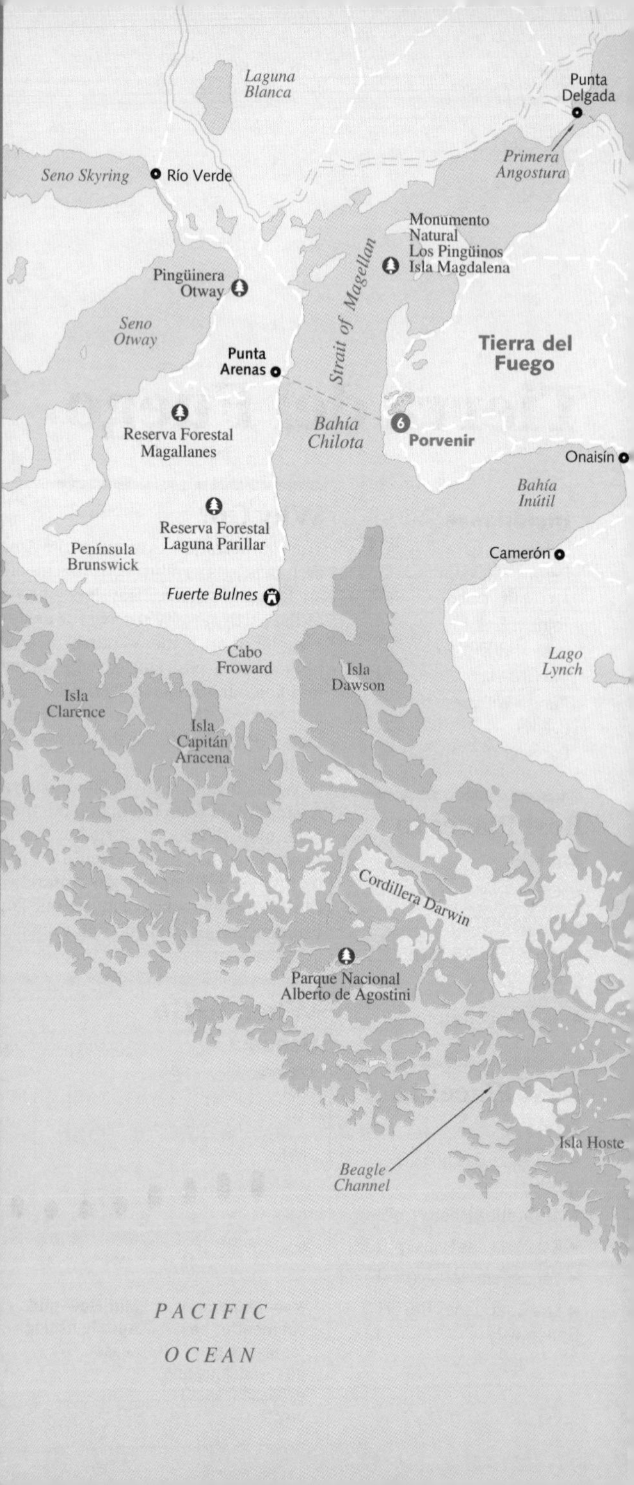

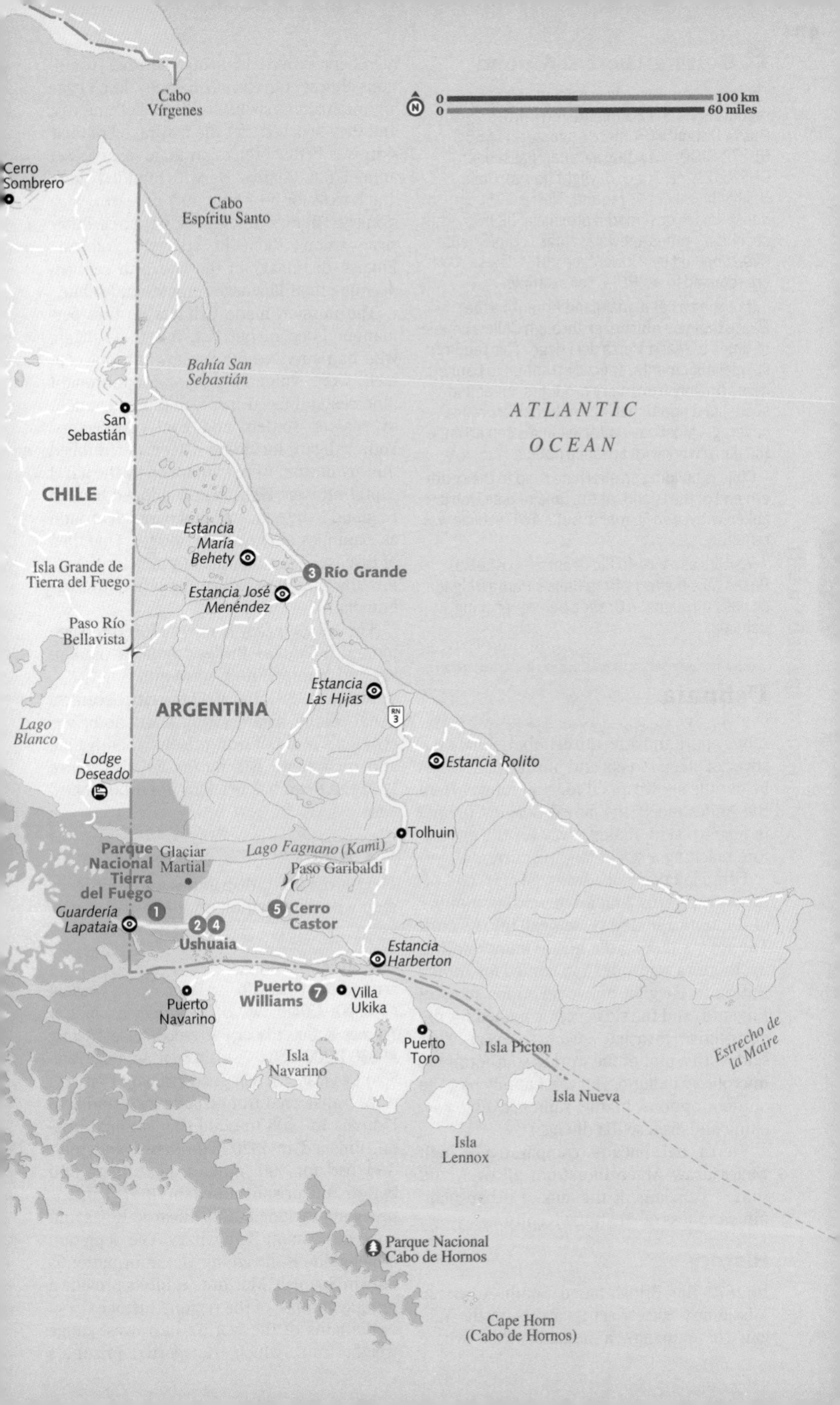

Cabo Vírgenes
100 km
60 miles
Cerro Sombrero
Cabo Espíritu Santo
Bahía San Sebastián
San Sebastián
ATLANTIC OCEAN
CHILE
Estancia María Behety
3 Río Grande
Isla Grande de Tierra del Fuego
Estancia José Menéndez
Paso Río Bellavista
Estancia Las Hijas
RN 3
ARGENTINA
Lago Blanco
Estancia Rolito
Lodge Deseado
Tolhuin
Parque Nacional Tierra del Fuego
Glaciar Martial
Lago Fagnano (Kami)
Paso Garibaldi
5 Cerro Castor
Guardería Lapataia
1
2 4
Ushuaia
Estancia Harberton
Puerto Williams 7
Villa Ukika
Puerto Navarino
Puerto Toro
Isla Picton
Estrecho de la Maire
Isla Navarino
Isla Nueva
Isla Lennox
Parque Nacional Cabo de Hornos
Cape Horn (Cabo de Hornos)

Getting There & Around

The most common overland route from Patagonia is via the 20-minute ferry crossing at **Punta Delgada** (Primera Angostura; ☎56 61-272-8100; www.tabsa.cl; car/passenger CH$15,000/1700; ⊙daylight hours), Chile. Unlike the rest of Argentina, Tierra del Fuego doesn't have designated provincial highways but secondary roads known as *rutas complementarias*, modified by a lowercase letter. These roads are referred to as 'RC-a,' for example.

If renting a car in mainland Argentina, be aware that you must pass through Chile a couple of times to reach Tierra del Fuego. This requires special documents, special attention to banned items (mainly fruit, dairy products, meat and seeds) and additional international insurance coverage. Most car-rental agencies can arrange the paperwork with advance notice.

Chile is building an alternate road to the southern end of the island. At the time of research it linked with Lago Fagnano, but a 4WD vehicle was required.

Visitors can fly into Río Grande or Ushuaia. Buses take the ferry from Chile's Punta Delgada; all pass through Río Grande before reaching Ushuaia.

Ushuaia

☎02901 / POP 57,000

A busy port and adventure hub, Ushuaia is a sliver of steep streets and jumbled buildings below the snowcapped Martial Range. Here the Andes meets the famed Beagle Channel in a sharp skid, making way for the city before reaching a sea of lapping currents.

Ushuaia takes full advantage of its end-of-the-world status, and an increasing number of Antarctica-bound vessels call into its port. The town's mercantile hustle knows no irony: there's a souvenir shop named for Jimmy Button (a Fuegian native taken for show in England) and the ski center is named for the destructive invasive *castor* (beaver). That said, with a pint of the world's southernmost microbrew in hand, you can happily plot the outdoor options: hiking, sailing, skiing, kayaking and even scuba diving.

Tierra del Fuego's comparatively high wages draw Argentines from all over, and some locals lament the lack of urban planning and loss of small-town culture.

History

In 1870 the British-based South American Missionary Society set its sights on the Yahgan (or Yámana), a nomadic tribe whose members thrived in brutal weather conditions almost entirely naked – they didn't have any permanent shelter to keep clothing dry, and they believed that the natural oil of their skin was better protection than soaking-wet animal fur. Charles Darwin branded them 'the lowest form of humanity on earth.' Missionary Thomas Bridges didn't agree. After years among them, he created a Yahgan-English dictionary in the late 19th century, deeming their language complex and subtle.

The mission made Ushuaia its first permanent Fuegian outpost, but the Yahgan, who had survived 6000 years without contact, were vulnerable to foreign-brought illnesses and faced increasing infringement by sealers, settlers and gold prospectors. Four Yahgan, including a teenager dubbed 'Jimmy Button,' were kidnapped by the naval captain Robert FitzRoy and shipped back to England to be educated and paraded around as examples of gentrified savages. One died of disease. After months of public criticism, FitzRoy agreed to return the others to their homeland.

The tribe's legacy is now reduced to shell mounds, Thomas Bridges' famous dictionary and Jimmy Button souvenirs.

Between 1884 and 1947 the city became a penal colony, incarcerating many notorious criminals and political prisoners, both here and on remote Isla de los Estados. Since 1950 the town has been an important naval base.

Sights

The tourist office distributes a free city-tour map with information on the historic houses around town.

Museo Marítimo & Museo del Presidio MUSEUM

(☎02901-437481; www.museomaritimo.com; cnr Yaganes & Gobernador Paz; adult/student/family AR$300/200/650; ⊙10am-8pm Apr-Nov, 9am-8pm Dec-Mar, last admission 7:30pm) Convicts were transferred from Isla de los Estados to Ushuaia in 1906 to build this national prison, finished in 1920. The depressing cells, designed for 380 inmates, held up to 800 before the prison closed in 1947. Famous prisoners include author Ricardo Rojas and anarchist Simón Radowitzky. The depiction of penal life is intriguing, but information is only in Spanish. Maritime exhibits provide a unique glimpse of the region's history.

Remains of the world's narrowest-gauge freight train, which transported prisoners

ANTARCTICA: THE ICE

For many travelers, a journey to Antarctica represents a once-in-a-lifetime adventure. Despite its high price tag, it's much more than just a continent to tick off your list. You will witness both land and ice shelves piled with hundreds of meters of undulating, untouched snow. Glaciers drop from mountainsides and icebergs form sculptures as tall as buildings. The wildlife is thrilling, with thousands of curious penguins and an extraordinary variety of flying birds, seals and whales.

More than 90% of Antarctic-bound boats pass through Ushuaia; in the 2014–15 season, that meant almost 40,000 tourists – a stunning contrast to the continent's population of 5000 (summer) or 1200 (winter), consisting of scientists and staff. But travel here is not without its costs. On November 23, 2007, the hull of the MV *Explorer* was gashed by ice, but the ship was evacuated before it sank. The circumstances were highly unusual, although the incident prompted further safety measures.

So long as you've got a couple of weeks to spare, hopping on board a cruise ship is not out of the question. Some voyages take in the Falkland Islands and South Georgia (human population 10 to 20, estimated penguin population two to three million); some go just to the Antarctic Peninsula; others focus on retracing historic expeditions. A small but growing handful of visitors reach Antarctica aboard private vessels. All are sailboats (equipped with auxiliary engines).

The season runs from mid-October to mid-March, depending on ice conditions. It used to be that just peak-season voyages sold out, but now most trips do. When shopping around, ask how many days you will actually spend in Antarctica – keep in mind that crossing the Southern Ocean takes up to two days each way – and how many landings there will be. The smaller the ship, the more landings there are per passenger (always depending on the weather, of course). Tour companies charge from US$7000 to US$70,000, although some ships allow walk-ons, which can cost as little as US$5000 for 10 days. Required insurance costs extra (around US$800). Check to see if your ship provides outdoor clothing.

Due to Ushuaia's proximity to the Antarctic Peninsula, most cruises leave from here. If you are chasing the discounts, it's best to check in with agencies a few weeks in advance, once you're actually in South America. Last-minute bookings can be made through the helpful crew at **Freestyle Adventure Travel** (☎02901-609792, 02901-606661; www.freestyleadventuretravel.com; Gobernador Paz 866), a 1% for the Planet member that also offers discount Cape Horn trips, and **Ushuaia Turismo** (☎02901-436003; www.ushuaia turismoevt.com.ar; Gobernador Paz 865). Other travel agencies and tour operators offering packages include **Rumbo Sur** (☎02901-421139; www.rumbosur.com.ar; Av San Martín 350; ⌚9am-7pm Mon-Fri), **All Patagonia** (☎02901-433622; www.allpatagonia.com; Juana Fadul 48; ⌚10am-7pm Mon-Fri, to 1pm Sat) and Canal Fun (p498), though there are many more.

Check that your company is a member of the **International Association of Antarctic Tour Operators** (IAATO; www.iaato.org), which mandates strict guidelines for responsible travel to Antarctica. The following are just a few companies that go to Antarctica:

Adventure Associates Cruise (☎61-2 6355 2022; www.adventureassociates.com) Australia's first tour company to Antarctica, with many ships and destinations.

National Geographic Expeditions (www.nationalgeographicexpeditions.com) Highly recommended, with quality naturalists and experts, and the 148-passenger *National Geographic Explorer*.

Peregrine Adventures (☎61-3 8594 3905; www.peregrineadventures.com) Offers unique trips that include visiting the Antarctic Circle, with kayaking and camping options.

WildWings Travel (www.wildwings.co.uk) UK-based company that focuses on bird watching and wildlife in Antarctica.

Check http://polarconservation.org for up-to-date information and articles. In Ushuaia, consult the very helpful Antarctica Tourist Office (p506) at the pier.

Ushuaia

between town and work stations, sit in the courtyard. From December to March, guided tours (also in English) are at 11:30am and 4:30pm.

Museo del Fin del Mundo MUSEUM
(☎02901-421863; www.tierradelfuego.org.ar/museo; cnr Av Maipú & Rivadavia; AR$130; ⊙10am-7pm) Built in 1903, this former bank, close to the port, contains exhibits on Fuegian natural history, stuffed birdlife, photos of natives and early penal colonies, and replicas of moderate interest. Information is provided in Spanish with English translations. Guided visits are at 11am and 3:30pm.

Parque Yatana PARK
(Fundación Cultiva; ☎02901-425212; cnr Magallanes & 25 de Mayo; ⊙9am-noon Mon-Fri) Part art project, part urban refuge, this city block of lenga forest is being preserved from encroaching development. The forest, whose name in Yaghan means 'weave,' is a spot for indigenous people to practice their crafts, which are shown at the art center in the park and throughout the hiking trails.

Activities

In addition to boating, which can be undertaken year round, there's also scuba diving in the Beagle Channel, horseback riding, zip lining and rock climbing, making Ushuaia one of the top outdoor-adventure areas in southern Argentina.

Aeroclub Ushuaia SCENIC FLIGHTS
(☎02901-421717, 02901-421892; www.aeroclubushuaia.com; Luis Pedro Fique 151; per person 15/60min US$70/205) Offers scenic flights over the channel and the Cordillera Darwin. Flights leave before 1pm; try to confirm three days ahead. The weather here can change rapidly, so your flight may have to be delayed or cancelled.

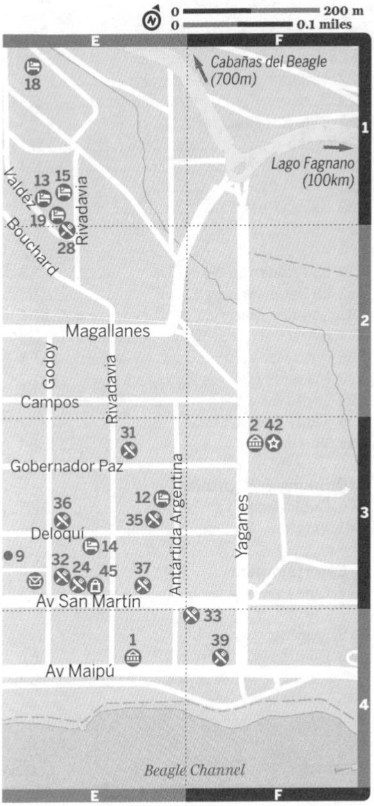

Cruceros Australis CRUISE
(☎in Buenos Aires 11-5128-4632; www.australis.com; 3 nights & 4 days per person from US$1190; ⏱late Sep-early Apr) Luxurious three- to four-night sightseeing cruises from Ushuaia to Punta Arenas (Chile), with the possibility of disembarking at Cape Horn.

Rayen Aventura ADVENTURE
(☎02901-15-580517, 02901-437005; www.rayenaventura.com; Av San Martín 611) Known for its upbeat 4x4 tours to Lago Fagnano, with trekking or kayaking options and *estancia* visits. Also has winter tours.

Hiking

Hiking possibilities aren't limited to Parque Nacional Tierra del Fuego: the entire mountain range behind Ushuaia, with its lakes and rivers, is a hiker's paradise. However, many trails are poorly marked or not marked at all, and some hikers who have easily scurried uphill have gotten lost trying to find the trail back down. For their safety, hikers going outside the national park are asked to register at the tourist office (p507) upon their departure and return. Club Andino Ushuaia (p507) has maps and good information. In an emergency, contact the **Civil Guard** (☎02901-22108, 103). Plan accordingly for rapid changes in weather.

Cerro Martial & Glaciar Martial OUTDOORS
The panoramas of Ushuaia and the Beagle Channel from here are more impressive than the smallish glacier. Weather is unpredictable, so take warm clothing and sturdy footwear. You can hike or do a canopy tour. To get here, catch a taxi or minivan to Cerro Martial; minivans leave from the corner of Av Maipú and Juana Fadul every half-hour from 8:30am to 6:30pm.

Skiing, Snowboarding & Sledging

With the surrounding peaks loaded with powder, winter visitors should jump at the chance to explore the local ski resorts. Accessed from RN 3, resorts offer both downhill and cross-country options. The ski season runs from June to September, with July (winter vacation) the busiest month. Sledding with huskies is another option and is perfect for families traveling with kids.

Cerro Castor SKIING
(☎02901-499301; www.cerrocastor.com; full-day lift ticket low/high season AR$885/1120; ⏱mid-Jun–mid-Oct) Incredibly scenic, this large resort 26km from Ushuaia via RN 3 has 15 runs spanning 400 hectares, beautiful cabins, and multiple restaurants. Rentals are available for skis and boards. Multiday and shoulder-season tickets are discounted. Clear windbreaks are added to lifts on cold days. August is the most reliable month for incredible snow conditions.

Tours

Many travel agencies sell tours around the region. You can go horseback riding, hiking or canoeing, visit Lagos Escondido and Fagnano, stay at an *estancia*, or spot birds and beavers.

Navigating the Beagle Channel's gunmetal-gray waters overlooking distant glaciers and rocky isles offers a fresh perspective and decent wildlife watching. Harbor cruises are usually four-hour morning or afternoon excursions to sea-lion and cormorant colonies. The number of passengers, and the extent of snacks and hiking options varies between operators. A highlight is an

Ushuaia

Sights
1 Museo del Fin del Mundo....E4
2 Museo Marítimo & Museo del Presidio....F3
3 Parque Yatana....D2

Activities, Courses & Tours
4 Canal Fun....D3
Che Turismo Alternativo....(see 5)
5 Patagonia Adventure Explorer....D4
6 Piratour....C3
7 Rayen Aventura....D3
8 Tierra....A3
9 Tolkar....E3
Tres Marías Excursiones....(see 5)
10 Turismo Comapa....D3
11 Ushuaia Turismo....C3

Sleeping
12 Antarctica Hostel....E3
13 Galeazzi-Basily B&B....E1
14 Hostel Cruz del Sur....E3
15 La Casa de Tere B&B....E1
16 Los Cormoranes....B1
17 Martín Fierro B&B....C3
18 Mysten Kepen....E1
19 Posada Fin del Mundo....E1
20 Torre al Sur....C3
21 Yakush....B3

Eating
22 Almacen Ramos Generales....C4
23 Bodegón Fueguino....C3
24 Cafe Bar Banana....E3
25 Chiko....D4
26 Christopher....C4
27 El Turco....A4
28 Kalma Resto....E2
29 Kaupé....D2
30 Küar 1900....D3
31 La Anónima....E3
32 La Estancia....E3
33 Lomitos Martinica....F4
34 María Lola Restó....B3
35 Paso Garibaldi....E3
36 Placeres Patagónicos....E3
37 Tante Sara....E3
38 Tante Sara....C3
39 Volver....F4

Drinking & Nightlife
40 Dublin Irish Pub....C3
41 Viagro....D4

Entertainment
42 Cine Pakawaia....F3

Shopping
43 Boutique del Libro....B4
44 Paseo de los Artesanos....D4
45 Quelhue Wine Shop....E3

island stop to hike and look at *conchales* (middens or shell mounds left by the native Yahgan). Tour operators offering cruises line the entrance to Ushuaia's pier.

★ **Tierra** ADVENTURE
(☎02901-15-486886, 02901-433800; www.tierraturismo.com; office 4C, Onas 235) Offering active tours and unusual tailored trips, this small agency was created by ultra-friendly, multilingual former guides who wanted to create a more personalized experience. Options include 4WD trips combining kayaking and hiking, treks in Parque Nacional Tierra del Fuego, and Estancia Harberton visits.

Canal Fun ADVENTURE
(☎02901-435777; www.canalfun.com; Roca 136;) Run by a group of younger, multilingual guides, these popular all-day outings include hiking and kayaking in Parque Nacional Tierra del Fuego, the famous 4WD adventure around Lago Fagnano, and a multi-sport outing around Estancia Harberton that includes kayaking and a visit by boat to the penguin colony.

Piratour BOATING
(☎02901-15-604646, 02901-435557; www.piratour.net; Av San Martín 847; penguin-colony tour AR$2500, plus port fee AR$20; ⏱9am-9pm) Runs 20-person tours to Isla Martillo for trekking and spotting Magellanic and Papúa penguins, plus a visit to Harberton. This is the only agency that gets you walking on the island – with others you have to penguin watch from the coast by boat. Also has boats to Puerto Williams (Chile; December to March). There's a second office at the Tourist Wharf.

Canopy Tours ADVENTURE
(☎02901-503767; www.canopyushuaia.com.ar; Refugio de Montaña, Cerro Martial; long/short route AR$600/450; ⏱10am-5pm Oct-Jun) These family-friendly canopy tours offer a long route (nine lines and two hanging bridges) and a shorter route (seven lines) that will get you zipping through the forest. By reservation only. The complex also has a cute cafe, with sandwiches, desserts and hot drinks, right before you start along the track to Glaciar Martial.

Patagonia Adventure Explorer BOATING
(☎02901-15-465842; www.patagoniaadvent.com.ar; Tourist Wharf) Comfortable boats with snacks and a short hike on Isla Bridges. For a more intimate experience on the Beagle Channel, set sail in the 18ft sailboat. Multiday trips and full-day sail trips with wine and gourmet snacks are also available.

Che Turismo Alternativo BOATING
(☎02901-15-517967; www.facebook.com/elcheturismoalternativo; Tourist Wharf; half-day tour AR$1200) This owner-run boat tour of the Beagle Channel includes a trek on Isla Bridges and local beer on tap to enjoy during the cruise back to the harbor – it's very popular with the hostel crowd. An additional AR$20 fee must be paid at the port before the boat leaves. Tours run daily from 10am and last four hours.

Compañía de Guías de Patagonia ADVENTURE
(☎02901-437753; www.companiadeguias.com.ar; full-day hike US$105) A reputable outfitter organizing expeditions and multiday treks around Ushuaia, Isla Navarino and further afield in remote Tierra del Fuego. Also offers glacier trekking, mountain biking and Antarctica trips with sea kayaking.

Turismo Comapa TOURS
(☎02901-430727; www.comapa.com; Av San Martín 409) Confirm Navimag and Cruceros Australis passages at this long-standing Chile-based agency. It also sells conventional tours and boat transfers to Puerto Williams (Chile).

Tierra Mayor ADVENTURE
(Anartur; ☎02901-430329; http://antartur.com.ar; RN 3, Km 3018; guided dogsledding US$50) Offers competitively priced adventure tours and has its own mountain base. Snowshoe a beautiful alpine valley or dogsled across Tierra Mayor. For a memorable night, combine either with an evening bonfire (US$130 to US$145). Also on offer are guided snowcat rides and a 4WD day trip to Lago Fagnano with canoeing and a barbecue. It's 19km from Ushuaia via RN 3.

Tres Marías Excursiones BOATING
(☎02901-15-611199, 02901-436416; www.tresmariasweb.com; Tourist Wharf) The only outfitter with permission to land on Isla 'H' in the Isla Bridges natural reserve, which has shell mounds and a colony of rock cormorants. Its small, picturesque sailboat takes only eight passengers.

Tolkar TOURS
(☎02901-431408, 02901-431412; www.tolkarturismo.com.ar; Roca 157) A helpful, popular, all-round agency, affiliated with Tecni-Austral buses (p507).

Festivals & Events

Festival Nacional de la Noche Más Larga CULTURAL
(Longest Night; mid-Jun) Coinciding with the winter solstice, this festival features shows and music recitals (ranging from tango to jazz to popular music), and free events throughout the city. Traditionally there's a 'Fuego de los Deseos,' in which participants write down obstacles blocking them from their dreams and then burn the notes in a big bonfire. For more, contact the Municipal Tourist Office (p507).

Marcha Blanca SPORTS
(www.marchablanca.com; mid-Aug) Running for a quarter of a century, this is Ushuaia's annual cross-country event, which recreates San Martín's historic August 17, 1817, crossing of the Andes. There's also a master class for ski enthusiasts, snow sculptures and a Nordic-ski marathon.

Sleeping

Reserve well ahead if you're planning a visit from January to early March. Check when booking for free arrival transfers. In winter, rates drop slightly and some places close, though visits at this time are becoming popular.

The Municipal Tourist Office has lists of B&Bs and *cabañas* (cabins). Hostels abound, all with kitchens and most with internet access. Rates typically drop 25% in low season (April to October).

★ **Antarctica Hostel** HOSTEL $
(☎02901-435774; www.antarcticahostel.com; Antártida Argentina 270; dm/d US$26/97; @ wifi) This friendly backpacker hub delivers with a warm atmosphere and helpful staff. The open floor plan and beer on tap are plainly conducive to making friends. Guests lounge and play cards in the common room and cook in a cool balcony kitchen. Cement rooms are clean and ample, with radiant floor heating.

Hostel Cruz del Sur HOSTEL $
(☎02901-434099; www.xdelsur.com.ar; Deloquí 242; dm US$25; @ wifi) This easygoing, organized hostel comprises two renovated houses (1920

OFF THE BEATEN TRACK

ESTANCIA HARBERTON

Tierra del Fuego's first *estancia*, **Harberton** (Skype estanciaharberton.turismo; www.estanciaharberton.com; entrance adult/child AR$240/free, dm US$50, s/d incl full board & activities US$325/580; 10am-7pm Oct 15-Apr 15), was founded in 1886 by missionary Thomas Bridges and his family. The location earned fame from a stirring memoir written by Bridges' son Lucas, titled *Uttermost Part of the Earth,* about his coming of age among the now-extinct Selk'nam and Yahgan people. Available in English, the book is an excellent introduction to the history of the region and the ways of its native peoples.

In a splendid location, the *estancia* is owned and run by Thomas Bridges' descendants. There's lodging available and day visitors can take guided tours (featuring the island's oldest house and a replica Yahgan dwelling), dine at the restaurant and visit the Reserva Yecapasela penguin colony. It's also a popular destination for bird watchers.

On-site, the impressive **Museo Acatushún** (www.estanciaharberton.com/museoacatushunenglish.html; entrance with estancia visit adult/child AR$240/free) was created by Natalie Prosser Goodall, a North American biologist who married into the extended Bridges family. Emphasizing the region's marine mammals, the museum has inventoried thousands of mammal and bird specimens; among the rarest is a Hector's beaked whale. Much of this vast collection was found at Bahía San Sebastián, north of Río Grande, where an 11km difference between high and low tide leaves creatures stranded. Confirm the museum's opening hours with Estancia Harberton.

Harberton is 85km east of Ushuaia via RN 3 and rough RC-j, a 1½- to two-hour drive. In Ushuaia, shuttles leave from the base of 25 de Mayo at Av Maipú at 9am, returning around 3pm. Day-long catamaran tours are organized by local agencies.

and 1926), painted tangerine and joined by a passageway. Dorm prices are based on room capacity, the only disadvantage being that your bathroom might be on another floor. There's a fine backyard patio, though indoor shared spaces are scant. Discounts are given for stays longer than four nights.

Torre al Sur HOSTEL $
(02901-430745; www.torrealsur.com.ar; Gobernador Paz 855; dm/d US$20/35;) The sister hostel to Cruz del Sur (p499) may not seem like much on the outside, but inside there's a welcoming, organized ambience, with colorful rooms, renovated bathrooms and a well-stocked kitchen. Marisa is the warm host.

La Posta HOSTEL $
(02901-444650; www.lapostahostel.com.ar; Perón Sur 864; dm/d US$22/65;) This cozy hostel and guesthouse on the outskirts of town is hugely popular with young travelers thanks to its warm service, homey decor and spotless open kitchen. The downside is that the place is far from the town center, but buses and taxis are plentiful.

Camping Municipal CAMPGROUND
(RN 3; campsites free) FREE About 10km west of town, en route to Parque Nacional Tierra del Fuego, this campground boasts a lovely setting but minimal facilities.

Los Cormoranes HOSTEL $
(02901-423459; www.loscormoranes.com; Kamshen 788; dm US$31-40, d/tr/q US$107/132/155;) This friendly, mellow HI hostel is a 10-minute (uphill) walk north of downtown. Six-bed dorms, some with private bathrooms, have radiant-heated floors and face outdoor plank hallways. Doubles have polished-cement floors and down duvets – the best is room 10, with bay views. Linens could use an update and common spaces are so-so. Breakfast includes DIY eggs and fresh-squeezed OJ.

Yakush HOSTEL $
(02901-435807; www.hostelyakush.com; Piedrabuena 118; dm US$23-25, d with/without bathroom US$85/75; mid-Oct–mid-Apr;) A colorful hostel that, while friendly and centrally located, seems a bit expensive for what you get.

★ **Galeazzi-Basily B&B** B&B $$
(02901-423213; www.avesdelsur.com.ar; Valdéz 323; s/d without bathroom US$45/65, 2-/4-person cabins US$110/140;) The best feature of this elegant wooded residence is its warm, hospitable family of owners, who will make you feel right at home. Rooms are small but offer a personal touch. Since beds are twin-size, couples may prefer a modern cabin out the back. It's a peaceful

spot, and where else can you practice your English, French, Italian and Portuguese?

Familia Piatti B&B B&B **$$**
(☎ 02901-15-613485, 02901-437104; www.familiapiatti.com; Bahía Paraíso 812, Bosque del Faldeo; d US$80, ste US$139-190; @ 🛜) If idling in the forest sounds good, head for this friendly B&B just five minutes outside town, with warm down duvets and native lenga-wood furniture. Hiking trails nearby lead up into the mountains. The friendly owners are multilingual (speaking English, Italian, Spanish and Portuguese) and can arrange transportation and guided excursions. Check the website for directions to get there.

Mysten Kepen GUESTHOUSE **$$**
(☎ 02901-430156, 02901-15-497391; http://mystenkepen.blogspot.com; Rivadavia 826; d/tr/q US$94/144/175; 🛜) If you want an authentic Argentine family experience, this is it. Hosts Roberto and Rosario recount stories of favorite guests from years past, and their immaculate two-kid home feels busy and lived in – in a good way. Rooms have newish installations, bright corduroy duvets and handy shelving for nighttime reading. Airport transfers and winter discounts are available.

Martín Fierro B&B B&B **$$**
(☎ 02901-430525; www.martinfierrobyb.com.ar; 9 de Julio 175; s/d US$70/110; ⏲ Sep-Apr; P 🛜) Spending a night at this charming inn feels like staying at the cool mountain cabin of a worldly friend who makes strong coffee and has a great book collection. The owner, Javier, personally built the interiors with local wood and stone; these days he cultivates a friendly, laid-back atmosphere where travelers get into deep conversations at the breakfast table.

Posada Fin del Mundo B&B **$$**
(☎ 02901-437345; www.posadafindelmundo.com.ar; cnr Rivadavia & Valdéz; d US$140) This expansive home exudes good taste and character, from the snug living room with folk art and expansive water views to the friendly chocolate lab. Of the nine distinctive rooms (some are small), the best are upstairs. Breakfast is abundant and there's also afternoon tea and cakes. The B&B is sometimes booked out by ski teams in winter.

La Casa de Tere B&B B&B **$$**
(☎ 02901-422312; www.lacasadetere.com.ar; Rivadavia 620; d with/without bathroom US$120/85) Tere showers guests with attention but also gives them the run of the place in this beautiful modern home with great views. The three tidy rooms fill up fast. Guests can cook, and there's cable TV and a fireplace in the living room. It's a short but steep walk uphill from the town center.

Arakur HOTEL **$$$**
(☎ 02901-442900; www.arakur.com; Cerro Alarken; d with valley/ocean view US$370/400; P ❄ @ 🛜 ≋) Towering over the city on a wooded promontory, Arakur is the town's latest luxury hotel, well known to locals for hosting an annual music festival. The look is sleek and modern, with neutral tones and personalized service, and the views are beyond comparison. Rooms feature electronic control panels and glass-walled bathrooms. The indoor-outdoor infinity pool is warm year-round.

Los Cauquenes Resort & Spa RESORT **$$$**
(☎ 02901-441300; www.loscauquenes.com; d from US$275; @ 🛜 ≋) This exclusive, sprawling wooden lodge sits directly on the Beagle Channel in a private neighborhood with gravel-road access. Rooms are tasteful and well appointed; special features include a playroom stocked with kids' games and outdoor terraces with glass windbreaks and stunning channel views. Free shuttles go downtown every few hours. It's 4km west of the airport.

There's also spa, sauna and indoor-outdoor pool. The spa features *yerba maté* scrubs and Andean peat masks.

Cabañas del Beagle CABIN **$$$**
(☎ 02901-15-511323, 02901-432785; www.cabanasdelbeagle.com; Las Aljabas 375; 2-person cabins US$140) Couples in search of a romantic hideaway delight in these rustic-chic cabins with heated stone floors, crackling fireplaces, and full kitchens stocked daily with fresh bread, coffee and other treats. Personable owner Alejandro wins high praise for his attentive service. It's 13 blocks uphill from the town center and accessed via Av Leandro Alem. Four-night minimum stay.

Cabañas Aldea Nevada CABIN **$$$**
(☎ 02901-422851; www.aldeanevada.com.ar; Martial 1430; 2/4-person cabins from US$140/190; @ 🛜) You expect the elves to arrive here any minute. This beautiful 6-hectare patch of lenga forest has 13 privately situated log cabins with outdoor grills. Interiors are rustic but modern, with functional kitchens, wood

FUEGIAN RITES OF PASSAGE

Part of traveling to Tierra del Fuego is searching for clues to its mystical, unknowable past. Souvenir shops sell a postcard of abstract intrigue: there's a naked man painted black. Fine horizontal white stripes cross his body from chest to foot. His face remains covered. So, what's this all about?

For people who lived exposed to the elements, dependent on their wits and courage, initiation ceremonies were a big deal. Those of the seafaring Yahgan (or Yámana) were surprisingly similar to those of the fierce northern neighbors they wanted little to do with, the nomadic hunters called Selk'nam (or Ona to the Yahgan). Both celebrated a male rite of passage that reenacted a great upheaval when the men stole the women's secrets to gain power over them. In the Kina, Yahgan men interpreted the spirits by painting their bodies with black carbon and striped or dotted patterns that used the region's white and red clays. The Selk'nam undertook their Hain ceremony similarly adorned, taking young men into huts where they were attacked by spirits. In related ceremonies men showed their strength to women by fighting the spirits in theatrical displays, each acting with the characteristics of a specific spirit. These manly displays did not always achieve their desired effect of subjugation: one account tells of spirits dispatched to menace female camps that instead evoked hilarity.

With European encroachment, these ceremonies became more abbreviated and much of their detailed significance was lost. When the last Hain was celebrated in the early 20th century in the presence of missionaries, it had already crossed over from ritual to theater.

stoves and hardwood details. Rough-hewn benches are contemplatively placed by the ponds, and there's a gazebo overlooking the Beagle Channel. Two-night minimum stay.

Cumbres del Martial INN $$$
(☎02901-424779; www.cumbresdelmartial.com.ar; Martial 3560; d/cabins US$220/340; @📶) This stylish place sits at the base of the Glaciar Martial. Standard rooms have a touch of English cottage, while the two-story wooden cabins are simply stunning, with stone fireplaces, Jacuzzis and dazzling vaulted windows. Lush robes, optional massages (extra) and your country's newspaper delivered to your mailbox are some of the fabulous details.

Eating

★**Almacen Ramos Generales** CAFE $
(☎02901-424-7317; Av Maipú 749; mains AR$73-175; ⌚9am-midnight) With its quirky memorabilia and postings about local environmental issues, this warm and cozy former general store is a peek inside the real Ushuaia. Locals hold their powwows here. Croissants and crusty baguettes are baked daily. There's also local beer on tap, a wine list, and light fare such as sandwiches, soups and quiche.

Cafe Bar Banana CAFE $
(☎02901-435035; Av San Martín 273; mains AR$80-150; ⌚8am-1am) Serving homemade burgers and fries, sandwiches, and steak and eggs, this is a local favorite for high-octane, low-cost dining with friends.

El Turco CAFE $
(☎02901-424711; Av San Martín 1410; mains AR$70-130; ⌚noon-3pm & 8pm-midnight) Nothing fancy, this classic, dated Argentine cafe nonetheless charms with inexpensive prices and swift-footed bow-tied waiters who want to try out their French on tourists. Standard dishes include *milanesa* (breaded meat), pizzas, crispy fries and roast chicken.

Lomitos Martinica ARGENTINE $
(☎02901-432134; Av San Martín 68; mains AR$85-125; ⌚11:30am-3pm & 8:30pm-midnight Mon-Sat) Cheap and cheerful, and full of locals getting take-out, this greasy spoon with grill-side seating serves enormous *milanesa* sandwiches and offers a cheap lunch special.

La Anónima SUPERMARKET $
(cnr Gobernador Paz & Rivadavia; ⌚9am-10pm) A grocery store with cheap take-out.

Volver SEAFOOD $$
(☎02901-423977; Av Maipú 37) Self-promoted as serving up *ceviche de la puta madre* (politely translated as 'fantastic seafood'), this place is run by a charismatic chef loved by locals. The food is served simply but is of incredible quality. Those who

think they don't like king crab should give it a second chance here: there are no added sauces and the crab's cooked to perfection.

Bodegón Fueguino PATAGONIAN **$$**
(☎02901-431972; Av San Martín 859; mains AR$130-250; ⏲noon-2:45pm & 8-11:45pm Tue-Sun) The spot to sample hearty home-style Patagonian fare or gather for wine and appetizers. Painted peach, this century-old Fuegian home is cozied up with sheepskin-clad benches, cedar barrels and ferns. A *picada* (shared appetizer plate) for two includes eggplant, lamb brochettes, crab and bacon-wrapped plums.

Christopher PARRILLA **$$**
(☎02901-425079; www.christopherushuaia.com.ar; Av Maipú 828; mains AR$120-280; ⏲noon-3pm & 8pm-midnight, to 1am Sat; Ⓟ) This classic grill and brewpub is deservedly popular with locals. Standouts include barbecue ribs, big salads and burgers. It's good value, with generous portions that you might want to share and a talented bartender mixing cocktails. Grab a table by the window for great harbor views.

Paso Garibaldi ARGENTINE **$$**
(☎02901-432380; Deloquí 133; mains AR$180-290; ⏲noon-2:30pm & 7-11:30pm Tue-Sat, 7-11:30pm Sun) Serving hearty local fare including black-bean stew, flavorful salads and roasted hake, this new addition is refreshingly without pretension. The recycled decor looks a little too improvised, but service couldn't be more attentive and dishes are well priced.

Placeres Patagónicos ARGENTINE **$$**
(☎02901-433798; www.facebook.com/PlaceresPatagonicos-Ushuaia-178544198846139; 289 Deloquí; snacks AR$65, tablas from AR$100; ⏲noon-midnight) This stylish cafe-deli serves *tablas* (wooden cutting boards) piled with homemade bread and mouthwatering local specialties like smoked trout and wild boar. It's a good place to sip *mate* (a bitter ritual tea) with a plate of *tortas fritas* (fry bread). Coffee arrives steaming in a bowl-sized mug.

La Estancia STEAK **$$**
(☎02901-431421; cnr Godoy & Av San Martín; mains AR$120-240; ⏲noon-3pm & 8-11pm) For authentic Argentine *asado* (barbecue), it's hard to beat this reliable, well-priced grill. There are many others along the main drag, but this is the one that consistently delivers. Enthusiastic appetites should go for the *tenedor libre* (all you can eat). Locals and travelers feast on whole roast lamb, juicy steaks, sizzling ribs and heaping salads.

Chiko SEAFOOD **$$**
(☎02901-431736; www.chikorestaurant.com.ar; 25 de Mayo 62; mains AR$140-300; ⏲noon-3pm & 7:30-11:30pm Mon-Sat) At this boon to seafood-lovers, crisp oversized calamari rings, *paila marina* (shellfish stew) and fish dishes like *abadejo a pil pil* (pollock in garlic sauce) are done so well that you might not mind the slowish service. An odd assemblage of homeland memorabilia suggests that the Chilean owners are a touch homesick.

Tante Sara CAFE **$$**
(☎02901-423912; www.tantesara.com; cnr Av San Martín & Juana Fadul; mains AR$154-265; ⏲8am-2am) This corner bistro, frequented by tourists and locals alike, serves the usual suspects in a warm atmosphere. For a late-night bite, this is your best bet – it's the only kitchen open until 2am. The burger menu is creative and extensive. Its **sister branch** (☎02901-433710; cnr Rivadavia & Av San Martín; mains AR$60-130; ⏲8am-8:30pm Mon-Thu, to 9pm Fri & Sat) offers nice pastries and weekend brunch.

Küar Resto Bar PUB FOOD **$$**
(☎02901-437396; http://kuar.com.ar; Av Perito Moreno 2232; mains AR$115-300; ⏲6pm-late) This chic log-cabin-style hangout offers local beer, cheese boards and tapas, as well as complete dinners with ample fresh seafood. The interior is stylish, but the highlight, especially at sunset, is the jaw-dropping view over the water. It's five minutes from the center by cab, or visit **Küar 1900** (☎02901-436807; http://kuar.com.ar; 2nd fl, Av San Martín 471; mains AR$120-180; ⏲noon-3:30pm & 6:30pm-midnight Mon-Sat), a smaller downtown venue focused on tapas.

★**Kalma Resto** INTERNATIONAL **$$$**
(☎02901-425786; www.kalmaresto.com.ar; Valdéz 293; mains AR$350-470, 5-course tasting menu AR$950; ⏲7-11pm Mon-Sat) This gem presents Fuegian staples like crab and octopus in a creative new context. Black sea bass wears a tart tomato sauce for contrast; there's stuffed lamb seasoned with pepper and rosemary; and the summer greens and edible flowers come fresh from the garden. It's gourmet at its least pretentious. The wine list is mind-blowing.

Service is stellar, with charismatic yet humble young chef Jorge making the rounds and sharing his enthusiasm for harvesting

1

RAPHAEL KOERICH/500PX ©

2

4

MATYAS REHAK/SHUTTERSTOCK ©

1. Snowboarding, Ushuaia (p497)
The peaks surrounding this city are loaded with powder, delighting winter visitors in search of a snow fix.

2. El Tren del Fin del Mundo (p508)
This train originally carted prisoners to work camps, now it takes tourists to the stunning Parque Nacional Tierra del Fuego.

3. Martial Range (p497)
Snowcapped mountains form a majestic backdrop to port city Ushuaia, which takes full advantage of its end-of-the-world status.

4. Estancia Harberton (p500)
Tierra del Fuego's first estancia, Harberton was founded in 1886 by missionary Thomas Bridges.

RAPHAEL KOERICH/500PX ©

local ingredients. For dessert, splurge with a not-too-sweet deconstructed chocolate cake.

★Kaupé INTERNATIONAL **$$$**
(☎02901-422704; www.kaupe.com.ar; Roca 470; mains AR$300-500) For an out-of-body seafood experience, make a reservation at this candlelit house overlooking the bay. Chef Ernesto Vivian employs the freshest of everything and service is impeccable. The tasting menu features two starters, a main dish and dessert, with standouts such as king crab and spinach chowder or black sea bass in blackened butter.

Chez Manu INTERNATIONAL **$$$**
(☎02901-432253; www.chezmanu.com; Martial 2135; mains AR$190-300) Heading to Glaciar Martial? Don't miss this quality place right on the way. It's just 2km from town, but you'll feel you're in the middle of nature. Chef Emmanuel adds a French touch to fresh local ingredients, such as Fuegian lamb or mixed plates of cold *fruits de mer*, and service is exceptional. The three-course set lunch is the best deal.

Incredible views are a welcome bonus.

María Lola Restó ARGENTINE **$$$**
(☎02901-421185; www.marialolaresto.com.ar; Deloquí 1048; mains AR$250-400; ⏲noon-midnight Mon-Sat; P) This creative cafe-style restaurant overlooks the channel. Locals pack in for homemade pasta with seafood or strip steak in rich mushroom sauce; the weekday set lunch or dinner with an included drink is AR$500. Service is good and portions tend toward the humongous: desserts can easily be split. It's among the few downtown restaurants with off-street parking.

Drinking & Nightlife

Dublin Irish Pub IRISH PUB
(☎02901-430744; 9 de Julio 168; ⏲7pm-4am) Dublin doesn't feel so far away at this dimly lit pub. Popular with the locals, it's the scene of lively banter and free-flowing drinks. Look out for occasional live music and be sure to try at least one of its three local Beagle beers. Arrive by 9pm if you want to score a seat.

Viagro BAR
(☎02901-421617; Roca 55; ⏲8pm-4am) If you can get past the unfortunate name, this cocktail nook is the perfect low-lit rendezvous spot, with exotic concoctions and appetizing tapas to fuel your night out. There's dancing on Saturday nights.

Entertainment

Cine Pakewaia CINEMA
(☎02901-436500; www.cinepackewaia.com; cnr Yaganes & Gobernador Paz; tickets AR$100) First-run movies are shown at the Museo del Presidio's fully restored hangar-style theater.

Shopping

Paseo de los Artesanos MARKET
(Plaza 25 de Mayo) This indoor artists market sells handmade jewelry, wool crafts, traditional *mates* and other household items. The majority of vendors only accept Argentine pesos, so bring cash. Hours vary depending on season and vendor, but most stalls are open between noon and 7pm. It's right next to the main port.

Quelhue Wine Shop WINE
(☎02901-435882; www.quelhue.com.ar; Av San Martín 253; ⏲9:30am-9:15pm) They don't seem to sell a bad bottle of wine in the whole place. This is a wine-lover's paradise, with floor-to-ceiling shelves stocked to the brim with Argentina's best reds, whites and sparklings. It also sells a solid selection of perfect picnic food: dried meats, a wide range of cheeses, and quality chocolates.

Boutique del Libro BOOKS
(☎02901-424750; Av San Martín 1120) Outstanding selection of Patagonia- and Antarctica-themed material, with literature, guidebooks and pictorials (also in English).

Information

IMMIGRATION

Immigration Office (☎02901-422334; Fuegia Basket 187; ⏲9am-noon Mon-Fri) Argentine office for immigration issues.

MEDICAL SERVICES

Hospital Regional (☎ext 107, 02901-423200; cnr Fitz Roy & 12 de Octubre) Emergency services. It's southwest of the center via Av Maipú.

MONEY

Several banks on Avs Maipú and San Martín have ATMs.

POST

Post Office (cnr Av San Martín & Godoy; ⏲9am-6pm Mon-Fri)

TOURIST INFORMATION

Antarctica Tourist Office (☎02901-430015; www.tierradelfuego.org.ar/antartida; Av Maipú 505; ⏲with ship in port 9am-5pm) Very helpful office at the pier.

Asociación Caza y Pesca (☎ 02901-422423, 02901-423168; www.cazaypescaushuaia.org; Av Maipú 822) Contact Asociación Caza y Pesca for a License 1, valid throughout the province, except in Parque Nacional Tierra del Fuego. Its website also has tidal charts.

Automóvil Club Argentino (ACA; www.aca.org.ar; cnr Malvina Argentinas & Onachaga) Argentina's auto club; good source for provincial road maps.

Club Andino Ushuaia (☎ 02901-422335, 02901-440732; www.clubandinoushuaia.com.ar; Refugio Wallner, LN Alem 2873; ⊙10am-1pm & 3-8pm Mon-Fri) Sells a map and bilingual trekking, mountaineering and mountain-biking guidebook. The club occasionally organizes hikes and can recommend guides. Located 5km west of Ushuaia.

Instituto Fueguino de Turismo (Infuetur; ☎ 02901-421423; www.tierradelfuego.org.ar; Av Maipú 505) Tourism office for Tierra del Fuego. Ask here about the development of island trekking routes called Huella del Fin del Mundo. It's on the ground floor of Hotel Albatros.

Municipal Tourist Office (☎ 02901-437666; www.turismoushuaia.com; Prefectura Naval 470; ⊙8am-9pm) Very helpful, with English- and French-speaking staff, a message board and multilingual brochures, as well as good lodging, activities and transport info. It also posts a list of available lodgings outside after closing time. There's a second office at the **airport** (☎ 02901-423970; www.turismoushuaia.com; airport; ⊙during flight arrivals).

National Parks Administration (☎ 02901-421315; Av San Martín 1395; ⊙9am-5pm Mon-Fri) Offers information on Parque Nacional Tierra del Fuego.

Getting There & Away

AIR

LAN is the best bet for Buenos Aires; purchase tickets through local travel agencies. **Aerolíneas Argentinas** (☎ 0810-2228-6527; www.aerolineas.com.ar; cnr Av Maipú & 9 de Julio) jets to Buenos Aires (one way 3½ hours) several times daily, sometimes stopping in El Calafate (70 minutes).

LADE (☎ 02901-421123, in Buenos Aires 011-5353-2387; www.lade.com.ar; Av San Martín 542) flies to Buenos Aires, El Calafate and Río Grande, and may serve other destinations.

BOAT

A few private yachts charter trips around the Beagle Channel, to Cape Horn and Antarctica. These trips must be organized well in advance.

For Puerto Williams (Chile), **Ushuaia Boating** (☎ 2901-609030; www.ushuaiaboating.com; Tourist Wharf s/n; 1 way US$120) goes daily in Zodiac boats. Tickets include a 40-minute crossing plus an overland transfer from Puerto Navarino. Note: inclement weather often means cancellations. Options include a 9:30am departure and sometimes (with sufficient demand) a 6pm departure. Another option to Puerto Williams is offered by **Piratour** (p498).

A small *tasa de embarque* (departure tax) is paid at the pier.

BUS

Ushuaia has no bus terminal. Book outgoing bus tickets as far in advance as possible; many readers have complained about getting stuck here in high season. Depending on your luck, long waits at border crossings can be expected.

Bus Sur (☎ 02901-430727; http://bussur.com; Av San Martín 245) has buses to Punta Arenas and Puerto Natales (Chile) three times weekly at 8am, connecting with Montiel services. It shares an office with Turismo Comapa, which also does tours and runs ferries in Chile.

Tecni-Austral (☎ 02901-431408; www.busbud.com; Roca 157) buses head daily to Río Grande and Río Gallegos via Tolhuin, and to Punta Arenas three times weekly. **Taqsa** (☎ 02901-435453; www.taqsa.com.ar; Juana Fadul 126) also has 7am buses to Río Grande and Rio Gallegos via Tolhuin; buses to Punta Arenas and Puerto Natales three times weekly; and buses to Río Gallegos, El Calafate and Bariloche daily.

Lider (☎ 02901-442264, 02901-436421; http://lidertdf.com.ar; Gobernador Paz 921) runs door-to-door minivans to Tolhuin and Río Grande six to eight times daily, with fewer departures on Sunday. **Montiel** (Transporte Montiel; ☎ 02901-421366; Gobernador Paz 605) has similar services.

Buses from Ushuaia

DESTINATION	COST (AR$)	TIME (HR)
El Calafate	1190	18
Punta Arenas, Chile	920	12
Río Gallegos	785	13
Río Grande	410	3½
Tolhuin	260	1½

Getting Around

Taxis to/from the modern airport, 4km southwest of downtown, cost AR$120. Taxis can be chartered for around AR$1300 for three hours. There's a local bus service along Av Maipú.

Rental rates for compact cars, including insurance, start at around AR$800 per day; try **Localiza** (☎ 02901-430739; www.localiza.com;

Av Maipú 768). Some agencies may not charge for drop-off in other parts of Argentine Tierra del Fuego.

Hourly ski shuttles (AR$250 roundtrip) leave from the corner of Juana Fadul and Av Maipú to resorts along RN 3 from 9am to 2pm daily. Each resort also provides its own transportation from downtown Ushuaia.

Parque Nacional Tierra del Fuego

Banked against the Beagle Channel, the hushed, fragrant southern forests of Tierra del Fuego are a stunning setting to explore. West of Ushuaia some 12km along RN 3, **Parque Nacional Tierra del Fuego** (www.parquesnacionales.gob.ar; AR$350, collected 8am-8pm) was Argentina's first coastal national park, extending 630 sq km from the Beagle Channel in the south to beyond Lago Fagnano in the north.

There's access to the southern edge of the park with scenic hikes along bays and rivers, or through dense native forests. For spectacular color, come in autumn, when hillsides of ñire glow red.

Birdlife is prolific, especially along the coastal zone. Keep an eye out for condors, albatross, cormorants, gulls, terns, oystercatchers, grebes, kelp geese and the comical, flightless, orange-billed steamer ducks. Common invasive species include the European rabbit and the North American beaver, both wreaking ecological havoc despite their cuteness. Gray and red foxes, enjoying the abundance of rabbits, may also be seen.

Sleeping & Eating

There is one *refugio* and various, mostly free campgrounds. Most get crowded, which means sites can become unreasonably messy. Do your part to take your trash out of the park and follow a leave-no-trace ethic.

There is plenty of availability for camping at wild sites. **Camping Ensenada** is 16km from the park entrance and nearest the Senda Costera trail; **Camping Río Pipo** is 6km from the entrance and easily accessed by either the road to Cañadon del Toro or the Senda Pampa Alta trail. **Camping Laguna Verde** and **Camping Los Cauquenes** are on the islands in Río Lapataia. There are no amenities at any of the sites; contact the park visitor center, **Centro de Visitantes Alakush** (9am-7pm, shorter hours Mar-Nov), for more information.

The park has closed the fee-based campground at Lago Roca but is planning a new campground with showers in a yet-to-be-determined location.

Bring your own provisions for picnics and camping. On-site there's a tiny (expensive) grocery store, open in high season.

Getting There & Away

Taxi fares here shared between groups can be the same price as bus tickets. Private tour buses also make the trip.

The most touristy and, beyond jogging, the slowest way to the park, **El Tren del Fin del Mundo** (02901-431600; www.trendelfindelmundo.com.ar; adult/child plus park entrance fee AR$790/150) originally carted prisoners to work camps. It departs (without the convicts) from the Estación del Fin del Mundo, 8km west of Ushuaia, three or four times daily in summer and once or twice daily in winter.

The one-hour, scenic narrow-gauge train ride has historical explanations in English and Spanish. Reservations are needed in January and February, when cruise-ship tours take over. You can take it one way and return via minibus, though the train fare is the same one way or roundtrip.

Hitchhiking to the park is feasible, but many cars may already be full.

Tolhuin & Lago Fagnano

02901

Named for the Selk'nam word meaning 'like a heart,' Tolhuin (population 2000) is a lake town nestled in the center of Tierra del Fuego, 132km south of Río Grande and 104km northeast of Ushuaia via smooth asphalt roads. Muddy streets and clear-cut forests mark this fast-growing frontier town that fronts the eastern shore of Lago Fagnano, also known as Lago Kami. Lago Fagnano, with low-key horseback riding, mountain biking, boating and fishing, is worth checking out as a tranquil lake spot.

Shared with Chile, the glacial-formed Lago Fagnano offers 117km of beaches, with most of its shoreline remote and roadless. Plans to create road access from Chile and put a catamaran here are developing.

Sights

Museo Histórico Kami MUSEUM

(tdf@gmail.com; Lago Fagnano s/n; 3-7pm Tue-Sun) FREE If you make one stop in Tolhuin, check out this museum, which is especially worthwhile for Spanish speakers. A former

Parque Nacional Tierra del Fuego – Lapataia Sector

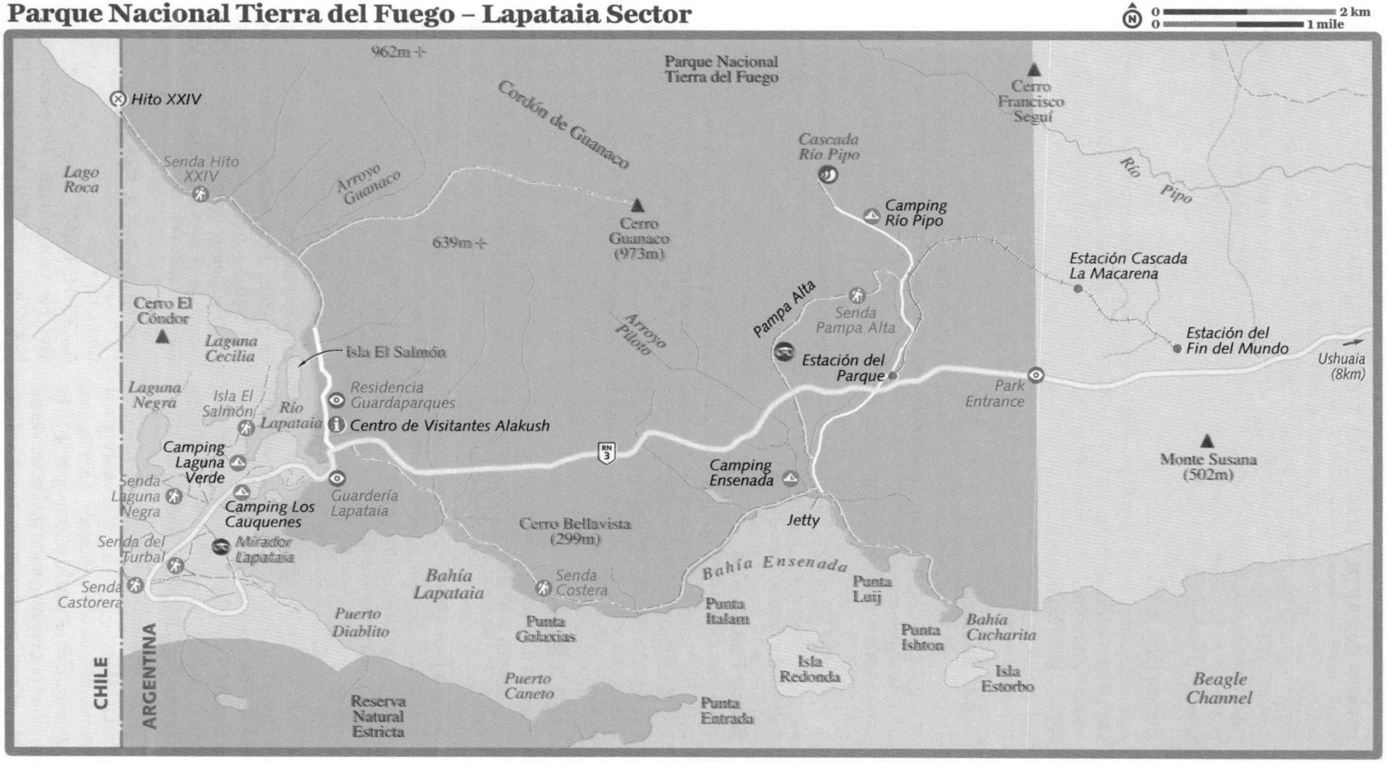

HIKING IN PARQUE NACIONAL TIERRA DEL FUEGO

After running 3242km from Buenos Aires, RN 3 reaches its terminus at the shores of Bahía Lapataia. From here, trails **Mirador Lapataia** (500m), with excellent views, and **Senda Del Turbal** (400m) lead through winding lenga forest further into the bay. Other short walks include the self-guided nature trail **Senda Laguna Negra** (950m), through peat bogs, and the **Senda Castorera** (400m), showcasing massive abandoned beaver dams on a few ponds.

Senda Hito XXIV

At the end of the road to Lago Roca, a flat trail (a 10km four-hour roundtrip) leads around Lago Roca's forested northeast shore to Hito XXIV – *veinticuatro* in Spanish – the boundary post that marks the Argentina–Chile frontier. It is illegal to cross the frontier, which is patrolled regularly.

From the same trailhead you can reach **Cerro Guanaco** (973m) via the steep and difficult 8km trail of the same name; it's a long, uphill haul, but the views are excellent.

Senda Costera

This 8km (four-hour) trek leads west from Bahía Ensenada along the coastline. Keep an eye out for old *conchales* (archaeologically important mounds of shells left by Yahgan inhabitants), now covered in grass. The trail meets RN 3 a short way east of the park administration *(guardería)* center at Lapataia. From here it is 1.2km further to Senda Hito XXIV.

It might be tempting to roll up the cuffs and go clamming, but be aware that occasional *marea roja* (red tides) contaminate mollusks (such as clams and mussels) along the shore of the Beagle Channel. This seasonal trail opens in December.

Senda Pampa Alta

The low heights of Pampa Alta (around 315m) grant long views across the Beagle Channel to Isla Navarino and Isla Hoste. RN 3 meets the trailhead 1.5km west of the Río Pipo and Bahía Ensenada road turnoffs (3km from the entrance gate). The 5km roundtrip trail first climbs a hill, passing a beaver dam along the way. Enjoy the impressive views at the lookout. A quick 300m further leads to a trail paralleling the Río Pipo and some waterfalls.

Laguna Negra

From the road 2km southwest of Lapataia, a trail leads north along the western side of Río Lapataia to a fishing spot opposite Isla El Salmón. Laguna Negra, a lovely lake in the forest, is easily accessible via a 1km circuit loop.

Senda Palestra

This 4km (three-hour) roundtrip trek from Bahía Ensenada follows a path eastward past an old copper mine to the popular rock-climbing wall of Palestra, near a *refugio* (rustic shelter) that is no longer in use.

1920s police post, the little house is now dedicated to regional history, starting with the Selk'nam people. One exhibit documents community members' stories of the still-recent pioneer times. It's next to Camping Hain, on Lago Fagnano. Don't be too shy to ask for a tour.

Parque Hain AMUSEMENT PARK
(Parque de Diversiones Reciclado; Lago Fagnano s/n; adult/child AR$50/20; 9am-5pm;) The product of a creative mind that never sleeps, this offbeat playground is styled entirely from recycled materials, namely 5000 wooden pallets, tires fashioned into playforms and bottles forming decorative motifs. Created by Roberto Barbel, who also owns the campground across the street with similar whimsy on display, it's a kick to take in.

Sleeping & Eating

Camping Hain CAMPGROUND $
(02964-15-603606; Lago Fagnano; campsites per person US$6, 3-/6-person refugios US$58/105) Located on Lago Fagnano,

Camping Hain has hot showers, grassy sites with wooden windbreaks, a huge barbecue pit and a *fogon* (sheltered fire pit and kitchen area). There's plenty of creative handiwork but no internet by design: unplug and enjoy. The owner can pick up guests from Panadería La Unión.

Hostería Ruta Al Sur HOTEL $$
(☎02901-492278; RN 3, Km2954; d incl breakfast US$125; ⊙mid-Oct–Apr; @ 📶 ✉) On the main road, this lovely lodge set among old beech trees is a bit of a surprise. So is the uneven service. There are sparkling rooms, a sprawling living room and a restaurant serving basic breakfasts. Confirm rates in advance since foreigners may be charged more (to be fair, it has rates for Tierra del Fuego residents and nonresidents too).

Panadería La Unión BAKERY $
(☎02901-492202; www.panaderialaunion.com.ar; Jeujepen 450; snacks AR$100; ⊙24hr) First-rate *facturas* (pastries) and second-rate instant cappuccinos keep this roadside attraction hopping. You may or may not recognize the Argentine celebrities gracing the walls (hint: the men are aging rock stars). Buses stop here to pick up passengers and hot water for *mate*.

Information

Banco de Tierra del Fuego (☎02901-492030; Minkiol s/n; ⊙10am-3pm Tue-Fri) Has an ATM.

Tourist Office (☎02901-492125; www.tierradelfuego.org.ar; Av de los Shelknam 80; ⊙8am-10pm Mon-Fri) Provides information on hiking, horseback-riding tours and gear rentals. It's located behind the gas station. Those coming from Ushuaia might get more complete info from Ushuaia's tourist office.

Getting There & Away

Throughout the day, buses and minivans passing along RN 3 (often already full in high season) stop at the Panadería La Unión bakery en route to Ushuaia or Río Grande (AR$280).

Río Grande

☎02964 / POP 66,500

A monster trout sculpture at the entrance to town announces the de facto fly-fishing capital of Tierra del Fuego, with world-class blue-ribbon angling for colossal sea-run trout. But nonfishers will likely blow through windswept Río Grande and hop a bus to Ushuaia, 230km southwest.

As wool baron José Menéndez' sheep stations developed, Río Grande grew as a makeshift service town. In 1893 the Salesian order, under the guidance of Monseñor Fagnano, set up a mission in an unsuccessful attempt to shelter the Selk'nam from the growing infringement. As a petroleum service center, the town has an industrial feel: even the public artworks look like giant, grim Tinkertoys. Geared to business travelers, Río Grande is pricey for visitors. Duty-free status, meant to foster development, has brought in electronics-manufacturing plants and wholesale appliance stores. During the Falklands War the military played an important role here; memorials pay tribute to fallen soldiers.

Activities

Hollywood stars, heads of state and former US presidents flock to desolate stretches around Río Grande in hope of landing the big one. Usually they are in luck. Rivers around Río Grande were stocked in the 1930s with brown, rainbow and brook trout. The region is now one of the world's best sea-run trout-fishing areas, with some local specimens weighing in at 16kg, rainbow trout reaching 9kg.

Fishing excursions are mostly organized through outside agents, many in the US. 'Public' fishing rivers, on which trips can be organized, include the Fuego, Menéndez, Candelaria, Ewan and MacLennan. Lodgings for many of the more elite angling trips are in *estancias* with exclusive use of some of the best rivers.

There are two types of fishing license. License 1 is valid throughout the province, except in Parque Nacional Tierra del Fuego. Contact Asociación Caza y Pesca (p507) in Ushuaia (its website also has tidal charts). License 2 is valid for Parque Nacional Tierra del Fuego and Patagonia. Contact the National Parks Administration office (p507) in Ushuaia or find more information on sport fishing in Argentina through the online portal **Pesca Argentina** (www.pescaargentina.com.ar). Other useful information:

Flies Rubber legs and woolly buggers.

License fees AR$270 per day or AR$1080 per season, depending on where you fish.

Limit One fish per person per day, catch and release.

Methods Spinning and fly casting; no night fishing.

Season November 1 to April 15, with catch-and-release restrictions from April 1 to April 15.

Sleeping & Eating

Hotel Villa HOTEL **$**
(☎02964-424998; www.hotelvilla-riogrande.com; Av San Martín 281; d/tr US$57/77; P@📶) Opposite Casino Status, this refurbished place has a dozen spacious and stylish rooms outfitted with down duvets, breakfast with *medialunas* (croissants) and a popular restaurant.

Posada de los Sauces HOTEL **$$**
(☎02964-432895; http://posadadelossauces.com; Elcano 839; d US$97; @📶) Catering mostly to high-end anglers, this warm and professional hotel fosters a lodge atmosphere, with fresh scents and woodsy accents. Deluxe rooms have Jacuzzis. The upstairs bar-restaurant, decked out in dark wood and forest green, is just waiting for stogies and tall tales to fill the air.

Don Peppone ITALIAN **$$**
(☎02964-432066; Perito Moreno 247; mains AR$180-250; ⊙noon-midnight Tue-Sun) On weekends there's a dose of madness in this busy pizzeria, with gooey brick-oven creations as well as a huge variety of pastas and meat dishes. Credit cards are accepted.

Tante Sara CAFE **$$**
(☎02964-421114; Av San Martín 192; mains AR$120-280; ⊙8am-1am Sun-Thu, to 2am Fri & Sat) An upscale chain in Tierra del Fuego, this nonetheless cozy spot hosts both ladies having tea and cake, and boys at the varnished bar downing beer and burgers. Salads (including romaine, egg, blue cheese and bacon) are surprisingly good, although service can be quite sluggish.

Information

Instituto Fueguino de Turismo (Infuetur; ☎02964-426805; www.tierradelfuego.org.ar; Av Belgrano 319; ⊙9am-9pm) Supplies tourist information for all of Argentine Tierra del Fuego.

Municipal Tourist Kiosk (turismo@riogrande.gob.ar; Rosales 350; ⊙9am-8pm) Helpful kiosk on Plaza Almirante Brown, with maps, *estancia* brochures and fishing details.

Getting There & Away

AIR

The **airport** (☎02964-420699) is a short taxi ride from town, off RN 3. **Aerolíneas Argentinas** (☎02964-424467; Av San Martín 607; ⊙9:30am-5:30pm Mon-Fri) flies daily to Buenos Aires. **LADE** (☎02964-422968; Lasserre 429; ⊙9am-3pm Mon-Fri) flies a couple of times weekly to Río Gallegos, El Calafate and Buenos Aires. New low-cost airlines plan to offer flights to Buenos Aires, Ushuaia and El Calafate. **Aviación Civil Argentina** (ANAC; www.anac.gob.ar) has a map with new routes and airlines.

BUS

The following bus companies depart from **Terminal Fuegina** (Finocchio 1194):

Buses Pacheco (☎02964-421554) Buses to Punta Arenas three times weekly at 10am.

Taqsa/Marga (☎02964-434316) Buses to Ushuaia via Tolhuin.

Bus Sur (☎02964-420997; www.bus-sur.cl; 25 de Mayo 712) Buses to Ushuaia, Punta Arenas and Puerto Natales three times weekly at 5:30am, connecting with Montiel. (Note that the separate ticket office is on 25 de Mayo.)

Tecni-Austral (☎02964-430610) Buses to Ushuaia via Tolhuin three times weekly at 8:30am; also to Río Gallegos and Punta Arenas three times weekly.

Other buses:

Lider (☎02964-420003; www.lidertdf.com.ar; Av Belgrano 1122) The best option for Ushuaia and Tolhuin is this door-to-door minivan service, with several daily departures. Call to reserve.

Montiel (☎02964-420997; 25 de Mayo 712) Buses to Ushuaia and Tolhuin.

Estancias Around Río Grande

Much of Tierra del Fuego held extensive sheep ranches known as *estancias*. Today, many have opened to small-scale tourism, offering a unique chance to learn about the region's history and enjoy its magic. They can also be an exclusive destination for fly fishing.

Activities

Estancia María Behety FISHING
(☎in USA 800-669-3474; www.theflyshop.com; 1 week fishing & lodging package per person US$7900; ⊙Dec-Apr) This highly exclusive lodge and working ranch caters to elite anglers. It's managed by The Fly Shop, a California-based outfitter. Wool baron José Menéndez founded this 1500-sq-km *estancia*, named after his wife. It's 17km west of Río Grande via RC-c. Besides boasting the world's largest shearing shed, it's considered the place to go to catch record-setting brown sea trout.

Sleeping

Estancia Las Hijas ESTANCIA $$
(☎02901-554462; www.estancialashijas.com.ar; RP 16; per person incl half-board overnight or day trip US$90, day trip incl transport US$300) This lauded *estancia* offers small-scale family visits for groups (inquire ahead, as different parties can combine). Indeed, the proprietors are known around these parts as *'locos divinos'* (crazy but fun). After horseback riding, sheep mustering and barbecues, guests stay in basic lodgings with shared bathrooms. For transportation from Ushuaia or Río Grande, there's a minimum of two people.

Estancia Las Hijas is located 33km north of Tolhuin, 7km in on the dirt road RP 16 (formerly 'G').

Estancia Rolito ESTANCIA $$$
(☎02901-432419, 02901-437351; RC-a, Km 14; s/d incl full board US$330/550) The rustic and charismatic Estancia Rolito is very Argentine and very inviting. Guests rave about the hikes through ñire and lenga forest. Day trips from Ushuaia (with Turismo de Campo) stop by for lunch or dinner and activities. Rates are based on double occupancy. Rolito is 100km from Río Grande and 150km from Ushuaia.

Getting There & Away

Visitors can arrive at *estancias* via private vehicle or on a package tour.

Puerto Williams (Chile)

☎061 / POP 1680

For authentic end-of-the-earth ambience, remote Isla Navarino wins the contest without even campaigning. Located south across the Beagle Channel from Ushuaia, it's a mostly uninhabited wilderness of peat bogs, southern beech forest and jagged, toothy spires known as Dientes del Navarino, also a famed trekking route. Puerto Williams is the only town, the official port of entry for vessels en route to Cape Horn and Antarctica, and home to the last living Yaghan speaker.

A permanent European presence was established on the island by mid-19th-century missionaries, who were followed by fortune seekers during the 1890s gold rush. Current inhabitants include the Chilean navy, municipal employees, and octopus and crab fishers. The remaining mixed-race descendants of the Yaghan people live in the small coastal village of Villa Ukika, a fifteen-minute walk east of town along the waterfront.

The island's 150km of trails are gaining international attention, though at points they're poorly marked and challenging. If hiking, take a companion, get directions from locals before heading out and register with the *carabineros* (police).

Sights

Museo Martín Gusinde MUSEUM
(☎61-262-1043; www.museomartingusinde.cl; cnr Araguay & Gusinde; donation requested; ⏲9:30am-1pm & 3-6:30pm Tue-Fri, 2:30-6:30pm Sat & Sun, reduced hours low season) An attractive museum honoring the German priest and ethnographer who worked among the Yaghan from 1918 to 1923. Focuses on ethnography and natural history. Public wifi is available in the library.

Club de Yates Micalvi LANDMARK
(⏲late Sep-May) A grounded German cargo boat, the *Micalvi* was declared a regional naval museum in 1976 but found infinitely better use as a floating bar, frequented by navy men and yachties. Unfortunately, the bar isn't open to the general public.

Yelcho Replica LANDMARK
Near the entrance to the military quarters is the original bow of the ship that rescued Ernest Shackleton's Antarctic expedition from Elephant Island in 1916.

Activities

Winter hikes are only recommended for experienced mountaineers.

★**Dientes de Navarino** HIKING
This trekking circuit offers impossibly raw and windswept vistas under Navarino's toothy spires. Beginning at the Virgin altar just outside of town, the five-day, 53.5km route winds through a spectacular wilderness of exposed rock and secluded lakes. Fit hikers can knock it out in four days in the (relatively) dry summer months. Markings are minimal: GPS, used in conjunction with marked maps, is a handy navigational tool.

Cerro Bandera HIKING
With expansive views of the Beagle Channel, this four-hour roundtrip covers the first approach of the Navarino Circuit. The trail ascends steeply through lenga to blustery

stone-littered hillside planted with a Chilean flag.

Lago Windhond HIKING

This remote lake is a lesser-known, but worthy, alternative to hiking the Dientes circuit, with sheltered hiking through forest and peat bogs. The four-day roundtrip is a better bet if there are high winds. For route details, ask at Turismo Shila or go with a guide.

Tours

Denis Chevallay TOURS

(cell 9-7876-6934; denischevallay@gmail.com; Ortiz 260; by appointment) For guided trekking or logistical support, Denis Chevallay guides in French, German and English and has a wealth of botanical and historical knowledge. Guiding includes porter support and a satellite emergency phone. Day trips to archaeological sites are also available.

Sleeping

Hostal Pusaki GUESTHOUSE $

(cell 9-9833-3248; pattypusaki@yahoo.es; Piloto Pardo 222; incl breakfast d US$75, r per person without bathroom US$28) With legendary warmth, Patty welcomes travelers into this cozy home with comfortable, carpeted rooms with private bathrooms. Patty also organizes group dinners, which are also available to nonguests.

Refugio El Padrino HOSTEL $

(61-262-1136, cell 9-8438-0843; Costanera 276; campsites per person US$25, dm incl breakfast US$13) Friendly and conducive to meeting others, this clean, self-service hostel doubles as a social hub hosted by the effervescent Cecilia. The small dorm rooms are located right on the channel.

Lakutaia Lodge HOTEL $$$

(61-262-1733; www.lakutaia.cl; s/d/tr US$233/292/349) About 3km east of town toward the airport, this modern lodge offers respite in a lovely, rural setting. There is a full-service restaurant and the library contains interesting history and nature references. There are also treks and horseback riding on offer. Its only disadvantage is its isolation; you might leave without getting much of a feel for the quirky town.

Eating & Drinking

Puerto Luisa Cafe CAFE

(cell 9-9934-0849; Costanera 317; snacks CH$3000; 10am-1pm & 4-9pm Mon-Fri, 8:30am-9pm Sat Nov-Mar;) Next to the dock, this welcoming haven offers espresso drinks, chocolates and pies in a cozy setting of oversized chairs with great sea views.

El Alambique PUB

(Piloto Pardo 217; 8pm-1am Tue-Sat) Covered in murals, this homespun pub delivers good homemade pastas (and pizzas on all-you-can-eat Fridays). It's the only venue with a pub atmosphere at night.

Information

Municipal Tourist Information (www.ptowilliams.cl/turismo.html; Centro Comercial; 9am-1pm & 2:30-6pm Mon-Fri, 9am-1pm Sat) Offers city and day-trek maps, as well as weather and route conditions for Lago Windhond and Dientes de Navarino treks. Located in a small kiosk.

Turismo Shila (cell 9-7897-2005; www.turismoshila.cl; O'Higgins 220; 9am-1:30pm & 4-8pm Mon-Sat) Very helpful stop for trekkers. Offers local guides, camping rentals, bicycle rentals, snowshoes, fishing gear and GPS maps. Also sells boat tickets and can arrange charter flights to Ushuaia.

Getting There & Away

Puerto Williams is accessible by plane or boat, though inclement weather can produce delays. Allow a cushion of extra travel time to get on or off the island.

Aerovías DAP (61-262-1052; www.aeroviasdap.cl; Centro Comercial s/n; 1 way CH$75,000; 9am-1pm & 2:30-6:30pm Mon-Fri, 10am-1:30pm Sat) Flies to Punta Arenas (CH$68,000, 1¼ hours) daily Monday to Saturday from November to March, with fewer winter flights. Reserve ahead since there's high demand. DAP flights to Antarctica may make a brief stopover here.

Transbordador Austral Broom (61-272-8100; www.tabsa.cl; reclining seat/bunk incl meals CH$108,000/151,000, 32hr) A ferry sails from the Tres Puentes sector of Punta Arenas to Puerto Williams four times a month on Thursdays, with departures from Puerto Williams back to Punta Arenas on Saturdays. Only bunk berths can be reserved ahead; the seats are reserved for locals until the last minute, although you can request one and will usually get it. Travelers rave about the trip: if the weather holds there are glacier views on the trip from Punta Arenas and the possibility of spotting dolphins or whales between December and April. From Puerto Williams, the glaciers are passed at night.

Ushuaia Boating (in Argentina 02901-436-193; www.ushuaiaboating.com; 1 way US$120; service Mon-Sat Oct-Apr) A sporadic service which usually goes daily in high season with Zodiac boats. Tickets include a sometimes bumpy and exposed 40-minute crossing plus an overland transfer to/from Puerto Navarino. Note: inclement weather often means cancellations and indefinite postponement.

Porvenir (Chile)

☎061 / POP 5910

If you want a slice of home-baked Fuegian life, this is it. Most visitors come on a quick day trip from Punta Arenas tainted by seasickness. But spending a night in this village of metal-clad Victorian houses affords you an opportunity to explore the nearby bays and countryside and absorb a little of the local life; bird watchers can admire the nearby king penguins, and lively populations of cormorants, geese and seabirds. Porvenir is known for its inaccessibility (there's no bus route here), but the completion of roads through the southern extension of Chilean Tierra del Fuego will open up a whole untouched wilderness to visitors.

Porvenir experienced waves of immigration, many from Croatia, when gold was discovered in 1879. Sheep *estancias* provided more reliable work, attracting Chileans from the island of Chiloé, who also came for fishing work. Today's population is a unique combination of the two.

Sights

Museo de Tierra del Fuego MUSEUM
(☎61-258-1800; Jorge Schythe 71; CH$1000; 8am-5pm Mon-Thu, to 4pm Fri, 10:30am-1:30pm & 3-5pm Sat & Sun) On the Plaza de Armas, the intriguing Museo de Tierra del Fuego has some unexpected materials, including Selk'nam skulls and mummies, musical instruments used by the mission Indians on Isla Dawson and an exhibit on early Chilean cinematography.

Tours

Gold panning, horseback riding and 4WD tours can be arranged through Porvenir's tourist office.

Far South Expeditions OUTDOORS
(www.fsexpeditions.com) High-end naturalist-run tours, with transportation available from Punta Arenas. Offers day trips and overnights to the king-penguin colony or all-inclusive packages.

Sleeping & Eating

Hotel Yagan GUESTHOUSE $
(☎61-258-0936; Philippi 296; s/d US$62/80;) Eleven clean and pleasant rooms offer heating and cable TV; some have wonderful views. The restaurant, serving fresh seafood and more, gets crowded for meals.

★ **Yendegaia House** B&B $$
(☎61-258-1919; http://yendegaiahouse.com; Croacia 702; s/d/tr incl breakfast US$67/100/120;) Everything a B&B should be, with naturalist books (some authored by the owner) to browse, abundant breakfast, views of the strait and spacious rooms with thick down duvets. This historic Magellanic home (Porvenir's first lodging) has been lovingly restored, and its family of hosts are helpful. Its tour agency, Far South Expeditions, runs naturalist-led trips. With bikes for rent.

The cafe features espresso drinks, sandwiches and pizza.

Club Croata SEAFOOD $$
(☎61-258-0053; Señoret 542; mains CH$5000-12,000; 11am-4pm & 7-10:30pm Tue-Sun) Formal by tradition, the town's most reliable restaurant serves good seafood at reasonable prices. There's also Croat specialties, such as pork chops with *chucrut* (sauerkraut). The pub is open to 3am.

Information

For tourism information, consult at the **kiosk** (Jan-Feb) in front of Parque Yugoslavo.

BancoEstado (cnr Philippi & Croacia; 10am-1pm Mon-Fri) has a 24-hour ATM.

The **post office** (Philippi 176; 9am-1pm & 3-5pm Mon-Fri) faces the plaza.

Getting There & Away

From Punta Arenas you can fly here with **Aerovías DAP** (☎061-261-6100; www.aeroviasdap.cl; cnr Señoret & Philippi) or take the ferry crossing with **Transbordador Austral Broom** (☎061-258-0089; www.tabsa.cl; passenger/vehicle Porvenir-Punta Arenas CH$6200/39,800).

A good gravel road (Rte 257) runs east along Bahía Inútil to the Argentine border at San Sebastián; allow about four hours. From San Sebastián (where there's gas and a motel), northbound motorists should avoid the heavily traveled and rutted truck route directly north and instead take the route from Onaisín to the petroleum-company town of Cerro Sombrero, en route to the crossing of the Strait of Magellan at Punta Delgada–Puerto Espora.

Uruguay

POP 3.4 MILLION

Includes ➡

Best Places to Eat

- Charco Bistró (p543)
- Café Picasso (p551)
- Parador La Huella (p558)
- Escaramuza (p529)
- La Fonda (p527)

Best Places to Stay

- La Posadita de la Plaza (p541)
- Estancia Panagea (p549)
- Casa Zinc (p557)
- El Galope Horse Farm & Hostel (p539)

Why Go?

Wedged like a grape between Brazil's gargantuan thumb and Argentina's long forefinger, Uruguay has always been something of an underdog. Yet after two centuries living in the shadow of its neighbors, South America's smallest country is finally getting a little well-deserved recognition. Progressive, stable, safe and culturally sophisticated, Uruguay offers visitors opportunities to experience everyday 'not made for tourists' moments, whether caught in a cow-and-gaucho traffic jam on a dirt road to nowhere or strolling with *mate*-toting locals along Montevideo's beachfront.

Short-term visitors will find plenty to keep them busy in cosmopolitan Montevideo, picturesque Colonia and party-till-you-drop Punta del Este. But it pays to dig deeper. Go wildlife watching along the Atlantic coast, hot-spring hopping up the Río Uruguay, or horseback riding under the big sky of Uruguay's interior, where vast fields spread out like oceans.

When to Go

Montevideo

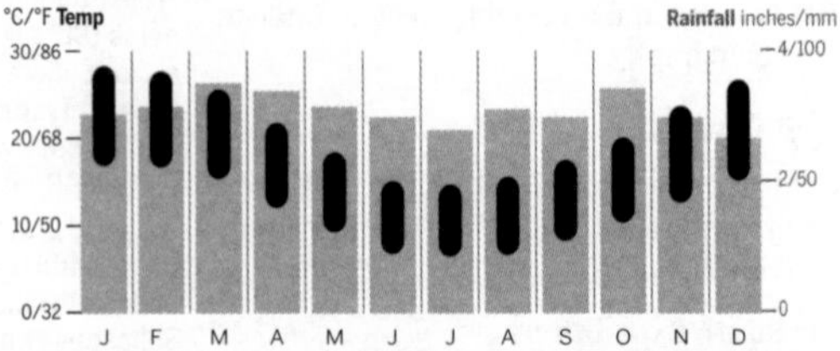

Feb Street theater and drumming consume Montevideo during Carnaval celebrations.

Mar Tacuarembó's gaucho festival, plus lower prices on the still-sunny Atlantic coast.

Oct Soak in Salto's hot springs, or channel Carlos Gardel at Montevideo's tango festival.

MONTEVIDEO

☎2 / POP 1.3 MILLION

The nation's capital and home to nearly half of Uruguay's population, Montevideo is a vibrant, eclectic place with a rich cultural life. Stretching 20km from east to west, the city wears many faces, from its industrial port to the exclusive beachside suburb of Carrasco near the airport. In the historic downtown business district, art deco and neoclassical buildings jostle for space alongside grimy, worn-out skyscrapers that appear airlifted from Havana or Ceauşescu's Romania, while to the southeast the shopping malls and modern high-rises of beach communities such as Punta Carretas and Pocitos bear more resemblance to those of Miami or Copacabana. Music, theater and the arts are alive and well here – from elegant older theaters and cozy little tango bars to modern beachfront discos – and there's a strong international flavor, thanks to the many foreign cultural centers and Montevideo's status as administrative headquarters for Mercosur, South America's leading trading bloc.

Sights

Note that many Montevideo museums are known by their acronyms. Most exhibits are in Spanish only.

Ciudad Vieja

★Teatro Solís THEATER

(Map p524; ☎1950-3323; www.teatrosolis.org.uy; Buenos Aires 678; tours UR$90, Wed free; ⏲tours 4pm Tue & Thu, 11am, noon & 4pm Wed, Fri & Sun, 11am, noon, 1pm & 4pm Sat) Just off Plaza Independencia, elegant Teatro Solís is Montevideo's premier performance space. First opened in 1856, and completely renovated during the past decade or so, it has superb acoustics. Regularly scheduled tours provide an opportunity to see the actual performance space without attending a show.

★Mercado del Puerto MARKET

(Map p524; Pérez Castellano) No visitor should miss Montevideo's old port market building, at the foot of Pérez Castellano, whose impressive wrought-iron superstructure shelters a gaggle of bustling *parrillas* (steak restaurants). On weekend afternoons in particular, it's a lively, colorful place where the city's artists, craftspeople and street musicians hang out.

Plaza Matriz PLAZA

(Map p524) Also known as Plaza Constitución, this leafy square was the heart of colonial Montevideo. On its west side stands the **Iglesia Matriz** (Map p524; Plaza Matriz), Montevideo's oldest public building, begun in 1784 and completed in 1799. Opposite is the **Cabildo** (Map p524; Juan Carlos Gómez 1362), a neoclassical stone structure finished in 1812. Benches under the trees and eateries along the adjacent sidewalk offer opportunities for a noon break.

Museo de los Andes MUSEUM

(Map p524; ☎2916-9461; www.mandes.uy; 619 Rincón; UR$200; ⏲10am-5pm Mon-Fri, to 3pm Sat) Opened in 2013, this unique museum documents the 1972 Andean plane crash (made famous in the book *Alive!*) that cost 29 Uruguayans their lives and profoundly impacted Uruguay's national psyche. Using original objects and photos from the crash site, it tells the story of the 16 survivors, who battled harrowing conditions for 72 days before returning alive to a stunned nation. The museum is a labor of love for director Jörg Thomsen, a personal friend of many of the families affected.

Museo del Carnaval MUSEUM

(Map p524; ☎2916-5493; www.museodelcarnaval.org; Rambla 25 de Agosto 218; UR$100; ⏲11am-5pm Thu-Sun Apr-Nov, daily Dec-Mar) This museum houses a wonderful collection of costumes, drums, masks, recordings and photos documenting the 100-plus-year history of Montevideo's Carnaval (p528). Behind the museum is a cafe and a courtyard where spectators can view performances during the summer months. Touch-screen displays added in 2014 offer limited English-language commentary.

Museo y Archivo Histórico Municipal MUSEUM

(Municipal Archive & Historical Museum; Map p524; ☎2915-9685; www.cabildo.montevideo.gub.uy; Juan Carlos Gómez 1362; ⏲noon-5:45pm Mon-Fri, 11am-5pm Sat) FREE This free historical museum on Ciudad Vieja's main square displays 18th-century paintings of Montevideo and other artifacts from the city's early days.

Museo de Arte Precolombino e Indígena MUSEUM

(MAPI; Map p524; ☎2916-9360; www.mapi.uy; 25 de Mayo 279; UR$100; ⏲10:30am-6pm Mon-Sat) This museum displays a permanent collection of artifacts and information about

Uruguay Highlights

1. **Carnaval** (p528) Dance to a different drummer during Montevideo's month-long festivities.
2. **Punta del Diablo** (p564) Catch a wave or a late-night beach party along Uruguay's untamed northern shoreline.
3. **Thermal Baths** (p548) Soak your weary muscles in hot springs near Salto.
4. **Valle del Lunarejo** (p566) Get off the beaten track in this remote nature preserve.
5. **Colonia del Sacramento** (p538) Sunbathe on the 18th-century town wall, or wander the leafy plazas and cobbled streets of this picturesque town on the Río de la Plata.
6. **Cabo Polonio** (p562) Lose yourself in the sand dunes and survey the sea lions from atop the lighthouse.
7. **Museo de la Revolución Industrial** (p547) Tour Uruguay's newest World Heritage site, the historic El Anglo meat-processing factory (maker of Oxo beef cubes) in easygoing Fray Bentos.
8. **Punta del Este** (p552) Hit the beaches by day and the clubs by night.
9. **Tacuarembó** (p549) Herd cattle on horseback and discover the simple joys of *estancia* (ranch) living under the stars.

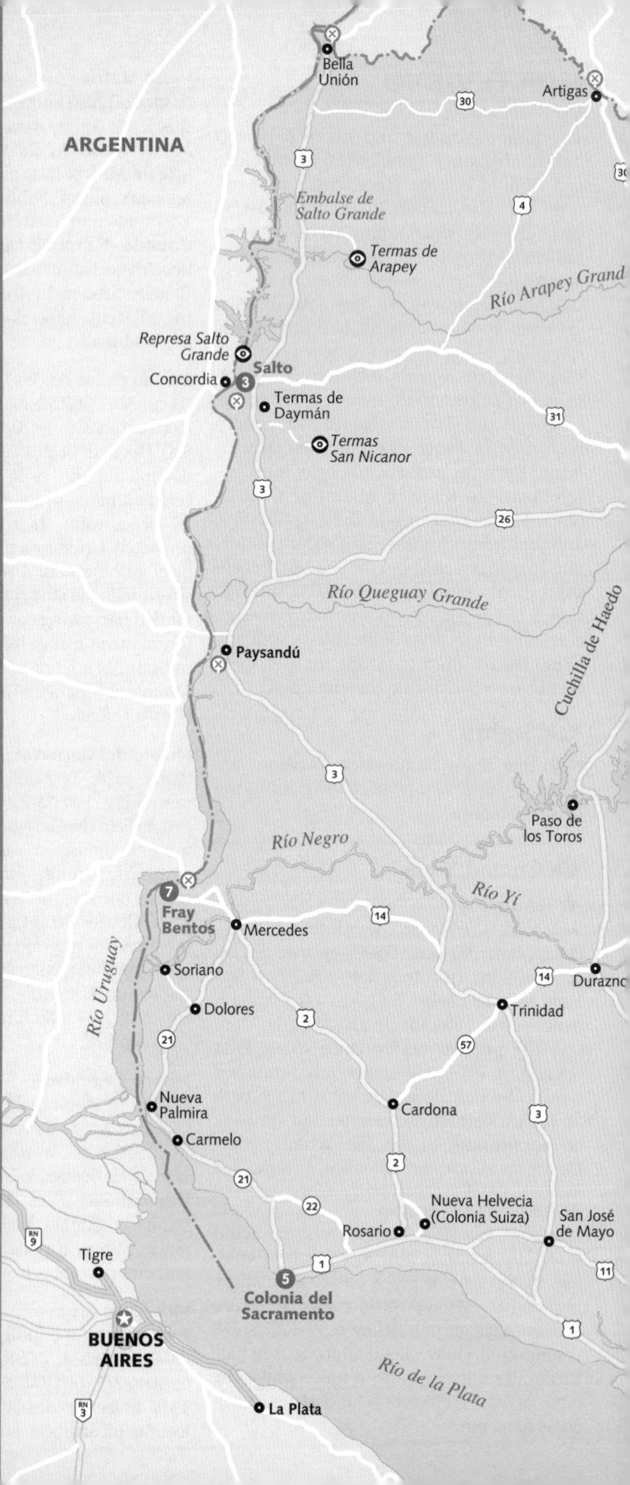

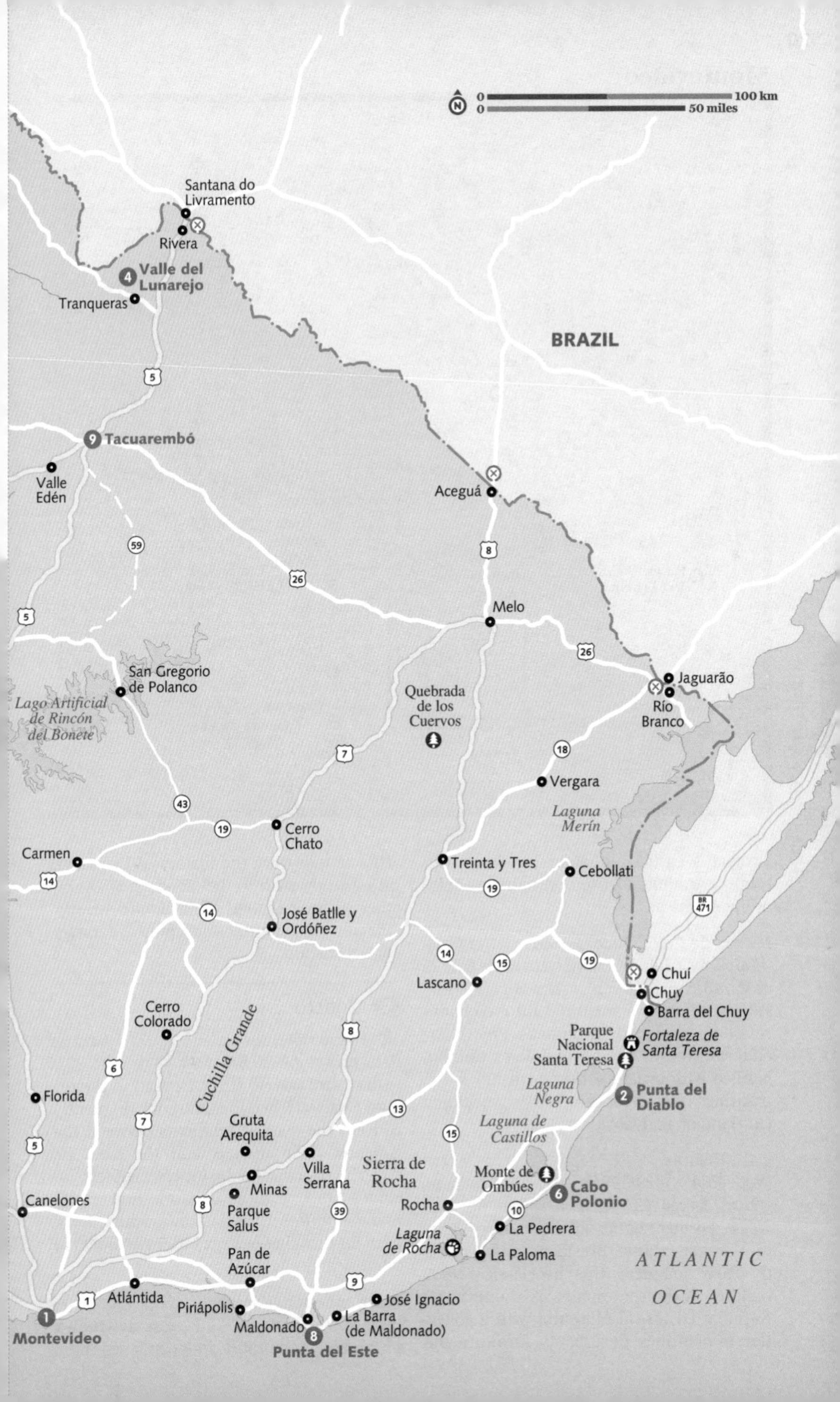
0 100 km
0 50 miles
Santana do Livramento
Rivera
4 Valle del Lunarejo
Tranqueras
BRAZIL
5
9 Tacuarembó
Valle Edén
59
Aceguá
8
26
5
Melo
26
Jaguarão
Río Branco
San Gregorio de Polanco
Lago Artificial de Rincón del Bonete
Quebrada de los Cuervos
7
18
Vergara
Laguna Merín
43
19
Cerro Chato
Carmen
Treinta y Tres
Cebollati
14
19
BR 471
14
José Batlle y Ordóñez
14
15
19
Lascano
Chuí
Chuy
Barra del Chuy
Cerro Colorado
Cuchilla Grande
8
Parque Nacional Santa Teresa
Fortaleza de Santa Teresa
6
Laguna Negra
2 Punta del Diablo
Florida
7
13
Laguna de Castillos
Gruta Arequita
15
5
Villa Serrana
Sierra de Rocha
Minas
Monte de Ombúes
6 Cabo Polonio
Canelones
8
Parque Salus
39
Rocha
10
La Pedrera
Laguna de Rocha
La Paloma
ATLANTIC OCEAN
Pan de Azúcar
9
Atlántida
1
José Ignacio
Piriápolis
1 Montevideo
Maldonado
La Barra (de Maldonado)
8 Punta del Este

Montevideo

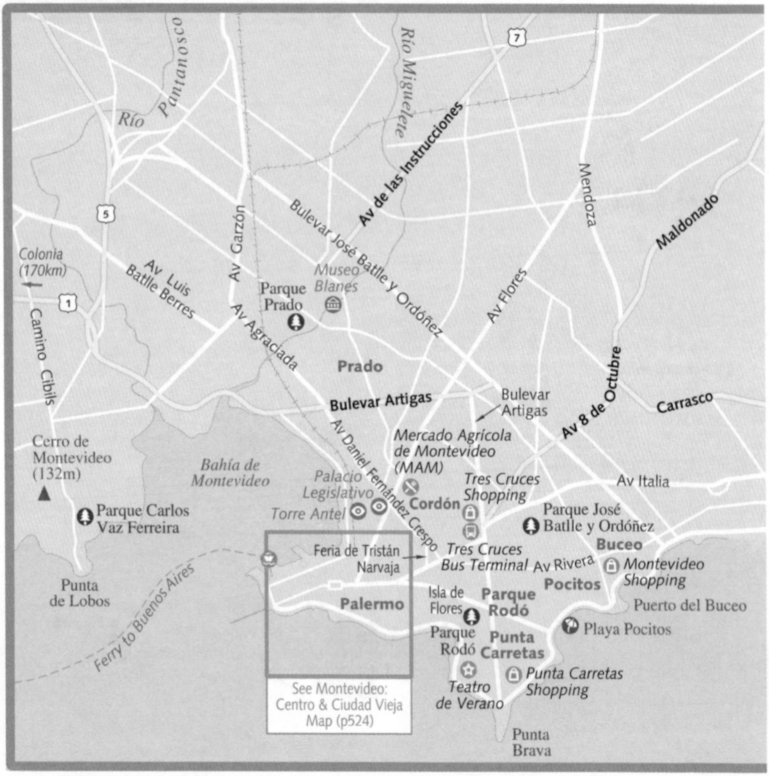

Uruguay's earliest inhabitants, along with rotating exhibits focused on native peoples of the Americas.

Museo de Artes Decorativas MUSEUM
(Map p524; ☎2915-1101; www.mec.gub.uy; Calle 25 de Mayo 376; ⏲12:30-5:30pm Mon-Fri) FREE The Palacio Taranco, a wealthy 1910 merchant's residence designed by famous French architects Charles Girault and Jules Chifflot, is filled with ornate period furnishings and paintings by European artists including Ghirlandaio and Goya.

Casa Rivera MUSEUM
(Map p524; ☎2915-1051; www.museohistorico.gub.uy; Rincón 437; ⏲noon-5:45pm Wed-Sun) FREE Former home of Fructuoso Rivera (Uruguay's first president and Colorado Party founder), this neoclassical 1802 building is the centerpiece of Montevideo's National Historical Museum, with a collection of paintings, documents, furniture and artifacts that trace the history of Uruguay's 19th-century path to independence. Several other historic Ciudad Vieja homes nearby, officially part of the museum, are rarely open to visitors.

Centro

★Museo del Gaucho MUSEUM
(Map p524; ☎2900-8764; Av 18 de Julio 998; ⏲10am-4pm Mon-Fri) FREE Housed in the ornate Palacio Heber, this museum eloquently conveys the deep attachments between the gauchos, their animals and the land. Its superb collection of historical artifacts includes horse gear, silver work, and *mates* and *bombillas* (metal straws with filters, used for drinking *mate*, a bitter ritual tea) in whimsical designs.

Plaza Independencia PLAZA
(Map p524) Montevideo's largest downtown plaza commemorates independence hero

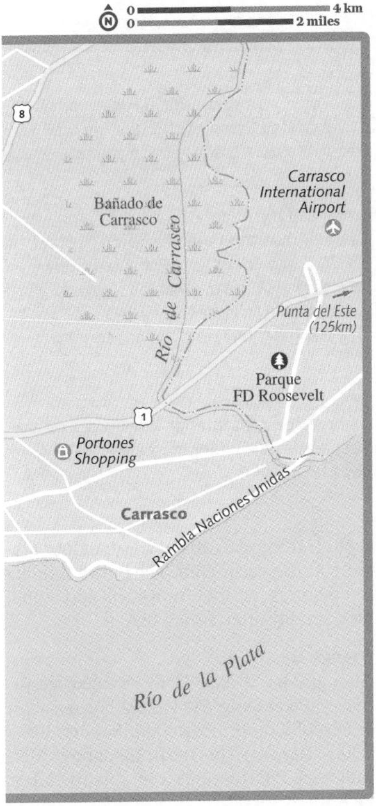

José Artigas with a 17m, 30-ton statue and the subterranean **Mausoleo de Artigas** (Map p524; 9am-5pm), where an honor guard keeps 24-hour vigil over Artigas' remains. Other notable structures surrounding the plaza include the stone gateway **Puerta de la Ciudadela** (Map p524), a lonely remnant of the colonial citadel demolished in 1833; the 19th-century **Palacio Estévez** (Map p524); and the 26-story **Palacio Salvo** (Map p524), the continent's tallest building when it opened in 1927, and still a classic Montevideo landmark.

North of Centro

Palacio Legislativo HISTORIC BUILDING
(2142; www.parlamento.gub.uy; Av General Flores s/n; tours US$3; 10:30am-3pm Mon-Fri) Dating from 1908, and still playing host to Uruguay's Asamblea General (legislative branch), the three-story neoclassical parliament building is also open for guided tours at 10:30am and 3pm Monday to Friday.

Torre Antel TOWER
(2928-8517; Guatemala 1075; tours half-hourly 3:30-5pm Mon, Wed & Fri, 10:30am-noon Tue & Thu) FREE For great views out across the city, take the elevator to the top of Montevideo's most dramatic modern skyscraper.

East of Centro

Museo del Fútbol MUSEUM
(2480-1259; www.estadiocentenario.com.uy/site/footballMuseum; Estadio Centenario, Av Ricaldoni s/n, Parque José Batlle y Ordóñez; UR$150; 10am-5pm Mon-Fri) A must-see for any *fútbol* (soccer) fan, this museum displays memorabilia from Uruguay's 1930 and 1950 World Cup wins. Visitors can also tour the stands.

Espacio de Arte Contemporáneo GALLERY
(2929-2066; www.eac.gub.uy; Arenal Grande 1930; 2-8pm Wed-Sat, 11am-5pm Sun) FREE This gallery makes thought-provoking use of the cells of a 19th-century prison, creating an avant-garde space for revolving exhibitions of contemporary art.

Parque Rodó, La Rambla & Eastern Beaches

La Rambla, Montevideo's multi-kilometer coastal promenade, is one of the city's defining elements, connecting downtown to the eastern beach communities of Punta Carretas, Pocitos, Buceo and Carrasco. This is Montevideo's social hub on Sunday afternoons, when the place is packed with locals cradling flasks of *mate* and mingling with friends.

★ **Museo Nacional de Artes Visuales** MUSEUM
(MNAV; 2711-6124; www.mnav.gub.uy; Giribaldi 2283, Parque Rodó; 2-7pm Tue-Sun) FREE Uruguay's largest collection of paintings is housed here in Parque Rodó. The spacious rooms are graced with works by Blanes, Cúneo, Figari, Gurvich, Torres García and other famous Uruguayans. For a closer look at some of these same artists, visit the **Museo Torres García** (Map p524; 2916-2663; www.torresgarcia.org.uy; Sarandí 683; UR$120; 10am-6pm Mon-Sat), **Museo Figari** (Map p524; 2915-7065; www.museofigari.gub.uy; Juan Carlos Gómez 1427; 1-6pm Tue-Fri, 10am-2pm Sat) FREE and **Museo Gurvich** (Map p524; 2915-7826; www.museogurvich.org; Sarandí 524; UR$150, Tue free; 10am-6pm Mon-Fri, 11am-3pm

URUGUAY IN...

Two Days

Just popping over from Buenos Aires for a couple of days? Don't overdo it! Focus your energy on the easygoing, picturesque historical river port of Colonia (p538) or the urban attractions of Montevideo (p517), both an easy ferry ride from the Argentine capital.

One Week

If you've got a week up your sleeve, continue north along the Atlantic coast and sample a few of Uruguay's best beaches: the early-20th-century resort of Piriápolis (p551), glitzy Punta del Este (p552), isolated Cabo Polonio (p562), surfer-friendly La Paloma (p560) and La Pedrera (p561), or the relaxed beach-party town of Punta del Diablo (p564). Alternatively, follow the Río Uruguay upstream toward Iguazú Falls via the wineries of Carmelo (p544), the quirky industrial museum at Fray Bentos (p547) and the hot springs of Salto (p548).

Two Weeks

With a whole two weeks to spare, get out and explore Uruguay's interior, ride horses on a tourist estancia (p553) and settle into a slower-paced lifestyle under the wide open skies of Tacuarembó (p549) or Valle del Lunarejo (p566).

Sat) in Ciudad Vieja, or the **Museo Blanes** (☎2336-2248; www.blanes.montevideo.gub.uy; Av Millán 4015; ⏰noon-5:45pm Tue-Sun) FREE in the Prado neighborhood north of Centro.

Castillo Pittamiglio HISTORIC BUILDING
(☎2710-1089; www.castillopittamiglio.org; Rambla Gandhi 633; guided tours UR$125) On the Rambla between Punta Carretas and Pocitos is this eccentric legacy of local alchemist and architect Humberto Pittamiglio. Its quirky facade alone is worth a look. Guided Spanish-language tours of the interior are available; see the website for monthly schedules.

Museo Naval MUSEUM
(☎2622-1084; cnr Rambla Presidente Charles de Gaulle & Av LA de Herrera; UR$60; ⏰9am-noon & 2-6pm Fri-Wed) Along the eastern waterfront in Buceo, this museum traces the role of boats and ships in Uruguayan history, from the indigenous Charrúa's canoe culture to the dramatic sinking of the German *Graf Spee* off Montevideo in 1939.

Activities

One of Montevideo's great pleasures is cruising along the walking-jogging-cycling track that follows the riverfront Rambla. A few kilometers east of the center you'll reach Playa Pocitos, which is best for **swimming** and where you should be able to jump in on a game of **beach volleyball**. A couple of bays further along at Buceo's Yacht Harbor you can get **windsurfing lessons** at the yacht club. The entire Rambla is a picturesque spot for a stroll and a popular Sunday-afternoon hangout.

Orange Bike CYCLING
(Map p524; ☎2908-8286; www.orangebike.com.uy; Pérez Castellano 1417bis; bike rental per 4/24hr US$10/20; ⏰9am-7pm Nov-Apr, 10am-5:30pm May-Oct) This outfit just above Mercado del Puerto rents out quality bikes. Pick up at its office, or it'll deliver one to your doorstep.

Courses

Academia Uruguay LANGUAGE
(Map p524; ☎2915-2496; www.academiauruguay.com; Juan Carlos Gómez 1408; group classes per week US$245, individual classes per hour US$30) One-on-one and group Spanish classes with a strong cultural focus. Also arranges homestays, private apartments and volunteer work.

Joventango DANCING
(Map p524; ☎2908-6813; www.joventango.com; Aquiles Lanza 1290; per class UR$225) Tango classes for all levels, from beginner to expert.

Festivals & Events

Much livelier than its Buenos Aires counterpart, Montevideo's late-summer **Carnaval** is the cultural highlight of the year.

At Parque Prado, north of downtown, Semana Criolla festivities during **Semana**

Santa (Holy Week) include displays of gaucho skills, *asados* (barbecues) and other such events.

In the last weekend of September or the first weekend of October, Montevideo's museums, churches and historic homes all open their doors free to the public during the **Días del Patrimonio** (National Heritage Days).

For 10 days in October, tango fills Montevideo's streets and performance halls during the **Festival 'Viva El Tango,'** organized by Joventango.

Sleeping

Montevideo boasts a growing number of stylish boutique and luxury hotels, a thriving hostel scene, and a host of dependable midrange options in the Centro. With more beds to choose from, competition is driving prices down; look online for the best deals.

Ciudad Vieja

★Hotel Palacio HOTEL $

(Map p524; ☎2916-3612; www.hotelpalacio.com.uy; Bartolomé Mitre 1364; r without breakfast & without/with balcony US$45/50; ❄📶) If you can snag one of the two 6th-floor rooms at this ancient family-run hotel one block off Plaza Matriz, go for it! Both feature air-conditioning and balconies with superb views of Ciudad Vieja's rooftops. The rest of the hotel also offers great value, with wood floors, antique furniture, a vintage elevator and old-school service reminiscent of a European *pensión*.

Spléndido Hotel HOTEL $

(Map p524; ☎2916-4900; www.splendidohotel.com.uy; Bartolomé Mitre 1314; d US$40-55, d without bathroom US$30-45, s without bathroom US$25-38; @📶) The faded, funky Spléndido offers decent value for budget travelers preferring privacy over a hostel-style party vibe. The better rooms have 5m-high ceilings and French doors opening to balconies; three rooms (106, 220 and 221) directly overlook Teatro Solís. Others are more cramped and considerably less inviting; survey the options before committing. Bars on the street below can get noisy.

Punto Berro Hostel Ciudad Vieja HOSTEL $

(Map p524; ☎2914-8600; www.puntoberrohostel.com; Ituzaingó 1436; dm/d incl dinner from US$17/33; @📶) Spread out over the two upper floors of an older Ciudad Vieja building, this hostel is only steps away from all of the old city's attractions. There's a nice roof deck upstairs where nightly *asados* (barbecues) are held. Downsides include a general lack of cleanliness and organization.

DON'T MISS

MONTEVIDEO WEEKEND HIGHLIGHTS

Weekends are the time to enjoy several of Montevideo's quintessential experiences. Note that Ciudad Vieja, outside of Mercado del Puerto, is a virtual ghost town on Sundays, when businesses are closed and the pulse of local life moves east to the long Rambla waterfront.

Saturday morning Browse the antiques market on Plaza Matriz (p517).

Saturday afternoon Discover your inner carnivore over lunch at Mercado del Puerto (p528).

Saturday night Attend a performance at Teatro Solís (p531) or Sala Zitarrosa (p531), sip *uvitas* (sweet wine drinks) and listen to live music at Fun Fun (p531), go for tapas and cocktails at Baker's Bar (p531) or party all night at the city's clubs.

Sunday morning Explore the labyrinth of market stalls at Feria de Tristán Narvaja (p532).

Sunday afternoon Join the parade of *mate*-toting locals strolling the 20km-long beachfront Rambla.

Sunday evening Catch a pre-Carnaval drumming rehearsal on the streets of Palermo or Parque Rodó, or attend Joventango's 7:30pm 'cafe-concert' of tango at the Mercado de la Abundancia (p532).

Montevideo: Centro & Ciudad Vieja

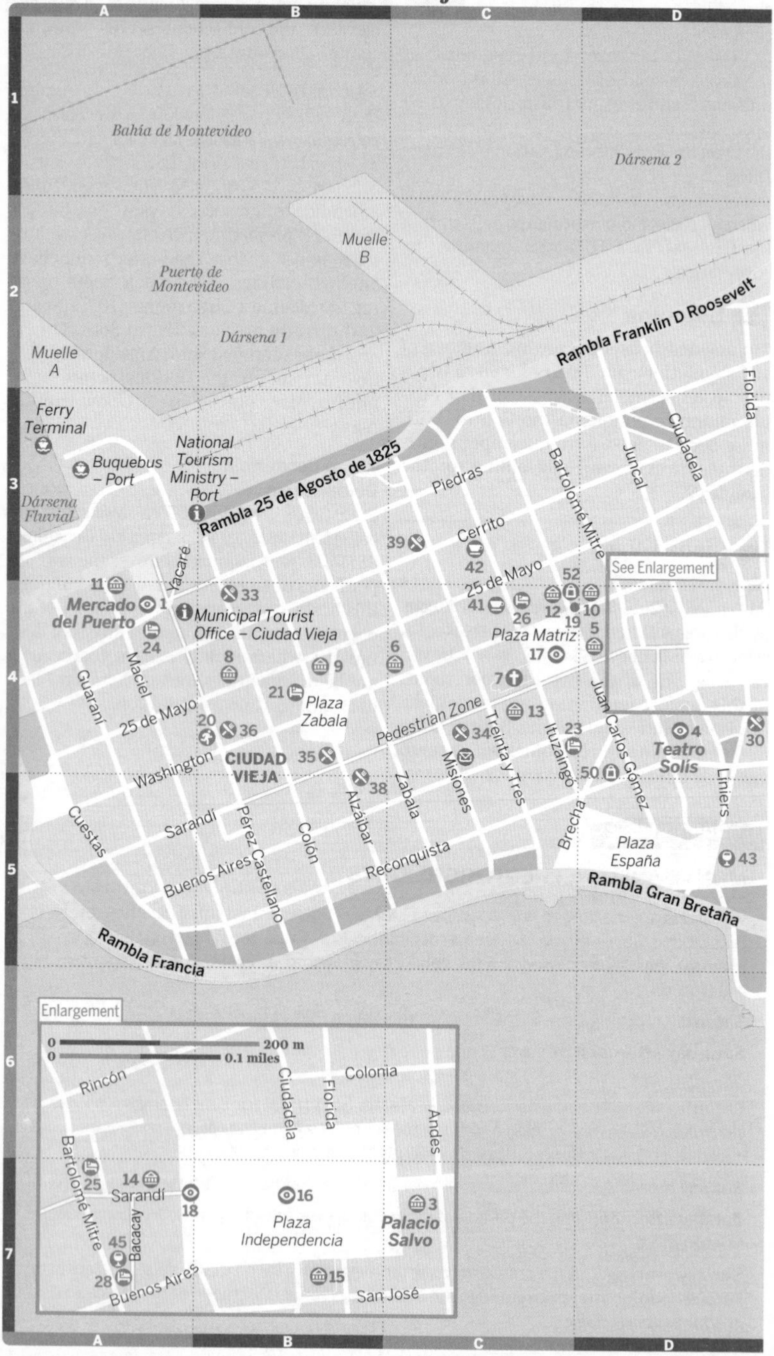

Bahía de Montevideo
Dársena 2
Muelle B
Puerto de Montevideo
Dársena 1
Muelle A
Rambla Franklin D Roosevelt
Ferry Terminal
Buquebus – Port
Dársena Fluvial
National Tourism Ministry – Port
Rambla 25 de Agosto de 1825
Piedras
Cerrito
25 de Mayo
Bartolomé Mitre
Juncal
Ciudadela
Florida
See Enlargement
Mercado del Puerto
Municipal Tourist Office – Ciudad Vieja
Yacaré
Plaza Matriz
Plaza Zabala
Pedestrian Zone
Guaraní
Maciel
Washington
CIUDAD VIEJA
Teatro Solís
Juan Carlos Gómez
Treinta y Tres
Itúzaingó
Misiones
Zabala
Alzáibar
Colón
Pérez Castellano
Sarandí
Cuestas
Buenos Aires
Reconquista
Brecha
Liniers
Plaza España
Rambla Gran Bretaña
Rambla Francia
Enlargement
0 200 m
0 0.1 miles
Rincón
Colonia
Ciudadela
Florida
Andes
Bartolomé Mitre
Sarandí
Bacacay
Plaza Independencia
Palacio Salvo
Buenos Aires
San José

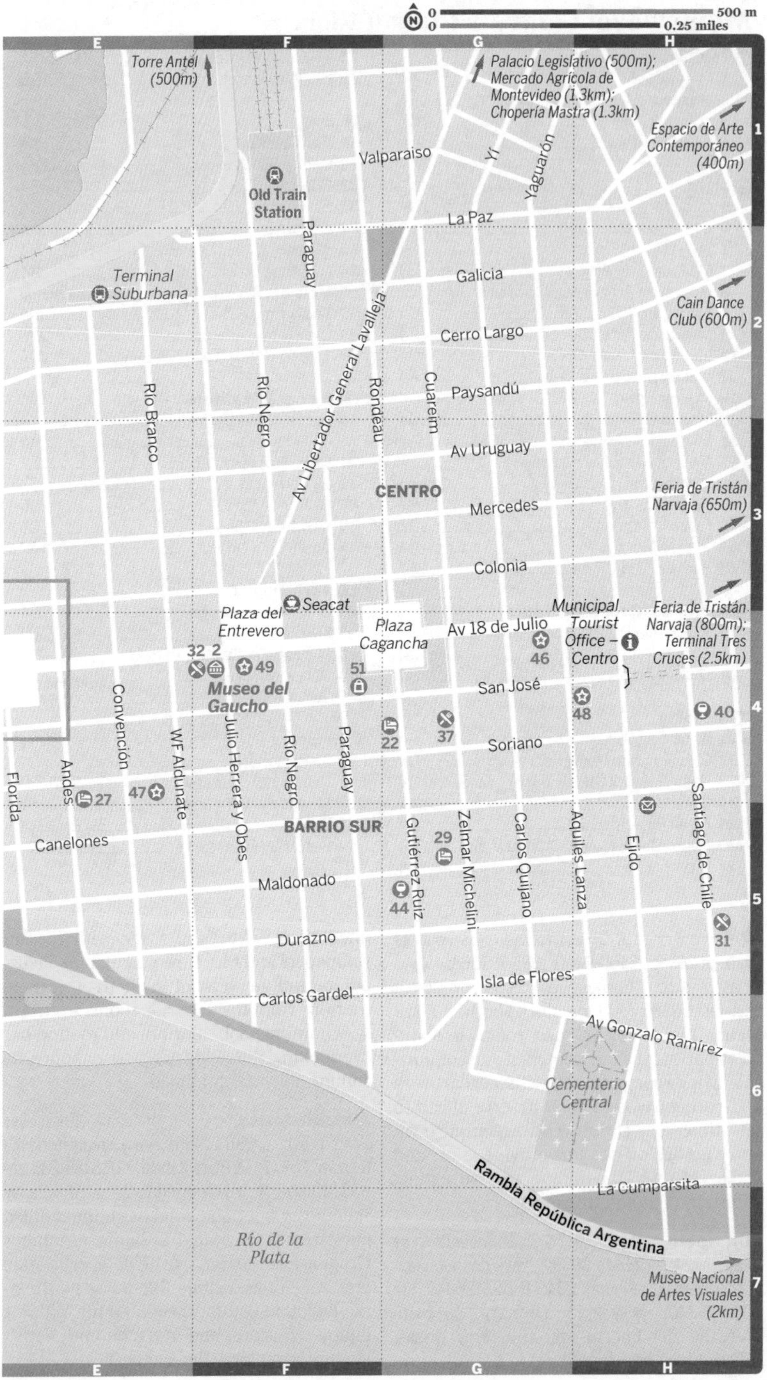

0 500 m
0 0.25 miles

Torre Antel (500m)

Palacio Legislativo (500m);
Mercado Agrícola de
Montevideo (1.3km);
Chopería Mastra (1.3km)

Espacio de Arte
Contemporáneo
(400m)

Valparaiso

Yi

Yaguarón

Old Train
Station

La Paz

Terminal
Suburbana

Galicia

Cain Dance
Club (600m)

Paraguay

Cerro Largo

Rondeau

Cuareim

Paysandú

Río Branco

Río Negro

Av Libertador General Lavalleja

Av Uruguay

CENTRO

Mercedes

Feria de Tristán
Narvaja (650m)

Colonia

Seacat

Plaza del
Entrevero

Plaza
Cagancha

Av 18 de Julio

Municipal
Tourist
Office –
Centro

Feria de Tristán
Narvaja (800m);
Terminal Tres
Cruces (2.5km)

32 2

49

51

46

Museo del
Gaucho

San José

48

40

22

37

Soriano

Convención

Andes

WF Aldunate

Julio Herrera y Obes

Río Negro

Paraguay

27

47

Gutiérrez Ruiz

Zelmar Michelini

Carlos Quijano

Aquiles Lanza

Ejido

Santiago de Chile

Florida

Canelones

BARRIO SUR

29

Maldonado

44

31

Durazno

Carlos Gardel

Isla de Flores

Av Gonzalo Ramírez

Cementerio
Central

Rambla República Argentina

La Cumparsita

Río de la
Plata

Museo Nacional
de Artes Visuales
(2km)

Montevideo: Centro & Ciudad Vieja

★ **Casa Sarandi Guesthouse** GUESTHOUSE $$
(Map p524; ☎2400-6460, 099-707068; www.casasarandi.com; Buenos Aires 558, 3rd fl; r without breakfast US$85;) One block south of Plaza Matriz, two attractive guest rooms in a vintage apartment share a kitchen and comfortable living room adorned with local artwork and parquet wood floors. Reserve ahead to set a time to meet the Welsh-Argentine owners, who live off-site but provide a key and oodles of up-to-the-minute tips on eating, entertainment and transport.

Don Hotel BOUTIQUE HOTEL $$
(Map p524; ☎2915-9999; www.donhotelmontevideo.com.uy; Piedras 234; d US$125-149, ste US$305-330;) Directly opposite Mercado del Puerto and the ferry docks, this modern boutique hotel is a study in refined black, white and silver, with Iberian wallpapers and tiles throughout, plus Jacuzzis and full-on views of the market's ornate rooftops from the superior rooms up front. A swimming pool, solarium and rooftop bar overlooking Montevideo's port enhance its comfortable, classy appeal.

Alma Histórica BOUTIQUE HOTEL $$$
(Map p524; ☎2914-7450; www.almahistoricahotel.com; Solis 1433, Plaza Zabala; r US$185-285, ste US$240-300;) Opened in 2014, this classy Italian-run boutique hotel has antique-filled guest rooms decorated in honor of famous Uruguayans (artists, writers, sports stars etc). Amenities include fine Swiss mattresses, Egyptian-cotton sheets, comfy pillows, laptop-size safes, and YouTube and Netflix streaming on large flat-screen TVs.

Other classy touches include an original 1900s marble staircase and an elegant library filled with art books and travel guides.

Centro

Caballo Loco Hostel HOSTEL $
(Map p524; ☎2902-6494; www.caballolocohostel.com; Gutierrez Ruiz 1287; dm US$14-24; ❄📶) This friendly hostel in a remodeled historic building enjoys an unbeatable downtown location, only steps from leafy Plaza Cagancha and the bus stops for Montevideo's bus station and beaches. Six spick-and-span four- to 10-bed dorms surround a welcoming, high-ceilinged common area with guest kitchen, pool table and TV lounge. Other pluses include friendly owners and on-site bike rentals.

Ukelele Hostel HOSTEL $
(Map p524; ☎2902-7844; www.ukelelehostel.com; Maldonado 1183; dm US$14-24, d US$40-70; @📶🏊) Attractive features at this 1920s family-home-turned-hostel include vintage architectural details and a grassy pool and patio area out back for lounging. It has a good mix of dorms and private rooms, and the inviting common areas include an on-site bar and a music room with high ceilings and wood floors.

Smart Hotel HOTEL $$
(Map p524; ☎2903-3222; www.smarthotelmontevideo.com; Andes 1240; r US$65-115; ❄📶) 'Smart' perfectly describes the modern lines, clean white furnishings and blond-wood decor of this well-positioned newcomer near Plaza Independencia. All rooms come with fridges, couches and coffee tables; pricier units add sofa beds, microwaves and/or terraces, while corner lofts have writing desks and ample extra space. It has an attached restaurant and a parking garage, and discounts apply for longer stays.

Parque Rodó, La Rambla & Eastern Beaches

Buenas Vibras Hostel HOSTEL $
(☎2407-5015; www.buenasvibrashostel.com; Maldonado 2077; dm US$14-17, d US$50; 📶) This newer, smaller hostel in trendy Parque Rodó doesn't immediately impress with its aesthetics, but the friendly reception more than compensates. Owner-manager Matias organizes barbecues, low-cost trips to local football matches and other events to bring people together and facilitate intercultural exchange. At research time, the 18-bed hostel was expanding to include a fourth dorm and one private room.

Cala di Volpe BOUTIQUE HOTEL $$
(☎2710-2000; www.hotelcaladivolpe.com.uy; cnr Rambla Gandhi & Parva Domus, Punta Carretas; r US$83-168, ste US$139-228; ❄@📶🏊) This classy place across from the beach abounds in boutique hotel features: comfy couches, writing desks, gleaming tile-and-marble bathrooms, and floor-to-ceiling picture windows with sweeping river views. It has a small rooftop pool and a nice restaurant.

Sofitel Montevideo Casino Carrasco & Spa CASINO HOTEL $$$
(☎2604-6060; www.sofitel.com; Rambla Republica de Mexico 6451, Carrasco; r US$220-357, ste from US$408; ❄@📶🏊) Renovated top to bottom and reopened as a luxury hotel in 2013, Carrasco's historic casino is easily the showiest sleep in town. The monumental early-20th-century building, long a major waterfront landmark in this well-heeled neighborhood, sports 116 rooms, including 23 distinctive suites, complemented by a casino, a spa with indoor and outdoor swimming pools, and Uruguay's most sumptuous breakfast spread.

Eating

Diners are spoiled for choice in Montevideo. The city offers everything from 19th-century cafes to trendy modern bistros, and from carnivore-centric *parrillas* to vegetarian- and vegan-friendly eateries, all interspersed with a wider choice of international cuisine than you'll find anywhere else in Uruguay. Ciudad Vieja's restaurant scene in particular is blossoming as old concerns about the neighborhood's security continue to wane.

Ciudad Vieja

★**La Fonda** VEGAN, HEALTH FOOD $$
(Map p524; ☎2917-1559; www.facebook.com/pg/lafondauy; Pérez Castellano 1422; mains UR$350-450; ⏰7-11pm Tue & Wed, noon-4pm & 7-11pm Thu-Sun; ✍) Grab a table on the pedestrianized street, or enter the high-ceilinged, brick-walled interior to watch the wild-haired chefs bantering to cool jazz as they roll out homemade pasta, carefully lay asparagus spears atop risotto or grab ingredients from the boxes of organic produce adorning their open kitchen. The ever-changing chalkboard menu always includes one vegan option.

DON'T MISS

CARNAVAL IN MONTEVIDEO

If you thought Brazil was South America's only Carnaval capital, think again! Montevideanos cut loose in a big way every February, with music and dance filling the air for a solid month.

Not to be missed is the early-February **Desfile de las Llamadas**, a two-night parade of *comparsas* (neighborhood Carnaval societies) through the streets of Palermo and Barrio Sur districts, just southeast of the Centro. *Comparsas* are made up of *negros* (persons of African descent) and *lubolos* (whites who paint their faces black for Carnaval, a long-standing Uruguayan tradition). Neighborhood rivalries play themselves out as wave after wave of dancers whirl to the electrifying rhythms of traditional Afro-Uruguayan *candombe* drumming, beaten on drums of three different pitches: the *chico* (soprano), *repique* (contralto) and *piano* (tenor). The heart of the parade route is Isla de Flores, between Salto and Gaboto. Spectators can pay for a chair on the sidewalk or try to snag a spot on one of the balconies overlooking the street.

Another key element of Montevideo's Carnaval are the *murgas*, organized groups of 15 to 17 gaudily dressed performers, including three percussionists, who perform original pieces of musical theater, often satirical and based on political themes. During the dictatorship in Uruguay, *murgas* were famous for their subversive commentary. All *murgas* use the same three instruments: the *bombo* (bass drum), *redoblante* (snare drum) and *platillos* (cymbals). *Murgas* play all over the city, and also compete throughout February in Parque Rodó at the Teatro de Verano (p532).

The fascinating history of Montevideo's Carnaval is well documented in the city's Museo del Carnaval (p517).

★Estrecho INTERNATIONAL **$$**
(Map p524; ☎2915-6107; www.estrecho.uy; Sarandí 460; mains UR$340-470; ⊙noon-4pm Mon-Sat) Grab a seat at the long stove-side counter and watch the chefs whip up delicious daily specials at this cozy Ciudad Vieja lunch spot. The international menu includes baguette sandwiches with steak or smoked salmon, a variety of salads, fresh fish of the day and divine desserts.

Sin Pretensiones CAFE **$$**
(Map p524; ☎2916-9972; www.sinpretensiones.com.uy; Peatonal Sarandí 366; mains UR$280-540; ⊙9:30am-6:30pm Mon-Fri) Enterprising young Argentine owner Guillermina has created this pleasingly unique cafe-boutique on Ciudad Vieja's main pedestrian street. The wide-open space invites people to settle in over breakfast pastries, glasses of wine or *grappamiel* (honey-infused grape brandy), afternoon tea or *mate*, and light meals any time of day (a real boon to foreigners who still haven't adjusted to Uruguay's late-night dinner schedule).

Toledo Bar de Tapas TAPAS **$$**
(Map p524; ☎2915-3006; www.facebook.com/pg/ToledoBardeTapas; Cerrito 499; tapas UR$195-410; ⊙noon-4pm Mon-Sat) Bringing a touch of Spain to the Ciudad Vieja, this corner bar serves a good mix of Iberian classics, from gazpacho and *arroz con mariscos* (rice with seafood) to *tortilla española* (potato omelette), *croquetas de jamón* (ham croquettes) and asparagus with romesco sauce. Yum!

★Mercado del Puerto PARRILLA **$$$**
(Map p524; www.mercadodelpuerto.com; Pérez Castellano; mains UR$300-700; ⊙noon-5pm daily year-round, to 11pm Tue-Fri Nov-Feb) This converted market on Ciudad Vieja's waterfront remains a Montevideo classic, even if the steady influx of cruise ships into the adjacent port has made it increasingly pricey. Take your pick of the densely packed *parrillas* and pull up a stool. Weekends are ideal for savoring the market's vibrant energy.

Es Mercat SEAFOOD **$$$**
(Map p524; ☎2917-0169; www.esmercat.com.uy; Colón 1550; mains UR$310-850; ⊙9am-5:30pm daily, 8pm-midnight Thu-Sat) If fish is your thing, Es Mercat is your place. Steer one block beyond the meat-crazed Mercado del Puerto to this Ciudad Vieja corner, where a rotating lineup of a half-dozen fresh-caught fish, from *merluza* (hake) to *abadejo* (pollock), gets scrawled on the blackboard daily. Your best bet? Solicit descriptions and recommendations from chef-owner Roberto and son Facundo.

Jacinto INTERNATIONAL $$$
(Map p524; www.jacinto.com.uy; cnr Sarandí & Alzáibar; sandwiches UR$280-390, mains UR$590-610; ⏲10am-midnight Mon-Sat) Lucía Soria's fresh-baked bread, flavorful salads and soups, savory tarts and sandwiches and other gastronomic delights have been pleasing Montevidean palates since 2012, when Soria first opened this high-ceilinged, checker-floored eatery in Ciudad Vieja. The food's as good as ever, and Soria's rise to fame as a *MasterChef* TV star in 2017 has added an extra dose of panache.

Centro

★Candy Bar TAPAS, BURGERS $
(Map p524; ☎2904-3179; www.facebook.com/CandyBarPalermo; Durazno 1402; tapas UR$120, mains UR$270-300; ⏲12:30pm-1am Tue-Sat, noon-2pm Sun) At this cool corner eatery, colorful folding chairs fill the sidewalk beneath a spreading sycamore tree, while the chefs inside mix drinks, whip up meals and juggle fresh-baked bread behind a countertop overhung with artsy lampshades. Reasonably priced tapas and burgers (carnivorous and vegetarian) rule the menu, complemented by artisan beers and mixed drinks. Sunday brunch is especially popular.

Shawarma Ashot MIDDLE EASTERN $
(Map p524; www.facebook.com/ShawarmaAshot; Zelmar Michelini 1295; sandwiches UR$150-230; ⏲11am-5pm Mon-Fri, noon-4pm Sat) Well-prepared Middle Eastern classics such as falafel and shawarma draw loyal lunchtime crowds at this unpretentious hole-in-the-wall. For a special treat, don't miss the UR$250 Saturday special: Uruguayan lamb with rice pilaf!

Bar Tasende PIZZA $
(Map p524; cnr Ciudadela & San José; pizza slices UR$100; ⏲10am-1am Sun-Thu, to 2am Fri & Sat) This classic high-ceilinged corner bar has been wooing patrons since 1931 with its trademark *muzzarella al tacho (*simple but tasty pizza slices laden with mozzarella) a perfect snack to accompany a beer any time of day.

Comi.K BRAZILIAN $$
(Map p524; ☎2902-4344; www.facebook.com/COMIKRestaurante; Av 18 de Julio 994, 2nd fl; specials incl drink & dessert UR$380; ⏲9am-9pm Mon-Fri, to 4pm Sat) Inside the Brazilian cultural center, reasonably priced meals – including the Saturday special *feijoada* (Brazil's classic meat-and-black-bean stew) – are served in an elegant 2nd-floor salon with high ceilings and stained glass. There's live Brazilian music most Friday evenings.

Parque Rodó, La Rambla & Eastern Beaches

El Club del Pan BAKERY $
(www.facebook.com/pg/clubdelpan; cnr Pablo de María & Muller; ⏲10am-7pm Tue-Fri, to 3pm Sat) After deriving inspiration from bakers around the world, Gonzalo Zubirí returned home to Montevideo to open this sweet corner spot, a stone's throw from Parque Rodó, in 2017. A cornucopia of sublime baked goods, from croissants to focaccia to *pain au chocolat*, emerges daily from the oven. At lunchtime, don't miss its daily sandwich specials, which range from vegan to carnivorous.

★Escaramuza CAFE $$
(☎2401-3475; www.escaramuza.com.uy; Pablo de María 1185; mains UR$250-430; ⏲9am-9pm Mon-Sat) Tucked into a beautifully restored Cordón home, Escaramuza impresses on many levels. Cross the threshold to discover one of Montevideo's most attractive bookshops. A few paces further and you've entered the seductive high-ceilinged cafe and back-patio restaurant, where patrons linger over superbly prepared, reasonably priced Uruguayan specials with health-food overtones; for example, *milanesas* (breaded cutlets) and buttery mashed potatoes, meet kale salad!

La Pulpería PARRILLA $$
(☎2710-8657; www.facebook.com/LaPulperiaMvdeo; cnr Lagunillas & Nuñez, Punta Carretas; mains UR$295-445; ⏲7pm-midnight Tue-Sat, noon-4pm Sun) The epitome of an intimate neighborhood *parrilla,* this corner place doesn't advertise its presence (drop by before 7pm and you won't even find a sign outside); instead, it focuses on grilling prime cuts of meat to perfection, and relies on word of mouth to do the rest. Grab a barstool by the blazing fire or a table on the sidewalk.

Casitanno URUGUAYAN $$
(☎2409-7236; www.facebook.com/casitanno; Maldonado 2051, Parque Rodó; mains UR$180-360; ⏲7pm-2am Sun, Mon & Wed, 8pm-3am Thu-Sat) With its colorful cocktail list, intimate bar area and street-facing front deck, this lively corner place draws a youthful late-night crowd for designer comfort food and drinks.

MERCADO AGRÍCOLA DE MONTEVIDEO

One of Montevideo's newer **foodie attractions** (MAM; ☎2200-9535; www.mam.com.uy; José Terra 2220; ⏲9am-10pm), this early-20th-century market building and national historic monument 2.5km north of the center was completely renovated and reopened in 2013. It now houses more than 100 merchants, including fruit and veggie vendors, cafes, restaurants, specialty food shops and a **microbrewery**.

Gourmet *chivitos* (Uruguay's classic fillet of beef sandwich with cheese, tomatoes, bacon, olives and mayonnaise) are the star attraction, served on ciabatta bread with tasty add-ons like arugula, caramelized onions and roasted peppers; vegetarians can sink their teeth into a meat-free version.

El Berretin URUGUAYAN **$$**
(☎2716-0609, 091-453131; www.facebook.com/elberretinbar; Guipuzcoa 496; ⏲noon-4pm & 8pm-1am) Serving a mix of Uruguayan grilled-meat classics and lighter fare such as Caesar salads, this historic art-deco corner grocery was converted into a popular resto-bar in 2016. Its most evocative feature is the *berretin* (secret underground hiding place used by 1970s Tupamaro rebels) discovered by workers during renovation, now preserved under glass in the restaurant's back room.

Foc FUSION **$$$**
(☎091-654227; www.facebook.com/restaurantefoc; Ramón Fernández 285, Punta Carretas; multicourse menus from UR$1000; ⏲8pm-midnight Mon-Sat) After nine years honing his culinary technique at Michelin-starred restaurants in Catalonia, chef Martín Lavecchia returned to Montevideo to open this divine restaurant. Five- to seven-course menus feature seafood delights like mussel-squid risotto or shrimp in coconut milk with cilantro, lime and guindilla peppers, followed by flamboyant desserts such as lemon mousse with mandarin ice cream and Pop Rock crumble.

La Perdiz PARRILLA **$$$**
(☎2711-8963; www.laperdizrestaurant.com; Guipúzcoa 350, Punta Carretas; mains UR$350-600; ⏲noon-4pm & 7:30pm-12:30am) Reserve ahead for this ever-popular *parrilla*, one block from the waterfront near Punta Carretas Shopping. Enjoy the best of Uruguay's carnivore culture at a fireside seat by the open grill, or spread out at one of the larger tables around the periphery. Save room for trademark desserts like *dulce de leche* (milk caramel) mousse and *frutillas con nata* (strawberries with whipped cream).

Drinking & Nightlife

Montevideo offers an intriguing mix of venerable cafes and trendy nightspots. Bars are concentrated on Bartolomé Mitre in Ciudad Vieja, south of Plaza Independencia in the Centro and near the corner of Canelones and Juan Jackson where the Parque Rodó and Cordón neighborhoods meet.

Ciudad Vieja

★ **Café Brasilero** CAFE
(Map p524; ☎2917-2035; www.facebook.com/cafebrasilerouy; Ituzaingó 1447; ⏲9am-8pm Mon-Fri, to 6pm Sat) This vintage 1877 cafe with dark wood paneling and historic photos gracing the walls makes a delightful spot for morning coffee or afternoon tea. It's also an excellent lunch stop, with good-value *menus ejecutivos* (all-inclusive daily specials for UR$400).

La Farmacia CAFE
(Map p524; Cerrito 550; ⏲9am-8pm Mon-Fri) Opened in 2017, this Ciudad Vieja cafe in a 19th-century pharmacy (circa 1870) oozes historic charm. Green marble tabletops, ornamental tiled floors and built-in wood cabinetry from its former incarnation make a splendid setting for morning coffee or mid-afternoon snacks.

Shannon Irish Pub PUB
(Map p524; www.theshannon.com.uy; Bartolomé Mitre 1318; ⏲6pm-late Mon-Fri, from 7pm Sat & Sun) Always hopping, the Shannon features a variety of Uruguayan microbrews plus a full complement of other beers from over a dozen countries. There's live music 365 days a year, from rock to traditional Irish bands.

Centro

Barón: la Barbería que Esconde un Secreto COCKTAIL BAR
(Map p524; Santiago de Chile 1270; ⏲6pm-2am Tue-Sat) Like a trip back to America's Prohibition days, 'the barbershop that hides a secret' is a clandestine cocktail bar tucked

behind an unassuming-looking storefront. Walk past the vintage barber chairs and open the secret doorway into one of Montevideo's coolest new nightspots. (And, yes, you can still get your hair cut too!)

La Ronda BAR

(Map p524; www.facebook.com/larondacafe; Ciudadela 1182; ⏲6pm-1am Sun-Thu, to 2am Fri & Sat) At this popular bar between Plaza Independencia and the riverfront, choose between the dark interior where the bartender spins vinyl or the sidewalk tables cooled by breezes off the Rambla.

Museo del Vino WINE BAR

(Map p524; ☎2908-3430; www.museodelvino.com.uy; Maldonado 1150; ⏲1-5pm & 9pm-1am Wed-Sat) A wine shop by day, this downtown venue also hosts frequent live tango performances in the evenings, accompanied by an excellent selection of Uruguayan wines.

North of Centro

Chopería Mastra MICROBREWERY

(www.mastra.com.uy; Mercado Agrícola de Montevideo, Local 17; ⏲11am-11pm) This convivial pub in Montevideo's agricultural market is the flagship outlet for Uruguay's beloved Mastra microbrewery. With a dozen varieties to choose from, you may prefer to opt for the *tabla degustación* (a four-beer sampler, available weekdays only). Mastra has several other pubs around town, including near the beach in **Pocitos** (www.mastra.com.uy; cnr 26 de Marzo & Pérez, ⏲7pm-2am Tue-Sat).

Cain Dance Club GAY

(www.caindance.com; Cerro Largo 1833, Cordón; ⏲12:30am-dawn Fri & Sat) Montevideo's premier gay nightspot (but also hetero-friendly), Cain is a multilevel club with two dance floors playing everything from techno to Latin beats.

Parque Rodó, La Rambla & Eastern Beaches

Montevideo Brew House MICROBREWERY

(☎2705-2763; www.mbh.com.uy; Libertad 2592; ⏲7pm-late Mon-Sat) Pouring six beers brewed on-site (including an excellent Guinness-like dry stout), along with half a dozen offerings from Montevideo's Davok microbrewery, this corner pub is one of Pocitos' most popular drinking spots.

Baker's Bar BAR

(☎098-652646; www.facebook.com/BakersBar; Pablo de María 1198; ⏲noon-2am Mon-Wed, to 3am Thu-Sat) One of Montevideo's newer drinking hot spots, Baker's sits smack in the heart of the Cordón–Parque Rodó nightlife district. Co-founders Santiago Urquhart and Charlie Sarli, transplants from superstar bar-restaurant La Huella on Uruguay's Atlantic coast, have infused the place with a cool, low-key energy, serving up well-mixed drinks, tasty tapas and good music.

Philomène TEAHOUSE

(☎2711-1770; www.philomenecafe.com; Solano García 2455, Punta Carretas; ⏲9am-8:30pm Mon-Fri, 11am-8:30pm Sat) This cozy spot specializes in big pots of tea served alongside cookies and light meals in a pair of gaily wallpapered parlor-sized rooms.

☆ Entertainment

Spanish-language websites with entertainment listings include www.cartelera.com.uy, www.vivomontevideo.com/cartelera, www.yamp.com.uy/agenda and www.socioespectacular.com.uy.

Live Music & Dance

Tango legend Carlos Gardel spent time in Montevideo, where the tango is no less popular than in Buenos Aires. Music and dance venues abound downtown.

★Fun Fun LIVE MUSIC

(Map p524; ☎2904-4859; www.barfunfun.com; Soriano 922, Centro; ⏲8pm-late Tue-Sat) Since 1895 this intimate, informal venue has been serving its famous *uvita* (a sweet wine drink) while hosting tango and other live music on a tiny stage. Temporarily moved to Calle Soriano in 2014, it's due to return four blocks west to its traditional location in Mercado Central once renovation work is finished.

★Teatro Solís PERFORMING ARTS

(Map p524; ☎1950-3323; www.teatrosolis.org.uy; Buenos Aires 678, Ciudad Vieja; from UR$150) The city's top performing-arts venue is home to the Montevideo Philharmonic Orchestra and hosts formal concerts of classical, jazz, tango and other music, plus music festivals, theater, ballet and opera.

Sala Zitarrosa PERFORMING ARTS

(Map p524; ☎1950-9241; www.salazitarrosa.com.uy; Av 18 de Julio 1012, Centro) Montevideo's

CARNAVAL DRUM SESSIONS

A great way to experience Carnaval out of season is by attending one of the informal candombe practice sessions that erupt in neighborhood streets throughout the year. A good place is in Parque Rodó, where the all-female group La Melaza gathers at the corner of Blanes and Gonzalo Ramírez and continues down San Salvador. Drumming usually starts Sundays around 6pm. Palermo and Barrio Sur are other good neighborhoods to see a session.

For a more complete list of Carnaval groups who hold regular weekend practice sessions in Montevideo's streets, see www.descubrimontevideo.uy/es/candombe-por-los-barrios.

best midsize auditorium venue for big-name music and dance performances, including tango, rock, flamenco, reggae and *zarzuela* (traditional Spanish musical theater).

Mercado de la Abundancia LIVE MUSIC
(Map p524; cnr San José & Aquiles Lanza, Centro; Sat free, UR$180 Sun; ⏲10pm-late Sat, 8pm-late Sun) On Saturday evenings from 10pm, locals throng the upper floor of this historic market to dance to live tango music. Join in, or watch from the sidelines at one of the adjacent restaurants. On Sundays, Montevideo's leading tango organization, Joventango (also based in the market), sponsors regular tango shows at 8pm, then opens its floor for dancing from 9:30pm.

Teatro de Verano LIVE MUSIC
(www.teatrodeverano.org.uy; from UR$210) Every January and February, *murgas* (Carnaval groups of 15 to 17 gaudily dressed performers, including three percussionists, who perform original pieces of political or satirical musical theater) compete at the Teatro de Verano in Parque Rodó. The competition has three rounds, with judges determining who advances and who gets eliminated.

Cinema

The three big shopping malls east of downtown (Punta Carretas, Montevideo and Portones) all have modern multiscreen cinemas.

Cinemateca Uruguaya CINEMA
(Map p524; ☎2900-9056; www.cinemateca.org.uy; Av 18 de Julio 1280, Centro; film tickets members/non-members free/UR$220) For art-house flicks, this film club charges a modest membership (UR$470 per month, plus UR$230 one-time sign-up fee), allowing unlimited viewing at its four cinemas; non-members pay a small entry fee per film. It hosts the two-week Festival Cinematográfico Internacional del Uruguay in March or April.

Spectator Sports

Fútbol, a Uruguayan passion, inspires large and regular crowds. The main stadium, the **Estadio Centenario** (Av Ricaldoni, Parque José Batlle y Ordóñez), opened in 1930 for the first World Cup, in which Uruguay defeated Argentina 4-2 in the final.

Fanáticos Fútbol Tours (☎099-862325; www.futboltours.com.uy) offers personalized tours led by knowledgeable, multilingual *fútbol* aficionados; prices include tickets to a match of your choosing, plus hotel transport. Alternatively, check with Matias at Buenas Vibras Hostel (p527) about his informal outings to watch local league matches.

Shopping

Central Montevideo's traditional downtown shopping area is Av 18 de Julio. Locals also flock to several large shopping malls east of downtown, including Punta Carretas Shopping, Tres Cruces Shopping (above the bus terminal) and Montevideo Shopping in Pocitos/Buceo.

Feria de Tristán Narvaja MARKET
(Tristán Narvaja, Cordón; ⏲9am-4pm Sun) This colorful Sunday-morning outdoor market is a decades-long tradition begun by Italian immigrants. It sprawls from Av 18 de Julio northwards along Calle Tristán Narvaja, spilling over onto several side streets. You can find used books, music, clothing, jewelry, live animals, antiques and souvenirs in its many makeshift stalls.

Saturday Flea Market MARKET
(Map p524; Plaza Matriz, Ciudad Vieja; ⏲8am-1pm Sat) Every Saturday, vendors take over Ciudad Vieja's central square, selling antique door knockers, saddles, household goods and just about anything else you can imagine. A smaller contingent of vendors appears on the plaza some weekdays.

Manos del Uruguay CLOTHING
(Map p524; ☎2914-5164; www.manos.com.uy; Sarandí 458; ⏲10am-6pm Mon-Fri, to 2pm Sat) This national cooperative, a member of the World Fair Trade Organization, is famous

for its quality woolen goods. In addition to its Ciudad Vieja branch, it also has an outlet downtown and shops in Montevideo Shopping and Punta Carretas Shopping east of downtown.

Pecarí FASHION & ACCESSORIES
(Map p524; ☎2915-6696; www.pecari.com.uy; Juan Carlos Gómez 1412; ⊙10am-7pm Mon-Fri, 10:30am-1:30pm Sat) For quality Uruguayan leather goods, including jackets, handbags, shoes and accessories, check out this shop just off Plaza Matriz in Ciudad Vieja.

La Pasionaria ARTS & CRAFTS
(Map p524; ☎2915-6852; www.lapasionaria.com.uy; Reconquista 587, Ciudad Vieja; ⊙10am-6pm Mon-Fri, 11am-5pm Sat) This colorful Ciudad Vieja shop sells clothing in its upstairs boutique and Uruguayan handicrafts downstairs. The attached cafe serves tasty soups, salads and daily specials, including vegetarian and vegan options.

Hecho Acá ARTS & CRAFTS
(☎2622-6683; www.hechoaca.com.uy; Montevideo Shopping, 1st fl, Local 147; ⊙10am-10pm) Woolen goods and other handicrafts from around the country are nicely displayed here.

Manos del Uruguay CLOTHING
(Map p524; ☎2900-4910; www.manos.com.uy; San José 1111, Centro; ⊙10:30am-6:30pm Mon-Fri, 10am-2pm Sat) Downtown outlet of Uruguay's national woolen-goods cooperative.

Orientation

Montevideo lies almost directly across the Río de la Plata from Buenos Aires. For many visitors, the most intriguing area is the Ciudad Vieja, the formerly walled colonial grid straddling the western tip of a peninsula between the sheltered port and the wide-open river. Just east of the old-town gate, the Centro (downtown) begins at Plaza Independencia, surrounded by historic buildings of the republican era. Avenida 18 de Julio, downtown Montevideo's commercial thoroughfare, runs east past Plaza del Entrevero, Plaza Cagancha and the Intendencia (town hall) toward Tres Cruces bus terminal, where it changes name to Avenida Italia and continues east toward Carrasco International Airport and the Interbalnearia highway to Punta del Este.

Westward across the harbor, 132m Cerro de Montevideo was a landmark for early navigators and still offers outstanding views of the city. Eastward, the Rambla hugs Montevideo's scenic waterfront, snaking past attractive Parque Rodó and through a series of sprawling residential beach suburbs – Punta Carretas, Pocitos, Buceo and Carrasco – that are very popular with the capital's residents in summer and on evenings and weekends.

Information

EMERGENCY

Ambulance (☎105)
Police (☎911)

INTERNET ACCESS

Most accommodations have a guest computer in the lobby, free in-room wi-fi, or both. Many restaurants and cafes also offer free wi-fi.

MEDIA

Newspapers Montevideo's leading dailies are *El País* (www.elpais.com.uy) and *El Observador* (www.elobservador.com.uy). The weekly *Búsqueda* (www.busqueda.com.uy) is another good news source.

MEDICAL SERVICES

Hospital Británico (☎2487-1020; www.hospitalbritanico.com.uy; Av Italia 2420) Highly recommended private hospital with English-speaking doctors; 2.5km east of downtown.

MONEY

Banks, ATMs and exchange houses such as **Indumex** (www.indumex.com; Terminal Tres Cruces; ⊙6am-midnight) are everywhere, including the airport and bus terminal; downtown they're concentrated along Av 18 de Julio.

POST

Convenient post offices:
Centro (Map p524; Canelones 1358; ⊙9am-6pm Mon-Fri)
Ciudad Vieja (Map p524; Misiones 1328; ⊙9am-6pm Mon-Fri)
Tres Cruces Bus Terminal (cnr Bulevar Artigas & Av Italia; ⊙9am-10pm Mon-Fri, 10am-10pm Sat & Sun)

SAFE TRAVEL

Montevideo is quite sedate by Latin American standards, although it's wise to exercise caution as in any large city. The installation of security cameras throughout Ciudad Vieja and the Centro in 2013 has led to a radical decrease in petty crime. Montevideo's *policia turística* (tourist police) patrol the streets and can help if you encounter any problems.

TELEPHONE

Uruguay's national telephone company Antel has branches all over town:
Centro (San José 1101; ⊙10am-5pm Mon-Fri)
Ciudad Vieja (Rincón 501; ⊙10am-5pm Mon-Fri)

1

BRUNO PEREIRA DA SILVA/SHUTTERSTOCK ©

MATYAS REHAK/SHUTTERSTOCK ©

1. Colonia del Sacramento (p538)
This irresistibly picturesque riverside town is a Unesco World Heritage site.

2. Punta del Este (p552)
Celebrity watchers have a full-time job here – this is one of South America's most glamorous resorts.

3. Museo de la Revolución Industrial (p547)
The former factory that produced the Oxo beef cube is now a fascinating museum.

4. Carnaval, Montevideo (p528)
The city cuts loose with music and dance every February.

KOBBY DAGAN/SHUTTERSTOCK ©

Tres Cruces Bus Terminal (Local 14B, Tres Cruces Bus Terminal; ⏲8am-10pm)

TOURIST INFORMATION

The Municipal Tourist Office has city maps, general Montevideo information and a downloadable visitor's guide to the city in English, Spanish and Portuguese.

Centro (Map p524; ☎1950-1830; www.descubrimontevideo.uy; cnr Av 18 de Julio & Ejido; ⏲9am-5pm) Downtown tourist office, on the ground floor of Montevideo's city hall.

Ciudad Vieja (Map p524; ☎2916-8434; www.descubrimontevideo.uy; Piedras 252; ⏲10am-4pm) Next to Mercado del Puerto.

The National Tourism Ministry (www.turismo.gub.uy) offers info about Montevideo and destinations throughout Uruguay.

Carrasco Airport (☎2604-0386; ⏲8am-8pm)

Port (Map p524; ☎2188-5111; Rambla 25 de Agosto & Yacaré; ⏲9am-5pm Mon-Fri)

Tres Cruces Bus Terminal (☎2409-7399; cnr Bulevar Artigas & Av Italia; ⏲8am-8pm)

USEFUL WEBSITES

guruguay.com Developed by Karen Higgs, owner of **Casa Sarandi Guesthouse** (p526), this is an excellent resource for English speakers. It's jam-packed with useful insider information about Montevideo and Uruguay as a whole.

Getting There & Away

AIR

Montevideo's stylishly modern Carrasco International Airport (p573) is served by direct flights from Madrid and Miami, and one-stop services from several other European and North American cities via Buenos Aires or São Paulo.

If you plan to visit both Argentina and Uruguay, note that Ezeiza airport in Buenos Aires offers more direct international flights than Carrasco, with a considerably wider range of airlines.

At the time of research there were no airlines offering domestic service within Uruguay.

BOAT

Buquebus (☎130; www.buquebus.com.uy) runs daily ferries direct from Montevideo to Buenos Aires on the high-speed *Francisco* boat (2¼ hours), named after Pope Francis. Full *turista*-class fares run UR$3485. Buquebus also offers less-expensive bus-boat combinations from Montevideo to Buenos Aires via Colonia (UR$1220 to UR$2259, 4½ hours). Better fares for all services above are available with online advance purchase; you can also buy direct from Buquebus counters at **Montevideo Port** (Map p524; Terminal Fluvio-Marítima; ⏲9am-7:30pm) and **Tres Cruces bus terminal** (ticket counters 28 & 29; ⏲6:30am-2am).

Seacat (Map p524; ☎2915-0202; www.seacatcolonia.com.uy; Río Negro 1400; ⏲9:30am-6:30pm Mon-Fri) and **Colonia Express** (☎2401-6666; www.coloniaexpress.com; Tres Cruces Bus Terminal, ticket counter 31A; ⏲5:30am-10:30pm) both offer more economical bus-boat connections from Montevideo to Buenos Aires via Colonia (4¼ hours). The cheapest one-way fares on both carriers start below UR$1000.

Cacciola Viajes (☎2407-9657; www.cacciolaviajes.com; Tres Cruces Bus Terminal, ticket counter 25B; ⏲8:30am-11:30pm) runs a scenic twice- to thrice-daily bus-launch service from Montevideo to Buenos Aires via the riverside town of Carmelo and the Argentine Delta suburb of Tigre. The eight-hour trip costs UR$900 one way.

BUS

Montevideo's modern **Tres Cruces Bus Terminal** (☎2401-8998; www.trescruces.com.uy; cnr Bulevar Artigas & Av Italia) is about 3km east of downtown. It has tourist information, clean toilets, luggage storage, ATMs and a shopping mall upstairs.

A taxi from the terminal to downtown costs between UR$170 and UR$200. To save your pesos, take city bus CA1, which leaves from directly in front of the terminal (on the eastern side), traveling to Ciudad Vieja via Av 18 de Julio (UR$24, 15 minutes).

For the beach neighborhoods of Punta Carretas and Pocitos, take city buses 174 and 183, respectively, from in front of the terminal (UR$33). A taxi to either neighborhood costs between UR$170 and UR$200.

All domestic destinations are served daily, and most several times a day. A small *tasa de embarque* (departure tax) is added to the ticket prices. Travel times are approximate.

EGA (☎2402-5164; www.ega.com.uy) provides the widest range of services to neighboring countries. Destinations in Argentina include Paraná, Santa Fe and Mendoza (all once weekly, on Friday), plus Córdoba and Rosario (each four times weekly). EGA also runs buses once weekly to Florianópolis and São Paulo, Brazil (Sunday); twice weekly to Asunción, Paraguay (Wednesday and Saturday); and daily to Porto Alegre, Brazil.

Service to Buenos Aires is more frequent, with **CITA** (☎2402-5425; www.cita.com.uy) and several competing companies offering multiple nightly departures.

Getting Around

TO/FROM THE AIRPORT

Carrasco International Airport Buses, shuttle vans, taxis and *remises* (private cars) make the 20km journey from the airport into Montevideo. Cheapest are the local Copsa and Cutcsa buses

(UR$58, 45 minutes) that leave from a stop directly in front of the arrivals hall, making frequent stops en route to **Terminal Suburbana** (Map p524; ☎1975; cnr Río Branco & Galicia), five blocks north of Plaza del Entrevero. Faster and more comfortable is COT's direct bus service between the airport (UR$181, 30 minutes) and Tres Cruces bus terminal. Look for the stop to the right as you exit the arrivals hall.

Shared shuttle vans (five-person minimum) also travel from the airport to the center (UR$400 per person); buy tickets from the taxisaeropuerto.com taxi counter in the airport arrivals hall.

Fixed-rate **airport taxis** (☎2604-0323; www.taxisaeropuerto.com) charge between UR$1200 and UR$1700 (depending on neighborhood) for the 30- to 45-minute ride from the airport into Montevideo. A less expensive and more comfortable way to get into the city is to pre-book a *remise* from a company like **B&B Remise** (☎096-603780; www.bybremises.com).

Ferry Terminal Ferries from Argentina dock just north of the Mercado del Puerto, within a five- to 15-minute walk of all Ciudad Vieja accommodations. Buses to other parts of the city (UR$33) run along Calle Cerrito, two blocks south of the port. Taxis queue just outside the ferry terminal and can take you anywhere in the city for UR$250 or less.

BUS

Montevideo's city buses, operated by **Cutcsa** (☎19333; www.cutcsa.com.uy), go almost everywhere for UR$33 per ride. For bus-connection info based on your point of origin and destination, see the Spanish-language website **Como Ir** (www.montevideo.gub.uy/aplicacion/como-ir).

CAR

Most international rental-car companies have counters at Carrasco Airport. In downtown Montevideo, you can also try the following Uruguayan companies (with nationwide branches):

Multicar (☎2902-2555; www.redmulticar.com; Colonia 1227, Centro; ⏲9am-7pm Mon-Fri, to 1pm Sat)

Punta Car (☎2900-2772; www.puntacar.com.uy; Cerro Largo 1383, Centro; ⏲9am-6:30pm Mon-Fri, to 1pm Sat)

TAXI

Montevideo's black-and-yellow taxis are all metered. Cabbies carry two official price tables, one effective on weekdays, the other (20% higher) used at night between 10pm and 6am, and on Sundays and holidays. It costs UR$39 to drop the flag (UR$49 nights and Sundays) and roughly UR$2 per city block thereafter. Even for a long ride, you'll rarely pay more than UR$200, unless you're headed to Carrasco Airport. To call a cab, dial **Radio Taxi 141** (☎141; www.141.com.uy) or

Buses from Montevideo

DESTINATION	COST (UR$)	TIME (HR)
INTERNATIONAL		
Asunción, Paraguay	4290-5240	20
Buenos Aires, Argentina	1512	10
Córdoba, Argentina	2915-3580	14
Florianópolis, Brazil	3995-4700	18
Porto Alegre, Brazil	2630-3375	11¾
São Paulo, Brazil	5630-7095	30
DOMESTIC		
Carmelo	501	3¼
Colonia	350	2¾
La Paloma	481	3½
La Pedrera	501	4
Mercedes	561	4
Paysandú	781	4½
Piriápolis	202	1½
Punta del Diablo	601	5
Punta del Este	282	2¼
Salto	1021	6½
Tacuarembó	781	4½

Radio Taxi Montevideo (☎1711; www.radiotaxi montevideo.com.uy). Taxis can also be hailed on any street corner by raising your hand – look for the illuminated red 'Libre' (Free) sign on the windshield.

WESTERN URUGUAY

From Colonia's tree-shaded cobblestone streets to the hot springs of Salto, the slow-paced river towns of western Uruguay have a universally relaxing appeal, with just enough urban attractions to keep things interesting. Here, the border with Argentina is defined by the Río de la Plata and the Río Uruguay, and the region is commonly referred to as *el litoral* (the shore).

Further inland you'll find the heart of what some consider the 'real' Uruguay – the gaucho country around Tacuarembó, with *estancias* sprinkled throughout the rural landscape and some beautiful, rarely visited nature preserves.

Colonia del Sacramento

☎452 / POP 26,230

On the east bank of the Río de la Plata, 180km west of Montevideo, but only 50km from Buenos Aires by ferry, Colonia is an irresistibly picturesque town enshrined as a Unesco World Heritage site. Its Barrio Histórico, an irregular colonial-era nucleus of narrow cobbled streets, occupies a small peninsula jutting into the river. Pretty rows of sycamores offer protection from the summer heat, and the riverfront is a venue for spectacular sunsets (it's a Uruguayan custom to applaud the setting sun). Colonia's charm and its proximity to Buenos Aires draw thousands of Argentine visitors; on weekends, especially in summer, prices rise and it can be difficult to find a room.

History

Colonia was founded in 1680 by Manuel Lobo, the Portuguese governor of Río de Janeiro, and occupied a strategic position almost exactly opposite Buenos Aires across the Río de la Plata. The town grew in importance as a source of smuggled trade items, undercutting Spain's jealously defended mercantile monopoly and provoking repeated sieges and battles between Spain and Portugal.

Although the two powers agreed over the cession of Colonia to Spain around 1750, it wasn't until 1777 that Spain took final control of the city. From this time, the city's commercial importance declined as foreign goods proceeded directly to Buenos Aires.

Sights

Barrio Histórico

Colonia's Barrio Histórico is filled with visual delights. Picturesque spots for wandering include the roughly cobbled 18th-century **Calle de los Suspiros** (Street of Sighs), lined with tile-and-stucco colonial houses, the **Paseo de San Gabriel**, on the western riverfront, the **Puerto Viejo** (Old Port) and the historic center's two main squares: sprawling **Plaza Mayor 25 de Mayo** and shady **Plaza de Armas** (the latter is also known as Plaza Manuel Lobo).

A single UR$50 ticket covers admission to Colonia's eight historical museums. All keep the same hours, but closing day varies by museum. Tickets are sold at Museo Municipal.

Faro LIGHTHOUSE
(UR$25; ⏱10am-sunset) One of the town's most prominent landmarks, Colonia's 19th-century working lighthouse provides an excellent view of the old town and the Río de la Plata. It stands within the ruins of the 17th-century **Convento de San Francisco**, just off the southwest corner of Plaza Mayor 25 de Mayo.

Portón de Campo GATE
(Manuel Lobo) The most dramatic way to enter the Barrio Histórico is via the reconstructed 1745 city gate. From here, a thick fortified wall runs south along the Paseo de San Miguel to the river, whose grassy banks are popular with sunbathers.

Museo Portugués MUSEUM
(☎4523-1237; www.museoscolonia.com.uy; Plaza Mayor 25 de Mayo 180; admission incl in historical museums ticket UR$50; ⏱11:15am-4:45pm, closed Wed & Fri) In this old house on Colonia's main square you'll find Portuguese relics including porcelain, furniture, maps, Manuel Lobo's family tree and the old stone shield that once adorned the Portón de Campo.

Museo Municipal MUSEUM
(☎4522-7031; www.museoscolonia.com.uy; Plaza Mayor 25 de Mayo 77; admission incl in historical museums ticket UR$50; ⏱11:15am-4:45pm, closed Tue) Houses an eclectic collection

WORTH A TRIP

ESTANCIA LIVING ON A LIMITED BUDGET

What do you get when you cross a tourist *estancia* and a hostel? Find out at **El Galope Horse Farm & Hostel** (☎099-105985; www.elgalope.com.uy; Colonia Suiza; dm US$25, d with/without bathroom US$75/68;), a unique country retreat 115km west of Montevideo and 60km east of Colonia. Experienced world travelers Mónica and Miguel offer guests a chance to 'get away from it all' and settle into the relaxing rhythms of rural life for a few days.

Horseback jaunts for riders of all levels (US$40 for beginners within the farm property, US$80 for experienced riders on longer rides) are expertly led by Miguel himself, and there's a sauna (US$10) and small pool to soothe those aching muscles at the end of the day. Breakfast is included; other meals, from lunches (US$9) to full-fledged *asados* (barbecues) or fondue dinners (US$15) are available. Taxi pickup from the bus stop in nearby Colonia Valdense is available upon request (US$10).

of treasures including a whale skeleton, a re-creation of a colonial drawing room, historical timelines and a scale model of Colonia (c 1762).

Casa Nacarello MUSEUM
(☎4523-1237; www.museoscolonia.com.uy; Plaza Mayor 25 de Mayo 67; admission incl in historical museums ticket UR$50; ⊙11:15am-4:45pm, closed Tue) This teeny colonial home is evocative of Colonia's early days, with period furniture, thick whitewashed walls, wavy glass and original lintels (duck if you're tall!).

Centro Cultural Bastión del Carmen CULTURAL CENTER
(www.facebook.com/centroculturalbastiondelcarmen; Rivadavia 223; ⊙noon-6pm) FREE Incorporating part of the city's historic fortifications, this theater and gallery complex adjacent to Colonia's Puerto Viejo hosts rotating art exhibits and periodic concerts. The grassy riverside grounds out back, with outdoor sculptures and an industrial chimney dating from 1880, make a picturesque spot for a midafternoon break.

Museo Indígena MUSEUM
(☎4523-1237; www.museoscolonia.com.uy; cnr Del Comercio & Av General Flores; admission incl in historical museums ticket UR$50; ⊙11:15am-4:45pm, closed Mon & Thu) Houses Roberto Banchero's personal collection of Charrúa stone tools, exhibits on indigenous history, and an amusing map upstairs showing how many European countries could fit inside Uruguay's borders (it's at least six!).

Museo del Azulejo MUSEUM
(☎4523-1237; www.museoscolonia.com.uy; cnr Misiones de los Tapes & Paseo de San Gabriel; admission incl in historical museums ticket UR$50; ⊙11:15am-4:45pm, closed Fri) This dinky 17th-century stone house has a small sampling of French and Catalan tilework.

Archivo Regional MUSEUM
(☎4523-1237; www.museoscolonia.com.uy; Misiones de los Tapes 115; admission incl in historical museums ticket UR$50; ⊙11:15am-4:45pm Mon-Fri) On the northwest edge of Plaza Mayor 25 de Mayo, the tiny Archivo Regional contains historical documents along with pottery and glass excavated from the 18th-century Casa de los Gobernadores nearby.

Iglesia Matríz CHURCH
(Plaza de Armas) Uruguay's oldest church – begun by the Portuguese in 1680, then completely rebuilt twice under Spanish rule – is the centerpiece of pretty Plaza de Armas. The plaza also holds the foundations of a house dating from Portuguese times.

Real de San Carlos

At the turn of the 20th century, Argentine entrepreneur Nicolás Mihanovich spent US$1.5 million building an immense tourist complex 5km north of Colonia at Real de San Carlos. The complex included a 10,000-seat bullring, a 3000-seat *frontón* (court) for the Basque sport of *jai alai*, a hotel-casino and a racecourse.

Only the racecourse functions today, but the ruins of the remaining buildings make an interesting excursion, and the adjacent beach is popular with locals on Sundays.

Museo Paleontológico MUSEUM
(☎4523-1237; www.museoscolonia.com.uy; José Roger Balet; admission incl in historical museums ticket UR$50; ⊙11:15am-4:45pm Thu-Sun) This two-room museum displays glyptodon shells, bones and other locally excavated

Colonia del Sacramento

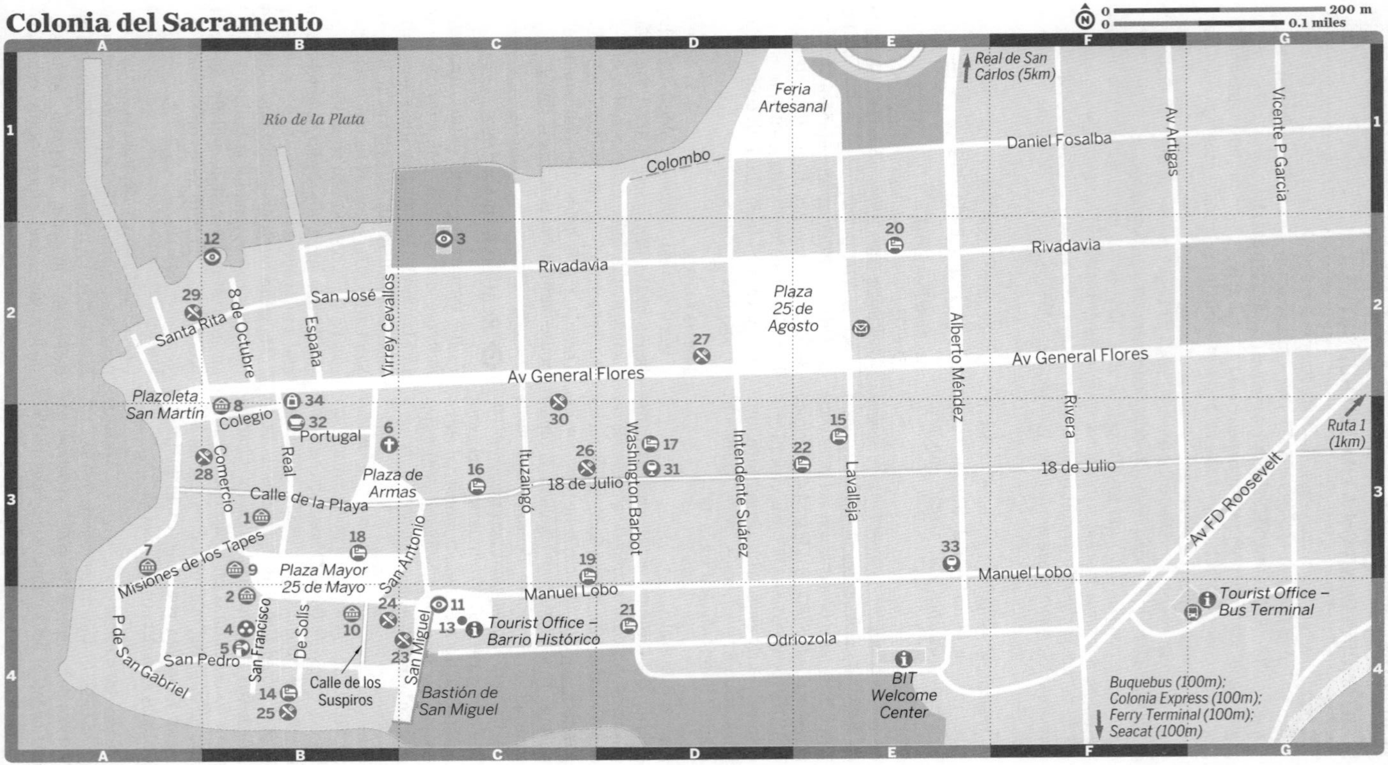

Colonia del Sacramento

Sights

1 Archivo Regional ... B3
2 Casa Nacarello ... B4
3 Centro Cultural Bastión del Carmen ... C2
4 Convento de San Francisco ... B4
5 Faro ... B4
6 Iglesia Matríz ... B3
7 Museo del Azulejo ... A3
8 Museo Indígena ... B3
9 Museo Municipal ... B3
10 Museo Portugués ... B4
11 Portón de Campo ... C4
12 Puerto Viejo ... B2

Activities, Courses & Tours

13 Walking Tours ... C4

Sleeping

14 Charco Hotel ... B4
15 Colonia Suite ... E3
16 El Capullo ... C3
17 El Viajero Hostel ... D3
18 La Posadita de la Plaza ... B3
19 Las Terrazas ... C3
20 Nova Posada ... E2
21 Posada del Ángel ... D4
22 Remus-Art Hostel ... E3

Eating

23 Bocadesanto ... C4
24 Buen Suspiro ... B4
25 Charco Bistró ... B4
26 Don Joaquín ... C3
27 El Portón ... D2
28 La Bodeguita ... B3
29 Lentas Maravillas ... A2
30 Los Farolitos ... C3

Drinking & Nightlife

31 Barbot ... D3
32 Ganache ... B3
33 Missfusion ... E3

Shopping

34 Malvón ... B2

finds from the private collection of self-taught paleontologist Armando Calcaterra.

Tours

Walking Tours WALKING
(☎099-379167; asociacionguiascolonia@gmail.com; tour per person in Spanish/other languages UR$150/200) The tourist office (p544) outside Colonia's old-town gate organizes good walking tours led by local guides. Spanish-language tours leave at 11am and 3pm daily year-round. Tours in other languages (English, French, Italian and Portuguese) can be arranged on request for a minimum of two people; ask at the tourist office.

Sleeping

Colonia has some great options for an overnight stay, though bear in mind that many hotels charge higher rates Friday through Sunday. Book in advance for summer weekends.

El Viajero Hostel HOSTEL $
(☎4522-2683; www.elviajerohostels.com; Washington Barbot 164; dm US$15-19, d US$50-70; ❄@📶) With bike rental, a bar for guests and air-con in all rooms, this hostel is brighter, fancier and somewhat cozier than the competition, and the location two blocks east of Plaza de Armas couldn't be better.

Remus-Art Hostel B&B $
(☎092-066985; www.facebook.com/remusarthostel; 18 de Julio 369; r US$80-90) This B&B in the home of German visual artist Christiane Brockmeyer has three comfortable, colorful rooms with shared bathroom and a spacious roof terrace where you can sunbathe, reach out and touch the overhanging sycamore leaves, or enjoy home-cooked candlelight dinners (per person US$25 including wine; specialties include raclette and fondue from Switzerland, where Christiane lived for 20 years).

★ **La Posadita de la Plaza** B&B $$
(☎4523-0502; www.posaditadelaplaza.com; Misiones de los Tapes 177; r US$125-180; 📶) At this whimsical guesthouse on Colonia's most historical square, friendly Brazilian photographer Eduardo has poured his creative genius into building a magical space resembling a life-size Joseph Cornell collage. Three guest rooms, an interior patio-deck with pretty old-town perspectives, and a cozy library-lounge are all decorated with found objects from Eduardo's world travels. Ample breakfasts feature freshly squeezed orange juice.

Le Moment BOUTIQUE HOTEL $$
(☎4520-2404; www.lemomentposadaboutique.com; Ruta 21, Km 186; r US$140-230; ❄📶🏊) On a clear day you can see Buenos Aires' skyscrapers glinting far across the river from

this classy country getaway, 15km north of Colonia. Friendly French expatriates (and veteran B&B owners) Sylvaine and Bruno woo guests with eight individually decorated, modern rooms, complemented by touches meant to invite relaxation: a swimming pool, an in-house resto-bar, and an intentional lack of TVs.

Las Terrazas BOUTIQUE HOTEL **$$**
(☎4522-4776; www.posadalasterrazas.com; Manuel Lobo 281; r US$115-150; ☎≋) This boutique hotel near picturesque Portón del Campo offers plenty of enticements: the friendly reception, the narrow, solar-heated outdoor pool and the spacious common area complete with free tea, *mate*, liqueurs and grappa made by the Argentine owner. It's worth paying extra for an upstairs room with one of the eponymous terraces, which boast cool views of Colonia's multicolored rooftops.

Nova Posada HOTEL **$$**
(☎4522-2952; www.novaposada.com; Rivadavia 463; d US$85-100, tr/q US$150/180; ❄@☎) With gleaming contemporary decor and spacious rooms with comfy beds, minibars and cable TV, this hotel is a good option for anyone who prefers modern comforts over colonial charm. It has a pretty garden with a breakfast patio and a cozy living room with a working fireplace, too. The ground-floor interconnected rooms are great for families.

Posada del Ángel HOTEL **$$**
(☎4522-4602; www.posadadelangel.net; Washington Barbot 59; r US$85-125; ❄@☎≋🐾) Conveniently located midway between the ferry port and Colonia's 18th-century town gate, this little hotel has down comforters for chilly nights, plus a leafy backyard with a pool for the summer heat. Inside, angels adorn the ceilings and walls. The cheapest rooms, facing an interior courtyard, lack charm; upstairs rooms are brighter with external windows; some have four-poster beds.

★**Colonia Suite** B&B **$$$**
(☎098-618966; www.coloniasuite.com; Lavalleja 169; r US$100-190; ❄☎) Incorporating three spacious upstairs suites and a 'garden house' bungalow out back, this is one of Colonia's most unique lodging options, abounding in homey features such as armchairs, colorful carpets, flat-screen TVs and local artwork. Enhancing the cozy vibe are a woodstove in one unit (Ateler) and well-equipped kitchenettes in two others (Joan Miró and Frida Kahlo).

Charco Hotel BOUTIQUE HOTEL **$$$**
(☎4523-5000; www.charcohotel.com; San Pedro 116; r US$210-400, Rancho US$383-450; ❄☎) Colonia's chicest hotel offers an incomparable old-town location, a waterfront restaurant-bar and beautifully landscaped grounds. Seven refined rooms in an elegantly remodeled historic building sport gleaming white decor and exposed stone and brickwork. Standouts include the suite with riverside terrace and the Rancho, a historic, kitchen-equipped Portuguese home sleeping up to six. Prepaid or multinight stays qualify for discounts.

El Capullo HOTEL **$$$**
(☎4523-0135; http://elcapullo.com; 18 de Julio 219; d US$135-180, apt US$205-250; ❄@☎≋) Tucked off a sycamore-shaded street in a prime Barrio Histórico location, El Capullo (the cocoon) offers guests a peaceful refuge from the surrounding bustle. The cheapest rooms lack external windows; it's worth paying extra for one upstairs or adjoining the grassy lawn out back. The bright communal spaces and spacious backyard with swimming pool are the big attractions here.

Eating

★**Don Joaquín** PIZZA **$**
(☎4522-4388; www.facebook.com/donjoaquinartesanalpizza; 18 de Julio 267; pizzas UR$155-240; ⏲8pm-midnight Tue-Sun) After 13 years in Europe, Colonia natives Yancí and Pierina returned home with a genuine Neapolitan pizza oven in tow. The result is this cheerful, high-ceilinged eatery where diners can watch the *pizzaiolo* (pizza chef) creating thin-crusted beauties with superb homemade sauce. Don't miss the carbonara with cheese, egg and delicately crunchy bacon, or the *pescatore* with mussels and shrimp.

Los Farolitos FAST FOOD **$**
(Av General Flores 272; sandwiches UR$45-225; ⏲12:30pm-1am) Renowned for its *chivitos*, this simple street-side stand also sells other low-cost, fast-food treats including hot dogs and *milanesas*.

Buen Suspiro URUGUAYAN **$$**
(☎4522-6160; www.buensuspiro.com; Calle de los Suspiros 92; picadas for 2 UR$360-670; ⏲11am-midnight) Duck under the wood beams into this cozy spot specializing in *picadas* (sharing boards of cheese and cold cuts). Sample local wines by the bottle or glass, accompanied by spinach and

leek tarts, ricotta-and-walnut 'truffles,' local cheese, sausage, soups and salads. Reserve ahead for a fireside table in winter, or while away a summer afternoon on the intimate back patio.

Bocadesanto BURGERS **$$**
(☎099-296022; www.bocadesanto.com; Paseo de San Miguel 81; burgers UR$390; ⏰noon-7pm Tue-Thu, to 4:30pm & 8-11pm Fri-Mon) Newcomer Bocadesanto pours all of its energy into creating Colonia's best burger: prime Uruguayan beef piled high with ingredients like home-roasted peppers, caramelized onions, Emmental cheese, bacon, arugula, pickles and sun-dried tomatoes, and complemented by good local microbrews on tap. Eat in the cozy colonial stone house, or on the sunny patio out back.

Lentas Maravillas INTERNATIONAL **$$**
(☎4522-0636; lentasmaravillas@gmail.com; Santa Rita 61; mains UR$300-395; ⏰1:30-6:30pm Mon, Tue & Fri, to 7:30pm Sat & Sun) Cozy as a friend's home, this is an agreeable spot to kick back with tea and cookies, or savor a homemade lemonade accompanied by soup, sandwiches or goulash. Flip through an art book from owner Maggie Molnar's personal library and enjoy the river views, either from the upstairs living room or the chairs on the grassy lawn below.

La Bodeguita INTERNATIONAL **$$**
(☎4522-5329; www.labodeguita.net; Del Comercio 167; mini pizzas UR$180, mains UR$340-550; ⏰8pm-midnight Tue-Fri, 12:30-4pm & 8pm-midnight Sat, 12:30-4pm Sun) Nab a table out back on the sunny two-level deck and soak up the sweeping river views while drinking sangria or munching on La Bodeguita's trademark mini pizzas, served on a cutting board. The wide-ranging menu also includes pasta, salads, steaks and *chivitos*.

El Portón PARRILLA **$$**
(☎4522-5318; www.facebook.com/parrilladaelporton; Av General Flores 333; mains UR$300-550; ⏰noon-3:30pm & 8pm-midnight Tue-Sat, noon-3:30pm Sun) With cheery reddish-orange and yellow decor inside and sidewalk seating out front, this is a long-standing local favorite for good-value grilled meats.

★**Charco Bistró** INTERNATIONAL **$$$**
(☎4523-5000; www.charcohotel.com; San Pedro 116; mains UR$420-680; ⏰noon-3:30pm & 8-11pm) Outstanding both for its location and its food, this bright and airy eatery with a contemporary aesthetic is tucked down a cobbled side street with a spacious deck overlooking the Río de la Plata's grassy shoreline. Tantalizing treats such as steak with chimichurri, grilled salmon and homemade ravioli come complemented by superb mixed drinks and ample glasses of local tannat wine.

Drinking & Nightlife

★**Missfusion** COCKTAIL BAR
(☎092-187501; www.barmissfusion.com; cnr Alberto Mendez & Manuel Lobo) Vivacious young owner-bartender Erika Valecillos Spinetti left her native Venezuela to open this brightly painted, high-ceilinged corner bar in 2016, and Colonia is much the better for it. Creative mixed drinks and homemade tapas from Erika's years as a caterer combine with a mix of contemporary and retro music to create an inviting vibe that may just keep you lingering longer than you intended.

Ganache CAFE
(☎4522-6386; www.facebook.com/GanacheColonia; Real 178; ⏰10am-8pm, closed Thu Apr-Oct) An inviting spot for a coffee break any time of year, Ganache lays tables out on the cobblestones in warm weather. Come winter or a rainy day, you'll be tempted by its sweet interior space with flowers on every table, cushiony chairs, parquet floors and a fireplace to ward off the Río de la Plata's chill breezes.

Barbot MICROBREWERY
(☎4522-7268; www.facebook.com/barbotcerveceria; Washington Barbot 160; ⏰6pm-2am Mon-Thu, noon-4am Fri-Sun; 📶) This sleek brewpub is well worth a visit for its ever-evolving collection of 15 home brews. If you can't chose between them, go for the four-beer tasting selection.

Shopping

Malvón CLOTHING
(☎4522-1793; Av General Flores 100; ⏰10am-7pm) Sells woolen blankets and clothing from the national cooperative Manos del Uruguay, along with other Uruguayan handicrafts.

Information

MONEY

BBVA (Av General Flores 299; ⏰1-5pm Mon-Fri) One of several ATMs along Av General Flores.

POST

Post Office (Lavalleja 226; ⊙10am-4pm Mon-Fri, 9am-noon Sat)

TELEPHONE

Antel (www.antel.com.uy; cnr Lavalleja & Rivadavia; ⊙10am-5pm Mon-Fri, 9am-2pm Sat)

TOURIST INFORMATION

BIT Welcome Center (☎4522-1072; www.bitcolonia.com; Odriozola 434; ⊙9am-6pm; 📶) In a sparkling glass-walled building opposite the port, this modern welcome center, operated by Uruguay's national tourism ministry, has tourist information, touch-screen displays and an overpriced (UR$50) 'Welcome to Uruguay' video presentation. It also has a travel agency and left-luggage lockers.

Tourist Office (☎4522-8506; www.coloniaturismo.com; Manuel Lobo 224; ⊙9am-6pm Mar-Dec, to 7pm Jan & Feb) On the edge of the Barrio Histórico is Colonia's municipal tourist office, which also organizes good walking tours (p541) led by local guides.

Tourist Office (cnr Manuel Lobo & Av FD Roosevelt; ⊙9am-6pm) There's another branch located at the bus station.

Getting There & Away

BOAT

From the ferry terminal at the foot of Rivera, **Buquebus** (☎130; www.buquebus.com.uy; ⊙9am-10pm) runs three or more fast boats (UR$920 to UR$2079, 1¼ hours) daily to Buenos Aires. The same company owns **Seacat** (☎4522-2919; www.seacatcolonia.com.uy; ⊙8am-9pm), which runs slightly faster, and often cheaper, ferry services along the same route (from UR$780, one hour).

A third operator offering similar service is **Colonia Express** (☎4522-9676; www.coloniaexpress.com; ⊙9am-10pm), which runs three fast ferries a day (from UR$773, 70 minutes).

All three companies offer child, senior and advance-purchase discounts.

Immigration for both countries is handled at the port before boarding.

BUS

Colonia's modern **bus terminal** (☎4523-0288; http://terminalcolonia.com.uy; cnr Manuel Lobo & Av FD Roosevelt) is conveniently located near the port and an easy 10-minute walk from the Barrio Histórico. It has tourist information and luggage-storage, money-changing and internet facilities.

Getting Around

Walking is enjoyable in compact Colonia, but motor scooters, bicycles and gas-powered buggies are popular alternatives. **Thrifty** (☎4522-2939; www.thrifty.com.uy; Av General Flores 172; bicycle/scooter/golf cart per hour US$6/12/18, per 24hr US$24/40/66; ⊙9am-7pm) rents everything from high-quality bikes to scooters to golf carts. Several other agencies rent cars and motorbikes near the bus and ferry terminals, including **Multicar** (☎4522-4893; www.multicar.com.uy; Manuel Lobo 505; ⊙9am-7pm), **Motorent** (☎4522-9665; www.motorent.com.uy; Manuel Lobo 505; ⊙9am-7pm), **Punta Car** (☎4522-2353; www.puntacar.com.uy; cnr 18 de Julio & Rivera), **Avis** (☎4522-9842; www.avis.com.uy; Bus Terminal; ⊙24hr) and **Europcar** (☎4522-8454; www.europcar.com.uy; Av Artigas 152; ⊙9am-7pm Mon-Fri, to 1pm Sat). The last two offer one-way car rentals between Colonia and Montevideo.

Local COTUC buses go to the beaches and bullring at Real de San Carlos (UR$22) from along Av General Flores.

Carmelo

☎454 / POP 18,040

Carmelo, dating from 1816, is a laid-back town of cobblestone streets and low old houses, a center for yachting, fishing and exploring the Paraná Delta. Surrounded by wine country, it has also increasingly become a destination for wine tourism. The town straddles the Arroyo de las Vacas, a stream that widens into a sheltered harbor just below the Río Uruguay's confluence with the Río de la Plata. The town center, seven blocks north of the arroyo, is Plaza Independencia. South of the arroyo across the bridge lies the pleasant beach of Playa Seré, backed by a large park with open space, camping, swimming and a huge casino. Daily launches connect Carmelo to the Buenos Aires suburb of Tigre.

Activities

The arroyo, with large, rusty boats moored along it, makes for a great ramble, as does the 30-minute stroll to the beach. Local wines have an excellent reputation, and vineyard visits are a popular activity.

Bodega Campotinto WINE
(☎4542-7744; www.campotinto.com; Camino de los Peregrinos, Colonia Estrella; tasting US$15; ⊙11am-7pm) Offering one of Carmelo's more enjoyable and reasonably priced wine-tasting experiences, Campotinto invites visitors to stroll a marked path 500m through the vines to a 19th-century family home,

which has been turned into a brand-new *sala de degustación* (tasting room).

Bodega El Legado WINE
(☎098-307193, 099-111493; Ramal Ruta 97; ⏰11am-7pm) The affable Bernardo Marzuca and María Marta Barberis, together with their sons, preside over this small but growing family-run winery north of Carmelo. Bernardo offers informal tours of the tannat and syrah vineyards, followed by tasting sessions (US$25 including a nice selection of cheeses and cold cuts) in the spacious and attractive tasting room up front.

Bodega Irurtia WINE
(☎4542-2323, 098-874281; www.irurtia.com.uy; Av Paraguay, Km 2.3) A couple of kilometers east of town, the region's largest winery, run by the Irurtia family since 1913, produces award-winning tannats and pinot noirs. With notice, visitors can take a 45-minute tour of the cellars (in English or French upon request), followed by tastings of one to five wines (US$10 to US$35, depending on the number of wines sampled).

Almacen de la Capilla WINE
(☎4542-7316; www.almacendelacapilla.wix.com/almacendelacapilla; Camino de los Peregrinos, Colonia Estrella; ⏰11am-6pm) Surrounded by vineyards, this historic general store sits at a country crossroads 5km north of Carmelo. The fifth-generation Cordano family has made wine here since 1870. Tastings (US$25) are available, but it's equally fun just to soak up the atmosphere while browsing the shelves of local products. Ask to see the diminutive wine cellar, hidden beneath a trap door behind the counter.

Look for the turnoff about 2km northwest of Carmelo, near the Km 257 marker on Ruta 21.

Sleeping & Eating

Ah'Lo Hostel Boutique HOSTEL $
(☎4542-0757; www.ahlo.com.uy; Treinta y Tres 270; dm US$30-35, d US$90-135, d without bathroom US$75-84, q without bathroom US$115-124; ❄📶) Carmelo's best downtown option, this combination hostel-posada delivers on its 'boutique' moniker, offering a comfortable seven-bed dorm with plush duvets and immaculate shared bathroom, plus nine private rooms, a well-equipped guest kitchen and a spacious central common area, all in an attractively restored colonial building seven blocks from the ferry terminal and two blocks from the main square.

Posada Campotinto INN $$
(☎4542-7744; www.campotinto.com; Camino de los Peregrinos, Colonia Estrella; r US$144-200; ❄📶) This tranquil spot on the grounds of Campotinto winery makes a delightful overnight getaway just 5km north of Carmelo. Four rooms in the main *casa de campo* (historic country home) are complemented by eight modern units out back, newly constructed in 2017. Within easy walking distance are the winery's tasting room and the picturesque 19th-century Capilla de San Roque.

Piccolino URUGUAYAN $
(☎4542-4850; cnr Calle 19 de Abril & Roosevelt; dishes UR$140-320; ⏰10:30am-midnight Wed-Mon) This corner place has decent *chivitos* and views of Carmelo's central square.

Comedor Lo'Korrea URUGUAYAN $$
(☎4542-6583, 099-530459; Colonia Estrella; fixed menu UR$470; ⏰8:30pm-midnight Sat, noon-3pm Sun) On Sunday afternoons, families flock to this quintessentially Uruguayan eatery in Carmelo's wine country to linger over Lo'Korrea's fixed menu of homemade ravioli, pâté and wine. Depending on the weather, people gravitate towards the cavernous interior dining room or install themselves at picnic tables on the lawn, while kids go wild on the adjacent bouncy castle.

★**Bodega y Granja Narbona** ITALIAN $$$
(☎4540-4778; www.narbona.com.uy; Hwy 21, Km 268; dishes US$25-34; ⏰noon-midnight) Set amid vineyards and orchards 13km from Carmelo, this restaurant in a restored 1908 farmstead serves gourmet pasta, Uruguayan beef, organic vegetables and fabulous tannat and *grappamiel* from Narbona's award-winning cellars. Inside, browse shelves stacked floor-to-ceiling with local olive oil, peach preserves and *dulce de leche*. The adjacent **Narbona Wine Lodge** (☎4540-4778; www.narbona.com.uy/en/lodge; Hwy 21, Km 268; ste US$242-363; 📶) offers luxurious overnight accommodations.

Information

Casa de la Cultura (☎4542-2001; www.carmeloturismo.com.uy; Calle 19 de Abril 246; ⏰9am-6pm Mar-Nov, to 7pm Dec-Feb) Three blocks south of the main square and eight blocks northeast of the launch docks.

Post Office (Uruguay 360; ⏰9am-5pm Mon-Fri)

Scotiabank (Uruguay 401; ⏲1-5pm Mon-Fri) One of several ATMs opposite the main square.

Getting There & Away

BOAT

Cacciola (☎4542-4282; www.cacciolaviajes.com; Wilson Ferreyra 263; ferry Carmelo-Tigre 1-way adult/child UR$770/670, shuttle bus Tigre-Buenos Aires UR$30; ⏲ticket office 3:30-4:30am & 8:30am-8pm) Runs twice-daily launches to the Buenos Aires suburb of Tigre, at 4:30am and 1:30pm Monday through Saturday and 12:30pm and 6:30pm on Sunday. Service is sometimes expanded to thrice-daily in summer. The 2½-hour trip through the Paraná Delta is the most scenic crossing between Uruguay and Argentina.

BUS

Both main bus companies are on or near Plaza Independencia. **Berrutti** (☎4542-2504; www.berruttiturismo.com/horarios.htm; Uruguay 337) has the most frequent service to Colonia; **Chadre** (☎4542-2987; www.agenciacentral.com.uy; Calle 18 de Julio 411) is the best bet for all other destinations.

Buses from Carmelo

DESTINATION	COST (UR$)	TIME (HR)
Colonia	161	1½
Mercedes	201	2
Montevideo	481	3½
Paysandú	481	5
Salto	715	7

Mercedes

☎453 / POP 42,000

Capital of the department of Soriano, Mercedes is a livestock center with cobblestone streets and a small pedestrian zone around an 18th-century cathedral on central Plaza Independencia. The town's most appealing feature is its leafy waterfront along the south bank of the Río Negro.

Sleeping & Eating

★**Estancia La Sirena** ESTANCIA $$$
(☎4530-2271, 099-532698; www.lasirena.com.uy/hosteria.html; Ruta 14, Km 4.5; r per person incl half/full board, horseback rides & other activities US$110/135) Surrounded by rolling open country 15km upriver from Mercedes, this *estancia* is one of Uruguay's oldest and most welcoming. The spacious 1830 ranch house, with its cozy parlor and fireplaces and end-of-the-road setting, makes a perfect base for relaxation, late-afternoon conversation under the eucalyptus trees, stargazing and horseback excursions to the nearby Río Negro. Homemade meals are included in rates.

Martiniano Parrilla Gourmet PARRILLA $$
(☎4532-2649; Rambla Costanera s/n; dishes UR$220-390; ⏲11am-3pm & 7:30pm-midnight Tue-Sun) The prime riverfront setting at the foot of 18 de Julio is complemented by a varied menu featuring homemade pasta, grilled meat, fish, gourmet burgers and *chivitos*.

Shopping

★**Lanas de Soriano** CLOTHING
(☎4532-2158; Colón 60; ⏲9am-noon & 3-6:30pm Mon & Wed-Fri, 9am-noon Tue) A rainbow of beautiful handmade woolens is available in this shop, hidden away in a residential neighborhood near the waterfront.

Information

Municipal Tourist Office (☎4532-2201, ext 2501; turismo@soriano.gub.uy; Plaza El Rosedal, Av Asencio btwn Colón & Artigas; ⏲9am-7pm Mon-Fri) In El Rosedal park, four blocks east of the bridge to Mercedes' campground.

Post Office (cnr Rodó & 18 de Julio; ⏲9am-5pm Mon-Fri)

Scotiabank (Giménez 719; ⏲1-5pm Mon-Fri) ATM on Plaza Independencia.

Getting There & Away

Mercedes' modern, air-conditioned **bus terminal** (Plaza General Artigas) is about 10 blocks from Plaza Independencia, in a shopping center with ATMs, a post office, free public bathrooms, luggage storage and an emergency medical clinic. A local bus (UR$22) stops just in front of the terminal, making a circuit around downtown at 10 minutes past the hour from 7:10am to 9:10pm.

Salto

☎473 / POP 104,000

Built near the falls where the Río Uruguay makes its 'big jump' (*'salto grande'* in Spanish), Salto is Uruguay's second-largest city and the most northerly crossing point to Argentina. It's a relaxed place with some 19th-century architecture and a pretty riverfront. People come here for the nearby hot springs and the recreation area above the enormous Salto Grande hydroelectric dam.

WORTH A TRIP

THE LITTLE BEEF CUBE THAT CIRCLED THE GLOBE

In 1865 the Liebig Extract of Meat Company located its pioneer South American plant near the river town of Fray Bentos, 35km west of Mercedes. It soon became Uruguay's most important industrial complex. British-run El Anglo took over operations in the 1920s and by WWII the factory employed 4000 people, slaughtering cattle at the astronomical rate of 2000 a day.

Looking at the abandoned factory today, you'd never guess that its signature product, the Oxo beef cube, once touched millions of lives on every continent. Oxo cubes sustained WWI soldiers in the trenches, Jules Verne sang their praises in his book *Around the Moon*, Stanley brought them on his search for Livingstone, and Scott and Hillary took them to Antarctica and Everest. More than 25,000 people from more than 60 countries worked here, and at its peak the factory was exporting nearly 150 products, using every part of the cow except its moo.

Enshrined as Uruguay's newest Unesco World Heritage site in July 2015, the former factory is now a museum – the **Museo de la Revolución Industrial** (museo.anglo@rionegro.gub.uy; UR$50, guided tour UR$120; ⌚9:30am-5pm Tue-Sun). Dozens of colorful displays, ranging from the humorous to the poignant, bring the factory's history vividly to life: a giant cattle scale where school groups are invited to weigh themselves; or the old company office upstairs, left exactly as it was when the factory closed in 1979, with grooves rubbed into the floor by the foot of an accountant who sat at the same desk for decades. Note that most signs are in Spanish only.

One- to two-hour guided tours (the schedule varies) grant access to the intricate maze of passageways, corrals and abandoned slaughterhouses behind the museum. At 11am on Thursdays, Saturdays and Sundays visitors can also tour the Casa Grande, a mansion that once housed the factory's manager.

The adjacent town of Fray Bentos, with its pretty riverfront promenade, is the southernmost overland crossing over the Río Uruguay into Argentina.

Fray Bentos is 45 minutes by bus from Mercedes (UR$60), two hours from Paysandú ($226), four hours from Colonia (UR$441) or Buenos Aires (UR$1450), and 4½ hours from Montevideo (UR$621).

Sights

Salto's museums all close during January.

Museo de Bellas Artes y Artes Decorativas MUSEUM

(Uruguay 1067; ⌚1-7pm Tue-Sat, 4-7pm Sun Feb-Dec) FREE Displays a nice collection of Uruguayan painting and sculpture in a historic two-story mansion with a grand staircase, stained glass and a back garden.

Museo del Hombre y la Tecnología MUSEUM

(cnr Av Brasil & Zorrilla; ⌚1-7pm Mon-Fri, 2-7pm Sat Feb-Dec) FREE Housed in a historic market building, this museum features excellent displays on local cultural development and history upstairs, and a small archaeological section downstairs.

Represa Salto Grande DAM

(www.saltogrande.org/visitas.php; ⌚7am-4pm) FREE A source of national pride, this massive hydroelectric dam 14km north of Salto provides over 50% of Uruguay's electricity. Free 90-minute guided tours (half-hourly) visit both the Uruguayan and Argentine sides. It's a 20-minute drive from Salto (UR$1200 roundtrip by taxi). En route, check out the stands selling homemade empanadas and freshly squeezed local orange juice 2L for UR$60!).

Sleeping & Eating

Gran Hotel Concordia HOTEL $

(☎4733-2735; www.facebook.com/granhotelconcordia; Uruguay 749; s/d US$31/58; ❄📶) This faded 1860s relic, a national historical monument, remains Salto's most atmospheric downtown budget option. A life-size cutout of Carlos Gardel, who once stayed in room 32, beckons you down a marble corridor into a leafy courtyard filled with murals and sculptures, surrounded by tired and musty rooms with tall French-shuttered windows.

★ **Art Hotel Deco** BOUTIQUE HOTEL $$

(☎4732-8585; www.arthoteldeco.com; Sarandí 145; s/d/ste US$90/120/150; ❄📶) Just paces from the city center, this classy boutique hotel easily outshines Salto's other downtown sleeping options. The lovingly renovated historic building abounds in period details, including high ceilings, polished wood floors, art deco door and window frames, an elegant sitting room and a lush back garden. Amenities include Egyptian-cotton sheets, cable TV, sauna and gym.

La Caldera PARRILLA $
(☎4732-4648; Uruguay 221; dishes UR$195-395; ⊙noon-3pm & 8pm-midnight Tue-Sun) With fresh breezes blowing in off the river and sunny outdoor seating, this *parrilla* makes a good lunch stop; at dinnertime, the cozy interior dining room, with its view of the blazing fire, is equally atmospheric.

Casa de Lamas URUGUAYAN $$
(☎4732-9376; Chiazzaro 20; dishes UR$225-495; ⊙8pm-midnight Wed, noon-2:30pm & 8pm-midnight Thu-Mon) Down near the riverfront, Salto's swankiest eatery is housed in a 19th-century building with pretty vaulted brick and stonework. The *menú de la casa* (set menu including appetizer, main dish, dessert and drink) goes for UR$475.

La Trattoria URUGUAYAN $$
(☎4733-6660; www.facebook.com/LaTrattoriasalto; Uruguay 754; dishes UR$225-495; ⊙noon-1am) Locals flock to this high-ceilinged downtown eatery for fish, meat and pasta. Sit in the wood-paneled dining room or people-watch from a sidewalk table on busy Calle Uruguay.

ℹ Information

BBVA (cnr Uruguay & Lavalleja; ⊙1-5pm Mon-Fri) One of several banks at this intersection.

Post Office (cnr Artigas & Sarandí; ⊙9am-5pm Mon-Fri)

Tourist Office – Bus Terminal (☎4733-4096; turismo@salto.gub.uy; Salto Shopping Center, cnr Avs Blandengues & Batlle; ⊙8am-10pm)

DON'T MISS

SALTO'S HOT SPRINGS

A whole slew of hot springs bubble up around Salto.

Termas San Nicanor (☎4730-2209; www.sannicanor.com.uy; Ruta 3, Km 475; campsites per person US$8.50, dm US$30-40, d US$110-150, 4-person cabins US$230; 📶🏊) Surrounded by a pastoral landscape of cows, fields and water vaguely reminiscent of a Flemish painting, this is the most tranquil of Salto's hot-springs resorts. It has two gigantic outdoor thermal pools, a restaurant, and accommodations for every budget, including campsites, no-frills dorms, four-person cabins, and private rooms in a high-ceilinged *estancia* with large fireplaces and peacocks strolling the grounds. Day use of the springs (8am to 10pm, available Friday to Sunday only) costs UR$150 (UR$100 in low season). The 12km unpaved access road leaves Ruta 3 10km south of Salto. Occasional **shuttles** (☎driver Martín Lombardo 099-732368; 1-way UR$500) to San Nicanor depart from Salto (corner of Larrañaga and Artigas) and Termas de Daymán. Schedules vary; phone ahead to confirm schedules.

Termas de Daymán (☎4736-9711; www.termasdedayman.com; UR$130; ⊙8am-10:30pm) About 8km south of Salto, Daymán is a heavily developed Disneyland of thermal baths complete with kids' water park. It's popular with Uruguayan and Argentine tourists, who roam the town's block-long main street in bathrobes. For comfortable accommodations adjacent to the springs, try **La Posta del Daymán** (☎camping 4736-9094, hotel 4736-9801; www.lapostadeldayman.com; campsites per person US$7, r per person incl breakfast US$37-55; 📶🏊). Empresa Cossa runs hourly buses between Salto and the baths (UR$32), leaving Salto's port via Av Brasil at 30 minutes past every hour (7:30am to 10:30pm), returning hourly from 7am to 11pm.

Termas de Arapey (☎4768-2101; www.termasarapey.com; UR$150; ⊙7am-11pm) About 90km northeast of Salto, Uruguay's oldest hot-springs resort offers multiple pools surrounded by gardens, fountains, and paths to the Río Arapey Grande. **Hotel Municipal** (☎4768-2441; www.viatermal.com/hotelarapey; s/d/tr US$57/78/92; ❄📶🏊), down near the river, offers the area's best-value accommodations. **Argentur** (☎099-734003, 4732-9931; www.minibusesargentur.blogspot.com) runs one or two buses daily from Salto (UR$190, 1½ hours).

Tourist Office – Centro (☎4733-4096; turismo@salto.gub.uy; Uruguay 1052; ⏰8am-7pm Mon-Sat)

Getting There & Away

BOAT

Transporte Fluvial San Cristóbal (☎4733-2461; cnr Av Brasil & Costanera Norte) runs launches across the river to Concordia, Argentina (adult/child UR$160/70, 15 minutes), three to four times daily between 8:45am and 6pm Monday through Saturday (no service on Sunday).

BUS

Buses from Salto

DESTINATION	COST (UR$)	TIME (HR)
Buenos Aires, Argentina	1155	7
Colonia	921	8
Concordia, Argentina	146	1
Montevideo	1021	6½
Paysandú	252	2
Tacuarembó	576	4

Salto's **bus terminal** (Salto Shopping Center, cnr Avs Blandengues & Batlle), in a spiffy modern shopping center 2km east of downtown, has a tourist-info kiosk, ATMs, internet facilities, free public restrooms and a supermarket.

Connect in Concordia for additional Argentine destinations, including Puerto Iguazú and Córdoba.

DON'T GET STRANDED IN SALTO ON SUNDAY!

Be advised that neither ferries nor buses run from Salto into Argentina on Sundays. If you're trying to cross the border, make sure to travel Monday through Saturday, or be prepared to pay a hefty taxi fare.

Tacuarembó

☎463 / POP 54,800

In the rolling hills along the Cuchilla de Haedo, Tacuarembó is gaucho country. Not your 'we pose for pesos' types, but your real-deal 'we tuck our baggy pants into our boots and slap on a beret just to go to the local store' crew. It's also the alleged birthplace of tango legend Carlos Gardel.

Capital of its department, Tacuarembó has pleasant sycamore-lined streets and attractive plazas. The town center is Plaza 19 de Abril, linked by the main thoroughfares 25 de Mayo and 18 de Julio.

Sights

Museo del Indio y del Gaucho MUSEUM
(cnr Flores & Artigas; ⏰10am-5pm Tue-Sat) FREE Paying romantic tribute to Uruguay's gauchos and indigenous peoples, this museum's collection includes stools made from horse and cow bones, elegantly worked silver spurs and other accessories of rural life.

Festivals & Events

Fiesta de la Patria Gaucha CULTURAL
(www.patriagaucha.com.uy; ⏰early Mar) This colorful, authentically home-grown five-day event is the planet's largest gaucho festival, attracting participants from Argentina, southern Brazil and all over Uruguay for exhibitions of traditional gaucho skills, music and other activities. It takes place in Parque 25 de Agosto, north of town.

Sleeping & Eating

Hotel Internacional HOTEL $
(☎4632-3324; Ituzaingó 211; s/d US$30/55) New owners at this centrally located downtown guesthouse have added a fresh coat of paint and air-conditioning in the en-suite units. It's still pretty bare bones, but it's a convenient place to lay your head if you find yourself spending the night in Tacuarembó.

★**Estancia Panagea** ESTANCIA $$
(☎099-836149, 4630-2670; www.panagea-uruguay.blogspot.com.uy; Ruta 31, Km 189; dm per person incl full board, farm activities, horseback riding & transport US$65) For a spectacular introduction to life on the Uruguayan land, head to this 970-hectare working *estancia* 40km northwest of Tacuarembó. Juan Manuel, who was born and raised here, his Swiss wife Susanne and gaucho Bilinga invite guests to get fully immersed in farm activities from the mundane (tagging and vaccinating animals) to the classic (herding cattle on horseback).

Guests sleep dorm-style in simple rooms, eat three home-cooked meals a day (including self-serve bacon and eggs cooked on the woodstove), hit the basketball and volleyball courts at sunset and congregate around the fireplace at night. Call ahead to coordinate dates and arrange transportation from Tacuarembó's bus station.

★Yvytu Itaty ESTANCIA **$$**
(☎099-837555, 4630-8421; www.viviturismorural.com.uy; s incl full board, farm activities & horseback riding US$85, per person with minimum of 2 people UR$75) Pedro and Nahir Clariget's unpretentious ranch-style home, 50km southwest of Tacuarembó, offers a first hand look at real gaucho life. Guests are invited to accompany Pedro and his friendly cattle dogs around the 636-hectare working *estancia* on horseback, participate in daily *estancia* routines and sip *mate* on the patio at sunset in anticipation of Nahir's tasty home cooking.

Call in advance for driving directions or to arrange pickup at Tacuarembó's bus station (UR$1700 roundtrip for a group of any size).

El Mirador Resto-Pub PUB FOOD **$**
(☎4634-2491; Sarandí 349; pub food from UR$250; ⏲7pm-3am Wed-Sun) This spiffy resto-pub pours eight varieties of Tacuarembó's home-grown Cabesas beer on tap, accompanied by *chivitos*, pizza, *picadas* (shared appetizer plates) and other pub food.

Information

Banco Santander (18 de Julio 258; ⏲1-5pm Mon-Fri) One of several ATMs near Plaza Colón.

Post Office (Ituzaingó 262; ⏲9am-5pm Mon-Fri)

Tourist Office (☎4632-7144; www.tacuarembo.gub.uy; cnr Ruta 5 & Av Victorino Pereira; ⏲7am-8pm Mon-Fri, 8am-noon Sat) Inside the bus terminal.

Getting There & Away

The **bus terminal** (☎4632-4441; cnr Ruta 5 & Av Victorino Pereira) is 1km northeast of the center. A taxi into town costs about UR$80.

Buses from Tacuarembó

DESTINATION	COST (UR$)	TIME (HR)
Montevideo	781	4½
Paysandú	483	3½
Salto	564	4

Valle Edén

Valle Edén, a lush valley 24km southwest of Tacuarembó, is home to the **Museo Carlos Gardel** (☎099-107303; UR$25; ⏲9:30am-5:30pm Thu-Sun). Reached via a drive-through creek spanned by a wooden suspension footbridge, and housed in a former *pulpería* (the general store and bar that used to operate on many *estancias*), the museum documents Tacuarembó's claim as birthplace of the revered tango singer – a claim vigorously contested by Argentina and France!

Sleeping

Accommodations in Valle Edén are available at **Camping El Mago** (☎4632-7144; campsites per tent/person US$3.50/1.50) or at **Posada Valle Edén** (☎4630-2345, 098-800100; www.posadavalleeden.com.uy; d US$50-74; ❄), where you can stay in the lovely historic mud-and-stone main inn, or sleep in one of the modern *cabañas* across the street.

Getting There & Away

Empresa Calebus runs an early-morning and a late-afternoon bus daily from Tacuarembó to Valle Edén (UR$68, 20 minutes), but these are inconveniently timed for visiting the museum on a day trip. Ideally, you'll want your own wheels.

EASTERN URUGUAY

The gorgeous 340km sweep of beaches, dunes, forests and lagoons stretching northeast from Montevideo to the Brazilian border is one of Uruguay's national treasures. Still largely unknown except to Uruguayans and their immediate neighbors, this region lies nearly dormant for 10 months of each year, then explodes with summer activity from Christmas to Carnaval. For sheer fun-in-the-sun energy, there's nothing like peak season, but if you can make it here slightly off-season (in March or the first three weeks of December), you'll experience its beauty for half the price.

Near the Brazilian border, abandoned hilltop fortresses and shipwrecks offer mute testimony to the era when Spain and Portugal struggled for control of the continent. Where lookouts once scanned the wide horizon for invading forces, a new wave of invaders has taken hold, from binocular-wielding whale watchers in Cabo Polonio to camera-toting paparazzi in Punta del Este.

Piriápolis

☎443 / POP 8800

With its grand old hotel and beachfront promenade backed by small mountains, Piriápolis is vaguely reminiscent of a Mediterranean beach town and exudes a certain old-school coastal-resort charm. It was developed for tourism in the early 20th century by Uruguayan entrepreneur Francisco Piria, who built the imposing landmark Argentino Hotel and an eccentric hillside residence known as Castillo de Piria (Piria's Castle).

Almost all the action happens in the 10-block stretch of beachfront between Av Artigas (the access road from Ruta 9) and Av Piria (where the coastline makes a broad curve southwards). Streets back from the beach quickly become residential.

The surrounding countryside holds many interesting features, including two of Uruguay's highest summits.

Sights & Activities

Swimming and **sunbathing** are the most popular activities, and there's good **fishing** off the rocks at the end of the beach, where Rambla de los Argentinos becomes Rambla de los Ingleses.

Sleeping & Eating

Hostel de los Colores HOSTEL $
(☎4432-6188; www.hosteldeloscolores.com.uy; Simón del Pino 1137; dm US$18-29, d US$50-90, d without bathroom US$45-80; @☜) Directly opposite Piriápolis' institutional 240-bed HI facility, this much smaller year-round hostel two blocks from the beach offers clean, colorful four- and six-bed dorms, plus three doubles. Bikes (UR$400 per day) and a kayak (UR$500 per day) are available for rent.

Argentino Hotel HISTORIC HOTEL $$$
(☎4432-2791; www.argentinohotel.com; Rambla de los Argentinos s/n; d incl breakfast/half-board from US$215/235; ❄@☜≋) Even if you don't stay here, you should visit this elegant 350-room European-style spa hotel with two heated river-water pools, a casino, an ice-skating rink and other luxuries.

★**Café Picasso** SEAFOOD $$
(☎4432-2597; cnr Rojas & Caseros; mains UR$270-590; ⊙noon-3:30pm Mon-Thu & Sun, noon-3:30pm & 8-11:30pm Fri & Sat May-Nov) Down a residential backstreet several blocks from the beach, septuagenarian chef-owner Carlos has converted his carport and front room into an informal, colorfully decorated restaurant with an open-air grill. Locals chat astride plastic chairs and listen to tango recordings while Carlos cooks up some of the best fish anywhere on Uruguay's Atlantic coast, along with paella (UR$590) on Sundays.

Information

Banco de la República (Rambla de los Argentinos, btwn Sierra & Sanabria; ⊙1-6pm Mon-Fri) Convenient ATM.

Post Office (Av Piria s/n; ⊙9am-5pm Mon-Fri) Two blocks in from the beachfront.

AROUND PIRIÁPOLIS

In the hills north of town, **Castillo de Piria** (☎4432-3268; Ruta 37, Km 4; ⊙8am-3:30pm Tue-Sun Apr-Nov, to 6pm Dec-Mar) FREE, Francisco Piria's opulent, castle-like former residence, has Spanish-language displays on the history of Piriápolis. About 1km further inland, hikers can climb Uruguay's fourth-highest 'peak,' **Cerro Pan de Azúcar** (Ruta 37, Km 5; ⊙7am-8:30pm) FREE (389m). The trail (2½ hours roundtrip) starts from the parking lot of the Reserva de Fauna Autóctona, narrowing from a gradual dirt road into a steep path marked with red arrows.

The private nature reserve **Sierra de las Ánimas** (☎SMS only 094-419891; www.sierradelasanimas.com; Ruta 9, Km 86; UR$130; ⊙9am-sunset Sat & Sun, plus Carnaval & Easter weeks, from 10am May-Oct) is just off the Interbalnearia (coastal highway), 25km toward Montevideo from Piriápolis. There are two good hiking trails, each three to four hours roundtrip: one leads to the 501m summit (Uruguay's second-highest), the other to the **Cañadón de los Espejos**, a series of waterfalls and natural swimming holes that are especially impressive after good rainfall. Other activities include rustic camping (UR$50 per person, by prior arrangement only) and mountain biking. Coming from Montevideo by bus, ask to be let off at Km 86 and cross the highway. In cold or rainy weather, send an SMS in advance to verify it's open.

Tourist Office (☎4432-5055; www.costaserrana.uy; Rambla de los Argentinos; ⌚10am-6pm Wed-Mon Apr-Nov, 9am-8pm daily Dec & Mar, to midnight Jan & Feb) Helpful staff and public toilets, on the waterfront near Argentino Hotel.

Getting There & Away

The **bus terminal** (☎4432-4526; cnr Misiones & Niza) is a few blocks back from the beach. COT and COPSA run frequent buses to Montevideo (UR$202, 1½ hours) and Punta del Este (UR$135, 50 minutes).

Punta del Este

☎42 / POP 9300

OK, here's the plan: tan it, wax it, buff it at the gym, then plonk it on the beach at 'Punta.' Once you're done there, go out and shake it at one of the town's famous clubs.

Punta del Este – with its many beaches, elegant seaside homes, yacht harbor, high-rise apartment buildings, pricey hotels and glitzy restaurants – is one of South America's most glamorous resorts, extremely popular with Argentines and Brazilians, and easily the most expensive place in Uruguay.

Celebrity watchers have a full-time job here. Punta is teeming with big names, and local gossipmongers keep regular tabs on who's been sighted where. Surrounding towns caught up in the whole Punta mystique include the famed club zone of La Barra to the east and Punta Ballena to the west.

Sights

★Casapueblo GALLERY

(☎4257-8041; www.carlospaezvilaro.com.uy/nuevo/museo-taller; UR$280; ⌚10am-sunset) Gleaming white in the sun and cascading nine stories down a cliffside, Uruguayan artist Carlos Páez Vilaró's exuberantly whimsical villa and art gallery sits atop Punta Ballena, a jutting headland 15km west of Punta del Este. Visitors can tour five rooms, view a film on the artist's life and travels, and eat up spectacular sunset views at the upstairs cafeteria-bar. There's a hotel and a restaurant adjacent. It's a 2km walk from the junction where Codesa's Línea 8 bus drops you.

★La Mano en la Arena SCULPTURE

(The Hand in the Sand; Playa Brava) Punta's most famous landmark is this monster-sized sculpted hand protruding from the sands of Playa Brava. Constructed in iron and cement by Chilean artist Mario Irarrázabal, it won first prize in a monumental art contest in 1982 and has been a Punta fixture ever since. The hand exerts a magnetic attraction over thousands of visitors every year, who climb and jump off its digits and pose for photos with it. Look for it just southeast of the bus station.

Town Beaches

On the peninsula's western (Río de la Plata) side, Rambla Gral Artigas snakes past calm **Playa Mansa**, then passes the busy **yacht harbor**, overflowing with boats, restaurants and nightclubs, before circling east to meet the open Atlantic Ocean. On the peninsula's eastern side, waves and currents are rougher, as reflected in the name **Playa Brava**, meaning Fierce Beach, and in the surfers flocking to **Playa de los Ingleses** and **Playa El Emir**.

Outlying Beaches

From Playa Mansa, west along Rambla Williman, the main beach areas are La Pastora, Marconi, Cantegril, Las Delicias, Pinares, La Gruta at Punta Ballena, and Portezuelo. Eastward, along Rambla Lorenzo Batlle Pacheco, the prime beaches are La Chiverta, San Rafael, La Draga and Punta de la Barra. In summer, all have *paradores* (small restaurants) with beach service.

Isla de Lobos ISLAND

About 10km offshore, this small island is home to the world's second-largest southern sea-lion colony (200,000 at last count), along with colonies of southern fur seals and South America's tallest lighthouse. The island is protected and can only be visited on an organized tour.

Isla Gorriti ISLAND

Boats leave every half-hour or so (daily in season, weekends in low season) from Punta del Este's yacht harbor for the 15-minute trip to this nearby island, which has excellent sandy beaches, a couple of restaurants and the ruins of Baterías de Santa Ana, an 18th-century fortification.

Activities

In summer, **parasailing**, **waterskiing** and **Jet Skiing** are possible on Playa Mansa. Operators set up on the beach along Rambla Claudio Williman between Paradas 2 and 20.

DON'T MISS

ESTANCIA TOURISM IN URUGUAY

Estancias, the giant farms of Uruguay's interior, are a national cultural icon. The Uruguayan Ministry of Tourism has designated 'Estancia Turística' as a distinct lodging category, and dozens of such places have opened their doors to tourists, from traditional working farms to historic rural hotels. Typically, *estancias* organize daily activities with a heavy emphasis on horseback riding; many also provide overnight accommodations. Most are difficult to reach without a vehicle, although they'll sometimes pick guests up with advance notice.

One of Uruguay's most impressive *estancias* is **San Pedro de Timote** (☎4310-8086; www.sanpedrodetimote.com; Ruta 7, Km 142, Cerro Colorado; r incl full board & all activities from US$340;), whose remarkable setting – 14km up a dirt road amid 253 hectares of rolling cattle country – is greatly enhanced by the complex of historic structures, some dating to the mid-19th century: a gracious white chapel, a courtyard with soaring palm trees, a library with gorgeous tilework and a circular stone corral. Common areas feature parquet floors, big fireplaces, comfy leather armchairs, two pools and a sauna. Full-board rates include three meals, afternoon tea and two daily horseback-riding excursions, plus occasional bonfires and full-moon walks. The turnoff is just outside the town of Cerro Colorado, 160km northeast of Montevideo on Ruta 7.

Other favorite tourist *estancias* include Estancia La Sirena (p546), near Mercedes; Guardia del Monte (p564), near the northern Atlantic coast; Estancia Panagea (p549), northwest of Tacuarembó; and Yvytu Itaty (p550), southwest of Tacuarembó.

In Montevideo, **Lares** (☎2901-9120; www.lares.com.uy; WF Aldunate 1341; ⊙9:30am-6:30pm Mon-Fri) is a travel agency specializing in *estancia* tourism.

Sunvalleysurf SURFING
(☎4248-1388; www.sunvalleysurf.com; Parada 3½, Playa Brava; ⊙11am-7pm) Wet suits, surfboards, bodyboards and lessons are available from the original shop on Playa Brava, plus branches on **Playa El Emir** (Calle 28, btwn Calles 24 & 26; ⊙11am-7pm) and in **La Barra** (☎4277-0943; Ruta 10, Km 160, La Barra; ⊙11am-11pm).

Tours

Dimar Tours BOATING
(☎094-410899; www.isladelobos.com.uy; Puerto; adult/child to Isla Gorriti UR$350/250, to Isla de Lobos US$50/30) Offers tours from Punta's port to Isla de Lobos and Isla Gorriti, daily in high season, weekends only in low season. A highlight of the Isla de Lobos tour is the chance to swim with sea lions. Other operators, including **Crucero Samoa** (☎099-545847; www.crucerosamoa.com; Puerto), have offices along the same boardwalk; take a wander to compare your options. Reserve ahead during peak season.

Sleeping

In summer Punta is jammed with people, and prices are astronomical; even hostels double their prices in January. In winter it's a ghost town, and places that stay open lower their prices considerably. During peak season, even places classified here as midrange tend to charge top-end rates. Low-season visitors will find prices more in keeping with standard ranges.

★**Tas D'Viaje Hostel** HOSTEL $
(☎4244-8789; www.tasdviaje.com; Calle 24 btwn Calles 28 & 29; dm US$15-35, d US$50-100;) Just one block from Playa El Emir, Punta's best – and best-located – hostel keeps improving, thanks to thoughtful owners and regular reinvestments in infrastructure. New in 2017, all dorms are now air-conditioned, and there's a spacious new deck, thatched-roof bar area out back and pizzeria up front to go with the pre-existing guest barbecue.

Seven private rooms with en-suite bath and flat-screen TV combine with seven dorms (three to 10 beds each), catering to a variety of budgets. It has a sea-facing breakfast deck, an inviting living room with fireplace, and an attractive guest kitchen. On-site bike and surfboard rentals cost US$15 each per day.

Hostel Punta Ballena HOSTEL $
(☎4257-7665; www.hostelpuntaballena.uy; cnr San Francisco & Sierra de la Ballena, Punta Ballena; dm US$14-22) In the hills above Punta Ballena, this secluded retreat is ideal for budget-minded travelers who prefer

Uruguay's Beaches

Stretching from Montevideo to Brazil, 300km of beaches hug the Río de la Plata and the Atlantic Ocean. Choose the style that suits: from Punta del Este's glitz to Cabo Polonio's rusticity.

Cabo Polonio

Its lighthouse beckoning from a lonely point dotted with lounging sealions and makeshift houses, Cabo Polonio (p562) is a nature-lover's dream. Getting here, on a pitching truck ride through the dunes, is half the fun.

La Paloma

Grab an ice cream and head for the waves. Family-friendly La Paloma (p560), tucked behind a wall of sand dunes, is the very picture of unadorned beachside fun.

Punta del Este

The dividing line between the Atlantic and the Río de la Plata, Punta del Este's (p552) tidy peninsula full of high-rises and perfect beaches morphs annually from sleepy beach town to summer playground for South America's 'see and be seen' party set.

Punta del Diablo

Punta del Diablo (p564) is the end of the line. A few steps down the beach and you're in Brazil, but most folks stay put, seduced by waves, seafood shacks, beach bonfires and the national park.

Piriápolis

A throwback to the 1930s, Piriápolis (p551) is about strolling the beachfront promenade past the grand hotel, or surveying the calm waters from the top of the chairlift.

La Pedrera

No view on Uruguay's entire Atlantic coast matches the wide-angle perspective from La Pedrera's (p561) cliffs. Join the surfers up top and contemplate your beach options for the day.

1. La Pedrera 2. Punta del Este 3. Piriápolis 4. Cabo Polonio

2

VICS/GETTY IMAGES ©

3

ELOJOTORPE/GETTY IMAGES ©

Punta del Este

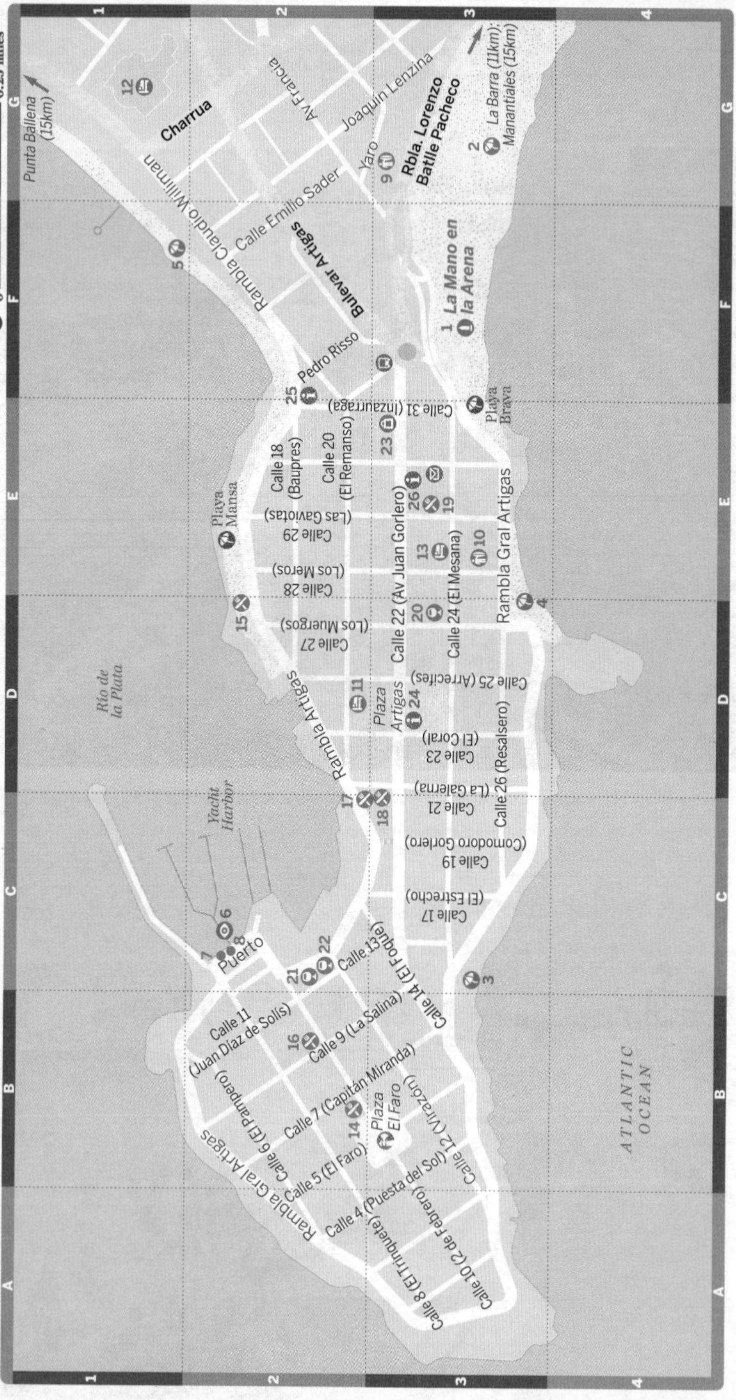

0 — 500 m
0 — 0.25 miles
Punta Ballena (15km)
La Barra (11km); Manantiales (15km)
Río de la Plata
Yacht Harbor
Puerto
ATLANTIC OCEAN
Charrua
Av Francia
Joaquin Lenzina
Rbla. Lorenzo Batlle Pacheco
Calle Emilio Sader
Yaro
Rambla Claudio Williman
Bulevar Artigas
La Mano en la Arena
Pedro Risso
Playa Brava
Playa Mansa
Calle 31 (Inzaurraga)
Calle 18 (Baupres)
Calle 20 (El Remanso)
Calle 29 (Las Gaviotas)
Calle 28 (Los Meros)
Calle 27 (Los Muergos)
Calle 22 (Av Juan Gorlero)
Calle 24 (El Mesana)
Rambla Gral Artigas
Calle 25 (Arrecifes)
Rambla Artigas
Plaza Artigas
Calle 23 (El Coral)
Calle 26 (Resalsero)
Calle 21 (La Galerna)
Calle 19 (Comodoro Gorlero)
Calle 17 (El Estrecho)
Calle 13
Calle 14 (El Foque)
Calle 11 (Juan Díaz de Solís)
Calle 9 (La Salina)
Calle 7 (Capitán Miranda)
Plaza El Faro
Calle 6 (El Pampero)
Calle 5 (El Faro)
Calle 12 (Virazon)
Calle 4 (Puesta del Sol)
Calle 10 (2 de Febrero)
Calle 8 (El Trinquete)
Rambla Gral Artigas

Punta del Este

Top Sights
1 La Mano en la Arena ... F3

Sights
2 Playa Brava ... G3
3 Playa de los Ingleses ... C3
4 Playa El Emir ... D3
5 Playa Mansa ... F1
6 Yacht Harbor ... C2

Activities, Courses & Tours
7 Crucero Samoa ... C2
8 Dimar Tours ... C2
9 Sunvalleysurf ... G3
10 Sunvalleysurf (Playa El Emir) ... E3

Sleeping
11 Bonne Étoile ... D2
12 Conrad Resort & Casino ... G1
13 Tas D'Viaje Hostel ... E3

Eating
14 Cuatro Mares ... B2
15 Guappa ... D2
16 Il Baretto ... B2
17 Lo de Tere ... C2
18 Olivia ... C3
Pizza al Taglio ... (see 13)
19 Rustic ... E3

Drinking & Nightlife
20 Capi Bar ... D3
21 Moby Dick ... C2
22 Soho ... C2

Shopping
23 Manos del Uruguay ... E3

Information
24 Municipal Tourist Office ... D3
25 Municipal Tourist Office – Playa Mansa ... F2
26 National Tourism Ministry ... E3

low-key fireside camaraderie to Punta-style partying. The six- to eight-bed dorms are pretty standard issue (and the triple-decker bunks may give pause to acrophobes), but the on-site bar-restaurant invites cozy conversation by the *parrilla*, and the beach (Playa Portezuelo) is a short walk downhill.

Camping San Rafael CAMPGROUND $
(☎4248-6715; www.campingsanrafael.com.uy; Saravia s/n; campsites per person US$12.50, plus per vehicle US$3; ⏰Nov-Easter) This campground, near the bridge to La Barra, has well-kept facilities on woodsy grounds, complete with store, restaurant, laundry, 24-hour hot water and other amenities.

Bonne Étoile HOTEL $$
(☎4244-0301; www.hotelbonneetoile.com; Calle 20, btwn Calles 23 & 25; d US$60-85 Mar-Dec, US$128-160 Jan & Feb; ❄@📶) In a 1940s beach house adjoining a more modern six-story tower, Bonne Étoile offers clean, spacious rooms, some with river views. Low-season rates are among the best in town, and the location between Gorlero and the port is hard to beat.

★**Casa Zinc** BOUTIQUE HOTEL $$$
(☎4277-3003, 099-620066; www.casazinc.com; Calle 9, La Barra; r US$140-260 Apr-Oct, US$235-470 Nov-Mar; @📶) Replete with vintage furniture, claw-foot bathtubs and checkerboard marble floors, this magical La Barra getaway features six luxurious high-ceilinged theme rooms, including the Library, the luminous Architect's Studio and Back to School, with its twin beds and old-fashioned blackboards. Guests can enjoy breakfast till 4pm, prepare dinners in the beautifully appointed kitchen, or pore over the hotel's collection of art books.

★**Las Cumbres** BOUTIQUE HOTEL $$$
(☎4257-8689; www.cumbres.com.uy; Ruta 12, Km 3.5, Laguna del Sauce; d US$160-308, ste US$287-533; ❄@📶🏊) Near Punta Ballena, this understatedly luxurious hilltop paradise is eclectically decorated with treasures from the owners' world travels. The spacious rooms abound with special features, such as writing desks, fireplaces and outdoor whirlpool tubs. Guests have access to spa treatments, beach chairs and umbrellas, and free mountain bikes, and the tearoom terrace (open to the public) has magnificent sunset views.

L'Auberge HOTEL $$$
(☎4248-8888; www.laubergehotel.com; cnr Carnoustie & Av del Agua; r US$200-490; ❄📶🏊) A venerable Punta del Este landmark, this visually striking 1940s hotel encompasses a cluster of faux-Tudor mansion houses, big grassy lawns, a 13-story fairy-tale tower and a teahouse serving afternoon tea and waffles (a tradition initiated by the hotel's Belgian founder). Upper-floor rooms in the tower are especially atmospheric, with windows overlooking the sea and the adjacent pine woods.

WORTH A TRIP

JOSÉ IGNACIO

The rich and famous flock to this highly fashionable beachside town with its pretty lighthouse and long expanses of powdery sand, 30km east of Punta. The entire surrounding coastline is dotted with exclusive homes and a small crop of high-end hotels and restaurants, yet the overall vibe here remains low-key. Unlike nearby Punta del Este, where priorities seem to revolve around 'seeing and being seen,' José Ignacio feels more like a place where celebrities come to get off the grid and slip under the radar.

If you're a mere mortal without a trust fund to spend, you can always linger on José Ignacio's lovely beaches for the day and return elsewhere to sleep, or scope out vacation rentals in the less exclusive adjoining residential neighborhood of La Juanita.

Local bus 14, operated by Codesa (p560), runs from Punta del Este to José Ignacio seven times daily (UR$70, 50 minutes). COPSA also runs two daily long-distance buses (UR$115, 40 minutes) along the same route.

For a classic taste of José Ignacio's rarefied atmosphere, drop in at chic beachside eatery **Parador La Huella** (☎4486-2279; www.paradorlahuella.com; Playa Brava; mains UR$520-760; ⊙noon-3pm & 8pm-midnight Fri & Sat, noon-3pm Sun May-Oct), where you can mingle with José Ignacio's beautiful people over sushi, grilled fish and clay-oven-fired pizza, all served up with dreamy ocean views and a soundtrack that ranges from Leonard Cohen to David Byrne.

Conrad Resort & Casino CASINO HOTEL **$$$**
(☎4249-1111; www.conrad.com.uy; Parada 4, Playa Mansa; d US$170-456, ste from US$488; ❄@🛜≋) A longtime downtown fixture, this high-rise five-star remains one of the focal points of Punta's summertime 'see and be seen' social life. Better rooms have terraces with sea views, the pool and spa complex is fabulous, and the casino offers entertainment extravaganzas.

Eating

Restaurant prices in Punta del Este tend toward the extortionate. This town knows it's got a captive audience and charges accordingly. That said, there are a few eateries that cater mainly to locals who work in town; Calle 29 between Gorlero and Calle 24 is one good place to find these.

Pizza al Taglio PIZZA, BURGERS **$**
(Calle 24 btwn Calles 28 & 29; mains UR$200-350; ⊙8pm-late Nov-Apr) Where to eat in Punta del Este without breaking the bank? In warm weather, this chilled-out pizzeria on the front patio of Tas D'Viaje Hostel is a no-brainer. The whole focus here is pizza, burgers, *chivitos* and fries – well made, reasonably priced and accompanied by draft beer. 'Nuff said!

Rustic INTERNATIONAL **$**
(☎092-007457; www.facebook.com/Rusticbarpuntadeleste; Calle 29, btwn Juan Gorlero & Calle 24; mains UR$250-390; ⊙11am-4pm daily year-round, plus 8pm-late Fri & Sat Mar-Nov, daily Dec-Feb) Rustic wood tables, exposed brick walls, retro decor, and tasty food at affordable prices make this one of the peninsula's most attractive lunch spots. Friendly young owners Luciana and Sebastian offer service with a smile, bustling from table to table with *chivitos*, *milanesas*, quesadillas, salads and fish of the day. There's a UR$200 daily lunch special (cash only).

Olivia INTERNATIONAL **$$**
(☎4244-5121; Calle 21, btwn Rambla Artigas & Gorlero; mains UR$370-540; ⊙noon-midnight) Popular for its varied menu and moderate (by Punta standards) prices, this bright little eatery decked out with blond-wood tables and red-and-white chairs serves tacos, salads, sandwiches and more substantial fish and meat dishes, along with caipirinhas, mojitos, sangria or fresh ginger-mint lemonade. In good weather sit on the scenic rooftop terrace overlooking the port.

El Chancho y la Coneja URUGUAYAN **$$$**
(☎4277-2497; Calle 12/Nina Miranda, La Barra; mains UR$460-600; ⊙8pm-midnight daily Dec-Feb, Fri & Sat only Mar-Nov) Owners Horacio (the pig) and Karina (the rabbit) named this rustic backstreet hideaway for their Chinese zodiac animals. Well-chosen blues and jazz numbers, yellow brick walls, artsy light fixtures and distressed-wood benches set an atmospheric backdrop for delicious grilled meat and fish, homemade pasta (try the ricotta, basil, walnut and bacon *pierogi*,

inspired by Karina's Polish grandmother) and more.

Lo de Tere INTERNATIONAL **$$$**
(☎4244-0492; www.lodetere.com; Rambla Artigas near Calle 21; mains UR$620-1290; ⌚noon-3pm & 7pm-midnight) Even with early-bird discounts (20% to 40% between noon and 1pm and 7pm to 8pm), Lo de Tere is hard on the wallet, but you won't find finer food anywhere in Punta. The wide-ranging menu includes black-crab ravioli, orange-scented shrimp risotto, Uruguayan steak with rock salt and homemade chimichurri, and rack of lamb, all accompanied by fine harbor views.

Cuatro Mares SEAFOOD **$$$**
(☎4244-8916; www.cuatromares.com.uy; cnr Calles 7 & 10; mains UR$500-800; ⌚8-11pm Wed-Fri, noon-11pm Sat & Sun) Fresh fish is the big draw at the 'Four Seas' restaurant, up near the lighthouse in the older residential part of Punta. Three or four deliciously grilled specials are on offer daily, but if you insist on something less fishy, there are also wild cards like chicken with polenta or leek, Brie and veggie omelettes.

Guappa URUGUAYAN **$$$**
(☎4244-0951; www.guappa.com.uy; Rambla Artigas btwn Calles 27 & 28; mains UR$540-1090; ⌚noon-midnight) For seafood, salads, pasta, panini or *chivitos* in one of Punta's prettiest waterfront settings, grab a spot on the beachside deck here, then enjoy watching the waiters try to look dignified as they cross the street with loaded trays. A popular spot to watch the sun go down.

Il Baretto ITALIAN **$$$**
(☎4244-5565; www.ilbarettopunta.com; cnr Calles 9 & 10; pizza UR$290-440, dishes UR$580-850; ⌚11am-4pm & 8pm-late daily mid-Dec–Carnaval, 11am-4pm Sat & Sun & 6pm-midnight Wed-Sun rest of year) Candlelit garden seating on plush chairs and couches provides a romantic setting for 'after-beach' drinks, along with homemade pasta, pizza and desserts.

Drinking & Nightlife

A cluster of clubs in Punta's port area stays open all year (weekends only in low season). During the super-peak season from Christmas through January, an additional slew of beach clubs with ever-changing names open along Playa Brava, on the beach road to La Barra.

Bear in mind that it's social suicide to turn up at a nightclub before 2am here. In general, Punta's bars stay open as long as there's a crowd and sometimes have live music on weekends.

Capi Bar BAR
(www.facebook.com/capipde; Calle 27, btwn Gorlero & Calle 24; ⌚6pm-3am Mon-Fri, 1pm-3am Sat & Sun) Launched in 2015, Punta del Este's first artisanal brewpub serves up its own Capitán home brew along with craft beers from all over Uruguay. The classy, low-lit interior also makes a nice place to linger over reasonably priced fish and chips, *rabas* (fried squid) and other bar snacks.

Moby Dick PUB
(www.mobydick.com.uy; Rambla Artigas, btwn Calles 10 & 12; ⌚6pm-5am Mon-Thu, noon-5am Fri-Sun) This classic pub near the yacht harbor is where Punta's dynamic social scene kicks off every evening. It's open year-round, with a mix of DJs and live music.

Ocean Club CLUB
(www.facebook.com/OceanClubPunta; Rambla Batlle Parada 12; ⌚1-7am) One of Punta's best and most reliable beach clubs, in the dunes between Punta and La Barra.

Soho CLUB
(www.facebook.com/SohoPuntaUy; Rambla Artigas, btwn Calles 10 & 12; ⌚11pm-6am) A dependable year-round dance spot featuring live bands and international DJs.

Entertainment

Medio y Medio JAZZ
(☎4257-8791; www.medioymedio.com; Av del Parador Viejo, Punta Ballena; ⌚noon-late daily Nov-Mar, noon-midnight Thu-Mon Apr-Oct) This jazz club and restaurant near the beach in Punta Ballena brings in top-name performers from Uruguay, Argentina and Brazil.

Shopping

Manos del Uruguay CLOTHING
(☎4244-1953; www.manos.com.uy; Gorlero btwn Calles 30 & 31; ⌚11am-7pm Mar-Dec, 10am-midnight Jan & Feb) The local branch of Uruguay's national cooperative, selling fine woolens.

Orientation

Punta itself is relatively small, confined to a narrow peninsula that officially divides the Río de la Plata from the Atlantic Ocean. The town has two separate grids: north of a constricted isthmus is the high-rise hotel zone; the southern area is largely residential. Street signs bear both names and numbers, though locals refer to most streets only by number. An exception is Av Juan Gorlero (Calle 22), the main commercial street, universally referred to as just 'Gorlero' (not to be confused with Calle 19, Comodoro Gorlero).

Information

Punta's many banks, ATMs and exchange offices are concentrated along Gorlero.

Banco de la República Oriental (cnr Gorlero & Calle 25; ⌚1-6pm Mon-Fri) One of two ATMs on this corner.

Municipal Tourist Office (☎4244-6510; www.maldonado.gub.uy; Plaza Artigas; ⌚8am-11pm mid-Dec–Feb, 10am-6pm rest of year) Full-service office on Punta's main square, with hotel-booking desk attached.

Municipal Tourist Office – Playa Mansa (Liga de Fomento; ☎4244-6519; cnr Calles 18 & 31; ⌚9am-10pm mid-Dec–Mar, 10am-4pm rest of year)

National Tourism Ministry (☎4244-1218; www.uruguaynatural.com; Gorlero 942; ⌚10am-5pm Mon-Sat)

Post Office (Calle 30, btwn Gorlero & Calle 24; ⌚9am-5pm Mon-Fri)

Getting There & Away

AIR

Punta del Este International Airport (p573) is at Laguna del Sauce, 20km west of Punta del Este. Direct international flights include Aerolíneas Argentinas to Buenos Aires' Aeroparque and **LATAM** (☎000-4019-0223; www.latam.com) to São Paulo.

BUS

From Punta's **bus terminal** (☎4249-4042; cnr Calle 32 & Bulevar Artigas), dozens of daily buses ply the coastal route to Montevideo. COT also runs two daily buses northeast up the coast to the Brazilian border, with intermediate stops at Rocha (transfer point for La Paloma, La Pedrera and Cabo Polonio) and Punta del Diablo.

Buses from Punta del Este

DESTINATION	COST (UR$)	TIME (HR)
Carrasco Airport	298	1¾
Montevideo	298	2¼
Piriápolis	135	1
Punta del Diablo	407	3
Rocha	213	1½

Getting Around

TO/FROM THE AIRPORT

Punta del Este International Airport AB Transporte (☎099-903433, 099-904420; transfer btwn airport & bus terminal or port UR$250, btwn airport & hotel UR$350) offers door-to-door minivan transfers to Punta del Este's airport. Alternatively, any Montevideo-bound bus can drop you at the airport entrance on the main highway (UR$94), about 250m from the terminal building.

BUS

Bus 14, operated by **Codesa** (☎4266-9129; www.codesa.com.uy), runs from Punta's bus terminal via the eastern beaches to La Barra (UR$57, 10 minutes) and José Ignacio (UR$60, 50 minutes); other Codesa buses run year-round to points west, including Punta Ballena.

CAR

Major international car-rental companies, along with Uruguayan rental agencies such as **Punta Car** (☎4248-2112; www.puntacar.com.uy; Bulevar Artigas 101; ⌚10am-6:30pm) and **Multicar** (☎4244-3143; www.redmulticar.com; Gorlero 860; ⌚9am-9pm Jan & Feb, 10am-7pm Mar-Dec), have counters at Punta del Este's airport. Downtown offices for all companies are concentrated along Gorlero and Calle 31.

La Paloma

☎447 / POP 3500

La Paloma sits on a small peninsula 225km east of Montevideo, in the pretty rural department of Rocha. The town itself is rather bland and sprawling, but the surrounding beaches offer some of Uruguay's best surfing. On summer weekends the town often hosts free concerts on the beach, making accommodations bookings essential.

Sights & Activities

Laguna de Rocha NATURE RESERVE

FREE An ecological reserve protected under Uruguay's SNAP program (p566), this vast and beautiful wetland 10km west of La Paloma has populations of black-necked swans, storks, spoonbills and other waterfowl.

El Faro del Cabo Santa María LIGHTHOUSE

(UR$25; ⌚3pm-sunset) The 1874 completion of this local lighthouse marked La Paloma's genesis as a summer beach resort. The unfinished first attempt collapsed in a violent storm, killing 17 French and Italian workers, who are buried nearby. Outside is a solar clock using shadows cast by the lighthouse.

Peteco Surf Shop
SURFING

(☑4479-6172; www.facebook.com/PetecoSurf Shop; Av Nicolás Solari, btwn Avs El Sirio & del Navío; ☺10am-8pm Thu-Mon, to 6pm Tue & Wed) This friendly surf shop rents all the necessary equipment (shortboards, longboards, bodyboards, sandboards, wet suits and kayaks) and can hook you up with good local instructors. The best surfing beaches are Los Botes, Solari and Anaconda southwest of town, and La Aguada and La Pedrera to the north.

🛏 Sleeping & Eating

Hostel Arazá
HOSTEL $

(☑4479-9710; www.facebook.com/HostelAraza LaPaloma; Orion s/n; dm US$12-23, d US$72-92; 🛜🏊) Conveniently located near La Paloma's bus station, this newer hostel stands out for its exceptional owners, who bend over backward to make guests feel welcome. A host of amenities invite interaction, including swimming pool, barbecue and volleyball court. Good breakfasts and high standards of cleanliness are the icing on the cake.

Beach Hostel
La Balconada
HOSTEL $

(☑4479-6273; www.labalconadahostel.com.uy; Centauro s/n; dm US$12-35, d US$50-80, d without bathroom US$40-65; 🛜) This surfer-friendly hostel has an enviable location a stone's throw from La Balconada beach, about 1km southwest of the center. Take a taxi from the bus station and the hostel will pick up the tab.

Hotel Bahía
HOTEL $$

(☑4479-6029; www.elbahia.com.uy; cnr Avs del Navío & del Sol; d US$65-130; 🛏🌀🛜) For its central location and overall comfort, Bahía is hard to beat. Rooms are clean and bright, with firm mattresses and bedside reading lights. The seafood restaurant downstairs (mains UR$325 to UR$575, closed Tuesday) has been in business since 1936 and regularly gets recommended by locals as La Paloma's best.

Punto Sur
SEAFOOD $$

(☑099-624630, 4479-9462; Centauro s/n; dishes UR$325-525; ☺noon-1am) For casual dining with an ocean view, this place on Playa La Balconada is the obvious choice, featuring tapas, paella, grilled fish and homemade pasta.

Lo de Edinson
PARRILLA, PIZZA $$

(☑4479-8178; www.facebook.com/LoDeEdinson; Av Nicolás Solari, btwn Antares & de la Virgen; mains UR$195-375; ☺8am-11pm Wed-Mon) Best known for its grilled meats, this popular eatery in the heart of La Paloma also does decent pizzas and has a well-stocked bakery selling takeaway treats.

ℹ Information

Banks, post and telephone offices are all on the main street, Avenida Nicolás Solari.

Tourist Office (☑4479-6088; www.lapalomauruguay.com.uy; Av Nicolás Solari; ☺10am-10pm daily mid-Dec–Easter, 10:30am-4:30pm Mon-Sat rest of year) On the traffic circle at the heart of town. A second office in the bus terminal opens seasonally.

ℹ Getting There & Away

From La Paloma's **bus terminal** (Aries s/n), 500m northwest of the center, COT, Cynsa and Rutas del Sol all run frequently to Montevideo (UR$481, four hours). There's also frequent local service to La Pedrera (UR$60, 15 minutes). Rutas del Sol runs twice daily to the Cabo Polonio turnoff (UR$120, 45 minutes) and once daily to Punta del Diablo (UR$240, two hours). For other destinations, take a bus to the departmental capital of Rocha (UR$65, 30 minutes, frequent), where hourly buses ply the coastal route in both directions.

La Pedrera

POP 230

Long a mecca for surfers, laid-back La Pedrera sits atop a bluff with magnificent sweeping views of the beaches stretching north toward Cabo Polonio and south toward La Paloma. The town typically sees a huge surge of visitors and second-home owners between Christmas and Carnaval, when everyone is here to celebrate sun, sand and surf. The rest of the year, La Pedrera gets downright sleepy, with most hotels and tourist services closing down altogether between April and November.

🛏 Sleeping & Eating

El Viajero La
Pedrera Hostel
HOSTEL $

(☑099-470542; www.elviajerolapedrera.com; Venteveo, btwn Pirincho & Zorzal; dm US$15-33, d US$62-83; ☺Dec–mid-Mar; @🛜) Part of Uruguay's largest hostel chain, this well-located seasonal hostel is tucked down a side street,

OFF THE BEATEN TRACK

HORSING AROUND IN THE HILLS

An hour inland from La Pedrera, the Sierra de Rocha is a lovely landscape of gray rocky crags interspersed with rolling rangeland. **Caballos de Luz** (☎099-400446; www.caballosdeluz.com; horseback rides per person from US$50, s/d incl horseback ride & full board US$150/270), run by the multilingual Austrian-Uruguayan couple Lucie and Santiago, offers hill-country horse treks lasting from 2½ hours to a week, complete with three delicious vegetarian meals daily and overnight accommodation in a thatched cottage, a dome or a private double room. Call for pickup at the bus station in Rocha (US$20), or drive there yourself (it's about 30 minutes off Hwy 9).

a five-minute walk from the bus stop and only 500m from the beach.

Brisas de la Pedrera BOUTIQUE HOTEL **$$$**
(☎093-955795; www.brisasdelapedrera.com; d US$150-300; ❄📶) La Pedrera's oldest lodging – completely remodeled in boutique style and reopened in 2009 by Argentine-American owner Laura Jauregui – woos guests with sunny, spacious rooms, high-end amenities (but no TVs), and spectacular ocean views from the upstairs units with private terraces.

La Pe SEAFOOD **$$**
(☎094-408955; www.facebook.com/RestaurantLaPe; Av Principal; mains UR$340-510; ⏲1-4pm & 8:30pm-12:30am Dec-Mar) 'P' is for pasta, paella and – in Spanish – *pescado* (fish). This popular place, smack in the heart of La Pedrera's main street, serves all three, with outdoor seating under the trees and a nice play area for kids. Look for the red, vine-covered building with the fish logo.

Costa Brava SEAFOOD **$$**
(mains UR$295-525; ⏲noon-3pm & 8pm-midnight daily Dec-Mar; 8pm-midnight Fri & Sat, noon-3pm Sat & Sun Apr-Nov) Perched atop the bluffs overlooking the Atlantic, Costa Brava is all about seafood accompanied by an unbeatable view.

Lajau MEDITERRANEAN, SEAFOOD **$$$**
(☎099-922091; mains UR$360-650; ⏲1-4pm & 9pm-1am) Presided over by a Santa Claus-bearded Basque chef, this cozy family-run spot one block from the waterfront has a short, sweet menu of pasta and seafood. Locally caught crab, rays, shark and shrimp make their way into house specialties like *fidegua* (a paella-like dish made with fish, shellfish and noodles instead of rice).

ℹ Information

The closest ATMs are in La Paloma.

Tourist Office (☎4472-3100; Av Principal s/n; ⏲10am-6pm Dec-Easter, to 10pm during Jan-Carnaval period) A seasonally operating office a few blocks in from the beach. It's in a tiny wooden kiosk next to the OSE water towers (the town's tallest landmark).

ℹ Getting There & Away

Buses southbound to Montevideo (UR$501) and northbound to the Cabo Polonio turnoff (UR$74) stop near the tourist office on La Pedrera's main street. Schedules vary seasonally; a list is posted at the tourist office. There are also frequent buses to Rocha (UR$100), where you can make connections north and south.

Cabo Polonio

POP 60

Northeast of La Paloma at Km 264.5 on Ruta 10 lies the turnoff to Cabo Polonio, one of Uruguay's wildest areas and home to its second-biggest sea-lion colony, near a tiny fishing village nestled in sand dunes on a windswept point crowned by a lonely lighthouse. In 2009 the region was declared a national park, under the protective jurisdiction of Uruguay's SNAP program (p566). Despite a growing influx of tourists (and an incongruously spiffy entrance portal), Cabo Polonio remains one of Uruguay's most rustic coastal villages. There are no banking services, and the town's limited electricity is derived from generators, and solar and wind power.

👁 Sights & Activities

In high season, Cabo Polonio's **surf school** (☎099-212542), operated by local residents Mario and Ruben, offers surfing classes and board rentals.

Faro Cabo Polonio LIGHTHOUSE
(UR$25; ⏲10am-1pm & 3pm-sunset) Built in 1881, Cabo Polonio's striking 27m-tall lighthouse provides a fabulous perspective on

the point, the sea-lion colony and the surrounding dunes and islands.

★Cabalgatas Valiceras HORSEBACK RIDING
(☎099-574685; www.cabalgatasvaliceras.com.uy; Barra de Valizas) Based in nearby Barra de Valizas, this excellent operator offers horseback excursions into the national park, through the dunes and along the beaches north of Cabo Polonio, including monthly full-moon rides.

Wildlife Watching

Wildlife viewing in Cabo Polonio is excellent year-round. Below the lighthouse, southern sea lions (*Otaria flavescens*) and South American fur seals (*Arctocephalus australis*) frolic on the rocks. You can also spot southern right whales from August to October, penguins on the beach between May and August, and the odd southern elephant seal (*Mirounga leonina*) between January and March on nearby Isla de la Raza.

Sleeping & Eating

Many locals rent rooms and houses. The hardest time to find accommodation is during the first two weeks of January. From April through November, prices drop dramatically (40% to 70%).

Cabo Polonio Hostel HOSTEL $
(☎099-445943; www.cabopoloniohostel.com; dm/d mid-Dec–Feb US$33/100, rest of year US$18/50; ⏲Oct-Apr) The affable Gabi presides over this rustic beachfront hostel, recently expanded to include a larger, brighter kitchen and a brand-new ocean-view dorm. A Polonio classic, it also features a hammock-strewn patio and a woodstove for stormy nights. The abandoned TV in the dunes out front and the custom-designed NoFi logo epitomize owner Alfredo's low-tech philosophy: slow down and unplug!

Casitas de Marta y Hector RENTAL HOUSE $
(☎098-533427; r US$30-70, houses Apr-Nov US$30, Dec-Mar US$150) Hector and Marta, a friendly local fishing couple, rent out two sweet double rooms and a self-contained house sleeping up to seven. All come with stoves, gas refrigerators and solar-powered outlets for charging phones. Look for the salmon-orange house with the green flag just north of where trucks stop (and the 'Hay Pescado' sign when they've got fish to sell!).

Pancho Hostal del Cabo HOSTEL $
(☎099-307870; dm Jan & Feb US$30, Mar-Dec US$11) Providing bare-bones dorms on two levels, Pancho's popular hostel is impossible to miss; look for the yellow corrugated roof, labeled with giant red letters, toward the beach from the 4WD truck stop. Nice features include a spacious new kitchen, a beachfront lounging area and the 2nd-floor dorm under the A-frame roof, with its small terrace looking straight out at the ocean.

Mariemar HOTEL $$
(☎099-875260, 4470-5164; posadamariemar@hotmail.com; d Dec-Feb US$150, Mar-Nov US$42) Tucked below the lighthouse, with beach access right outside the back door, this hotel-restaurant is one of Polonio's oldest year-round businesses. The simple rooms all have ocean views, with upstairs units preferable to those down below. The attached restaurant (mains UR$320 to UR$570) serves everything from afternoon snacks (seaweed fritters and cold beer) to full seafood meals.

Lo de Dany URUGUAYAN $$
(mains UR$160-420; ⏲9am-10pm) This straightforward orange snack shack near the 4WD truck stop is run by one of Polonio's few year-round resident families. It's a welcoming, affordable spot for everything from homemade *buñuelos de algas* (seaweed fritters) to *rabas* (fried squid), to *chivitos*.

El Club PARRILLA, INTERNATIONAL $$
(☎098-353165; www.facebook.com/elclubcabopolonio; mains UR$300-480; ⏲11am-late mid-Dec–Easter) This colorfully decorated, eco-conscious eatery combines the creative efforts of Colombian artist Camila, her Uruguayan partner Fernando and various local chefs. Specialties include grilled fish, artisanal beer, wood-fired pizza and fondue cooked atop recycled tin cans. It doubles as a social club where people gather to play chess and enjoy live music. *Platos del día* (UR$420) include some vegetarian options.

Drinking & Nightlife

Lo de Joselo BAR
(⏲6pm-late) For a quintessential Polonio experience, head to this ramshackle bar, overgrown with dense shrubbery and flowering vines. Blind bartender Joselo presides over the funky candlelit interior, serving up *licor de butia* (alcohol made from local palm fruit), *grappamiel* and stiff shots of *caña*

WORTH A TRIP

LAGUNA DE CASTILLOS

Northwest of Cabo Polonio is the Laguna de Castillos, a vast coastal lagoon that shelters Uruguay's largest concentration of *ombúes*, graceful treelike plants whose anarchic growth pattern results in some rather fantastic shapes. In other parts of Uruguay the *ombú* is a solitary plant, but specimens here – some of them centuries old – grow in clusters, insulated by the lagoon from the bovine trampling that has spelled their doom elsewhere.

Rutas del Sol buses heading north from Cabo Polonio can drop you at the Monte de Ombúes dock, just north of the bridge over the Arroyo Valizas (Km 267 on Ruta 10).

Monte de Ombúes (099-295177; tours per person with 5-person minimum from UR$500) On Laguna de Castillos' western shore (near Km 267 on Ruta 10), brothers Marcos and Juan Carlos Olivera, whose family received this land from the Portuguese crown in 1793, lead two- to three-hour nature excursions. Tours begin with a 20-minute boat ride through a wetland teeming with cormorants, ibis, cranes and black swans, followed by a hike through the *ombú* forest.

Departures are frequent in summer (anytime five people show up); other times of year, reserve ahead. With advance notice, longer bird-watching tours of the lagoon can be arranged in the low season.

Guardia del Monte (099-872588, 4470-5180; www.guardiadelmonte.com; Ruta 9, Km 261.5; r per person incl breakfast/half-board/full board US$110/150/180) Overlooking Laguna de Castillos' northern shore is this tranquil hideaway, originally established in the 18th century as a Spanish guard post to protect the Camino Real and the coastal frontier from pirates and Portuguese marauders. The lovely *estancia* house oozes history, from the parlor displaying 18th-century maps and bird drawings to the kitchen's Danish woodstove salvaged from an 1884 shipwreck.

Overnight rates include afternoon tea and meals served on the old brick patio or by the fireplace in the cozy dining room. Activities include horseback excursions (US$30) and walks along the lakeshore or into the surrounding *ombú* forest. It's at the end of a 10km dead-end road, off Ruta 9, 4km south of the town of Castillos.

(sugarcane alcohol). It's a few paces from the 4WD truck stop toward the lighthouse.

Getting There & Away

Rutas del Sol runs two to five buses daily from Montevideo to the Cabo Polonio entrance portal on Ruta 10 (UR$601, 4½ hours). Here you'll pile onto a 4WD truck for the lurching, bumpy ride across the dunes into town (UR$218 roundtrip, 30 minutes each way).

There's a **stop** for 4WD trucks in the town center.

Punta del Diablo

POP 820

Once a sleepy fishing village, Punta del Diablo has long since become a prime summer getaway for Uruguayans and Argentines, and the epicenter of Uruguay's backpacker beach scene. Waves of uncontrolled development have pushed further inland and along the coast in recent years, but the stunning shoreline and laid-back lifestyle still exert their age-old appeal. To avoid the crowds, come outside the Christmas-to-February peak season; in particular, avoid the first half of January, when as many as 30,000 visitors inundate the town.

From the town's traditional center, a sandy 'plaza' 200m inland from the ocean, small dirt streets fan out in all directions.

Sights & Activities

During the day you can rent surfboards or horses along the town's main beach, or trek an hour north to Parque Nacional Santa Teresa. In the evening there are sunsets to watch, spontaneous bonfires and drum sessions to drop in on…you get the idea.

Sleeping

Punta del Diablo offers a plethora of lodging options, from hostels to posadas to *cabañas*; this latter term applies to everything from rustic-to-a-fault shacks to custom-built designer condos with all modern conveniences. Most *cabañas* have kitchens; some require you to bring your own bedding. For help finding something, ask at Supermercado El Vasco in the heart of town, or check online at www.portaldeldiablo.com.uy. Rates skyrocket between Christmas and February.

★El Diablo Tranquilo HOSTEL $
(☎4477-2647; www.eldiablotranquilo.com; Av Central; dm US$28-40, d Dec-Easter US$80-160, dm/d rest of year from US$14/44; @☎) Follow the devilish red glow into one of South America's most seductive hostels, whose endless perks include inviting chill-out areas, bike and surfboard rentals, yoga and language classes, horseback excursions and more. At the beachside Playa Suites annex, upstairs rooms have full-on ocean views, while the attached bar-restaurant offers meals, beach service and a late-night party scene.

La Casa de las Boyas HOSTEL $
(☎4477-2074; www.lacasadelasboyas.com.uy; Playa del Rivero; dm US$15-35, d Dec-Mar US$60-120, Apr-Nov US$50-70; @☎≋) A stone's throw from the beach and a 10-minute walk north from the town center, this hostel offers a pool, two guest kitchens, summer-only dorms of varying size, and year-round apartments and lofts equipped with en-suite bathrooms, kitchenettes and satellite TV. Other enticements include restaurant, game room, bike and surfboard rentals, and horseback excursions.

Posada Nativos BOUTIQUE HOTEL $$
(☎099-641394; www.nativos.com.uy; cnr Santa Teresa & General San Martín; r US$88-154; ☎) Artist Eduardo Vigliola's labor of love, this thatch-roofed boutique hotel incorporates local stone and wood details, surrounded by landscaped grounds dotted with water lilies, papyrus, edible and medicinal plants, a small stream and a Japanese-style pond. The four-bedroom Casa Nativos out back, complete with living room and kitchen, doubles as part of the hotel and as a stand-alone vacation rental.

Eating & Drinking

Punta del Diablo's drinking scene revolves around Playa de los Pescadores, where you'll find a number of beachside bars.

★Resto-Pub 70 ITALIAN $
(☎099-103367; www.facebook.com/pub70; Playa de los Pescadores; mains UR$260-350; ⊙noon-3pm & 7:30-11pm daily late Dec-Mar, Sat & Sun only rest of year) Run by an Italian family from the Veneto, this portside eatery serves divine, reasonably priced homemade pasta such as *lasagne alle cipolle* (veggie lasagna with walnuts and caramelized onions), accompanied by UR$50 glasses of house wine. Afterwards, don't miss the *cantucci con vino dolce* (almond biscotti dipped in sweet wine) and *limoncino* (an artisanal liqueur made with fragrant Uruguayan lemons).

Empanada Stands EMPANADAS $
(Feria Artesanal, Playa de los Pescadores; empanadas UR$75; ⊙10am-4pm daily Jan & Feb, Sat & Sun only Mar-Dec) Tucked in among the artisan stalls down by the port, sisters Alba, Mónica and Noelia Acosta operate three no-frills stands that serve up Punta del Diablo's tastiest low-cost snack: hot-from-the-fryer empanadas filled with fish, mussels, meat, cheese, olives and other savory goodies.

Cero Stress INTERNATIONAL $$
(☎4477-2220; Av de los Pescadores; mains UR$320-490; ⊙noon-midnight; ☎☎) By far the greatest asset of this laid-back eatery is its deck, which offers amazing ocean views. It's the perfect place to sip a caipirinha (Brazilian cocktail with sugarcane alcohol) at sunset while contemplating your evening plans. There's also occasional live music.

Il Tano INTERNATIONAL $$$
(☎096-589389; www.iltanocucina.com; Calle 5 btwn Calles 20 & Coronilla; mains UR$370-530; ⊙7-10pm Mon-Thu, 7-11pm Fri, noon-4pm & 7-11pm Sat, noon-4pm Sun) Punta del Diablo's classiest restaurant is this cozy house with a wraparound porch, overlooking a pretty garden whose veggies and herbs complement the Italian-influenced menu of pasta, meat and seafood. Specialties include homemade shrimp-and-zucchini ravioli, ham-and-cheese agnolotti with a creamy wild-mushroom sauce, and pork shoulder with a sweet-and-sour sauce featuring fruit from local butiá palms.

Information

Punta del Diablo has no cash machines other than the temporary **Redbrou ATM** (Calle 9) set up at Paseo del Rivero each summer. Bring cash with you; only some businesses accept credit cards, and the nearest banks are an hour away in Castillos (40km southwest) or Chuy (45km north).

OFF THE BEATEN TRACK

URUGUAY'S OFF-THE-BEATEN-TRACK NATURE PRESERVES

Uruguay's vast open spaces are a naturalist's dream. The Uruguayan government has designated several natural areas for protection under its **SNAP program** (Sistema Nacional de Áreas Protegidas; www.mvotma.gub.uy/portal/snap). Funding remains minimal and tourist infrastructure rudimentary, but intrepid travelers will be rewarded for seeking out these little-visited spots. **Valle del Lunarejo** and **Quebrada de los Cuervos** are the two preserves that best capture the spirit of Uruguay's wild gaucho country. Other SNAP preserves along the Atlantic coast include Cabo Polonio, Cerro Verde and Laguna de Rocha.

Quebrada de los Cuervos

This small hidden canyon cuts through the rolling hill country 40km northwest of Treinta y Tres (325km northeast of Montevideo), providing an unexpectedly moist and cool habitat for a variety of plants and birds. There are two self-guided hiking trails: a 2½-hour loop through the canyon (UR$50 park admission fee required), and a privately owned trail to the Cascada de Olivera waterfall just outside the park (30 minutes each way, UR$30).

A perfect base for exploring this region is **Cañada del Brujo** (☎099-297448, 4452-2837; www.pleka.com/delbrujo; per person incl breakfast/half-board/full board US$25/42/57), a rustic hostel in an old schoolhouse 8km from the park and 14km from Ruta 8. Hostel owner Pablo Rado leads hikes (UR$300) and horseback rides (UR$500) to the nearby Salto del Brujo waterfall and enjoys introducing guests to the joys of gaucho life: drinking *mate*, eating simple meals cooked on the woodstove and watching spectacular sunsets under the big sky. With advance notice, he can provide transportation to the hostel from Treinta y Tres or from the highway turnoff at Km 306.7 on Ruta 8.

Nuñez (nunez.com.uy) and **EGA** (www.ega.com.uy) run frequent buses from Montevideo to Treinta y Tres (UR$581, 4¼ hours).

Valle del Lunarejo

This gorgeous valley, 95km north of Tacuarembó, is a place of marvelous peace and isolation, with birds and rushing water providing the only soundtrack.

Visitors can spend the night at enchanting **Posada Lunarejo** (☎4650-6400; www.facebook.com/posada.lunarejo.7; Ruta 30, Km 238; r per person incl full board Mon-Thu US$69, Fri-Sun US$79), a restored 1880 building 2km off the main road, 3km from the river and a few steps from a bird colony teeming with *garzas* (cranes) and *espátulas rosadas* (roseate spoonbills). The posada organizes nearby hikes and horseback rides.

CUT (www.cutcorporacion.com.uy) offers the most convenient bus schedule to Valle del Lunarejo on its daily Montevideo–Tacuarembó–Artigas bus, leaving Montevideo at noon (UR$933, six hours) and leaving Tacuarembó at 4:50pm (UR$159, 1½ hours). Posada Lunarejo can meet your bus if you call ahead.

Getting There & Away

Rutas del Sol, COT and Cynsa all offer service to Punta del Diablo's bus terminal, 2.5km west of town. From here it's a five- to 10-minute shuttle (UR$25) or taxi (UR$100) ride into town.

Buses run daily to Montevideo and Chuy on the Brazilian border; for other coastal destinations, you'll usually need to change buses in Castillos or Rocha.

Buses from Punta del Diablo

DESTINATION	COST (UR$)	TIME (HR)
Castillos	79	1
Chuy	99	1
Montevideo	601	5
Punta del Este	407	3
Rocha	200	1½

Parque Nacional Santa Teresa

This army-administered **national park** (☎4477-2101; www.sepae.webnode.es; Ruta 9, Km 302; ⏲8am-8pm Dec-Mar, to 6pm Apr-Nov) FREE, 35km south of the Brazilian border, attracts many Uruguayan and Brazilian visitors to its relatively uncrowded beaches, including **Playa Grande**, **Playa del Barco** and **Playa de las Achiras**.

The **Capatacía** (park headquarters), 1km east of Ruta 9, has an Antel phone office, a post office, s market, a bakery and a restaurant, along with a very small zoo and a plant conservatory.

The park's star attraction, 4km north of park headquarters on Ruta 9, is the impressive hilltop **Fortaleza de Santa Teresa** (UR$30; ⏲10am-7pm daily Dec-Mar, to 5pm Wed-Sun Apr-Nov), a fortress begun by the Portuguese in 1762 and finished by the Spaniards after they captured the site in 1793.

At the park's northeastern corner is **Cerro Verde**, a coastal bluff providing important sea-turtle habitat. Directly opposite the park entrance, on the west side of Ruta 9, a 5km dead-end dirt road leads to **Laguna Negra**, a vast lagoon where flamingos, capybaras and other wildlife can be spotted.

Sleeping & Eating

The park offers 2000 dispersed campsites in eucalyptus and pine groves, along with a simple hostel and a variety of four- to 10-person *cabañas* for rent.

Capatacia Restaurant URUGUAYAN $
(mains UR$150-420; ⏲10am-10pm) At the Capatacía (Parque Nacional Santa Teresa park headquarters) is this restaurant, serving no-frills Uruguayan fare such as *chivitos*, steaks and *milanesas*.

Getting There & Away

Buses from Punta del Diablo (UR$53, 15 minutes) will drop you off at Km 302 on Ruta 9; from here, it's a flat 1km walk east to the Capatacía (park headquarters).

Alternatively, walk north along the beach a couple of kilometers from Punta del Diablo to reach the park's southern edge at Playa Grande.

UNDERSTAND URUGUAY

Uruguay Today

Currently, hot topics of conversation include the continued implementation of Uruguay's groundbreaking marijuana law, the revitalization of the Ciudad Vieja and the bright future prospects of Uruguay's national football team.

Uruguay's move toward legalized marijuana, first authorized in 2013, cleared another hurdle in 2017 as government-approved pharmacies began selling pot to Uruguayan citizens. In mid-July, 16 pharmacies provided over 5000 registered users with their first legally approved dose of 10g of government greenhouse-grown weed (total price tag? UR$187, or about US$6.50, per person). All went smoothly on the local level; however, an international wrinkle emerged when US banks, citing concerns about the drug trade, threatened sanctions against any Uruguayan bank who did business with the participating pharmacies. As a result, the pharmacies and their marijuana-loving customers have been obliged to conduct all business in cash until further notice.

Montevideo's Ciudad Vieja has seen a surge of revitalization in the past two years as municipal-government efforts to eliminate petty crime in the neighborhood have begun to bear fruit. Several new restaurants and hotels have moved in, and businesses are keeping longer hours as concerns about security have waned. This has all translated into an uptick in tourism to Montevideo's historic center.

Meanwhile, Uruguayan soccer fans are jazzed at the team's emerging crop of young new players, including Federico Valverde and Rodrigo Bentancur, both of whom seem poised to continue making an impact at 2022's Qatar World Cup and well beyond.

History

Uruguay's aboriginal inhabitants were the Charrúa along the coast and the Guaraní north of the Río Negro. The hunting-and-gathering Charrúa discouraged European settlement for more than a century by killing Spanish explorer Juan de Solís and most of his party in 1516. In any event there was little to attract the Spanish, who valued these lowlands along the Río de la Plata only as an access route to gold and other quick riches further inland.

FESTIVALS & EVENTS

Uruguay's Carnaval lasts for more than a month and is livelier than Argentina's. Semana Santa (Holy Week) has become known as Semana Turismo – many Uruguayans travel out of town, and finding accommodations is tricky during this time. Other noteworthy events include Tacuarembó's Fiesta de la Patria Gaucha (p549) and the nationwide Días del Patrimonio in early October, during which visitors are invited to tour Uruguay's most important historical and cultural monuments free of charge.

The first Europeans to settle on the Banda Oriental (Eastern Shore) were Jesuit missionaries near present-day Soriano, on the Río Uruguay. Next came the Portuguese, who established present-day Colonia in 1680 as a beachhead for smuggling goods into Buenos Aires. Spain responded by building its own citadel at Montevideo in 1726. The following century saw an ongoing struggle between Spain and Portugal for control of these lands along the eastern bank of the Río de la Plata.

Napoleon's invasion of the Iberian peninsula in the early 19th century precipitated a weakening of Spanish and Portuguese power and the emergence of strong independence movements throughout the region. Uruguay's homegrown national hero, José Gervasio Artigas, originally sought to form an alliance with several states in present-day Argentina and southern Brazil against the European powers, but he was ultimately forced to flee to Paraguay. There he regrouped and organized the famous '33 Orientales,' a feisty band of Uruguayan patriots under General Juan Lavalleja, who, with Argentine support, crossed the Río Uruguay on April 19, 1825, and launched a campaign to liberate modern-day Uruguay from Brazilian control. In 1828, after three years' struggle, a British-mediated treaty established Uruguay as a small independent buffer between the emerging continental powers.

For several decades, Uruguay's independence remained fragile. There was civil war between Uruguay's two nascent political parties, the Colorados and the Blancos (named, respectively, for the red and white bands they wore); Argentina besieged Montevideo from 1838 to 1851; and Brazil was an ever-present threat. Things finally settled down in the second half of the 19th century, with region-wide recognition of Uruguay's independence and the emergence of a strong national economy based on beef and wool production.

In the early 20th century, visionary president José Batlle y Ordóñez introduced such innovations as pensions, farm credits, unemployment compensation and the eight-hour work day. State intervention led to the nationalization of many industries, the creation of others, and a new era of general prosperity. However, Batlle's reforms were largely financed through taxing the livestock sector, and when exports faltered mid-century, the welfare state crumbled. A period of military dictatorship began in the early 1970s, during which torture became routine, and more than 60,000 citizens were arbitrarily detained, before the 1980s brought a return to democratic traditions.

The past decade has seen remarkable developments in Uruguayan culture and politics. After nearly two centuries of back-and-forth rule between the two traditional parties, Blancos and Colorados, Uruguayans voted the leftist Frente Amplio (Broad Front) into power in 2004 and again in 2009 and 2014. Over that span, the Frente Amplio government has presided over numerous social changes, including the legalization of marijuana, abortion and same-sex marriage.

ESSENTIAL FOOD & DRINK

Asado Uruguay's national gastronomic obsession, a mixed grill cooked over a wood fire featuring various cuts of beef and pork, chorizo, *morcilla* (blood sausage) and more.

Chivito A cholesterol bomb of a steak sandwich piled high with bacon, ham, fried or boiled egg, cheese, lettuce, tomato, olives, pickles, peppers and mayonnaise.

Ñoquis The same plump potato dumplings the Italians call *gnocchi*, traditionally served on the 29th of the month.

Buñuelos de algas Savory seaweed fritters, a specialty along the coast of Rocha.

Tannat Uruguay's beloved, internationally acclaimed red wine.

Grappamiel Strong Italian-style grappa (grape brandy), sweetened and mellowed with honey.

Culture

The one thing Uruguayans will tell you is that they're *not* anything like their *porteño* cousins across the water. Where Argentines can be brassy and sometimes arrogant, Uruguayans tend to be more humble and relaxed. Where the former have always been a regional superpower, the latter have always lived in the shadow of one. Those jokes about Punta del Este being a suburb of Buenos Aires don't go down so well on this side of the border. There are plenty of similarities, though: the near-universal appreciation for the arts, the Italian influence and the gaucho heritage.

Uruguayans like to take it easy and pride themselves on being the opposite of the hotheaded Latino type. Sunday's the day for family and friends, to throw half a cow on the *parrilla,* and to sit back and sip some *mate.* The population is well educated, and the gap between rich and poor is much less pronounced than in most other Latin American countries.

Population

With 3.4 million people, Uruguay is South America's smallest Spanish-speaking country. The population is predominately white (88%), with 8% mestizo (people with mixed Spanish and indigenous blood) and 4% black. Indigenous peoples are practically nonexistent. The average life expectancy (77 years) is one of Latin America's highest. The literacy rate is also high, at 98.5%, while population growth is a slow 0.27%. Population density is roughly 19 people per square kilometer.

Religion

Uruguay has more self-professed atheists and agnostics per capita (17%) than any other Latin American country. Some 47% identify themselves as Roman Catholic, with 11% claiming affiliation with other Christian denominations. There's a small Jewish minority, numbering around 20,000.

Sports

Uruguayans, like just about all Latin Americans, are crazy about *fútbol* (soccer). Uruguay has won the World Cup twice, including the first tournament, played in Montevideo in 1930. The national team (known commonly as La Celeste) has continued to excel periodically at the international level, winning the 2011 Copa America, appearing in the 2014 World Cup, and placing second only to Brazil in the South American qualifying rounds for the 2018 World Cup.

The most notable teams are Montevideo-based Nacional and Peñarol. If you go to a match between these two, sit on the sidelines, not behind the goal, unless you're up for some serious rowdiness.

Asociación Uruguayo de Fútbol (www.auf.org.uy), in Montevideo, can provide information on matches and venues.

Arts

Despite its small population, Uruguay has an impressive literary and artistic tradition. The country's most famous philosopher and essayist is José Enrique Rodó, whose 1900 essay *Ariel,* contrasting North American and Latin American civilizations, is a classic of the country's literature. Major contemporary writers include Juan Carlos Onetti, Mario Benedetti and Eduardo Galeano. Theater is also popular and playwrights like Mauricio Rosencof are prominent.

Uruguay's most renowned painters are Juan Manuel Blanes, Pedro Figari and Joaquín Torres García, each of whom has a museum dedicated to their works in Montevideo. Sculptors include José Belloni, whose life-size bronzes can be seen in Montevideo's parks.

Tango is big in Montevideo – Uruguayans claim tango legend Carlos Gardel as a native son, and one of the best-known tangos, 'La Cumparsita,' was composed by Uruguayan Gerardo Matos Rodríguez. During Carnaval, Montevideo's streets reverberate to the energetic drumbeats of *candombe,* an African-derived rhythm brought to Uruguay by slaves from 1750 onwards, and to the sounds of *murgas,* satirical musical-theater groups who perform throughout the city. On the contemporary scene, several Uruguayan rock bands have won a following on both sides of the Río de la Plata, including Buitres, La Vela Puerca and No Te Va Gustar.

Food & Drink

Uruguayan cuisine revolves around grilled meat. *Parrillas* (restaurants with big racks of meat roasting over a wood fire) are everywhere, and weekend *asados* are a national tradition. *Chivitos* are hugely popular, as are

EATING PRICE RANGES

The following price ranges are for a standard main course.

$ less than UR$300

$$ UR$300–500

$$$ more than UR$500

SLEEPING PRICE RANGES

The following price ranges refer to a double room with bathroom in high season. Breakfast is usually included in the price.

$ less than US$75

$$ US$75–150

$$$ more than US$150

chivitos al plato (served with fried potatoes instead of bread). In rural Uruguay, vegetarians often have to content themselves with the ubiquitous pizza and pasta, although vegetarian- and vegan-friendly restaurants are increasingly emerging in places like Montevideo and Colonia del Sacramento. Seafood is excellent on the coast. Desserts are heavy on meringue, *dulce de leche*, burnt sugar and custard.

Tap water is fine to drink in most places. Uruguayan wines (especially tannats) are excellent, and a small but growing lineup of craft brews is now appearing alongside traditional mass-produced beers like Patricia, Pilsen and Zillertal.

Uruguayans consume even more *mate* (a bitter tea-like beverage indigenous to South America) than Argentines. If you get the chance, try to acquire the taste – there's nothing like whiling away an afternoon with new-found friends passing around the *mate*.

Most restaurants charge *cubiertos* – small 'cover' charges that theoretically pay for the basket of bread offered before your meal.

Environment

Though one of South America's smallest countries, Uruguay is not so small by European standards. Its area of 176,215 sq km is greater than England and Wales combined, or slightly bigger than the US state of Florida.

Uruguay's two main ranges of interior hills are the Cuchilla de Haedo, west of Tacuarembó, and the Cuchilla Grande, south of Melo; neither exceeds 500m in height. West of Montevideo the terrain is more level. The Río Negro flowing through the center of the country forms a natural dividing line between north and south. The Atlantic coast has impressive beaches, dunes, headlands and lagoons. Uruguay's grasslands and forests resemble those of Argentina's pampas or southern Brazil, and patches of palm savanna persist in the east, along the Brazilian border.

The country is rich in birdlife, especially in the coastal lagoons of Rocha department. Most large land animals have disappeared, but the occasional ñandú (rhea) still races across northwestern Uruguay's grasslands. Whales, fur seals and sea lions are common along the coast.

SURVIVAL GUIDE

Directory A–Z

ACCESSIBLE TRAVEL

Uruguay is increasingly providing for travelers with special needs. In Montevideo, for example, you'll find newly constructed ramps and dedicated bathrooms in high-profile destinations such as Plaza Independencia and Teatro Solís, disabled access on some bus lines and a growing number of ATMs for the visually impaired. However, there's still a long way to go. Spanish-language websites providing useful resources for those with disabilities include pronadis.mides.gub.uy, www.accesibilidad.gub.uy and discapacidad.gub.uy.

ACCOMMODATIONS

Uruguay has an excellent network of hostels and campgrounds, especially along the Atlantic coast. Other low-end options include *hospedajes* (family homes) and *residenciales* (budget hotels).

Posadas (inns) are available in all price ranges and tend to be homier than hotels. Hotels are ranked from one to five stars, according to amenities.

Country *estancias turísticas* (marked with blue National Tourism Ministry signs) provide lodging on farms.

ACTIVITIES

Punta del Diablo, La Paloma, La Pedrera and Punta del Este all get excellent surfing waves, while Cabo Polonio and the coastal lagoons of Rocha department are great for whale-and bird-watching, respectively. Punta del Este's beach scene is more upmarket, with activities such as parasailing, windsurfing and Jet Skiing.

Horseback riding is very popular in the interior and can be arranged on most tourist *estancias*.

ELECTRICITY

Uruguay uses the same electrical plug as Argentina.

EMBASSIES & CONSULATES

The following missions are located in Montevideo.

Argentine Embassy (☎2902-8166; www.eurug.cancilleria.gov.ar; Cuareim 1470; ⏰10am-6pm Mon-Fri); **Consulate** (☎2902-8623; www.cmdeo.mrecic.gov.ar; WF Aldunate 1281; ⏰1-3pm Mon-Fri)

Australian Consulate (☎098-451451; www.dfat.gov.au/missions/countries/uy.html; 25 de Mayo 455, Piso 2; ⏰11:30am-3:30pm Mon-Fri)

Brazilian Embassy (☎2707-2119; http://montevideu.itamaraty.gov.br; Artigas 1394; ⏰10am-1pm & 3-6pm Mon-Fri); **Consulate** (☎2901-2024; http://cgmontevideu.itamaraty.gov.br; Convención 1343, 6th fl; ⏰9am-3pm Mon-Fri)

Canadian Embassy (☎2902-2030; www.uruguay.gc.ca; Plaza Independencia 749, Oficina 102; ⏰9-11am & 2-4:30pm Mon-Thu, 9-11am Fri)

French Embassy (☎1705-0000; www.ambafranceuruguay.org; Av Uruguay 853; ⏰8:30am-12:30pm & 1:30-5:30pm Mon-Thu, 8:30am-4:30pm Fri)

German Embassy (☎2902-5222; www.montevideo.diplo.de; La Cumparsita 1435; ⏰9-11:30am Mon & Wed-Fri, 1-3:30pm Tue)

New Zealand Consulate (☎2916-0900; ricardo.shaw.uy@gmail.com; Alzáibar 1305; ⏰by arrangement)

UK Embassy (☎2622-3630; www.gov.uk/world/uruguay; Marco Bruto 1073; ⏰9am-1pm & 2-5:30pm Mon-Thu, 9am-2pm Fri)

US Embassy (☎1770-2000; https://uy.usembassy.gov; Lauro Müller 1776; ⏰9am-5:30pm Mon-Fri)

HEALTH

There's a good public-health system in Uruguay. Tap water is safe to drink and there are no vaccinations required for travel here.

INSURANCE

Worldwide travel insurance is available at www.lonelyplanet.com/travel-insurance. You can buy, extend and claim online anytime – even if you're already on the road.

INTERNET ACCESS

Wi-fi zones are commonplace in cities and larger towns. Antel (state telephone company) offices sell SIM cards with reasonably priced data plans for unlocked phones, and also provide free wi-fi in many cases.

LEGAL MATTERS

Uruguay has some of Latin America's most lenient drug laws. Possession of small amounts of marijuana or other drugs for personal use has been decriminalized, but their sale remains illegal.

LGBTIQ+ TRAVELERS

Uruguay is widely considered the most LGBTIQ+-friendly nation in Latin America. In 2008 it became the first Latin American country to recognize same-sex civil unions, and in 2013 same-sex marriage was legalized. In Montevideo, look for the pocket-sized **Friendly Map** (www.friendlymap.com.uy) listing LGBTIQ+-friendly businesses throughout the country.

MONEY

ATMs widespread; credit cards widely accepted

ATMs

In all but the smallest interior towns, getting cash with your ATM card is easy. Machines marked with the green Banred or blue Redbrou logo serve all major international banking networks. ATMs dispense bills in multiples of 100 pesos. Many also dispense US dollars, designated as US$, but only in multiples of US$100.

Credit Cards

Most upmarket hotels, restaurants and shops accept credit cards. Visa is most commonly accepted, followed by MasterCard. American Express cards are of more limited use.

Exchange Rates

Argentina	AR$1	UR$1.66
Australia	A$1	UR$22.50
Brazil	R$1	UR$8.92
Canada	C$1	UR$22.76
Chile	CH$100	UR$4.63
Euro zone	€1	UR$34.00
Japan	¥100	UR$25.56
New Zealand	NZ$1	UR$20.16
UK	UK£1	UR$38.08
USA	US$1	UR$29.15

Money Changers

There are *casas de cambio* in Montevideo, Colonia, the Atlantic beach resorts and border towns such as Chuy. They typically keep longer hours than banks but may offer lower rates.

Tipping

Restaurants Leave 10% of the bill.

Taxis Round up the fare a few pesos.

WHAT'S THE BUZZ: URUGUAY'S NEW MARIJUANA LAW

In December 2013 Uruguay became the first country in the world to fully legalize cannabis. Uruguayan citizens are now allowed to grow up to six marijuana plants for personal use each year, and are entitled to purchase up to 40g per month at local pharmacies through the government's national distribution system.

Meanwhile, smoking pot in public is already legal – for anyone, foreigners included – in the same places where cigarette smoking is permitted. Paradoxically, however, non-Uruguayans are not allowed to purchase weed.

OPENING HOURS

Banks 1–6pm Monday to Friday

Bars, pubs and clubs 6pm–late; things don't get seriously shaking until after midnight

Restaurants noon–3pm and 8pm–midnight or later; if serving breakfast, open around 8am

Shops 9am–1pm and 3–7pm Monday to Saturday; in larger cities, many stay open at lunchtime and/or on Sunday

POST

Correo Uruguayo (www.correo.com.uy), the national postal service, has offices throughout Uruguay.

PUBLIC HOLIDAYS

Año Nuevo (New Year's Day) January 1

Día de los Reyes (Epiphany) January 6

Viernes Santo/Pascua (Good Friday/Easter) March/April (dates vary)

Desembarco de los 33* (Return of the 33 Exiles) April 19; honors the exiles who returned to Uruguay in 1825 to, with Argentine support, liberate the country from Brazil

Día del Trabajador (Labor Day) May 1

Batalla de Las Piedras* (Battle of Las Piedras) May 18; commemorates a major battle in the fight for independence

Natalicio de Artigas* (Artigas' Birthday) June 19

Jura de la Constitución (Constitution Day) July 18

Día de la Independencia (Independence Day) August 25

Día de la Raza* (Columbus Day) October 12

Día de los Muertos (All Souls' Day) November 2

Navidad (Christmas Day) December 25

Holidays marked with an asterisk may be celebrated on the nearest Monday to create a *puente* (long weekend).

TELEPHONE

Uruguay's country code is 598. **Antel** (www.antel.com.uy) is the state telephone company, with offices in every town.

All Uruguayan landline numbers are eight digits long, beginning with 2 for Montevideo or 4 for elsewhere in the country. Cell (mobile) phone numbers consist of a three-digit prefix (most commonly 099) followed by a six-digit number. If dialing internationally, drop the leading zero.

Cell Phones

Three companies – **Antel** (www.antel.com.uy), **Claro** (www.claro.com.uy) and **Movistar** (www.movistar.com.uy) – provide cell-phone service in Uruguay. Rather than use expensive roaming plans, many travelers bring an unlocked cell phone (or buy a cheap one here) and insert a local pay-as-you-go SIM card. SIMs can readily be purchased at Antel offices and recharged at service stations, shopping malls and streetside kiosks throughout Uruguay.

TIME

Uruguay Standard Time is three hours behind GMT, as in Argentina. Daylight-saving time was abolished in 2015.

TOURIST INFORMATION

The **National Tourism Ministry** (Ministerio de Turismo y Deporte; www.turismo.gub.uy) operates 10 offices around the country. It distributes excellent free maps for each of Uruguay's 19 departments, along with specialized information on *estancia* tourism, Carnaval, surfing and other subjects of interest to travelers. Most towns also have a municipal tourist office on the plaza or at the bus terminal.

VISAS

Nationals of Western Europe, Australia, the USA, Canada and New Zealand automatically receive a 90-day tourist card, renewable for another 90 days. Other nationals may require visas. For an official list of current visa requirements by nationality, see https://migracion.minterior.gub.uy.

VOLUNTEERING

All Uruguayan organizations that accept volunteers require a minimum commitment of one month, and many also expect at least basic Spanish proficiency.

One worthwhile group that regularly seeks international volunteers is **Karumbé** (www.karumbe.org), which promotes sea-turtle conservation in Parque Nacional Santa Teresa.

WOMEN TRAVELERS

Women are generally treated with respect, and traveling alone is safer here than in many other Latin American countries.

Getting There & Away

Most visitors cross by ferry from Buenos Aires, arriving in Colonia, Montevideo or Carmelo. A few airlines, including American, Iberia and Air Europa, offer direct international flights to Montevideo; several others connect through Buenos Aires or São Paulo. Land links include three international bridges across the Río Uruguay to Argentina, and six main border crossings into Brazil.

Border Crossings

FROM	TO	ROUTE
ARGENTINA		
Buenos Aires	Montevideo	Boat (Buquebus)
Buenos Aires	Colonia	Boat (Buquebus, Colonia Express, Seacat)
Tigre	Carmelo	Boat (Cacciola)
Gualeguaychú	Fray Bentos	Puente General San Martín (bridge)
Colón	Paysandú	Puente General Artigas (bridge)
Concordia	Salto	Represa Salto Grande (dam)
Concordia	Salto	Boat (Transporte Fluvial San Cristóbal)
BRAZIL		
Chuí	Chuy	Hwy BR-471/UR-9
Jaguarão	Río Branco	Hwy BR-116/UR-26
Aceguá	Aceguá	Hwy BR-153/UR-8
Santana do Livramento	Rivera	Hwy BR-293/UR-5
Quaraí	Artigas	Hwy BR-377/UR-30
Barra do Quaraí	Bella Unión	Hwy BR-472/UR-3

AIR

Montevideo's **Carrasco International Airport** (☎2604-0329; www.aeropuertodecarrasco.com.uy) is the main port of entry. A few direct flights from Argentina and Brazil also serve **Punta del Este International Airport** (Aeropuerto de Punta del Este; ☎4255-9777; www.puntadeleste.aero).

With the failure of former carriers Pluna and Alas Uruguay, the country no longer has a national airline, and there are no commercial domestic flights.

LAND

Uruguay shares borders with the Argentine province of Entre Ríos and the southern Brazilian state of Rio Grande do Sul. Major highways and bus services are generally good, although buses from Montevideo to Buenos Aires are slower and less convenient than the ferries across the Río de la Plata. For Iguazú Falls, traveling via Argentina is faster, cheaper and more straightforward than traveling through Brazil.

SEA

There are several ferry routes between Argentina and Uruguay, with the most popular being the one-hour crossing of the Río de la Plata between Buenos Aires and Colonia del Sacramento. Other routes include Buenos Aires to Montevideo, Tigre to Carmelo and Concordia to Salto.

Getting Around

ARRIVING IN URUGUAY

Carrasco International Airport (Montevideo) Local buses (UR$58), express buses (UR$181), shuttle vans (UR$400), taxis (UR$1200 to UR$1700) and *remises* make the 20km journey from the airport into Montevideo in 30 to 45 minutes.

Ferry Terminal (Colonia del Sacramento) Most Colonia hotels are within a 10- to 15-minute walk or a five-minute taxi ride of the ferry terminal. The long-distance bus station is one block northeast of the port. Rental-car agencies are clustered between the ferry terminal and the bus station.

Ferry Terminal (Montevideo) Ferries from Argentina dock just north of the Mercado del Puerto in Ciudad Vieja. Taxis queue outside the ferry terminal and can take you anywhere in the city within five to 15 minutes (UR$100 to UR$250, depending on destination).

BUS

Buses are comfortable, the government-regulated fares are reasonable and distances are short. Many companies offer free wi-fi on board. In the few cities that lack terminals, all companies are within easy walking distance of each other, usually around the main plaza.

Reservations are unnecessary except during holiday periods. On peak travel dates a single company may run multiple departures at the same hour, in which case they'll mark a bus number on your ticket; check with the driver to make sure you're boarding the right bus, or you may find yourself in the 'right' seat on the wrong bus!

Most towns with central bus terminals have a reasonably priced left-luggage facility.

CAR & MOTORCYCLE

Visitors to Uruguay who are staying less than 90 days need only bring a valid driver's license from their home country. Uruguayan drivers are extremely considerate, and even bustling Montevideo is quite sedate compared with Buenos Aires.

Due to government regulation, all service stations, including the ubiquitous state-owned Ancap, charge the same price for fuel. At the time of research, regular unleaded gasoline cost UR$45.90 per liter, premium UR$47.60 per liter.

Car Hire

Economy cars rent locally for upwards of UR$1500 a day in high season, with tax and insurance included. Advance online bookings are often significantly cheaper than in-country rentals. Most credit-card companies' automatic LDW (loss-damage-waiver) insurance covers rentals in Uruguay.

Road Rules & Hazards

Drivers are required to turn on their headlights during the daytime on all highways. In most towns, alternating one-way streets are the rule, with an arrow marking the allowed direction of travel.

Outside Montevideo, most intersections have neither a stop sign nor a traffic light; right of way is determined by who reaches the corner first. This can be nerve-racking for the uninitiated!

Main highways fanning out from Montevideo are generally in excellent condition, especially Ruta 1 to Colonia del Sacramento and Ruta 9 (the Interbalnearia) to Punta del Este. Outside the capital and coastal tourist areas, traffic is minimal and poses few problems, though some interior roads can be rough. Keep an eye out for livestock and wildlife.

Speed limits are clearly posted but rarely enforced. Arbitrary police stops are rare.

LOCAL TRANSPORTATION

Taxis, *remises* and local buses are similar to those in Argentina. Taxis are metered; between 10pm and 6am, and on Sundays and holidays, fares are 20% higher. There's a small additional charge for luggage, and passengers generally tip the driver by rounding fares up to the next multiple of five or 10 pesos. Uber and similar ride-sharing services are also widely used in Montevideo. City bus service is excellent in Montevideo and other urban areas, while *micros* (minibuses) form the backbone of the local transit network in smaller coastal towns such as La Paloma.

Understand Argentina

History

A vast country holding a diverse population, Argentina has a tumultuous past, at points tainted by periods of despotic rule, corruption and hard times. But its history is also illustrious, the story of a country that fought off Spanish colonial rule to become a world economic powerhouse – for a while. Argentina gave birth to international icons such as the gaucho, Evita Perón and Che Guevara. Understanding its past is essential to understanding its present and even Argentines themselves.

Native Peoples

Many different native peoples ranged throughout what became Argentina. On the pampas lived the hunter-gatherer Querandí, and in the north the Guaraní were semisedentary agriculturalists and fishermen. In the Lake District and Patagonia, the Pehuenches and Puelches gathered the pine nuts of the araucaria, while the Mapuche entered the region from the west as the Spanish pushed south. Today there are several Mapuche reservations, mostly in the area around Junín de los Andes.

Until they were wiped out by Europeans, there were indigenous inhabitants as far south as Tierra del Fuego (Land of Fire), where the Selk'nam, Haush, Yahgan and Alacaluf peoples lived as mobile hunters and gatherers. Despite frequently inclement weather, they wore little or no clothing; frequent fires kept them warm and gave the region its name.

Of all of Argentina, the northwest was the most developed. Several indigenous groups, notably the Diaguita, practiced irrigated agriculture in the valleys of the eastern Andean foothills. Inhabitants were influenced by the Tiahuanaco empire of Bolivia and by the great Inca empire, which expanded south from Peru from the early 1480s. In Salta province the ruined city of Quilmes is one of the best-preserved pre-Incan sites.

Argentina's native peoples hunted guanaco and ñandú (a large bird resembling an emu) with various weapons, including *boleadoras*. These weighted balls were thrown to ensnare a prey's legs. Today, replica *boleadoras* are sold at artisan shops throughout the country.

Enter the Spanish

Just over a decade after Christopher Columbus accidentally encountered the Americas, other European explorers began probing the Río de la Plata estuary. Most early explorations of the area were motivated by rumors of vast quantities of silver. Spaniard Sebastian Cabot optimistically

TIMELINE

10,000 BCE

Humans, having crossed the Bering Strait approximately 20,000 years earlier, finally reach the area of modern-day Argentina. The close of one of the world's greatest human migrations nears.

7370 BCE

Toldense culture makes its first paintings of hands inside Patagonia's famous Cueva de las Manos. The paintings prove humans inhabited the region this far back.

4000 BCE

The indigenous Yahgan, later referred to as Fuegians by the English-speaking world, begin populating the southernmost islands of Tierra del Fuego. Humans could migrate no further south.

named the river Río de la Plata (River of Silver), and to drive the rumors home, part of the new territory was even given the Latin name for silver *(argentum)*. But the mineral riches that the Spanish found in the Inca empire of Peru never panned out in this misnamed land.

The first real attempt at establishing a permanent settlement on the estuary was made in 1536, by Spanish aristocrat Pedro de Mendoza. He landed at present-day Buenos Aires, but after the colonists tried pilfering food from the indigenous Querandí, the natives turned on them violently. Within four years Mendoza had fled back to Spain without a lick of silver, and the detachment of troops he left behind headed upriver to the gentler environs of Asunción, present-day capital of Paraguay.

Northwest Supremacy

Although Spanish forces had re-established Buenos Aires by 1580, it remained a backwater in comparison to Andean settlements founded by a separate and more successful Spanish contingent moving south from Alto Perú (now Bolivia). With ties to the colonial stronghold of Lima and financed by the bonanza silver mine at Potosí, the Spanish founded some two dozen cities as far south as Mendoza (1561) during the latter half of the 16th century.

The two most important centers were Tucumán (founded in 1565) and Córdoba (1573). Tucumán lay in the heart of a rich agricultural region and supplied Alto Perú with grains, cotton and livestock. Córdoba became an important educational center, and Jesuit missionaries established *estancias* (ranches) in the sierras to supply Alto Perú with mules, foodstuffs and wine. Córdoba's Manzana Jesuítica (Jesuit Block) is now the finest preserved group of colonial buildings in the country, and several Jesuit *estancias* in the Central Sierras are also preserved. These sites, along with the central plazas of Salta (founded in 1582), boast the finest colonial architecture.

The Mission (1986), starring Robert De Niro and Jeremy Irons, is an epic film about the Jesuit missions and missionaries in 18th-century South America. It's the perfect kickoff for a trip to northern Argentina's missions.

Buenos Aires: Bootlegger to Boomtown

As the northwest prospered, Buenos Aires suffered the Crown's harsh restrictions on trade for nearly 200 years. But because the port was ideal for trade, frustrated merchants turned to smuggling, and contraband trade with Portuguese Brazil and nonpeninsular European powers flourished. The wealth passing through the city fueled its initial growth.

With the decline of silver mining at Potosí in the late 18th century, the Spanish Crown was forced to recognize Buenos Aires' importance for direct transatlantic trade. Relaxing its restrictions, Spain made Buenos Aires the capital of the new viceroyalty of the Río de la Plata – which included Paraguay, Uruguay and the mines at Potosí – in 1776.

1480s CE

The Inca empire expands into present-day Argentina's Andean northwest. At the time the region was inhabited by Argentina's most advanced indigenous cultures, including the Diaguita and Tafí.

1536

Pedro de Mendoza establishes Puerto Nuestra Señora Santa María del Buen Aire on the Río de la Plata. But the Spaniards anger the indigenous Querandí, who soon drive the settlers out.

1553

Francisco de Aguirre establishes Santiago del Estero, furthering Spain's expansion into present-day Argentina from Alto Perú. Today the city is the country's oldest permanent settlement.

1561

The city of Mendoza is founded by Spaniards during their push to establish access to the Río de la Plata, where Spanish ships could deliver more troops and supplies.

The new viceroyalty had internal squabbles over trade and control issues, but when the British raided the city in 1806 and again in 1807 (in an attempt to seize control of Spanish colonies during the Napoleonic Wars), the response was unified. Locals rallied against the invaders without Spanish help and chased them out of town.

The Spanish slave trade in the 18th and 19th centuries brought a significant African population to Argentina, particularly Buenos Aires province, to labor in agriculture, livestock and domestic work. While cholera and yellow fever epidemics, as well as their participation in the Argentine War of Independence, wiped out much of the population, Africans made significant contributions to Argentine culture.

The late 18th century also saw the emergence of the gauchos of the pampas. The South American counterpart to North America's cowboys, they hunted wild cattle and broke in wild horses whose numbers had multiplied after being left behind by expeditions on the Río de la Plata.

One of the best-known contemporary accounts of post-independence Argentina is Domingo Faustino Sarmiento's *Life in the Argentine Republic in the Days of the Tyrants* (1868). Also superb is his seminal classic *Facundo: Civilization and Barbarism* (1845).

Independence & Infighting

Toward the end of the 18th century, criollos (Argentine-born colonists) became increasingly dissatisfied and impatient with Spanish authority. The expulsion of British troops from Buenos Aires gave the people of the Río de la Plata new confidence in their ability to stand alone. After Napoleon invaded Spain in 1808, Buenos Aires finally declared its independence on May 25, 1810.

Independence movements throughout South America soon united to expel Spain from the continent by the 1820s. Under the leadership of General José de San Martín and others, the United Provinces of the Río de la Plata (the direct forerunner of the Argentine republic) declared formal independence at Tucumán on July 9, 1816.

Despite achieving independence, the provinces were united in name only. With a lack of any effective central authority, regional disparities within Argentina – formerly obscured by Spanish rule – became more obvious. This resulted in the rise of the *caudillos* (local strongmen), who resisted Buenos Aires as strongly as Buenos Aires had resisted Spain.

Argentine politics was divided between the Federalists of the interior, who advocated provincial autonomy, and the Unitarists of Buenos Aires, who upheld the city's central authority. For almost 20 years bloody conflicts between the two factions left the country nearly exhausted.

The Reign of Rosas

In the first half of the 19th century Juan Manuel de Rosas came to prominence as a *caudillo* in Buenos Aires province, representing the interests of rural elites and landowners. He became governor of the province in 1829 and, while he championed the Federalist cause, he also helped cen-

1573

The city of Córdoba is founded by Tucumán governor Jerónimo Luis de Cabrera, establishing an important link on the trade routes between Chile and Alto Perú.

1580

Buenos Aires is re-established by Spanish forces, but the city remains a backwater for years, in comparison with the growing strongholds of Mendoza, Tucumán and Santiago del Estero.

1609

Jesuits begin building missions in northeast Argentina, including San Ignacio Miní (1610), Loreto (1632) and Santa Ana (1633), concentrating the indigenous Guaraní into settlements known as *reducciones.*

1767

The Spanish Crown expels the Jesuits from all of New Spain, and the mission communities decline rapidly.

tralize political power in Buenos Aires and proclaimed that all international trade be funneled through the capital. His reign lasted more than 20 years (to 1852), and he set ominous precedents in Argentine political life, creating the infamous mazorca (his ruthless political police force) and institutionalizing torture.

Under Rosas, Buenos Aires continued to dominate the new country, but his extremism turned many against him, including some of his strongest allies. Finally, in 1852 a rival *caudillo* named Justo José de Urquiza (once a staunch supporter of Rosas) organized a powerful army and forced Rosas from power. Urquiza's first task was to draw up a constitution, which was formalized by a convention in Santa Fe on May 1, 1853.

Between 1833 and 1835, Charles Darwin explored Argentina during his voyage around the world as a young naturalist. He observed human customs, local flora and fauna, fossils and geological aspects of the region.

The Fleeting Golden Age

Elected the Republic of Argentina's first official president in 1862, Bartolomé Mitre was concerned with building the nation and establishing infrastructure. His goals, however, were subsumed by the War of the Triple Alliance (or Paraguayan War), which lasted from 1864 to 1870. Not until Domingo Faustino Sarmiento, an educator and journalist from San Juan, became president did progress in Argentina really kick in.

Buenos Aires' economy boomed and immigrants poured in from Spain, Italy, Germany and Eastern Europe. The new residents worked in the port area, lived tightly in the tenement buildings and developed Buenos Aires' famous dance – the tango – in the brothels and smoky nightclubs of the port. Elsewhere in the country, Basque and Irish refugees became the first shepherds, as both sheep numbers and wool exports increased nearly tenfold between 1850 and 1880.

Still, much of the southern pampas and Patagonia were inaccessible for settlers because of resistance from indigenous Mapuche and Tehueche. In 1878 General Julio Argentino Roca carried out an extermination campaign against the indigenous people, in what is known as the Conquista del Desierto (Conquest of the Desert). The campaign doubled the area under state control and opened Patagonia to settlement and sheep.

By the turn of the 20th century Argentina had a highly developed rail network (financed largely by British capital), fanning out from Buenos Aires in all directions. Still, the dark cloud of a vulnerable economy loomed. Industry could not absorb all the immigration, labor unrest grew and imports surpassed exports. Finally, with the onset of the worldwide Great Depression, the military took power under conditions of considerable social unrest. An obscure but oddly visionary colonel, Juan Domingo Perón, was the first leader to try to come to grips with the country's economic crisis.

Tomás Eloy Martínez' *The Perón Novel* (1998) is a fascinating, fictionalized version of the life of ex-president Juan Perón, culminating in his return to Buenos Aires in 1973.

1776

Spain names Buenos Aires the capital of the new viceroyalty of the Río de la Plata. The territory includes the areas of present-day Paraguay, Uruguay and the mines at Potosí (Bolivia).

1806–07

Attempting to seize control of Spanish colonies, British forces raid Buenos Aires in 1806 and in 1807. Buenos Aires militias defeat British troops without Spain's help, which kindles ideas of independence.

May 25, 1810

Buenos Aires declares its independence from Spain, although actual independence is still several years off. The city names the Plaza de Mayo in honor of the event.

July 9, 1816

After successful independence movements throughout South America, the United Provinces of the Río de la Plata (Argentina's forerunner) declares formal independence from Spain at Tucumán.

Juan Perón

Juan Perón emerged in the 1940s to become Argentina's most revered, as well as most despised, political figure. He first came to national prominence as head of the National Department of Labor, after a 1943 military coup toppled civilian rule. With the help of his second wife, Eva Duarte (Evita), he ran for and won the presidency in 1946.

During previous sojourns in fascist Italy and Nazi Germany, Perón had grasped the importance of spectacle in public life and also developed his own brand of watered-down Mussolini-style fascism. He held massive rallies from the balcony of the Casa Rosada, with the equally charismatic Evita at his side. Although they ruled by decree rather than consent, the Peróns legitimized the trade-union movement, extended political rights to working-class people, secured voting rights for women and made university education available to any capable individual. Of course, many of these social policies made him disliked by conservatives and the rich classes.

Many Nazi fugitives, including former SS officials, were welcomed to Argentina by Perón. Most assumed quiet lives of anonymity. In 1960 Adolf Eichmann, the mastermind of the Nazi final solution logistics, was taken off the streets by Mossad agents to stand trial in Israel. Josef Mengele fled onward to Paraguay.

Economic hardship and inflation undermined Juan Perón's second presidency in 1952, and Evita's death the same year dealt a blow to both the country and the president's popularity. In 1955 a military coup sent him into exile in Spain. Thirty years of catastrophic military rule would follow.

During his exile, Perón plotted his return to Argentina. In the late 1960s increasing economic problems, strikes, political kidnappings and guerrilla warfare marked Argentine political life. In the midst of these events, Perón returned to Argentina and was voted president again in 1973; however, after an 18-year exile, there was no substance to his rule. Chronically ill, Perón died in mid-1974, leaving a fragmented country to his ill-qualified third wife, Isabel.

The Military Dictatorship & the Disappeared

In the late 1960s and early 1970s, antigovernment feeling was rife and street protests often exploded into all-out riots. Armed guerrilla organizations emerged as radical opponents of the military, the oligarchies and US influence in Latin America. With increasing official corruption exacerbating Isabel Perón's incompetence, Argentina found itself plunged into chaos.

1829

Federalist *caudillo* Juan Manuel de Rosas becomes governor of Buenos Aires province and de facto ruler of the Argentine Confederation. He rules with an iron fist for more than 20 years.

1852

Federalist and former Rosas ally Justo José de Urquiza defeats Rosas at the Battle of Caseros and, in 1853, draws up Argentina's first constitution.

1862

Bartolomé Mitre is elected president of the newly titled Republic of Argentina and strives to modernize the country by expanding the railway network, creating a national army and postal system, and more.

1864–70

The War of the Triple Alliance is fought between Paraguay and the allied countries of Argentina, Brazil and Uruguay. Paraguay is defeated and loses territory.

On March 24, 1976, a military coup led by army general Jorge Rafael Videla took control of the Argentine state apparatus and ushered in a period of terror and brutality. Videla's sworn aim was to crush the guerrilla movements and restore social order. During what the regime euphemistically labeled the Process of National Reorganization (known as 'El Proceso'), security forces went about the country arresting, torturing and killing anyone on their hit list of suspected leftists.

During the period between 1976 and 1983, human-rights groups estimate that 30,000 people 'disappeared.' Ironically, the dictatorship ended only when the Argentine military attempted a real military operation: liberating the Falkland Islands (Islas Malvinas) from British rule.

EVITA, LADY OF HOPE

'I will come again, and I will be millions.'

Eva Perón, 1952

From her humble origins in the pampas to her rise to power beside President Juan Perón, María Eva Duarte de Perón is one of history's most revered political figures. Known affectionately as Evita, Argentina's most beloved First Lady even eclipsed the legacy of her husband, who governed Argentina from 1946 to 1955.

At the age of 15 Eva Duarte left her hometown of Junín for Buenos Aires. Looking for work as an actor, she eventually landed a job in radio. In 1944 she attended a benefit at Buenos Aires' Luna Park and met Colonel Juan Perón. He fell in love with her and they married in 1945.

Shortly after Perón won the presidency in 1946, Evita went to work in the office of the Department of Labor and Welfare. During Perón's two terms, Evita empowered her husband through her charisma and outreach to the nation's poor, who came to love her dearly. She built housing for the poor, created programs for children, and distributed clothing and food items to needy families. She campaigned for the aged, offered health services to the poor and advocated for a law extending suffrage to women.

Perón won his second term in 1952, but that same year Evita – at age 33 and at the height of her popularity – died of cancer. It was a blow to Argentina and her husband's presidency.

Although remembered for extending social justice to those she called the country's *descamisados* (shirtless ones), Evita and her husband ruled with an iron fist. They jailed opposition leaders and newspapers, and banned *Time* magazine when it referred to her as an 'illegitimate child.' However, there is no denying the extent to which she empowered women at all levels of Argentine society and helped the country's poor.

Today Evita enjoys near-saint status. Get to know her at Museo Evita, or visit her tomb in the Recoleta cemetery; both are in Buenos Aires. Or read her ghostwritten autobiography *La razón de mi vida* (My Mission in Life; 1951).

1865

More than 150 Welsh immigrants traveling aboard the clipper *Mimosa* land in Patagonia and establish Argentina's first Welsh colony in the province of Chubut.

1868

Domingo Faustino Sarmiento, an educator and journalist from San Juan, is elected president. He encourages immigration to Argentina, ramps up public education and pushes to Europeanize the country.

1869–95

The Argentine economy booms, immigration skyrockets as Italian and Spanish immigrants flood in, and Buenos Aires' population grows from 90,000 to 670,000. The tango emerges in Buenos Aires.

1926

Novelist and poet Ricardo Güiraldes publishes *Don Segundo Sombra*, a classic work of gaucho literature evoking the spirit of the gaucho and its impact on Argentine society.

The Falklands War

In late 1981 General Leopoldo Galtieri assumed the role of president. To stay in power amid a faltering economy and mass social unrest, Galtieri played the nationalist card and launched an invasion in April 1982 to dislodge the British from the Falkland Islands, which had been claimed by Argentina as its own Islas Malvinas for nearly 150 years. Since it had been a British colony from 1841, a majority of the islands' residents were English speakers who favored British sovereignty.

However, Galtieri underestimated the determined response of British Prime Minister Margaret Thatcher. After only 74 days Argentina's ill-trained, poorly motivated and mostly teenaged forces surrendered ignominiously. The military regime collapsed, and in 1983 Argentines elected civilian Raúl Alfonsín to the presidency.

The Falklands War is still a somewhat touchy subject in Argentina. To avoid any verbal brawls, it's polite to call them the 'Malvinas' instead of the 'Falklands.'

Aftermath of the Military Dictatorship

In his successful 1983 presidential campaign, Alfonsín pledged to prosecute military officers responsible for human-rights violations during the military dictatorship of 1976 to 1983. He convicted high-ranking junta officials for kidnapping, torture and homicide, but when the government attempted to try junior officers, these officers responded with uprisings in several parts of the country. The timid administration succumbed to military demands and produced the Ley de la Obediencia Debida (Law of Due Obedience), allowing lower-ranking officers to use the defense that they were following orders, as well as the Ley de Punto Final (Full Stop Law), declaring dates beyond which no criminal or civil prosecutions could take place. At the time these measures prevented the prosecution of notorious individuals; in 2003, however, they were repealed.

Military dictatorship crime cases have since been reopened. Since 2003, several officers have been convicted for crimes. Despite these arrests, many of the leaders of El Proceso remained free, both in Argentina and abroad. In late 2017 the federal court in Buenos Aires made a final reckoning in the several-years-long ESMA detention center trials, indicting 54 people and sentencing 29 former military officials to life in prison for kidnapping, torture and murder.

The Menem Years

Carlos Saúl Menem was elected president in 1989, and quickly embarked on a period of radical free-market reform. In pegging the peso to the US dollar, he effectively created a period of false economic stability, one that would create a great deal of upward mobility among Argentina's middle class. However, his policies – which included privatization of state-owned companies – are widely blamed for Argentina's economic collapse in 2002, when the overvalued peso was considerably devalued.

1946

Juan Perón is elected president and makes changes to the Argentine political structure. Eva Perón embarks on her social-assistance programs to help lower-class women and children.

1952

Eva Perón dies of cancer on July 26 at age 33, one year into her husband's second term as president. Her death would severely weaken the political might of her husband.

1955

After the economy slides into recession President Perón loses further political clout and is finally thrown from the presidency and exiled to Spain after another military coup.

1976–83

Under the leadership of General Jorge Videla, a military junta takes control of Argentina. In eight years an estimated 30,000 people 'disappear.'

Menem's presidency ran until 1999, and in 2003 he made another presidential bid – only to withdraw after the first round. He then became a senator for his home province of La Rioja in 2005 (but two years later failed to win the governorship). All the while, Menem's post-presidential career was characterized by scandals. In 2013 he was sentenced to seven years in prison for illegally dealing arms to Croatia and Ecuador (the conviction was overturned in 2018), and in 2015 he was sentenced to 4½ years in prison for embezzling public funds back in the 1990s. However, his position as senator granted him immunity from incarceration. Menem remained a senator for La Rioja until his death in February 2021 at the age of 90.

Carlos Menem's Syrian ancestry earned him the nickname 'El Turco' (The Turk). In 2001 he married Cecilia Bolocco, a former Miss Universe who is 35 years his junior; they're now divorced.

LAS MADRES DE LA PLAZA DE MAYO

In 1977, after a year of brutal human-rights violations under the leadership of General Jorge Rafael Videla, 14 mothers marched into the Plaza de Mayo in Buenos Aires. They did this despite the military government's ban on public gatherings and despite its reputation for torturing and killing anyone it considered dissident. The mothers, wearing their now-iconic white head scarves, demanded information about their missing children, who had 'disappeared' as part of the government's efforts to quash political opposition.

The group, which took on the name Las Madres de la Plaza de Mayo (The Mothers of Plaza de Mayo), developed into a powerful social movement and was the only political organization that overtly challenged the military government. Las Madres were particularly effective as they carried out their struggle under the banner of motherhood, which made them relatively unassailable in Argentine culture. Their movement showed the power of women – at least in a traditional role – in Argentine culture, and they are generally credited with helping to kick-start the re-establishment of the country's civil society.

After Argentina's return to civilian rule in 1983, thousands of Argentines were still unaccounted for, and Las Madres continued their marches and their demands for information and retribution. In 1986 Las Madres split into two factions. One group, known as the Línea Fundadora (Founding Line), dedicated itself to recovering the remains of the disappeared and to bringing military perpetrators to justice. The other, known as the Asociación Madres de Plaza de Mayo, held its last yearly protest in January 2006, saying it no longer had an enemy in the presidential seat. Línea Fundadora, however, still holds a silent vigil every Thursday afternoon in remembrance of the disappeared – and to protest other social causes.

And there is hope: in 2014 one of the most famous and respected grandmothers, Estela Carlotto, finally found her grandson after 36 years of searching. Argentina cried with her in joy – and perhaps in the hope of more future reunions.

1982

With the economy on the brink of collapse once again, General Leopoldo Galtieri invades the Falkland Islands/Islas Malvinas, unleashing a wave of nationalism and distracting the country from its problems.

1983

After the failure of the Falklands War and with an economy on the skids, Raúl Alfonsín is elected the first civilian leader of the country since 1976.

1989

Peronist Carlos Menem succeeds Alfonsín as president and overcomes the hyperinflation that reached nearly 200% per month by instituting free-market reforms.

1999–2000

Fernando de la Rua succeeds Menem as president, inheriting a failing economy. Agricultural exports slump and strikes begin throughout the country. The IMF grants Argentina US$40 million in aid.

Nunca más (Never Again; 1984), the official report of the National Commission on the Disappeared, systematically details military abuses from 1976 to 1983 during Argentina's Dirty War.

'La Crisis'

Fernando de la Rua succeeded Menem in the 1999 elections, inheriting an unstable economy and US$114 billion in foreign debt. With the Argentine peso pegged to the US dollar, Argentina was unable to compete on the international market and exports slumped. A further decline in international prices of agricultural products pummeled the Argentine economy, which depended heavily on farm-product exports.

By 2001 the Argentine economy teetered on the brink of collapse, and the administration, with Minister of Economy Domingo Cavallo at the wheel, took measures to end deficit spending and slash state spending. After attempted debt swaps and talk of devaluing the peso, middle-class Argentines began emptying their bank accounts. Cavallo responded by placing a cap of US$250 per week on withdrawals, but it was the beginning of the end.

By mid-December unemployment hit 18.3% and unions began a nationwide strike. Things came to a head on December 20 when middle-class Argentines took to the streets in protest against de la Rua's handling of the economic situation. Rioting spread throughout the country and President de la Rua resigned. Three interim presidents had resigned by the time Eduardo Duhalde took office in January 2002, becoming the fifth president in two weeks. Duhalde devalued the peso and announced that Argentina would default on US$140 billion in foreign debt, the biggest default in world history.

Enter Néstor Kirchner

Duhalde's minister of economy, Roberto Lavagna, negotiated a deal with the IMF in which Argentina would pay only the interest on its debts. Simultaneously, devaluation of the peso meant that Argentina's products were suddenly affordable on the world market, and by 2003 exports were booming. The surge was great for the country's GNP, but prices at home skyrocketed, plunging more of Argentina's already shaken middle class into poverty.

A presidential election was finally held in April 2003, and Santa Cruz Governor Néstor Kirchner emerged victorious after his opponent, former president Carlos Menem, bowed out of the election.

By the end of his term in 2007, Kirchner had become one of Argentina's most popular presidents. He reversed amnesty laws that protected members of the 1976–83 junta against being charged for atrocities committed during the military dictatorship of 1976 to 1983. He took a strong stance against government corruption and steered the economy away from strict alignment with the US (realigning it with Argentina's South American neighbors). And in 2005 he paid off Argentina's entire debt

2002

Interim president Eduardo Duhalde devalues the peso, and Argentina defaults on a US$140-billion international debt (US$800 million owed to the World Bank), the largest default in history.

2003

Néstor Kirchner is elected president of Argentina after Carlos Menem bows out of the presidential race, despite winning more votes in the first round of elections.

2007

Former First Lady Cristina Fernández de Kirchner is elected president.

2010

Néstor Kirchner dies suddenly, dealing a serious blow to the Kirchner dynasty. Many thought he would run for president in 2011, and likely win.

to the IMF in a single payment. By the end of Kirchner's presidency in 2007, unemployment had fallen to just under 9% – from a high of nearly 25% in 2002.

But not everything was bread and roses. The fact that Argentina had repaid its debt was fantastic news indeed, but economic stability didn't necessarily follow. In fact, a series of problems ensued during Kirchner's presidency: high inflation rates caused by a growing energy shortage, unequal distribution of wealth, and a rising breach between rich and poor that was slowly obliterating the middle class.

However, things were going well enough for Kirchner. When the presidential seat was up for grabs in 2007, Argentines expressed their satisfaction with Kirchner's policies by electing his wife, well-known senator Cristina Fernández de Kirchner, as president. Cristina won the presidency with a whopping 22% margin over her nearest challenger and became Argentina's first elected female president.

Hectór Olivera's 1983 film *Funny Dirty Little War* is an unsettling but excellent black comedy set in a fictitious town just before the 1976 military coup.

The Trials & Tribulations of Cristina

Weak opposition and her husband's enduring clout contributed to Cristina's clear-cut victory, despite the lack of straightforward policies during her campaign. While this was not the first time Argentina had had a female head of state (Isabel Perón held a brief presidency by inheriting her husband's term), Cristina was the first woman to be elected president by popular vote in Argentina. As a lawyer and senator she was often compared to Hillary Clinton; as a fashion-conscious political figure with a penchant for chic dresses and designer bags, she also evoked memories of Evita.

On October 27, 2010, Néstor Kirchner died suddenly of a heart attack. It was a disaster for the Kirchner dynasty, but the country rallied around Cristina's sorrow and she was easily re-elected in early 2011. Her platform appealed to the populist vote, promising to raise incomes, restore industry and maintain Argentina's economic boom. The approach worked like a charm, but her acclaim wasn't to last.

From October 2011, in an effort to curb capital heading overseas, the government required Argentines to substantiate their purchases of US dollars. This is what had created the black market for US dollars, which are highly sought after as a stable currency. And the real-estate market stalled, since purchases were pretty much always transacted in US dollars.

Cristina's tumultuous presidency was laced with scandals, unpopular decisions and roller-coaster approval ratings, along with inflation unofficially estimated at up to 30%. Yet her presidency also saw some positive sides, including a stronger economy during the first part of her

At least two terms came about due to Argentina's economic crisis: *el corralito* (a small enclosure) refers to the cap placed on cash withdrawals from bank accounts during 'La Crisis,' while *cacerolazo* (from the word *cacerola*, meaning pan) is the street protest where angry people bang pots and pans.

2011

Cristina Kirchner wins the presidential re-election race; her politics move away from the traditional Justicialist Party, favoring young upstarts La Cámpora, led by her son Máximo Kirchner.

2012

Inflation is running at about 25%, though the government's official figures say that it's less than 10%. Kirchner passes a law restricting the sale of US dollars, creating huge black-market demand.

January 2015

State prosecutor Alberto Nisman is found shot dead in his apartment. He had accused Cristina Kirchner of covering up 1994's AMIA (Jewish community center) bombing investigation.

November 2015

Buenos Aires mayor Mauricio Macri wins the presidential election against Daniel Scioli, in Argentina's first-ever presidential run-off vote.

tenure, the strengthening of certain social programs, and the legalization of same-sex marriage in July 2010.

An Argentine Pope & Progressive Change

After Cardinal Jorge Mario Bergoglio, the archbishop of Buenos Aires, was named pope in March 2013 he took the name Francis I. In Argentina national pride swelled: Francis was the first pope from the Americas and no doubt also the first to have grown up drinking *mate* and ardently supporting San Lorenzo *fútbol* club. As pope, he criticized capitalism and consumerism, and supported action on climate change. Nonetheless, his views still opposed the ordination of women, abortion and same-sex marriage, though he notably addressed homosexuality by asking, 'Who am I to judge?'

Meanwhile, the narrow victory of pro-business, free-market-reform candidate Mauricio Macri in the 2015 presidential election looks to have been no more than a neoliberal blip in the long run of populist governments in Argentina. In 2019 Macri was beaten at the polls by center-left candidate Alberto Fernández and his running mate, Cristina Kirchner, who returned to the role of vice president. The legalization of abortion had been among Fernández's election promises, and in December 2020 the senate voted to approve the new law. Momentum for change had been building in the form of a grassroots movement which saw women take to the streets to demand an end to violence against women and access to legal abortions. In 2021 the Fernández government also introduced new public sector jobs quotas for transgender people, adding to what was already some of the world's most progressive trans rights legislation.

November 2017

A naval submarine with 44 crew members disappears off the coast of Patagonia: its fatal malfunction alerts the public to the deteriorating military infrastructure.

October 2019

Center-left candidate Alberto Fernández defeats incumbent Mauricio Macri in the presidential race. Cristina Fernández de Kirchner returns to office as vice president.

November 2020

Three days of national mourning are declared after footballer Diego Maradona dies of a heart attack, aged 60. Thousands of grieving fans gather in Buenos Aires to pay their respects.

December 2020

The senate approves legislation that legalizes abortion in Argentina. The new law follows a five-year campaign by Argentina's grassroots women's rights movement.

Life in Argentina

Throughout Latin America, Argentines endure a reputation for being cocky. 'How does an Argentine commit suicide?' goes the old joke. 'By jumping off his ego.' And while you might find a nugget of truth in this stereotype – which applies mainly to *porteños* (Buenos Aires residents) – you'll also realize that a warm and gregarious social nature more accurately defines the Argentine psyche. In addition, Argentines are survivors who gracefully persevere through the many ups and downs of their economy with aplomb.

Regional Identity

Opinionated, brash and passionate, Argentines are quick to engage in conversation and will talk after dinner or over coffee until the wee hours of the morning. For outsiders, there's charm in their quickness to engage and their human warmth. They are probably the most loquacious of South Americans, but they also hold a subtle broodiness to their nature that manifests everywhere from the country's melancholy tangos to its atmospheric literature. This characteristic stems from a cynicism they've acquired as they've watched their country, one of the world's economic powerhouses during the late 19th and early 20th centuries, descend into a morass of international debt. Argentines are fighters, always working to improve their situation, but every financial recovery feels precarious. They've endured military coups and severe government repression, while witnessing their nation plundered by corrupt politicians. But their melancholy is just a part of the picture. Add everything together and you get a society full of people who are fun, fiery and proud. And you'll come to love them for it.

Argentines almost always exchange a kiss on the cheek in greeting – even between men. In formal and business situations, though, it is better to go with a handshake.

Lifestyle

Although Buenos Aires holds more than one-third of the country's population, it's surprisingly unlike the rest of Argentina or, for that matter, much of Latin America. As is the case throughout the country, one's lifestyle in the capital depends mostly on money. A modern flat rented by a young advertising creative in Buenos Aires' Las Cañitas neighborhood differs greatly from a family home in one of the city's impoverished *villas* (shantytowns), where electricity and clean water are luxuries.

Geography and ethnicity also play important roles. Both of these Buenos Aires homes have little in common with that of an indigenous family living in an adobe house in a desolate valley of the Andean Northwest, where life is eked out through subsistence agriculture. In regions such as the pampas, Mendoza province and Patagonia, a provincial friendliness surrounds a robust, outdoor lifestyle. In Patagonia, many residents feel more affinity for their Chilean counterparts living at the same latitude with ranching traditions than for their brethren living in the capital.

Argentina's workforce is 55% female, and women currently occupy 40% of Argentina's congressional seats.

Argentina has a reasonably sized middle class, though it has been shrinking significantly in recent years, and poverty has grown. Nonetheless, compared with much of the region, the country boasts decent public education and access to healthcare and higher education. At the other end of the spectrum, wealthy city dwellers have moved into *countries* (gated communities) in surprising numbers and live lifestyles more on a par with those of their international counterparts.

One thing that all Argentines have in common is their devotion to family. City executives join family for weekend dinners, and the cafe owner in San Juan meets friends out at the family *estancia* (ranch) for a Sunday *asado* (barbecue). Children commonly live with their parents until they're married, especially within households of limited means.

The Sporting Life

Fútbol (soccer) is an integral part of Argentines' lives, and on game day you'll know it by the cheers and yells emanating from shops and cafes. The national team has reached the World Cup final five times and has triumphed twice, in 1978 and 1986. The Argentine team also won Olympic gold twice, at the 2004 and 2008 games. The most popular teams are Boca Juniors and River Plate (there are around two dozen professional teams in Buenos Aires alone) and the fanatical behavior of the country's *barra brava* (hooligans) rivals that of their European counterparts. Among the best-known *fútbol* players are Diego Maradona, Gabriel Batistuta, and of course Lionel Messi, who has been voted FIFA's best player of the year five times.

Jimmy Burns' *Hand of God* (1997) is the definitive book about football legend Diego Maradona and makes a great read – even if you're not a soccer fanatic.

Rugby's popularity has increased in Argentina ever since Los Pumas, the national team, beat France in the first game of the 2007 Rugby World Cup and again in the play-off for third place. The Pumas also made it to the semifinals of the 2015 World Cup, another huge accomplishment.

Horse racing, tennis, basketball, golf and boxing are also popular. Argentina has the top polo horses and players in the world, and the Dakar Rally has been taking place partly or mostly in Argentina since 2009.

Pato is Argentina's traditional sport, played on horseback and mixing elements from both polo and basketball. It was originally played with a duck (a '*pato*'), but now, thankfully, uses a ball encased in leather handles. Despite its long history and tradition, however, relatively few people follow it.

SOCIAL DOS & DON'TS

When it comes to etiquette, knowing a few intricacies will keep you on the right track.

Dos

- Greet people you encounter with *buenos días* (good morning), *buenas tardes* (good afternoon) or *buenas noches* (good evening).
- In small villages, greet people on the street and when walking into a shop.
- Greet all people in a group individually with a kiss.
- Accept and give *besos* (kisses) on the cheek.
- Use *usted* (the formal term for 'you') when addressing elders and in formal situations.
- Dress for the occasion; only tourists and athletes wear shorts in Buenos Aires.

Don'ts

- Don't refer to the Islas Malvinas as the Falkland Islands, and don't talk to strangers about the Dirty War.
- Don't suggest that Brazil is better than Argentina at *fútbol*, or that Pelé is better than Maradona. And don't refer to *fútbol* as soccer.
- Don't show up at bars before midnight, or nightclubs before 3am, or dinner parties right on time (be fashionably late).
- Don't refer to people from the United States as Americans or *americanos;* use the term *estadounidenses* (or even *norteamericanos*) instead. Most Latin Americans consider themselves 'American' (literally from America, whether it be North, Central or South).

The Sounds of Argentina

A variety of music genres are well represented in Argentina, especially when it comes to the country's most famous export, the tango. It is notably a rock-n-roll culture, heavily influenced by the rebel tradition put forth in the UK and US, with intense respect for rock's bluesy roots. But the country also grooves to different sounds, be it *chamamé* in Corrientes, *cuarteto* in Córdoba or *cumbia villera* in the poor neighborhoods of Buenos Aires.

Tango

There's no better place to dive into tango than through the music of the genre's most legendary performer, singer Carlos Gardel (1887–1935). A French-Argentine born in Toulouse, his tragic death in a plane crash at the peak of his career sealed his status as a national hero. Many of his tangos, like *Volver, Por una Cabeza* and *Madreselva,* have been re-recorded throughout the years by diverse artists and have become national treasures.

Murga is a form of athletic musical theater composed of actors and percussionists. Primarily performed in Uruguay, *murga* in Argentina is more heavily focused on dancing than singing. You're most likely to see this exciting musical art form at Carnaval celebrations.

Violinist Juan D'Arienzo's orchestra reigned over tango throughout the 1930s and into the 1940s. Osvaldo Pugliese and Héctor Varela are important bandleaders from the 1940s, but the real giant of the era was *bandoneón* (small type of accordion) player Aníbal Troilo.

Modern tango is largely dominated by the work of Astor Piazzolla, who moved the *tango nuevo* (traditional tango music infused with modern elements) genre from the dance halls into the concert halls. Also a master *bandoneón* player, Piazzolla paved the way for the tango fusion, which emerged in the 1970s and is popularized by neo-tango groups such as Gotan Project, Bajofondo Tango Club and Tanghetto.

While in Buenos Aires, keep an eye out for Orquesta Típica Fernández Fierro, who put a new twist on traditional tango songs but also perform original creations. Other orchestras to watch out for are Orquesta Típica Imperial and El Afronte.

Contemporary influential tango singers include Susana Rinaldi, Daniel Melingo, Adriana Varela and the late Eladia Blásquez.

Folk Music

The folk (*folklore* or *folklórico*) music of Argentina takes much of its inspiration from the northwestern Andean region and countries to the north, especially Bolivia and Peru. Its roots are indigenous and colonial Afro-Hispanic, spanning a variety of styles, including *chacarera, chamamé* and zamba. Tango and European folk have also influenced the genre.

The late Atahualpa Yupanqui (1908–92) was Argentina's most important *folklórico* musician of the 20th century. Yupanqui's music emerged with the *nueva canción* ('new song') movement that swept Latin America in the 1960s. *Nueva canción* was rooted in folk music and its lyrics often dealt with social and political themes. The genre's grande dame was Argentina's Mercedes Sosa (1935–2009) of Tucumán, winner of several Latin Grammy awards. Considered the voice of the voiceless, she brought attention to the struggles of the forgotten throughout the continent. She spent the years

Top: Chango Spasiuk performing in Buenos Aires

Bottom: Traditional folk dancing, Mendoza

of the military dictatorship in exile in Europe. Her best-known recording, *Gracias a La Vida*, is a tribute to Chilean songstress Violeta Parra.

Another contemporary *folklórico* musician is accordionist Chango Spasiuk, a virtuoso of Corrientes' *chamamé* music. Singer-songwriter-guitarist Horacio Guarany's 2004 album *Cantor de Cantores* was nominated for a Latin Grammy in the Best Folk Album category.

Mariana Baraj is a singer and percussionist who experiments with Latin America's traditional folk music as well as elements of jazz, classical music and improvisation. Soledad Pastorutti's first two albums have been Sony's top sellers in Argentina – ever!

Other big names in *folklórica* are Eduardo Falú, Víctor Heredia, Los Chalchaleros, and León Gieco (aka 'the Argentine Bob Dylan').

Rock & Pop

Argentina has always been a rock-n-roll culture, unlike many of its Latin American neighbors that favor the tropical beats of salsa and merengue. In this way, the country has been a leader in the region, bringing clever and thrilling *rock en español* to every corner of Latin America. Its heyday was the 1980s. Musicians such as Charly García, Fito Páez and Luis Alberto Spinetta are *rock nacional* (Argentine rock) icons. Soda Stereo, Sumo, Los Pericos and Grammy winners Los Fabulosos Cadillacs rocked Argentina throughout the 1980s. Bersuit Vergarabat endures as one of Argentina's best rock bands, with a musical complexity that is arguably without peer. R&B-influenced Ratones Paranoicos opened for the Rolling Stones in 1995, while La Portuaria – who fuse Latin beats with jazz and R&B – collaborated with David Byrne in 2006.

Other big-name groups are offbeat Babasónicos, punk rockers Attaque 77, fusion rockers Los Piojos, plus Los Redonditos de Ricota, Los Divididos, Catupecu Machu and Gazpacho. Illya Kuryaki and the Valderramas are metal-meets-hip-hop, while catchy Miranda! has an electro-pop style. Finally, eclectic Kevin Johansen sings in both English and Spanish.

Born in Córdoba in the early 1940s, *cuarteto* is Argentina's original pop music: despised by the middle and upper classes for its arresting rhythm and offbeat musical pattern, as well as its working-class lyrics, it is definitely music from the margins. Although definitively *cordobés* (from Córdoba), it's played in working-class bars, dance halls and stadiums throughout the country.

Electrónica & More

Electrónica exploded in Argentina in the 1990s and has taken on various forms in popular music. Heavyweights in DJ-based club and dance music include Aldo Haydar (progressive house), Bad Boy Orange (drum 'n' bass), Diego Ro-K ('the Maradona of Argentine DJs') and Gustavo Lamas (blending ambient pop and electro house). Award-winning Hernán Cattáneo has played with Paul Oakenfold and at Burning Man.

Música tropical – a lively, Afro-Latin sound of salsa, *merengue* and especially *cumbia* – has swept Argentina in recent years. Originating in Colombia, *cumbia* combines an infectious dance rhythm with lively melodies.

One of Buenos Aires' most interesting music spectacles is La Bomba de Tiempo, a collective of percussionists whose explosive performances are improvisational, tribal and even simulate electronic dance music. Check them out at Ciudad Cultural Konex in Buenos Aires on Monday evenings.

Argentine music has experienced the phenomenon of blending electronic music with more traditional sounds. Onda Vaga's smooth harmonies add a jazzy feel to traditional *folklore,* while Juana Molina's ambient-electronic music with a dose of the avant-garde has been compared to Björk's sound. Finally, there's Chancha Via Circuito, who fuses electronic music with *cumbia.*

Cumbia villera is a relatively recent musical phenomenon: a fusion of *cumbia* and gangsta posturing with a punk edge and reggae overtones. Born of Buenos Aires' shantytowns, its aggressive lyrics deal with marginalization, poverty, drugs, sex and the Argentine economic crisis.

Literature & Cinema

Argentina has a strong literary heritage, with many contemporary writers using the country's darkest moments as inspiration for their complex and sometimes disturbing novels. Argentina also has a vibrant, evolving film industry. The country has won two Oscars for Best Foreign Language Film (in 1985 and 2009) – the only Latin American country ever to have won the award – and continues to produce excellent directors and movies.

Literature

Journalist, poet and politician José Hernández (1831–86) gave rise to the *gauchesco* literary tradition with his epic poem *Martín Fierro* (1872), which acknowledged the role of the gauchos in Argentina's development. Argentine writing only reached an international audience during the 1960s and 1970s, when the stories of Jorge Luis Borges, Julio Cortázar, Ernesto Sabato, Adolfo Bioy Casares and Silvina Ocampo, among many others, were widely translated for the first time.

Jorge Luis Borges (1899–1986), the brightest light of Argentine literature, is best known for the complex labyrinthine worlds and sophisticated mind teasers constructing his stories. His early stories, such as *Death and the Compass* and *Streetcorner Man,* offer a metaphysical twist on Argentine themes, while his later works – including *The Lottery in Babylon, The Circular Ruins* and *Garden of the Forking Paths* – are works of fantasy. *Collected Fictions* (1999) is a complete set of his stories.

Victoria Ocampo (1890–1979) was a famous writer, publisher and intellectual who founded Sur, a renowned cultural magazine of the 1930s. You can visit her mansion near Buenos Aires.

Despite being discovered and influenced by Borges in the 1940s, Julio Cortázar (1914–84) produced writing that was considerably different. His short stories and novels are more anthropological and concern people living seemingly normal lives in a world where the surreal becomes commonplace. Cortázar's most famous book is *Hopscotch.*

Another great writer is Ernesto Sabato (1911–2011), whose complex and uncompromising novels have been extremely influential on later Argentine literature. *The Tunnel* (1948) is Sabato's engrossing existentialist novella about an obsessed painter and his distorted personal take on reality.

Adolfo Bioy Casares' (1914–99) sci-fi novella *The Invention of Morel* (1940) not only gave Alain Resnais the plot for his classic film *Last Year at Marienbad,* but also introduced the idea of the holodeck decades before *Star Trek* existed.

The work of the contemporary, post-boom generation of Argentine writers is more reality based, often reflecting the influence of popular culture and directly confronting the political angles of 1970s authoritarian Argentina. One of the most famous post-boom Argentine writers is Manuel Puig (1932–90; author of *Kiss of the Spider Woman*). In the Argentine tradition, Puig did much of his writing in exile, fleeing Argentina during the Perón years and ultimately settling in Mexico.

Osvaldo Soriano (1943–97), perhaps Argentina's most popular contemporary novelist, wrote *A Funny Dirty Little War* (1986) and *Winter Quarters* (1989). Juan José Saer (1937–2005) penned short stories and crime novels, while Rodrigo Fresán (1963–), the youngster of the post-boom generation, wrote the international bestseller *The History of Argentina* (1991).

The novel *Zama* by Antonio Di Benedetto (1956) was adapted into a film released in 2017. Other notable contemporary writers include Ricardo Piglia, Tomás Eloy Martínez, Andrés Neuman, César Aira, Oliverio Coelho, Pedro Mairal, Iosi Havilio and Samanta Schweblin.

Cinema

One of Argentina's major contributions to cinema is Luis Puenzo's *The Official Story* (1985), which deals with the Dirty War. Another well-known international movie is Héctor Babenco's *Kiss of the Spider Woman* (1985), based on the novel by Manuel Puig. Both movies won Oscars.

New Argentine Cinema developed in the 1990s, brought about by economic and political unrest. Films that spearheaded this movement include Martín Rejtman's *Rapado* (1992) and *Pizza, birra, faso* (Pizza, Beer, Cigarettes; 1998) by Adrián Caetano and Bruno Stagnaro.

Metegol (Underdogs; 2013) is a 3D film directed by Juan José Campanella; it cost US$22 million, making it the most expensive Argentine movie ever produced.

Pablo Trapero is one of Argentina's foremost filmmakers. Among his works are award-winning *Mundo grúa* (Crane World; 1999), the ensemble road movie *Familia rodante* (Rolling Family; 2004) and *Nacido y criado* (Born and Bred; 2006), a stark story about a Patagonian man's fall from grace. His 2010 film noir *Carancho* played at the Cannes Film Festival, and in 2015 *The Clan* won the Silver Lion award at the Venice international Film Festival.

Daniel Burman's films include *Esperando al mesías* (Waiting for the Messiah; 2000), *El abrazo partido* (Lost Embrace; 2004) and *Derecho de familia* (Family Law; 2006). His most recent effort, *El misterio de la felicidad* (The Mystery of Happiness; 2015), is a warm comedy about love, friendship and happiness. Burman's other claim to fame is his co-production of Walter Salles' Che Guevara–inspired *The Motorcycle Diaries*.

Another director to have made a mark on Argentine cinema is the late Fabián Bielinsky. He left behind a small but powerful body of work that includes his award-winning feature *Nueve reinas* (Nine Queens; 2000). His last film, the 2005 neo-noir flick *El aura,* screened at Sundance and was the official Argentine entry for the 2006 Oscars.

Lucrecia Martel's 2001 debut *La Ciénaga* (The Swamp) and *La Niña Santa* (The Holy Girl; 2004) deal with the themes of social decay, the Argentine bourgeoisie and sexuality in the face of Catholic guilt. Her powerful *La Mujer sin Cabeza* (The Headless Woman; 2008) was showcased at Cannes. Another acclaimed director, Carlos Sorin, bases his dramas – which include *Historias Mínimas* (Minimal Stories; 2002), *Bombón el Perro* (Bombón the Dog; 2004), *La Ventana* (The Window; 2008) and *Días de Pesca* (Gone Fishing; 2012) – in Patagonia.

Juan José Campanella's *El Hijo de la Novia* (Son of the Bride) received an Oscar nomination for Best Foreign Language Film in 2001, while *Luna de Avellaneda* (Moon of Avellaneda; 2004) is a clever story about a social club and those who try to save it. In 2009 he won the Oscar for best Foreign Language Film with *El Secreto de sus Ojos* (The Secret in Their Eyes). That same year, Mariano Cohn and Gastón Duprat's *El Hombre de al Lado* (The Man Next Door; 2009) won a cinematography award at the 2010 Sundance Film Festival.

Operation Finale by director Chris Weitz is a highly anticipated film on the capture of Adolf Eichmann in Buenos Aires, due for release in 2018.

Other noteworthy films include Lucía Puenzo's *XXY* (2007), the tale of a 15-year-old hermaphrodite, and Juan Diego Solanas' *Nordeste* (Northeast; 2005), which tackles difficult social issues such as child trafficking; both were screened at Cannes. In 2013 Puenzo directed *Wakolda* (The German Doctor), the true story of the family who unknowingly lived with Josef Mengele during his exile in South America. *Vino para Robar* (To Fool a Thief; 2013) is another worthwhile tale of competing thieves. Finally, Damián Szifron's black comedy *Relatos Salvajes* (Wild Tales; 2014) was Oscar nominated for Best Foreign Language Film.

The Natural World

Argentina. For anyone raised on *National Geographic* and adventure stories, the name is loaded with wild images: Magellanic penguins off the Atlantic coast, the windswept of expanses of Patagonia and Tierra del Fuego, the vast grasslands of the pampas, the towering Andes and raging Iguazú Falls. Reaching from the subtropics to the Beagle Channel, the country is simply unmatched in natural wonders.

The Land

With a total land area of about 2.8 million sq km, Argentina is the world's eighth-largest country. It stretches from La Quiaca on the Bolivian border, where summers can be brutally hot, to Ushuaia in Tierra del Fuego, where winters are experienced only by seasoned locals and the nuttiest of travelers. It's a distance of nearly 3500km, an expanse that encompasses a vast array of environments and terrain.

Above: Iguazú Falls (p193)

The Central & Northern Andes

In the extreme north, the Andes are basically the southern extension of the Bolivian *altiplano,* a thinly populated high plain between 3000m and 4000m in altitude, punctuated by even higher volcanic peaks. Although days can be surprisingly hot, frosts occur almost nightly. The Andean Northwest is also known as the puna.

Further south, in the arid provinces of San Juan and Mendoza, the Andes climb to their highest altitudes, with 6962m Cerro Aconcagua topping out as the highest point in the western hemisphere. Here, the highest peaks lie covered in snow through the winter. Although rainfall on the eastern slopes is inadequate for crops, perennial streams descend from the Andes and provide irrigation water, which has brought prosperity to the wine-producing provinces of Mendoza, San Juan and San Luis. Winter in San Juan province is the season of the *zonda,* a hot, dry wind descending from the Andes that causes dramatic temperature increases.

At its mouth the Río de la Plata is an amazing 200km wide, making it the widest river in the world – though some consider it more like a river estuary.

The Chaco

East of the Andes and the Andean foothills, much of northern Argentina consists of subtropical lowlands. This arid area, known as the Argentine Chaco, is part of the much larger Gran Chaco, an extremely rugged, largely uninhabited region that extends into Bolivia, Paraguay and Brazil. The Argentine Chaco encompasses the provinces of Chaco, Formosa and Santiago del Estero, the easternmost reaches of Jujuy, Catamarca and Salta provinces, and the northernmost parts of Santa Fe and Córdoba.

The Chaco has a well-defined winter dry season, and summer everywhere in the Chaco is brutally hot. Rainfall decreases as you move east to west. The wet Chaco, which encompasses the eastern parts of Chaco and Formosa provinces, and the northwestern part of Santa Fe, receives more rain than the dry Chaco, which covers central and western Chaco and Formosa provinces, most of Santiago del Estero and parts of Salta.

Mesopotamia

Also referred to as the Litoral (as in littoral), Mesopotamia is the name for the region of northeast Argentina between the Río Paraná and Río Uruguay. Here the climate is mild and rainfall is heavy in the provinces of Entre Ríos and Corrientes, which make up most of Mesopotamia. Hot and humid Misiones province, a politically important province surrounded on three sides by Brazil and Paraguay, contains part of Iguazú Falls, whose waters descend from southern Brazil's Paraná Plateau. Shallow summer flooding is common throughout Mesopotamia and into the eastern Chaco, but only the immediate river floodplains become inundated in the west.

Iguazú Falls consists of more than 275 individual falls that tumble from heights as great as 80m. They stretch for nearly 3km and are arguably the most amazing waterfalls on earth.

The Pampas & Atlantic Coast

Bordered by the Atlantic Ocean and Patagonia and stretching nearly to Córdoba and the Central Sierras, the pampas are Argentina's agricultural heartland. Geographically, this region covers the provinces of Buenos Aires and La Pampa, as well as southern chunks of Santa Fe and Córdoba.

This area can be subdivided into the humid pampas, along the Litoral, and the arid pampas of the western interior and the south. More than a third of the country's population lives in and around Buenos Aires. Annual rainfall exceeds 900mm, but several hundred kilometers westward it's less than half that.

The absence of nearly any rises in the land makes some parts of this area vulnerable to flooding from the relatively few, small rivers that cross it. Only the granitic Sierra de Tandil (484m) and the Sierra de la Ventana (1273m), in southwestern Buenos Aires province, and the Sierra de Lihué Calel disrupt the otherwise monotonous terrain.

Parque Nacional Tierra del Fuego (p508)

Along the Atlantic coast, the province of Buenos Aires features the sandy, often dune-backed beaches that attracted the development of seaside resorts. South of Viedma, cliffs begin to appear, but the landscape remains otherwise desolate for its entire stretch south through Patagonia.

The largest dinosaur ever discovered (so far!) is *Patagotitan mayorum*, uncovered in Chubut province; the herbivore measured a massive 37m long and 6m high, and weighed 85 tons.

Patagonia & the Lake District

Ever-alluring Patagonia is the region of Argentina south of the Río Colorado, which flows southeast from the Andes and passes just north of the city of Neuquén. The Lake District is a subregion of Patagonia. Province-wise, Patagonia consists of Neuquén, Río Negro, Chubut and Santa Cruz. It's separated from Chilean Patagonia by the Andes.

The Andean cordillera is high enough that Pacific storms drop most of their rain and snow on the Chilean side. In the extreme southern reaches of Patagonia, however, enough snow and ice still accumulate to form the largest southern-hemisphere glaciers outside of Antarctica.

East of the Andean foothills, the cool, arid Patagonian steppes support huge flocks of sheep. For such a southerly location, temperatures are relatively mild, even in winter, when more uniform atmospheric pressure moderates the strong gales that blow most of the year.

Except for urban centers such as Comodoro Rivadavia and Río Gallegos, Patagonia is thinly populated. Tidal ranges along the Atlantic coast are too great for major port facilities. In the valley of the Río Negro and at the outlet of the Río Chubut (near the town of Trelew), people farm and cultivate fruit orchards.

Tierra del Fuego

The world's southernmost permanently inhabited territory, Tierra del Fuego ('Land of Fire') consists of one large island (Isla Grande), unequally divided between Chile and Argentina, and many smaller ones. When

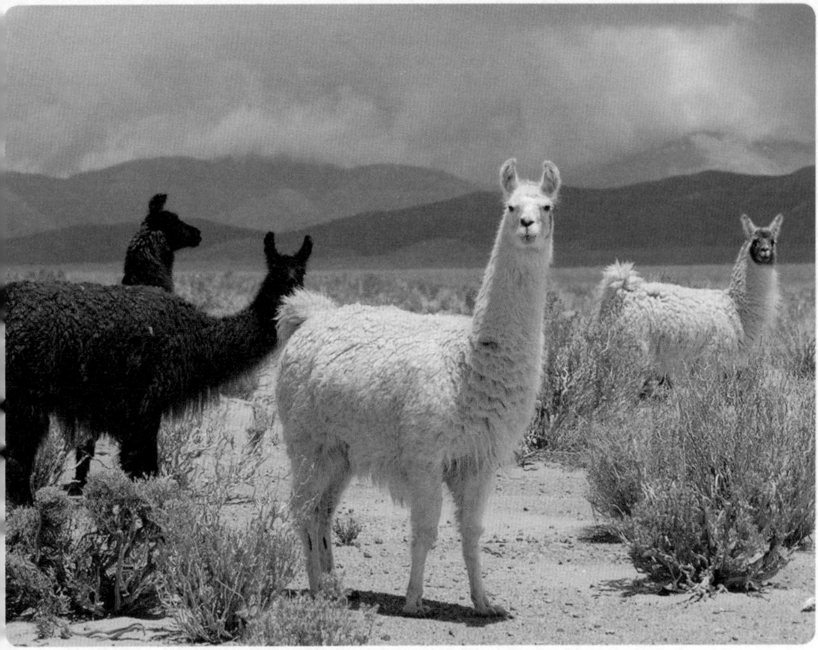

Llamas

Europeans first passed through the Strait of Magellan (which separates Isla Grande from the Patagonian mainland), the fires of the now endangered Yahgan people gave this land its name.

The northern half of Isla Grande, resembling the Patagonian steppes, is devoted to sheep grazing, while its southern half is mountainous and partly covered by forests and glaciers. As in Patagonia, winter conditions are rarely extreme.

Wildlife

With such variances in terrain over great distances, it's no wonder Argentina boasts a wide range of flora and fauna. Subtropical rainforests, palm savannas, high-altitude deserts and steppes, humid-temperate grasslands, alpine and sub-Antarctic forests and rich coastal areas all support their own special life forms.

Península Valdés is one of the few places on earth where killer whales (orcas) have been seen hunting sea lions by beaching themselves. You'd be *very* lucky to witness this phenomenon, however.

Animals

Northeast Argentina boasts the country's most diverse animal life. One of the best areas on the continent to enjoy wildlife is the swampy Esteros del Iberá, in Corrientes province, where animals such as swamp deer, capybaras and caimans, along with many large migratory birds, are common. It's comparable – arguably even better – than Brazil's more famous Pantanal.

In the drier northwest the most conspicuous animal is the domestic llama, but its wild cousins, the guanaco and vicuña, can also be seen. Your odds of seeing them are excellent if you travel by road through Parque Nacional Los Cardones to Salta. Their yellow fur is often an extraordinary puff of color against the cactus-studded backdrop. Many migratory birds, including flamingos, inhabit the high saline lakes of the Andean Northwest.

In less densely settled areas, including the arid pampas of La Pampa province, guanacos and foxes are not unusual sights. Many bodies of water, both permanent and seasonal, provide migratory-bird habitats.

Most notable in Patagonia and Tierra del Fuego, the wealth of coastal wildlife ranges from Magellanic penguins, cormorants and gulls to sea lions, fur seals, elephant seals, orcas and whales. Several coastal reserves, from Río Negro province south to Tierra del Fuego, are home to enormous concentrations of wildlife that are one of the region's greatest visitor attractions. Inland on the Patagonian steppe, as in the northwest, the guanaco is the most conspicuous mammal, but the flightless rhea, resembling the ostrich, runs in flocks across the plains.

Plants

When it comes to plant life, the country's most diverse regions are in northeast Argentina, the Lake District, the Patagonian Andes and the subtropical forests of northwest Argentina.

The high northern Andes are dry and often barren, and vegetation is limited to sparse bunch grasses and low, widely spaced shrubs. In Jujuy and La Rioja provinces, however, huge, vertically branched cardón cacti add a rugged beauty to an otherwise empty landscape. In the Andean *precordillera,* between the Chaco and the Andes proper, lies a strip of dense, subtropical montane cloud forest known as the Yungas. This area sees heavy summertime rains and is one of the most biologically diverse regions in the country.

The wet Chaco is home to grasslands and gallery forests with numerous tree species, including the quebracho colorado and caranday palm. The dry Chaco, although extremely parched, is still thick with vegetation. It hosts taller trees and a dense understory of low-growing spiny trees and shrubs.

In Mesopotamia rainfall is sufficient to support swampy lowland forests and upland savanna. Misiones' native vegetation is dense subtropical forest, though its upper elevations are studded with araucaria pines.

The once lush native grasses of the Argentine pampas have suffered under grazing pressure and the proliferation of grain farms that produce cash crops such as soy beans. Today very little native vegetation remains, except along watercourses like the Río Paraná.

Most of Patagonia lies in the rain shadow of the Chilean Andes, so the vast steppes of southeastern Argentina resemble the sparse grasslands of the arid Andean highlands. Closer to the border there are pockets of dense *Nothofagus* (southern beech), *Araucaria araucana* (aka monkey puzzle trees) and coniferous woodlands that owe their existence to the winter storms that sneak over the cordillera. Northern Tierra del

CAPYBARAS

Treading, with its webbed feet, a very fine line between cute and ugly, the capybara is a sizable semiaquatic beast that you're bound to encounter in the Esteros del Iberá area. Weighing in at up to 75kg, the *carpincho,* as it's known in Spanish, is the world's largest rodent.

Very much at home both on land and in the water, the gentle and vaguely comical creatures eat aquatic plants and grasses in great quantity. They form small herds, with a dominant male living it up with four to six females. The male can be recognized by a protrusion on its forehead that emits a territory-marking scent. The lovably roly-poly babies are born in spring.

Though protected in the Iberá area, the capybara is farmed and hunted elsewhere for its skin, which makes a soft, flexible leather. The meat is also considered a delicacy in traditional communities.

Top: Sea lion, Tierra del Fuego

Bottom: Cactus, Purmamarca (p248)

ESTIVILLML/GETTY IMAGES ©

Glaciar Perito Moreno (p464)

Fuego is a grassy extension of the Patagonian steppe, but the heavy rainfall of the mountainous southern half supports verdant southern-beech forests.

Argentina's National Parks

Argentina's national and provincial parks offer a huge variety of environments, from the sweltering tropics of Parque Nacional Iguazú to the crashing glaciers of Parque Nacional Los Glaciares to the animal-rich coastal waters of Reserva Faunística Península Valdés.

One of Latin America's first national-park systems, Argentina's dates from the turn of the 20th century, when explorer and surveyor Francisco P Moreno donated 75 sq km near Bariloche to the state in return for guarantees that the parcel would be preserved for the enjoyment of all Argentines. In 1934 this area became part of Parque Nacional Nahuel Huapi, Argentina's first national park.

Since then the country has established many other parks and reserves, mostly but not exclusively in the Andean region. There are also important provincial parks and reserves, such as Reserva Faunística Península Valdés, which do not fall within the national-park system but deserve attention. Some national parks are more visitor oriented than the provincial parks, but there are exceptions.

Visitors in Buenos Aires can stop at the national parks administration (www.parquesnacionales.gob.ar) for maps and brochures, which are sometimes in short supply in the parks.

Drones are prohibited in the parks.

Survival Guide

Directory A–Z

Accessible Travel

- Negotiating Argentina as a disabled traveler is not the easiest of tasks. Those in wheelchairs in particular will quickly realize that many cities' narrow, busy and uneven sidewalks are difficult to negotiate. Crossing streets is also a problem, since not every corner has ramps (and those that exist are often in need of repair) and traffic can be ruthless when it comes to pedestrians and wheelchair users.
- A few buses do have *piso bajo* – they 'kneel' and have extra-large spaces – but the Subte in Buenos Aires does not cater to the mobility-impaired.
- International hotel chains often have wheelchair-accessible rooms, as do other less-fancy hotels. Some restaurants, tourist sights and public buildings have ramps, but bathrooms are not always wheelchair-accessible (in bigger cities, shopping malls are a good bet for these).
- In Buenos Aires, **QRV Transportes Especiales** (☎011-15-6863-9555, 011-4306-6635; www.qrvtransportes.com.ar) offers private transportation and city tours in vans fully equipped for wheelchair users.
- Other than the use of Braille on ATMs, little effort has been dedicated to bettering accessibility for the vision impaired. Stoplights are rarely equipped with sound alerts.
- The **Biblioteca Argentina Para Ciegos** (Argentine Library for the Blind, BAC; ☎011-4981-0137; www.bac.org.ar; Lezica 3909; ⏲noon-7pm Mon-Fri; Ⓢ Línea A Castro Barros) in Buenos Aires maintains a Braille collection of books in Spanish, as well as other resources.
- Download Lonely Planet's free Accessible Travel guides from http://lptravel.to/AccessibleTravel.

Also check out the following international organizations:

Flying Wheels Travel (www.flyingwheelstravel.com)

Mobility International USA (www.miusa.org)

Society for Accessible Travel & Hospitality (www.sath.org)

Accommodations

Accommodations range from campgrounds to five-star luxury hotels. Wi-fi is common and breakfast is usually included. Reservations are advisable for regional high seasons. Payment in cash (usually at midrange to top-end hotels) sometimes results in a 10% discount. Likewise, you can be charged a 'fee' for using credit cards.

Hotels From basic to luxury, with a wide range in pricing.

B&Bs Common in cities and tourist destinations, usually midrange.

Hospedajes Homey accommodations, sometimes with private bathrooms. Similar to a pensión or *residencial*.

Estancias Accommodations on a ranch ranging from basic to luxurious.

Hostels Budget dormitories aimed at younger travelers.

Cabañas

- Some tourist destinations, especially at the beach or in the country, have *cabañas* (cabins) for rent. These are usually stand-alone cabin-type accommodations, and nearly always have a

PLAN YOUR STAY ONLINE

For more accommodations reviews by Lonely Planet authors, check out www.lonelyplanet.com. You'll find independent reviews, as well as recommendations on the best places to stay.

stocked kitchen. They are a great deal for groups or families (as they often have several rooms), though sometimes their off-the-beaten-track location means you'll need a vehicle to reach them. A destination's tourist office is a good place to find a list of local *cabañas*.

Camping & Refugios

➡ Camping can be a splendid way to experience Argentina, particularly the Lake District and Patagonia, where there are many good campgrounds.

➡ Many Argentine cities or towns have a fairly central municipal campground, but these are hit-and-miss – sometimes delightfully woodsy, sometimes crowded and ugly.

➡ Private campgrounds usually have good facilities: hot showers, toilets, laundry, barbecue for grilling, restaurant or *confitería* (cafe) and small grocery store. Free campgrounds are often excellent, especially in the Lake District, although they lack facilities. Municipal campgrounds are cheap, but can become party central on weekends.

➡ Argentine camping equipment is often more expensive and inferior than you may be used to.

➡ Camp stoves take locally available butane cartridges (which should *not* be taken on airplanes).

➡ There are definitely mosquitoes in Argentina, but mosquito repellent is widely available.

➡ Backpacking and backcountry camping opportunities abound in and around the national parks, especially those in the Lake District and the south. Some parks have free or cheap *refugios* (basic shelters), which have cooking facilities and rustic bunks.

SLEEPING PRICE RANGES

The following price ranges refer to the cost of a double room during high season. Unless otherwise stated, double rooms include bathroom, and breakfast is included in the price.

$ less than US$75

$$ US$75–150

$$$ more than US$150

Many hotels take payment in US dollars and may also change them at a rate close to the official.

Estancias

➡ Few experiences feel more typically Argentine than staying at an *estancia* (a traditional ranch, often called *fincas* in the northwest). Some are very basic in their amenities, particularly if they are faithful to their roots as rustic country estates. *Estancias* are a wonderful way to spend time in remote areas of the country – and wine, horses and *asados* (traditional barbecues) are almost always involved.

➡ *Estancias* are especially common in the area around Buenos Aires, near Esteros del Iberá, and throughout the Lake District and Patagonia, where they're often geared toward anglers. They're not cheap, but rates generally include room, board and some activities.

Hospedajes, Pensiones & Residenciales

➡ Aside from hostels, these are Argentina's cheapest accommodations, and the differences among them are sometimes ambiguous.

➡ A *hospedaje* is usually a large family home with a few extra bedrooms (and, generally, a shared bathroom).

➡ Similarly, a pensión offers short-term accommodations in a family home but may also have permanent lodgers.

➡ *Residenciales* generally occupy buildings designed for short-stay accommodations, although some (known euphemistically as *albergues transitorios*) cater to clientele who intend only *very* short stays – of two hours maximum. These are mostly used by young Argentine couples.

➡ Rooms and furnishings at these accommodations are modest, often basic and usually clean, and rooms with shared bathrooms are the cheapest.

Hostels

➡ Hostels are common in Argentina, and range from basic no-frills deals to beautiful, multi-perk offerings more luxurious than your basic hotel. Most fall in between, but all have common kitchens, living areas, shared bathrooms and dorm rooms. Most have a few private rooms with or without bathroom.

➡ Hostels are a great way to meet other travelers, both Argentines and foreigners, especially if you're by yourself. Social events such as *asados* often take place, and local tours can be offered. However, remember that Argentines are night owls and hostelers tend to follow suit, so earplugs can be handy indeed.

➡ Hostel organizations, which offer discounts with membership, include

HIGH SEASON

High season is generally January and February (when Argentines take their summer breaks), Semana Santa (Easter week) and July and August. In Patagonia, high season is October through March. Reserve ahead during these times. Outside these times, prices can drop anywhere from 20% to 50%.

Hostelling International (www.hihostels.com) and HoLa (www.holahostels.com).

Hotels

- Argentine hotels vary from depressing, utilitarian one-star places to luxurious five-star hotels with all the usual top-tier services. Oddly enough, many one- and two-star hotels can prove better value than three- and four-star lodgings.
- In general, hotels provide a room with private bathroom, often a telephone and usually a TV with cable; some have microwaves and/or kitchenettes. Sometimes they have a *confitería* or restaurant and almost always include breakfast, whether it be a few *medialunas* (croissants) with coffee or full American-style buffet.

Rentals & Homestays

- House and apartment rentals often save you money if you're staying in one place for an extended period. This can be an especially good deal during high season at resort locations, such as Bariloche or beach cities along the Atlantic coast (just book way ahead) – especially for groups. Tourist offices can be good sources for listings in addition to internationally used apps.
- During the tourist season, mostly in the interior, families rent rooms to visitors. Often these are excellent bargains, permitting access to cooking and laundry facilities while encouraging contact with Argentines. Tourist offices in many smaller towns or cities sometimes maintain lists of such accommodations.

Courses

- Argentina is a hot destination for studying Spanish. Most Spanish-language courses are based in Buenos Aires, though larger cities such as Mendoza and Córdoba are also excellent.
- Tango classes are hugely popular in Buenos Aires, where cooking classes – for both Argentine and international cuisine – are also available.
- Asking fellow travelers for recommendations is the best way to pick a good institute, or tango and cooking classes that cater to your needs.

Customs Regulations

- Argentine officials are generally courteous and reasonable toward tourists. Electronic items, including laptops, cameras and cell (mobile) phones, can be brought into the country duty free, provided they are not intended for resale. If you have a lot of electronic equipment, however, it may be useful to have a typed list of the items you are carrying (including serial numbers) or a pile of purchase receipts.
- If you're entering Argentina from a neighboring country, officials focus on different things. Travelers southbound from the central Andean countries may be searched for drugs, while those from bordering countries will have fruits and vegetables confiscated. Carrying illegal drugs will pretty much get you into trouble no matter which country you're coming from.

Discount Cards

- The International Student Identity Card (ISIC) is available through www.isic.org. It can help travelers obtain discounts on public transportation and admissions to museums. Any official-looking university identification may (or may not) be accepted as a substitute.
- An HI card, available at any HI hostel (www.hihostels.com), will get you discounts on your stay at any HI facility. The HoLa (www.holahostels.com) card works in a similar way for a different network of hostels.
- Travelers over the age of 60 can sometimes obtain senior-citizen discounts on museum admissions and the like. Usually a passport with date of birth is sufficient to use as evidence of age.

Electricity

- Argentina's electric current operates on 220V, 50Hz. Adapters are readily available from almost any *ferretería* (hardware store).
- Most electronic equipment (such as cameras, telephones and computers) are dual/multi-voltage, but if you're bringing something that's not (such as a hairdryer), use a voltage converter or you might short out your device.

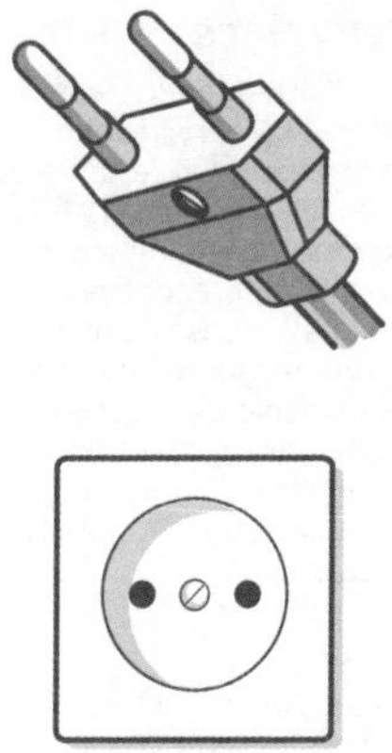

Type C
220V/50Hz

Type H
230V/50Hz

Embassies & Consulates

Embassies and consulates are found in Buenos Aires. Some other cities around Argentina (especially near the borders) also have the consulates of certain countries.

Australian Embassy (011-4779-3500; www.argentina.embassy.gov.au; Villanueva 1400; 8:30am-5pm Mon-Fri; Línea D Olleros)

Bolivian Embassy (011-4394-1463; www.embajadadebolivia.com.ar; Av Corrientes 545; 9:30am-5:30pm Mon-Fri; Línea B Florida)

Brazilian Consulate (011-4515-6500; www.conbrasil.org.ar; Carlos Pellegrini 1363, 5th fl; 9am-1pm Mon-Fri; Línea C San Martín)

Canadian Embassy (011-4808-1000; www.embassy-canada.com; Tagle 2828; 8:30am-12:30pm & 1:30-5:30pm Mon-Thu, 8:30am-2pm Fri; 130, 62, 33)

Chilean Embassy (011-4808-8601; www.chile.gob.cl/argentina; Tagle 2762; 9am-1pm & 2-5pm Mon-Fri; Línea H Las Heras)

Dutch Embassy (011-4338-0050; http://argentina.nlembajada.org; Olga Cossettini 831, 3rd fl; 9am-5pm Mon-Thu, to 1pm Fri; Línea B Alem)

French Embassy (011-4515-7030; www.embafrancia-argentina.org; Cerrito 1399; 9am-12:30pm & 2-4pm Mon-Fri; Línea C San Martín)

German Embassy (011-4778-2500; www.buenosaires.diplo.de; Villanueva 1055; 8:30-11am Mon-Fri; Línea D Olleros)

Italian Consulate (011-4114-4800; www.consbuenosaires.esteri.it; Reconquista 572; 8am-2pm Mon, Tue, Thu & Fri; Línea B Alem)

New Zealand Embassy (011-5070-0700; www.nzembassy.com/argentina; Carlos Pellegrini 1427, 5th fl; 9am-5pm Mon-Fri; Línea C San Martín)

Spanish Embassy (011-4809-4900; www.exteriores.gob.es/Embajadas/buenosaires; Av Figueroa Alcorta 3102; 9am-2:30pm Mon-Fri; 130, 62, 93)

UK Embassy (011-4808-2200; www.ukinargentina.fco.gov.uk; Dr Luis Agote 2412; 9am-1pm Mon-Fri; 63, 130, 93)

Uruguayan Embassy (011-6009-4020; www.embajadadeluruguay.com.ar; Paraguay 1571; 9am-3pm Mon-Fri; Línea D Tribunales)

US Embassy (011-5777-4533; https://ar.usembassy.gov; Colombia 4300; 9am-5:30pm Mon-Fri; Línea D Plaza Italia)

EATING PRICE RANGES

The following price ranges refer to a standard main course.

$ less than AR$165

$$ AR$165–260

$$$ more than AR$260

Health

Public health care in Argentina is reasonably good and free, even if you're a foreigner. Waits can be long, however, and quality inconsistent. Those who can afford it usually opt for the superior private-care system, and here most doctors and hospitals will expect payment in cash. Many medical personnel speak English.

Bringing a signed and dated note from your doctor, describing your medical conditions and medications (with their generic or scientific names) is a good idea. It's also a good idea to bring medications in their clearly labeled, original containers. Most pharmacies in Argentina are well supplied.

Dengue Fever

➡ Dengue fever is a viral infection found throughout South America. It is transmitted by Aedes mosquitoes, which prefer to bite during the daytime and breed primarily in artificial water containers, such as cans, cisterns, plastic containers and discarded tires. As a result, dengue is especially common in densely populated urban environments.

➡ In Misiones and Formosa provinces, almost 5000

TAXES

Foreigners are exempt from the 21% IVA (value-added tax) on lodging when paying by credit card or with US dollars. While this is the law, smaller establishments often argue that they don't have a card reader (or that it's broken).

cases were reported in 2017, the most since nearly 27,000 cases of dengue were reported during the last outbreak in northern Argentina in 2009.

- Dengue usually causes flu-like symptoms, including fever, muscle aches, joint pains, headaches, nausea and vomiting, often followed by a rash. The body aches may be quite uncomfortable, but most cases resolve uneventfully in a few days.

Insurance

- A travel insurance policy to cover theft, loss, medical problems and trip cancellation or delays is a good idea. Some policies specifically exclude dangerous activities such as scuba diving, skiing, rock climbing and even trekking; read the fine print. Check that the policy covers ambulances or an emergency flight home.
- Keep all your paperwork in case you have to file a claim later. Paying for your flight with a credit card often provides limited travel insurance – ask your credit-card company what it is prepared to cover.
- Worldwide travel insurance is available at www.lonelyplanet.com/travel-insurance. You can buy, extend and claim online anytime – even if you're already on the road.

Internet Access

- Wi-fi is available at many (if not most) hotels and cafes, restaurants and airports, and it's generally good and free.
- Internet cafes and *locutorios* (telephone centers) with very affordable internet access can be found in practically all Argentine towns and cities.
- To find the @ *(arroba)* symbol on keyboards, try holding down the Alt key and typing 64, or typing AltGr-2. You can also ask the attendant *'¿Cómo se hace la arroba?'* ('How do you make the @ sign?').
- In remote spots like El Chaltén and other parts of Patagonia wi-fi may be uniformly poor.

Legal Matters

- Police can demand identification at any moment and for whatever reason, though it's unlikely to happen. Always carry photo ID or a copy of your passport, and – most importantly – *always* be courteous and cooperative.
- Drugs and most other substances that are illegal in the USA and many European countries are also illegal here, though marijuana has been somewhat decriminalized in Argentina (and is legal in Uruguay).
- If arrested, you have the constitutional right to a lawyer, to a telephone call and to remain silent (beyond giving your name, nationality, age and passport number). Don't sign anything until you speak to a lawyer. If you don't speak Spanish, a translator should be provided for you.

LGBTIQ+ Travelers

- In 2010 Argentina was the first country in Latin America to legalize same-sex marriage. The country has become increasingly gay-friendly over recent years. Buenos Aires is one of the world's top gay destinations – with dedicated hotels and B&Bs, bars and nightclubs. The capital is home to South America's largest annual gay pride parade.
- Although Buenos Aires (and, to a lesser extent, Argentina's other large cities) is becoming increasingly tolerant, most of the rest of Argentina still feels uncomfortable with same-sex relationships. Homophobia rarely takes the form of physical violence, however, and gay people regularly travel throughout the country to return home with nothing but praise.
- When it comes to public affection, Argentine men are more physically demonstrative than their North American and European counterparts. Behaviors such as kissing on the cheek in greeting or a vigorous embrace are innocuous even to those who express unease with same-sex relationships. Lesbians walking hand in hand should attract little attention, since heterosexual Argentine women frequently do so, but this would be very conspicuous behavior for men. When in doubt, it's best to be discreet.

Maps

- Tourist offices throughout the country provide free city maps that are good enough for tooling around town.
- Download a maps app, like maps.me, with the requisite regional maps for handy use offline.

➡ With offices in nearly every Argentine city, the **Automóvil Club Argentino** (ACA; ☎011-4808-4040; www.aca.org.ar; Av del Libertador 1850; ⏱9am-4pm Mon-Fri; 🚌130, 62, 93) publishes excellent maps of provinces and cities that are particularly useful for driving. Card-carrying members of foreign automobile clubs can get discounts.

➡ Geography nerds will adore the topographic maps available from the **Instituto Geográfico Nacional** (Map p74; ☎011-4576-5545; www.ign.gob.ar; Av Cabildo 381; ⏱8am-2pm Mon-Fri; Ⓢ Línea D Ministro Carranza) in Buenos Aires.

Money

ATMs are widely available, though tend to run out of money in tourist destinations. Credit cards are accepted in most hotels and restaurants.

ATMs

➡ *Cajeros automáticos* (ATMs) are found in nearly every city and town in Argentina and can also be used for cash advances on major credit cards. They're the best way to get money, and nearly all have instructions in English. Limits on withdrawal can be very low –sometimes as low as US$115, though the withdrawal fee can be relatively high (not including charges by your home bank). You can withdraw several times per day, but beware these charges – which are per transaction. Banelco ATMs tend to allow larger withdrawals.

➡ Not all foreign cards work in ATMs. Bring more than one option and be sure to alert your home bank that you are traveling in Argentina.

➡ In Patagonia, places like like El Calafate and El Chaltén quickly run out of cash in high season.

Cash

➡ The Argentine unit of currency is the peso (AR$).

➡ Notes come in denominations of two, five, 10, 20, 50, 100, 200, 500 and 1000 pesos.

➡ One peso equals 100 *centavos*; coins come in denominations of five, 10, 25 and 50 *centavos*, as well as one and two pesos.

➡ At present, US dollars are accepted by many tourist-oriented businesses, but you should always carry some pesos.

➡ Don't be dismayed if you receive dirty and hopelessly tattered banknotes; they'll be accepted everywhere. Some places refuse torn or marked foreign banknotes, however, so make sure you arrive in Argentina with pristine bills.

➡ Counterfeiting, of both local and US bills, has become a problem in recent years, and merchants are very careful when accepting large denominations. You should be, too; look for a clear watermark or running thread on the largest bills, and get familiar with the local currency *before* you arrive in Argentina. See www.landingpadba.com/ba-basics-counterfeit-money. Being aware of fake bills is especially important in dark places like nightclubs or taxis.

➡ Getting change from large denominations can be a problem for small purchases. Large supermarkets and restaurants are your best bet. Always keep a stash of change with you, in both small bills and coins.

Credit Cards

➡ Many (but not all!) tourist services, larger stores, hotels and restaurants – especially in the bigger cities – take credit cards such as Visa and MasterCard.

➡ The most widely accepted credit cards are Visa and MasterCard, though American Express and a few others are valid in some establishments. Before you leave home, warn your credit-card company that you'll be using it abroad.

➡ Some businesses add a *recargo* (surcharge) of 5% to 10% toward credit-card purchases. Also, the actual amount you'll eventually pay depends upon the official exchange rate not at the time of sale but when the purchase is posted to an overseas account, sometimes weeks later.

➡ If you use a credit card to pay restaurant bills, be aware that tips can't usually be added to the bill. Many lower-end hotels and private tour companies will not accept credit cards. Many places will

INFLATION-SAVVY PLANNING

Lonely Planet aims to give its readers as precise an idea as possible of what things cost. Rather than just slapping hotels or restaurants into vague budget categories, we publish the actual rates and prices that businesses quote to us during research. The problem is that Argentina's inflation was running at an official rate of around 20% at the time of writing, and some unofficial estimates are more than double this. But we've found that readers prefer to have real numbers in their hands and do compensatory calculations themselves.

Argentina remains a decent-value destination, but don't expect our quoted prices to necessarily reflect your own experience. Our advice: call or check a few hotel or tour-operator websites before budgeting for your trip, just to make sure you're savvy about current rates.

PRACTICALITIES

Addresses In Argentine addresses, the word *local* refers to a suite or office. If an address has 's/n' – short for *sin numero* (without number) – the address has no street number.

Laundry Affordable *lavanderías* are widely available in Argentina.

Newspapers Argentina's biggest papers are centrist *Clarín* (www.clarin.com), conservative *La Nación* (www.lanacion.com.ar) and lefty *Página 12* (www.pagina12.com.ar). The *Argentina Independent* (www.argentinaindependent.com) is an excellent English-language online newspaper.

Photography Many photo stores can affordably transfer images from your digital camera to a memory stick; you can also get them printed out. Old-fashioned print and slide film are available, as is developing.

Smoking Smoking is banned in workplaces, all public indoor areas, schools, hospitals, museums and theaters, and on all public transportation.

Weights and measures The metric system is used.

give you a small discount if you pay in cash rather than use a credit card.

Money Changers

- US dollars are by far the preferred foreign currency, although Chilean and Uruguayan pesos can be readily exchanged at the borders.
- Cash dollars and euros can be changed at banks and *cambios* (exchange houses) in most larger cities, but other currencies can be difficult to change outside Buenos Aires.
- You'll need your passport to change money; it might be best to avoid any sort of street-tout money changer.

Tipping

An interesting note: when your server is taking your bill with payment away, saying '*gracias*' usually implies that the server should keep the change as a tip. If you want change back, don't say '*gracias*' – say '*cambio, por favor*' instead.

Note that tips can't be added to credit-card bills, so carry cash for this purpose. Also note that the *cubierto* that some restaurants charge is not a tip; it's a sort of 'cover charge' for the use of utensils and bread.

Restaurants and cafes It's customary to tip about 10% of the bill for decent service.

Hotel staff, bus porters, delivery people, hotel porters and taxi drivers Give a few bills.

Restaurant servers and spas Tip 15%.

Opening Hours

General opening hours:

Banks 8am to 3pm or 4pm Monday to Friday; some till 1pm Saturday

Bars 8pm or 9pm to between 4am and 6am nightly

Cafes 6am to midnight or much later; open daily

Clubs 1am to 2am to between 6am and 8am Friday and Saturday

Office business hours 8am to 5pm

Post offices 8am to 6pm Monday to Friday, 9am to 1pm Saturday

Restaurants Noon to 3:30pm and 8pm to midnight or 1am (later on weekends)

Shops 9am or 10am to 8pm or 9pm Monday to Saturday

Post

- The often unreliable Correo Argentino (www.correoargentino.com.ar) is the government postal service.
- Essential overseas mail should be sent *certificado* (registered).
- You can send packages less than 2kg from any post office, but anything heavier needs to go through *aduana* (a customs office). In Buenos Aires, this office is near Retiro bus terminal and is called Correo Internacional. Take your passport and keep the package open, as you'll have to show its contents to a customs official.
- Domestic couriers, such as Andreani (www.andreani.com.ar) and **OCA** (Map p58; ☎011-4311-5305; www.oca.com.ar; Viamonte 526; ⏲8am-6pm Mon-Fri; Ⓢ Línea C Lavalle), and international couriers such as DHL and FedEx are far more dependable than the post office. But they're also far more expensive. The last two have offices only in the largest cities, while the first two usually serve as their connections to the interior of the country.
- If a package is being sent to you, expect to wait awhile before receiving notification of its arrival. Nearly all parcels sent to Buenos Aires go to the international Retiro office, near the Buquebus terminal. To collect the package you'll have to wait (sometimes hours), first to get it and then to have it checked by customs.

There's also a processing fee. Don't expect any valuables to make it through.

Public Holidays

Government offices and businesses are closed on Argentina's numerous public holidays. If the holiday falls on a midweek day or weekend day, it's often bumped to the nearest Monday; if it falls on a Tuesday or Thursday, then the in-between days of Monday and Friday are taken as holidays.

Public-transportation options are more limited on holidays, when you should reserve tickets far in advance. Hotel booking should also be done ahead of time.

The following list does not include provincial holidays, which may vary considerably.

January 1 Año Nuevo; New Year's Day.

February/March Carnaval. Dates vary; a Monday and Tuesday become holidays.

March 24 Día de la Memoria; Memorial Day. Anniversary of the day that started the 1976 dictatorship and subsequent Dirty War.

March/April Semana Santa; Easter week. Dates vary; most businesses close on 'Good Thursday' and Good Friday; major travel week.

April 2 Día de las Malvinas; honors the fallen Argentine soldiers from the Islas Malvinas (Falkland Islands) war in 1982.

May 1 Día del Trabajador; Labor Day.

May 25 Día de la Revolución de Mayo; commemorates the 1810 revolution against Spain.

June 20 Día de la Bandera; Flag Day. Anniversary of the death of Manuel Belgrano, creator of Argentina's flag and military leader.

July 9 Día de la Independencia; Independence Day.

August (third Monday in August) Día del Libertador San Martín; marks the anniversary of José de San Martín's death in 1850.

October 12 (second Monday in October) Día del Respeto a la Diversidad Cultural; a day to respect cultural diversity

November 20 (fourth Monday in November) Día de la Soberanía Nacional; Day of National Sovereignty.

December 8 Día de la Concepción Inmaculada; celebrates the immaculate conception of the Virgin Mary.

December 25 Navidad; Christmas Day.

Note that Christmas Eve and New Year's Eve are treated as semi-holidays, and you will find some businesses closed for the latter half of those days.

Safe Travel

➡ For tourists, Argentina is one of the safest countries in Latin America. This isn't to say you should skip down the street drunk with your long-lens camera dangling, but with a little common sense you can visit Argentina's big cities as safely as you could London, Paris or New York. That said, crime has been on the rise.

Petty Crime

➡ The economic crisis of 1999–2001 plunged a lot of people into poverty, and street crime (pickpocketing, bag-snatching and armed robbery) has subsequently risen, especially in Buenos Aires. Here, be especially watchful for pickpockets on crowded buses, on the Subte (subway) and at busy *ferias* (street markets). Still, most people feel perfectly safe in the big cities, more so in the small towns of the provinces.

➡ Bus terminals are common places where tourists become separated from their possessions. For the most part bus terminals are safe, as they're usually full of families traveling and saying goodbyes, but they can also be prime grounds for bag-snatchers. Always keep an eagle eye on your belongings. This is especially true in Buenos Aires' Retiro station.

➡ At sidewalk cafe or restaurant tables, always have your bag close to you, preferably touching your body. You can also place the strap around your leg or tie it around the furniture. Be careful showing off expensive electronics like laptops, iPods or iPads. Other places to be wary are tourist destinations and on crowded public transportation.

➡ In Buenos Aires the **Tourist Police** (Comisaría del Turista; ☎0800-999-5000, 011-4309-9000, ext 6422; turista@policiafederal.gov.ar; Av Corrientes 436; ⏰24hr; Ⓢ Línea B Florída) provide interpreters and help victims of robberies and rip-offs.

Pickets & Protests

➡ Street protests have become part of daily life in Argentina, especially in Buenos Aires' Plaza de Mayo area. Generally these have little effect on tourists other than blocking traffic or making it difficult to see Buenos Aires' Plaza de Mayo and the Casa Rosada.

➡ The country has many *gremios* or *sindicatos* (trade unions), and it seems that one of them is always on strike. Transportation unions sometimes go on strike, which can affect travelers directly by delaying domestic flights and bus services. It's always a good idea to keep your eye on the news before traveling.

Drivers

➡ Being a pedestrian in Argentina is perhaps one of the country's more difficult ventures. Many Argentine drivers jump the gun when the traffic signal is about to change to green, drive extremely fast and change lanes unpredictably. Even though pedestrians at corners and crosswalks have the legal right of way, very few drivers respect this and will hardly slow down when you are crossing. Be especially careful of buses, which can be recklessly driven and, because of their large size, particularly dangerous.

Police & Military

➡ The police and military have a reputation for being corrupt or irresponsible, but both are generally helpful and courteous to tourists. If you feel you're being patted down for a bribe (most often if you're driving), you can respond by tactfully paying up or asking the officer to accompany you to the police station to take care of it. The latter will likely cause the officer to drop it – though it could also lead you into the labyrinthine bureaucracy of the Argentine police system. Pretending you don't understand Spanish may also frustrate a potential bribe.

Telephone

➡ To use street phones, you'll pay with regular coins or *tarjetas telefónicas* (magnetic phone cards available at many kiosks). You'll only be able to speak for a limited time before you get cut off, so carry enough credit.

➡ Toll-free numbers begin with 0800; these calls can only be made within Argentina. Numbers that start with 0810 are charged at a local rate only, no matter where (in Argentina) you are calling from.

➡ The cheapest way to make an international call is to use an online service (such as Skype or Google Voice) or use a phone card. International calls can be made at *locutorios*, but they're more expensive this way. When dialing abroad, dial 00, followed by the code of the country you're calling, then the area code and number.

Directory Assistance	☎110
Fire	☎100
Medical Emergency	☎107
Police	☎911 in some larger cities, ☎101
Tourist Police (Buenos Aires)	☎011-4346-5748, ☎0800-999-5000

Cell Phones

It's best to bring your own unlocked tri- or quad-band GSM cell phone to Argentina, then buy an inexpensive SIM chip (you'll get a local number) and credits (or *carga virtual*) as needed.

➡ All SIM cards now must be registered to users before they can be activated. In theory, a foreigner can activate a SIM card with identification, but in our experience, knowing a local willing to register the phone under their own name, address and DNI made the process possible.

➡ Both SIM chips and credits can be bought at many kiosks or *locutorios*; look for '*recarga facil*' or '*saldo virtual*' signs. Phone unlocking services are available; ask around. You can also buy cell phones that use SIM chips.

➡ Be careful renting phones as they're not usually a better deal than outright buying a cell phone.

➡ If you plan not to use a local SIM card, purchase an international plan to avoid being hit with a huge bill for roaming costs.

Phone Cards

➡ Telephone calling cards sold at kiosks make domestic and international calls far cheaper than calling direct. However, they must be used from a fixed line such as a home or hotel telephone (provided you can dial outside the hotel).

➡ When purchasing one, tell the clerk the country you will call so they give you the right card.

Locutorios & Internet Cafes

➡ Most common in more remote places where internet and phone services are poor, a *locutorio* is a small telephone office with private calling cabins.

➡ When making international calls from *locutorios* ask about off-peak discount hours, which generally apply after 10pm and on weekends. Making international calls over the internet using Skype is a cheap option; many internet cafes have this system in place.

Time

➡ Argentina is three hours behind GMT and generally does not observe daylight-saving time (though this situation can easily change). When it's noon in Argentina, it's 7am in San Francisco, 10am in New York, 3pm in London and 1am the next day in Sydney (add one hour to these destinations during their daylight-saving times).

➡ Argentina uses the 24-hour clock in written communications, but both the 12- and 24-hour clocks can be used conversationally.

ELECTRONICS WARNING

Note that buying a smart phone, and especially an iPhone, is extremely expensive in Argentina due to import restrictions – and they are not widely available. This makes them easy targets for theft. If you do bring your smart phone, don't flash it around unnecessarily or leave it unprotected somewhere. This goes for tablet computers and laptop computers, too.

Toilets

- Public toilets in Argentina are better than in most of South America, but there are certainly exceptions. For the truly squeamish, the better restaurants and cafes are good alternatives. Large shopping malls often have public bathrooms, as do international fast-food chains.
- Always carry your own toilet paper, since it often runs out in public restrooms, and don't expect luxuries such as soap, hot water and paper towels either.
- In smaller towns, some public toilets charge a small fee for entry. Changing facilities for babies are not always available.
- Some may find bidets a novelty; they are those shallow, ceramic bowls with knobs and a drain, often accompanying toilets in hotel bathrooms. They are meant for between-shower cleanings of nether regions. Turn knobs slowly, or you may end up spraying yourself or the ceiling.

CALLING ARGENTINA

To call a number in Argentina from another country, dial your international exit code, then the country code for Argentina, then the area code (without the zero) and number. For example, if you're calling a Buenos Aires landline number from the United States, you'd dial:

- 011-54-11-xxxx-xxxx
- 011 is the United States' international exit code
- 54 is Argentina's country code
- 11 is Buenos Aires' city code without the beginning zero
- xxxx-xxxx is your local Buenos Aires phone number, usually eight digits

When dialing an Argentine cell phone from another country, dial your international exit code, then 54, then 9, then the area code without the 0, then the number – leaving out the 15 (which most Argentine cell phone numbers start with). For example, if you're calling a Buenos Aires cell phone number from the United States, you'd dial:

- 011-54-9-11-xxxx-xxxx

Cell-phone dialing is a bit more complicated in Argentina than in other countries. Cell-phone numbers in Argentina are always preceded by '15.' If you're calling a cell phone number from a landline, you'll have to dial '15' first (add the area code before the '15' as necessary). However, if you're calling a cell phone from another cell phone, you don't need to dial '15.' You also don't need to dial '15' to send text messages.

WhatsApp is a popular way of sending free texts and voice messages.

Tourist Information

- Argentina's national tourist board is the **Ministerio de Turismo** (www.turismo.gob.ar); its main office is in Buenos Aires.
- Almost every destination city or town has a tourist office, usually on or near the main plaza or at the bus terminal. Each Argentine province also has its own representation in Buenos Aires. Most of these are well organized, often offering a computerized database of tourist information, and can be worth a visit before heading for the provinces.

Visas

- Nationals of Canada, most Western European countries, Australia and New Zealand do not need a visa to visit Argentina. Upon arrival, most visitors get a 90-day stamp in their passport. Canadians must pay a significant 'reciprocity fee' before arriving.
- Dependent children traveling without *both* parents theoretically need a notarized document certifying that both parents agree to the child's travel. Parents may also wish to bring a copy of the custody form; however, there's a good chance they won't be asked for either document.
- Depending on your nationality, very short visits to neighboring countries sometimes do not require visas; e.g. you *might* not be asked for a Brazilian visa to cross from the Argentine town of Puerto Iguazú to Foz do Iguaçu, as long as you return the same day – but doing so is at your own risk.
- The same is true at the Bolivian border town of Villazón, near La Quiaca. Officials at Paraguayan crossings can give day stamps, however. Check current regulations for the latest situation.

Visa Extensions

- For a 90-day extension on your tourist visa, get ready for bureaucracy and visit Buenos Aires' immigration office **Dirección Nacional de Migraciones** (www.migraciones.gov.ar). The fee is currently AR$600 for non-Mercosur nationals

ARGENTINA'S RECIPROCITY FEE

Citizens from some countries have to pay a reciprocity fee *(tasa de reciprocidad)* before arriving in Argentina; ideally you'll be reminded of this when you buy your airplane ticket. This fee is equal to what Argentines are charged for visas to visit those countries. You'll need to pay this fee online via credit card; see www.migraciones.gov.ar/accesibleingles and click on 'Reciprocity Fee.'

Fees are US$78 for Canadians (good until a month before your passport expires). Check current regulations as rules can change quickly.

(those from countries other than Argentina, Brazil, Paraguay and Uruguay). Interestingly enough, the fee for overstaying your visa is also AR$600 (but this can change).

➡ If you're staying more than three months, consider crossing into Colonia or Montevideo (both in Uruguay; Colonia can be an easy day trip) or into Chile for a day or two before your visa expires, then return with a new 90-day visa. However, this only works if you don't need a visa to enter the other country.

Volunteering

There are many opportunities for volunteering in Argentina, from food banks to *villas miserias* (shantytowns) to organic farms. Some ask for just your time, or a modest fee – and some charge hundreds of dollars (with likely a low percentage of money going directly to those in need). Before choosing an organization, it's good to talk to other volunteers about their experiences.

Aldea Luna (www.aldealuna.com.ar) Work on a farm in a nature reserve.

Anda Responsible Travel (www.andatravel.com.ar/en/volunteering) Buenos Aires travel agency supporting local communities.

Centro Conviven (http://centroconviven.blogspot.com) Helps kids in Buenos Aires' *villas*.

Conservación Patagonica (www.conservacionpatagonica.org) Help to create a national park.

Eco Yoga Park (www.ecoyogavillages.org/volunteer-programs) Work on an organic farm, construct ecobuildings and teach local communities.

Fundación Banco de Alimentos (www.bancodealimentos.org.ar) Short-term work at a food bank.

Habitat for Humanity Argentina (www.hpha.org.ar) Building communities.

WWOOF Argentina (www.wwoofargentina.com) Organic farming in Argentina.

Women Travelers

➡ Being a woman traveling in Argentina can sometimes be a challenge, especially if you are young or alone. In some ways Argentina is a safer place for a woman than Europe, the USA and most other Latin American countries, but dealing with its machismo culture can be a real pain in the ass.

➡ Catcalling can be highly irritating. Verbal comments include crude language, hisses, whistles and *piropos* (flirtatious comments), which are often vulgar .

➡ As tempting as it may be to respond, the best thing to do is completely ignore the comments.

➡ Chivalry is part of the fabric of life. Men frequently hold the door open for women and let them enter first, offer bus seats when people are standing or seat their female companions when dining.

Work

➡ Unless you have a special skill, business and/or speak Spanish, it's hard to find paid work in Argentina other than teaching English or working at a hostel or expat bar.

➡ Native English speakers usually work out of language institutes. Twenty hours a week of actual teaching is about enough for most people (note you aren't paid for prep time or travel time, which can add another hour or two for each hour of teaching). Frustrations include dealing with unpleasant institutes, time spent cashing checks at the bank, classes being spread throughout the day and cancelled classes. Institute turnover is high and most people don't teach for more than a year.

➡ A TEFL certification can certainly help but isn't mandatory for all jobs (check out www.teflbuenosaires.com). You'll make more money teaching private students, but it takes time to gain a client base. And you should take into account slow periods, such as December through February, when many locals leave town on summer vacation.

➡ To find a job, call up the institutes or visit expat bars and start networking. March is when institutes are ramping up their courses, so it's the best time to find work. Many teachers work on tourist visas (which is not a big deal), heading over to Uruguay every three months for a new visa or visiting the immigration office for a visa extension.

➡ There are job postings at http://buenosaires.en.craigslist.org and you can try posting on expat Facebook groups or website forums such as www.baexpats.org.

Transportation

GETTING THERE & AWAY

Entering Argentina

- Entering Argentina is straightforward; immigration officials at airports are generally quick and to the point, while those at border crossings may take more time scrutinizing your documents and belongings.
- Citizens from Canada have to pay a reciprocity fee (p612) before entering Argentina.

Passports

- Anyone entering Argentina should have a passport valid for at least six months from date of entry, and ideally past the date the passport holder leaves the country.
- Once you're in Argentina, police can still demand identification at any moment (but rarely do without reason), so carry at least a photocopy of your passport around at all times (when it will also come in handy for entering government buildings, getting tax-free purchases, changing money at a bank etc).

Onward Ticket

- When entering by air, you officially must have a return ticket, though this is rarely asked for by officials once you're in Argentina. However, it is commonly asked for by the airline in the country of origin. Most airlines prohibit the boarding of any passengers without proof of onward travel, regardless of whether the person was sold a one-way ticket or not. They do this because they'd be responsible for flying you back home should you be denied entry once you're in Argentina. Check with your airline for details.

Air

- Argentina has direct flights between North America, the UK, Europe, Australia and South Africa, and from nearly all South American countries. You can also fly to a neighboring country, such as Brazil or Chile, and continue overland to Argentina.
- If you plan to enter Argentina and fly directly to the provinces, be sure that your tickets are booked for the same airport. Otherwise, plan sufficient time between flights, calculating 40 minutes to two hours to drive or shuttle between airports.

Airports & Airlines

- Most international flights arrive at Buenos Aires' **Aeropuerto Internacional Ministro Pistarini** (Ezeiza; ☎011-5480-6111; www.aa2000.com.ar), which is a 40- to 60-minute shuttle-bus or taxi ride out of town (35km).

CLIMATE CHANGE & TRAVEL

Every form of transport that relies on carbon-based fuel generates CO_2, the main cause of human-induced climate change. Modern travel is dependent on airplanes which might use less fuel per kilometer per person than most cars but travel much greater distances. The altitude at which aircraft emit gases (including CO_2) and particles also contributes to their climate change impact. Many websites offer 'carbon calculators' that allow people to estimate the carbon emissions generated by their journey and, for those who wish to do so, to offset the impact of the greenhouse gases emitted with contributions to portfolios of climate-friendly initiatives throughout the world. Lonely Planet offsets the carbon footprint of all staff and author travel.

ARRIVAL TIPS: AEROPUERTO INTERNACIONAL MINISTRO PISTARINI (EZEIZA)

- Citizens from Canada pay a 'reciprocity fee' (p612) *(tasa de reciprocidad)* before flying into Argentina.
- If you want to change money at Ezeiza, note that the *cambios* (exchange houses) there generally offer poor rates. Better rates are found at the local bank branch; after exiting customs into the reception hall, make a U-turn to the right to find Banco de la Nación's small office. Its also has an ATM and is open 24 hours, though long lines are common. There are other ATMs at Ezeiza, too, all of which offer the official exchange rate.
- There's a tourist-information booth just beyond the city's 'Taxi Ezeiza' stand.
- Shuttle buses and taxis frequently run from Ezeiza to the center. If you have a connecting regional flight through a different airport, check with the airline to see if your ticket includes the shuttle between airports.
- When flying out of Ezeiza, get there at least two to three hours before your international flight. Security and immigration lines can be long, and be aware that traffic is often bad getting to Ezeiza – it can take an hour or more to go the 35km from downtown Buenos Aires.

- Close to downtown Buenos Aires is **Aeroparque Internacional Jorge Newbery** (☎011-5480-6111; www.aa2000.com.ar; Av Rafael Obligado; 🚌33, 45), which handles mostly domestic flights but also a few international ones from neighboring countries.
- There are several other international airports around Argentina. Basic information on most Argentine airports can be found online at Aeropuertos Argentina 2000 (www.aa2000.com.ar).
- **Aerolíneas Argentinas** (www.aerolineas.com.ar) is the national carrier and has a decent international reputation.

Land

Border Crossings

There are numerous border crossings from neighboring Bolivia, Brazil, Chile, Paraguay and Uruguay. Border formalities are generally straightforward as long as all your documents are in order (p611).

BOLIVIA

La Quiaca to Villazón Many buses go from Jujuy and Salta to La Quiaca, where you walk across a bridge to the Bolivian border.

Aguas Blancas to Bermejo From Orán, reached by bus from Salta or Jujuy, take a bus to Aguas Blancas and then Bermejo, where you can catch a bus to Tarija.

Salvador Mazza (Pocitos) to Yacuiba Buses from Jujuy or Salta go to Salvador Mazza at the Bolivian border, where you cross and grab a shared taxi to Yacuiba.

BRAZIL

The most common crossing is from Puerto Iguazú to Foz do Iguaçu. Check both cities for more information on the peculiarities of this border crossing, especially if you're crossing the border into Brazil only to see the other side of Iguazú Falls.

There is also a border crossing from Paso de los Libres to Uruguaiana (Brazil).

CHILE

There are numerous crossings between Argentina and Chile. Except in far southern Patagonia, every land crossing involves crossing the Andes. Due to weather, some high-altitude passes close in winter; even the busy Mendoza–Santiago route over RN 7 can close for several days (sometimes longer) during a severe storm. Always check road conditions, especially if you have a flight scheduled on the other side of the mountains. The following are the most commonly used crossings:

Bariloche to Puerto Montt This border crossing over the Andes to Chile is usually no fuss; a popular 'tour' crossing is the famous, scenic 12-hour bus-boat combination. It takes two days in winter.

El Calafate to Puerto Natales and Parque Nacional Torres del Paine Probably the most beaten route down here, heading from the Glaciar Perito Moreno (near El Calafate) to Parque Nacional Torres del Paine (near Puerto Natales). Several buses per day in summer; one to two daily in the low season.

Los Antiguos to Chile Chico Those entering Argentina from Chile can access the rugged RN 40 from here and head down to El Chaltén and El Calafate. Best in summer, when there's actually public transportation available.

Mendoza to Santiago The most popular crossing between the two countries, passing 6962m Aconcagua en route.

Salta to San Pedro de Atacama (via Jujuy, Purmamarca and Susques) A 10-hour bus ride through the altiplano with stunningly beautiful scenery.

Ushuaia to Punta Arenas Daily buses in summer, fewer in winter, on this 10- to 12-hour trip (depending on weather conditions), which includes a ferry crossing at either Porvenir or Punta Delgada/Primera Angostura.

PARAGUAY & URUGUAY

➡ There are two direct border crossings between Argentina and Paraguay: Clorinda to Asunción, and Posadas to Encarnación. From Puerto Iguazú, Argentina, you can also cross through Brazil into Ciudad del Este, Paraguay.

➡ Border crossings from Argentine cities to Uruguayan cities include Gualeguaychú to Fray Bentos; Colón to Paysandú; and Concordia to Salto. All involve crossing bridges. Buses from Buenos Aires to Montevideo and other waterfront cities, however, are slower and less convenient than the ferries (or ferry-bus combinations) across the Río de la Plata.

Bus

➡ Travelers can bus to Argentina from most bordering countries. Buses are usually comfortable, modern and fairly clean. Crossing over does not involve too many hassles; just make sure that you have any proper visas beforehand.

River

There are several river crossings between Uruguay and Buenos Aires that involve ferry or hydrofoil, and often require combinations with buses.

➡ **Buenos Aires to Colonia** Daily ferries (one to three hours) head to Colonia, with bus connections to Montevideo (an additional three hours).

➡ **Buenos Aires to Montevideo** High-speed ferries carry passengers from downtown Buenos Aires to the Uruguayan capital in only 2¼ hours.

➡ **Tigre to Carmelo** Regular passenger launches speed from the Buenos Aires suburb of Tigre to Carmelo in 2½ hours (services also go to Montevideo from Tigre).

Sea

Access to Argentina by sea is primarily through cruise ships. **Cruceros Australis** (☎in Buenos Aires 11-5128-4632; www.australis.com; 3 nights & 4 days per person from US$1190; ⊙late Sep-early Apr) travels between Ushuaia and Punta Arenas on a scenic four-day cruise.

GETTING AROUND

Air

➡ The national carrier, **Aerolíneas Argentinas** (www.aerolineas.com.ar), offers the most domestic flights, but it's not necessarily better than its competitors.

➡ Other airlines with domestic flights include **LATAM** (www.latam.com), Andes (www.andesonline.com) and Líneas Aéreas del Estado (LADE; www.lade.com.ar), the air force's passenger service. Norwegian Air (www.norwegian.com/ar) was also planing to add regional flights at the time of research.

➡ At the time of research, a spate of new low-cost airlines were in the process of implementing regional flights between provinces, a service that is changing travel patterns throughout Argentina. For listings, see individual cities.

➡ Demand for flights around the country can be heavy, especially during some holidays (such as Christmas or Easter) and the vacation months of January, February and July. Seats are often booked out well in advance, so reserve as far ahead as possible.

➡ Nearly all domestic flights land at **Aeroparque Internacional Jorge Newbery** (☎011-5480-6111; www.aa2000.com.ar; Av Rafael Obligado; 🚌33, 45), a short distance north of downtown Buenos Aires. It's worth noting that Argentina's domestic flight system can be very unreliable – flights are often cancelled or delayed, and there can be frequent labor strikes. It might be a good idea to avoid tight itineraries; for example, leave a day's cushion in between your domestic and international flights.

Bicycle

➡ If you dig cycling your way around a country, Argentina has potential. You'll see the landscape in greater detail, have far more freedom than you would if beholden to public transportation, and likely meet more locals.

➡ Road bikes are suitable for many paved roads, but byways are often narrow and surfaces can be rough. A *todo terreno* (mountain bike) is often safer and more convenient, allowing you to use the unpaved shoulder and the very extensive network of gravel roads throughout the country. Argentine bicycles are

DEPARTURE TAX

Departure tax is included in the price of a ticket.

improving in quality but are still far from equal to their counterparts in Europe or the USA.

➡ There are several drawbacks to long-distance bicycling in Argentina. One is the wind, which in Patagonia can slow your progress to a crawl. Finding water sources in some areas can also be an issue. Finally, Argentine motorists can be a serious hazard to cyclists, particularly on many of the country's straight, narrow, two-lane highways. Make yourself as visible as possible, and wear a helmet.

➡ Bring an adequate repair kit and extra parts and stock up on good maps, which is usually easier to do once you're in Argentina. Always confirm directions and inquire about conditions locally. In Patagonia, a windbreaker, shelter and warm clothing are essential. Don't expect much traffic on some back roads.

Boat

➡ Opportunities for boat or river travel in and around Argentina are limited, though there are regular international services to/from Uruguay and to/from Chile via the Lake District. Further south, from Ushuaia, operators offer boat trips on the Beagle Channel in Tierra del Fuego.

➡ The Buenos Aires suburb of Tigre has numerous boat excursions around the delta of the Río de la Plata.

Bus

➡ If you're doing any serious traveling around Argentina, you'll become very familiar with the country's excellent bus network. Long-distance buses (known as *micros*) are fast and surprisingly comfortable and can be a rather luxurious experience. It's the way most Argentines get around. Larger luggage is stowed in the hold below, security is generally good (especially on the 1st-class buses) and attendants tag your bags. If you have a long trip – say, Buenos Aires to Mendoza – overnight buses are the way to go, saving you a night's accommodations.

➡ Most cities and towns have a central bus terminal where each company has its own ticket window. Some companies post schedules prominently, and the ticket price and departure time are always on the ticket you buy. Expect restrooms, left luggage, fast-food stalls, kiosks and newspaper vendors inside or near almost every large terminal. In tourist-destination cities they'll often have a tourist information office. There are generally few if any hotel touts or other traveler-hassling types at terminals; El Calafate is one notable exception.

➡ Websites that sell long-distance bus tickets online (and without commission) are www.plataforma10.com.ar, centraldepasajes.com.ar and www.omnilineas.com.

➡ Some long-distance bus services face reduced services as low-cost airlines offer stiff competition.

Classes & Costs

➡ Most bus lines have modern coaches with spacious, comfortable seats, large windows, air-conditioning, TVs, toilets (bring toilet paper) and sometimes an attendant serving coffee and snacks.

➡ On overnight trips it's well worth the extra pesos to go *coche cama* (sleeper class); seats are wide, recline almost flat and are very comfortable. For even more luxury there's *ejecutivo* (executive), which is available on a few popular runs. For less luxury, *semi-cama* (semisleeper) seats are manageable. If pinching pesos, *común* (common) is the cheapest class. For trips less than about five hours, there's usually no choice and buses are *común* or *semi-cama*, which are both usually just fine.

➡ Bus fares vary widely depending on the season, class and company. Patagonia runs tend to be the most expensive. Many companies accept credit cards.

Reservations

➡ Often you don't need to buy bus tickets beforehand unless you're traveling on a Friday between major cities, when overnight *coche cama* services sell out fast. During holiday stretches, such as late December through February, July, and August, tickets sell quickly. As soon as you arrive somewhere, especially if it's a town with limited services, find out which companies go to your next destination and when, and plan your trip.

➡ When the bus terminal is on the outskirts of a big town or city, there are often downtown agencies selling tickets without commission.

Seasonal Services

➡ In the Lake District and northern Patagonia, bus services are good during summer (November through March), when there are many microbus routes to campgrounds, along lake circuits, to trailheads and to other destinations popular with tourists. Outside summer, however, these services slow way down.

➡ In Patagonia the famed stretch of RN 40, or Ruta Nacional Cuarenta (Rte 40), was once infrequently traveled and rough – though most of it is now paved (it's still good to have a 4WD for side roads, however). But there's still little public transportation despite the road improvements, and it's mostly via expensive, summertime microbus 'tours.'

A HANDY WEBSITE FOR DRIVERS

A very handy website for those driving around Argentina is www.ruta0.com. Among other things, you can punch in two destinations and get the recommended routes (and whether they're paved or not), distances in kilometers, driving times and even how much it will cost in gas consumption.

Car & Motorcycle

➡ Because Argentina is so large, many parts are accessible only by private vehicle, despite the country's extensive public-transportation system. This is especially true in Patagonia, where distances are great and buses can be infrequent.

Automobile Associations

➡ Whenever driving in Argentina, it's worth being a member of the **Automóvil Club Argentino** (ACA; ☎011-4808-4040; www.aca.org.ar; Av del Libertador 1850; ⏲9am-4pm Mon-Fri; 🚌130, 62, 93), which has offices, gas stations and garages throughout the country and offers road service and towing in and around major destinations. ACA recognizes members of most overseas auto clubs and grants them privileges including road service and discounts on maps and accommodations. Bring your card.

Bringing Your Own Vehicle

➡ Chile is probably the best country on the continent for shipping a vehicle from overseas, though Argentina is feasible. Getting the vehicle out of customs typically involves routine but time-consuming paperwork.

Driver's License & Documents

➡ An International Driving Permit can supplement your national or state driver's license, though car-rental agencies are unlikely to ask you for one. If you are stopped, police will inspect your automobile registration and insurance and tax documents, all of which must be up to date.

➡ Drivers of Argentine vehicles must carry their title document (*tarjeta verde* or 'green card'); if it's a rental, make sure it's in the glove box. For foreign vehicles, customs permission is the acceptable substitute.

➡ Liability insurance is obligatory, and police often ask to see proof of insurance at checkpoints.

Fuel

➡ *Nafta* (gas) prices are more expensive than in the US. Avoid *común* (regular) as it's usually low quality. Super and premium are better choices. In Patagonia gas prices are about a third less than elsewhere.

➡ *Estaciones de servicio* (gas stations) are fairly common, but outside the cities keep an eye on your gas gauge. In Patagonia it's a good idea to carry extra fuel.

Rental

➡ To rent a car, you must be at least 21 years of age and have a credit card and valid driver's license from your country. Agencies rarely ask for an International Driving Permit.

➡ When you rent a vehicle find out how many kilometers are included. Unlimited-kilometer deals exist but can be much more expensive, depending on the destination.

➡ Reserving a car with one of the major international agencies in your home country often gets you lower rates; you can also try online sites such as www.despegar.com.

➡ One of the cheapest places to rent a car is Bariloche; if you're heading to Patagonia, for example, this is a good place to rent. Taking a rental car into Chile might be allowed for an extra fee.

➡ For motorcycle rentals, you must be at least 25 years of age; head to **Motocare** (☎011-4761-2696; www.motocare.com.ar/rental; Esteban Echeverría 738, Vicente López) located in Buenos Aires (or Neuquén). Honda Transalp 700s are available; bring your own helmet and riding gear. For driving outside big cities only.

➡ If renting a car in Argentina and crossing into Chile, or vice versa, most rental-car companies require you to return the car to the country of origin.

Purchase

➡ Purchasing a vehicle in Argentina can be complicated for foreigners. This usually involves having a permanent local address, obtaining a CDI (a tax ID number) and paying for the vehicle in cash. To buy a used vehicle, you must transfer the title at a title-transfer office, with the current owner and all their proper papers present. Make sure all licenses, tickets and taxes have been paid.

➡ Speaking Spanish helps. Getting insurance without a DNI (national document) can be difficult but not impossible. As a foreigner without a DNI you may own a vehicle in Argentina; however, you theoretically cannot take it out of the country without a notarized authorization, which can be difficult to obtain.

➡ It's wise to supplement this information with your own current research.

Insurance

➡ Liability insurance is obligatory in Argentina, and police ask to see proof of insurance at checkpoints.

➡ If you plan on taking the car to neighboring countries, make sure it will remain covered (you'll have to pay extra).

➡ Among reputable insurers in Argentina are Mapfre (www.mapfre.com.ar) and ACA (www.aca.org.ar).

Road Rules & Hazards

➡ Anyone considering driving in Argentina should know that Argentine drivers are aggressive and commonly ignore speed limits, road signs and even traffic signals.

➡ Night driving is not recommended; in many regions animals hang out on the road for warmth.

➡ Have on hand some emergency reflectors *(balizas)* and a fire extinguisher *(matafuego)*.

➡ Headrests are required for the driver and passengers, and seatbelts are obligatory (though few wear them).

➡ Motorcycle helmets are also obligatory, although this law is rarely enforced.

➡ You won't often see police patrolling the highways, but you might meet them at major intersections and roadside checkpoints where they conduct meticulous document and equipment checks. Sometimes these checks are pretexts for graft. If you are uncertain about your rights, politely state your intention to contact your embassy or consulate. If you *do* want to pay a bribe for the sake of expediency, ask *'¿Puedo pagar la multa ahora?'* ('Can I pay the fine now?').

Hitchhiking

➡ Along with Chile, Argentina is probably the best country for hitchhiking *(hacer dedo)* in all of South America. The major drawback is that Argentine vehicles are often stuffed full with families and children, but truckers will sometimes pick up backpackers. A good place to ask is at *estaciones de servicio* on the outskirts of large Argentine cities, where truckers gas up their vehicles.

➡ In Patagonia, where distances are great and vehicles few, hitchers should expect long waits and carry warm, windproof clothing and refreshments.

➡ Having a sign will improve your chances for a pickup, especially if it says something like *visitando Argentina de Canada* ('visiting Argentina from Canada'), rather than just a destination. Argentines are fascinated by foreigners.

➡ Be aware that hitchhiking is never entirely safe in any country in the world, and we don't recommend it. Travelers who decide to hitch should understand that they are taking a small but potentially serious risk. People who do choose to hitch will be safer if they travel in pairs. Always let someone know where you are planning to go.

Local Transportation

Bus

➡ Local Argentine buses, called *colectivos*, are notorious for charging down the street and spewing clouds of black smoke while traveling at breakneck speeds. Riding on them is a good way to see the cities and get around, providing you can sort out the often complex bus systems. Buses are clearly numbered and usually carry a placard indicating their final destination. Sometimes, identically numbered buses serve slightly different routes (especially in big cities), so pay attention to the placards. To ask 'Does this bus go (to the town center)?' say *'¿Va este colectivo (al centro)?'*

➡ Some city buses operate on coins; pay as you board.

➡ In big cities, such as Buenos Aires, Mendoza or Mar del Plata, you must buy transportation cards, purchased at many kiosks. *Sube* cards can be credited once and used in any of the cities where they are valid. Some cities use other card systems that are not connected.

➡ If you are in a city for a short time, most Argentine commuters will cheerfully swipe their card for you if you offer to pay them the fare.

Subway

➡ Buenos Aires is the only Argentine city with a subway system (known as the Subte), and it's the quickest and cheapest way of getting around the city center.

Taxi & Remise

➡ The people of Buenos Aires make frequent use of taxis, which are digitally metered and cheap by US and European standards. Outside the capital, meters are common but not universal, and you'll need to agree on a fare in advance.

➡ *Remises* are unmarked radio taxis, usually without meters, that have fixed fares (comparable to those of taxis) within a given zone. Any business will phone one for you if you ask.

➡ Where public transportation is scarce it's possible to hire a taxi or *remise* with a driver for the day. This can be especially convenient and economical for a group, especially for taking an area tour. Always negotiate the fee in advance.

Train

- For many years there were major reductions in long-distance train services in Argentina, but recent years have seen some rail lines progressively reopened.
- Good sources for information are www.seat61.com/southamerica.htm and www.sofse.gob.ar.
- Trains serve most of Buenos Aires and some surrounding provinces. During the holiday periods, such as Christmas or national holidays, buy tickets in advance.
- Train fares tend to be lower than comparable bus fares, but trains are slower and there are fewer departure times and destinations.
- Long-distance trains have sleepers.
- Train buffs will want to take the narrow-gauge *La Trochita,* which runs 20km between Esquel and Nahuel Pan. Another legendary ride is Salta's touristy but spectacular *Tren a las Nubes* (Train to the Clouds), which at one point spans a desert canyon at an altitude of 4220m – though it's famously unreliable. And finally, the scenic *Tren Patagónico* connects Bariloche to Viedma.

Language

Latin American Spanish pronunciation is easy, as most sounds have equivalents in English. Read our colored pronunciation guides as if they were English, and you'll be understood. Note that kh is a throaty sound (like the 'ch' in the Scottish *loch*), v and b are like a soft English 'v' (between a 'v' and a 'b'), and r is strongly rolled. Also note that the letters *ll* (pronounced ly or simplified to y in most parts of Latin America) and *y* are pronounced like the 's' in 'measure' or the 'sh' in 'shut' in Argentina, which gives the language its very own local flavor. In this chapter, we've used the symbol sh to represent this sound. You'll get used to this very quickly listening to and taking your cues from the locals.

The stressed syllables are indicated with an acute accent in written Spanish (eg *días*) and with italics in our pronunciation guides.

The polite form is used in this chapter; where both polite and informal options are given, they are indicated by the abbreviations 'pol' and 'inf'. Where necessary, both masculine and feminine forms of words are included, separated by a slash and with the masculine form first, eg *perdido/a* (m/f).

BASICS

Hello.	*Hola.*	*o*·la
Goodbye.	*Adiós./Chau.*	a·*dyos*/chow
How are you?	*¿Qué tal?*	ke tal
Fine, thanks.	*Bien, gracias.*	byen *gra*·syas
Excuse me.	*Perdón.*	per·*don*

WANT MORE?

For in-depth language information and handy phrases, check out Lonely Planet's *Latin American Spanish Phrasebook*. You'll find it at **shop.lonelyplanet.com**, or you can buy Lonely Planet's iPhone phrasebooks at the Apple App Store.

Sorry.	*Lo siento.*	lo *syen*·to
Please.	*Por favor.*	por fa·*vor*
Thank you.	*Gracias.*	*gra*·syas
You're welcome.	*De nada.*	de *na*·da
Yes./No.	*Sí./No.*	see/no

My name is ...
Me llamo ... — me *sha*·mo ...

What's your name?
¿Cómo se llama usted? — *ko*·mo se *sha*·ma oo·*ste* (pol)
¿Cómo te llamas? — *ko*·mo te *sha*·mas (inf)

Do you speak English?
¿Habla inglés? — *a*·bla een·*gles* (pol)
¿Hablas inglés? — *a*·blas een·*gles* (inf)

I don't understand.
Yo no entiendo. — yo no en·*tyen*·do

ACCOMMODATIONS

I'd like a ... room.	*Quisiera una habitación ...*	kee·*sye*·ra *oo*·na a·bee·ta·*syon* ...
single	*individual*	een·dee·vee·*dwal*
double	*doble*	*do*·ble

How much is it per night/person?
¿Cuánto cuesta por noche/persona? — *kwan*·to *kwes*·ta por *no*·che/per·*so*·na

Does it include breakfast?
¿Incluye el desayuno? — een·*kloo*·she el de·sa·*shoo*·no

campsite	*terreno de cámping*	te·*re*·no de *kam*·peeng
hotel	*hotel*	o·*tel*
guesthouse	*hostería*	os·te·*ree*·a
youth hostel	*albergue juvenil*	al·*ber*·ge khoo·ve·*neel*
air-con	*aire acondicionado*	*ai*·re a·kon·dee·syo·*na*·do

bathroom	*baño*	*ba*·nyo
bed	*cama*	*ka*·ma
window	*ventana*	ven·*ta*·na

DIRECTIONS

Where's ...?
¿Dónde está ...? — *don*·de es·*ta* ...

What's the address?
¿Cuál es la dirección? — kwal es la dee·rek·*syon*

Could you please write it down?
¿Puede escribirlo, por favor? — *pwe*·de es·kree·*beer*·lo por fa·*vor*

Can you show me (on the map)?
¿Me lo puede indicar (en el mapa)? — me lo *pwe*·de een·dee·*kar* (en el *ma*·pa)

at the corner	*en la esquina*	en la es·*kee*·na
at the traffic lights	*en el semáforo*	en el se·*ma*·fo·ro
behind ...	*detrás de ...*	de·*tras* de ...
in front of ...	*enfrente de ...*	en·*fren*·te de ...
left	*izquierda*	ees·*kyer*·da
next to ...	*al lado de ...*	al *la*·do de ...
opposite ...	*frente a ...*	*fren*·te a ...
right	*derecha*	de·*re*·cha
straight ahead	*todo recto*	*to*·do *rek*·to

EATING & DRINKING

Can I see the menu, please?
¿Puedo ver el menú, por favor? — *pwe*·do ver el me·*noo* por fa·*vor*

What would you recommend?
¿Qué me recomienda? — ke me re·ko·*myen*·da

Do you have vegetarian food?
¿Tienen comida vegetariana? — *tye*·nen ko·*mee*·da ve·khe·ta·*rya*·na

I don't eat (red meat).
No como (carne roja). — no *ko*·mo (*kar*·ne *ro*·kha)

That was delicious!
¡Estaba buenísimo! — es·*ta*·ba bwe·*nee*·see·mo

Cheers!
¡Salud! — sa·*loo*

The bill, please.
La cuenta, por favor. — la *kwen*·ta por fa·*vor*

I'd like a table for ...	*Quisiera una mesa para ...*	kee·*sye*·ra *oo*·na *me*·sa *pa*·ra ...
(eight) o'clock	*las (ocho)*	las (*o*·cho)
(two) people	*(dos) personas*	(dos) per·*so*·nas

LUNFARDO

Below are some of the spicier *lunfardo* (slang) terms you may hear on your travels in Argentina.

boliche – disco or nightclub

boludo – jerk, asshole, idiot; often used in a friendly fashion, but a deep insult to a stranger

bondi – bus

buena onda – good vibes

carajo – asshole, prick; bloody hell

chabón/chabona – kid, guy/girl (term of endearment)

che – hey

diez puntos – OK, cool, fine (literally '10 points')

fiaca – laziness

guita – money

laburo – job

macanudo – great, fabulous

mango – one peso

masa – a great, cool thing

mina – woman

morfar – eat

pendejo – idiot

piba/pibe – cool young guy/girl

piola – cool, clever

pucho – cigarette

re – very, eg *re interestante* (very interesting)

trucho – fake, imitation, bad quality

¡Ponete las pilas! – Get on with it! (literally 'Put in the batteries!')

Me mataste. – I don't know; I have no idea. (literally 'You've killed me')

Le faltan un par de jugadores. – He's not playing with a full deck (literally 'He's a couple of players short')

che boludo – The most *porteño* phrase on earth. Ask a friendly local youth to explain.

Key Words

appetisers	*aperitivos*	a·pe·ree·*tee*·vos
bottle	*botella*	bo·*te*·sha
bowl	*bol*	bol
breakfast	*desayuno*	de·sa·*shoo*·no
children's menu	*menú infantil*	me·*noo* een·fan·*teel*
(too) cold	*(muy) frío*	(mooy) *free*·o
dinner	*cena*	*se*·na
food	*comida*	ko·*mee*·da

fork	*tenedor*	te·ne·*dor*
glass	*vaso*	*va*·so
hot (warm)	*caliente*	ka·*lyen*·te
knife	*cuchillo*	koo·*chee*·yo
lunch	*almuerzo*	al·*mwer*·so
main course	*plato principal*	*pla*·to preen·see·*pal*
plate	*plato*	*pla*·to
restaurant	*restaurante*	res·tow·*ran*·te
spoon	*cuchara*	koo·*cha*·ra
with/without	*con/sin*	kon/seen

Meat & Fish

beef	*carne de vaca*	*kar*·ne de *va*·ka
chicken	*pollo*	*po*·sho
duck	*pato*	*pa*·to
fish	*pescado*	pes·*ka*·do
lamb	*cordero*	kor·*de*·ro
pork	*cerdo*	*ser*·do
turkey	*pavo*	*pa*·vo
veal	*ternera*	ter·*ne*·ra

Fruit & Vegetables

apple	*manzana*	man·*sa*·na
apricot	*damasco*	da·*mas*·ko
artichoke	*alcaucil*	al·*kow*·seel
asparagus	*espárragos*	es·*pa*·ra·gos
banana	*banana*	ba·*na*·na
beans	*chauchas*	*chow*·chas
beetroot	*remolacha*	re·mo·*la*·cha
cabbage	*repollo*	re·*po*·sho
carrot	*zanahoria*	sa·na·*o*·rya
celery	*apio*	*a*·pyo
cherry	*cereza*	se·*re*·sa
corn	*choclo*	*cho*·klo
cucumber	*pepino*	pe·*pee*·no
fruit	*fruta*	*froo*·ta
grape	*uvas*	*oo*·vas
lemon	*limón*	lee·*mon*
lentils	*lentejas*	len·*te*·khas
lettuce	*lechuga*	le·*choo*·ga
mushroom	*champiñón*	cham·pee·*nyon*
nuts	*nueces*	*nwe*·ses
onion	*cebolla*	se·*bo*·sha
orange	*naranja*	na·*ran*·kha
peach	*durazno*	doo·*ras*·no
peas	*arvejas*	ar·*ve*·khas
(red/green) pepper	*pimiento (rojo/verde)*	pee·*myen*·to (*ro*·kho/*ver*·de)
pineapple	*ananá*	a·na·*na*
plum	*ciruela*	seer·*we*·la
potato	*papa*	*pa*·pa
pumpkin	*zapallo*	sa·*pa*·sho
spinach	*espinacas*	es·pee·*na*·kas
strawberry	*frutilla*	froo·*tee*·sha
tomato	*tomate*	to·*ma*·te
vegetable	*verdura*	ver·*doo*·ra
watermelon	*sandía*	san·*dee*·a

Other Foods

bread	*pan*	pan
butter	*manteca*	man·*te*·ka
cheese	*queso*	*ke*·so

EL VOSEO

Spanish in the Río de la Plata region differs from that of Spain and the rest of the Americas, most notably in the use of the informal form of 'you'. Instead of *tuteo* (the use of *tú*), Argentines commonly speak with *voseo* (the use of *vos*), a relic from 16th-century Spanish requiring slightly different grammar. All verbs change in spelling, stress and pronunciation. Examples of verbs ending in *-ar*, *-er* and *-ir* are given below – the *tú* forms are included to illustrate the contrast. Imperative forms (commands) also differ, but negative imperatives are identical in *tuteo* and *voseo*.

The Spanish phrases in this chapter use the *vos* form. An Argentine inviting a foreigner to address him or her informally will say *Me podés tutear* (literally 'You can address me with *tú*'), even though they'll use the *vos* forms in subsequent conversation.

Verb	Tuteo	Voseo
hablar (speak): You speak./Speak!	*Tú hablas./¡Habla!*	*Vos hablás./¡Hablá!*
comer (eat): You eat./Eat!	*Tú comes./¡Come!*	*Vos comés./¡Comé!*
venir (come): You come./Come!	*Tú vienes./¡Ven!*	*Vos venís./¡Vení!*

egg	*huevo*	we·vo
honey	*miel*	myel
jam	*mermelada*	mer·me·*la*·da
oil	*aceite*	a·*sey*·te
pasta	*pasta*	*pas*·ta
pepper	*pimienta*	pee·*myen*·ta
rice	*arroz*	a·*ros*
salt	*sal*	sal
sugar	*azúcar*	a·*soo*·kar
vinegar	*vinagre*	vee·*na*·gre

Drinks

beer	*cerveza*	ser·*ve*·sa
coffee	*café*	ka·*fe*
(orange) juice	*jugo (de naranja)*	*khoo*·go (de na·*ran*·kha)
milk	*leche*	*le*·che
tea	*té*	te
(mineral) water	*agua (mineral)*	*a*·gwa (mee·ne·*ral*)
(red/white) wine	*vino (tinto/ blanco)*	*vee*·no (*teen*·to/ *blan*·ko)

EMERGENCIES

Help!	*¡Socorro!*	so·*ko*·ro
Go away!	*¡Vete!*	*ve*·te

Call ...!	*¡Llame a ...!*	*sha*·me a ...
a doctor	*un médico*	oon *me*·dee·ko
the police	*la policía*	la po·lee·*see*·a

I'm lost.
Estoy perdido/a. es·*toy* per·*dee*·do/a (m/f)

I'm ill.
Estoy enfermo/a. es·*toy* en·*fer*·mo/a (m/f)

I'm allergic to (antibiotics).
Soy alérgico/a a (los antibióticos). soy a·*ler*·khee·ko/a a (los an·tee·*byo*·tee·kos) (m/f)

Where are the toilets?
¿Dónde están los baños? *don*·de es·*tan* los *ba*·nyos

QUESTION WORDS

How?	*¿Cómo?*	*ko*·mo
What?	*¿Qué?*	ke
When?	*¿Cuándo?*	*kwan*·do
Where?	*¿Dónde?*	*don*·de
Who?	*¿Quién?*	kyen
Why?	*¿Por qué?*	por ke

SIGNS

Abierto	Open
Cerrado	Closed
Entrada	Entrance
Hombres/Varones	Men
Mujeres/Damas	Women
Prohibido	Prohibited
Salida	Exit
Servicios/Baños	Toilets

SHOPPING & SERVICES

I'd like to buy ...
Quisiera comprar ... kee·*sye*·ra kom·*prar* ...

I'm just looking.
Sólo estoy mirando. *so*·lo es·*toy* mee·*ran*·do

Can I look at it?
¿Puedo verlo? *pwe*·do *ver*·lo

How much is it?
¿Cuánto cuesta? *kwan*·to *kwes*·ta

That's too expensive.
Es muy caro. es mooy *ka*·ro

Can you lower the price?
¿Podría bajar un poco el precio? po·*dree*·a ba·*khar* oon *po*·ko el *pre*·syo

There's a mistake in the bill.
Hay un error en la cuenta. ai oon e·*ror* en la *kwen*·ta

ATM	*cajero automático*	ka·*khe*·ro ow·to·*ma*·tee·ko
credit card	*tarjeta de crédito*	tar·*khe*·ta de *kre*·dee·to
internet cafe	*cibercafé*	see·ber·ka·*fe*
market	*mercado*	mer·*ka*·do
post office	*correos*	ko·*re*·os
tourist office	*oficina de turismo*	o·fee·*see*·na de too·*rees*·mo

TIME & DATES

What time is it?	*¿Qué hora es?*	ke *o*·ra es
It's (10) o'clock.	*Son (las diez).*	son (las dyes)
It's half past (one).	*Es (la una) y media.*	es (la *oo*·na) ee *me*·dya
morning	*mañana*	ma·*nya*·na
afternoon	*tarde*	*tar*·de
evening	*noche*	*no*·che
yesterday	*ayer*	a·*sher*
today	*hoy*	oy
tomorrow	*mañana*	ma·*nya*·na

Monday	*lunes*	*loo*·nes
Tuesday	*martes*	*mar*·tes
Wednesday	*miércoles*	*myer*·ko·les
Thursday	*jueves*	*khwe*·ves
Friday	*viernes*	*vyer*·nes
Saturday	*sábado*	*sa*·ba·do
Sunday	*domingo*	do·*meen*·go

TRANSPORTATION

boat	*barco*	*bar*·ko
bus	*colectivo/ micro*	ko·lek·*tee*·vo/ *mee*·kro
plane	*avión*	a·*vyon*
train	*tren*	tren

first	*primero*	pree·*me*·ro
last	*último*	*ool*·tee·mo
next	*próximo*	*prok*·see·mo

A ... ticket, please.	*Un boleto de ..., por favor.*	oon bo·*lee*·to de ... por fa·*vor*
1st-class	*primera clase*	pree·*me*·ra *kla*·se
2nd-class	*segunda clase*	se·*goon*·da *kla*·se
one-way	*ida*	*ee*·da
return	*ida y vuelta*	*ee*·da ee *vwel*·ta

I want to go to ...
Quisiera ir a ... kee·*sye*·ra eer a ...

Does it stop at ...?
¿Para en ...? *pa*·ra en ...

What stop is this?
¿Cuál es esta parada? kwal es *es*·ta pa·*ra*·da

What time does it arrive/leave?
¿A qué hora llega/sale? a ke *o*·ra *she*·ga/*sa*·le

Please tell me when we get to ...
¿Puede avisarme cuando lleguemos a ...? *pwe*·de a·vee·*sar*·me *kwan*·do she·*ge*·mos a ...

I want to get off here.
Quiero bajarme aquí. *kye*·ro ba·*khar*·me a·*kee*

airport	*aeropuerto*	a·e·ro·*pwer*·to
bus stop	*parada de colectivo*	pa·*ra*·da de ko·lek·*tee*·vo
platform	*plataforma*	pla·ta·*for*·ma
ticket office	*taquilla*	ta·*kee*·sha
timetable	*horario*	o·*ra*·ryo
train station	*estación de trenes*	es·ta·*syon* de *tre*·nes

NUMBERS

1	*uno*	*oo*·no
2	*dos*	dos
3	*tres*	tres
4	*cuatro*	*kwa*·tro
5	*cinco*	*seen*·ko
6	*seis*	seys
7	*siete*	*sye*·te
8	*ocho*	*o*·cho
9	*nueve*	*nwe*·ve
10	*diez*	dyes
20	*veinte*	*veyn*·te
30	*treinta*	*treyn*·ta
40	*cuarenta*	kwa·*ren*·ta
50	*cincuenta*	seen·*kwen*·ta
60	*sesenta*	se·*sen*·ta
70	*setenta*	se·*ten*·ta
80	*ochenta*	o·*chen*·ta
90	*noventa*	no·*ven*·ta
100	*cien*	syen
1000	*mil*	meel

I'd like to hire a ...	*Quisiera alquilar ...*	kee·*sye*·ra al·kee·*lar* ...
4WD	*un todo-terreno*	oon to·do·te·*re*·no
bicycle	*una bicicleta*	*oo*·na bee·see·*kle*·ta
car	*un coche/ auto*	oon *ko*·che/ *aw*·to
motorcycle	*una moto*	*oo*·na *mo*·to

helmet	*casco*	*kas*·ko
hitchhike	*hacer dedo*	a·*ser de*·do
mechanic	*mecánico*	me·*ka*·nee·ko
petrol/gas	*nafta*	*naf*·ta
service station	*estación de servicio*	es·ta·*syon* de ser·*vee*·syo

Is this the road to ...?
¿Se va a ... por esta carretera? se va a ... por es·ta ka·re·*te*·ra

Can I park here?
¿Puedo estacionar acá? *pwe*·do e·sta·syo·*nar* a·*ka*

The car has broken down.
El coche se ha averiado. el *ko*·che se a a·ve·*rya*·do

I've run out of petrol.
Me he quedado sin nafta. me e ke·*da*·do seen *naf*·ta

I have a flat tyre.
Tengo una goma pinchada. *ten*·go *oo*·na ·*go*·ma peen·*cha*·da

GLOSSARY

aerosilla – chairlift

alcalde – mayor

alerce – large coniferous tree, resembling a California redwood, from which Argentina's Parque Nacional Los Alerces takes its name

arbolito – literally 'little tree'; a street moneychanger and to be avoided

arroyo – creek, stream

autopista – freeway or motorway

baliza – emergency reflector

balneario – any swimming or bathing area, including beach resorts

bandoneón – an accordion-like instrument used in tango music

barrio – neighborhood or borough of the city

cabildo – colonial town council; also, the building that housed the council

cajero automático – ATM

cambio – money-exchange office; also *casa de cambio*

campo – the countryside; alternately, a field or paddock

cartelera – an office selling discount tickets

casa de cambio – money-exchange office, often shortened to *cambio*

casa de familia – family accommodations

casa de gobierno – a government building

castellano – the term used for the Spanish language spoken throughout Latin America

catarata – waterfall

cerro – hill, mountain

certificado – certified mail

chacra – small, independent farm

coche cama – sleeper class on a train

coima – a bribe; one who solicits a bribe is a *coimero*

colectivo – local bus

combi – long-distance bus

común – common class on a train

correo – post office

costanera – seaside, riverside or lakeside road or walkway

criollo – a term used for any Latin American of European descent

cruce – crossroads

dique – a dam; the resultant reservoir is often used for recreational purposes; can also refer to a drydock

edificio – a building

ejecutivo – executive class on a train

esquina – street corner

estacion de servicio – gas station

estancia – extensive ranch for cattle or sheep; some are now open to tourists

este – east

feria – a street fair or street market

fútbol – soccer

horario – schedule

locutorio – private long-distance telephone office, often with fax and internet

manzana – literally 'apple'; also used to define one square block of a city

mercado artesanal – handicraft market

mestizo – a person of mixed Indian and Spanish descent

mirador – scenic viewpoint, usually on a hill but often in a building

municipalidad – city hall

nafta – gasoline or petrol

neumático – spare tire

norte – north

oeste – west

parada – a bus stop

paseo – an outing, such as a walk in the park or downtown

peatonal – pedestrian mall, usually in the downtown area of major Argentine cities

peña – club that hosts informal folk-music gatherings

piropo – a flirtatious remark

piso – floor

primera – 1st class on a train

propina – a tip, for example, in a restaurant or theater

pulpería – a country store or tavern

quebrada – a canyon

rambla – boardwalk

rancho – a rural house, generally of adobe, with a thatched roof

recargo – additional charge, usually 10%, that many Argentine businesses add to credit-card transactions

refugio – a usually rustic shelter in a national park or remote area

remise – taxi

ripio – gravel

rotisería – takeout shop

rotonda – traffic circle, roundabout

RN – Ruta Nacional; a national highway

RP – Ruta Provincial; a provincial highway

s/n – sin número, indicating a street address without a number

semi-cama – semisleeper class on a train or long-distance bus

sendero – a trail in the woods

sur – south

tarjeta magnética – magnetic bus card, such as a SUBE card

tarjeta telefónica – telephone card

turista – 2nd class on a train, usually not very comfortable

zona franca – duty-free zone

zonda – a hot, dry wind descending from the Andes

FOOD GLOSSARY

a punto – cooked medium well (referring to steak)
agua de la canilla – tap water
agua mineral – mineral water, usually available *con/sin gas* (sparkling/still)
ajo – garlic
alfajor – two flat, soft cookies filled with *dulce de leche* and covered in chocolate or meringue
almuerzo – lunch
amargo – bitter
asado – Argentine barbecue (both the food and the event), often a family event on Sunday

bien cocido – well done (referring to steak)
bife (de chorizo/costilla/lomo) – (sirloin strip/T-bone/tenderloin) steak
bombilla – metal straw with filter for drinking *mate*
bondiola – cured pork shoulder
budín de pan – bread pudding

café – coffee
casero – homemade
carne – meat (usually beef)
cerdo – pork
cena – dinner
cerveza – beer
chimichurri – a spicy marinade for meat, usually made of parsley, garlic, spices and olive oil
chinchulines – intestines
choclo – corn
chopp – draft beer
choripán – a spicy sausage served in a bread roll
chorizo – sausage (note the difference from *bife de chorizo*)
comedor – basic cafeteria
confitería – a shop that serves quick meals
cortado – espresso with steamed milk added
costillas – short ribs
crudo – raw
cubierto – in restaurants, the cover charge you pay for utensil use and bread

desayuno – breakfast
dulce – sweet
dulce de leche – Argentina's national sweet, found in many desserts; a type of thick, milky caramel

empanada – meat or vegetable hand pie; popular Argentine snack
entrada – appetizer
entraña – skirt steak

facturas – pastries; also receipts
frito/a – fried
fruta – fruit
frutos secos – nuts (nuts are also called *nueces*)

helado – ice cream
heladería – an ice-cream shop
hielo – ice
hígado – liver
hongo – mushroom (also called champignon)
huevos – eggs

jamón – ham
jarra – pitcher
jengibre – ginger
jugo (exprimido) – juice (freshly squeezed)
jugoso – medium rare (referring to steak); also general term for juicy

lengua – tongue
lenguado – flounder (fish)
licuado – fruit shake
locro – a traditional meat and corn stew from northern Argentina
lomito – a steak sandwich
lomo – tenderloin

manteca – butter
mariscos – seafood
matambre – a thin cut of beef, sometimes made into a stuffed roll *(matambre relleno)*
mate – a gourd used for drinking *yerba mate* or the tea itself
medialuna (de manteca/de grasa) – croissant (sweet/savory)
merienda – afternoon tea
merluza – hake (fish)
mermelada – jam or jelly
miel – honey
milanesa – breaded cutlet (usually beef)
minuta – in a restaurant or *confitería*, a short order such as spaghetti or *milanesa*
mollejas – sweetbreads
morcilla – blood sausage

ñoquis – gnocchi

ojo de bife – rib-eye steak

pancho – hot dog
papas frita – french fries
parrillada – a mixed grill of steak and other beef cuts
parrilla – a restaurant specializing in steak dishes
pescado – fish
picada – a cheese and cured meat sample plate
pollo – chicken
postre – dessert
propina – tip (gratuity)
puchero – soup combining vegetables and meats, often served with rice

recargo – an additional charge (such as for use of a credit card, usually about 10%)
rotisería – takeout shop

sandwiches de miga – thin sandwiches made from crustless white bread
sorrentino – a stuffed pasta, like ravioli but large and round
submarino – hot milk served with a bar of dark chocolate

tallarines – noodles
tenedor libre – literally 'free fork'; an all-you-can-eat restaurant
tira de asada – grilled beef ribs

vacio – flank steak
verduras – vegetables
vegetariano/a – (m/f) vegetarian
vinoteca – wine bar
vino (blanco/tinto) – (red/white) wine

yerba mate – 'Paraguayan tea' *(Ilex paraguariensis),* which Argentines and Uruguayans consume in very large amounts

Behind the Scenes

SEND US YOUR FEEDBACK

We love to hear from travelers – your comments keep us on our toes and help make our books better. Our well-traveled team reads every word on what you loved or loathed about this book. Although we cannot reply individually to your submissions, we always guarantee that your feedback goes straight to the appropriate authors, in time for the next edition. Each person who sends us information is thanked in the next edition – the most useful submissions are rewarded with a selection of digital PDF chapters.

Visit **lonelyplanet.com/contact** to submit your updates and suggestions or to ask for help. Our award-winning website also features inspirational travel stories, news and discussions.

Note: We may edit, reproduce and incorporate your comments in Lonely Planet products such as guidebooks, websites and digital products, so let us know if you don't want your comments reproduced or your name acknowledged. For a copy of our privacy policy visit lonelyplanet.com/legal.

OUR READERS

Many thanks to the travelers who used the last edition and wrote to us with helpful hints, useful advice and interesting anecdotes: Andrew Kitzrow, Cintia Barraza, Denise Sasaki, Diego Echandi, Evana Stanonik, Felipe Ferraro, Gonçalo Correia, Miguel Prohaska, Nicolas Léonard, Olga Cirera, Patxi García Collado & Janire Gonzalez Echevarría, Rodrigo Machado, Sean O'Donnell, Sergio Rodriguez, Susan Ottenweller, Thomas Hammond, Virginia Mortari

WRITER THANKS

Isabel Albiston

Huge thanks to MaSovaida Morgan, Patricio Santos, Cé Martínez, Jessica Pollack, Madi Lang, Miles Lewis, Sorrel Moseley-Williams, Jazmín Arellano, Mercedes Fauda, Lorena Polo, Alan Seabright, Bárbara Poey, Patricia Franco, Nano Aznarez, Maria Elia Capella, Magda Dobrajska and my family. Your insider tips, friendship and support are greatly appreciated. *Besos* for Facundo, Verita, Felipe, Ciro and Lottie and Alice, and special thanks to *asadores* Marcelo Larroque and Julian Mule – *un aplauso*!

Cathy Brown

I'd like to thank my kiddos for always being supportive as I take off to end-of-the-world destinations and my dad for never missing a chance to make it known how proud of me he is for ending up a travel writer. I'd also like to thank Juan and Ignacio of Tierra Turismo for friendship, great wine, Guns N' Roses karaoke, *asados*, magical lupine fields, Tolhuin randomness and, basically, the best road trip ever helping me to get to know their beloved Tierra del Fuego.

Gregor Clark

Muchísimas gracias to the many Uruguayans and resident expatriates who shared their love of the country and local knowledge with me, especially Gloria, Tino, Miguel, Monica, Alain, Cecilia, Eduardo, Aaron, Victoria, Karen, Juan Manuel, Nahir and Pedro. Back home, *besos y abrazos* to Gaen, Meigan and Chloe, who always make coming home the best part of the trip.

Alex Egerton

Props to all of those on the ground in Argentina who lent a hand to make a daunting research trip work, including Hada, Alejandra, Natalia, Marian, the team in Misiones, Laura, Pablo, Paula and, especially, Ariadna for the phenomenal research efforts. And big thanks to Olga and Nick for their patience and support.

Michael Grosberg

Thanks to the following for their graciousness, hospitality and insight: Charlie O'Malley, Ricardo Paez, Adam Stern, Kai and Mercedes, Maria Ines Arroyo from Cachueta, María Marta Guisasola and Edmundo Day. Also, thanks to Rosie and Carly for joining me on part of the trip and sharing the joys of Mendoza.

Anna Kaminski

I'd like to thank MaSovaida Morgan for entrusting me with Bariloche & the Lake District, and everyone who helped me along the way. In particular, the super-helpful Club Andino staff in Bariloche, El Bolson and Junin de los Andes; Julio and Adriana in Bariloche; Gloria and Sebastian in Villa la Angostura; the staff at the Chos Malal tourist office; the very helpful park ranger at Lago Trome; Juanita in Neuquen's wine region; and Roberto in San Martin.

Carolyn McCarthy

Many thanks go out to all who helped me on this latest research trip. First, to my co-pilots Leif and Sergio, who helped me tackle 6000km of Patagonian roads in the wettest and snowiest spring in years. Hugs to Graciela, who climbed mountains to join me on my birthday (*gracias hermana!*). I'm very grateful to Gaston for his tireless dedication to helping travelers, the crew at Cabo Raso for their fine hospitality, Alvaro at Puesto Cagliero, Anita and Walter O.

Anja Mutić

Gracias to all the great people who helped me on the road in Argentina: Viviana in Capilla del Monte, Mabel in San Marcos Sierras, and the amazing Agus in Córdoba. MaSovaida – I'm so grateful to have shared the road with you! Most of all, *hvala* to Kweli, my 'little big maestro', who makes the big journey worth it.

Adam Skolnick

Special thanks to Co-Pilot Maximus April Wong: without you, I would have been lost in Argentina. With you, I got lost in Argentina! Thanks also to my Argentine family: Mercedes Martinez and Chris Weitz. Thanks to MaSovaida Morgan for sending me out into the wilderness, and to the rest of the Lonely Planet team. It's always a pleasure to collaborate with such smart, passionate people. Thanks to Aurelia Monnier at Palo Santo in Buenos Aires. And thanks especially to beautiful Argentina!

ACKNOWLEDGEMENTS

Climate map data adapted from Peel MC, Finlayson BL & McMahon TA (2007) 'Updated World Map of the Köppen-Geiger Climate Classification', Hydrology and Earth System Sciences, 11, 163344.

Cover photograph: Macaw at Iguazú Falls, Junior Braz/Shutterstock ©

THIS BOOK

This 12th edition of Lonely Planet's *Argentina* guidebook was curated by Isabel Albiston, and researched and written by Isabel, Cathy Brown, Gregor Clark, Alex Egerton, Michael Grosberg, Anna Kaminski, Carolyn McCarthy, Anja Mutić and Adam Skolnick. The previous edition was also written by Isabel, Cathy, Gregor, Alex, Michael, Anna, Carolyn, Anja and Adam. This guidebook was produced by the following:

Senior Product Editor Daniel Bolger

Product Editors Bruce Evans

Cartographer Corey Hutchison

Book Designer Catalina Aragón

Assisting Editors Nigel Chin, Andrea Dobbin, Samantha Forge, Jennifer Hattam, Jodie Martire, Monique Perrin, Simon Williamson

Cover Researcher Ania Bartoszek

Thanks to Hannah Cartmel, Victoria Harison, Karen Henderson

Index

Map Pages **000**
Photo Pages **000**

C

Map Pages **000**
Photo Pages **000**

Map Pages **000**
Photo Pages **000**

Map Pages **000**
Photo Pages **000**

Map Pages **000**
Photo Pages **000**

Map Legend

Sights
- Beach
- Bird Sanctuary
- Buddhist
- Castle/Palace
- Christian
- Confucian
- Hindu
- Islamic
- Jain
- Jewish
- Monument
- Museum/Gallery/Historic Building
- Ruin
- Shinto
- Sikh
- Taoist
- Winery/Vineyard
- Zoo/Wildlife Sanctuary
- Other Sight

Activities, Courses & Tours
- Bodysurfing
- Diving
- Canoeing/Kayaking
- Course/Tour
- Sento Hot Baths/Onsen
- Skiing
- Snorkeling
- Surfing
- Swimming/Pool
- Walking
- Windsurfing
- Other Activity

Sleeping
- Sleeping
- Camping
- Hut/Shelter

Eating
- Eating

Drinking & Nightlife
- Drinking & Nightlife
- Cafe

Entertainment
- Entertainment

Shopping
- Shopping

Information
- Bank
- Embassy/Consulate
- Hospital/Medical
- Internet
- Police
- Post Office
- Telephone
- Toilet
- Tourist Information
- Other Information

Geographic
- Beach
- Gate
- Hut/Shelter
- Lighthouse
- Lookout
- Mountain/Volcano
- Oasis
- Park
- Pass
- Picnic Area
- Waterfall

Population
- Capital (National)
- Capital (State/Province)
- City/Large Town
- Town/Village

Transport
- Airport
- Border crossing
- Bus
- Cable car/Funicular
- Cycling
- Ferry
- Metro station
- Monorail
- Parking
- Petrol station
- Subway/Subte station
- Taxi
- Train station/Railway
- Tram
- Underground station
- Other Transport

Routes
- Tollway
- Freeway
- Primary
- Secondary
- Tertiary
- Lane
- Unsealed road
- Road under construction
- Plaza/Mall
- Steps
- Tunnel
- Pedestrian overpass
- Walking Tour
- Walking Tour detour
- Path/Walking Trail

Boundaries
- International
- State/Province
- Disputed
- Regional/Suburb
- Marine Park
- Cliff
- Wall

Hydrography
- River, Creek
- Intermittent River
- Canal
- Water
- Dry/Salt/Intermittent Lake
- Reef

Areas
- Airport/Runway
- Beach/Desert
- Cemetery (Christian)
- Cemetery (Other)
- Glacier
- Mudflat
- Park/Forest
- Sight (Building)
- Sportsground
- Swamp/Mangrove

Note: Not all symbols displayed above appear on the maps in this book